THE RĀGAS OF SOUTH INDIA

THE RĀGAS OF SOUTH INDIA

A Catalogue of Scalar Material

By WALTER KAUFMANN

INDIANA UNIVERSITY PRESS
BLOOMINGTON · LONDON

The publication of this work has been supported in part by funds made available through the Indiana University Humanities Series.

Published in Canada by Fitzhenry & Whiteside Limited, Don Mills, Ontario

Manufactured in the United States of America

Library of Congress Cataloging in Publication Data
Kaufmann, Walter, 1907-
The rāgas of South India.
Bibliography
1. Music--India--History and criticism. 2. Music, Karnatic--History and criticism. 3. Music, Karnatic--Thematic catalogs. I. Title.
ML338.K373 781.7'54'8 75-1941
ISBN 0-253-39508-9 1 2 3 4 5 80 79 78 77 76

To
CHARLES H. WEBB
Dean, School of Music
Indiana University

CONTENTS

The register lists the names and numbers of all the *mēḷas* and *janya rāgas*. The *mēḷas* and *rāgas* are set forth in numerical order in the text and may be located easily by means of the page headings.

PREFACE

This book is intended to serve as a second part to my *The Rāgas of North India* (from now on referred to as RNI).[1] I have endeavoured to deal particularly with the tone materials of the *rāgas* of South India, surveying beside the 72 *mēḷas* the colossal material of *janya rāgas* (derivative *rāgas*). The emphasis on a survey of scales is necessitated by the fact that there exist already numerous books and articles that describe historical and theoretical matters of Indian music. These lengthy, often obscure and confusing offerings have been stated and restated more than frequently and there is little reason to repeat them again in detail. With the exception of various works written in Sanskrit and in the vernacular languages of the South, those written in European languages, although describing the scales of the 72 primary *mēḷas*, usually present only an astonishingly small number of well-known *janya rāgas* and ignore the overwhelming and fascinating wealth of the rest. Another reason for paying attention primarily to these scales is the fact that during the last few centuries southern musicians in their theoretical deliberations have concentrated more and more on the various scalar formations and on aspects of classifying this material in a systematic manner. Many subtleties of interpretation of the past, such as the uses of the *aṃśa* (predominant note), *nyāsa* (final note), and *graha* (initial note), ornaments, special microtonal intonations, and various other features gradually lost their importance, and theorists of the present time mention them only occasionally or not at all. However, it would be erroneous to find fault with this attitude. The aim of defining scales and grouping them into families is characteristic of the theoretical reflections of southern musicians of recent periods.

My effort to present over 2000 *rāgas* of the South, by no means an exhaustive one, resulted in this work which may provide information concerning the immense multitude of *janyas* and serve also as a catalog offering details of scales and, in some instances, melody examples of specific *rāgas*.

In contrast to my descriptions of North Indian *rāgas* in RNI, where numerous subtle musical details had to be shown in order to achieve clear definitions, this study emphasizes, as already mentioned, the presentation of the scales in their manifold configurations. Musical embellishments, however, are shown only if their uses appear to be of importance at the present time.

Theoretical works of the South written by Indian authors demonstrate the scale degrees by merely using Indian tone syllables (*SA*, *RI*, *GA*, etc., or simply *s*, *r*, *g*, etc.) without any notational indications of changes of pitch of certain notes, a method fully acceptable to the informed Indian musician. A western reader, however, not always well aware of the changing notes (*vikṛta svaras*) as they appear in the scales of the 72 *mēḷas*, will require some time before he can determine them. If the note *SA* is considered to be the western note C, the tone syllable *RI* can mean Db in one group of *mēḷas*, D in another, D# in a third one; similarly *GA* can be Ebb, Eb, or E; *MA* will be F in *mēḷas* 1-36 and F# in *mēḷas* 37-72; *DHA* can be Ab, A, or A#; and *NI* may be interpreted as Bbb, Bb, or B. In order to simplify matters I have presented all scales, song examples, and other musical illustrations in western staff notation where all tonal alterations are clearly recognizable.

Three of the many recent works dealing with South Indian music deserve to be mentioned here: in the front row stands Professor P. Sambamoorthy's unfinished *Dictionary of South Indian Music and Musicians* (see below under SD), a work consisting of two slim volumes that cover a wealth of items, unfortunately only from A to K. Another work, dealing with the listing of *rāgas* is *A Key to Hindu Music* by Chittibabu Naidu (see under N). Naidu used Arabic numbers instead of tone syllables. A third book mentioning *rāgas* of the South is N. S. Ramachandran's *The Ragas of Karnatic Music* (see under R).

As already mentioned, the representations of scale degrees in these and other South Indian works are generally made by means of Indian tone syllables, a method somewhat complex for the western reader. Any scholar, well versed in South Indian music, particularly in the correct interpretation of the tone syllables within the 72 *mēḷas*, is referred to the works listed above (SD, N, R). It is obvious that the numerous scales representing *rāgas* are in their overwhelming majority common knowledge of South Indian musicians and cannot be considered to be the personal property of a particular scholar. Exceptions can be made in a few instances where the creation of specific *rāgas* is ascribed to a particular musician.

All song examples, melody patterns (*varṇams*), and other musical specimens presented in the following survey are my own transcriptions into western staff notation and are derived from various sources. One source, in this book represented by unmarked musical examples, is a large number of fine musicians, mainly from the staff of All India Radio (Bombay, Madras, Delhi, Calcutta, etc.). They gave me song examples either notated in Tamil, Telugu, or Nagari scripts, or they performed for me in order to enable me to write them in staff notation. In many instances these musicians told me that, according to their knowledge, the true origins of the songs were unknown and many have been described as being traditional. There were so many musicians during the almost fifteen years of my work as Director of Music at All India Radio (Bombay) that I am unable to list their names. I am profoundly grateful for their excellent and valuable help.

In later years, long after my return from India, I found a few of these songs in printed form in some Tamil publications. The melodies were not always fully identical with the material I had received in India and documentation concerning the real sources was not always reliable. I nevertheless endeavoured to refer to the later published material whenever possible. For instance, the song example of *Tōḍi* (8,1): in a comparison of my transcription with the song shown in SPC, III, 54 (see below), several small differences can be noticed. In this instance the differences were of special significance and I cited SPC (III, 54) as the available source. The reader will, of course, observe the differences between my version and that shown in the SPC.

Beside expressing my obligation to numerous South Indian musicians of thirty years ago, it is my pleasant duty to thank Professor P. Sambamoorthy (Madras) for his extremely kind help and for his generous permission to quote from his works. Furthermore I wish to acknowledge the excellent assistance I received from my friends Professor Wayne Howard (Kent State University), and Miss Laura Youens and Mr. James Griesheimer (both of

Indiana University). Finally I want to express my gratitude to the Department of Research and Advanced Studies of Indiana University.

Indiana University — Walter Kaufmann
Bloomington, Indiana

SOURCES

Veṅkaṭamakhin. *Caturdaṇḍi Prakāśika* (in Sanskrit and Tamil). Madras, 1933.

Singaracharyulu, Perungulam, and Alaha (Chinna). *Gāya Locanam* (in Sanskrit and Tamil). Madras, 1902.

Ayyangar, Perungulam, Śrinivāsa. *Gāna Vīdya Prakāśin* (in Tamil). Tirunelveli, ca. 1908.

Johannes, T. C. R. (Yogi Sundarajam). *Bharata Saṅgīta Svayambōdhini* (in Tamil). Madras, 1913.

JMA *The Journal of the Music Academy*. Madras.

MNO Kaufmann, Walter. *Musical Notations of the Orient*. Bloomington: Indiana University Press, 1967.

RNI ______________. *The Rāgas of North India*; Bloomington: Indiana University Press, 1968.

N Naidu, Chittibabu. *A Key to Hindu Music*. Madras, 1925. (Naidu lists his *rāgas* in alphabetical order on pp. 36-98. He indicates the twelve *svarasthanas* by the use of the numbers 1 to 12.)

Pallavi Seshayyar's Manuscripts (in Telugu), written ca. 1800; unpublished; preserved by Prof. P. Sambamoorthy, Madras.

R Ramachandran, N. S. *The Rāgas of Karnatic Music*. Madras, 1938.

S Sambamoorthy, P. *South Indian Music* (6 Vols.). Madras, 1951-69.

SCM *Samgraha Cūḍā Maṇi of Govinda*; *Veṅkaṭa Kavi*. *Bahattara Mēḷakartā*. Adyar Library, Madras, 1938.

SD (I and II) Sambamoorthy, P. *A Dictionary of South Indian Music and Musicians* (2 Vols., containing items from A to K). Madras, 1952, 1959.

SPC (II and III) ______________. *A Practical Course in Karnatic Music* (Vols. II and III). Madras, 1960, 1963.

INTRODUCTION

In informal conversations with northern musicians about the art music of the South, occasional remarks can be heard that imply that at present the music of the South shows a remarkable lack of the subtleties which when seen from a northern point of view are essential for the formation and character of the majority of *rāgas*. Southern musicians, when involved in similar conversations, maintain that their own music is older than that of the North, that it was less exposed to foreign influences, that, therefore, it is less distorted and that its system of 72 *mēḷas* is better organized than corresponding features of the North. They would add that in contrast to northern habits, where the names of composers are almost never mentioned because the performer himself usually is his own composer in his improvisations, southern musicians show greater respect toward individual composers and often mention their names and the titles of celebrated songs.

The importance of these arguments need not be taken too seriously. Yet, they do show that there exist certain differences between northern and southern music. An impartial observer will have to add that there are numerous parallels and similarities that are of importance to the music of the North and South. The *rāga* principle is the same, the formal structures of art songs and instrumental pieces are more or less the same. The rhythms differ to some degree but possess the same underlying nature of employing groups of measures (*āvartas*) in contrast to the western custom of lining up single individual measures, one after the other.[2] The use of drone and drums (*mṛdanga* or *tablas*), the manner of accompaniment at the present time is the same, and even extra-musical matters of the past, such as the fixed performance times and the ancient concept of magic powers believed to be inherent in certain *rāgas*, are more or less of the same kind.

Despite the few differences between the music of the North and South and despite the not always pertinent critical opinions uttered by northern and southern musicians, several instances can be observed where certain *rāgas* of the North have become favorites in southern performances, and conversely. This can be observed in numerous broadcast performances and recordings when northern musicians perform southern pieces, and southern musicians northern pieces. This feature can also be noticed in the names of several *rāgas*: in the South there appear names such as *Hindusthān Behāg* or *Hindusthān Kāpi*, *rāgas* of more or less clearly defined northern character as distinguished from the *rāgas* *Karnāṭaka Behāg* or *Karnāṭaka Kāpi*, where the word *Karnāṭaka* indicates southern music.

Although I have tried to curtail the consideration of historical matters, sources, and theoretical deliberations, it has been necessary to mention briefly a few authors, works, and musical features of the past in order to offer at least a sketchy background to the subsequent array of southern *rāgas*. As already stated, many musicians of the North may argue that the music of the South, having been less subject to changes, shows less foreign-influenced phenomena than the music of the North. It is difficult to agree or disagree with this view, because there are arguments for and against it. One against the northern view is the fact that during the centuries following the Islamic invasions of the North the migrations of southern musicians to the North and a smaller number of similar migrations of northern musicians to the South have altered the picture of noticeable differences between northern and southern musical phenomena. For example, Hindu musicians, many converted to the Islamic faith and employed at the courts of the Muslim rulers of the North, had to compete with Mohammedan musicians whereby new *rāgas* (e.g., *Miyan ki Mallār*)[3] were created. Several of these court musicians wrote books about the music of their newly adopted home, probably with the aim of impressing their princely employers with their musical knowledge. More than often these musician-authors used in their descriptions of *rāgas* terminologies of their original homeland and they paraphrased or, more frequently, copied faithfully lengthy passages from other, earlier sources. Gradually musical terminologies became so obscure that by the sixteenth century they had lost their meanings almost entirely, a situation that contributed greatly to a remarkable confusion in music theory. This habit of paraphrasing and quoting pages and pages of earlier sources lasted far beyond the sixteenth century. As a matter of fact it still can be observed in works written at the present time.

Indian writers on music had to deal with three problems in their deliberations: the determination of the various scale degrees which required some method of measuring the sizes of intervals between the seven basic notes within the octave; setting up scales, basic and derivative; and grouping the various scales into families. The oldest known endeavour in India of grouping certain musical phenomena, not yet scales, but songs (*sāmans*), appears in the *Puṣpasūtra* (9,26) which was written some time between the fifth and second centuries B.C. In this work, which originated several centuries before the first music-theory treatise, the writer groups the songs into five-, six-, and seven-note types. Reference is made to the number of notes within the octave but the intervals between them are not yet clearly defined. Since about 200 A.D., beginning with the theoretical chapters and treatises by Bharata, Mataṅga, Nānyadeva, Nārada, and others, up to Śārṅgadeva (thirteenth century), the intervals between the scale degrees were determined by means of the twenty-two *śrutis*,[4] and the scales were grouped from various points of view. An early grouping showed the *SA*- and *MA*-*grāmas*; other groupings dealt with heavenly (*mārga*) and secular (*deśi*) types; and a fourteenth-century grouping (Locanakavi)[5] and several later ones placed the *rāgas* into father, wife, and son types. Only since the sixteenth century, particularly in the South, have groupings of *rāgas* from a musical point of view appeared.

A survey of southern sources that contain some information about music could be started with an epic written in Tamil in the second century. It can be considered to be a contemporary work to Bharata's often quoted *Nāṭyaśāstra*. This southern epic, the *Śilappadikāram* ("The Ankle Bracelet") was written by prince Ilangō Adigal, a brother of king Shenguttuvan of western South India.[6] This work has been provided with two commentaries, an early one in incomplete form, by Arumpadavuraiyār, and a fifteenth-century one by Aḍiyārkunallār. As in the North the seven scale degrees were determined by means of the twenty-two *śrutis*. The intervals between the degrees were referred to in both commentaries by terms such as *dvi-śruti* (two-*śruti*), *tri-śruti* (three-*śruti*), and *catuḥ-śruti* (four-*śruti*). Eventually also *pañc-śruti* (five-*śruti*) and *ṣaṭ-śruti* (six-*śruti*) were employed. In southern works there gradually emerged the concept of twelve *svarasthanas* (available places within the octave for the seven basic notes), while northern theorists, still following in the footsteps of Bharata, relied on the *śrutis* which provided twenty-two *svarasthanas*, a cumbersome method that could easily lead to misunderstandings. In all instances the seven basic scale degrees were described by the number of *śrutis*. In the late nineteenth century Raja S. Tagore insisted that the *śrutis* had to be placed above the basic notes, a method that did not clarify but that confused the determination of scale degrees. Śārṅgadeva (thirteenth century) employed nineteen *svarasthanas* within the octave, and other writers referred to different *śruti* numbers. The general number was twenty-two and in the South in later periods twenty-four.

A real history of music of the South begins during the second half of the sixteenth century with Rāmāmātya, who replaced the ancient system (*grāma-mūrchhanā-jāti-paddhati*) with his new *mēḷa-paddhati*. He was the first theorist to try to establish a link between an old theory filled with countless obscure quotations from various sources and the actual performance practice of his own time. His important work, the *Svaramēḷa-kalānidhī*,[7] written in 1550, contains a sentence that shows his attitude toward the music theory before his famous work was created. He states that "the knowledge about music is theoretical and in practical aspects has become obscure and causes contradictory opinions" (I, 24). It may be of some interest to mention that in I (27) Rāmāmātya speaks about his grandfather on the mother's side (mahamata), whose name was Kallapa Deśika. This grandfather may have been identical with Chatura Kallinātha, the author of the famous *Saṅgītarat-nākaratika*, a commentary to the *Saṅgītaratnākara* by Śārṅgadeva.[8] Rāmāmātya aimed at a simplification of the earlier system and employed only seven of the old *vikṛta svaras* (sharp and flat notes), maintaining that the other five were merely enharmonic sounds of them.

Rāmāmātya called his head *rāgas*, *janakas* ("parents") or *mēḷakas* (abbr.: *mēḷas*—"unifiers"). The *mēḷa* is, similar to the North Indian *thāṭa*,[9] a plain seven-tone scale, representing the tone material of a group of subordinate *janya rāgas*. The *mēḷa* serves as an impersonal headline, without strong and weak notes, without any embellishments, and without any *vakra* (zigzag) features, in the process of classifying the *janyas*. Rāmāmātya postulates twenty *mēḷas* and over sixty *janyas*:[10]

MĒḶAS	*JANYAS*
Mukhārī	*Mukhārī* and several *grāma rāgas*
Mālavagaula	*Mālavagaula*, *Lalitā*, *Baulikā*, *Saurāṣṭra*, *Gurjarī*, *Mechabaulī*, *Patamañjarī*, *Guṇḍakriyā*, *Sindhu-rāmakriyā*, *Chāyagaula*, *Kuranjī*, *Kannada-vangāla*, *Mangala*, *Kauśika*, *Malharī*, and others
Śrī-rāga	*Śrīrāga*, *Bhairavī*, *Gaulī*, *Dhanyāsī*, *Śuddha-bhairavī*, *Velāvalī*, *Mālavaśrī*, *Śankarābharana*, *Āndolī*, *Deva-gāndhārī*, *Madhyamādi*, and others
Sāranganāṭa	*Sāranganāṭa*, *Sāverī*, *Sārangabhairavī*, *Naṭṭanārāyaṇī*, *Śuddha-vasanta*, *Pūrvagaula*, *Kuntalavarālī*, *Bhinnaṣaḍja*, *Nārāyaṇī*, and others
Hiṇḍola	*Hiṇḍola*, *Mārga-hiṇḍola*, *Bhūpāla*, and others
Śuddha-rāmakriyā	*Śuddha-rāmakriyā*, *Pāḍi*, *Ārdradeśī*, *Dīpaka*
Deśakṣī	*Deśakṣī*
Kannaḍa-gaula	*Kannaḍa-gaula*, *Ghaṇṭārava*, *Śuddha-vangāla*, *Chāyānāṭa*, *Turuṣka-toḍī*, *Nāgadhvani*, *Devakriyā*, and others
Śuddhanāṭa	*Śuddhanāṭa* and others
Āhirī	*Āhirī* and others
Nādarāmakriyā	*Nādarāmakriyā* and others
Śuddhavarālī	*Śuddhavarālī* and others
Rītigaula	*Rītigaula* and others
Vasanta-bhairavī	*Vasanta-bhairavī*, *Somarāga*, and others
Kedāragaula	*Kedaragaula*, *Nārāyaṇagaula*, and others
Hejjuji	*Hejjuji* and others
Sāmavarālī	*Sāmavarālī* and others
Revagupti	*Revagupti* and others
Sāmanta	*Sāmanta* and others
Kāmbhoji	*Kāmbhoji* and others

The reason for naming the first *janya rāga* after the *mēḷa* is the fact that originally one or the other favorite *rāga* was employed to stand as headline for other derivative *rāgas*. In several instances the *mēḷa-rāgas*, genuine *rāgas* that function as *mēḷas*, can be considered to have been the forerunners of the impersonal *mēḷas*. Rāmāmātya's basic scale of *śuddha* notes (*Mukhārī*) corresponds with the modern *Kanakāṅgī* (C-Db-Ebb-F-G-Ab-Bbb-c). Many of Rāmāmātya's *mēḷas* are identical with those stated in Somanātha's impressive list shown in his *Rāgavibodha*, written in 1609. This important work describes and demonstrates numerous *rāga* types which may have southern or northern origin. The terminology used by the author is southern, but there is some disagreement whether the *rāgas* refer to the North or South.[11]

In the fifth chapter of the *Svaramēḷakalānidhī*, Rāmāmātya informs the reader about some prescribed performance times of the following *rāgas*:[12]

Early morning: *Mallārī*, *Velāvalī*, *Sāverī*, *Lalitā*, *Dhanyāsī*, *Nārāyanī*, *Karnāṭa-vangāla*, *Vasanta-bhairavī*, *Bhūpalī*
Late morning: *Deśakṣī* *Baulī* *Gauṇḍakriyā*
Early afternoon: *Śuddha-rāmakriyā*
Afternoon: *Nāṭī*, *Sāranga-nāṭa*, *Bhairavī*, *Karnāṭa-gauda*, *Hejjuji*, *Madhyamādi*, *Revaguptī*
Late afternoon: *Sāmanta*, *Śuddha-vasanta*, *Kedāragaula*, *Nādarāmakriyā*, *Pāḍī*
Evening: *Mālavagauḍa*, *Śrīrāga*, *Kāṃbhojī*, *Rītigaula*, *Saurāṣṭra*
At all times: *Varālī*, *Mukhārī*, *Mālavaśrī*, *Hiṇdola*, *Sāmavarālī*, *Nāgadhvani*, *Somarāga*, *Ghaṇṭārava*, *Bhinnaṣaḍja*

Written at the same time as Somanātha's *Rāgavibodha* is the *Saṅgīta Sūdha* (or *Saṅgīta Sūdhanidhī*)[13] of 1614, a work by Govinda Dīkṣita (Ayyan). It mentions fifteen *mēḷas* and fifty *rāgas* in its four chapters extant. Although it is written in excellent and superbly polished Sanskrit, a quality usually not found in other works of a similar nature, it shows no progress of Rāmāmātya's ideas. The author returns to earlier theoretical considerations and quotes frequently and extensively from Dattila, Nārada, Kohala, Mataṅga, Bharata, all the way up beyond Śārṅgadeva to Kesava, Kallinātha, and others. Even the old terminology is employed again. Among these quotations appears a reference to a fourteenth-century source, a *Saṅgīta Sāra* by a certain Vidyārana. It mentions the term *mēḷadhikara*, about two hundred years before Rāmāmātya allegedly invented and, to a certain degree, elaborated the concept of *mēḷa*.

Noticeable progress in the evolution of Carnatic

music was made by Veṅkaṭamakhin in his *Caturdaṇḍi Prakāśika.*[14] This work was written in Sanskrit verses in 1620 under the auspices of prince Vijayarāghava Nāyak of Tanjore. Veṅkaṭamakhin was the son of Govinda Dīkṣita and lived, like his father, in Tanjore. He was no innovator in the determination of the scale degrees. His *śuddha* notes are again those of *mēḷa Mukhārī*, and his *vikṛta* notes are *sādhāraṇa* and *antara GA* (Eb and E), *varali* (or *prati*) *MA* (F#), and *kaiśika* and *kākalī NI* (Bb and B). In *RI* and *DHA* forms he uses the terms *pañcśruti* (five-*śruti*) and *ṣaṭśruti* (six-*śruti*). He also substitutes *catuḥśruti* (four-*śruti*) for *pañcśruti*, a matter of little or no consequence to the performing musician. But he does make a distinction between the *pañcśruti* and *ṣaṭśruti* intervals. For instance, the *pañcśruti DHA* in *rāga Deśakṣī* and the *ṣaṭśruti DHA* in *rāga Nāṭa* represent different pitches although according to Veṅkaṭamakhin they differ only by one *śruti*. It is probable that Veṅkaṭamakhin used the old *śruti* measurements as a more or less handy tool for his descriptions without aiming at mathematical and acoustical accuracy. An important point in his work is his use of twelve *svarasthanas* in the octave:

SA	e.g.,	C	
Śuddha RI		Db	
Śuddha GA or *catuḥśruti RI* or *pañcśruti RI*		Ebb	(D)
Sādhāraṇa GA or *ṣaṭśruti RI*		Eb	(D#)
Antara GA		E	
MA		F	
Varali or *prati MA*		F#	
PA		G	
Śuddha DHA		Ab	
Śuddha NI or *catuḥśruti DHA* or *pañcśruti DHA*		Bbb	(A)
Kaiśika NI or *ṣaṭśruti DHA*		Bb	(A#)
Kākalī NI		B	

The most important feature of the *Caturdaṇḍī Prakāśika* appears in chapter IV (slokas 81-92), in which the author states that he has created a system of 72 *janaka mēḷas* and that not even Śiva could find any fault with it. He remarks that in the formation of the *mēḷas* all 72 permutations of notes are unnecessary, because only several *mēḷas* are in general use. Thus, although he drafts the outlines of all 72 *mēḷas* (without establishing all their names), he describes the following nineteen in the following manner:

	SA	RI	GA	MA	PA	DHA	NI
Mukhārī	C	*śuddha* Db	*śuddha* Ebb	F	G	*śuddha* Ab	*śuddha* Bbb
Sāma-varāli	C	*śuddha* Db	*sādh.* Eb	F	G	*śuddha* Ab	*kākalī* B
Bhūpāla	C	*śuddha* Db	*sādh.* Eb	F	G	*śuddha* Ab	*kaiśika* Bb
Hejjuji	C	*śuddha* Db	*antara* E	F	G	*śuddha* Ab	*śuddha* Bbb
Vasanta-bhairavī	C	*śuddha* Db	*antara* E	F	G	*śuddha* Ab	*kaiśika* Bb
Gauḷa	C	*śuddha* Db	*antara* E	F	G	*śuddha* Ab	*kākalī* B
Bhairavī	C	5-*śruti* D	*sādh.* Eb	F	G	*śuddha* Ab	*kaiśika* Bb
Āhirī	C	5-*śruti* D	*sādh.* Eb	F	G	*śuddha*	*kaiśika* Bb
Śrīrāga	C	5-*śruti* D	*sadh.* Eb	F	G	5-*śruti* A	*kaiśika* Bb
Kāṃbhojī	C	5-*śruti* D	*antara* E	F	G	5-*śruti* A	*kaiśika* Bb
Śankarā-bharana	C	5-*śruti* D	*antara* E	F	G	5-*śruti* A	*kākalī* B
Sāmanta	C	5-*śruti* D	*antara* E	F	G	6-*śruti* A#	*kākalī* B
Deśākṣī	C	6-*śruti* D#	*antara* E	F	G	5-*śruti* A	*kākalī* B
Nāṭa	C	6-*śruti* D#	*antara* E	F	G	6-*śruti* A#	*kākalī* B
Śuddha-varālī	C	*śuddha* Db	*śuddha* Ebb	*varali* F#	G	*śuddha* Ab	*kākalī* B
Pantu-varālī	C	*śuddha* Db	*sādh.* Eb	*varali* F#	G	*śuddha* Ab	*kākalī* B
Śuddha-rāmakriyā	C	*śuddha* Db	*antara* E	*varali* F#	G	*śuddha* Ab	*kākalī* B
Simharava (created by Veṅkaṭamakhin)	C	5-*śruti* D	*sādh.* Eb	*varali* F#	G	5-*śruti* A	*kaiśika* Bb
Kalyāṇī	C	5-*sruti* D	*antara* E	*varali* F#	G	5-*śruti* A	*kākalī* B

Veṅkaṭamakhin is one of the few theorists of South India who still indicate in a number of *rāgas* the formerly important notes (*graha*, *aṃśa*, and *nyāsa*). He states, however, that these notes are not and need not be respected any more.

Later musicians and writters have erroneously ascribed to Veṅkaṭamakhin the invention and use of the *kaṭapayādi* prefixes (see below). It can be assumed that musicians before Veṅkaṭamakhin may have had similar ideas toward the creation of an orderly system of *mēḷas*. In 1934, during one of the conferences of the Music Academy of Madras, Nazir Uddin Khan of Lahore informed the assembled scholars that "something like the system of Veṅkaṭamakhin" had already existed in the fourteenth century. Nazir Uddin was able to show that the names of the 72 *mēḷas* did indeed appear in the texts of four *dhrūpads*[15] created by the poet-singer Bijou Naik, a southerner who had come to the North and served at the court of Alla-ud-din (1296-1316). N. S. Ramachandran[16] reports that another source, a work of a certain Somanārya, probably a contemporary of Naik, also deals with the names of the 72 *mēḷas*.[17]

Veṅkaṭamakhin's nineteen *mēḷas* represented no newly created forms. They were genuine *rāgas*, the majority of which did not have *krama sampūrṇa* (straight seven-tone) scales in ascent and descent. Veṅkaṭamakhin's important step was his suggesting the feasibility of creating 72 *mēḷas* by applying chromatic alterations of five scale degrees in an orderly rotating manner. He never went any further than to propose this method. Nevertheless, he indicated the spots where in his proposed system of 72 *mēḷas* his nineteen *mēḷas* had to be placed:
1. *Mukhārī*; 3. *Sāmavarālī*; 8. *Bhūpāla*; 13. *Hejjuji*; 14. *Vasanta-bhairavī*; 15. *Gauḷa*; 20. *Bhairavī*; 21. *Āhirī*; 22. *Śrī*; 28. *Kāmbhojī*; 29. *Śankarābharaṇa*; 30. *Sāmanta*; 35. *Deśakṣī*; 36. *Nāṭa*; 39. *Śuddhavarālī*; 45. *Pantuvarālī*; 51. *Śuddharāmakriyā*; 58. *Simharava*; 65. *Kalyāṇī*.

The elaboration and the naming of all the 72 *mēḷas* were made by one Muddu Veṅkaṭamakhin, probably a grandson of the master, who "beginning [the list of *meḷas*] with *Kanakāmbari*, catalogued [them] in the *anubandha* (appendix) of the published edition of the *Caturdaṇḍi Prakāśikā*, in addition to certain *rāgas* that were not current in Veṅkaṭamakhin's time, but had since invaded the South."[18]

This system and a second one to be mentioned below did not become popular immediately. There were numerous musicians and writers who opposed this "dehumanized" manner of artificially creating scales and ignoring the many subtleties, the real refinement of the *rāgas*. The storm of objections abated to some degree when it became known that the great Tyāgarāja (1767-1847) used some of the new scales in his (approximately) two-thousand *kīrtaṇas* and *kṛtis*. Originally these songs were transmitted from mouth to ear. Some songs have been preserved by the master's pupils in notated form on cadjan leaves (palm-leaf manuscripts, preserved in the Adyar Library, Madras) and in recent time have appeared in print, mostly in Tamil notation. In the palm-leaf manuscripts the *mēḷa* names often appear in distorted forms, many beginning with the letter R. Instead of *Kharaharapriya* is written *Rakhapriyaraya*; instead of *Kīravāṇi* appears *Rakiniva*; instead of *Mararanjani* stands *Ramam-ṅijama*; instead of *Charukeśi* appears *Rukechasi*; and so forth. Distortions of this kind destroy the *kaṭapayādi* organization and show that the writers of the palm-leaf manuscripts aimed at keeping the correct *mēḷa* names secret, an attitude of concealment that can be observed in various musical cultures of the East.

Śrī Tyāgarāja's use of some of Veṅkaṭamakhin's scales was carried on by his contemporaries and followers, such as Śyāma Śāstri (1763-1827), Muthuswami Dīkṣitar (1775-1835), and others. The characteristic of Veṅkaṭamakhin's system was the fact that each of his *mēḷa-rāgas* could employ the seven notes within the octave not necessarily in a strict step-by-step scale form.

A second system that later was to become widely popular showed the 72 *mēḷas* in rigid scale form. These scales were no *rāgas* but, as already mentioned, served as headlines for groups of *janyas* that employed fully or partly the materials of the *mēḷas*. The *mēḷa* names were given *kaṭapayādi* prefixes (to be shown below). This system appeared for the first time in an unusual work called the *Saṃgraha Cūḍa Maṇi*, probably written by one Govinda in the late eighteenth or early nineteenth century. Almost nothing is known about it.[19] The writer of its preface, T. R. Śrinivāsa Ayyangār, reports that Pandit Subrahmaṇya Śāstri (the editor) had found the manuscript written in Telugu script on palm leaves. The first printed edition had been provided with a second part, a *Lakṣaṇa Gīta*, presentations of the *mēḷas* in the form of melody patterns that can serve as material for the composition of real songs. I have transcribed into western staff notation specimens (frequently I have used only fragments) of melody patterns from Govinda's disputed work. This source, as already stated, originated two or three hundred years ago and when the Adyar Library (Madras) made it accessible in Sanskrit (only the Preface is in English) in 1938, it appeared without any copyright restrictions, a fact that deserves the gratitude of researchers. However, in order to assist the reader in finding the specimens in the publication of the Adyar Library, I have provided all my subsequent (now transcribed) quotations from this work with the abbreviation SMC and the appropriate page numbers.

Despite the numerous objections raised by various scholars to this work, it is indeed the first tangible and distinct source of the *Kanakāṅgī-Ratnāṅgī* system which today is the generally accepted basis of Carnatic art music. The theoretical works of the later nineteenth century and those of the present time offer no new information and need not be mentioned in this brief survey. The only exception is the large number of books and articles written by Professor P. Sambamoorthy of Madras.

Before describing the *Kanakāṅgī-Ratnāṅgī* system, the *kaṭapayādi* prefixes have to be considered. Although the *kaṭapayādi sankhya* (*kaṭapayādi* numbering) was described in my MNO (pp. 204-7), I have taken the liberty of presenting it again for the convenience of the reader.

Between every *mēḷa* name and its number in the *Kanakāṅgī-Ratnāṅgī* system exists a close relationship. If a traveller from the West asks a southern musician, not necessarily a highly educated person, for the correct number of a certain *mēḷa*, the musician will, with very little hesitation, invariably come forth with the accurate number. This feat, which first was admired as a great mnemonic achievement, is based upon an ingenious system. It rests upon the proper order of consonants as they appear in the Sanskrit alphabet, an alphabet that serves as foundation for all other Indian alphabets. In contrast to European alphabets its order of consonants consists of four groups:

(a) *Kādinava* group:

K	*KH*	*G*	*GH*	*NG*	*CH*	*CHH*	*J*	*JH*	(*JN*)
1	2	3	4	5	6	7	8	9	0

(b) *Ṭādinava* group:

Ṭ	*ṬH*	*Ḍ*	*ḌH*	*Ṇ*	*T*	*TH*	*D*	*DH*	(*N*)
1	2	3	4	5	6	7	8	9	0

(c) *Pādipancha* group:

P	*PH*	*B*	*BH*	*M*
1	2	3	4	5

(d) *Yādiashṭa* group:

Y	*R*	*L*	*V*	*S*	*SH*	*S*	*H*	(*LH*	*KSH*	*DNY*)
1	2	3	4	5	6	7	8	0	0	0

The first letters of the four groups, *ka*, *ṭa*, *pa*, and *ya* have been used to form the term *kaṭapayādi*. The letters in each of the four groups are numbered: in the first two groups from 1 to 9, in the third from 1 to 5, and in the fourth from 1 to 8. Some of the letters at the end of the first, second, and fourth groups are not counted and are provided with the number 0.

The relationship between *mēḷa* number and *mēḷa* name is determined in the following manner: the first two consonants (prefixes) of the *mēḷa* name are taken and their numbers in the alphabet established. It is of no consequence whether the consonants belong to the first, second, third, or fourth groups. These two numbers are then read in reversed order (right to left). These two digits will represent the correct number of the *mēḷa* in the system of the 72. A few examples may illustrate this procedure. Supposing the number of *mēḷa* *Harikāṃbhoji* has to be found. The first letter of the *mēḷa* name is *H*, which is 8 in the *yādiashṭa* group; the second consonant is *R*, which, by chance, is 2 in the same group of letters. If the numbers 8, 2 are reversed, the result is 28, the correct number of *Harikāṃbhoji* is obtained. Another example may be *Kiravāṇī*: *K* is 1 in the *kādinava* group, and *R* is 2 in the *yādiashṭa* group. If the digits 1, 2 are reversed to 21, the correct number of *Kiravāṇī* is established.

Some *mēḷa* names have double consonants in either the first or second syllables. In the following instances the first letter of the double consonants has to be considered:

Chakravāka: *CH* and *K*, 6 1, reversed: 16
Divyamaṇī: *D* and *V*, 8 4, reversed: 48
Viśvambarī: *V* and *Ś*, 4 5, reversed: 54
Śyāmalāṅgī: *Ś* and *M*, 5 5, reversed: 55
Simhendramadhyāma: *S* and *M*, 7 5, reversed: 57
Chitrāmbarī: *CH* and *T*, 6 6, reversed: 66

In the following *mēḷa* names the second letter of each double consonant has to be taken:

Dharmavatī: *DH* and *M*, 9 5, reversed: 59
Gāṅgeyabhūṣaṇī: *G* and *G*, 3 3, reversed: 33
Jhaṅkāradhvanī: *JH* and *K*, 9 1, reversed: 19
Ratnāṅgī: *R* and *N*, 2 0, reversed: 02
Ṣaḍvidhamārgiṇī: *Ṣ* and *V*, 6 4, reversed: 46
Ṣaṇmukhapriyā: *Ṣ* and *MA*, 6 5, reversed: 56
Sūryakānta: *S* and *Y*, 7 1, reversed: 17

The 72 *mēḷas* are organized into twelve *chakras* ("wheels," groups of six scales each, and each *chakra* has its own name. Occasionally six syllables (*pa*, *śrī*, *go*, *bhu*, *ma*, and *sha*) are used that represent the sequence of six *mēḷas* within each *chakra*. When these syllables are combined with the *chakra* names they assist the musician in determining the number of the *mēḷa*. For instance *veda-śrī*: *veda* is the name of the fourth *chakra*, and *śrī* represents its second *mēḷa*. As the first three *chakras* represent eighteen *mēḷas*, *veda-śrī* will refer to the twentieth *mēḷa* (the second *mēḷa* of the fourth *chakra*).

Some writers employed the *kaṭapayādi sankhya* in the determination of rhythmic units in the *tālas* (rhythmic modes), also at times in the numbering of the *śrutis* and in several extra-musical matters. None of these procedures became popular.

The classification of *janya rāgas* subordinated to the *mēḷas* is by far not as distinct as that of the *mēḷas*. Southern music theory generally groups the *janyas* into eight types, not counting those that employ *krama sampūrṇa* (complete, straight seven-tone scales) in ascent and descent. The first type represents *rāgas* with five notes in ascent and descent; the second type has five notes in ascent and six in descent; the third uses five notes in ascent and seven in descent. The fourth, fifth, and sixth types employ six notes in ascent and five, six, and seven notes in descent, respectively. The seventh and eighth types have seven notes in ascent and five and six respectively in descent. This method of classifying the *janyas* is used only for educational purposes. Another grouping of the *janyas* takes into consideration the numbers of *vakra* (zig-zag) features in ascent and descent. Further endeavours to classify the *janyas* combine the numbers of notes in ascent and descent and the various *vakra* features. None of these classifications is used in musical practice. The concepts of strong and weak notes, ornaments, special phrases, etc., play no role in any method of classification.

Below are shown three lists of the 72 *mēḷas*. The first represents the modern system (*Kanakāṅgī-Ratnāṅgī*) in which the *mēḷas* are shown as rigid, "impersonal" seven-tone scale forms (*krama sampūrṇa*), in which the *mēḷa* names are provided with *kaṭapayādi* prefixes. List two shows the earlier 72 *mēḷa-rāgas* (*Kanakāmbarī-Phenadyuti*) in *asampūrṇa* form (containing five, six, also seven notes in ascent or descent, and *vakra* types). Their tone materials do not necessarily appear in step-by-step scale forms and their names are without any *kaṭapayādi* prefixes. List three shows a later version of *asampūrṇa* types provided with *kaṭapayādi* prefixes.

	List I	*List II*	*List III*
	Sampūrṇa mēḷas (The modern system with *kaṭapayādi* prefixes)	*Asampūrna mēla-rāgas* (without *katapayādi* prefixes)	*Asampūrna mēla-rāgas* (with *katapayādi* prefixes)
1.	*Kanakāṅgī*	*Kanakāmbarī*	*Kanakāmbarī*
2.	*Ratnāṅgī*	*Phenadyuti*	*Phenadyuti*
3.	*Gānamūrti*	*Sāmavarāli*	*Gānasāmavārali*
4.	*Vanaspāti*	*Bhānumātī*	*Bhānumātī*
5.	*Mānavātī*	*Manoranjanī*	*Manoranjanī*
6.	*Tānarūpi*	*Tanukīrti*	*Tanukīrti*
7.	*Senāvati*	*Senāgraṇī*	*Senāgraṇī*
8.	*Hanumaṭṭoḍi*	*Toḍi*	*Janatoḍi*
9.	*Dhenukā*	*Bhinnaṣaḍja*	*Dhunibhinna-ṣaḍja*
10.	*Nāṭakapriyā*	*Nāṭābharaṇam*	*Nāṭābharaṇam*
11.	*Kokilapriyā*	*Kokilārāvam*	*Kokilārāvam*
12.	*Rūpāvatī*	*Raupyanāgam*	*Rūpāvatī*
13.	*Gāyakapriya*	*Hejjuji*	*Geyahejjaji*
14.	*Vakulābharanam*	*Vasantabhairavi*	*Vāṭivasanta-bhairavi*
15.	*Māyāmālavagauḷa*	*Mālavagauḷa*	*Māyāmālavagauḷa*
16.	*Chakravākam*	*Vegavāhiṇi*	*Toyavegavāhiṇi*
17.	*Sūryakāntam*	*Supradīpam*	*Chhāyavati*
18.	*Hāṭakāmbari*	*Śuddhamālavi*	*Jayaśuddha-mālavi*
19.	*Jhaṅkāradhvanī*	*Jhaṅkāra-bhramarī*	*Jhaṅkāra-bhramarī*
20.	*Nāṭabhairavī*	*Bhairavī*	*Nārirītigauḷa*
21.	*Kiravāṇī*	*Kiraṇāvali*	*Kiraṇāvali*
22.	*Kharaharapriyā*	*Śrīrāga*	*Śrīrāga*
23.	*Gaurīmanoharī*	*Velāvali*	*Gaurīvelāvali*
24.	*Varuṇapriyā*	*Vīravasantam*	*Vīravasantam*
25.	*Mārarañjanī*	*Śarāvati*	*Śarāvati*
26.	*Chārukeśī*	*Taraṅgiṇī*	*Taraṅgiṇī*
27.	*Sarasāṅgī*	*Surasena*	*Saurasena*
28.	*Harikāṃbhojī*	*Kāṃbhojī*	*Harikedāragauḷa*
29.	*Dhīraśankarā-bharaṇa*	*Śankarābharaṇam*	*Dhīraśankarā-bharaṇa*
30.	*Nāgānandinī*	*Sāmantam*	*Nāgābharaṇam*
31.	*Yāgapriyā*	*Kalahaṃsa*	*Kalāvati*
32.	*Rāgavardhanī*	*Rāgachūḍāmani*	*Rāgachūḍāmani*
33.	*Gāṅgeyabhūṣaṇī*	*Gāṅgātaraṅgiṇī*	*Gāṅgātaraṅgiṇī*
34.	*Vāgadhīśvarī*	*Chhāyānāṭa*	*Bhogachhāyānāṭa*
35.	*Śūlinī*	*Deśākṣī*	*Sailadeśākṣī*

	List I	*List II*	*List III*
36.	*Chalanāṭa*	*Nāṭa*	*Chalanāṭa*
37.	*Sālagam*	*Sālava*	*Saugandhinī*
38.	*Jalārṇavam*	*Jaganmohana*	*Jaganmohana*
39.	*Jhālavarāli*	*Varāli*	*Dhālivarāli*
40.	*Navanītam*	*Nabhomani*	*Nabhomani*
41.	*Pāvani*	*Prabhāvati*	*Kumbhinī*
42.	*Raghupriyā*	*Raghulīla*	*Ravikriyā*
43.	*Gavāmbodhi*	*Gīrvāna*	*Gīrvāni*
45.	*Śubhapantu-varālī*	*Pantuvarālī*	*Śaivapantu-varālī*
46.	*Śaḍvidhamārgiṇī*	*Tivravāhini*	*Sthavarājam*
47.	*Suvarṇāṅgī*	*Sauvīra*	*Sauvīra*
48.	*Divyamaṇī*	*Jīvantini*	*Jivantikā*
49.	*Dhavalāmbarī*	*Dhavalāṅgī*	*Dhavalāṅgam*
50.	*Nāmanārāyaṇī*	*Narmada*	*Nāmadeśi*
51.	*Kāmavardhanī*	*Rāmakriyā*	*Kāśirāmakriyā*
52.	*Rāmapriyā*	*Rāmamanohari*	*Rāmamanohari*
53.	*Gamanaśrama*	*Gamakakriyā*	*Gamakakriyā*
54.	*Viśvambarī*	*Vaiśākha*	*Vamśavatī*
55.	*Śyāmalāṅgī*	*Śāmala*	*Śāmala*
56.	*Śaṇmukhapriyā*	*Trimūrti*	*Chāmaram*
57.	*Simhendra-madhyāma*	*Sīmantinī*	*Sumadyuti*
58.	*Hemavatī*	*Simhārava*	*Deśisimhāravam*
59.	*Dharmavatī*	*Dhaumyarāga*	*Dhāmavatī*
60.	*Nītimatī*	*Nishādarāga*	*Nishādam*
61.	*Kāntāmaṇi*	*Kuntala*	*Kuntala*
62.	*Riṣabhapriyā*	*Ratnabhānu*	*Ratipriyā*
63.	*Latāṅgī*	*Gotrāri*	*Gītapriyā*
64.	*Vāchaspati*	*Bushāvali*	*Būshāvati*
65.	*Mechakalyāṇī*	*Kalyāṇī*	*Śāntakalyāṇī*
66.	*Chitrāmbarī*	*Chaturaṅgiṇī*	*Chaturaṅgiṇī*
67.	*Sucharitra*	*Satyavati*	*Santānamanjari*
68.	*Jyotisvarūpini*	*Jotishmati*	*Jotirāga*
69.	*Dhātuvardhani*	*Dhautapancham*	*Dhautapanchama*
70.	*Nāsikabhūṣaṇī*	*Nāsāmaṇi*	*Nāsāmaṇi*
71.	*Kosalam*	*Kusumāvali*	*Kusumākara*
72.	*Rasikapriyā*	*Rasamanjarī*	*Rasamanjarī*

All subsequent presentations and discussions of *mēḷas* and *rāgas* refer to the first list, the widely popular *Kanakāṅgī-Ratnāṅgī* system of the present time.

As already mentioned, the 72 *mēḷas* are organized into twelve *chakras*, each containing six *mēḷas*:

Chakras:		Mēḷas:
I.	*Indu chakra*	1 - 6
II.	*Netra chakra*	7 - 12
III.	*Agni chakra*	13 - 18
IV.	*Veda chakra*	19 - 24
V.	*Bāṇa chakra*	25 - 30
VI.	*Rutu chakra*	31 - 36
VII.	*Rishi chakra*	37 - 42
VIII.	*Vāsu chakra*	43 - 48
IX.	*Brahma chakra*	49 - 54
X.	*Diśi chakra*	55 - 60
XI.	*Rūdra chakra*	61 - 66
XII.	*Āditya chakra*	67 - 72

The names of the twelve *chakras* are chosen in such a manner that they can serve the musician as a mnemonic device toward establishing the number of each *chakra*. The word *Indu* signifies the moon, a single phenomenon; hence *Indu* means number one, or the first *chakra*. *Netra* means the (two) eyes, hence it implies the second *chakra*. *Agni* ("fire") refers to the three sacred fires (*agni trayam*); *Veda* signifies the four Vedas; *Bāṇa* points to the five Banas of Manmatha; *Rutu* to the six seasons; there are seven *Rishis*, eight *Vāsus*, nine *Prajāpatis* (*Brahmas*), ten *Diśis* (directions), eleven *Rūdras*, and twelve *Ādityas* (suns) as mentioned in the legends (*pūraṇas*).

Instead of outlining the lengthy methods that theorists employed for the determination of the degrees of the 72 scales, a summarizing simplification will achieve the same results as will be shown in the two tables seen below. All twelve *chakras*, that is, all 72 *mēḷas*, have the following notes in their lower tetrachords. It may be stated here again that the unchanged notes of the first six *chakras* (*mēḷas* 1-36) are C, F, and G, while the unchanged notes of the second six *chakras* (*mēḷas* 37-72) are C, F#, and G.

Chakra I:	C	Db	Ebb	F	*Chakra* VII:	C	Db	Ebb	F#
Chakra II:	C	Db	Eb	F	*Chakra* VIII:	C	Db	Eb	F#
Chakra III:	C	Db	E	F	*Chakra* IX:	C	Db	E	F#
Chakra IV:	C	D	Eb	F	*Chakra* X:	C	D	Eb	F#
Chakra V:	C	D	E	F	*Chakra* XI:	C	D	E	F#
Chakra VI:	C	D#	E	F	*Chakra* XII:	C	D#	E	F#

The scales of the first to the sixth *mēḷas*, within each *chakra*, change in the upper tetrachord in the following manner:

Chakra:

I	II	III	IV	V	VI	VII	VIII	IX	X	XI	XII				
Mēḷas:															
1	7	13	19	25	31	37	43	49	55	61	67:	G	Ab	Bbb	c
2	8	14	20	26	32	38	44	50	56	62	68:	G	Ab	Bb	c
3	9	15	21	27	33	39	45	51	57	63	69:	G	Ab	B	c
4	10	16	22	28	34	40	46	52	58	64	70:	G	A	Bb	c
5	11	17	23	29	35	41	47	53	59	65	71:	G	A	B	c
6	12	18	24	30	36	42	48	54	60	66	72:	G	A#	B	c

The two foregoing tables, which I have presented for the first time in my MNO (p. 202), will provide the necessary means to enable the reader to determine the scale degrees of any of the 72 *mēḷas*. For instance, if the scale of *mēḷa* 21 is to be ascertained, the second table shows that the 21. *mēḷa* (*Kiravāṇī*) belongs in the fourth *chakra*. The first table presents the notes of the lower tetrachord, placed to the right side of number IV: C D Eb F. The note G remains unaltered throughout the system. The notes of the upper tetrachord of the 21. *mēḷa* appear in the second table at the right end of the third line, in which the number 21 appears: G Ab B c. Thus the entire scale of *mēḷa* 21 is C D Eb F G Ab B c.

The formal structures of art songs (and instrumental pieces) and the various *tālas* (rhythmic modes) have been discussed by me elsewhere (MNO, p. 461, n.226; and pp. 188-94). As they have no direct pertinence to the *rāga* material under consideration, they have been omitted in this study.

THE RĀGAS OF SOUTH INDIA

MĒḶAS AND JANYA RĀGAS

In the following survey each *mēḷa* (with a few exceptions) is followed by brief descriptions of its subordinate *janya rāgas*. The quantity of *janyas* is a comparatively good indicator of the importance and popularity of the primary *mēḷa*. Some of the frequently performed *mēḷa-rāgas* have large numbers of *janyas*, such as *mēḷas* 8, 15, 20, 22, 28, and 29. These basic scales and their subordinate forms are particularly favored by South Indian performers and their audiences. Other scales, particularly those of *mēḷas* with a small number of *janyas* enjoy little popularity and are often described as being too artificial.

As already indicated, the *Saṃgraha Cūḍa Maṇi* (SCM) is followed by a *Lakṣaṇa Gīta*, a section dealing with melody patterns that can be used for the composition of genuine song melodies. Each melody pattern appears in *trisra jāti* of *triputa tāla*, a rhythmic mode with seven metric units (3+2+2). If the word *triputa* is used without any *jāti* indication, it invariably signifies the *trisra* form (see MNO, 193-4).

In my descriptions of *rāgas* reference to a specific *janya rāga* is made in the following manner: for instance, *janya rāga Mitrarañjāni* will be represented by the numbers 25 and 16. The first number (25) indicates the primary *mēḷa*, and the second number (16) shows the place where *Mitrarañjāni* appears among the various *janyas* of *mēḷa* 25.

A systematic transliteration of *raga* names, names of authors, titles of books, and various other terms, poses a problem, because in sources written in the English language, such as the compilations of Sambamoorthy and Chitti Babu Naidu, the spelling of numerous *rāga* names differs. Similar phenomena occur also in Sanskrit, Marathi, Tamil, and Telugu where the discrepancies generally concern the transliteration or interpretation of certain vowels (long or short), of consonants (*sh*, *ṣ*, *ś*, *ksh*, *kṣ*, *m*, *ṃ*, *ṁ*, *n*, *ṇ*, *ṅ*, *l*, *ḷ*, *ch*, *c*, *chh*, and others), the use or omission of end syllables, and the linking or not linking of constituent words that form several *rāga* names. One can observe *Śuddha Mālavi*, *Śuddhamālavi*, *Shuddha Mālavi*, or *Shuddhamālavi*; *Cintāmaṇi* or *Chintāmaṇi*; *chāyā* or *chhāyā* (where the ch sound is aspirated); *bhūṣaṇi* or *bhūshaṇi*; *niṣāda(m)* or *nishāda*; *Bhairavi* or *Bhairavī*; *Simantini* or *Simandini*; *Vasant*, *Vasanta*, or *Vasantam*; and numerous other instances. Although all *e*'s and *o*'s are considered long (unless specially marked) I have indicated this somewhat unnecessary feature, imitating the method of transliteration employed in sources written in English by Indian scholars.

The terminology used in the following descriptions has been reduced to a minimum. Beside the tone names I have used the terms *sampūrṇa*, *asampūrṇa*, *krama sampūrṇa*, and *vakra*. These terms have been explained in the foregoing Introduction. I have used the term *vakra* in all instances where the ascending or descending lines are to be performed in a zigzag manner, although Indian music theory employs other terms (for instance *bhadrā*, which is used to indicate brief passages such as CDC, DED, EFE, etc.).

Chakra I

1. *MĒḶA KANAKĀṄGĪ*

Kanakāṅgī represents the modern *śuddha* scale, the "natural" notes of Karnatic music. Veṅkaṭamakhin calls this *rāga Kanakāmbarī* and equates it with the ancient *Mukhārī*, one of his nineteen *mēḷas* which were well known in his time. The western way of notating the *Kanakāṅgī* scale is (C-Db-Ebb, etc.). If treated as a *raga*, *Kanakāṅgī* assumes some modifications: according to Veṅkaṭamakhin the notes *GA* (Ebb) and *NI* (Bbb) are avoided in ascent:

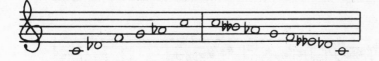

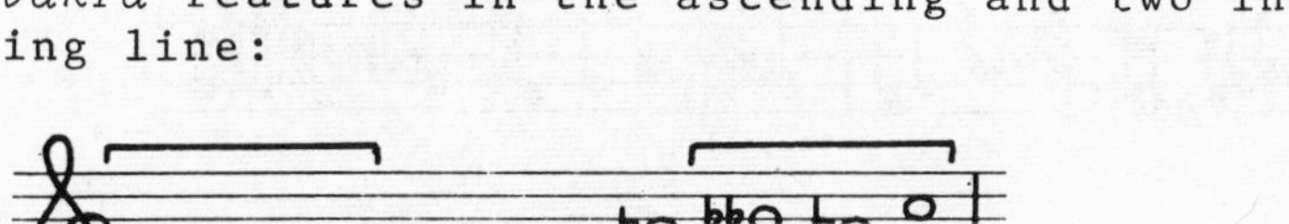

Govinda (SCM), however, states that the *sampūrṇa* form is employed in both ascent and descent with two *vakra* features in the ascending and two in the descending line:

Kanakāṅgī, as a *rāga*, is rarely performed. Its performance time is supposed to be in the morning. Occasionally musicians state that the notes *RI* (Db), *MA* (F), and *NI* (Bbb) have some importance. The note *NI* (Bbb), forbidden in ascent by Veṅkaṭamakhin, does appear in the modern form of the *rāga* and is often executed with a slight vibrato.

The following specimen, a fragment, composed by Śrī Tyāgarāja, is the only known song (*kṛti*) in the *rāga*. Its text, not shown here, is in Sanskrit. The fragment shows the *pallavi*, which is followed immediately by a *charana*. The *anupallavi* is omitted. After the *charana* the *pallavi* has to be repeated.

KANAKĀṄGĪ (*Ādi-tāla*)

Pallavi

Charana

Janya Rāgas of the First Mēḷa

The general opinion is that no *janyas* are ascribed to the first *mēḷa*. The *Lakṣaṇa Gīta* (SCM) mentions two, and during the last two centuries several additional *janya rāgas* have appeared under the heading of *Kanakāṅgī*, all of which are little known and rarely performed.

(1) *Kanakāmbarī*

As stated before, *Kanakāmbarī* is Veṅkaṭamakhin's name of Govinda's *Kanakāṅgī*, and the scales of the two *rāgas* are identical. It can appear with one of the following forms of ascent:

(a)

(b)
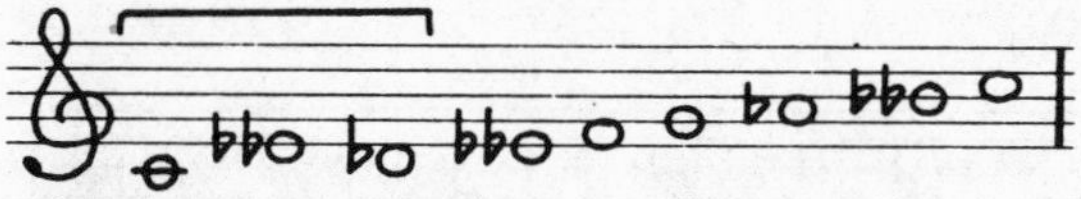

(c)

The descent is *krama sampūrṇa* in all instances:

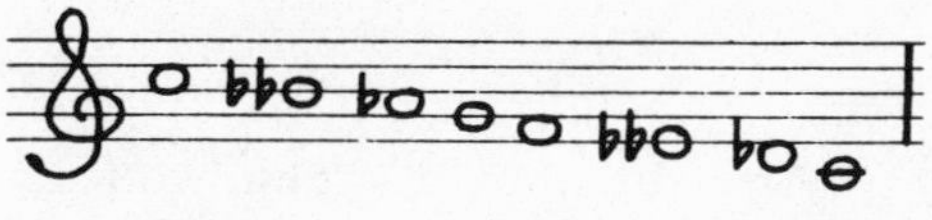

The list of scales appended to the *Bāhattara Mēḷakartā* of Veṅkaṭa Kavi (also listed in SCM) shows the following *Kanakāmbarī* material with the two *Kanakāṅgī vakra* features in ascent:

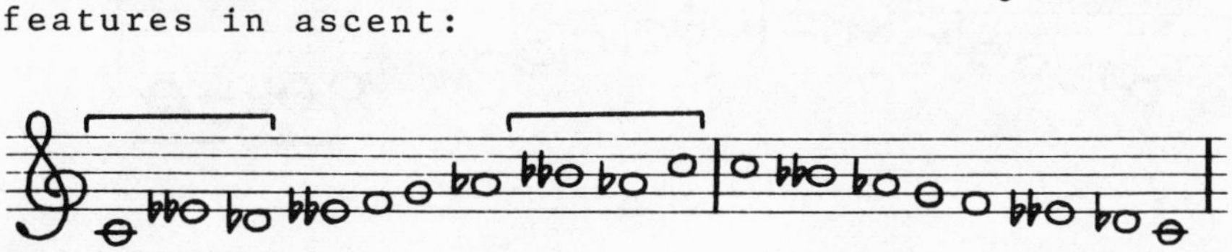

The following melody specimen is taken from SCM, 2.

KANAKĀMBARĪ RĀGA (*Triputa-tāla*),

(2) *Śuddhamukhārī*

This is the second *janya rāga* listed in the SCM. Its scale is *krama sampūrṇa* in ascent and avoids the note *PA* (G) in descent.

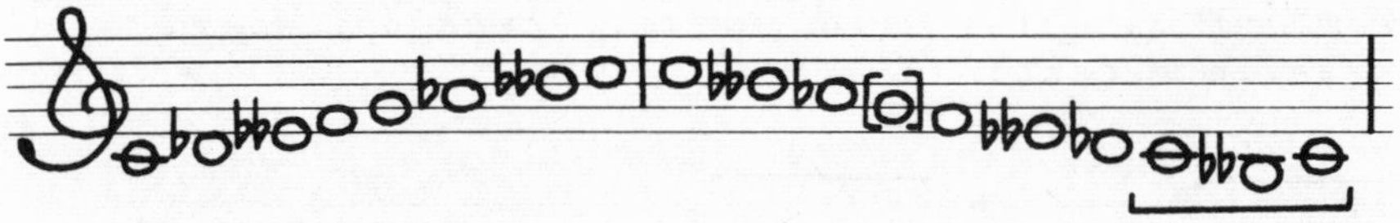

ŚUDDHAMUKHĀRĪ (*Triputa-tāla*) SCM, 2-3

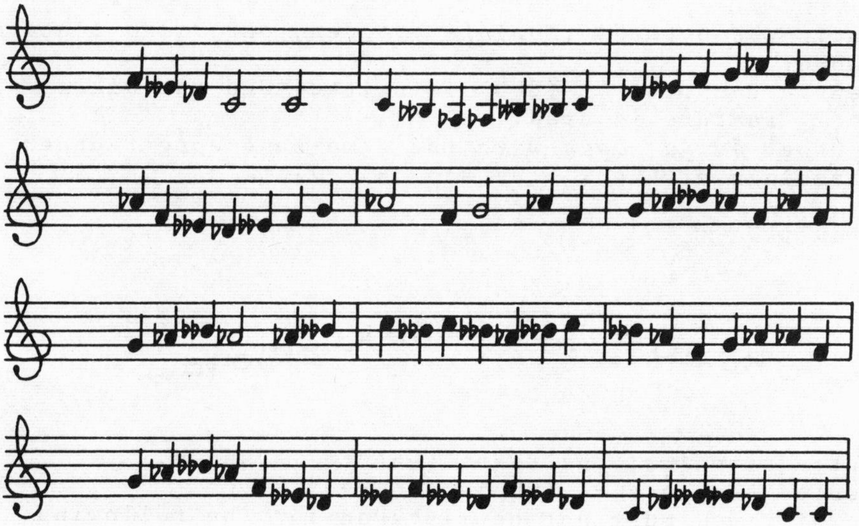

Another *janya rāga* with the name *Mukhārī* appears under the heading of the 22. *mēḷa* (99).

(3) *Auravaśēyapriya*

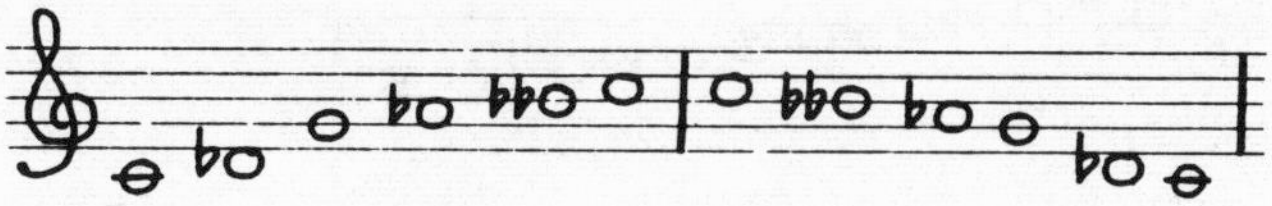

The notes *GA* (Ebb) and *MA* (F) are avoided entirely.

(4) *Bhanupriya*

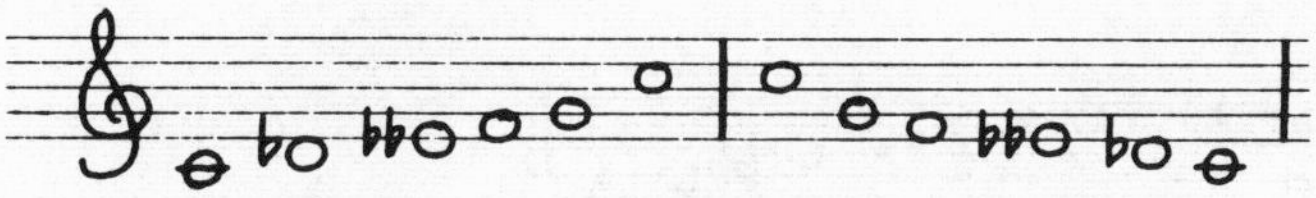

The notes *DHA* (Ab) and *NI* (Bbb) are avoided entirely.

Another *rāga* with the same name appears under the heading of the 21. *mēḷa* (6); (cf. SSPS as quoted in SD I, 49).

(5) *Bhōga Cintāmaṇi* (*Chintāmaṇi*)

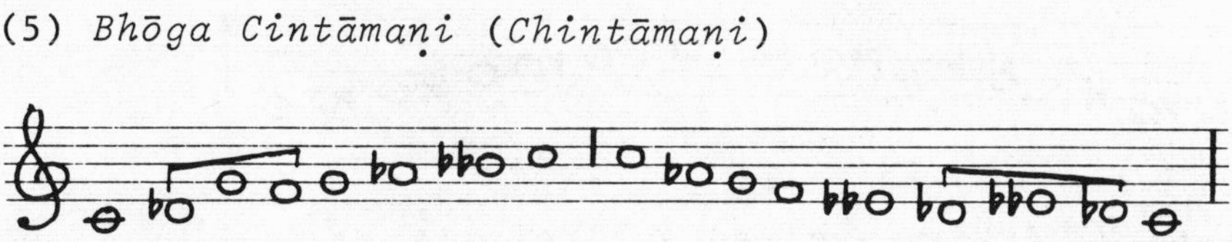

Ascent: the note *GA* (Ebb) is avoided; one *vakra* feature is shown.
Descent: the note *NI* (Bbb) is omitted and one *vakra* (*bhadrā*) feature is used.

Other *janya rāgas* with the same name appear under the headings of the 7. (3) and 56. (7) *mēḷas*.

(6) *Ḍaulikā*

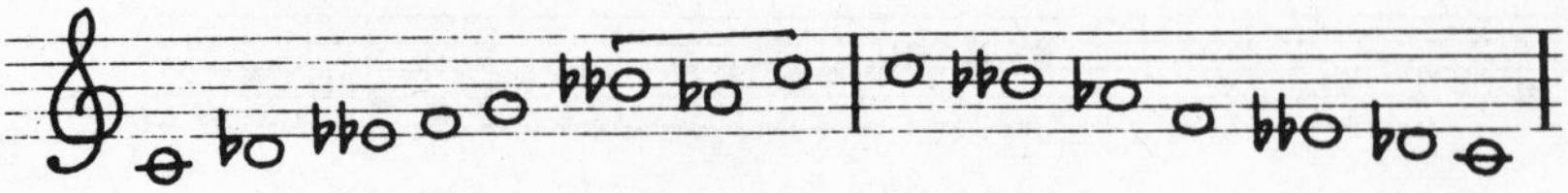

Ascent: *sampūrṇa*; one *vakra* feature is shown.
Descent: the note *PA* (G) is avoided.

This *rāga* must not be mistaken for the following *janya Dhaulikā*:

(7) *Dhaulikā*

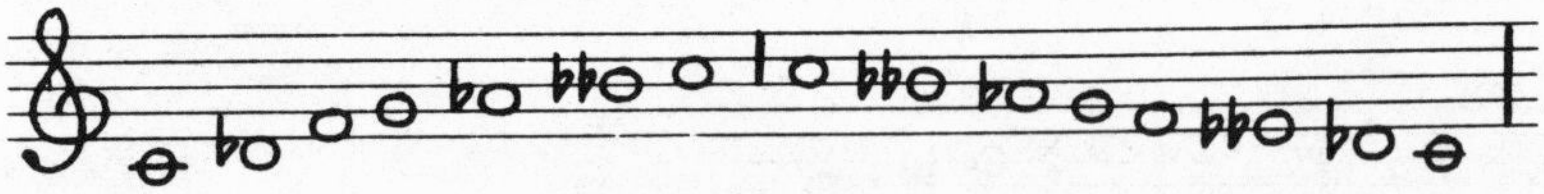

Ascent: the note *GA* (Ebb) is avoided.
Descent: *krama sampūrṇa*.

(8) *Dokā*

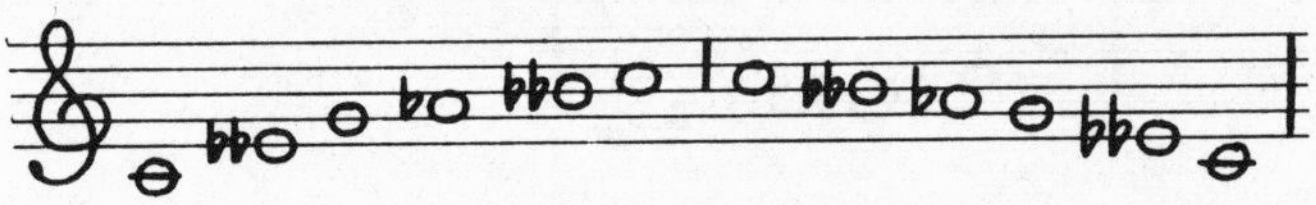

The notes *RI* (Db) and *MA* (F) are avoided entirely.

(9) *Gautami*

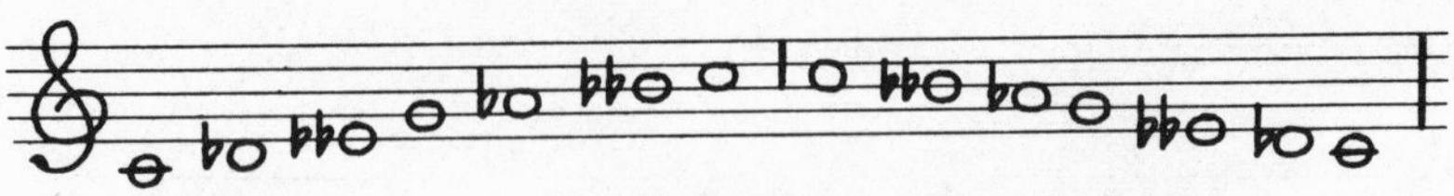

The note *MA* (F) is avoided entirely.

(10) *Indrapriya*

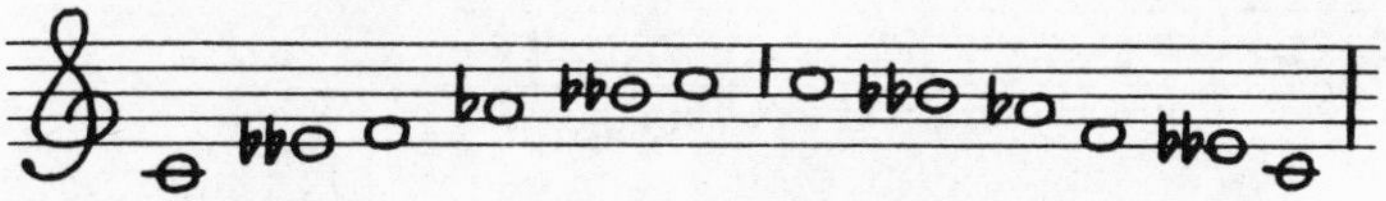

The notes *RI* (Db) and *PA* (G) are avoided entirely.
There are two other *janya rāgas*, both called *Indrapriya* that are listed under the headings of the 24.(14) and 54.(8) *mēḷas*.

(11) *Kamalini*

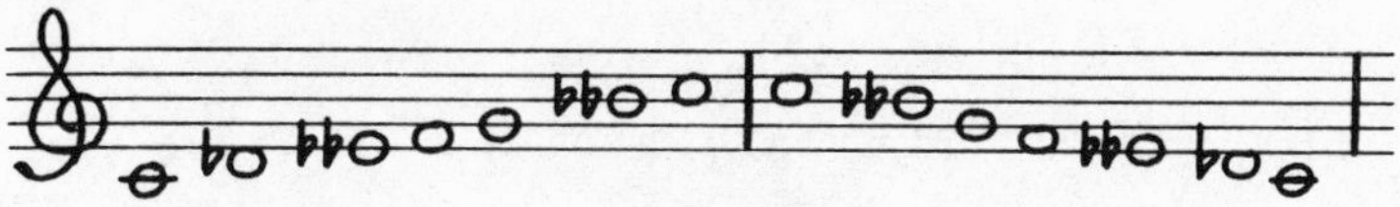

The note *DHA* (Ab) is avoided entirely.
Another *rāga* with the same name appears under the heading of the 30. *mēḷa* (12).

(12) *Kāntāraka Pāṇi*

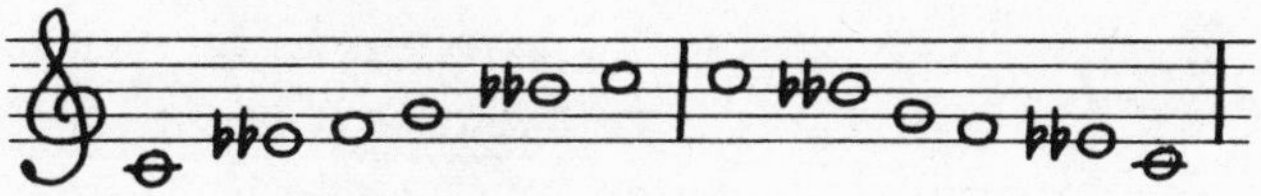

The notes *RI* (Db) and *DHA* (Ab) are avoided entirely. A remark in SD (II, 299) states that "since *śuddha gāndhāra* [Ebb] and *śuddha nishāda* [Bbb] will in effect be the equivalents of *chatuśśruti RI* [D] and *chatuśśruti DHA* [A] this *rāga* when rendered will sound as *Śuddha Sāveri rāga*."

(13) *Katakapriya* (*Khadgapriya*)

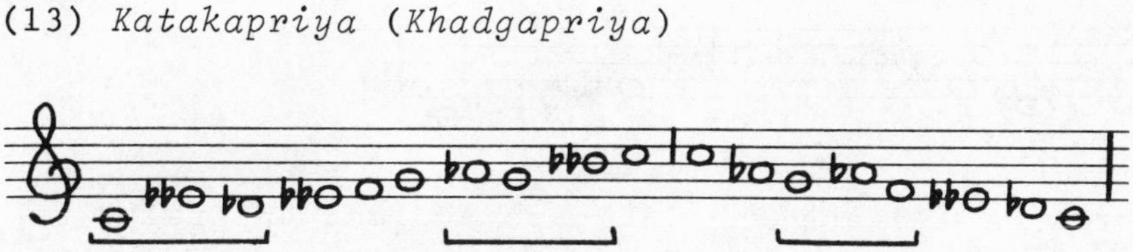

Ascent: *sampūrṇa*; two *vakra* features are shown.
Descent: the note *NI* (Bbb) is avoided; one *vakra* feature is shown.

(14) *Kīrtipriya*

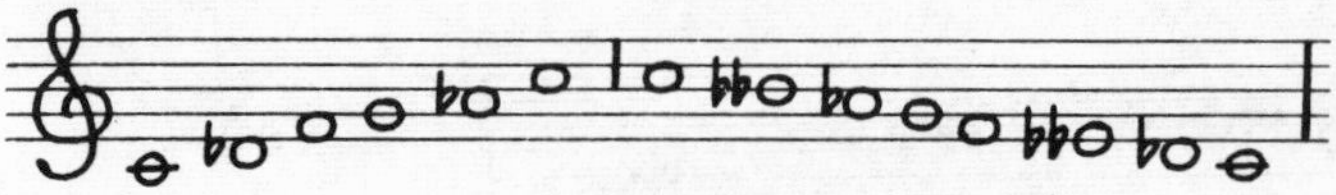

Ascent: the notes *GA* (Ebb) and *NI* (Bbb) are avoided.
Descent: *krama sampūrṇa*.

(15) *Kshana Prabha* (*Kṣana Prabha*)

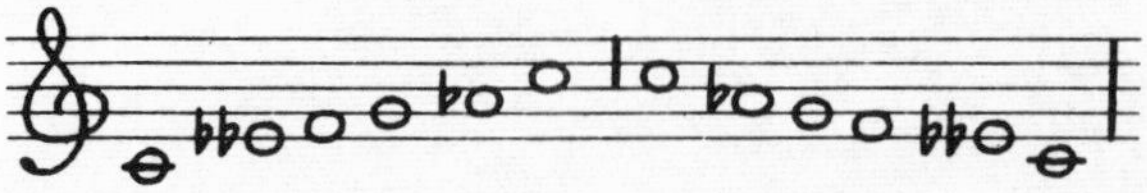

The notes *RI* (Db) and *NI* (Bbb) are avoided entirely.

(16) *Kūlaṃkasha* (*Kūlaṃkaṣa*)

The notes *GA* (Ebb) and *PA* (G) are avoided entirely.

(17) *Latāntapriya*

The notes *GA* (Ebb) and *NI* (Bbb) are avoided entirely.

(18) *Mandākini*

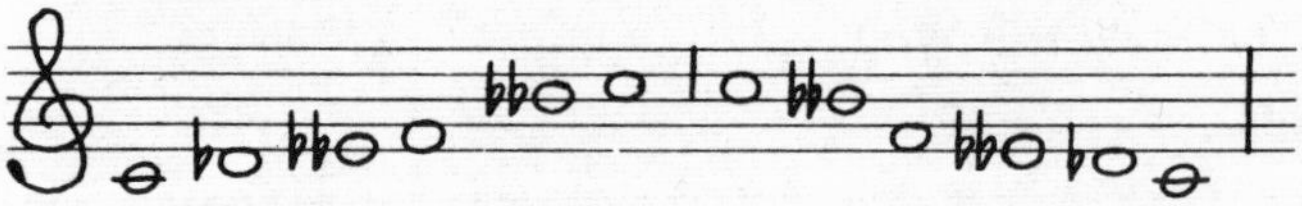

The notes *PA* (G) and *DHA* (Ab) are avoided entirely.

(19) *Mānya*

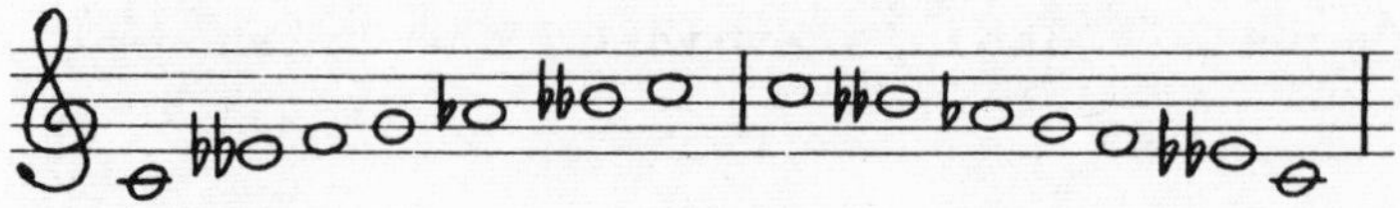

The note *RI* (Db) is avoided entirely.

(20) *Mōhanamallār*

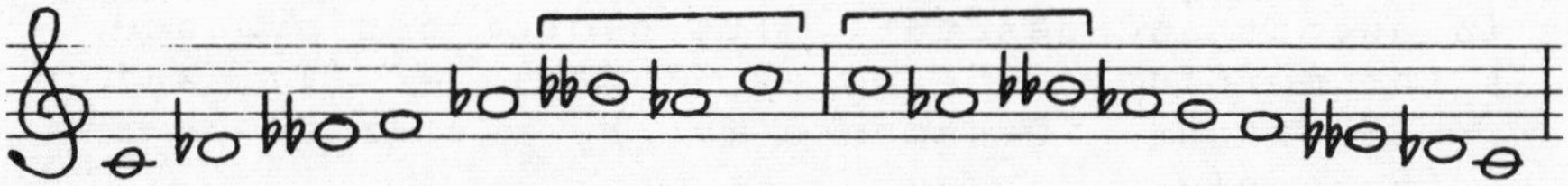

Ascent: the note *PA* (G) is avoided; one *vakra* feature is shown.
Descent: *sampūrṇa*; one *vakra* feature is used.

(21) *Muktāmbari*

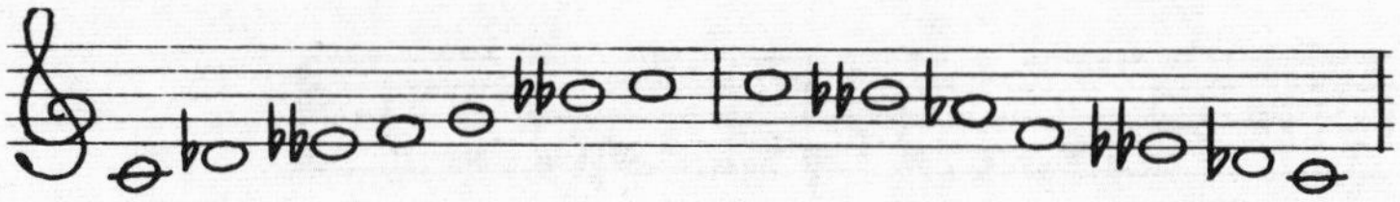

Ascent: the note *DHA* (Ab) is avoided.
Descent: the note *PA* (G) is omitted.

(22) *Raṅganāyaki*

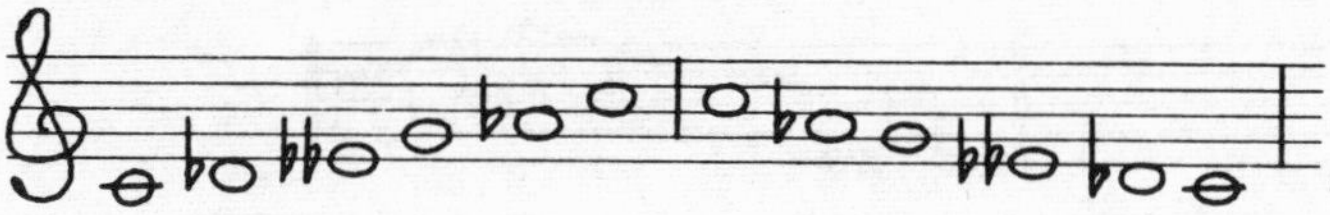

The notes *MA* (F) and *NI* (Bbb) are avoided entirely.

(23) *Rasagucham*

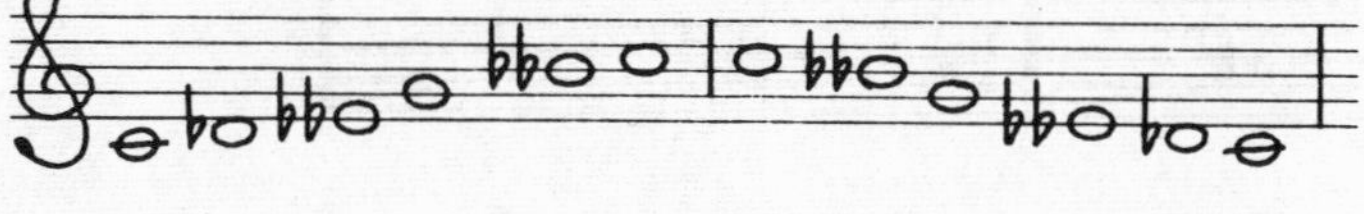

The notes *MA* (F) and *DHA* (Ab) are avoided entirely.

2. *MĒḶA RATNĀṄGĪ*

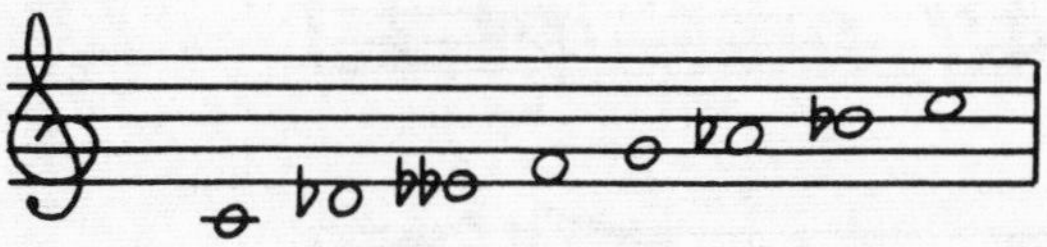

Veṅkaṭamakhin calls this *mēḷa Phenadyuti* and states

that it has to avoid the note *GA* (Ebb) in ascent and that *NI* (Bb) should appear in a vakra *passage*.

The *Rāga Ratnāṅgī* of the present time is not subject to Veṅkaṭamakhin's rules and employs all seven notes in ascent and descent. Its proper performance time is the morning. The notes *RI* (Db), *MA* (F), and *DHA* (Ab) are important. Ornaments may be performed on any note of the scale.

The following song example is a *kīrtana* by L. Muthiah Bhagavathar of Mysore:[1]

RATNĀṄGĪ (*Rūpaka-tāla*)

Pallavi

Repeat the first *avarta* of the *pallavi*

Anupallavi

Repeat the first and third *avartas* of the *pallavi*

Charana

Repeat the first and third *avartas* of the *pallavi*

Janya Rāgas of the Second Mēḷa

(1) *Phenadyuti*

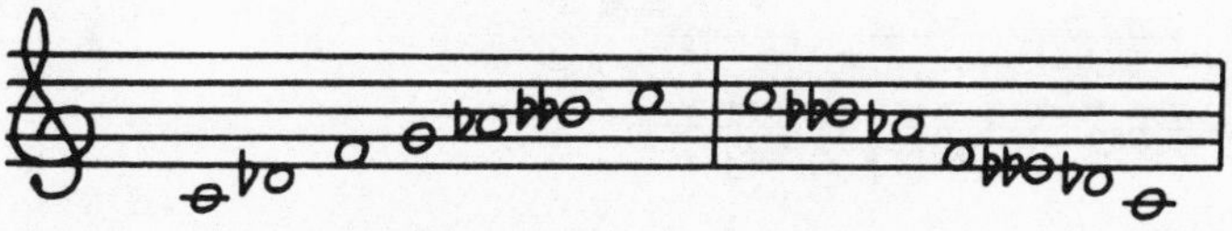

Veṅkaṭamakhin's rule of omitting the note *GA* (Ebb) in ascent is still observed at the present time. His other rule, to treat the note *NI* (Bb) in ascent in a *vakra* manner, is occasionally observed in the passage *NI-DHA-sa* (Bb-Ab-c). At the present time the note *PA* (G) is avoided in descent.

The following part of a melody pattern illustrates not only the two rules but also the *vakra* passage:

PHENADYUTI RĀGA (*Triputa-tāla*) SCM, 4

(2) *Śrīmani*

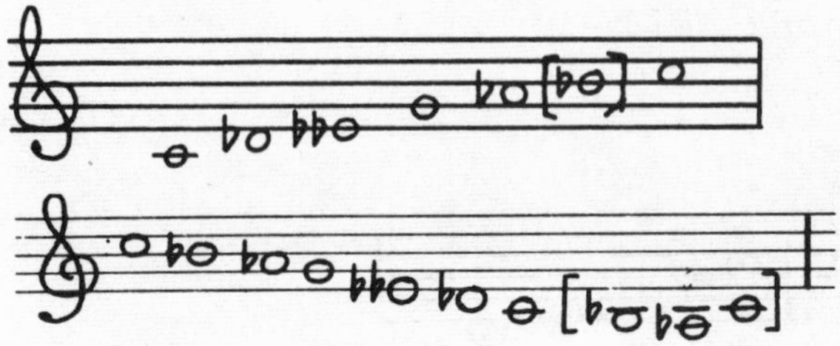

The scale of this *rāga* avoids the note *MA* (F) entirely and occasionally omits the note *NI* (Bb) in ascent. The strong notes are *GA* (Ebb), *PA* (G), and *DHA* (Ab). In the descending progression *PA-GA-RI-SA* the note *GA* is intoned as *sādharana GA* (Eb), while in all other instances this note remains *śuddha GA* (Ebb), occasionally described as *catuḥśruti RI* (D).

ŚRIMANI RĀGA (*Ādi-tāla*)

Pallavi

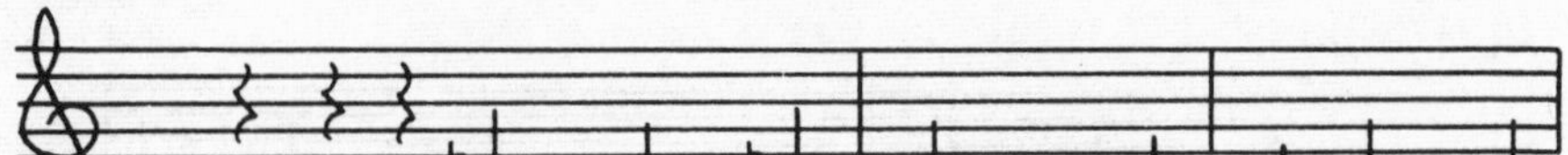

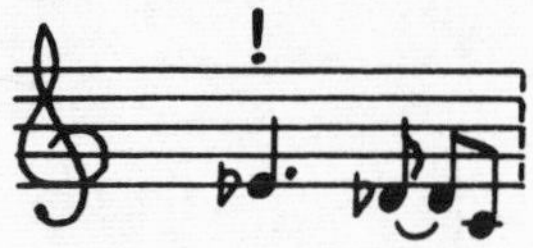

Repeat the whole *pallavi*

Anupallavi

Repeat the *pallavi*

Charana

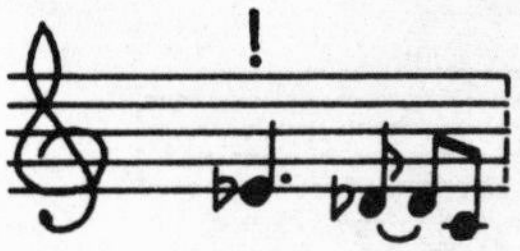

Repeat the *pallavi*

(3) *Ghaṇṭārava*

This rare *rāga* can also be placed under the heading of the 8. *mēḷa* (9).

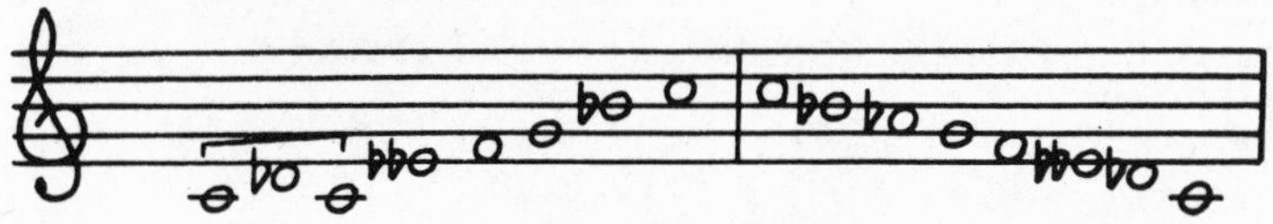

The sequence *SA-RI-SA* (C-Db-C) is characteristic and the note *DHA* (Ab) is avoided in ascent. The descent is *sampūrṇa*.

The following melody pattern is taken from SCM, 6:

GHAṆṬĀRAVA RĀGA (*Triputa-tāla*)

(4) *Ānanda Nāṭani*

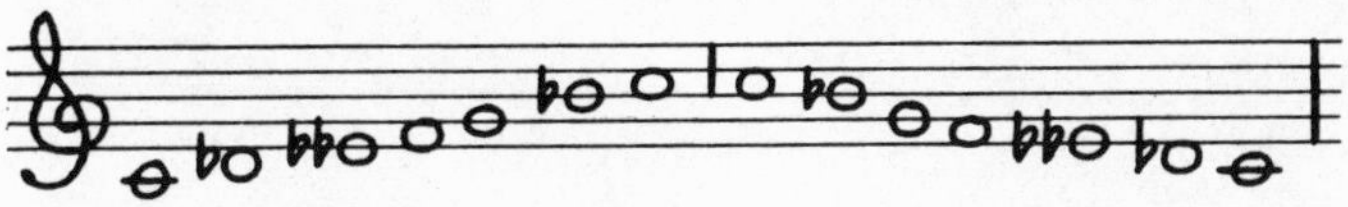

The note *DHA* (Ab) is avoided entirely.

(5) *Bhūpaḷa Cintāmaṇi*

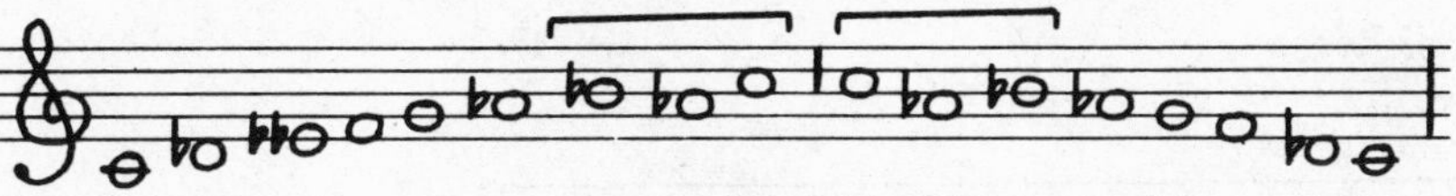

Ascent: *sampūrṇa*; one *vakra* feature is shown.
Descent: the note *GA* (Ebb) is avoided; one *vakra* feature is used.

(6) *Gaurī Gāndhāri*

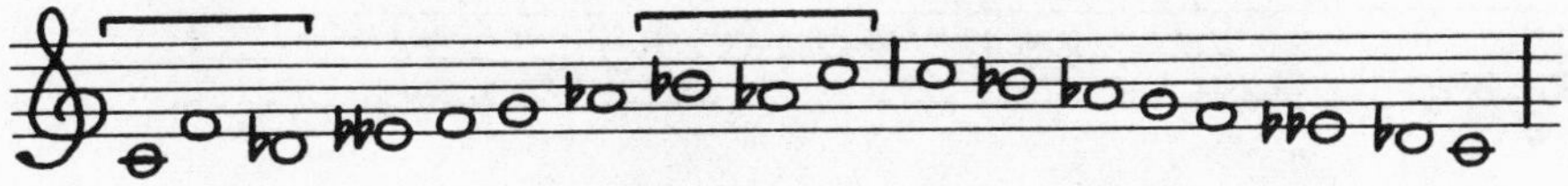

Ascent: *sampūrṇa*; two *vakra* features are shown.
Descent: *krama sampūrṇa*.

(7) *Jaya Sindhu*

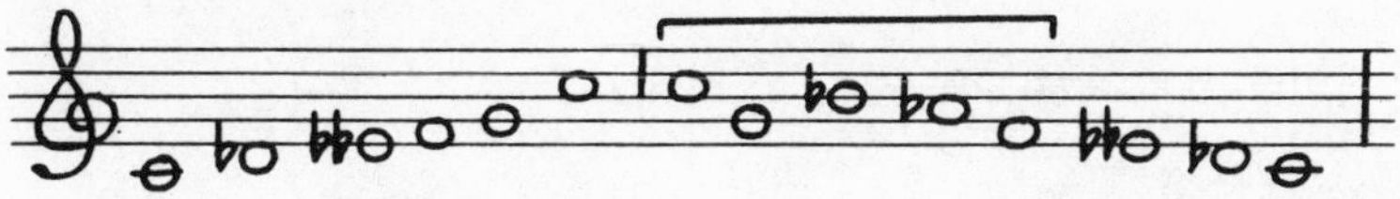

Ascent: the notes *DHA* (Ab) and *NI* (Bb) are avoided.
Descent: *sampūrṇa*; one extended *vakra* passage is shown.

(8) *Jīvarañjani*

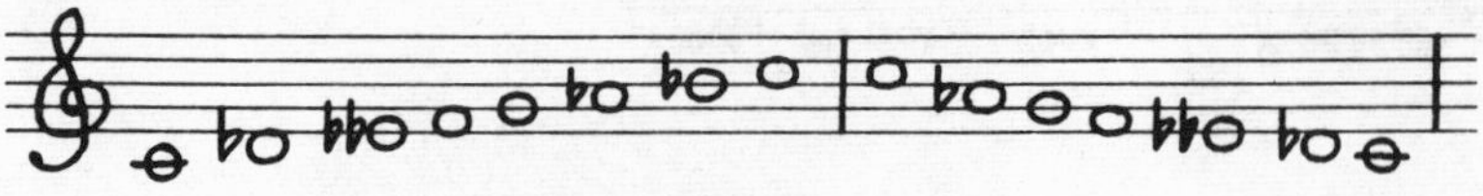

Ascent: *krama sampūrṇa*
Descent: the note *NI* (Bb) is avoided.

(9) *Kāmini*

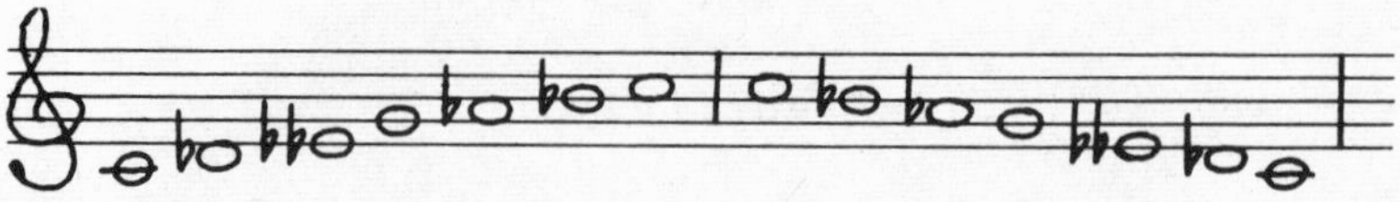

The note *MA* (F) is avoided entirely.

(10) *Kumbhini*

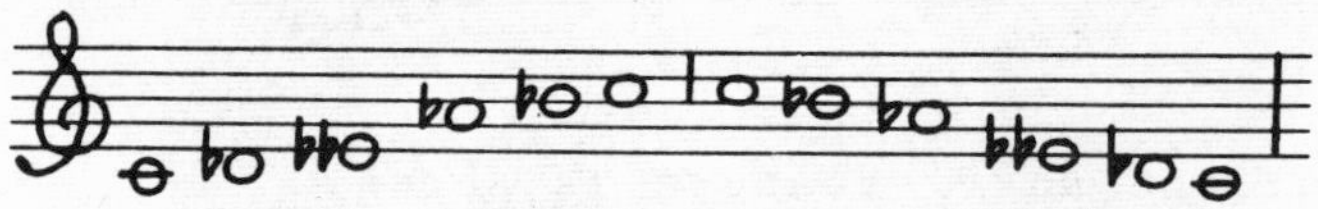

The notes *MA* (F) and *PA* (G) are avoided entirely.
Kumbhini represents also the 41. *mēḷa* of the *asampūrṇa paddhati*, where it has the following material:

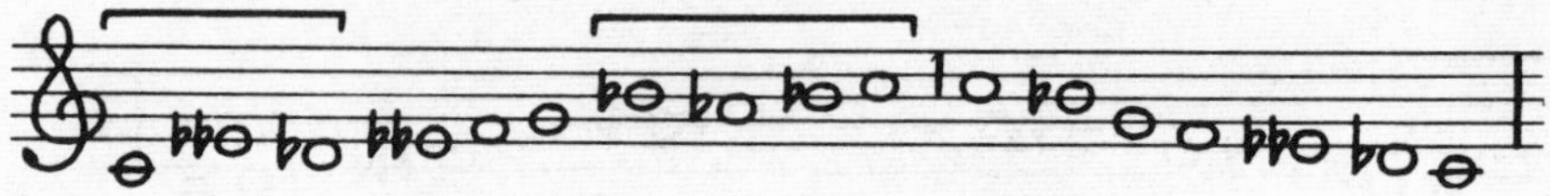

(See also 41,7)

(11) *Marāladhvani*

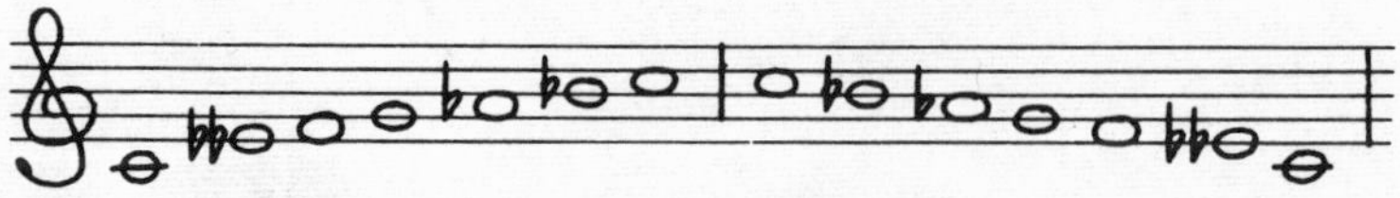

The note *RI* (Db) is avoided entirely.

(12) *Nīharādri*

The notes *RI* (Db) and *MA* (F) are avoided entirely.

(13) *Pāñchālika*

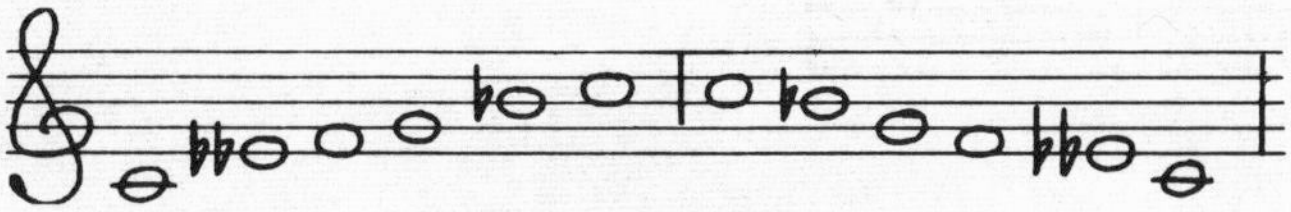

The notes *RI* (Db) and *DHA* (Ab) are avoided entirely.

(14) *Pushpavasantam* (*Puṣpavasantam*)

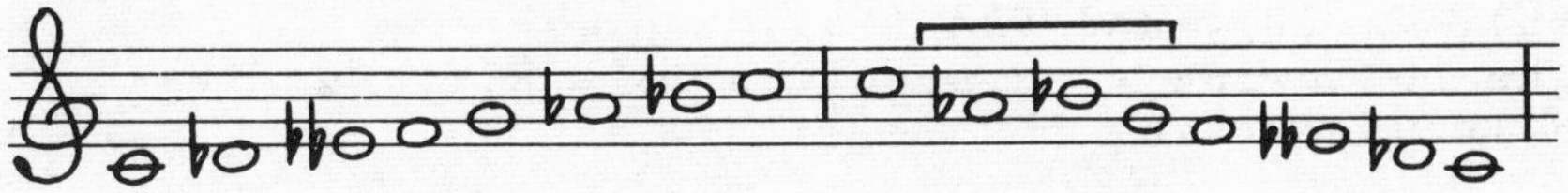

Ascent: *krama sampūrṇa*
Descent: *sampūrṇa*; one *vakra* feature is shown.

(15) *Rēvati*

The notes *GA* (Ebb) and *DHA* (Ab) are avoided entirely.

(16) *Vasantabhūpālam*

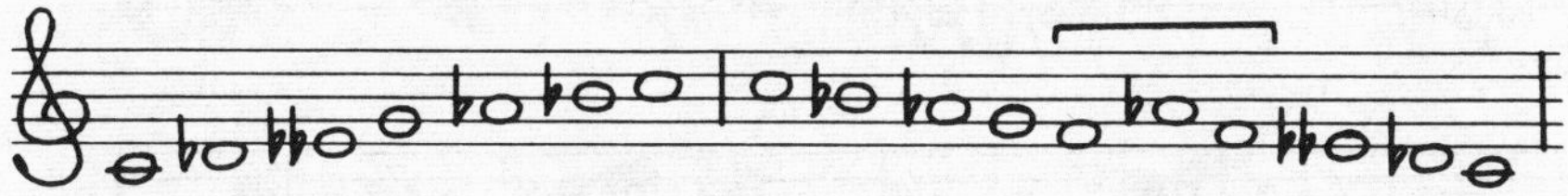

Ascent: the note *MA* (F) is avoided.
Descent: *sampūrṇa*; one *vakra* feature is shown.

(17) *Vasantamanōharī*

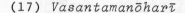

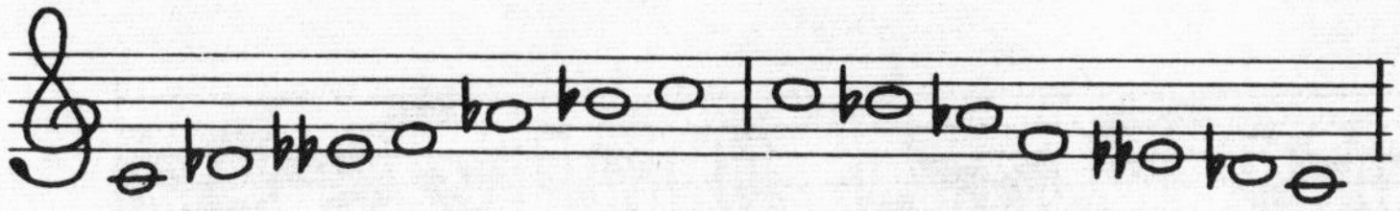

The note *PA* (G) is avoided entirely.

3. *MĒḶA GĀNAMŪRTI*

Veṅkaṭamakhin calls this *mēḷa Sāmāvarāḷi*. *Gānamūrti* has, as do all modern *mēḷas*, *krama sampūrṇa* form in ascent and descent. In the songs of *rāga Gānamūrti* various liberties (e.g., *vakra* features) can be observed, which, not strictly obligatory, are left to the discretion of the performers. The strong notes are *GA* (Ebb), *MA* (F), and *DHA* (Ab).

The following song specimen is a *kīrtana*; its origin is uncertain.

GĀNAMŪRTI (*Ādi-tāla*)

Pallavi

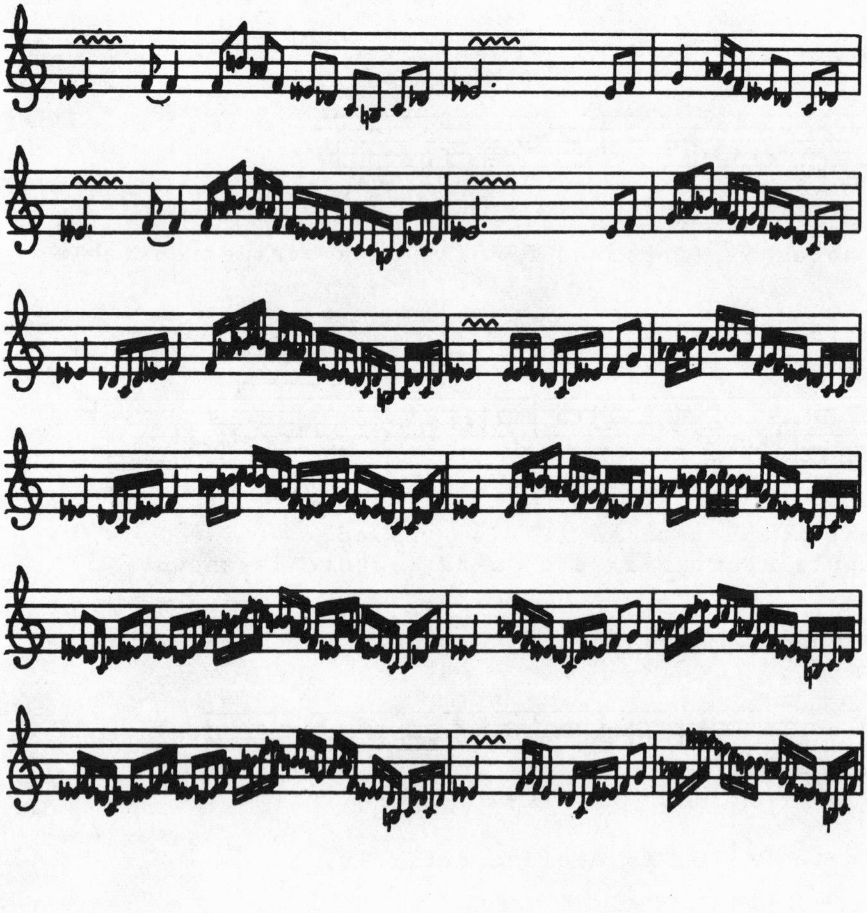

Repeat the first measure of the *pallavi*. This is followed by two measures holding the note *GA*.

Anupallavi

Repeat the first measure of the *pallavi*, which is followed by two measures holding the note *GA*

Charana

Repeat again the first measure of the *pallavi* which is to be followed by either the note *GA* or *SA*.

Janya Rāgas of the Third Mēḷa

(1) *Sāmavarāḷi*

As already indicated this *janya rāga* is Veṅkaṭamakhin's version of *Gānamūrti*, in which the note *GA* (Ebb) is avoided in ascent. The descent is *sampūrṇa* and may contain one or more vaguely defined *vakra* steps that need not be used at all.

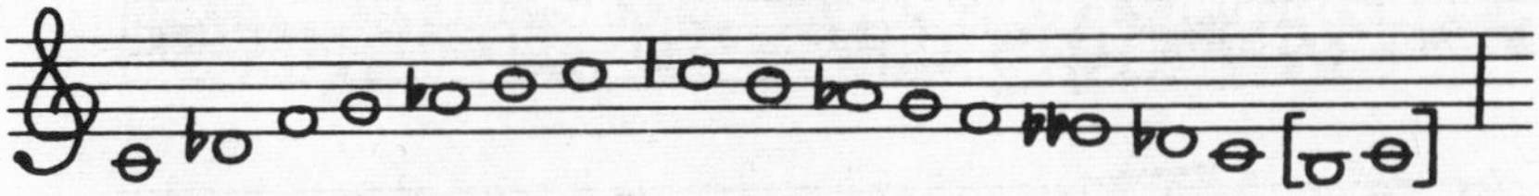

The following fragment of a melody pattern is taken from SCM, 7:

SĀMAVARĀLI RĀGA (*Triputa-tāla*)

(2) *Bhinnapañcama*

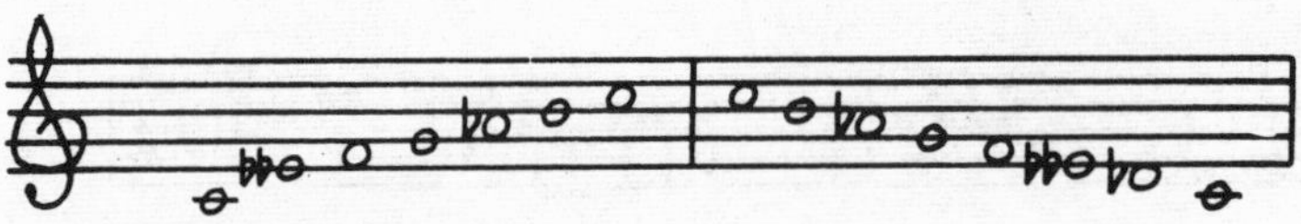

Ascent: the note *RI* (Db) is avoided.
Descent: *sampūrṇa*.

BHINNAPAÑCHAM RĀGA (*Triputa-tāla*) SCM, 8

(3) *Bhāvajapriya*

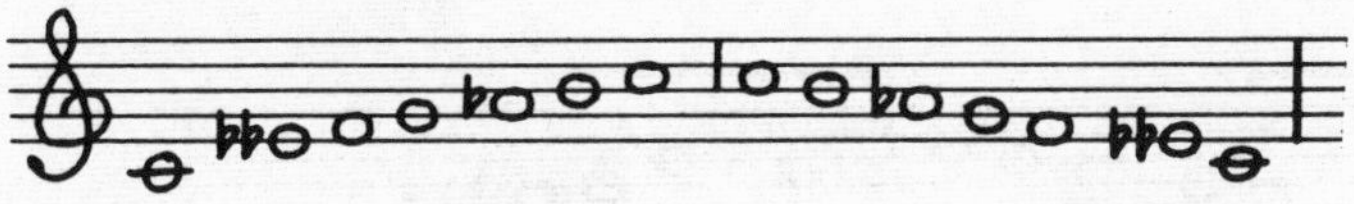

The note *RI* (Db) is avoided entirely.

(4) *Bhēri Karṇīka*

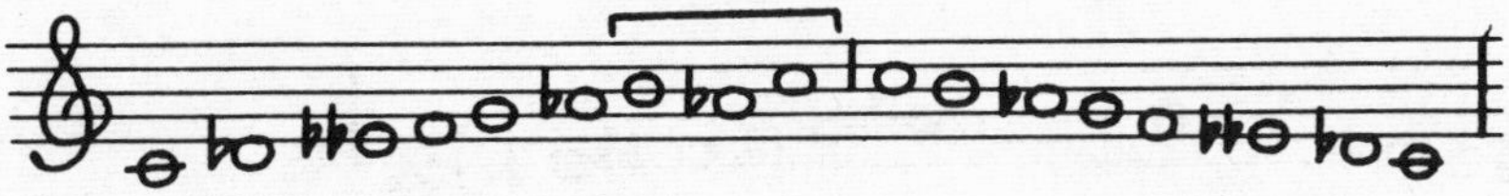

Ascent: *sampūrṇa*; one *vakra* feature is shown.
Descent: *krama sampūrṇa*

(5) *Bhujangi*

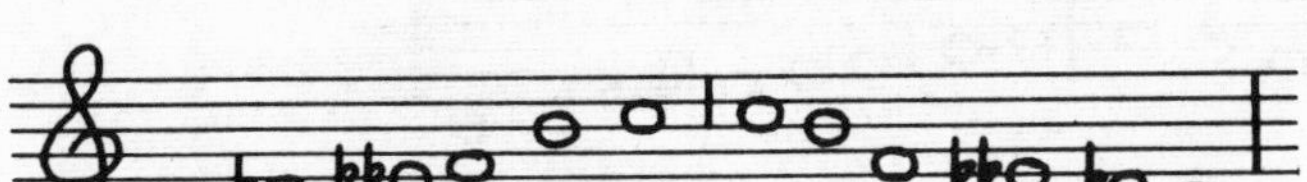

The notes *PA* (G) and *DHA* (Ab) are avoided entirely.

(6) *Chandana Gandhi*

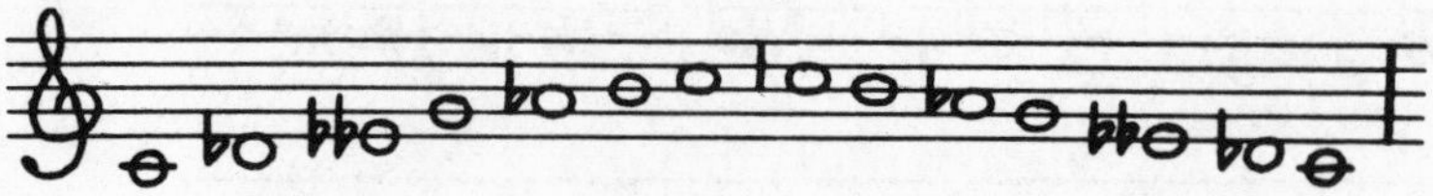

The note *MA* (F) is avoided entirely.

(7) *Chhāyā Gauḷa*

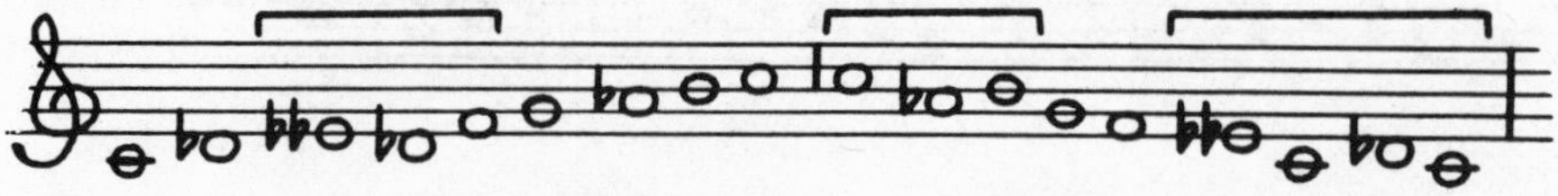

The scale is *sampūrṇa* and shows three *vakra* features, one in ascent and two in descent. Another *rāga* with the same name appears under the heading of the 15. *mēḷa* (49).

(8) *Chhāyā Vēḷa*

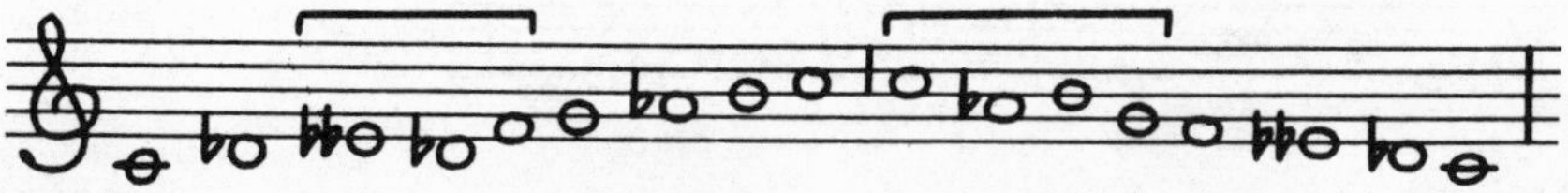

The scale is *sampūrṇa* and shows one *vakra* feature in ascent and one in descent.

(9) *Gāna Lalita*

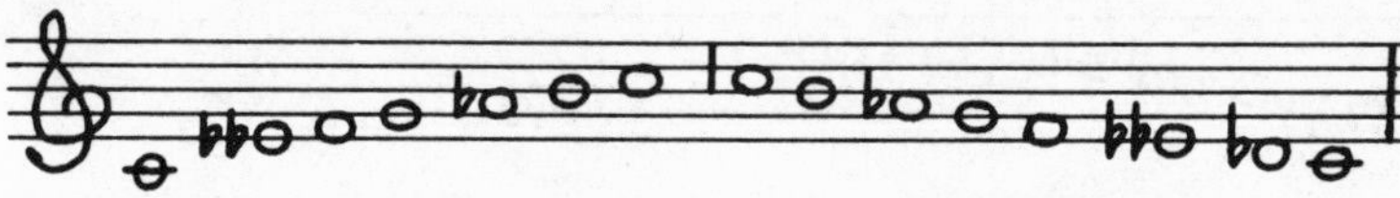

The note *RI* (Db) is avoided in ascent. The descent is *krama sampūrṇa*.

(10) *Girikarṇika*

The note *GA* (Ebb) is avoided in ascent. The descent is *krama sampūrṇa*.

(11) *Kumārapriya*

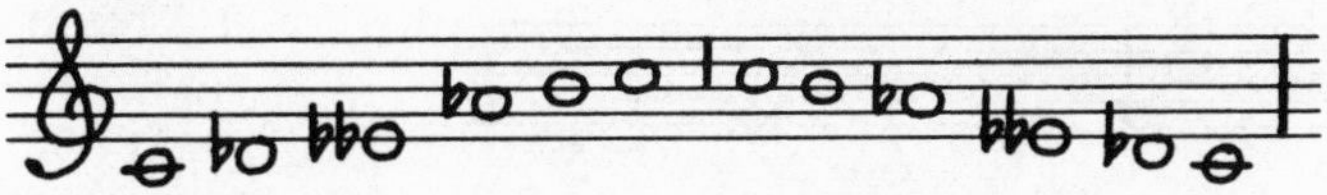

The notes *MA* (F) and *PA* (G) are avoided entirely.

(12) *Kurañjalōchani*

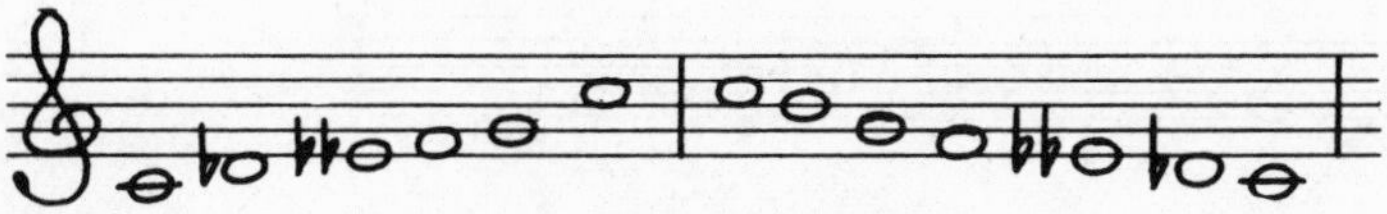

The note *DHA* (Ab) is avoided entirely. The note *NI* (B) is omitted in ascent.

(13) *Lalitatōḍi*

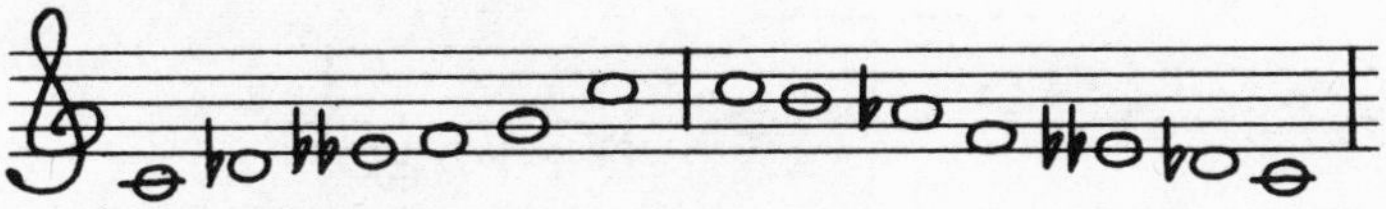

Ascent: the notes *DHA* (Ab) and *NI* (B) are avoided.
Descent: the note *PA* (G) is omitted.

(14) *Maṅgalagauri*

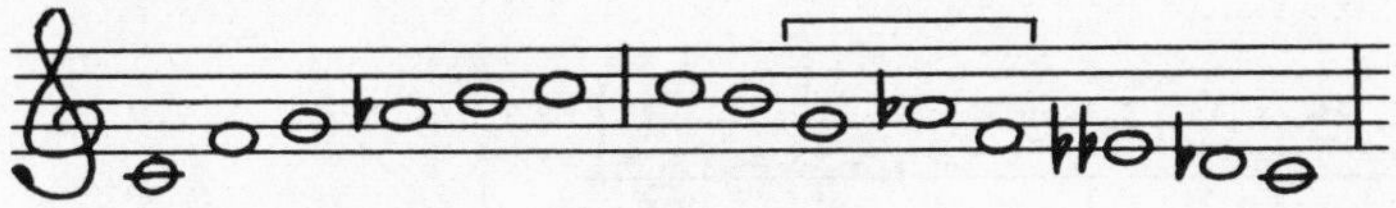

Ascent: the notes *RI* (Db) and *GA* (Ebb) are avoided.
Descent: *sampūrṇa*; one *vakra* feature is shown.

(15) *Pūrvavarāḷi*

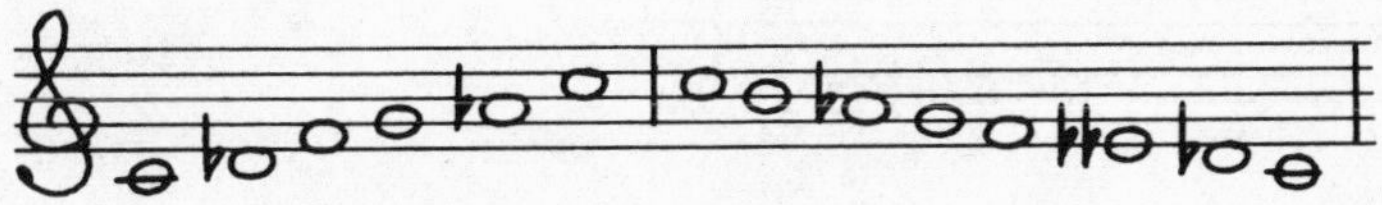

Ascent: the notes *GA* (Ebb) and *NI* (B) are avoided.
Descent: *krama sampūrṇa*.

(16) *Rāgamūrti*

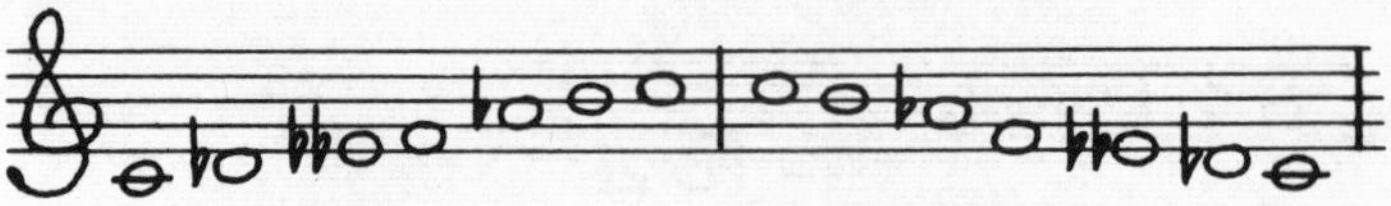

The note *PA* (G) is avoided entirely.

(17) *Sāraṅgalalita*

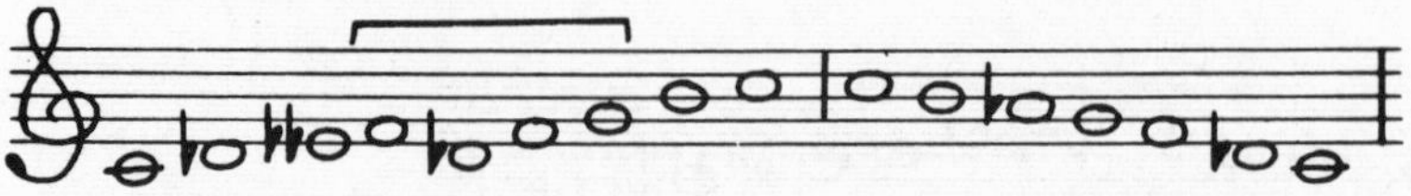

Ascent: the note *DHA* (Ab) is avoided and one *vakra* feature is shown.
Descent: the note *GA* (Ebb) is omitted.

(18) *Triyambakapriya*

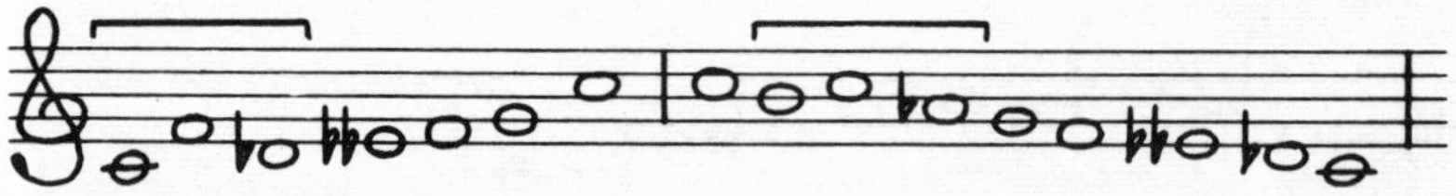

Ascent: the notes *DHA* (Ab) and *NI* (B) are avoided; one *vakra* feature is shown.
Descent: *sampūrṇa*; one *vakra* feature is used.

(19) *Varavarṇini*

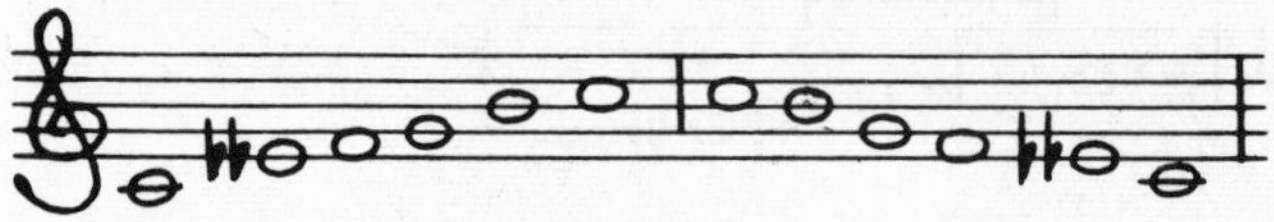

The notes *RI* (Db) and *DHA* (Ab) are avoided entirely.

(20) *Vishārata* (*Viśārata*)

The note *DHA* (Ab) is avoided entirely. *GA* (Ebb) is omitted in ascent and *RI* (Db) in descent.

4. *MĒḶA VANASPĀTI*

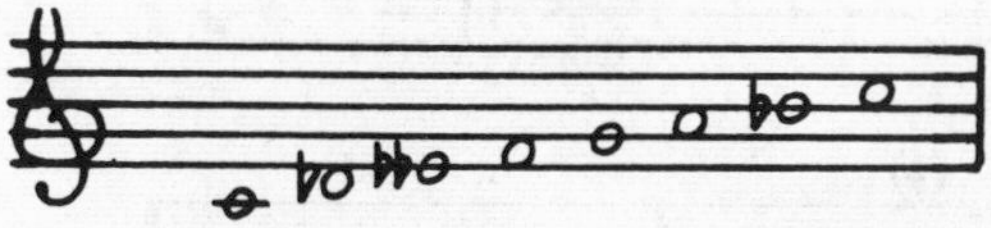

Veṅkaṭamakhin calls this *mēla Bhānumātī* in his *asampūrṇa mēḷas*. *Vanaspāti*, as a *rāga*, has three strong notes: *RI* (Db), *GA* (Ebb), and *DHA* (A). In the ascending sequence *SA-RI-GA* (C-Db-Ebb) it has become a habit to extend the duration of the middle note (*RI*) even when the notated melody does not specifically indicate such a prolongation. Of interest is also the descending sequence *MA-GA-RI* (F-Ebb-Db). Its middle note (*GA*) is often replaced by a distinctly low intoned *MA* ($\overset{\flat}{F}$) which can approximate the pitch of E, in rare instances even Eb. In the following *kīrtana* it is represented as *MA-MA-RI* (in Nagari script) which I have transcribed as F-$\overset{\flat}{F}$-Db.

VANASPĀTI (*Rūpaka-tāla*)

Pallavi

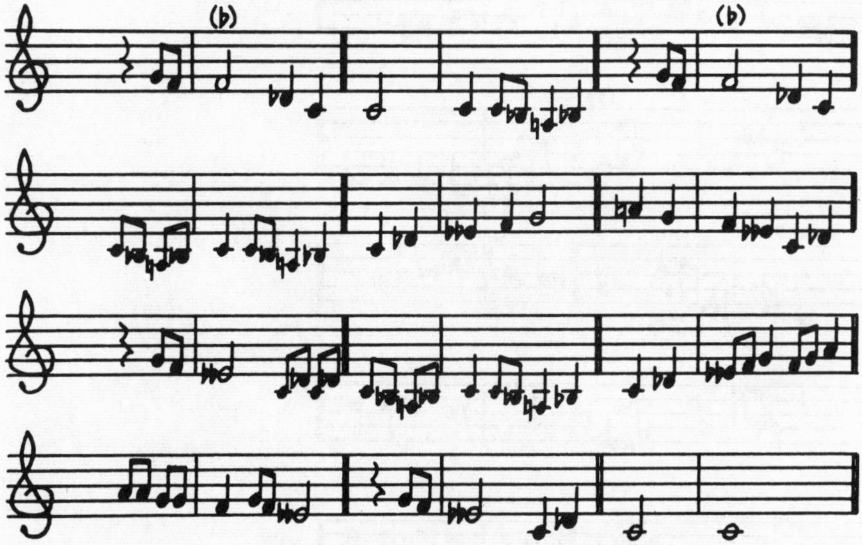

Anupallavi

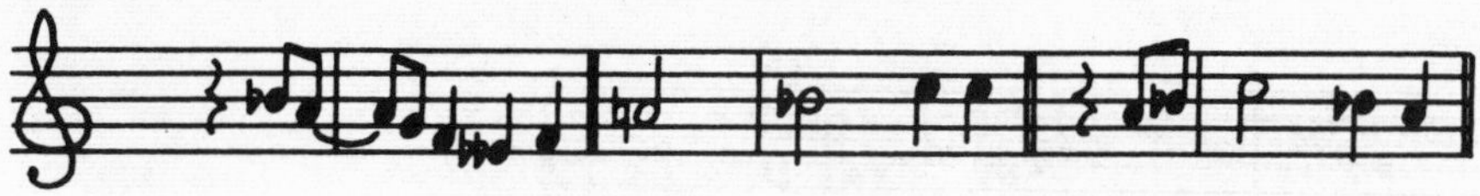

Charana

Repeat the entire *pallavi*

Janya Rāgas of the Fourth Mēḷa

(1) *Bhānumātī*

As a *rāga*, *Bhānumātī* avoids in ascent the notes *DHA* (A) and *NI* (Bb) and shows one *vakra* feature. The descent is *krama sampūrṇa*.

BHĀNUMĀTĪ RĀGA (*Triputa-tāla*) SMC, 9-10

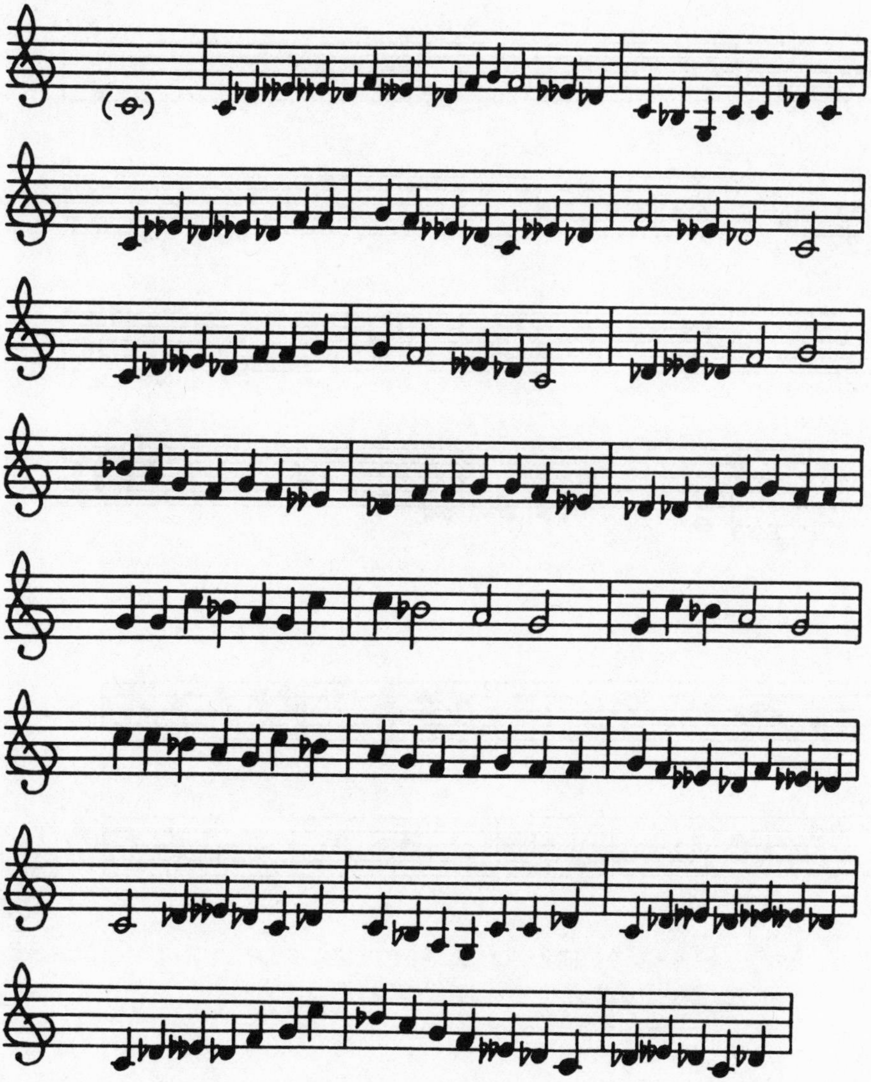

(2) *Rasali* (*Rasāvali*)

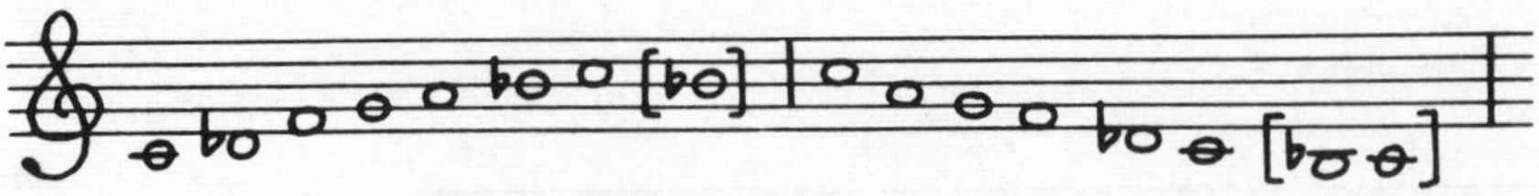

The note *GA* (Ebb) is avoided entirely and the note *NI* (Bb) is omitted in descent. The notes *RI* (Db), *MA* (F), and *DHA* (A) are strong.

The following song specimen is a *kīrtana*:

RASALI RĀGA (*Ādi-tala*)

Pallavi

A

B

Anupallavi

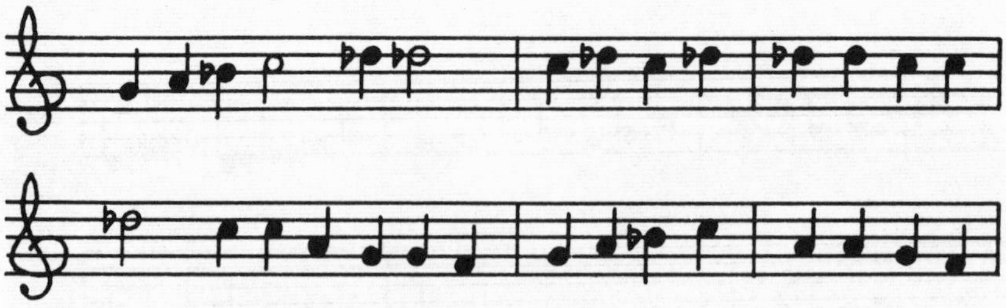

Repeat here lines A and B of the *pallavi*

Charana

Repeat here the lines A and B of the *pallavi*

(3) *Bhūvanēśvari*

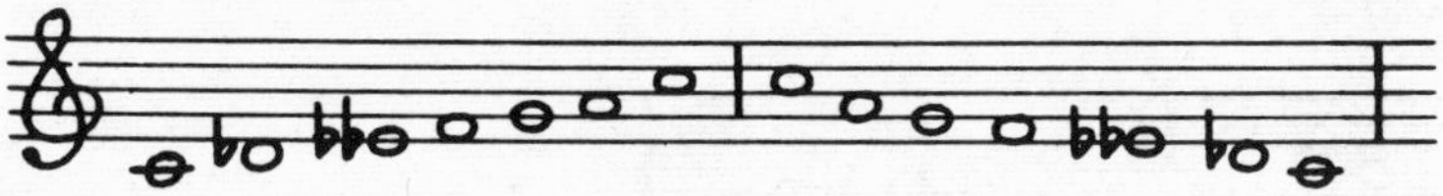

The note *NI* (Bb) is avoided entirely.

(4) *Chitrarūpi*

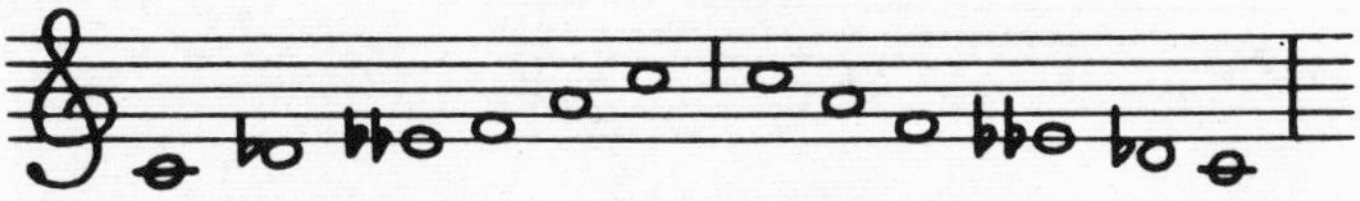

The notes *PA* (G) and *NI* (Bb) are avoided entirely.

(5) *Indu Sītala* (*Indu Sītalī*)

The entire scale is *sampūrṇa* and shows two *vakra* features, one in ascent and one in descent.

(6) *Jñānadāyaki (Jñānadāyiki)*

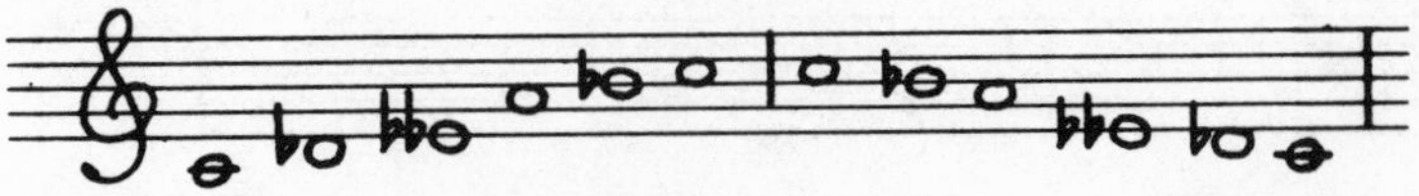

The notes *MA* (F) and *PA* (G) are avoided entirely.

(7) *Karṇāṭaka Suraṭi*

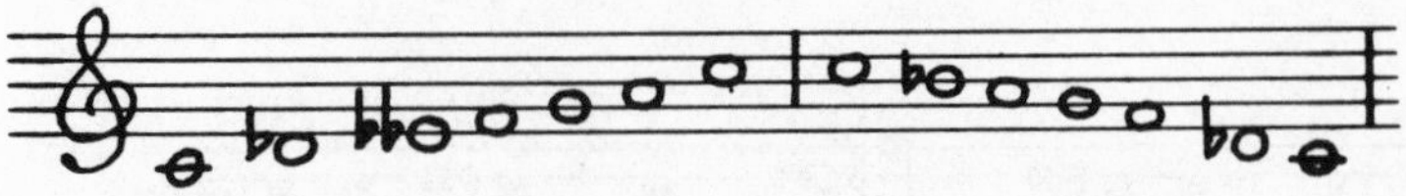

Ascent: the note *NI* (Bb) is avoided.
Descent: the note *GA* (Ebb) is omitted.

(8) *Kāyapriya*

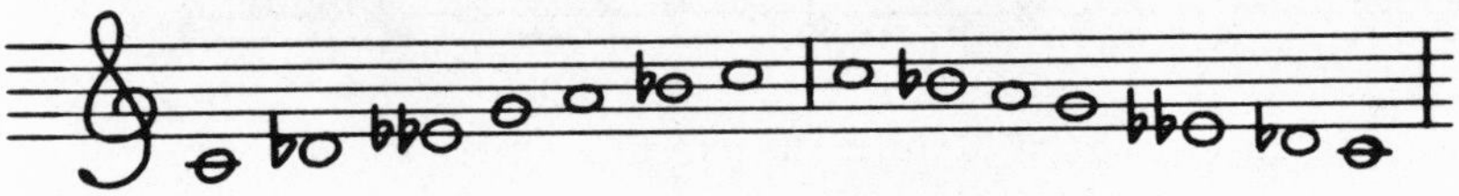

The note *MA* (F) is avoided entirely.

(9) *Himavāluka*

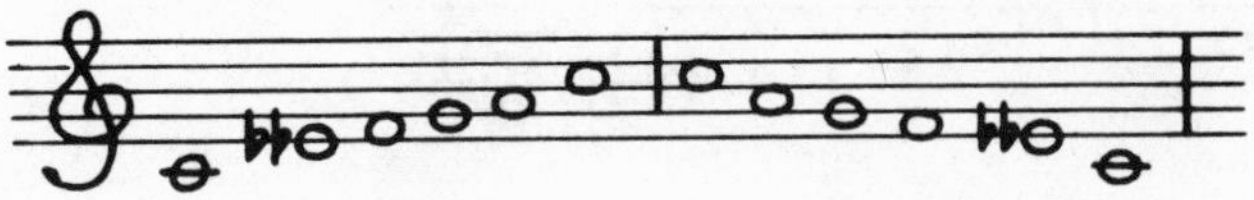

The notes *RI* (Db) and *NI* (Bb) are avoided entirely.

(10) *Krajavali*

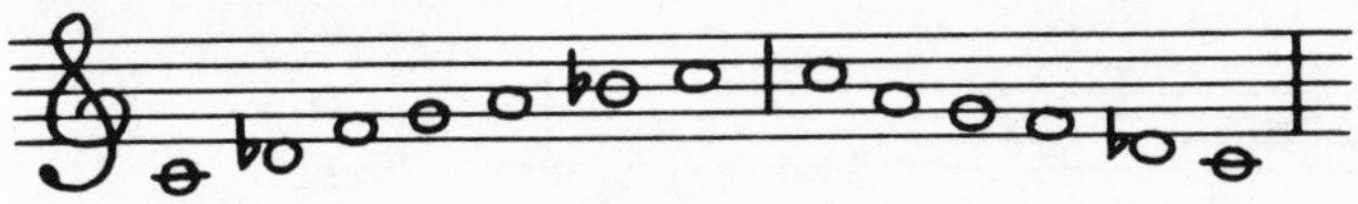

The note *GA* (Ebb) is avoided entirely. In descent the note *NI* (Bb) is omitted.

(11) *Līlāraṅgani*

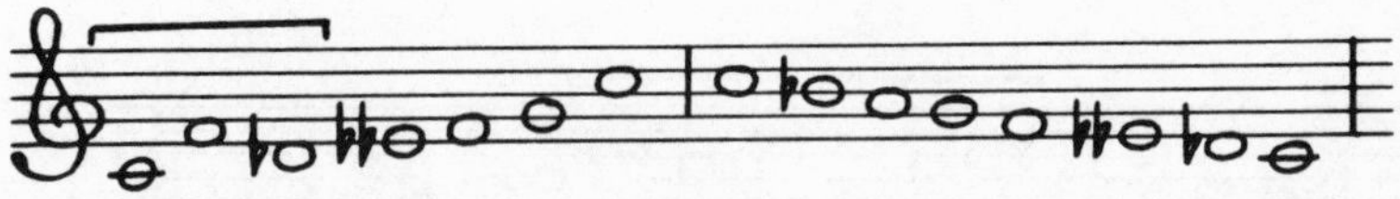

Ascent: the notes *DHA* (A) and *NI* (Bb) are avoided; one *vakra* feature is shown.
Descent: *krama sampūrṇa*.

(12) *Sāradhālaṅgi*

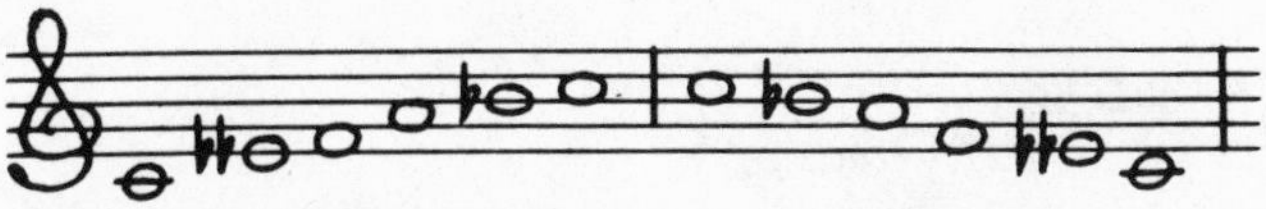

The notes *RI* (Db) and *PA* (G) are avoided entirely.

(13) *Sugātra*

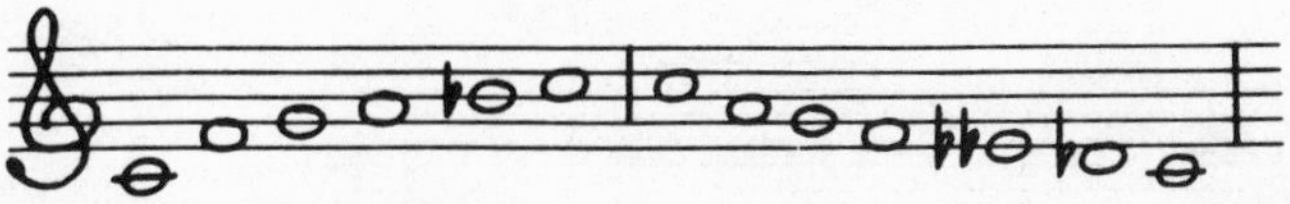

Ascent: the notes *RI* (Db) and *GA* (Ebb) are avoided.
Descent: the note *NI* (Bb) is omitted.

(14) *Surabhūṣaṇi*

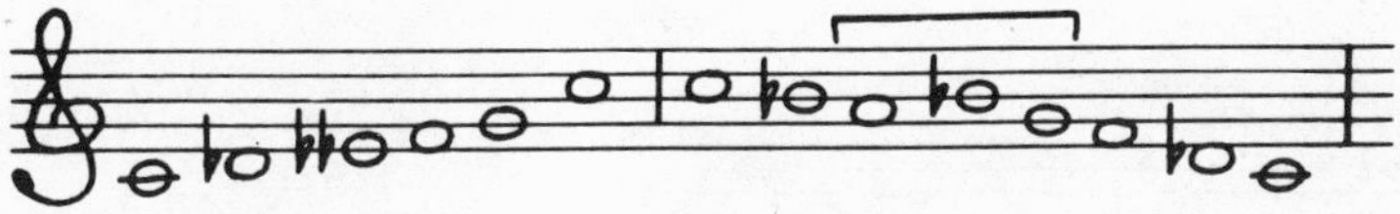

Ascent: the notes *DHA* (A) and *NI* (Bb) are avoided.
Descent: the note *GA* (Ebb) is omitted and one *vakra* feature is shown.

(15) *Śuddhamañjari*

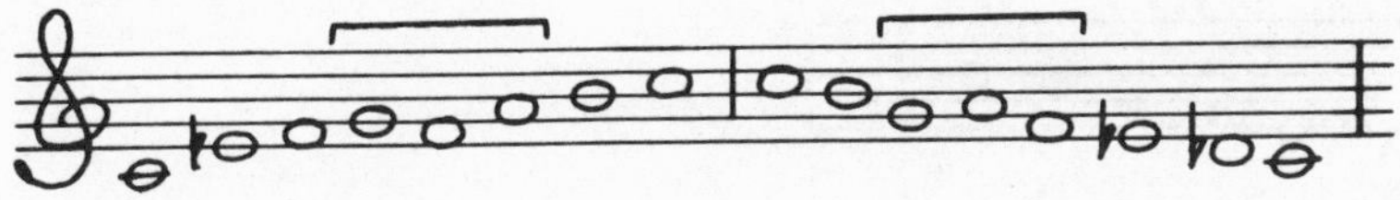

Ascent: the note *RI* (Db) is avoided and one *vakra* feature is shown.
Descent: *sampūrṇa*; one *vakra* feature is used.

(16) *Tamasvini*

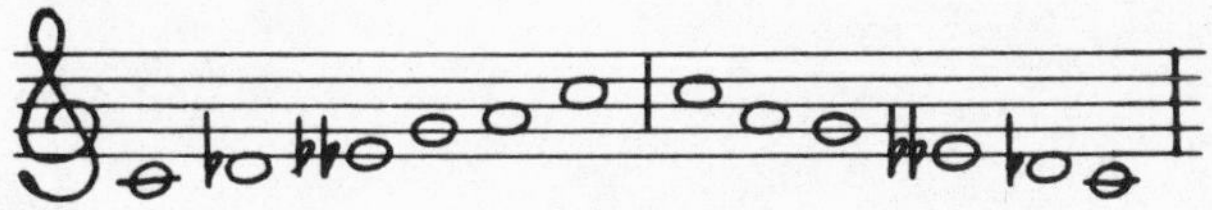

The notes *MA* (F) and *NI* (Bb) are avoided entirely.

(17) *Vallika*

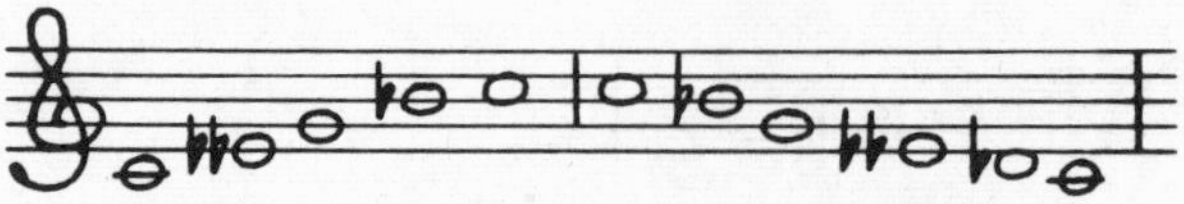

The notes *MA* (F) and *DHA* (A) are avoided entirely. *RI* (Db) is omitted in ascent.

(18) *Vīravikramam*

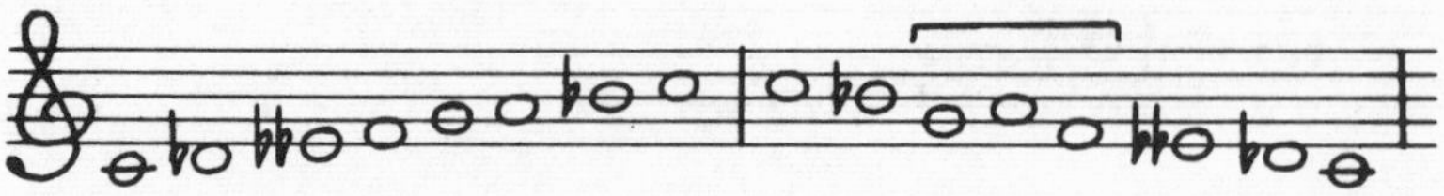

Ascent: *krama sampūrṇa*.
Descent: *sampūrṇa*; one *vakra* feature is shown.

(19) *Vitapi*

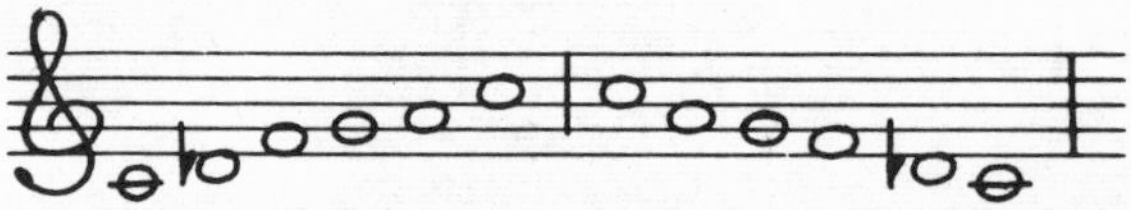

The notes *GA* (Ebb) and *NI* (Bb) are avoided entirely.

5. *MĒḶA MĀNAVĀTĪ*

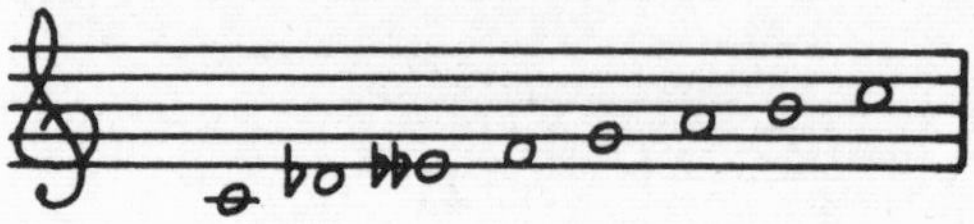

Veṅkaṭamakhin's name for this *mēla* is *Manōrañjanī*. In *rāga Mānavātī* the notes *GA* (Ebb), *ṀA* (F), *DHA* (A), and *NI* (B) are strong. *RI* (Db) is often approached from *SA* (C). *Mānavātī* can be performed at any time.

The following song specimen is a *kīrtana*:

MĀNAVĀTĪ (*Ādi-tāla*)

Pallavi

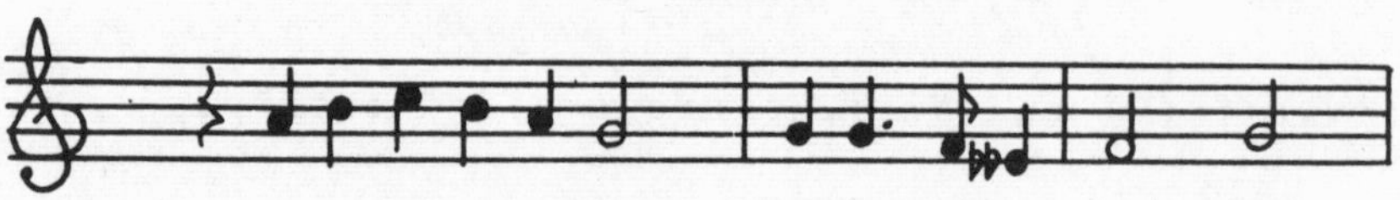

A

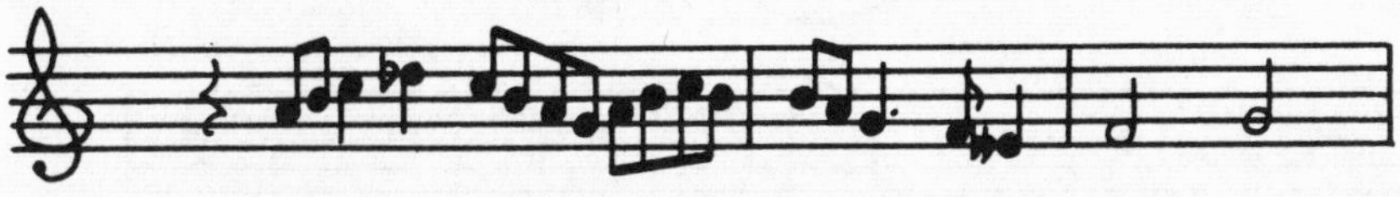

B

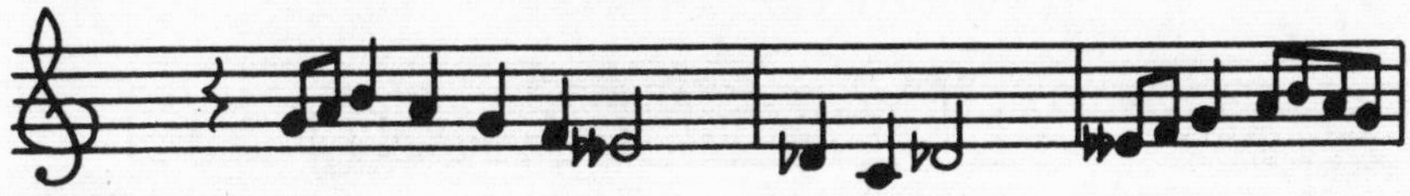

Repeat lines A and B of *pallavi*

Anupallavi

Repeat lines A and B of the *pallavi*

Charana

Repeat lines A and B of the *pallavi* and conclude the song with the note *MA* (F)

Janya Rāgas of the Fifth Mēḷa

(1) *Manōrañjanī*

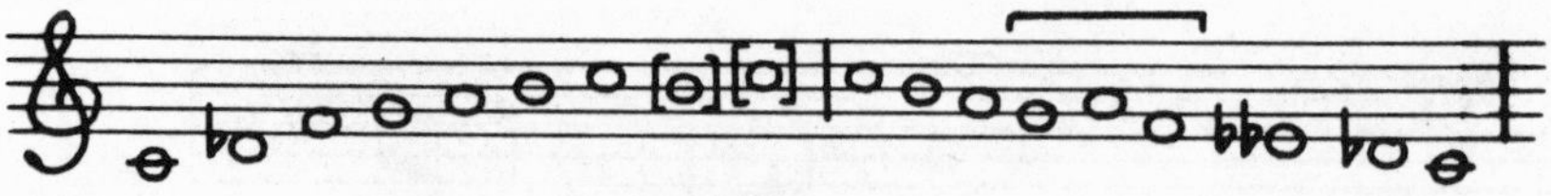

Ascent: the note *GA* (Eb) is avoided.
Descent: *sampūrṇa*; one *vakra* feature is shown.

MANŌRAÑJANĪ RĀGA (*Triputa-tāla*) SCM, 12

(2) *Abhimānini*

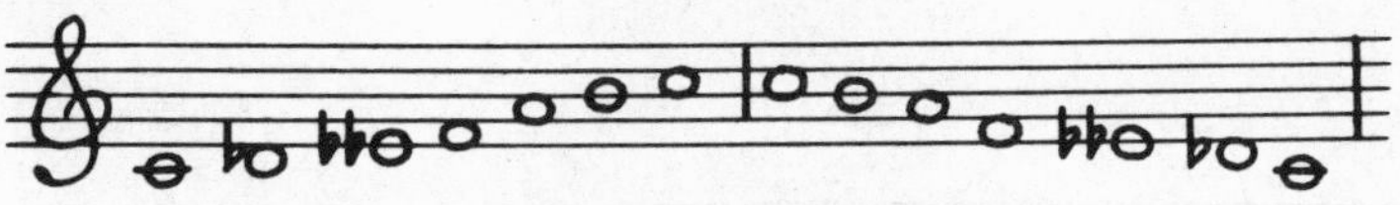

The note *PA* (G) is avoided entirely.

(3) *Bhūpāḷa Manōhari*

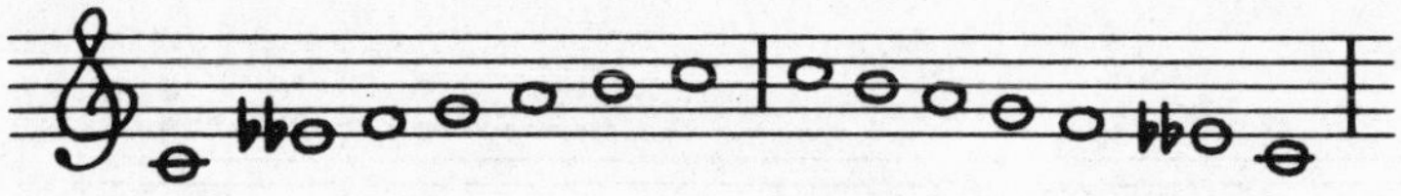

The note *RI* (Db) is avoided entirely.

(4) *Dēśya Gauri*

The scale is *sampūrṇa* and shows two *vakra* features, one in ascent and one in descent.

(5) *Ghana Śyāmaḷa*

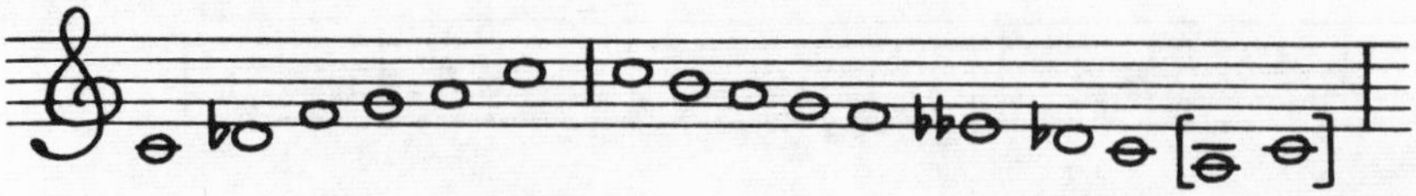

Ascent: the notes *GA* (Ebb) and *NI* (B) are avoided.
Descent: *sampūrṇa*.
Another version of the ascent uses the note *GA* (Ebb) and avoids *RI* (Db). This second form is shown in the SCM (86) where it is called *Ghana Śyāmaḷanāṭaka*.

(6) *Jayasāveri*

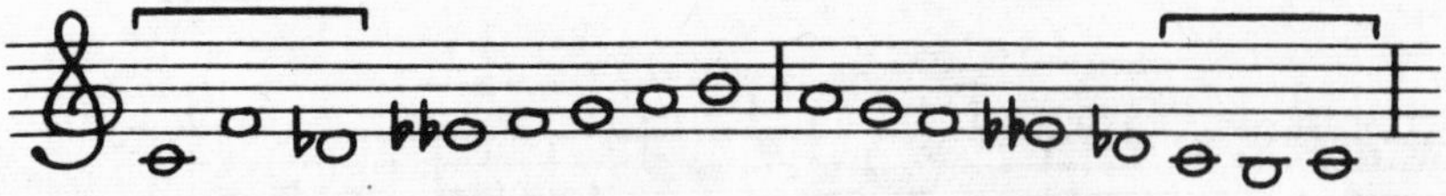

The scale is *niṣādāntya*, meaning that its highest note is *NI*. It shows two *vakra* features, one in ascent and one in descent.

(7) *Jñotnāpriya*

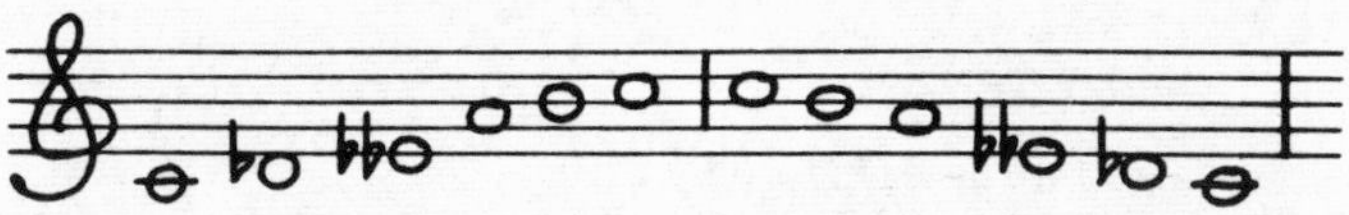

The notes *MA* (F) and *PA* (G) are avoided entirely.

(8) *Kāmya*

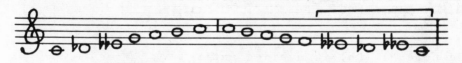

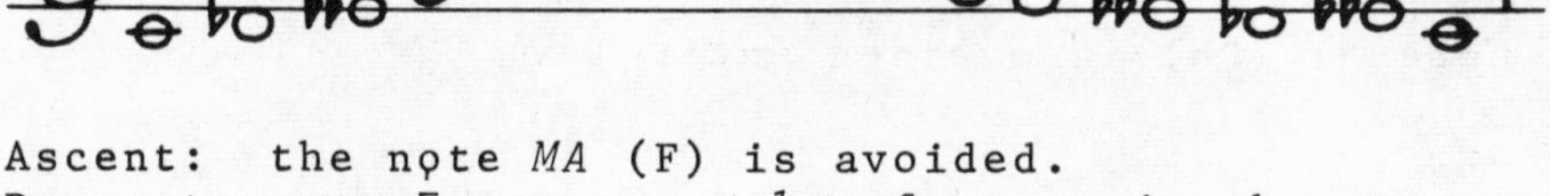

Ascent: the note *MA* (F) is avoided.
Descent: *sampūrṇa*; one *vakra* feature is shown.

(9) *Kandarpa Manōhari*

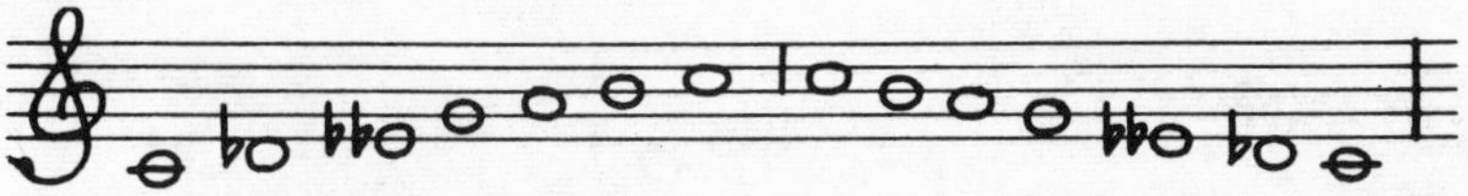

The note *MA* (F) is avoided entirely.

(10) *Kaumati*

Ascent: the note *MA* (F) is avoided.
Descent: *sampūrṇa*.

(11) *Minalōchana*

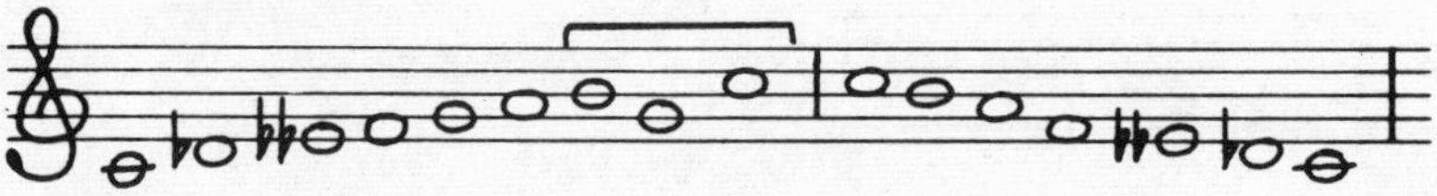

Ascent: *sampūrṇa*; one *vakra* feature is shown.
Descent: the note *PA* (G) is avoided.

(12) *Pūrvakannaḍa*

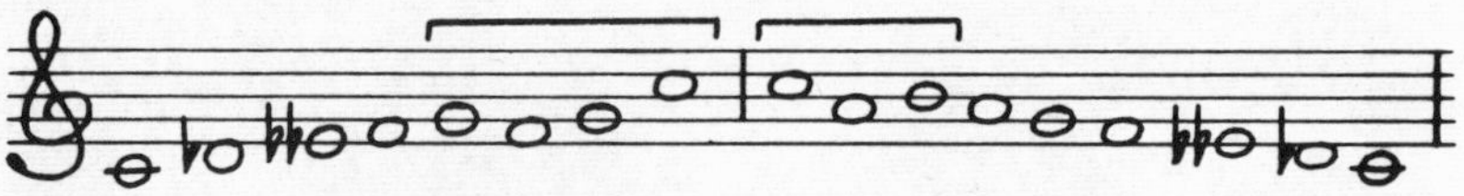

Ascent: the notes *DHA* (A) and *NI* (B) are avoided; one *vakra* feature is shown.
Descent: *sampūrṇa*; one *vakra* feature is used.

(13) *Pūrvasindhu*

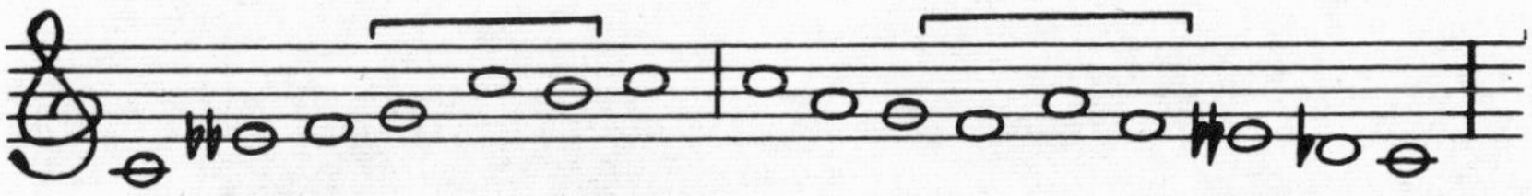

Ascent: the notes *RI* (Db) and *DHA* (A) are avoided; one *vakra* feature is shown.
Descent: the note *NI* (B) is omitted. One *vakra* feature is used.

(14) *Sāgu*

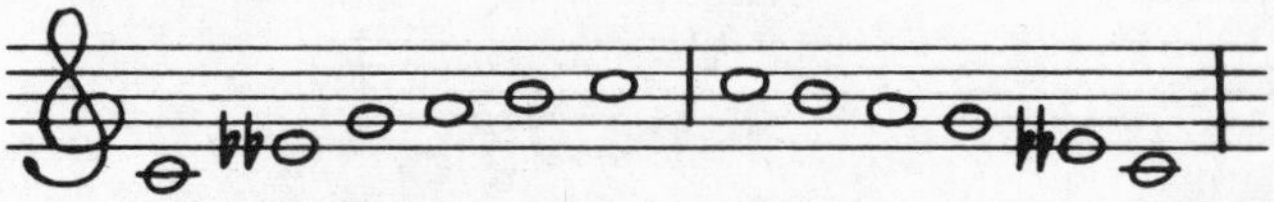

The notes *RI* (Db) and *MA* (F) are avoided entirely.

(15) *Śravanti*

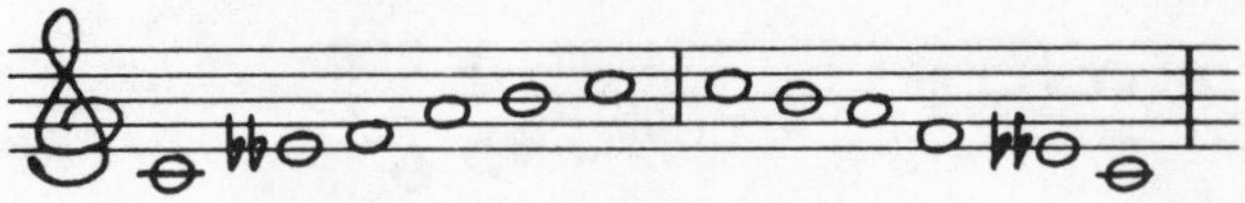

The notes *RI* (Db) and *PA* (G) are avoided entirely.

6. *MĒḶA TĀNARŪPI*

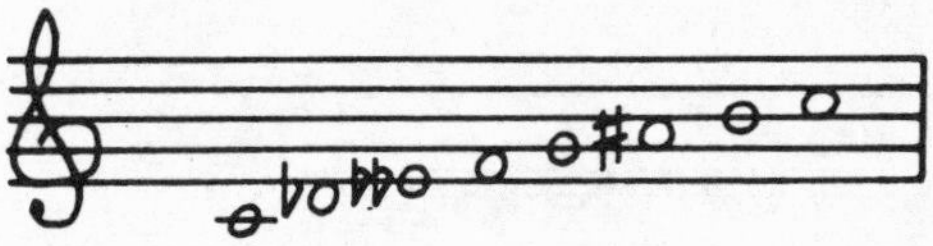

Veṅkaṭamakhin calls the *mēḷa*, *Tanukīrti*. *Rāga Tānarūpi* should be performed in the morning. The notes *RI* (Db), *MA* (F), and *NI* (B) are strong.

The following song specimen is a *kīrtana*:

TĀNARŪPI (*Ādi-tāla*)

Pallavi

Repeat the *pallavi*

Anupallavi

Repeat the *pallavi*

Charana

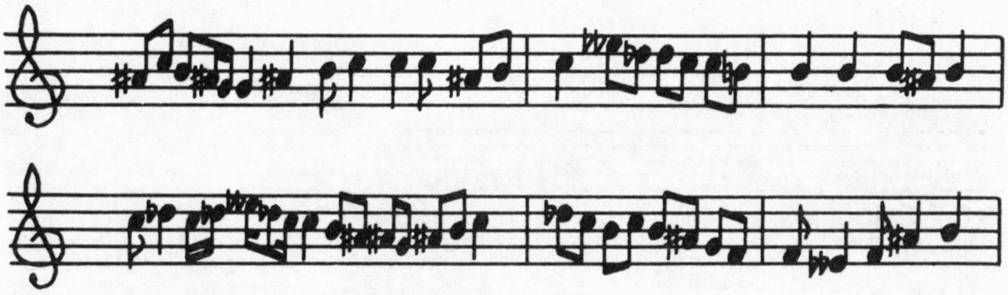

Repeat the *pallavi*. The song ends with the note *SA* (c).

Janya Rāgas of the Sixth Mēḷa

(1) *Tanukīrti*

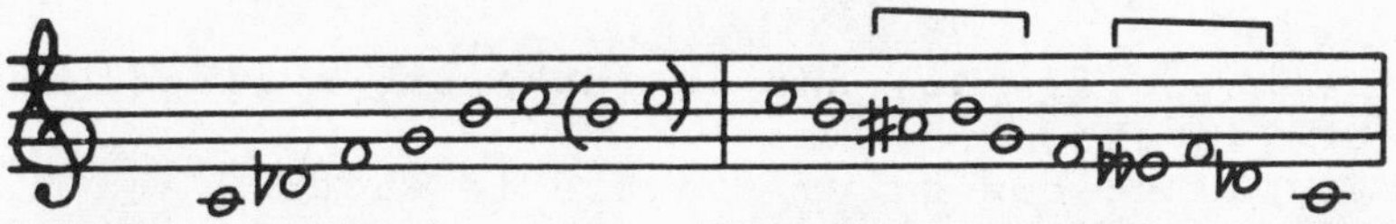

Tanukīrti, as *janya rāga* of the 6. *mēḷa* avoids the notes *GA* (Ebb) and *DHA* (A#) in ascent. The *sampūrṇa* descent shows two *vakra* features.

TANUKĪRTI RĀGA (*Triputa-tāla*) SCM, 14-15

(2) *Bhinnaniṣāda*

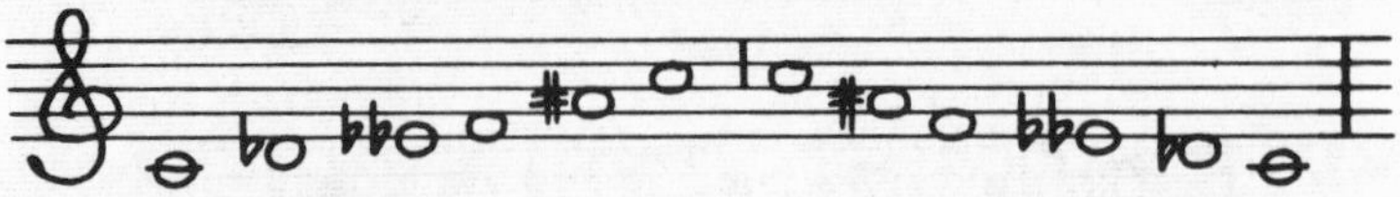

The notes *PA* (G) and *NI* (B) are avoided entirely.

Another *Bhinnaniṣāda* appears under the heading of the 63. *mēḷa* (1) where it is a *niṣādāntya rāga*.

(3) *Chhāyā Nārāyaṇi*

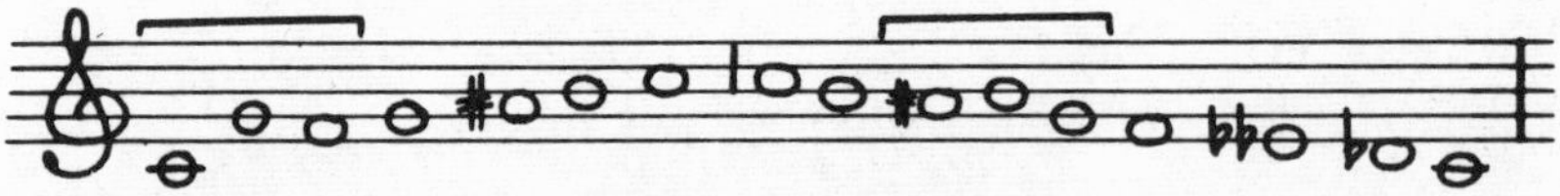

Ascent: the notes *RI* (Db) and *GA* (Ebb) are avoided; one *vakra* feature is shown.
Descent: *sampūrṇa*; one *vakra* feature is shown.

(4) *Dēśya Nārāyaṇi*

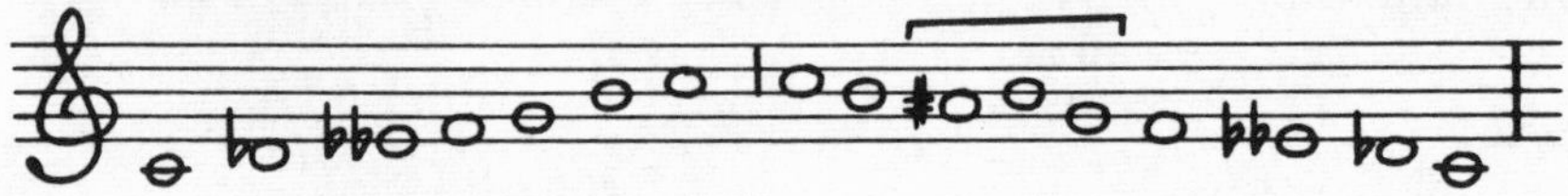

Ascent: the note *DHA* (A#) is avoided.
Descent: *sampūrṇa*; one *vakra* feature is shown.

(5) *Dēśya Suraṭi*

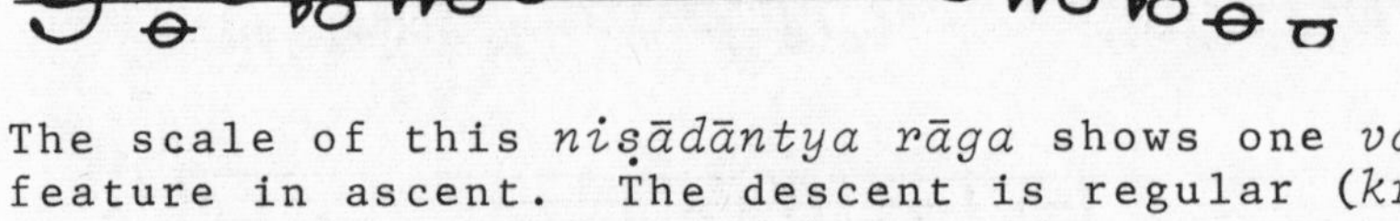

The scale of this *niṣādāntya rāga* shows one *vakra* feature in ascent. The descent is regular (*krama*), but begins with the note *PA* (G) and extends to the low *NI* (B).

(6) *Dharaṇi Priya*

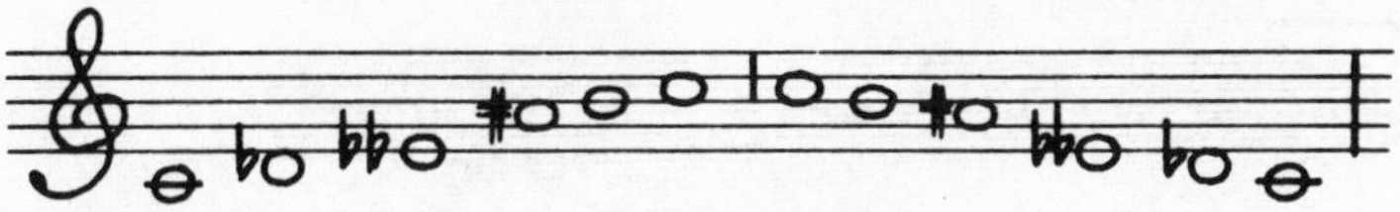

The notes *MA* (F) and *PA* (G) are avoided entirely.

(7) *Gauḷa Māḷavi*

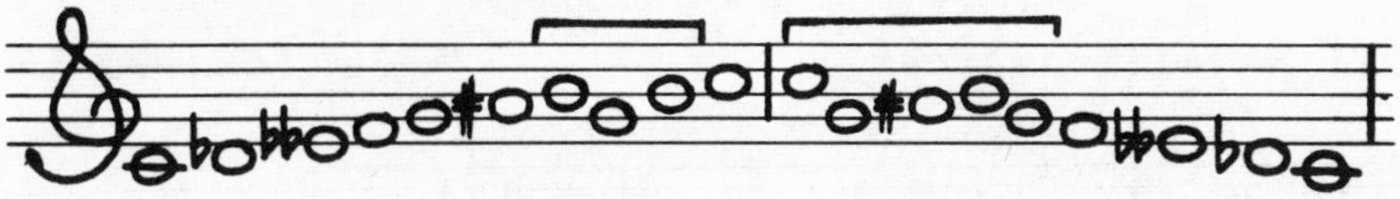

The scale is *sampūrṇa* and shows two *vakra* features, one in ascent and one in descent.

(8) *Īśvarī*

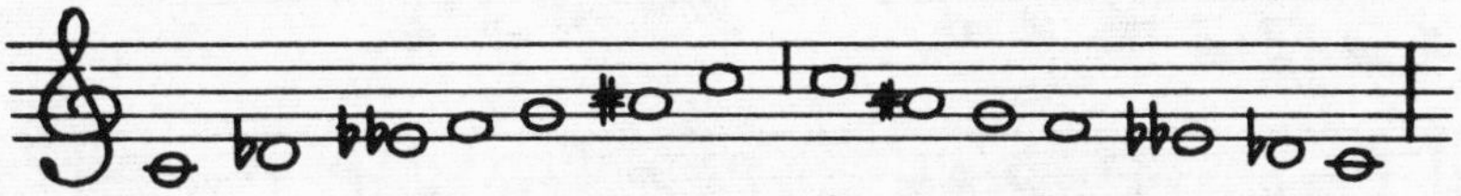

The note *NI* (B) is avoided entirely.

(9) *Jñānasvarūpiṇī*

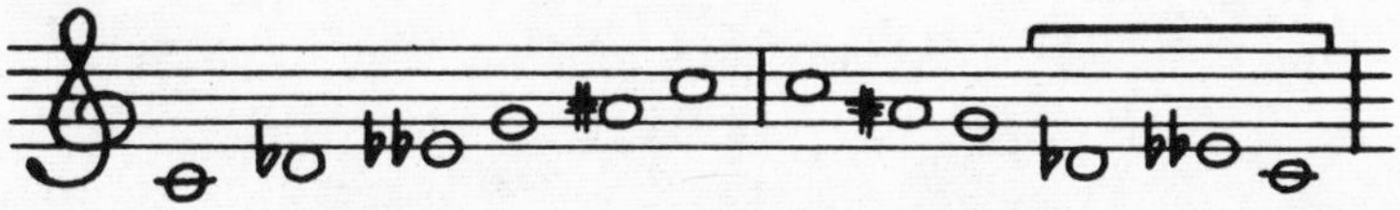

The notes *MA* (F) and *NI* (B) are avoided entirely. In descent appears one *vakra* feature.

(10) *Kamālapati*

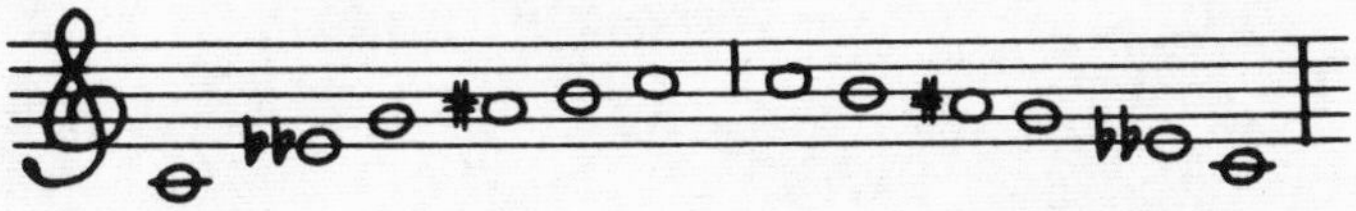

The notes *RI* (Db) and *MA* (F) are avoided entirely.

(11) *Kāśmīra*

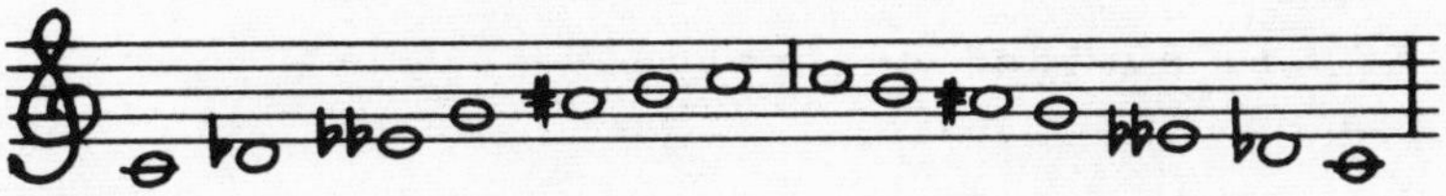

The note *MA* (F) is avoided entirely.

(12) *Śṛṅgāriṇī*

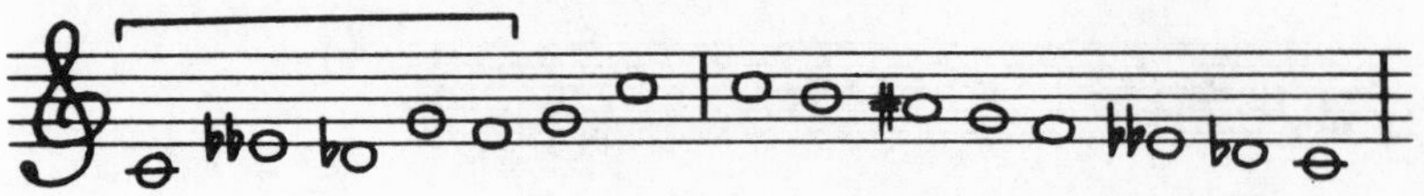

Ascent: the notes *DHA* (A#) and *NI* (B) are avoided; one *vakra* feature is shown.
Descent: *krama sampūrṇa*.

ŚṚṄGĀRIṆĪ RĀGA (Triputa-tāla) SCM, 15-16

(13) *Mahila*

The note *RI* (Db) is avoided entirely.

(14) *Nādarūpi*

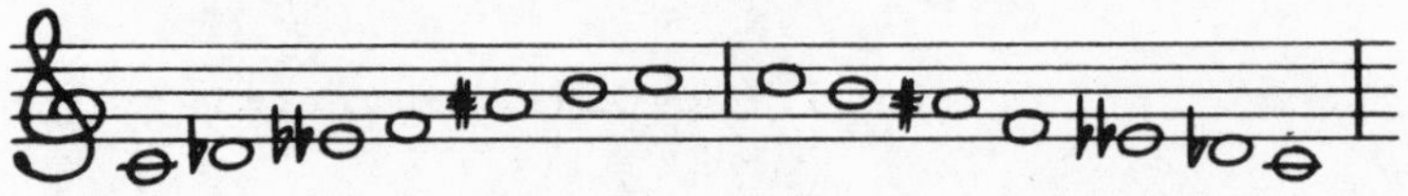

The note *PA* (G) is avoided entirely.

(15) *Śrīmālavi*

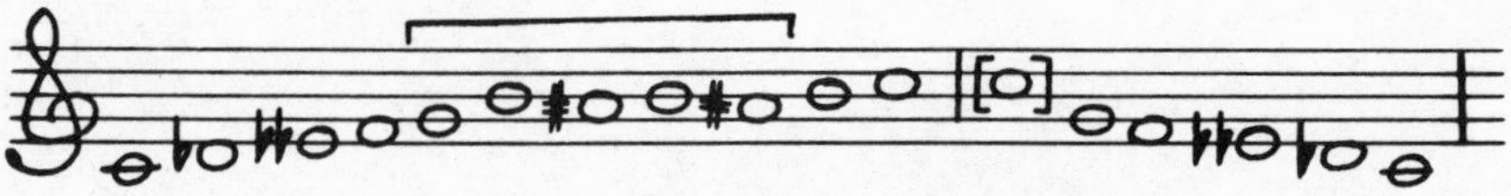

Ascent: *sampūrṇa*; one extended *vakra* feature is shown.
Descent: the notes *NI* (B) and *DHA* (A#) are avoided.

(16) *Taraṇipriya*

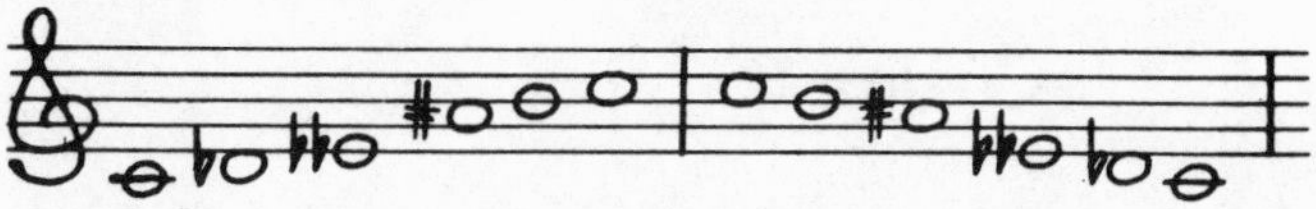

The notes *MA* (F) and *PA* (G) are avoided entirely.

(17) *Tilakaprakāśini*

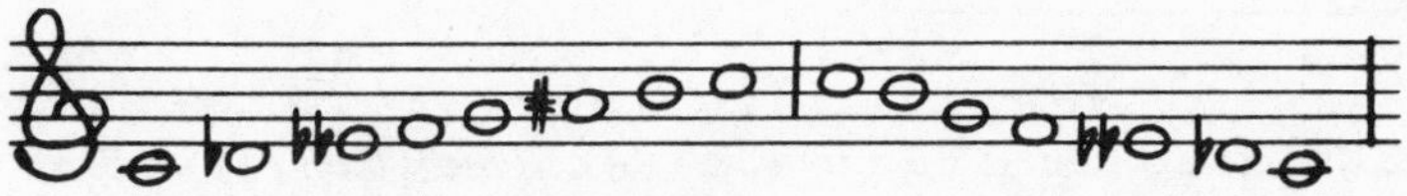

Ascent: *krama sampūrṇa*.
Descent: the note *DHA* (A#) is avoided.

(18) *Vibhāvari*

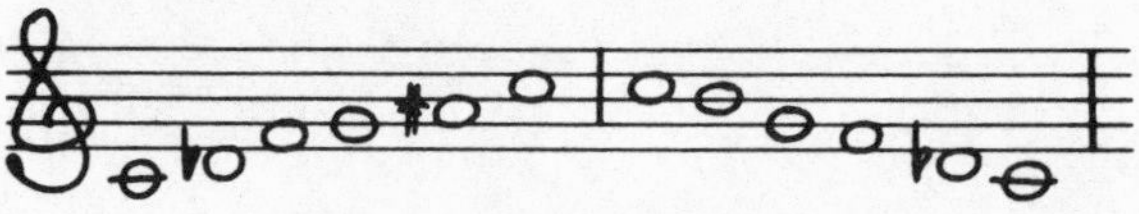

The note *GA* (Ebb) is avoided entirely. *NI* (B) is omitted in ascent and *DHA* (A#) in descent.

Chakra II

7. *MĒḶA SENĀPĀTI (SENĀVATI)*

Veṅkaṭamakhin calls this *mēḷa Senāgraṇī*. In *rāga Senāpāti* the note *GA* (Eb) is almost always approached from below (from *RI*, Db) and shows a slight vibrato. The strong notes in this *rāga* are *RI* (Db), *GA* (Eb), and *DHA* (Ab). *Senāpāti* is to be performed in the morning.

The following song specimen is a *kīrtana*:

SENĀPĀTI (*Ādi-tāla*)

Pallavi

Repeat the *pallavi*

Anupallavi

Repeat the *pallavi*

Charana

Repeat the *pallavi*

Janya Rāgas of the Seventh Mēḷa

(1) *Senāgraṇī*

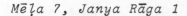

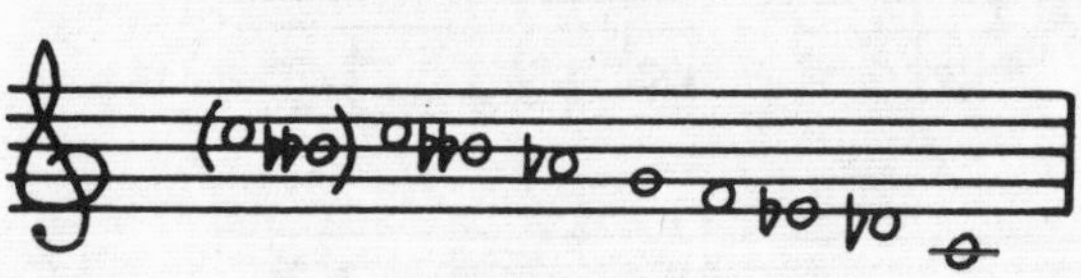

Ascent: the note *PA* (G) is avoided; one *vakra* feature is shown.
Descent: *krama sampūrṇa*.

SENĀGRAṆĪ RĀGA (*Triputa-tāla*) SCM, 17

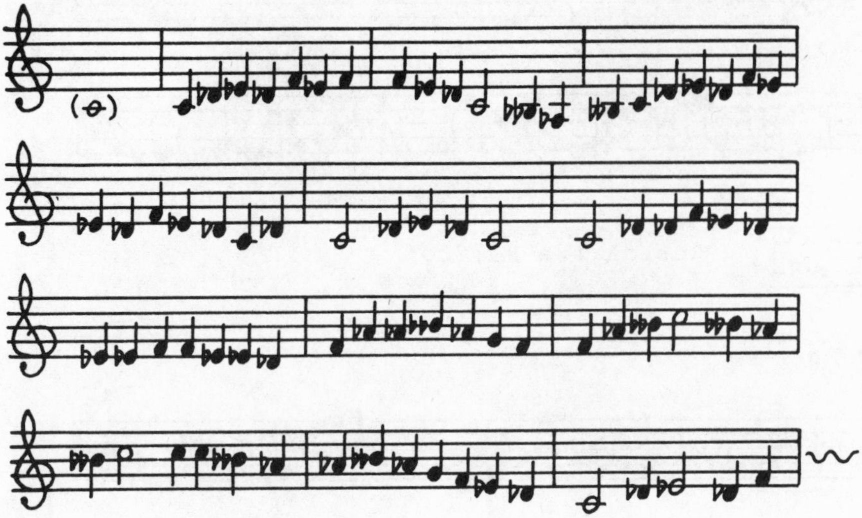

(2) *Bhōgi*

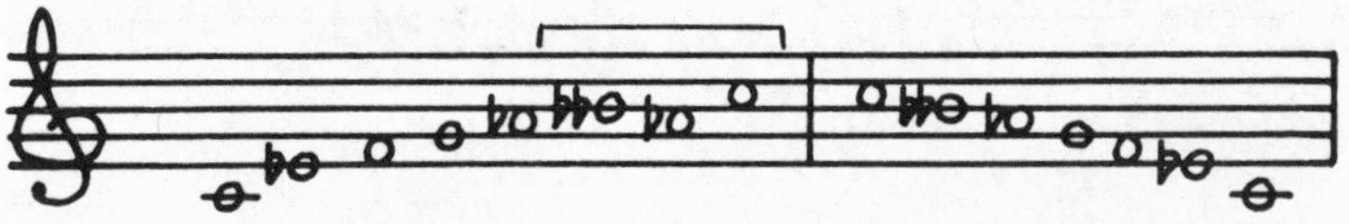

The note *RI* (Db) is avoided entirely. One *vakra* feature is shown in ascent.

BHŌGI RĀGA (*Triputa-tāla*) SCM, 17-18

(3) *Chintāmaṇi* (*Cintāmaṇi*, *Bhōga-Chintāmaṇi*, *Jaṭshrintāmaṇi*)

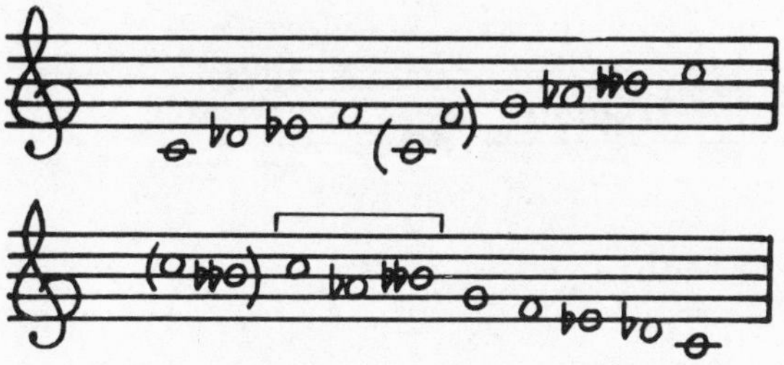

The scale of this *rāga* is *sampūrṇa* and shows one *vakra* feature in descent.

CHINTĀMAṆI RĀGA (*Triputa-tāla*) SCM, 18

Other *janya rāgas* with the same name appear under the headings of the 1. (5) and 56. (7) *mēḷas*.

(4) *Aṅguru*

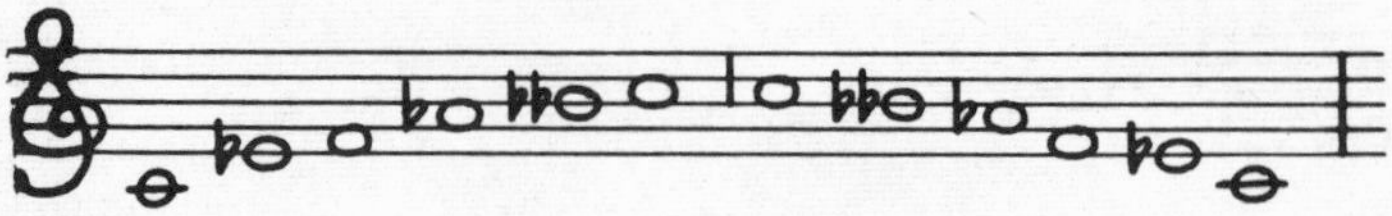

The notes *RI* (Db) and *PA* (G) are avoided entirely.

(5) *Anīkini*

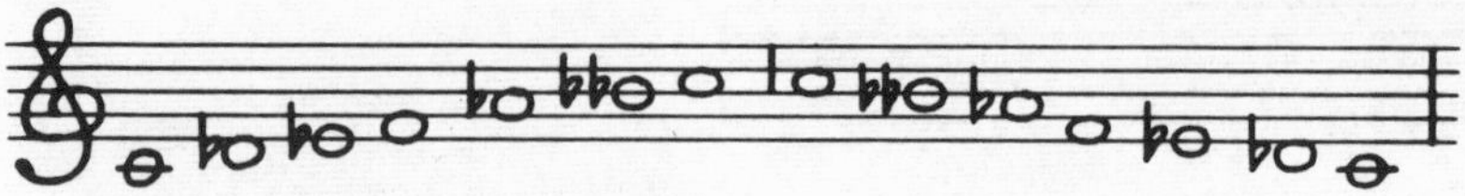

The note *PA* (G) is avoided entirely.

(6) *Bhānugauḷa*

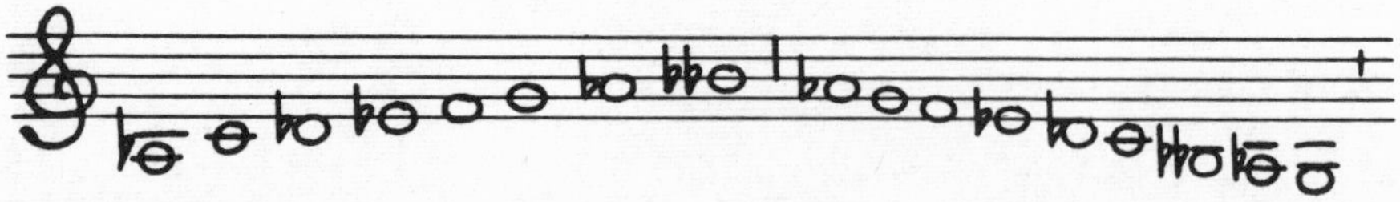

The scale of this *rāga* is *niṣādāntya*.

(7) *Bhōga Rañjani*

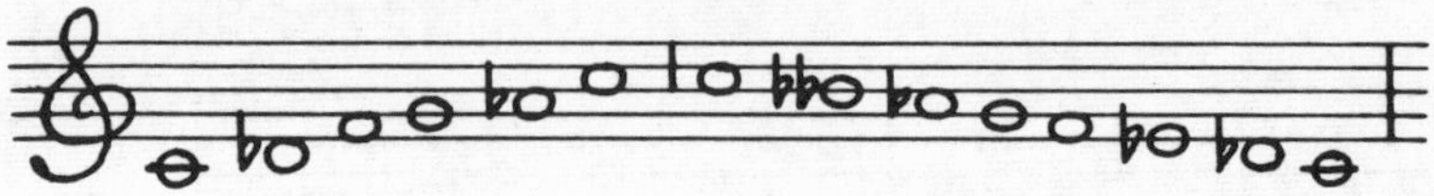

Ascent: the notes *GA* (Eb) and *NI* (Bbb) are avoided.
Descent: *krama sampūrṇa*.

(8) *Bhōga Śikhāmaṇi*

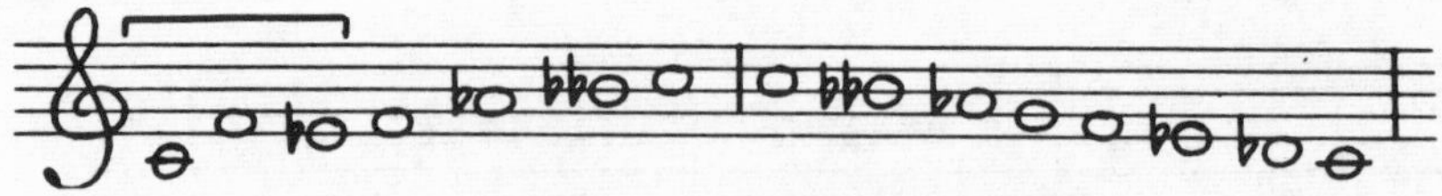

Ascent: the notes *RI* (Db) and *PA* (G) are avoided; one *vakra* feature is shown.
Descent: *krama sampūrṇa*.

(9) *Bōtika*

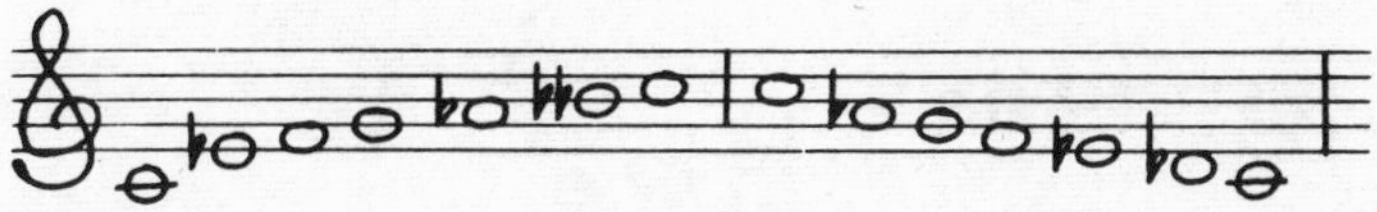

Ascent: the note *RI* (Db) is avoided.
Descent: the note *NI* (Bbb) is omitted.

(10) *Chhāyā Gauri*

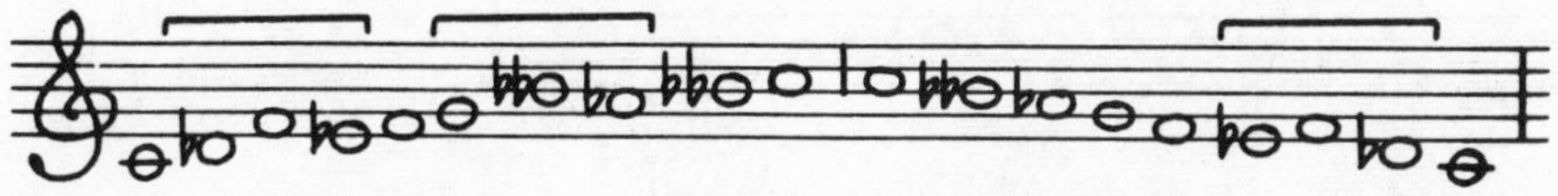

The scale is *sampūrṇa* and shows two *vakra* features in ascent and one in descent. SD (I, 84) remarks that *Chhāyā Gauri* is listed as a *janya rāga* of the 15. *mēḷa* in *Rāga Tāla Cintāmaṇi* (n.d.; see SD I, viii), a work in Telugu.

(11) *Chhāyā Māḷavi*

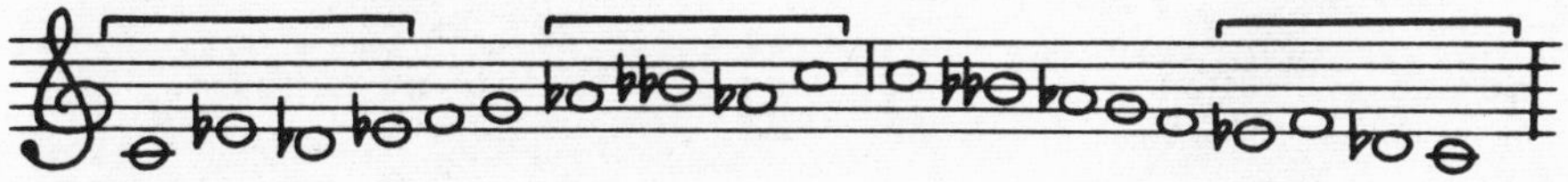

The scale is *sampūrṇa* and shows two *vakra* features in ascent and one in descent.

(12) *Chiraṇṭi*

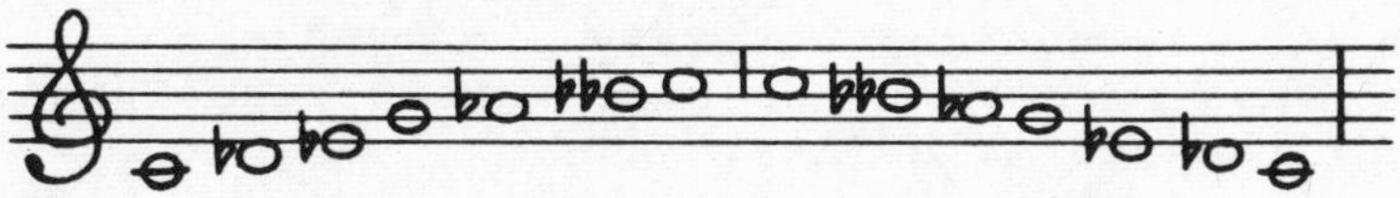

The note *MA* (F) is avoided entirely.

(13) *Chittākarshiṇi*

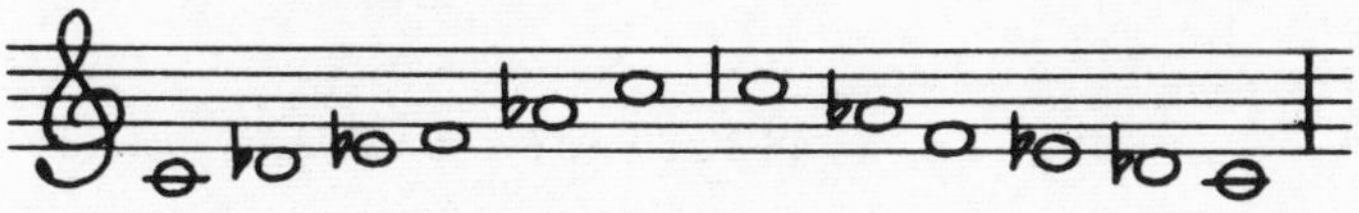

The notes *PA* (G) and *NI* (Bbb) are avoided entirely.

(14) *Dīrghika*

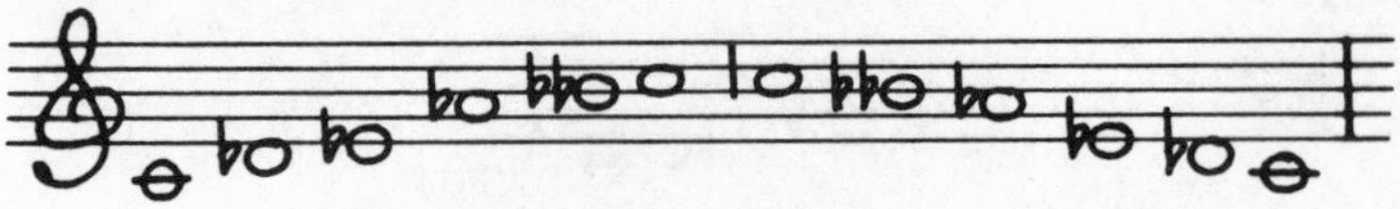

The notes *MA* (F) and *PA* (G) are avoided entirely.

(15) *Gauḷa Chandrika*

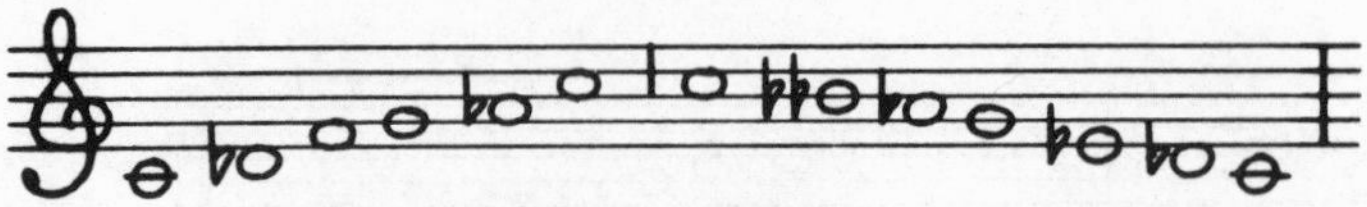

Ascent: the notes *GA* (Eb) and *NI* (Bbb) are avoided.
Descent: the note *MA* (F) is omitted.

(16) *Kalākaṇṭha*

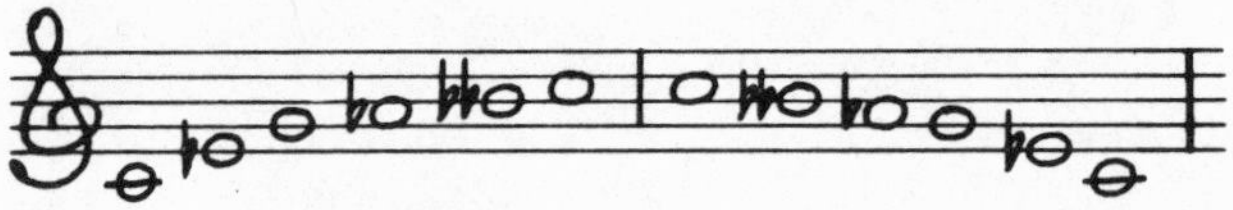

The notes *RI* (Db) and *MA* (F) are avoided entirely.

(17) *Karatoyam*

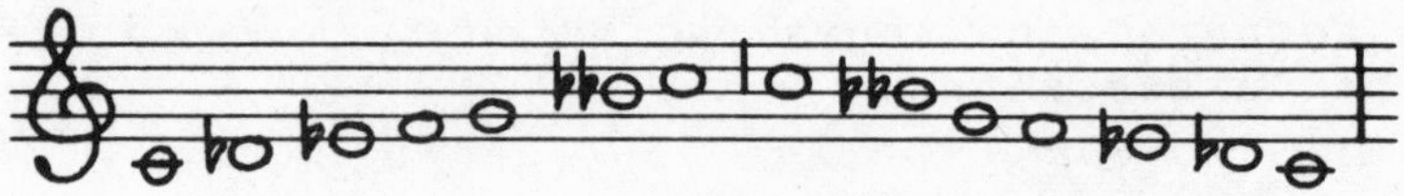

The note *DHA* (Ab) is avoided entirely.

Another *janya rāga* with the same name appears under the heading of the 56. *mēḷa* (14).

(18) *Īśagauḷa*

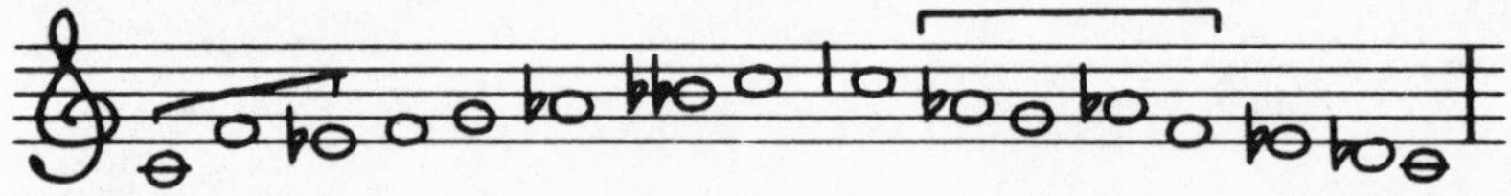

Ascent: the note *RI* (Db) is avoided; one *vakra* feature is shown.
Descent: the note *NI* (Bbb) is omitted; one *vakra* feature is used.

(19) *Malayajālapini*

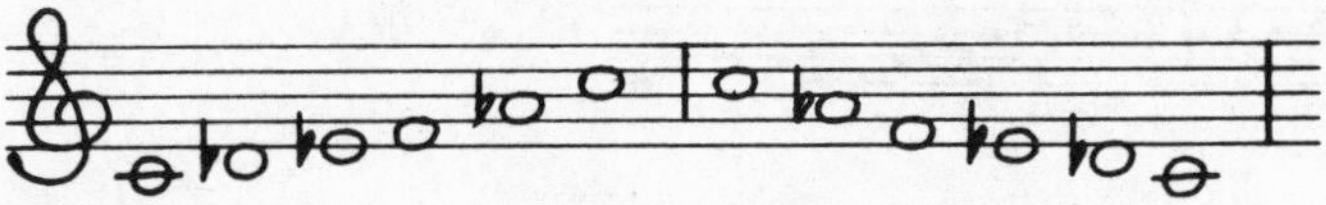

The notes *PA* (G) and *NI* (Bbb) are avoided entirely.

(20) *Rāgarañjani*

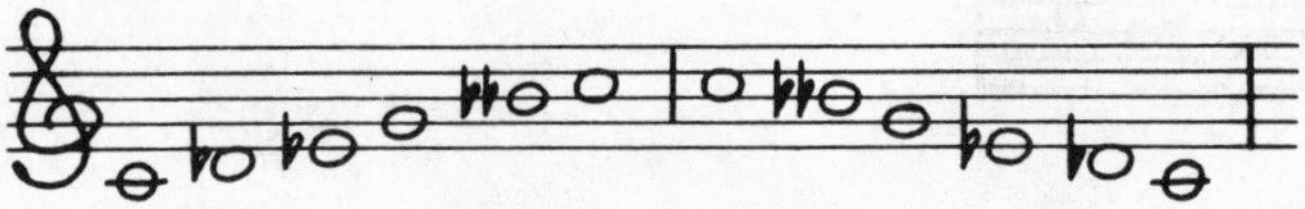

The notes *MA* (F) and *DHA* (Ab) are avoided entirely.

(21) *Saindhavagauḷi*

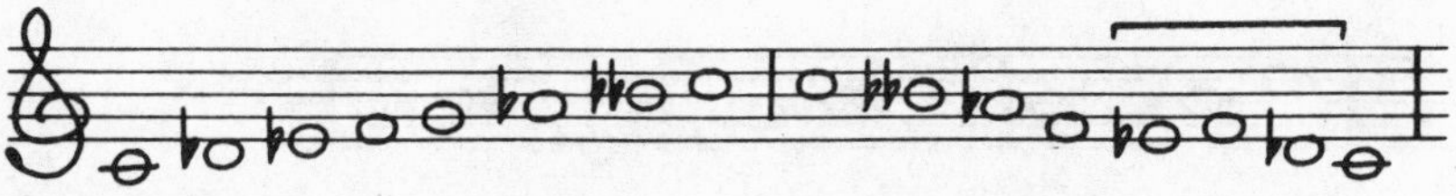

Ascent: *krama sampūrṇa*.
Descent: the note *PA* (G) is avoided; one *vakra* feature is shown.

(22) *Sindhugauri*

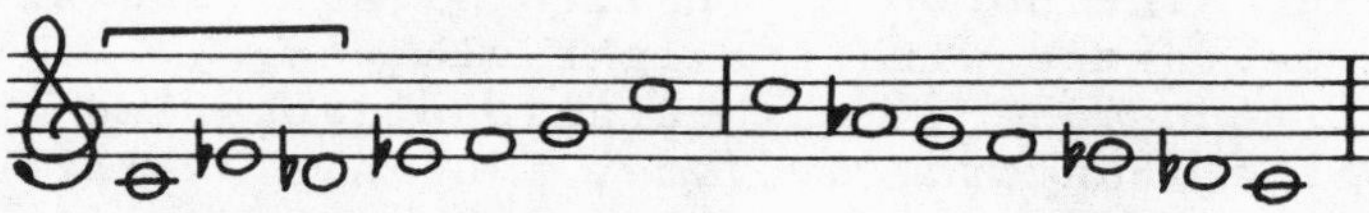

The note *NI* (Bbb) is avoided entirely. *DHA* (Ab) is omitted in ascent. One *vakra* feature is shown in ascent.

(23) *Tīrghika*

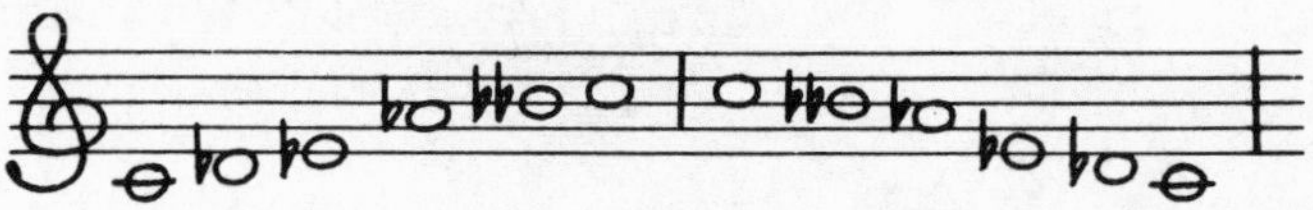

The notes *MA* (F) and *PA* (G) are avoided entirely.

(24) *Vitika*

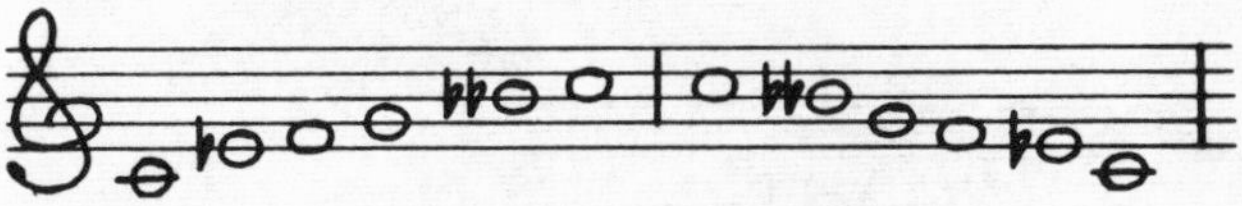

The notes *RI* (Db) and *DHA* (Ab) are avoided entirely.

8. *MĒḶA HANUMATTŌḌI* (*HANUMATŌḌI*, *HANUMANTŌḌI*)

Hanumattōḍi is a popular *rāga* with numerous *janya rāgas*. It is to be performed in the evening. S (III, 26), however, states, that it can be performed at any time. The strong (*aṃśa*) notes are *MA* (F) and *PA* (G).

Characteristic phrases in this *rāga* are supposed to be:

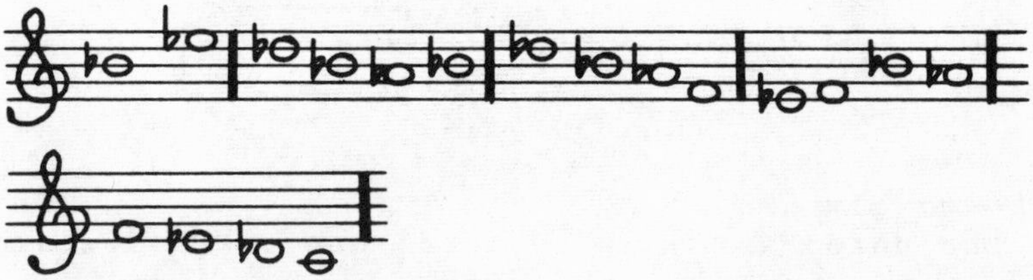

Melodies in *Hanumattōḍi* can begin with *SA* (C), *GA* (Eb), *MA* (F), *PA* (G), *DHA* (Ab), and *NI* (Bb); only *RI* (Db) is excluded. The notes *GA* (Eb), *DHA* (Ab), and *NI* (Bb) are often performed with a slight vibrato.

In the past *Hanumattōḍi* was occasionally called *Janatōḍi*. Ahobala (*Saṅgīta Pārijāta*, 1700 A.D.) states that in this *rāga* the note *DHA* (Ab) is the *nyāsa* ("finalis") and *GA* (Eb) the *aṃśa* (strong note). Govinda calls this *rāga*, in which the note *PA* (G) is avoided, *Śuddha Tōḍi*. Even at the present time it can be observed that the note *PA* (G) is weak in *Hanumattōḍi* and is avoided entirely in its first *janya rāga Tōḍi*.

HANUMATTŌḌI (*Ādi-tāla*) SPC III, 54

Pallavi

Anupallavi

Charana

The foregoing *kīrtana*, composed by Pattanam Subrahmanya Aiyer (1845-1902), a well-known musician of the Madras region, appears under the heading *Tōḍi*. At the present time there is indeed no difference between the primary *rāga* (*Hanumattōḍi*) and its first *janya* (*Tōḍi*). The SCM makes a distinction which will be observed when the *janya rāga* is presented. But there is little doubt that *Tōḍi* can stand for *Hanumattōḍi*.

HANUMATTŌḌI (*Triputa-tāla*) SCM, 19

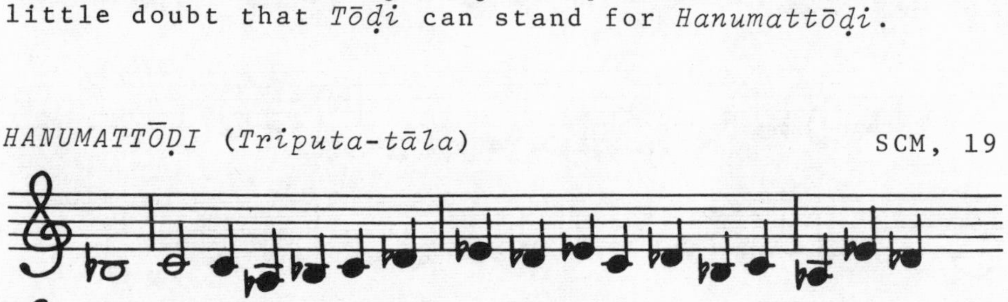

Janya Rāgas of the Eighth Mēḷa

Many *janya rāgas* of this *mēḷa* have become as popular as the primary *rāga*. The frequency of their performances shows different interpretations and, as with the other popular *mēḷas* and *rāgas*, changes from given materials and patterns cannot be called exceptions but represent more or less widely accepted habits.

(1) *Tōḍi* (*Janatōḍi*, *Śuddhatōḍi*)

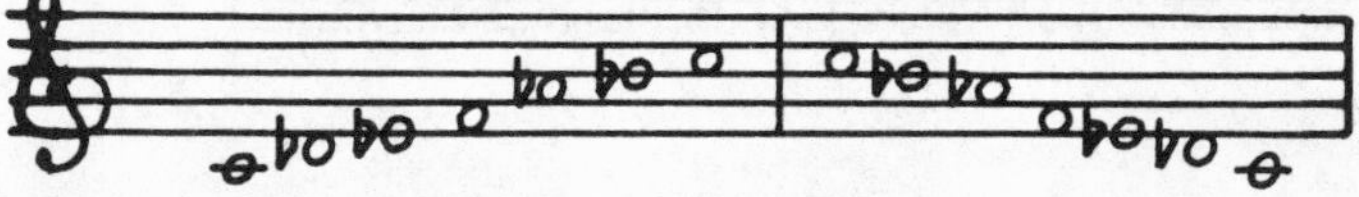

As already mentioned, the *janya rāga Tōḍi*, as shown in the SCM, avoids the note *PA* (G) entirely. But there are other *Tōḍi* interpretations that employ this note and thus lose their distinction from the primary *rāga* (*Hanumattōḍi*).

RAGA TODI (*Triputa-tāla*) SCM, 20

The following song specimen, composed by the Maharaja Swati Tirunal of Travancore (1813-47) employs the note *PA* (G) and thus shows no difference from *Hanumattōḍi*:

TŌḌI RAGA (*Ādi-tāla*) SPC II, 53

Pallavi

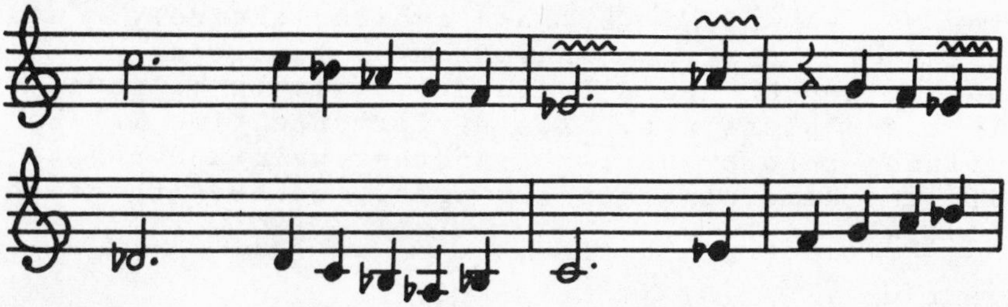

Charana

(2) *Bhūpāḷa(m)*

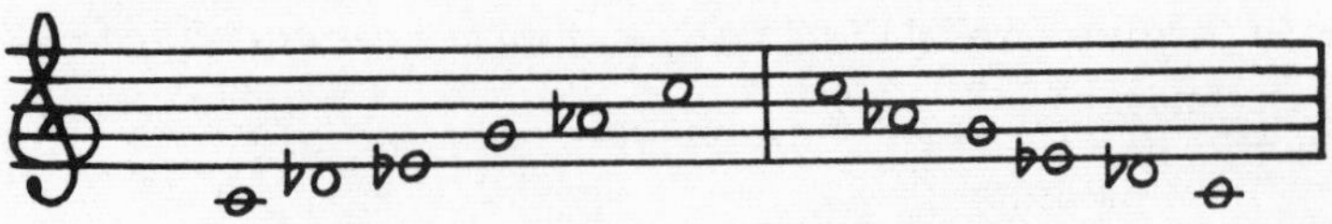

The notes *MA* (F) and *NI* (Bb) are avoided entirely. *GA* (Eb) is said to be strong, having *aṃśa* function.

Bhūpāḷa can be heard frequently. It is believed to bring luck and blessings. Its performance time is the early morning before sunrise. Another well-known *janya rāga* with the same name appears under the heading of the 15. *mēḷa* (24).

BHŪPĀLAM RĀGA (*Ādi-tāla*)

Pallavi

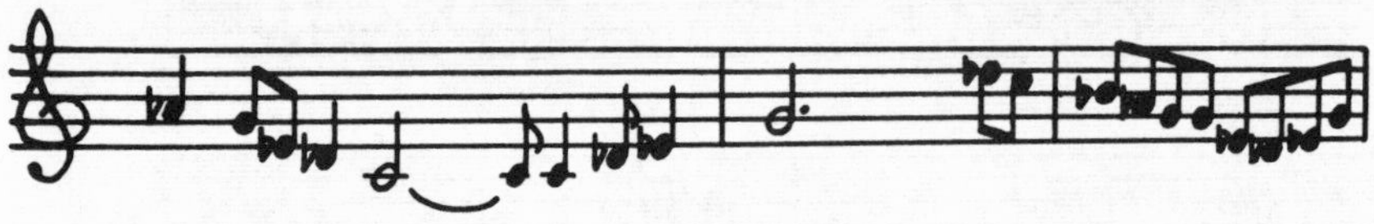

Anupallavi

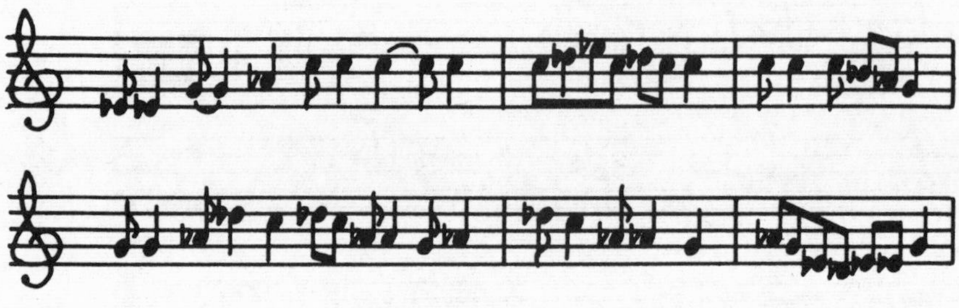

Charana

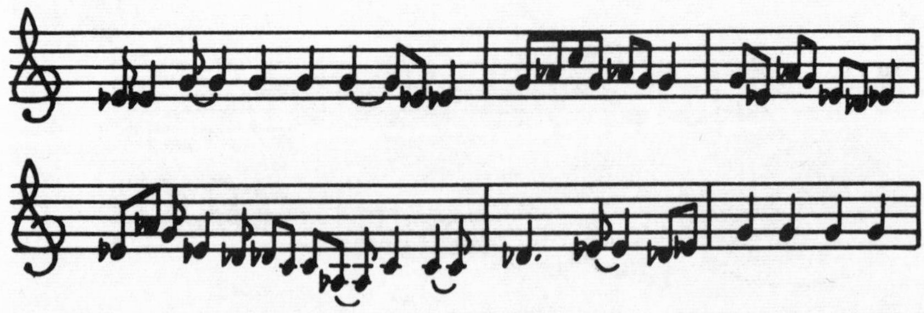

In the performance of the foregoing song the soloist usually adds a second *charana* which consists of the two lines of the *anupallavi*.

RĀGA BHŪPAḶA (*Triputa-tāla*) SCM, 20

(3) *Nāgavarāḷi*

The scale is a *dhaivatāntya* type, meaning that its highest note is *DHA* (Ab). *Nāgavarāḷi*, not to be mistaken for *Nāgasvarāḷi* (a *janya* of the 28. *mēḷa*), shows two *vakra* features, one in ascent and one in descent.

Govinda describes the scale of this *rāga* in the following manner:

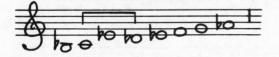

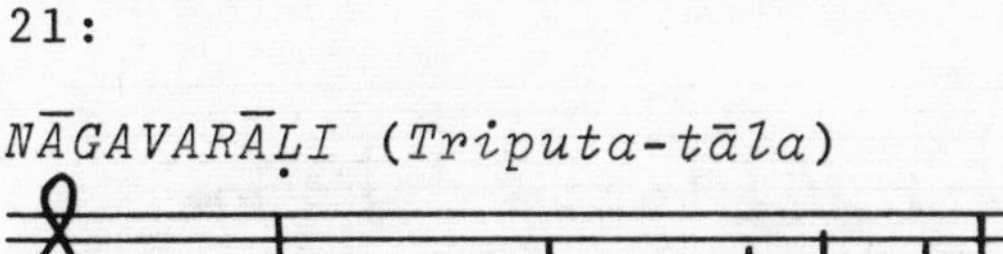

The descent is identical with the one shown above.

The following melody specimen is taken from SCM, 21:

NĀGAVARĀḶI (*Triputa-tāla*)

(4) *Śuddhasamant* (*Śuddhasīmantī*, *Śuddhasīmantinī*)

This obscure *janya rāga* is identical with *Nāgavarāli*. Govinda, however, presents the scale in a different form:

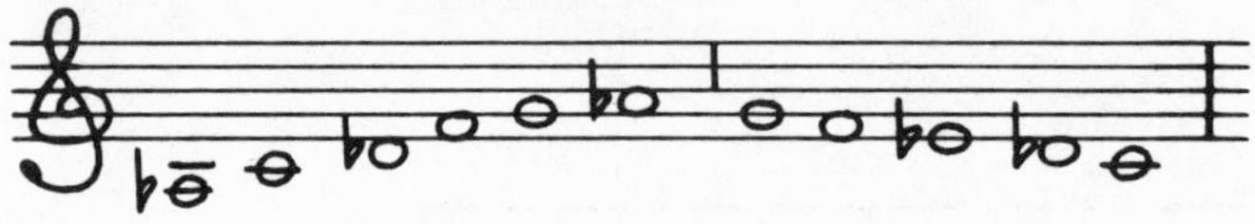

Veṅkaṭamakhin does not describe this *janya* at all. The note *ṄI* (Bb) is avoided entirely and *GA* (Eb), according to Govinda, is omitted in ascent; it appears, however, in the following melody specimen:

RĀGA ŚUDDHASĪMANTĪ (*Triputa-tāla*) SCM, 24

Another form of the scale, occasionally and not reliably referred to as *Śuddhasīmantinī*, avoids the note *NI* (Bb) entirely but stresses the notes *GA* (Eb) and *DHA* (Ab) in contrast to Govinda's rule which prescribes the omission of *GA* (Eb) in ascent.

ŚUDDHASĪMANTINĪ RĀGA (*Ādi-tāla*)

Pallavi

Anupallavi

Charana

(5) *Āsāvēri*

Ascent: the notes *GA* (Eb) and *NI* (Bb) are avoided.
Two forms of descent: (a) *sampūrṇa*; (b) the note *MA* (F) is omitted and one *vakra* feature is shown.
Strong notes are *RI* (Db), *GA* (Eb), and *DHA* (Ab).

In the passages *GA-RI-MA* and *RI-MA-PA* the note *RI* is intoned about a semitone higher to *catuḥśruti RI* (D natural) whereby the two passages become Eb-D-F and D-F-G.

Another *Āsāvēri*, usually written *Āsāvari*, derived from the North Indian *rāga* (see RNI, 463-69) can appear under the heading of the 20. *mēḷa*. This *rāga* is not shown in this study because it represents a North Indian form.

ĀSĀVĒRI RĀGA (*Ādi-tāla*)

Pallavi

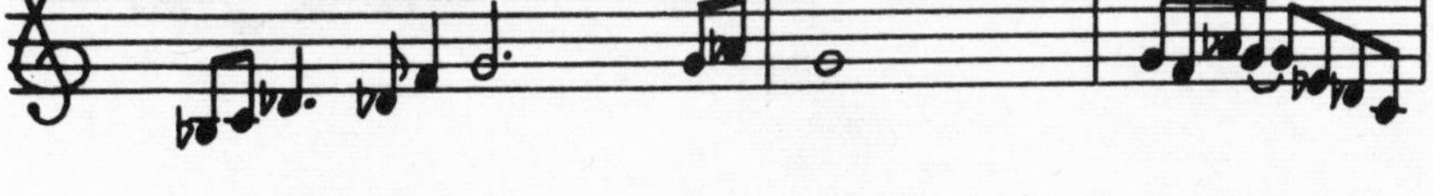

Anupallavi

Charana

The foregoing song example offers a comparatively clear, although abbreviated, picture of the formal structure of *kīrtanas*.

Pallavi: The first line is usually repeated, often with some minor modifications, as can be observed in the second line. The third line is repeated in the fourth in a manner similar to the way the first and second lines are performed. The fifth line is repeated only occasionally. This repetition is optional and has not been notated in the example.
Anupallavi: The sixth and seventh lines are not repeated. They often are followed by a repetition of the *pallavi* (not shown in the transcription).
Charana: This section is not repeated. It is followed either by the entire *pallavi* or by its first three lines. The final note of the song has to be a strong note, either *SA* (C) or *PA* (G).

In numerous *kīrtanas* the second half of the *charana* either imitates the material of the *anupallavi* or merely repeats the *anupallavi*, and the first half of the *charana* either imitates or repeats the material of the *pallavi*.

A further form of *Āsāvēri* is *Āsāvēri Tōḍi*. It differs from *Āsāvēri* by the use of the note *ṄI* (Bb) in ascent:

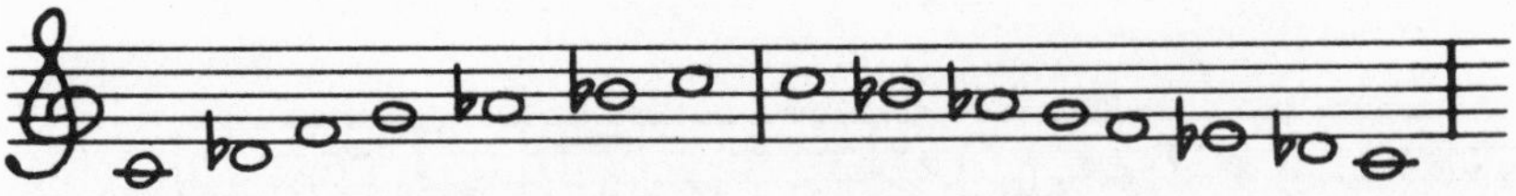

(6) *Punnāgavarāḷi*

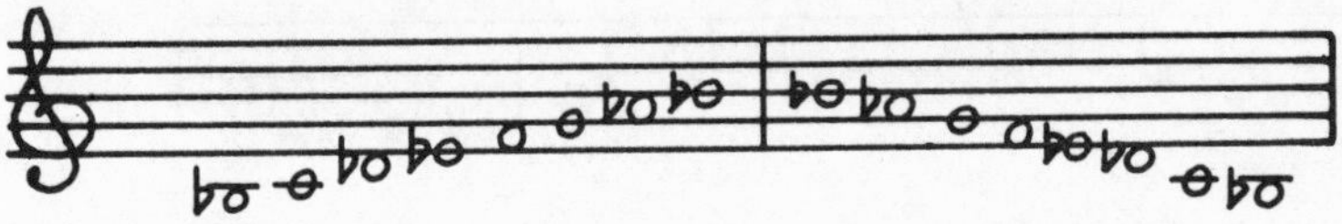

This *rāga* is to be performed in the morning. Its scale has *niṣādāntya* character. In the following passage the note *RĪ* is intoned high as *catuḥśruti RI* (D natural): *GA-RI-GA-MA-PA* (Eb-D-Eb-F-G). Strong notes are *GA* (Eb), *MA* (F), *DHA* (Ab), and *NI* (Bb).

The following song specimen represents a *varadi kīrtana*, a simple one-section song without an *anupallavi*. After the first *charana* the singer repeats the *pallavi*. Then follows the second *charana*.

PUNNĀGAVARĀḶI RĀGA (Ādi-tāla)

Pallavi

First charana

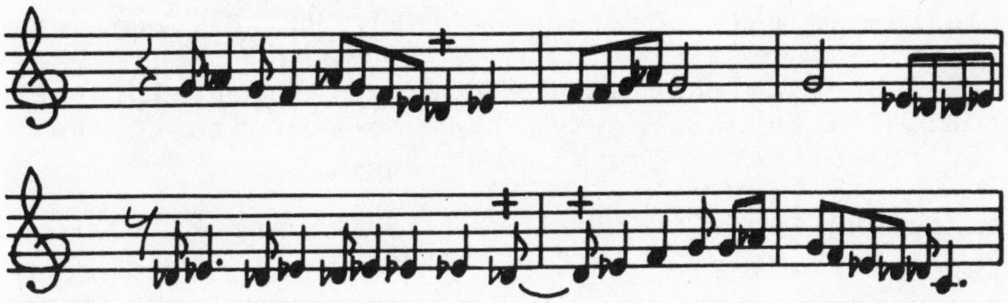

Second charana

After the first *charana* the soloist usually repeats the *pallavi*; then follows the second *charana*.

(7) *Āhiri Tōḍi (Āhiri)*

This *rāga*, frequently called simply *Āhiri*, can be interpreted in various ways. Therefore it is called a *bhaṣanga rāga*, a "mixed form," in which notes foreign to its basic tone material may be employed. This is the reason why *Āhiri* can be ascribed not only to the 8. but also to the 14. *mēḷa*. In the past, Veṅkaṭamakhin had placed this *janya* under the heading of his 20. *mēḷa*.

Āhiri is an evening *rāga* and has, despite its frequent use in religious songs, a popular character. Musicians of the older generation will remember the saying that if this *rāga* is performed at the wrong time, in the morning, for instance, the singer will be unable to find food for the rest of the day.

The basic *Āhiri* scale is:

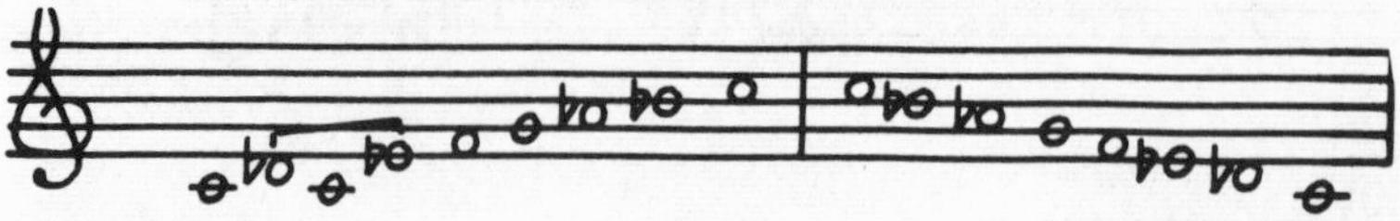

Strong notes in this *rāga* are *GA* (Eb), *MA* (F), *DHA* (Ab), and *NI* (Bb).

Āhiri phrases that employ not only the basic notes of the 8. *mēḷa* but also notes that are foreign to the scale of the primary *rāga* can be:

śuddha RI (Db)

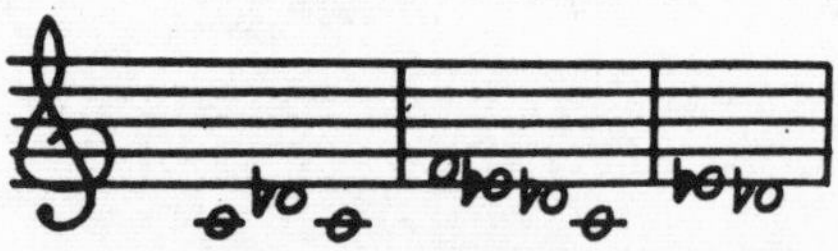

catuḥśruti RI (D)

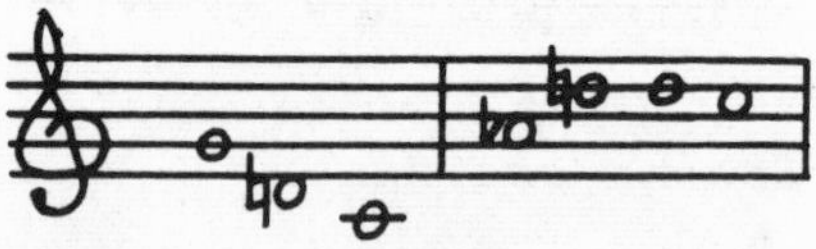

sādhāraṇa GA (Eb)

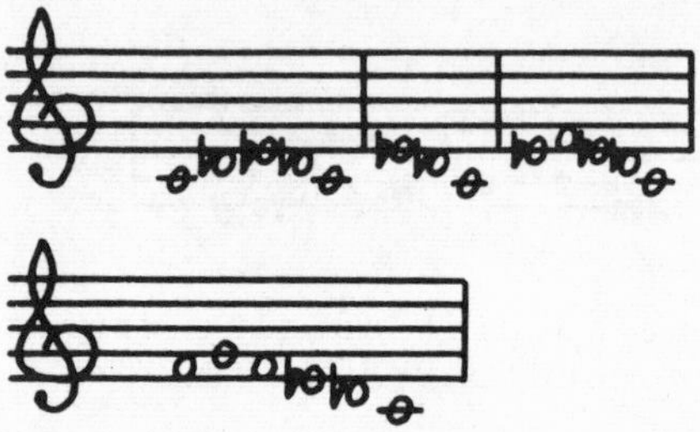

antara GA (E)

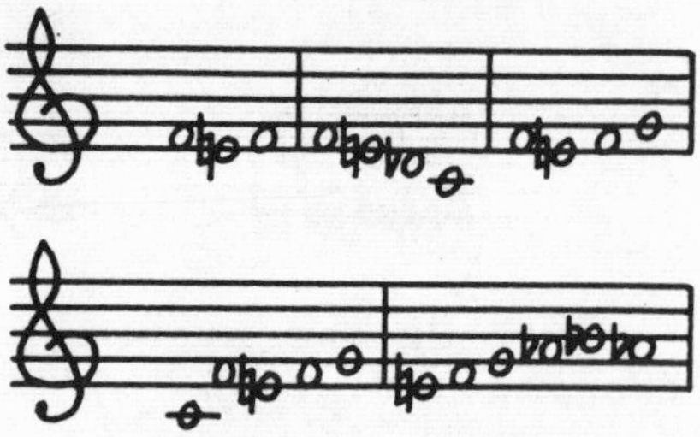

śuddha DHA (Ab)

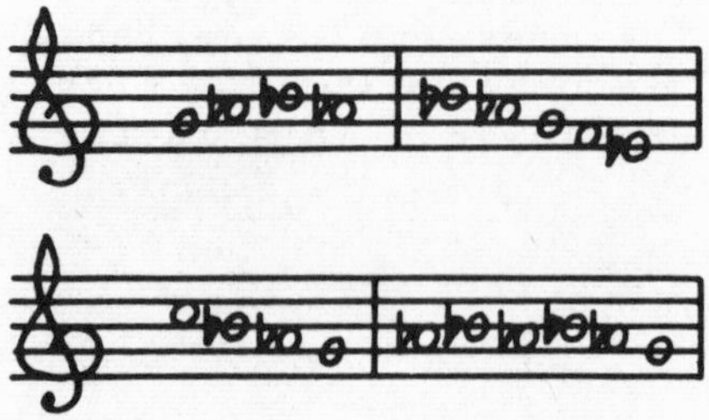

catuḥśruti DHA (A)

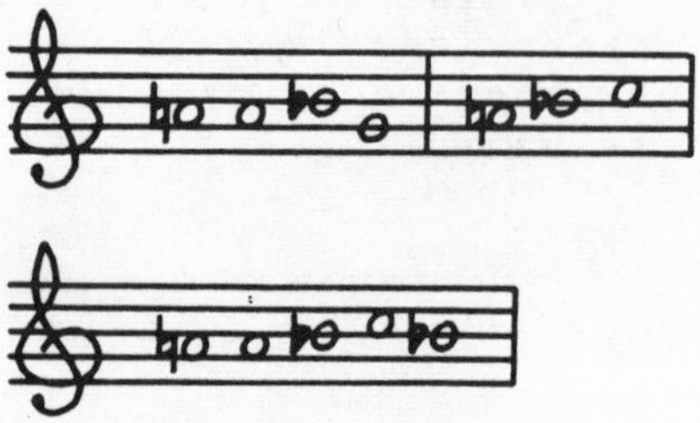

kaiśiki NI (Bb)

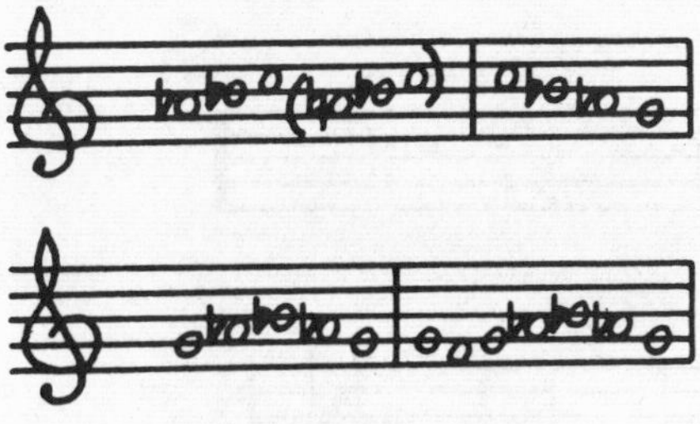

kākalī NI (B)

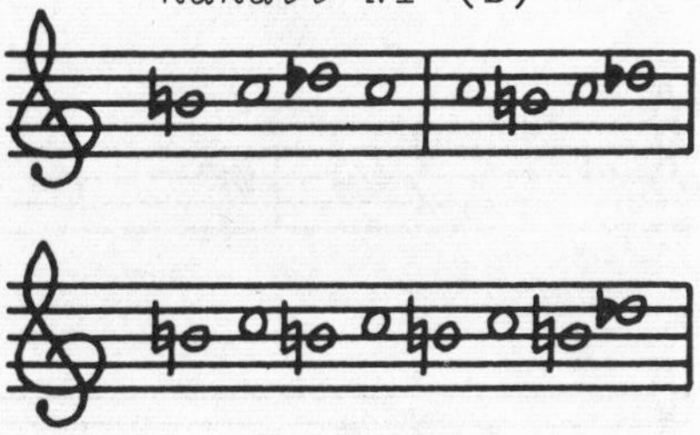

The rules concerning the use of regular and foreign notes are vague, and performers allow themselves various liberties.

A general survey of the *Āhiri* material shows the following dispositions:

śuddha RI (Db): usually employed in descent
catuḥśruti RI (D): used in skips
sādhāraṇa GA (Eb): mainly in descent
antara ĠA (E): usually in ascent, particularly before *MA* (F)
śuddha DHA (Ab): used in descent
catuḥśruti DHA (A): appears in ascent, usually before *ṆI* (Bb).
kaiśiki NI (Bb): can appear in ascent and descent
kākalī NI (B): used in ascent before *SA* (c)

The variety of using these notes is unusually large. It may be added that these phenomena appear in all *Āhiri* types, and at times there arise difficulties of classifying the resulting melodies under the headings of specific *mēḷas*.

The following song example, a *kīrtana* in the popular *chāpu tāla*,[2] shows a simple form of *Āhiri* in which none of the altered notes occurs:

ĀHIRI RĀGA (Chapu-tāla)

First pallavi

Second pallavi

Repeat the first pallavi

Charana

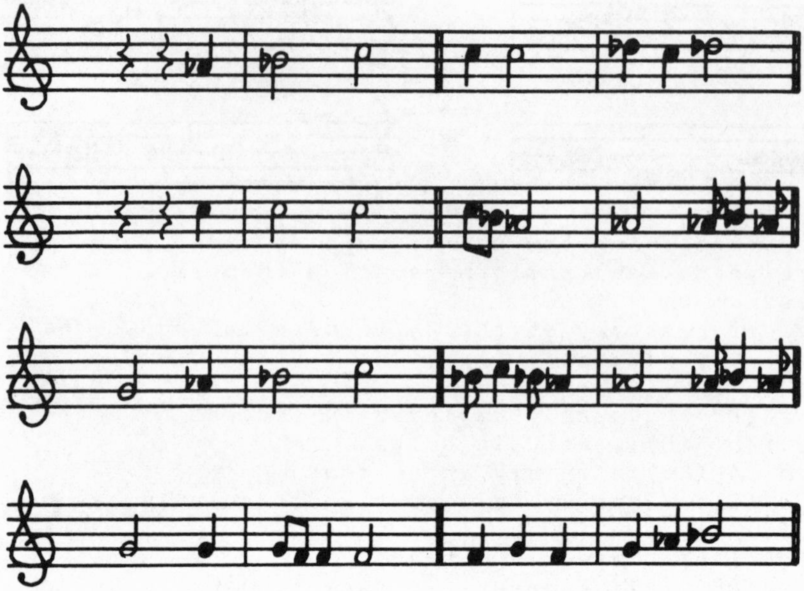

(8) *Dēśyatōḍi*

There are several opinions concerning the tone material and performance practice of this *janya rāga*. The most frequently offered description shows a scale that avoids the note *RI* (Db) in ascent and is *sampūrṇa* in descent.

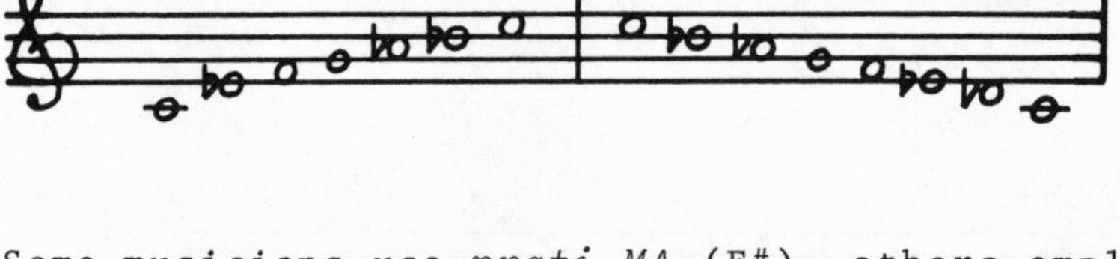

Some musicians use *prati MA* (F#), others employ both forms of *MA* (F and F#), and others oppose one or the other method. *Dēśyatōḍi*, also known as *Turuṣka Tōḍi* ("Turkish Tōḍi"), is believed to be of northern origin. In the South there exists allegedly only one *kṛti* in this *rāga*, composed by Tyāgarāja. This song is usually sung in such a manner that the listener has the impression of hearing *rāga Śubhapantuvarāḷī* (45. *mēḷa*).

According to S (VI, 185) *Divyamalati*, a recently created *janya rāga* appears to be closely related to *Dēśyatōḍi*. Its scale avoids the note *RI* (Db) entirely.

(9) *Ghaṇṭā*

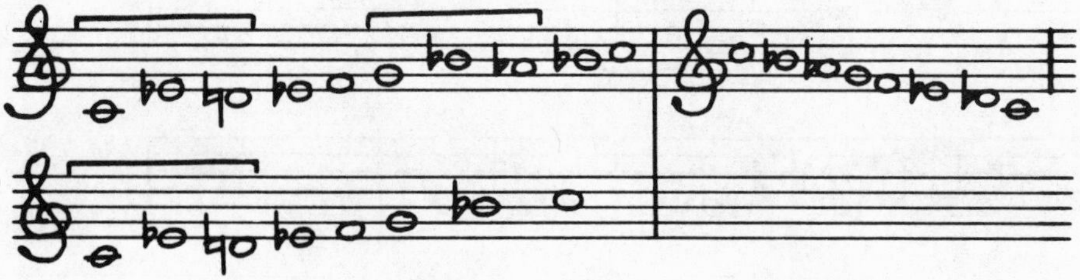

The scale of this *rāga* has two ascending forms. The first one is *sampūrṇa* and shows two *vakra* features; the second one avoids the note *DHA* (Ab) and shows one *vakra* feature. In both forms appears the note *catuḥ-śruti RI* (D), a remarkable feature because the note is foreign to the tone material of the 8. *mēḷa*. The descending scale of *Ghaṇṭā* is *sampūrṇa*; it generally uses the note *RI śuddha* (Db), but there are instances when musicians raise the Db to D, whereby the *rāga* can be ascribed to the 20. *mēḷa*. Beside altering Db to D, a similar raise was applied to the note *DHA* (Ab changed to A).

Occasionally, particularly in the past, melodies in this *rāga* began with the low note *NI* (Bb). *Ghaṇṭā* is a very rare *rāga* and there are musicians who maintain that *Ghaṇṭā* is not in use any more. SD (II, 190) states that "this *rāga* is known by other names [such] as *Ghaṇṭāravam* and *Ghaṇṭāṇam*;" (see also 2,3 and 56, 8).

(10) *Dhanyāsi*

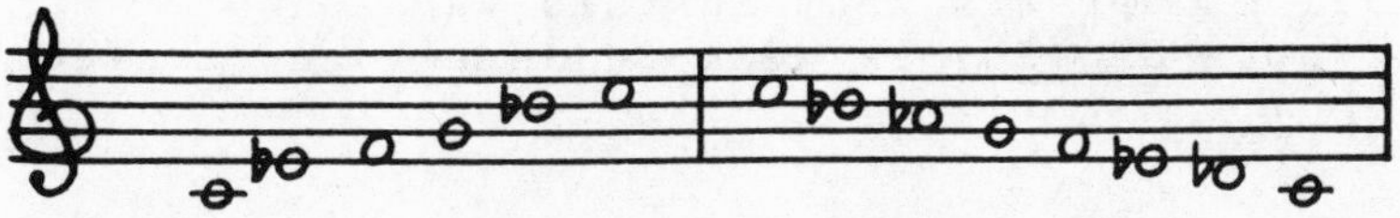

Ascent: the notes *RI* (Db) and *DHA* (Ab) are avoided.
Descent: *sampūrṇa*.
Strong notes are *GA* (Eb) and *DHA* (Ab). *GA* is often performed with a small vibrato. *Dhanyāsi* should be sung in the morning.

The following song specimen is a *kīrtana* composed by Mysore Sadasivarayar, a court musician of Mysore, famous for his *varnas*, *kṛtis*, and other songs (dates are uncertain). The specimen is quoted from SPC (III, 104-5).

DHANYĀSI RĀGA (*Ādi-tāla*)

Pallavi

Anupallavi

According to a recording of the *Gīta Govinda* (twenty-four famous religious song texts of the twelfth-century saint and poet Jayadēva) made by Wayne Howard in Kerala in 1971 it appears that in this version of *Dhanyāsi* the note *GA* (Eb) is weak in ascent and avoided in descent.

(11) *Amrita Dhanyāsi*

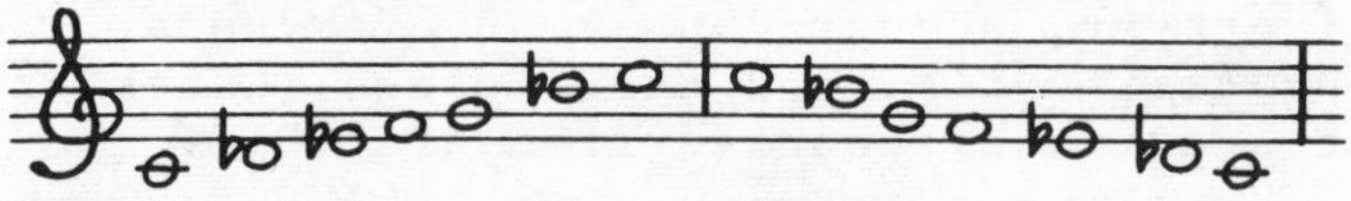

The note *DHA* (Ab) is avoided entirely.

(12) *Adbhodam*

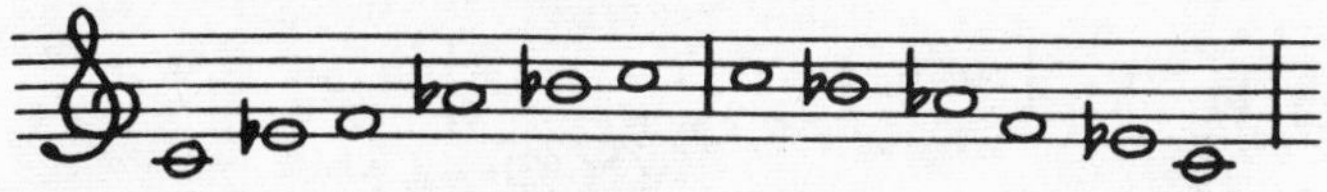

The notes *RI* (Db) and *PA* (G) are avoided entirely.

(13) *Bhānu Chandrikā*

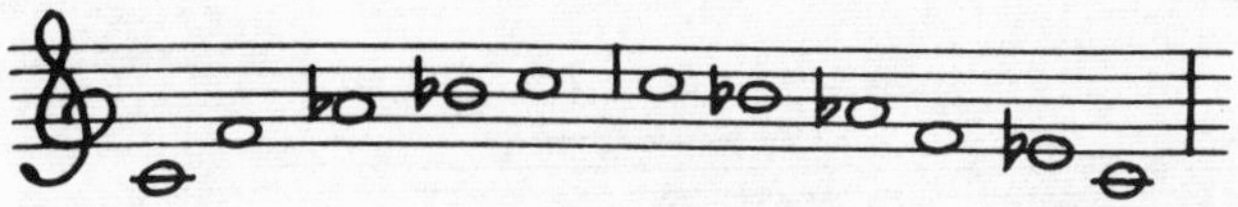

The notes *RI* (Db), *GA* (Eb), and *PA* (G) are avoided entirely.

(14) *Bhīshmāvaḷi*

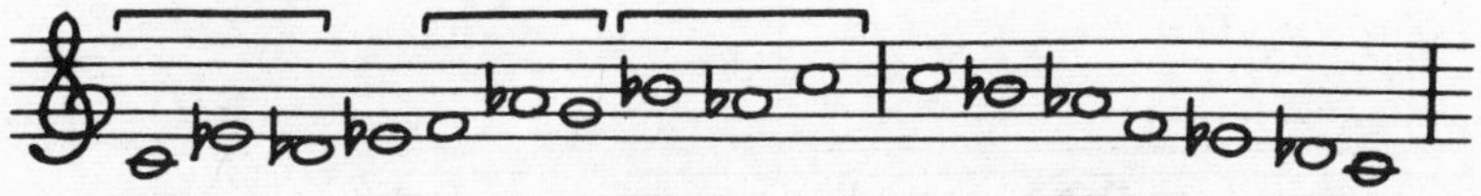

Ascent: *sampūrṇa*; three *vakra* features are shown.
Descent: the note *PA* (G) is avoided.

(15) *Bhramara Kētanam*

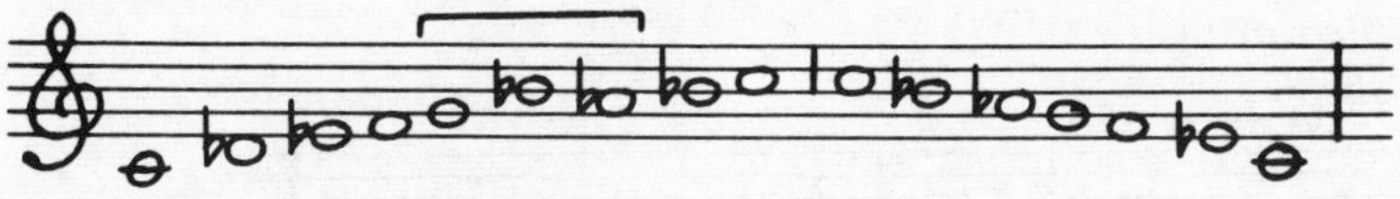

Ascent: *sampūrṇa*; one *vakra* feature is shown.
Descent: the note *RI* (Db) is avoided.

(16) *Chandra Gāndhāram*

The notes *PA* (G) and *DHA* (Ab) are avoided entirely. *NI* (Bb) is omitted in ascent.

(17) *Chandrikā Gauḷa*

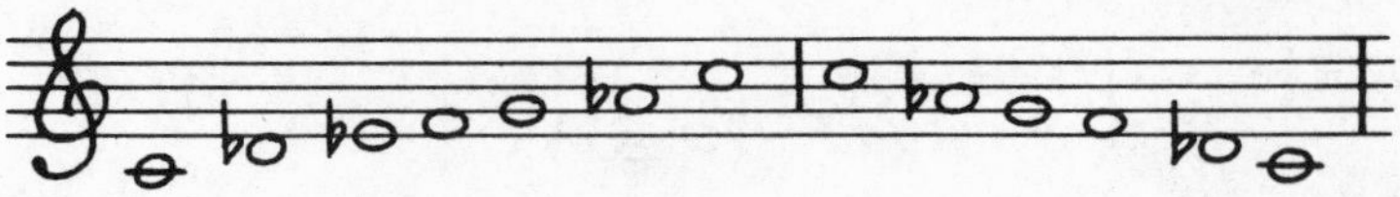

The note *NI* (Bb) is avoided entirely. *GA* (Eb) is omitted in descent. See also *Chandrikā Dhavaḷi* (*Chandrikā Gauḷa*) (8, 17).

(18) *Chhāyā Bauḷi*

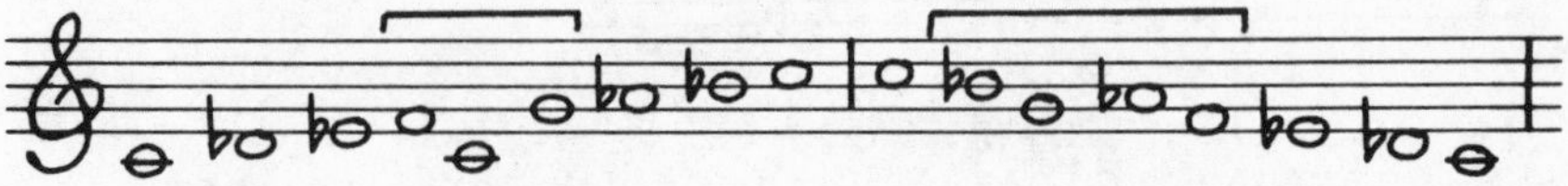

The scale is *sampūrṇa* and shows two *vakra* features, one in ascent and one in descent.

(19) *Dēśika Baṅgāḷa*

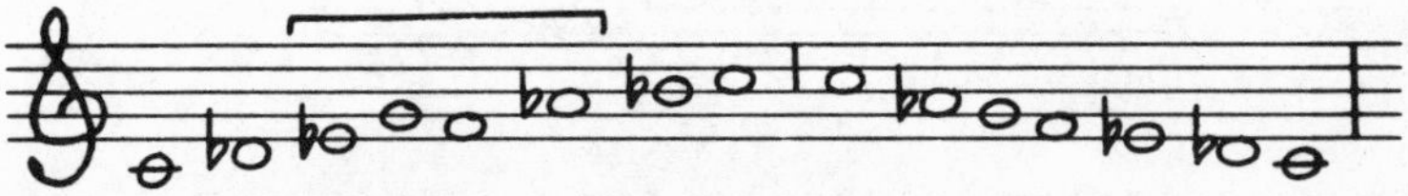

Ascent: *sampūrṇa*; one *vakra* feature is shown.
Descent: the note *NI* (Bb) is avoided.

(20) *Dēśya Bangāḷa*

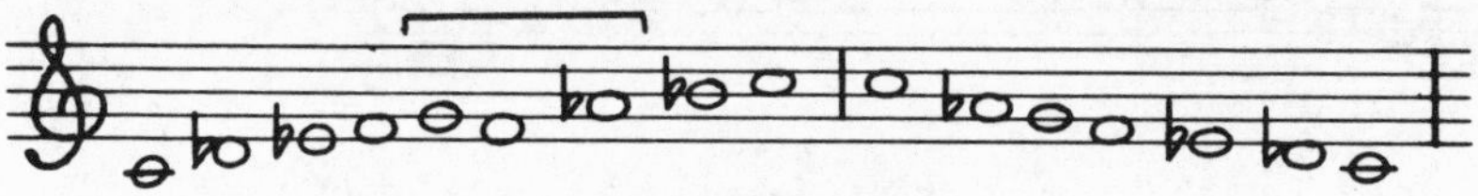

With the exception of placing the *vakra* feature in the ascending line beyond *MA* (F), there is no difference between this *rāga* and *Dēśika Baṅgāḷa*

(21) *Dhanāsari*

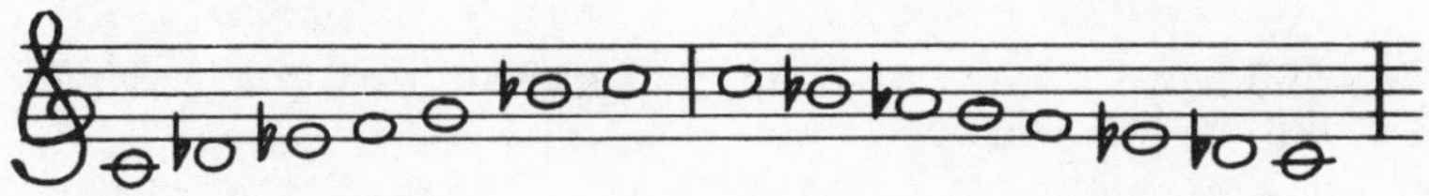

Ascent: the note *DHA* (Ab) is avoided.
Descent: *krama sampūrṇa*.

(22) *Dhavaḷa Kēsarī*

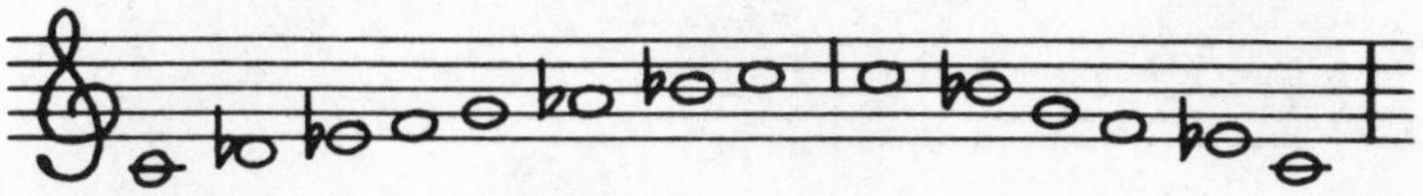

Ascent: *krama sampūrṇa.*
Descent: the notes *DHA* (Ab) and *RI* (Db) are avoided.

(23) *Gambhīra Vasantam*

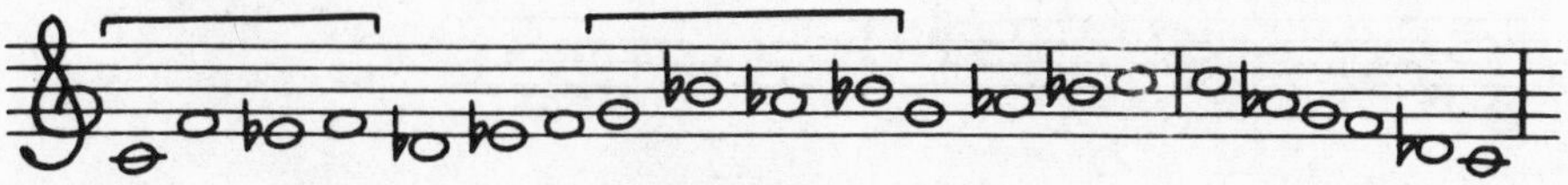

Ascent: *sampūrṇa*; two *vakra* features are shown.
Descent: the notes *NI* (Bb) and *GA* (Eb) are avoided.

(24) *Gōmūtrakam*

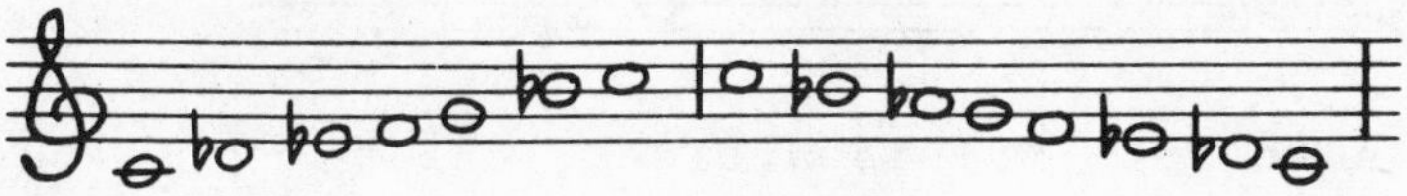

Ascent: the note *DHA* (Ab) is avoided.
Descent: *krama sampūrṇa.*

(25) *Haṃsānandi*

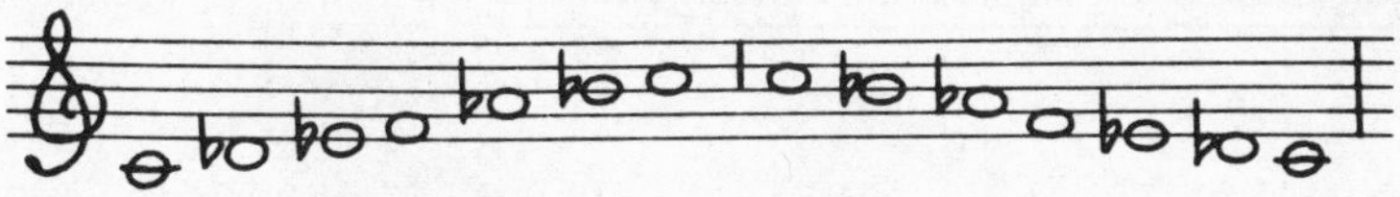

The note *PA* (G) is avoided entirely.

Another *janya rāga* with the same name appears under the heading of the 53. *mēḷa* (14).

(26) *Indu Sāraṅganāṭa*

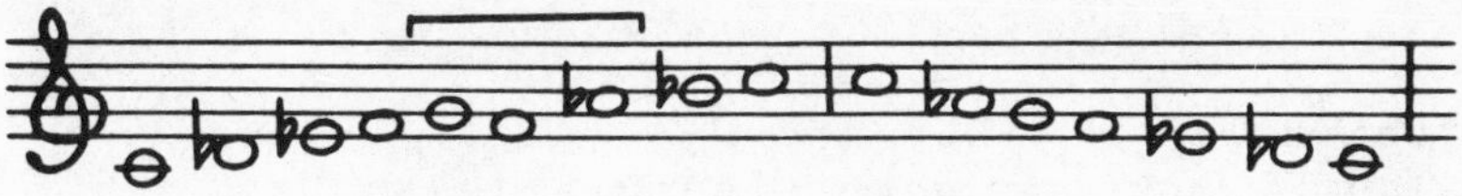

Ascent: *sampūrṇa*; one *vakra* feature is shown.
Descent: the note *NI* (Bb) is avoided.

(27) *Kalāhaṃsagāmini*

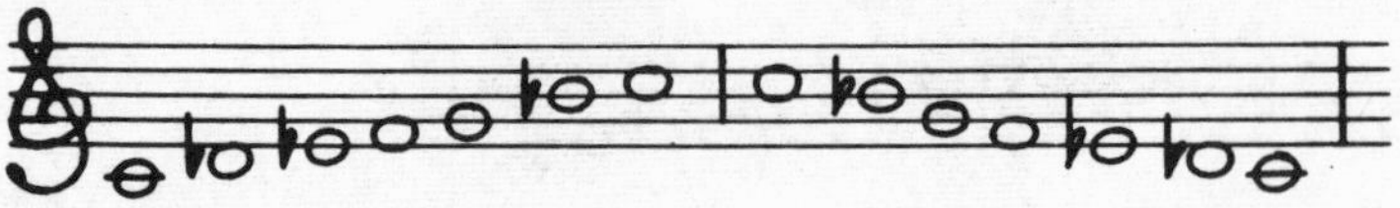

The note *DHA* (Ab) is avoided entirely.

(28) *Kalāsāvēri*

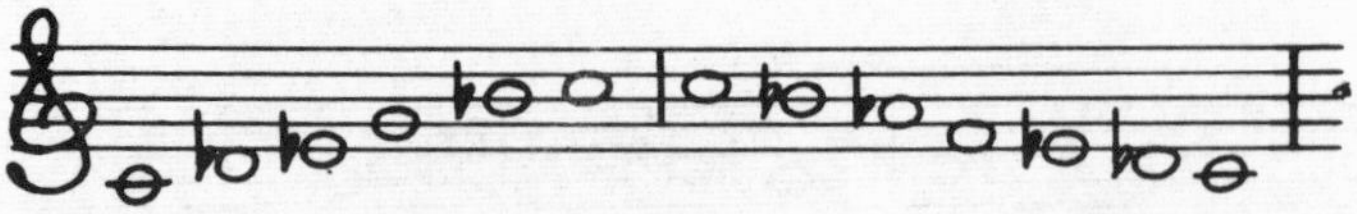

Ascent: the notes *MA* (F) and *DHA* (Ab) are avoided.
Descent: the note *PA* (G) is omitted.

(29) *Kaṃsāri*

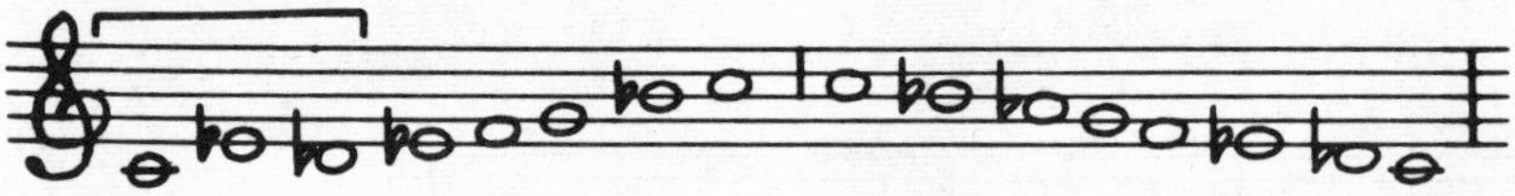

Ascent: the note *DHA* (Ab) is avoided; one *vakra* feature is shown.
Descent: *krama sampūrṇa*.

(30) *Kannaḍa Sālavi*

Ascent: the notes *RI* (Db) and *NI* (Bb) are avoided.
Descent: the note *PA* (G) is omitted.

(31) *Kānta Dhanyāsi*

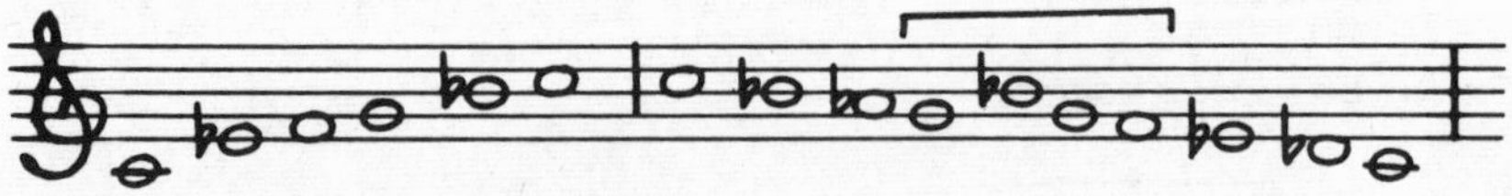

Ascent: the notes *RI* (Db) and *DHA* (Ab).
Descent: *sampūrṇa*; one *vakra* feature is shown.

(32) *Kāshyapī* (*Kāśyapī*)

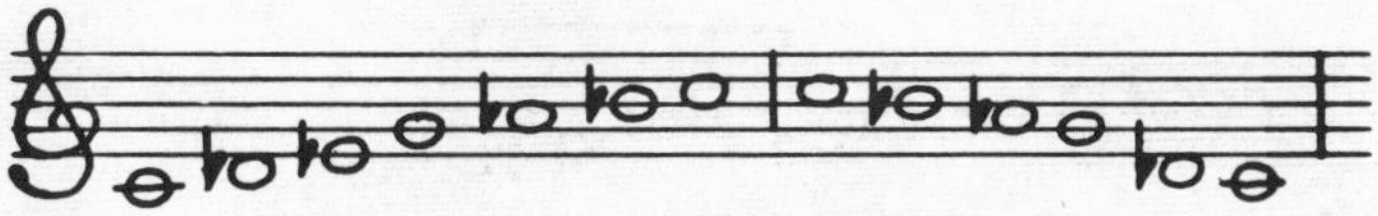

The note *MA* (F) is avoided entirely. *GA* (Eb) is omitted in descent.

(33) *Khaḍgadhāriṇi*

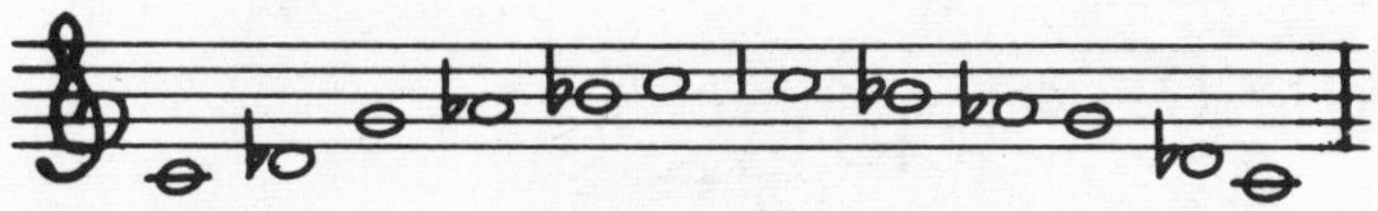

The notes *GA* (Eb) and *MA* (F) are avoided entirely.

(34) *Khadyōtapriya*

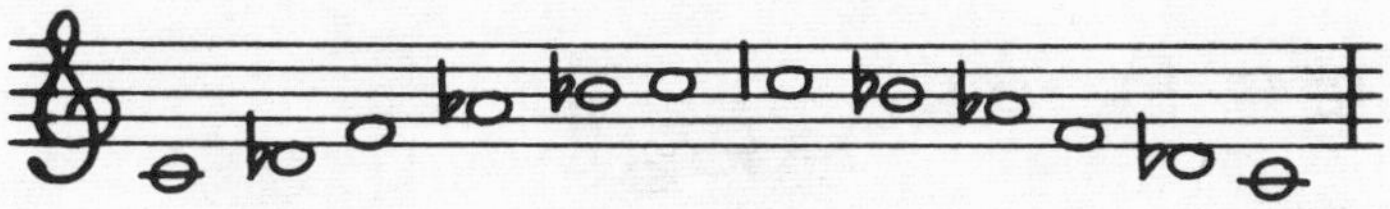

The notes *GA* (Eb) and *PA* (G) are avoided entirely.

(35) *Kshaṇika* (*Kṣaṇika*)

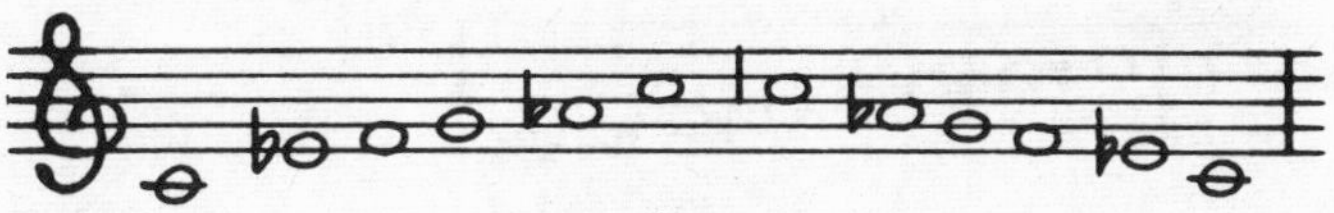

The notes *RI* (Db) and *NI* (Bb) are avoided entirely.

(36) *Himāṅgi*

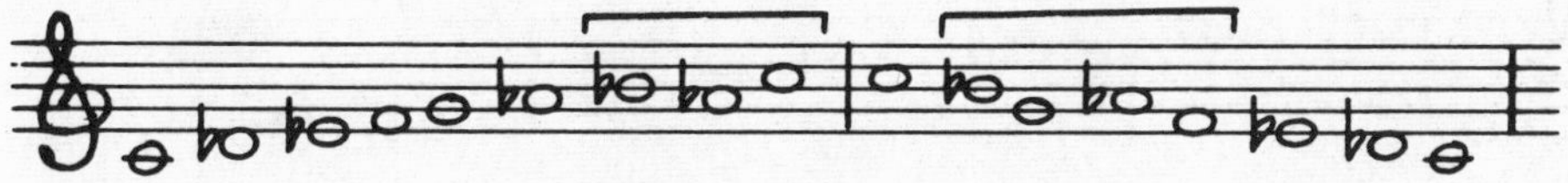

The scale is *sampūrṇa* and shows one *vakra* feature in ascent and one in descent.

(37) *Himavardhani*

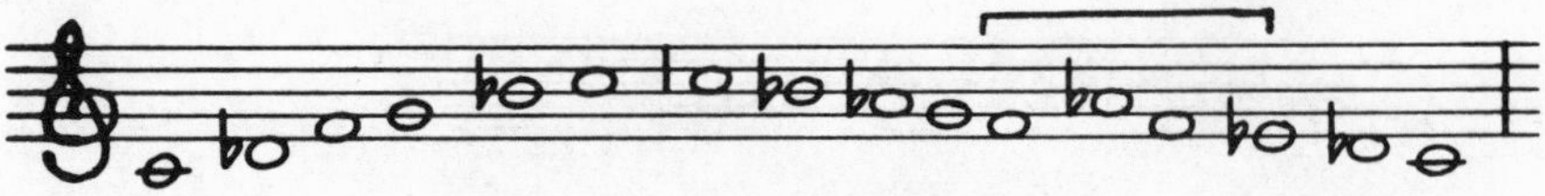

Ascent: the notes *GA* (Eb) and *DHA* (Ab) are avoided.
Descent: *sampūrṇa*; one *vakra* feature is shown.

(38) *Mrugākshi* (*Mrugākṣi*)

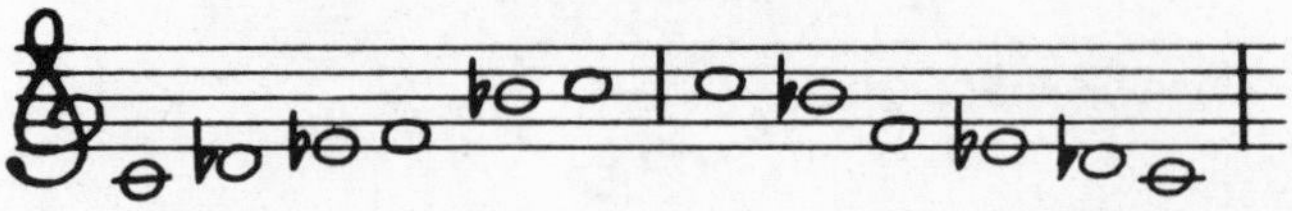

The notes *PA* (G) and *DHA* (Ab) are avoided entirely.

(39) *Navasūtika*

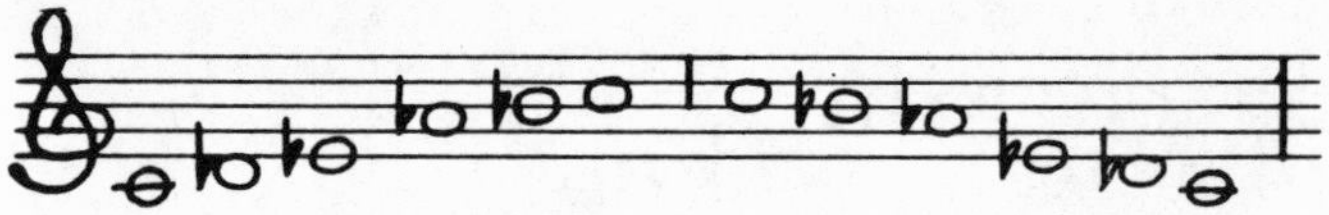

The notes *MA* (F) and *PA* (G) are avoided entirely.

(40) *Nādanāli*

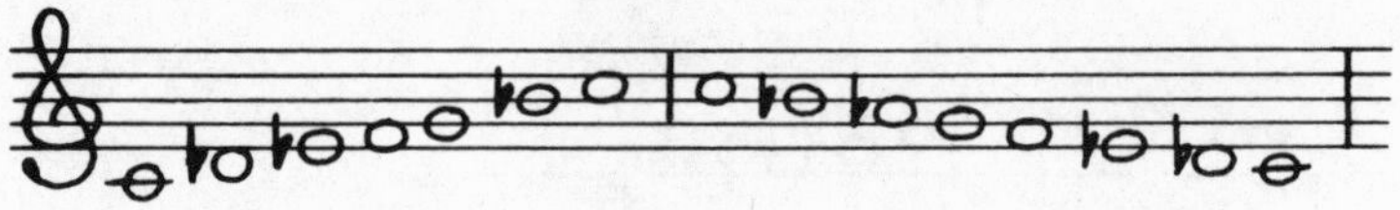

Ascent: the note *DHA* (Ab) is avoided.
Descent: *krama sampūrṇa*.

(41) *Pushkaraṇī* (*Puṣkaraṇī*)

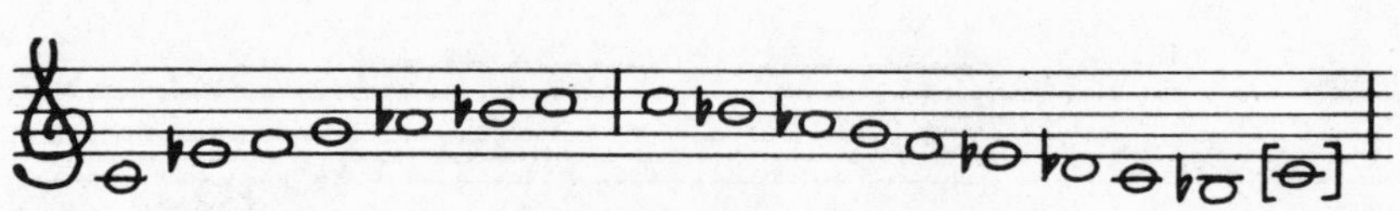

Ascent: the note *RI* (Db) is avoided.
Descent: *krama sampūrṇa*.

(42) *Rukmāṅgi*

The notes *MA* (F) and *DHA* (Ab) are avoided entirely.

(43) *Śuddhamāruva*

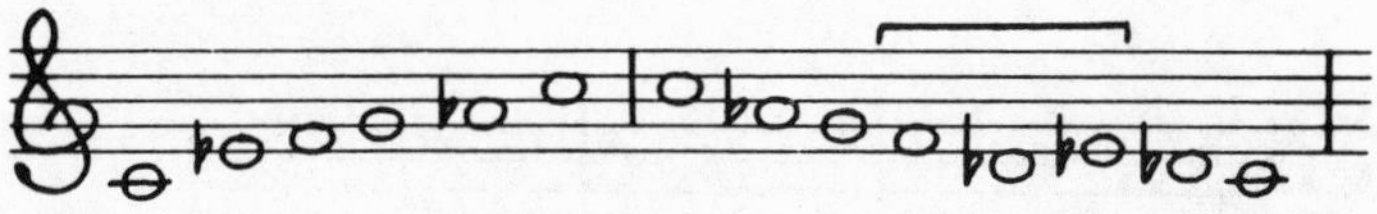

The note *NI* (Bb) is avoided entirely. *RI* (Db) is avoided in ascent. The descent shows one *vakra* feature.

9. *MĒḶA DHĒNUKA*

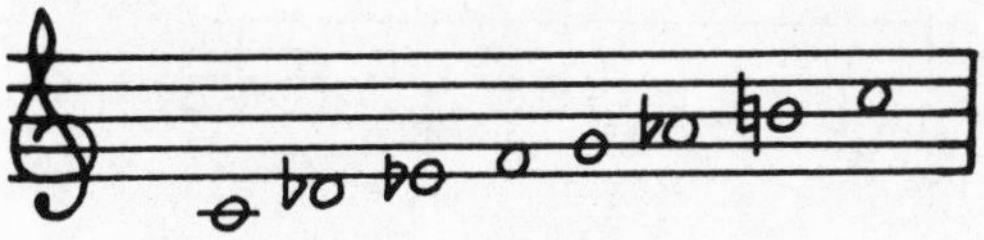

Veṅkaṭamakhin calls this *rāga Dhunnibhinnaṣaḍja*. *Rāga Dhēnuka*, which is to be performed in the morning, stresses the notes *GA* (Eb) and *NI* (B). The note *GA* (Eb) is supposed to be extended in duration even if the notated song does not indicate such a prolongation.

The following song specimen is a *kīrtana*:

DHĒNUKA (*Triputa catusra-jāti tāla*)

Pallavi

Anupallavi

Charana

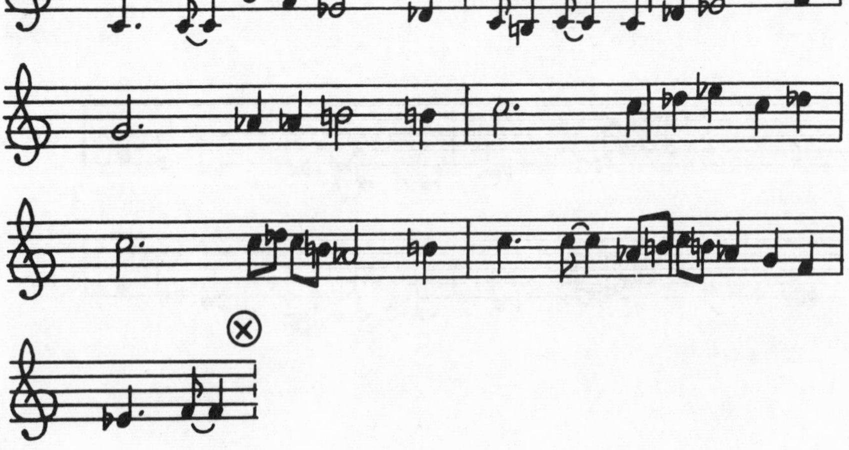

When the singer reaches the sign ⊗ he returns to the beginning of the *pallavi*. The second time he continues the melody through the *charana* and then returns to the last line of the *anupallavi* (marked with ⊗). The song ends after a final repetition of the first line of the *pallavi* with the note *GA* (Eb), the first note of the second line of the *pallavi*.

Janya Rāgas of the Ninth Mēḷa

(1) *Bhinnaṣaḍja(m)*

The ascent of this scale can be performed in two ways. The note *DHA* (Ab) is avoided in both instances. The descent omits the note *NI* (B). The stressed notes of *Bhinnaṣaḍja* are *RI* (Db), *GA* (Eb), and *NI* (B). The *rāga* can be performed at any time.

BHINNA-ṢAḌJA RĀGA (Ādi-tāla)

Pallavi

Anupallavi

Repeat the entire *pallavi*

Charana

Repeat the entire *pallavi*

When performing this song the singer, when repeating the *pallavi* after the *anupallavi* adds as final note *SA* (C).

(2) *Takka*

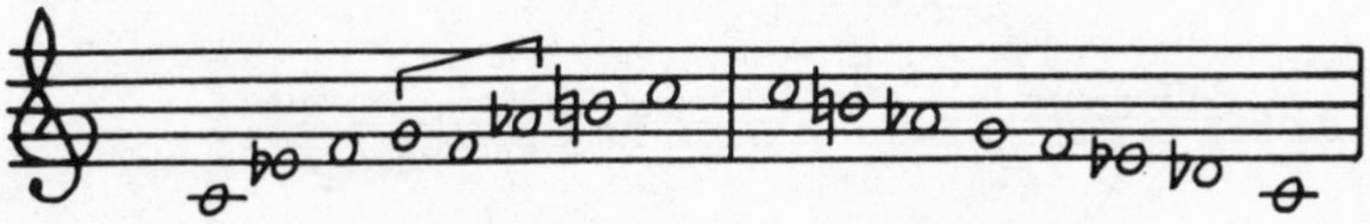

Ascent: the note *RI* (Db) is avoided; one *vakra* feature is shown.
A second form of ascent avoids the progression *GA-MA-PA* (Eb-F-G) by omitting the middle note *MA* (F):

Descent: *sampūrṇa*.

Veṅkatamakhin places this *rāga* under the heading of his 15. *mēḷa* and states that the note *RI* (Db) has to be avoided in ascent and that *NI* (B) be omitted in descent. The note *PA* (G) is to be treated weakly.

At the present time the note *NI* (B) is employed in the descending line. There are musicinas who use notes foreign to the material of the 9. *mēḷa* in their *Takka* performances, a sign of the popularity of this *rāga*. *Takka* can be sung or played at any time.

TAKKA RĀGA (*Triputa-tāla*) SCM, 29

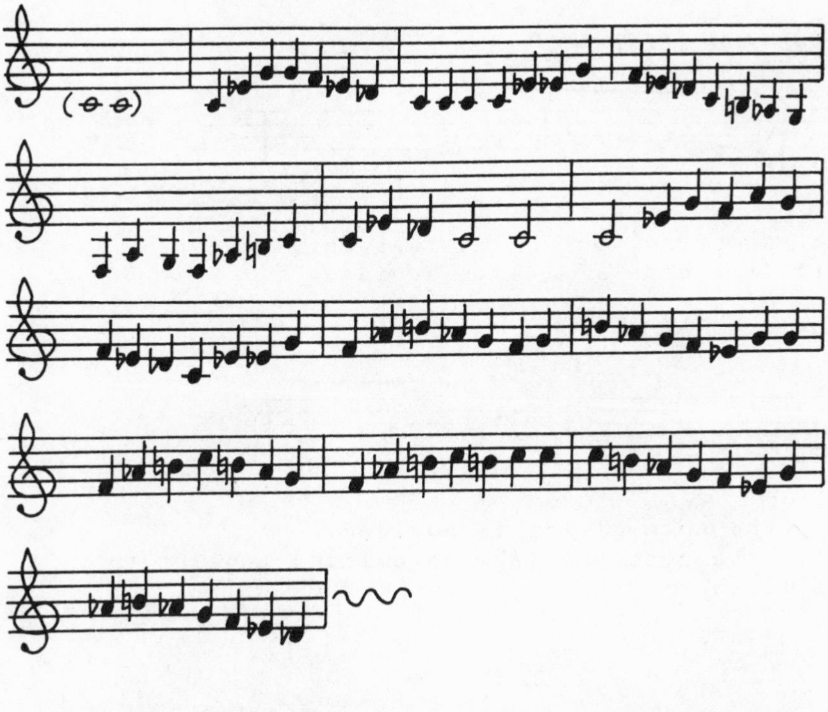

(3) *Bāgēsari Bahār*

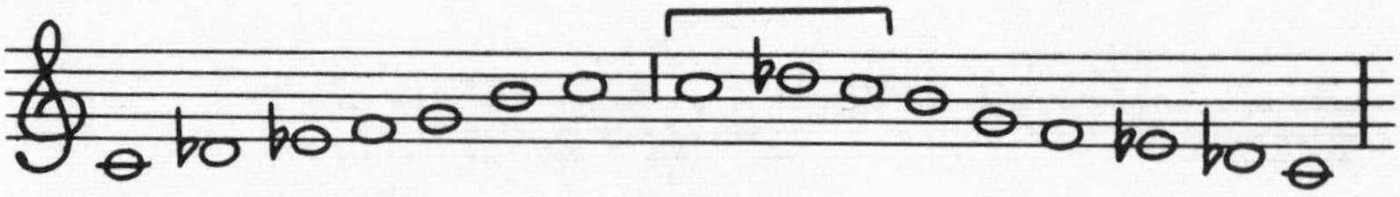

The note *DHA* (Ab) is avoided entirely. The *sampūrṇa* descent shows one *vakra* feature.

(4) *Bhārgavī*

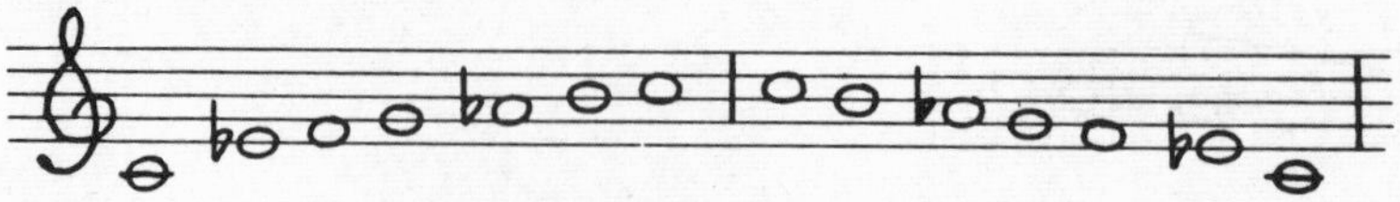

The note *RI* (Db) is avoided entirely. Another *rāga* with the same name appears under the heading of *mēḷa* 37 (3).

(5) *Dēśika Rudri*

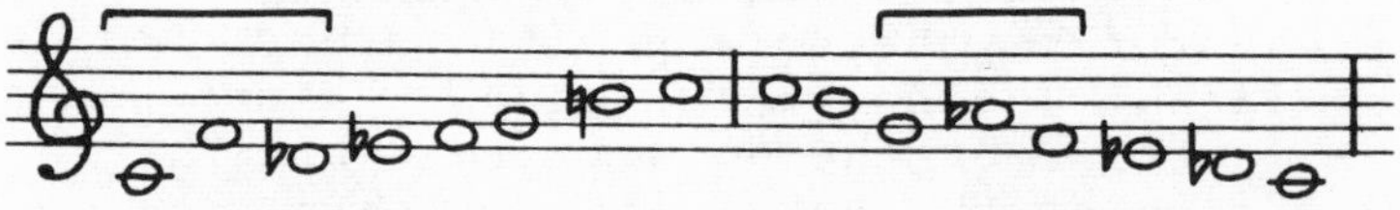

Ascent: the note *DHA* (Ab) is avoided; one *vakra* feature is shown.
Descent: *sampūrṇa*; one *vakra* feature is used.

(6) *Dēśya Āndhāli*

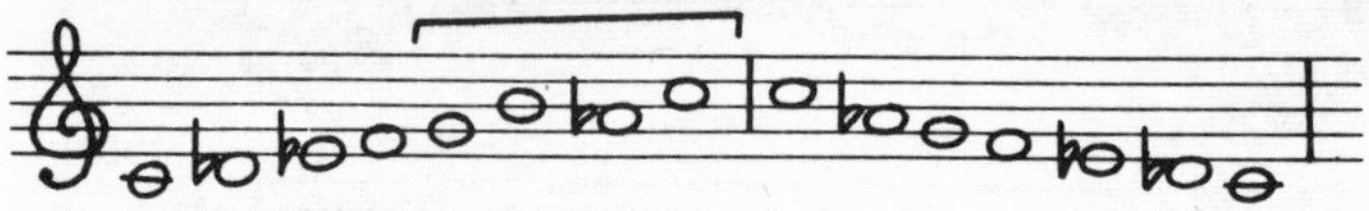

Ascent: *sampūrṇa*; one *vakra* feature is shown.
Descent: the note *NI* (B) is avoided.

(7) *Dhairyamukhi*

Ascent: the note *NI* (B) is avoided.
Descent: the note *DHA* (Ab) is omitted; one *vakra* feature is shown.

(8) *Gaja Sāri*

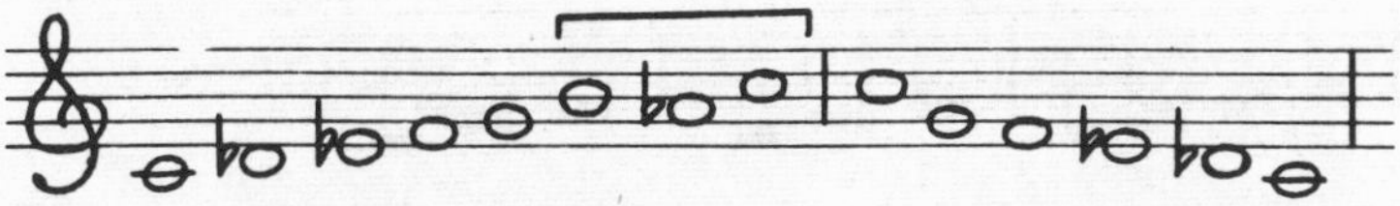

Ascent: *sampūrṇa*; one *vakra* feature is shown.
Descent: the notes *NI* (B) and *DHA* (Ab) are avoided.

(9) *Gaurī Baṅgāḷa*

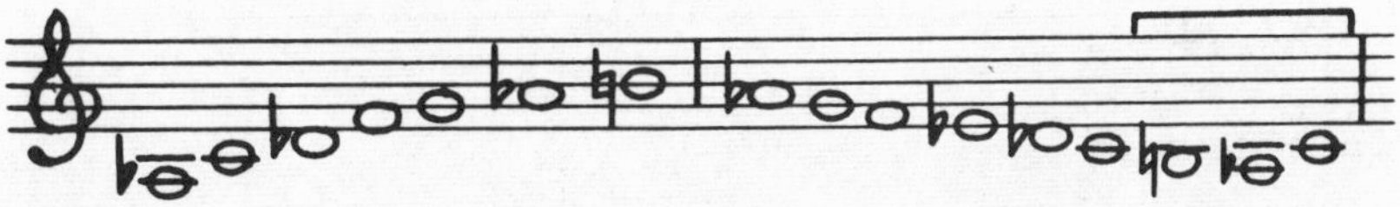

The ascending scale of this *rāga* begins with the note *DHA* (Ab) of the *mandra saptaka* (low octave range) and, having *niṣādāntya* character, has as its highest note *NI* (B).
Ascent: the note *NI* (B) of the low octave range and *GA* (Eb) are avoided.
Descent: one *vakra* feature is shown.

(10) *Kanakādri*

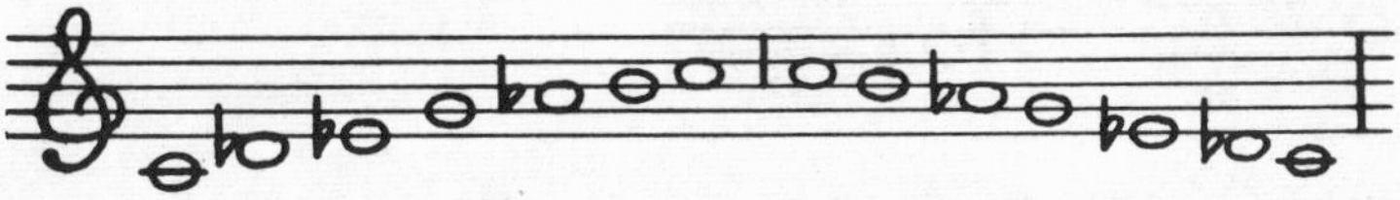

The note *MA* (F) is avoided entirely.

(11) *Shokavāḷi* (*Śokavāḷi*)

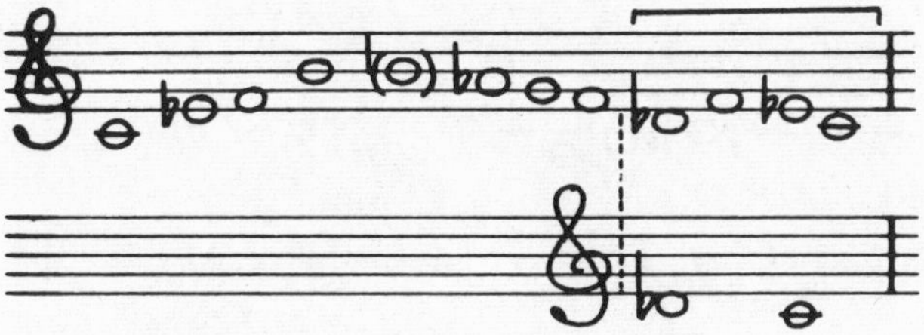

The scale has *niṣādāntya* character.
Ascent: the notes *RI* (Db), *PA* (G), and *DHA* (Ab) are avoided.
Descent: one version shows one *vakra* feature, the other appears in a straight form.

SHOKAVĀLI RĀGA (*Triputa-tāla*) SCM, 28

(12) *Lalitaśrīkanti*

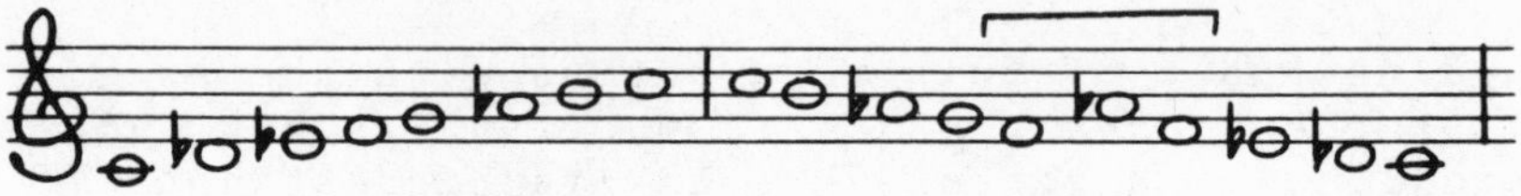

Ascent: *Krama sampūrṇa*.
Descent: *sampūrṇa*; one *vakra* feature is shown.

(13) *Lalitasiṃhāravam*

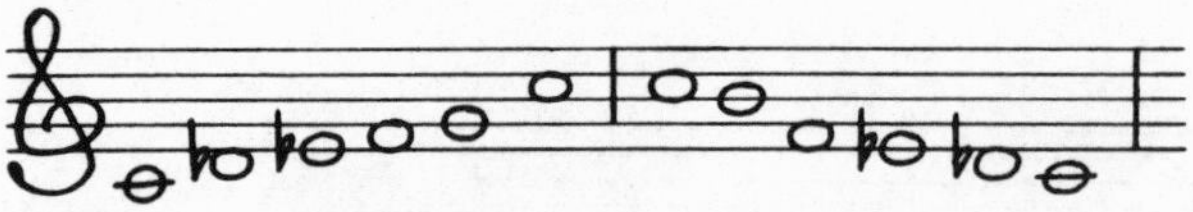

The note *DHA* (Ab) is avoided entirely. *NI* (B) is omitted in ascent.

Another *rāga* with the same name appears under the heading of the 59. *mēḷa* (11).

(14) *Marālagāmini*

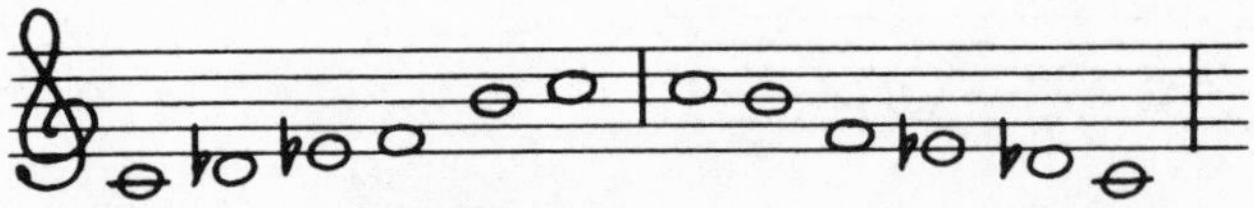

The notes *PA* (G) and *DHA* (Ab) are avoided entirely.

(15) *Mōhananāṭa*

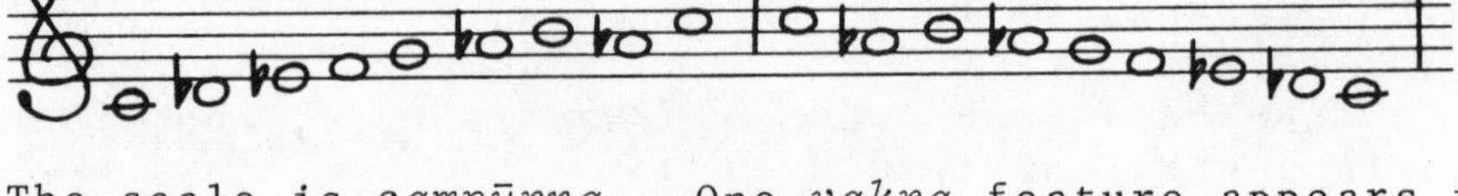

The scale is *sampūrṇa*. One *vakra* feature appears in ascent, the other in descent.

(16) *Sindhuchintāmaṇi*

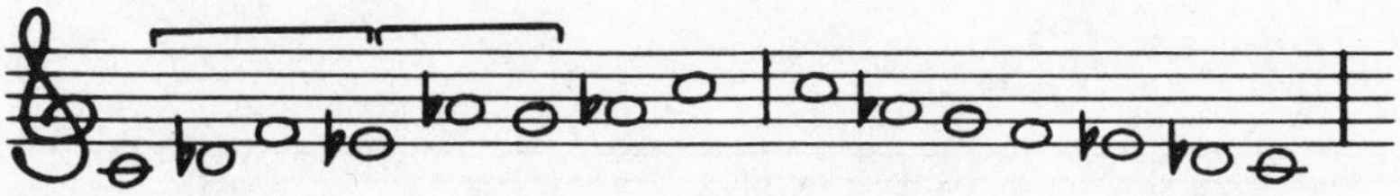

The note *NI* (B) is avoided entirely. The ascent shows two *vakra* features.

(17) *Śālmali*

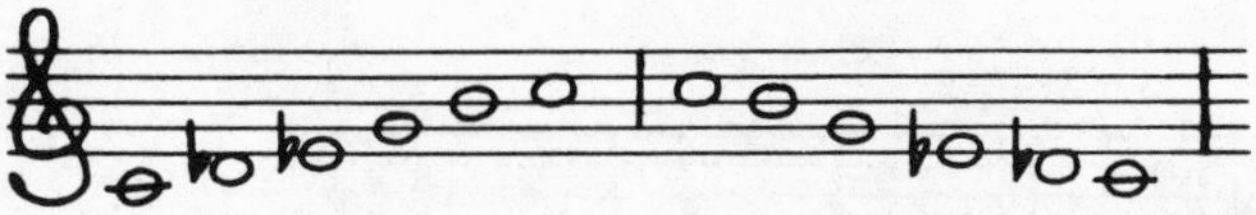

The notes *MA* (F) and *DHA* (Ab) are avoided entirely.

(18) *Trimūrtipriya*

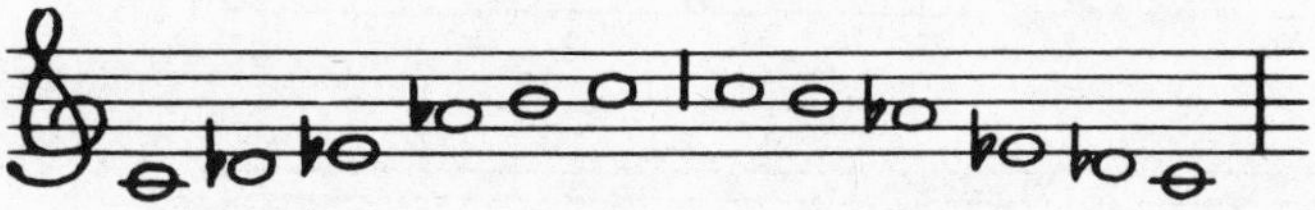

The notes *MA* (F) and *PA* (G) are avoided entirely.

10. *MĒḶA NĀṬAKAPRIYA*

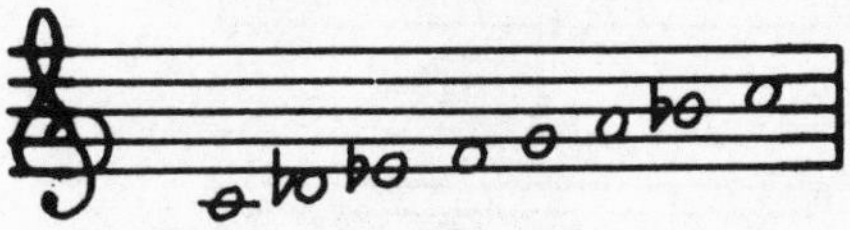

Veṅkaṭamakhin calls this *rāga Naṭābharaṇam* and states that it avoids the note *RI* (Db) entirely and that the note *DHA* (A) appears in *vakra* features in ascent and descent.

The present *rāga Nāṭakapriya* and its first *janya rāga Naṭābharaṇam* (see below) employ the note *RI* (Db) and there appears no *vakra* feature in the primary *rāga*; but there is one in the ascending line, beginning with *DHA* (A), in *Naṭābharaṇam*. However, Veṅkaṭamakhin's rule of avoiding *RI* (Db) entirely is not in use any more. In the present *rāga Nāṭakapriya* the note *RI* (Db) is not only used but stressed, together with the notes *MA* (F), *DHA* (A), and *NI* (Bb).

Nāṭakapriya is to be performed in the evening or at night. The following song specimen is a *kīrtana*:

NĀṬAKAPRIYĀ (Ādi-tāla)

Pallavi

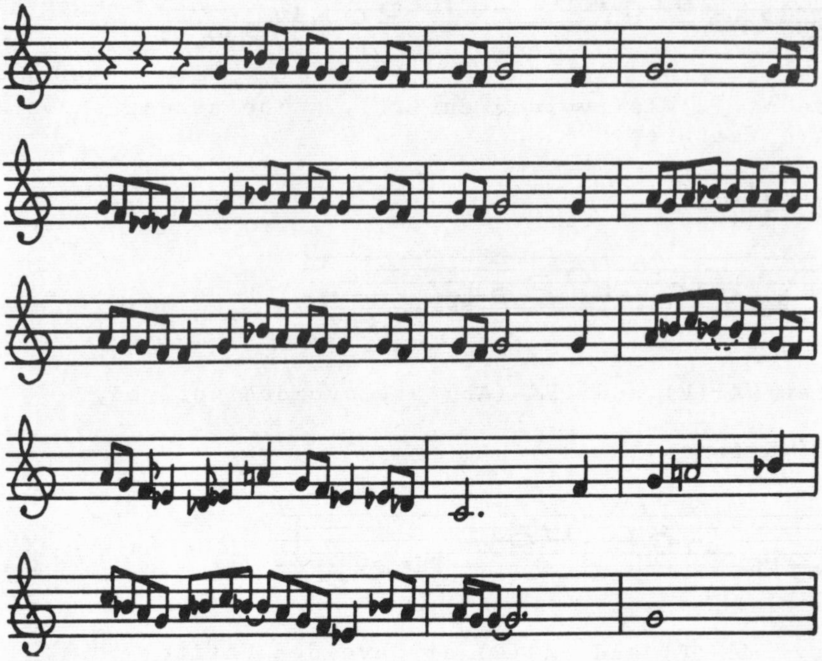

Anupallavi

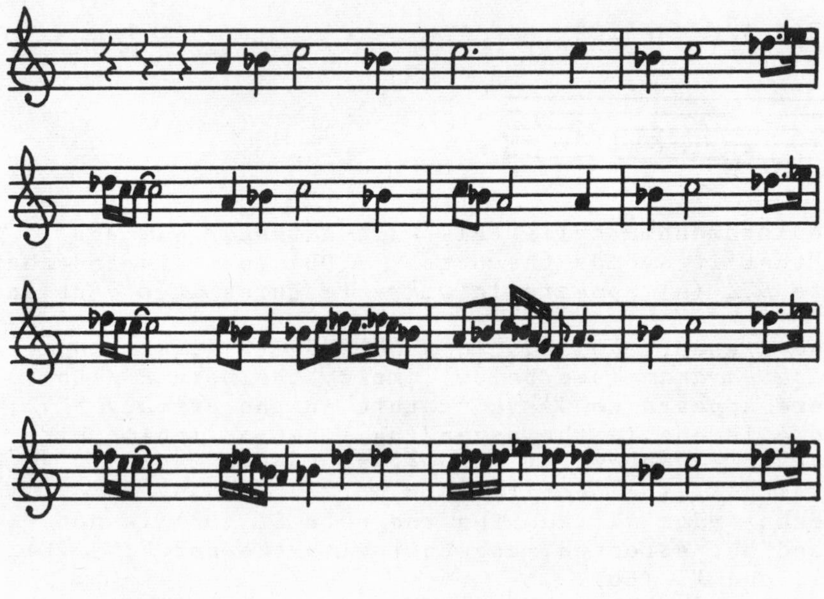

The *pallavi* is repeated

Janya Rāgas of the Tenth Mēḷa

(1) *Nāṭabharaṇam*

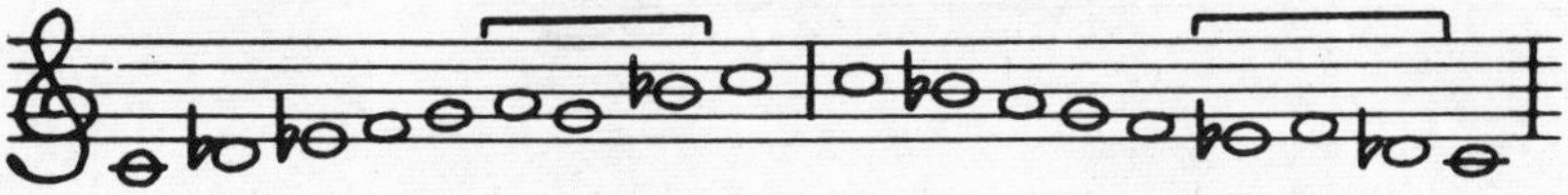

The scale is *sampūrṇa* and shows two *vakra* features; one in ascent and one in descent.

(2) *Dīparam* (*Dīpar*)

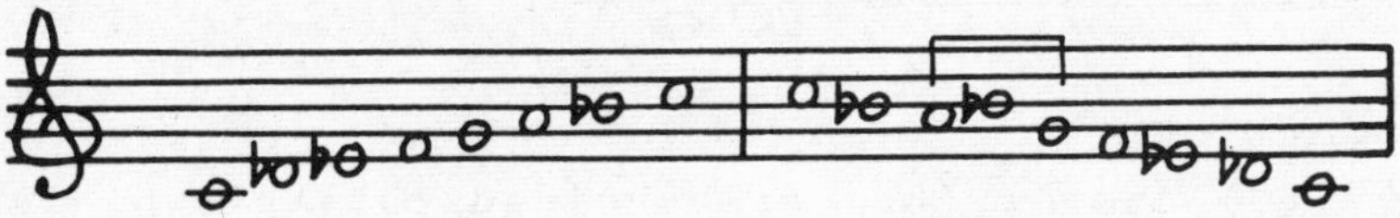

The scale is *sampūrṇa* and shows one *vakra* feature in descent.

(3) *Mālavaśrī*

This recently created *janya rāga* is ascribed to Tiruvaiyar Subrahmaṇya Aiyar (acc. to R, 222).

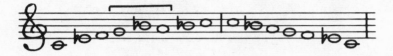

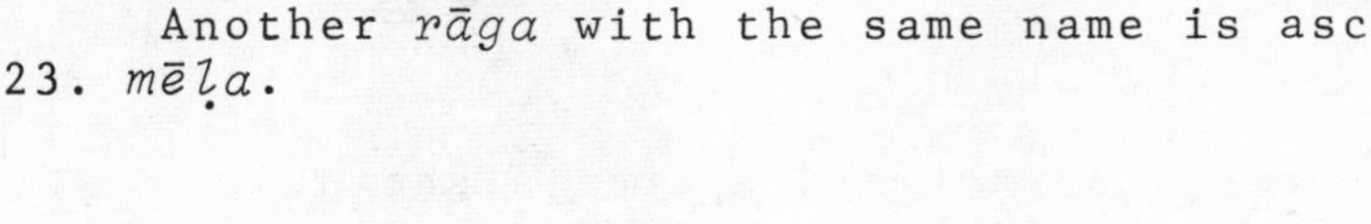

The note *RI* (Db) is avoided entirely. The ascent shows one *vakra* feature.

Another *rāga* with the same name is ascribed to the 23. *mēḷa*.

(4) *Alankārapriya*

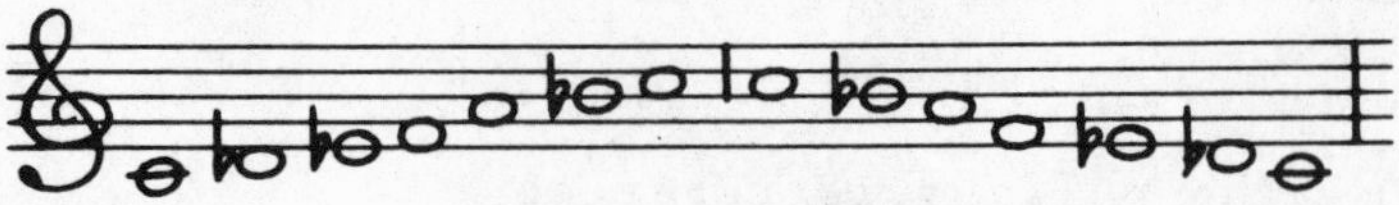

The note *PA* (G) is avoided entirely.

(5) *Bhramara Vardhani*

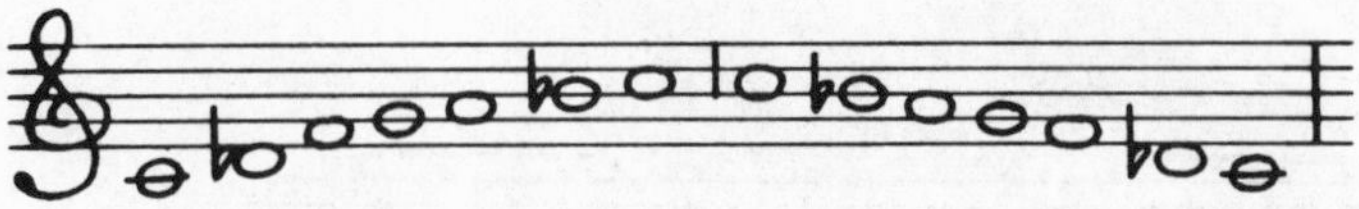

The note *GA* (Eb) is avoided entirely.

(6) *Chitta Mōdiṇi* (*Chitta Mōhiṇi*)

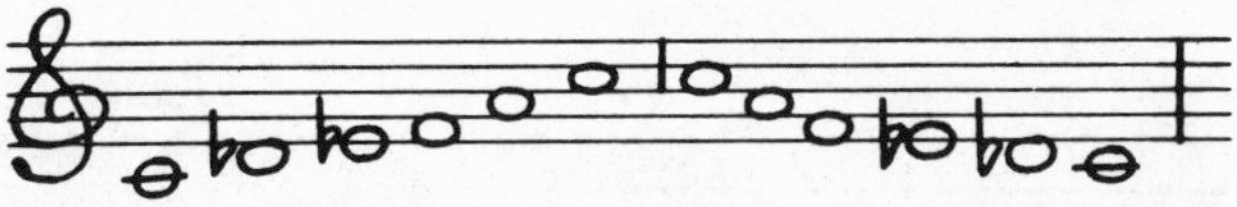

The notes *PA* (G) and *NI* (Bb) are avoided entirely.

(7) *Jñānabōdhini*

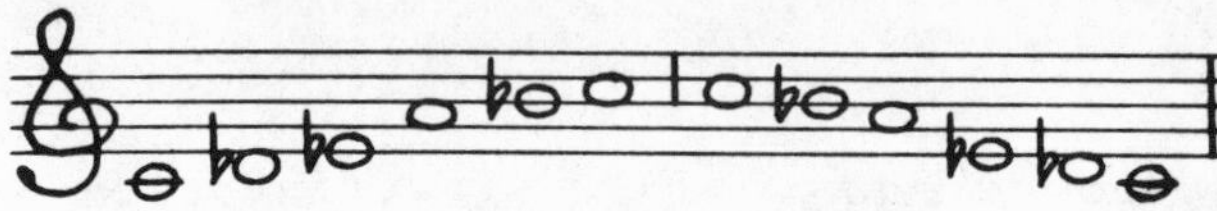

The notes *MA* (F) and *PA* (G) are avoided entirely.

(8) *Kannaḍa Saurāshṭram* (*Kannaḍa Saurāṣṭram*)

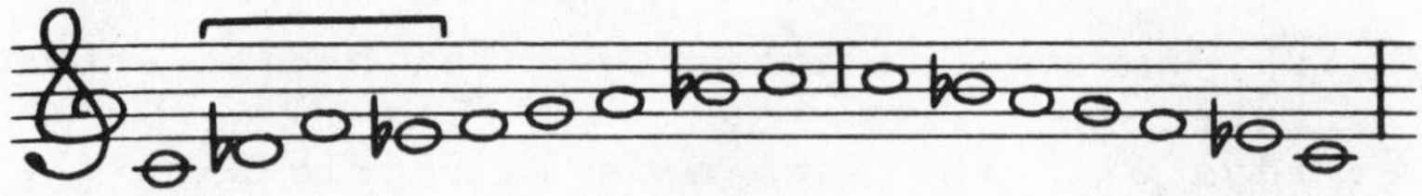

Ascent: *sampūrṇa*; one *vakra* feature is shown.
Descent: the note *RI* (Db) is avoided.

(9) *Kinnarēśapriya*

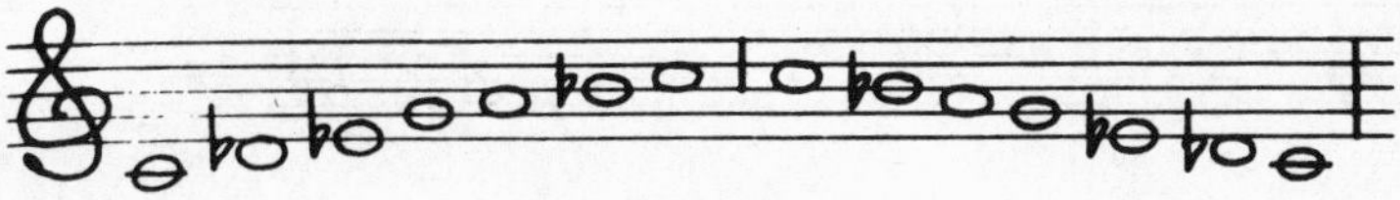

The note *MA* (F) is avoided entirely.

(10) *Hindōḷa Dēśika*

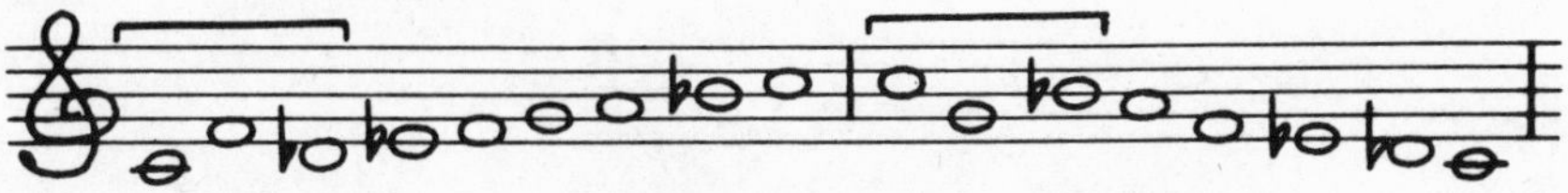

The scale is *sampūrṇa* and shows two *vakra* features, one in ascent and one in descent.

(11) *Mataṅgagāmini*

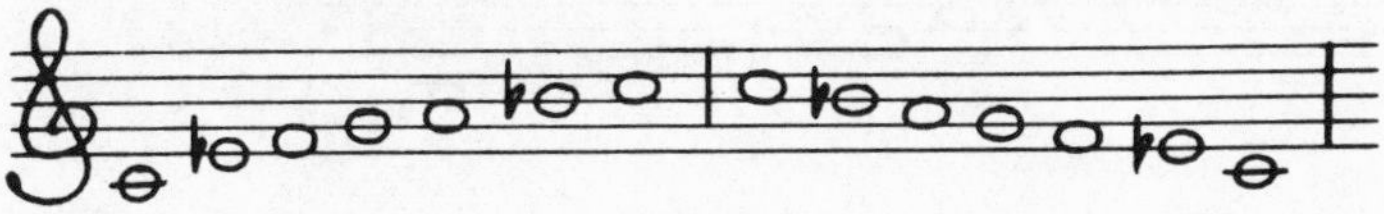

The note *RI* (Db) is avoided entirely. (N shows two forms of *DHA* (A and Ab) in ascent).

(12) *Nāgamani*

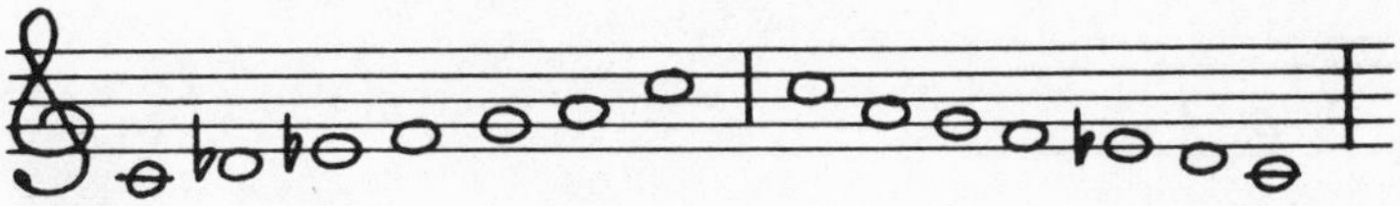

The note *NI* (Bb) is avoided entirely.

(13) *Nirañjani*

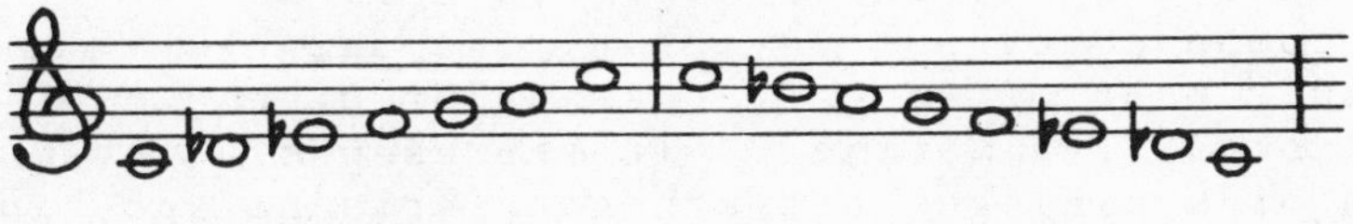

Ascent: the note *NI* (Bb) is avoided.
Descent: *krama sampūrṇa*.

(14) *Pūrvarāmakriya*

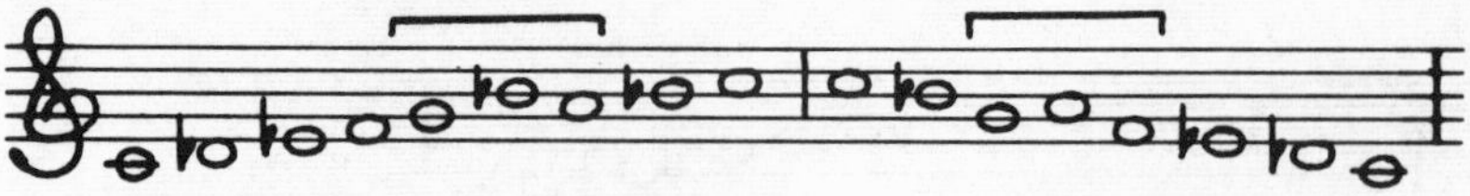

Ascent: *sampūrṇa*; one *vakra* feature is shown.
Descent: *sampūrṇa*; one *vakra* feature is used.

(15) *Sindhubhairavī*

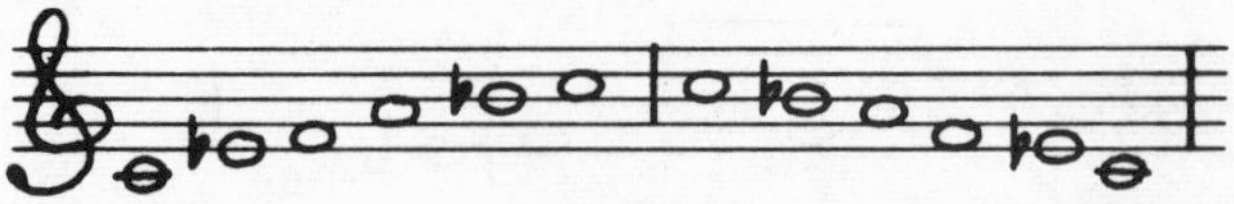

The notes *RI* (Db) and *PA* (G) are avoided entirely.

(16) *Vasantakannaḍa*

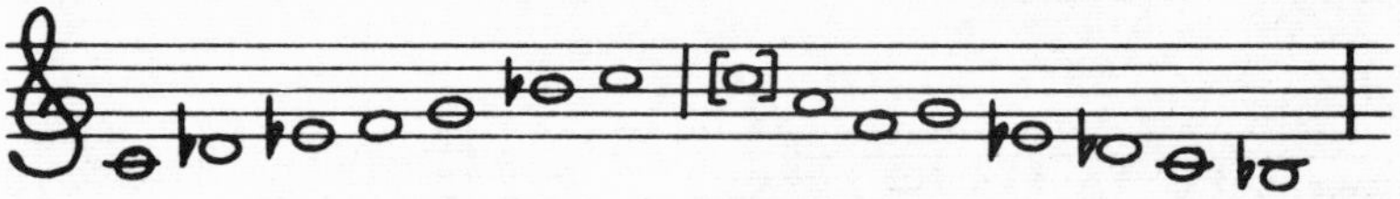

Ascent: the note *DHA* (A) is avoided.
Descent: the note *NI* (Bb) is omitted; one *vakra* feature is shown.

11. *MELA KOKILAPRIYA*

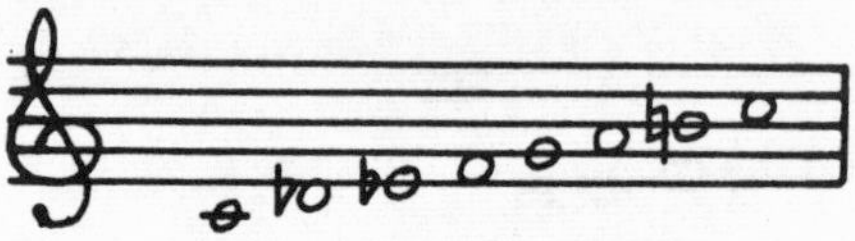

Veṅkaṭamakhin, who calls this *rāga Kokilāṛāva(m)*, states that the note *GA* (Eb) is to be avoided in ascent. Govinda and other (*lakṣaṇa*) sources describe this *rāga* as *sampūrṇa*. Stressed notes are *MA* (F) and *DHA* (A).

The following specimen is a simple *kṛti* in *Kokilapriya* composed by Śrī Jayadeva, the saintly twelfth-century poet of Bengal, the author of the already mentioned *Gīta Govinda*. It represents a love song in form of a dialogue between Lord Krishna and his beloved Rukmiṇī. At the present time this song is used as a simple *bhajan* (devotional song) in which all textual verses are sung to the same melody.

KOKILAPRIYA (*Chapu-tāla*)

Pallavi

Janya Rāgas of the 11. Mēḷa

(1) *Kokilārāva(m)*

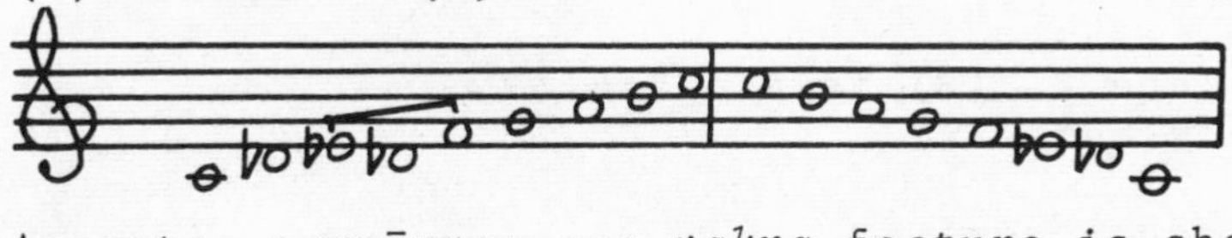

Ascent: *sampūrṇa*; one *vakra* feature is shown.
Descent: *krama sampūrṇa*.

(2) *Vardhani*

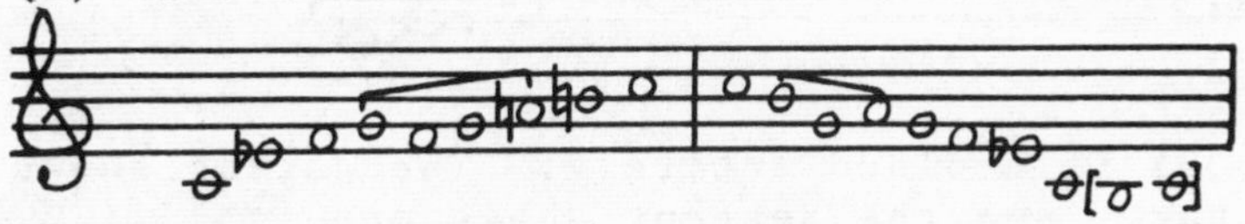

The note *RI* (Db) is avoided entirely. Two *vakra* features are shown, one in ascent and one in descent.

(3) *Chaturānanapriya*

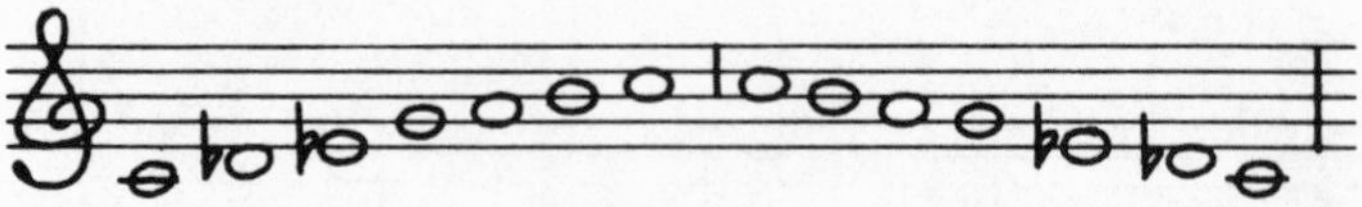

The note *MA* (F) is avoided entirely.

(4) *Chhāyā Saindhavi*

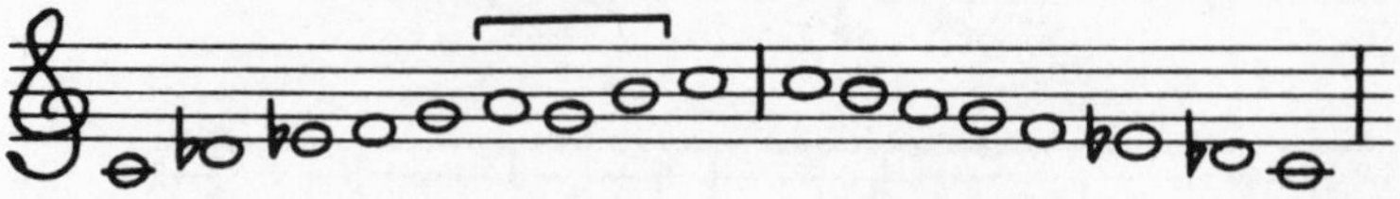

The scale is *sampūrṇa* and shows one *vakra* feature in ascent.

(5) *Chitra Maṇi*

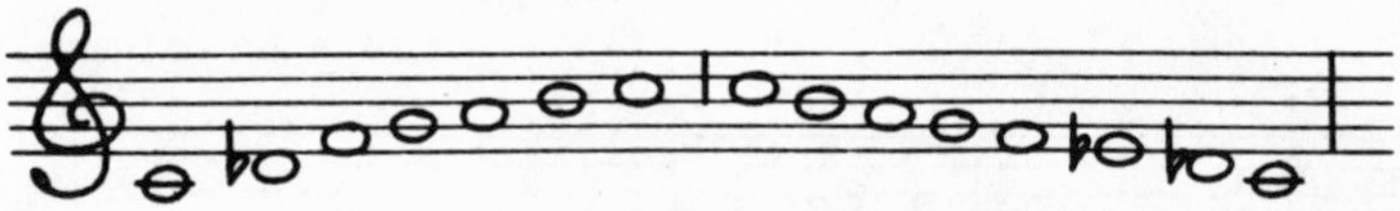

Ascent: the note *GA* (Eb) is avoided.
Descent: *krama sampūrṇa*.

(6) *Kaumāri*

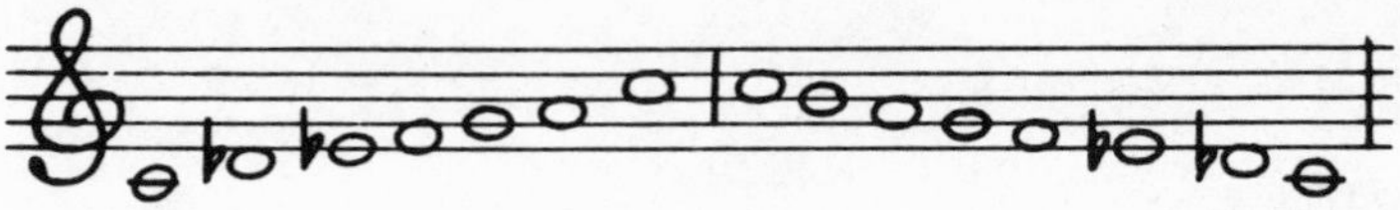

Ascent: the note *NI* (B) is avoided.
Descent: *krama sampūrṇa*.

(7) *Kōkila Kāmavardhani*

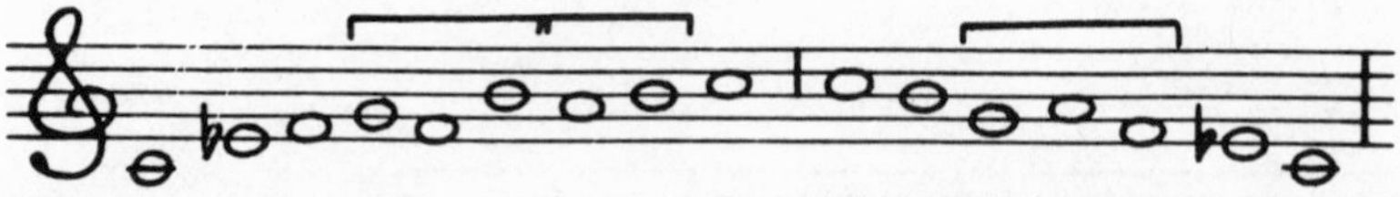

The note *RI* (Db) is avoided entirely. The ascent shows two *vakra* features and the descent shows one.

(8) *Māruvadēśika*

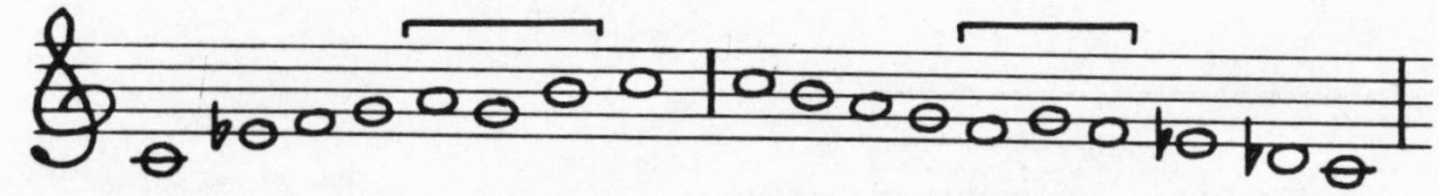

Ascent: the note *RI* (Db) is avoided; one *vakra* feature is shown.
Descent: *sampūrṇa*; one *vakra* feature is used.

(9) *Mukhapriya*

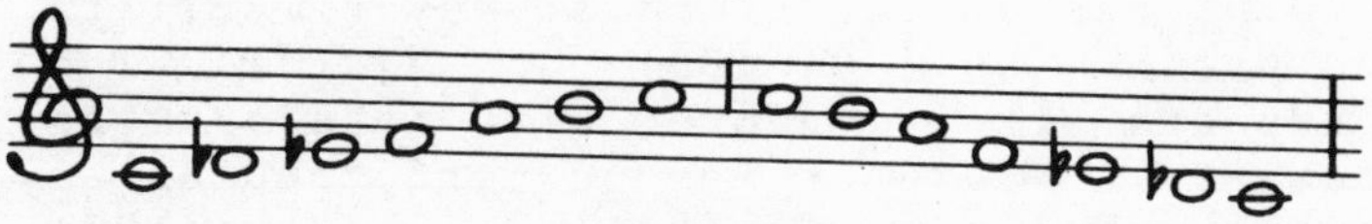

The note *PA* (G) is avoided entirely.

(10) *Sindhukriya*

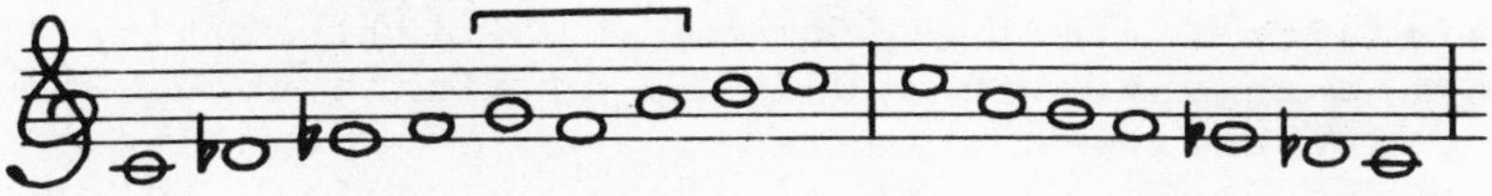

Ascent: *sampūrṇa*; one *vakra* feature is shown.
Descent: the note *NI* (B) is avoided.

(11) *Tittibhadhvani*

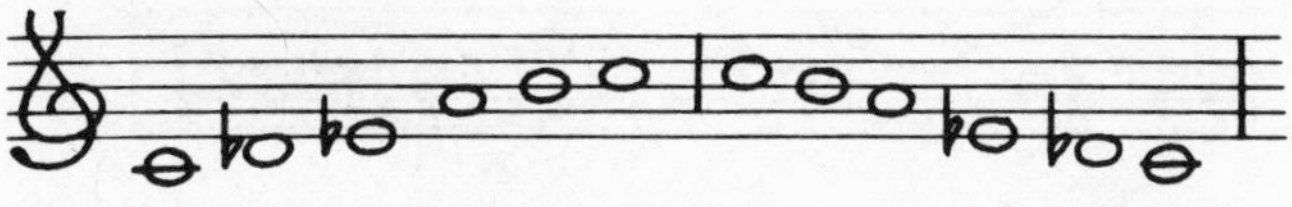

The notes *MA* (F) and *PA* (G) are avoided entirely.

(12) *Vasantanārāyani*

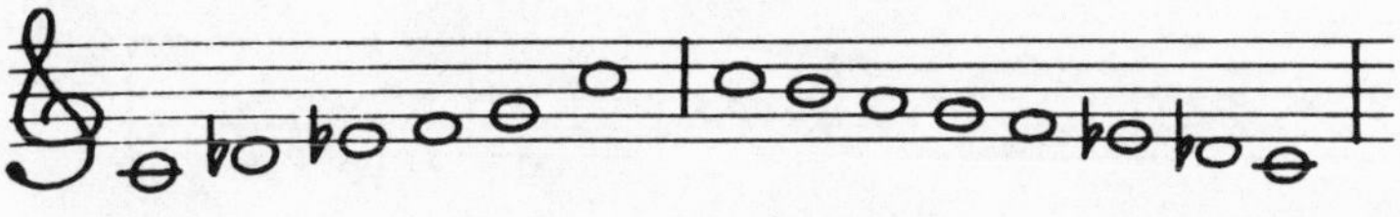

Ascent: the notes *DHA* (A) and *NI* (B) are avoided.
Descent: *krama sampūrṇa*.

12. *MĒḶA RŪPĀVATĪ*

Veṅkaṭamakhin calls this *rāga Rūpaciti* (*Rūpacati*, also *Rūpyanaga* or *Raupyanaga*) and states that the notes *GA* (Eb), *DHA* (A#), and *NI* (B) are avoided in ascent and that *DHA* (A#) has to appear in a *vakra* feature in descent.

Raga Rūpāvatī can be performed at any time. Its stressed notes are *RI* (Db), *GA* (Eb), and *MA* (F). The latter two notes are often rendered with more or less elaborate ornaments. Vibratos may be performed on any note of the scale. The note *NI* (B) is to be treated weakly. In the following song specimen, a *kīrtana*, the note *PA* (G) is also treated weakly.

The *kīrtana* shown below is in *jhampa tāla*. As already mentioned, if the word *jhampa* appears alone, it always refers to its *misra jāti* form (7+1+2). I have transcribed each rhythmical unit as an eighth note, and instead of presenting a detailed *misra jāti* organization, have made each measure of the song contain ten units (10/8).

RŪPĀVATĪ (*Jhampa-tāla*)

Pallavi

Anupallavi

Repeat the *pallavi*

Janya Rāgas of the 12. Mēḷa

(1) *Raupyanaga*

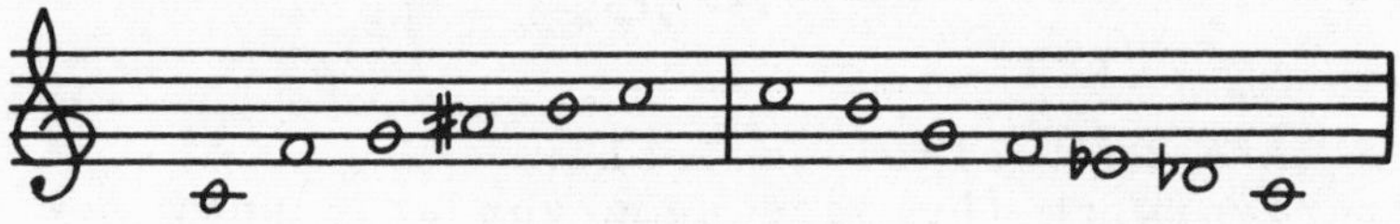

Ascent: the notes *RI* (Db) and *GA* (Eb) are avoided.
Descent: the note *DHA* (A#) is omitted.

A second version of the *Raupyanaga* descent is:

This second version is *sampūrṇa* and shows one *vakra* feature.

RAUPYANAGA RĀGA (*Triputa-tāla*) SCM, 35

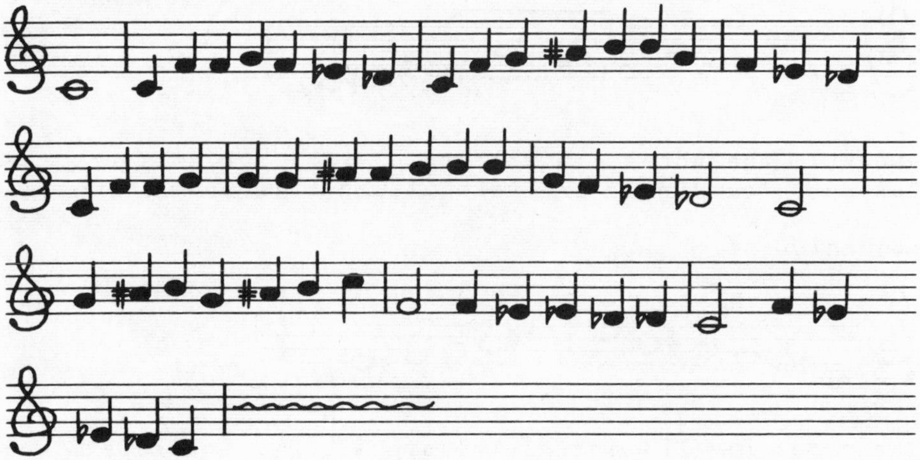

(2) *Bhanūkōkila*

The note *RI* (Db) is avoided entirely. *GA* (Eb) is omitted in ascent. The descent shows one *vakra* feature.

(3) *Bhōga Varāḷi*

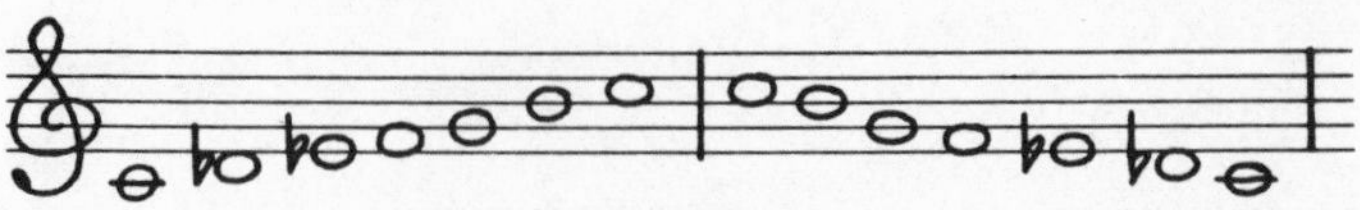

The note *DHA* (A#) is avoided entirely.

Another *rāga* with the same name appears under the heading of the 37. *mēḷa* (5).

(4) *Bhōgavati*

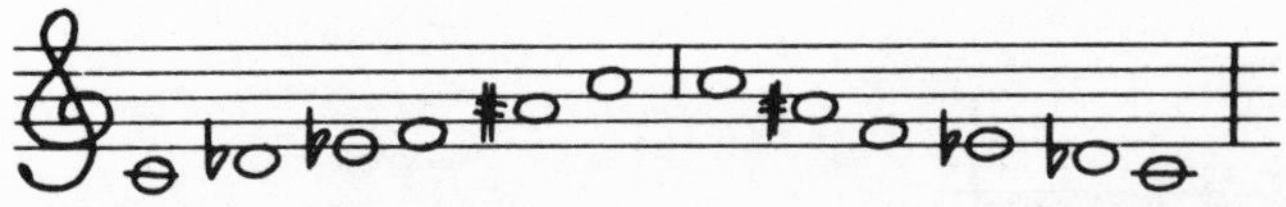

The notes *PA* (G) and *NI* (B) are avoided entirely.

Another *rāga* with the same name appears under the heading of the 22. *mēḷa* (17).

(5) *Gāpriyanagam*

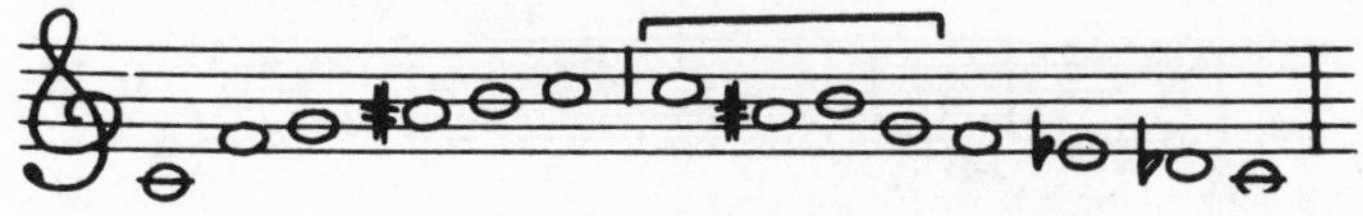

Ascent: the notes *RI* (Db) and *GA* (Eb) are avoided.
Descent: *sampūrṇa*; one *vakra* feature is shown.

(6) *Kalāpini*

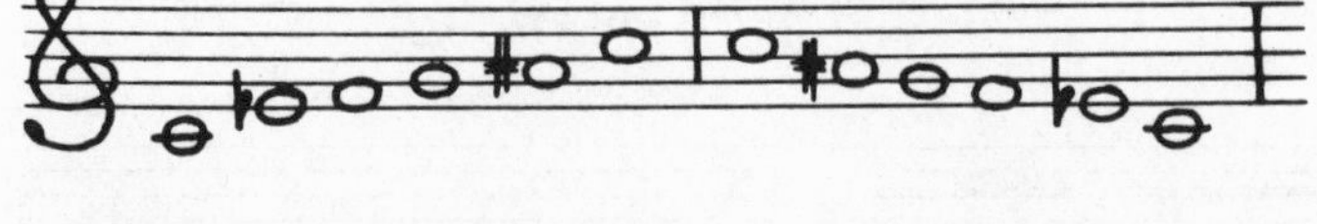

The notes *RI* (Db) and *NI* (B) are avoided entirely.

(7) *Kapila*

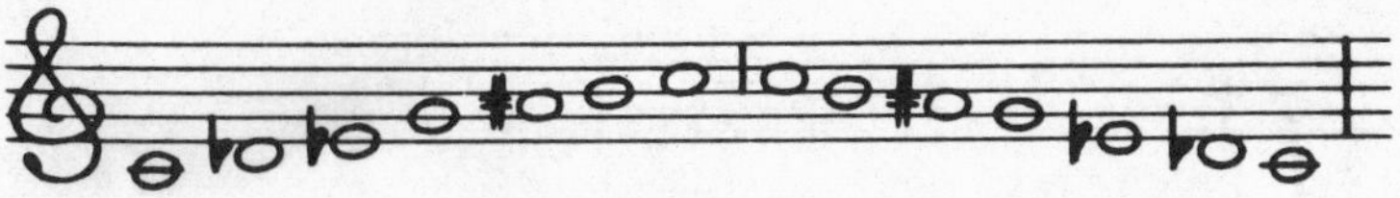

The note *MA* (F) is avoided entirely.

(8) *Kāpyā Nagam*

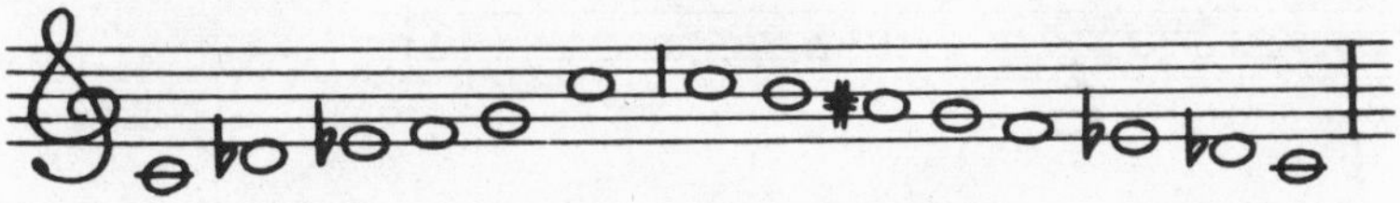

Ascent: the notes *DHA* (A#) and *NI* (B) are avoided.
Descent: *sampūrṇa*.

(9) *Kshēpiṇi* (*Kṣēpiṇi*)

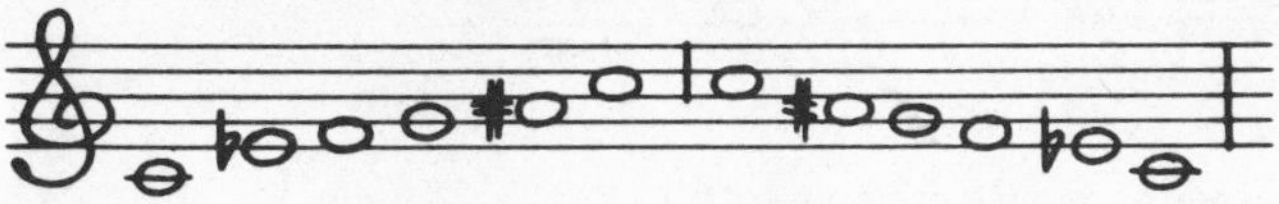

The notes *RI* (Db) and *NI* (B) are avoided entirely.
Compare with *rāga Kalāpini* (6) of *mēḷa* 12.

(10) *Lavayuvati*

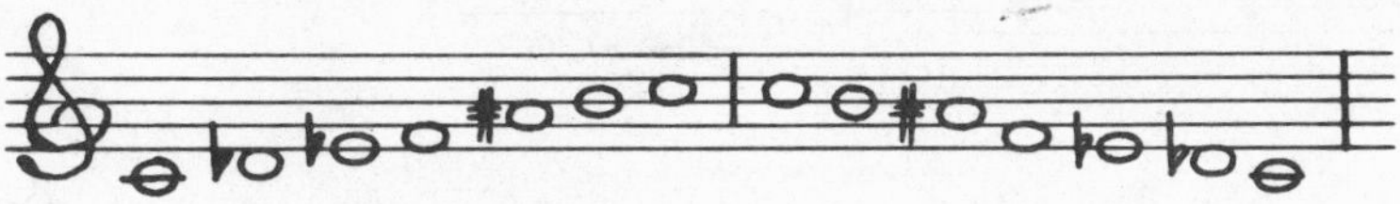

The note *PA* (G) is avoided entirely.

(11) *Mādhavapriya*

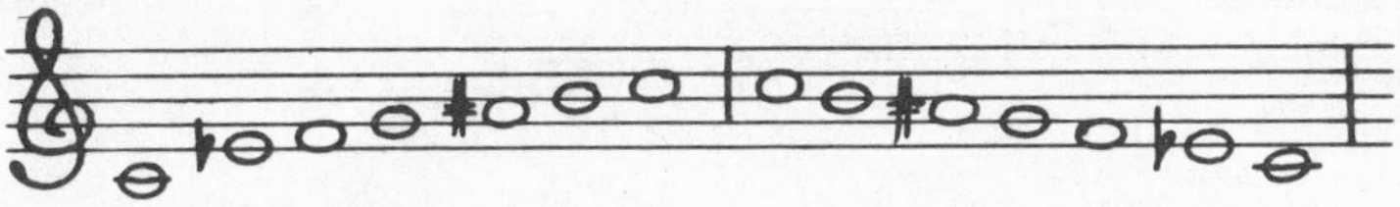

The note *RI* (Db) is avoided entirely.

(12) *Nāgarājam*

The note *NI* (B) is avoided entirely.

(13) *Pūrṇasvarāvali*

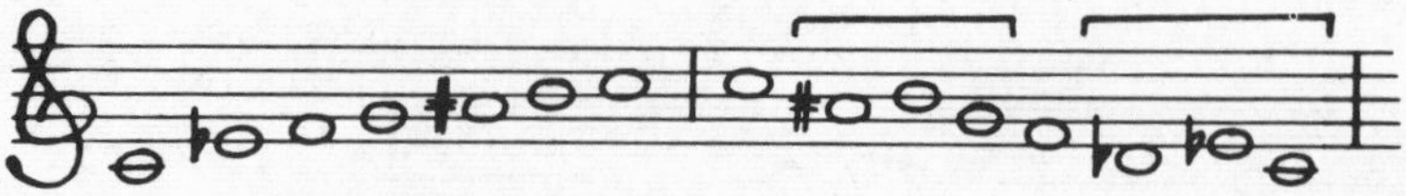

Ascent: the note *RI* (Db) is avoided.
Descent: *sampūrṇa*; two *vakra* features are shown.

(14) *Pratāpavasantam*

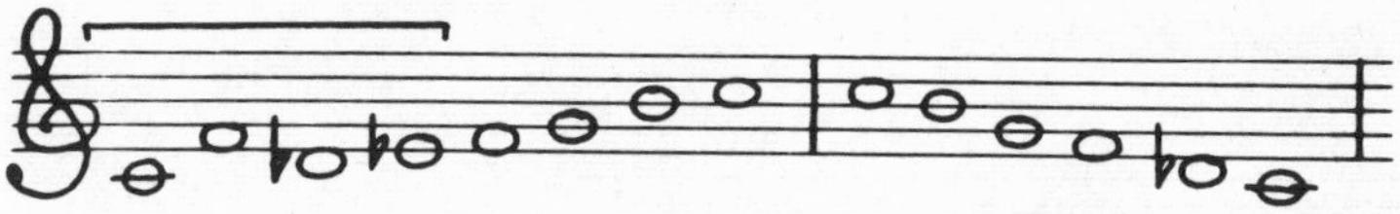

The note *DHA* (A#) is avoided entirely.
The ascent shows one *vakra* feature and the descent omits the note *GA* (Eb).

(15) *Sāmakurañji*

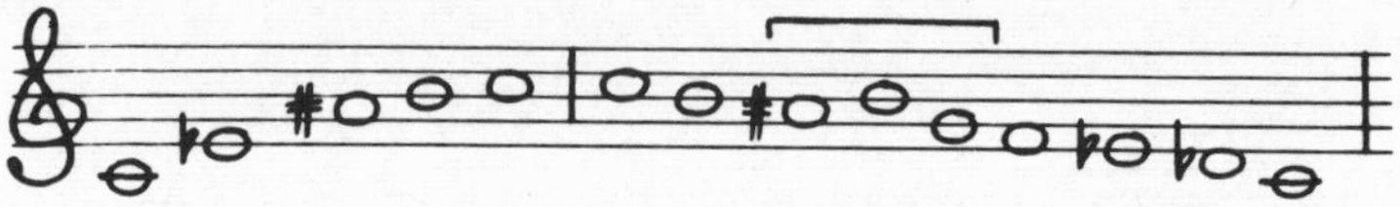

Ascent: the notes *RI* (Db), *MA* (F), and *PA* (G) are avoided.
Descent: *sampūrṇa*; one *vakra* feature is shown.

(16) *Sōmabhairavī*

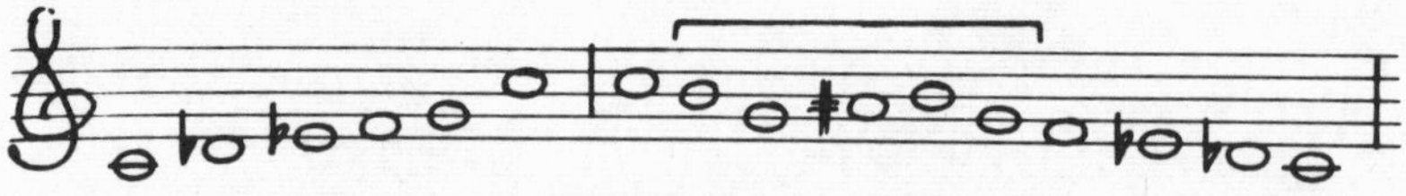

Ascent: the notes *DHA* (A#) and *NI* (B) are avoided.
Descent: *sampūrṇa*; one extended *vakra* feature is shown.

(17) *Śaśaṅkakiraṇi*

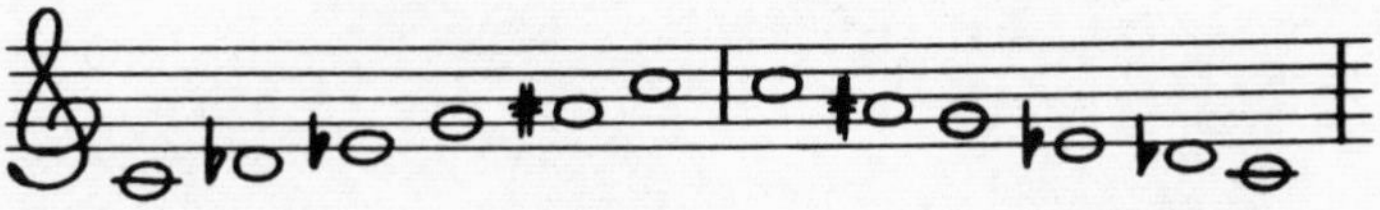

The notes *MA* (F) and *NI* (B) are avoided entirely.

Chakra III

13. *MELA GĀYAKAPRIYA*

In the earlier system of *asampūrṇa mēḷas* this *mēḷa* was called *Hejjujji*. In the later system, when *kaṭapayādi* prefixes were employed, its name was *Geyahejjajji*. Veṅkaṭamakhin states that this *rāga* avoids the note *NI* (Ḃbb) entirely (see below: *Janya Rāga Hejjujji*).

Rāga Gāyakapriya is heptatonic, as are all *mēla-rāgas* of the present time. Its strong notes are *RI* (Db), *MA* (F), and *NI* (Bbb). *Gāyakapriya* is supposed to be performed in the morning, although it can be heard at other times as well.

The following song specimen is a *kṛti* in *khanda chapu tāla* (2+3):

GĀYAKAPRIYA (*Khanda chapu-tāla*)

Pallavi

A

B

Repeat the entire *pallavi*

Anupallavi

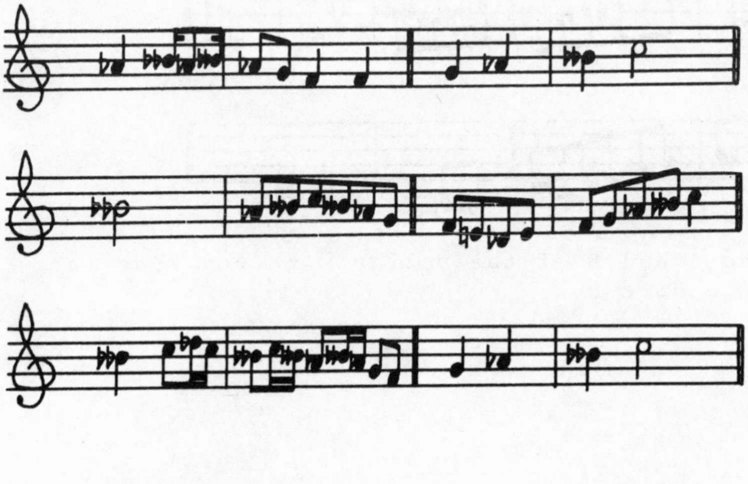

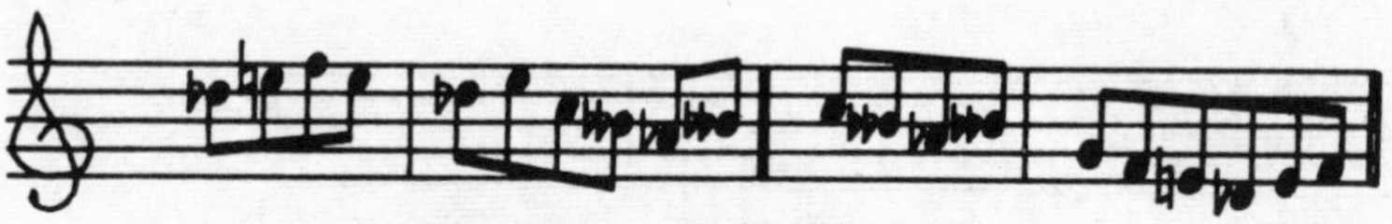

Repeat lines A and B of the *pallavi*

Charana

Repeat lines A and B of the *pallavi* and conclude the song with the note *PA*

Janya Rāgas of the 13. Mēḷa

(1) *Hejjujji* (*Hejjajji*)

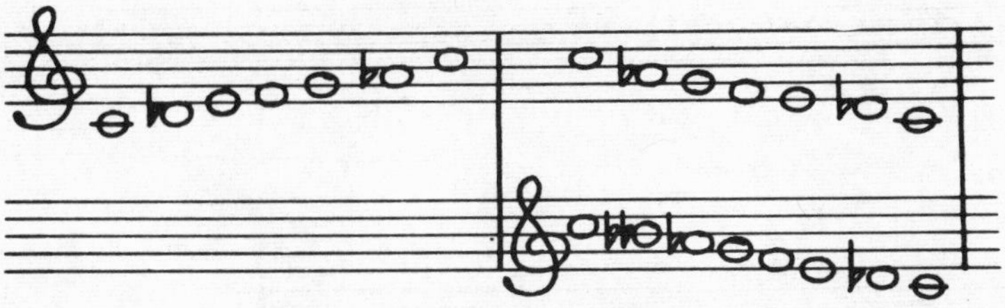

The traditional form of the scale avoids the note *NI* (Bbb) entirely. The second version of descent shown above appears in SD (II, 227); it employs the note *NI* (Bbb).

The following passages are believed to be characteristic of this *rāga*:

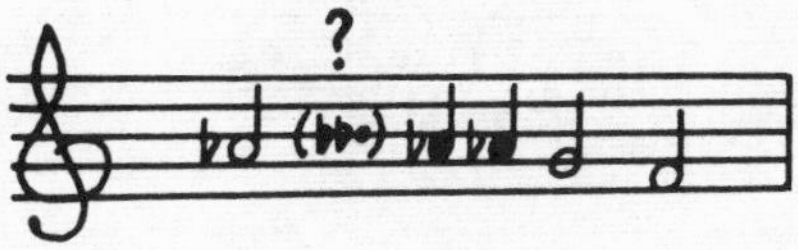

The melody specimen shown below employs the note *NI* (Bbb) in descent:

RĀGA HEJJUJJI (*Triputa-tāla*) SCM, 36-37

(2) *Megh* (*Megha*)

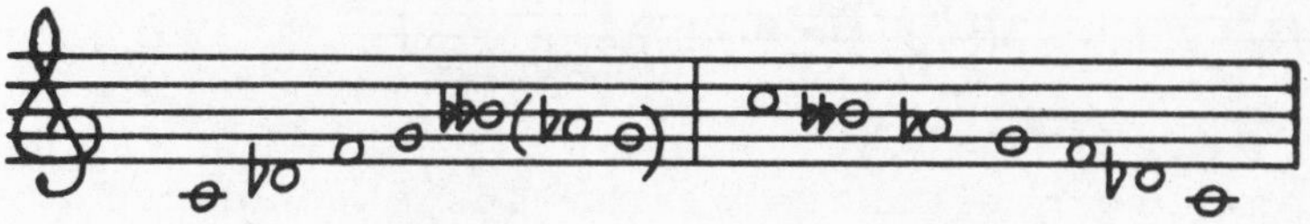

The note *GA* (E) is avoided entirely.

MEGHA RĀGA (*Triputa-tāla*) SCM, 37

(3) *Jujāvaḷi*

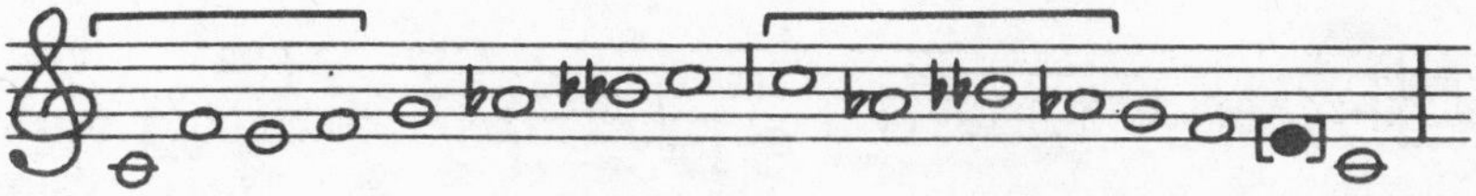

The note *RI* (Db) is avoided entirely. The scale shows two *vakra* features, one in ascent and one in descent. R (174) reports that a *Rāga Lakṣaṇa* manuscript of Tanjore calls this *rāga Jujāhuḷi* or *Sujaskāvaḷi* with the following descending scale:

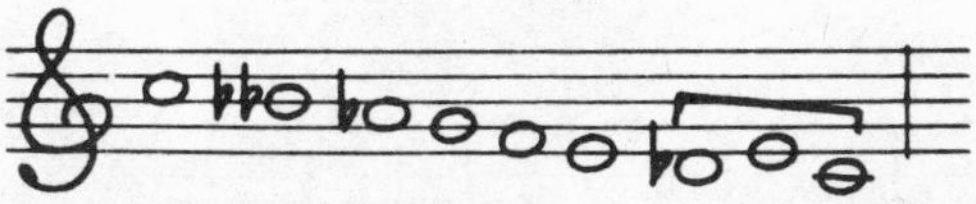

R also states that a fragment of a work, a *Saṅgīta Viṣaya*, preserved in the Government Oriental Manuscripts Library of Madras, defines this *rāga*, called *Jujāhuri*, as follows:

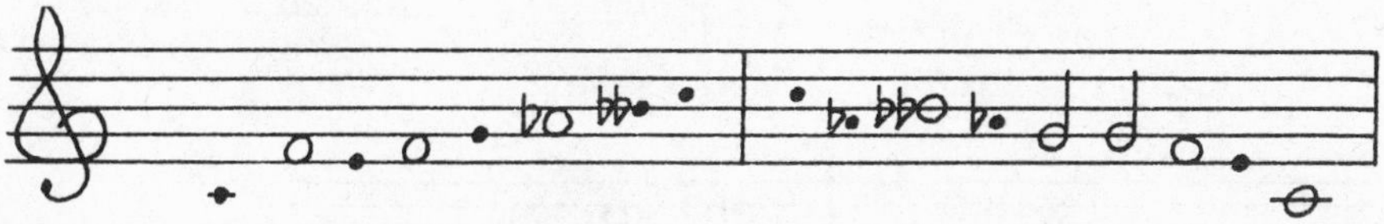

The material is shown here with its strong and weak notes.

Compare this latter scale with that of another *rāga Jujāhuḷi* ascribed to the 28. *mēḷa*. The following specimen represents *Jujāvaḷi* of the 12. *mēḷa*:

RĀGA JUJĀVAḶI (*Triputa-tāla*) SCM, 38

(4) *Kalakaṇṭhi*

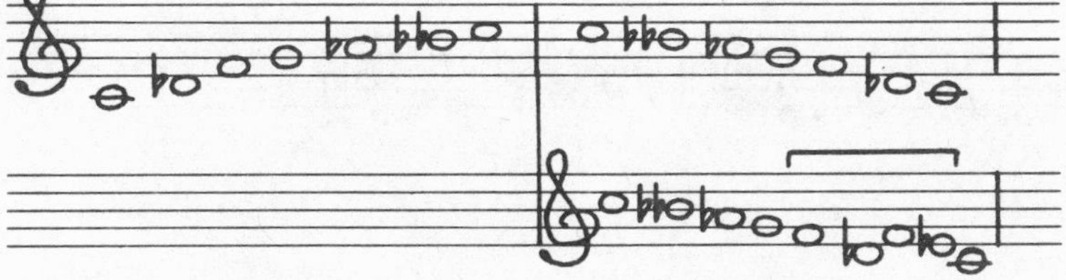

There are two forms of the *Kalakaṇṭhi* scale: (a) in which the note *GA* (Eb) is avoided entirely, and (b) in which *GA* (Eb) is omitted in ascent while it is used in the *sampūrṇa* descent. The descent of the second version shows one *vakra* feature.

RĀGA KALAKAṆṬHI (*Triputa-tāla*) SCM, 38-39

(5) *Kalagaḍā* (*Kaltadā*)

The note *MA* (F) is omitted entirely.
Veṅkaṭamakhin does not describe this *rāga* at all. Another *rāga* with the same name appears under the heading of the 16. *mēḷa* (5), where the notes *DHA* and *NI* represent A and Bb respectively.

RĀGA KALAGAḌĀ (*Triputa-tāla*) SCM, 39

(6) *Davvi*

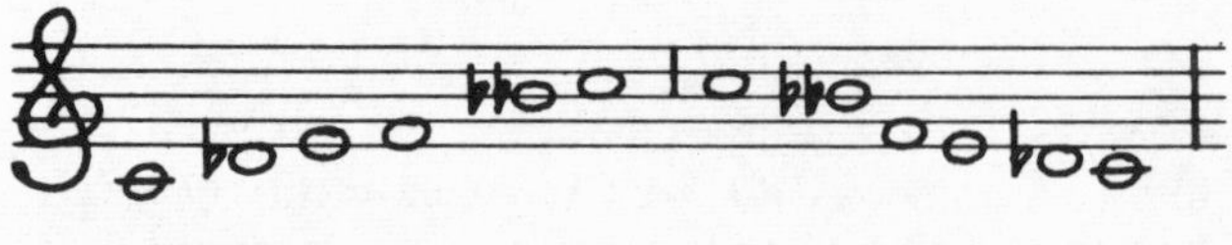

The notes *PA* (G) and *DHA* (Ab) are avoided entirely.

(7) *Dhīramati*

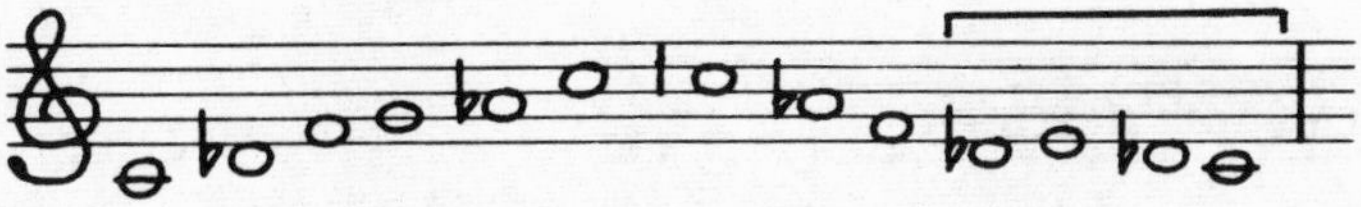

The note *NI* (Bbb) is avoided entirely. In ascent *GA* (E) and in descent *PA* (G) are omitted. The descending line shows one *vakra* feature.
Another *rāga* with the same name appears under the heading of the 29. *mēḷa* (34).

(8) *Domka* (*Ḍhomka*)

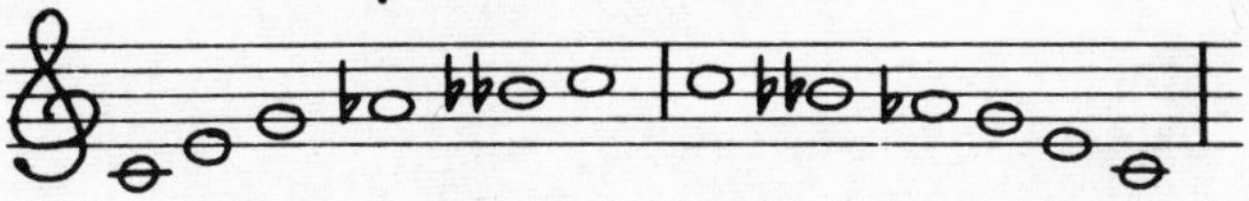

The notes *RI* (Db) and *MA* (F) are omitted entirely.

(9) *Esāri*

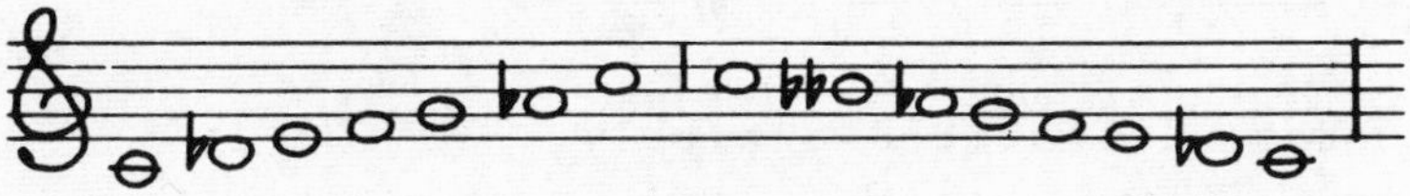

Ascent: the note *NI* (Bbb) is avoided.
Descent: *krama sampūrṇa*.

(10) *Gītapriya*

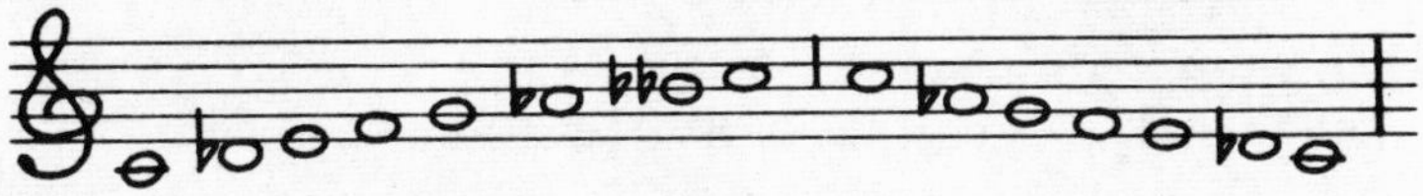

Ascent: *krama sampūrṇa*.
Descent: the note *NI* (Bbb) is avoided.
Another *rāga* with the same name appears under the heading of the 63. *mēḷa* (8).

(11) *Haṃsa Naṭani*

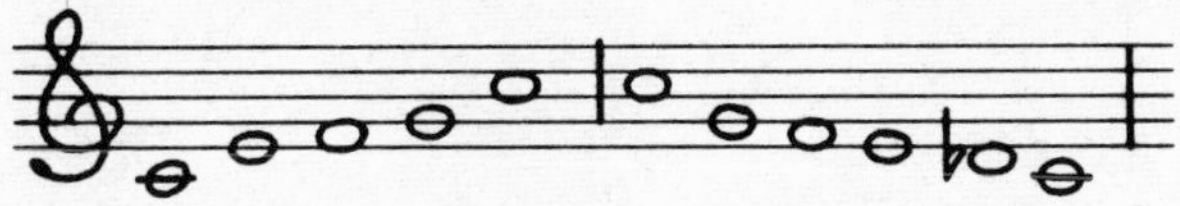

The notes *DHA* (Ab) and *NI* (Bbb) are avoided entirely.
The note *RI* (Db) is omitted in ascent.

(12) *Haṃsa Vāridhi*

The notes *GA* (E) and *NI* (Bbb) are avoided entirely.

(13) *Kaliki*

Ascent: *krama sampūrṇa*.
Descent: the note *GA* (E) is avoided.

(14) *Kalyāṇa Kēsari*

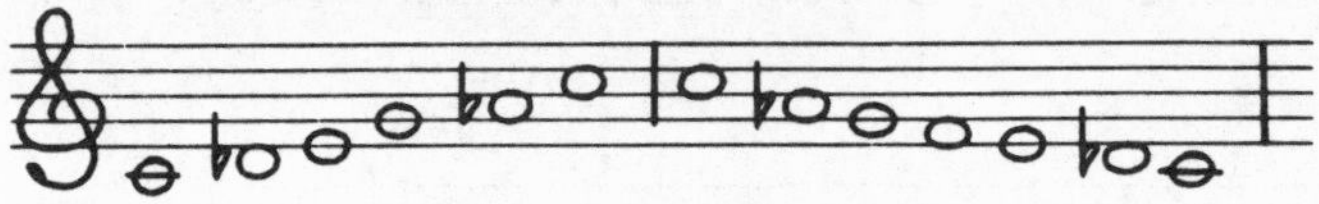

The note *NI* (Bbb) is avoided entirely. *MA* (F) is omitted in ascent.

(15) *Kaṇaka*

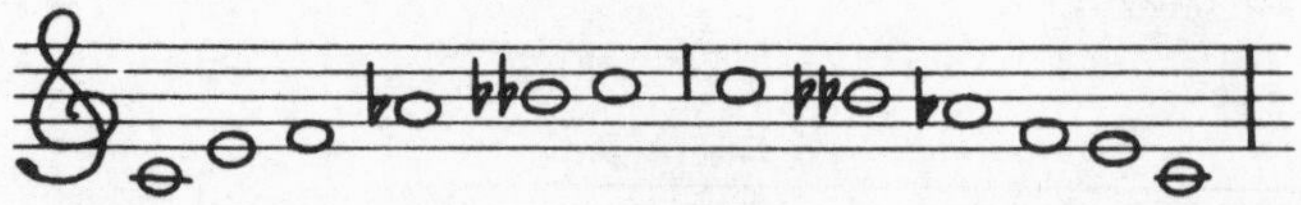

The notes *RI* (Db) and *PA* (G) are avoided entirely.

(16) *Kuntala Kāmbhōji*

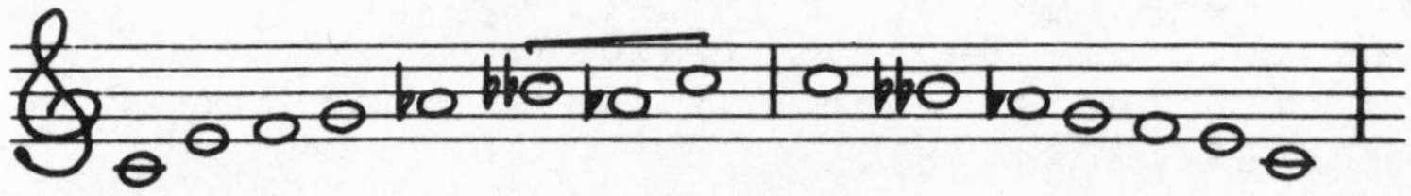

The note *RI* (Db) is avoided entirely. The ascent shows one *vakra* feature.

(17) *Bhujaga Chintāmaṇi*

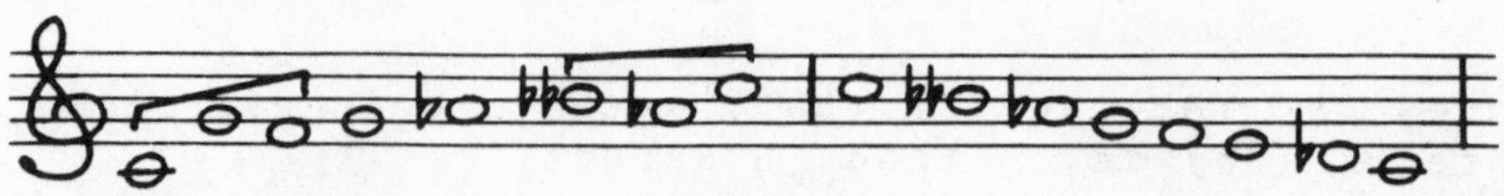

Ascent: the notes *RI* (Db) and *GA* (E) are avoided; two *vakra* features are shown.
Descent: *krama sampūrṇa*.

(18) *Lōkapriya*

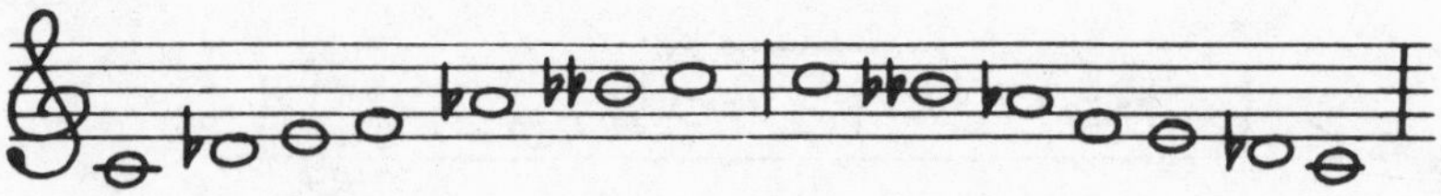

The note *PA* (G) is avoided entirely.

(19) *Marīchika*

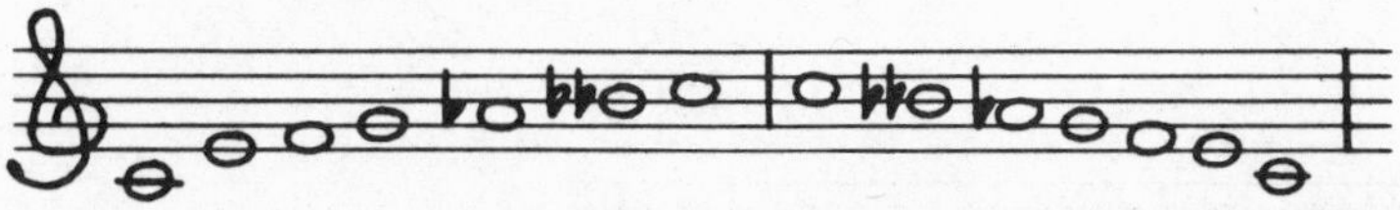

The note *RI* (Db) is avoided entirely.

(20) *Mēgharagam* (*Mēgharañjani*)

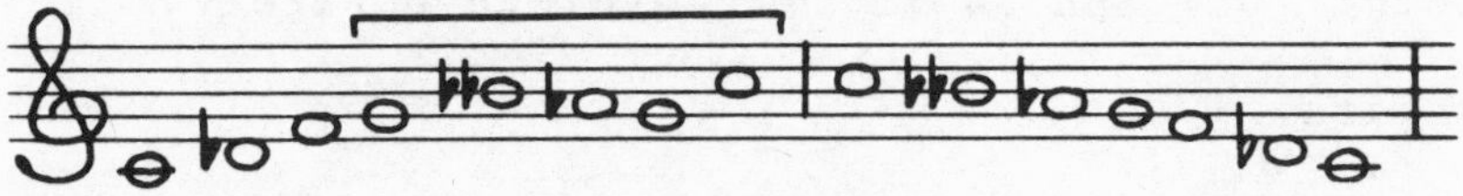

The note *GA* (E) is avoided entirely. The ascent shows one extended *vakra* feature.

(21) *Nāgasāmantam*

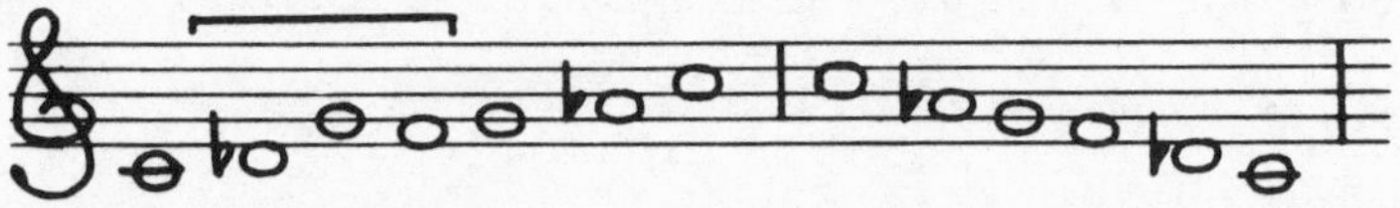

The notes *GA* (E) and *NI* (Bbb) are avoided entirely. The ascent shows one *vakra* feature.

(22) *Ratnabhūṣaṇi*

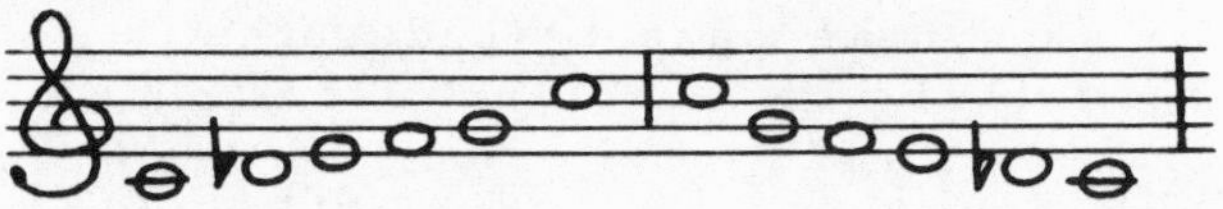

The notes *DHA* (Ab) and *NI* (Bbb) are avoided entirely.

(23) *Sāmanārāyaṇi*

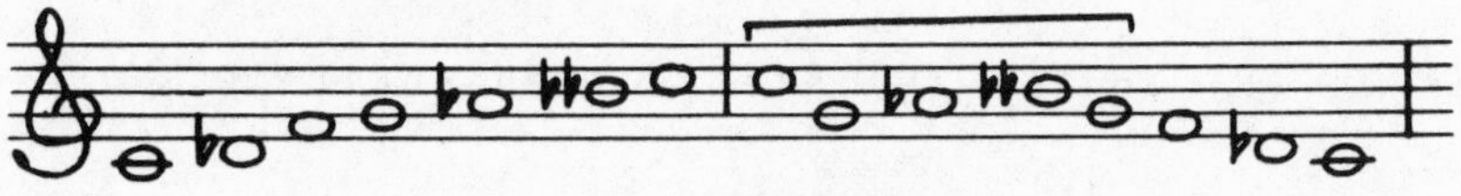

The note *GA* (E) is avoided entirely. The descent shows one extended *vakra* feature.

(24) *Sujaskāvali*

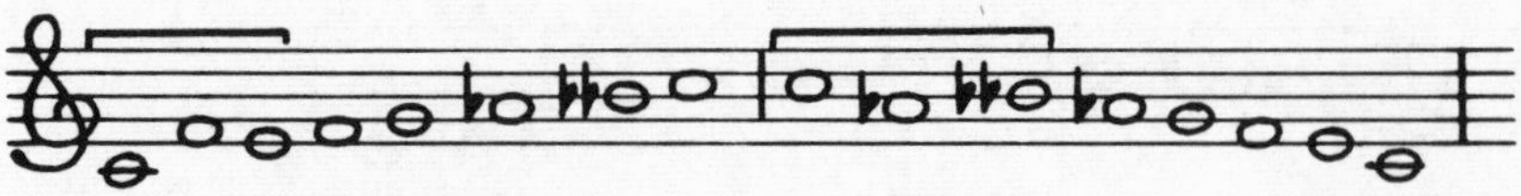

The note *RI* (Db) is avoided entirely. Ascent and descent show one *vakra* feature each.

(25) *Suravarāli*

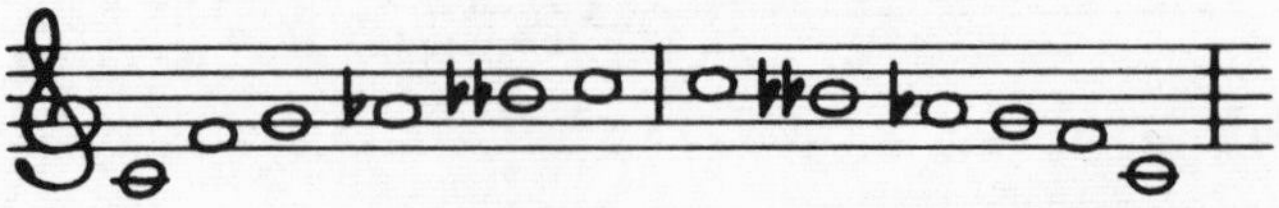

The notes *RI* (Db) and *GA* (E) are avoided entirely.

(26) *Suvarata*

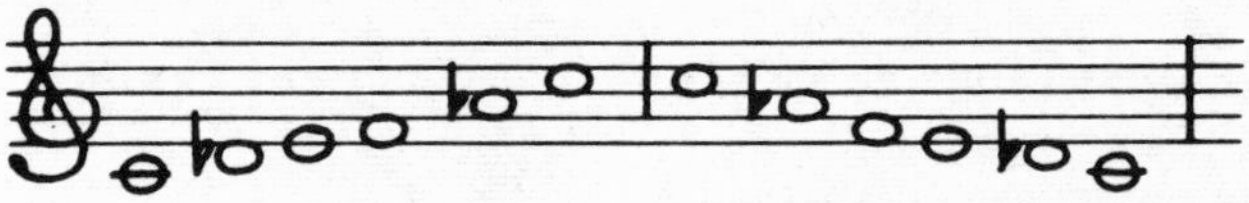

The notes *PA* (G) and *NI* (Bbb) are avoided entirely.

(27) *Śukhavāni*

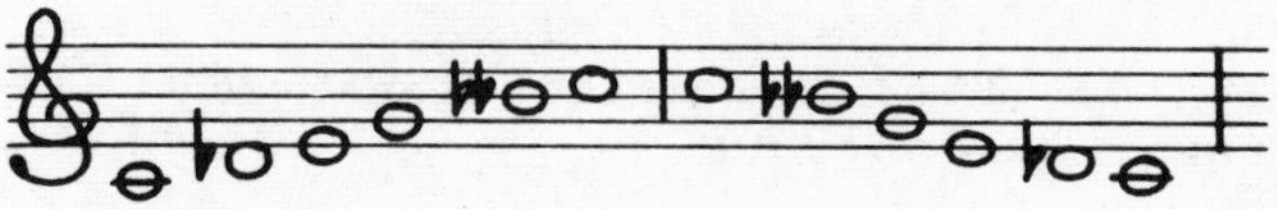

The notes *MA* (F) and *DHA* (Ab) are avoided entirely. Another *rāga* with the same name appears under the heading of the 21. *mēḷa* (19).

(28) *Tridaśarañjani*

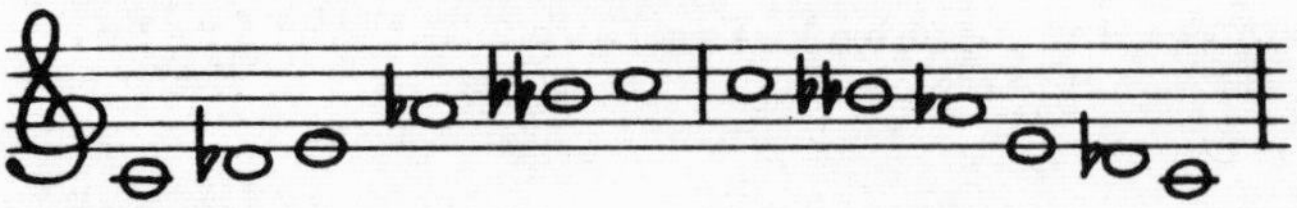

The notes *MA* (F) and *PA* (G) are avoided entirely.

14. *MELA VAKUḶĀBHARAṆAM*

Rāga Vakuḷābharaṇam may be performed at any time. Stressed notes are *GA* (E) and *NI* (Bb), which should be slightly extended (even if not notated in a prolonged manner) and performed with a slight vibrato. Veṅkaṭamakhin calls this *rāga Vaṭivasantabhairavī* and states that the note *PA* (G) has to be used sparingly. Tuḷajā in his description of this *rāga* remarks that the ascending passage *SA-RI-GA-MA* (C-Db-E-F) must not be used and that the note *PA* (G) has to be avoided in descent. At present both rules are ignored. The following example is a *kīrtana* in *Vakuḷābharaṇam*:

VAKUḶĀBHARAṆAM (*Triputa-tāla*)

Pallavi

A

B
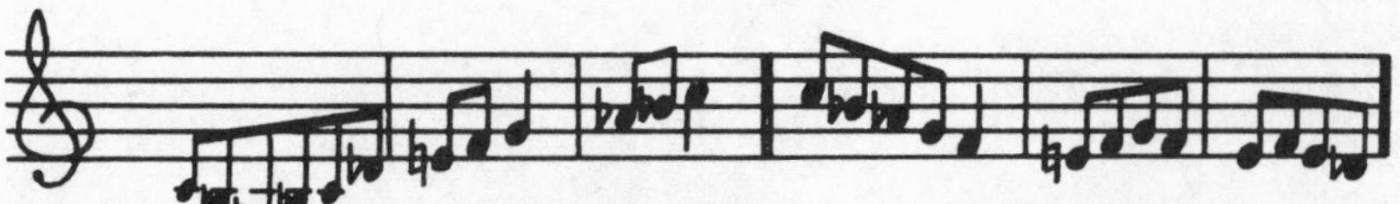

C

Repeat lines A, B, and C of the *pallavi*

Anupallavi

Repeat lines A, B, and C of the *pallavi*

Charana

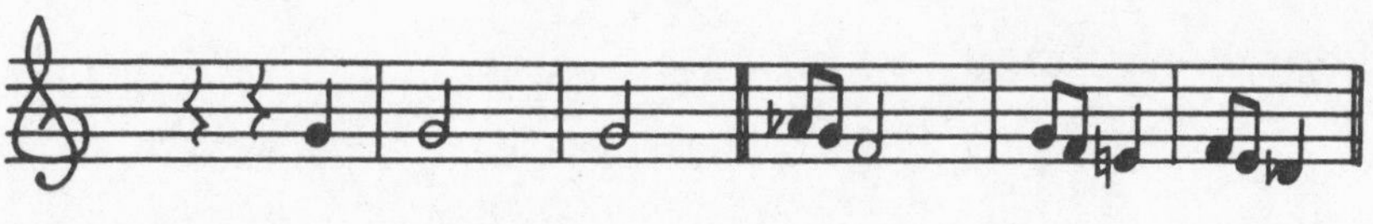

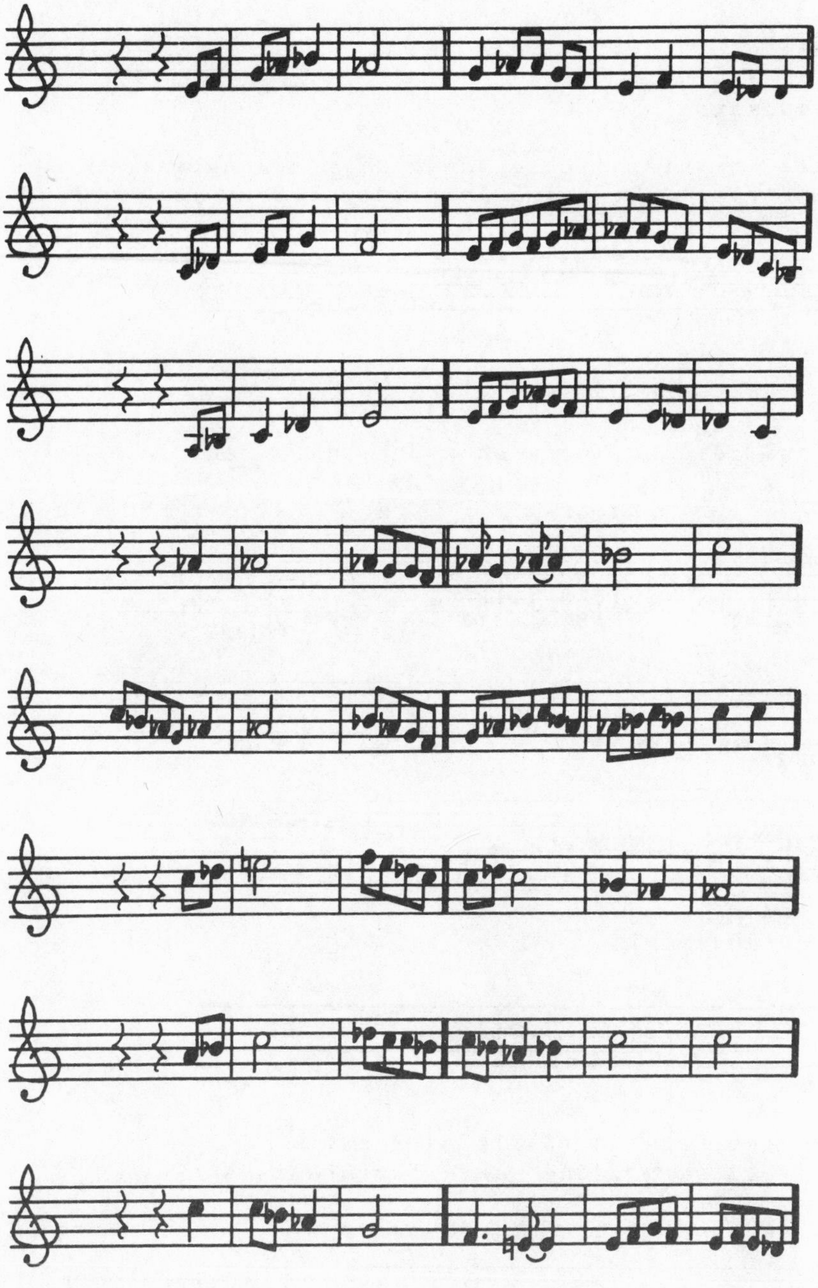

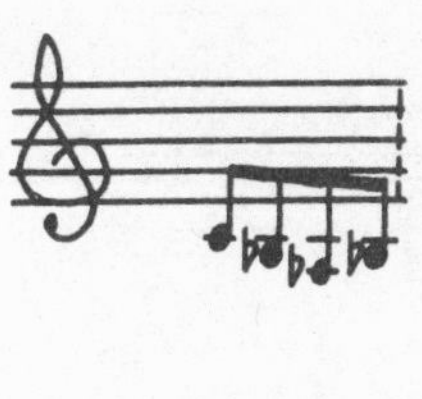

Repeat lines A, B, and C of the *pallavi* and conclude the song with the note *SA* (C).

Janya Rāgas of the 14. Mēḷa

(1) *Rāgavasant*

The scale of this obscure *janya rāga* can appear in several forms. The commonly accepted form is:

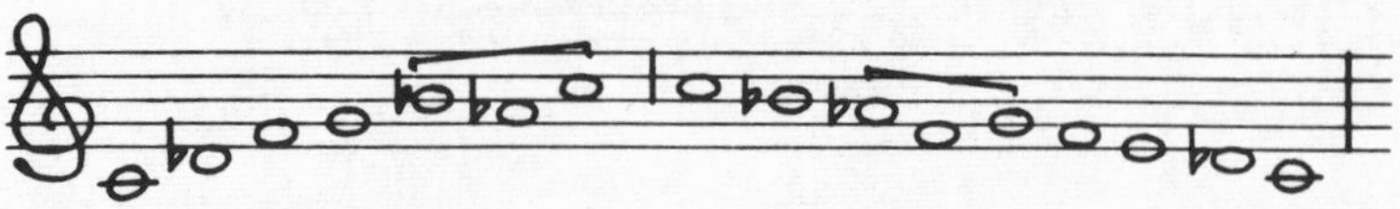

Ascent: the note *GA* (E) is avoided.
Descent: *sampūrṇa*.
Ascent and descent, each show one *vakra* feature.

RĀGAVASANT (*Triputa-tāla*) SCM, 40-41

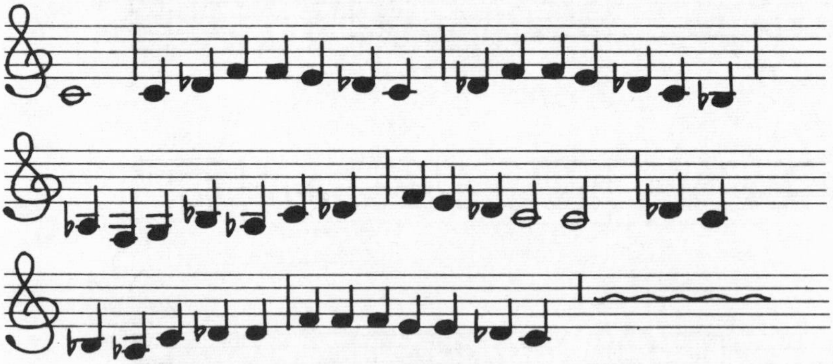

(2) *Vasantbhairavī*

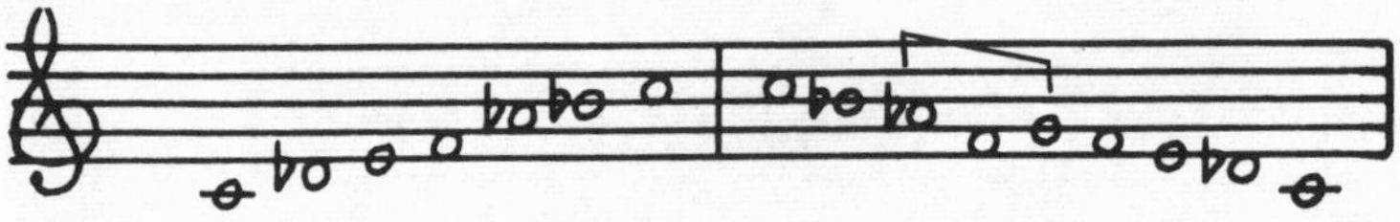

Ascent: the note *PA* (G) is avoided.
Descent: *sampūrṇa*; one *vakra* feature is shown.

RĀGA VASANTABHAIRAVĪ (*Triputa-tāla*) SCM, 41

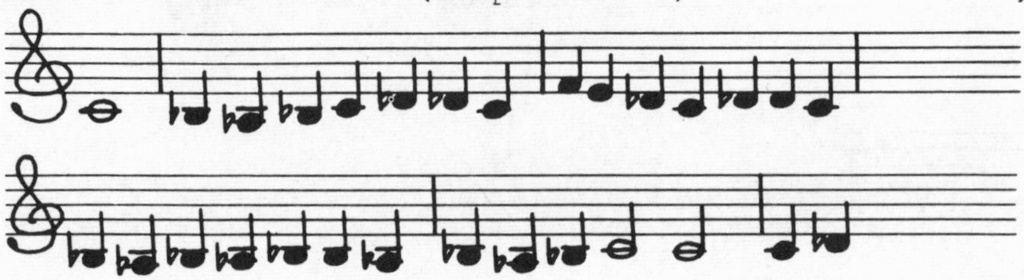

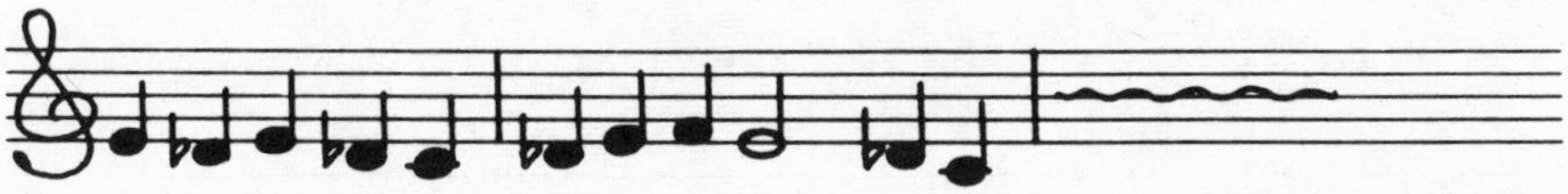

(3) *Āhiri*

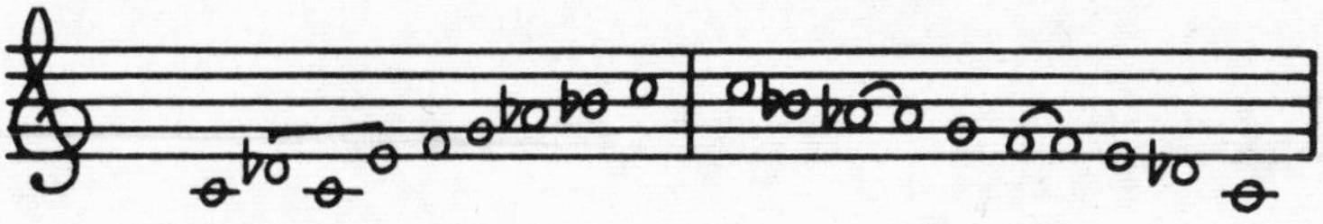

The *sampūrṇa* scale of this *rāga* shows one *vakra* feature in ascent. The notes *DHA* (Ab) and *MA* (F) are stressed.

Another *rāga* with the same name appears under the heading of the 8. *mēḷa* (7). The similarity between the two *rāgas* is obvious.

In the foregoing *Āhiri* specimen (*ādi tāla*) the characteristic *vakra* feature in ascent is not observed. Furthermore, the note *RI* (Dd) is avoided in ascent. No particular stressing of the notes *DHA* (Ab) and *MA* (F) can be noticed.

(4) *Vasantmukhāri*

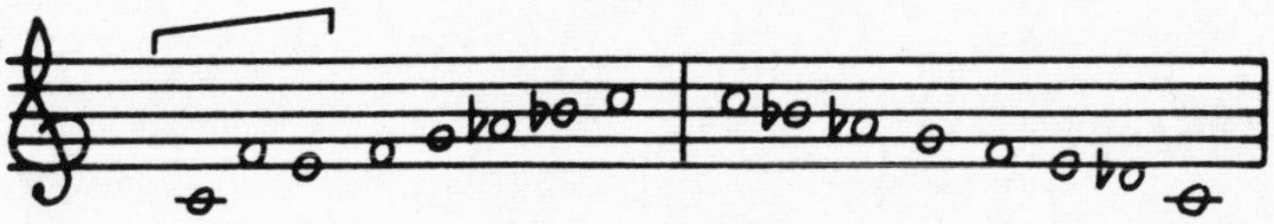

Ascent: the note *RI* (Db) is avoided. One *vakra* feature is shown.
Descent: *krama sampūrṇa*

RĀGA VASANTMUKHĀRI (*Triputa-tāla*) SCM, 43

(5) *Soma*

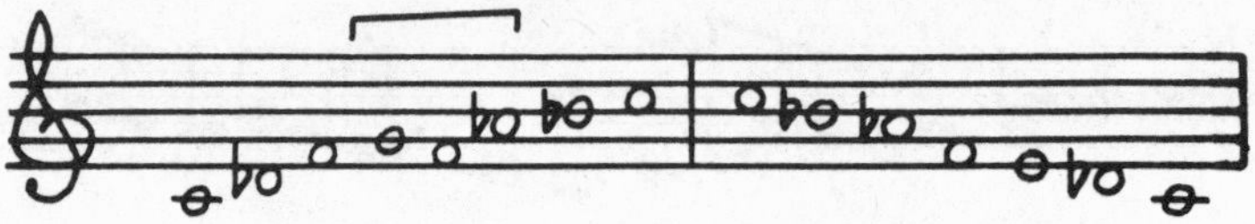

Ascent: the note *GA* (E) is avoided; one *vakra* feature is shown.
Descent: the note *PA* (G) is omitted.

SOMARĀGA (*Triputa-tāla*) SCM, 42

(6) *Bhūvana Rañjani*

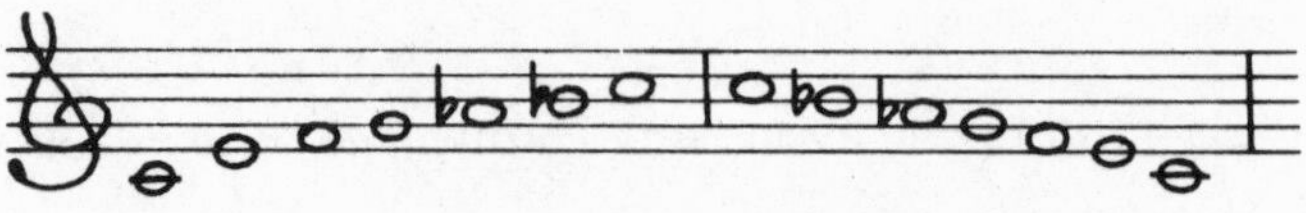

The note *RI* (Db) is avoided entirely.

(7) *Chandraśēkharapriya*

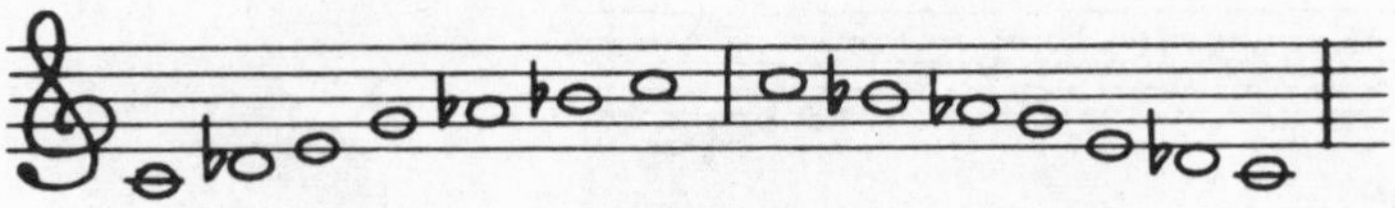

The note *MA* (F) is avoided entirely.

(8) *Ghana Śobhitam*

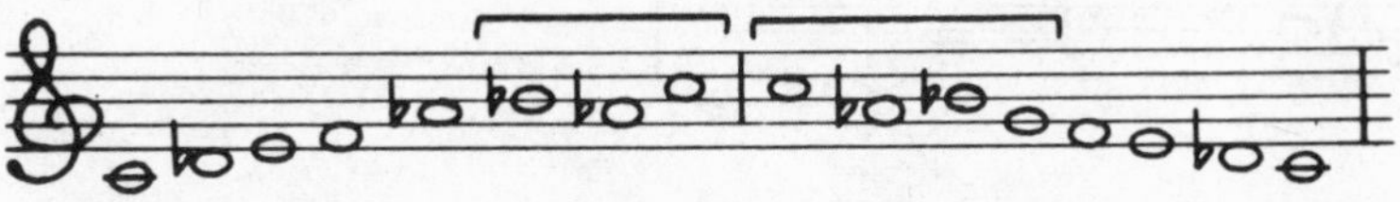

Ascent: the note *PA* (G) is avoided; one *vakra* feature is shown.
Descent: *sampūrṇa*; one *vakra* feature is used.

(9) *Haṃsa Kāmbhōji*

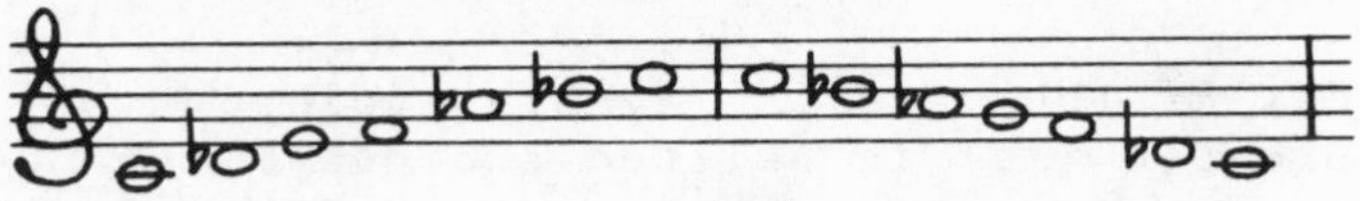

Ascent: the note *PA* (G) is avoided.
Descent: the note *GA* (E) is omitted.

(10) *Kalindaja*

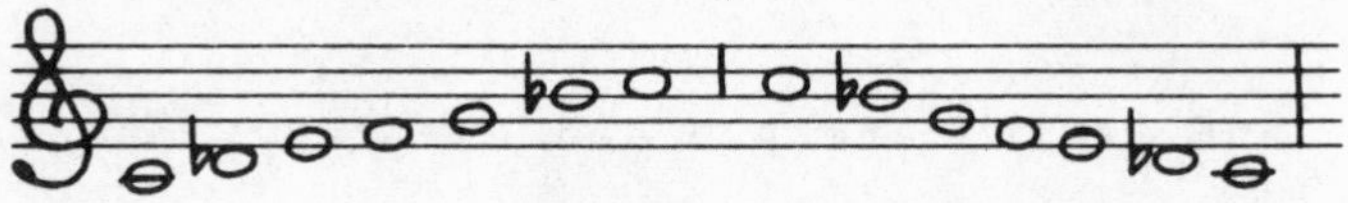

The note *DHA* (Ab) is avoided entirely.

(11) *Karṇāṭaka Andhāḷi*

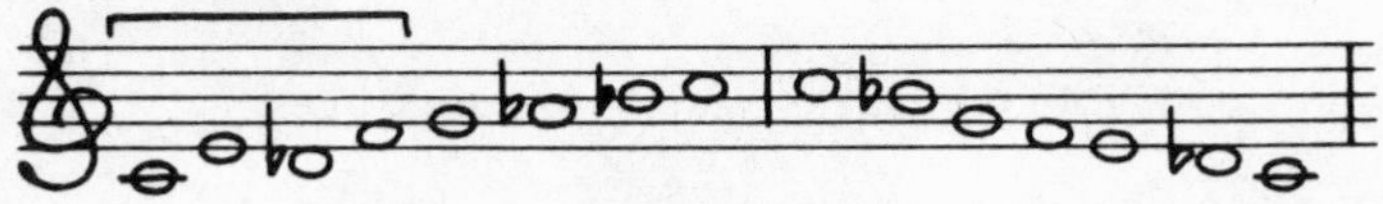

Ascent: *sampūrṇa*; one *vakra* feature is shown.
Descent: the note *DHA* (Ab) is avoided.

(12) *Kuvalayābharaṇam*

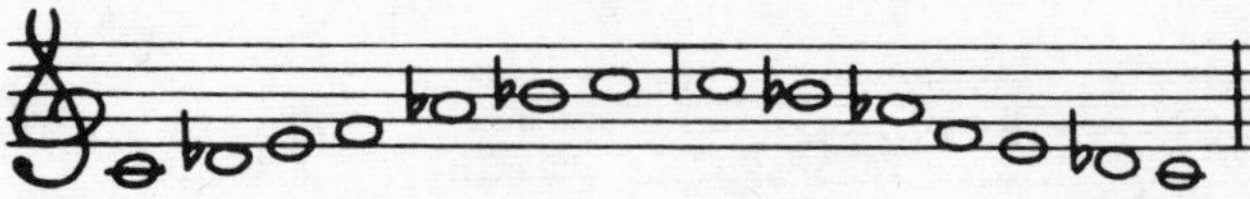

The note *PA* (G) is avoided entirely.

(13) *Lāsaki*

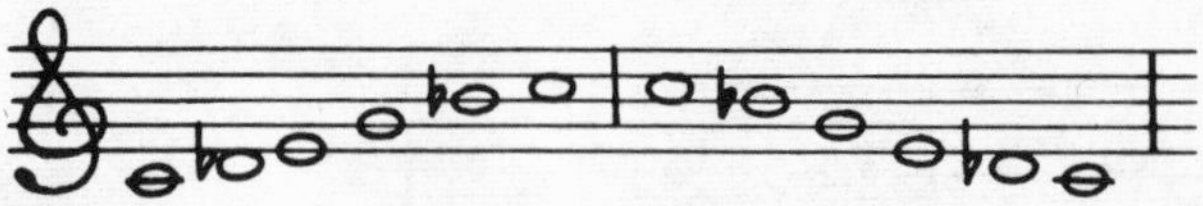

The notes *MA* (F) and *DHA* (Ab) are avoided entirely.

(14) *Nitalaprakāśini*

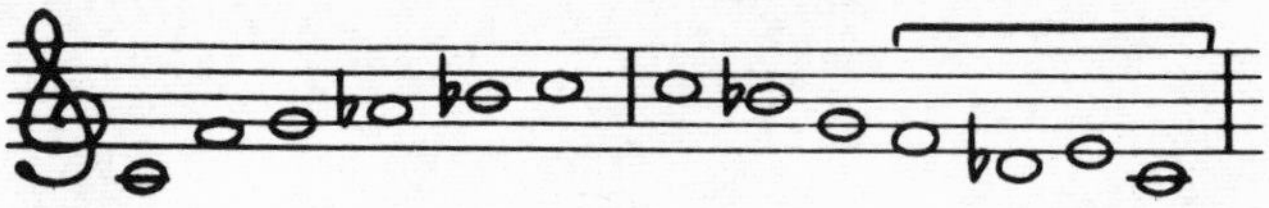

Ascent: the notes *RI* (Db) and *GA* (E) are avoided.
Descent: the note *DHA* (Ab) is omitted and one *vakra* feature is shown.

(15) *Pālini*

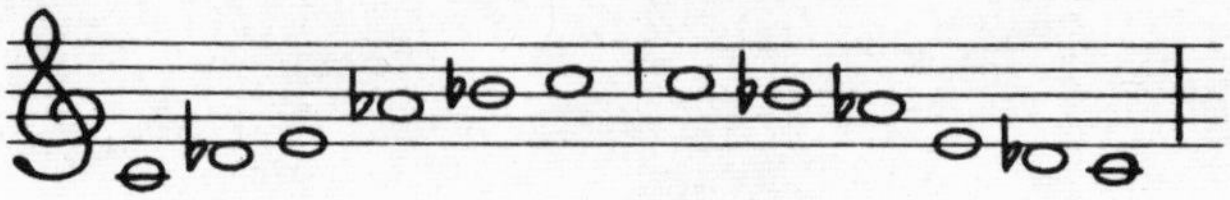

The notes *MA* (F) and *PA* (G) are avoided entirely.

(16) *Salāpam*

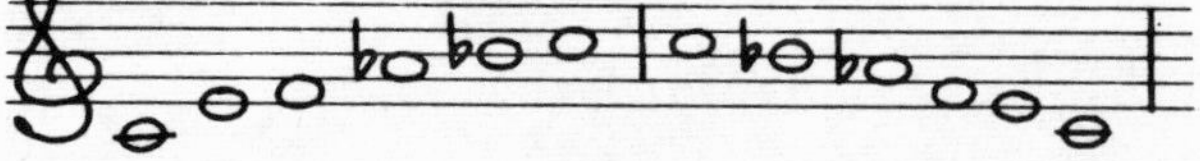

The notes *RI* (Db) and *PA* (G) are avoided entirely.

(17) *Śuddhakāmbhōji* (*Śudhakāmbhōji*)

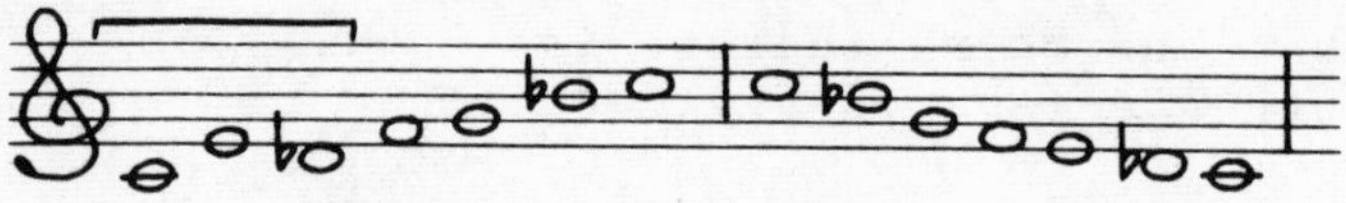

The note *DHA* (Ab) is avoided entirely. The ascent shows one *vakra* feature.

(18) *Tāpa*

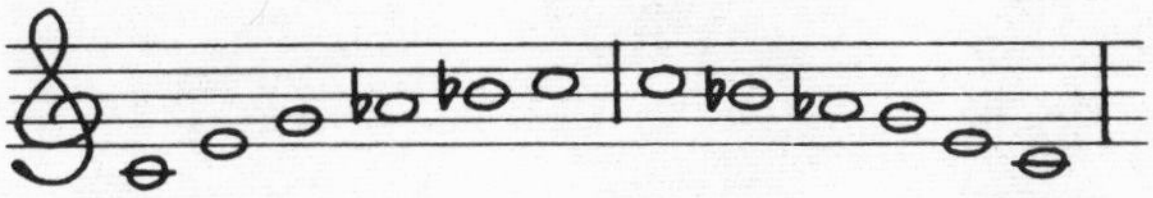

The notes *RI* (Db) and *MA* (F) are avoided entirely.

(19) *Tāpasapriya*

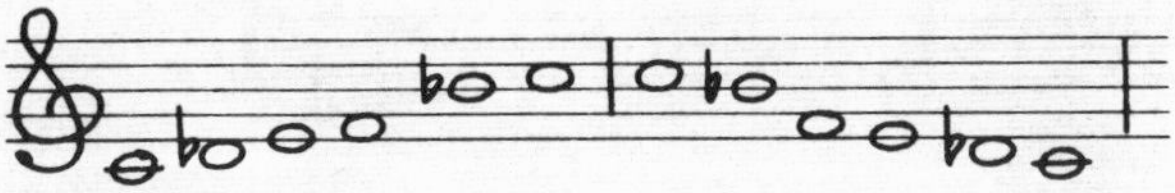

The notes *PA* (G) and *DHA* (Ab) are avoided entirely.

15. *MĒḶA MĀYĀMĀḶAVAGAUḶA (MĀYĀMĀḶAVAGAUḌA)*

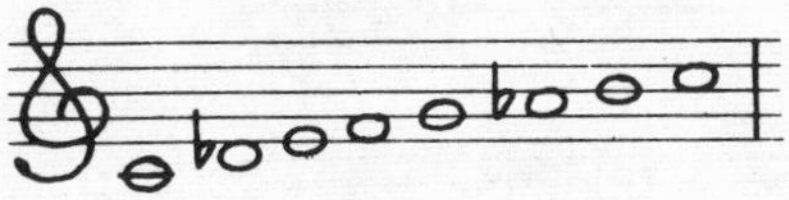

Māyāmāḷavagauḷa is one of the frequently performed *rāgas*. Its popularity is also shown by the large number of *janya rāgas* ascribed to it. Its tone material is the same as that of *rāga Bhairav* of North India (see RNI, 233-37). In contrast to the northern *rāga*, *Māyāmāḷavagauḷa* may be performed at any time. Stressed notes are *GA* (E) and *NI* (B), both often rendered with a small vibrato. This popular southern *rāga* is often used in light, entertaining music, and musicians occasionally alter one or the other note of its material by a semitone. Students of South Indian music usually begin their studies with this comparatively simple *rāga*.

The following song specimen is a *kīrtana*:

MĀYĀMĀḶAVAGAUḶA (*Rūpaka-tāla*)

Pallavi

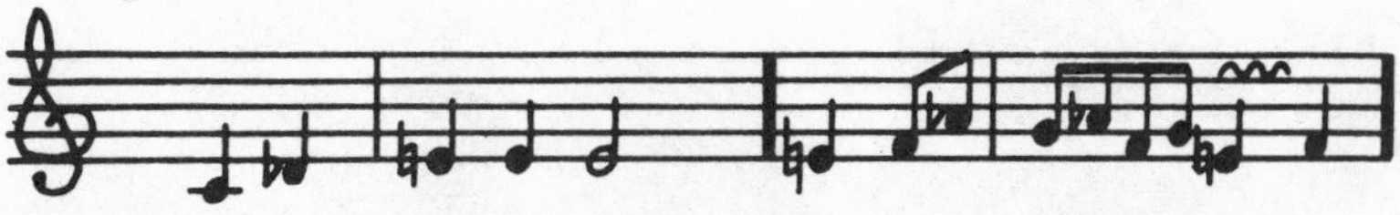

Repeat the entire *pallavi*

[variations]

A

B

C

D

Anupallavi

Repeat lines A, B, C, D of the *pallavi*

Charana

Repeat lines A, B, C, D of the *pallavi*

Janya Rāgas of the 15. Mēḷa

Some of the *janya rāgas* show distinctly their relation with the material of the primary *rāga*. There are others which are vague in interpretation, and their scales can be ascribed not only to *Māyāmāḷavagauḷa* but to other *mēḷas* as well.

(1) *Sāveri*

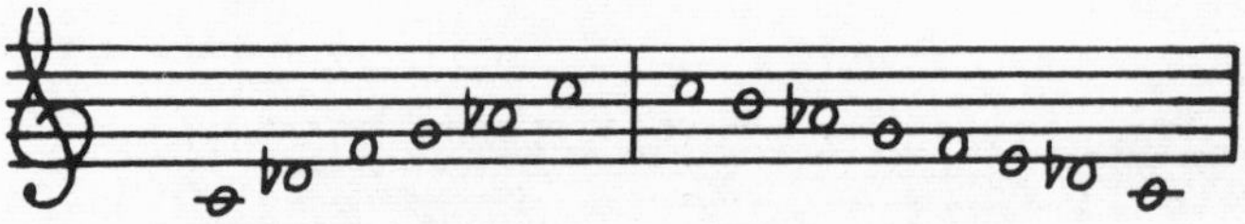

Ascent: the notes *GA* (E) and *NI* (B) are avoided.
Descent: *krama sampūrṇa*; the notes *GA* (E) and *NI* (B), although used, are often intoned slightly low, particularly in the passages *SA-RI-MA-GA* (C-Db-F-E) and *SA-NI-SA* (C-B-C). *Sāveri* should be performed in the early morning.

SĀVERI RĀGA (*Ādi-tala*)

Pallavi

A

B

C
D

E

Repeat the lines A, B, C, D, and E of the *pallavi*

Anupallavi

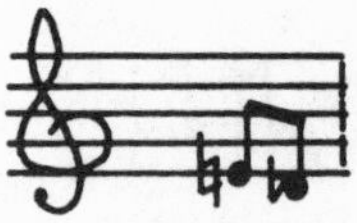

Repeat the lines A, B, C, D, and E of the *pallavi*

Charana

Repeat the lines A, B, C, D, and E of the *pallavi*

(2) *Gauḷa*

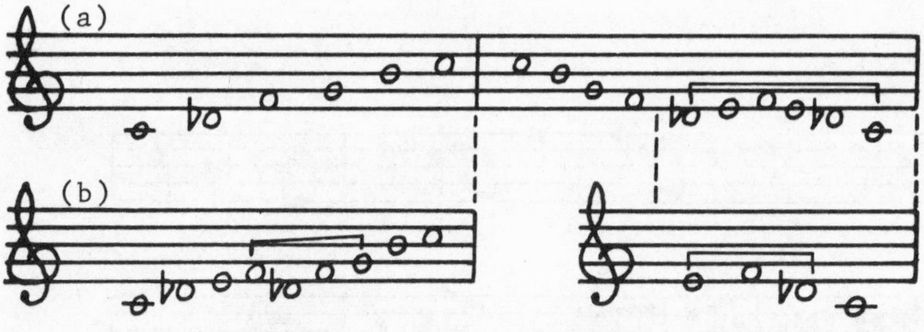

This *janya rāga* can be represented by two scales: The first one (a) the common *Gauḷa* scale, has been stated already by Veṅkaṭamakhin. The second one (b) is the scale stated by Ġovinda.
The first scale, generally in use at the present time, avoids the note *DHA* (Ab) entirely. *GA* (E) is omitted in ascent, and one extended *vakra* feature is shown in descent. Stressed notes are *RI* (Db), *MA* (F), *PA* (G), and *NI* (B).
The second scale (b), rarely used at the present time, avoids the note *DHA* (Ab) entirely. One *vakra* feature appears in ascent and one in descent.

The following song specimen is one of the *Pañcharatna Kīrtana*, "The Five Diamond Kirtanas" composed by Tyāgarāja. These five *kīrtanas*, actually *kṛtis*, are performed in the *rāgas Gauḷa*, *Ārabhī*, *Nāṭa*, *Śrī*, and *Varāḷi*. With the exception of the *kṛti* in *raga Nāṭa* which has Sanskrit words, they have Telugu texts (further details about these *kṛtis* may be found in M. R. Shankaramurti, *Śrī Tyāgarāja's Pañcharatna Kīrtanas*, written in Kanarese, Bangalore: Sudershanam, 1961 [?].

GAUḶA RĀGA (Ādi-tāla)

Pallavi

Anupallavi

Repeat the entire *pallavi*.

Charana

In the text of the last line of this song appears the name of the composer.

RĀGA GAUḶA (*Rūpaka-tāla*) SPC II, 39

(3) *Rēvagupti*

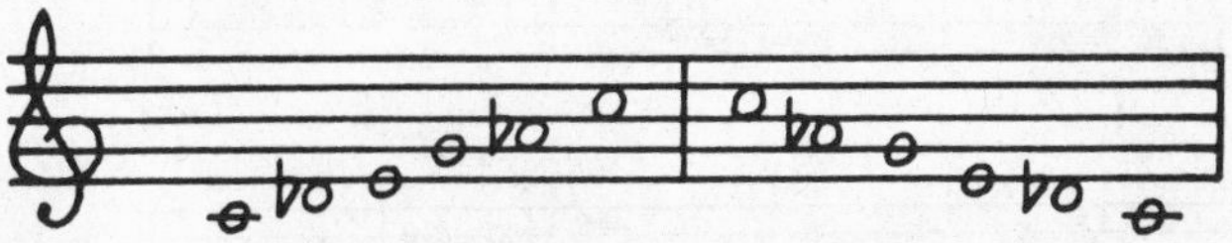

This *janya rāga* can be performed at any time. Its scale avoids the notes *MA* (F) and *NI* (B) entirely. Stressed notes are supposed to be *RI* (Db), *GA* (E), and *DHA* (Ab).

See also *Bhūpāḷam* (*Bibāsu*) 15,24; these *rāgas* have identical features, but as they have been mentioned separately in SD (I, 61; 64) and N (under the names of *Rēygupti* and *Bēbās*), the same method has been adopted in this study.

RĒVAGUPTI RĀGA (*Ādi-tāla*)

Pallavi

Anupallavi

Charana

Repeat the entire *pallavi*

(4) *Malahari*

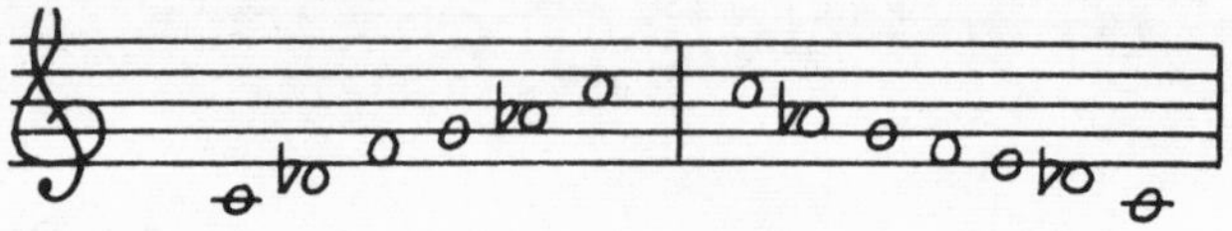

The note *NI* (B) is avoided entirely. *GA* (E) is omitted in ascent.

The following song specimen was composed by the saintly Purandra Dasa (1480-1564), a celebrated Krishna bhakta, often called "the father of Carnatic music:"

MALAHARI RĀGA (*Rupaka-tāla*) SPC II, 35

(5) *Gauḷīpantu* (*Gauḍīpantu*)

(a)

(b)

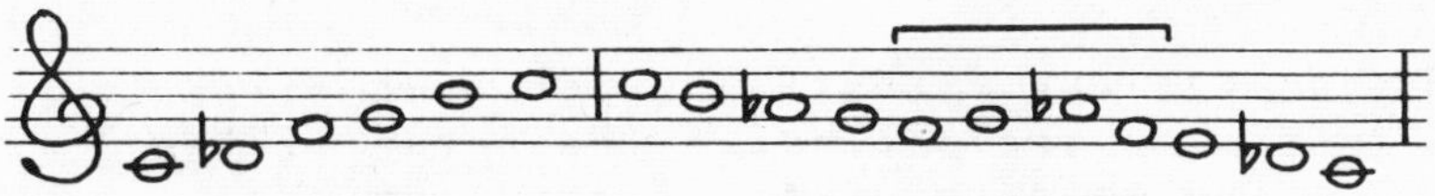

This *janya rāga* can be performed at any time. Musicians of the older generation, however, maintain that the appropriate performance time is midday.

According to Veṅkaṭamakhin, the ascent of scale (a) is *sampūrṇa* and shows two *vakra* features. Its descent is *krama sampūrṇa*. Scale (b), more frequently used at the present time, avoids the notes *GA* (E) and *DHA* (Ab) in ascent. Occasionally these two notes are omitted entirely. The note *MA* (F) in ascent is often intoned slightly sharp. The descent of scale (b) is generally *sampūrṇa* and shows one *vakra* feature. There are several variants in the interpretation of this *rāga*.

South Indian musicians and writers have woven the following legend about this *rāga*: One day, we are told, Tyāgarāja wanted to pay homage to the statue of the sacred Veṅkaṭaramanaswami in the temple of Tirupati, but he was not permitted to enter. Tyāgarāja, standing in front of the building, sang the following song in which he begged the Saint to open the gate for him. When the song came to an end, the temple gates burst open of their own accord and the great singer was able to enter the sacred place and offer his prayers.

GAUḶĪPANTU RĀGA (*Ādi-tāla*)

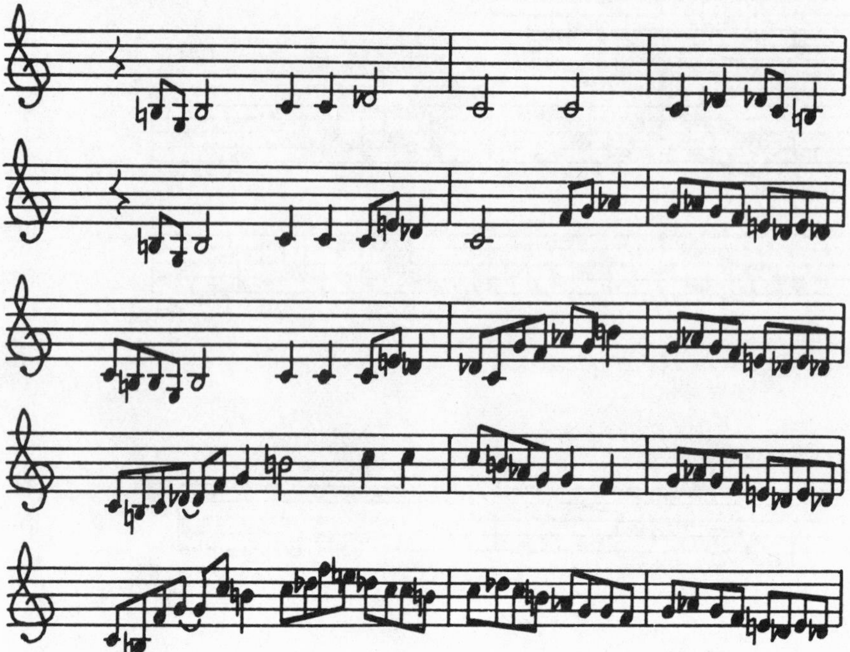

Repeat the first measure of the first line of the *pallavi*. The notes of the third measure of the first line are changed to the held note *SA* as it appears in the second measure of the first line

Anupallavi

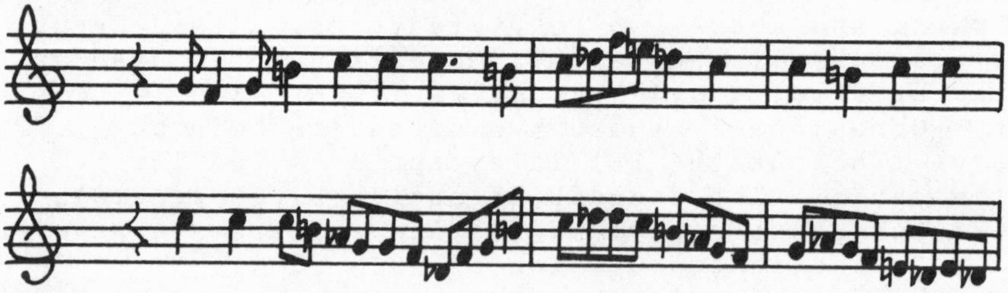

Repeat the altered first line of the *pallavi* as described above

Charana

Repeat the altered first line of the *pallavi* as described above

(6) *Jaganmōhinī* (*Jaganmōhanī*)

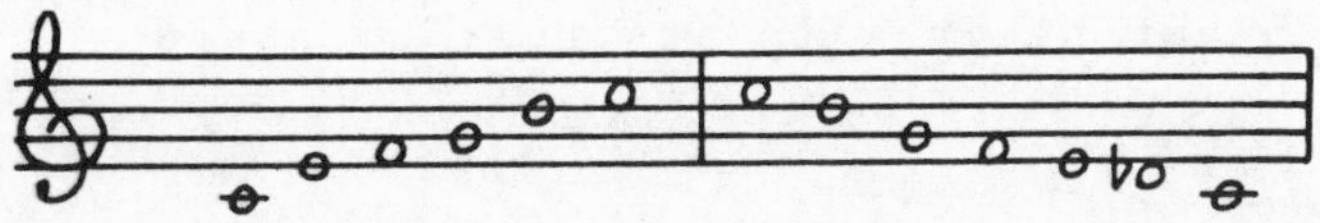

The scale of this popular *janya rāga*, which can be performed at any time, avoids the note *DHA* (Ab) entirely and *RI* (Db) in ascent. Stressed notes are *GA* (E) and *NI* (B). Veṅkaṭamakhin does not describe this *rāga*.

The following song specimen is a *kīrtana* in *rūpaka tāla* (2+4):

JAGANMŌHINĪ RĀGA (*Rūpaka-tāla*)

Pallavi

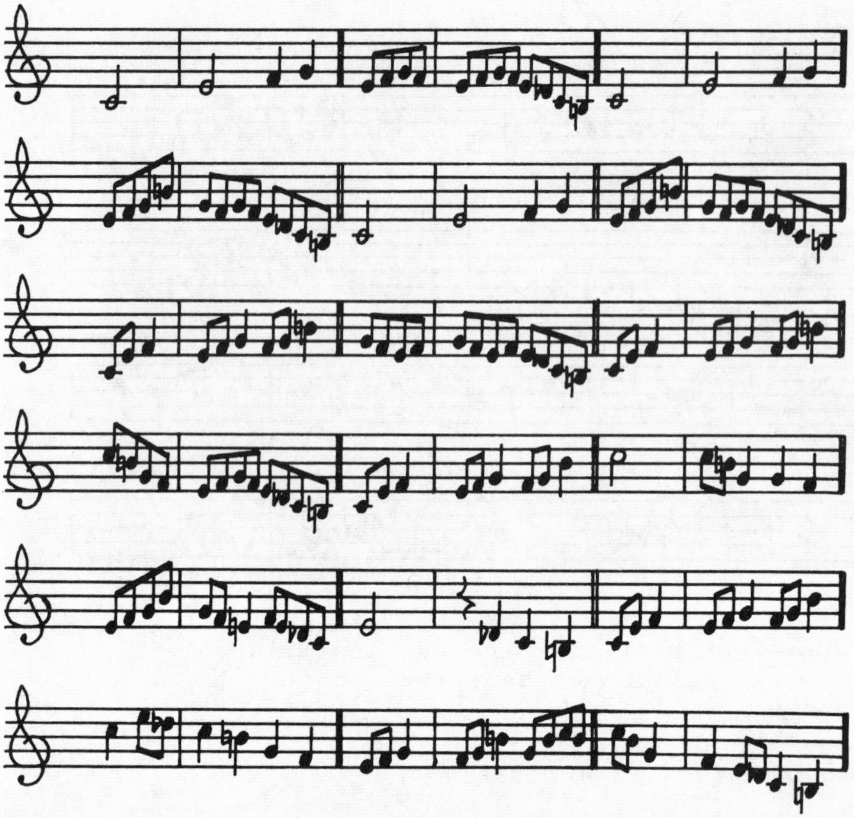

Repeat the *pallavi* but begin with its third measure

Anupallavi

Repeat the *pallavi* but begin with its third measure

Charana

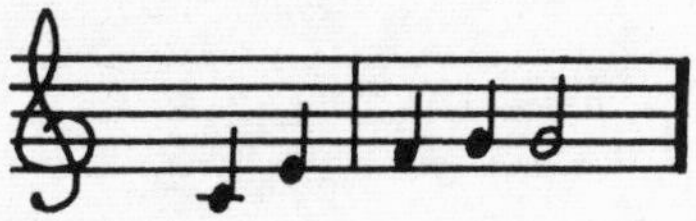

Repeat the *pallavi* but begin with its third measure

(7) *Vasanta*

This *janya rāga*, not to be mistaken for *Rāgavasant*, a *janya* subordinated to the 14. *mēḷa* (1), can be performed at any time. Indian music theory of the past employed some involved sophistry in the definitions of scales that caused manifold misunderstandings in later times. In *rāga Vasanta*, we are informed, appears the note *cyuta PA*, also called "*śuddha PA*." This note was by no means a pure *PA* (G natural), but the terms represented a slight lowering in pitch of this now unchangeable note. SD (I, 93) in the explanation of the term *chyuta panchama* [*cyuta PA*] states that "with the emergence of the concept of *PA* as an *avikruta svara* [a note that cannot be altered in pitch], the *chyuta panchama* came to denote the sharpened form of *prati madhyama* [F#]." In notated pieces of recent times *cyuta* or *śuddha PA* is not represented by F# but by an F[!] natural. In actual performances this note is intoned slightly higher than F.

Another change of pitch can be observed in the intonation of the note *DHA* (theoretically: Ab) particularly in the passage *MA-DHA-MA* (F-Ab-F), where the middle note can appear sharp. Repeated hearings of this *rāga* showed little or even no difference between the Ab and A natural. It appears that the matter of intonation of *DHA* is left, more or less, to the discretion of the performing artist.

The scale of *Vasanta*, without showing the occasional microtonal alterations, is:

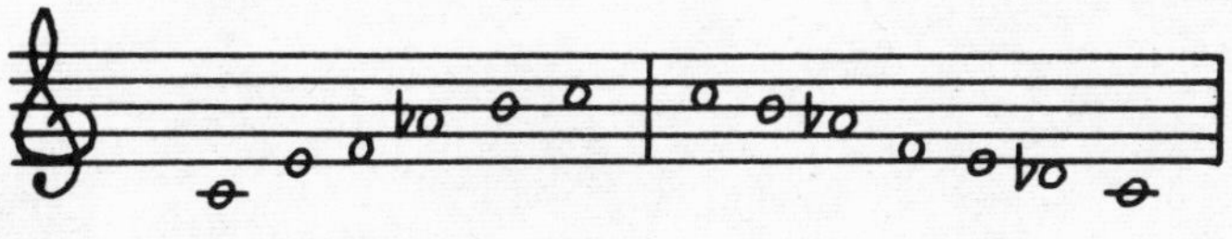

The note *PA* (G) is avoided entirely and *RI* (Db) is generally omitted in ascent.
Another *rāga* with the same name appears under the heading of the 17. *mēḷa* (3).

VASANTA RĀGA (Ādi-tāla)

Pallavi

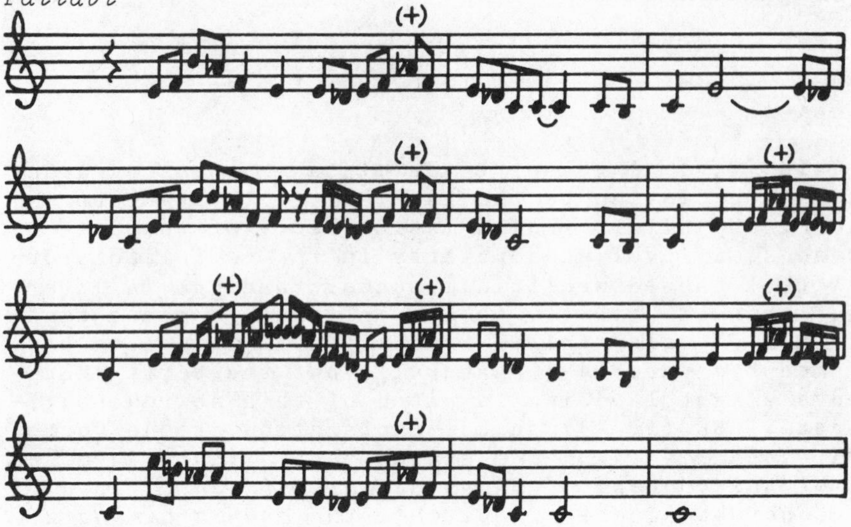

Anupallavi

Repeat the entire *pallavi*

Charana

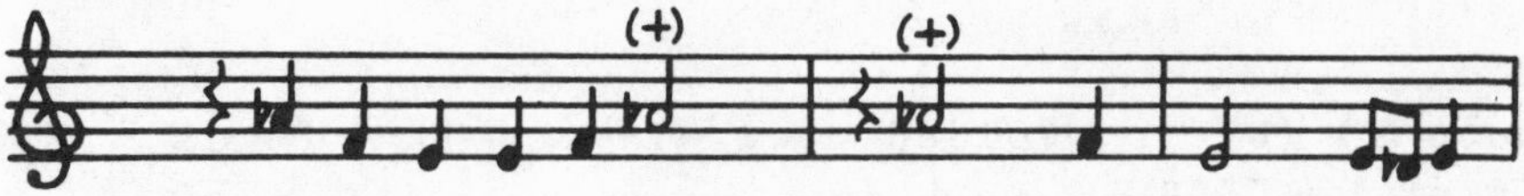

Repeat the entire *pallavi*

(8) *Sindhurāmakriyā*

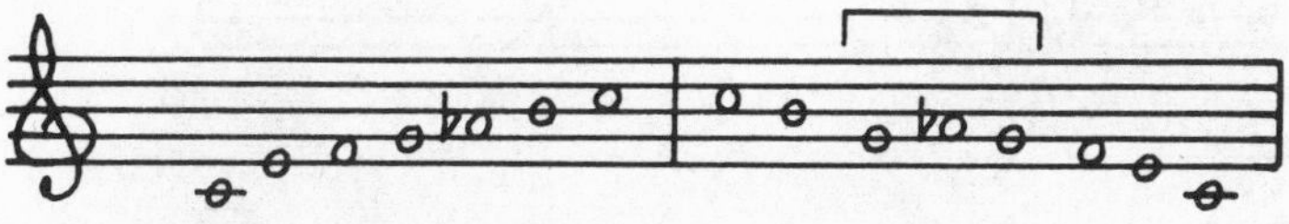

This *janya rāga* can be performed at any time. It became popular in the last thirty or forty years. The note *RI* (Db) is avoided entirely, and in descent one *vakra* feature is shown.

The following song specimen is a *kīrtana* in *ādi tāla*.

SINDHURĀMAKRIYĀ RĀGA (*Ādi-tāla*)

Pallavi

Anupallavi

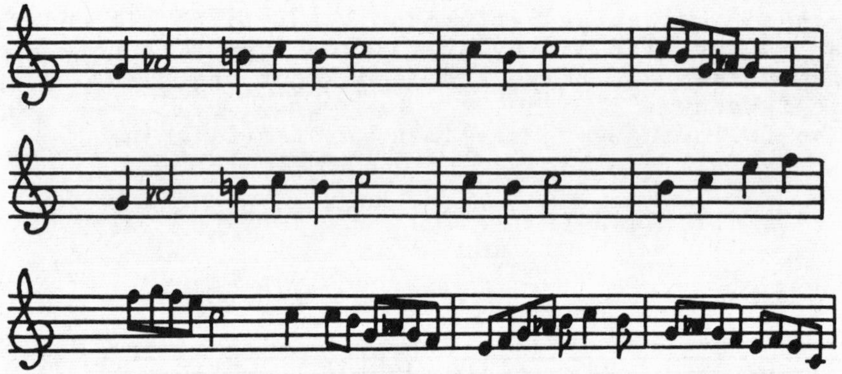

Repeat the last four lines of the *pallavi*

Charana

Repeat the last four lines of the *pallavi*

(9) *Nādanāmakriyā*

The scale of this light and popular *rāga*, which is usually performed in the late afternoon or in the early evening, has *nisādāntya* character. There are two versions of rendering the lower tetrachord of the ascent. The descent is *sampūrṇa*.

In a *Gīta Govinda* performance in Kerala the scale of this *rāga* employs the upper note *SA* (c). If the scale of *Nādanāmakriyā* always and everywhere used the upper *SA* (c), there would be no difference between it and *Māyāmāḷavagauḷa*.

Ahobala in his *Saṅgīta Pārijāta* (ca. 1700) relates that the note *PA* (G) has to be stressed and, contrary to present practice, prescribes that the note *GA* (E) be avoided in ascent. Govinda Dīkṣita (*Saṅgīta Sudhā*) calls this *rāga Nādarāmakriyā*. Its stressed notes are believed to be *RI* (Db), *MA* (F), and *DHA* (Ab).

NĀDANĀMAKRIYA RĀGA (*Ādi-tāla*)

Pallavi

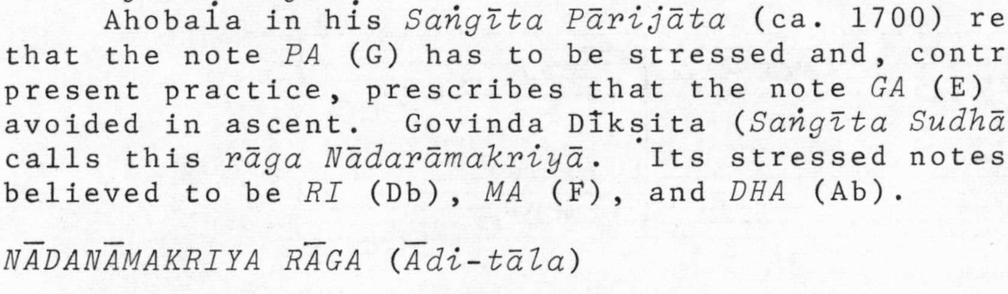

The *pallavi* is repeated and stands for an *anupallavi*

(10) *Gurjari* (*Gujjari*, *Ghūrjari*)

SD (II) presents two *rāgas*: *Ghūrjari* (p. 191) with the descent:

avoiding the note *NI* (B), and *Gujjari* (p. 216) with the *sampūrṇa* descent:

showing one *vakra* feature. This creates the impression of two different *rāgas*. But as the SD (II, 191 and 216) illustrates both *rāgas* with the same *kṛti* of Tyāgarāja ("*Varalandu kommani*"), it can be assumed that we are dealing here with one single *rāga* despite the variant shown in descent.

The entire scale, showing both forms of descent, is thus:

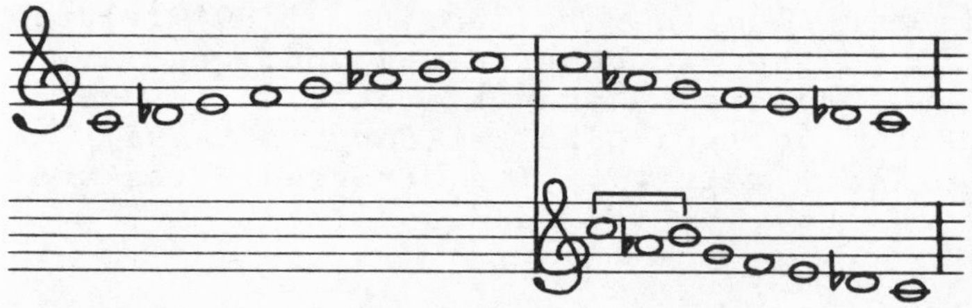

Veṅkaṭamakhin states that the note *DHA* (theoretically Ab) often appears as a *pañcaśruti DHA* ("five-*śruti DHA*") which means that the note stands five *śrutis* above *PA* (G), approximating in pitch an A natural. This intonation can still be observed at various occasions. Stressed notes are supposed to be *MA* (F), *DHA* (Ab or, in some instances, A), and *NI* (B). Ahobala speaks about omitting the notes *MA* (F) and *NI* (B) in descent, a procedure that is not observed at the present time.

GURJARI RĀGA (Ādi-tāla)

Pallavi

Anupallavi

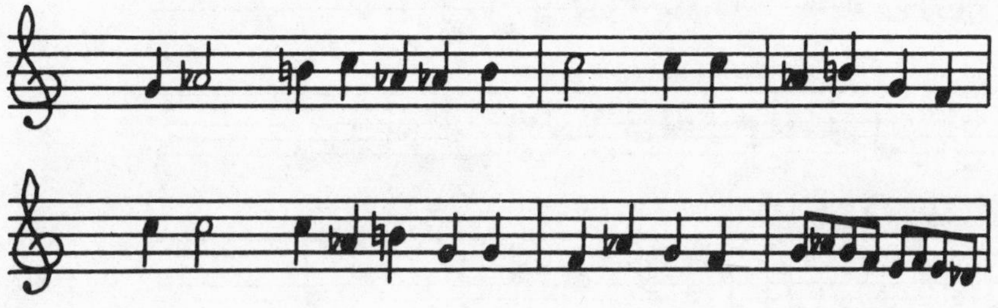

Repeat the entire *pallavi*

Charana

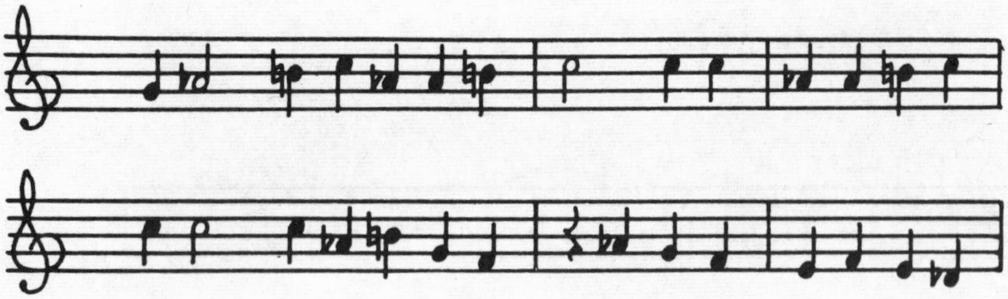

Repeat the entire *pallavi*

(11) *Bauḷi*

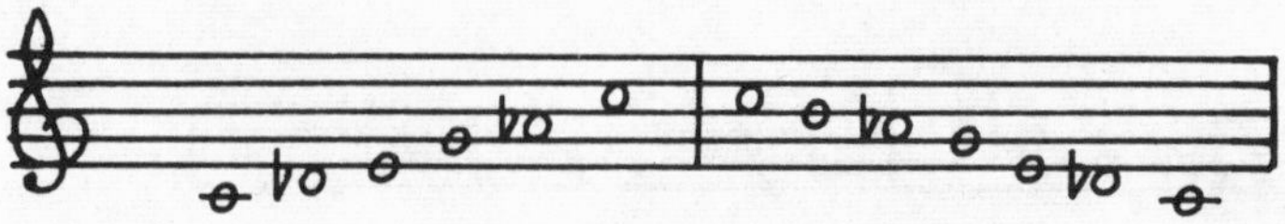

The note *MA* (F) is avoided entirely and *NI* (B) is omitted in ascent. Tuḷajā calls this *rāga Bahuḷī*.

RĀGA BAUḶI (*Triputa-tāla*) SMC, 43-44

According to a recording of the *Gīta Govinda* made by Wayne Howard in Kerala in 1971, the performance of *Bauḷi*

shows that the notes *RI* (Db) and *DHA* (Ab) are avoided in ascent:

(12) *Gaurī*

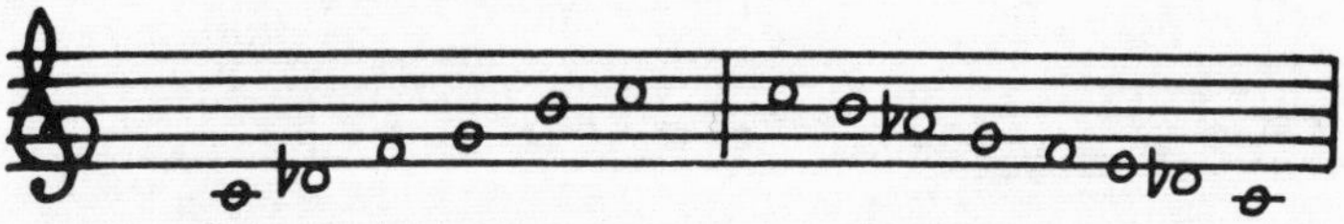

Gaurī, a *rāga* that can be performed at all times, avoids the notes *GA* (E) and *DHA* (Ab) in ascent. The descent is *krama sampūrṇa*.

The intonation and use of the note *PA* (G) were, and occasionally still are, subject to dispute: according to Veṅkaṭamakhin this note can become a *cyuta PA* (cf. *Vasanta* 15, 7). Even at the present time it can happen that *PA* is intoned remarkably low. My term "remarkably low" is used purposely because every performer, whenever he deals with microtonal (or larger) pitch alterations has his own way of intonation. I have discussed this matter in detail in RNI (9-10), where it is shown that it would be useless to determine exact intervallic distances that show the extent of these peculiar alterations.

Returning to the disputable note *PA* (G) it may be added that there are instances when it is not used at all in descent. The passage

using *PA* (G) in descent and the allegedly forbidden *GA* (E) in ascent is believed to be characteristic of this *rāga*.

RĀGA GAURĪ (*Triputa-tāla*) SCM, 29

(13) *Maṅgalakaiśika*

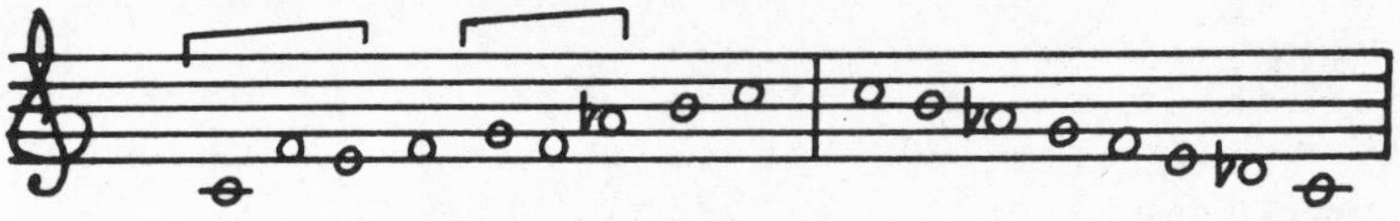

Ascent: *RI* (Db) is avoided; two *vakra* features are shown.
Descent: *krama sampūrṇa*.

RĀGA MAṄGALAKAIŚIKA (*Triputa-tāla*) SCM, 52

(14) *Mārgadēśika*

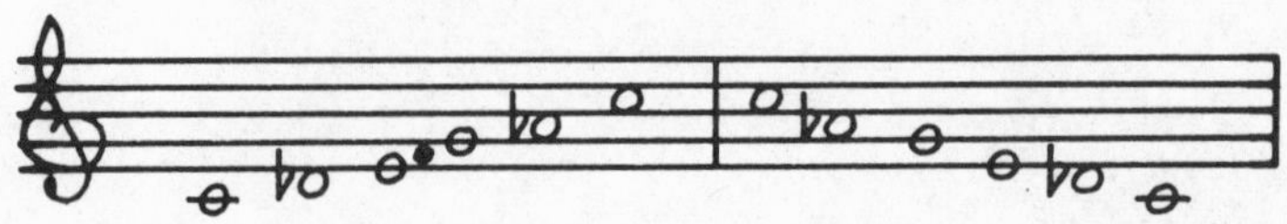

The note *NI* (B) is avoided entirely. *MA* (F) is used very sparingly in ascent and is omitted in descent.

Another *Mārgadēśika* (with a different descent) appears as 15,90.

RĀGA MĀRGADĒŚIKA (*Triputa-tāla*) SCM, 64

(15) *Mēchabauḷi*

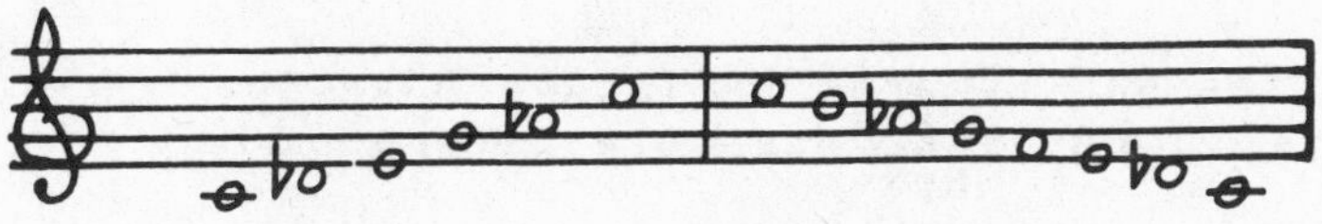

Ascent: the notes *MA* (F) and *NI* (B) are avoided.
Descent: *krama sampūrṇa*.

RĀGA MĒCHABAUḶI (*Triputa-tāla*) SCM, 48-49

(16) *Megharañji*

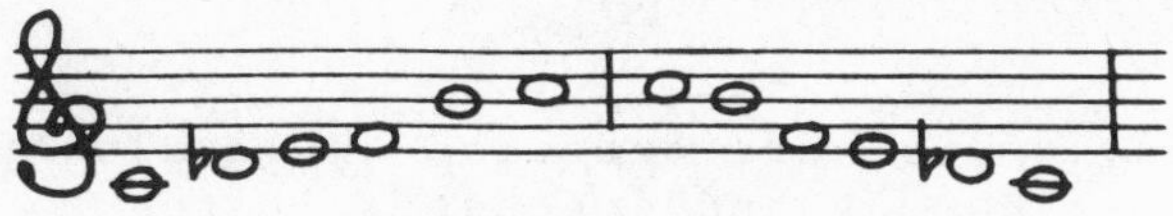

The notes *PA* (G) and *DHA* (Ab) are avoided entirely.

RĀGA MEGHARAÑJI (*Triputa-tāla*) SCM, 55-56

(17) *Pādi* (*Pahāḍi*)

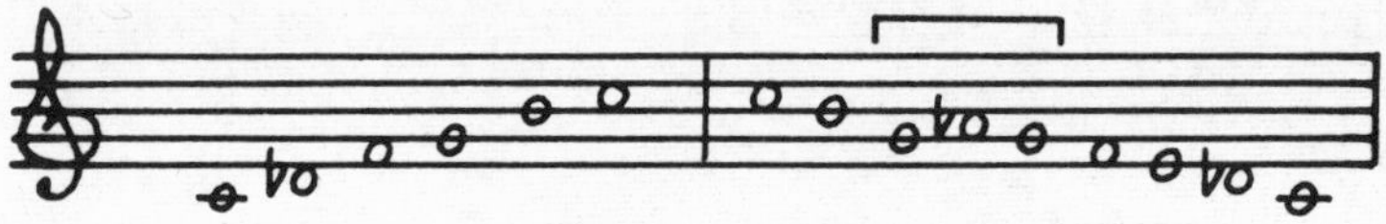

Ascent: the notes *GA* (E) and *DHA* (Ab) are avoided.
Descent: *sampūrṇa*; one *vakra* feature is shown.

RĀGA PĀDI (*Triputa-tāla*) SCM, 56

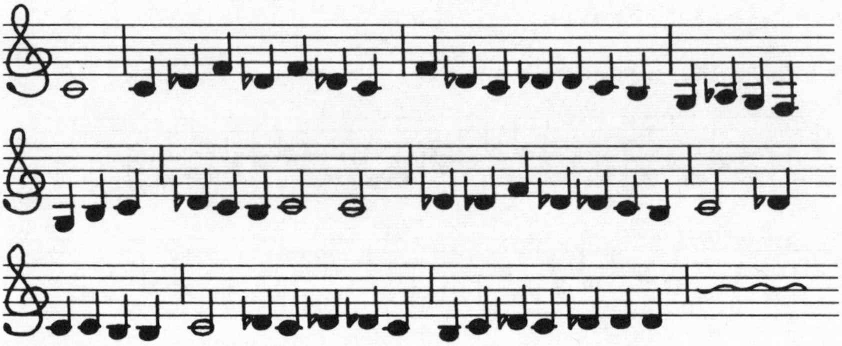

(18) *Paraju*

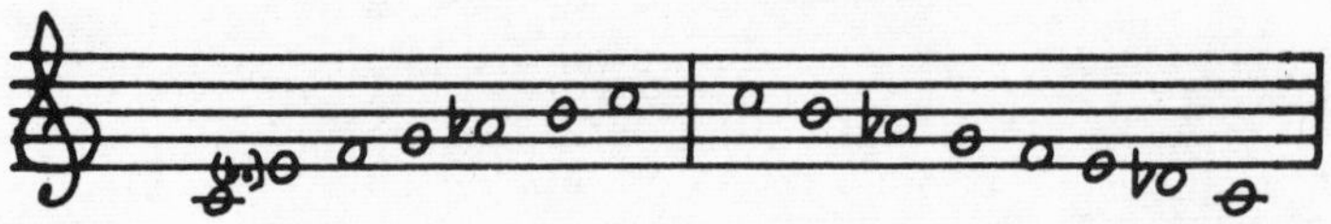

Veṅkaṭamakhin, Govinda, and others describe the scale of this *rāga* as *sampūrṇa* in ascent and descent. At the present time it has become a habit to avoid the note *RI* (Db) in ascent. The descent retains its old *sampūrṇa* form.

The following melody specimen employs the note *RI* (Db) in ascent:

RĀGA PARAJU (*Triputa-tāla*) SCM, 65

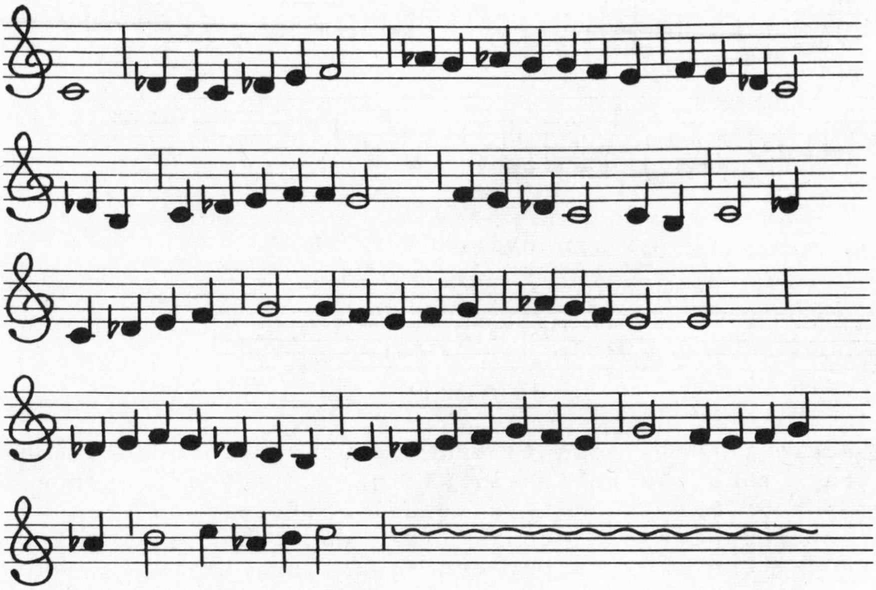

(19) *Pūrvī*

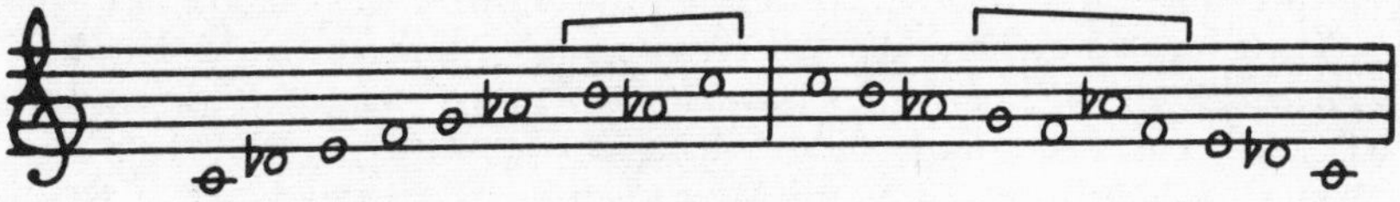

The scale of this *rāga* is *sampūrṇa* and shows two *vakra* features, one in ascent and one in descent.

Tuḷajā presents the following version of the *Pūrvī* scale:

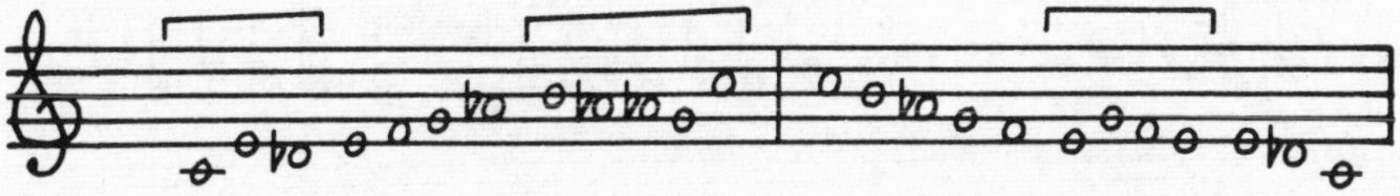

Beside the indicated *vakra* features, the notes *DHA* (Ab) and *GA* (E) are to be stressed.

RĀGA PŪRVĪ (*Triputa-tāla*) SCM, 66

(20) *Saurāshṭra(m)* (*Saurāṣṭram*)

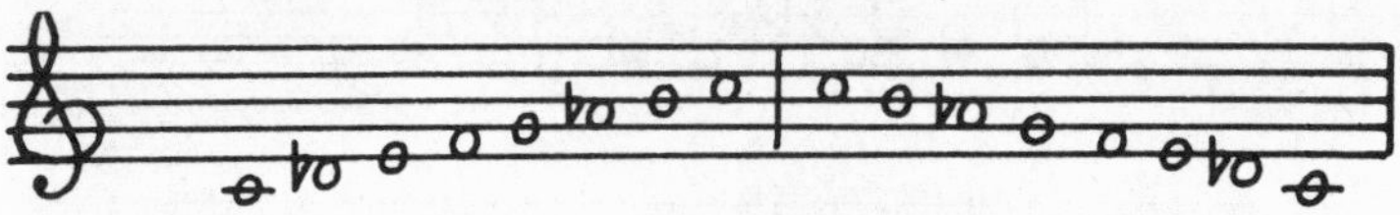

The scale of this *rāga* is *krama sampūrṇa* in ascent and descent, thus theoretically wiping out any difference from the primary *rāga*. In actual performances, however, some differences can occur. The descending scale, for instance, can show one or even two *vakra* features, a phenomenon that may or may not happen. If it does, the features can appear at various places of the descending line. Another difference from the material of the primary *rāga* is the occasional high intonation of the note *DHA* (theoretically Ab). Already Veṅkaṭamakhin in his *Caturdaṇḍī Prakāśika* is aware of the high *DHA* and speaks of the occasional use of a *pañcaśruti DHA*. Another, but minor, difference can be observed at times when the note *NI* (B) is treated "weakly."

RĀGA SAURĀSHṬRAM (*Triputa-tāla*) SCM, 61

(21) *Lalitā*

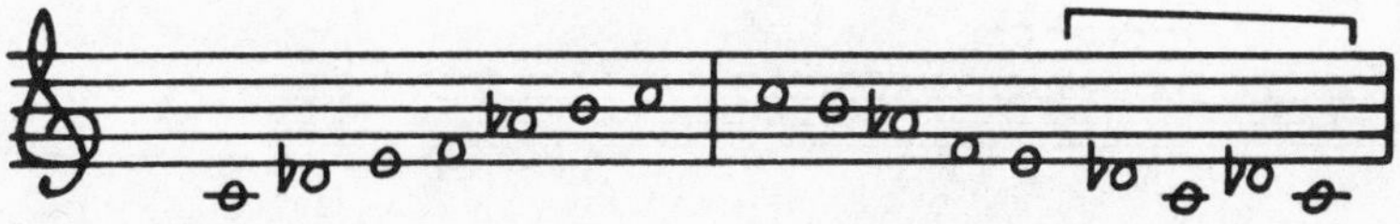

The scale of this *rāga* avoids the note *PA* (G) entirely. The wavering motion of *RI-SA-RI-SA* (Db-C-Db-C) in descent is used frequently.

Numerous South Indian musicians were or are of the opinion (cf. Report on the Madras Music Conference, Dec. 26, 1939) that the note *DHA* has to be used in its *śuddha* form (Ab). Despite this officially acknowledged view there are many other musicians who employ occasionally a highly intoned *DHA* the pitch of which approximates the A natural.

There exists another *Lalitā* in which the note *DHA* always maintains the pitch of A. It appears under the heading of the 17. *mēḷa* (21).

(22) *Lalitapañcham*

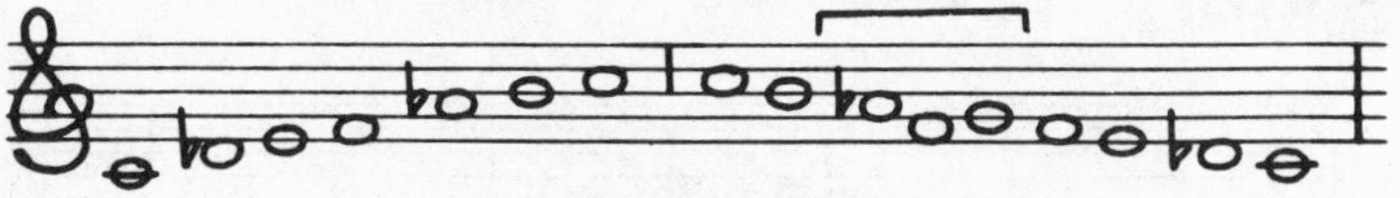

As in *rāga Lalitā* (15,21) the note *PA* (G) is avoided in ascent. However, this note is used in the indicated *vakra* feature in the *sampūrṇa* descent.

RĀGA LALITAPAÑCHAM (*Triputa-tāla*) SCM, 53

(23) *Ārdradēśī* (*Ārdradēśika*)

There are two versions of the ascending scale of this *rāga*. The first one, (a) shows the commonly used form. Version (b) appears less frequently. The ascent of version (b) avoids the note *GA* (E) and occasionally also *NI* (B). The descent of both versions omits the note *NI* (B).

Ārdradēśī can be performed at any time.

RĀGA ĀRDRADĒŚI (*Triputa-tāla*) SCM, 62

(24) *Bhūpāḷam* (*Rēvagupti*, *Bibāsu*)

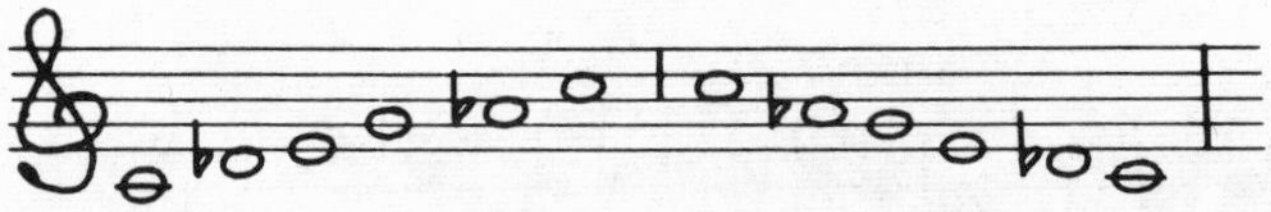

The tone syllables *SA*, *RI*, *GA*, *PA*, *DHA* of this *rāga* are the same as those of the solemn and important *rāga* *Bhūpāli* of North India, where they indicate the notes C, D, E, G, A.

In this *janya rāga*, often also called *Rēvagupti* (15,3) or *Bibāsu* (15,42), the notes *MA* (F) and *NI* (B) are omitted entirely as in the North Indian *rāga*.

Bhūpāḷam has also been listed under the heading of the 8. *mēḷa* (2) where, as already pointed out, the note *GA* is Eb. In order to avoid any confusion it is of importance for the reader to see also 15,3 and 15,42.

(25) *Dēśyagauḷa*

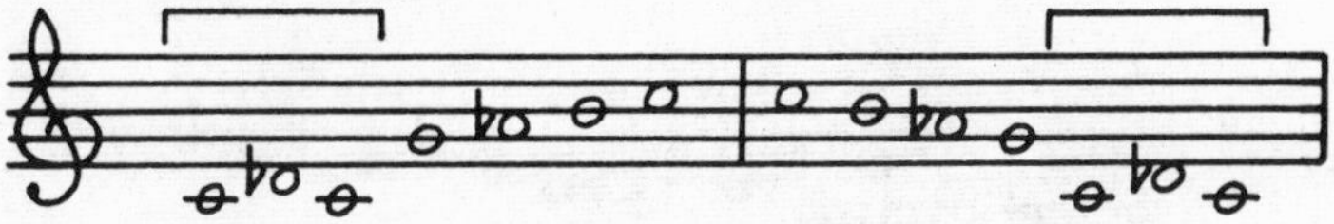

The notes *GA* (E) and *MA* (F) are avoided entirely. At the beginning of the ascent and at the end of the descent appears a characteristic passage *SA-RI-SA* (C-Db-C).

RĀGA DĒŚYAGAUḶA (*Triputa-tāla*) SCM, 58

(26) *Gummakāmbhōji*

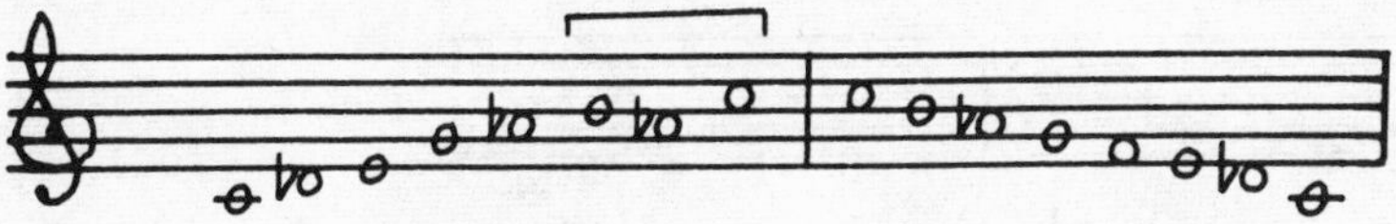

Ascent: the note *MA* (F) is avoided; the indicated *vakra* feature is used occasionally.
Descent: *krama sampūrṇa*.

RĀGA GUMMAKĀMBHŌJI (*Triputa-tāla*) SCM, 49

(27) *Guṇḍakriya*

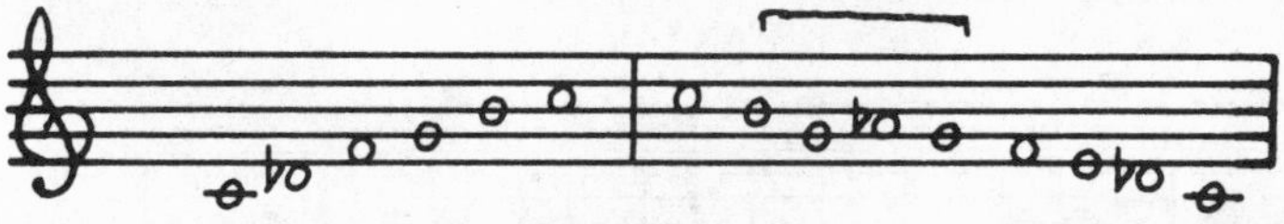

Ascent: the notes *GA* (E) and *DHA* (Ab) are avoided.
Descent: *sampūrṇa*; one *vakra* feature is shown.

SD (II, 217) states that "Tyāgarāja's *Intanuchu varnimpa* is a well-known *kriti* in this *rāga*. This is an ancient *rāga*. Tradition has it that Āñjanēya once sang this *rāga* and "made the rocks around him melt." A similar legend can be observed concerning the magical effects of *rāga Kedar* of North India (see RNI, 88).

(28) *Kannaḍa Baṅgāḷa*

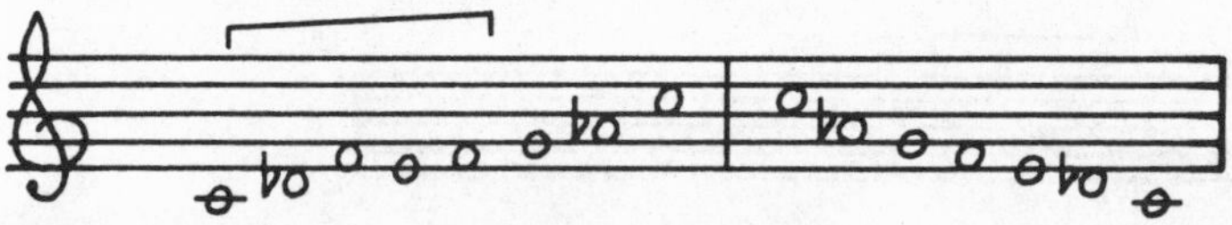

The note *NI* (B) is avoided entirely. The ascent shows one *vakra* feature.
A second ascent can be:

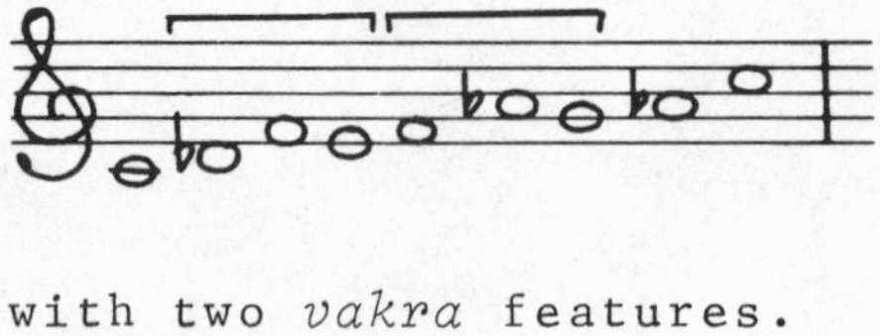

with two *vakra* features.

RĀGA KANNAḌA BANGĀḶA (*Triputa-tāla*) SCM, 63

(29) *Krishṇaveni* (*Kṛṣṇaveni*)

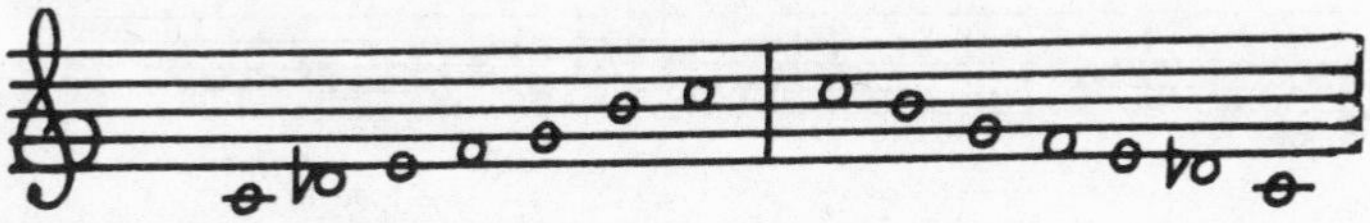

The note *DHA* (Ab) is avoided entirely.

(30) *Mallikāvasantam*

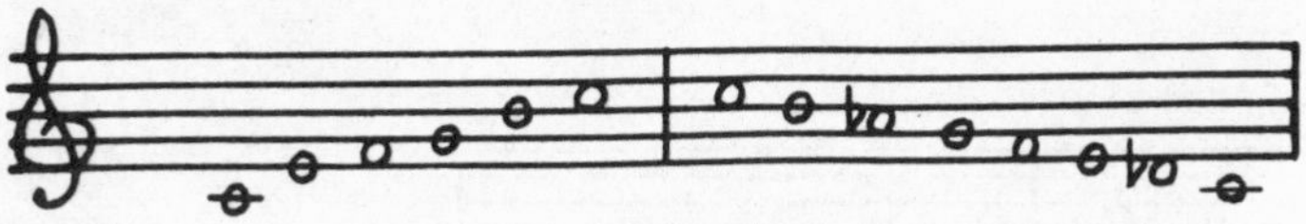

Ascent: the notes *RI* (Db) and *DHA* (Ab) are avoided.
Descent: *krama sampūrṇa*.

(31) *Māruva*

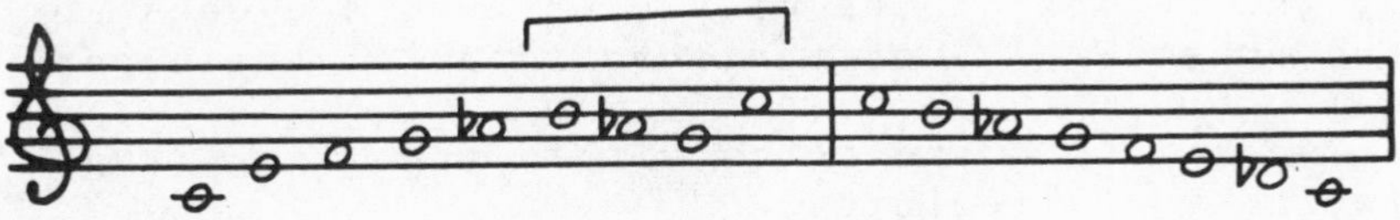

Ascent: the note *RI* (Db) is avoided and one *vakra* feature is shown.
Descent: *krama sampūrṇa*.

Another form of descent is:

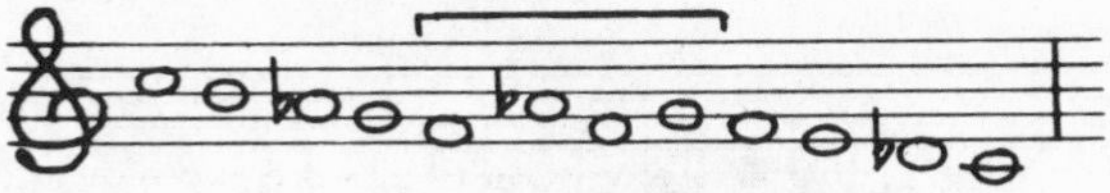

It is *sampūrṇa* and shows one extended *vakra* feature.

Another *Māruva* appears under the heading of the 51. *mēḷa* (28).

RĀGA MĀRUVA (Triputa-tāla) SCM, 54

(32) *Pūrnapañcham*

Pūrnapañcham is a *dhaivatāntya* or *madhya rāga* because its highest note is *DHA* (Ab). The term *madhya rāga* implies that the range extends only into the *madhya saptaka*, the region of the middle octave, and does not reach the upper *SA* (c) of the *tara saptaka*, the upper octave.

The scale avoids no notes within the given range and shows no *vakra* features.

RĀGA PURÑAPANCHAM (Triputa-tāla) SCM, 57

(33) *Sāraṅganāṭa*

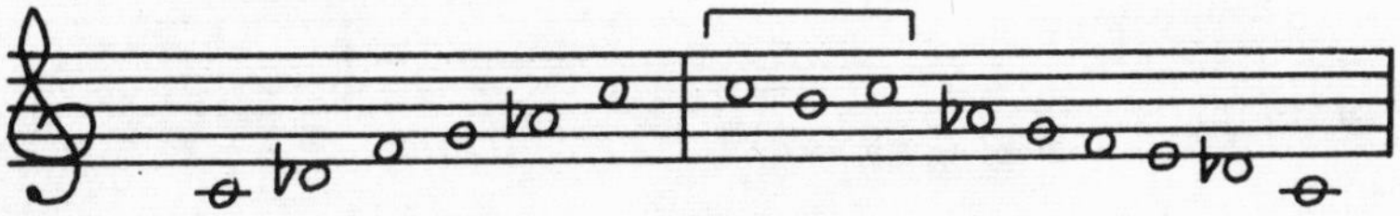

Ascent: the notes *GA* (E) and *NI* (B) are avoided.
Descent: *sampūrṇa*; one *vakra* feature is shown.

RĀGA SĀRAṄGANĀṬA (*Triputa-tala*) SCM, 47

Occasionally a *janya rāga* with the name *Sālanganāṭa* of the 15. *mēḷa* is mentioned which is supposed to have the following ascent:

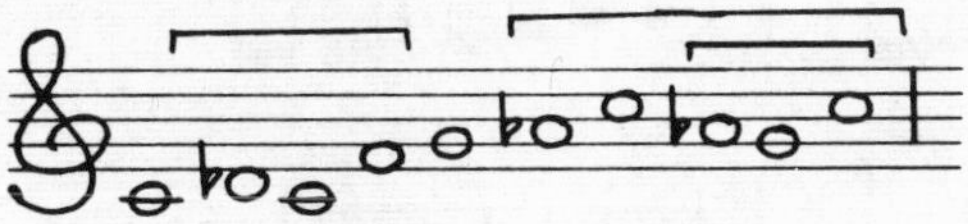

It is not clear whether *Sāraṅganāṭa* and *Sālaṅganāṭa* are two different *rāgas* with remarkably similar names or whether one is merely a variant of the other. The second assumption appears to be plausible because *raga Sāraṅganāṭa* of Govinda was the same as *Sālaṅganāṭa* of Veṅkaṭamakhin.

The following is a part of a melody specimen of *Sālaṅganāṭa*:

RĀGA SĀLAṄGANĀṬA (*Triputa-tāla*) SCM, 52-53

(34) *Śuddhakriya*

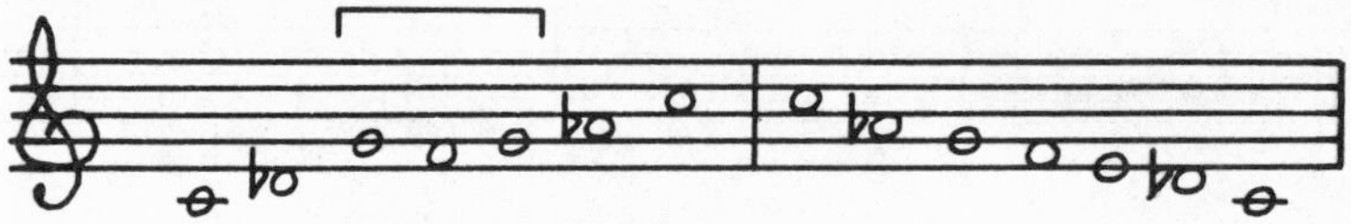

The note *NI* (B) is avoided entirely. *GA* (E) is omitted in ascent where one *vakra* feature can be used.

RĀGA ŚUDDHAKRIYA (*Triputa-tāla*) SCM, 54-55

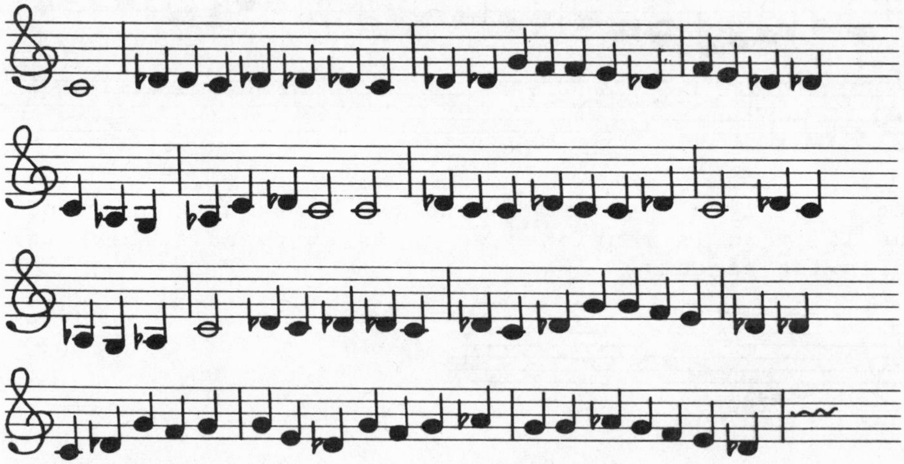

(35) *Surasindhu*

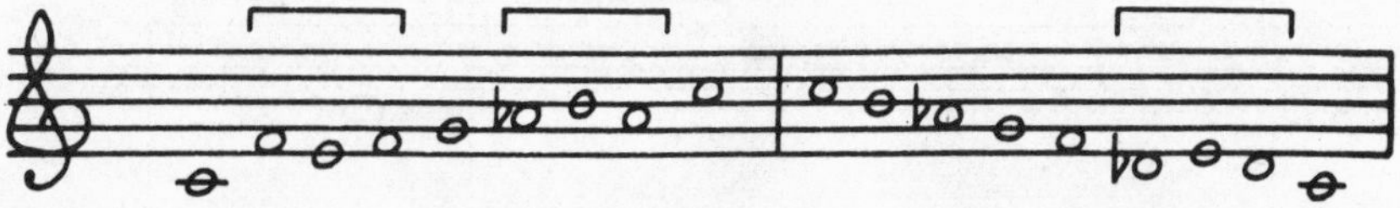

Ascent: the note *RI* (Db) is avoided; two *vakra* features are shown.
Descent: *sampūrṇa*; one *vakra* feature is used.

RĀGA SURASINDHU (*Triputa-tāla*) SCM, 57-58

(36) *Āndhra Dēśika*

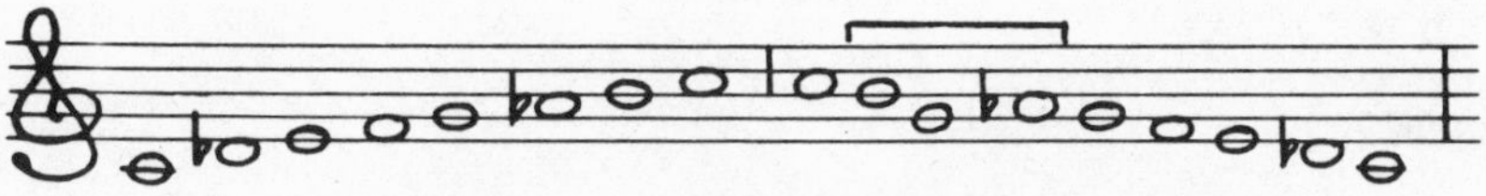

Ascent: *krama sampūrṇa*.
Descent: *sampūrṇa*; one *vakra* feature is shown.

(37) *Bālikāvasantam*

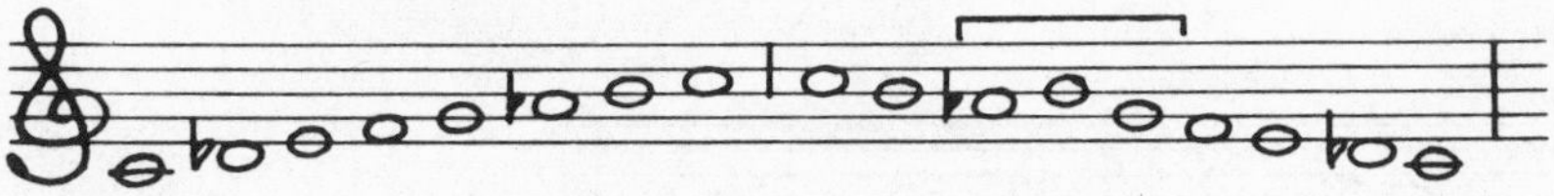

Ascent: *krama sampūrṇa*.
Descent: *sampūrṇa*; one *vakra* feature is shown.

(38) *Basamāna*

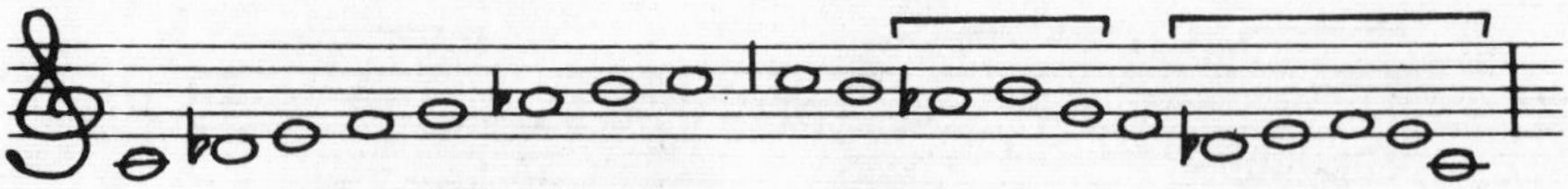

Ascent: *krama sampūrṇa.*
Descent: *sampūrṇa*; two *vakra* features are shown.

(39) *Bhāmāmaṇi*

Ascent: the note *PA* (G) is avoided and one *vakra* feature is shown.
Descent: the notes *NI* (B) and *MA* (F) are omitted.

Another *janya rāga* with the same name and with a similar scale structure appears under the heading of the 61. *mēḷa* (1).

(40) *Bhāva Haṃsa*

The note *RI* (Db) is avoided entirely and *MA* (F) is omitted in ascent.

(41) *Bhāvini*

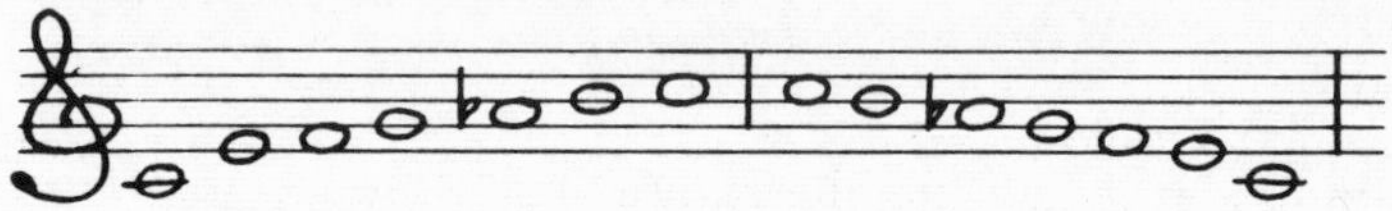

The note *RI* (Db) is avoided entirely.

(42) *Bibāsu*

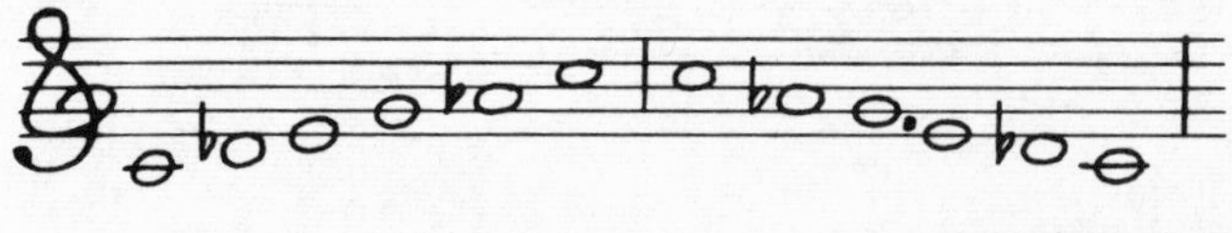

As already mentioned in the remarks added to the descriptions of *janya rāgas Rēvagupti* (*Rēgupti*) (15,3) and *Bhūpāḷam* (*Bibāsu*) (15,24), all have identical tone material.

A slight difference from *Rēvagupti* and *Bhūpāḷam* may occur in the descending scale of *Bibāsu* where at times a faint trace of the note *MA* (F) can be employed.

(43) *Bindu Hērāḷi*

Ascent: *sampūrṇa*; two *vakra* features are shown.
Descent: *krama sampūrṇa*.

(44) *Brahma Līlā*

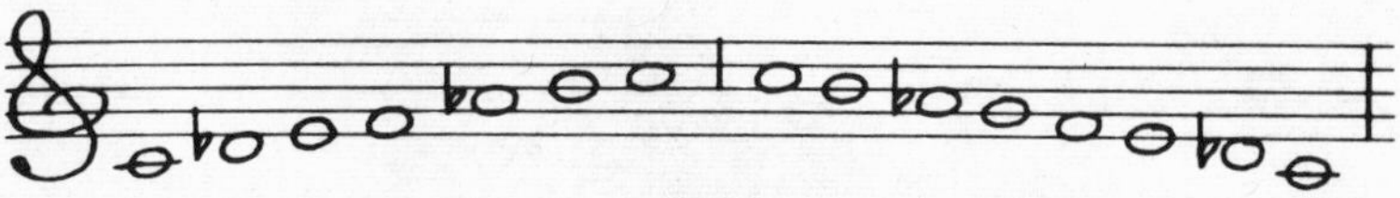

Ascent: the note *PA* (G) is avoided.
Descent: *krama sampūrṇa*.

(45) *Chammarakriya*

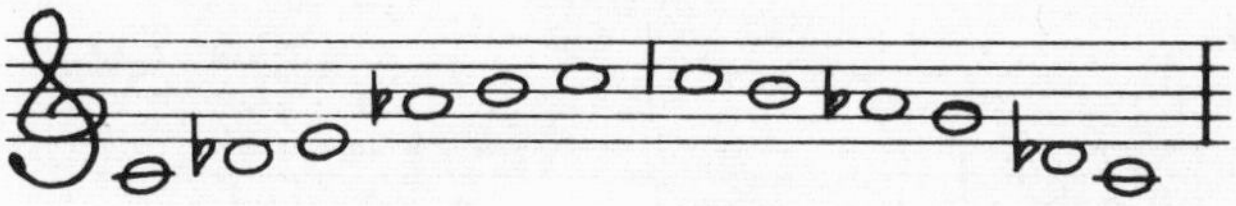

The note *MA* (F) is avoided entirely. *PA* (G) is avoided in ascent and *GA* (E) in descent.

(46) *Chandrarēkhā*

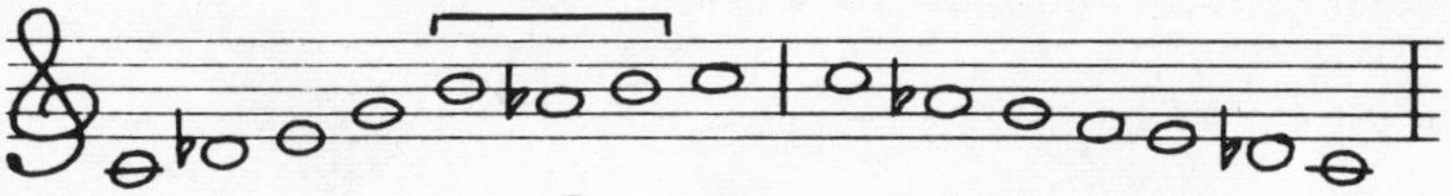

Ascent: the note *MA* (F) is avoided and one *vakra* feature is shown.
Descent: the note *NI* (B) is omitted.

Another *rāga* with the same name appears under the heading of the 58. *mēḷa* (3).

(47) *Chandrikā Dhavaḷi* (*Chandrikā Gauḷa*)

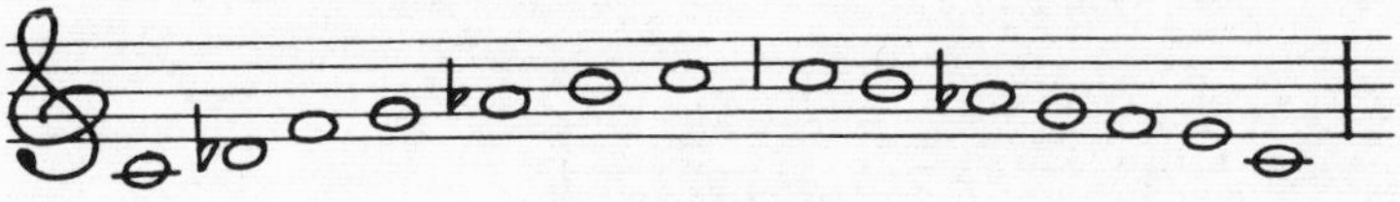

Ascent: the note *GA* (E) is avoided.
Descent: the note *RI* (Db) is omitted.

Another *rāga* with the name *Chandrikā Gauḷa* appears under the heading of the 8. *mēḷa* (17).

(48) *Chāru Vardhanī*

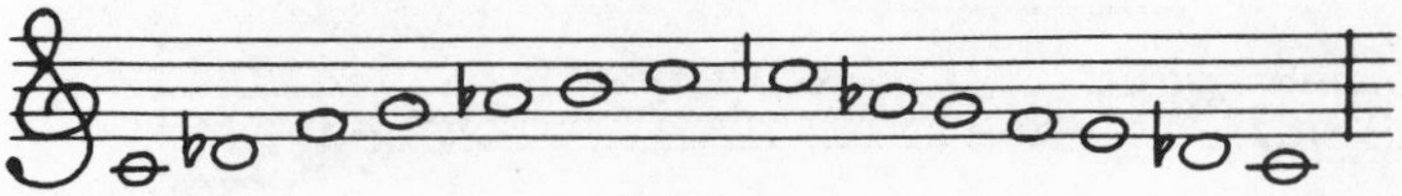

Ascent: the note *GA* (E) is avoided.
Descent: the note *NI* (B) is omitted.

(49) *Chhāyā Gauḷa*

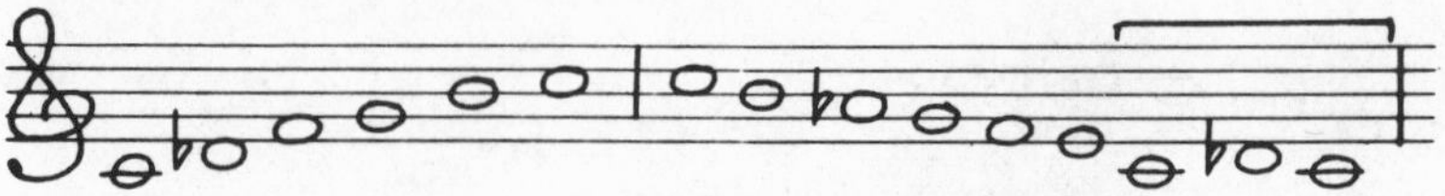

Ascent: the notes *GA* (E) and *DHA* (Ab) are avoided.
Descent: *sampūrṇa*; one *vakra* feature is shown.

Another *rāga* with the same name appears under the heading of the 3. *mēḷa* (7).

(50) *Chhāyā Kauśīka*

Ascent: the note *DHA* (Ab) is avoided and one *vakra* feature is shown.
Descent: *krama sampūrṇa*.

(51) *Chitra Mandīra*

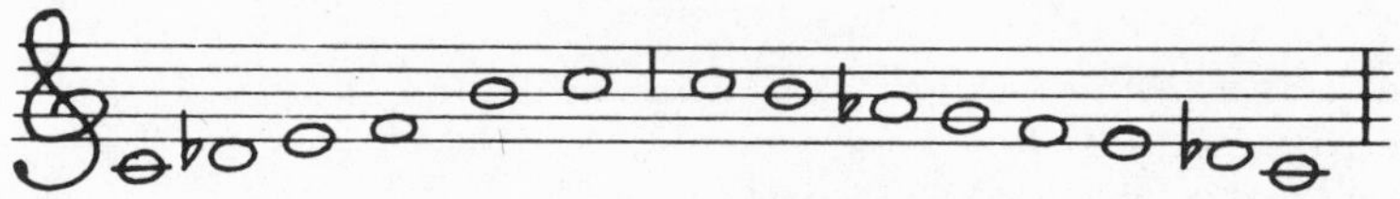

Ascent: the notes *PA* (G) and *DHA* (Ab) are avoided.
Descent: *krama sampūrṇa*.

(52) *Dākshāyaṇi* (*Dākṣāyaṇi*)

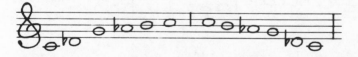

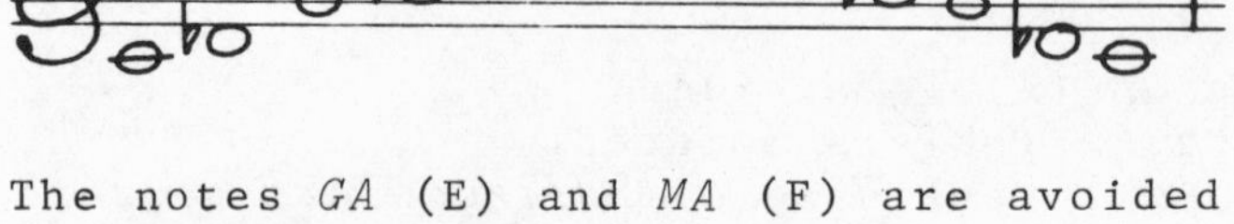

The notes *GA* (E) and *MA* (F) are avoided entirely.

Another *rāga* with the same name appears under the heading of the 29. *mēḷa* (30).

(53) *Dāraka Vasanta*

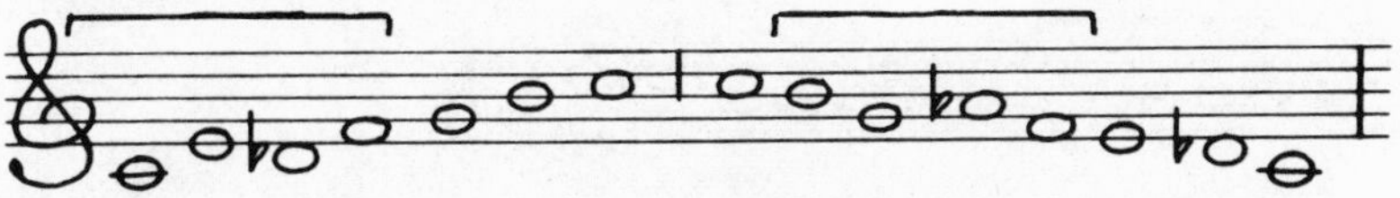

Ascent: the note *DHA* (Ab) is avoided.
Descent: *sampūrṇa*; one *vakra* feature is shown.

(54) *Dēśya Rēvagupti* (*Dēśya Rēgupti*)

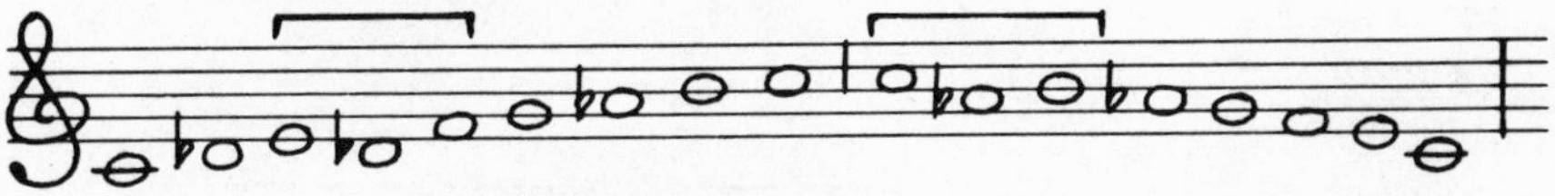

Ascent: *sampūrṇa*; one *vakra* feature is shown.
Descent: the note *RI* (Db) is avoided and one *vakra* feature is shown.

(55) *Dēvarañji*

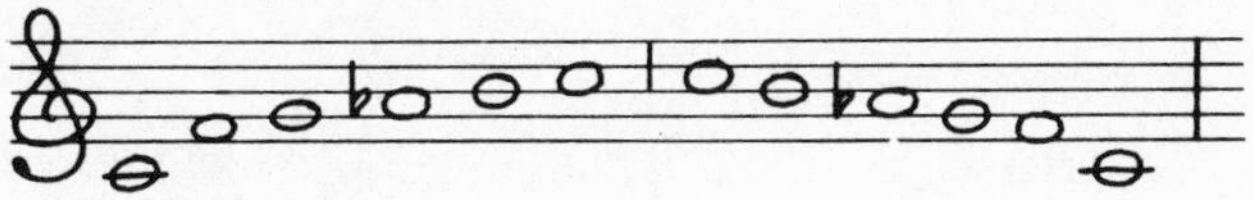

The notes *RI* (Db) and *GA* (E) are avoided entirely.

(56) *Dhāma Rañjani*

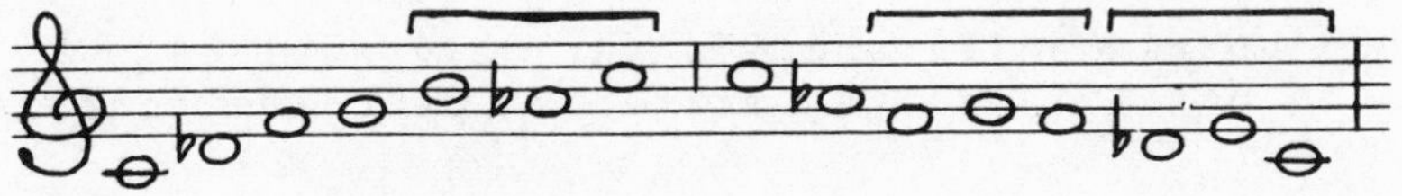

Ascent: the note *GA* (E) is avoided; one *vakra* feature is shown.
Descent: the note *NI* (B) is omitted and two *vakra* features are used.

(57) *Dhātakunda*

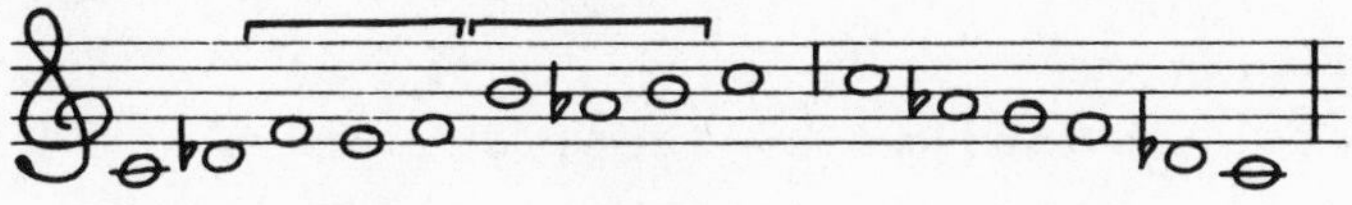

Ascent: the note *PA* (G) is avoided; two *vakra* features are shown.
Descent: the notes *NI* (B) and *GA* (E) are omitted.

(58) *Dhavaḷāṅgi*

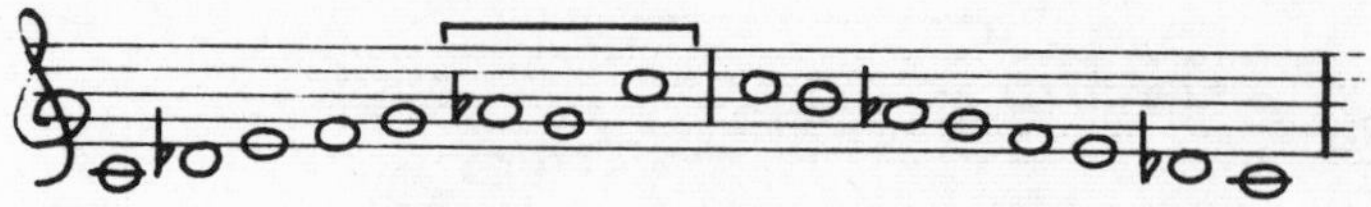

Ascent: the note *NI* (B) is avoided and one *vakra* feature is shown.
Descent: *krama sampūrṇa*.

Another *rāga* with the same name appears under the heading of the 49. *mēḷa* (8).

(59) *Dīshaṇārati* (*Dīṣaṇārati*)

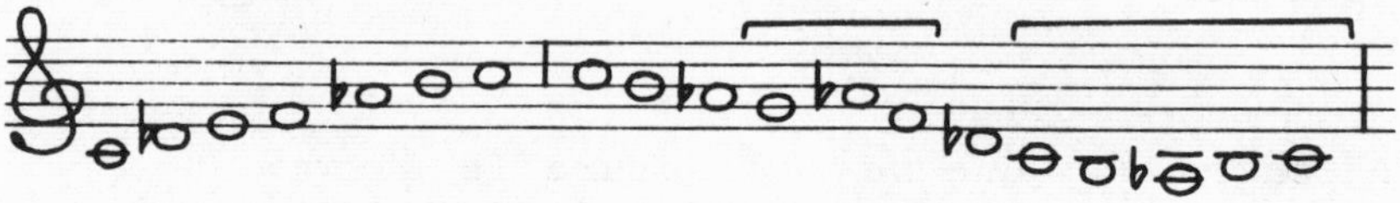

Ascent: the note *PA* (G) is avoided.
Descent: the note *GA* (E) is omitted. Two *vakra* features (the second one considerably extended) are shown.

(60) *Divya Bauḷi*

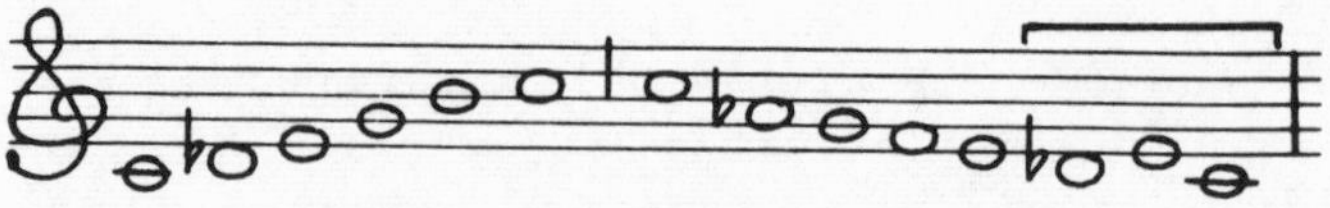

Ascent: the notes *MA* (F) and *DHA* (Ab) are avoided.
Descent: the note *NI* (B) is omitted. One *vakra* feature is shown.

(61) *Ēkākshari* (*Ēkākṣari*)

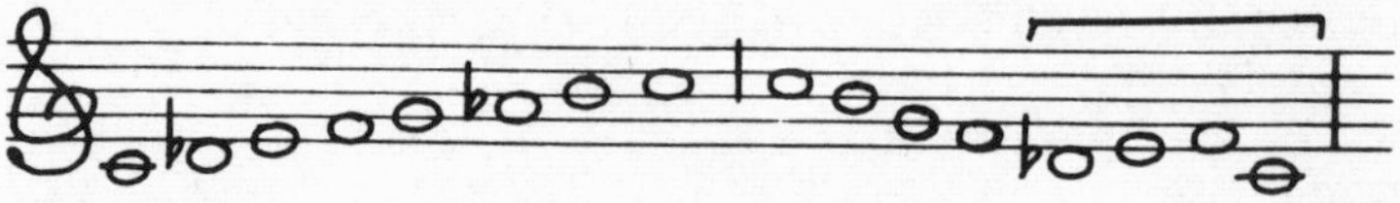

Ascent: *krama sampūrṇa*.
Descent: the note *DHA* (Ab) is avoided; one *vakra* feature is shown.

(62) *Ēkalīla*

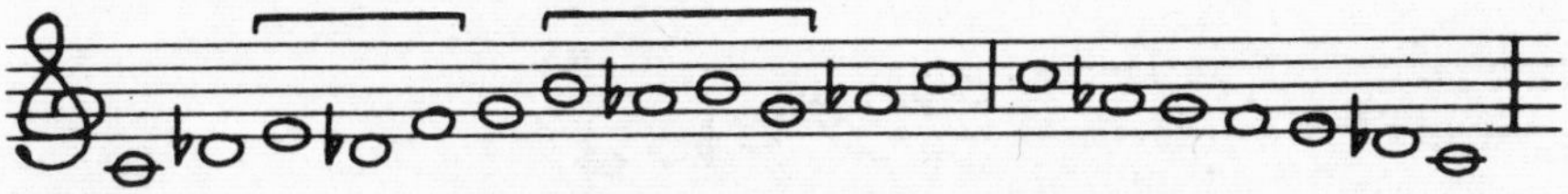

Ascent: *sampūrṇa*; two *vakra* features are shown.
Descent: the note *NI* (B) is avoided.

(63) *Ēkanika*

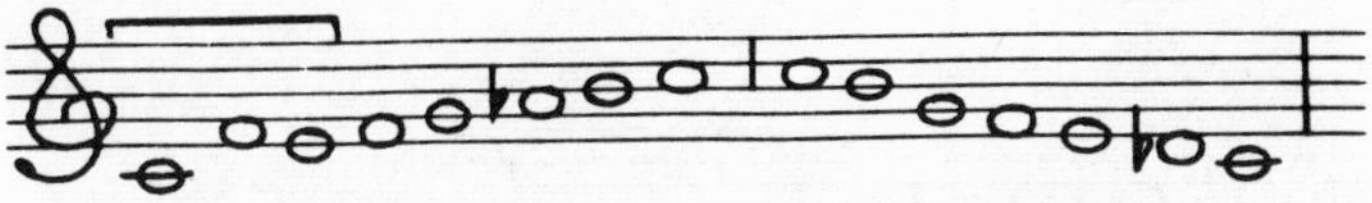

Ascent: the note *RI* (Db) is avoided; one *vakra* feature is shown.
Descent: the note *DHA* (Ab) is omitted.

(64) *Gamana Lalita*

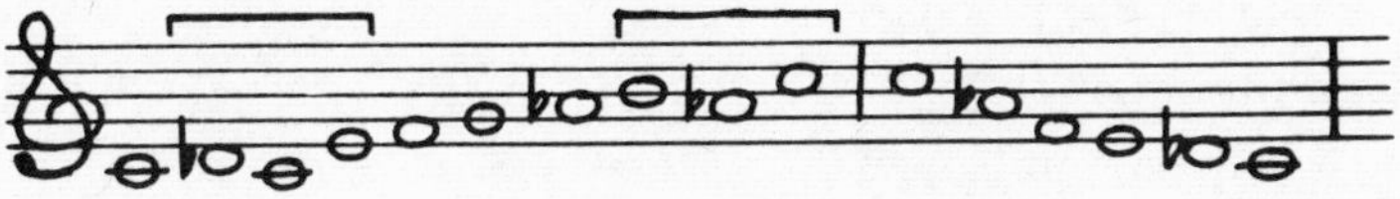

Ascent: *sampūrṇa*; two *vakra* features are shown.
Descent: the notes *NI* (B) and *PA* (G) are avoided.

(65) *Gāna Sindhu* (*Ghāna Sindhu*)

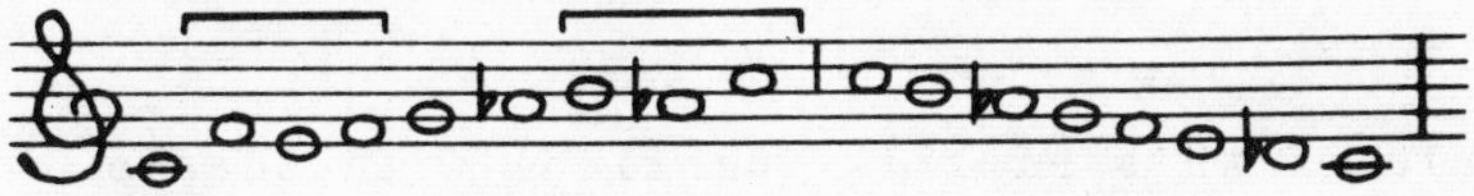

Ascent: the note *RI* (Db) is avoided and two *vakra* features are shown.
Descent: *krama sampūrṇa*.

(66) *Gāna Svabhāva*

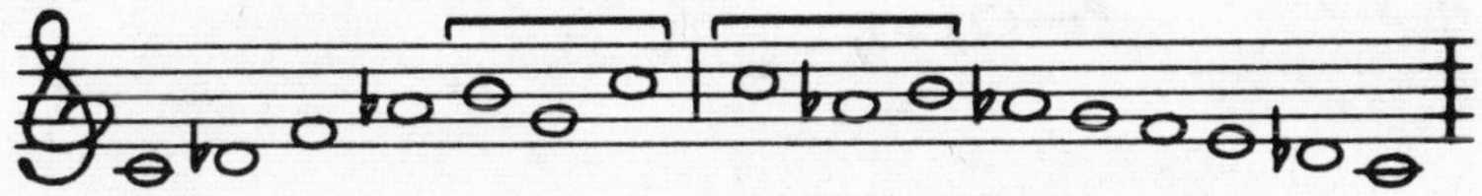

Ascent: the note *GA* (E) is avoided. One *vakra* feature is shown.
Descent: *sampūrṇa*; one *vakra* feature is used.

(67) *Gāndhāra Gauḷa*

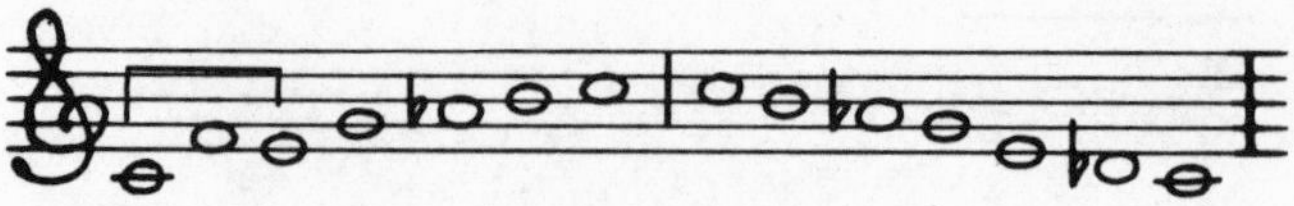

Ascent: the note *RI* (Db) is avoided; one *vakra* feature is shown.
Descent: the note *MA* (F) is omitted.

(68) *Gōmukhi*

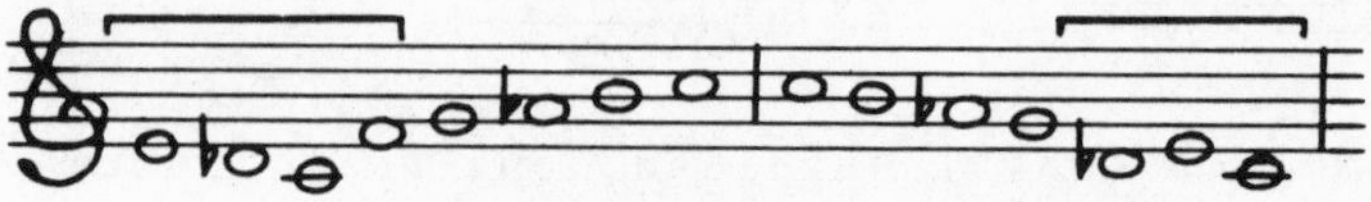

Ascent: *sampūrṇa*; one extended *vakra* feature is shown.
Descent: the note *MA* (F) is avoided. One *vakra* feature is shown.

(69) *Gōpikabhūṣaṇam*

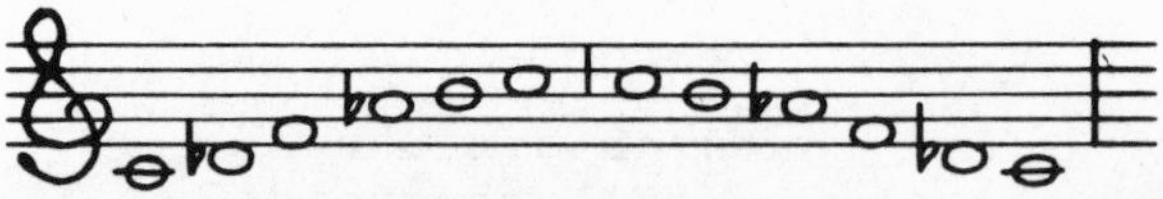

The notes *GA* (E) and *PA* (G) are avoided entirely.

(70) *Gōpikā Kusumam*

The scale of this *rāga* is identical with that of *Gōpikabhūṣaṇam* (15,69) but is mentioned separately in SD (II, 200).

(71) *Haṃsa*

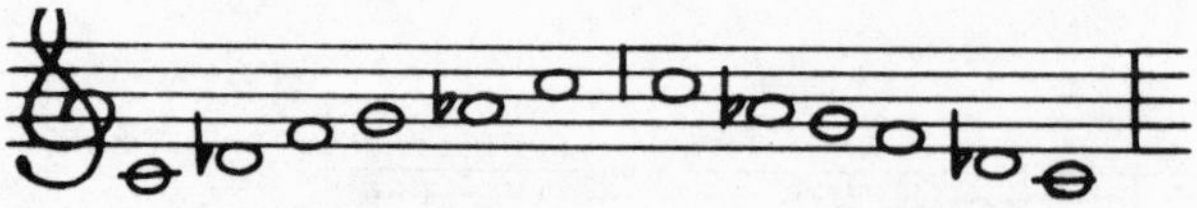

The notes *GA* (E) and *NI* (B) are avoided entirely.

(72) *Haṃsa Mañjari*

Ascent: the notes *MA* (F) and *NI* (B) are avoided.
Descent: the notes *DHA* (Ab) and *GA* (E) are omitted.

(73) *Janavarāḷi*

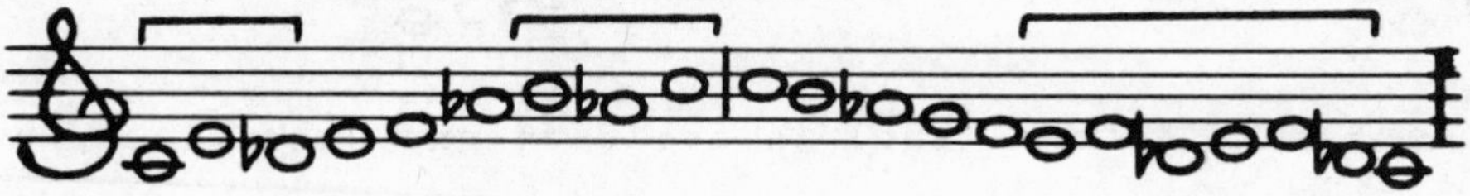

Ascent: the note *PA* (G) is avoided; two *vakra* features are shown.
Descent: *sampūrṇa*; one extended *vakra* feature is used.

(74) *Jharapuñjari*

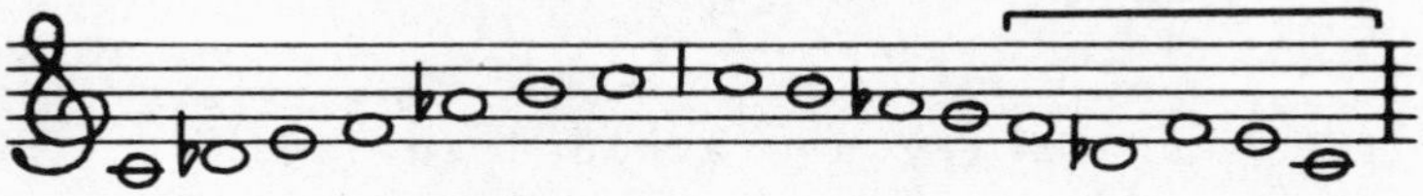

Ascent: the note *PA* (G) is avoided.
Descent: *sampūrṇa*; one extended *vakra* feature is shown

(75) *Jōgī*

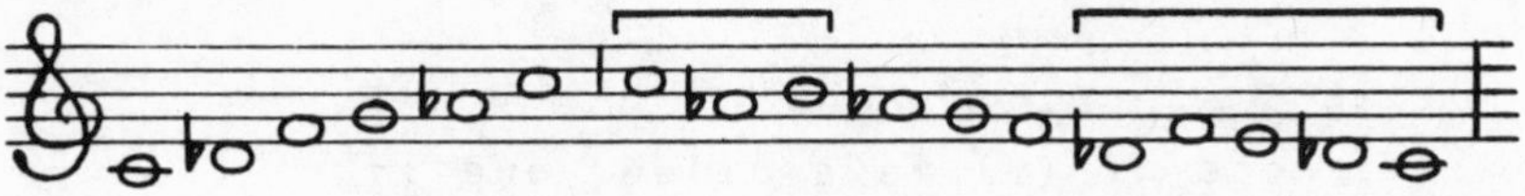

Ascent: the notes *GA* (E) and *NI* (B) are avoided.
Descent: *sampūrṇa*; two *vakra* features are shown—one short, one extended.

(76) *Jōgisāvēri*

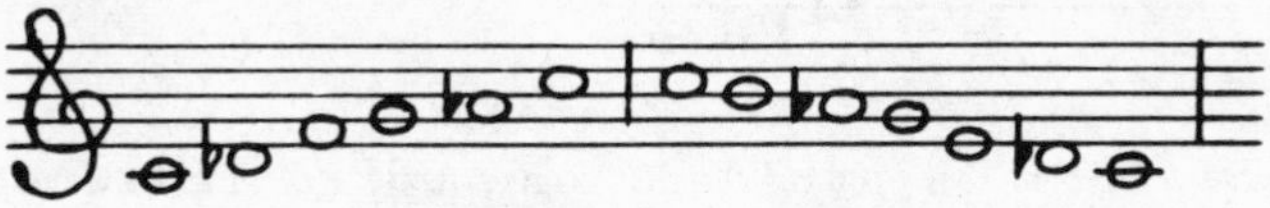

Ascent: the notes *GA* (E) and *NI* (B) are avoided.
Descent: the note *MA* (F) is omitted.

(77) *Kālindi*

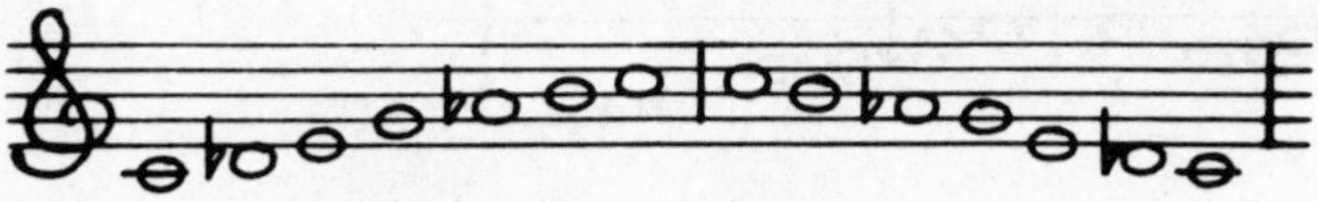

The note *MA* (F) is avoided entirely.
Another *rāga* with the same name appears under the heading of the 22. *mēḷa* (67).

(78) *Kamala Pañchamam*

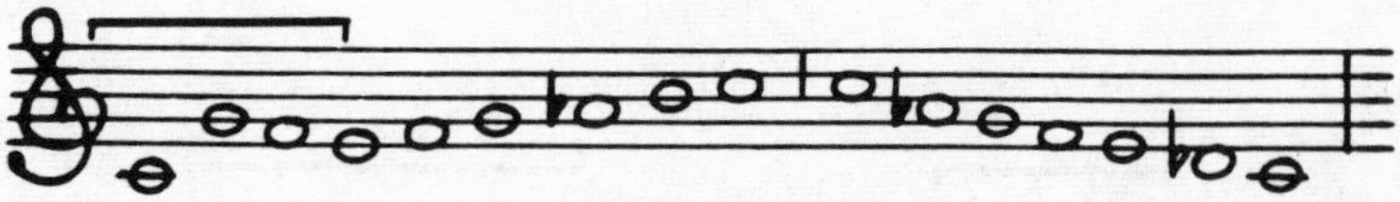

Ascent: the note *RI* (Db) is avoided; one *vakra* feature is shown.
Descent: the note *NI* (B) is omitted.

(79) *Karaka*

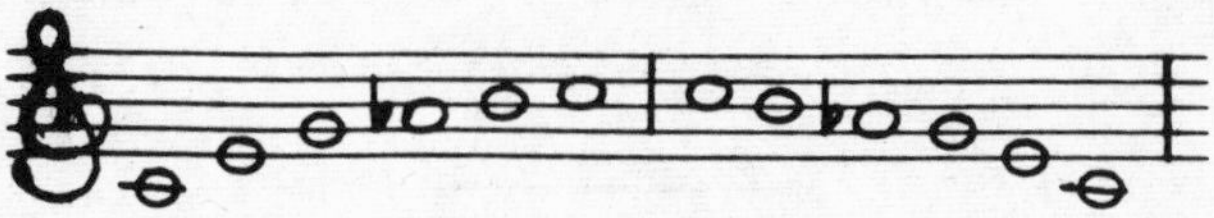

The notes *RI* (Db) and *MA* (F) are avoided entirely.

(80) *Karṇāṭaka Sāraṅga*

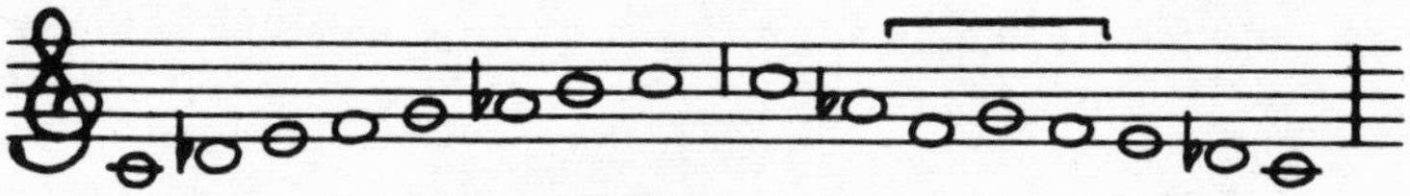

Ascent: *krama sampūrṇa.*
Descent: the note *NI* (B) is avoided; one *vakra* feature is shown.

(81) *Kōkila Vardhani*

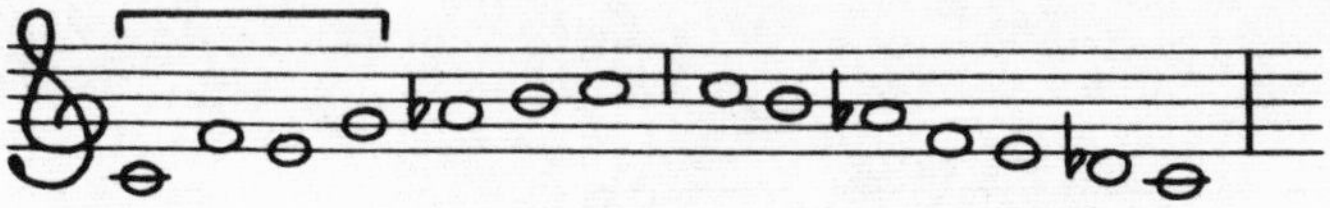

Ascent: the note *RI* (Db) is avoided; one *vakra* feature is shown.
Descent: the note *PA* (G) is omitted.

(82) *Kukuḍa*

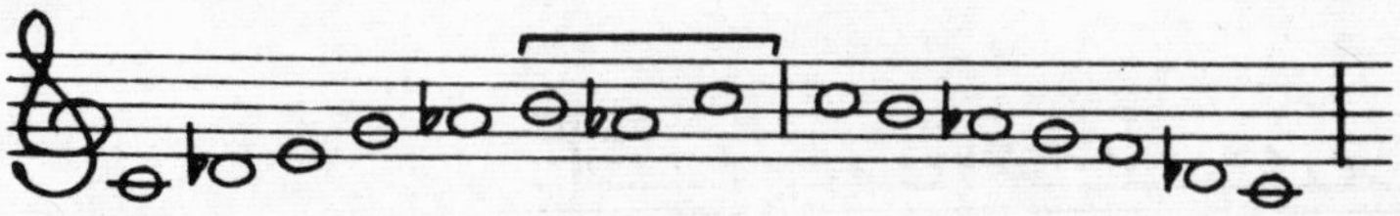

Ascent: the note *MA* (F) is avoided; one *vakra* feature is shown.
Descent: the note *GA* (E) is omitted.

(83) *Kuṅkumāmbari*

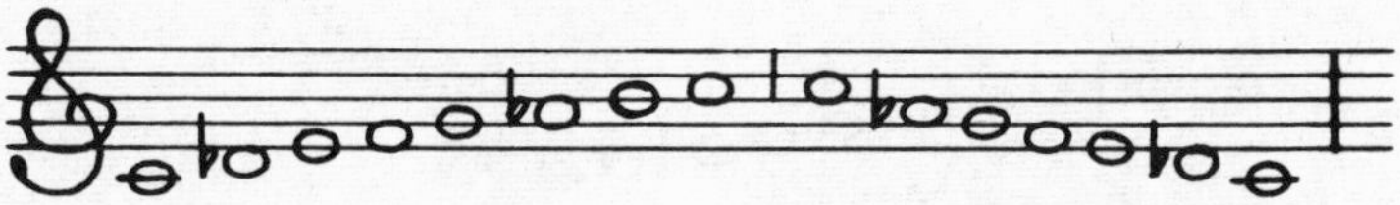

Ascent: *krama sampūrṇa*.
Descent: the note *NI* (B) is avoided.
The phrase *SA-NI-DHA-NI-SA* (c-B-Ab-B-c), also using the note *NI* (B) in descent, is believed to be characteristic for this *rāga*.

(84) *Khecharāṅgi*

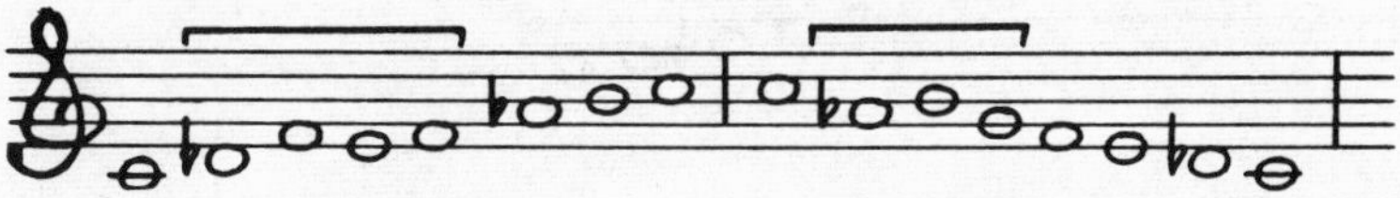

Ascent: the note *PA* (G) is avoided. One *vakra* feature is shown.
Descent: *sampūrṇa*; one *vakra* feature is used.

(85) *Lalitagauri*

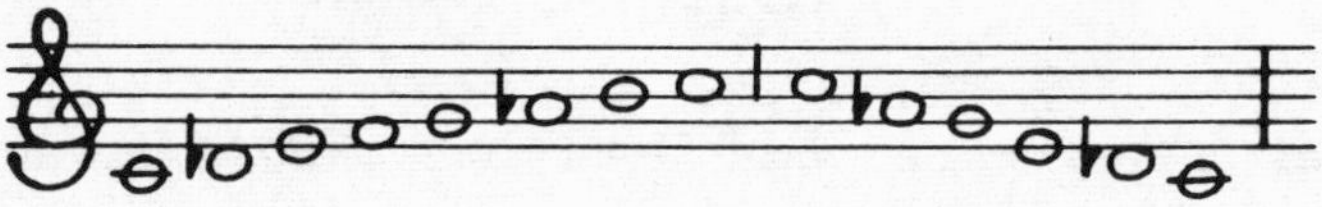

Ascent: *krama sampūrṇa*.
Descent: the notes *NI* (B) and *MA* (F) are avoided.

(86) *Lalitakriya*

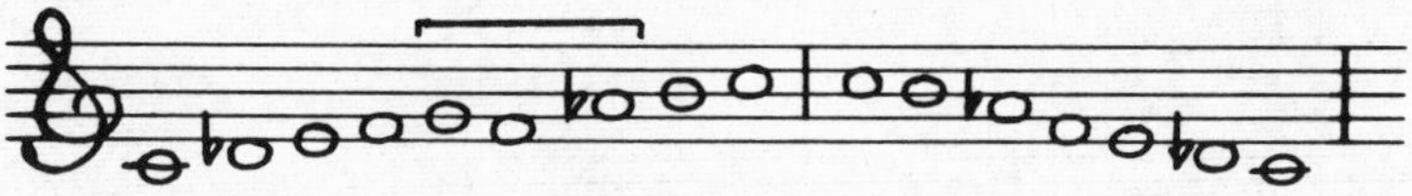

Ascent: *krama sampūrṇa*; one *vakra* feature is shown.
Descent: the note *PA* (G) is avoided.

(87) *Makarālapriya*

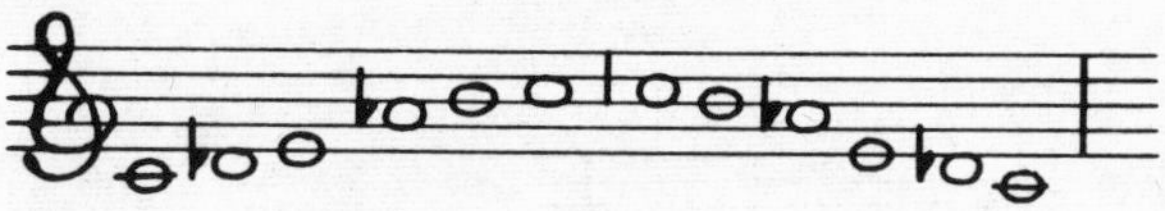

The notes *MA* (F) and *PA* (G) are avoided entirely.

(88) *Mālava*

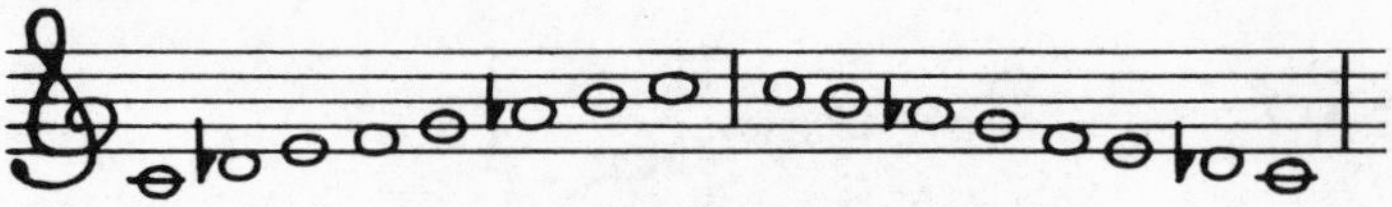

The scale of this *rāga* is *krama sampurṇa* and is identical with that of the primary *rāga Māyāmāḷavagauḷa*. (N lists it separately.)

(89) *Mālavapañchamam*

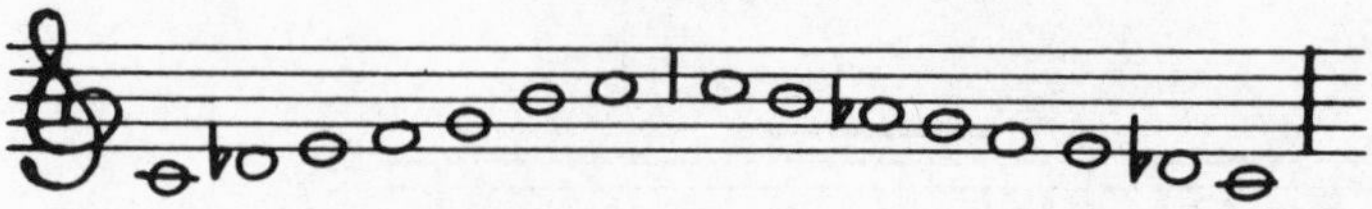

Ascent: the note *DHA* (Ab) is avoided.
Descent: *krama sampūrṇa.*

(90) *Mārgadēṡika*

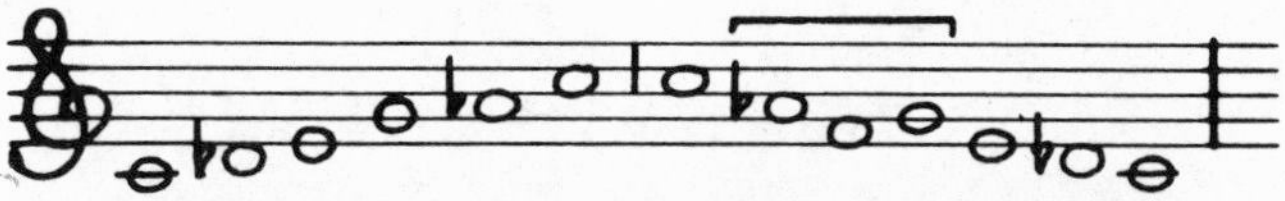

Although listed as a separate *rāga*, this *Mārgadēṡika* can be considered to be a variant of 15,14. The difference between the two forms can be noticed in the descending scale. In the *Mārgadēṡika* under consideration (15,90) the note *NI* (B) is avoided entirely. The note *MA* (F) is omitted in ascent and one *vakra* feature is shown in descent.

(91) *Mitrakiraṇi*

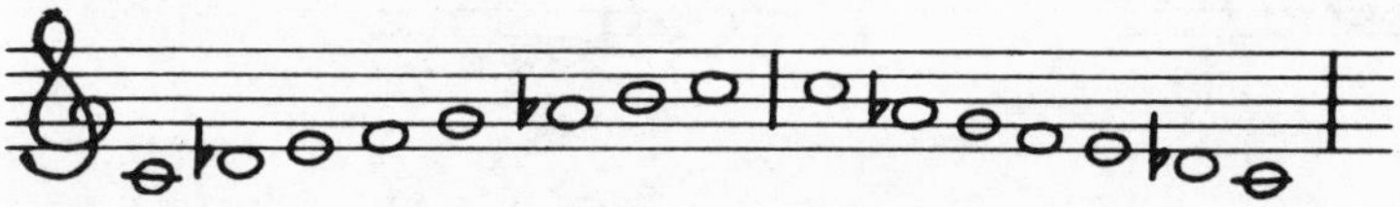

Ascent: *krama sampūrṇa.*
Descent: the note *NI* (B) is avoided.

(92) *Nēpālagauḷa*

The note *PA* (G) is avoided entirely.

(93) *Pāñchali*

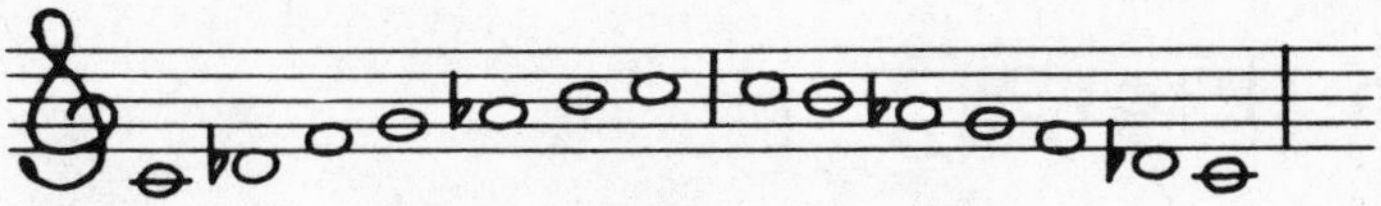

The note *GA* (E) is avoided entirely.

(94) *Rukmāmbari*

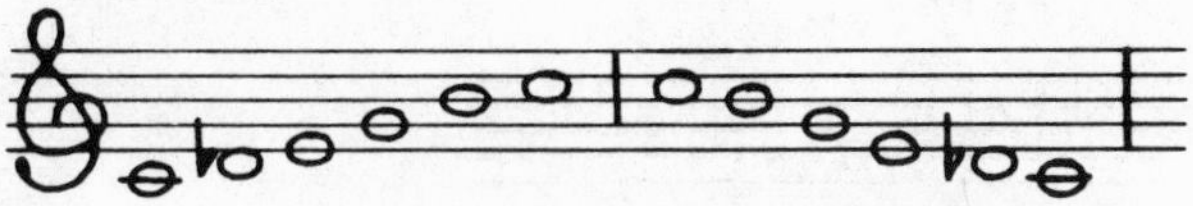

The notes *MA* (F) and *DHA* (Ab) are avoided entirely.

(95) *Sindhurāmakriya*

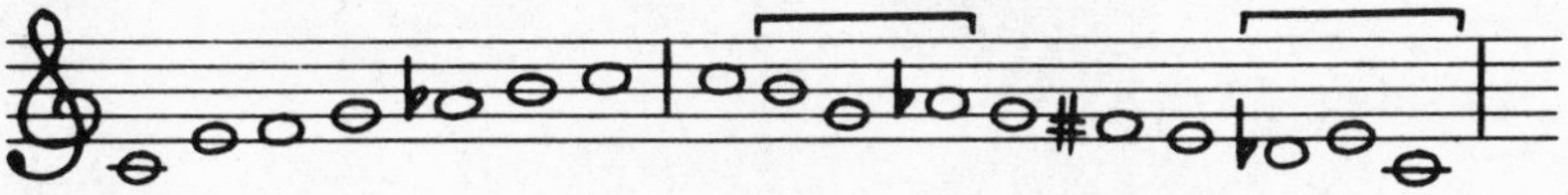

Ascent: the note *RI* (Db) is avoided.
Descent: *sampūrṇa*; two *vakra* features are shown.

Compare this *rāga* with *Sindhurāmakriya* (15,8). N indicates the use of F# in descent (of 15,95), a note foreign to the basic material of *mēḷa* 15.

(96) *Śrī*

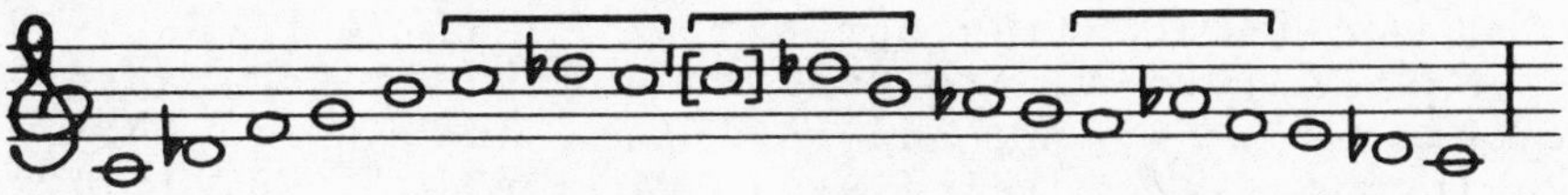

This *rāga* is a variant of *Śrīrāga* (22,1).
Ascent: the notes *GA* (E) and *DHA* (Ab) are avoided. At the end of the theoretical ascent and the beginning of the descent the upper *SA* (c) can veer in a *vakra* feature to *RI* (db) of the *tara saptaka*.
Descent: *sampūrṇa*; one additional *vakra* feature is shown.

(97) *Śuddhamalahari*

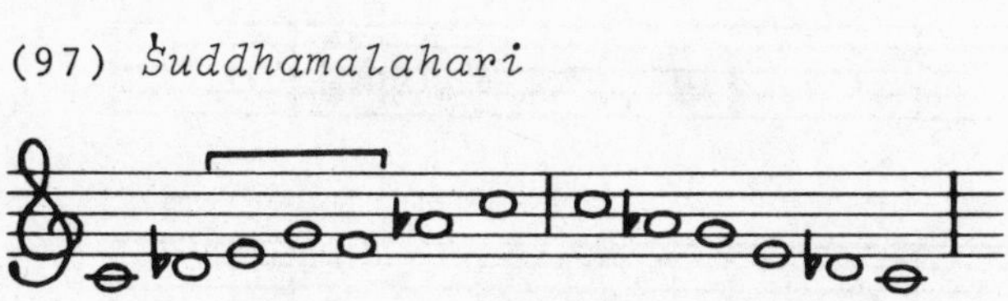

The note *NI* (B) is avoided entirely. The ascent shows one *vakra* feature and the descent omits the note *MA* (F).

(98) *Tāravam*

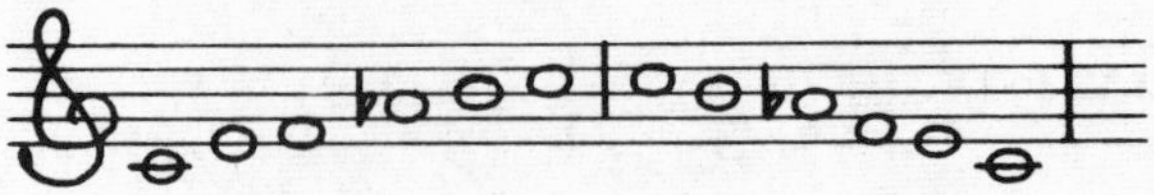

The notes *RI* (Db) and *PA* (G) are avoided entirely.

(99) *Vasantapriya*

Ascent: *sampūrṇa*; one *vakra* feature is shown.
Descent: the notes *DHA* (Ab) and *GA* (E) are avoided.

16. *MĒḶA CHAKRAVĀKA*(*M*)

Chakravāka can be performed at any time. Veṅkaṭamakhin calls this *rāga Toyavegavāhini*.

Sambamoorthy relates that "*RI* [Db] and *NI* [Bb] are *jīva svaras* [stressed notes]; *RI* [Db] and *PA* [G] are *nyāsa svaras* [concluding notes]; *GA-MA-RI-SA* [E-F-Db-C] and *PA-MA-DHA* [G-F-A] are *viṡesha sanchāras* [characteristic phrases]; *SA*, *GA*, and *PA* [C, E, and G] are the commencing notes for melodies in this *rāga*" (SD, I, 72).

In present-day practice these matters are treated very lightly or are ignored, as can be observed, in part, in the following song specimen:

CHAKRAVĀKA (*Triputa-tāla*)

Pallavi

Repeat the *pallavi* beginning from A

Anupallavi

Repeat the *pallavi* beginning from A

Charana

Repeat the *pallavi* beginning from A

Janya Rāgas of the 16. Mēḷa

(1) *Vegavāhini*

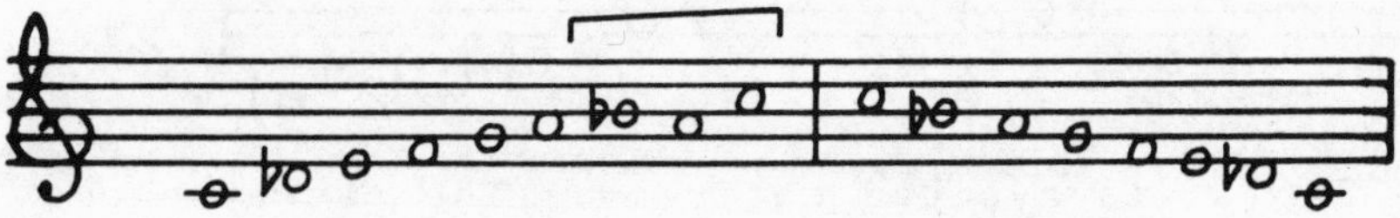

Ascent: *sampūrṇa*; one *vakra* feature is shown.
Descent: *krama sampūrṇa*

RĀGA VEGAVĀHINI (*Triputa-tāla*) SCM, 69

(2) *Kalāvati*

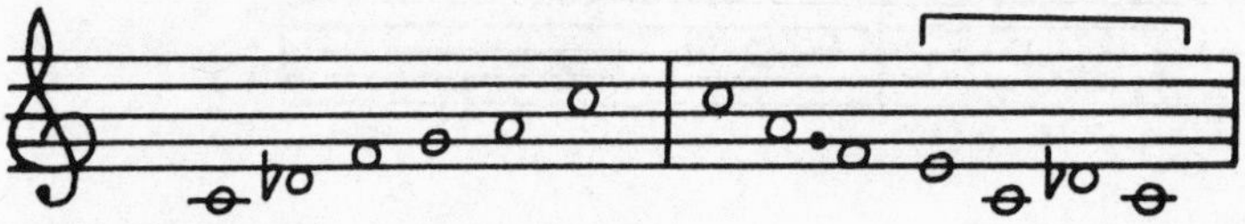

The note *NI* (Bb) is avoided entirely. *GA* (E) is omitted in ascent and *PA* (G) in descent, although there are some musicians who employ the latter. One *vakra* feature is shown in descent. *Kalāvati* can be performed at any time.

The name *Kalāvati* is used by Veṅkaṭamakhin to denote the *rāga* which at the present time is called *Yāgapriyā* (31. *mēḷa*). Veṅkaṭamakhin's scale shows some modifications which are shown below in the description of *Yāgapriyā*.

(3) *Bhūjaṅgiṇi*

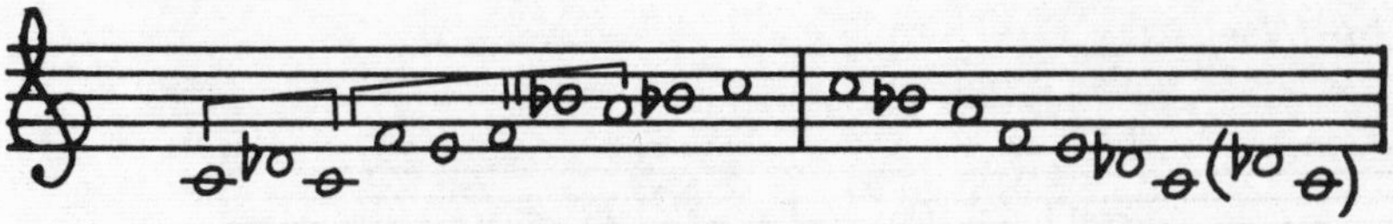

The note *PA* (G) is avoided entirely. The ascent shows three *vakra* features and the two characteristic steps: *SA-MA* (C-F) and *MA-NI* (F-Bb).

RĀGA BHŪJAṄGIṆI (*Triputa-tāla*) SCM, 69-70

(4) *Bindumālini*

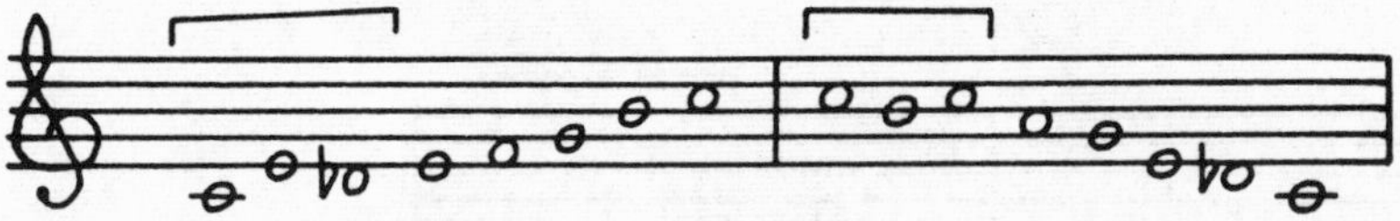

Ascent: the note *DHA* (A) is avoided; one *vakra* feature is shown.
Descent: the note *MA* (F) is omitted; one *vakra* feature is used.

(5) *Kalagaḍa*

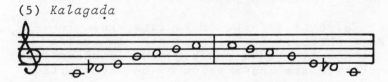

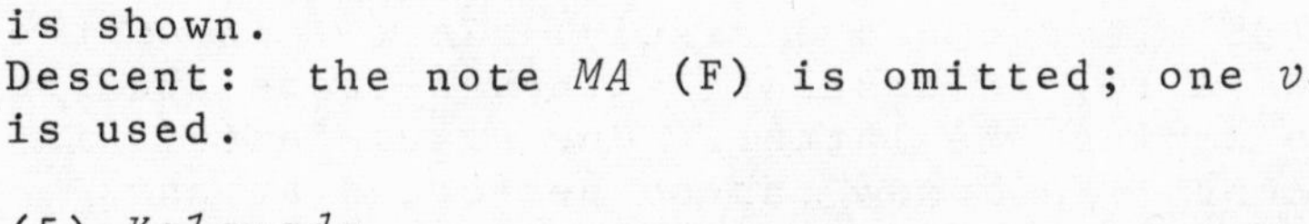

The note *MA* (F) is omitted entirely. Another form of *Kalagaḍa* appears under the heading of the 13. *mēḷa* (5). It has the same scale structure but differs in the intonation of the notes *DHA* and *NI*.

Kalagaḍa can be performed at any time.

(6) *Malayamāruta*

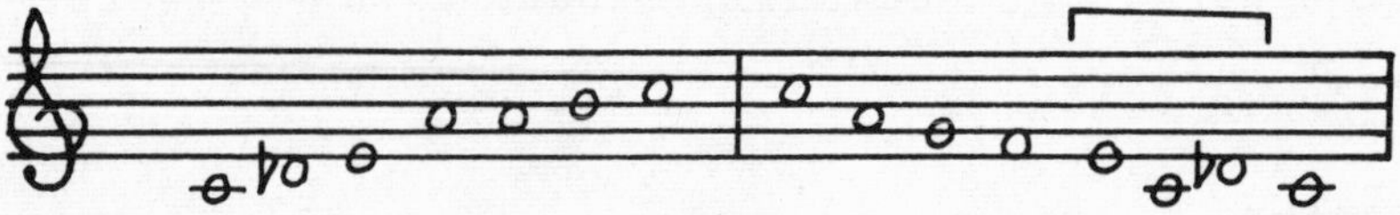

Ascent: the notes *MA* (F) and *PA* (G) are avoided. *DHA* (A) is stressed.
Descent: the note *NI* (Bb) is omitted; one *vakra* feature is shown.

(7) *Ballāti* (*Bhallādi*)

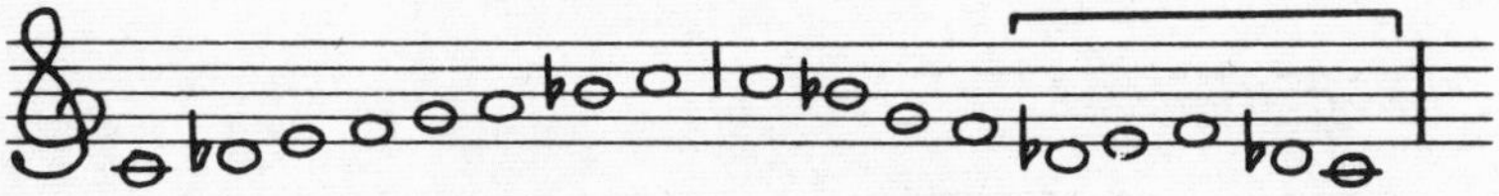

Ascent: *krama sampūrna*.
Descent: the note *DHȦ* (A) is avoided and one extended *vakra* passage is shown.

SD (I, 48) lists *Bhallādi* separately, but there is no doubt that the two listings merely represent two names of the same *rāga*.

(8) *Bhaktapriya*

Ascent: the note *RI* (Db) is avoided.
Descent: *sampūrṇa*; one extended *vakra* feature is shown.

(9) *Bhavyalīlā*

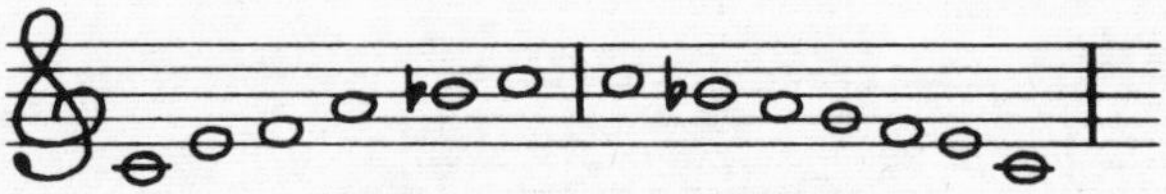

The note *RI* (Db) is avoided entirely. *PA* (G) is omitted in ascent.

(10) *Bhūjagamiṇi*

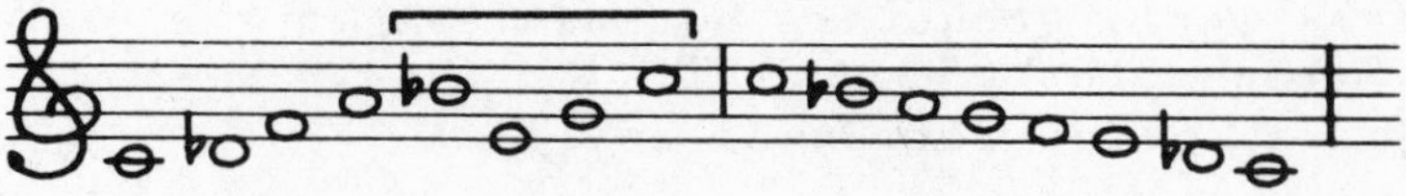

Ascent: *sampūrṇa*; one unusually expanded *vakra* feature is shown.
Descent: *krama sampūrṇa*.

(11) *Bhūpāḷika*

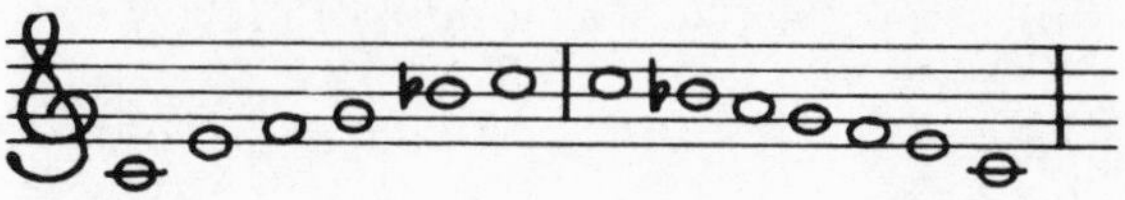

The note *RI* (Db) is avoided entirely. *DHA* (A) is omitted in ascent.

(12) *Bhūvana Mōhiṇi*

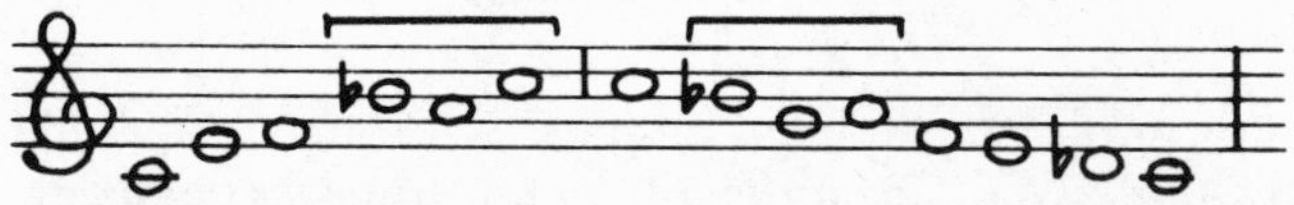

Ascent: the notes *RI* (Db) and *PA* (G) are avoided; one *vakra* feature is shown.
Descent: *sampūrṇa*; one *vakra* feature is used.

(13) *Bindu Kalaṅga*

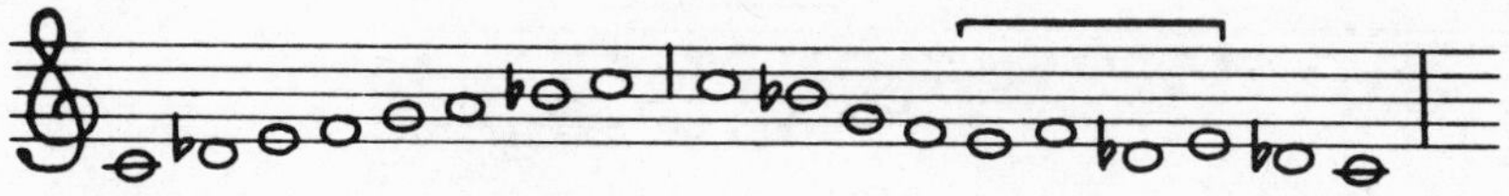

Ascent: *krama sampūrṇa*.
Descent: the note *DHA* (A) is avoided; one *vakra* feature is shown.

(14) *Chandra Kiraṇi*

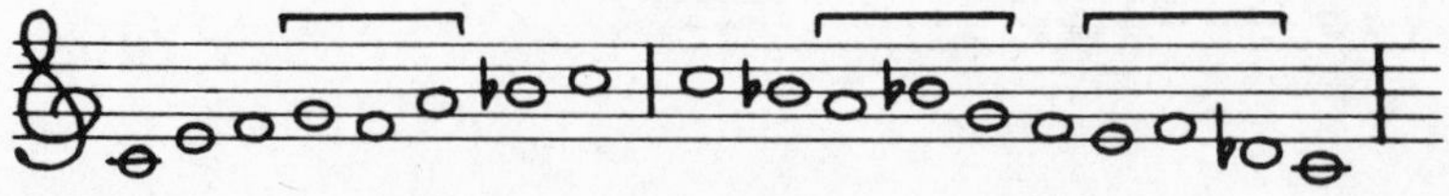

Ascent: the note *RI* (Db) is avoided; one *vakra* feature is shown.
Descent: *sampūrṇa*; two *vakra* features are used.

(15) *Chinmayi*

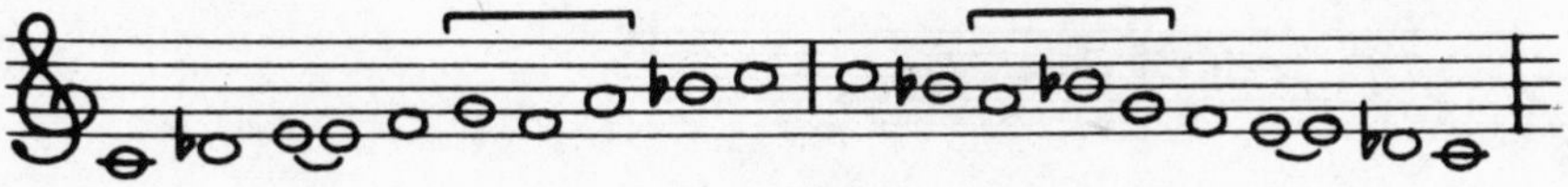

Ascent and descent are *sampūrṇa*; each shows one *vakra* feature. The note *GA* (E) can be stressed.

(16) *Dehāḷi*

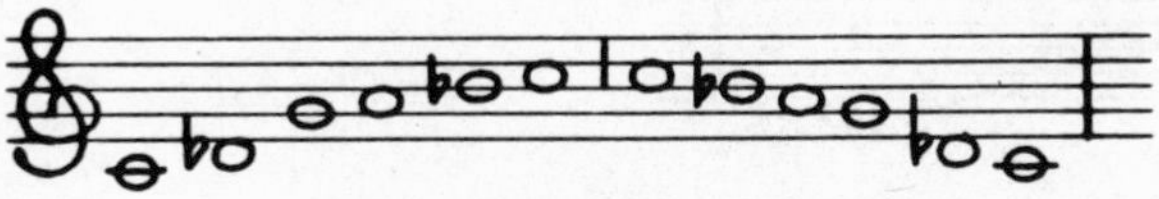

The notes *GA* (E) and *MA* (F) are avoided entirely.

(17) *Dhana Pālinī*

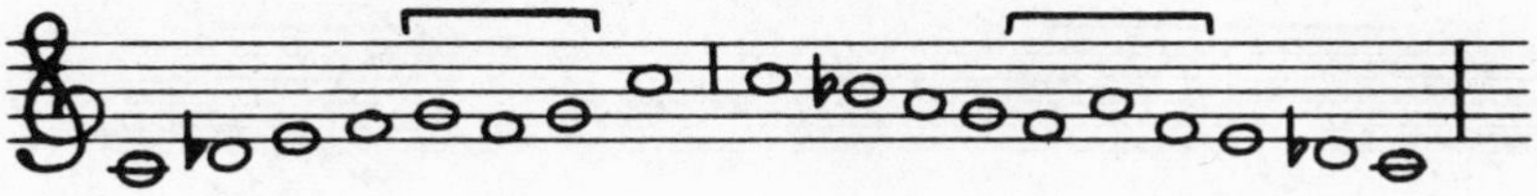

Ascent: the notes *DHA* (A) and *NI* (Bb) are avoided. One *vakra* feature is shown.
Descent: *sampūrṇa*; one *vakra* feature is used.

(18) *Gaṇita Vinōdiṇi*

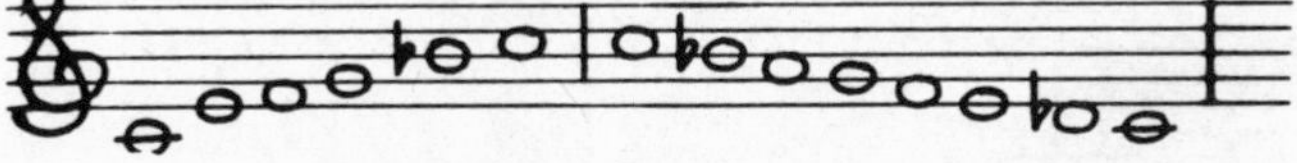

Ascent: the notes *RI* (Db) and *DHA* (A) are avoided.
Descent: *krama sampūrṇa*.
(See also 16,23)

(19) *Ghōshaṇi* (*Ghōshiṇi*, *Ghōṣaṇi*, *Ghōṣiṇi*)

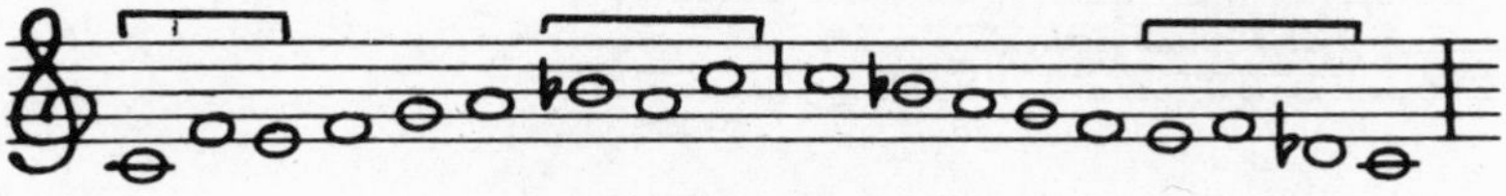

Ascent: the note *RI* (Db) is avoided. Two *vakra* features are shown.
Descent: *sampūrṇa*; one *vakra* feature is used.

(20) *Ghrutāchi*

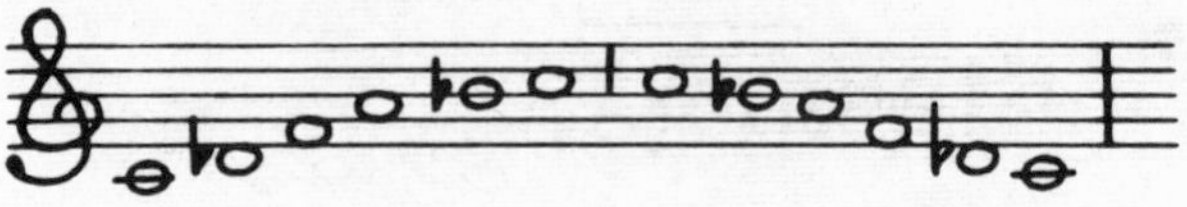

The notes *GA* (E) and *PA* (G) are avoided entirely.

(21) *Grīṣmāvaḷi*

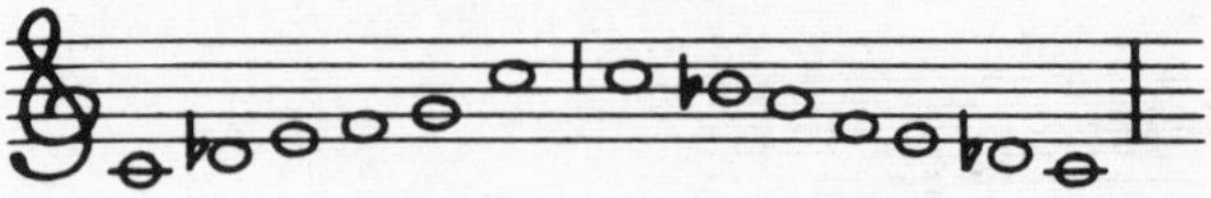

Ascent: the notes *DHA* (A) and *NI* (Bb) are avoided.
Descent: the note *PA* (G) is omitted.

(22) *Guhapriya*

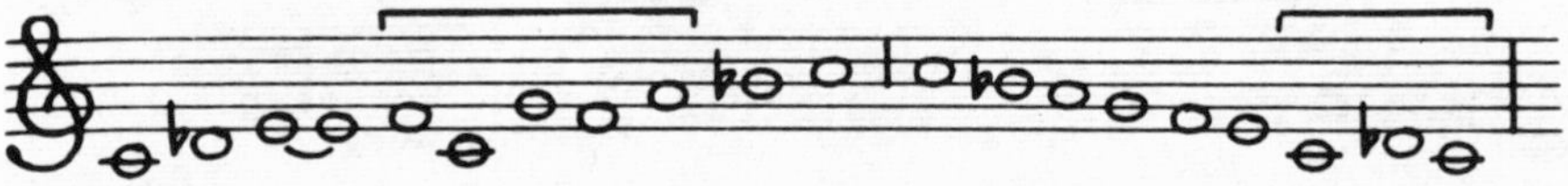

Ascent: *sampūrṇa*; one extended *vakra* feature is shown. The note *GA* (E) can be stressed.
Descent: *sampūrṇa*; one *vakra* feature is shown.

A *rāga* called *Guṇapriya* appears to be identical with *Guhapriya*; the descent of *Guṇapriya* has been given as

which may be only a variant of that of *Guhapriya*.

(23) *Guṇita Vinōdiṇi*

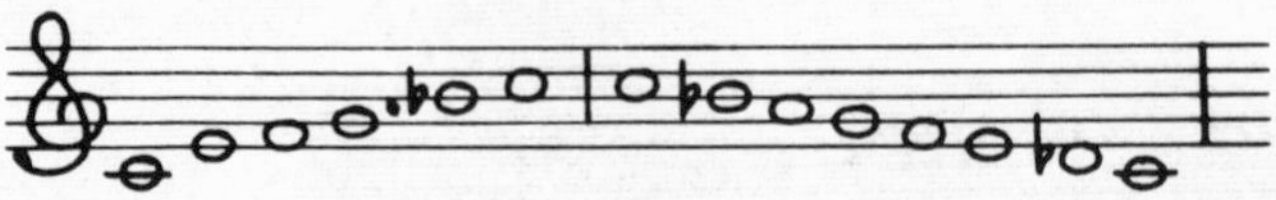

Ascent: the notes *RI* (Db) and, almost always, *DHA* (A) are avoided.
Descent: *krama sampūrṇa*.

This *rāga* appears to be identical with *Gaṇita Vinōdiṇi* (16,18). SD (II, 217) lists the two *rāgas* separately. One slight difference had been reported to me by an unreliable source that states that the ascent of *Guṇita Vinōdiṇi* can employ at times a faint trace of the note *DHA* (A).

(24) *Janākarṣaṇi*

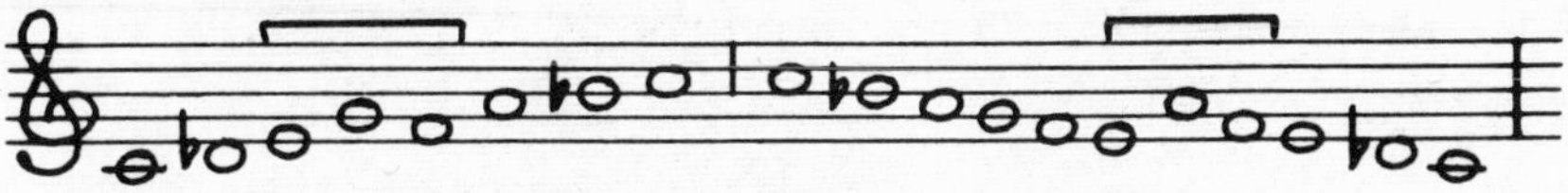

The *sampūrṇa* scale of this *rāga* shows one *vakra* feature in ascent and one in descent.

(25) *Kādambiṇi*

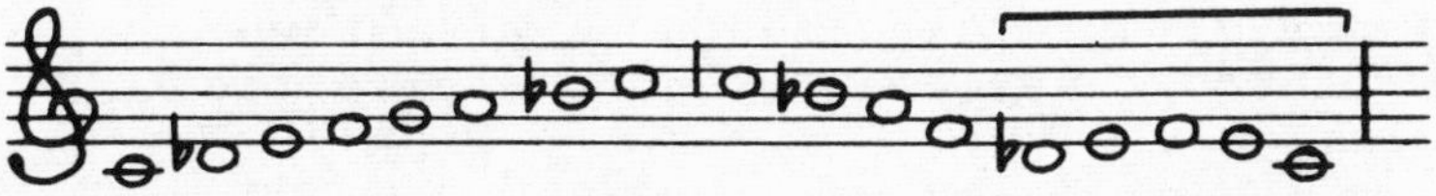

Ascent: *krama sampūrṇa*
Descent: the note *PA* (G) is avoided; one extended *vakra* feature is shown.

Another *rāga* with the same name appears under the heading of the 19. *mēḷa* (13).

(26) *Karṇabhūṣaṇi*

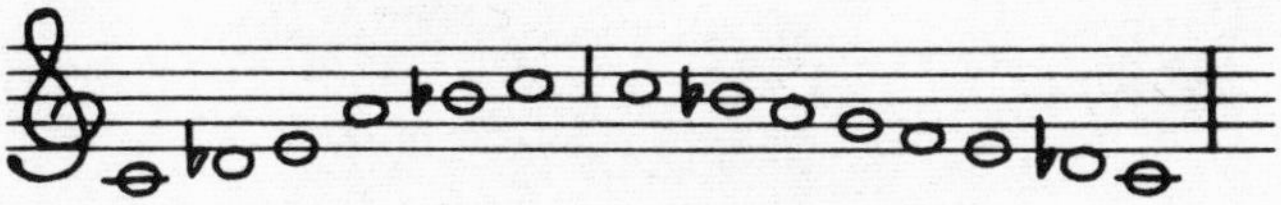

Ascent: the notes *MA* (F) and *PA* (G) are avoided.
Descent: *krama sampūrṇa*.

Another *rāga* with the same name appears under the heading of the 70. *mēḷa* (6).

(27) *Kōkilam*

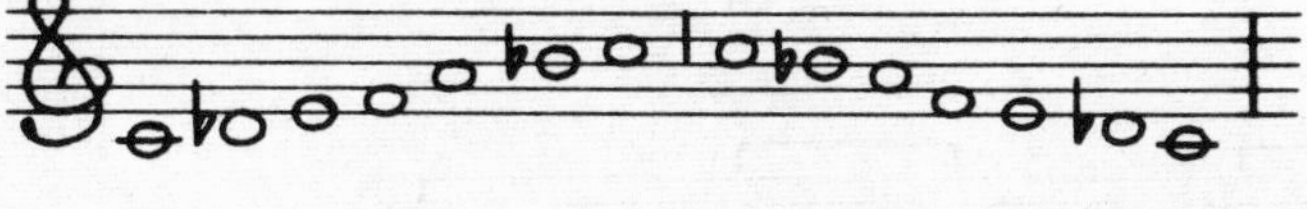

The note *PA* (G) is avoided entirely.

Kōkilam has become remarkably popular in recent times.

(28) *Kujanmōhanam*

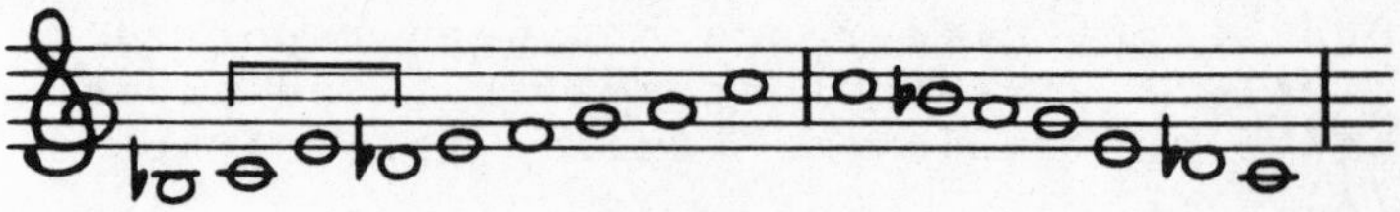

Ascent: the note *NI* (Bb) (of the middle octave range) is avoided and one *vakra* feature is shown.
Descent: the note *MA* (F) is omitted.

(29) *Kuntala*

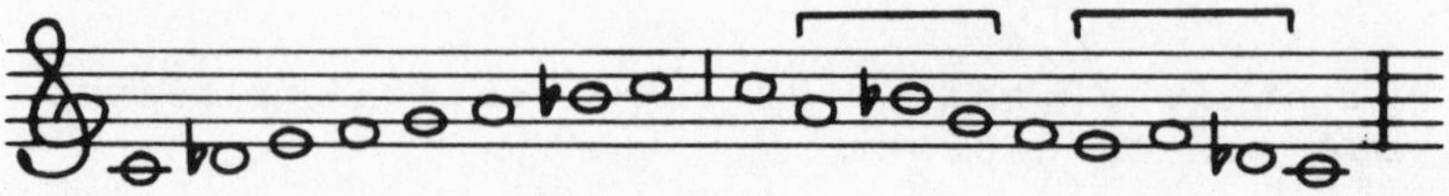

Ascent: *krama sampūrṇa*.
Descent: *sampūrṇa*; two *vakra* features are shown.
The name *Kuṅtala* was also used to denote the 61. *asampūrṇa mēḷa*.

(30) *Kusumāṅgi*

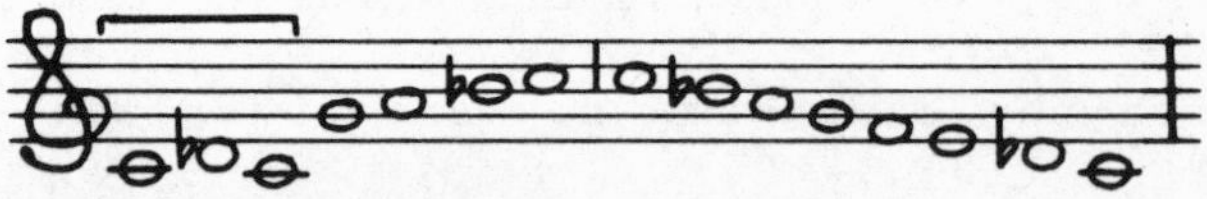

Ascent: the notes *GA* (E) and *MA* (F) are avoided; one *vakra* feature is shown.
Descent: *krama sampūrṇa*.

(31) *Kuvalayānandi*

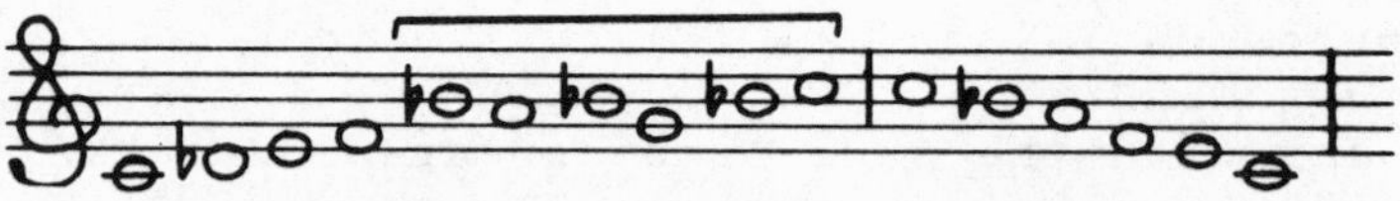

Ascent: *sampūrṇa*; one extended *vakra* passage is shown.
Descent: the notes *PA* (G) and *RI* (Db) are avoided.

(32) *Manasijapriya*

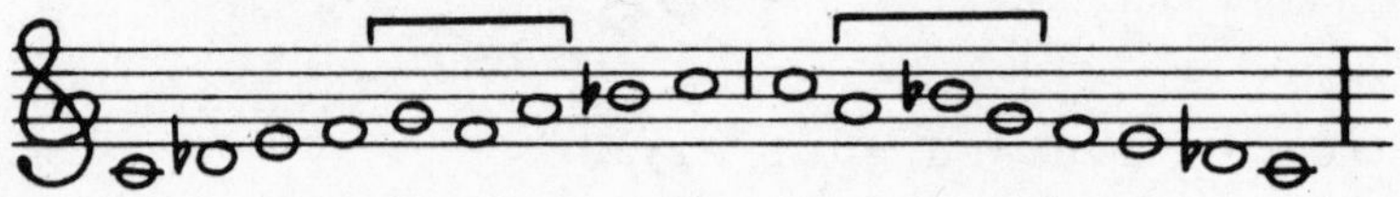

The scale of this *rāga* is *sampūrṇa* and shows one *vakra* feature in ascent and one in descent.

(33) *Mānaskagāmiṇī*

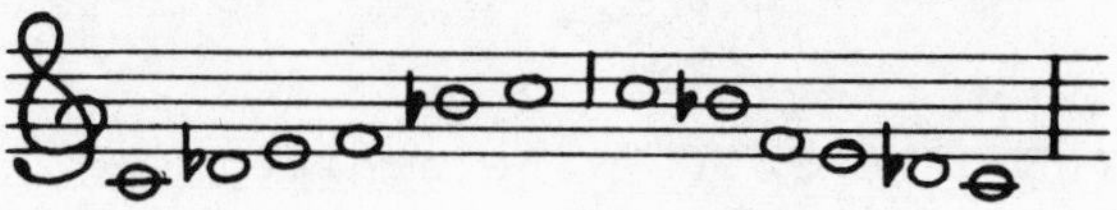

The notes *PA* (G) and *DHA* (A) are avoided entirely.

(34) *Nabhōmārgiṇi*

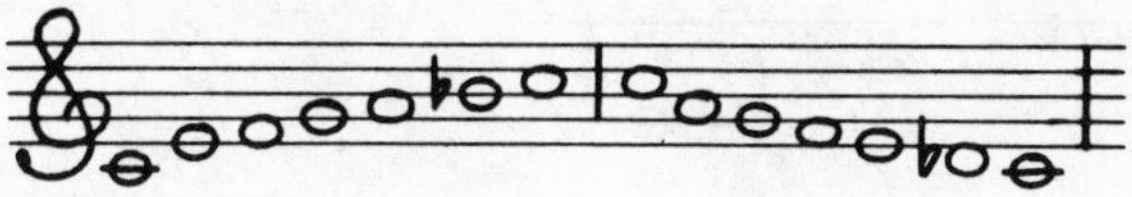

Ascent: the note *RI* (Db) is avoided.
Descent: the note *NI* (Bb) is omitted.

(35) *Padmini*

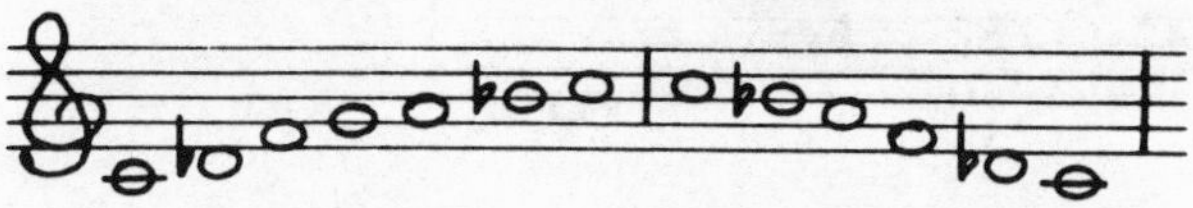

The note *GA* (E) is avoided entirely. *PA* (G) is avoided in descent.

(36) *Rasakalānidhi*

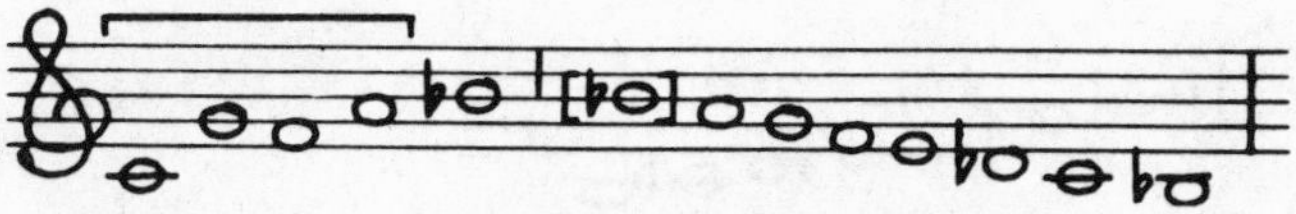

This is a *niṣādāntya rāga*. Its ascent shows one *vakra* feature and avoids the notes *RI* (Db) and *GA* (E).

(37) *Rasikarañjani*

The notes *MA* (F) and *NI* (Bb) are avoided entirely.

(38) *Ravikiraṇi*

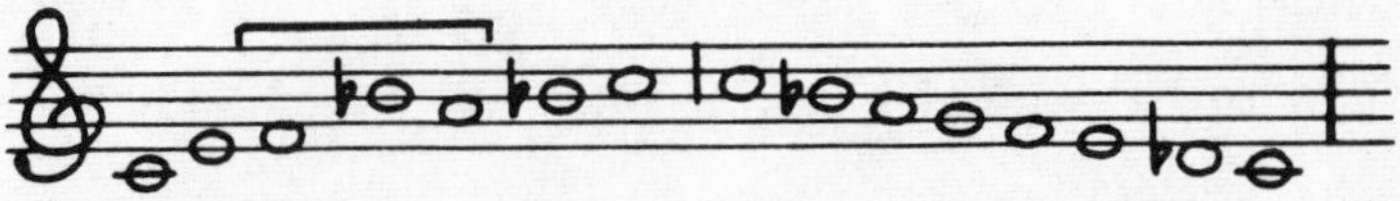

Ascent: the notes *RI* (Db) and *PA* (G) are avoided and one *vakra* feature is shown.
Descent: *krama sampūrṇa*.

(39) *Śasiprakāśini*

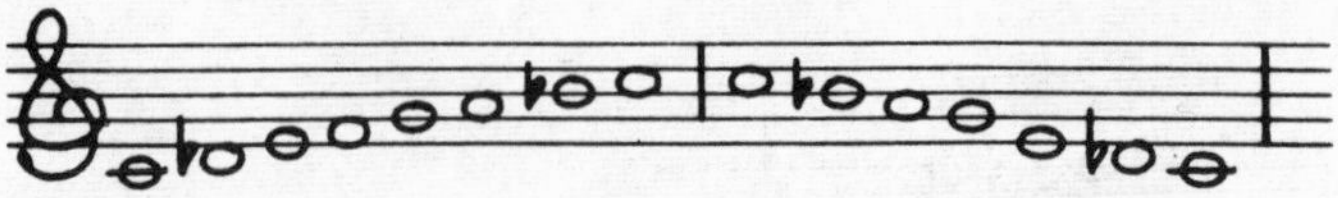

Ascent: *krama sampūrṇa*.
Descent: the note *MA* (F) is avoided.

(40) *Śāntasvarūpi*

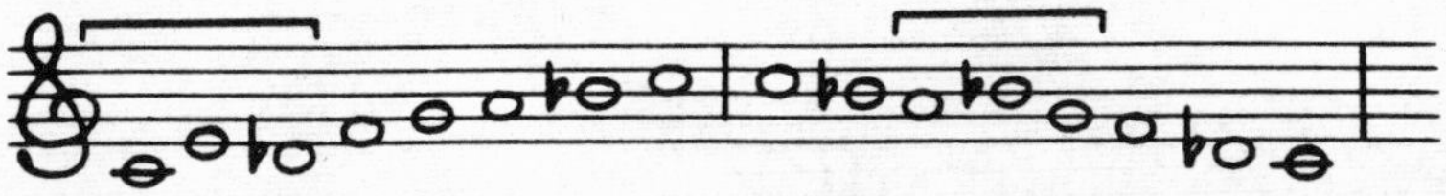

Ascent: *sampūrṇa*; one *vakra* feature is shown.
Descent: the note *GA* (E) is avoided and one *vakra* feature is used.

(41) *Śivānandi*

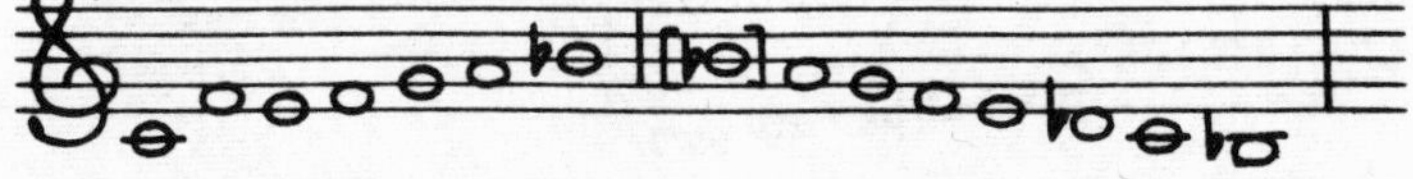

This scale has *niṣādāntya* character and shows in ascent one *vakra* feature where the note *RI* (Db) is omitted.

(42) *Śuddhaśyāmala*

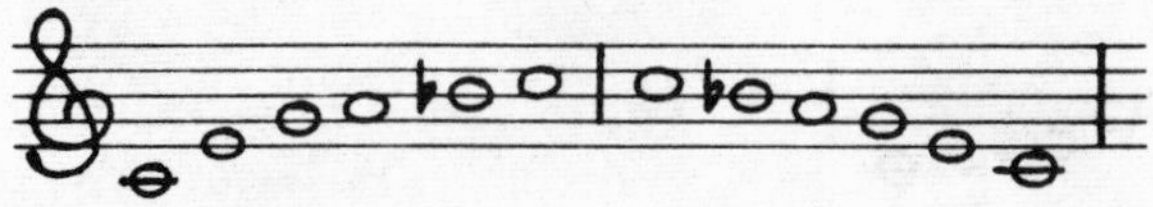

The notes *RI* (Db) and *MA* (F) are avoided entirely.

(43) *Vīṇādharī*

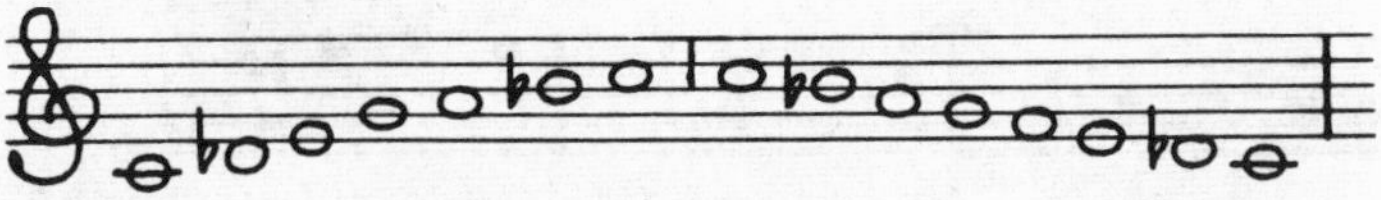

Ascent: the note *MA* (F) is avoided.
Descent: *krama sampūrṇa*.

This *rāga*, recently created, was introduced by Muthiah Bhāgavathar (see note 1 to the 2. *mēḷa*).

17. *MĒḶA SŪRYAKĀNTA*

Sūryakānta may be performed at any time. Stressed notes are *RI* (Db), *DHA* (A), and *NI* (B).

Veṅkaṭamakhin calls this *rāga Chhāyāvatī* and states that the note *PA* (G) is to be avoided in ascent.

The following song specimen in *Sūryakānta* is a *kīrtana* in which the note *PA* (G) is employed:

SŪRYAKĀNTA (*Ādi-tāla*)

Pallavi

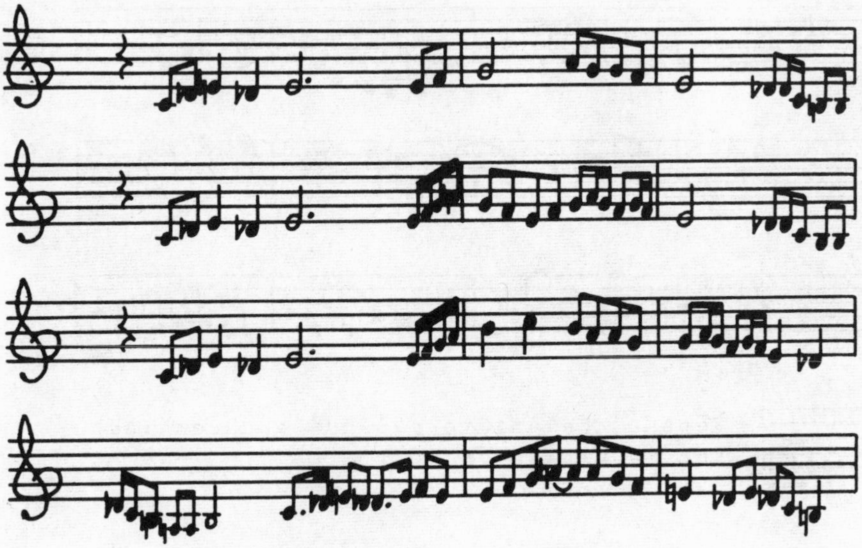

Anupallavi

Repeat the entire *pallavi*

Charana

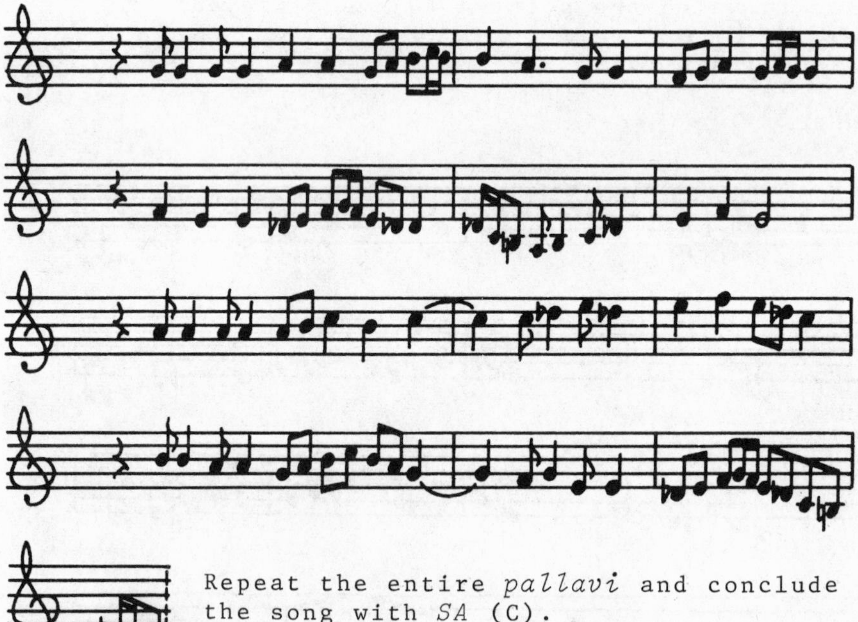

Repeat the entire *pallavi* and conclude the song with *SA* (C).

Janya Rāgas of the 17. Mēḷa

(1) *Bhairava*

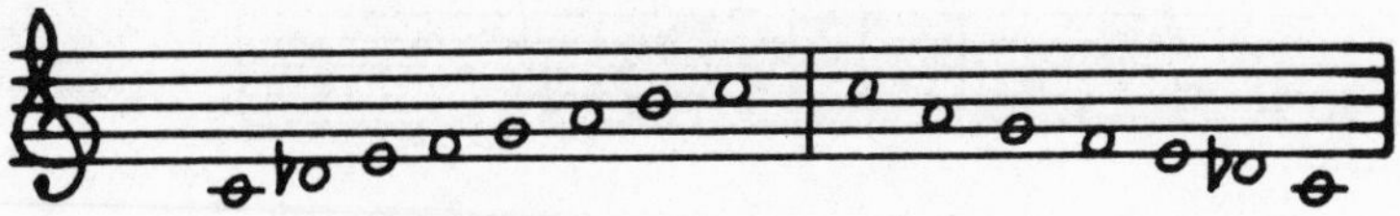

Ascent: *krama sampūrṇa*
Descent: the note *NI* (B) is avoided. *DHA* (A) can be stressed.

R (181) reports that Subbarāma Dīkṣitar uses the following descent:

The following song specimen is a *kṛti* by Tyāgarāja:

BHAIRAVA RĀGA (*Ādi-tala*)

Pallavi

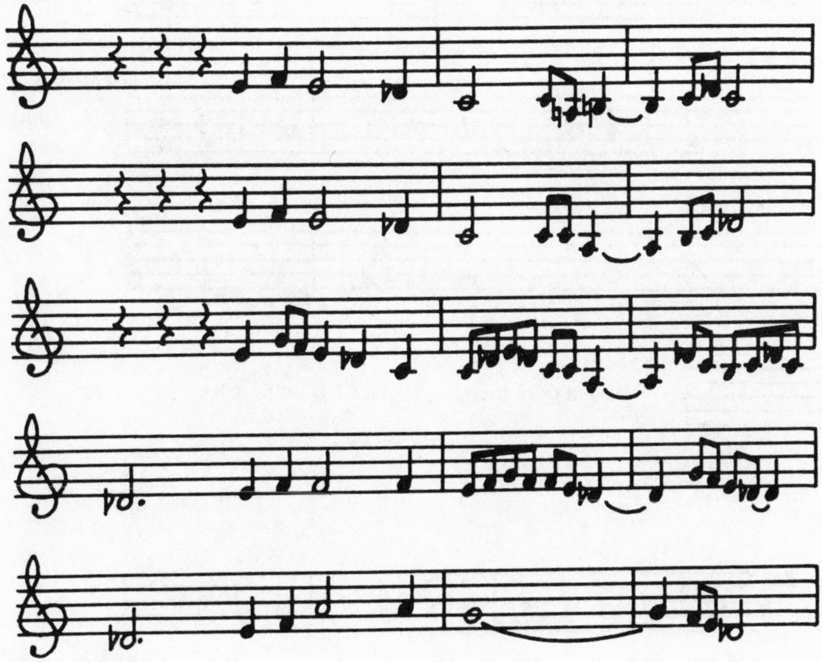

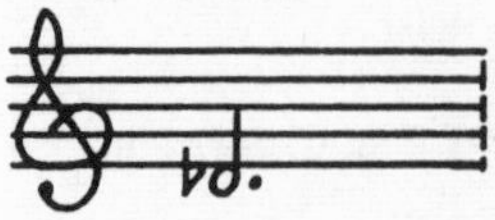

Repeat lines A and B of the *pallavi*

Anupallavi

Repeat lines A and B of the *pallavi*

Charana

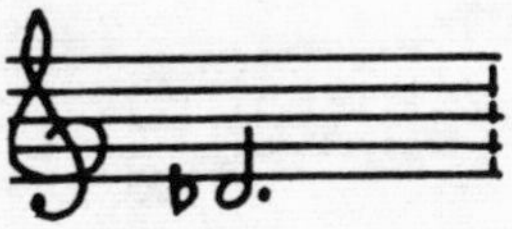

Repeat lines A and B of the *pallavi* and conclude the song either with *RI* (Db) or with *SA* (C)

(2) *Supradipa(m)*

Ascent: the note *GA* (E) is avoided.
Descent: *sampūrṇa*; one *vakra* feature is shown.

RĀGA SUPRADIPA (*Triputa-tāla*) SCM, 71

(3) *Vasanta*

This *rāga* employs the same scale degrees as *Vasanta* (15, 7). The difference between the two scales can be observed in the use of the note *DHA*, which is Ab in the 15. and A in the 17. *mēḷa*.

The following song fragment appears in SPC (III, 101). It is in *Ādi tāla*, and the composer's name is Singarachariar.

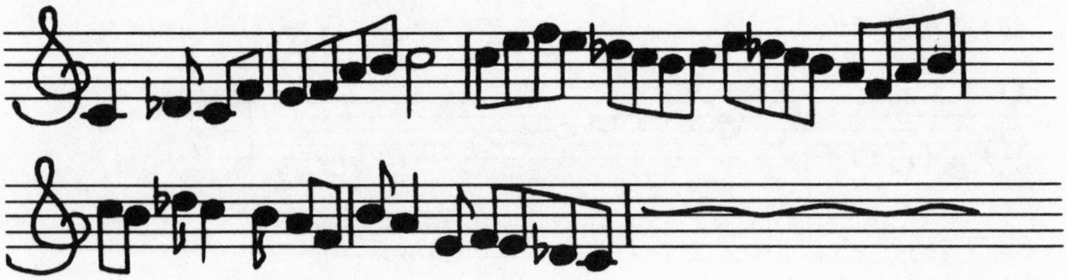

(4) *Alivardhani*

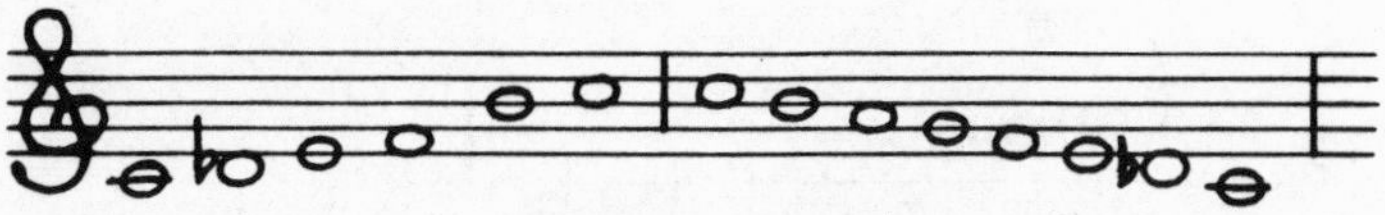

Ascent: the notes *PA* (G) and *DHA* (A) are avoided.
Descent: *krama sampūrṇa*.

(5) *Ananta*

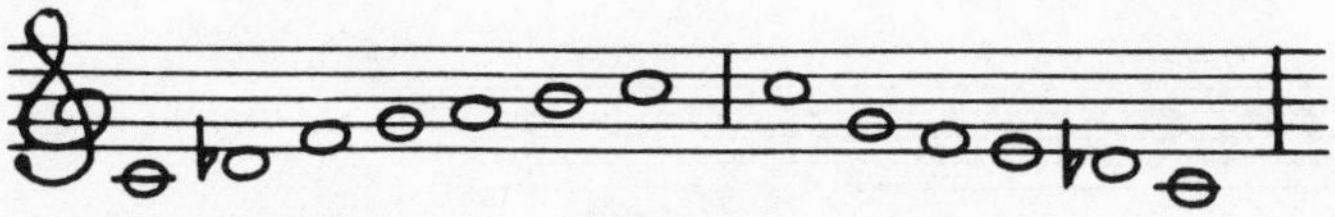

Ascent: the note *GA* (E) is avoided.
Descent: the notes *NI* (B) and *DHA* (A) are omitted.

(6) *Bhadraśrī*

The notes *MA* (F) and *PA* (G) are avoided entirely.

(7) *Champaka Māli*

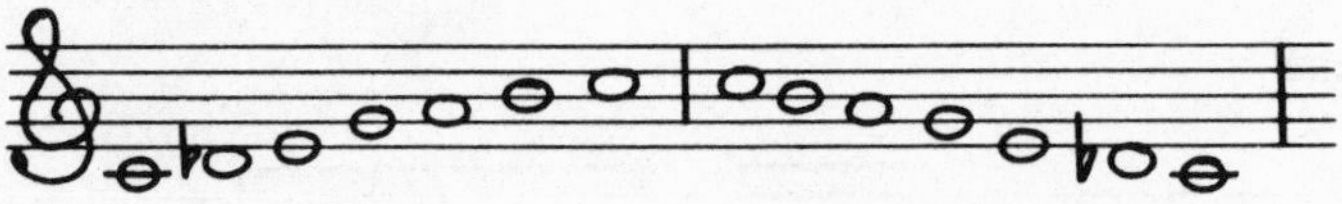

The note *MA* (F) is avoided entirely.

(8) *Chhāyāvati*

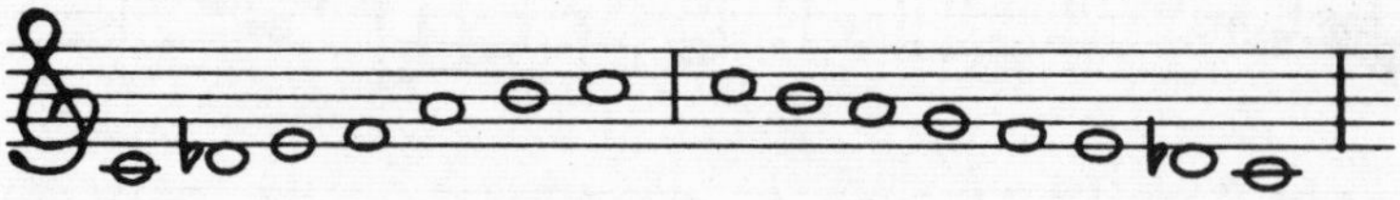

Ascent: the note *PA* (G) is avoided.
Descent: *krama sampūrṇa.*

(9) *Divya Taraṅgiṇī*

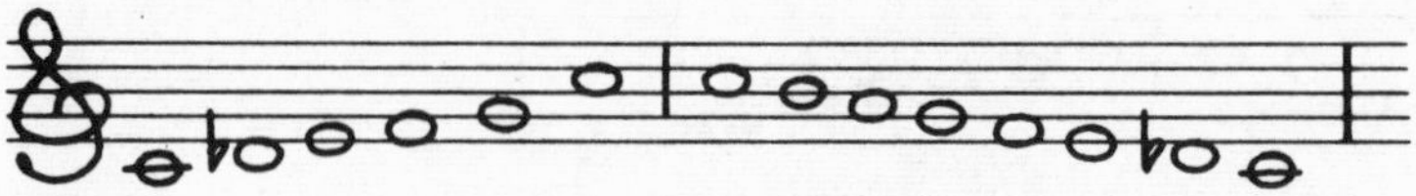

Ascent: the notes *DHA* (A) and *NI* (B) are avoided.
Descent: *krama sampūrṇa.*

(10) *Garjam*

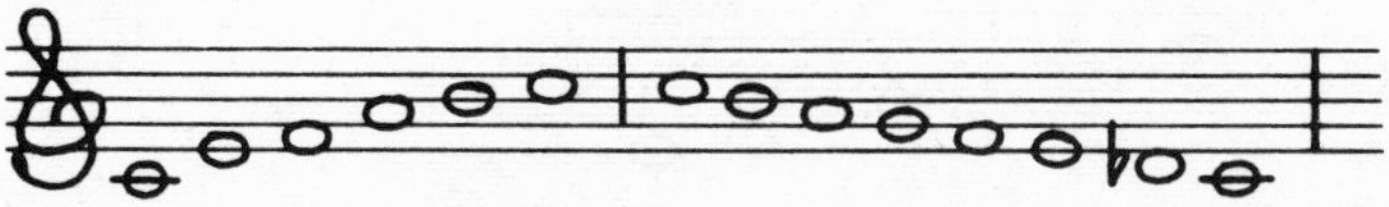

Ascent: the notes *RI* (Db) and *PA* (G) are avoided.
Descent: *krama sampūrṇa.*

(11) *Hayagati*

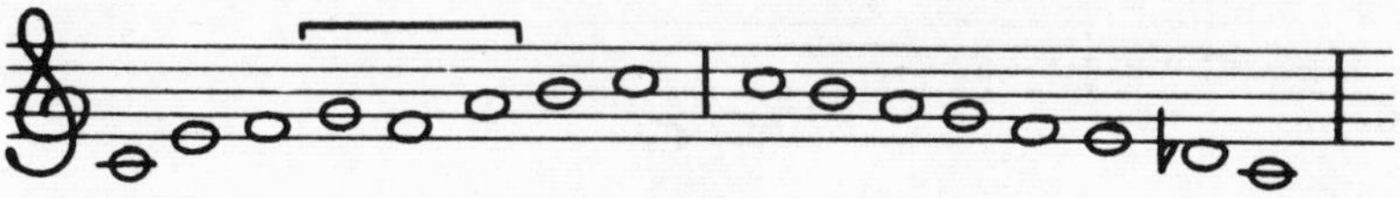

Ascent: the note *RI* (Db) is avoided; one *vakra* feature is shown.
Descent: *krama sampūrṇa.*

(12) *Jayābharaṇam*

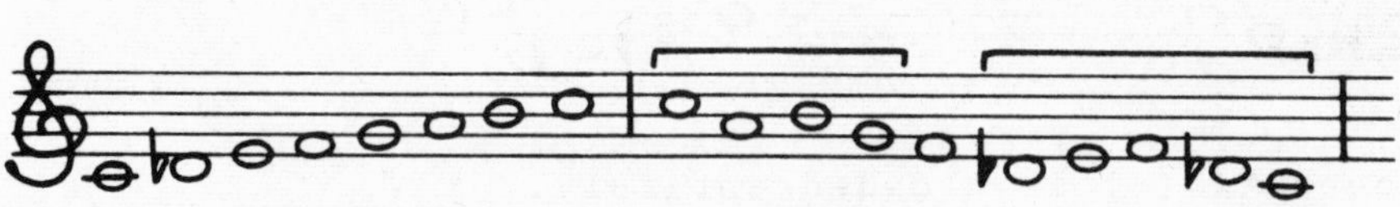

Ascent: *krama sampūrṇa.*
Descent: *sampūrṇa*; two extended *vakra* features are shown.

This *rāga* must not be mistaken for the *janya rāga Jayābharaṇi* ascribed to the 27. *mēḷa* (15).

(13) *Jindu*

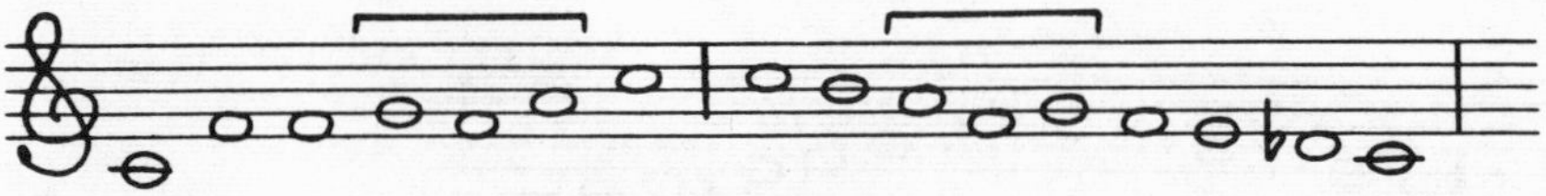

Ascent: the notes *RI* (Db), *GA* (E), and *NI* (B) are avoided. One *vakra* feature is shown.
Descent: *sampūrṇa*; one *vakra* feature is used.

(14) *Jivantika*

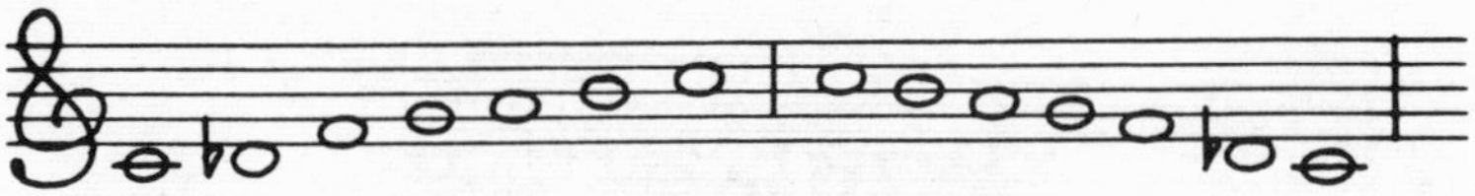

The note *GA* (E) is avoided entirely.

(15) *Kallōla Dhvani*

The scale of this *rāga* is *sampūrṇa* and shows in ascent two and in descent two *vakra* features.

(16) *Karṇāṭa Jōgi*

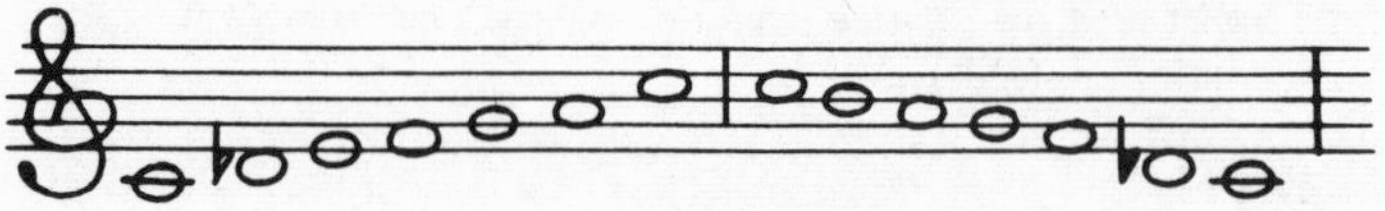

Ascent: the note *NI* (B) is avoided.
Descent: the note *GA* (E) is omitted.

(17) *Kēsāravaḷi*

Ascent: the note *GA* (E) is avoided.
Descent: the notes *NI* (B) and *MA* (F) are omitted.

(18) *Kriyā Virāmam*

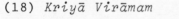

The scale of this *rāga* is *sampūrṇa* and shows in ascent two and in descent one *vakra* feature.

(19) *Kuntala Sāraṅga*

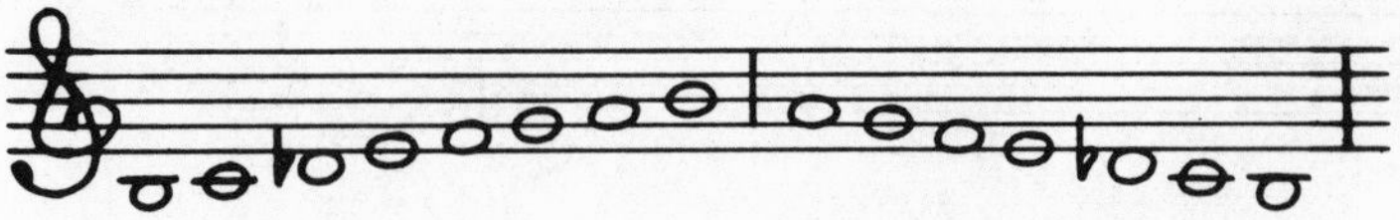

The scale of this *rāga* has *niṣādāntya* character. It is *sampūrṇa*.

(20) *Kusuma Mārutam*

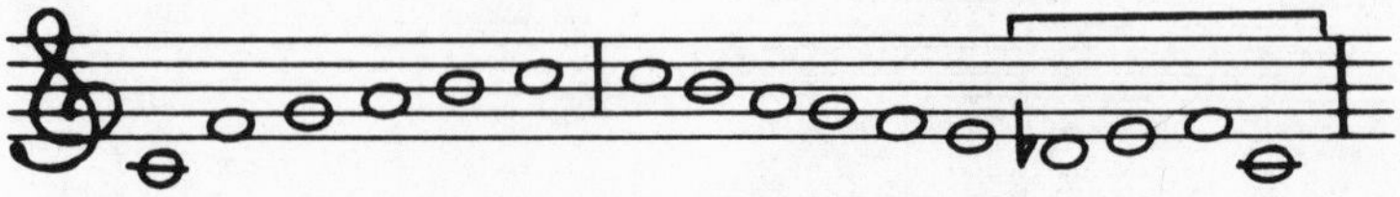

Ascent: the notes *RI* (Db) and *GA* (E) are avoided.
Descent: *sampūrṇa*; one *vakra* feature is shown.

(21) *Lalitā*

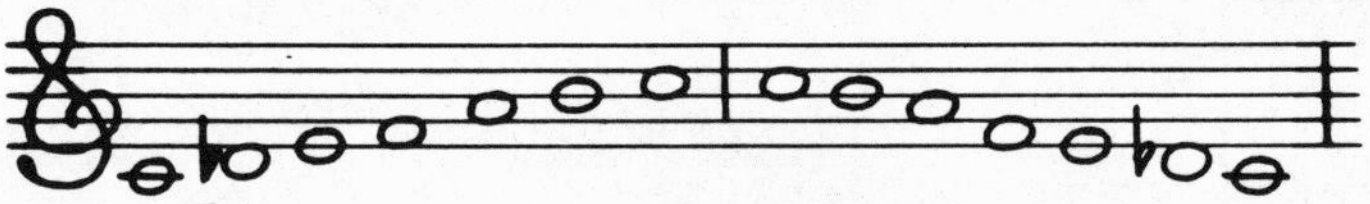

The note *PA* (G) is avoided entirely.

Another *rāga* with the same name appears under the heading of the 15. *mēḷa* (21).

(22) *Maṇḍalāgrapāṇi*

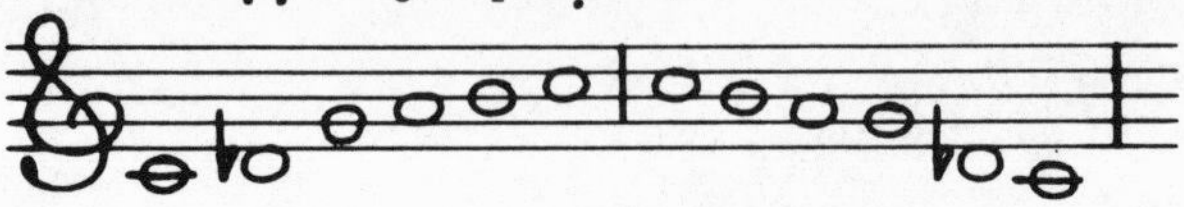

The notes *GA* (E) and *MA* (F) are avoided entirely.

(23) *Nāgachandrika* (*Nāgachudāman*)

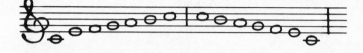

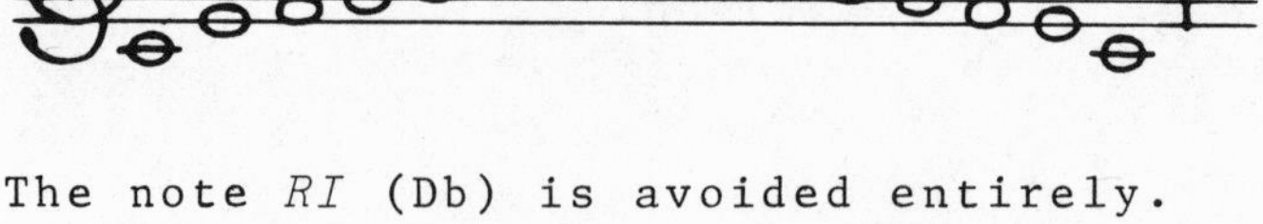

The note *RI* (Db) is avoided entirely.

(24) *Rāgachandrikā*

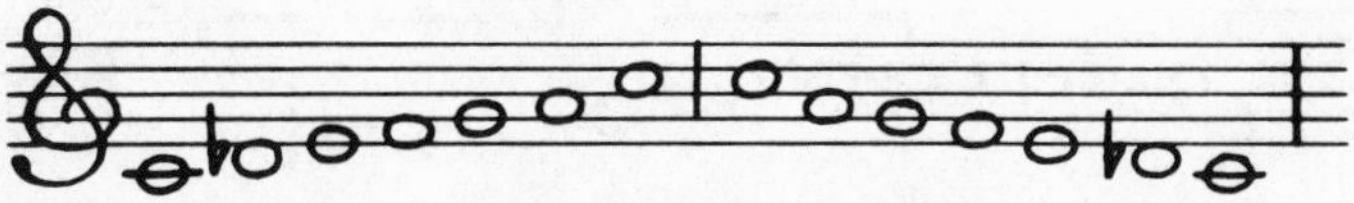

The note *NI* (B) is avoided entirely.

(25) *Sāmakannaḍa*

Ascent: *sampūrṇa*; one *vakra* feature is shown.
Descent: the notes *NI* (B) and *GA* (E) are avoided.

(26) *Sāmantamallār*

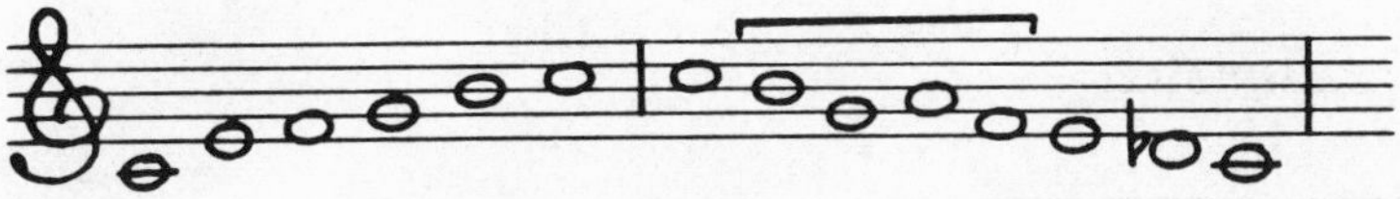

Ascent: the notes *RI* (Db) and *DHA* (A) are avoided.
Descent: *sampūrṇa*; one *vakra* feature is shown.

(27) *Sēnāmani*

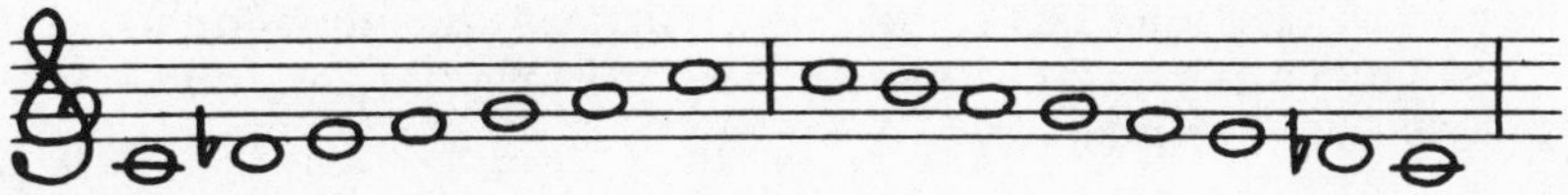

Ascent: the note *NI* (B) is avoided.
Descent: *krama sampūrṇa*.

(28) *Śuddhalalitā*

Rāga Śuddhalalitā is identical with *rāga Lalitā* (17, 21). Under the name of *Śuddhalalitā* the *rāga Lalitā* experienced a revival, inspired greatly by the work of Muthiah Bhagavathar (1877-1945; see note 1 to the 2. *mēḷa*).

(29) *Sōmataraṅgiṇī*

Ascent: the note *RI* (Db) is avoided; one *vakra* feature is shown.
Descent: *sampūrṇa*; two *vakra* features are used.

(30) *Timiratāriṇi*

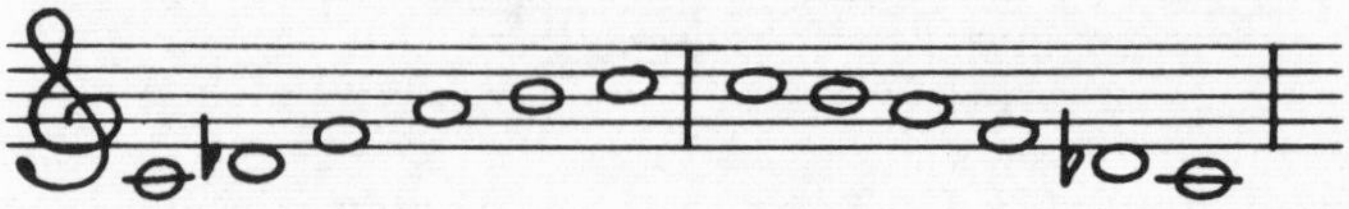

The notes *GA* (E) and *PA* (G) are avoided entirely.

18. *MĒḶA HĀṬAKĀMBARĪ*

Hāṭakāmbarī can be performed at any time. Stressed notes are *RI* (Db), *MA* (F), and *NI* (B).

Veṅkaṭamakhin calls this *rāga Jayaśuddhamāḷavi*.

The following song example is a *kīrtana* in *ādi tāla*. It has no *anupallavi*.

HĀṬAKĀMBARĪ (*Ādi-tāla*)

Pallavi

Repeat the first line of the *pallavi*

Charana

Repeat the entire *pallavi* and conclude the song with the note *SA* (C).

Janya Rāgas of the 18. Mēḷa

(1) *Śuddha Māḷavi*

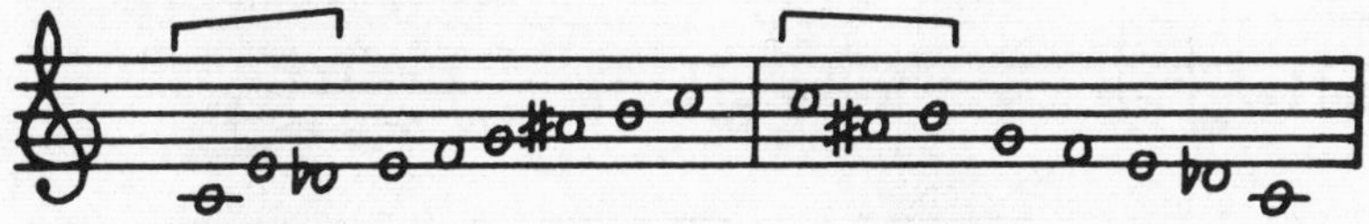

The scale of this *rāga* is *sampūrṇa* and shows two *vakra* features, one in ascent and one in descent.

RĀGA ŚUDDHA MĀḶAVI (*Triputa-tāla*) SCM, 73

(2) *Sinhela (Siṃhela)*

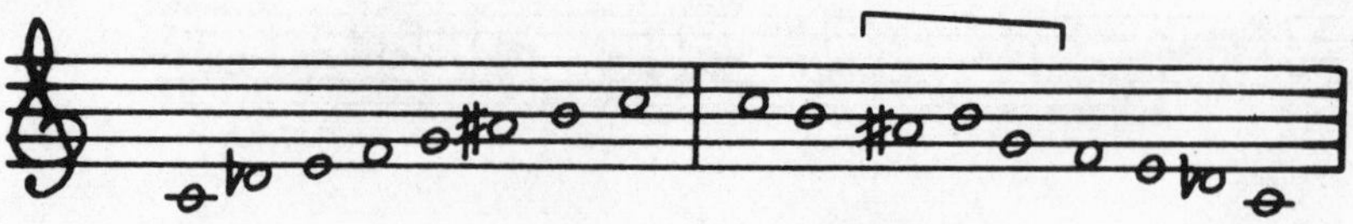

Ascent: *krama sampūrṇa.*
Descent: *sampūrṇa*; one *vakra* feature is shown.

RĀGA SINHELA (Triputa-tāla) SCM, 74

(3) *Kallōla(m)*

The note *RI* (Db) is avoided entirely. The ascent can be performed in two ways:
(a) avoiding *RI* (Db), *GA* (E), and *MA* (F),
(b) avoiding only *RI* (Db).
The descent shows one *vakra* feature.

Melodies in this *rāga* usually begin with the note *SA* (c) of the *tāra saptaka* (upper octave region).

RĀGA KALLŌLA (Triputa-tāla) SCM, 75

(4) *Bhanu Chūḍāmaṇī (Bhanu Cūḍāmaṇī)*

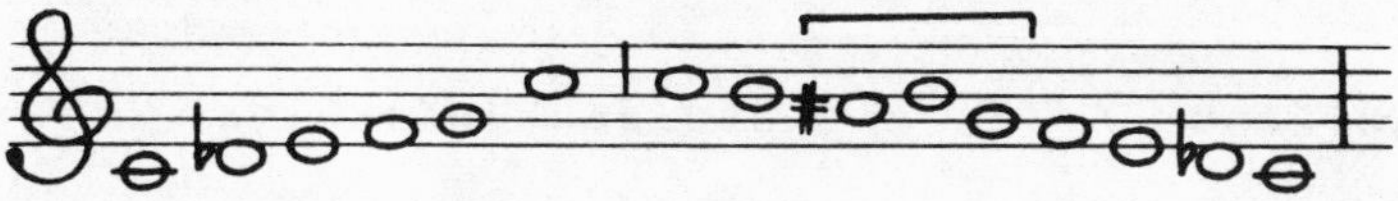

Ascent: the notes *DHA* (A#) and *NI* (B) are avoided.
Descent: *sampūrṇa*; one *vakra* feature is shown.

(5) *Bhūpāḷa Taraṅgiṇi*

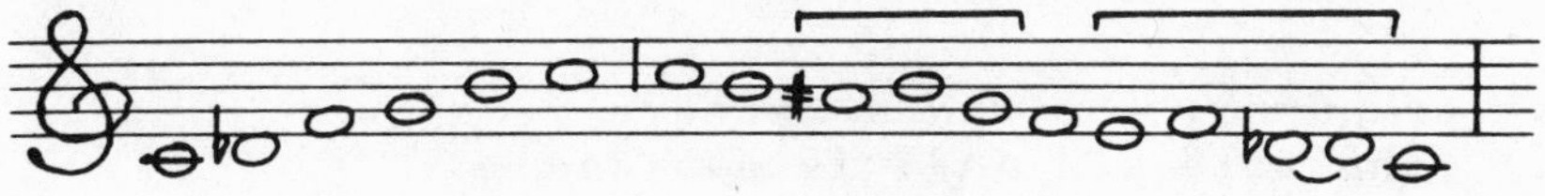

Ascent: the notes *GA* (E) and *DHA* (A#) are avoided.
Descent: *sampūrṇa*; two *vakra* features are shown.

(6) *Chandra Chūḍapriya*

Ascent: the note *RI* (Db) is avoided. One *vakra* feature is shown.
Descent: the notes *DHA* (A#) and *GA* (E) are omitted.

(7) *Chandrikā*

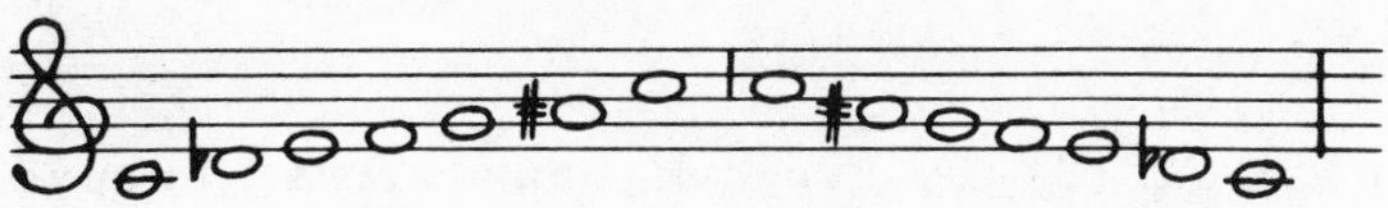

The note *NI* (B) is avoided entirely.

Another *rāga* with the same name appears under the heading of the 21. *mēḷa* (7).

(8) *Divya Gāndhāram*

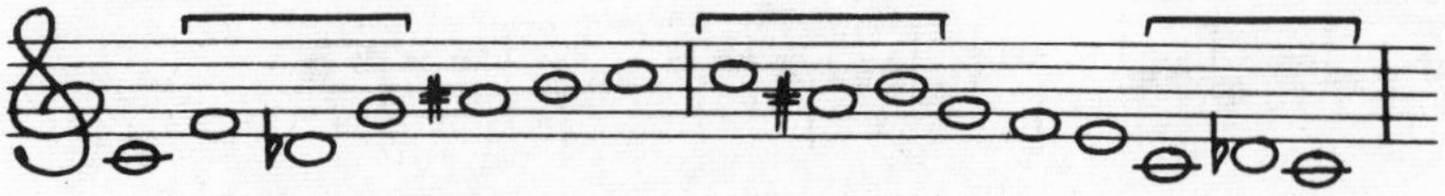

Ascent: the note *GA* (E) is avoided; one *vakra* feature is shown.
Descent: *sampūrṇa*; two *vakra* features are used.

(9) *Druhiṇa Priya*

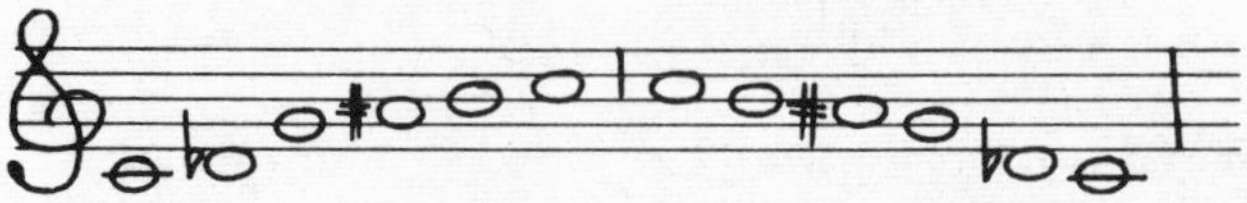

The notes *GA* (E) and *MA* (F) are avoided entirely.

(10) *Hitabhāsini*

Ascent: *sampūrṇa*; one *vakra* feature is shown.
Descent: the note *DHA* (A#) is avoided.

(11) *Javanika*

The note *MA* (F) is avoided entirely.

(12) *Kandarapriya*

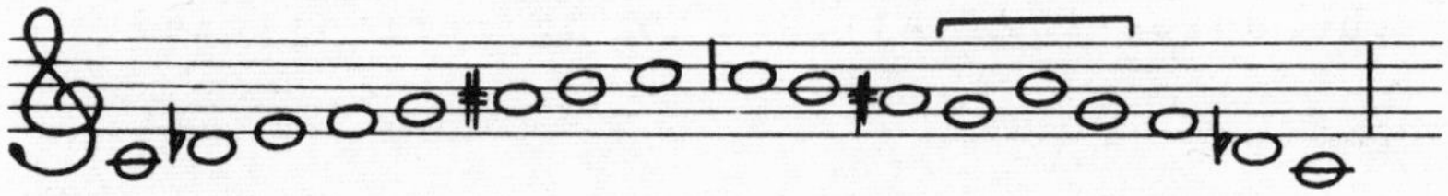

Ascent: *krama sampūrṇa*.
Descent: the note *GA* (E) is avoided; one *vakra* feature is shown.

(13) *Nakshatramāla* (*Nakṣatramāla*)

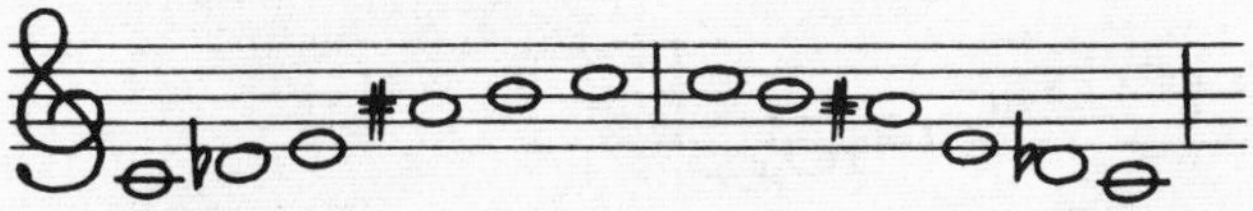

The notes *MA* (F) and *PA* (G) are avoided entirely.

(14) *Nāgatarañjiṇi*

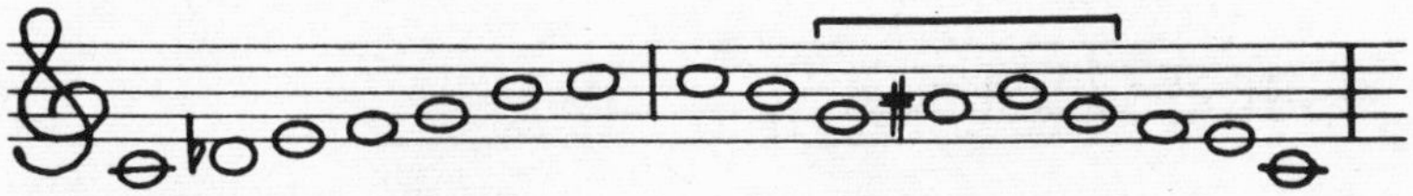

Ascent: the note *DHA* (A#) is avoided.
Descent: the note *RI* (Db) is omitted; one *vakra* feature is shown.

(15) *Nārāsam*

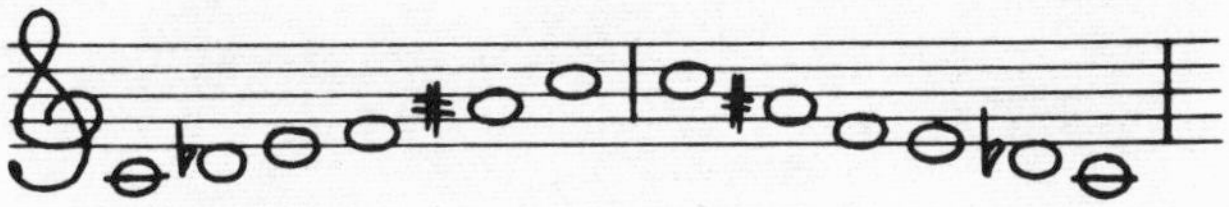

The notes *PA* (G) and *NI* (B) are avoided entirely.

(16) *Pinākiṇi*

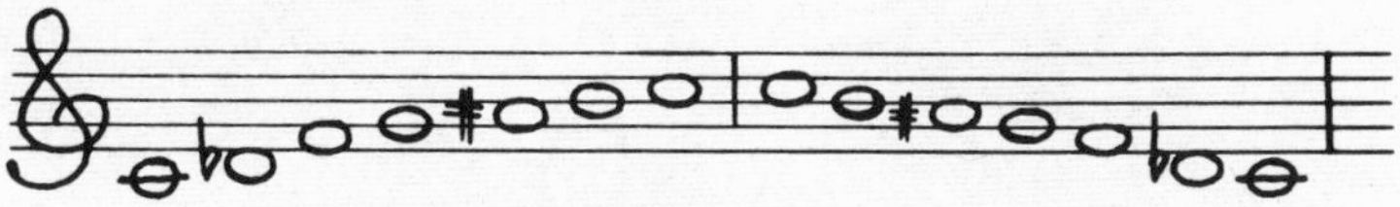

The note *GA* (E) is avoided entirely.

(17) *Śuddhakannaḍa*

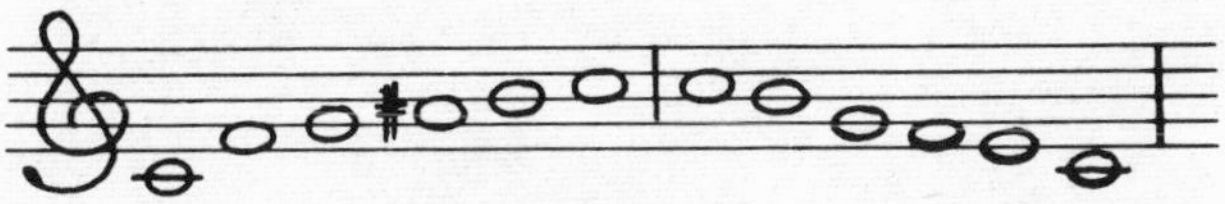

The note *RI* (Db) is avoided entirely. In ascent *GA* (E) is omitted and in descent *DHA* (A#).

(18) *Triyāma*

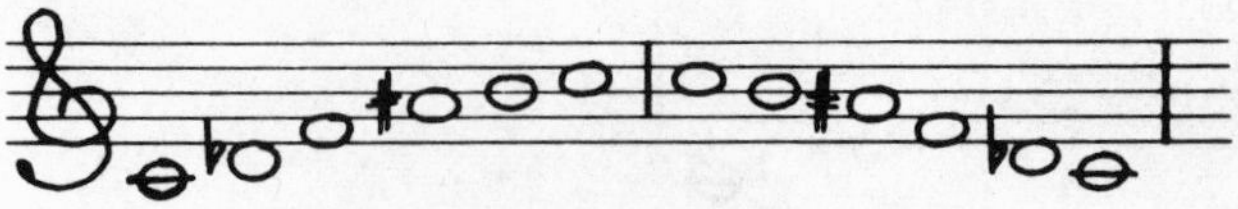

The notes *GA* (E) and *PA* (G) are avoided entirely.

(19) *Varṇarūpiṇi*

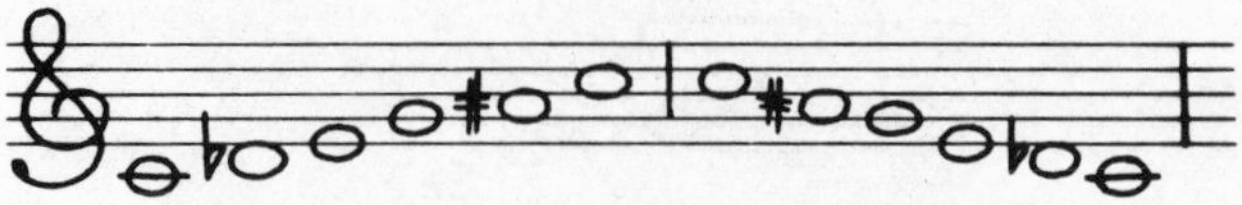

The notes *MA* (F) and *NI* (B) are avoided entirely.

Chakra IV

19. *MĒḶA JHAṄKĀRADHVANI*

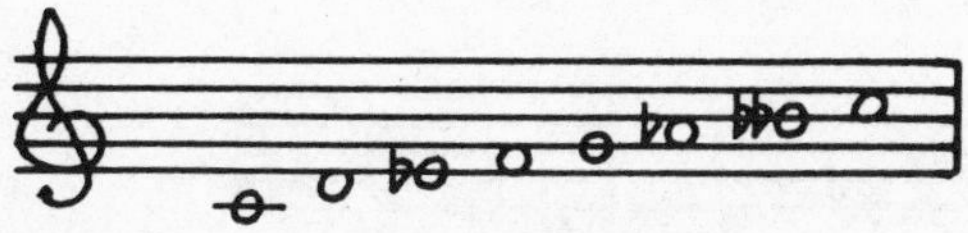

This *rāga* can be performed at any time. Its stressed notes are *GA* (Eb), *MA* (F), and *NI* (Bbb).

Veṅkaṭamakhin called this *rāga Jhaṅkārabhramarī*, in which the note *NI* (Bbb) was to be avoided in ascent.

The following song examples is a *kīrtana* by Tyāgarāja:

JHAṄKĀRADHVANI (*Ādi-tāla*)

Pallavi

Repeat the entire *pallavi*

Anupallavi

Repeat the entire *pallavi*

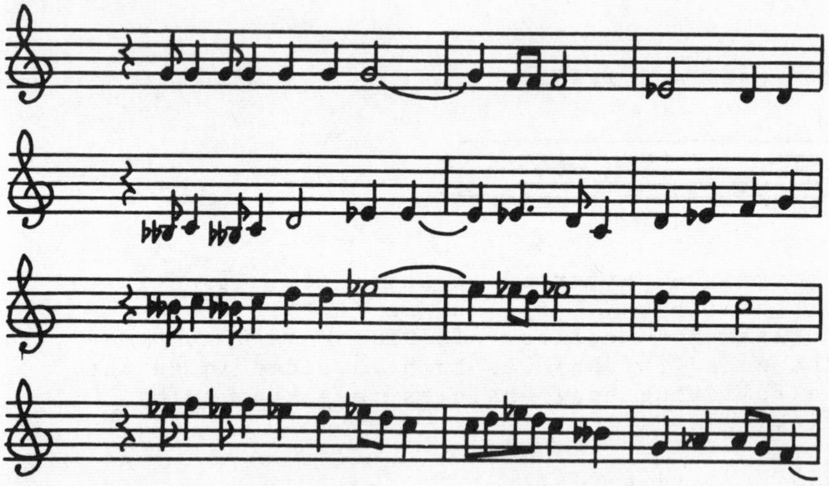

Repeat the entire *pallavi*. The song may end either with *MA* (F) or with *PA* (G).

Janya Rāgas of the 19. Mēḷa

(1) *Jhaṅkārabhramarī*

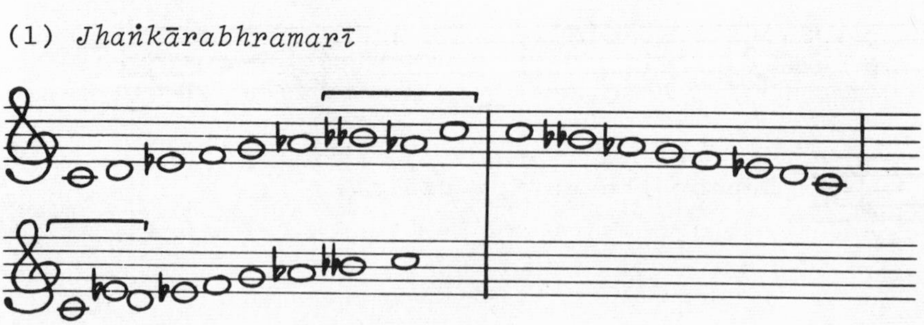

The scale of this *rāga* is *sampūrṇa*. There are two possible forms of ascent, each one showing one *vakra* feature.

RĀGA JHAṄKĀRABHRAMARĪ (*Triputa-tāla*) SCM, 77

(2) *Pūrṇalalita*

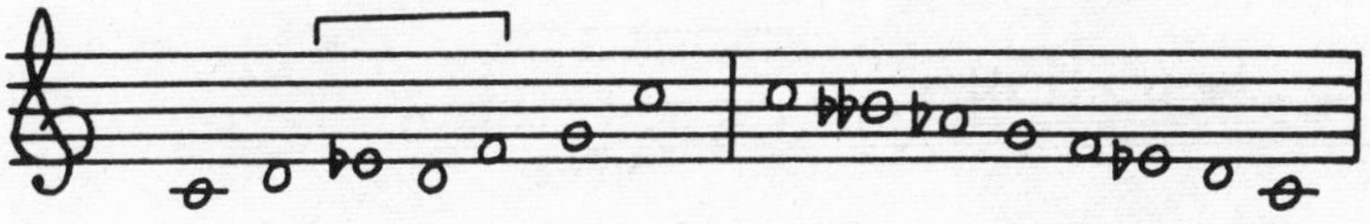

Ascent: the notes *DHA* (Ab) and *NI* (Bbb) are avoided; one *vakra* feature is shown.
Descent: *krama sampūrṇa*.

RĀGA PŪRṆALALITA (*Triputa-tāla*) SCM, 77

(3) *Amrita Taraṅgiṇī* (*Amrita Rañjaṇī*)

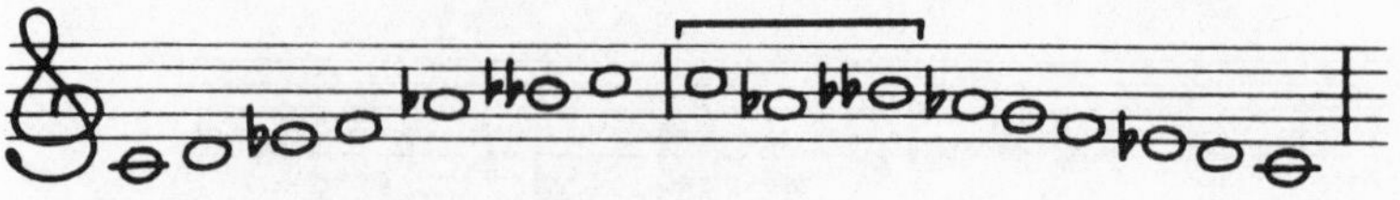

Ascent: the note *PA* (G) is avoided.
Descent: *sampūrṇa*; one *vakra* feature is shown.

(4) *Bhramara*

The note *PA* (G) is avoided entirely.

(5) *Champaka Latā*

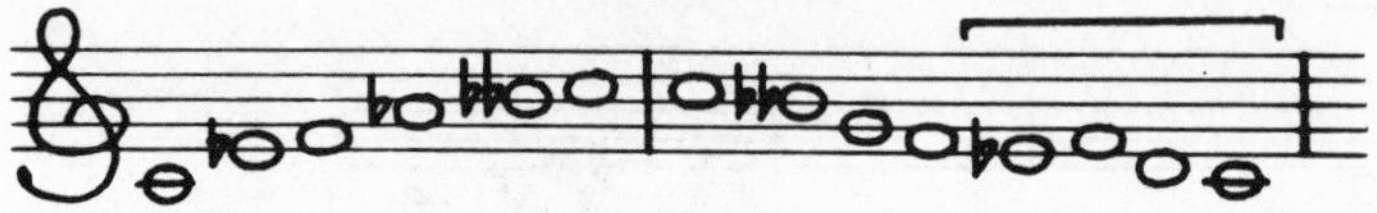

Ascent: the notes *RI* (D) and *PA* (G) are avoided.
Descent: the note *DHA* (Ab) is omitted; one *vakra* feature is shown.

(6) *Chhāyā Sindhu*

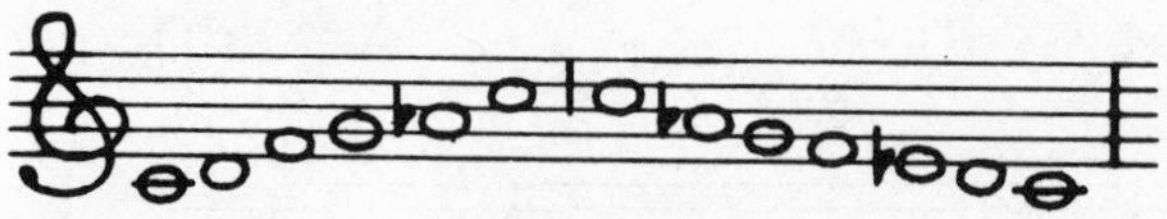

The note *NI* (Bbb) is avoided entirely. *GA* (Eb) is omitted in ascent.

(7) *Dēśya Bēgaḍa*

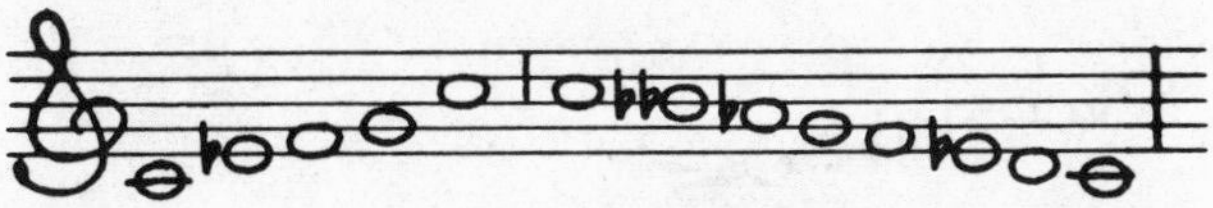

Ascent: the notes *RI* (D), *DHA* (Ab), and *NI* (Bbb) are avoided.
Descent: *krama sampūrṇa*.

(8) *Dēśya Byāgaḍa*

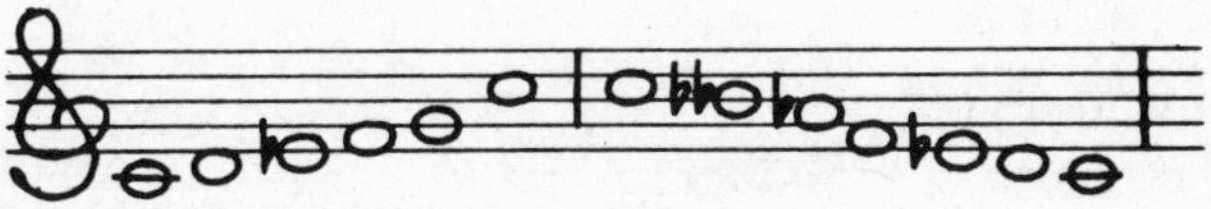

Although the names *Dēśya Bēgaḍa* (19,7) and *Dēśya Byāgaḍa* are almost identical, the examination of the two scales shows a distinct difference between the two *rāgas*. The scale of *Dēśya Byāgaḍa* avoids the notes *DHA* (Ab) and *NI* (Bbb) in ascent, and *PA* (G) in descent.

(9) *Dhūsaravarṇi*

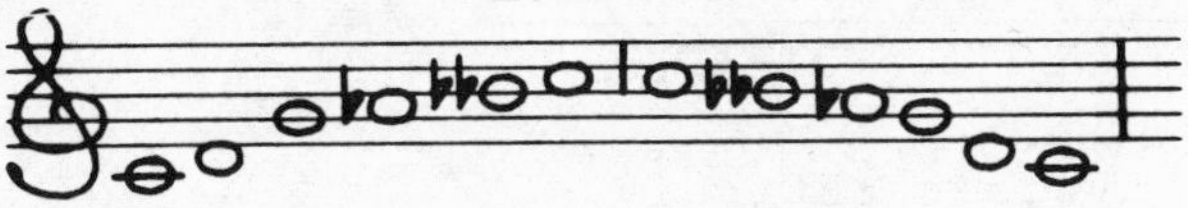

The notes *GA* (Eb) and *MA* (F) are avoided entirely.

(10) *Gānapriya*

The notes *PA* (G) and *NI* (Bbb) are avoided entirely.

(11) *Haimavati*

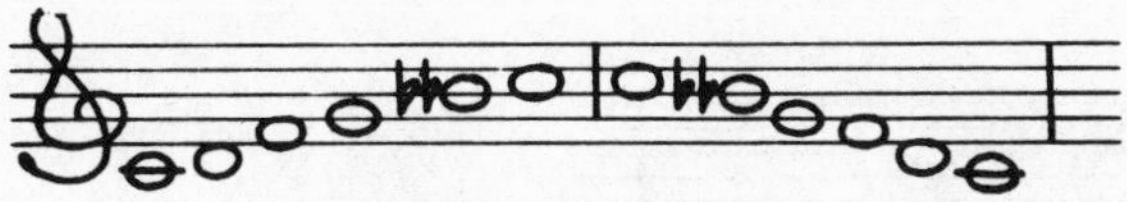

The notes *GA* (Eb) and *DHA* (Ab) are avoided entirely.

(12) *Jhaṅkāri*

The note *NI* (Bbb) is avoided entirely.

SD (II, 260) states that another *rāga Jhaṅkāri* appears under the heading of the 20. *mēḷa*. This is an error: the *rāga* referred to is *Jhaṅkāravāṇi* (20, 64).

(13) *Kādambiṇi*

The note *MA* (F) is avoided entirely.

Another *rāga* with the same name appears under the heading of the 16. *mēḷa* (25).

(14) *Kāñchanāṅgi* (*Kāñcanāṅgi*)

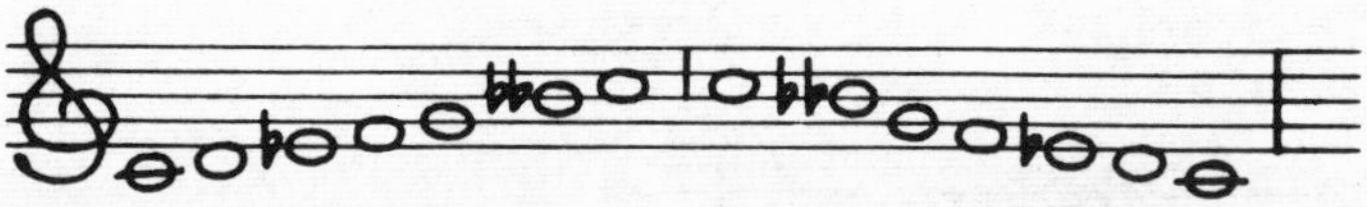

The note *DHA* (Ab) is avoided entirely.

Another *rāga* with the same name appears under the heading of the 55. *mēḷa* (11).

(15) *Kusumajā*

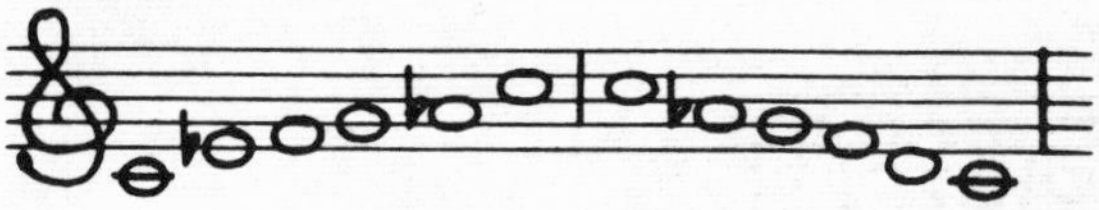

The note *NI* (Bbb) is avoided entirely. *RI* (D) is omitted in ascent and *GA* (Eb) in descent.

(16) *Pūrvasālavi*

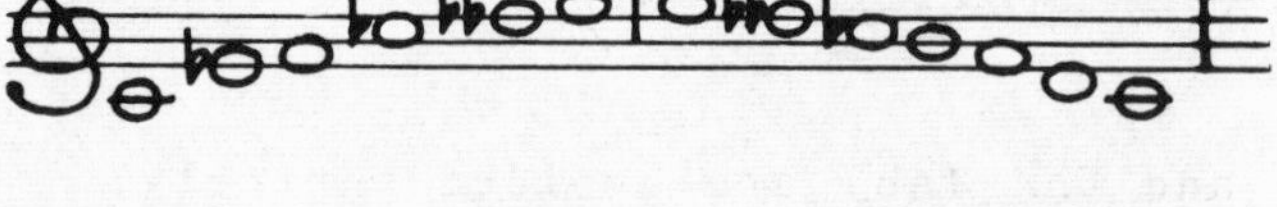

Ascent: the notes *RI* (D) and *PA* (G) are avoided.
Descent: the note *GA* (Eb) is omitted.

(17) *Sindhusālavi*

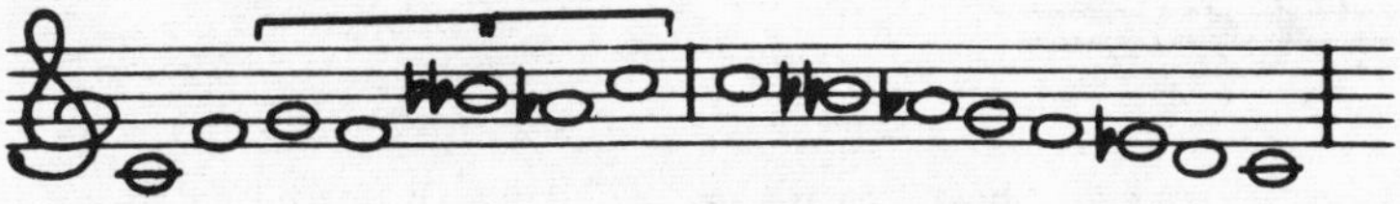

Ascent: the notes *RI* (D) and *GA* (Eb) are avoided. Two *vakra* features are shown.
Descent: *krama sampūrṇa*.

(18) *Tiraskaraṇi*

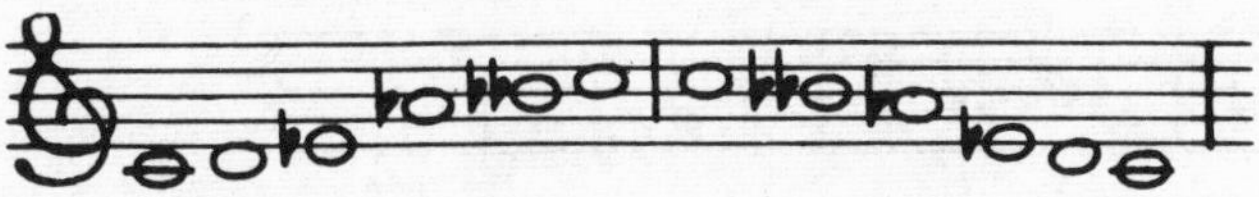

The notes *MA* (F) and *PA* (G) are avoided entirely.

(19) *Tripādaka*

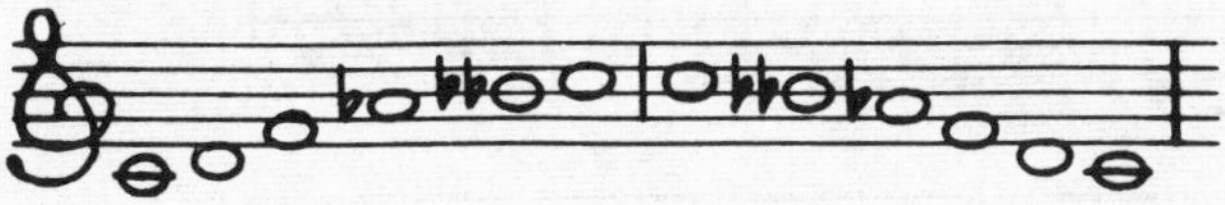

The notes *GA* (Eb) and *PA* (G) are avoided entirely.

20. *MĒḶA NAṬABHAIRAVĪ (NARABHAIRAVĪ)*

Rāga Naṭabhairavī may be performed at any time. At present it is rarely used in its pure form. Instead one can hear its *janya rāga Bhairavī* (20,1), which differs from the primary *rāga* in the use of the note *DHA* (A natural instead of Ab).

Veṅkaṭamakhin calls this *rāga Narirītigauḷa*, in which he forbids the use of the note *DHA* (Ab) in ascent.

The stressed notes of *Naṭabhairavī* are *RI* (D), *GA* (Eb), *MA* (F), and *NI* (Bb). In the comparatively rare performances of this *rāga*, musicians have the habit of repeating each note twice within brief ascending passages in the following manner:

Among several passages that appear to be characteristic of *rāga Naṭabhairavī* are:

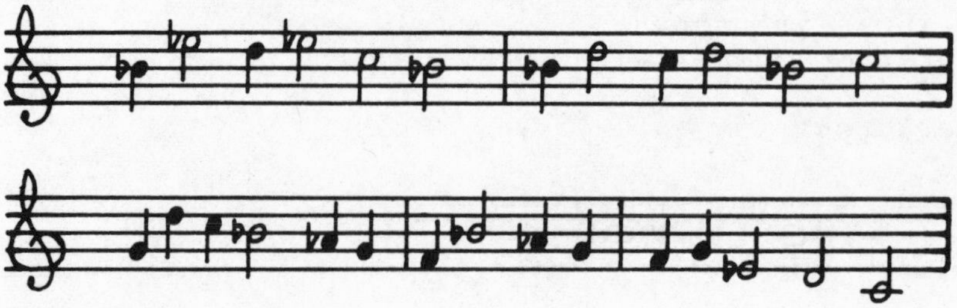

NAṬABHAIRAVĪ (*Triputa-tāla*) SCM, 78

Janya Rāgas of the 20. Mēḷa

(1) *Bhairavī*

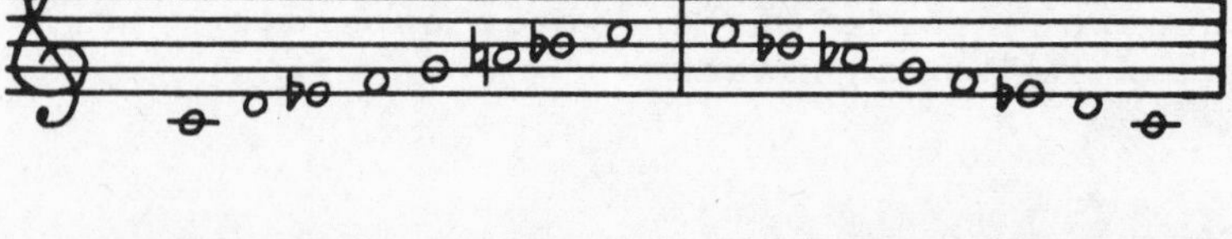

Bhairavī is much more frequently performed than its primary *rāga*, *Naṭabhairavī*. Its scale is *krama sampūrṇa* in ascent and descent. Its sixth scale degree, Ab according to the material of the 20. *mēḷa*, is often intoned high (described by the theorists as *catuḥśruti* or *pañcśruti DHA*, which comes very close to the western A natural). In descent the note *DHA* always shows its dependence on *Naṭabhairavi* and remains Ab. This *anya svara* ("foreign note") in ascent represents the noticeable difference from *Naṭabhairavī* (where *DHA* stays Ab in ascent and descent) and appears in passages such as:

although there are occasions when the performer, not bound by a strict rule, prefers the use of Ab in ascent.

Bhairavī can be performed at all times. Stressed notes of this *rāga* are the same as those of the primary *rāga*. The following example is a *varna*, a didactic song specimen which shows some characteristic features of the *rāga*. I have transcribed the metrical units of *Āta tāla* (*khaṇḍa jāti*) of this piece with half notes in order to show a clear picture of the many fast-moving passages.

BHAIRAVĪ RĀGA (*Āta-tāla*)

Pallavi

Repeat the section between A and B of the *pallavi*

Anupallavi

Repeat the section between A and B of the *pallavi*

Charana

only if the *charana*
is repeated

Repeat ad. lib. the section between
C and D of the *charana*

only if the *charana*
is repeated

Repeat ad. lib. the section between
C and D

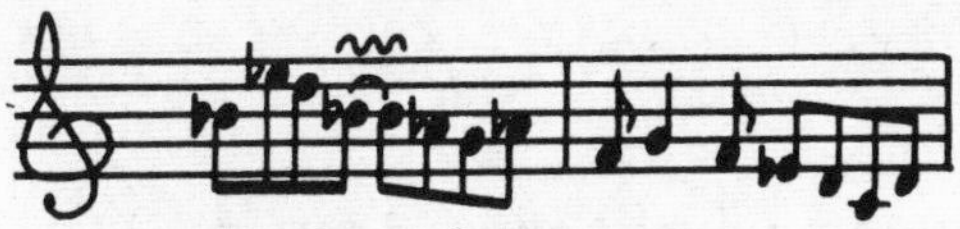

only if the *charana*
is repeated

Repeat ad. lib. the section between
C and D

Repeat the section between C and FINE

The following *Bhairavī* passages were taken from a *Gīta Govinda* performance in Kerala (recorded by Wayne Howard in 1972):

The two following examples show another version of *Bhairavī* in which the note *PA* (G) is avoided entirely. The scale example shows also a frequently used *vakra* feature in ascent.

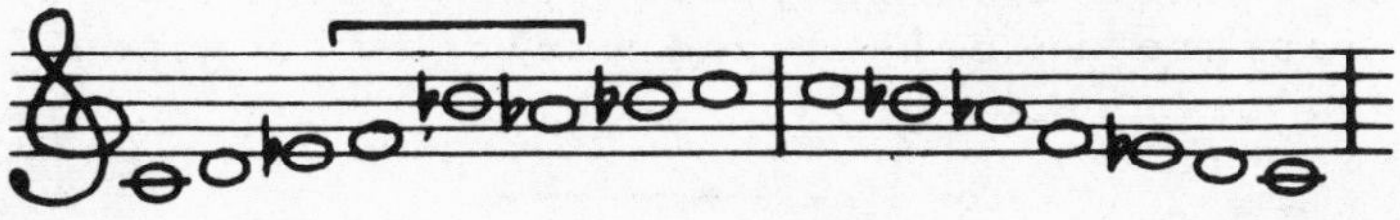

RĀGA BHAIRAVĪ (*Triputa-tāla*) SCM, 79

(2) *Rītigauḷa*

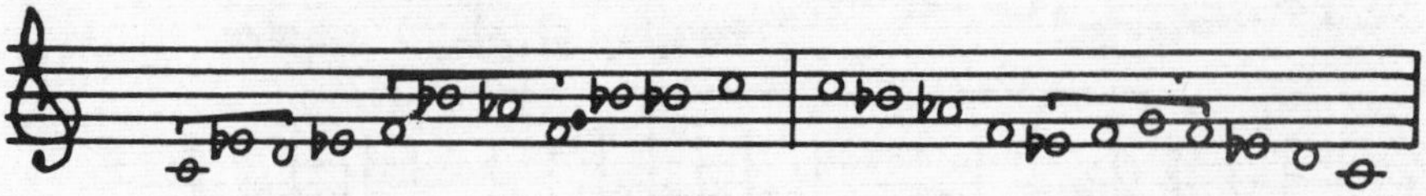

The scale is *sampūrṇa* and shows two *vakra* features in ascent and one in descent. The note *PA* (G) is avoided almost entirely, but may appear in the following and similar descending passages:

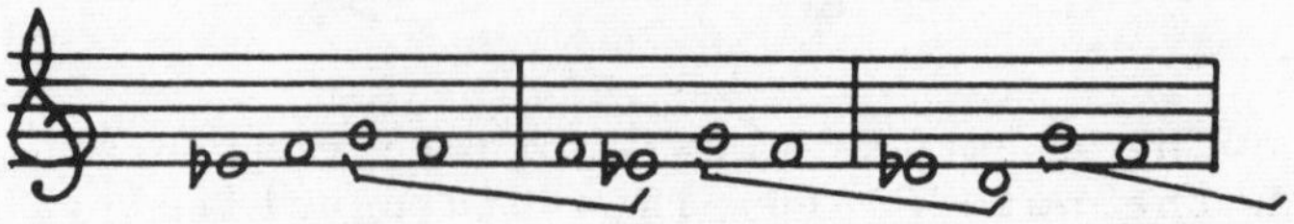

Rītigauḷa, to be performed in the evening, is subject to several interpretations. The following version shows only one *vakra* feature in ascent and employs the note *PA* (G) in the ascending line:

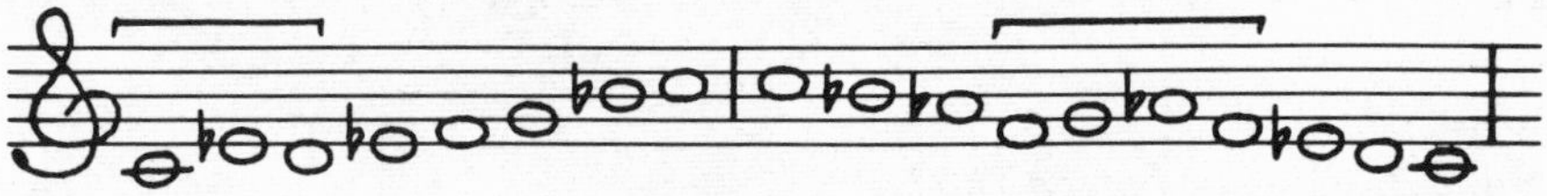

In this version of *Rītigauḷa* the note *DHA* (Ab) is avoided in ascent. The descent is similar to that of the first version. Stressed notes are to be *GA* (Eb), *MA* (F), and *NI* (Bb).

There are musicians who insist that the note *PA* (G) be avoided in ascent. In some districts, particularly in Kerala, the note *DHA* is intoned so high that the sound of A natural is achieved. This shows the reason why this *rāga* is ascribed occasionally to the 22. *mēḷa*.

The following song example is a *kīrtana*. Each rhythmic unit has been transcribed with an eighth note. The song is in *chapu tāla* (3+4) and has no *anupallavi*. The textual lines are sung to the repeated *pallavi*, thus producing a distinctly strophic character.

RĪTIGAULA RĀGA (*Chapu-tāla*)

Pallavi

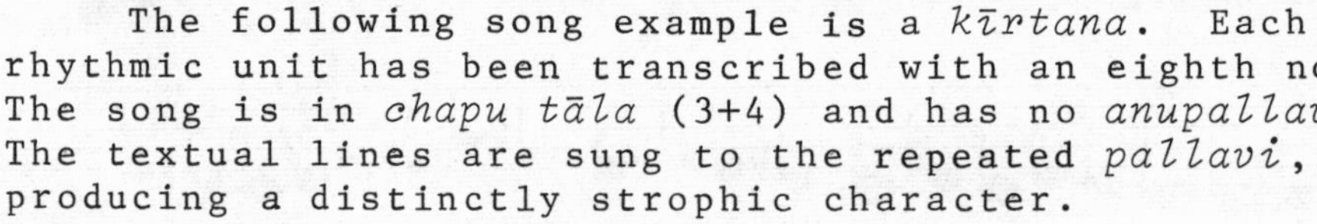

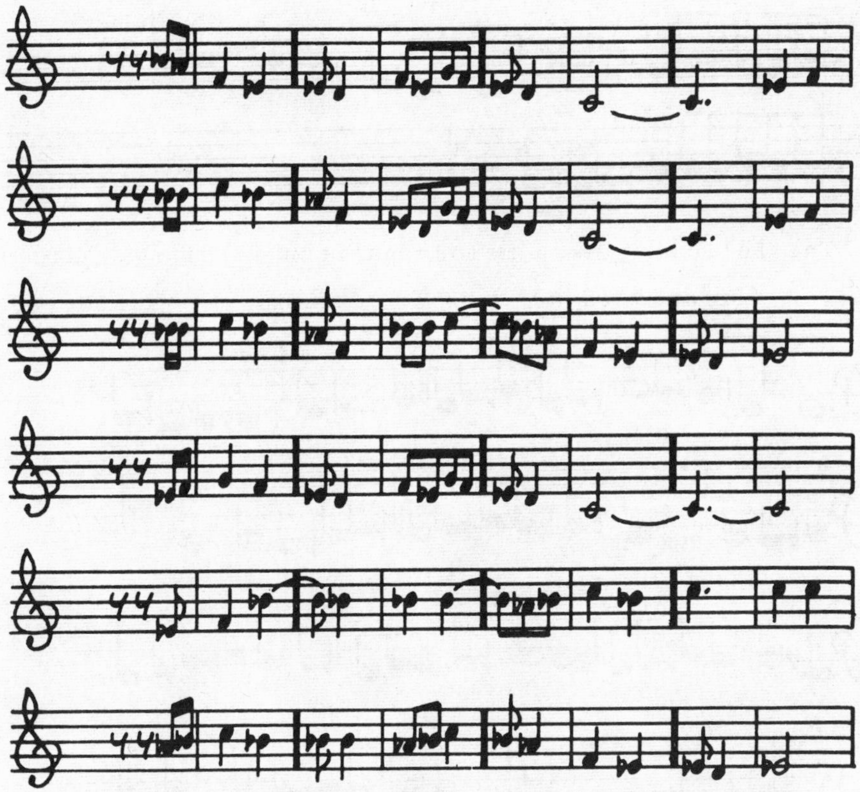

The following *Rītigauḷa* passages taken from a Śyāma Śāstrī performance, recorded by Wayne Howard in 1972, interpret the note *DHA*, in the few instances when it appears, as A natural and ignore the traditional *vakra* features:

The following is a melody pattern in *Rītigauḷa*:

RĪTIGAUḶA (*Triputa-tāla*) SCM, 80

The first song example in *Rītigauḷa* (*kīrtana* in *chapu tāla*) shows the use of the note *ṖA* (G) in descent:

The last melody pattern (SCM) shown above uses *PA* (G) also in ascent:

(3) *Saraṅgakāpi*

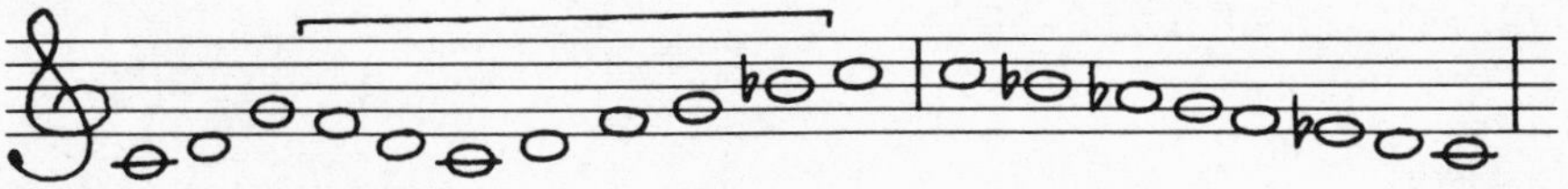

Ascent: the notes *GA* (Eb) and *DHA* (Ab) are avoided. One large *vakra* feature is shown.
Descent: *krama sampūrṇa*.

A second version of this *rāga* is shown below as 20, 22.

SARAṄGAKĀPI RĀGA (20,3) (*Triputa-tāla*) SCM, 95

(4) *Śuddhadēśi*

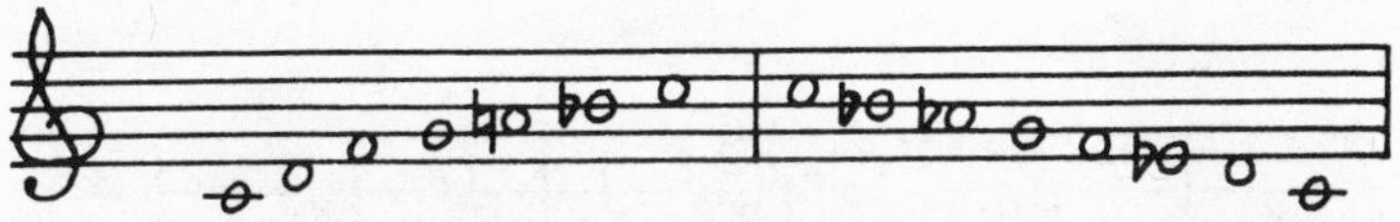

This *rāga* can be performed at any time. Its scale avoids the note *GA* (Eb) in ascent. The descent is *krama sampūrṇa*. The note *DHA* generally becomes A natural in ascent. In some instances this note is described as a *triśruti DHA* [*three-śruti DHA*] which would indicate a pitch slightly lower than A and a little higher than Ab. This note is always executed with a slight vibrato. In descent, however, *DHA* appears in its *śuddha form* (Ab). There are, as to be expected, some musicians who insist on employing a slightly sharp *DHA* (A or $\overset{+}{\text{A}}$b) also in descent.

Veṅkaṭamakhin's presentation of the following (*sampūrṇa*) descent of this *rāga* would read in western staff notation approximately:

The following example represents a *kīrtana*:

ŚUDDHADĒŚI RĀGA (Ādi-tāla)

Pallavi

A

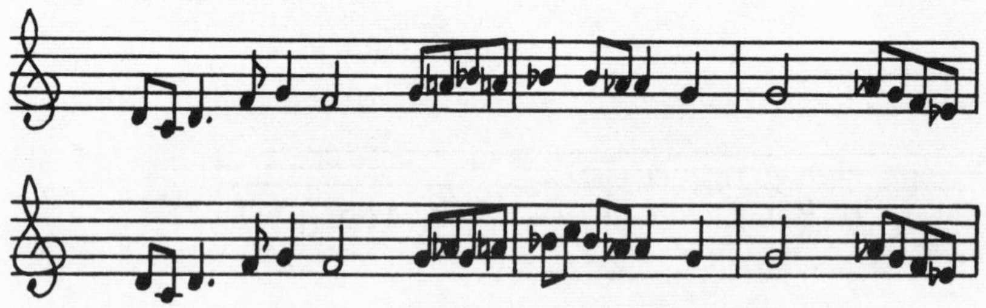

B

Repeat lines A and B of the *pallavi*

Anupallavi

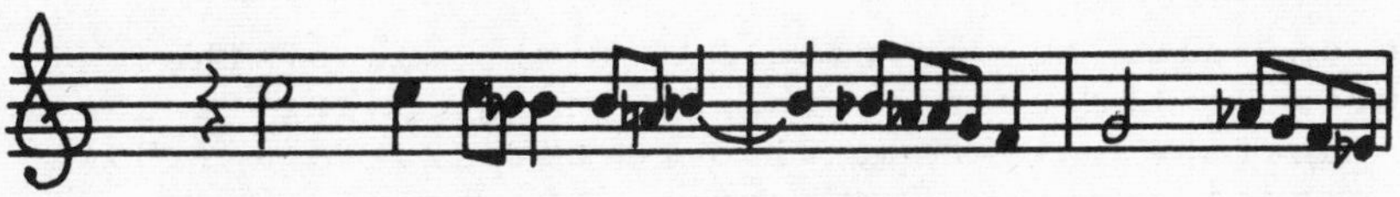

Repeat lines A and B of the *pallavi*

Charana

Repeat lines A and B of the *pallavi* and conclude the song with *RI-SA* (D-C)

(5) *Pūrṇaṣaḍja*

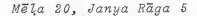

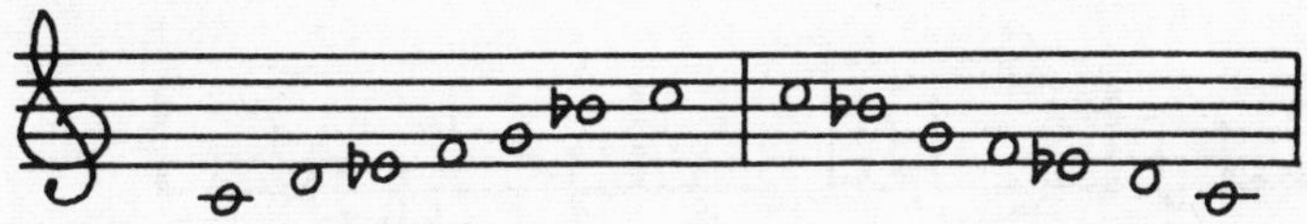

The note *DHA* (Ab) is avoided entirely. Stressed notes in this *rāga* are *GA* (Eb), *MA* (F), and *NI* (Bb).

The omission of the note *DHA* (Ab), one of the characteristic features of the 20. *mēḷa*, makes it possible to ascribe this *rāga* also to the 22. *mēḷa* (109). The difference between *Pūrṇaṣaḍja* (20, 5) and *Pūrṇaṣaḍja* (22, 109) can be observed in the note *PA* (G): in the former *rāga* it is used, in the latter it is avoided in ascent.

The following song specimen is a *kīrtana*:

PŪRṆAṢAḌJA (*Rūpaka-tāla*)

Pallavi

Anupallavi

Repeat the entire *pallavi*

Charana

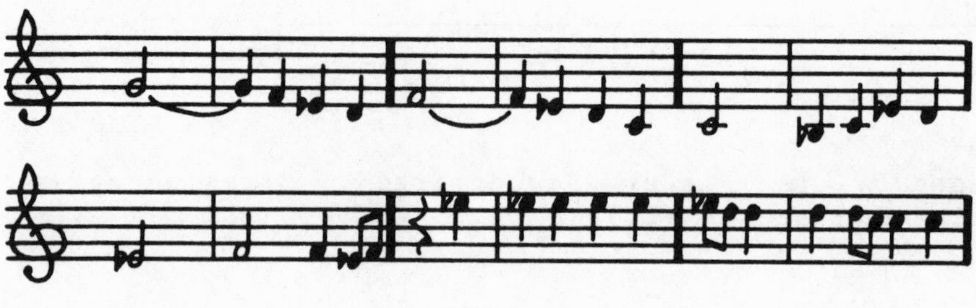

Repeat the entire *pallavi*

Another form of *Pūrṇaṣaḍja* can be:

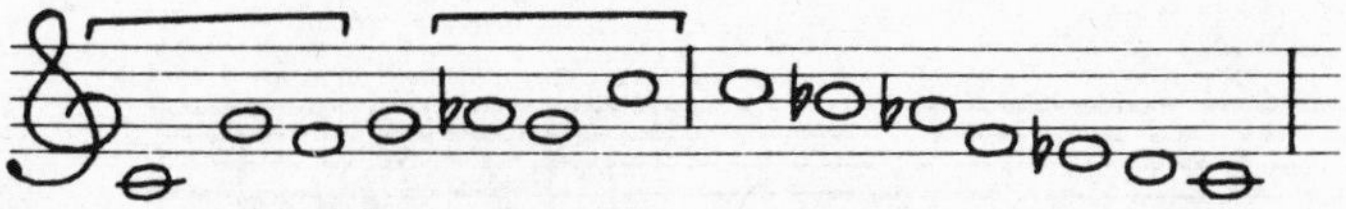

Ascent: the notes *RI* (D) and *NI* (Bb) are avoided; two *vakra* features are shown.
Descent: the note *PA* (G) is omitted.

SMC, 92

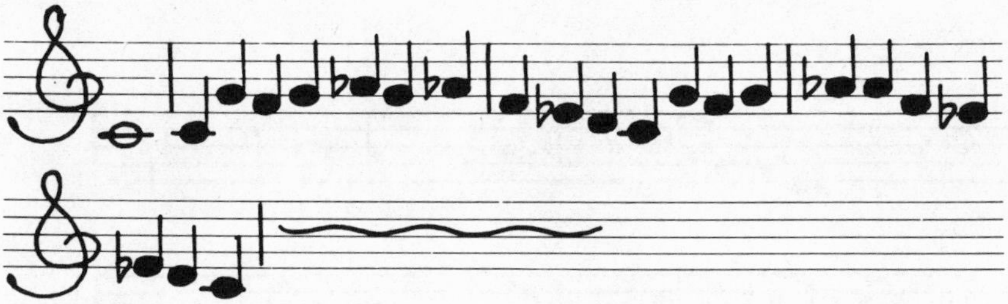

(6) *Mārgahindōḷa*

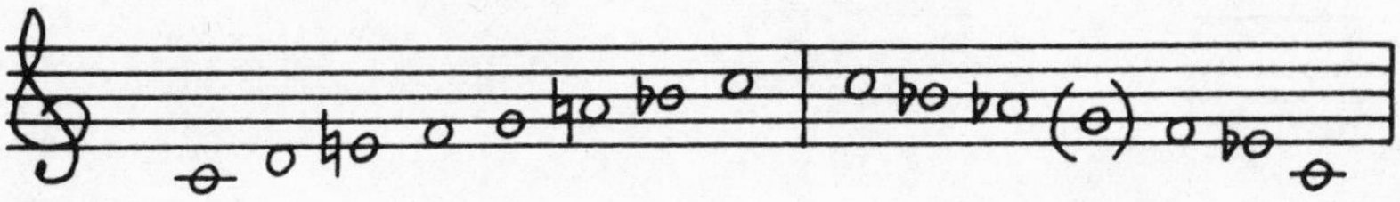

This *rāga* can be performed at any time. Its ascent shows high intonations of the notes *GA* (from Eb to E) and *DHA* (from Ab to A) which occur almost always in *Mārgahindōḷa* performances at the present time. This distinct change of these two notes alienates *Mārgahindōḷa* from its primary *rāga*.
Ascent: *kṛama sampūrṇa*.
Descent: the note *RI* (D) is avoided.
PA (G) is treated very weakly, often to such a degree that it is omitted.

There are musicians who use the notes *antara GA* (E) and *catuḥśruti DHA* (A) not only in ascent but also in descent, whereby the relationship of *Mārgahindōḷa* with the 20. *mēḷa* becomes very weak.

Another *Mārgahindōḷa* is listed under the heading of the 22. *mēḷa* (96).

The following song example, a *kīrtana*, represents *Mārgahindōḷa* of the 20. *mēḷa*:

MĀRGAHINDŌḶA RĀGA (Ādi-tāla)

Pallavi

Repeat the *pallavi*

Anupallavi

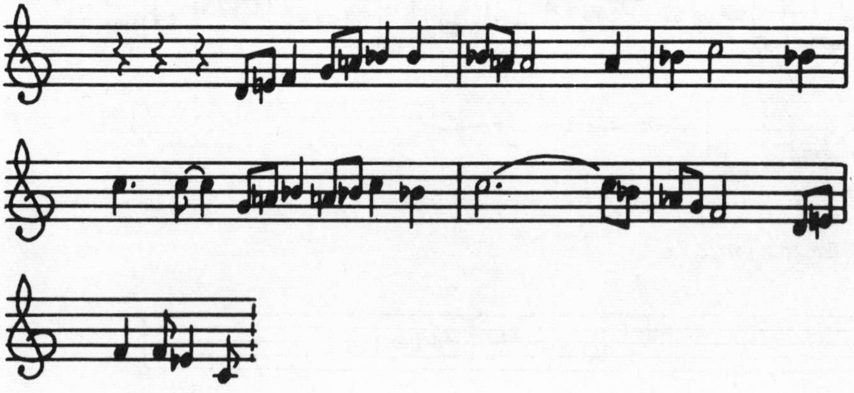

Charana

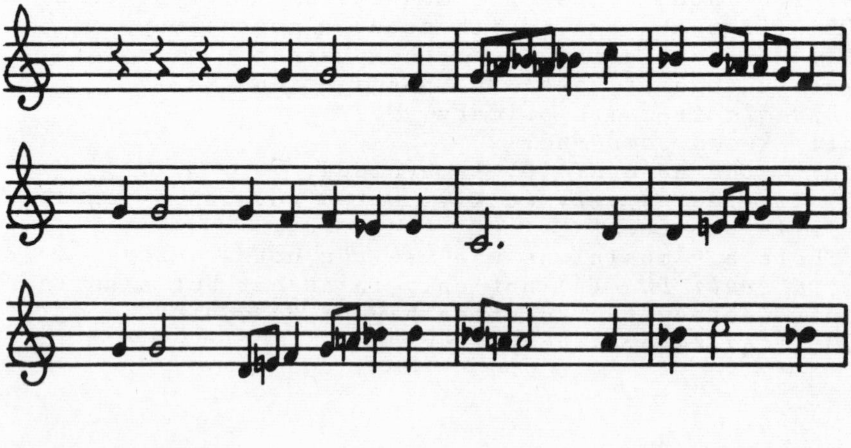

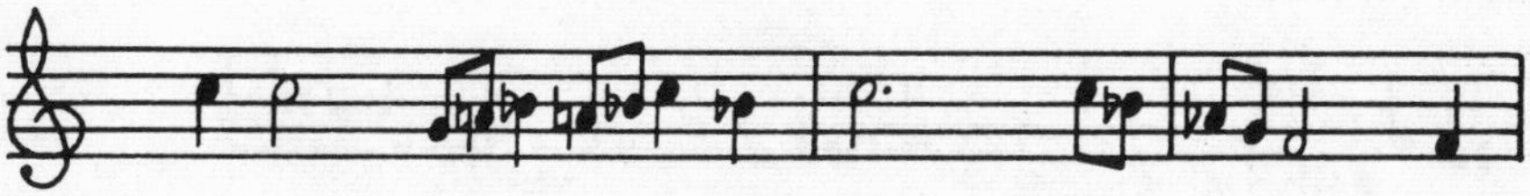

Repeat the *pallavi* and conclude the song with *MA* (F)

(7) *Hindōḷa* (*m*)

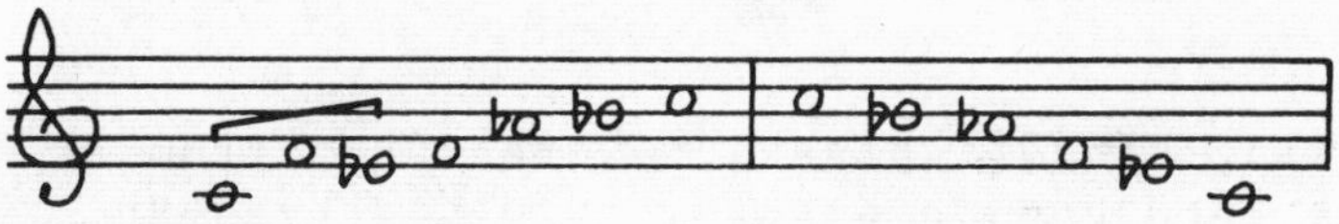

The notes *RI* (D) and *PA* (G) are avoided entirely. The ascent shows one characteristic *vakra* feature.

Despite the plain difference between the scales of *Māргahindōḷa* and *Hindōḷa*, the two *rāgas* are often and erroneously described as being identical. While the descents are indeed similar and at times can become identical, the ascents differ in the use and omission of the note *PA* (G) respectively.

There are some musicians who speak about the high intonation of the notes *GA* and *DHA* (Eb to E; Ab to A), there is no doubt that they refer to *Māргahindōḷa*. In *Hindōḷa* these notes are never intoned high and the *rāga* shows clearly its strong relationship to *Naṭabhairavī*, its primary *rāga*.

HINDŌḶA RĀGA (*Triputa-tāla*) SCM, 82

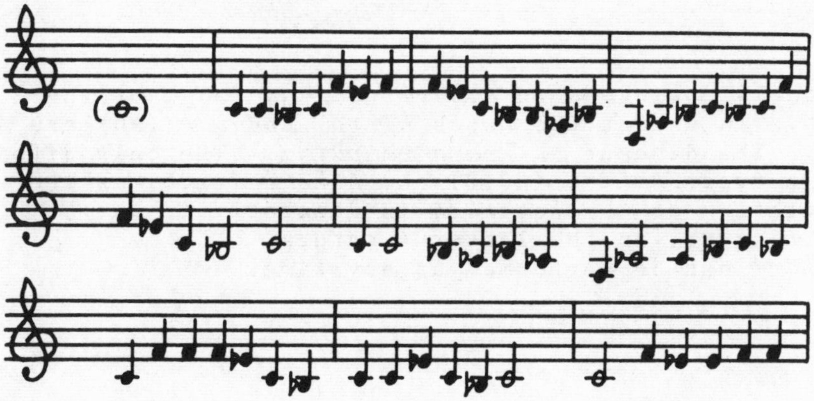

The following *Hindōḷa* passages were taken from a *Gīta Govinda* performance in Kerala, recorded by Wayne Howard in 1972:

These passages illustrate the strict omission of the note *PA* (G). The characteristic *vakra* feature in ascent has been ignored.

(8) *Ābhēri*

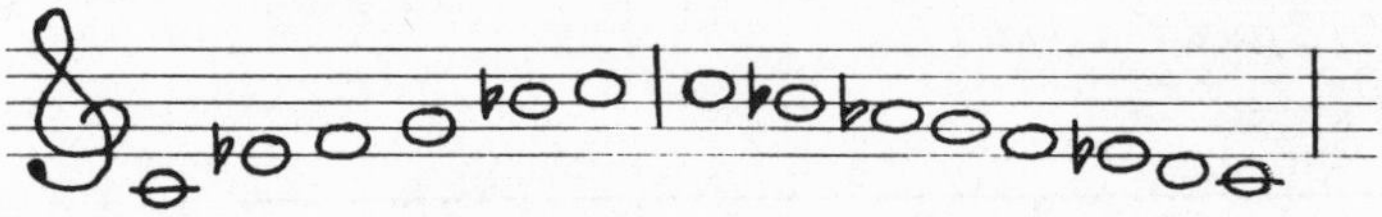

This *rāga* is analogous to *Ābhēri*, a *janya rāga* of the 22. *mēḷa*. In ascent the notes *RI* (D) and *DHA* (Ab) are avoided. The descent is *krama sampūrṇa*. The only difference between *Ābhēri* (20,8) and *Ābhēri* (22,6) is the interpretation of the note *DHA* in descent. In the former it is Ab, in the latter A natural.

Ābhēri can be performed at any time.

RĀGA ĀBHĒRI (*Triputa-tāla*) SCM, 83

(9) *Ānandabhairavī*

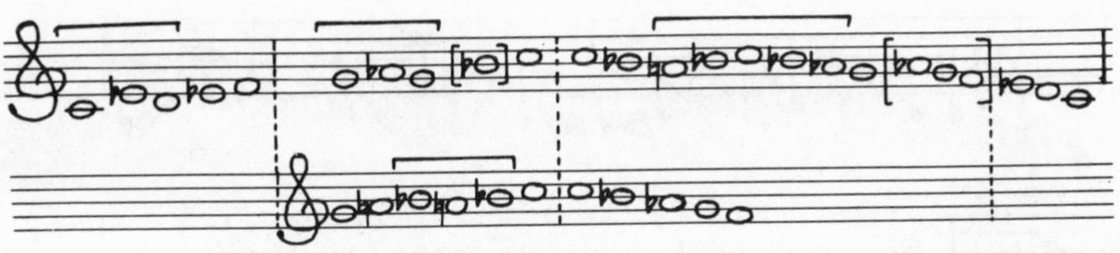

This *rāga* may be performed at any time. Its scale which is shown in two versions is *sampūrṇa* and shows two *vakra* features in ascent. One extended *vakra* feature may appear in descent. The note *DHA* usually becomes A natural in ascent and is Ab in descent. Occasionally one phrase may occur with the note A in descent:

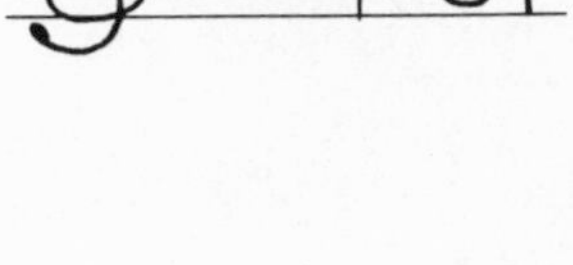

Numerous simple melodies, folk-songs, children's songs, marriage songs, etc., exist in this *rāga*.

The stressed note of *Ānandabhairavī* are *GA* (Eb), *MA* (F), and *NI* (Bb), and melodies in this *rāga* never descend to a note lower than *NI* (Bb) of the *mandra saptaka* (low octave range).

The following song specimen is a *pada* (*pada varna*, *chauka varna*, or *ata varna*), a dance song by Kshetrayya:[3]

ĀNANDABHAIRAVĪ RĀGA (*Triputa-tāla*)

Pallavi

Repeat the first line of the *pallavi* up to A. The last two measures of the first line after A are changed to the held note *SA* (C).

Anupallavi

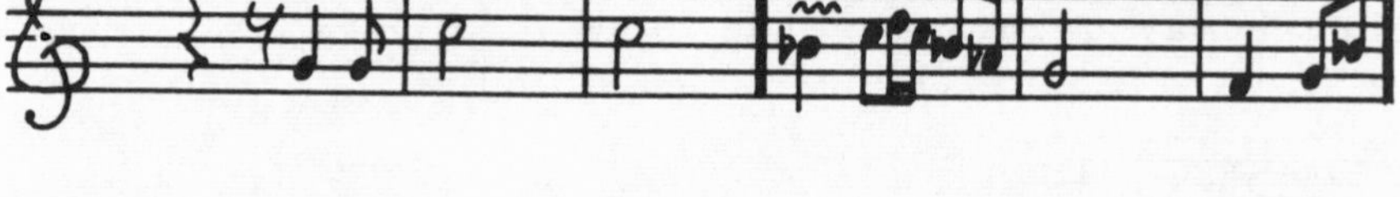

Repeat the first line of the *pallavi* up to A. The last two measures of the first line after A are changed to the held note *SA* (C).

Charana

Repeat the first line of the *pallavi* up to A. The song concludes with the note *SA* (C).

The following passages are taken from an *Ānanda-bhairavī* section of a *Gīta Govinda* performance in Kerala, recorded by Wayne Howard in 1972:

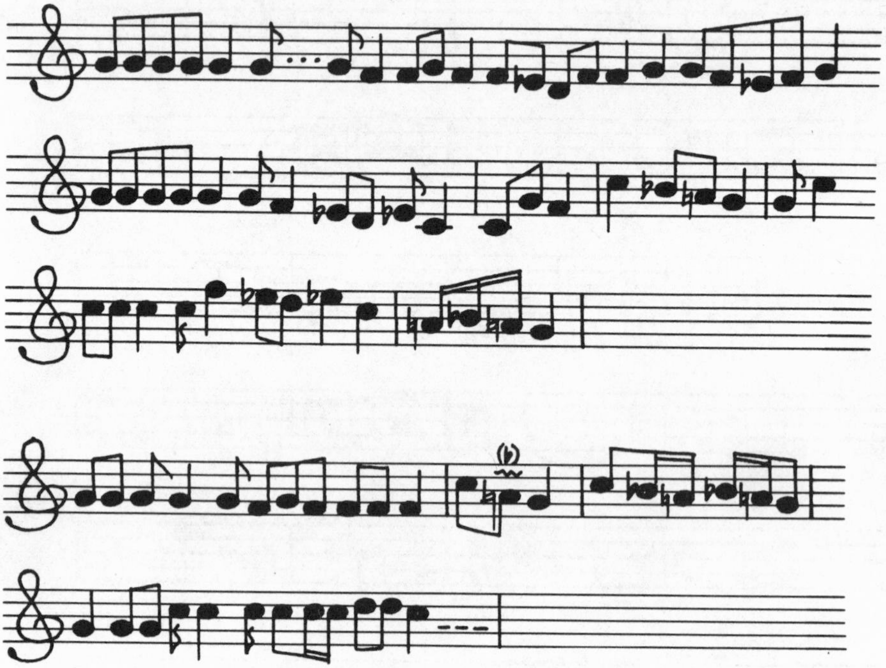

(10) *Jayantaśrī*

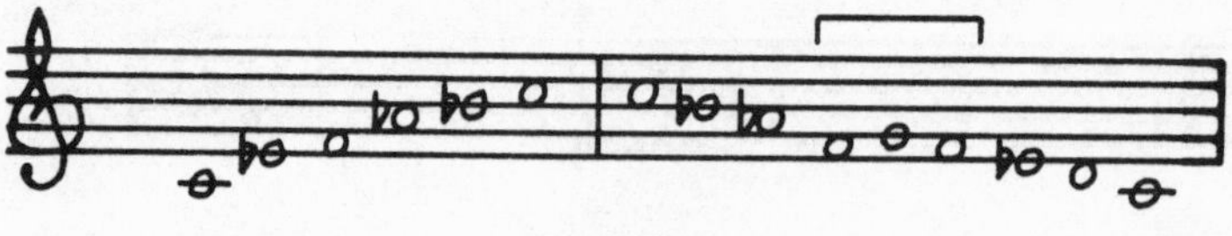

The note *RI* (D) is avoided in ascent. *PA* (G) is generally omitted in ascent; it appears in one *vakra* feature in descent.

RĀGA JAYANTAŚRĪ (*Triputa-tāla*) SCM, 80-81

(11) *Udayaravichandrikā*

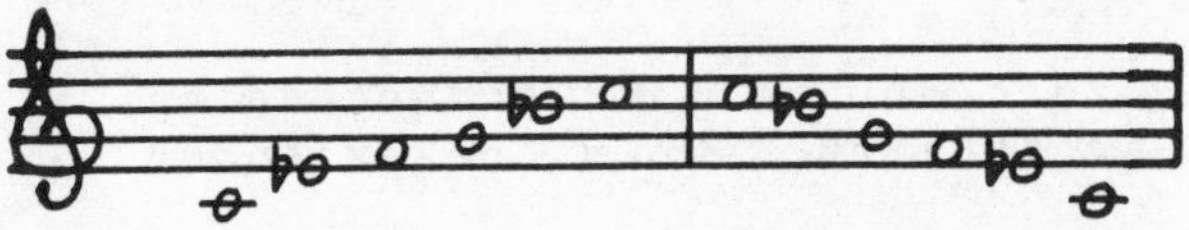

The notes *RI* (D) and *DHA* (Ab) are avoided entirely. The omission of these two notes (particularly *DHA*) allows this *rāga* to be listed also under the headings of other *mēḷas*. *Udayaravichandrikā* will be considered again as 22, 131. The opinions are still divided as to where to place this *rāga*. Some musicians subordinate it not only under the 20. and 22. *mēḷas* but also under *Dhenuka*, the 9. *mēḷa*. This advocates the use of the note *kākali NI* (B). In practice, however, this *rāga* is generally not performed with this note but with *kaiśika NI* (Bb) whereby *Udayaravichandrikā* comes dangerously close to the *rāga Śuddhadhanyasi* (22, 122).

In the Madras Music Conference of December 25, 1933, the question whether *kākali* or *kaiśika NI* is to be used in this *rāga* was put to a vote and the scholars present preferred the *kākali* form by eight against six votes. A discussion connected with this vote showed that in the phrase *SA-NI-SA* the note *NI* would be sharp and approach in pitch *kākali NI* (B), while in the descending phrase *SA-NI-PA* the middle note would veer distinctly toward or become *kaiśika NI* (Bb).

RĀGA UDAYARAVICHANDRIKĀ (*Triputa-tāla*) SCM, 83

(12) *Gōpika Vasanta*

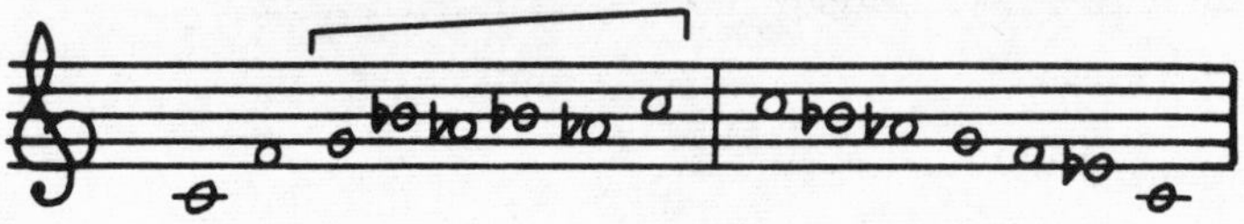

The note *RI* (D) is avoided entirely. The ascending scale omits the note *GA* (Eb) and shows one extended *vakra* feature.

RĀGA GŌPIKA VASANTA (*Triputa-tāla*) SCM, 93

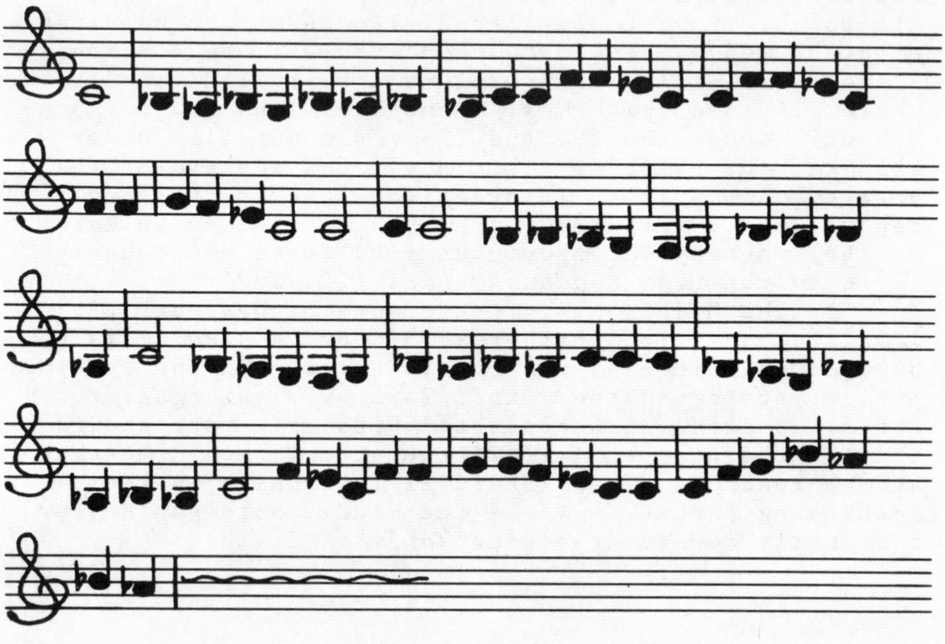

(13) *Nārāyaṇadēśadi*

The scale of this *rāga* is vaguely defined. A possible form shows *sampūrṇa* ascent and descent. The ascent has two *vakra* features, and one form of the descent has one *vakra* feature.

RĀGA NĀRĀYAṆADĒŚADI (Triputa-tāla) SCM, 81

(14) *Dēvakriyā*

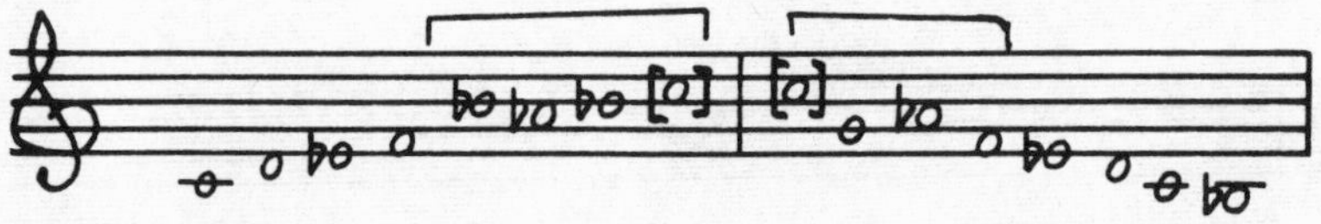

SD I, 109, quoting SSPS, states that the highest note of the *Dēvakriyā* ascent is *NI* (Bb), that the note *PA* (G) is avoided, and that the descent begins with the note *PA* (G) and ends with the lower *NI* (Bb). Both ascent and descent show one *vakra* feature.

R (184) calls *Dēvakriyā* of the 20. *mēḷa* a *madhya rāga* because its scale does not reach up to *SA* (c) of the *tāra saptaka*. We must add here that there are instances when the full range, including the upper *SA* (c) and even notes beyond it, is used.

R (ibid.) substantiates this by reporting that a *Rāga Lakṣaṇa*, a manuscript from Tanjore (publ. in Poona, n.d.) presents the following scale that avoids the note *PA* (G) entirely and extends its range to the upper *SA* (c): C-D-Eb-F-Ab-Bb-c, c-Bb-Ab-F-Eb-D-C.

The note *DHA* (Ab) in the *vakra* feature of the ascent (shown above) is often interpreted as a *catuḥ-śruti DHA* (A natural). In descent the note *DHA* is always Ab. The note *NI* (Bb) is avoided in descent only in the middle octave region, but may be used in the *mandra saptaka* (low octave).

SD (I, 109) remarks that "in the Dikshitar school, the *rāga Śuddhasāveri* [see 29, 103] goes by the name *Dēvakriya*...."

Another *rāga* with the same name is listed under heading of the 22. *mēḷa* (32).

RĀGA DĒVAKRIYĀ (20,14) (*Triputa-tāla*) SCM, 85

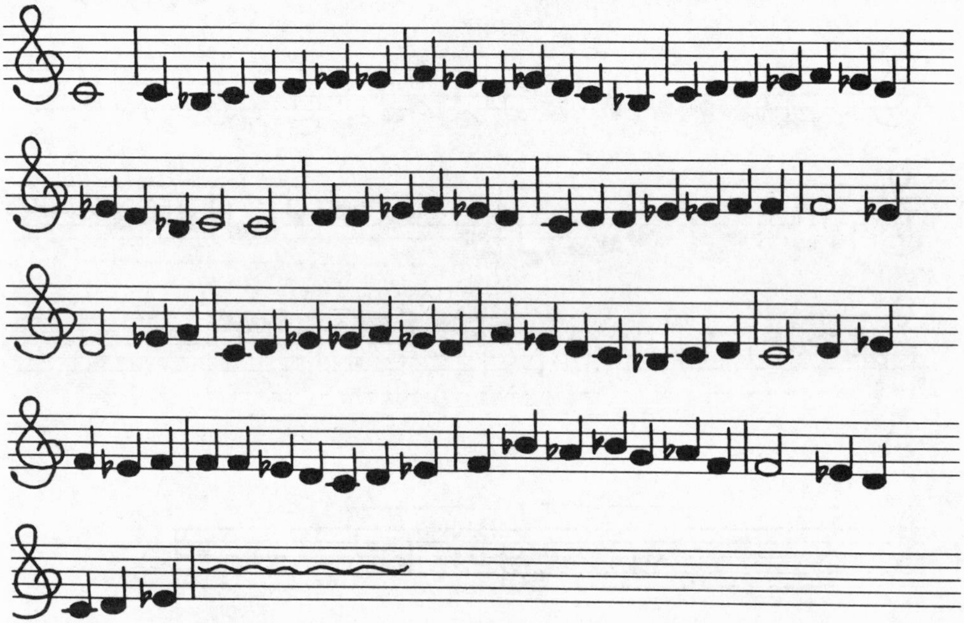

(15) *Indughaṇṭārava*(m)

The scale of this *rāga* has *niṣādāntya* character, avoids the note *RI* (D) in ascent, and has one *vakra* feature. The descent is *sampūrṇa*, extending from *madhya NI* (Bb of the middle octave to *mandra NI* (Bb of the lower octave range).

RĀGA INDUGHAṆṬĀRAVA (Triputa-tāla) SCM, 86

(16) *Vasantavarāḷi*

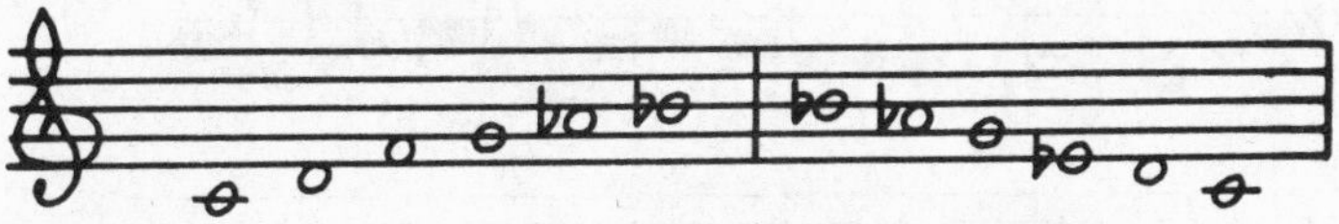

The scale is *niṣādāntya* and avoids the note *GA* (Eb) in ascent and *MA* (Ḟ) in descent.

RĀGA VASANTAVARĀḶI (Triputa-tāla) SCM, 86-87

(17) *Nagagāndhāri*

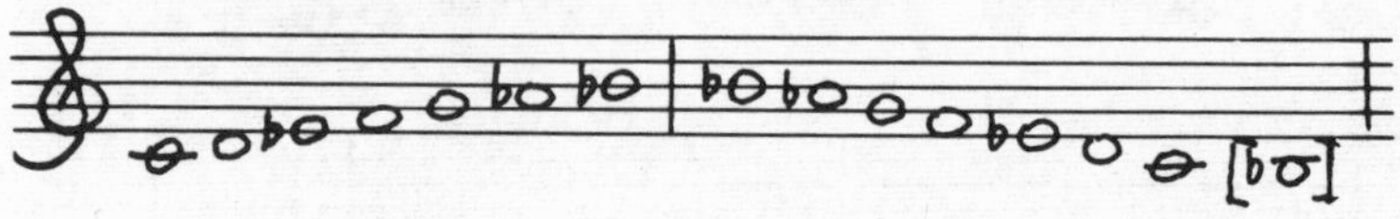

The scale of this *rāga*, quoted from the *SCM* (*Rāga Lakṣaṇa*, 84-5), has *niṣādāntya* character. There are certain performers who avoid the note *MA* (F) in descent.

NAGAGĀNDHĀRI (*Triputa-tāla*) SCM, 87-88

(18) *Nāyakī*

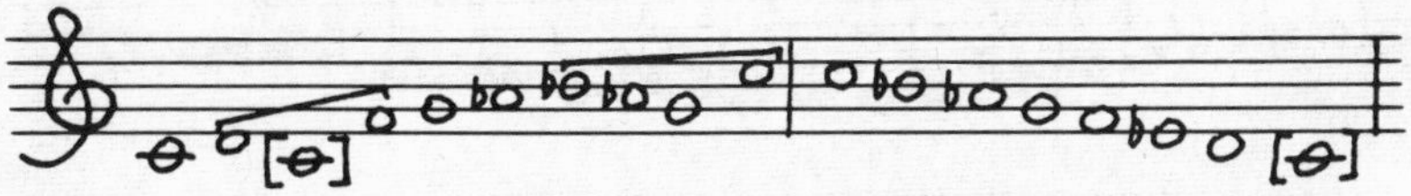

The scale of this *rāga* avoids the note *GA* (Eb) in ascent and shows two *vakra* features. The descent is *sampūrṇa*. The note *DHA* in ascent can be sharp so that its pitch approximates or becomes A natural.

Another *rāga* with the same name appears under the heading of the 22. *mēḷa* (5).

NAYAKI (*Triputa-tāla*) SCM, 90-91

(19) *Kanakavasantam*

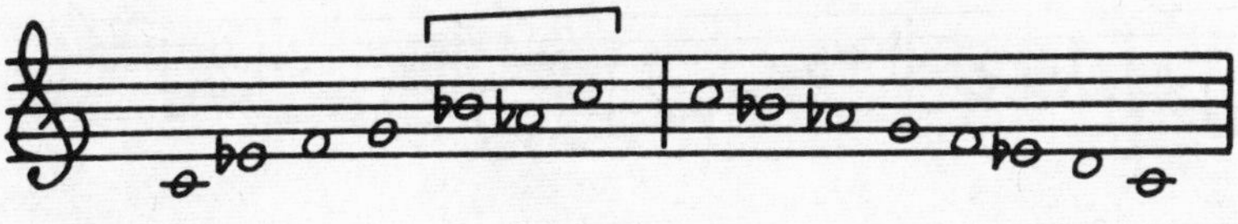

Ascent: the note *RI* (D) is avoided; one *vakra* feature is shown.
Descent: *krama sampūrṇa*.

KANAKAVASANTAM (*Triputa-tāla*) SCM, 91

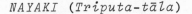

(20) *Chāpa Ghanṭ̤āravam*

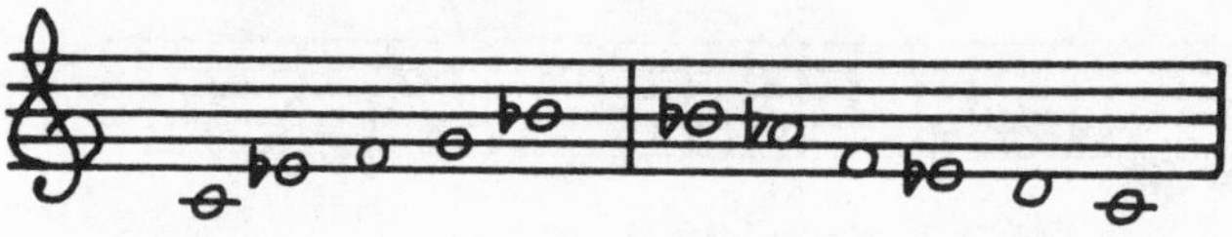

Chāpa Ghanṭ̤āravam is a *niṣādāntya* (or *madhya*) *rāga*.
Ascent: the notes *RI* (D) and *DHA* (Ab) are avoided.
Descent: the note *PA* (G) is omitted.

CHĀPA GHANṬ̤ĀRAVAM (*Triputa-tāla*) SCM, 93

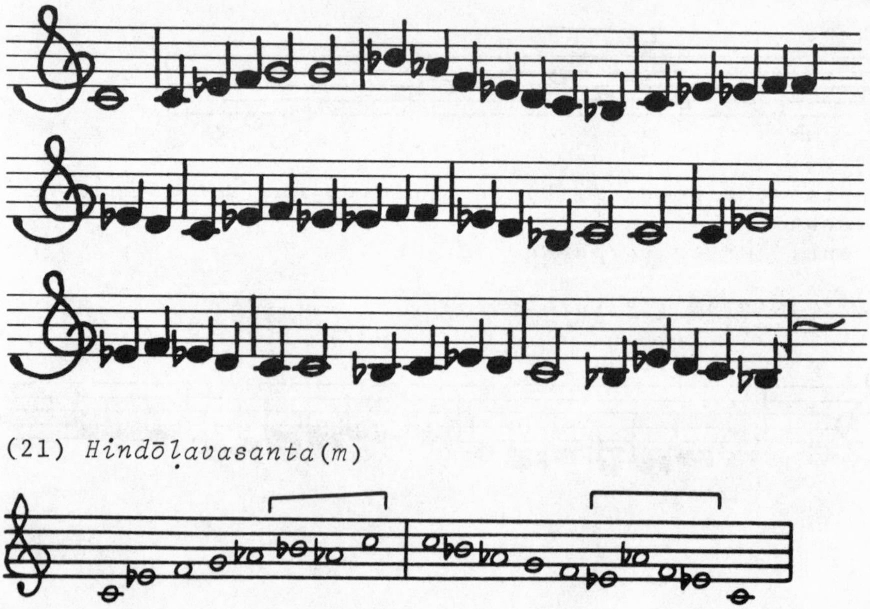

(21) *Hindōḷavasanta(m)*

This scale avoids the note *RI* (D) entirely and shows two *vakra* features, one in ascent and one in descent.

Another *rāga* with the same name is listed under the heading of the 22. *mēḷa* (55).

RĀGA HINDŌḶAVASANTA (Triputa-tāla) SCM, 94

(22) *Sāraṅgakāpi* (second form)

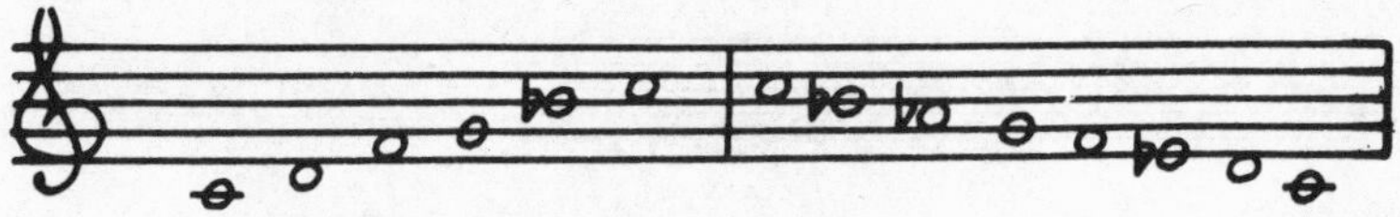

This second form of *Sāraṅgakāpi* (the first one is 20,3) avoids the notes *GA* (Eb) and *DHA* (Ab) in an ascent that is free of any *vakra* feature. The *krama sampūrṇa* descent is identical with that of the first form.

RĀGA SĀRAṄGAKĀPI (20,22) (*Triputa-tāla*) SCM, 95

(23) *Jiṅgla*

The *sampūrṇa* scale of this *rāga* shows one *vakra* feature in ascent. The note *GA* (Eb) is supposed to be stressed.

RĀGA JIṄGLA (*Triputa-tāla*) SCM, 96

(24) *Amritavāhini*

This *rāga* can be performed at any time.
Ascent: the note *GA* (Eb) is avoided.
Descent: the note *PA* (G) is omitted.

RĀGA AMRITĀVAHINI (*Triputa-tāla*) SCM, 96

(25) *Māñji*

The *sampūrṇa* scale of this *rāga* uses in ascent the *catuḥśruti DHA* (A natural) and in descent *DHA śuddha* (Ab).

There are several versions of *Māñji*:

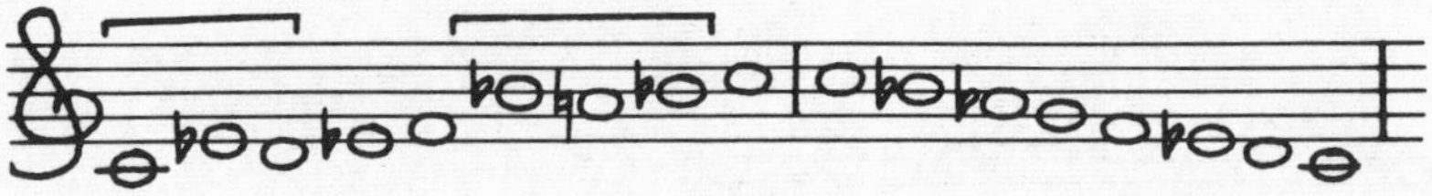

This version avoids the note *PA* (G) in ascent and shows two *vakra* features. The descent is *krama sampūrṇa*. Another version of *Māñji* can be observed in the descending scale:

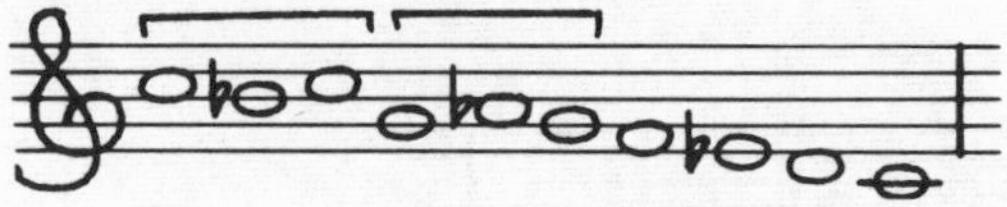

It is *sampūrṇa* and shows two *vakra* features.

RĀGA MĀÑJI (Triputa-tāla)   SCM, 88

(26) *Sāramati* (*Rati*)

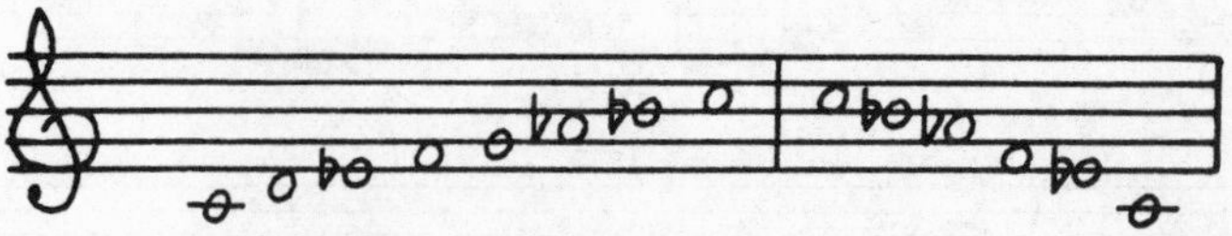

Ascent: *krama sampūrṇa*.
Descent: the notes *PȦ* (G) and *RI* (D) are avoided.

(27) *Ādi Bhairavī*

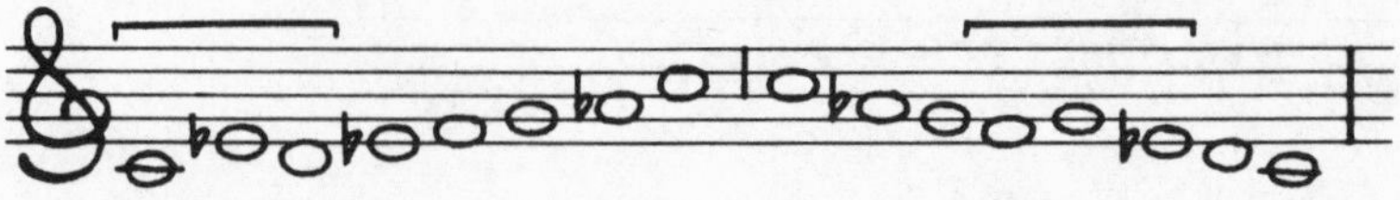

The note *NI* (Bb) is avoided entirely. One *vakra* feature is shown in ascent and one in descent.

(28) *Agnikōpam*

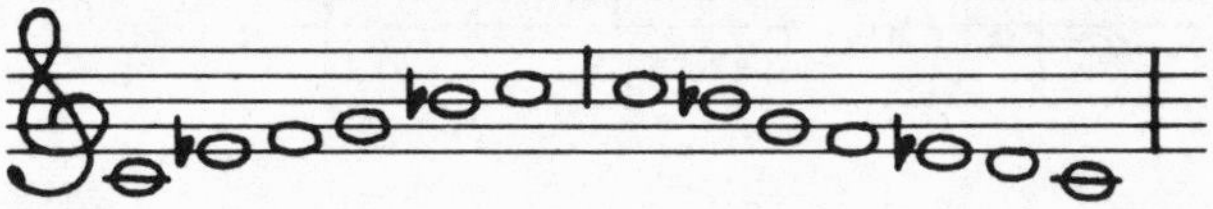

The note *DHA* (Ab) is avoided entirely. *RI* (D) is omitted in ascent.

(29) *Āhōri*

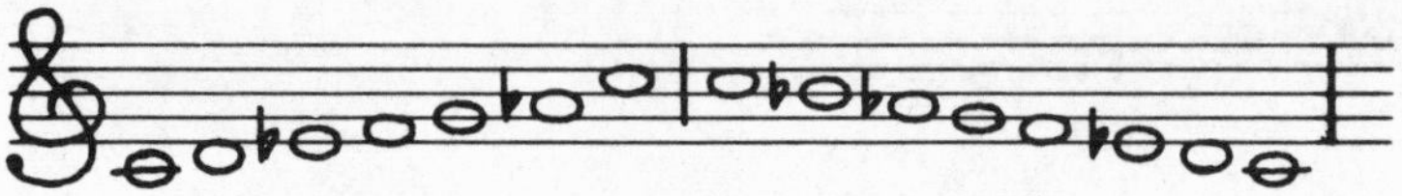

Ascent: the note *NI* (Bb) is avoided.
Descent: *krama sampūrṇa*.

(30) *Ashṭavādam* (*Aṣṭavādam*)

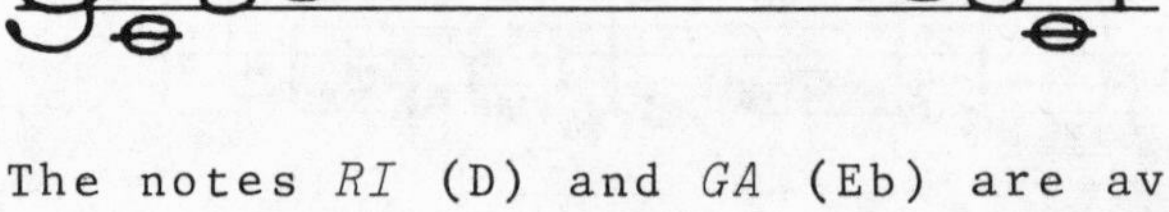

The notes *RI* (D) and *GA* (Eb) are avoided entirely.

(31) *Bhāgīrati*

The notes *MA* (F) and *PA* (G) are avoided entirely.

(32) *Bhēndrūla*

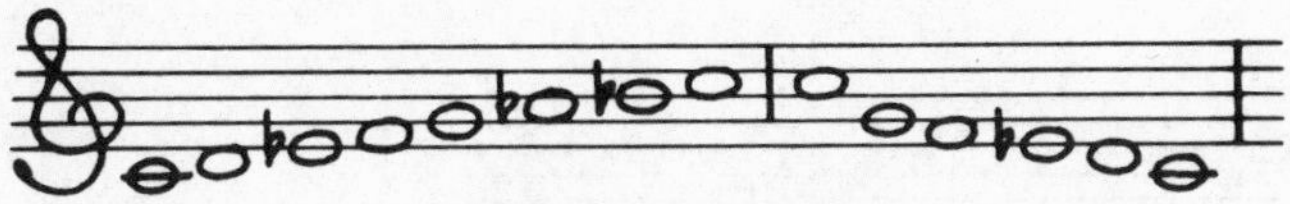

Ascent: *krama sampūrṇa*
Descent: the notes *NI* (Bb) and *DHA* (Ab) are avoided.

(33) *Bhṛṅga Vilasitā*

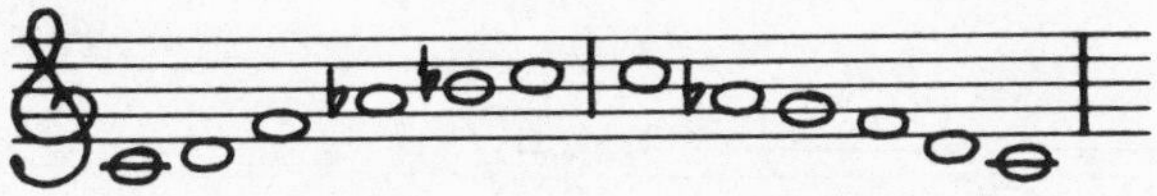

The note *GA* (Eb) is omitted entirely. *PA* (G) is avoided in ascent and *NI* (Bb) in descent.

(34) *Bhūvana Gāndhāri*

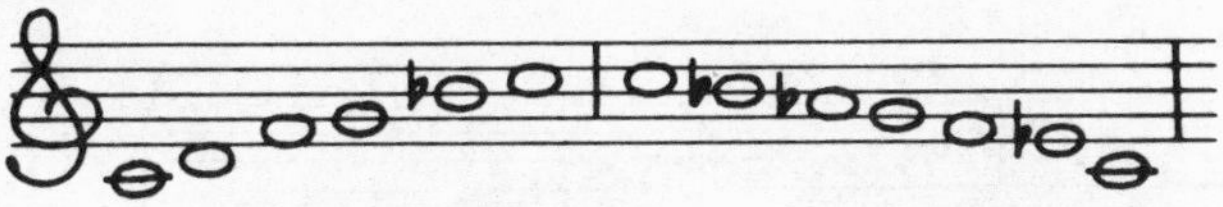

Ascent: the notes *GA* (Eb) and *DHA* (Ab) are avoided.
Descent: the note *RI* (D) is omitted.

(35) *Brūravi*

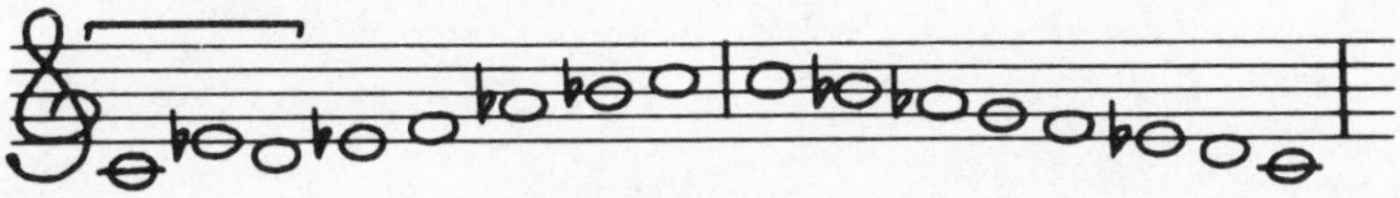

Ascent: the note *PA* (G) is avoided; one *vakra* feature is shown.
Descent: *krama sampūrṇa*.

(36) *Chakradhari*

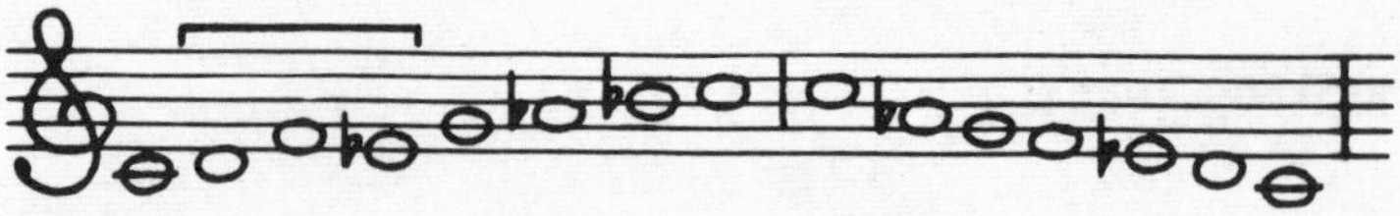

Ascent: *sampūrṇa*; one *vakra* feature is shown.
Descent: the note *NI* (Bb) is avoided.

(37) *Chalanavarāḷi*

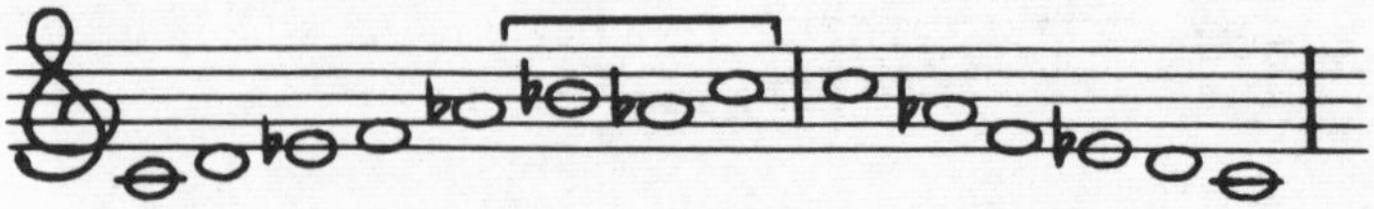

The note *PA* (G) is avoided entirely. The ascent shows one *vakra* feature and the descent avoids the note *NI* (Bb).

(38) *Chaṇḍika*

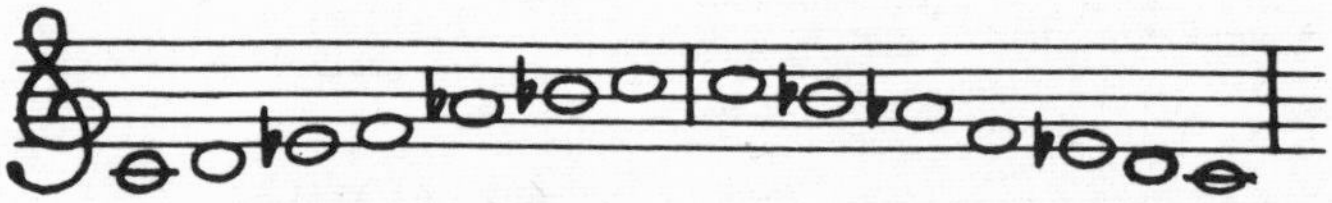

The note *PA* (G) is avoided entirely.

(39) *Chhāyā*

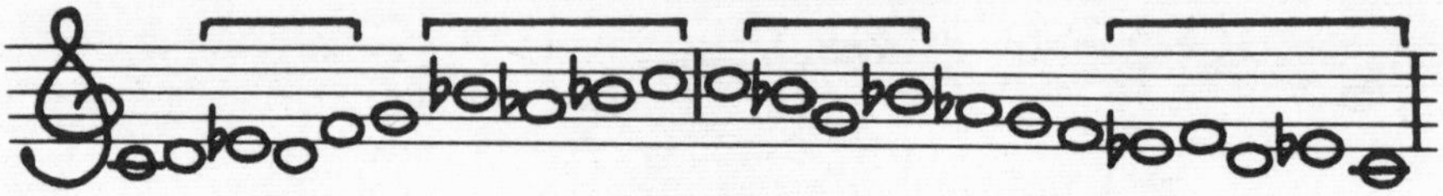

The scale of this *rāga* is *sampūrṇa*. SD (I, 84) describes *Chhāyā* as an "*ubhāya vakra rāga*," implying that the two *vakra* features of the ascent are related to those shown in descent.

(40) *Chitra Varāḷi*

Ascent: *sampūrṇa*; one *vakra* feature is shown.
Descent: the notes *DHA* (Ab) and *PA* (G) are avoided.

(41) *Dhairyōdari*

Ascent: the notes *RI* (D) and *DHA* (Ab) are avoided.
Descent: the note *NI* (Bb) is omitted; one *vakra* feature is shown.

(42) *Dhanakriya Dhātu*

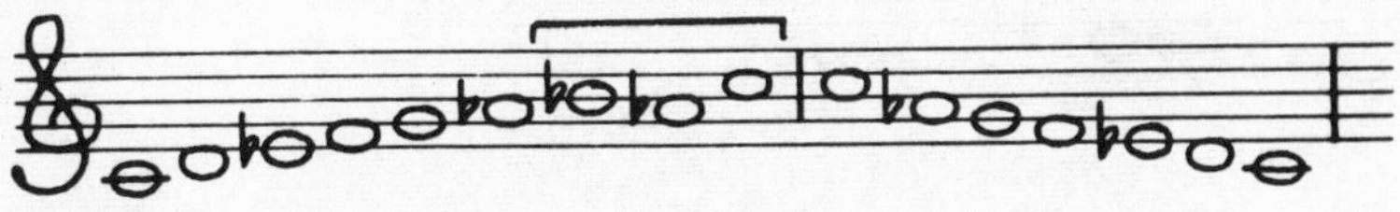

Ascent: *sampūrṇa*; one *vakra* feature is shown.
Descent: the note *NI* (Bb) is avoided.

(43) *Dharma Prakāśini*

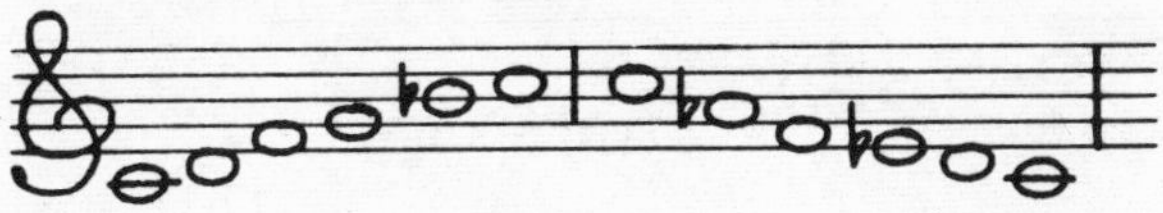

Ascent: the notes *GA* (Eb) and *DHA* (Ab) are avoided.
Descent: the notes *NI* (Bb) and *PA* (G) are omitted.

(44) *Dhaulikā Gauḷa*

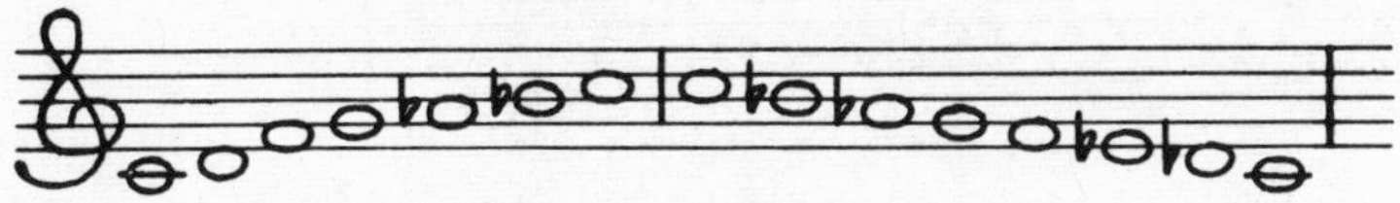

Ascent: the note *GA* (Eb) is avoided.
Descent: *krama sampūrṇa*.

(45) *Dhavaḷa Vāhini*

Ascent: the notes *MA* (F) and *DHA* (Ab) are avoided.
Descent: *krama sampūrṇa*.

(46) *Dinadyuti*

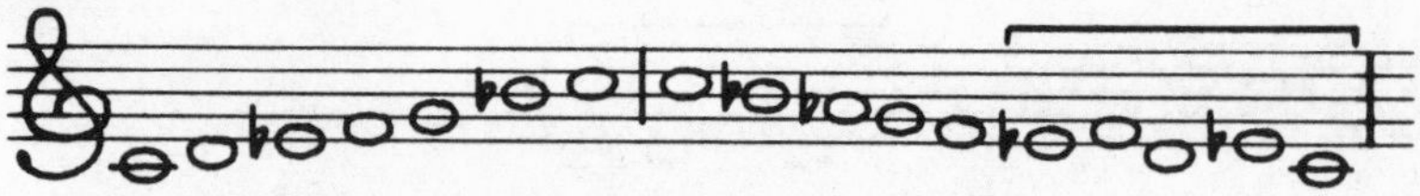

Ascent: the note *DHA* (Ab) is avoided.
Descent: *sampūrṇa*; one *vakra* feature is shown.

(47) *Dīpika Vasantam*

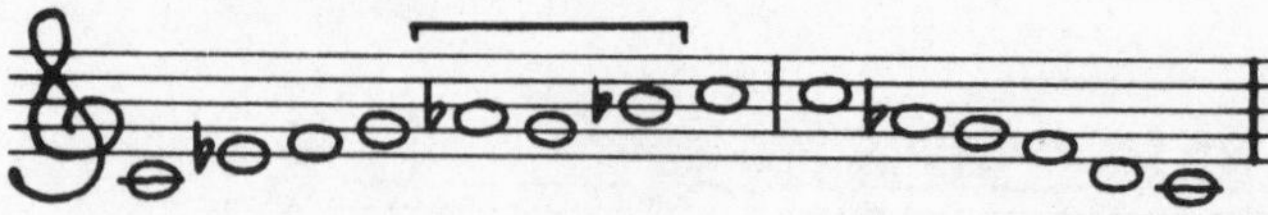

Ascent: the note *RI* (D) is avoided; one *vakra* feature is shown.
Descent: the notes *NI* (Bb) and *GA* (Eb) are avoided.

(48) *Dīrghataraṅgiṇi*

Ascent: the notes *RI* (D) and *PA* (G) are avoided.
Descent: *sampūrṇa*; one extended *vakra* feature is shown.

(49) *Divikāmantini*

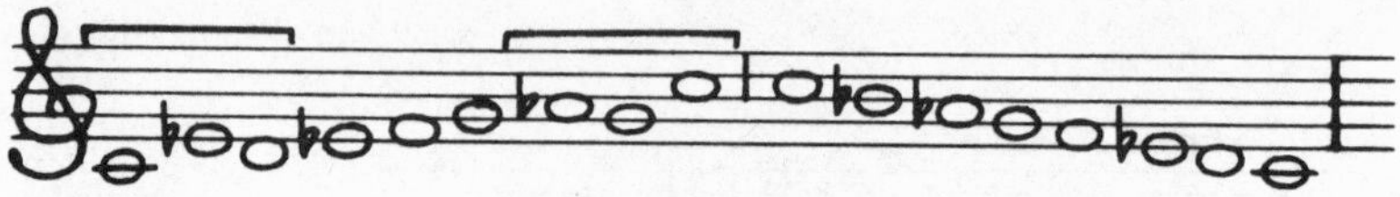

Ascent: the note *NI* (Bb) is avoided; two *vakra* features are shown.
Descent: *krama sampūrṇa*.

(50) *Divyagāndhāri*

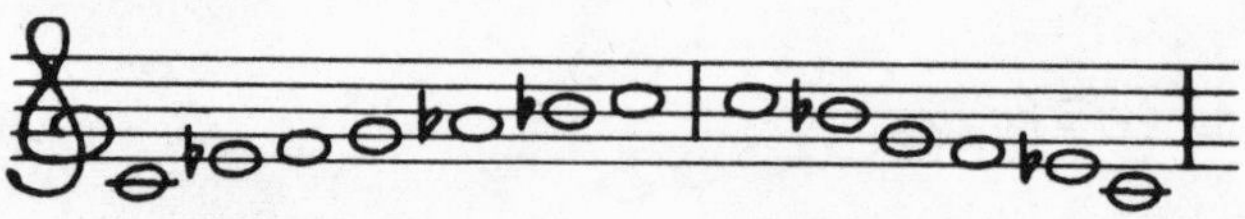

The note *RI* (D) is avoided entirely. *DHA* (Ab) is omitted in descent. SD (I, 120) states that according to Perungulam Srīnivasa Ayyangār's *Gāna Vidyā Prakāśini*, there is "another *rāga* of the same name under this *mēḻa* [20]...with the following *ārōhaṇa* and *avarōhaṇa* [ascent and descent]:"

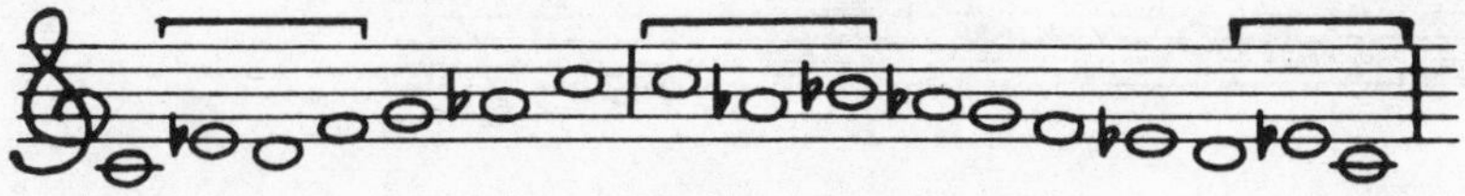

Ascent: the note *NI* (Bb) is avoided; one *vakra* feature is shown.
Descent: *sampūrṇa*; two *vakra* features are used.

(51) *Dyuti Mālini*

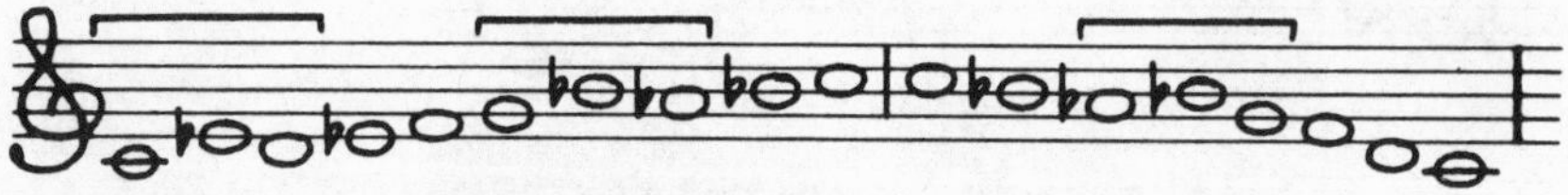

Ascent: *sampūrṇa*; two *vakra* features are shown.
Descent: the note *GA* (Eb) is avoided; one *vakra* feature is used.

(52) *Gamana Taraṅgiṇi*

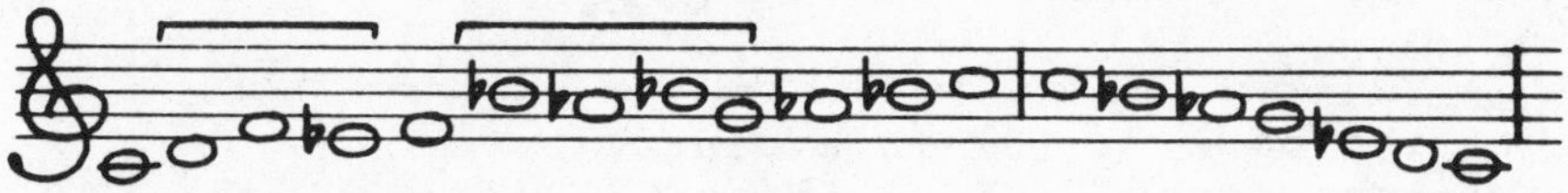

Ascent: *sampūrṇa*; two *vakra* features are shown.
Descent: the note *MA* (F) is avoided.

(53) *Gānāṅgi*

The scale of this *rāga* is *sampūrṇa* and shows in ascent one, in descent two *vakra* features.

(54) *Gāndhārapriya*

Ascent: the note *DHA* (Ab) is avoided. One *vakra* feature is shown.
Descent: *sampūrṇa*; one extended *vakra* feature is used.

(55) *Gītamōhini*

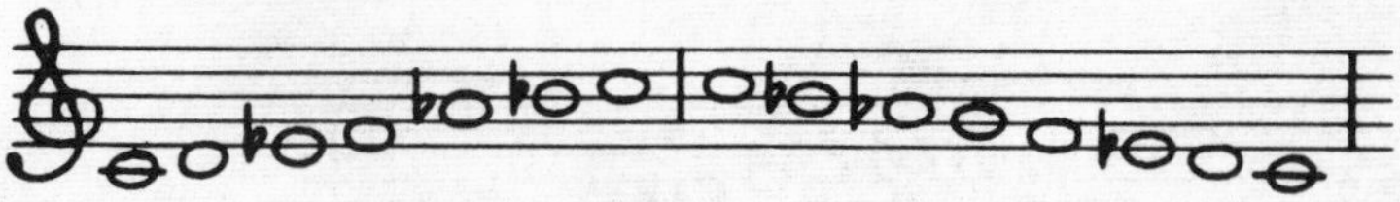

Ascent: the note *PA* (G) is avoided.
Descent: *krama sampūrṇa*.

(56) *Gōmētikapriya*

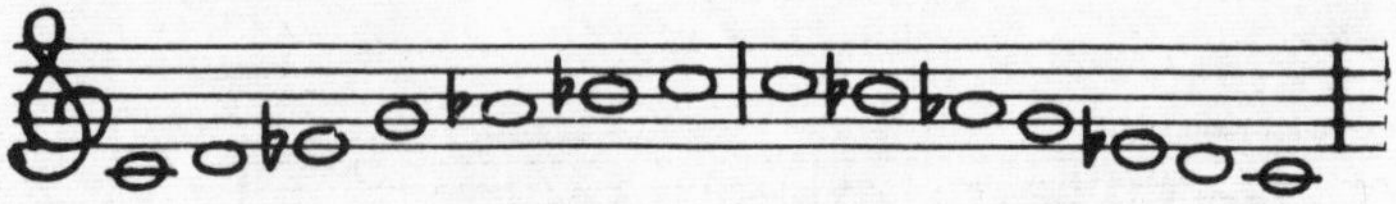

The note *MA* (F) is avoided entirely.

(57) *Goviḍambini*

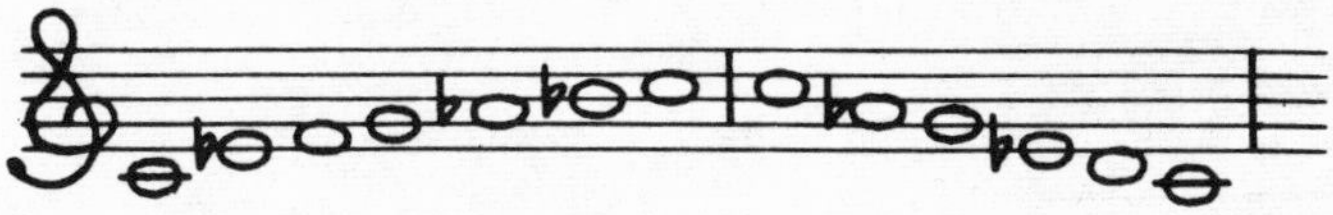

Ascent: the note *RI* (D) is avoided.
Descent: the notes *NI* (Bb) and *MA* (F) are omitted.

(58) *Guruprakāśi*

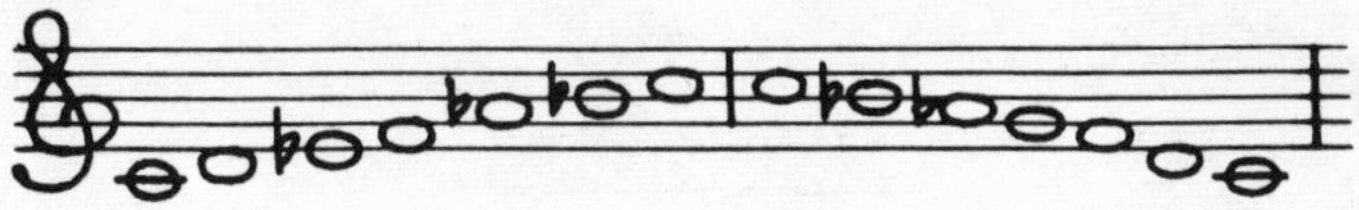

Ascent: the note *PA* (G) is avoided.
Descent: the note *GA* (Eb) is omitted.

(59) *Hāhōri* (*Hāhūri*)

Ascent: *sampūrṇa*; two *vakra* features are shown.
Descent: the note *PA* (G) is avoided.

(60) *Haṃsa Ghanṭāravam*

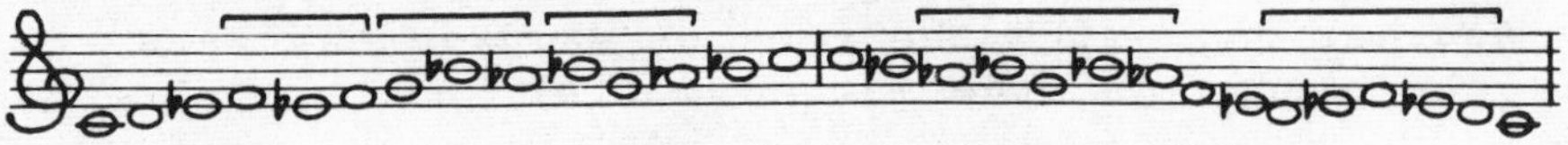

This scale is *sampūrṇa* and shows three *vakra* features in ascent and two extended ones in descent.

(61) *Hēmakriya*

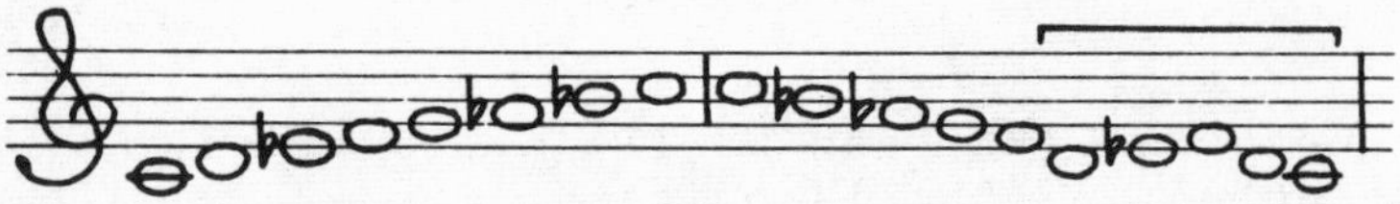

Ascent: *krama sampūrṇa*
Descent: *sampūrṇa*; one extended *vakra* feature is shown.

(62) *Jagamaṇi*

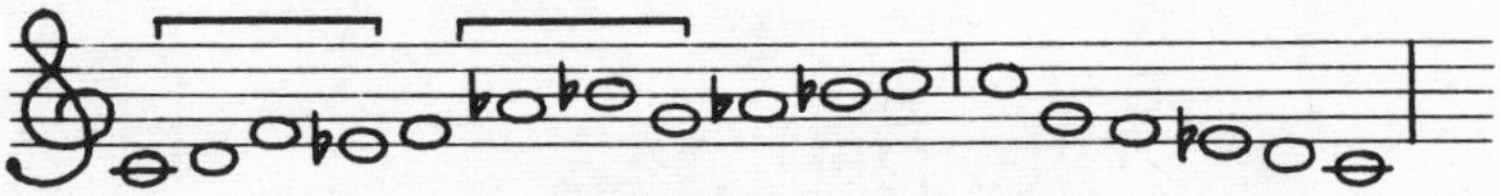

Ascent: *sampūrṇa*; two *vakra* features are shown.
Descent: the notes *NI* (Bb) and *DHA* (Ab) are avoided.

(63) *Janānandini*

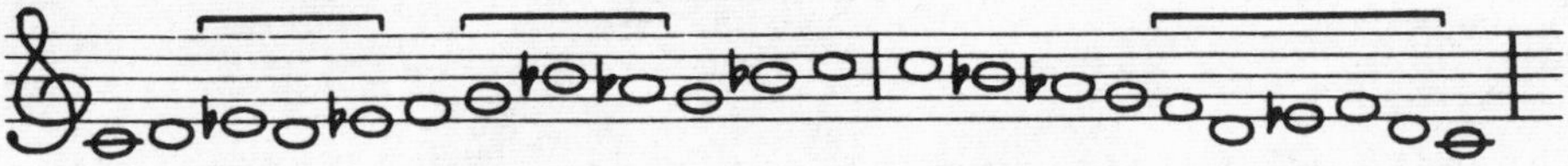

The scale is *sampūrṇa* and shows two *vakra* features in ascent and one extended *vakra* passage in descent.

(64) *Jhaṅkāravāṇi*

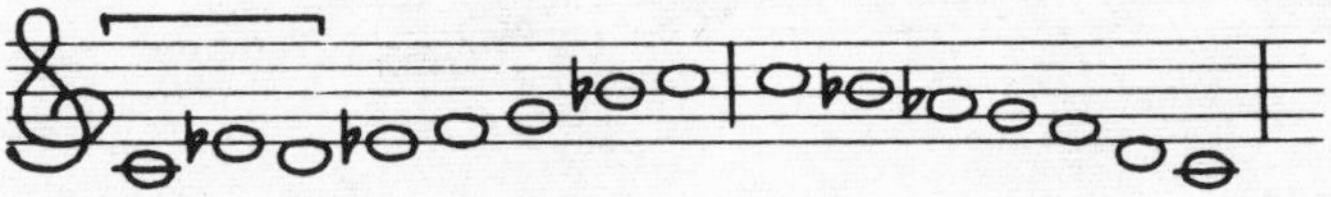

Ascent: the note *DHA* (Ab) is avoided and one *vakra* feature is shown.
Descent: the note *GA* (Eb) is omitted.

SD (II, 60) mentions another *rāga* with the name of *Jhaṅkāri*, which is identical with *Jhaṅkāravāṇi*.

Another *rāga* with the name of *Jhaṅkāri* appears under the heading of the 19. *mēḷa* (12).

(65) *Jōsīla*

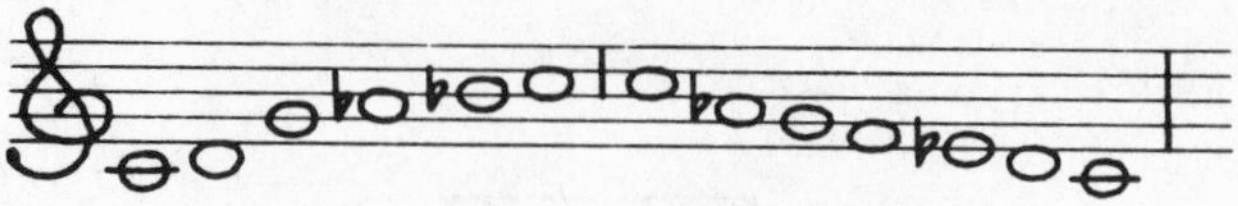

Ascent: the notes *GA* (Eb) and *MA* (F) are avoided.
Descent: the note *NI* (Bb) is omitted.

(66) *Kamalataraṅgiṇi*

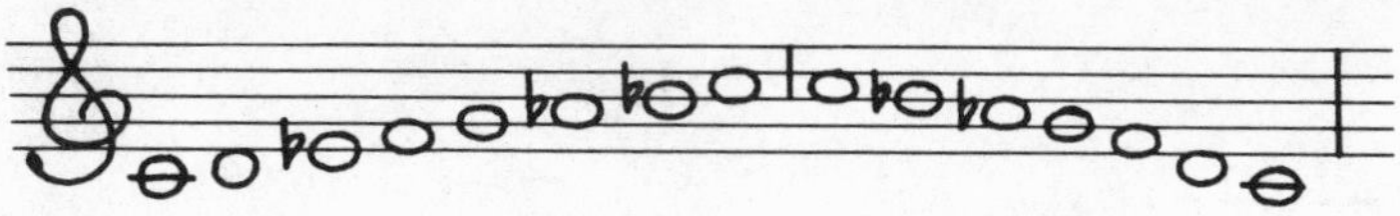

Ascent: *krama sampūrṇa*.
Descent: the note *GA* (Eb) is avoided.

(67) *Kannaḍa Mallār*

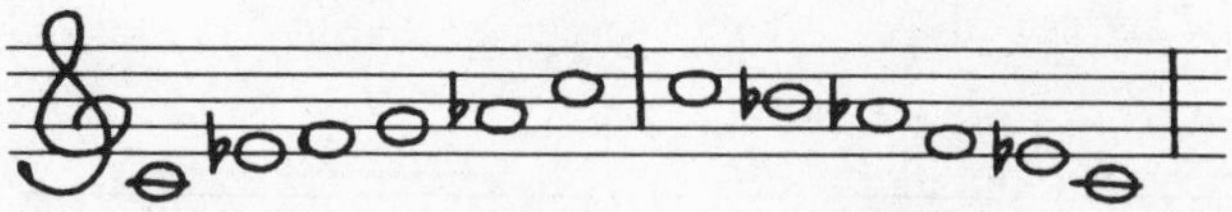

The note *RI* (D) is avoided entirely. *NI* (Bb) is omitted in ascent and *PA* (G) in descent.

(68) *Karṇikādhari*

Ascent: *krama sampūrṇa*.
Descent: *sampūrṇa*; one *vakra* feature is shown.

(69) *Karṇika Rañjani*

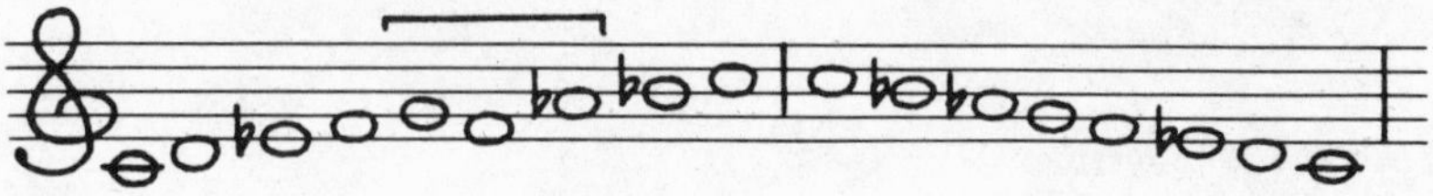

Ascent: *sampūrṇa*; one *vakra* feature is shown.
Descent: *krama sampūrṇa*.

(70) *Kāryamati*

Ascent: the notes *MA* (F) and *NI* (Bb) are avoided.
Descent: *sampūrṇa*; one *vakra* feature is shown.

(71) *Kauśikikanada*

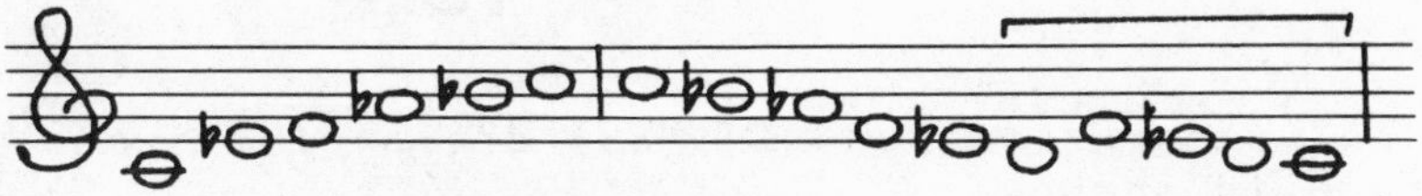

The note *PA* (G) is avoided entirely. *RI* (D) is omitted in ascent. The descent shows one extended *vakra* feature.

(72) *Kauśilakam*

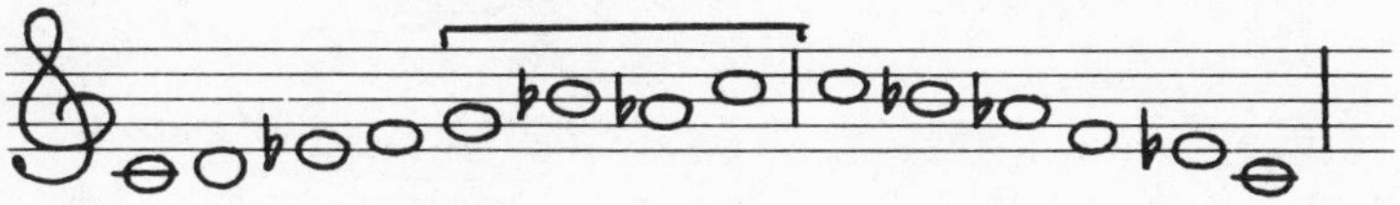

Ascent: *sampūrṇa*; one *vakra* feature is shown.
Descent: the notes *PA* (G) and *RI* (D) are avoided.

(73) *Kāvya Chitra*

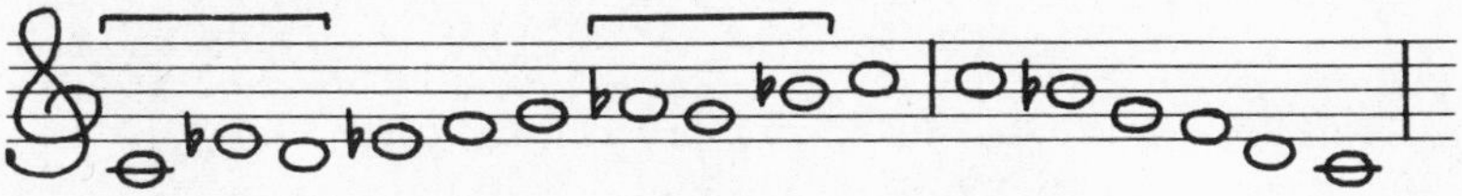

Ascent: *sampūrṇa*; two *vakra* features are shown.
Descent: the notes *DHA* (Ab) and *GA* (Eb) are avoided.

(74) *Kēyachāradhāriṇi*

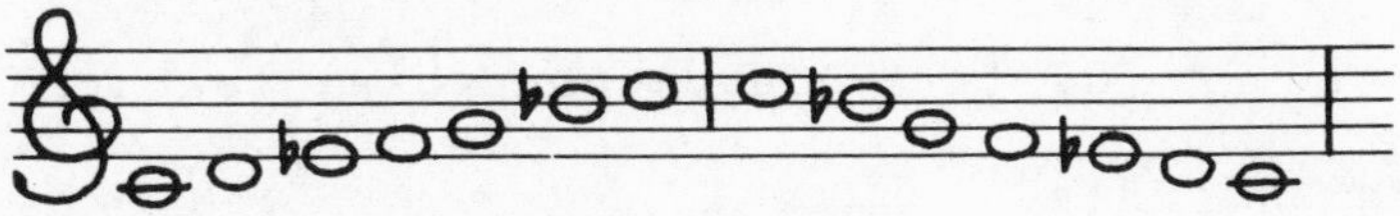

The note *DHA* (Ab) is avoided entirely.

(75) *Khagarājitam*

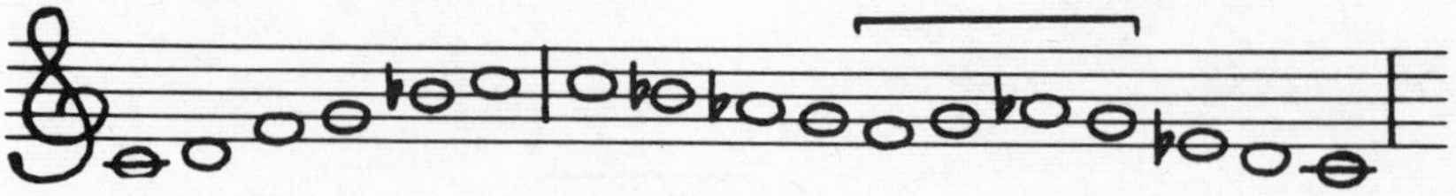

Ascent: the notes *GA* (Eb) and *DHA* (Ab) are avoided.
Descent: *sampūrṇa*; one *vakra* feature is shown.

(76) *Kumāra Lila*

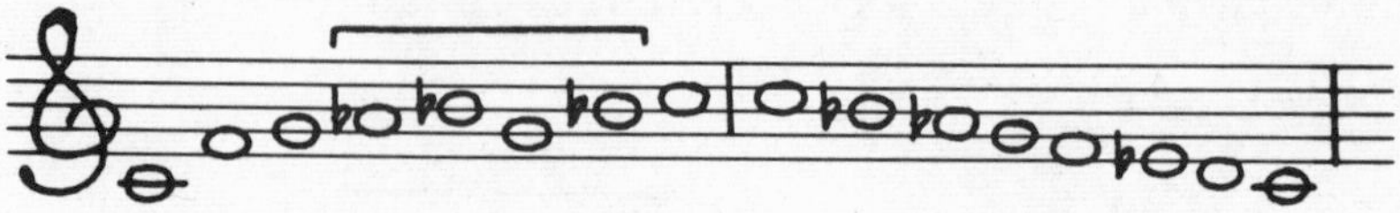

Ascent: the notes *RI* (D) and *GA* (Eb) are avoided; one *vakra* feature is shown.
Descent: *krama sampūrṇa*.

(77) *Nīlavēni*

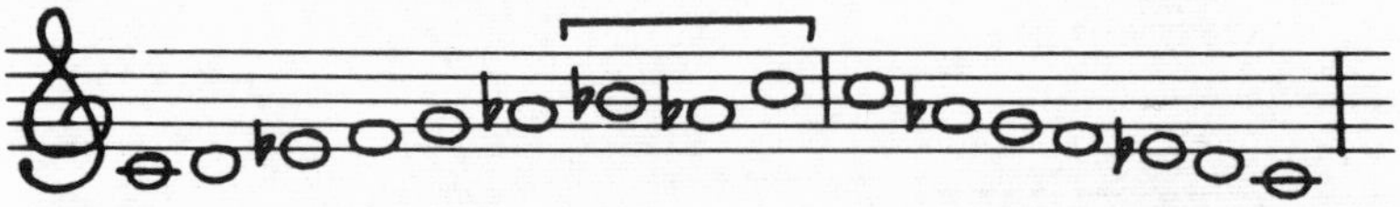

Ascent: *sampūrṇa*; one *vakra* feature is shown.
Descent: the note *NI* (Bb) is avoided.

(78) *Parabhrutāviṇi*

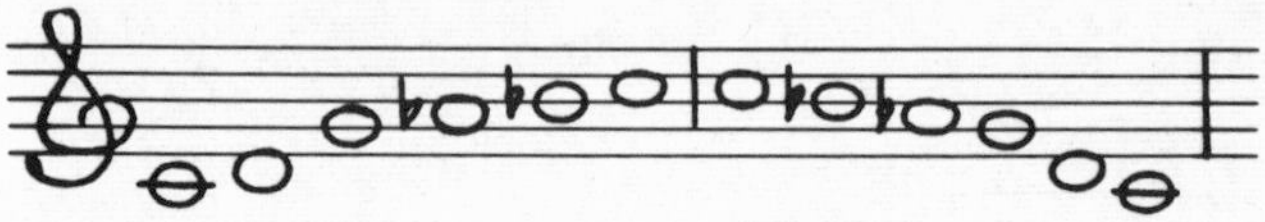

The notes *GA* (Eb) and *MA* (F) are avoided entirely.

(79) *Pūrṇabhairavī*

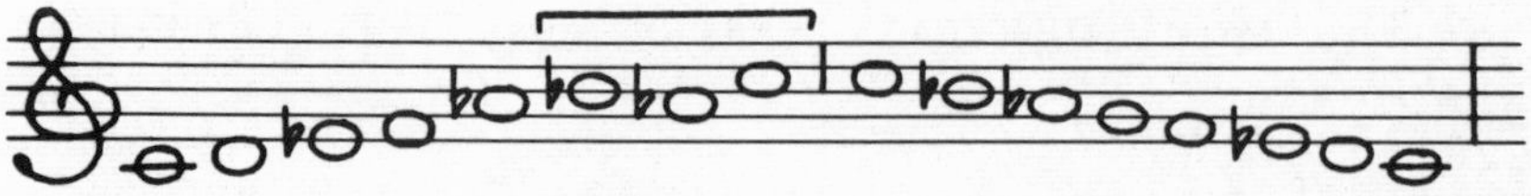

Ascent: the note *PA* (G) is avoided; one *vakra* feature is shown.
Descent: *krama sampūrṇa*.

(80) *Ratipatipriya*

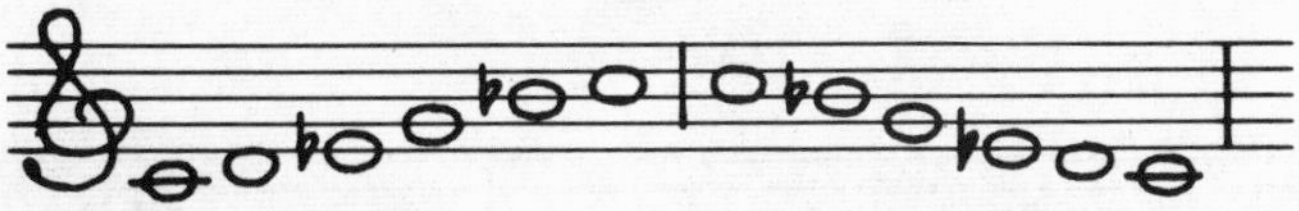

The notes *MA* (F) and *DHA* (Ab) are avoided entirely.

(81) *Sindhudhanyāsi*

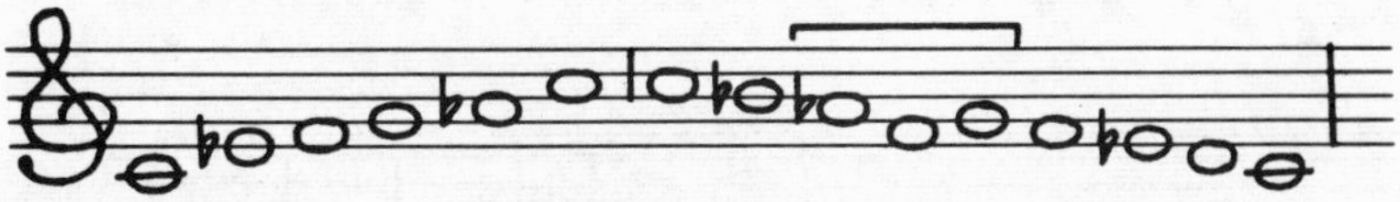

Ascent: the notes *RI* (D) and *NI* (Bb) are avoided.
Descent: *sampūrṇa*; one *vakra* feature is shown.

(82) *Śuddhasālavi*

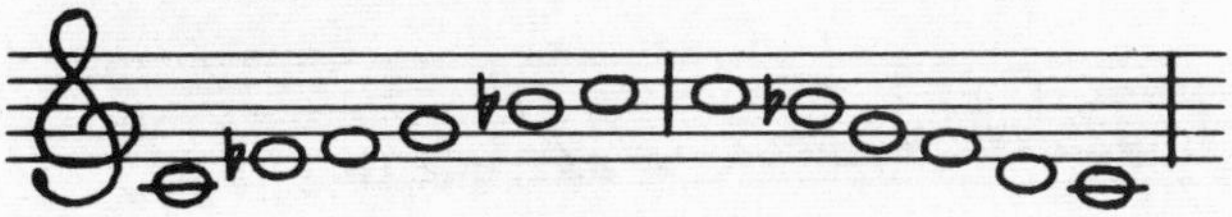

The note *DHA* (Ab) is avoided entirely. The ascent avoids *RI* (D) and the descent *GA* (Eb).

21. *MĒḶA KIRAVĀṆI*

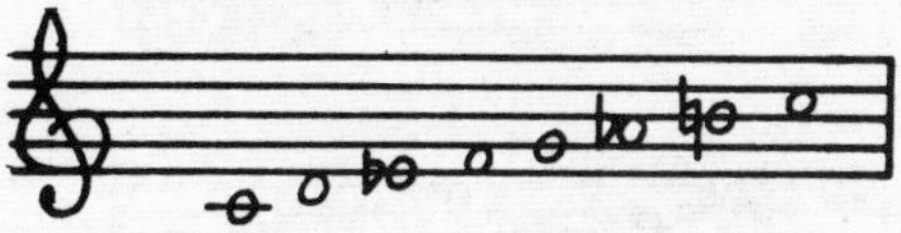

Kiravāṇi can be performed at any time and appears frequently in light and popular music. Its stressed notes are said to be *RI* (D), *GA* (Eb), *MA* (F), and *NI* (B).

Veṅkaṭamakhin calls this *rāga Kiraṇāvali* and states that its scale avoids the note *MA* (F) in ascent. He remarks that *vakra* features appear on the notes *PA* (G) in ascent and on *DHA* (Ab) and *MA* (F) in descent.

The following song example is a *kṛti* in *Ādi tāla*, composed by Tyāgarāja:

KIRAVĀṆI (Ādi-tāla)

Pallavi

A

B

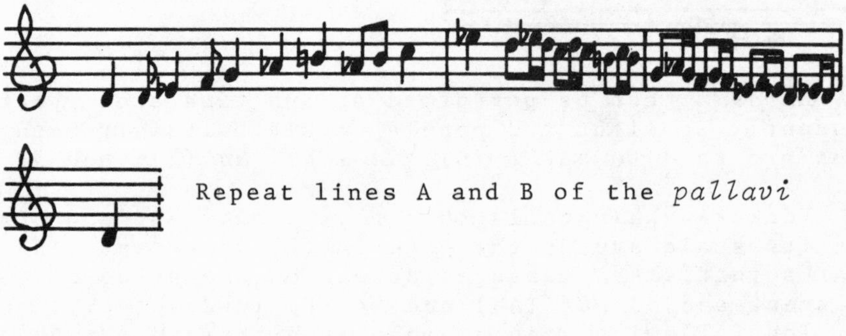

Repeat lines A and B of the *pallavi*

Anupallavi

Repeat lines A and B of the *pallavi*

Charana

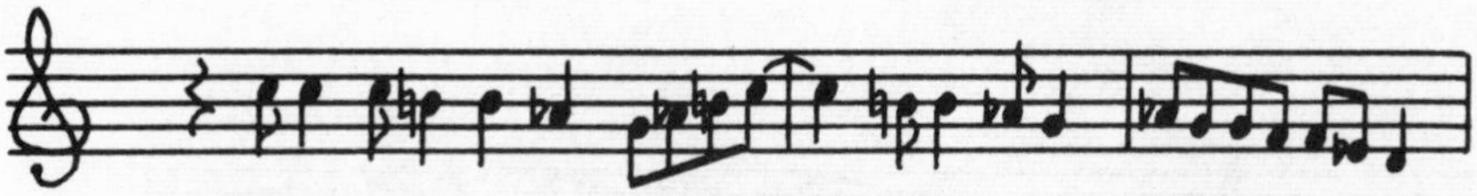

Repeat lines A and B of the *pallavi*. The song concludes with *RI* (D) or *SA* (C).

RĀGA KIRAVĀṆI (*Triputa-tāla*) SCM, 97

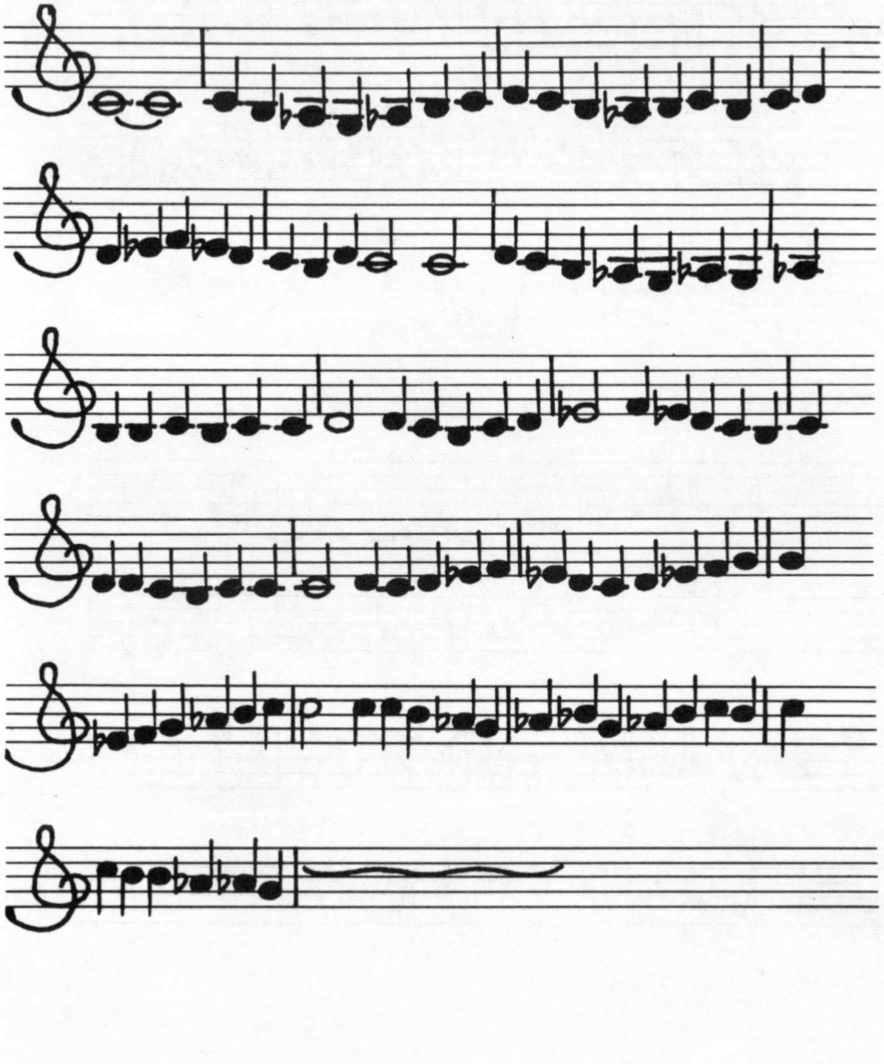

Janya Rāgas of the 21. Mēḷa

(1) *Jayaśrī*

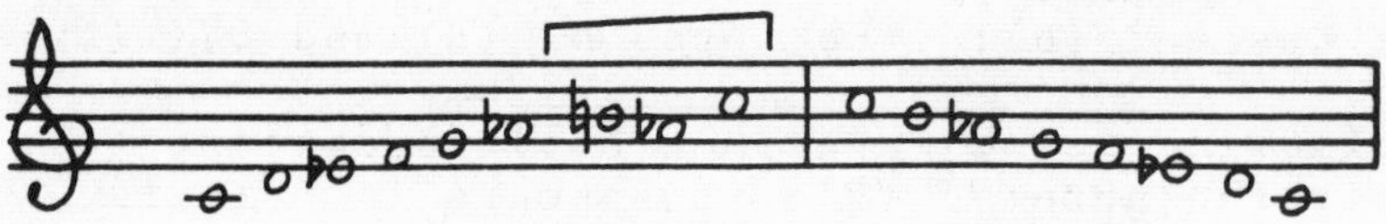

This scale is *sampūrṇa* and shows one *vakra* feature in ascent.

RĀGA JAYAŚRĪ (*Triputa-tāla*) SCM, 98

(2) *Kiraṇāvaḷi*

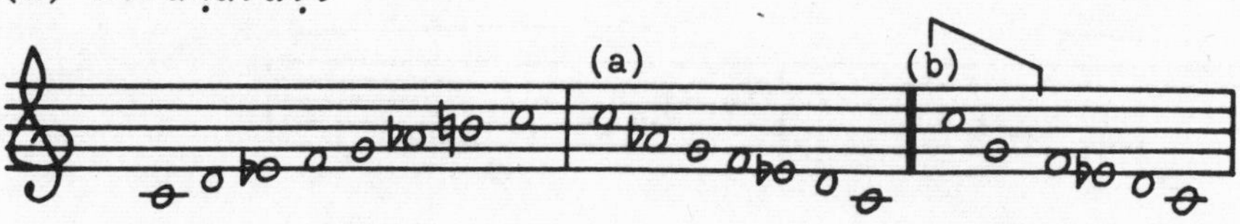

Although this *rāga* bears the name of Veṅkaṭamakhin's 21. *mēḷa*, it does not follow his descriptions (cf. remark to the 21. *mēḷa*).
Ascent: *krama sampūrṇa*
Descent (a): the note *NI* (B) is avoided.
Alternative descent (b): the notes *NI* (B) and *DHA* (Ab) are omitted.

The following melody specimen employs descent (a), avoiding only the note *NI* (B); it appears in *triputa tāla* and is taken from SCM, 99:

(3) *Madhavi*

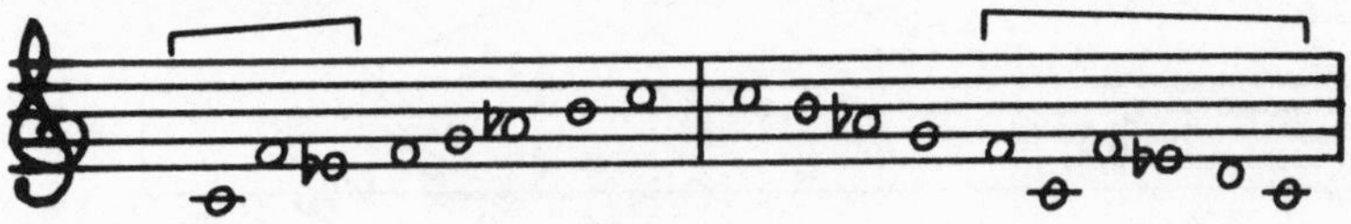

Ascent: the note *RI* (D) is avoided; one *vakra* feature is shown.
Descent: *sampūrṇa*; one extended *vakra* feature is used.

RĀGA MADHAVI (Triputa-tāla) SCM, 99-100

(4) *Kalyāṇa Vasanta*

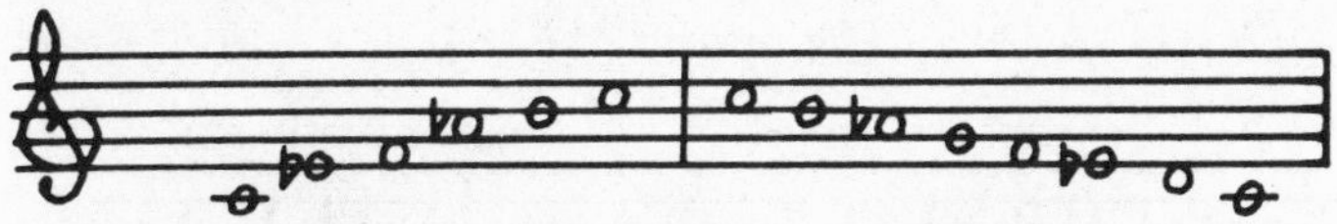

Ascent: the notes *RI* (D) and *PA* (G) are avoided.
Descent: *krama sampūrṇa.*

Another *rāga* with the same name is listed under the heading of the 22. *mēḷa* (69).

RĀGA KALYĀṆA VASANTA (Triputa-tāla) SCM, 101

(5) *Karnāṭaka Dēvagāndhāri*

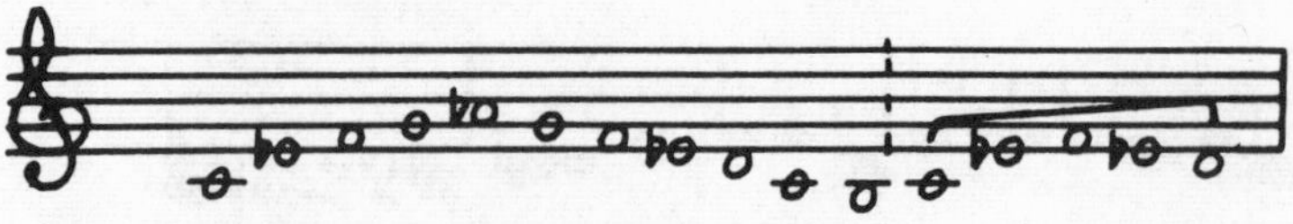

This *rāga* has *dhaivatāntya* character, because its highest note is *DHA* (Ab) of the *madhya saptaka* (middle octave range). The scale can be shown in two ways: one that begins the ascent with the low *NI* (B), avoids (in ascent) the note *RI* (D), and stops with *DHA* (Ab); its descent progresses in a step-by-step manner from *DHA* (Ab) back to the low *NI* (B); another presentation of the scale appends to the lowest note of the descent the passage *SA-GA-MA-GA-RI* (C-Eb-F-Eb-D).

Another *rāga* with the same name appears under the heading of the 22. *mēḷa* (76).

RĀGA KARNĀṬAKA DĒVAGĀNDHĀRI (*Triputa-tāla*) SCM, 101

(6) *Bhānupriya*

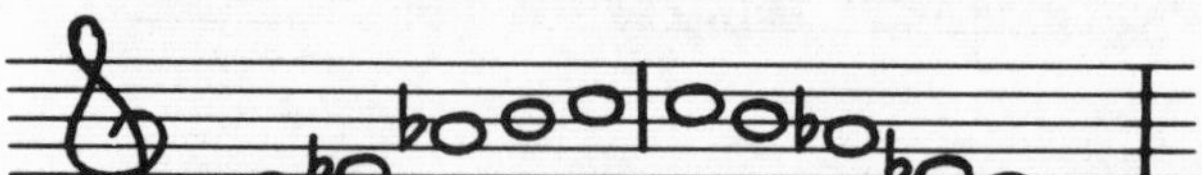

The notes *MA* (F) and *PA* (G) are avoided entirely.

Another *rāga* with the same name is listed under the heading of the 1. *mēḷa* (4).

(7) *Chandrikā*

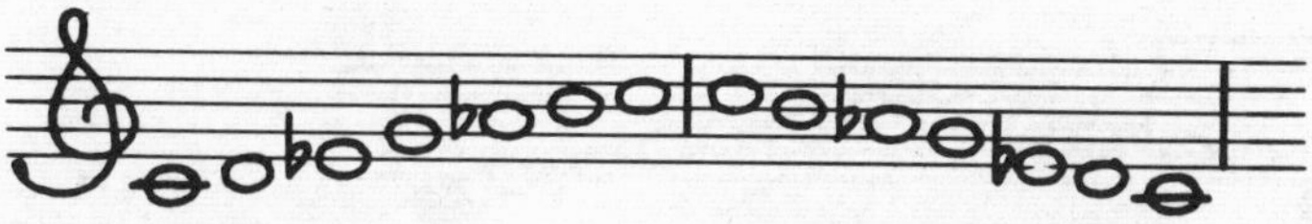

The note *MA* (F) is avoided entirely.

Another *rāga* with the same name appears under the heading of the 18. *mēḷa* (7).

(8) *Divyābharaṇam*

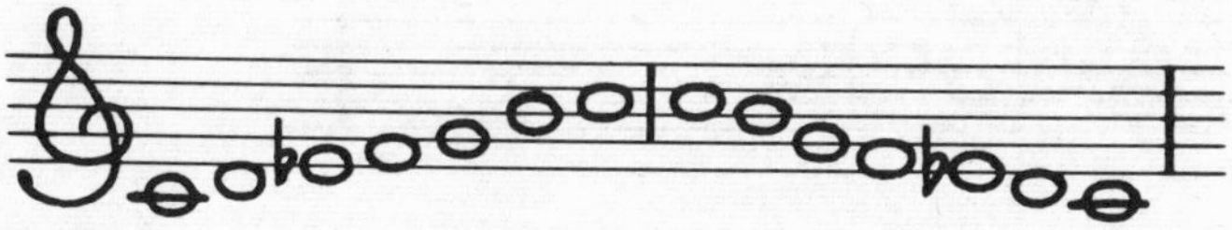

The note *DHA* (Ab) is avoided entirely.

(9) *Gagana Bhūpāḷam* (*Gagana Bhūpāḷi*)

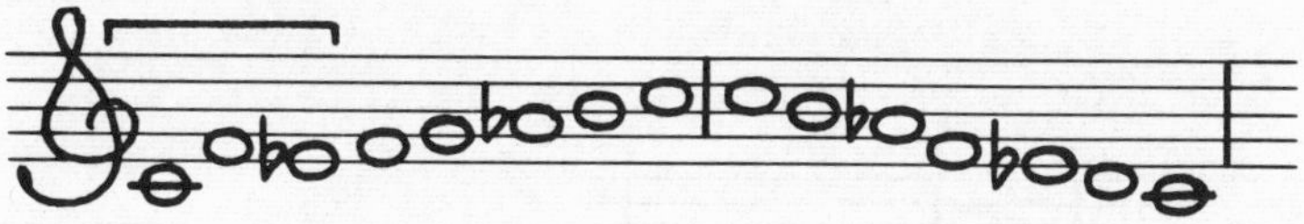

Ascent: the note *RI* (D) is avoided; one *vakra* feature is shown.
Descent: the note *PA* (G) is omitted.

(10) *Haṃsa Pañchamam*

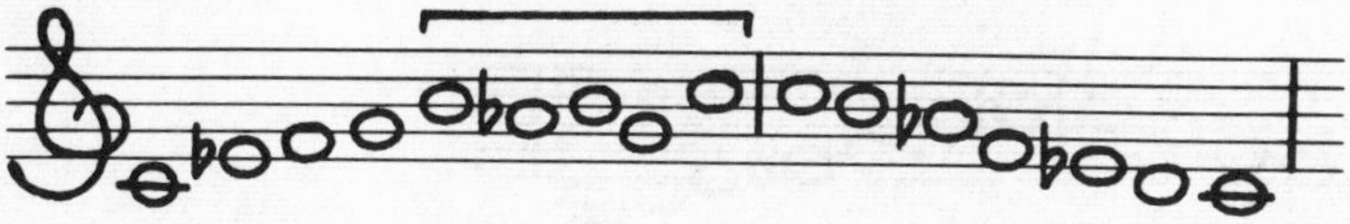

Ascent: *sampūrṇa*; one extended *vakra* feature is shown.
Descent: the note *PA* (G) is avoided.

(11) *Hāṭakabharaṇam*

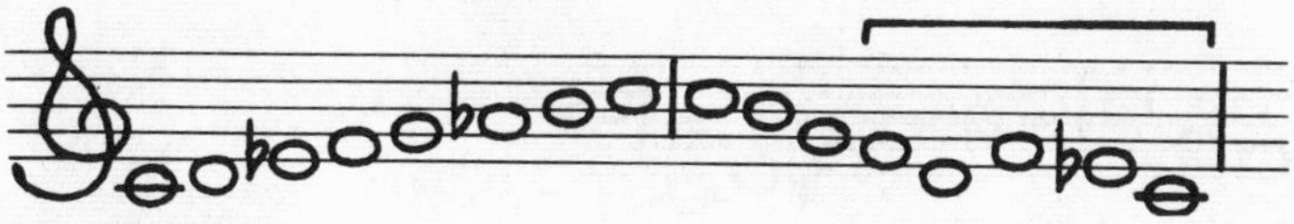

Ascent: *krama sampūrṇa*.
Descent: the note *DHA* (Ab) is avoided; one extended *vakra* feature is shown.

(12) *Indu Dhavaḷi*

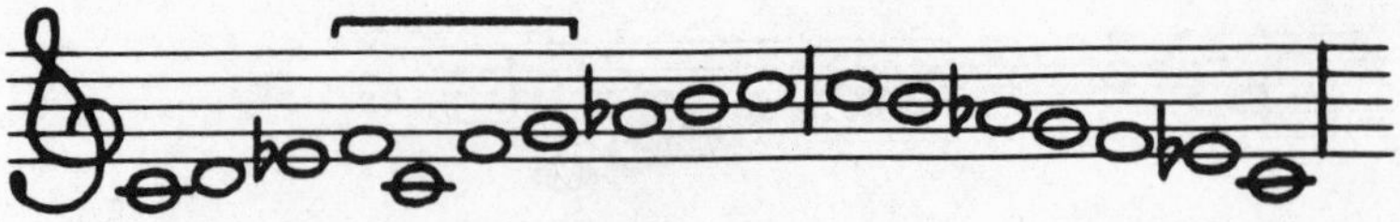

Ascent: *sampūrṇa*; one *vakra* feature is shown.
Descent: the note *RI* (D) is avoided.

(13) *Indu Hāvaḷi*

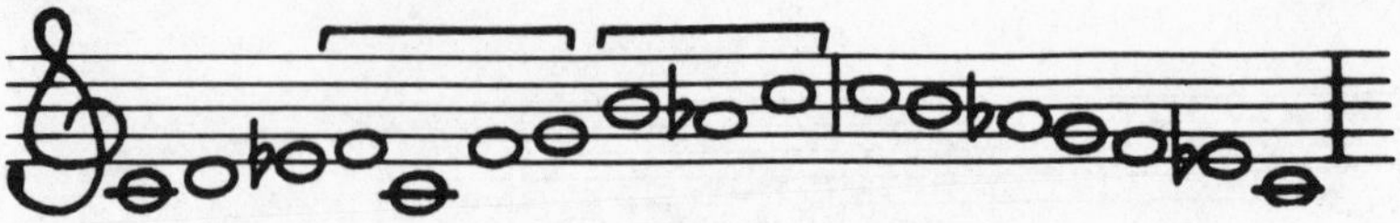

This *rāga* differs from *Indu Dhavali* (21,22) only by the use of a second *vakra* feature in ascent: *NI-DHA-SA* (B-Ab-c). In all other aspects the two *rāgas* are identical.

(14) *Kadaram*

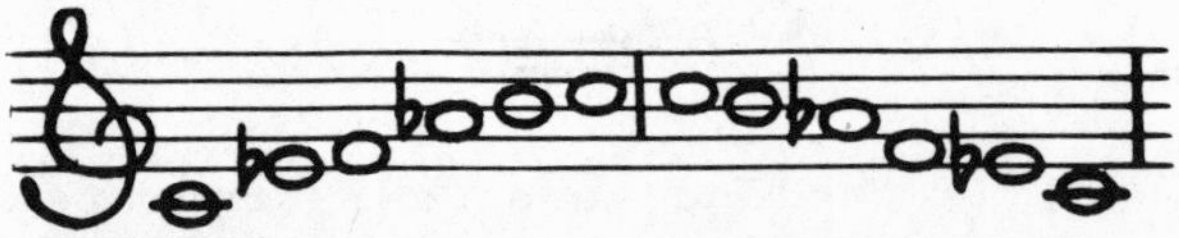

The notes *RI* (D) and *PA* (G) are avoided entirely.

(15) *Kula Bhūshaṇi* (*Kula Bhūṣani*)

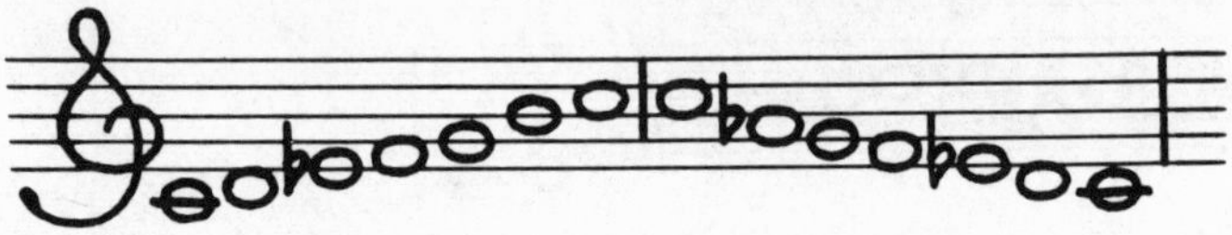

Ascent: the note *DHA* (Ab) is avoided.
Descent: the note *NI* (B) is omitted.

(16) *Nāgadīpakam*

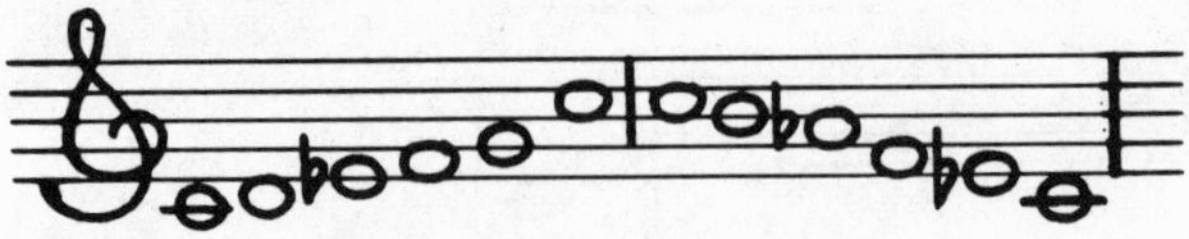

Ascent: the notes *DHA* (Ab) and *NI* (B) are avoided.
Descent: the notes *PA* (G) and *RI* (D) are omitted.

(17) *Sāmantasālavi*

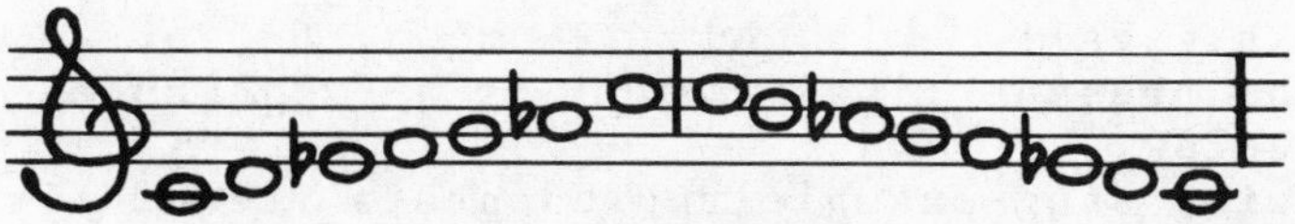

Ascent: the note *NI* (B) is avoided.
Descent: *krama sampūrṇa.*

(18) *Sōmagiri*

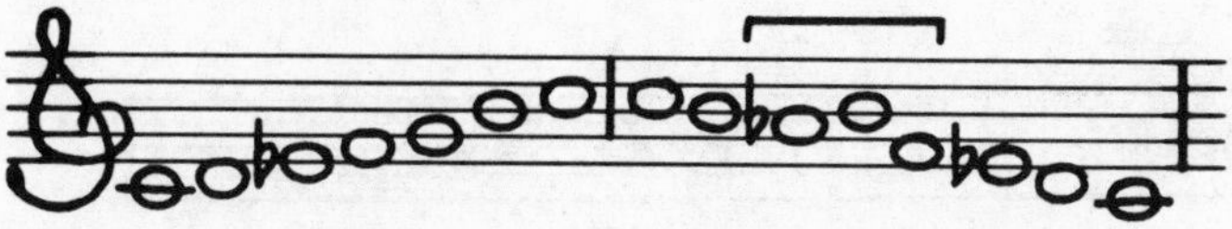

Ascent: the note *DHA* (Ab) is avoided.
Descent: the note *PA* (G) is omitted; one *vakra* feature is shown.

(19) *Śukhavāni*

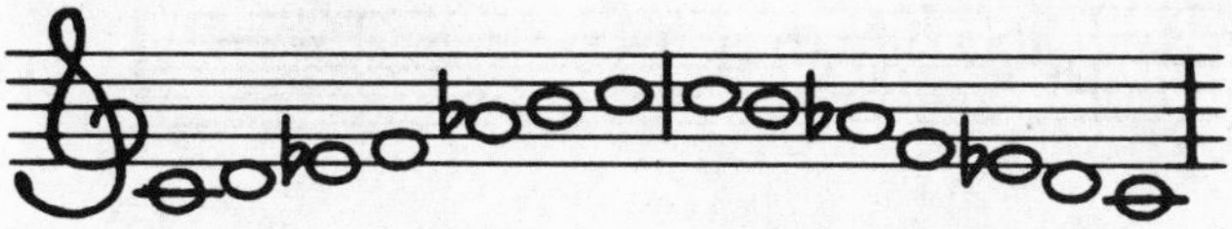

The note *PA* (G) is avoided entirely.

Another *rāga* with the same name appears under the heading of the 13. *mēḷa* (27).

(20) *Vasumati*

The notes *GA* (Eb) and *MA* (F) are avoided entirely.

22. *MĒḶA KHARAHARAPRIYĀ* (*KARAHARAPRIYĀ*)

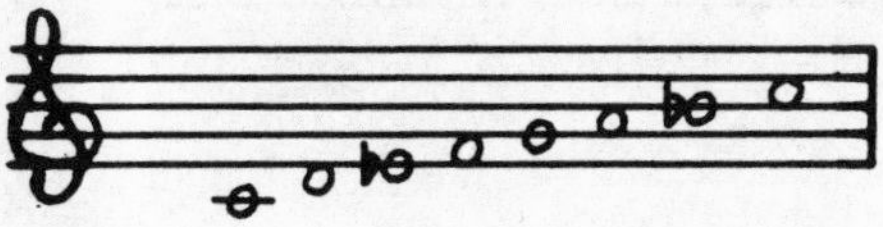

Kharaharapriyā is a remarkably popular *rāga* and may be

performed at any time. It possesses a large number of *janya rāgas*.

Veṅkaṭamakhin calls this, his 22. *mēḷa*, *Śrī* or *Śrīrāga*. At the present time *Śrīrāga* is a *janya* and will be shown below.

The following song example represents a frequently performed *kīrtana* by Tyāgarāja:

KARAHARAPRIYĀ (*Triputa-tāla*)

Pallavi

Anupallavi

Charana

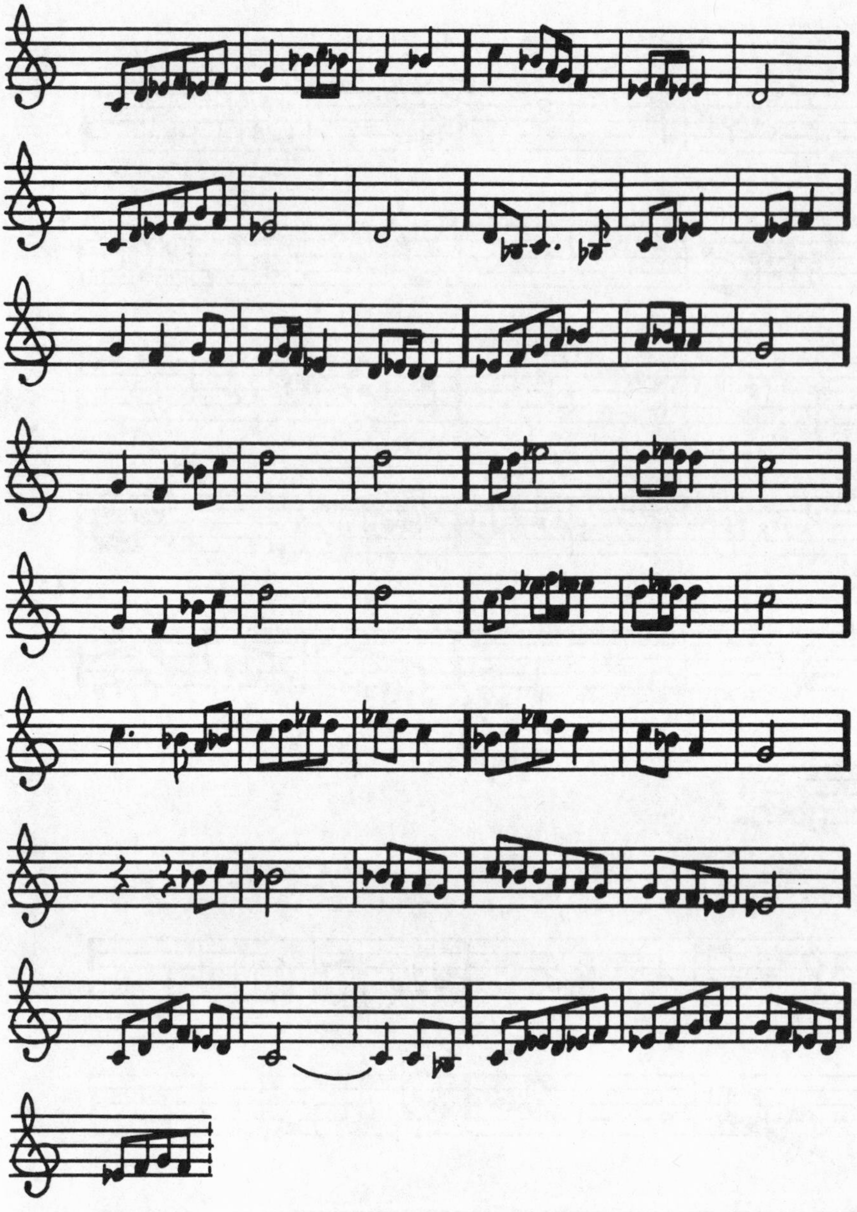

The following is a melody specimen in *Kharahara-priyā* (*Triputa-tāla*), from SCM, 102:

Janya Rāgas of the 22. Mēḷa

(1) *Śrīrāga*

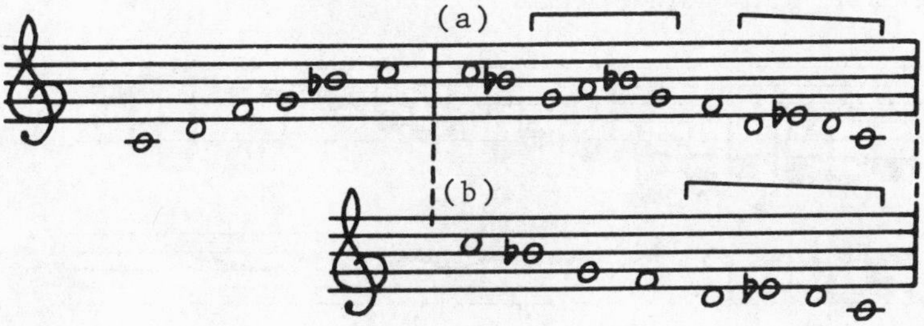

Ascent: the notes *GA* (Eb) and *DHA* (A) are avoided.
Descent (a): *sampūrṇa*; two *vakra* passages are shown. The note *DHA* (A) may occur, but always in a "weak" form.
Descent (b): the note *DHA* (A) is omitted; one *vakra* feature is used.

Musicians allow themselves various liberties when performing this *rāga*, hence the scale may become modified, particularly in its descending form. The ascent remains more or less unchanged.[4]

The following is a song fragment composed by a musician named Garbapuriyar:[5]

ŚRĪ RĀGA (*Ādi-tāla*) SPC III, 95-96

Pallavi

Anupallavi

Śrīrāga specimen from SCM, 102-3:

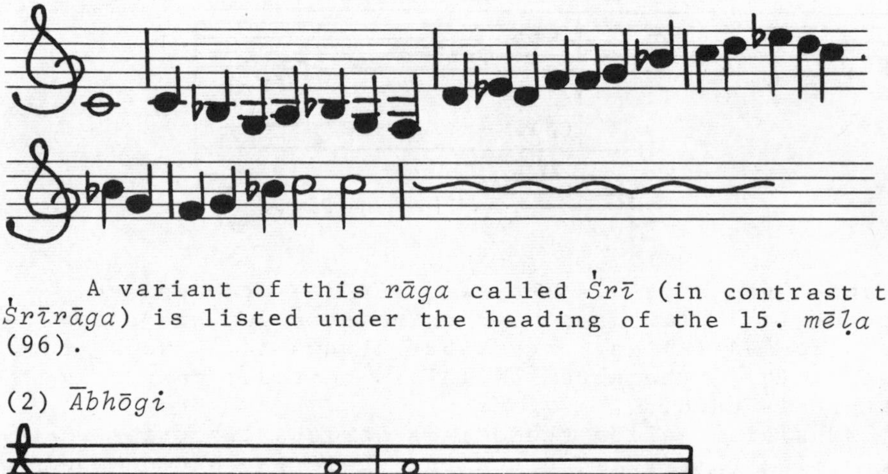

A variant of this *rāga* called *Śrī* (in contrast to *Śrīrāga*) is listed under the heading of the 15. *mēḷa* (96).

(2) *Ābhōgi*

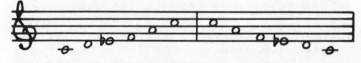

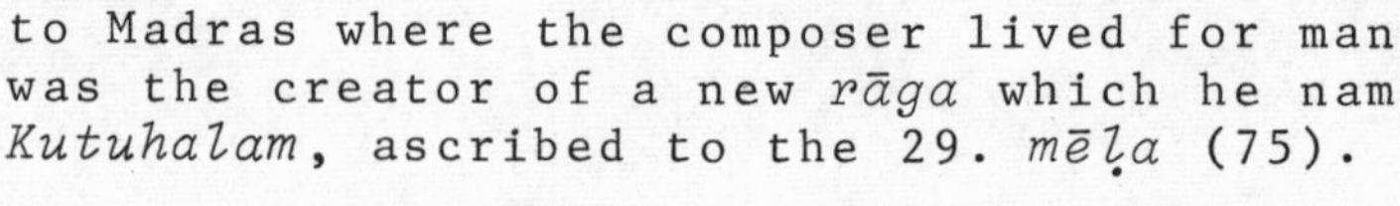

The notes *PA* (G) and *NI* (Bb) are avoided entirely. The following song specimen was composed by Pattaṇam Subramanya Ayyar (1845-1902). The name Pattanam refers to Madras where the composer lived for many years. He was the creator of a new *rāga* which he named *Kadana Kutuhalam*, ascribed to the 29. *mēḷa* (75).

ĀBHŌGI RĀGA (Ādi-tāla) SPC, III, 62

Pallavi

Anupallavi

ĀBHŌGI (Triputa-tāla) SCM, 110-11

(3) *Kānaḍa*

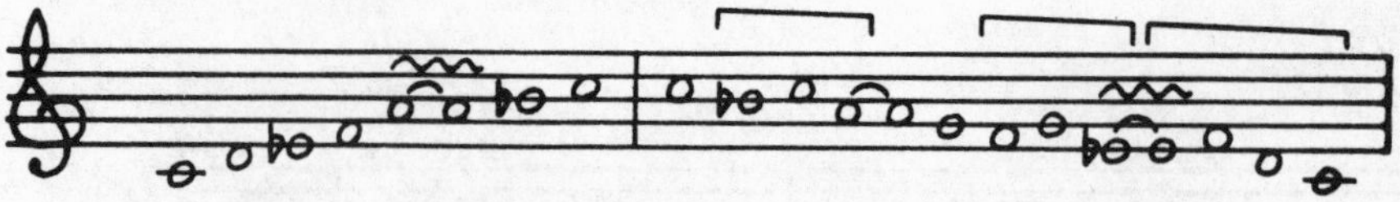

Ascent: the note *PA* (G) is avoided.
Descent: *sampūrna*; three *vakra* features are shown.

The note *DHA* (A) in ascent and descent is frequently performed with a small narrow-ranged vibrato. The same practice is applied to the note *GA* (Eb), but only in descent.

As *Kānaḍa*, like its primary *rāga*, enjoys considerable popularity, musicians take various liberties, particularly in the descending line. However, the last four notes of the *Kānaḍa* descent, forming the *vakra* feature *GA-MA-RI-SA* (Eb-F-D-C) have to be maintained. This feature is not only characteristic for *Kānaḍa* of the South but also for *Kānaḍa* types of the North (see RNI, 499).

Melodies in this *rāga* often begin with the note *RI* (D), or with *PA* (G), or *DHA* (A). SD II, 293 mentions also the note *NI* (Bb) as an initial feature. *Kānaḍa* can be performed at all times.

Another *rāga* with the same name (or *Kannaḍa*) appears under the heading of the 29. *mēḷa* (79).

KĀNAḌA RĀGA (*Ādi-tāla*) SPC III, 97

Pallavi

Anupallavi

(4) *Darbār(u)*

Ascent: the note *GA* (Eb) is avoided.

The descent is subject to various interpretations, as is usual in popular *rāgas*. The two forms of descent shown above as (a) and (b) are the most frequently employed. Both are *sampūrṇa*; descent (a) contains an extended *vakra* passage, and descent (b) is *krama sampūrṇa*. The note *GA* (Eb), occasionally also *RI* (D), is performed with slight vibratos in descent.

Melodies in this *rāga* often begin with the note *RI* (D), or with *PA* (G), also with *DHA* (A). *Darbar* can be performed at any time.

The following song example is composed by Tiruvarur Thiagaiyer:[6]

DARBĀR RĀGA (*Ādi-tāla*) SPC III, 94

Pallavi

Anupallavi

DARBĀR (*Triputa-tāla*) SCM, 121

(5) *Nāyakī*

There are various scales that are said to represent the material of *Nāyakī*. The two scales shown below are commonly in use:

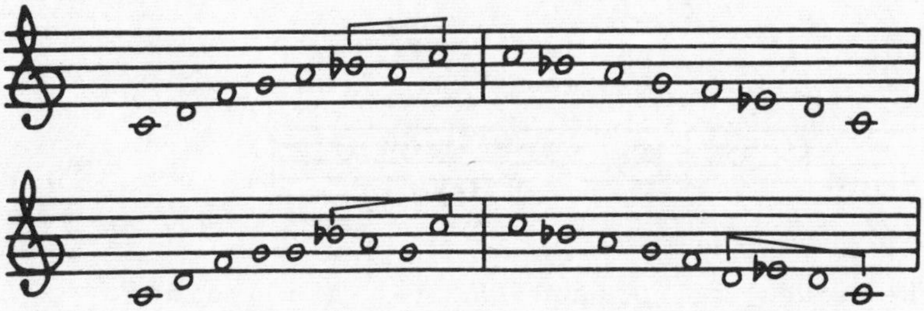

Both scales avoid the note *GA* (Eb) in ascent and both have *sampūrṇa* descents. Each scale shows one *vakra* feature in ascent. The descent of the first scale is *krama sampūrṇa*; that of the second shows one *vakra* feature.

The following song example shows no *vakra* features in ascent; the straight ascending progression *NI-SA* (Bb-c) can be observed in measures 4, 5, 7, 9, and 10. In descent, however, the *vakra* feature of the second scale, *RI-GA-RI-SA* (D-Eb-D-C) can be seen in measures 3, 4, 6, 10, and 12.

Nāyakī appears also under the heading of the 20. *mēḷa* (18) in which the note *DHA* is interpreted as Ab.

NĀYAKĪ RĀGA (*Khanda-jāti triputa-tāla*) SPC III, 85-86

Pallavi

Anupallavi

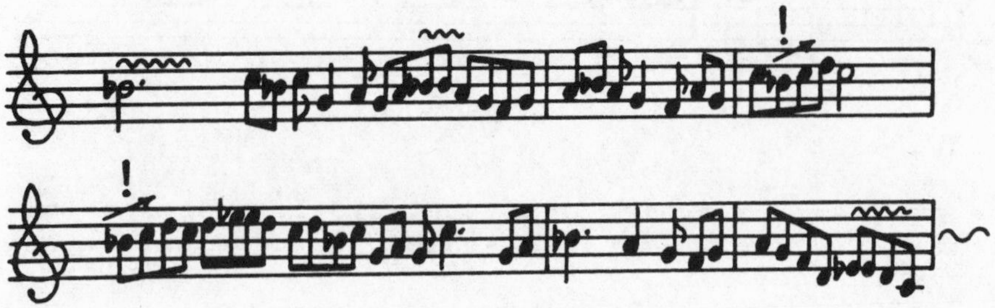

(6) *Ābhēri*

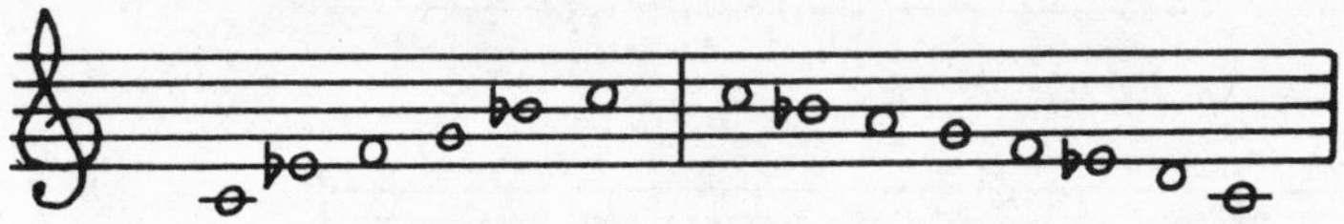

Ascent: the notes *RI* (D) and *DHA* (A) are avoided.
Descent: *krama sampūrṇa*.

In the phrase *PA-ḌHA-PA* the middle note is intoned low whereby the phrase sounds G-Ab-G.

Ābhēri can be performed at any time.
Another *rāga* with the same name appears under the heading of the 20. *mēḷa* (6).

(7) *Ānanda Vāridhi*

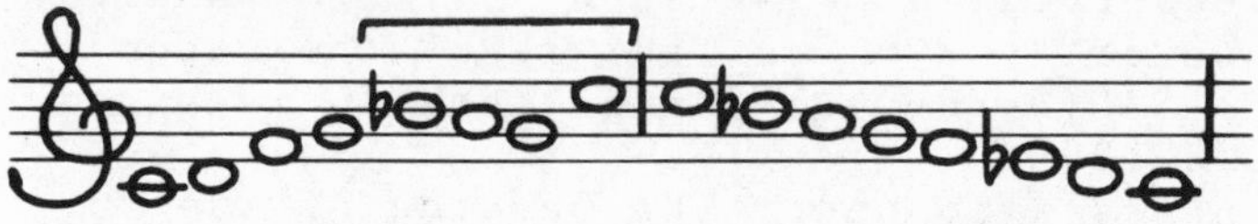

Ascent: the note *GA* (Eb) is avoided. One characteristic *vakra* feature is shown.
Descent: *krama sampūrṇa*.

(8) *Āndōlikā*

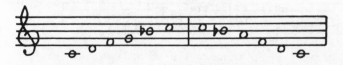

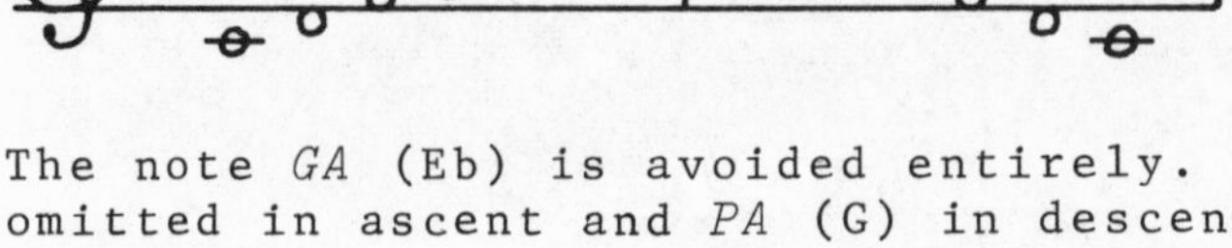

The note *GA* (Eb) is avoided entirely. *DHA* (A) is omitted in ascent and *PA* (G) in descent.

(9) *Anilāvaḷi*

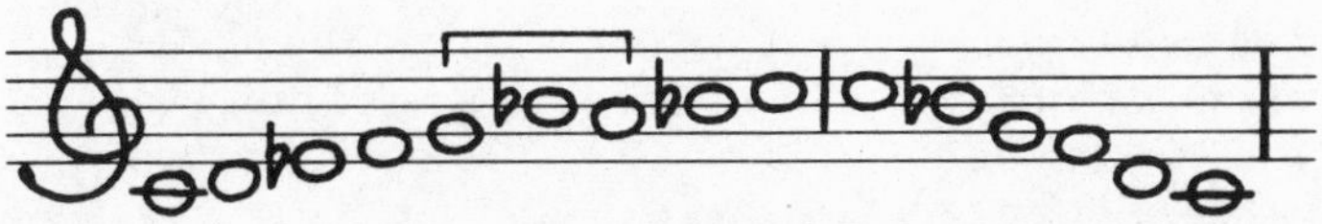

Ascent: *sampūrṇa*; one *vakra* feature is shown.
Descent: the notes *DHA* (A) and *GA* (Eb) are avoided.

(10) *Aruṇa Chandrikā*

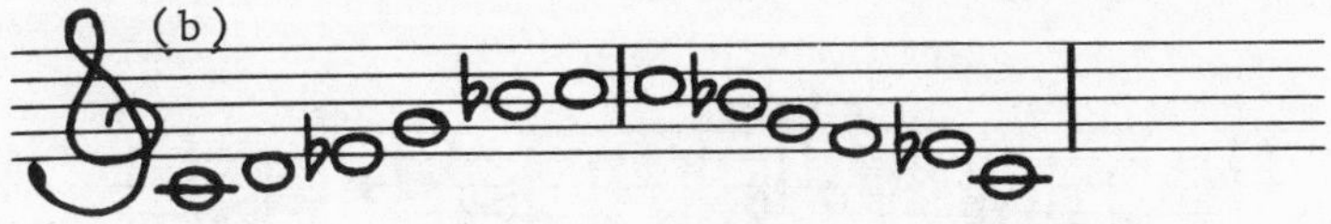

SD (I, 28) mentions two separate *rāgas* with the same name, subordinated to the same *mēḷa*.
Another opinion considers scales (a) and (b) as representations of one *rāga*, a phenomenon that shows the latitude of interpretation of *rāgas* derived from a remarkably popular primary *rāga*.

Scale (a) avoids the notes *RI* (D) and *DHA* (A) in ascent. Its descent is *sampūrṇa* and shows one *vakra* feature. Scale (b) employs the note *RI* (D) in ascent but avoids the notes *MA* (F) and *DHA* (A). The descent shows no *vakra* feature and omits the notes *DHA* (A) and *RI* (D).

(11) *Bālachandrikā*

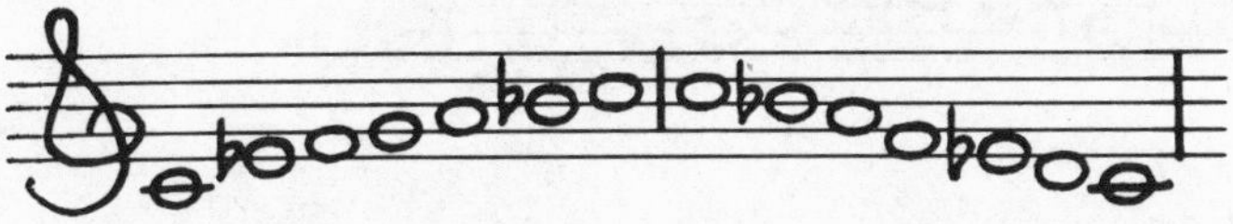

Ascent: the note *RI* (D) is avoided.
Descent: the note *PA* (G) is omitted.

(12) *Bālaghōshi* (*Bālaghōshiṇi*, *Bālaghōṣi*, *Bālaghōṣiṇi*)

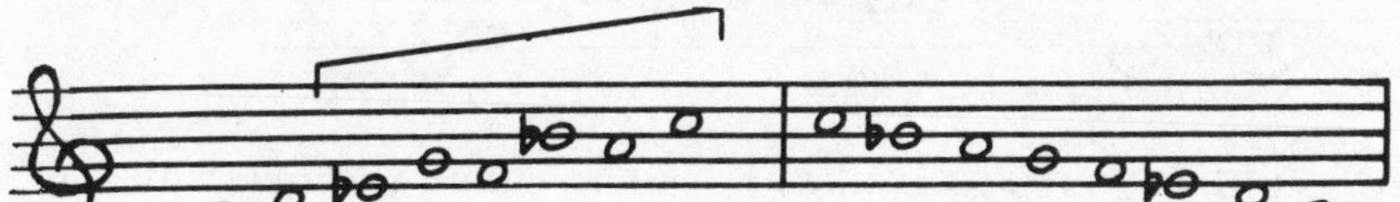

Ascent: *sampūrṇa*; one characteristic *vakra* passage is shown.
Descent: *krama sampūrṇa*.

The following fragment of a melody specimen is taken from SCM, 126:

BĀLAGHŌSHI (*Triputa-tāla*) SCM, 126

(13) *Bhadra Sāraṅga Līla*

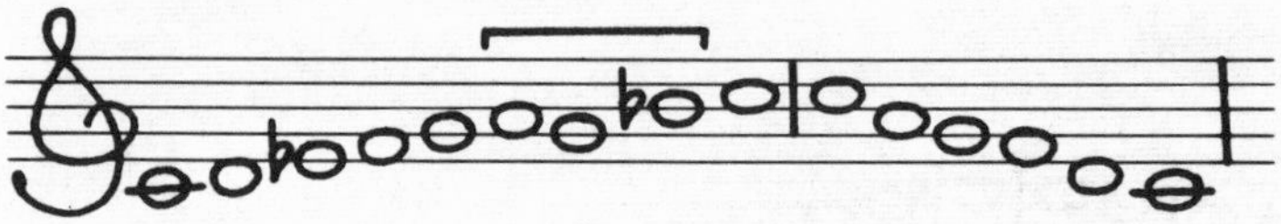

Ascent: *sampūrṇa*; one *vakra* feature is shown.
Descent: the notes *NI* (Bb) and *GA* (Eb) are avoided.

(14) *Bhāgavatapriya*

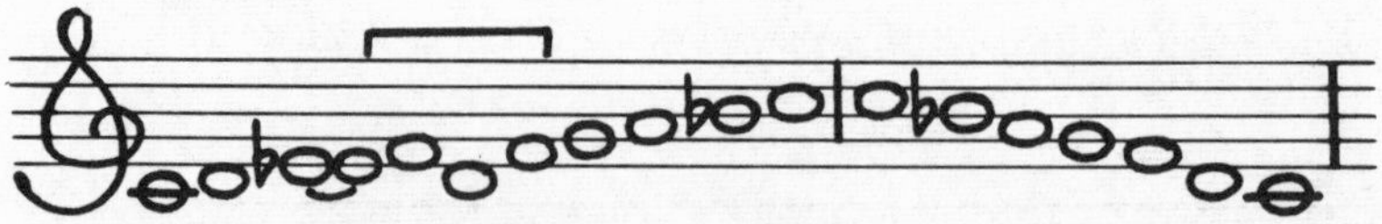

Ascent: *sampūrṇa*; one *vakra* feature is shown; the note *GA* (Eb) is to be stressed.
Descent: the note *GA* (Eb) is avoided.

(15) *Bhāgya Rañjaṇi*

Ascent: the note *PA* (G) is avoided.
Descent: the notes *NI* (Bb) and *DHA* (A) are omitted.

(16) *Bhōga Kannaḍā*

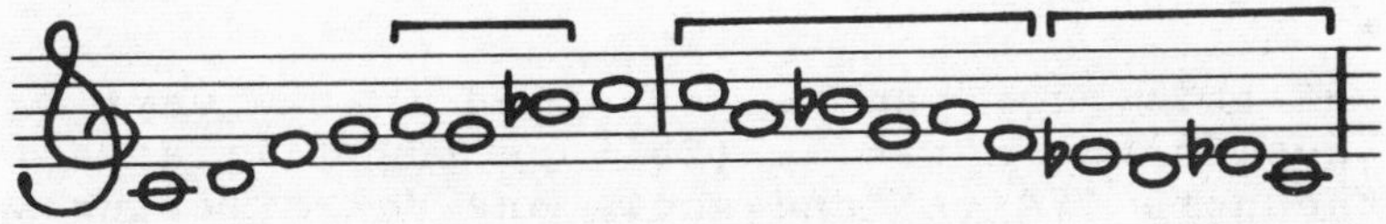

Ascent: the note *GA* (Eb) is avoided; one *vakra* feature is shown.
Descent: *sampūrṇa*; two extended *vakra* features are used.

(17) *Bhōgavati*

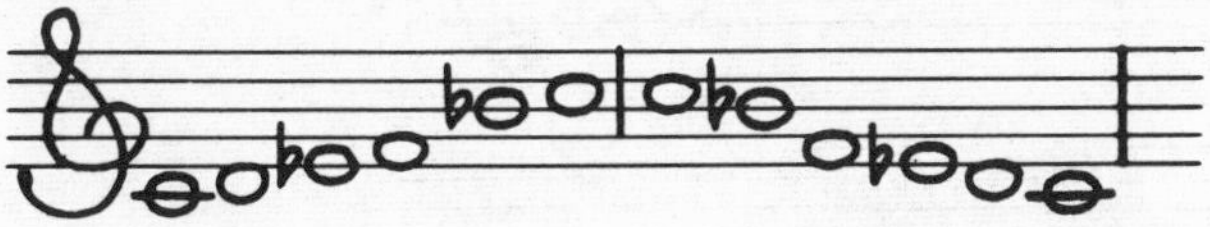

The notes *PA* (G) and *DHA* (A) are avoided entirely.

Another *rāga* with the same name appears under the heading of the 12. *mēḷa* (4).

(18) *Bhramarikā Mañjari*

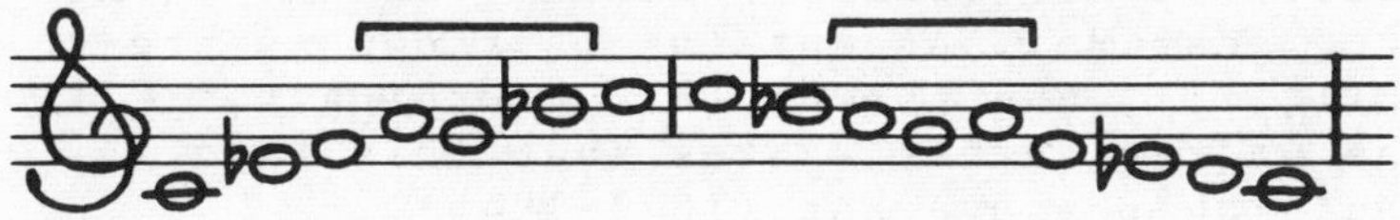

Ascent: the note *RI* (D) is avoided; one *vakra* feature is shown.
Descent: *sampūrṇa*; one *vakra* feature is used.

(19) *Bhūyōmaṇi*

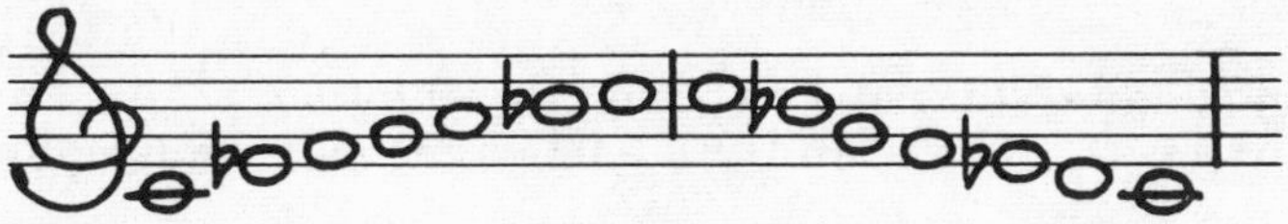

Ascent: the note *RI* (D) is avoided.
Descent: the note *DHA* (A) is omitted.

(20) *Bṛndāvana Sāraṅga*

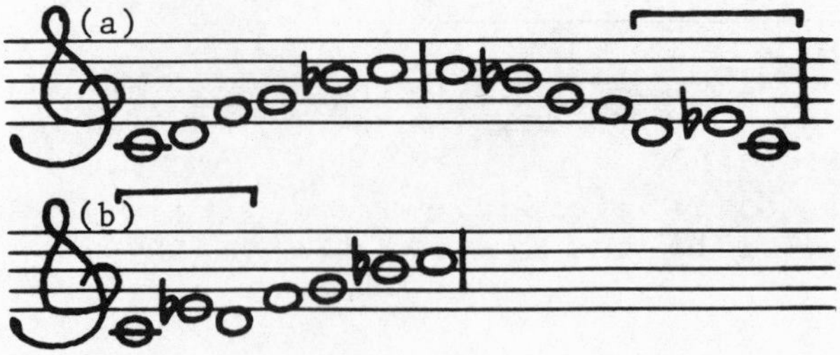

The ascent of this *rāga* can be performed in two ways. Ascent (a) avoids the notes *GA* (Eb) and *DHA* (A); ascent (b) omits the note *DHA* (A) and shows one *vakra* feature. The descent avoids the note *DHA* (A) and shows one *vakra* feature.

(21) *Chakra Pradīptā*

The scale of this recently created *rāga* is *sampūrṇa* in ascent and avoids the notes *PA* (G) and *RI* (D) in descent. There are two forms of ascent, both showing the same *vakra* feature. Ascent (a) is shown as presented in SD(I, 71), and ascent (b) according to R (223). The latter author states that this *rāga* was created by Muthiah Bhagavathar (1877-1945).[7]

(22) *Chandrakalā*

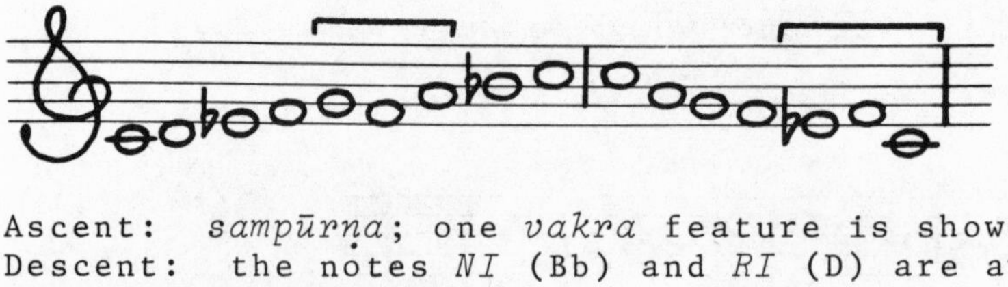

Ascent: *sampūrṇa*; one *vakra* feature is shown.
Descent: the notes *NI* (Bb) and *RI* (D) are avoided; one *vakra* feature is used.

(23) *Chandramaṇḍana*

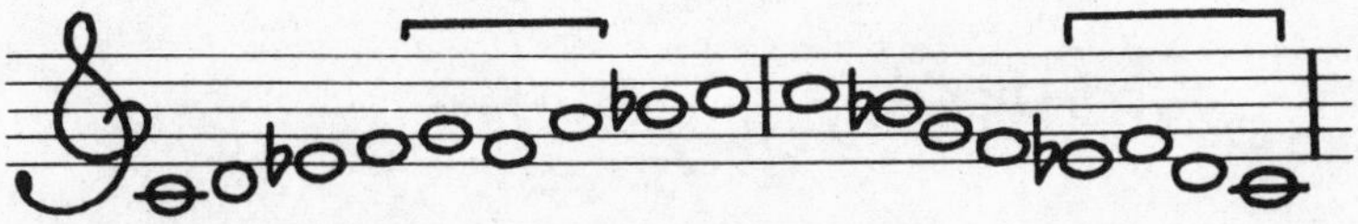

Ascent: *sampūrṇa*; one *vakra* feature is shown.
Descent: the note *DHA* (A) is avoided; one *vakra* feature is used.

(24) *Charāvaḷi*

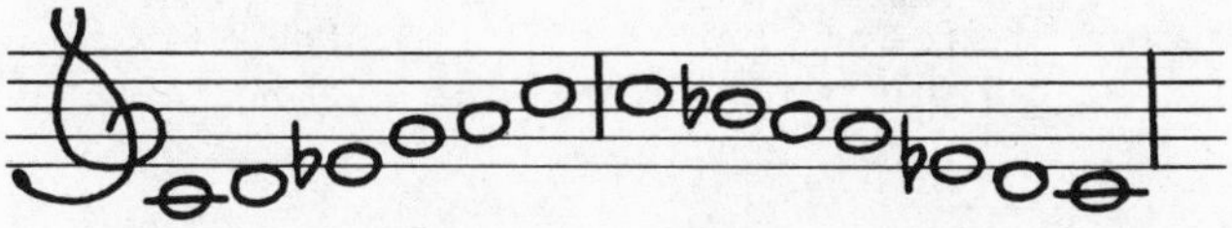

The note *MA* (F) is avoided entirely. *NI* (Bb) is omitted in ascent.

(25) *Chātam*

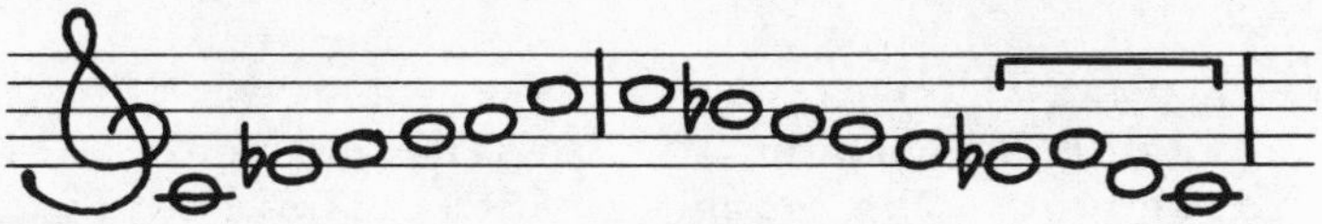

Ascent: the notes *RI* (D) and *NI* (Bb) are avoided.
Descent: *sampūrṇa*; one *vakra* feature is shown.

(26) *Chhandōdharī*

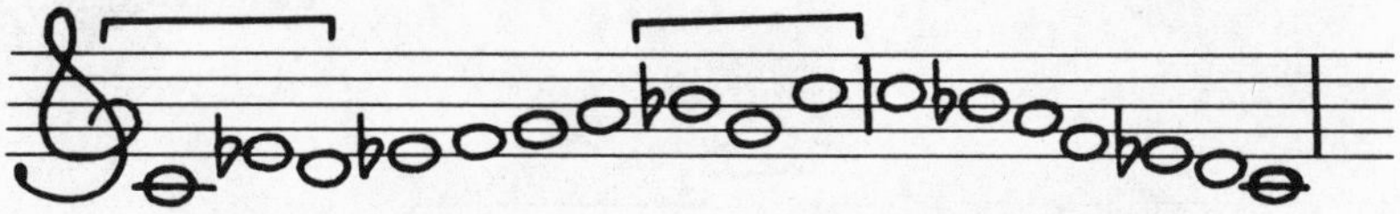

Ascent: *sampūrṇa*; two *vakra* features are shown.
Descent: the note *PA* (G) is avoided.

(27) *Chhāyā Ṡobhitam*

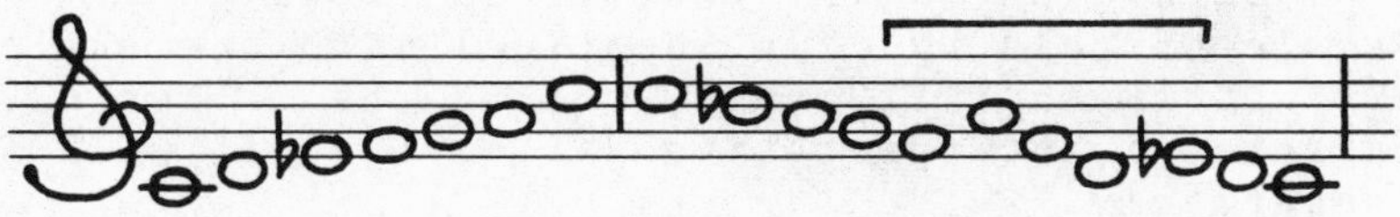

Ascent: the note *NI* (Bb) is avoided.
Descent: *sampūrṇa*; one extended *vakra* passage is shown.

(28) *Chitta Rañjaṇi*

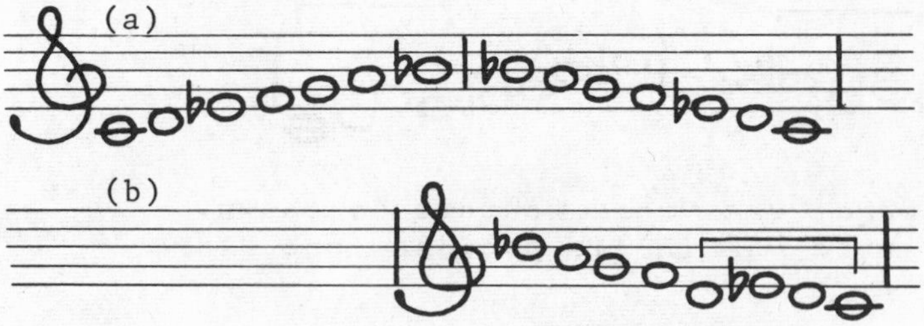

The ascent of this *niṣādāntya* scale is *krama sampūrṇa*. There are two forms of descent in use: (a) is *krama sampūrṇa* and (b) is *sampūrṇa* and shows one *vakra* feature.

(29) *Dēśya Kānaḍā*

Ascent: the note *PA* (G) is usually avoided.
Descent: the notes *DHA* (A) and *MA* (F) are omitted; one *vakra* feature is shown. The note *GA* (Eb) is stressed.

The following two passages, using *PA* (G) in ascent, are characteristic:

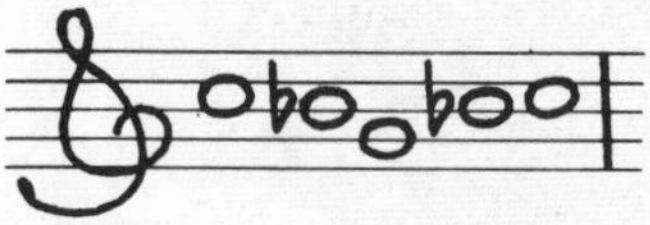

(30) *Dēśya Kāpi*

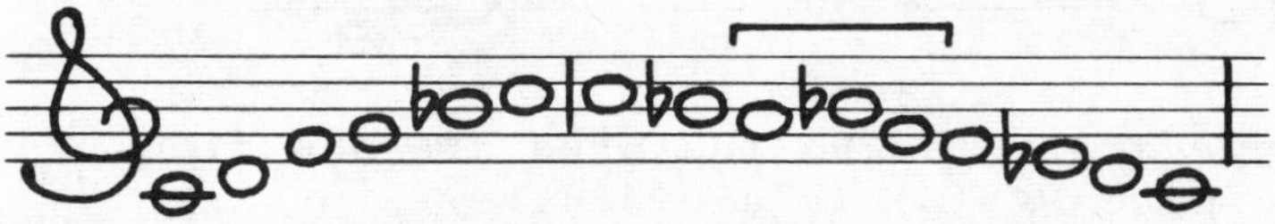

Ascent: the notes *GA* (Eb) and *DHA* (A) are avoided.
Descent: *sampūrṇa*; one *vakra* feature is shown.

The scale of this *rāga* is identical with one scale form of *Hindusthan Kāpi* (22, 51), but as the latter *rāga* shows several interpretative differences it will be shown separately.

(31) *Dēśya Manoharī*

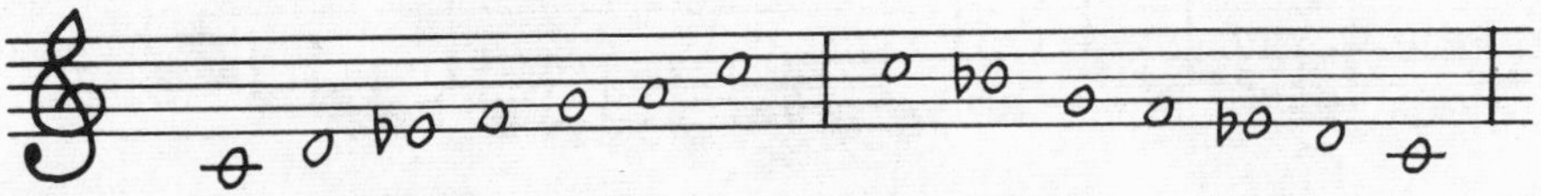

Ascent: the note *NI* (Bb) is avoided.
Descent: the note *DHA* (A) is omitted.

(32) *Dēvakriya*

Both scales are presented as representatives of *Dēvakriya*. Scale (a) is given by S (III, 307), and scale (b) by SD (I, 109).

Scale (a) avoids the notes *GA* (Eb) and *DHA* (A) in ascent. Its descent is *sampūrṇa* and shows one *vakra* feature.

Scale (b) is *sampūrṇa* in *ascent* and *descent* and shows two *vakra* features in ascent and one in descent.

Another *rāga* with the same name appears under the heading of the 20. *mēḷa* (14).
The SD (I, 109) remarks that "in the Dikshitar school the *rāga Śuddha Sāveri* goes by the name *Dēvakriya*. The Song "Śrī Guruguhatārayaśumām" by Muthuswamy Dikshitar is given as *Dēvakriya*. It is set in *Śuddha Sāveri*."

(33) *Dēvamanōharī*

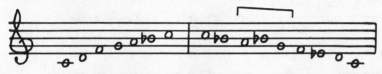

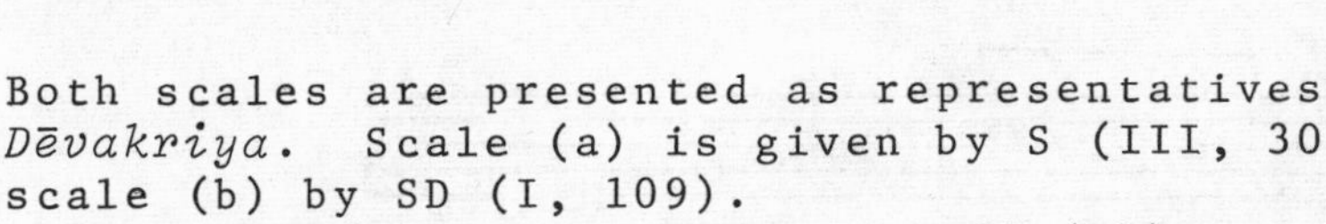

The note *GA* (Eb) is avoided in ascent. The *sampūrṇa* descent shows one *vakra* feature.
The following melody pattern comes from SCM, 125:

DĒVAMANŌHARĪ (*Triputa-tāla*)

(34) *Dēvamrita Varshiṇi* (*Dēvamṛta Varṣiṇi*)

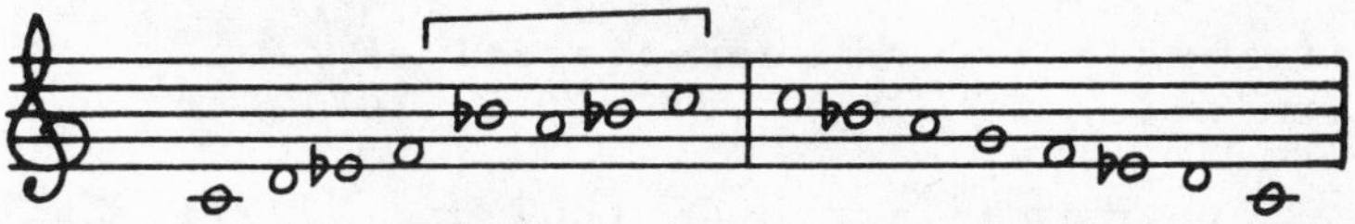

Ascent: the note *PA* (G) is avoided; one *vakra* feature is shown.
Descent: *krama sampūrṇa*

(35) *Dēva Mukhāri*

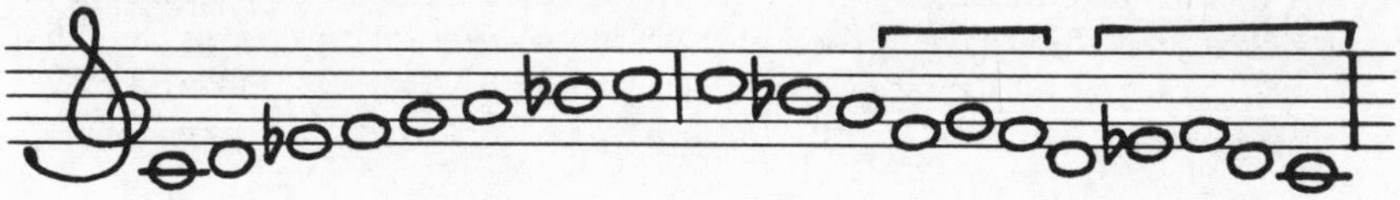

Ascent: *krama sampūrṇa*.
Descent: *sampūrṇa*; two *vakra* features are shown.

(36) *Dēvarañjaṇi*

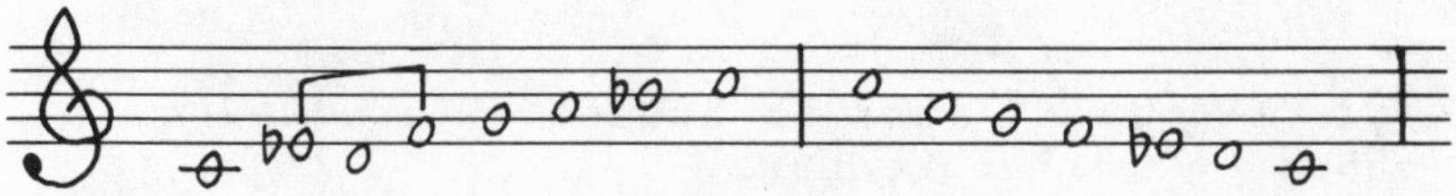

Ascent: *sampūrṇa*; one *vakra* feature is shown.
Descent: the note *NI* (Bb) is avoided.

Another *rāga* with the same name appears under the heading of the 28. *mēḷa* (77).

(37) *Dhātu Manōhari* (*Dhāta Manōhari*)

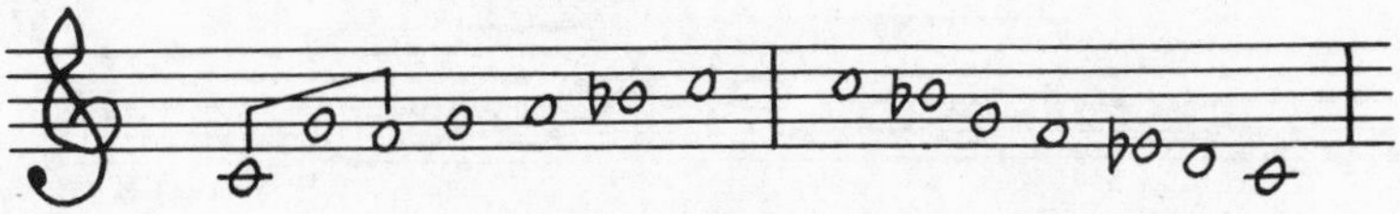

Ascent: the notes *RI* (D) and *GA* (Eb) are avoided; one *vakra* feature is shown.
Descent: the note *DHA* (A) is omitted.

(38) *Dhīra Kaḷā*

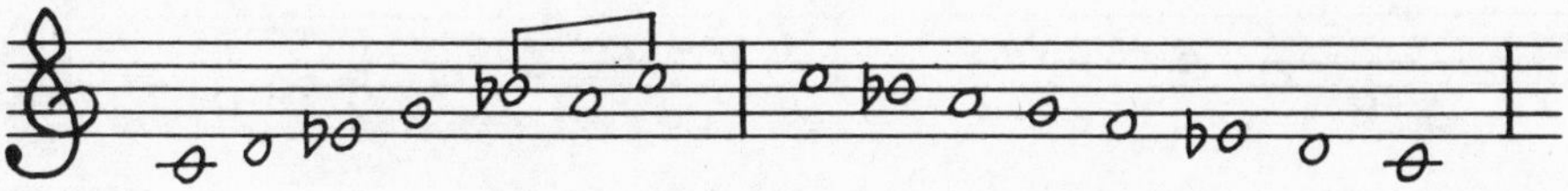

Ascent: the note *MA* (F) is avoided; one *vakra* feature is shown.
Descent: *krama sampūrṇa*.

(39) *Dilīpaka(m)*

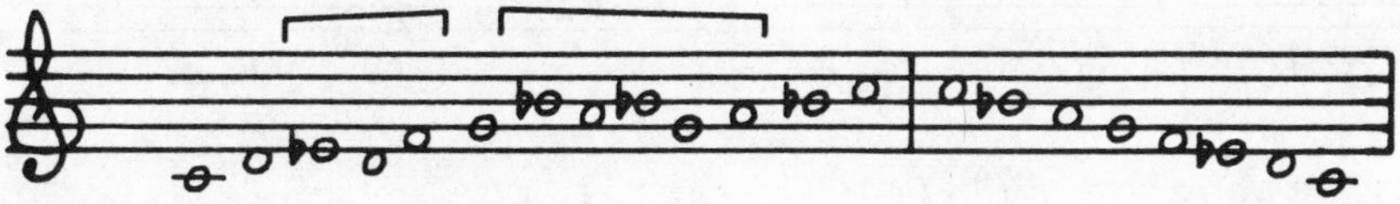

Ascent: *sampūrṇa*; two *vakra* features are shown.
Descent: *krama sampūrṇa*.

Occasionally a simple scale form of this *rāga* can be observed:

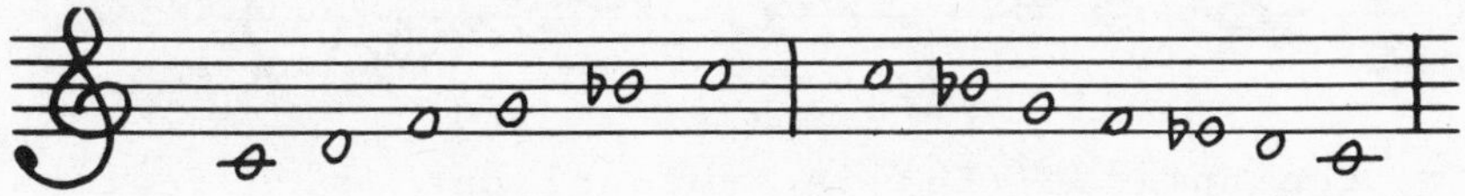

In this scale the note *DHA* (A) is avoided entirely and *GA* (Eb) is omitted in ascent.

(40) *Gāna Vasantam*

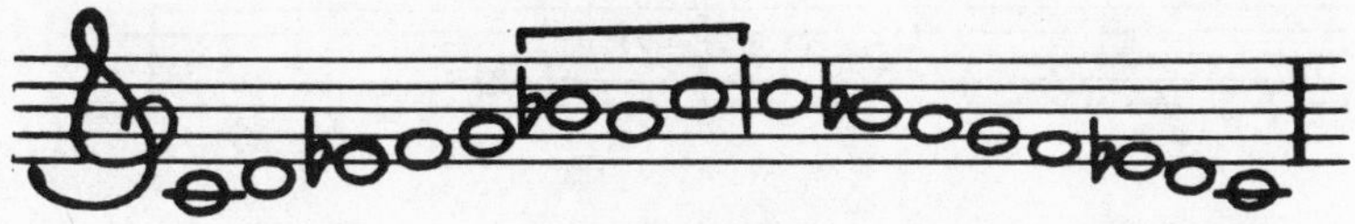

Ascent: *sampūrṇa*; one *vakra* feature is shown.
Descent: *krama sampūrṇa*.

(41) *Gārava Siṃhala*

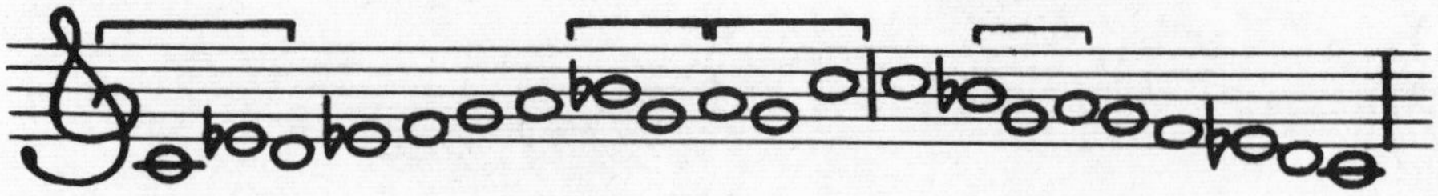

This scale is *sampūrṇa* in ascent and descent. In ascent appear three, and in descent one *vakra* feature.

(42) *Gaurī Vasantam*

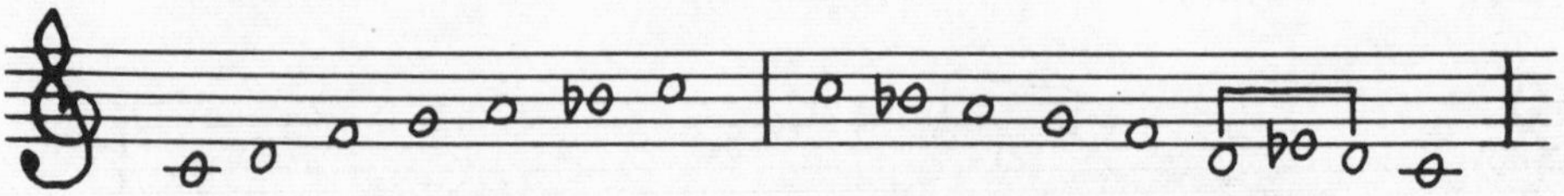

Ascent: the note *GA* (Eb) is avoided.
Descent: *sampūrṇa*; one *vakra* feature is shown.

(43) *Ghana Kēśi*

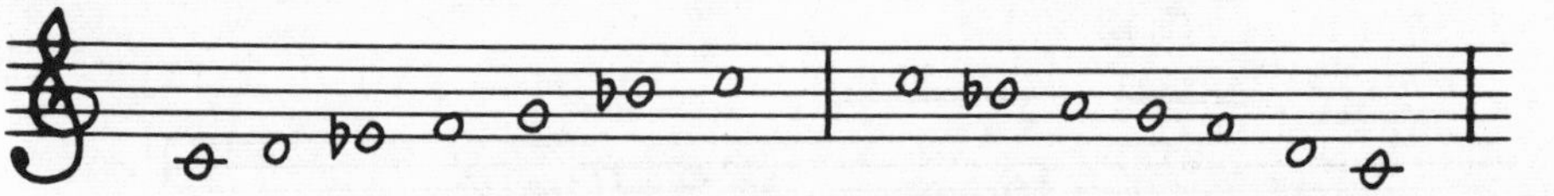

Ascent: the note *DHA* (A) is avoided.
Descent: the note *GA* (Eb) is omitted.

(44) *Ghanaja Ghana*

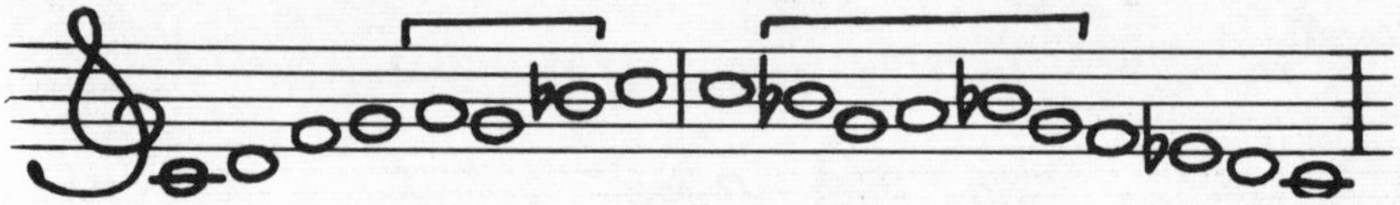

Ascent: the note *GA* (Eb) is avoided; one *vakra* feature is shown.
Descent: *sampūrṇa*; one extended *vakra* passage is used.

(45) *Grandha Vikṣēpam*

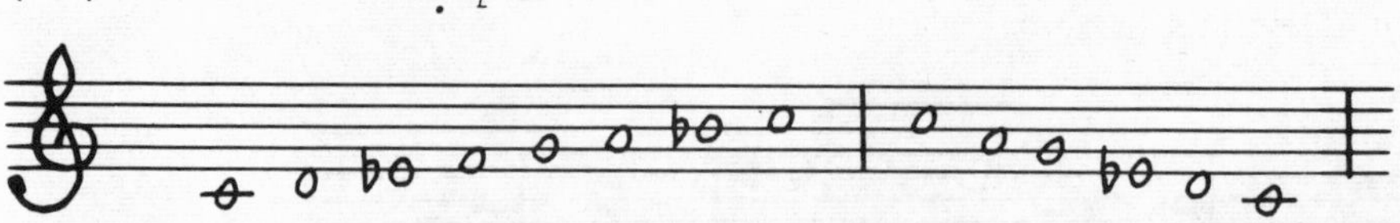

Ascent: *krama sampūrṇa*.
Descent: the notes *Nİ* (Bb) and *MA* (F) are avoided.

(46) *Hanokahā*

This scale is *sampūrṇa*. It shows two *vakra* features in ascent and two in descent.

(47) *Hariharamōhiṇi*

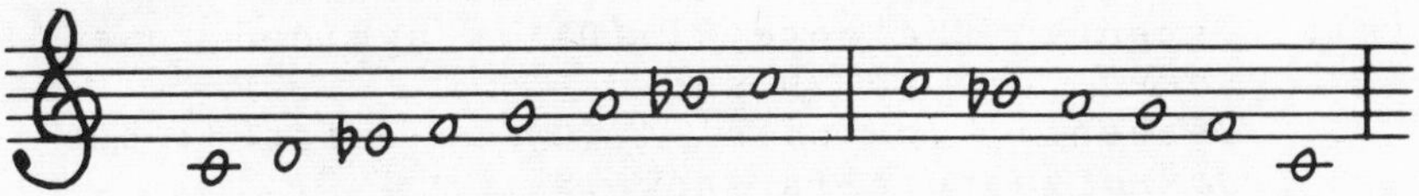

Ascent: *krama sampūrṇa*.
Descent: the notes *GA* (Eb) and *RI* (D) are avoided.

(48) *Harinārāyaṇi*

This *rāga* can be represented by two different scales: Scale (a) is *sampūrṇa* in ascent and shows two *vakra* features. Its descent avoids the note *DHA* (A). Scale (b), according to SSPS, as reported in SD (II, 225), shows a *sampūrṇa* ascent with one *vakra* feature. Its descent is identical with that of scale (a).

Another *rāga* with the same name appears under the heading of *mēḷa* 28 (94).

(49) *Hēmāvaḷi*

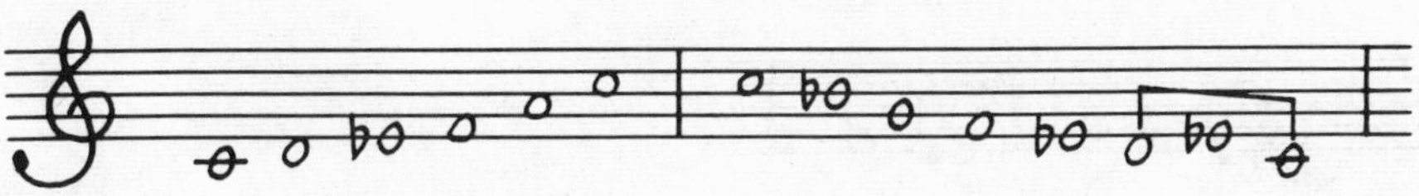

Ascent: the notes *PA* (G) and *NI* (Bb) are avoided.
Descent: the note *DHA* (A) is omitted; one *vakra* feature is shown.

(50) *Hindōḷavasantam*

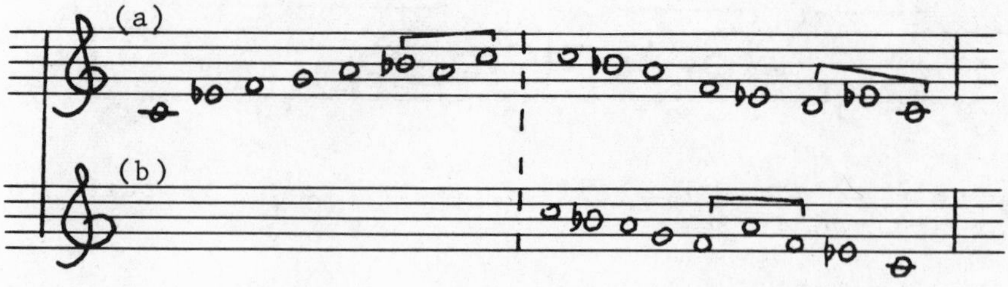

There are two scales that represent this *rāga*.

Scale (a): Ascent: the note *RI* (D) is avoided; one *vakra* feature is shown.
Descent: the note *PA* (G) is omitted; one *vakra* feature is shown.

Scale (b): Ascent: identical with that of scale (a).
Descent: the note *RI* (D) is avoided; one *vakra* feature is shown.

Another *rāga* with the same name appears under the heading of the 20. *mēḷa* (21).

(51) *Hindustan Kāpi* (*Hindusthāni Kāpi*)

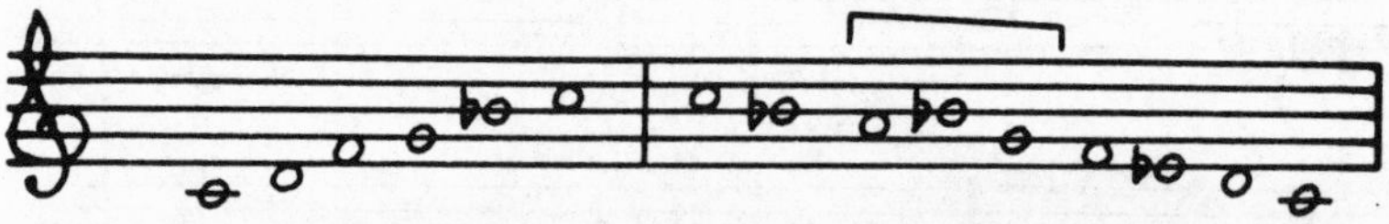

Ascent: the notes *GA* (Eb) and *DHA* (A) are avoided.
Descent: *sampūrṇa*; one *vakra* feature is shown. The note *GA* (Eb) is stressed.

This *rāga*, its name and material pointing to *rāga Kāfi* of North India (see RNI, 359-62), is a popular form of the southern *Kāpi rāgas* (22,73; 22,78). As in all popular *rāgas*, changes can occur within the prescribed material that may vary from one performance to the next. Frequent changes are:

i) An insertion of "*antara GA*" (E) in ascent; for instance:

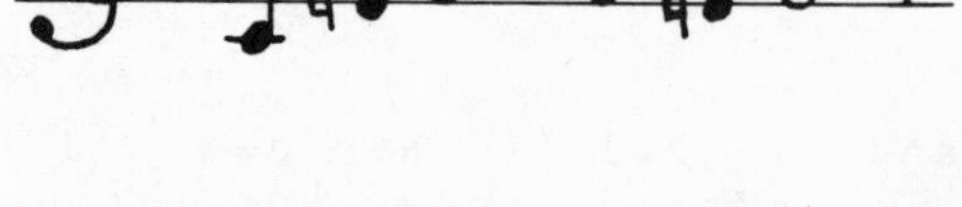

ii) The use of "*śuddha DHA*" (Ab) in descent; for instance:

iii) The use of "*kākali NI*" (B), particularly in ascent:

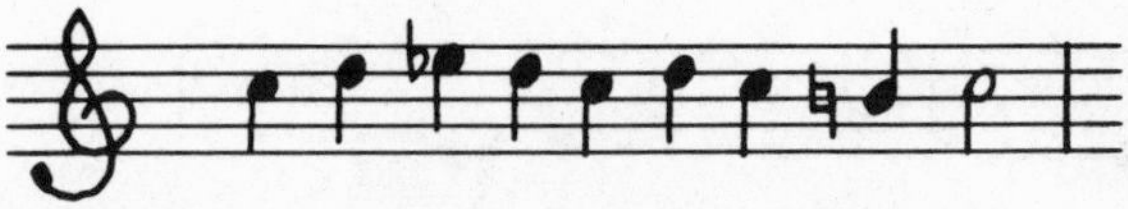

The descending scale of this *rāga* can also show two *vakra* features:

(52) *Husēni* (*Huśāni*, *Uśāni*, *Uśēni*)

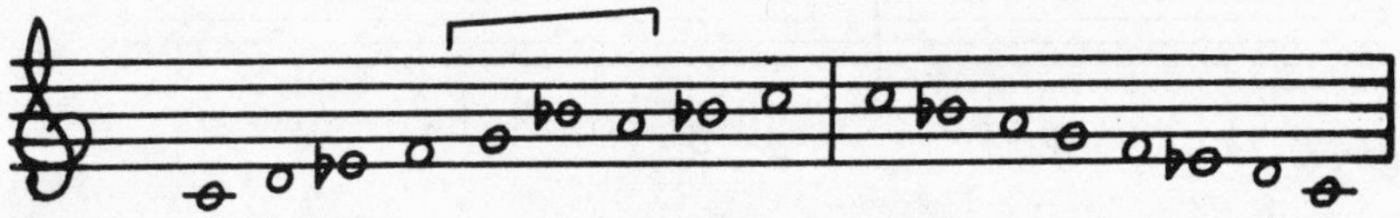

Ascent: *sampūrṇa*; one *vakra* feature is shown.
Descent: *krama sampūrṇa*.

Like *Hindustan Kāpi* the name of this *rāga* points to the North (see RNI, 50). As *Husēni* is performed frequently, particularly in dance and drama, changes in its tone material can occur often.

Another version of the *Husēni* scale is:

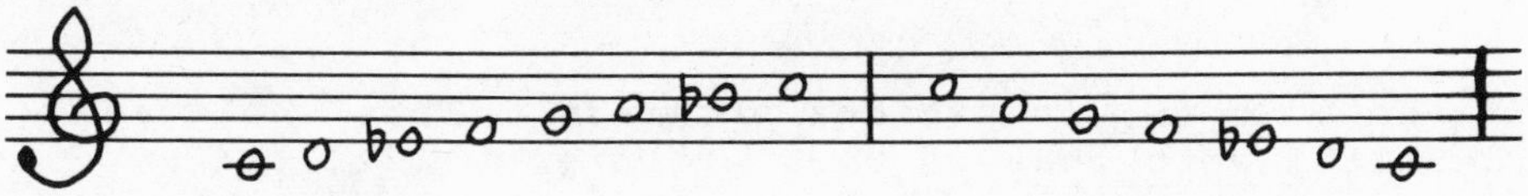

Ascent: *krama sampūrṇa*.
Descent: the note *NI* (Bb) is avoided.

The note "*śuddha DHA*" (Ab) can appear, for instance, in:

Melodies in this *rāga* usually begin with one of the following notes: *SA* (C), *RI* (D), or *NI* (Bb).

The following melody specimen comes from SCM, 118:

(53) *Inakapriya*

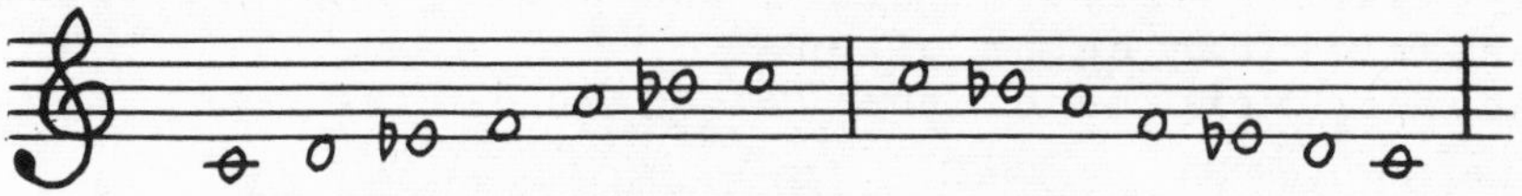

The note *PA* (G) is avoided entirely. This scale is identical with that of *rāga Śrīrañjani* (22, 118).

(54) *Janāndōḷika*

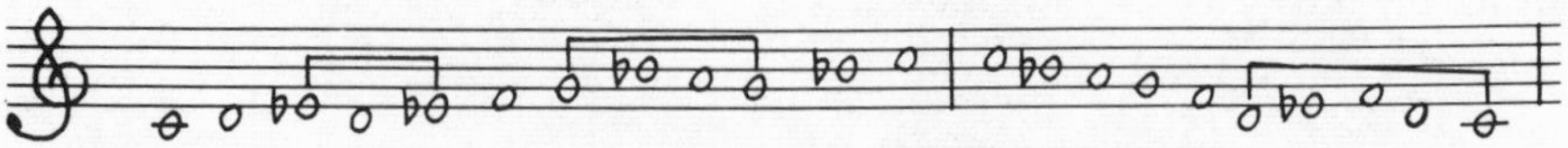

Ascent: *sampūrṇa*; two *vakra* features are shown.
Descent: *sampūrṇa*; one extended *vakra* feature is shown.

(55) *Jayākṣari*

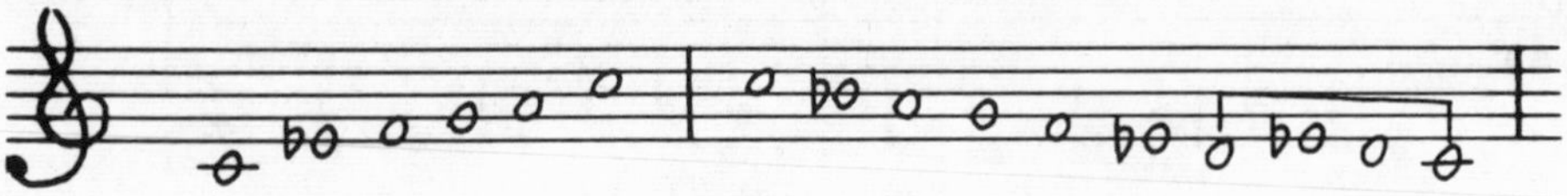

Ascent: the notes *RI* (D) and *NI* (Bb) are avoided.
Descent: *sampūrṇa*; one *vakra* feature is shown.

(56) *Jayamañjari*

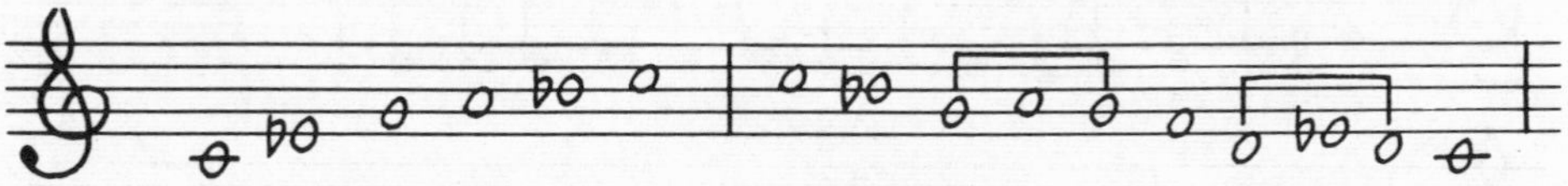

Ascent: the notes *RI* (D) and *MA* (F) are avoided.
Descent: *sampūrṇa*; two *vakra* features are shown.

(57) *Jayamanōharī*

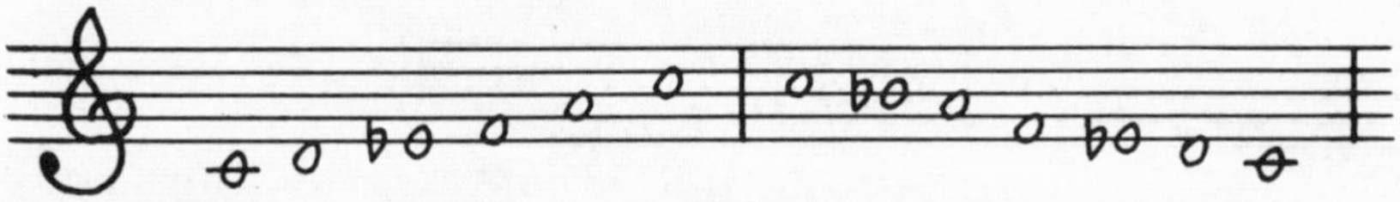

The note *PA* (G) is avoided entirely. *NI* (Bb) is omitted in ascent.

A second form of the *Jayamanōharī* scale avoids also the note *GA* (Eb) in descent.

The notes *MA* (F), *DHA* (A), occasionally also *GA* (Eb), are to be stressed.

(58) *Jayanārāyaṇi*

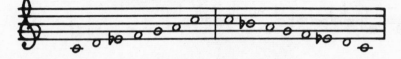

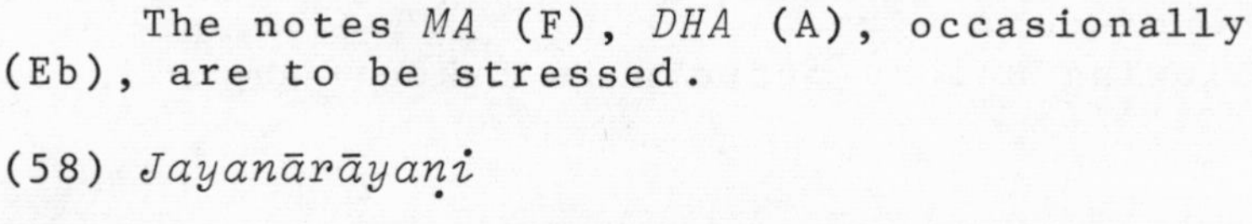

Ascent: the note *NI* (Bb) is avoided. *GA* (Eb) is to be stressed.
Descent: *krama sampūrṇa*.

The following melody specimen comes from SCM, 112:

(59) *Jayanta Sēna*

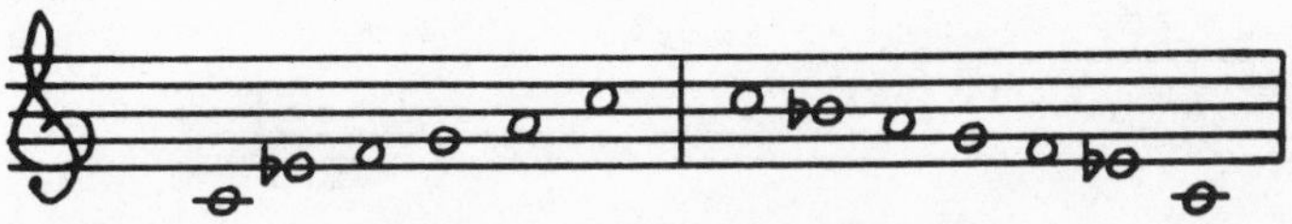

The note *RI* (D) is avoided entirely. *NI* (Bb) is omitted in ascent.

SD (II, 257) states that "Raghunata Naik, the ruler of Tanjore (early seventeenth century) is credited with the invention of this *rāga*."

The following melody pattern is taken from SCM, 107:

(60) *Jhālamañjari*

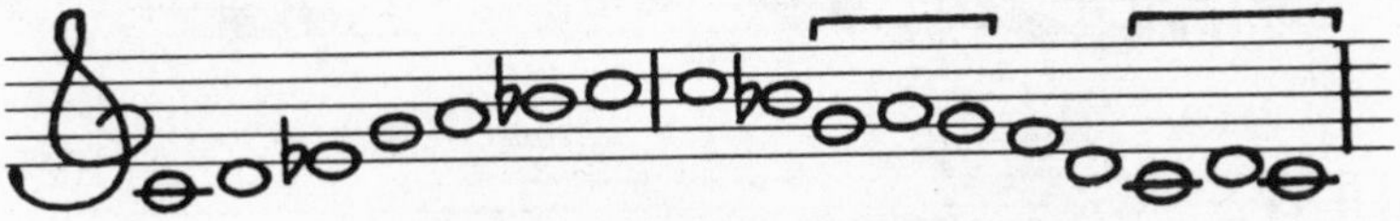

Ascent: the note *MA* (F) is avoided.
Descent: the note *GA* (Eb) is omitted; two *vakra* features are shown.

(61) *Jīvikā Vasanta*

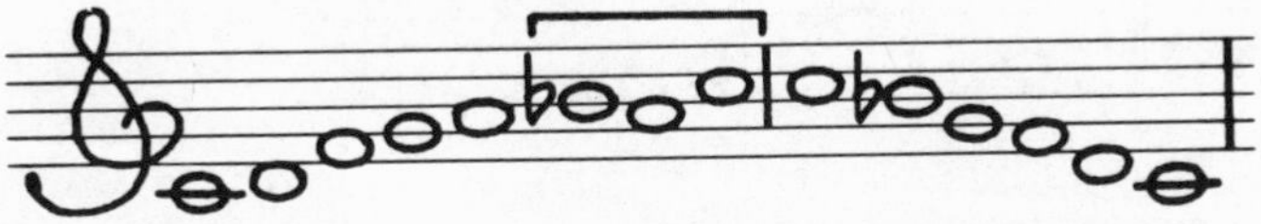

The note *GA* (Eb) is avoided entirely. One *vakra* feature is shown in ascent. *DHA* (A) is omitted in descent.

(62) *Kaiśika*

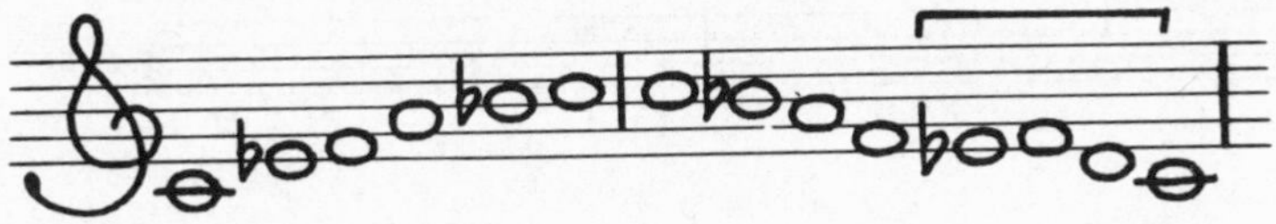

The note *PA* (G) is avoided entirely. *RI* (D) is omitted in ascent and the descent shows one *vakra* feature.

(63) *Kaḷānidhi*

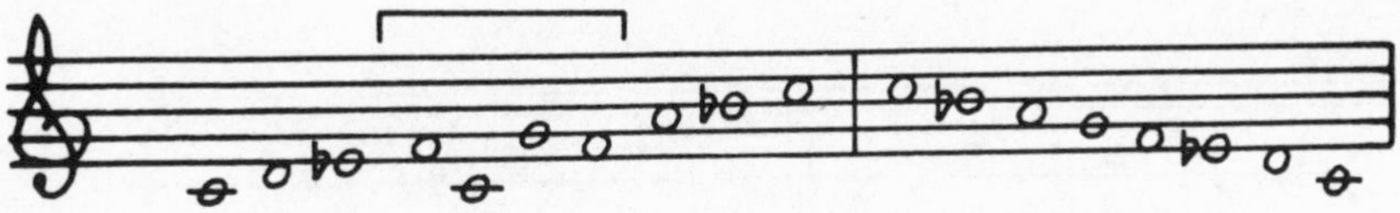

Ascent: *sampūrṇa*; one *vakra* feature is shown.
Descent: *krama sampūrṇa*.
The following melody specimen is taken from SCM, 114-15:

(64) *Kalāsvarūpi*

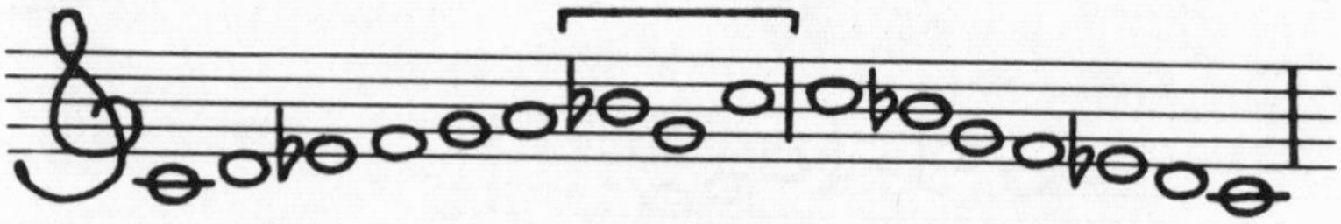

Ascent: *sampūrṇa*; one *vakra* feature is shown.
Descent: the note *DHA* (A) is avoided.

(65) *Kalhāru*

The note *NI* (Bb) is avoided entirely. The ascent shows two *vakra* features and the descent omits the note *GA* (Eb).

(66) *Kālika*

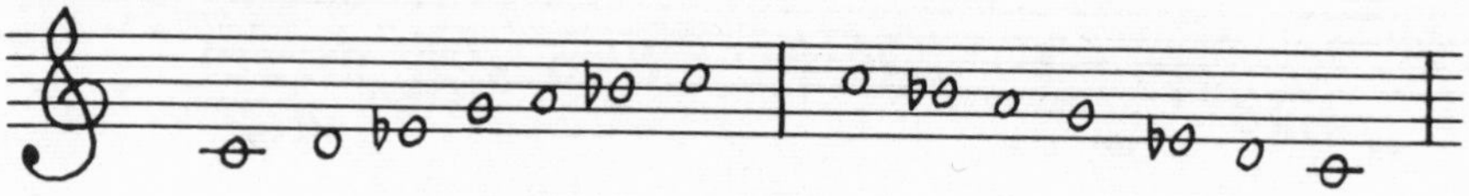

The note *MA* (F) is avoided entirely.

(67) *Kālindi*

The note *DHA* (A) is avoided entirely.

Another *rāga* with the same name appears under the heading of the 15. *mēḷa* (77).

(68) *Kalyāṇa Taraṅgini*

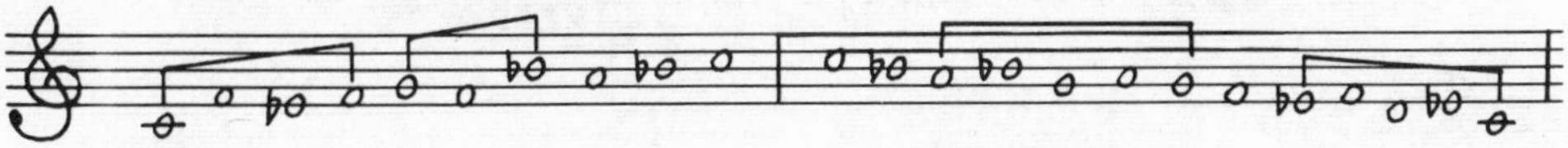

Ascent: the note *RI* (D) is avoided; two *vakra* features are shown.
Descent: *sampūrṇa*; two *vakra* features are used.

(69) *Kalyāṇa Vasanta*

Ascent: the note *RI* (D) is avoided.
Descent: *sampūrṇa*; one *vakra* feature is shown.

(70) *Kanaka Varāḷi*

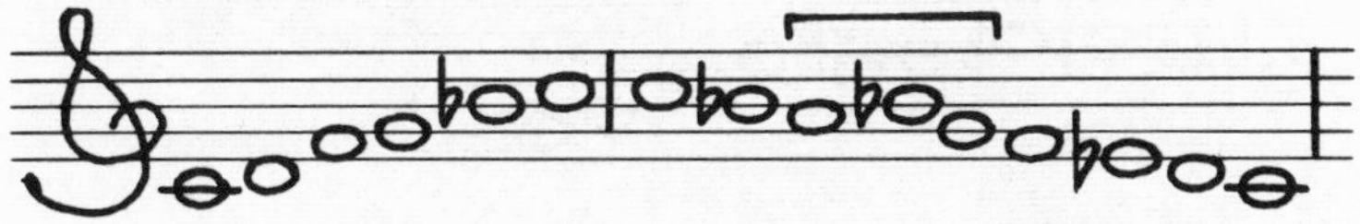

Ascent: the notes *GA* (Eb) and *DHA* (A) are avoided.
Descent: *sampūrṇa*; one *vakra* feature is shown.

(71) *Kannaḍa Gauḷa* (*Kannaḍa Gauḷi*)

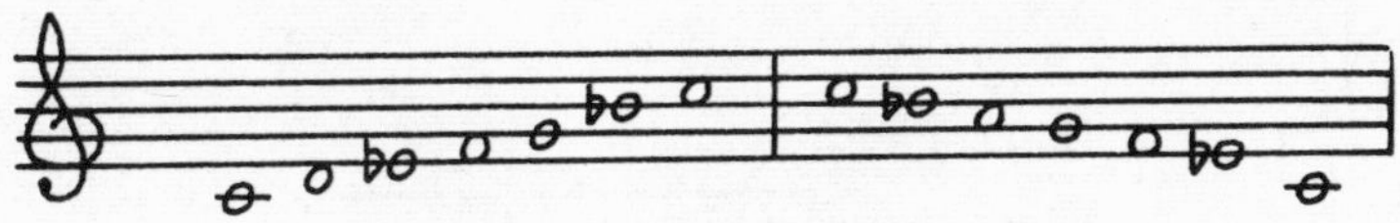

Ascent: the note *DHA* (A) is avoided.
Descent: the note *RI* (D) is omitted.

This *rāga* can be performed at all times. According to SD (II, 298) the notes *kaiśiki NI* (Bb) in ascent and *sādhārana GA* (Eb) in descent are of importance and have to be stressed.

The following melody specimen is taken from SCM, 104:

KANNAḌA GAUḶA (*Triputa-tāla*)

(72) *Kannaḍa Varāḷi*

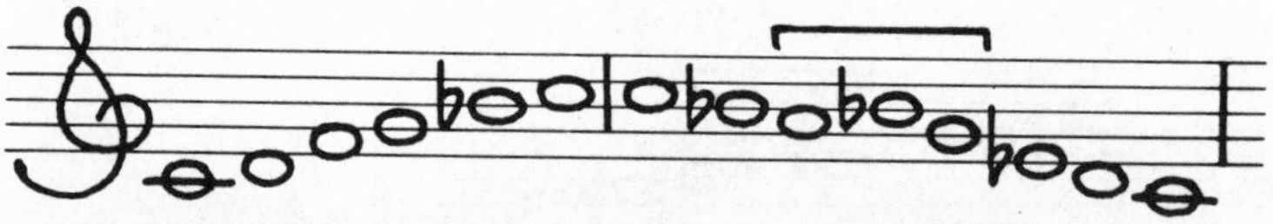

Ascent: the notes *GA* (Eb) and *DHA* (A) are avoided. Descent: the note *MA* (F) is omitted; one *vakra* feature is shown.

(73) *Kāpi*
See *Karṇāṭaka Kāpi* (22, 78)

(74) *Kāpi Jaṅgla*

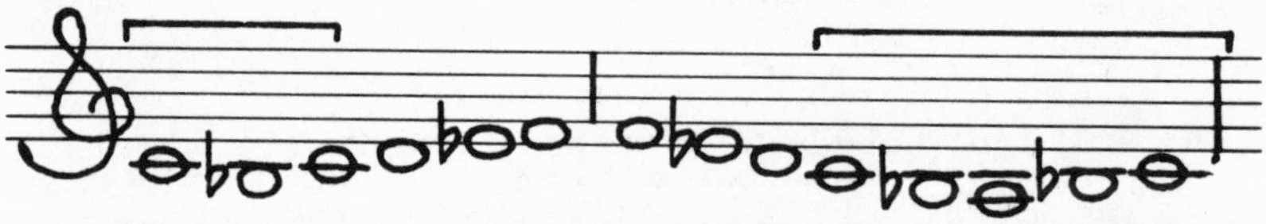

This *rāga* is represented by a short-ranged scale showing one *vakra* feature in ascent and one extended one in descent.

The SD (II, 300) remarks that "Vina Kuppayyar [n.d.] has composed a Divyanama Kīrtana [a simple song of praise containing the name of the deity, sung by the entire congregation at various occasions such as the circumambulation of the sacred lamp]....There is no other composition in this *rāga*."

(75) *Karaṇi*

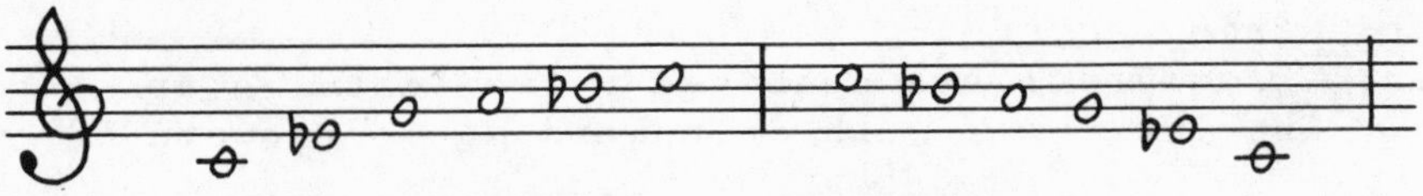

The notes *RI* (D) and *MA* (F) are avoided entirely.

(76) *Karṇāṭaka Dēvagāndhāri*

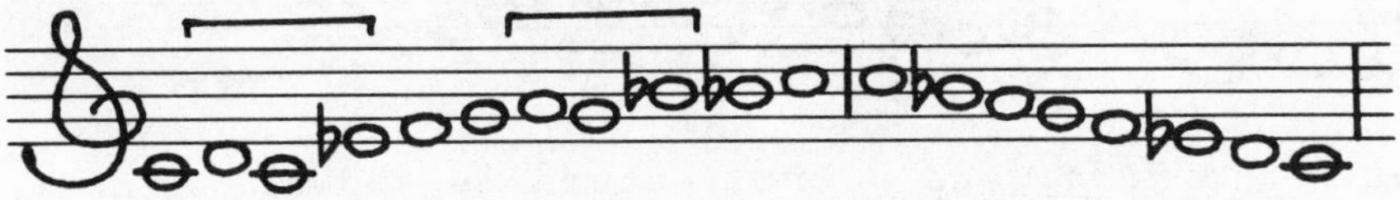

Ascent: *sampūrṇa*; two *vakra* features are shown.
Descent: *krama sampūrṇa*.

Another *rāga* with the same name appears under the heading of the 21. *mēḷa* (5).

The SD (II, 302) remarks that "in practice there is no difference between this *Karṇāṭaka Dēvagāndhāri* and *Ābhēri* [22, 6]." A comparison of the two scales shows a similarity, but identicalness cannot be observed.

The following passages are taken from a recording of the *Gīta Govinda* made in Kerala by Wayne Howard in 1972:

(77) *Karṇāṭa Kāpi*
(not to be mistaken for *Karṇāṭaka Kāpi*, 22, 78)

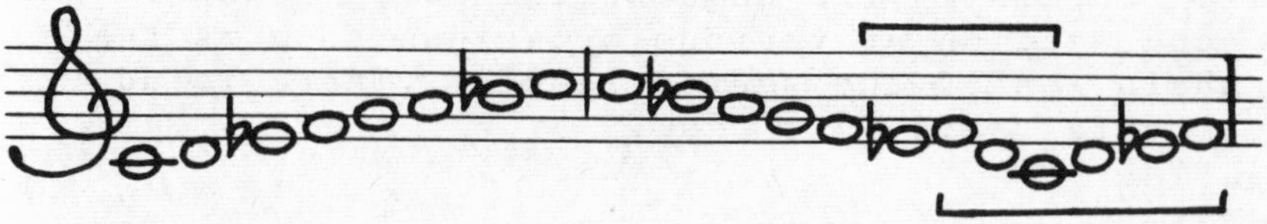

Ascent: *krama sampūrṇa*.
Descent: *sampūrṇa*; two combined *vakra* features are shown. The line ends with an upward motion toward *MA* (F).

(78) *Karṇāṭaka Kāpi* (*Kāpi*)

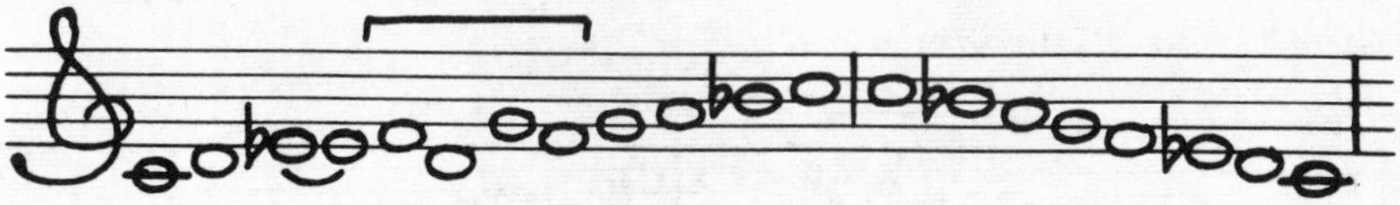

Ascent: *sampūrṇa*; one *vakra* feature is shown.
Descent: *krama sampūrṇa*.

A second form of this *rāga* is:

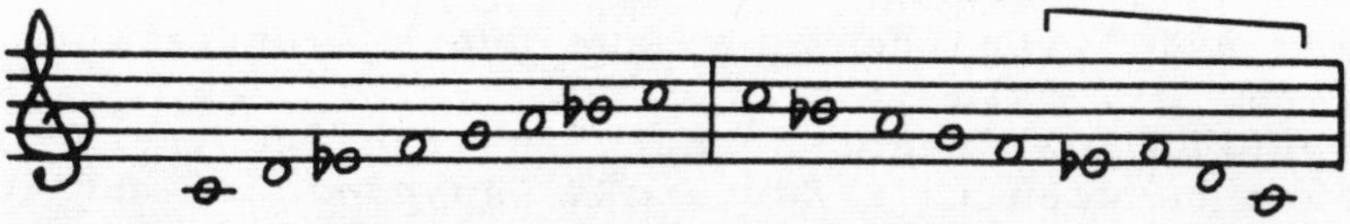

Ascent: *krama sampūrṇa*.
Descent: *sampūrṇa*; one frequently used *vakra* feature is shown.

The following melody specimen is taken from SCM, 118:

KĀPI (*Triputa-tāla*)

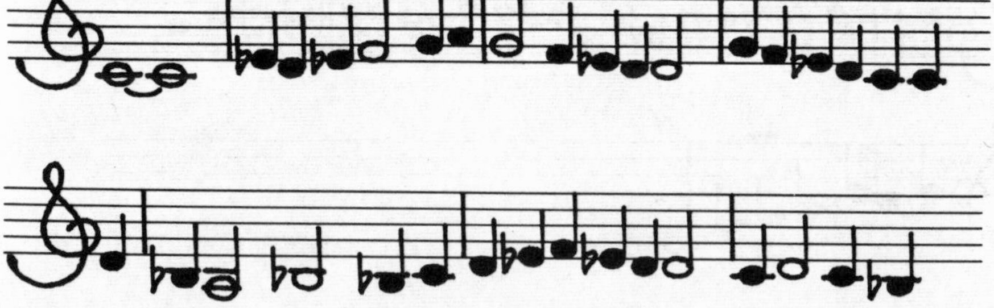

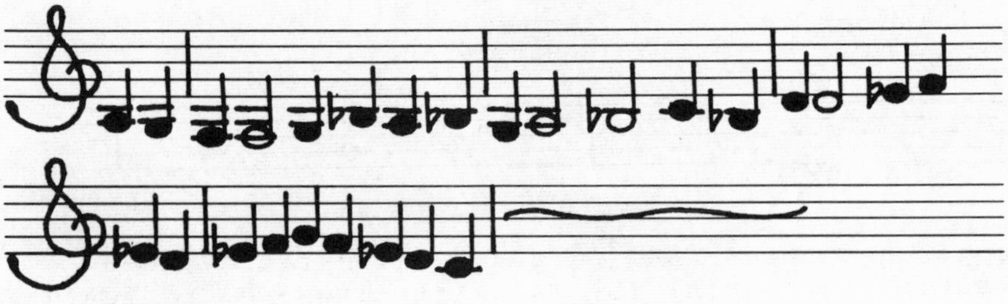

(79) *Kaṭhinya*

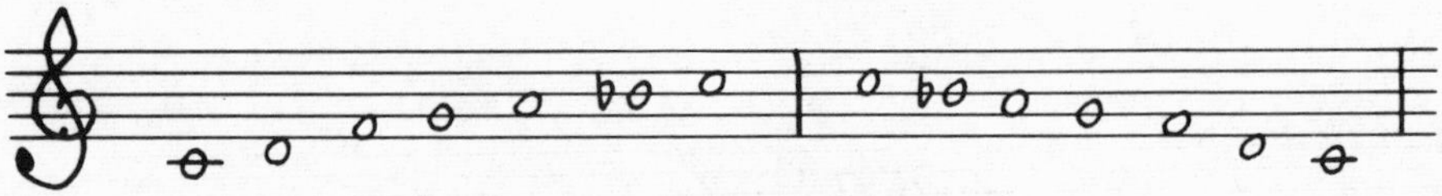

The note *GA* (Eb) is avoided entirely.

(80) *Karṇarañjaṇi*

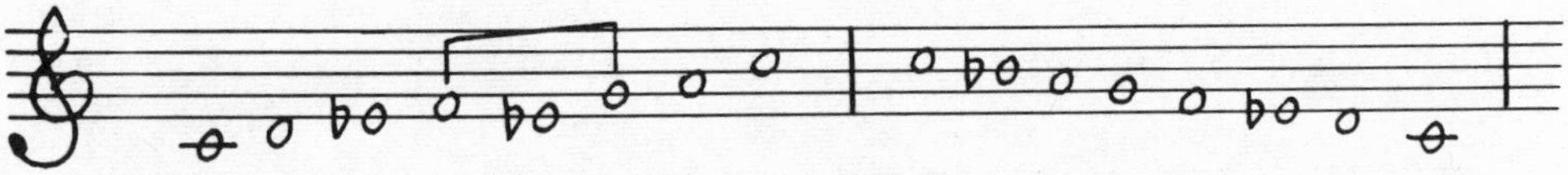

This recently created *rāga* was introduced by Muthiah Bhagavathar (see n. 1 of this chapter).
Ascent: the note *NI* (Bb) is avoided and one *vakra* feature is shown.
Descent: *krama sampūrṇa*

(81) *Khilāvaḷi*

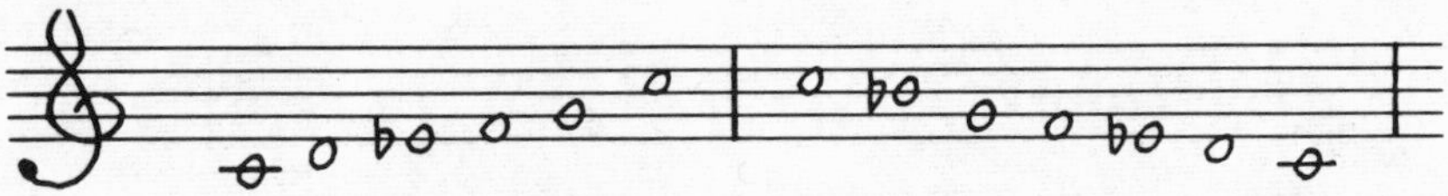

The note *DHA* (A) is avoided entirely; *NI* (Bb) is omitted in ascent.

(82) *Kiraṇa Bhāskara*

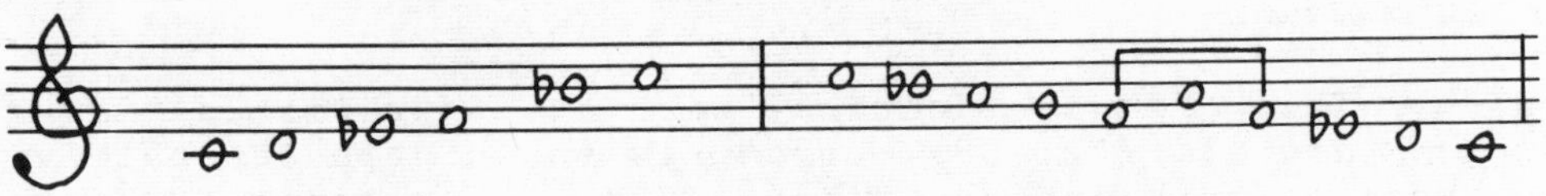

Ascent: the notes *PA* (G) and *DHA* (A) are avoided.
Descent: *sampūrṇa*; one *vakra* feature is shown.

(83) *Kumudapriya*

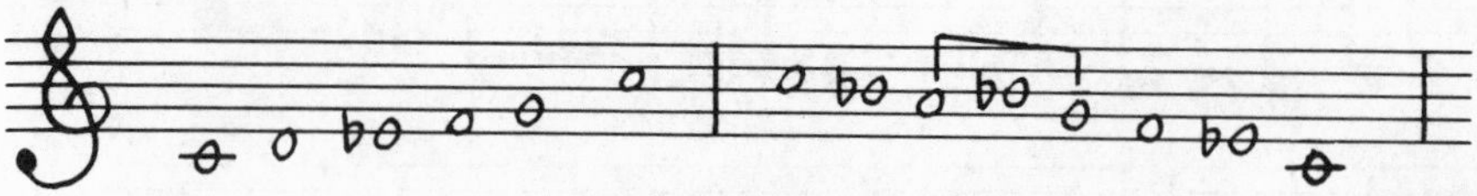

Ascent: the notes *DHA* (A) and *NI* (Bb) are avoided.
Descent: the note *RI* (D) is omitted; one *vakra* feature is shown.

Another *rāga* with the same name is 51,26.

(84) *Kundamālika*

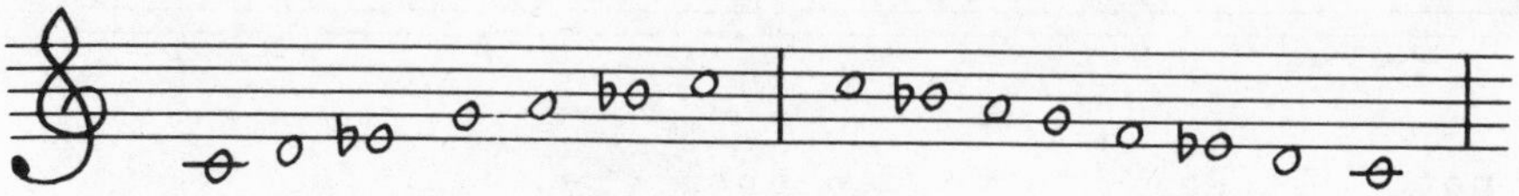

Ascent: the note *MA* (F) is avoided.
Descent: *krama sampūrṇa*.

(85) *Lalitagāndhari*

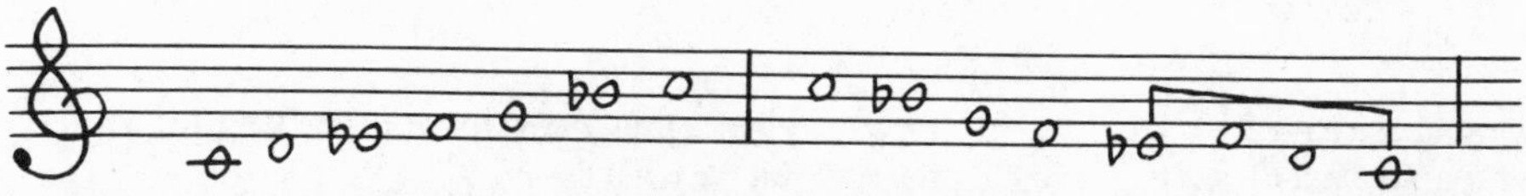

The note *DHA* (A) is avoided entirely. One *vakra* feature is shown in descent.

(86) *Lalitamanōharī*

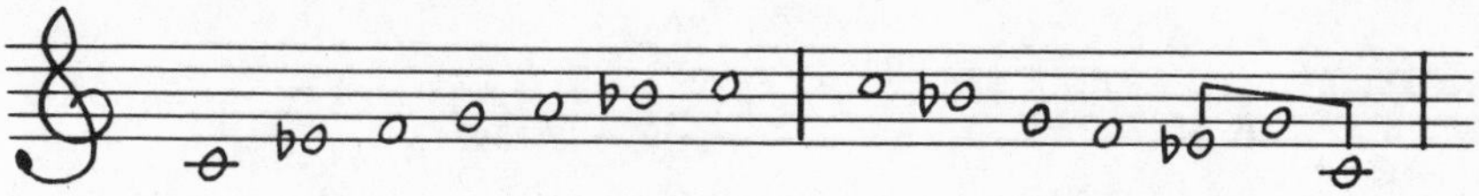

The note *RI* (D) is avoided entirely. In descent the note *DHA* (A) is omitted and one *vakra* feature is shown.

(87) *Mādhi*

This *rāga* is identical with the next listed *rāga* *Madhyamāvati* (22, 88). *Mādhi* is shown here separately because South Indian writers (e.g., N) present the two *rāgas* in this manner, implying that there may exist some differences in their performances. As far as I know there are none.

(88) *Madhyamāvati*

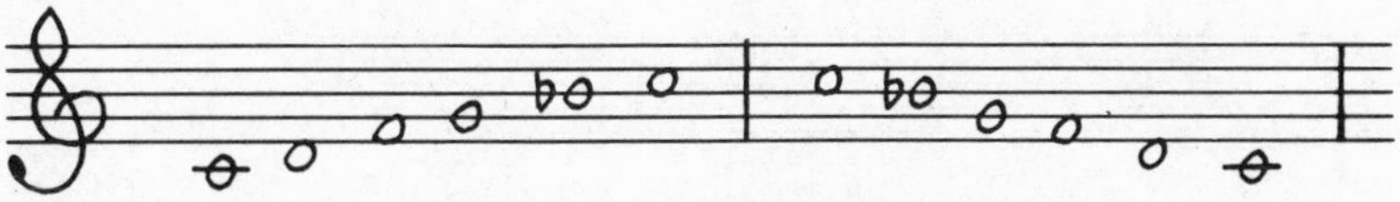

The notes *GA* (Eb) and *DHA* (A) are avoided entirely. The notes *RI* (D), *MA* (F), and *NI* (Bb) are to be stressed.

This *rāga* seems to be identical with *rāga Mādhi* (22, 87).

The following melody specimen is taken from SCM, 105.

The three passages shown below are from a *Gīta Govinda* performance in Kerala, recorded by Wayne Howard in 1972:

(89) *Makutadhāriṇi*

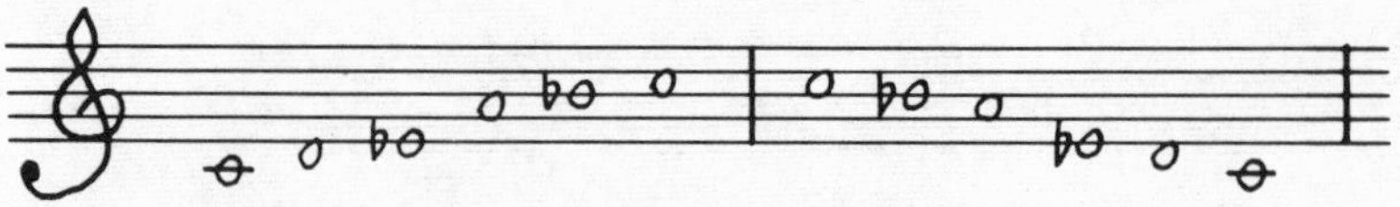

The notes *MA* (F) and *PA* (G) are avoided entirely.

(90) *Mālavaśrī*

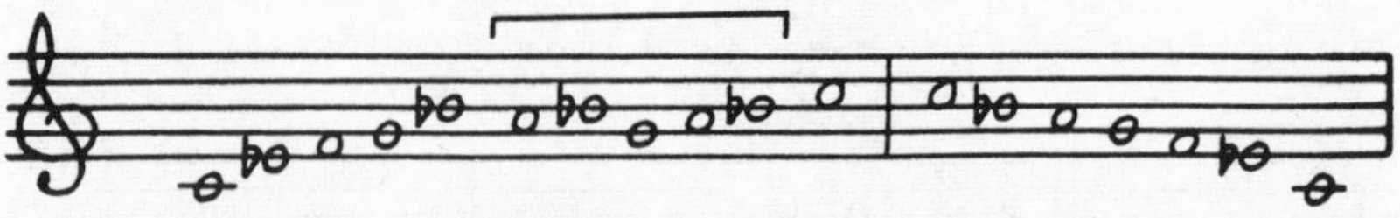

The note *RI* (D) is avoided entirely. The ascent shows one extended *vakra* passage.

The following melody specimen is taken from SCM, 103.

(91) *Mallār(u)*

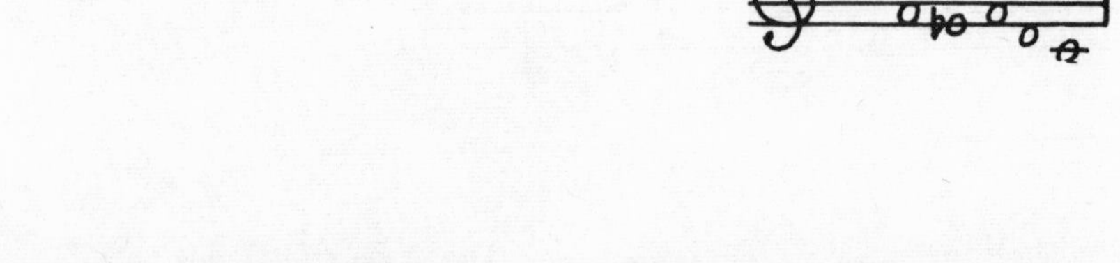

The note *NI* (Bb) is avoided entirely. Two *vakra* features appear in ascent; one is shown in the descent of the second form of the scale. A slight similarity between this *rāga* and the North Indian *Mallār* types (see RNI, 394-435) can be observed, particularly in the second form of the descending scale.

The following melody specimen is taken from SCM, 123-24:

(92) *Mandamari*

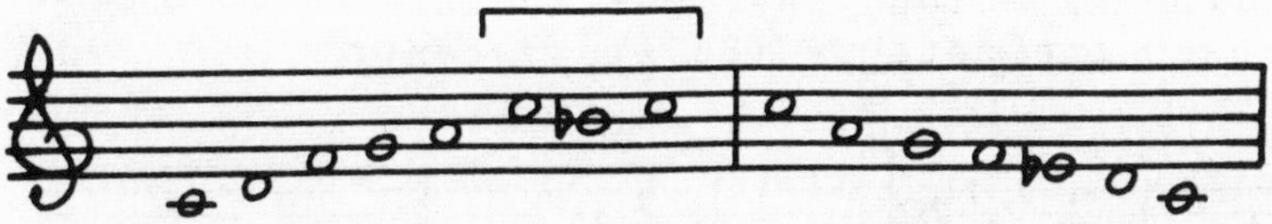

Ascent: the note *GA* (Eb) is avoided; one *vakra* feature is shown.
Descent: the note *NI* (Bb) is omitted.

The following melody specimen is taken from SCM, 122:

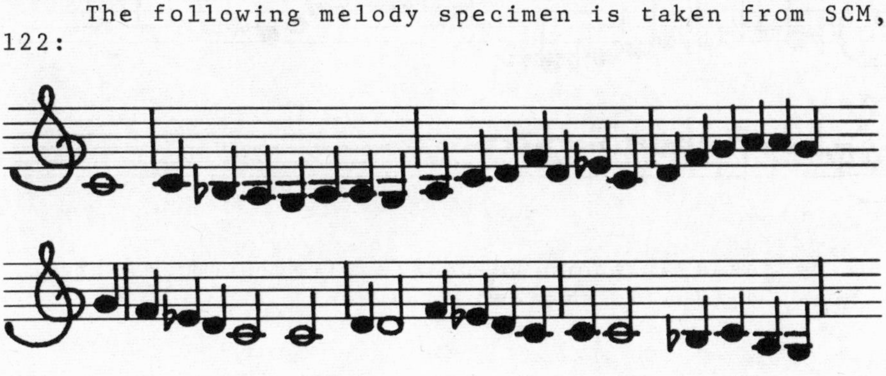

(93) *Maṇiraṅgu*

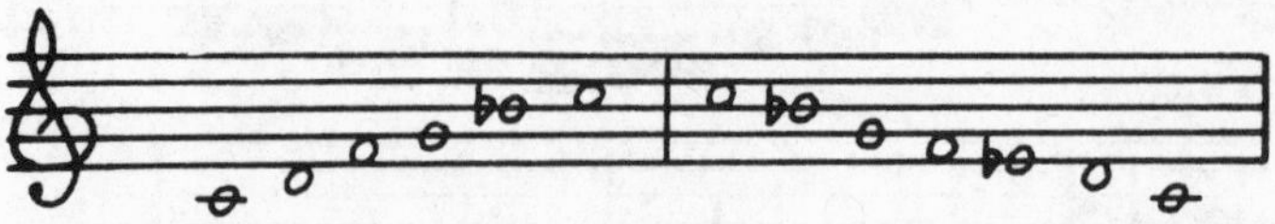

The note *DHA* (A) is avoided entirely. *GA* (Eb) is omitted in ascent.

Occasionally musicians use the note *DHA* (A) in descent. Govinda employs the note *GA* (Eb) also in ascent. A second ascent of this *rāga*, showing the note *GA* (Eb) and one *vakra* feature, is:

The following melody specimen is taken from SCM, 106-07; it uses the note *GA* (Eb) in ascent:

The passages shown below are often used; in them the note *GA* (Eb) is avoided in ascent.

(94) *Mañjari*

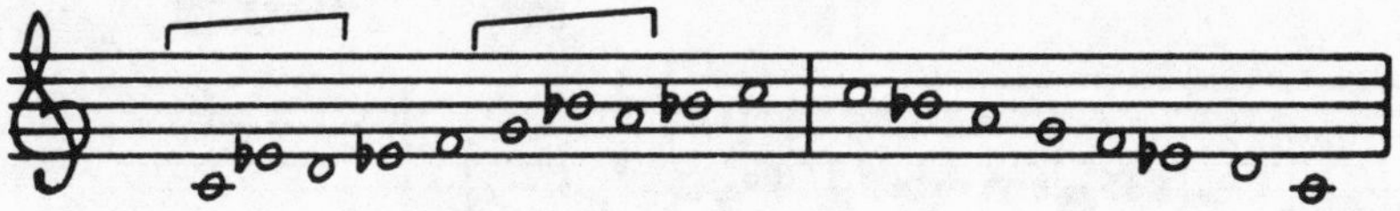

Ascent: *sampūrṇa*; two *vakra* features are shown.
Descent: *krama sampūrṇa*.

The following melody specimen is taken from SCM, 117:

MAÑJARI (*Triputa-tāla*)

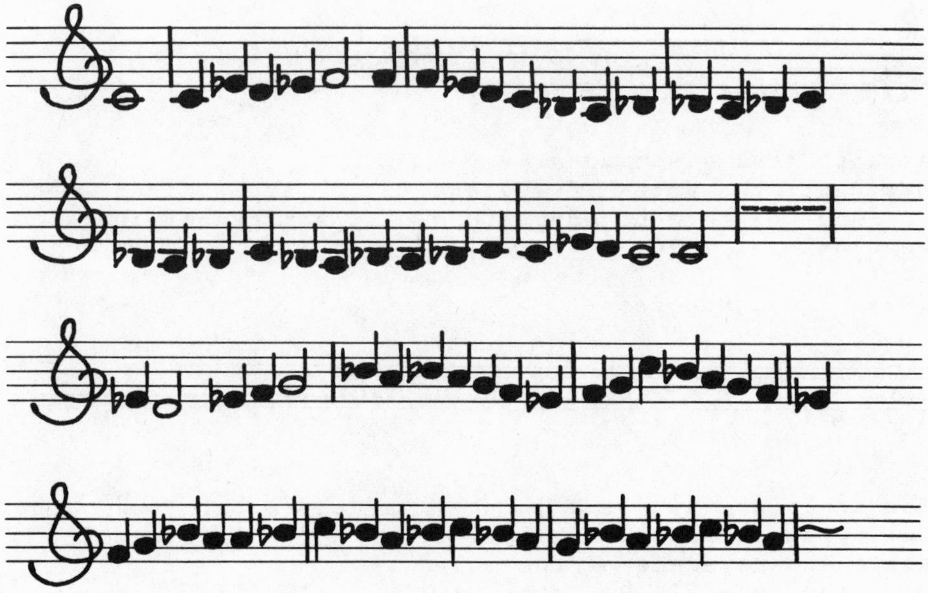

(95) *Manōharī*

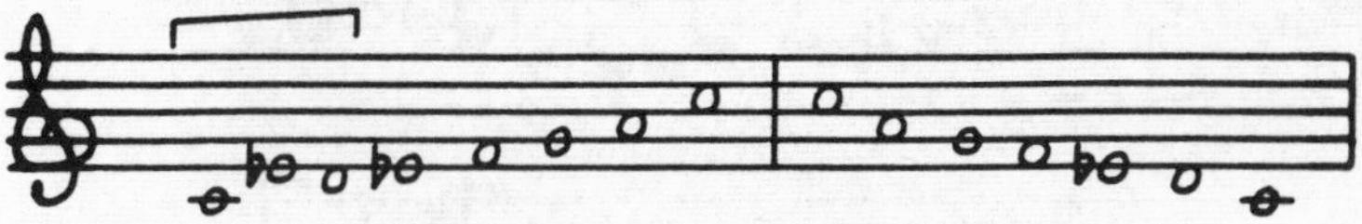

The note *NI* (Bb) is avoided entirely. The ascent shows one *vakra* feature.

RĀGA MANŌHARĪ (*Triputa-tāla*) SCM, 113

(96) *Mārgahindōḷa*

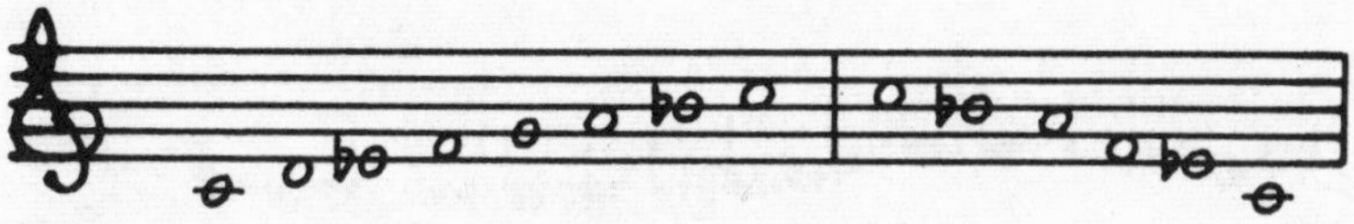

Ascent: *krama sampūrṇa*.
Descent: the notes *PȦ* (G) and *RI* (D) are avoided.

Another form of *Mārgahindōḷa* appears under the heading of the 20. *mēḷa* (6).

(97) *Māruvadhanyāsi*

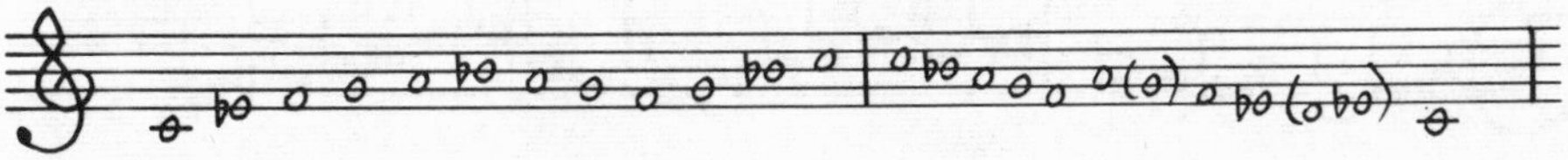

The scale of this *rāga* is only vaguely determined. The following shows a rough outline of a combination of scale and movement of the melody.

The note *RI* (D) is generally avoided in ascent but may appear in descent.

The following melody specimen is taken from SCM, 114:

Occasionally a *rāga Mārudhanyāsi* is mentioned which probably is, if not the same, closely related to *Māruvadhanyāsi*. The *Mārudhānyasi* scale is supposed to be:

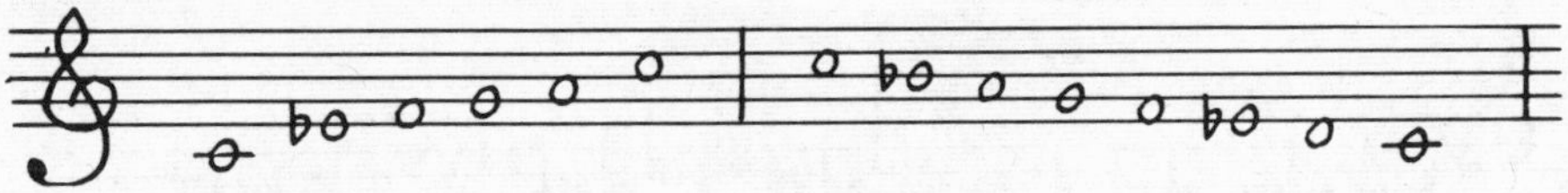

Ascent: the notes *RI* (D) and *NI* (Bb) are avoided.
Descent: *krama sampūrṇa*.

(98) *Māyāpratīpam*

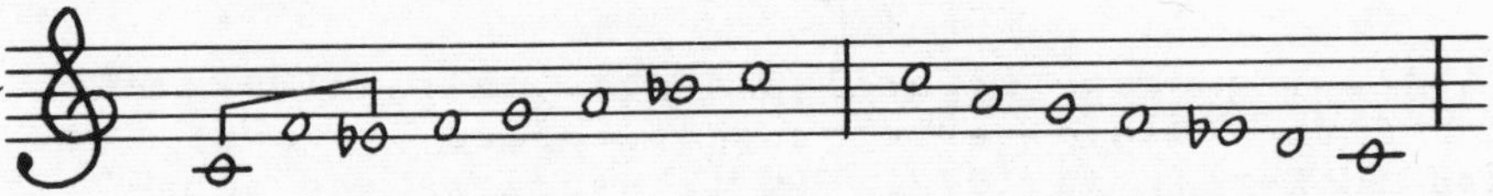

According to R (222-23) this is a recently created *rāga*. Its originator is believed to be Muthiah Bhagavathar (see n. 1, this chapter).
Ascent: the note *RI* (D) is avoided and one *vakra* feature is shown.
Descent: the note *NI* (Bb) is omitted.

(99) *Mukhārī*

The scale of this *rāga* has two forms of ascent. The note *GA* (Eb) is avoided in both. Form (a) shows one *vakra* feature and form (b) avoids the note *DHA* (A). The *sampūrṇa* descent is the same in both forms.

At the present time the note *DHA* is often lowered to *śuddha DHA* (Ab) in descent. There are some performers who lower the note *RI* to *śuddha RI* (Db) in descent and raise *NI* to *kākali NI* (B) in ascent. These deviations from the basic scale are typical for the popular character of this *rāga*.

The following melody specimen is taken from SCM, 124:

The following shows several passages in raga *Mukhārī* from a *Gīta Govinda* performance recorded by Wayne Howard in Kerala in 1972. It illustrates the occasional use of the note *śuddha DHA* (Ab) in ascent and descent.

(100) *Nadāchintāmaṇi* (*Nadācintāmaṇi*)

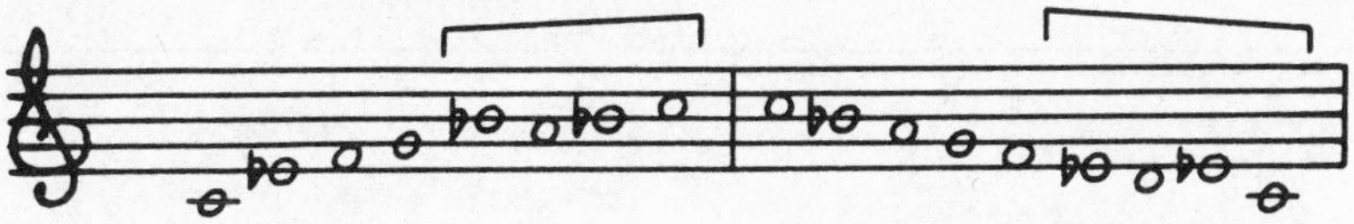

Ascent: the note *RI* (D) is avoided; one *vakra* feature is shown.
Descent: *sampūrṇa*; one *vakra* feature is used.

(101) *Nādāmūrti*

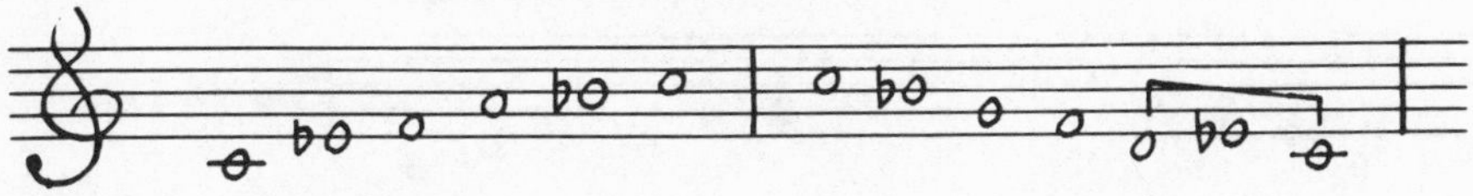

Ascent: the notes *RI* (D) and *PA* (G) are avoided.
Descent: the note *DHA* (A) is omitted; one *vakra* feature is shown.

(102) *Nādataraṅgiṇī*

The scale of this rare *rāga* is obscure. Sambamoorthy (S, III, 312) offers the following material:

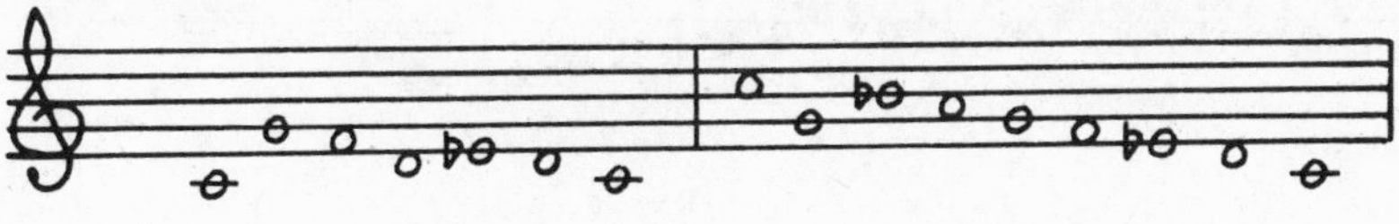

(103) *Nādanapriya*

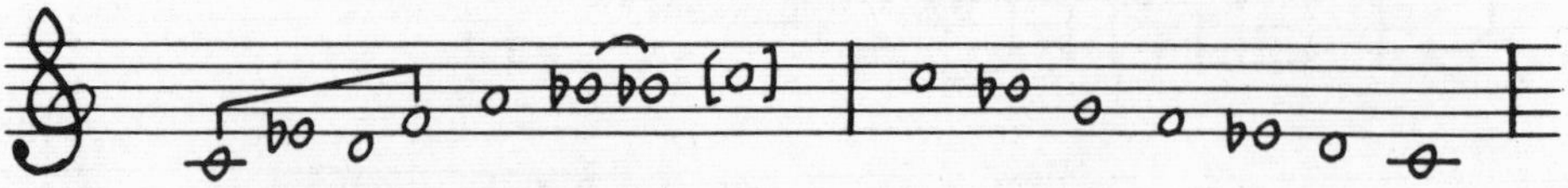

Ascent: the note *PA* (G) is avoided; *NI* (Bb) is stressed and one *vakra* feature is shown.
Descent: the note *DHA* (A) is omitted.

(104) *Navaratnavilāsam*

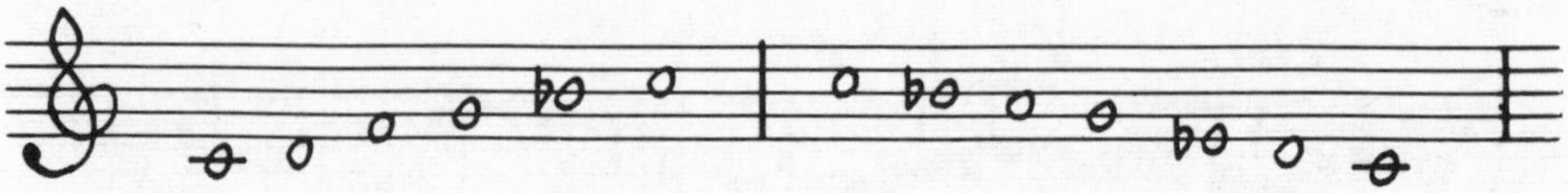

Ascent: the notes *GA* (Eb) and *DHA* (A) are avoided.
Descent: the note *MA* (F) is omitted.

According to R (223) this *rāga* was first introduced by Muthiah Bhagavathar (see n.1, this chapter).

(105) *Nāgari*

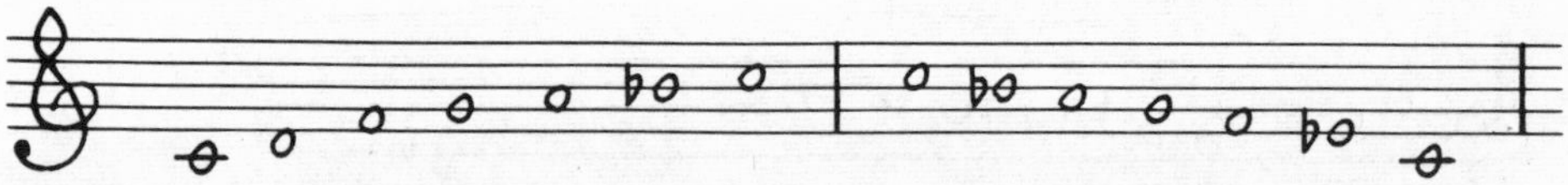

Ascent: the note *GA* (Eb) is avoided.
Descent: the note *RI* (D) is omitted.

(106) *Palamajarī* (*Phalamañjarī*)

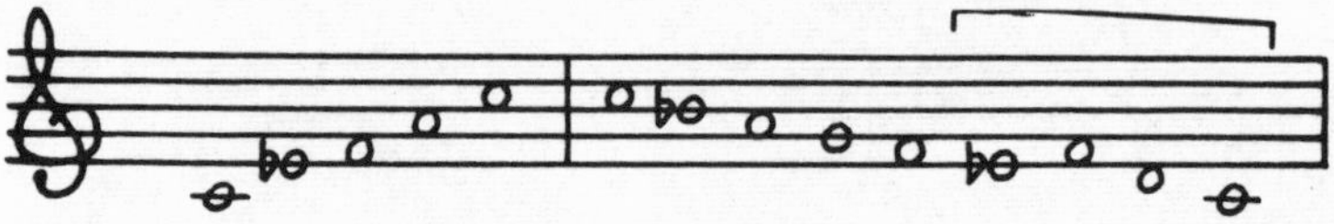

Ascent: the notes *RI* (D), *PA* (G), and *NI* (Bb) are avoided.
Descent: *sampūrṇa*; one *vakra* feature is shown.

The following melody specimen is taken from SCM, 106:

(107) *Pañchama* (*Pañcama*)

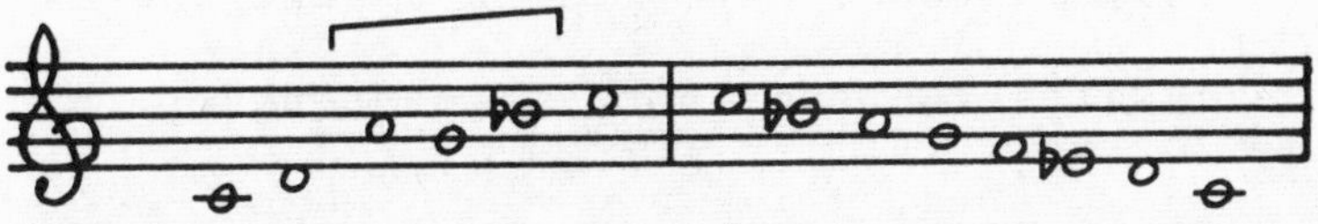

Ascent: the notes *GA* (Eb) and *MA* (F) are avoided; one *vakra* feature is shown.
Descent: *krama sampūrṇa*.

The following melody specimen comes from SCM, 115-16:

(108) *Pūrṇakalānidhi*

Ascent: the note *RI* (D) is avoided.

Descent: the note *NI* (Bb) is omitted. According to N the note *RI* (D) is intoned as Db.

(109) *Pūrṇaṣaḍja*

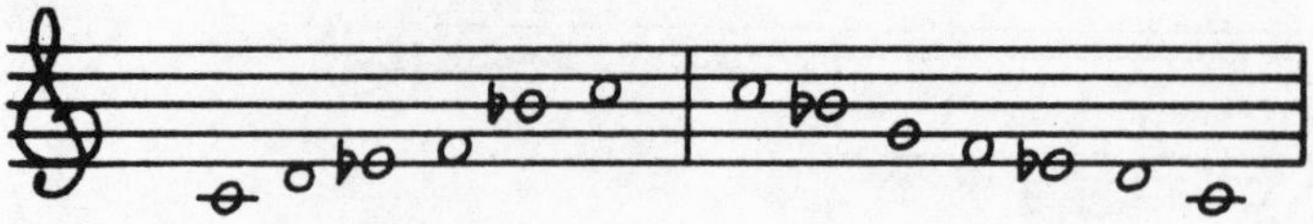

The note *DHA* (A) is avoided entirely. *PA* (G) is omitted in ascent. *NI* (Bb) is to be stressed in ascent and *GA* (Eb) in descent.

Another *rāga* with the same name appears under the heading of the 20. *mēḷa* (5).

(110) *Pūrvamukhāri*

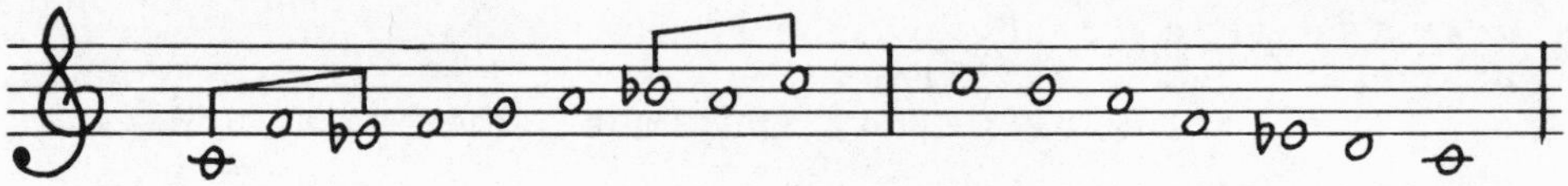

Ascent: the note *RI* (D) is avoided; two *vakra* features are shown.
Descent: the note *PA* (G) is omitted. According to N the note *NI* is intoned sharply, approximately B.

(111) *Pushpalatīkā* (*Puṣpalatīkā*)

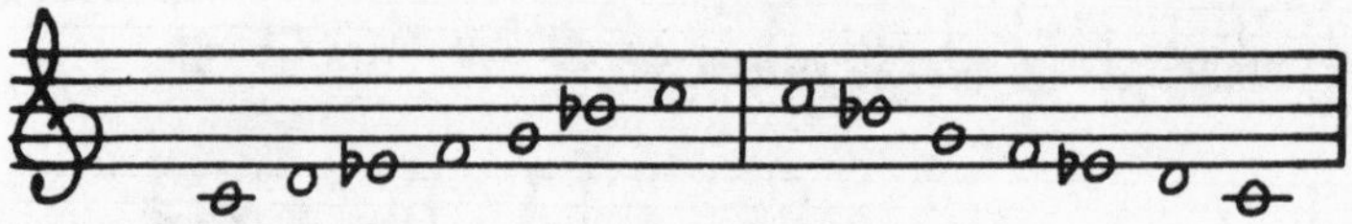

The note *DHA* (A) is avoided entirely.

(112) *Rudrapriya*

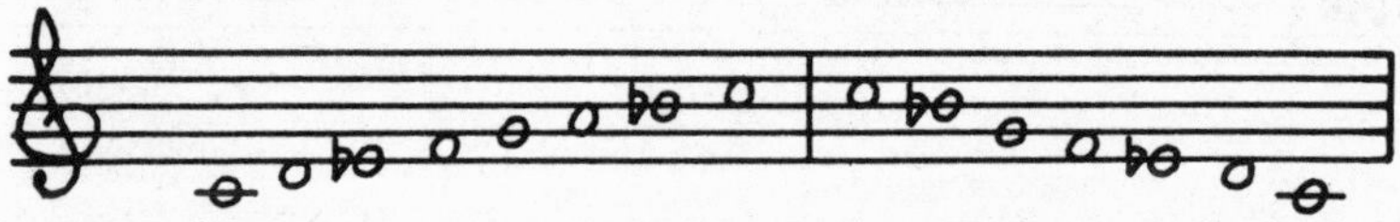

Ascent: *krama sampūrṇa*.
Descent: the note *DHA* (A) is avoided.

The note *GA* (Eb) is to be stressed, particularly in descent.

(113) *Saindhavi* (*Saindhvi*)

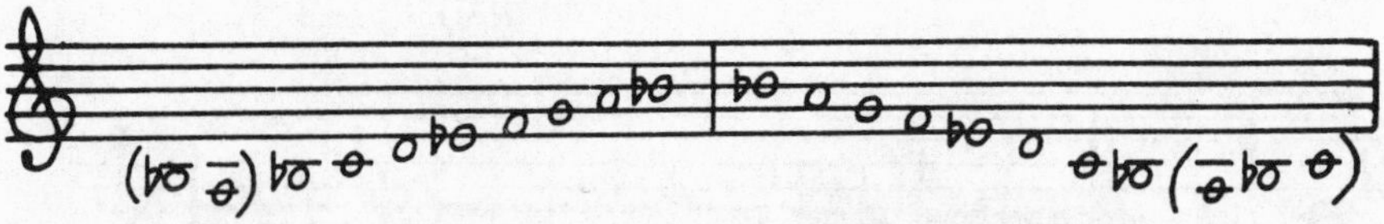

R (187) describes this *rāga* as a *madhya rāga* ("middle-range *rāga*"). The scale has *niṣādāntya* character because its highest note is *NI* (Bb) and its range is generally confined to the middle octave with the exception of the notes *NI* (Bb) and *DHA* (A) of the *mandra saptaka* (low octave range). Veṅkaṭamakhin speaks about a certain irregularity of *DHA* (A) in ascent (which refers to the note *DHA* of the low octave range). Tuḷajā states that if this *rāga* is sung by a warrior he will be victorious.

Another form of *Saindhvi* is:

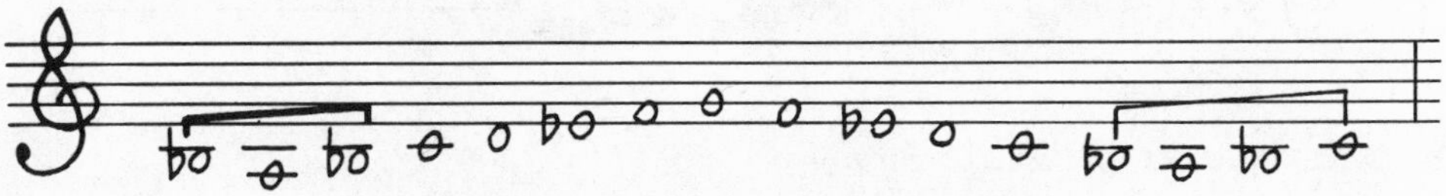

The following melody specimen is taken from SCM, 111-12:

(114) *Sālaga Bhairavī*

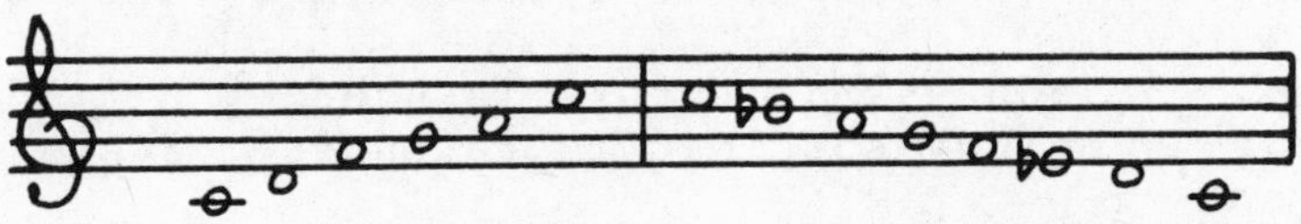

Ascent: the notes *GA* (Eb) and *NI* (Bb) are avoided.
Descent: *krama sampūrṇa*.

The following melody specimen is taken from SCM, 111-12:

(115) *Saṃkrantanapriya*

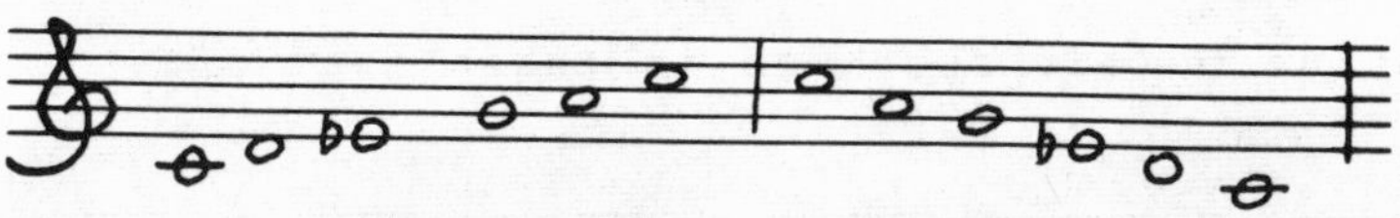

The notes *MA* (F) and *NI* (Bb) are avoided entirely.

(116) *Siddhasēna*

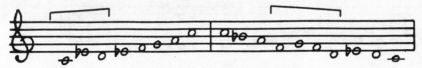

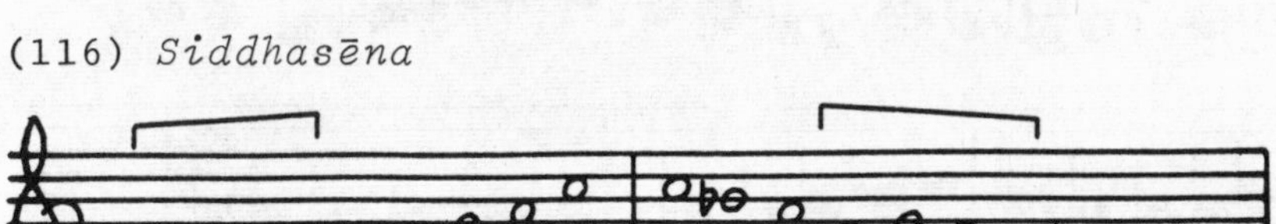

Ascent: the note *NI* (Bb) is avoided; one *vakra* feature is shown.
Descent: *sampūrṇa*; one *vakra* feature is used.

The following melody specimen is taken from SCM, 122-23:

(117) *Śrīmanōhari*

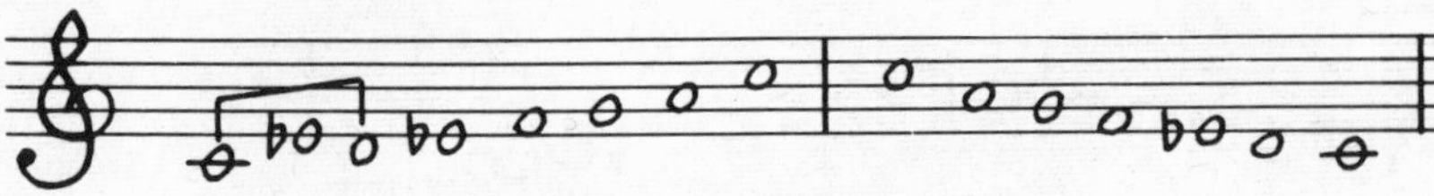

The note *NI* (Bb) is avoided entirely. The ascent shows one *vakra* feature.

(118) *Śrīrañjaṇi*

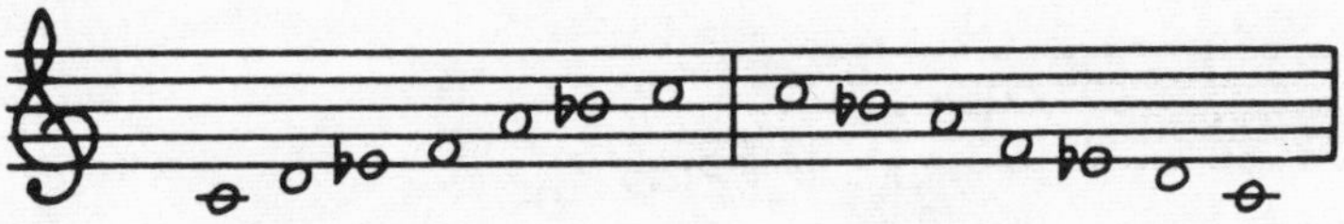

The note *PA* (G) is avoided entirely.
Songs in this *rāga* generally begin with one of the following notes: *SA* (C), *RI* (D), *MA* (F), or *NI* (Bb). *Śrīrañjaṇi* can be performed at any time. Its scale is identical with that of *rāga Inakapriya* (22, 53).

The following melody specimen is taken from SCM, 119-20:

ŚRĪRANJANI (*Triputa-tāla*)

(119) *Śubhāṅgi*

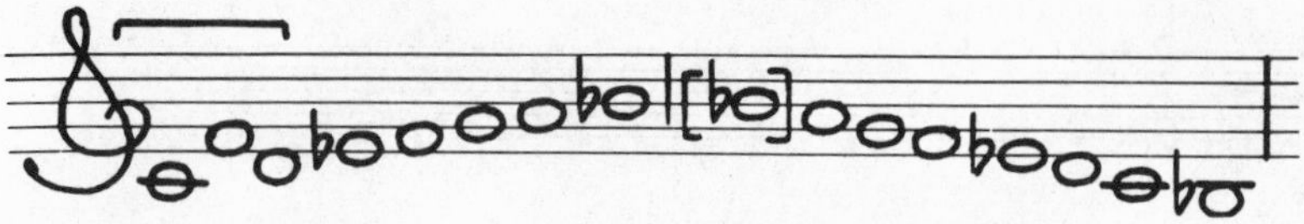

This *rāga* has *niṣādāntya* character and shows in ascent one *vakra* feature.

(120) *Śuddhabaṅgāḷa*

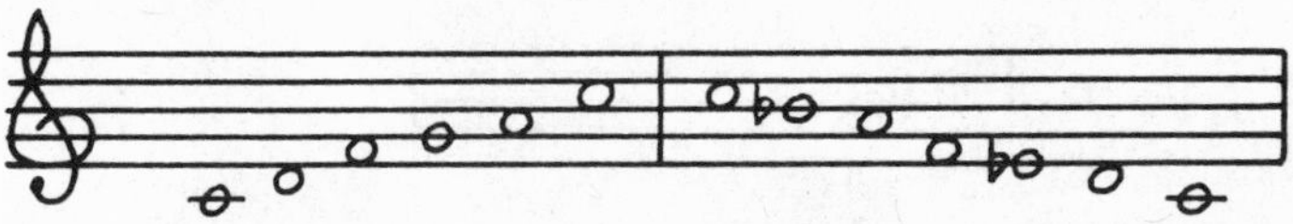

Ascent: the notes *GA* (Eb) and *NI* (Bb) are avoided.
Descent: the note *PA* (G) is omitted.

Another form of the *Śuddhabaṅgāḷa* descent is:

The following melody specimen is taken from SCM, 116:

ŚUDDHABAṄGĀḶA (*Triputa-tāla*)

(121) *Śuddhabhairavī*

The note *PA* (G) is avoided entirely. The ascent omits the note *RI* (D) and shows one *vakra* feature.

The following melody specimen is taken from SCM, 110:

ŚUDDHABHAIRAVĪ (*Triputa-tāla*)

(122) *Śuddhadhanyāsi*

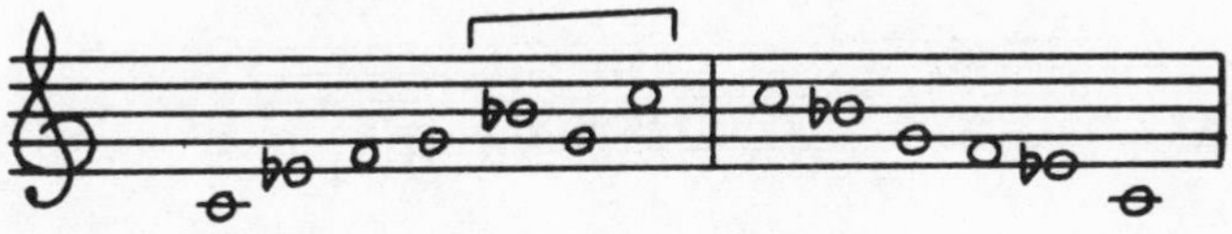

The notes *RI* (D) and *DHA* (A) are avoided entirely. The ascent shows one *vakra* feature.

The following melody specimen is taken from SCM, 109:

ŚUDDHADHANYĀSI (*Triputa-tāla*)

(123) *Śuddhamadhyamam*

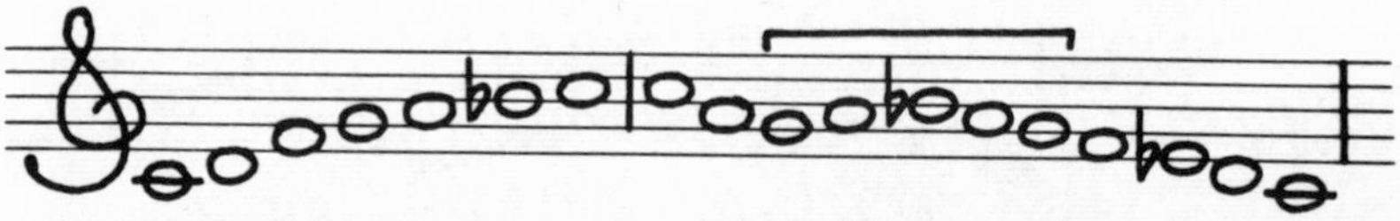

Ascent: the note *GA* (Eb) is avoided.
Descent: *sampūrṇa*; one extended *vakra* feature is shown.

(124) *Śuddhamanōharī*

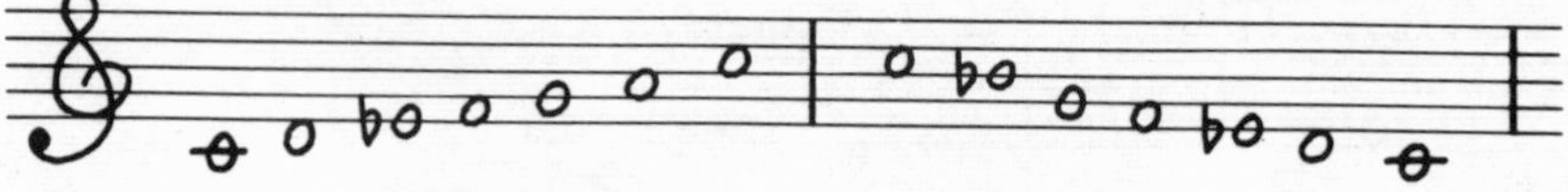

Ascent: the note *NI* (Bb) is avoided.
Descent: the note *DHA* (A) is omitted.

(125) *Śuddhavelāvalī*

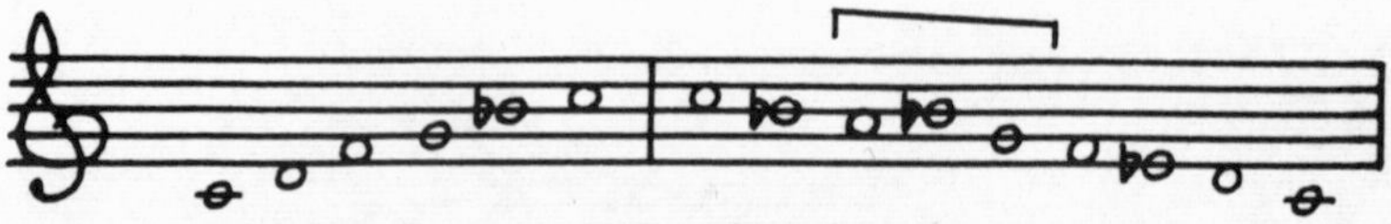

Ascent: the notes *GA* (Eb) and *DHA* (A) are avoided.

Descent: *sampūrṇa*; one *vakra* feature is shown.

The following melody specimen is taken from SCM, 120:

ŚUDDHAVELĀVALĪ (*Triputa-tāla*)

(126) *Sugunabhūṣaṇi*

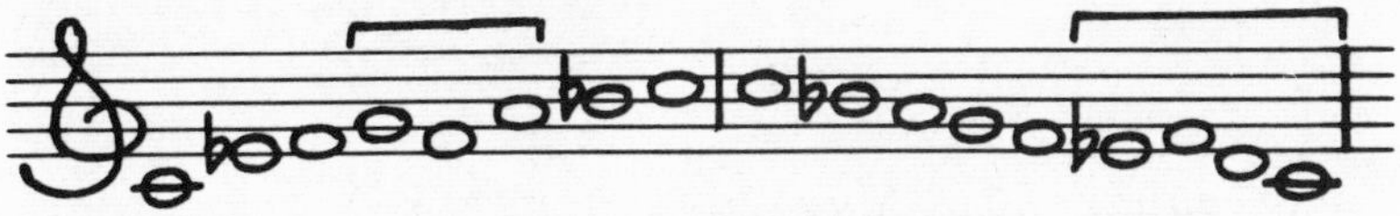

Ascent: the note *RI* (D) is avoided; one *vakra* feature is shown.
Descent: *sampūrṇa*; one *vakra* feature is used.

(127) *Sujaris*

The note *DHA* (A) is avoided entirely. There are two *vakra* features in ascent and two in descent.

(128) *Svarabhuṣaṇi*

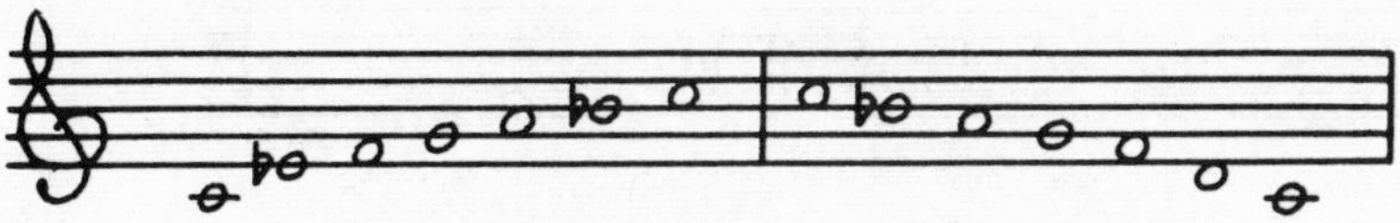

Ascent: the note *RI* (D) is avoided.
Descent: the note *GA* (Eb) is omitted.

(129) *Svarakalānidhi*

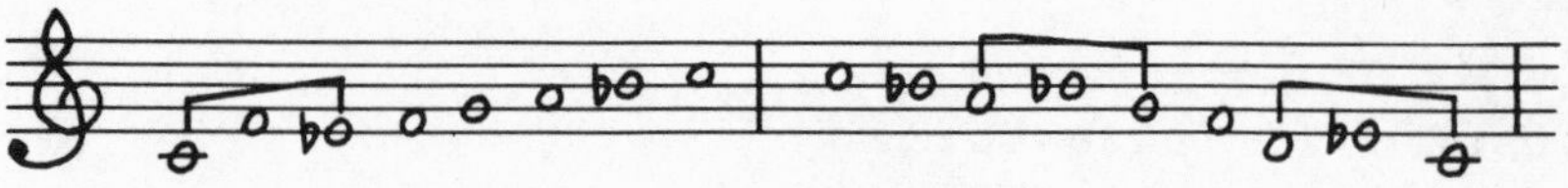

Ascent: the note *RI* (D) is avoided; one *vakra* feature is shown.
Descent: *sampūrṇa*; two *vakra* features are used.

(130) *Svrararañjaṇi*

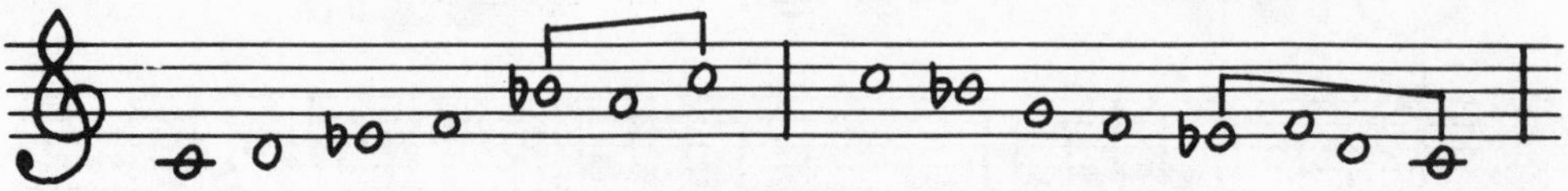

Ascent: the note *PA* (G) is avoided; one *vakra* feature is shown.
Descent: the note *DHA* (A) is omitted; one *vakra* feature is used.

(131) *Udayaravicandrikā* (*Udayaravichandrikā*)

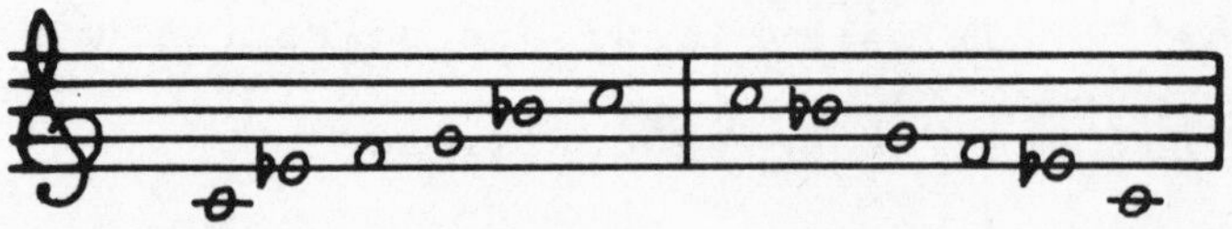

This *rāga* has the same tone material as *rāga Śuddhadhanyāsi* (22, 122). The difference between the two *rāgas* lies in the fact that *Udayaravicandrikā* has no *vakra* features.

Udayaravicandrikā is also listed under the heading of the 20. *mēḷa* (11).

(132) *Varamu*

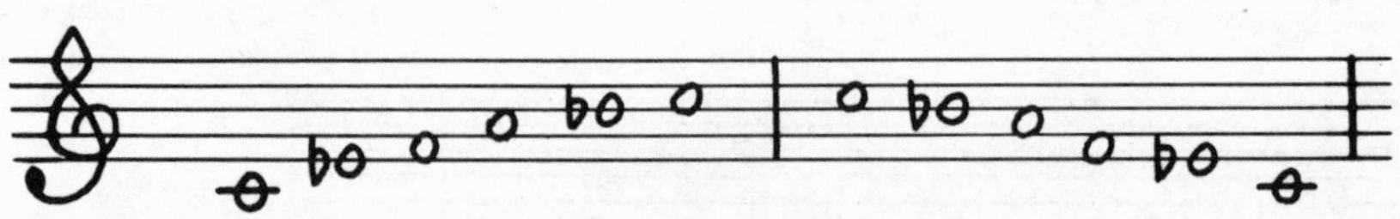

The notes *RI* (D) and *PA* (G) are avoided entirely.

23. *MĒḶA GAURĪMANŌHARĪ* (*GAURĪMONŌHARĪ*)

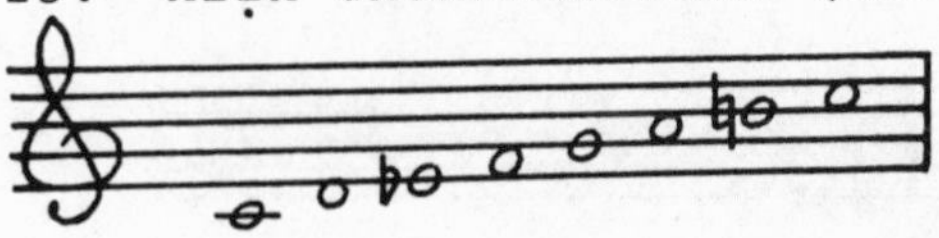

Rāga Gaurīmanōharī can be performed at any time. Its stressed notes are *GA* (Eb), *MA* (F), and *NI* (B).

Veṅkaṭamakhin calls this *rāga Gaurīvelāvaḷī*, in which the notes *GA* (Eb) and *NI* (B) are avoided in ascent.

The following song example is a *kīrtana* by Tyāgarāja:

GAURĪMANŌHARĪ (*Jhampa-tāla*)

Pallavi

Repeat the entire *pallavi*

Anupallavi

Repeat the entire *pallavi*

Charana

Repeat the entire *pallavi*

The following passages are taken from a *Gīta Govinda* performance recorded by Wayne Howard in Kerala in 1972:

Janya Rāgas of the 23. Mēḷa

This *mēḷa* is not as popular as the 22. *mēḷa* and only eighteen *janya rāgas* are listed under its heading.

(1) *Veḷāvaḷī*

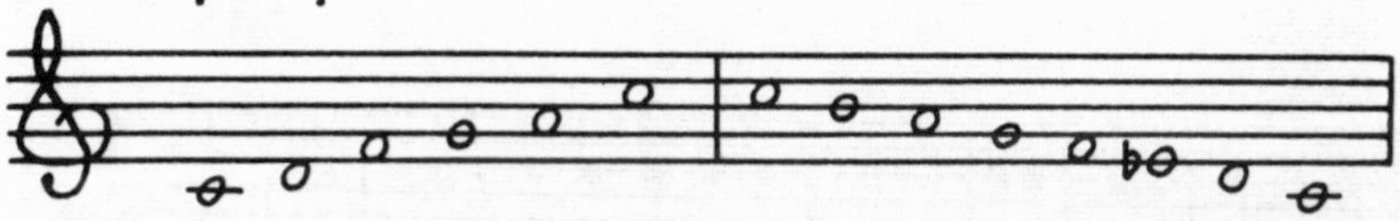

Ascent: the notes *GA* (Eb) and *NI* (B) are avoided.
Descent: *krama sampūrṇa*.

This *rāga* conforms with Veṅkaṭamakhin's *Gaurīveḷāvaḷī*. The following melody specimen is taken from SCM, 127:

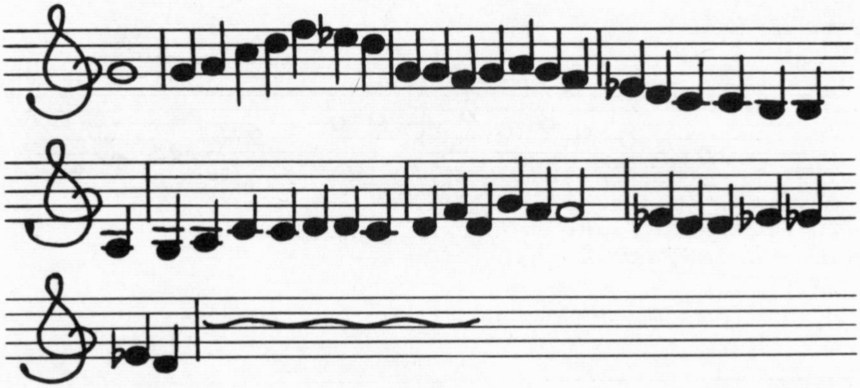

(2) *Ambāmanōharī*

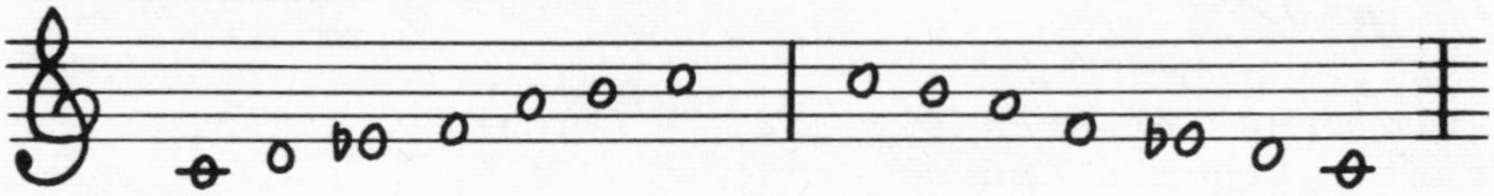

The note *PA* (G) is avoided entirely.

(3) *Chitra Mālikā* (*Citra Mālikā*)

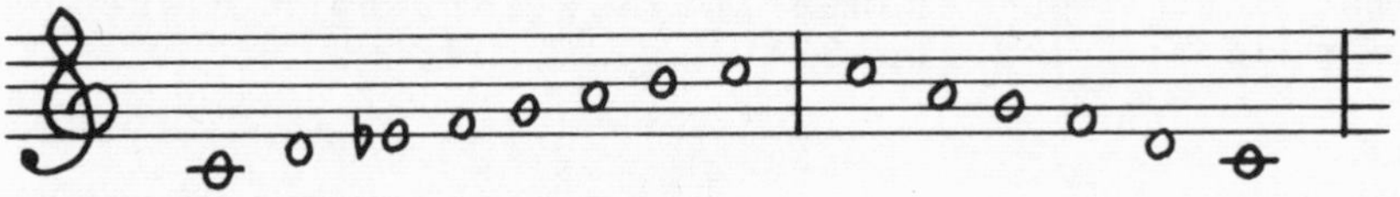

Ascent: *krama sampūrṇa*.
Descent: the notes *NĪ* (B) and *GA* (Eb) are avoided.

(4) *Darbhakūlam*

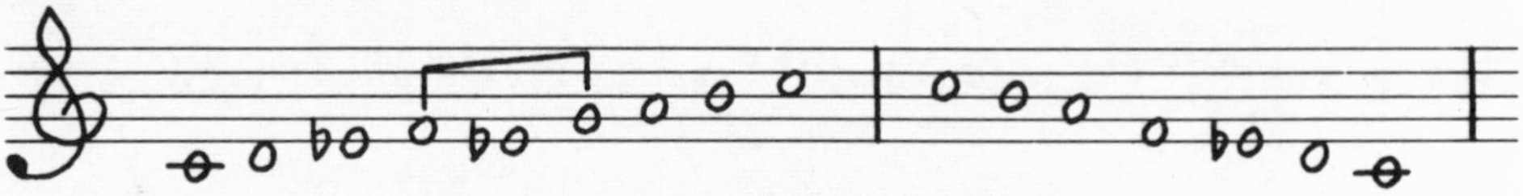

Ascent: *sampūrṇa*; one *vakra* feature is shown.
Descent: the note *PA* (G) is avoided.

(5) *Gāmākyam*

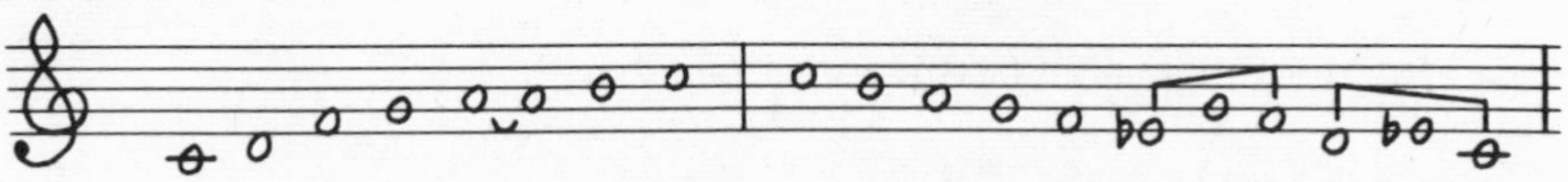

Ascent: the note *GA* (Eb) is avoided. *DHA* (A) is stressed.
Descent: *sampūrṇa*; two *vakra* features are shown.

(6) *Gambhīriṇi*

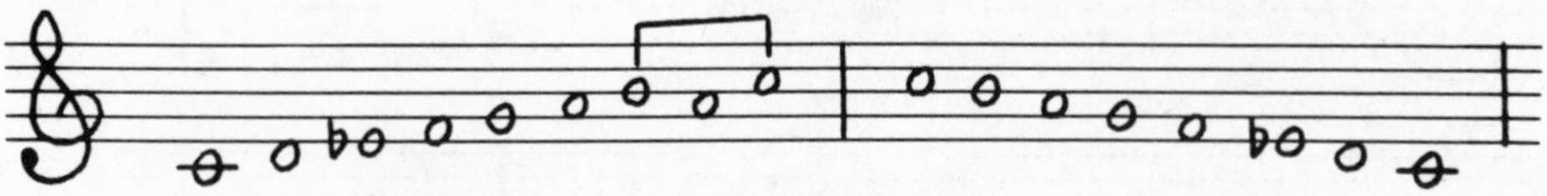

Ascent: *sampūrṇa*; one *vakra* feature is shown.
Descent: *krama sampūrṇa*.

(7) *Haṃsa Dīpakam*

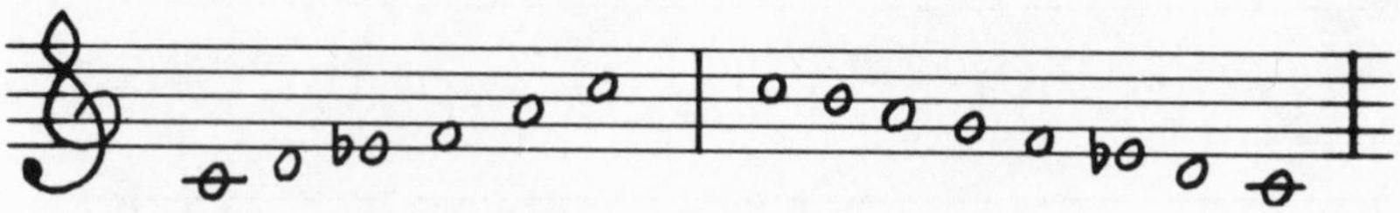

Ascent: the notes *PA* (G) and *NI* (B) are avoided.
Descent: *krama sampūrṇa*.

(8) *Hāsya Dīpakam*

This *rāga* is identical with *Haṃsa Dīpakam* (23,7). It is mentioned here because the SD lists both *rāgas* separately on pp. 222 and 371.

(9) *Kamala*

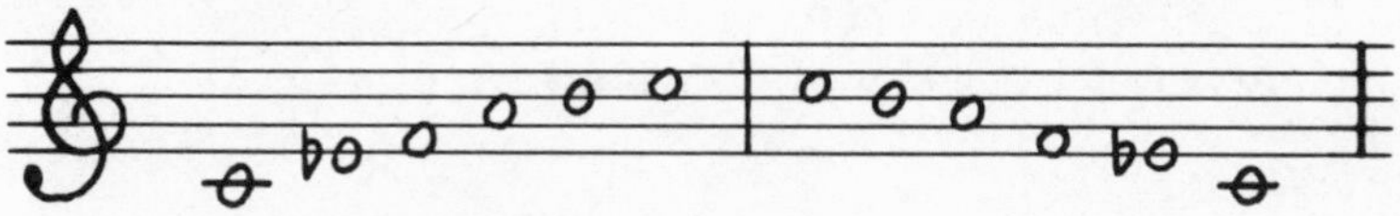

The notes *RI* (D) and *PA* (G) are avoided entirely.

(10) *Karapāni*

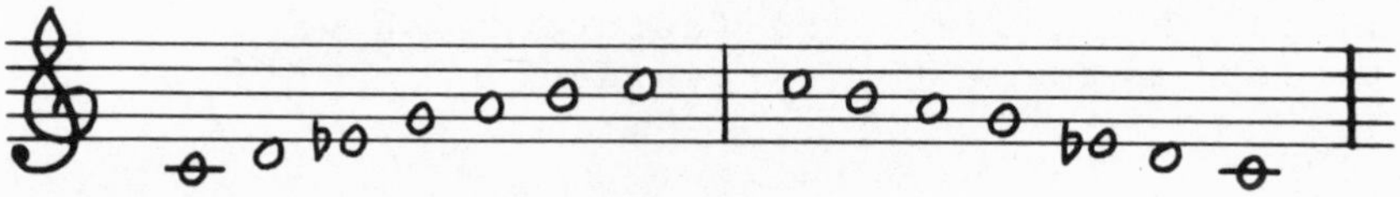

The note *MA* (F) is avoided entirely.

(11) *Kōkila Dīpakam*

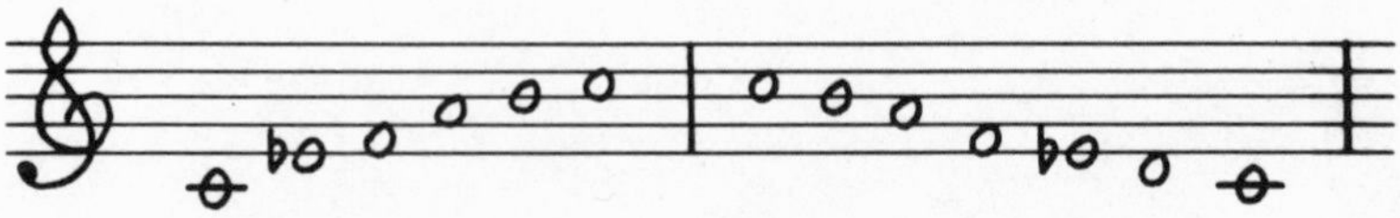

The note *PA* (G) is avoided entirely. *RI* (D) is omitted in ascent.

(12) *Nāgabhūpāḷam*

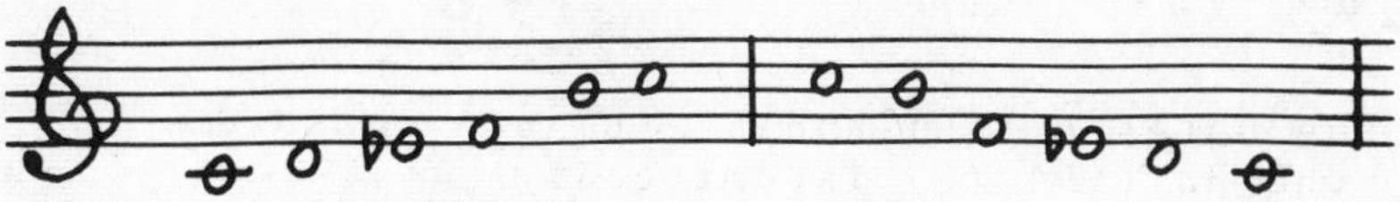

The notes *PA* (G) and *DHA* (A) are avoided entirely.

(13) *Nāgapañchamam (Nāgapañcamam)*

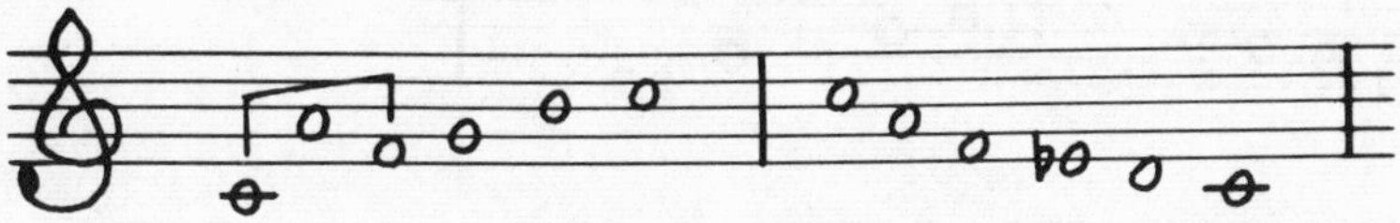

Ascent: the notes *RI* (D) and *GA* (Eb) are avoided; one *vakra* feature is shown.
Descent: the notes *NI* (B) and *PA* (G) are omitted.

(14) *Pālika*

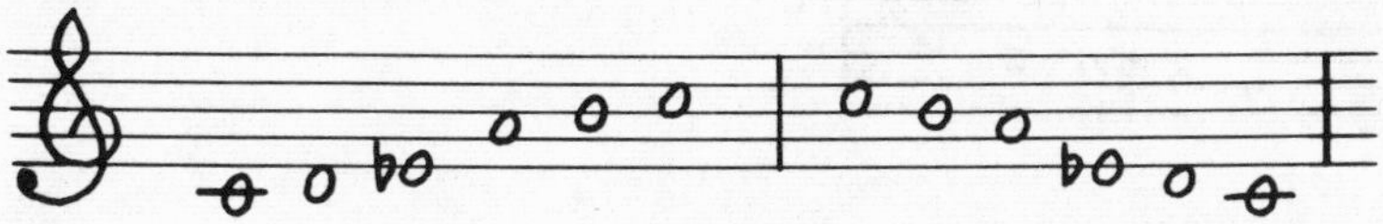

The notes *MA* (F) and *PA* (G) are avoided entirely.

(15) *Sālavibaṅgāla*

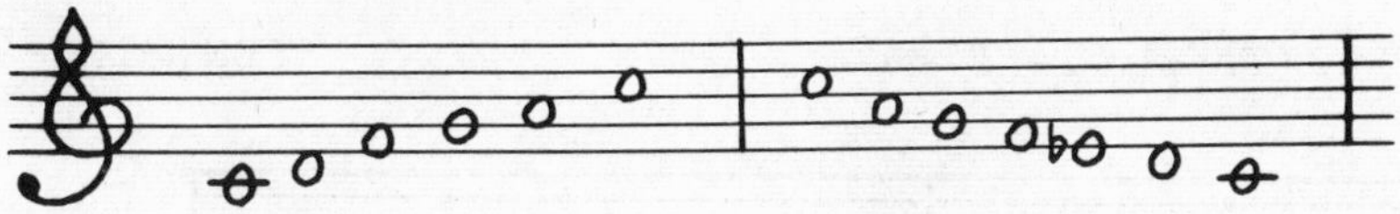

The note *NI* (B) is avoided entirely. *GA* (Eb) is omitted in ascent.

(16) *Sāmasālavi*

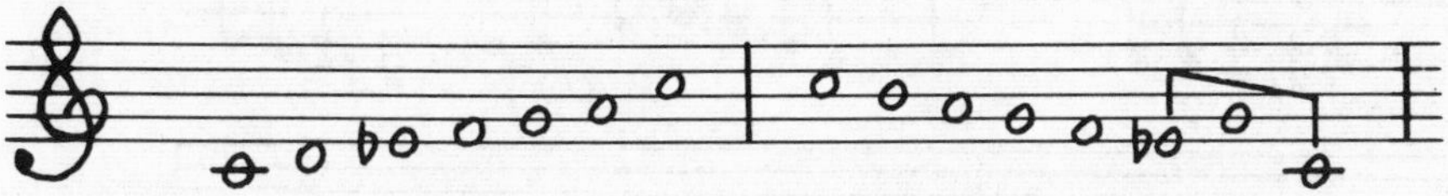

Ascent: the note *NI* (B) is avoided.
Descent: the note *RI* (D) is omitted; one *vakra* feature is shown.

(17) *Siṃhēlabhairavī*

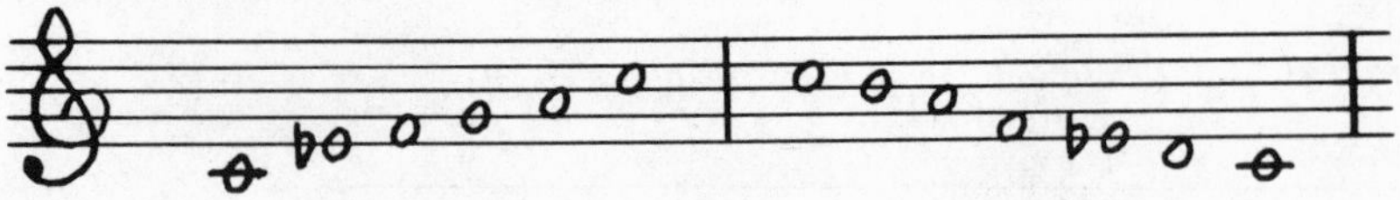

Ascent: the notes *RI* (D) and *NI* (B) are avoided.
Descent: the note *PA* (G) is omitted.

(18) *Varudham*

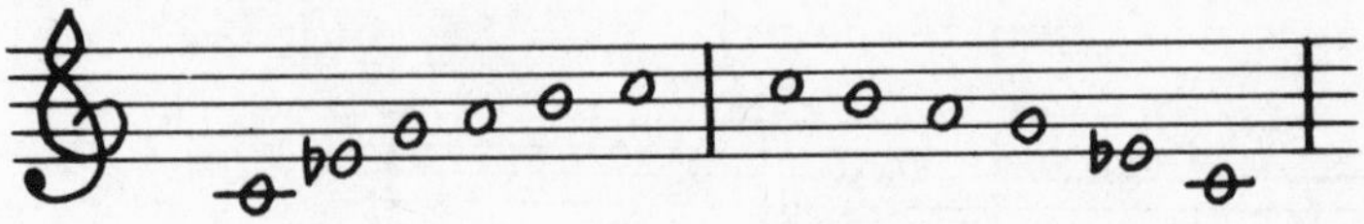

The notes *RI* (D) and *MA* (F) are avoided entirely.

24. *MĒḶA VARUṆAPRIYĀ*

Veṅkaṭamakhin called this *rāga Vīravasantam*. As in numerous other instances Veṅkaṭamakhin'a *rāga* name appears in the modern system as the name of the first *janya rāga* subordinated to the primary *rāga*.

VARUṆAPRIYĀ (*Triputa-tāla*) SCM, 128-9

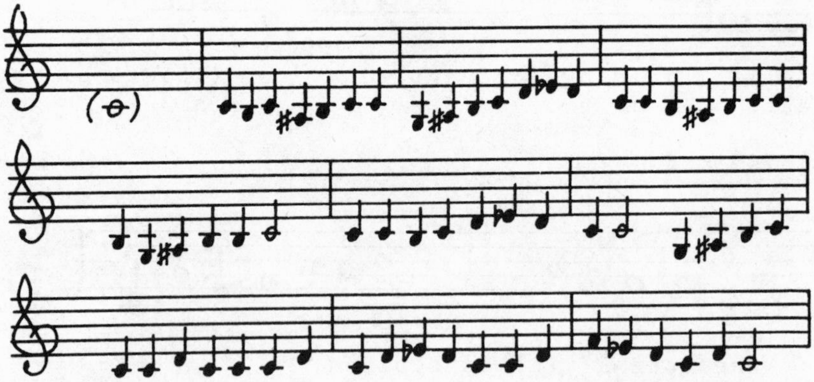

Janya Rāgas of the 24. Mēḷa

(1) *Vīravasantam*

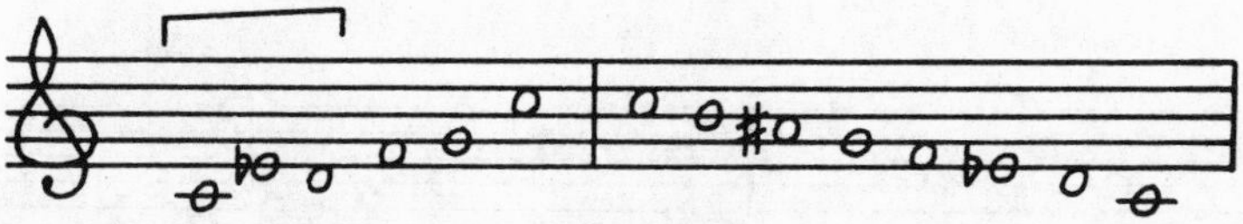

Ascent: the notes *DHA* (A#) and *NI* (B) are avoided; one *vakra* feature is shown.
Descent: *krama sampūrṇa*.

The following melody specimen is taken from SCM, 129:

(2) *Ashṭi (Aṣṭi)*

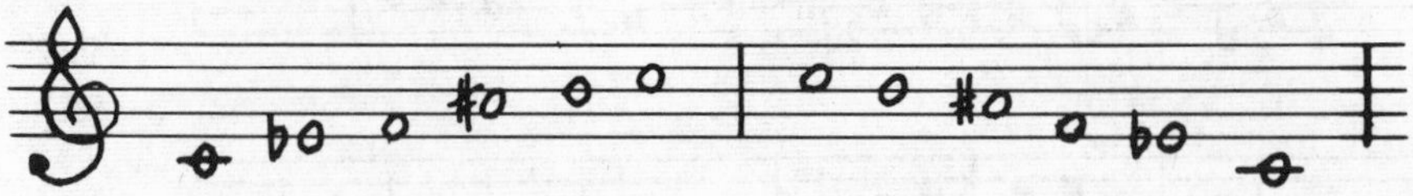

The notes *RI* (D) and *PA* (G) are avoided entirely.

(3) *Bhānu Dīpakam*

Ascent: *krama sampūrṇa*.
Descent: the notes *DHA* (A#) and *GA* (Eb) are avoided.

(4) *Bhṛṅgu Kuṅga*

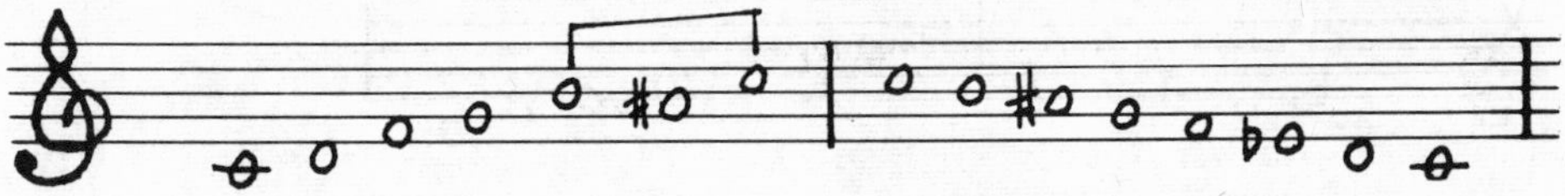

Ascent: the note *GA* (Eb) is avoided; one *vakra* feature is shown.
Descent: *krama sampūrṇa*.

(5) *Brudūvaka*

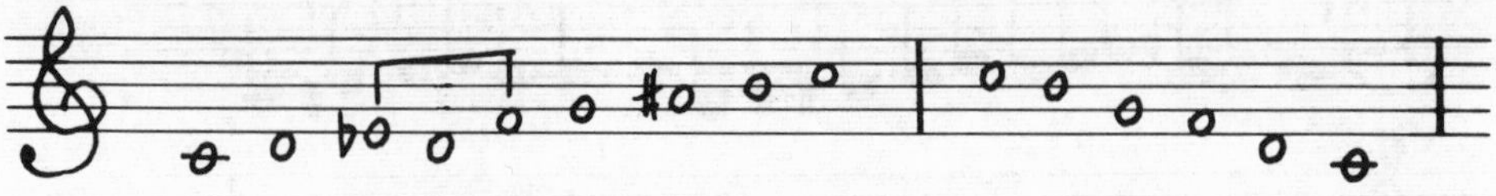

Ascent: *sampūrṇa*; one *vakra* feature is shown.
Descent: the notes *DHA* (A#) and *GA* (Eb) are avoided.

(6) *Gāndharva Nārāyaṇi*

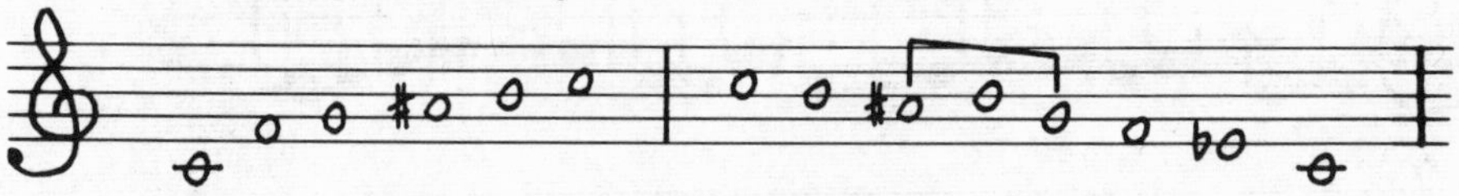

The note *RI* (D) is avoided entirely. *GA* (Eb) is omitted in ascent. The descent shows one *vakra* feature.

(7) *Gaula Pañchamam (Gaula Pañcamam)*

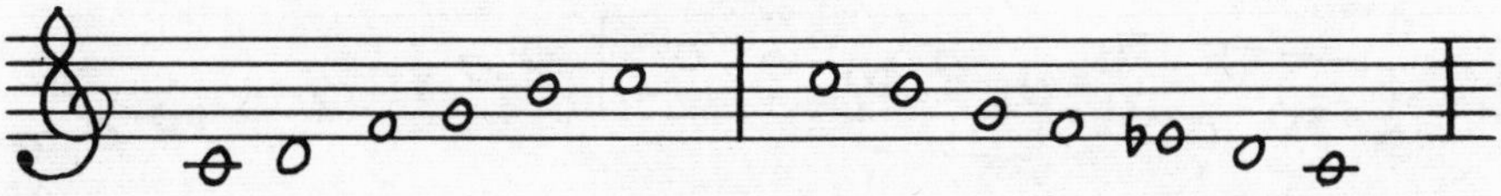

The note *DHA* (A#) is avoided entirely. *GA* (Eb) is omitted in ascent.

(8) *Haṃsa Bhāṣiṇi*

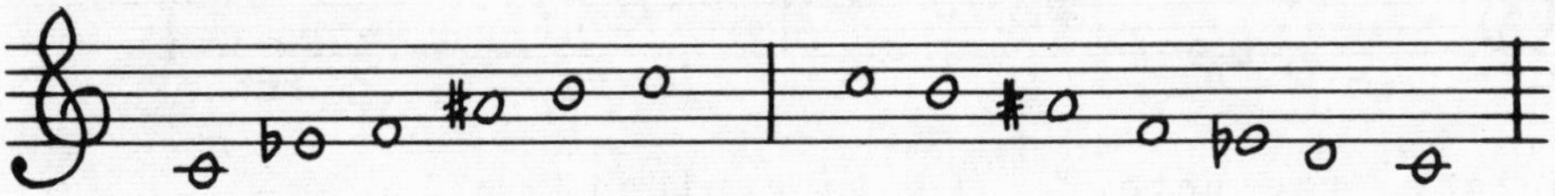

The note *PA* (G) is avoided entirely. *RI* (D) is omitted in ascent.

(9) *Haṃsa Bhūṣaṇi*

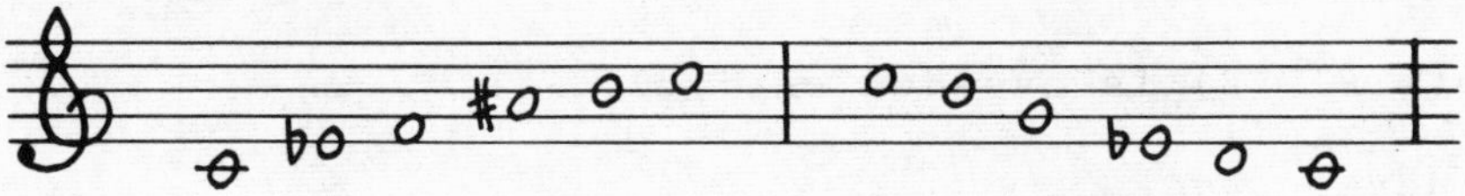

Ascent: the notes *RI* (D) and *PA* (G) are avoided.
Descent: the notes *DHA* (A#) and *MA* (F) are omitted.

Many musicians maintain that the *rāgas Haṃsa Bhāṣiṇi* (24,8) and *Haṃsa Bhūṣaṇi* are identical. SD (II, 222), however, shows different descents in the two *rāgas*. In the former the descent is c-B-A#-F-Eb-D-C, while in the latter it is c-B-G-Eb-D-C. Therefore *Haṃsa Bhūṣaṇi* is shown here separately.

(10) *Haṃsa Bhūpāḷam*

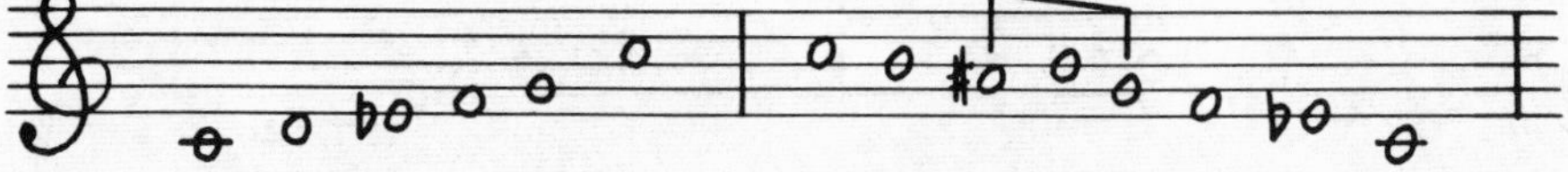

Ascent: the notes *DHA* (A#) and *NI* (B) are avoided.
Descent: the note *RI* (D) is omitted; one *vakra* feature is shown.

(11) *Haṃsapriya*

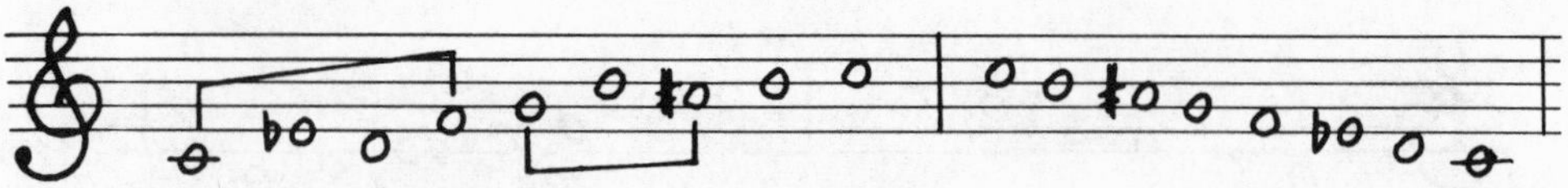

The scale of this *rāga* is *sampūrṇa* in ascent and shows two *vakra* features. The descent is *krama sampūrṇa*.

(12) *Hāsya Bhūṣaṇi*

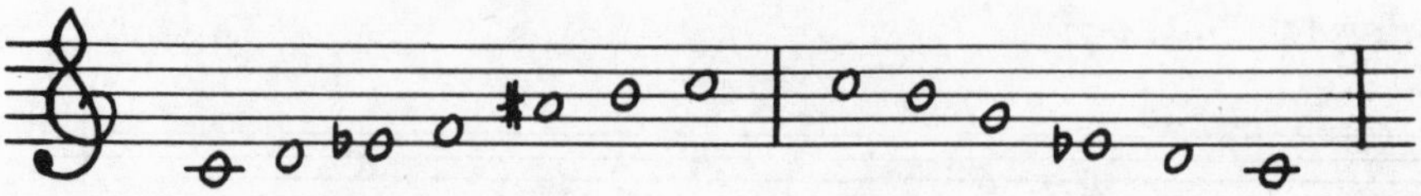

Ascent: the note *PA* (G) is avoided.
Descent: the notes *DHA* (A#) and *MA* (F) are omitted.

(13) *Hīṃkāri*

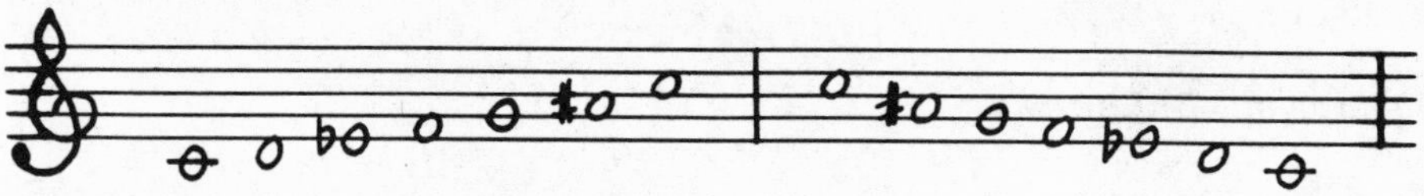

The note *NI* (B) is avoided entirely.

(14) *Indrapriya*

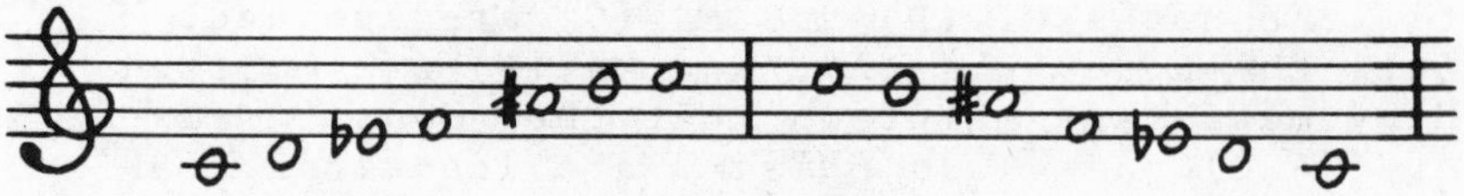

The note *PA* (G) is avoided entirely.

There are two other *rāgas* with the same name: one is 1,10 and the other 54,8.

(15) *Kamalāsanapriya*

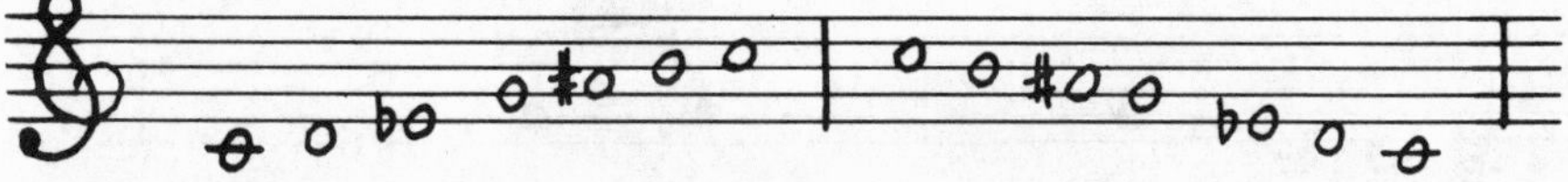

The note *MA* (F) is avoided entirely.

(16) *Karuvali*

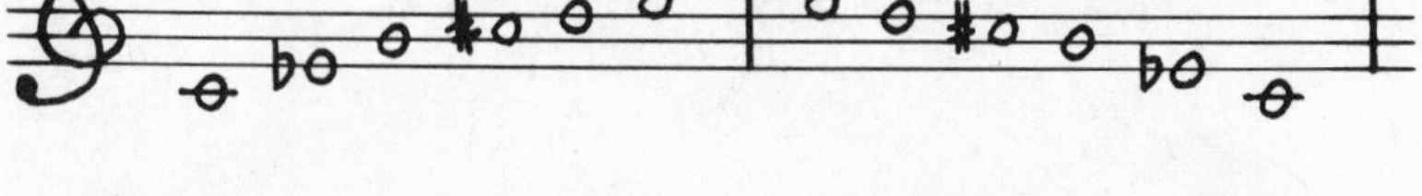

The notes *RI* (D) and *MA* (F) are avoided entirely.

(17) *Mukurapōla*

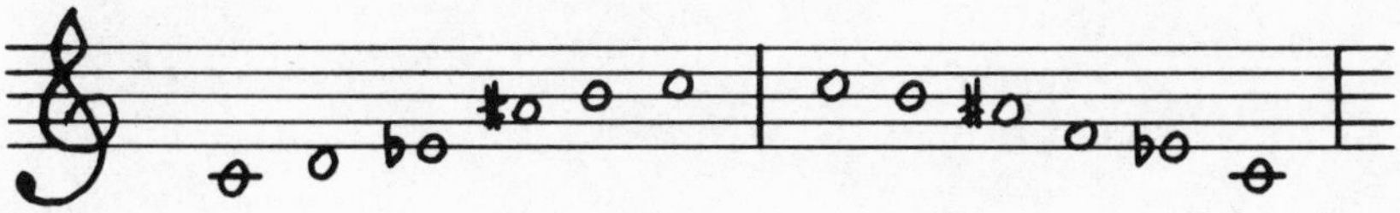

The note *PA* (G) is avoided entirely. *MA* (F) is omitted in ascent and *RI* (D) in descent.

(18) *Navanītapañchamam* (*Navanitapañcamam*)

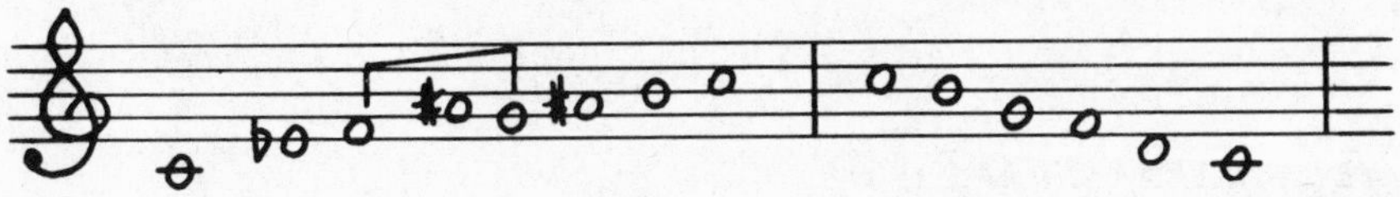

Ascent: the note *RI* (D) is avoided; one *vakra* feature is shown.
Descent: the notes *DHA* (A#) and *GA* (Eb) are omitted.

(19) *Simhēlakāpi*

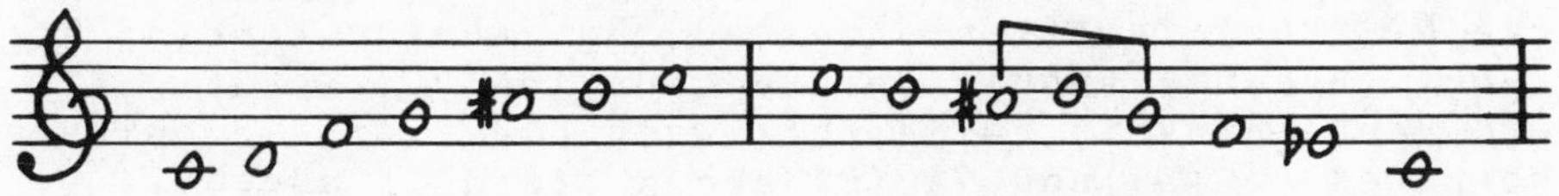

Ascent: the note *GA* (Eb) is avoided.
Descent: the note *RI* (D) is omitted; one *vakra* feature is shown.

(20) *Sōmadīpakam*

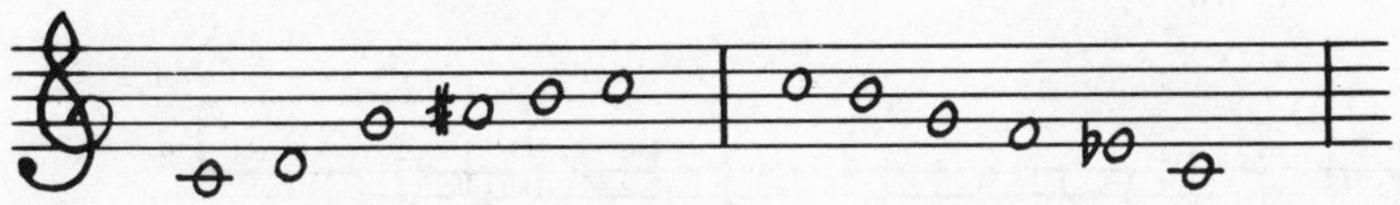

Ascent: the notes *GA* (Eb) and *MA* (F) are avoided.
Descent: the notes *DHA* (A#) and *RI* (D) are omitted.

(21) *Shūlatāriṇi* (*Śūlatāriṇi*)

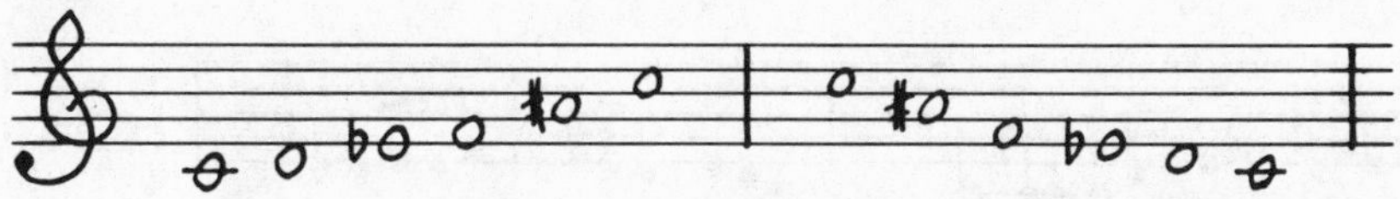

The notes *PA* (G) and *NI* (B) are avoided entirely.

Chakra V

25. *MĒḶA MĀRARAÑJANĪ*

Rāga Mārarañjanī can be performed at any time. The note *NI* (Bbb) is often stressed, but the descending step *NI-DHA* (Bbb-Ab) should be used sparingly.

Veṅkaṭamakhin calls this *rāga Śarāvati*, in which the notes *RI* (D) and *GA* (E) are avoided in ascent.

The following song specimen is a *kīrtana* by Tyāgarāja:

MĀRARAÑJANĪ (*Ādi-tāla*)

Pallavi

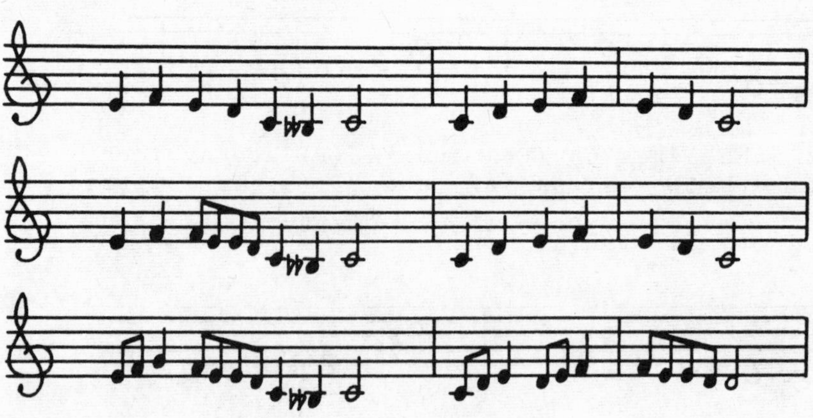

A

B

Anupallavi

Repeat lines A and B of the *pallavi*

Charana

Repeat lines A and B of the *pallavi*. The song ends with the note *SA* (C).

Janya Rāgas of the 25. Mēḷa

(1) *Śaraddyuti*

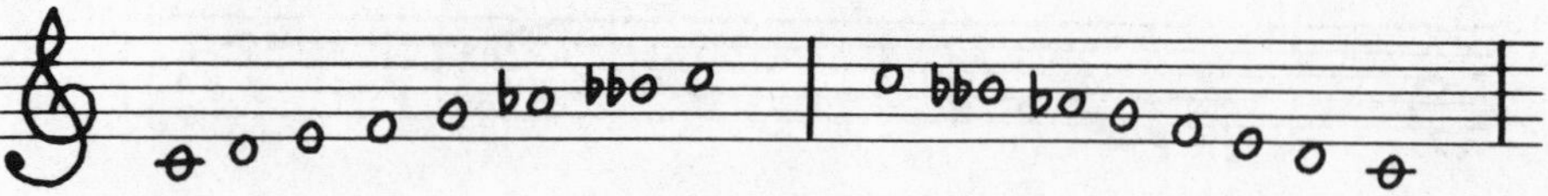

The scale of this *rāga* is *krama sampūrṇa* in ascent and descent and reveals no difference from the material of its primary *rāga*. There is, however, another *sampūrṇa* ascent in use which shows one *vakra* feature:

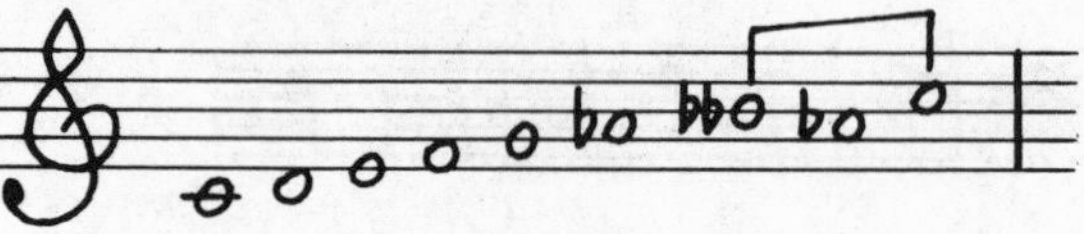

ŚARADDYUTI (*Triputa-tāla*) SCM, 131

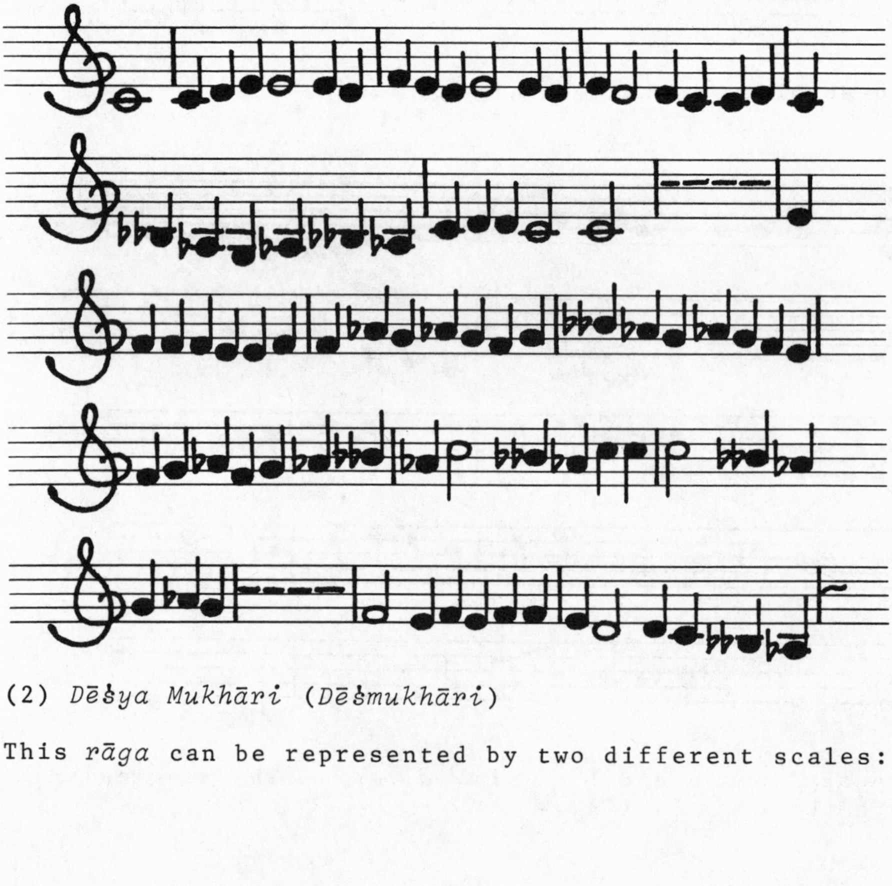

(2) *Dēśya Mukhāri* (*Dēśmukhāri*)

This *rāga* can be represented by two different scales:

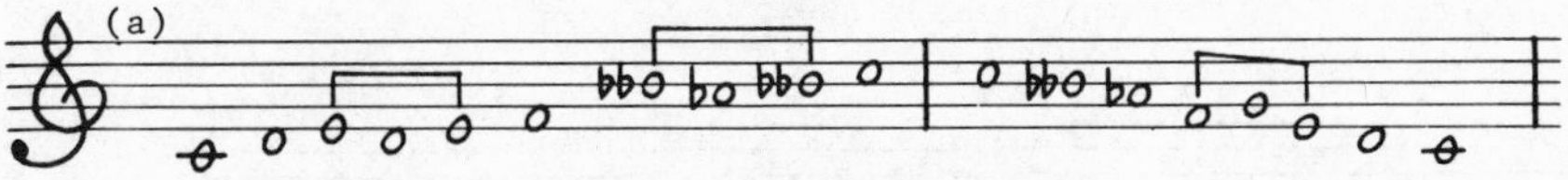

Scale (a) is stated in SD (I, 107). It avoids the note *PA* (G) entirely and shows two *vakra* features in ascent and one in descent.

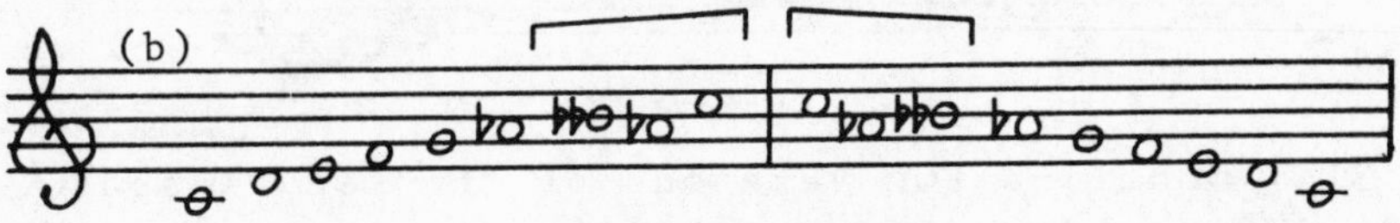

Scale (b), generally called *Dēśmukhāri*, appears more often than scale (a). It is *sampūrṇa* in ascent and descent and shows one *vakra* feature in ascent and one in descent.

DĒŚMUKHĀRI (*Triputa-tāla*) SCM, 132

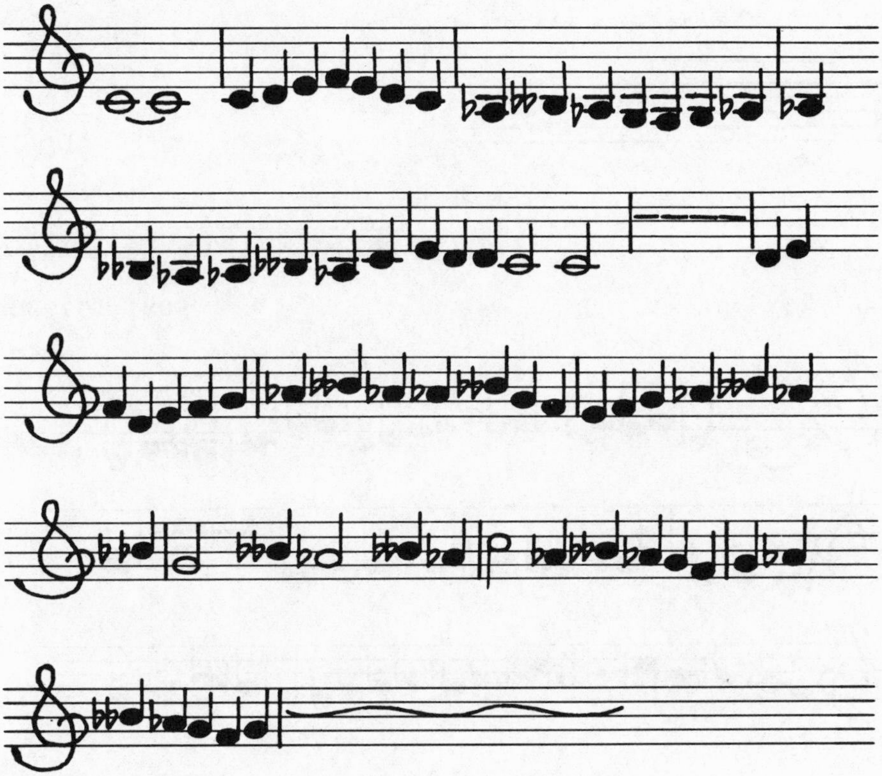

(3) *Kēsarī*

SD (II, 314) mentions two versions of the *Kēsarī* scale. Scale (a) avoids the note *NI* (Bbb) in ascent and shows one *vakra* feature. The descent is *krama sampūrṇa*. Scale (b) also avoids the note *NI* (Bbb) in ascent and shows the same ascending *vakra* feature as scale (a). The two ascents differ in the use of the two upper notes of the scale. In scale (a) appear *PA-SA* (G-c) and in scale (b) *DHA-SA* (Ab-c). The descent of scale (b) is *sampūrṇa* and shows one *vakra* feature.

In the Appendix to the SCM (331) the following ascent of the *Kēsarī* scale is given:

The descent of this version is identical with that of scale (b).

KĒSARĪ (*Triputa-tāla*) SCM, 132-33

(4) *Bhadra*

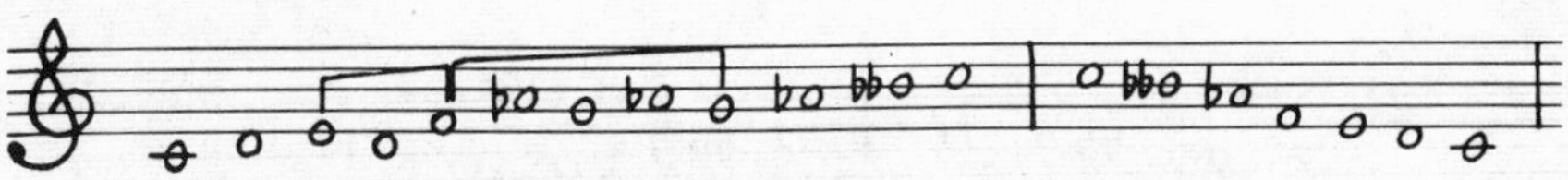

Ascent: *sampūrṇa*; two *vakra* features are shown.
Descent: the note *PA* (G) is avoided.

(5) *Bhānukānti*

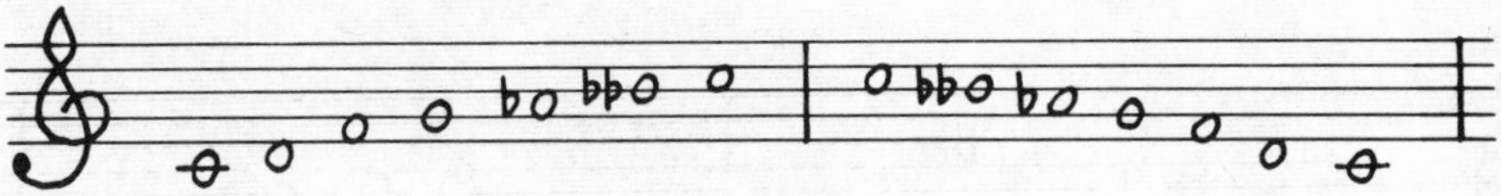

The note *GA* (E) is avoided entirely.

(6) *Bhānupratāpam*

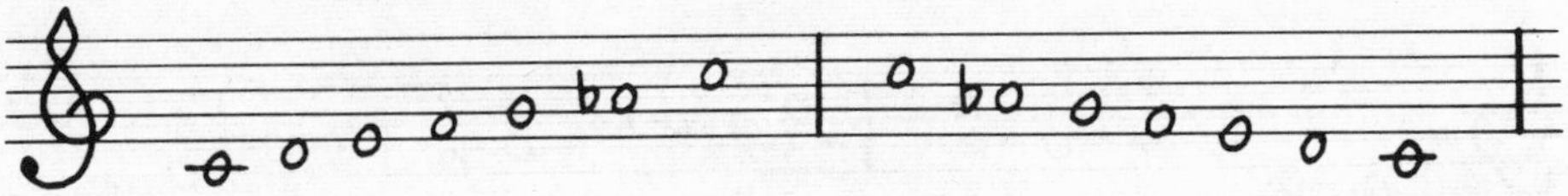

The note *NI* (Bbb) is avoided entirely.

(7) *Bhargapriya*

The notes *MA* (F) and *PA* (G) are avoided entirely.

(8) *Dēva Kūṭam*

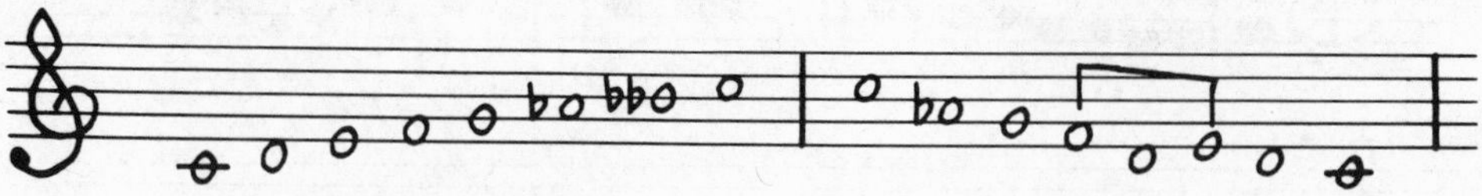

Ascent: *krama sampūrṇa.*
Descent: the note *NI* (Bbb) is avoided; one *vakra* feature is shown.

(9) *Dēva Sālagam*

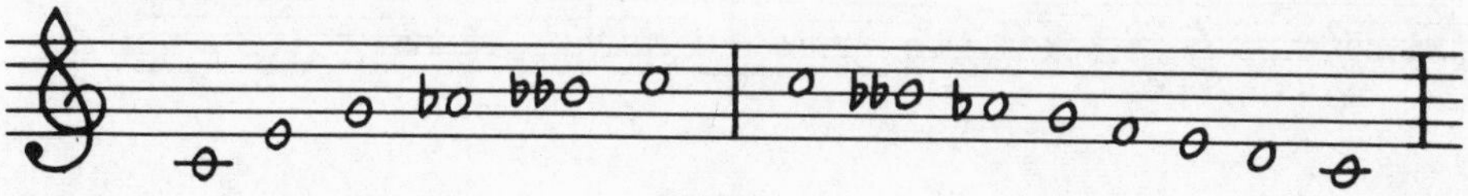

Ascent: the notes *RI* (D) and *MA* (F) are avoided.
Descent: *krama sampūrṇa.*

(10) *Gāyakamandini*

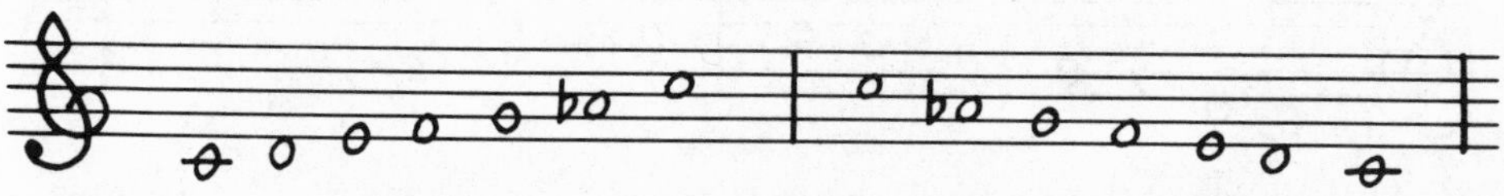

The note *NI* (Bbb) is avoided entirely.

(11) *Haṃsa Gāndhāri*

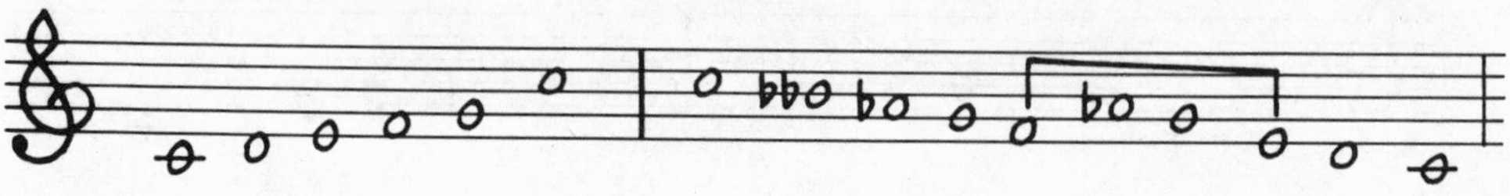

Ascent: the notes *DHA* (Ab) and *NI* (Bbb) are avoided.
Descent: *sampūrṇa*; one *vakra* feature is shown.

(12) *Hāsya Gāndhāri*

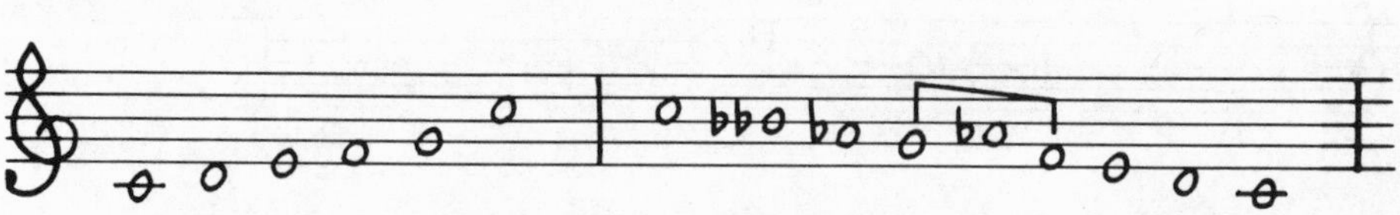

This *rāga* appears to be the same as *Haṃsa Gāndhāri* (25, 11). The only difference between the two *rāgas* can be observed in their descents: in *Hamsa Gāndhāri* the *vakra* feature is *MA-DHA-PA* (F-Ab-Ġ), while in *Hāsya Gāndhāri* it is *PA-DHA-MA* (G-Ab-F).

(13) *Kallōla Sāvēri*

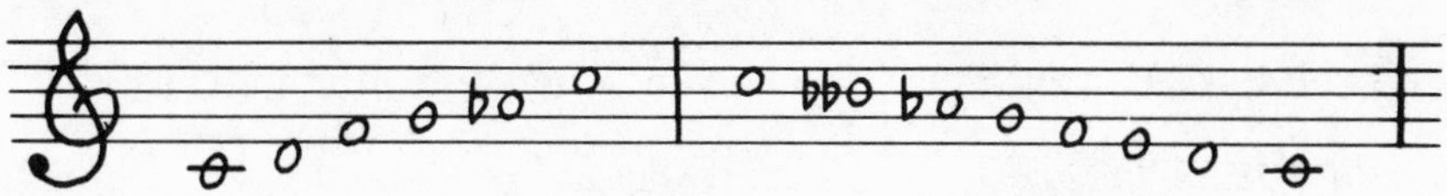

Ascent: the notes *GA* (E) and *NI* (Bbb) are avoided.
Descent: *krama sampūrṇa*.

(14) *Kumāra Rañjaṇi*

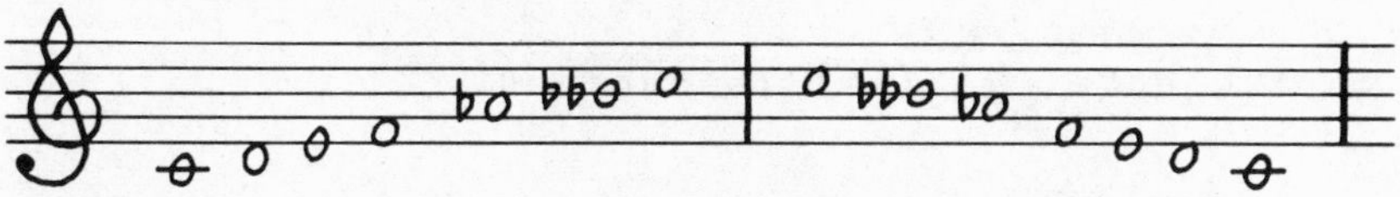

The note *PA* (G) is avoided entirely.

(15) *Kusuma Dhāriṇi*

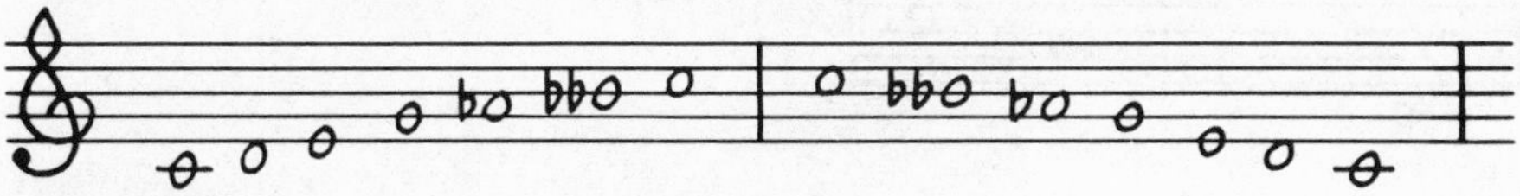

The note *MA* (F) is avoided entirely.

(16) *Mitrarañjāni*

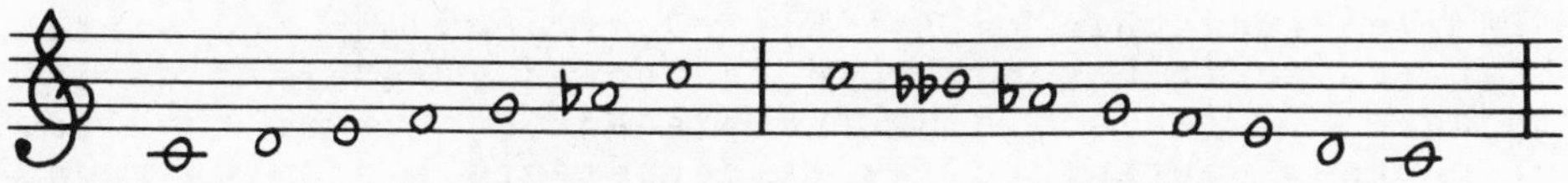

Ascent: the note *NI* (Bbb) is avoided.
Descent: *krama sampūrṇa*.

(17) *Murajavādhini*

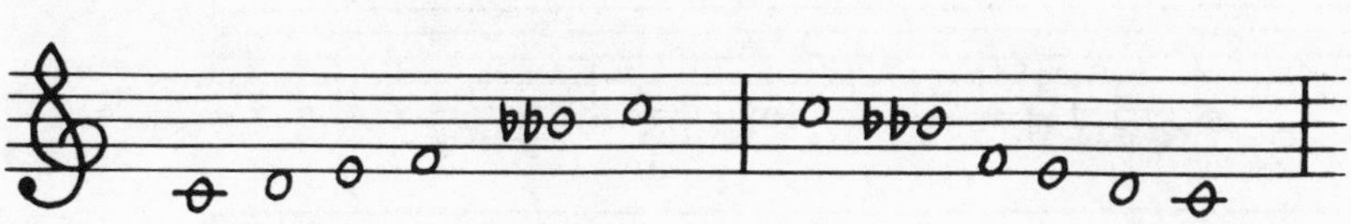

The notes *PA* (G) and *DHA* (Ab) are avoided entirely.

(18) *Rāgamañjari*

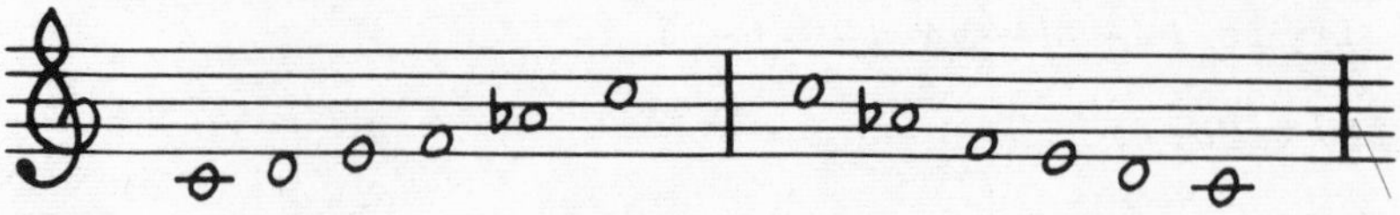

The notes *PA* (G) and *NI* (Bbb) are avoided entirely.

(19) *Siṃhēlavasantam*

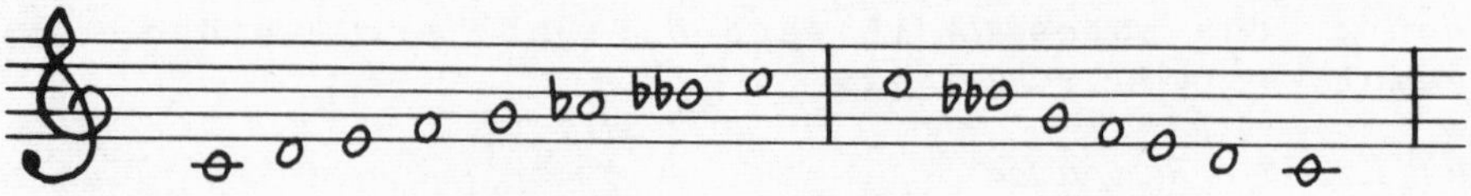

Ascent: *krama sampūrṇa.*
Descent: the note *DHA* (Ab) is avoided.

26. *MĒḶA CHĀRUKEŚĪ* (*CĀRUKEŚĪ*)

Chārukeśī is a rarely performed *rāga*, and comparatively few *janya rāgas* are subordinated to the 26. *mēḷa*. Tyāgarāja was the first among the great southern musicians who used this *rāga* which can be performed at any time of the day.

Veṅkaṭamakhin calls this *rāga Taraṅgiṇī* and states that its scale has to avoid the notes *RI* (D) and *GA* (E) in ascent. The scale of the present *Chārukeśī rāga* is, of course, heptatonic, as it represents a primary *rāga* form.

CHĀRUKEŚĪ (*Triputa-tāla*) SCM, 133-4

Janya Rāgas of the 26. Mēḷa

(1) *Taraṅgiṇī*

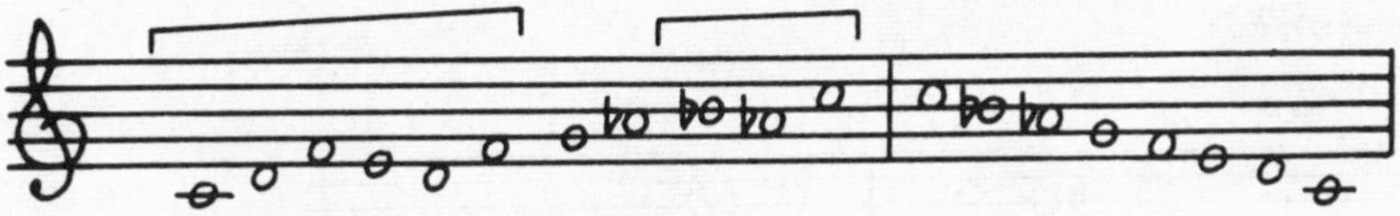

The present *Taraṅgiṇī* scale, in contrast to the one postulated by Veṅkaṭamakhin, is *sampūrṇa* and shows in ascent two *vakra* features. The descent is *krama sampūrṇa*.

TARAṄGIṆĪ (*Triputa-tāla*) SCM, 134

(2) *Badari*

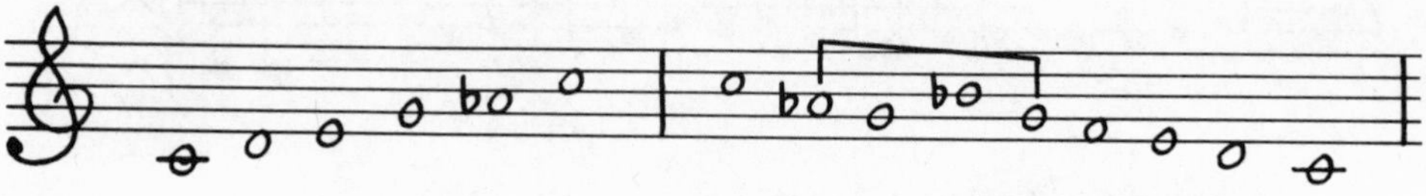

Ascent: the notes *MA* (F) and *NI* (Bb) are avoided.
Descent: *sampūrṇa*; one *vakra* feature is shown.

(3) *Bhagavati*

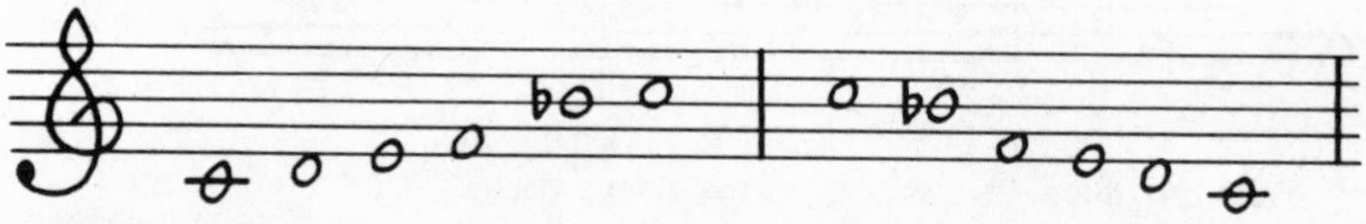

The notes *PA* (G) and *DHA* (Ab) are avoided entirely.

(4) *Chārukuntaḷa* (*Cārukuntaḷa*)

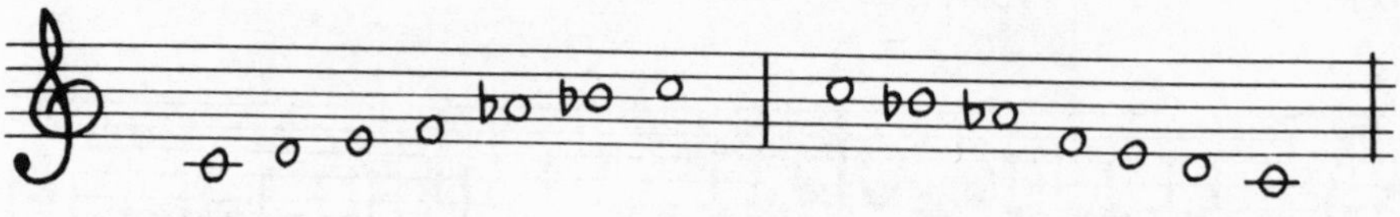

The note *PA* (G) is avoided entirely.

(5) *Chitsvarūpi* (*Chitsvarūpiṇi*)

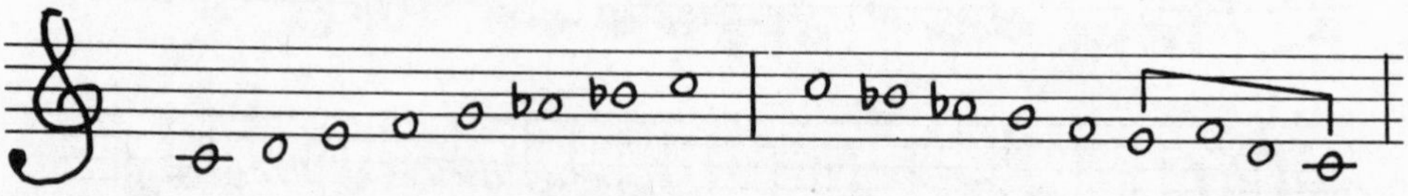

Ascent: *krama sampūrṇa*.
Descent: *sampūrṇa*; one *vakra* feature is shown.

(6) *Gāndharva Manōharī*

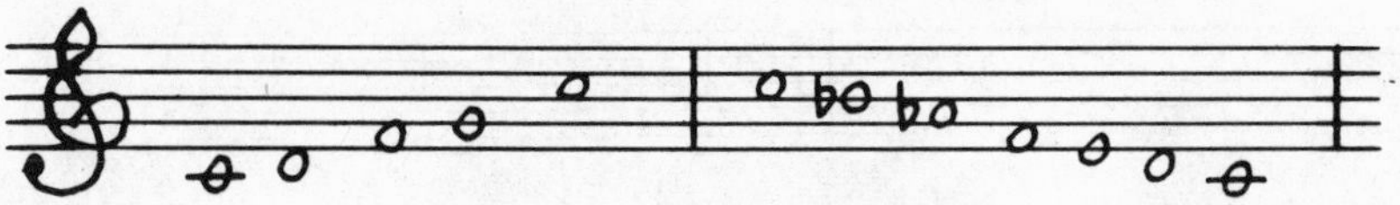

Ascent: the notes *GA* (E), *DHA* (Ab), and *NI* (Bb) are avoided.
Descent: the note *PA* (G) is omitted.

(7) *Kalākaṇṭhatvani*

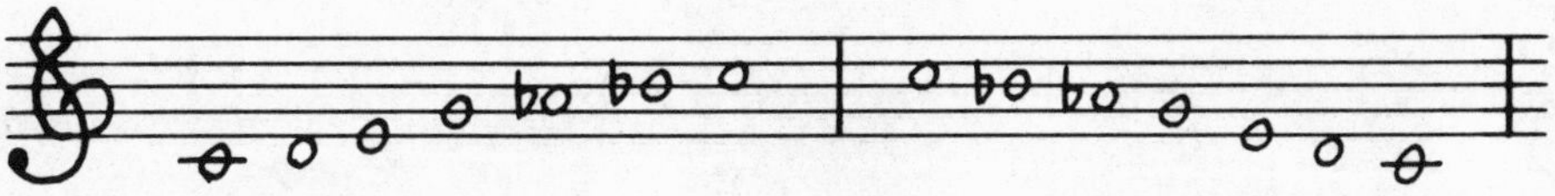

The note *MA* (F) is avoided entirely.

(8) *Kannaḍa Pañchama* (*Kannaḍa Pañcama*)

The SD (II, 298) shows two versions of this *rāga*:

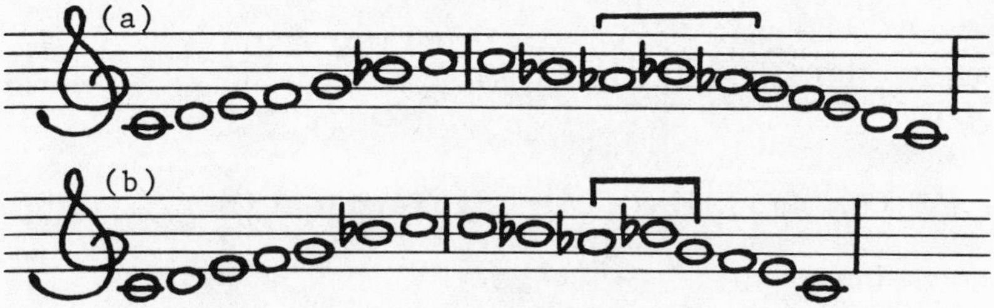

Both versions have the same ascent and avoid the note *DHA* (Ab). The descent of version (a) is *sampūrṇa* and shows the *vakra* feature *DHA-NI-DHA* (Ab-Bb-Ab), while the descent of version (b) avoids the note *RI* (D) and shows the *vakra* feature *DHA-NI-PA* (Ab-Bb-G).

(9) *Kōkila Pratāpam*

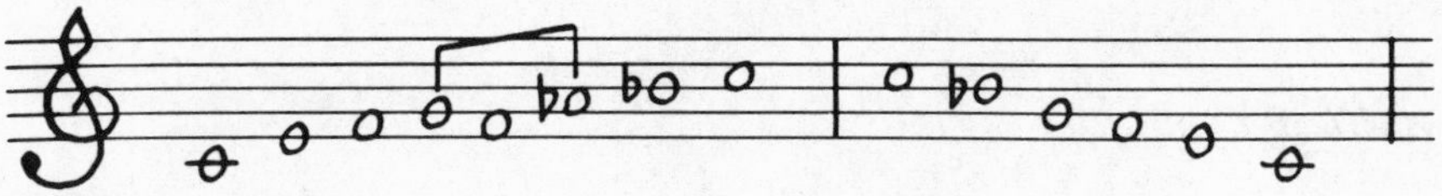

The note *RI* (D) is avoided entirely. The ascent shows one *vakra* feature and the descent omits also the note *DHA* (Ab).

(10) *Kōmalāṅgi*

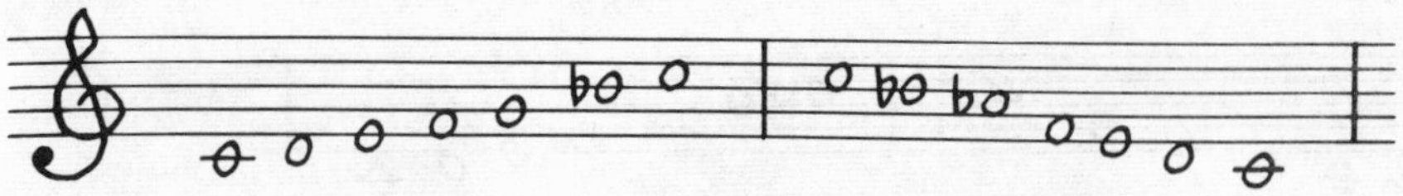

Ascent: the note *DHA* (Ab) is avoided.
Descent: the note *PA* (G) is omitted.
Another *rāga* with the same name is listed under the heading of *mēḷa* 27 (20).

(11) *Matulika*

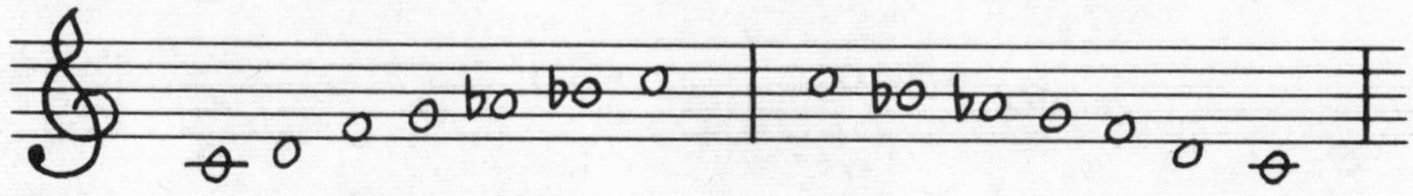

The note *GA* (E) is avoided entirely.
Another *rāga* with the same name appears under the heading of the 27. *mēḷa* (25).

(12) *Mṛdāni*

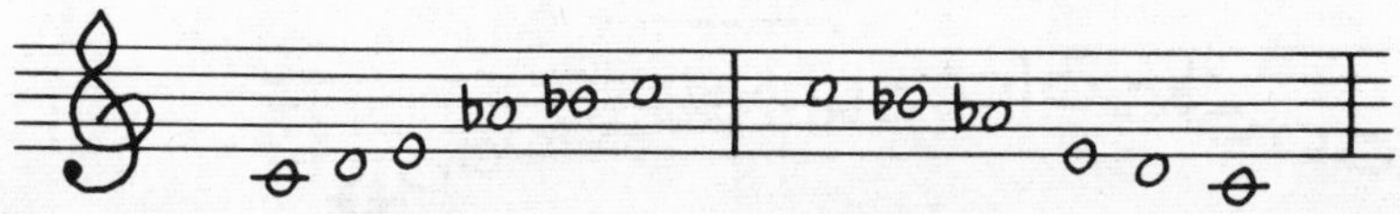

The notes *MA* (F) and *PA* (G) are avoided entirely.

(13) *Sōmapratāpam*

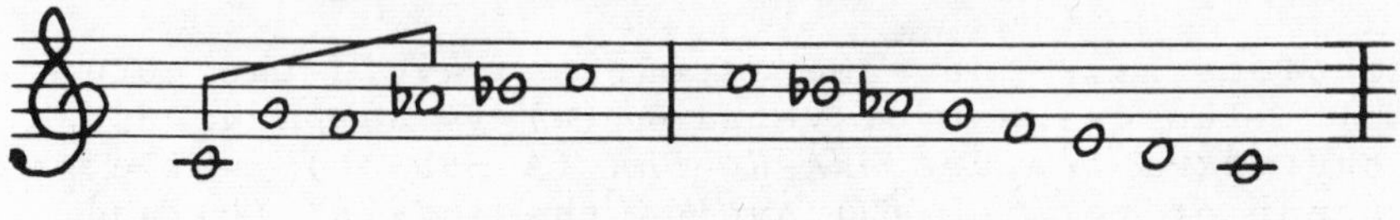

Ascent: the notes *RI* (D) and *GA* (E) are avoided; one *vakra* feature is shown.
Descent: *krama sampūrṇa*.

27. *MĒḶA SARASĀṄGĪ*

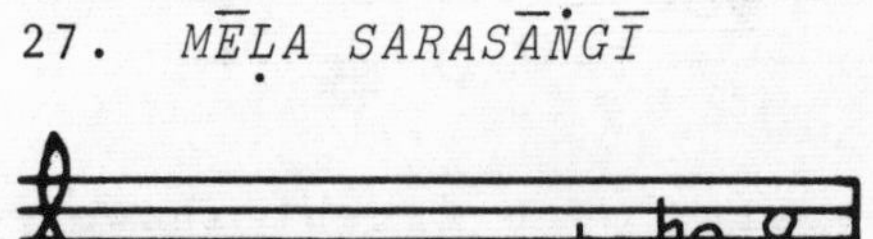

Rāga Sarasāṅgī can be performed at any time. Veṅkaṭamakhin calls this *rāga Saurasena* (*Surasena*), which avoids the note *RI* (D) in descent.

SARASĀṄGI *Triputa-tāla* SCM, 135

Janya Rāgas of the 27. Mēḷa

(1) *Surasena* (*Saurasena*)

At the present time the scale of this *rāga* avoids the note *GA* (E) in ascent and shows one *vakra* feature. The descent usually omits the note *NI* (B). There are, however, several other forms of the *Surasena* scale which can vary from one performer to the other. One of these forms is:

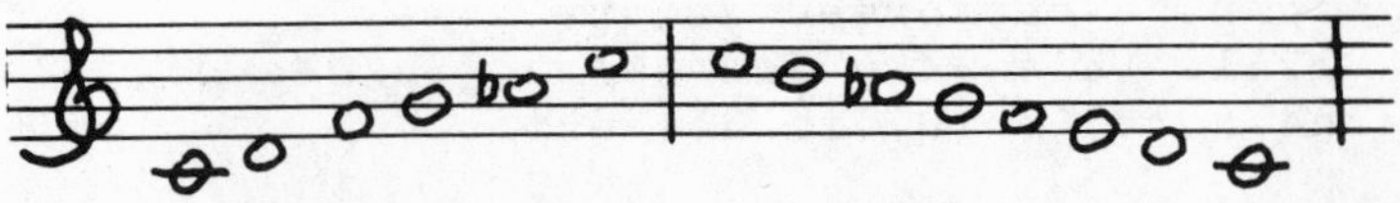

Ascent: the notes *GA* (E) and *NI* (B) are avoided.
Descent: *krama sampūrṇa*.

SURASENA (*Triputa-tāla*) SCM, 135-36

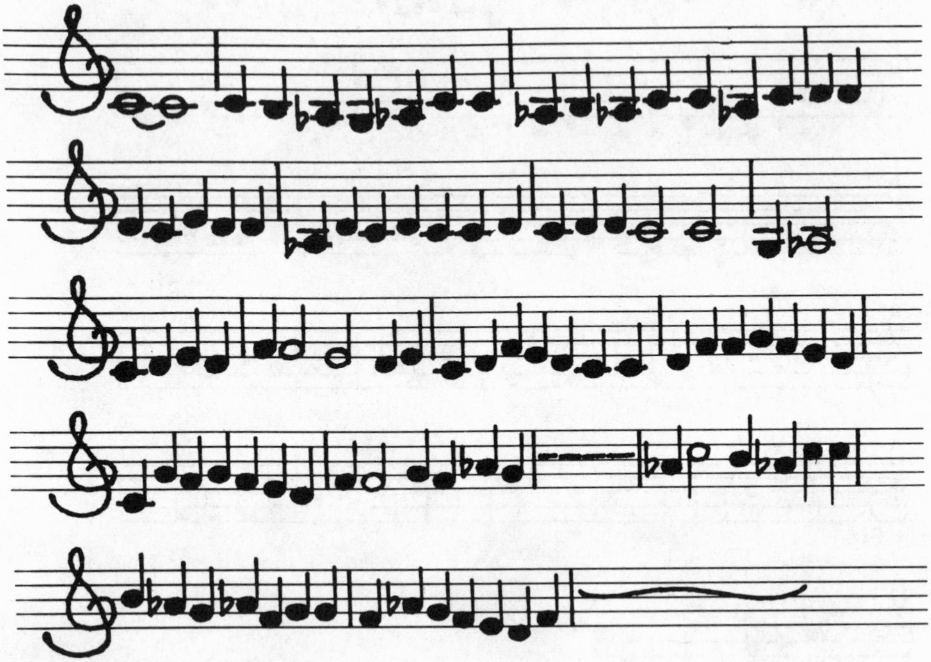

(2) *Divya Pañchama*(*m*) (*Divya Pañcam*)

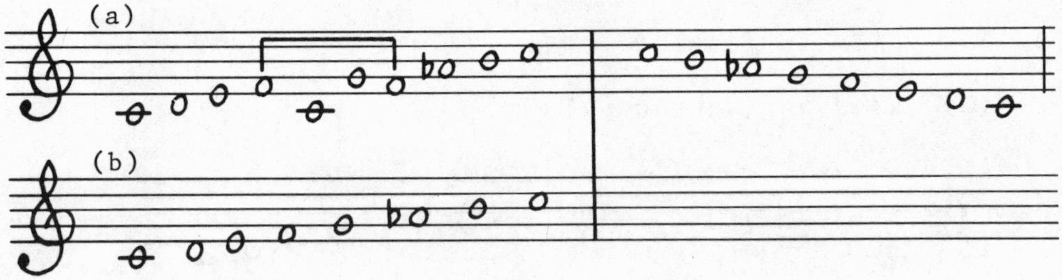

Two forms of ascent are in use. Form (a) is *sampūrṇa* and shows one *vakra* feature. Form (b) is *krama sampūrṇa*. The descent of both forms is *krama sampūrṇa*.

DIVYA PAÑCHAMA (*Triputa-tāla*) SCM, 136-37

(3) *Kamalāmanōharī*

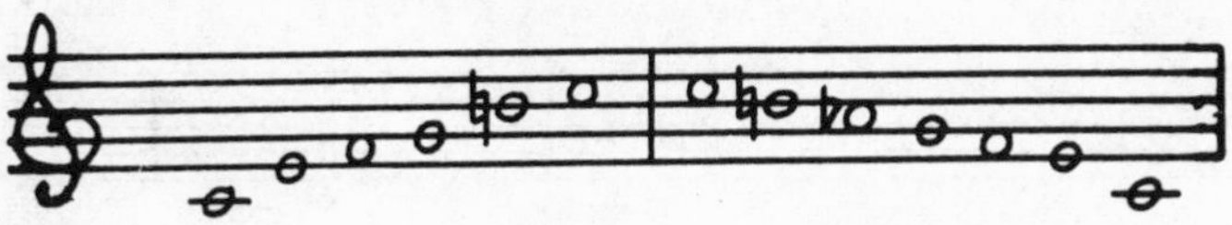

The note *RI* (D) is avoided entirely. *DHA* (Ab) is omitted in ascent.
This *rāga* must not be mistaken for *Manōharī* of the 22. *mēḷa* (95).

KAMALĀMANŌHARĪ (*Triputa-tāla*) SCM, 137

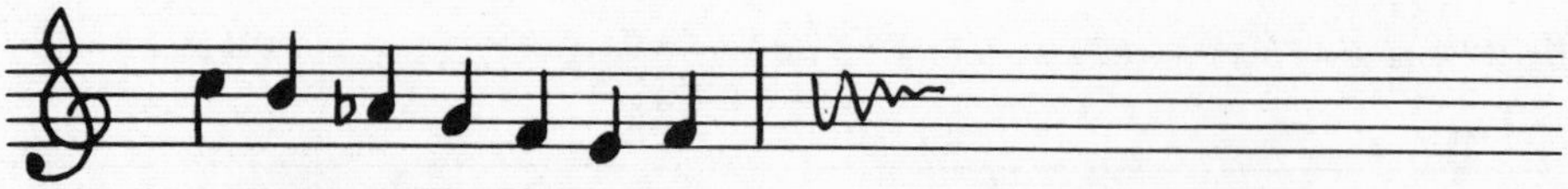

(4) *Nalikānti*

The note *DHA* (Ab) is avoided entirely. The ascent shows one *vakra* feature.

(5) *Bhānukiraṇi*

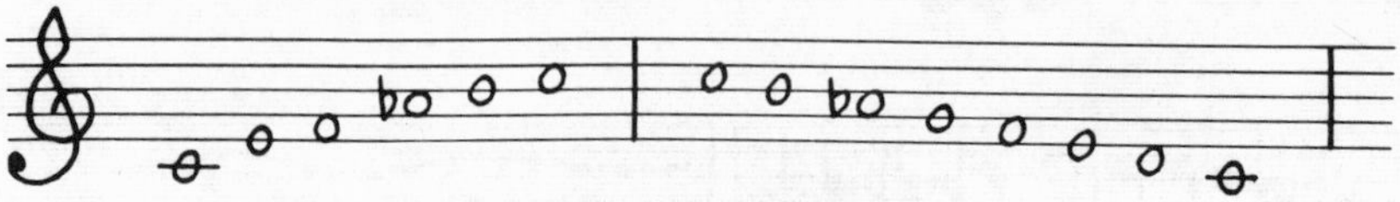

Ascent: the notes *RI* (D) and *PA* (G) are avoided.
Descent: *krama sampūrṇa*.

(6) *Bhinna Gāndhāri*

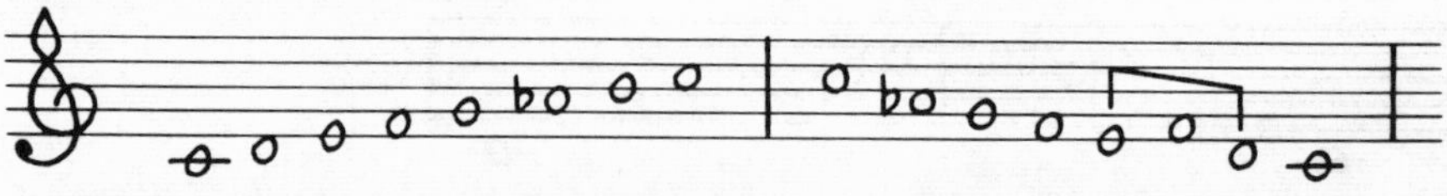

Ascent: *krama sampūrṇa*.
Descent: the note *NI* (B) is avoided and one *vakra* feature is shown.

(7) *Bhōga Līlā*

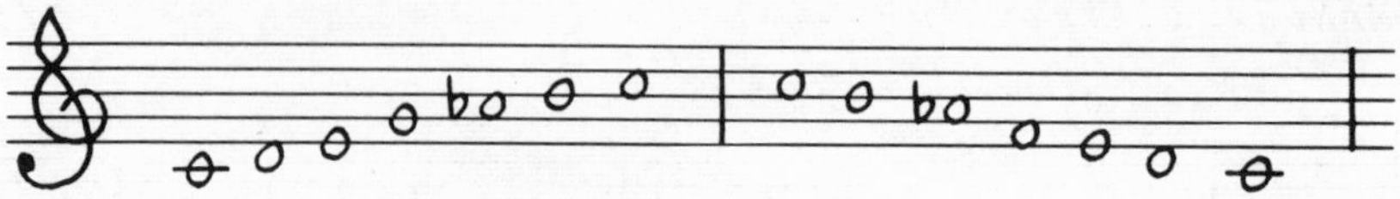

Ascent: the note *MA* (F) is avoided.
Descent: the note *PA* (G) is omitted.

(8) *Dēvakurañji*

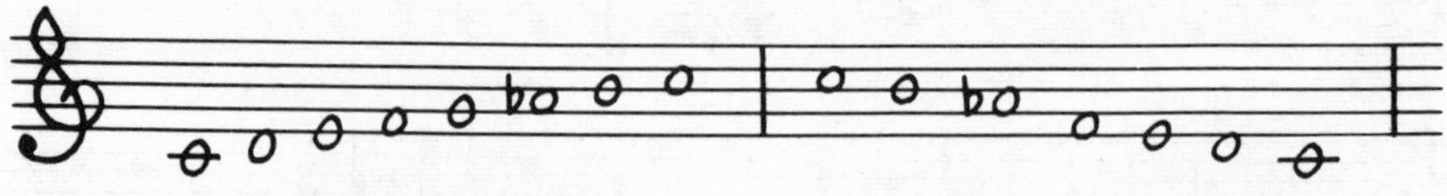

Ascent: *krama sampūrṇa*.
Descent: the note *PA* (G) is avoided.

(9) *Dhvajakriyā*

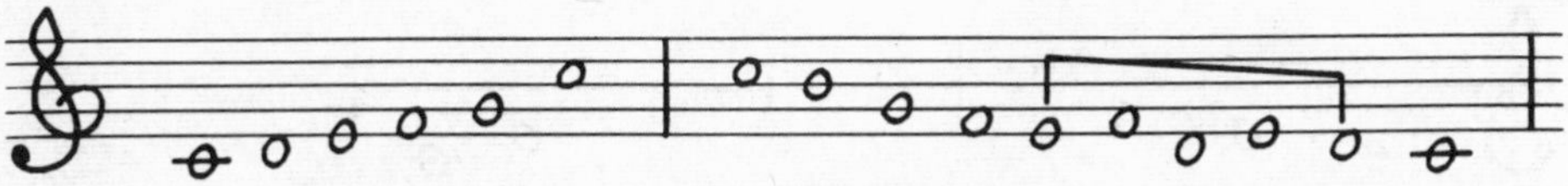

The note *DHA* (Ab) is avoided entirely. The ascent avoids also *NI* (B) and the descent shows an extended *vakra* feature.

(10) *Dinakarakāntī*

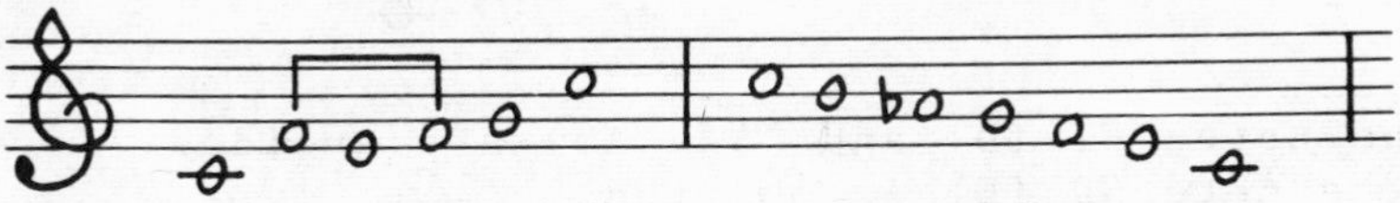

The note *RI* (D) is avoided entirely. The ascent avoids also the notes *DHA* (Ab) and *NI* (B) and shows one *vakra* feature.

(11) *Divya Gandhi*

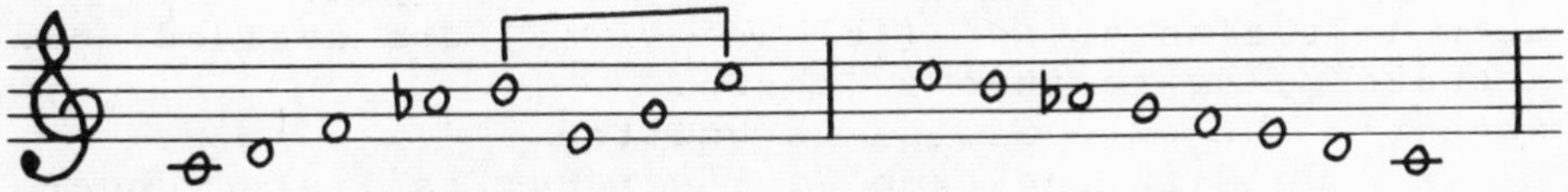

Ascent: *sampūrṇa*; one extended *vakra* feature is shown.
Descent: *krama sampūrṇa*.

(12) *Divyāmbari*

Ascent: the notes *RI* (D) and *GA* (E) are avoided; one *vakra* feature is shown.
Descent: *sampūrṇa*; one *vakra* feature is used.

Another *rāga* with the same name appears under the heading of the 40. *mēḷa* (3).

(13) *Haripriya*

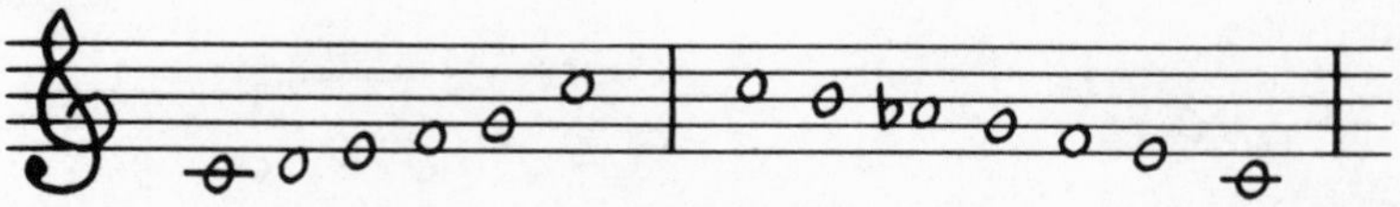

Ascent: the notes *DHA* (Ab) and *NI* (B) are avoided.
Descent: the note *RI* (D) is omitted.

(14) *Jalajavāsini*

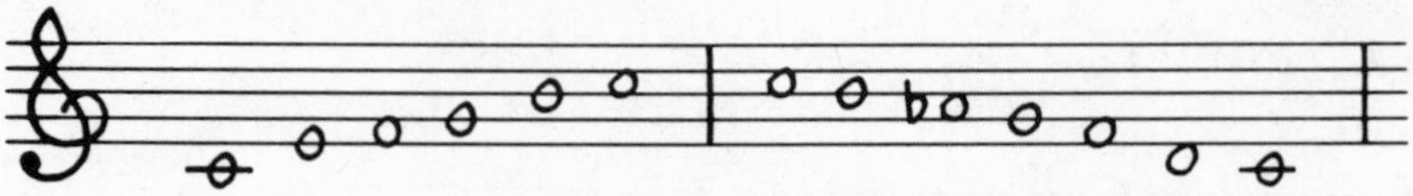

Ascent: the notes *RI* (D) and *DHA* (Ab) are avoided.
Descent: the note *GA* (E) is omitted.

(15) *Jayābharaṇi*

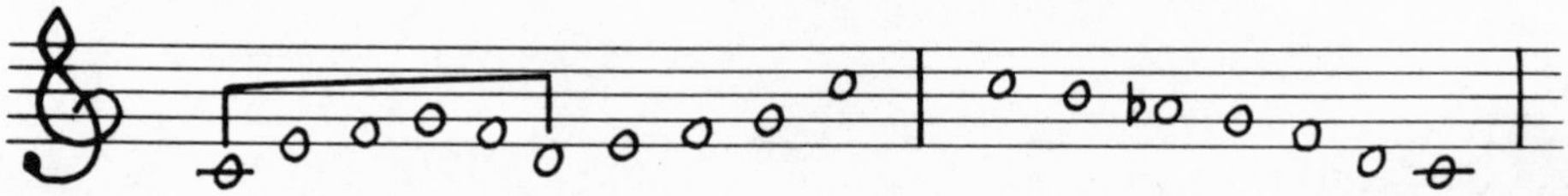

Ascent: the notes *DHA* (Ab) and *NI* (B) are avoided; one extended *vakra* feature is shown.
Descent: the note *GA* (E) is omitted.

A *rāga* with the name *Jayābharaṇam* is listed under the heading of *mēḷa* 17 (12).

(16) *Kacha Rāga (Kacarāga)*

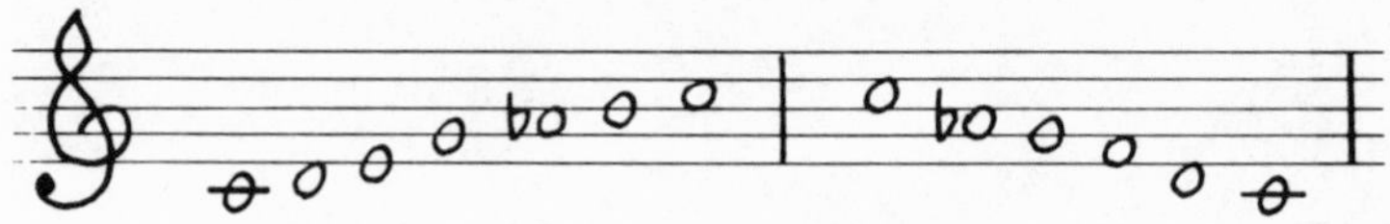

Ascent: the note *MA* (F) is avoided.
Descent: the notes *NI* (B) and *GA* (E) are omitted.

(17) *Kadanam*

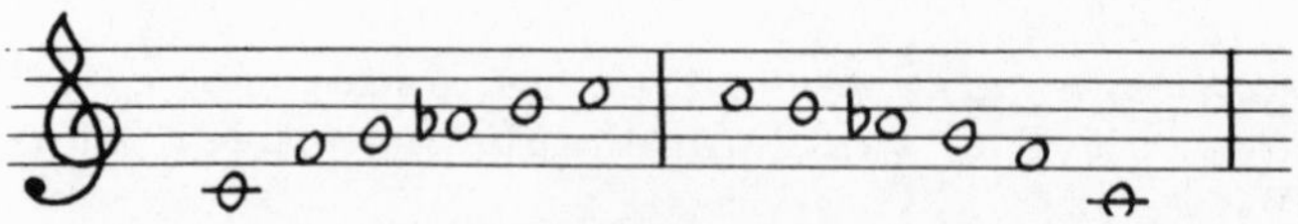

The notes *RI* (D) and *GA* (E) are avoided entirely.

(18) *Kedāranāṭa*

The note *DHA* (Ab) is avoided entirely. The ascent shows one *vakra* feature.

(19) *Kēsaranāṭa*

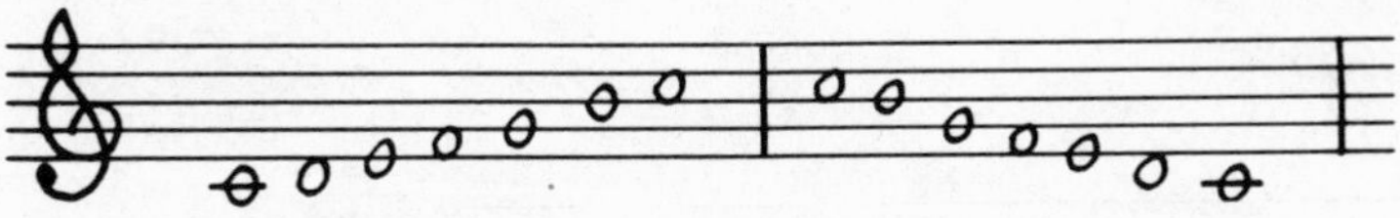

The note *DHA* (Ab) is avoided entirely.

(20) *Kōmalāṅgi*

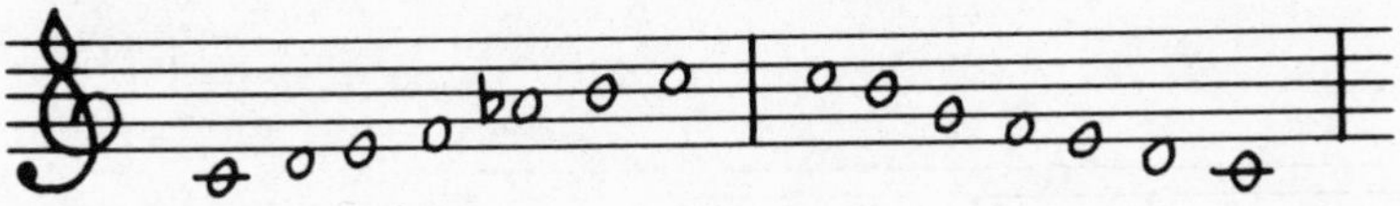

Ascent: the note *PA* (G) is avoided.
Descent: the note *DHA* (Ab) is omitted.

Another *rāga* with the same name appears under the heading of the 26. *mēḷa* (10).

(21) *Kusumapriya*

Ascent: *krama sampūrṇa*.
Descent: the note *DHA* (Ab) is avoided.

(22) *Kusumasāraṅga*

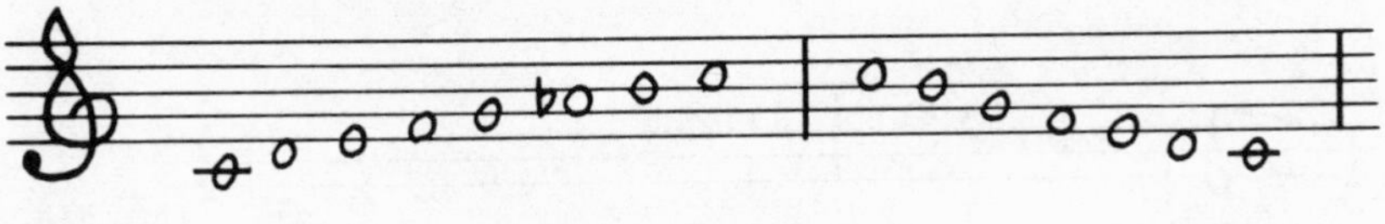

Ascent: *krama sampūrṇa*.
Descent: the note *DHA* (Ab) is avoided.

Another *rāga* with the same name appears under the heading of the 56. *mēḷa* (16).

(23) *Manimāyi*

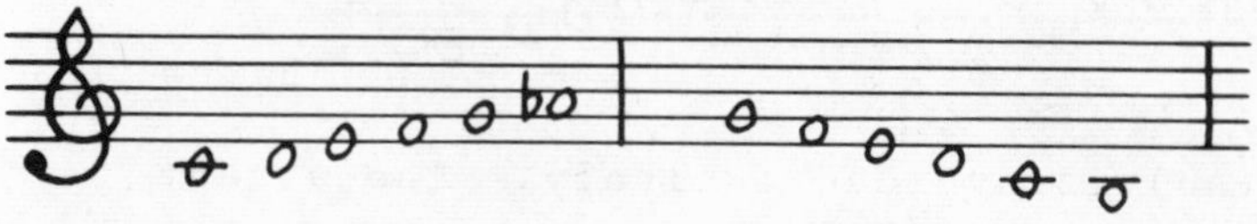

Manimāyi is a *dhaivatāntya rāga*. Its highest note is *DHA* (Ab) and its lowest (in descent) is *NI* (B) of the *mandra saptaka* (lowest octave range).

(24) *Mattakāsini*

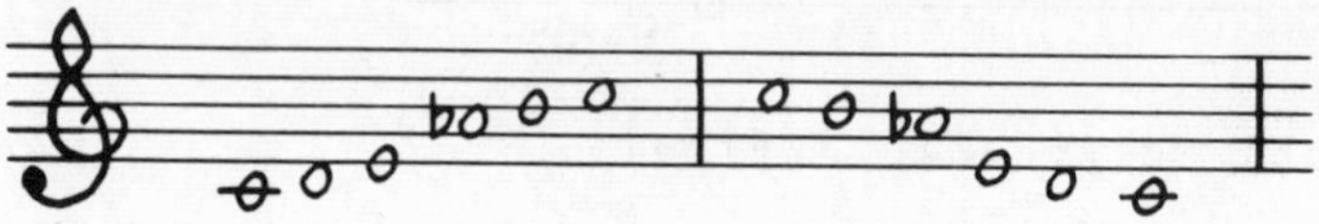

The notes *MA* (F) and *PA* (G) are avoided entirely.

(25) *Matulika*

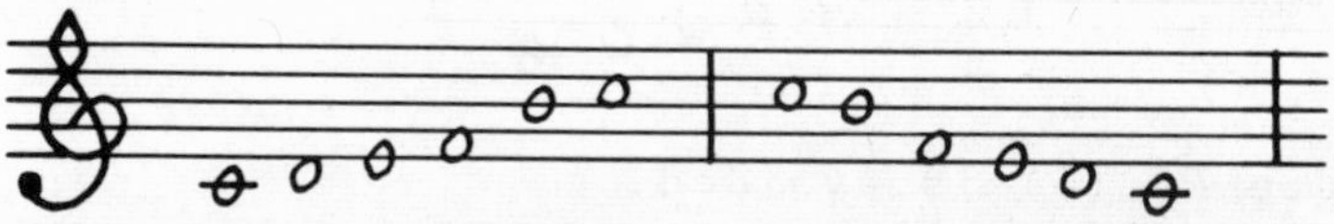

The notes *PA* (G) and *DHA* (Ab) are avoided entirely.
Another *rāga* with the same name appears under the heading of the 26. *mēḷa* (11).

(26) *Mānābharaṇi*

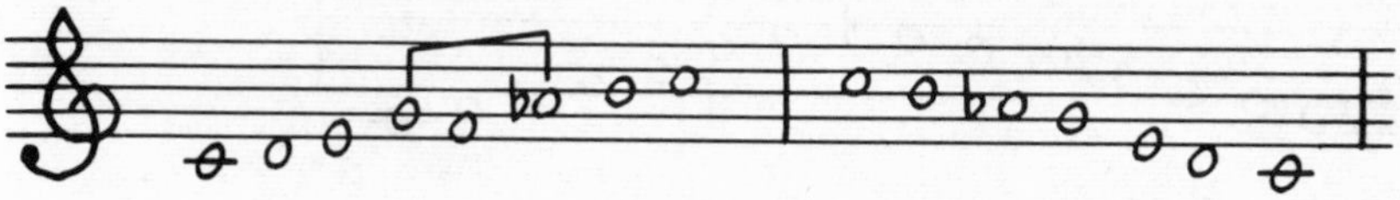

Ascent: *sampūrṇa*; one *vakra* feature is shown.
Descent: the note *MA* (F) is avoided.

(27) *Nādapriya*

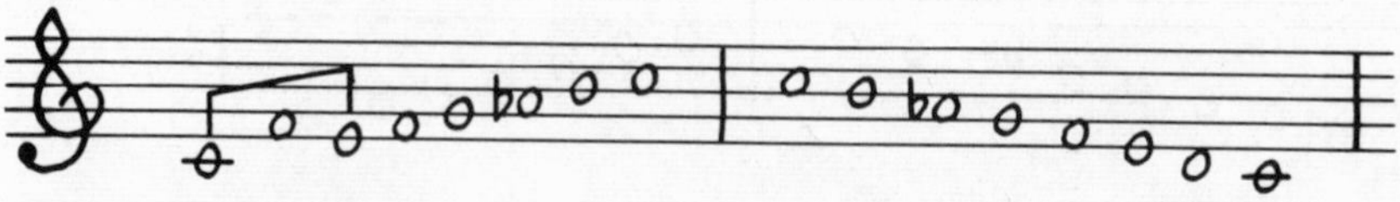

Ascent: the note *RI* (D) is avoided; one *vakra* feature is shown.

Descent: *krama sampūrṇa.*

(28) *Nādasvarūpi*

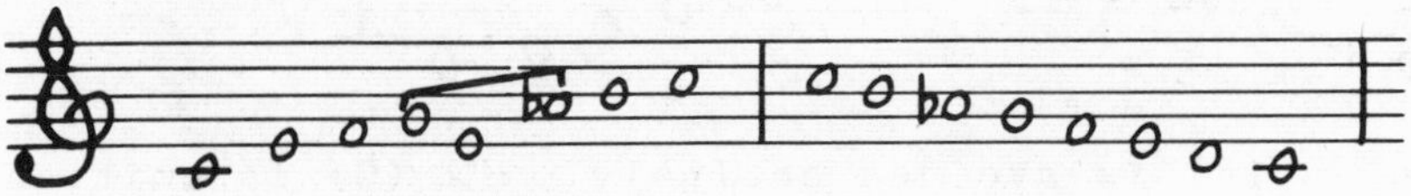

Ascent: the note *RI* (D) is avoided; one *vakra* feature is shown.
Descent: *krama sampūrṇa.*

(29) *Nādavinōdini*

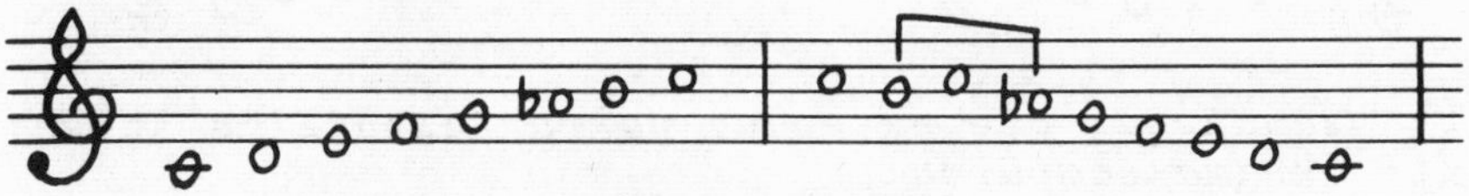

Ascent: *krama sampūrṇa.*
Descent: *sampūrṇa*; one *vakra* feature is shown.

(30) *Nāgabharaṇi* (*Nāgabharṇi*)

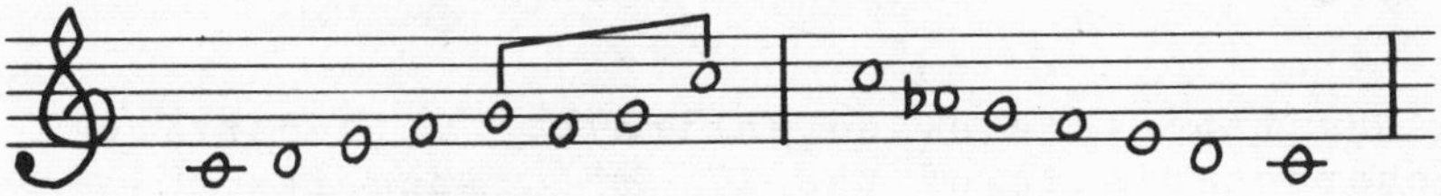

Ascent: the notes *DHA* (Ab) and *NI* (B) are avoided; one *vakra* feature is shown.
Descent: *krama sampūrṇa.*

(31) *Nīlamani*

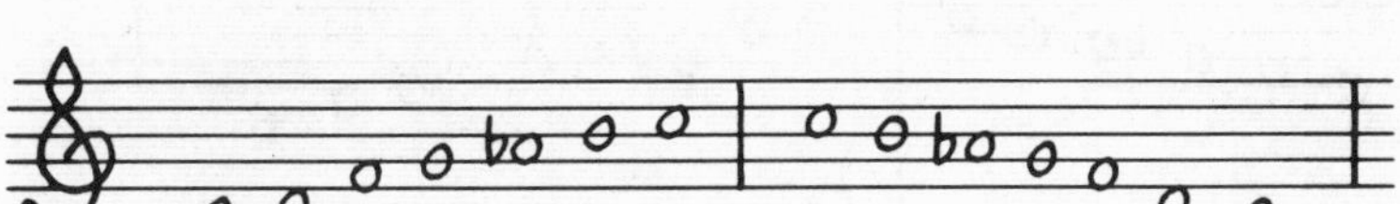

The note *GA* (E) is avoided entirely.

(32) *Padmarāgam*

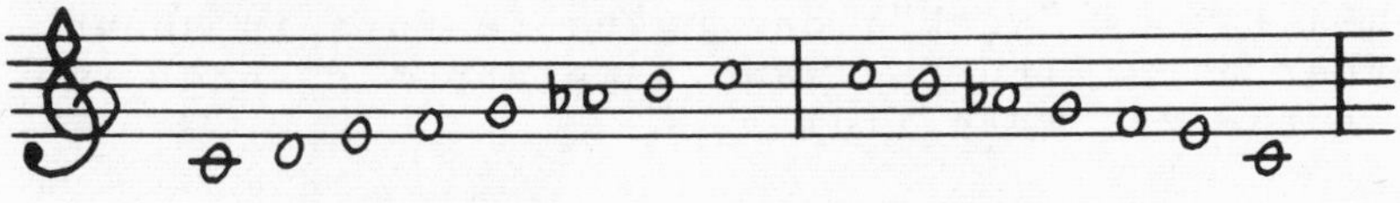

Ascent: *krama sampūrṇa.*
Descent: the note *RI* (D) is avoided.

(33) *Priyatarshaṇi* (*Priyatarṣaṇi*)

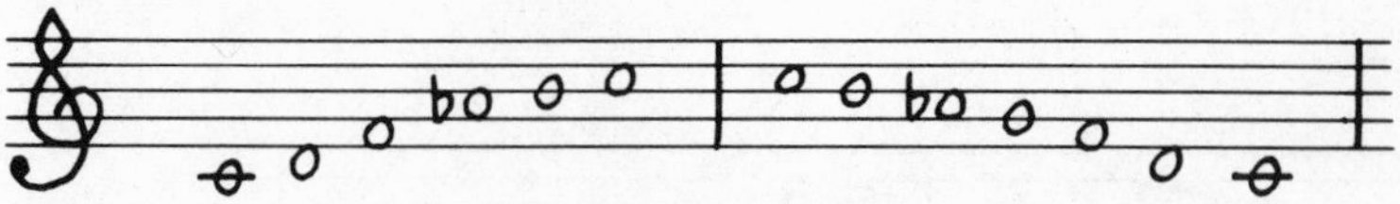

The note *GA* (E) is avoided entirely. *PA* (G) is omitted in ascent.

(34) *Ratnamani*

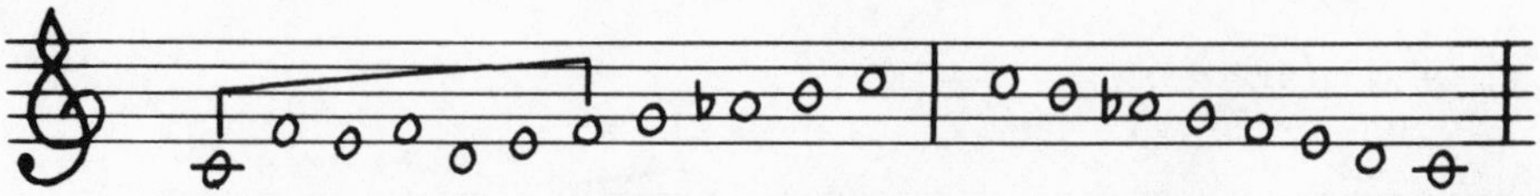

Ascent: *sampūrṇa*; one extended *vakra* feature is shown.
Descent: *krama sampūrṇa*.

(35) *Ruṣyakētupriya*

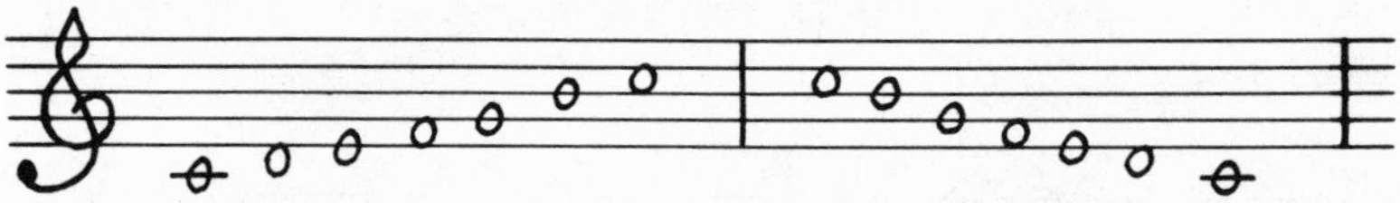

The note *DHA* (Ab) is avoided entirely. This particular note is characteristic of the 27. *mēḷa*, and its omission would allow a placing of this *rāga* under the headings of the 29. and 30. *mēḷas*.

(36) *Sarasapriya*

Ascent: *krama sampūrṇa*.
Descent: (a) *sampūrṇa*; one *vakra* feature is shown. (b) the note *PA* (G) is "weak"; one *vakra* feature is shown.

Another *rāga* with the same name appears under the heading of the 72. *mēḷa* (10).

(37) *Siṃhavāhinī*

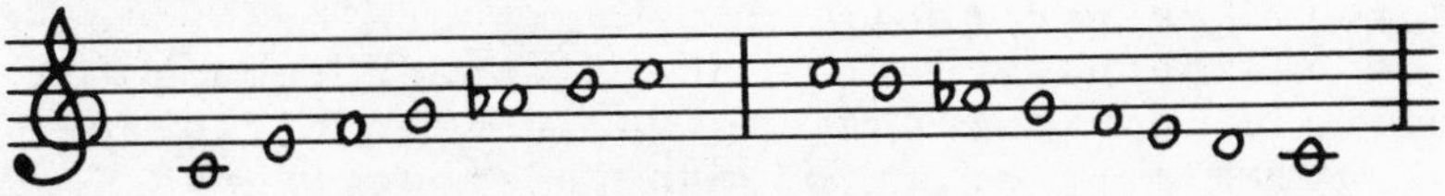

Ascent: the note *RI* (D) is avoided.
Descent: *krama sampūrṇa*.

According to R (p. 223) this *rāga* is of recent origin and was introduced by Muthiah Bhāgavathar (see n. 1, Mēḷa and Rāga chapter).

(38) *Sōmamukhi*

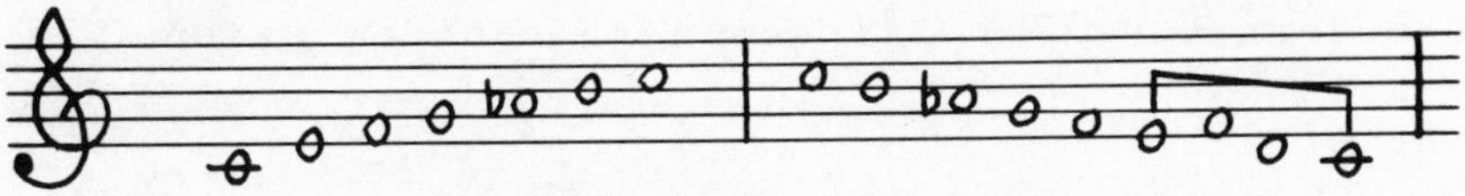

Ascent: the note *RI* (D) is avoided.
Descent: *sampūrṇa*; one *vakra* feature is shown.

(39) *Sūtradhari*

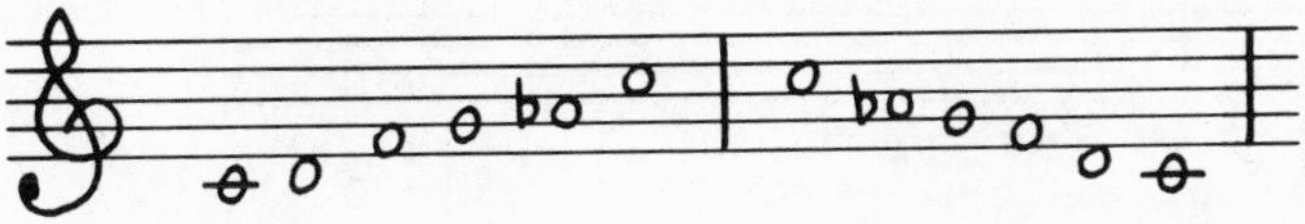

The notes *GA* (E) and *NI* (B) are avoided entirely.

(40) *Taralam*

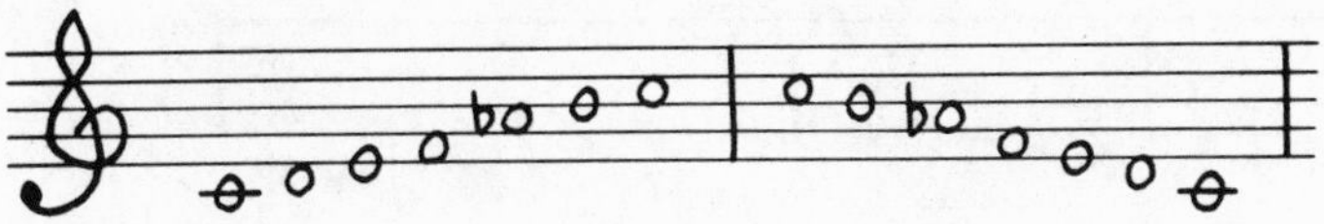

The note *PA* (G) is avoided entirely.

28. *MĒḶA HARIKĀMBHŌJI*

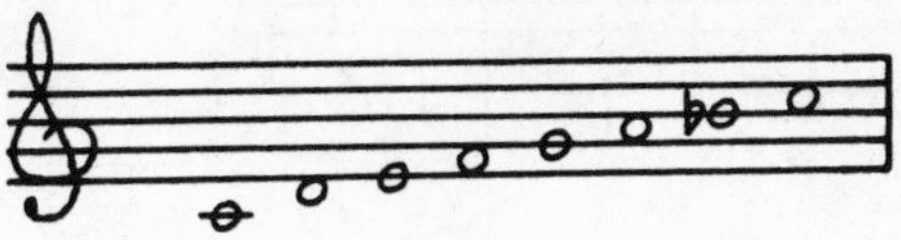

The *janya rāgas* subordinated to the 28. and 29. *mēḷas* represent two giant *rāga* families in South Indian music. Both *mēḷas* and their *rāga* forms are exceptionally famous and popular, hence there appear remarkably large numbers of *janya rāgas* listed under their headings. The great popularity of many of these *janya rāgas* is shown not only by frequent performances but also by the varying inter·retations which may change from one singer or player to the next.

As it is impossible to examine these countless variants, below will be shown the "generally accepted standard" forms of the *rāgas*.

The present *Harikāmbhōji* was called by Veṅkaṭamakhin, *Harikēdaragauḷa*, in which the notes *GA* (E) and *DHA* (A) were supposed to be avoided in ascent. In the modern *Harikāmbhōji* scale no such omissions are in use.

HARIKĀMBHŌJI (*Triputa-tāla*) SCM, 138

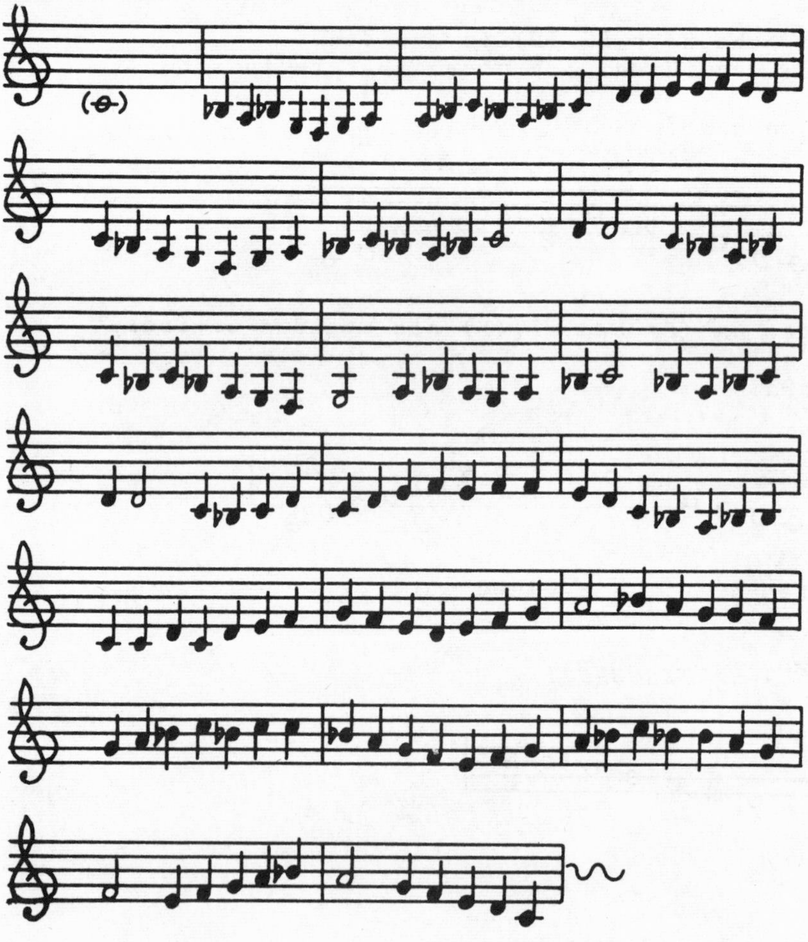

Janya Rāgas of the 28. Mēḷa

(1) *Kāmbhōji*

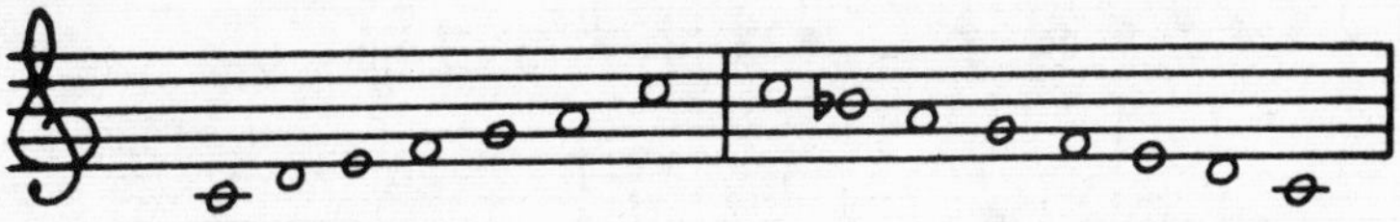

Ascent: the note *NI* (Bb) is avoided.
Descent: *krama sampūrṇa*.

Kāmbhōji, an ancient *rāga*, is often performed at the beginning of, or during, theatrical representations. According to S (III, 281) this *rāga* is identical with a *rāga Kāmōdari* (or *Kāmōdani*) which occurs in the Kathakali performances of Kerala.

In the descending passage *SA-NI-PA* (c-$\overset{+}{\text{B}}$b-G) the note *NI* is often taken so sharply that it can be interpreted as B natural.

The author of the following song example bears the name Fiddle Ponnuswami.[8] There are numerous musicians in the South who adopted the names of musical instruments for their first names. One can observe English and Indian names, such as "fiddle," or vīṇā" and others.

KĀMBHŌJI RĀGA (*Ādi-tāla*) SPC III, 47

Pallavi

Anupallavi

KĀMBHŌJI (*Triputa-tāla*) SCM, 139

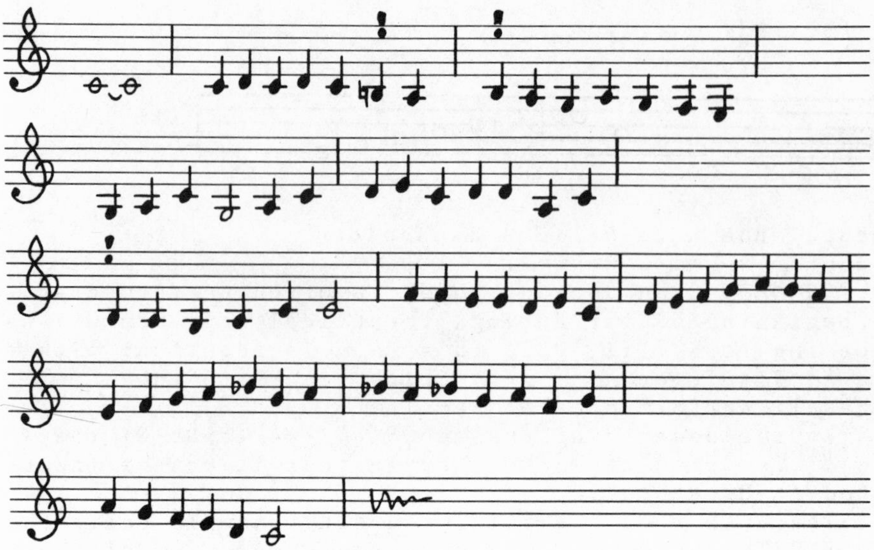

(2) *Kēdāragauḷa*

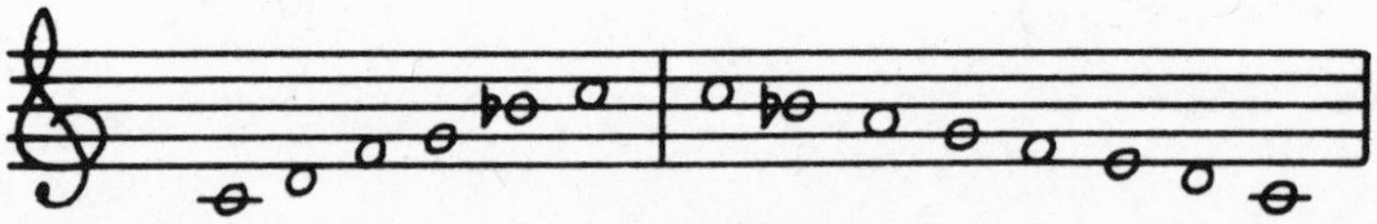

Ascent: the notes *GA* (E) and *DHA* (A) are avoided.
Descent: *krama sampūrṇa*.

The performance time of this *rāga* is at night. SD (II, 313) remarks that "the *rāga*'s identity is straightaway revealed when the *tāra sthāyi rishabha* [the note d of the high octave range, a ninth above middle C] is rendered as a stressed and prolonged note."

The notes *RI* (D) and *NI* (Bb) are generally performed with a slight vibrato.

The following song example was composed by Tiruvarur Thiagaiyer (1767-1847) of Tiruvarur, Tanjore District, Madras State; Thiagaiyer was one of the important musicians of the South.

KĒDĀRAGAUḶA RĀGA (*Ādi-tāla*) SPC III, 92-93

Pallavi

Anupallavi

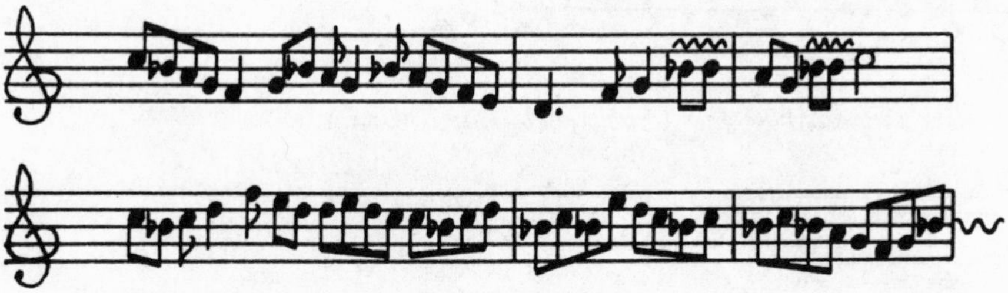

(3) *Mohana* (*Mohanakalyāṇi*)

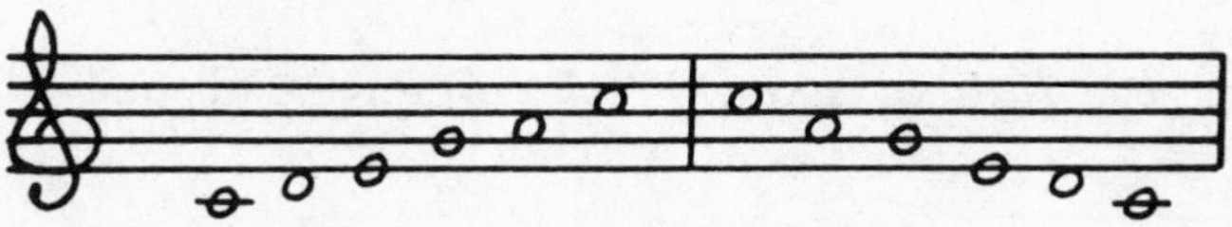

The notes *MA* (F) and *NI* (Bb) are avoided entirely, thus producing an anhemitonic pentatonic scale in ascent and descent. *Mohana* is a popular *rāga* and can often be heard in theatrical performances. It is believed to bring luck and may be performed at any time.

Veṅkaṭamakhin places this *raga* into his 65. *mēḷa*. Tulaja calls this *rāga Mohanakalyāṇi*.

Another *rāga Mohanakalyāṇi* (or *Śuddhakalyāṇi*) with the same ascending but a different descending scale, is listed under the heading of the 65. *mēḷa* (40).

MOHANA RĀGA (*Rūpaka-tāla*) SPC II, 42-43

Pallavi

(4) *Yadukulakāmbhōji* (*Yarukulakāmbhōji*)

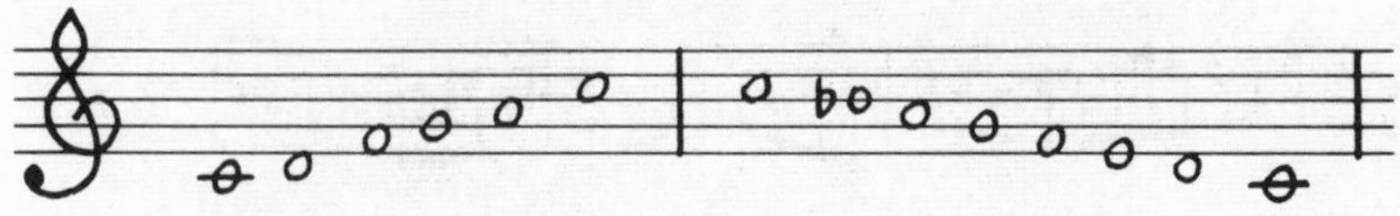

Ascent: the notes *GA* (E) and *NI* (Bb) are avoided.
Descent: *krama sampūrṇa*.
The notes *RI* (D) and *DHA* (A) are generally performed with a slight vibrato.

A second form of *Yadukulakāmbhōji* ascent can be:

in which only the note *NI* (Bb) is avoided and the note *GA* (E) appears in one *vakra* feature.

The following song example was composed by the famous Śyāma Śāstri (1762-1827) of Tanjore. The song under consideration is in *Sabu tāla* (7+7+7+7), transcribed in the present instance as four times seven eighth notes.

YADUKULAKĀMBHŌJI RĀGA (*Sabu-tāla*) SPC III, 44

Pallavi

Charana

YADUKULAKĀMBHŌJI (*Triputa-tāla*) SCM, 162-3

(5) *Khamās* (*Kamasu*)

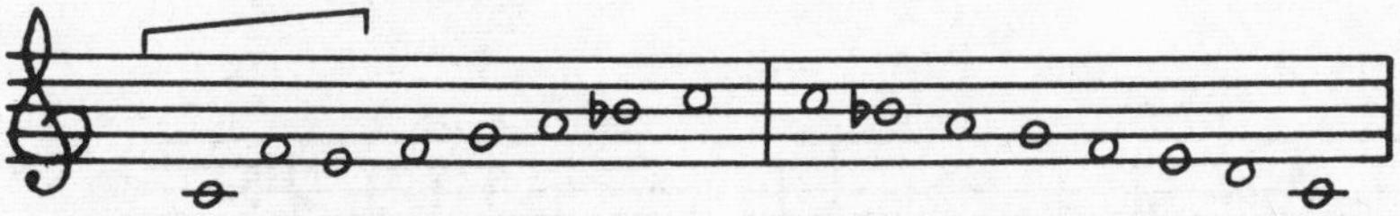

Ascent: the note *RI* (D) is avoided; one *vakra* feature is shown.
Descent: *krama sampūrṇa*.
When the note *NI* (Bb) appears between two *SA* (C or c), it is usually taken sharp and can be interpreted as B natural:

Stressed notes in this *rāga* are supposed to be *MA* (F) and *PA* (G).

Khamās is considered to be a pleasant and popular *rāga*. It seems that the characteristic *vakra* feature in ascent, as it appears in *Khamās* performances of the present time, did not exist or was not in use at Govinda's time. Govinda postulates his *Khamās* scale in the following manner:

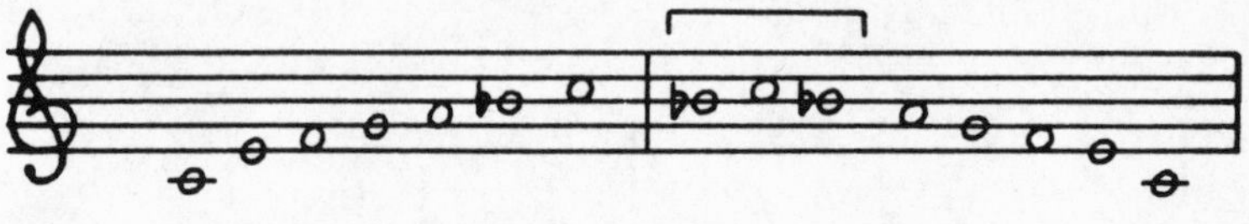

The note *RI* (D) is avoided entirely. SD (II, 303) describes the *rāga Karṇāṭaka Khamās* as follows:

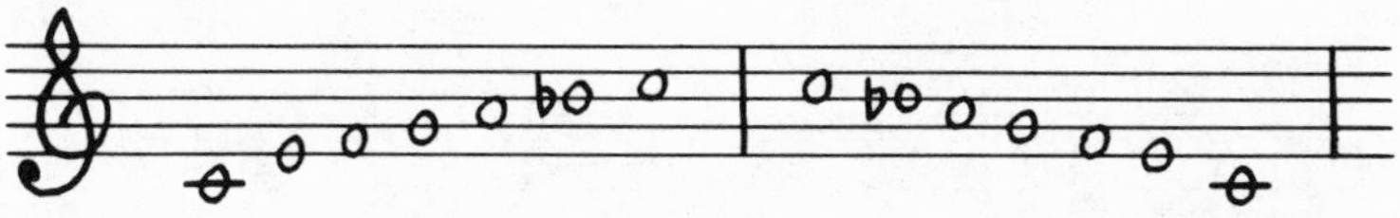

Again, the note *RI* (D) is avoided entirely and SD (ibid) states that "the introduction of the *kākali nishāda* [B natural] in the phrase s n s [*SA-NI-SA*, C-B-C] began after Tyāgarāja's time." There is little doubt that *Khamās* and *Karṇāṭaka Khamās* represent the same *rāga*.

The following song example was composed by Chinnikrishna Dasar (1828-81):

KHAMĀS (KAMĀS) RĀGA Ādi-tāla SPC II, 50-51

Pallavi

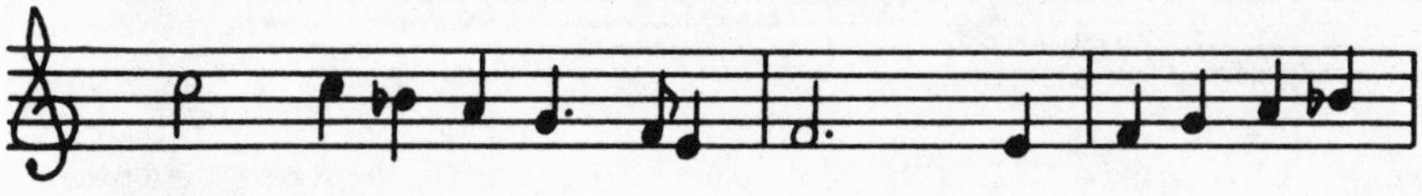

Anupallavi

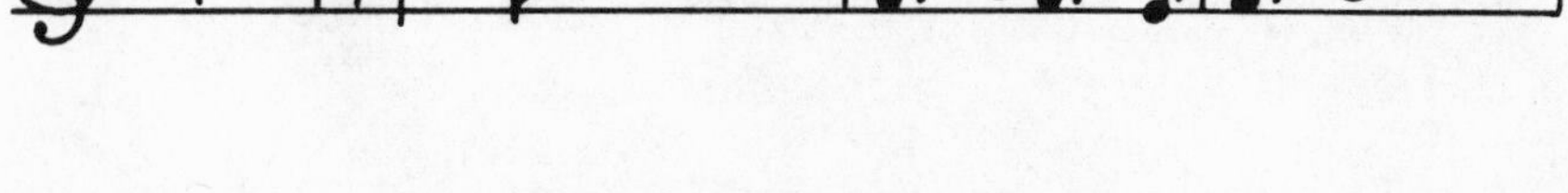

Charana

KHAMĀS (*Triputa-tāla*) SCM, 164

(6) *Nāṭakurañji*

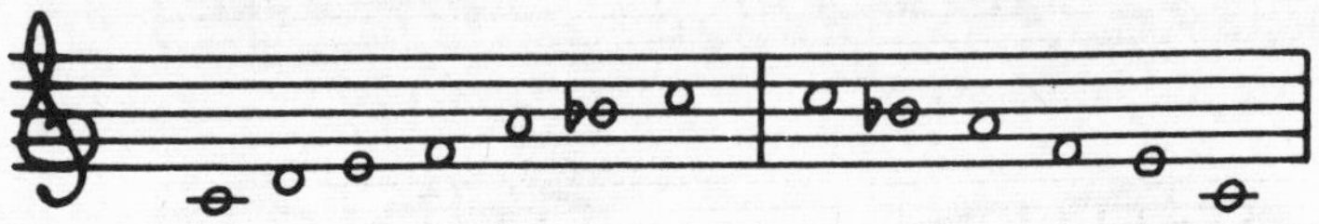

The note *PA* (G) is avoided entirely and *RI* (D) is omitted in descent. In some instances, e.g., in the Sanskrit work *Saṅgīta Kaumudī* (see R, 164) the use of the note *PA* (G) is permitted in descent.

Another form of the *Nāṭakurañji* scale is:

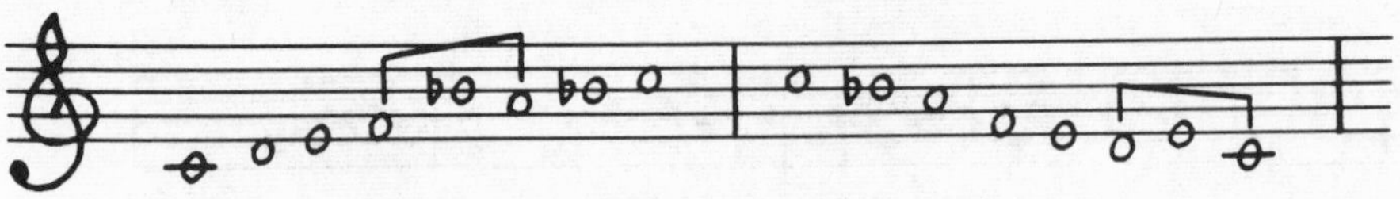

The note *PA* (G) is avoided entirely as in the first form. *RI* (D), however, appears in descent, and both ascent and descent show one *vakra* feature.

The following song specimen was composed by Kuppuswami;[9] in this song appears the forbidden note *PA* (G) in ascent and descent (see measures 1, 4, 5, 7, 9, 10).

NĀṬAKURAÑJI RĀGA (*Ādi-tāla*) SPC III, 102-3

Pallavi

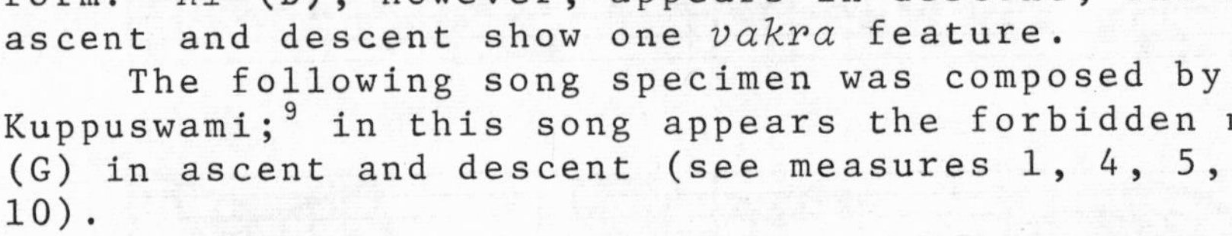

Anupallavi

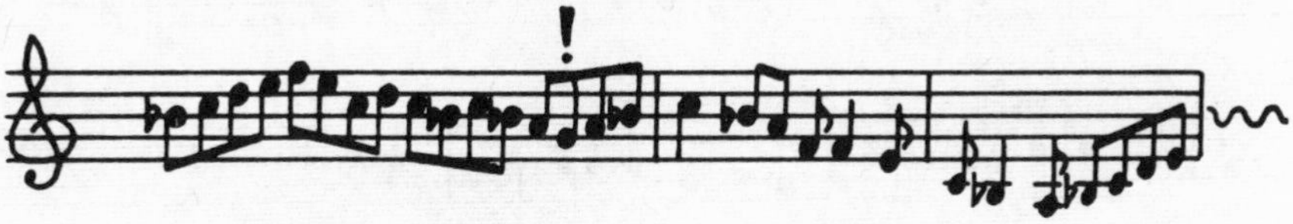

Of some interest is the following melody pattern. It avoids the note *PA* (G) but uses *RI* (D) in descent.

NĀṬAKURAÑJI (*Triputa-tāla*) SCM, 165

(7) *Bahudāri*

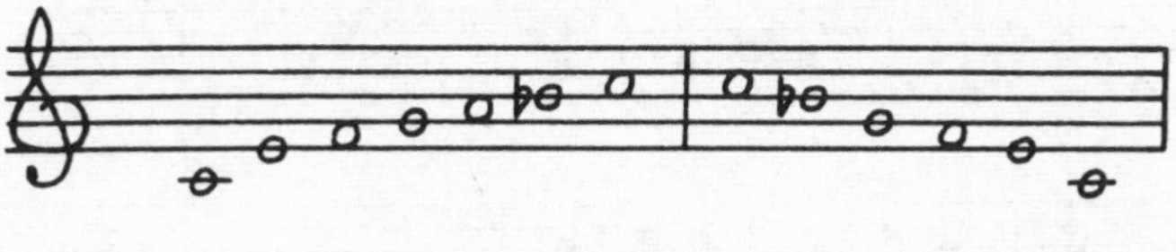

The note *RI* (D) is avoided entirely and *DHA* (A) is omitted in descent.

BAHUDĀRI (*Triputa-tāla*) SCM, 161

(8) *Balahaṃsa*

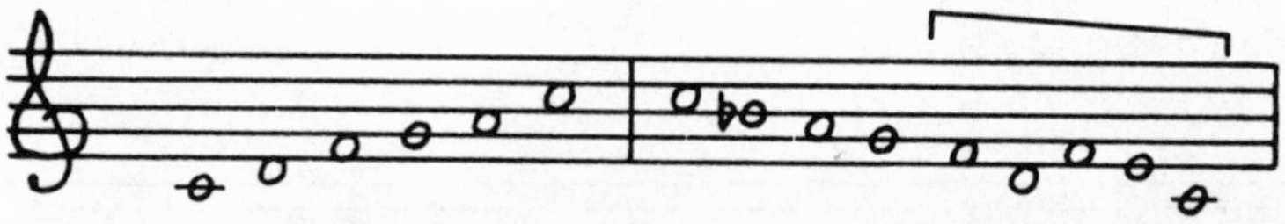

Ascent: the notes *GA* (E) and *NI* (Bb) are avoided.
Descent: *sampūrṇa*; one *vakra* feature is shown.

BALAHAṂSA (*Triputa-tāla*) SCM, 143-4

(9) *Budhamanoharī*

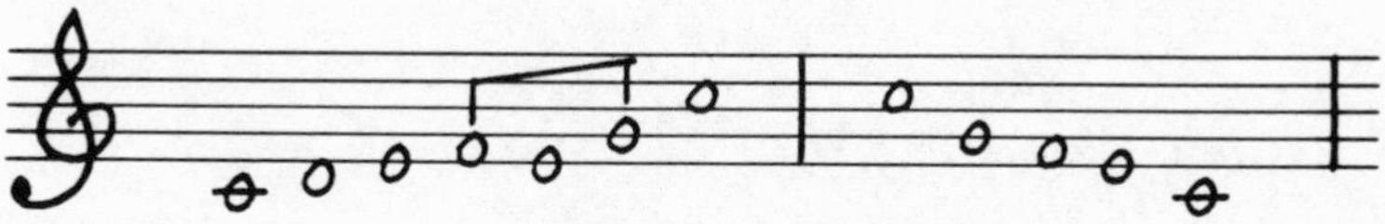

The notes *DHA* (A) and *NI* (Bb) are avoided entirely and *RI* (D) is omitted in descent. The one *vakra* feature in ascent is characteristic.

According to R (222-3) this recent *rāga* was introduced by Muthiah Bhagavathar.

Another *rāga* with the same name and the same scale structure, excepting the omission or use of the note *RI* (D), appears under the heading of the 29. *mēḷa* (21).

(10) *Chhāyatarangiṇi*

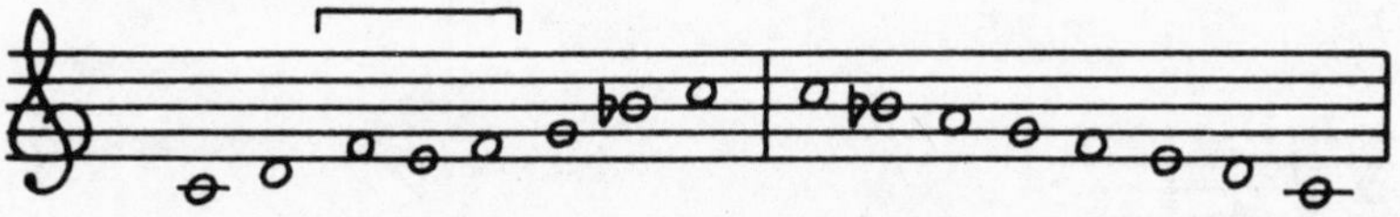

Ascent: the note *DHA* (A) is avoided; one *vakra* feature is shown.
Descent: *krama sampūrṇa*.

CHHĀYĀTARANGIṆI (*Triputa-tāla*) SCM, 143

(11) *Dēśakshi* (*Dēśakṣi*)

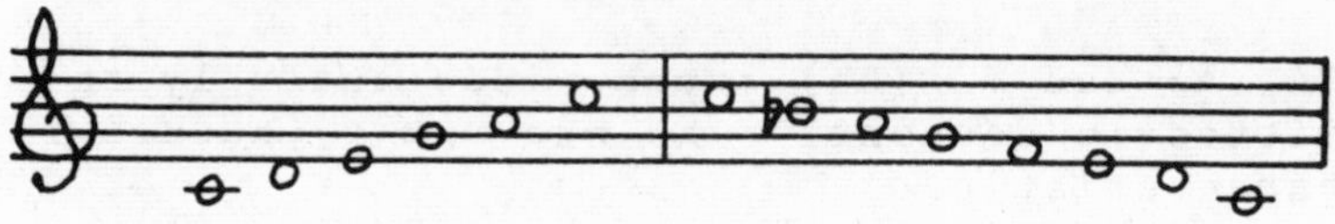

Ascent: the notes *MA* (F) and *NI* (Bb) are avoided.
Descent: *krama sampūrṇa*.

This same *rāga* can also be ascribed to the 29. *mēḷa* (31) because the note characteristic of the 28. *mēḷa*, *NI* (Bb), does not appear in ascent and is in many instances interpreted as B natural, as in the descending phrase:

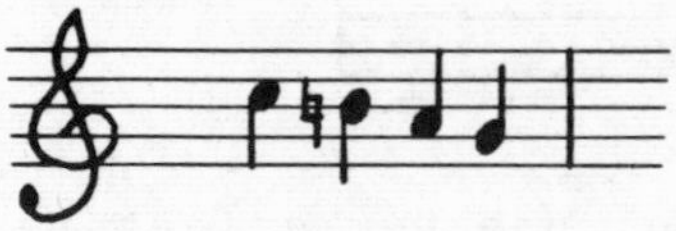

There are several versions of *Dēśakshi*. For instance:

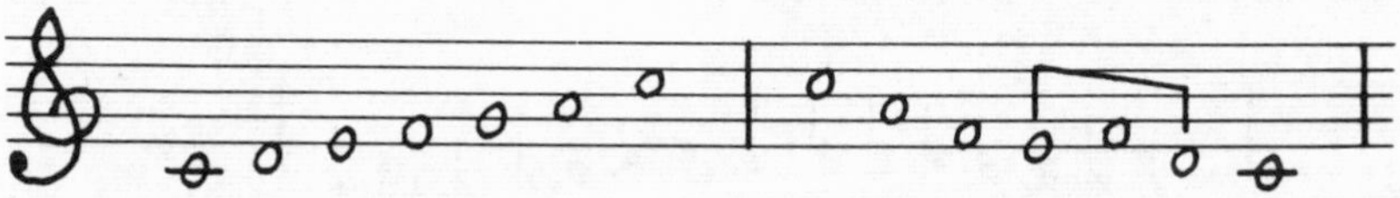

in which the crucial note *NI* (Bb) is avoided entirely and *PA* (G) is omitted in descent. Other versions are subject to the tastes of individual performers. They not only treat the note *NI* either as Bb or B, but they include diverse *vakra* features and at times omit certain notes altogether.

Another *rāga*, occasionally with the same name but generally called *Dēśākṣirī*, ascribed to the 35. *mēḷa* (3), must not be mistaken for the *rāga* under consideration. One characteristic of all types of *Dēśakshi* is the frequent use of notes in the *tāra saptaka* (high octave region).

DĒŚAKSHI (*Triputa-tāla*) SCM, 165-6

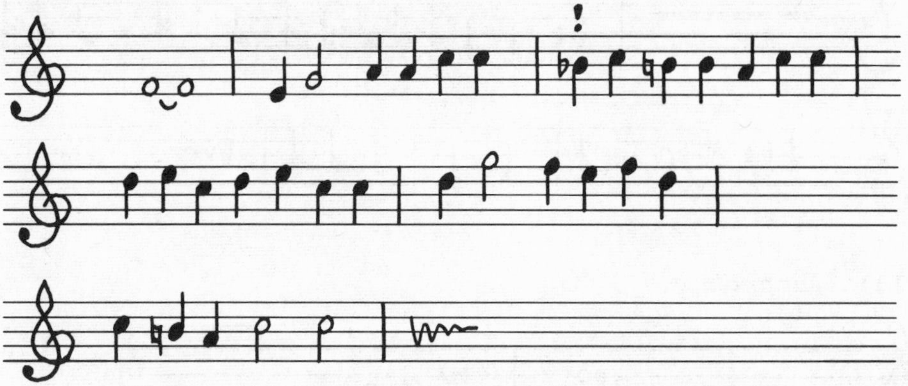

(12) *Dvijāvanti*

The ascent can be performed in two ways: either with one *vakra* feature and the avoidance of the note *NI* (Bb), or in *krama sampūrṇa* form. The descent is *sampūrṇa* and shows one *vakra* feature.

The note *GA*, particularly in the descending motion *GA-RI*, is frequently interpreted as Eb, while in straight ascent *GA* generally remains E.

DVIJĀVANTI (*Triputa-tāla*) SCM, 154

(13) *Īśamanōhari*

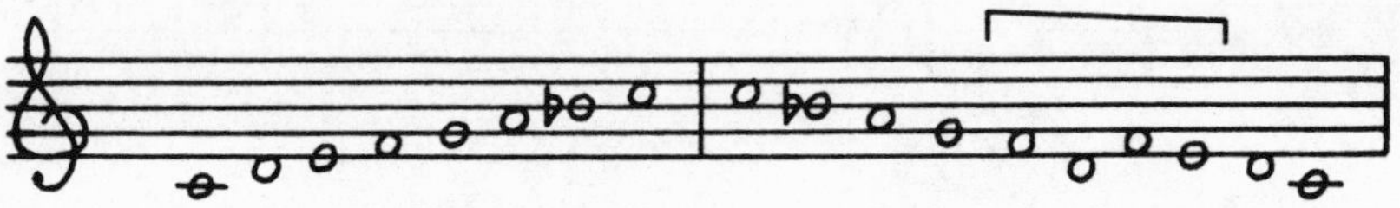

Ascent: *krama sampūrṇa*.
Descent: *sampūrṇa*; one *vakra* feature is shown.

In the sequences *SA-NI-SA* or *RI-NI-SA* the (rising) middle note is generally interpreted as B natural.

ĪŚAMANŌHARI (*Triputa-tāla*) SCM, 148-9

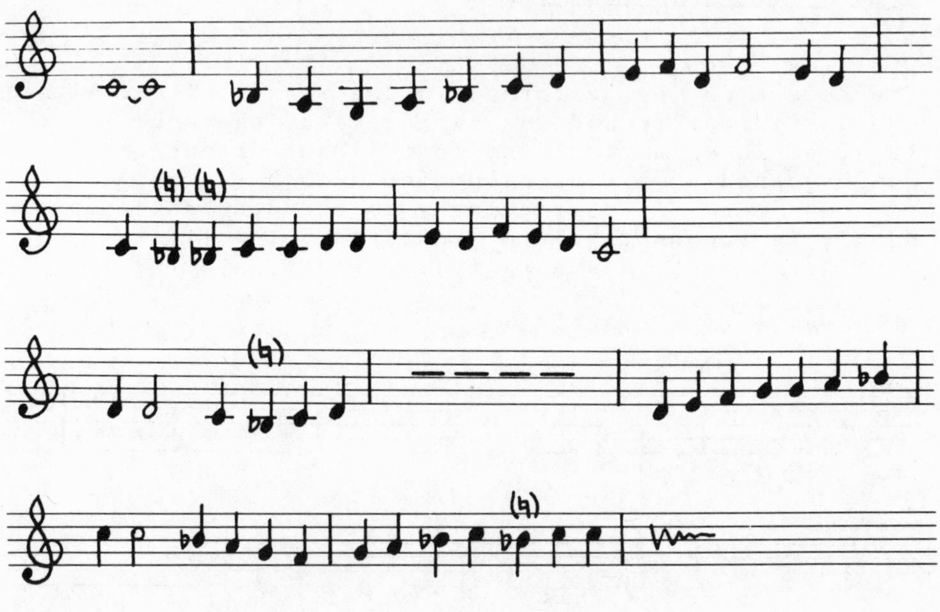

(14) *Jañjhūṭi* (*Juñjhūṭi*)

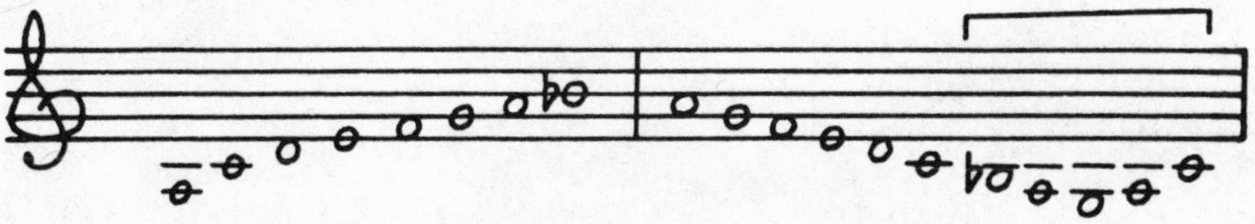

This is a *madhya* or *niṣādantya rāga* because the highest note to be used is *NI* (Bb) of the *madhya saptaka* (middle octave range). The ascent begins with the low *DHA* (A), avoids the note *NI* (Bb) of the lower range, and extends one octave to *NI* (Bb) of the middle octave. The descent, as shown, begins with *DHA* (A) of the middle range and employs, in an extended *vakra* passage, notes of the low octave range.

The note *GA*, particularly in descending motion, is often interpreted as Eb.

JAÑJHŪṬI (*Triputa-tāla*) SCM, 147

(15) *Jujāhuḷi*

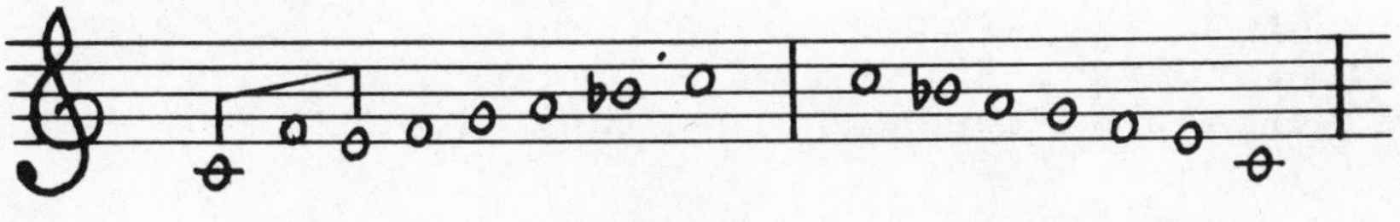

The note *RI* (D) is avoided entirely. The ascent shows one *vakra* feature. Compare with *rāga Jujāvaḷi* (*Jujāhuri*) of *mēḷa* 13 (3).

(16) *Kāpinārāyaṇi*

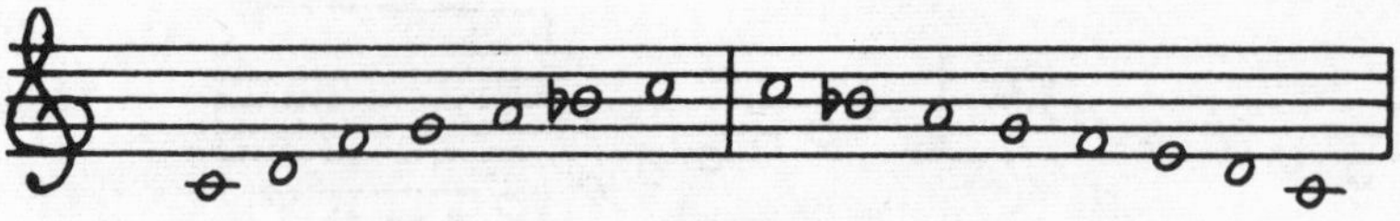

Ascent: the note *GA* (E) is avoided.
Descent: *krama sampūrṇa*.

KĀPINĀRĀYAṆI (*Triputa-tāla*) SCM, 146

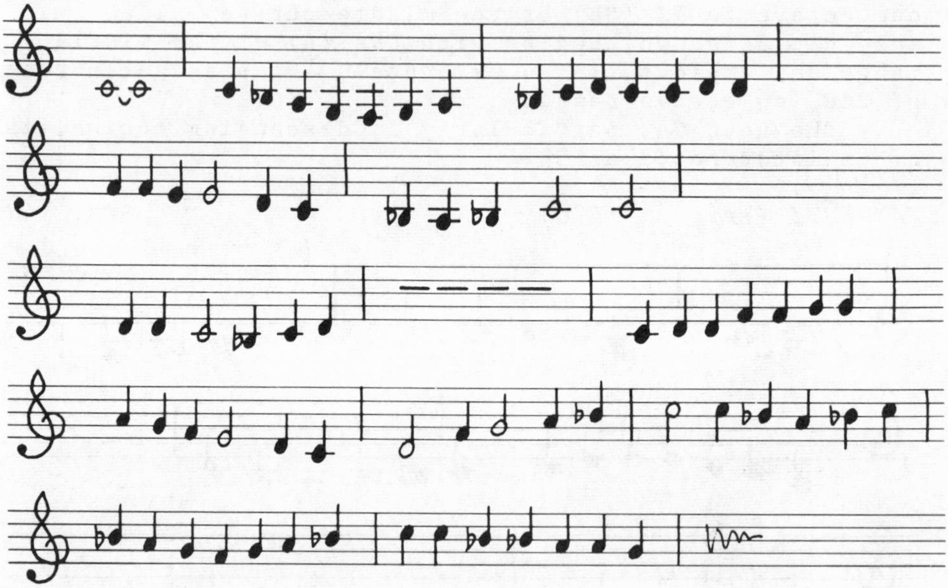

(17) *Karṇāṭaka Byāg* (*Karṇāṭaka Behāg*)

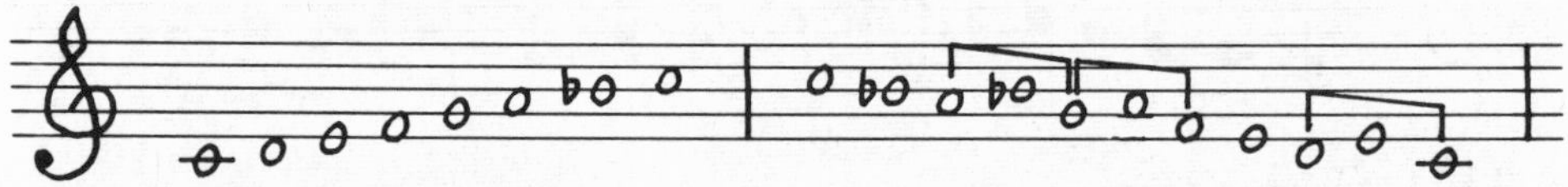

Ascent: *krama sampūrṇa*.
Descent: *sampūrṇa*; three *vakra* features are shown.

A variant of the *Karṇāṭaka Byāg* descent is:

(18) *Kōkiladhvani*

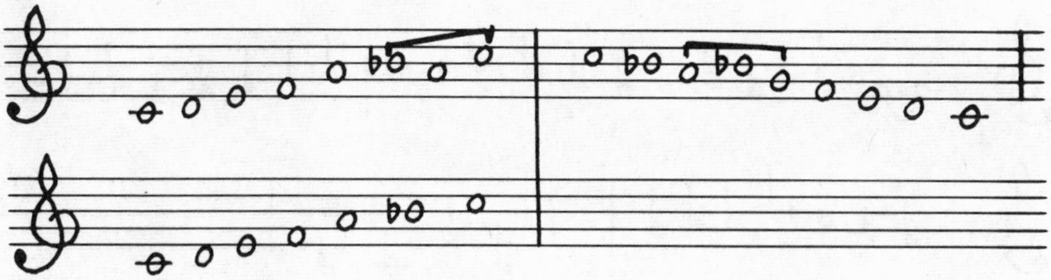

Two ascents are in use; both avoid the note *PA* (G). One ascent shows one *vakra* feature, the other does not. Descent: *sampūrṇa*; one *vakra* feature is shown.

KŌKILADHVANI (*Triputa-tāla*) SCM, 158

(19) *Kuntalavarāḷi*

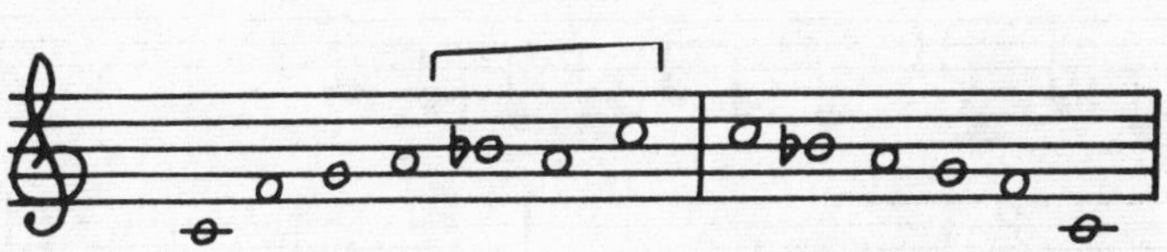

The notes *RI* (D) and *GA* (E) are avoided entirely. The ascent shows one *vakra* feature.

KUNTALAVARĀḶI (*Triputa-tāla*) SCM, 150

(20) *Mālavi*

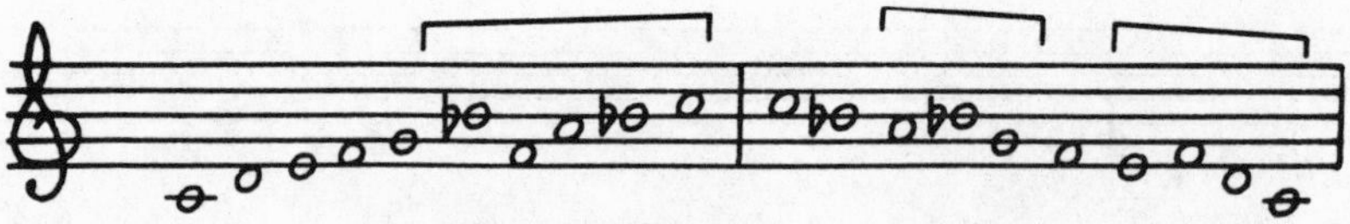

Ascent: *sampūrṇa*; one extended *vakra* feature is shown.
Descent: *sampūrṇa*; two *vakra* features are used.

MĀLAVI (*Triputa-tāla*) SCM, 142

(21) *Mattakōkila*

The scale of this rarely performed *rāga* is vaguely defined as:

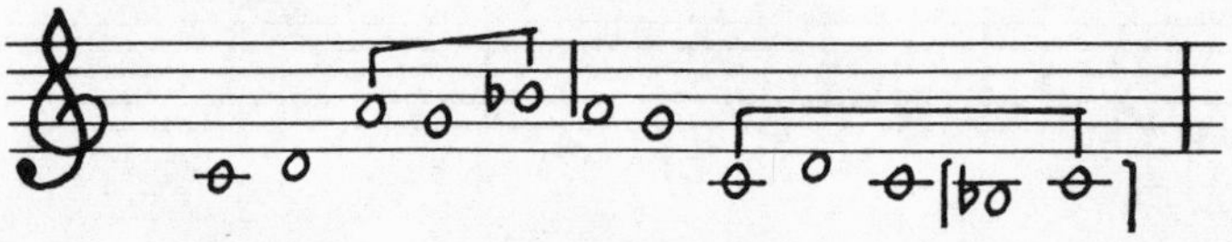

The notes *GA* (E) and *MA* (F) are avoided entirely. The scale shows two *vakra* features, one in ascent and one in descent.

MATTAKŌKILA (*Triputa-tāla*) SCM, 155

(22) *Nāgasvarāvali*

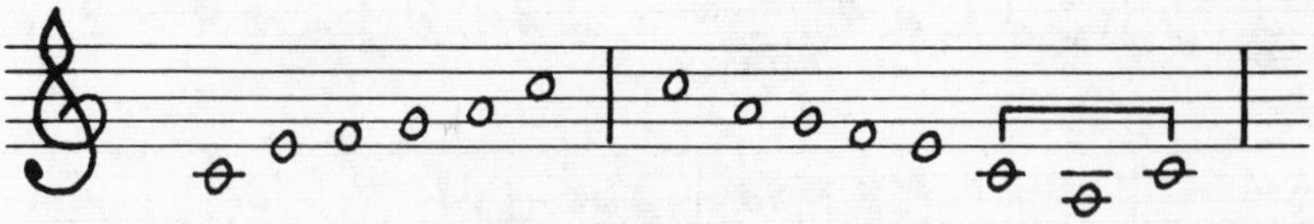

The notes *RI* (D) and *NI* (Bb) are avoided entirely. The *vakra* feature at the end of the descending scale appears only occasionally.

NĀGASVARĀVALI (*Triputa-tāla*) SCM, 160-61

The following passages in *Nāgasvarāvali*, being part of a *Gīta Govinda* performance, were recorded in Kerala by Wayne Howard in 1972:

(23) *Nārāyaṇagauḷa*

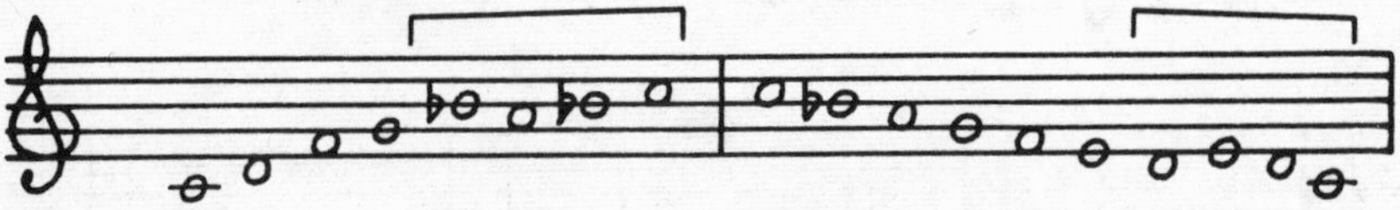

Ascent: the note *GA* (E) is avoided; one *vakra* feature is shown.
Descent: *sampūrṇa*; one *vakra* feature is used. There are instances when this latter *vakra* feature is omitted and the descent is *krama sampūrṇa*.

NĀRĀYAṆAGAUḶA (Triputa-tāla) SCM, 141

(24) *Nārāyaṇi*

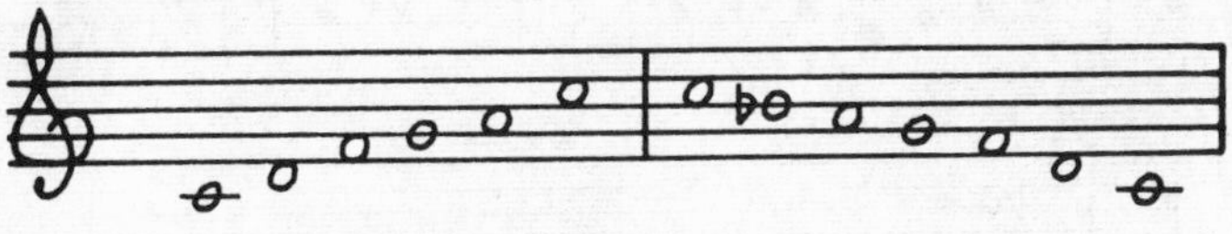

The note *GA* (E) is avoided entirely. In ascent the note *NI* (Bb) is omitted.

NĀRĀYAṆI (*Triputa-tāla*) SCM, 140-41

(25) *Nāṭanāyāraṇi*

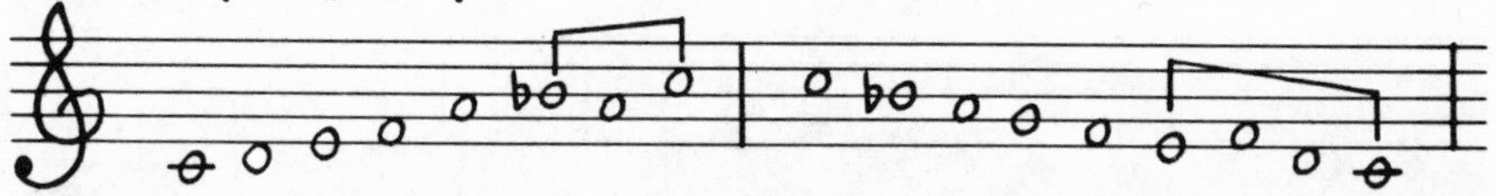

Ascent: the note *PA* (G) is avoided; one *vakra* feature is shown.
Descent: *sampūrṇa*; one *vakra* feature is used.

NĀṬANĀRĀYAṆI (*Triputa-tāla*) SCM, 144-45

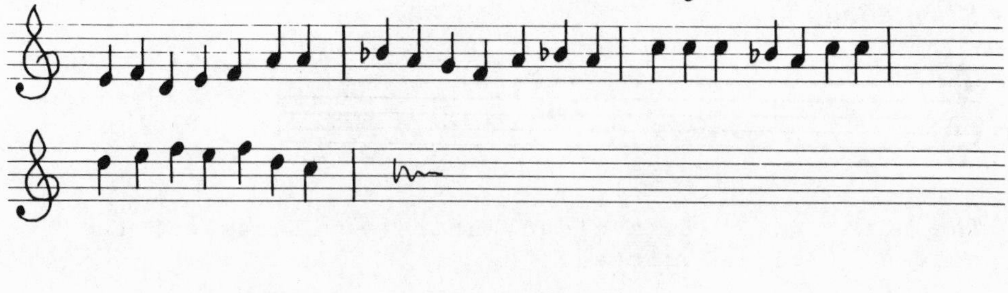

(26) *Navarasakalānidhi*

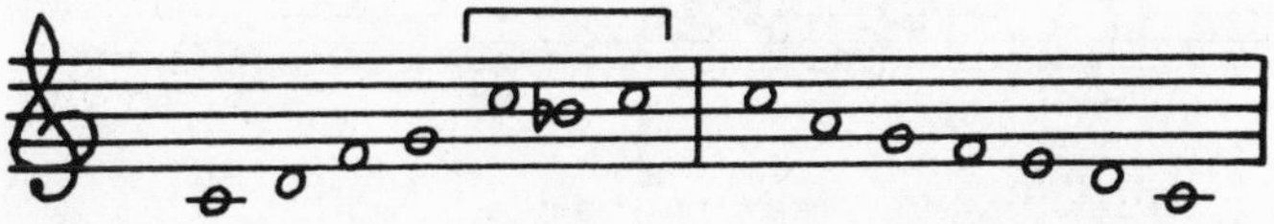

Ascent: the notes *GA* (E) and *DHA* (A) are avoided. One *vakra* feature is shown.
Descent: the note *NI* (Bb) is omitted.

(27) *Navarasakannaḍa*

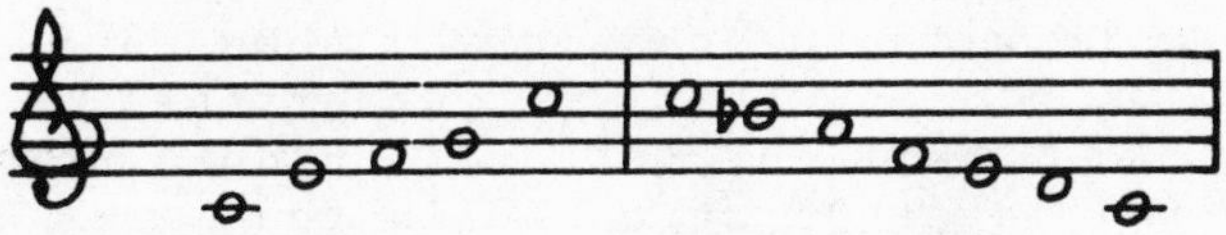

Ascent: the notes *RI* (D), *DHA* (A), and *NI* (Bb) are avoided.
Descent: the note *PA* (G) is omitted.

NAVARASAKANNAḌA (*Triputa-tāla*) SCM, 159

(28) *Nīlāmbari*

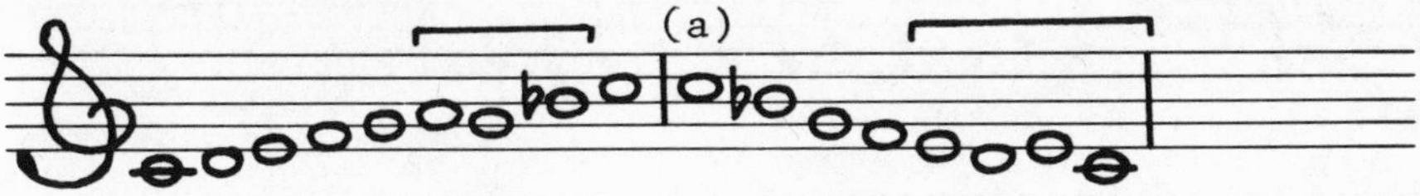

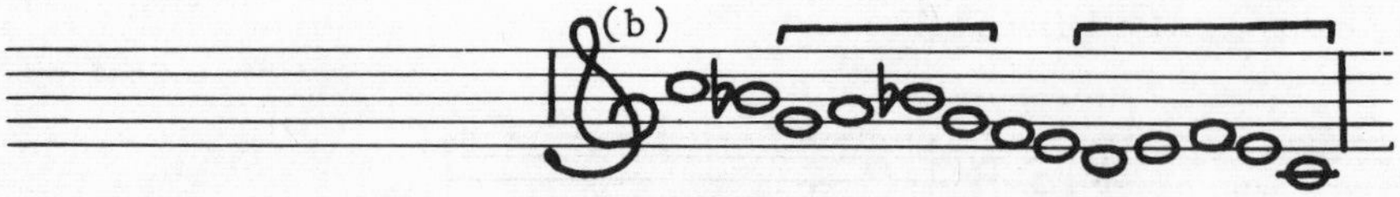

Ascent: *sampūrṇa*; one *vakra* feature is shown.
Descent: (a) the note *DHA* (A) is avoided and one *vakra* passage is used. (b) *sampūrṇa*; two extended *vakra* passages are used.

In addition to the two versions of descent there are other changes that can occur in *Nīlāmbari* performances. A frequent change happens in the rendition of the ascending note *NI* (originally Bb) which can be raised to B natural. This is the reason why some musicians feel justified in placing this *rāga* under the heading of the 29. *mēḷa*, where the pitch of Bb does not occur. The note *PA* (Ġ) is often stressed in the descending progression *PA-MA* (G-F); the lower note is performed with a vibrato and at times may be raised slightly in pitch.

NĪLĀMBARI (*Triputa-tāla*) SCM, 151-52

(29) *Pratāpavarāli*

The note *NI* (Bb) is avoided entirely and in ascent *GA* (E) is omitted and one *vakra* feature is shown.

Occasionally an ascent of this *rāga* can be observed that omits the *vakra* feature and avoids the note *DHA* (A):

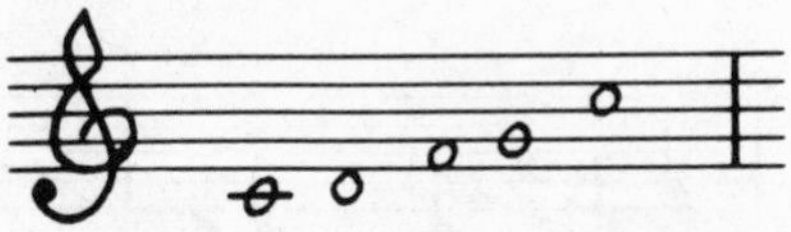

PRATĀPAVARĀLI (*Triputa-tāla*) SCM, 149

(30) *Pravālajoti*

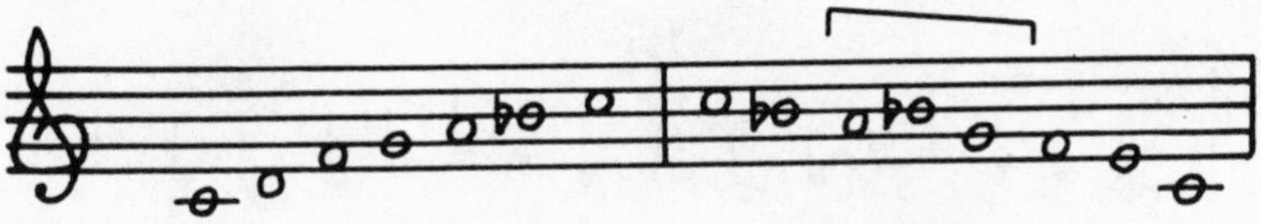

Ascent: the note *GA* (E) is avoided.
Descent: the note *RI* (D) is omitted; one *vakra* feature is shown.

(31) *Rāgapañcharam* (*Rāgapañcaram*)

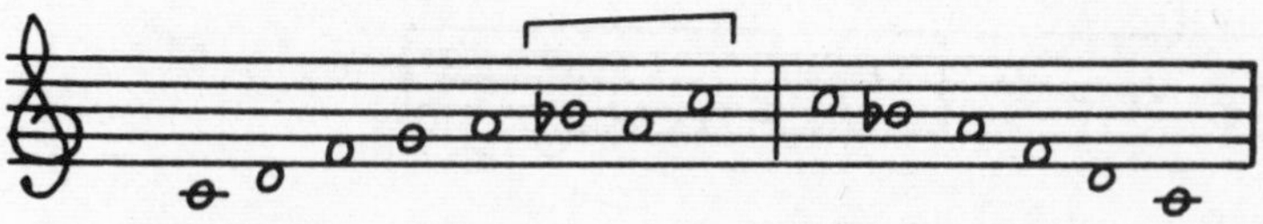

The note *GA* (E) is avoided entirely.
Ascent: one *vakra* feature is shown.
Descent: the note *PA* (G) is omitted.

RĀGAPAÑCHARAM (*Triputa-tāla*) SCM, 156-57

(32) *Ravichandrikā* (*Ravicandrikā*)

The note *PA* (G) is avoided entirely. The ascent shows one *vakra* feature.

RAVICHANDRIKĀ (*Triputa-tāla*) SCM, 157-58

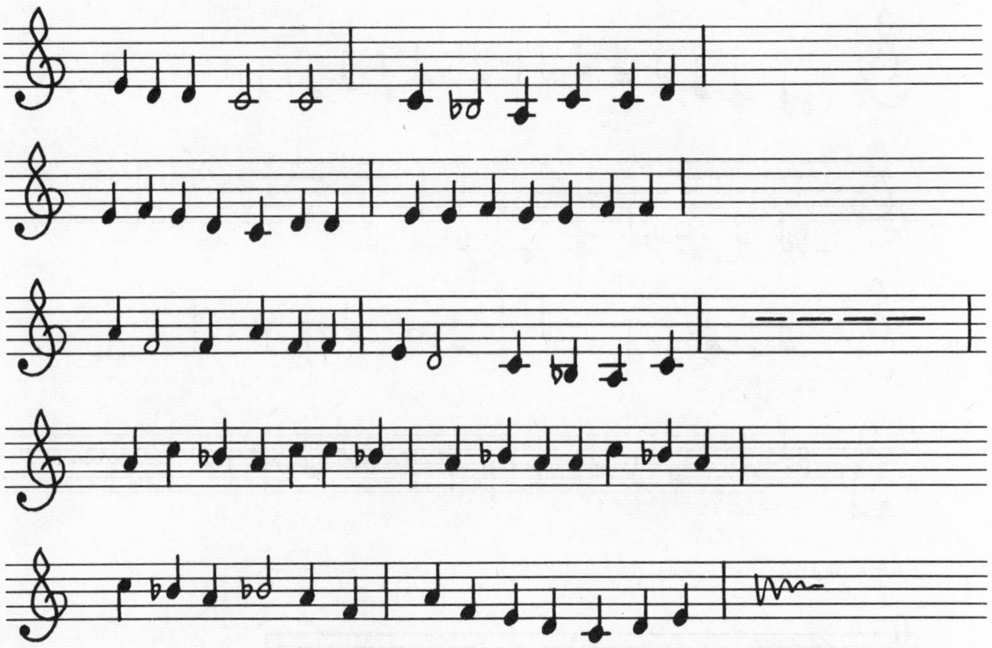

(33) *Śahāna*

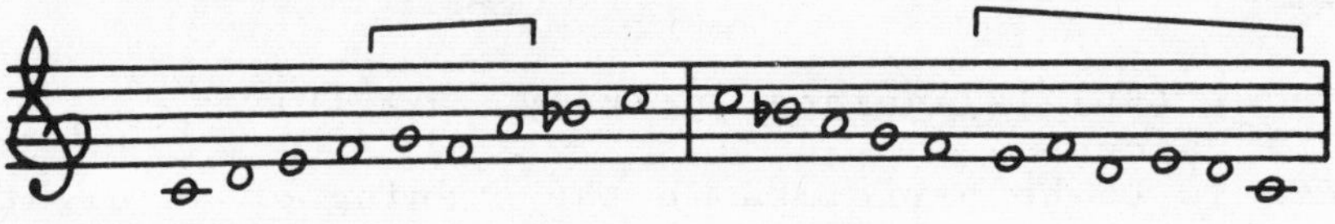

The scale of this *rāga* is *sampūrṇa*. One *vakra* feature appears in ascent, another extended one in descent.

At the present time some musicians have the habit of using both forms of *NI* (Bb and B) and of *GA* (Eb and E), a procedure not acceptable to the orthodox musicians. The correct notes employed in *Śahāna* are *antara GA* (E) and *kaiśika NI* (Bb). The latter note originally had *amśa* function, a feature that is only rarely noticed at the present time.

Another form of the *Śahāna* descent can be:

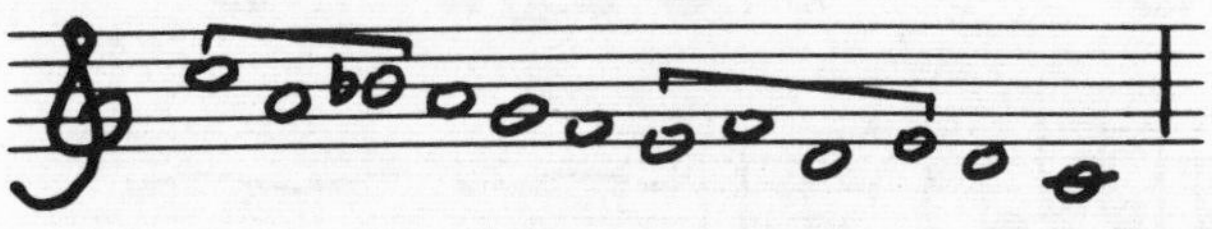

ŚAHĀNA (*Triputa-tāla*) SCM, 147-48

(34) *Sāma*

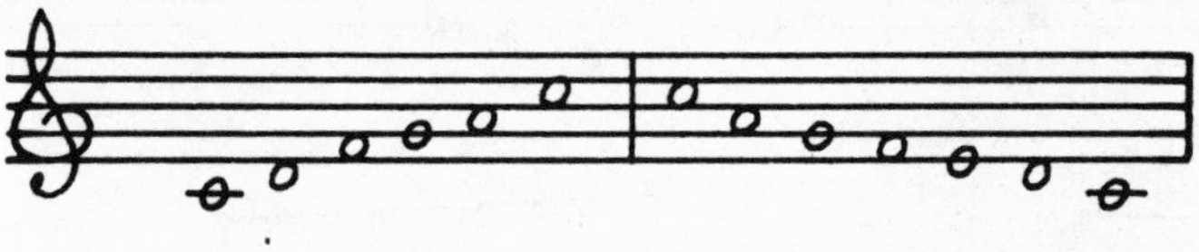

The note *NI* (Bb) is avoided entirely. *GA* (E) is omitted in ascent.

Sāma is to be performed in the evening or at night but in the present time no fixed performance time is observed.

SĀMA (*Triputa-tāla*) SCM, 152-53

(35) *Sarasvati Manoharī*

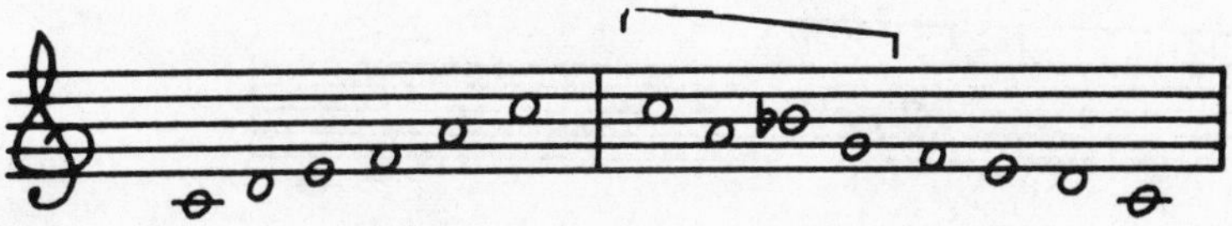

Ascent: the notes *PA* (G) and *NI* (Bb) are avoided.
Descent: *sampūrṇa*; one *vakra* feature is shown.

SARASVATI MANOHARĪ (*Triputa-tāla*) SCM, 151

(36) *Sindhu Kannaḍa*

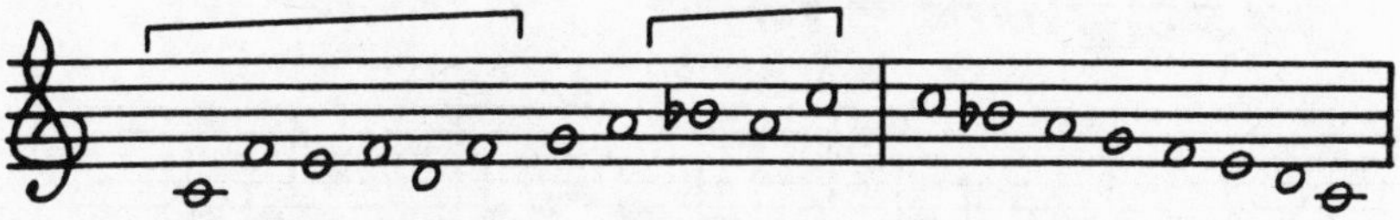

Ascent: *sampūrṇa*; two *vakra* features are shown.
Descent: *krama sampūrṇa*.

(37) *Śuddhataraṅgiṇī*

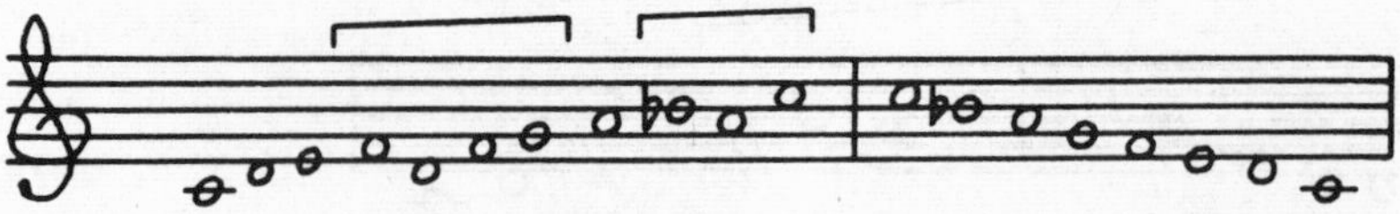

Ascent: *sampūrṇa*; two *vakra* features are shown.
Descent: *krama sampūrṇa*.

(38) *Suposhiṇi* (*Supoṣiṇi*)

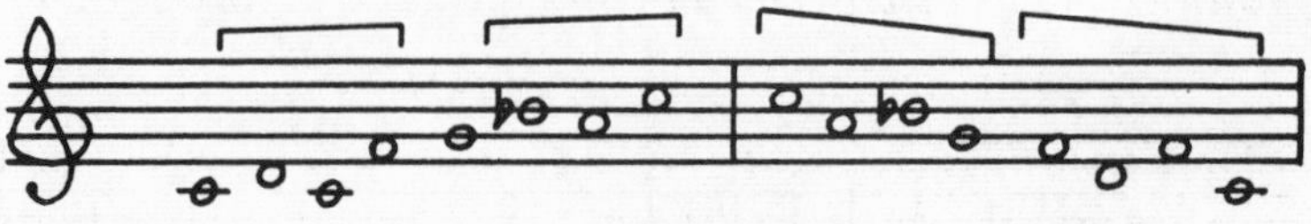

The note *GA* (E) is avoided entirely. Ascent and descent show two *vakra* features.

(39) *Suraṭi*

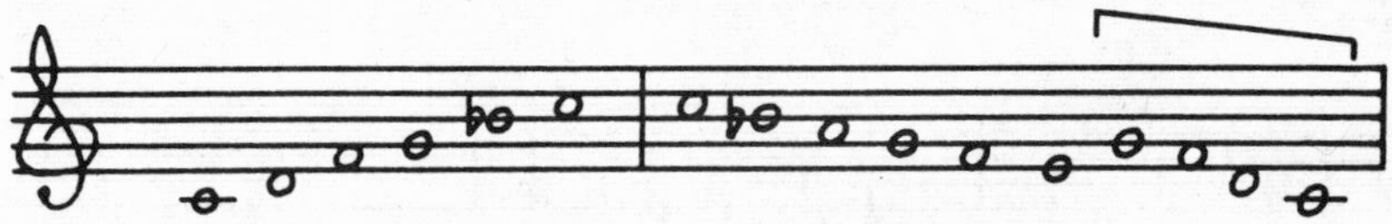

Ascent: the notes *GA* (E) and *DHA* (A) are avoided.
Descent: *sampūrṇa*; one extended *vakra* feature is shown. There are some musicians who avoid the note *GA* (E) entirely.

Another descent of this *rāga* avoids the *vakra* passage and appears in *krama sampūrṇa* form.

SURAṬI (*Triputa-tāla*) SCM, 163

In the following example which represents the opening measures of a *kṛti* the note *GA* (E) is avoided at first. Later in the song, in a few instances, not shown here, this note is used in a weak form.

SURATI Adi-tāla

(40) *Svarāvali*

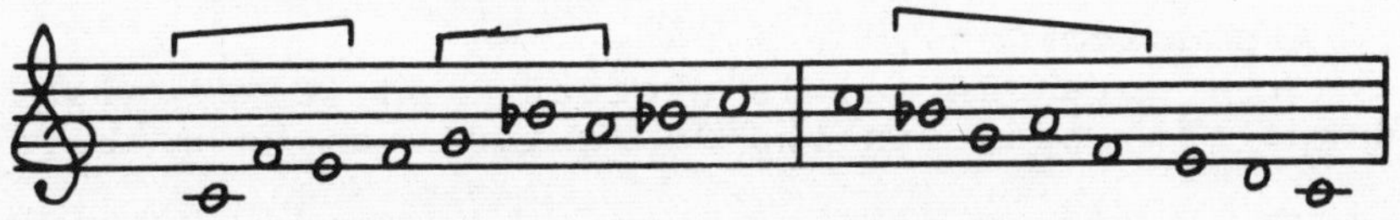

Ascent: the note *RI* (D) is avoided; two *vakra* features are shown.
Descent: *sampūrṇa*; one extended *vakra* feature is used.

SVARĀVALI (*Triputa-tāla*) SCM, 160

(41) *Svaravēdi*

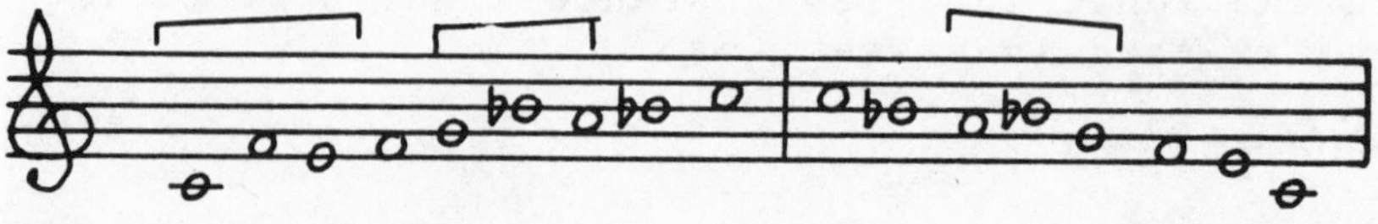

The note *RI* (D) is avoided entirely. The ascent of this *rāga* is identical with that of *Svarāvali rāga* (28, 40). The descent shows one *vakra* feature.

(42) *Umābharaṇam*

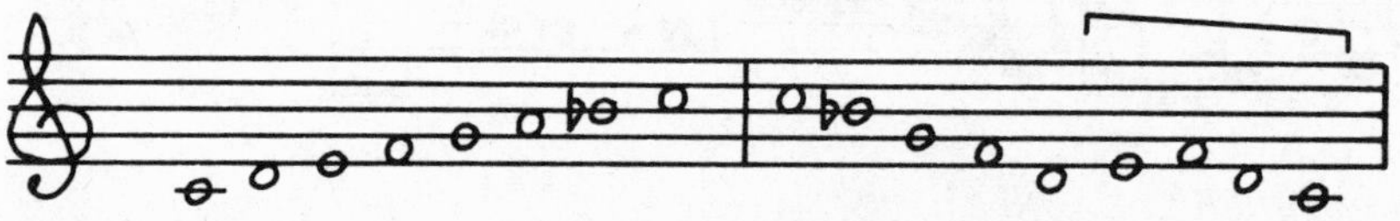

Ascent: *krama sampūrṇa*.
Descent: the note *DHȦ* (A) is avoided. *GA* (E) is also avoided but can appear in the *vakra* feature shown above.

(43) *Valaji*

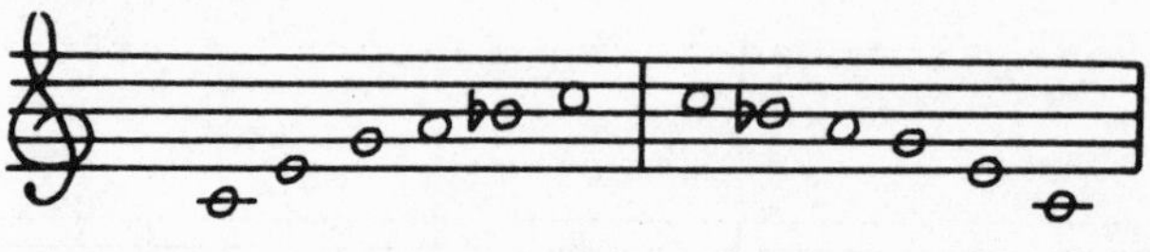

In recent times this *rāga* has become increasingly popular. The notes *RI* (D) and *MA* (F) are avoided entirely.

The following two brief passages in *Valaji* occur in a *Gīta Govinda* performance recorded by Wayne Howard in Kerala in 1972:

(44) *Vivardhini*

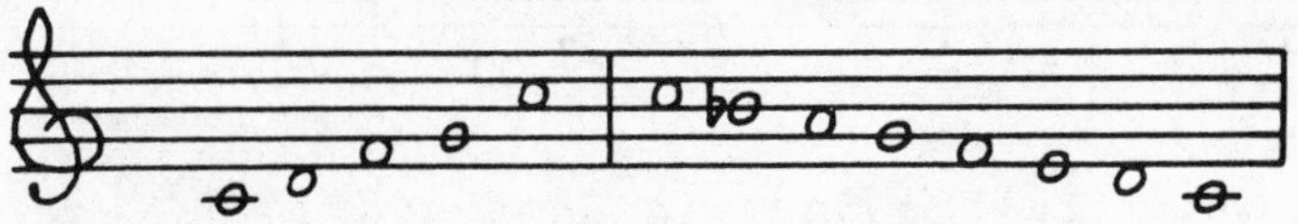

Ascent: the notes *GA* (E), *DHA* (A), and *NI* (Bb) are avoided.
Descent: *krama sampūrṇa*.

(45) *Alakavarāḷi*

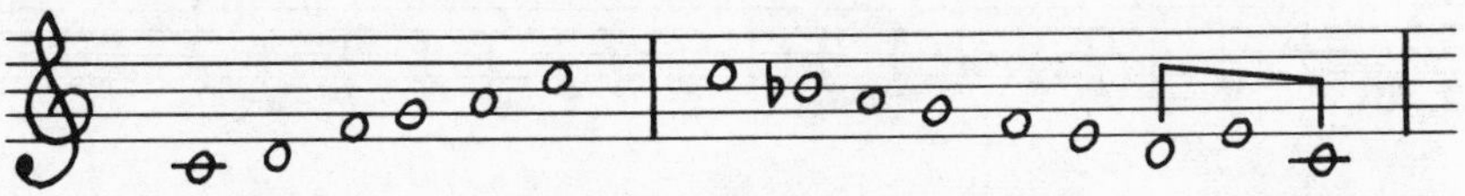

Ascent: the notes *GA* (E) and *NI* (Bb) are avoided.
Descent: *sampūrṇa*; one *vakra* feature is shown.

(46) *Amarāvaḷi*

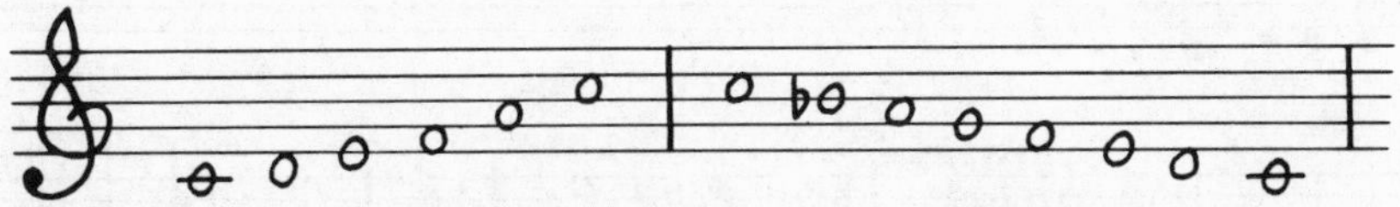

Ascent: the notes *PA* (G) and *NI* (Bb) are avoided.
Descent: *krama sampūrṇa*.

(47) *Ambhōgini*

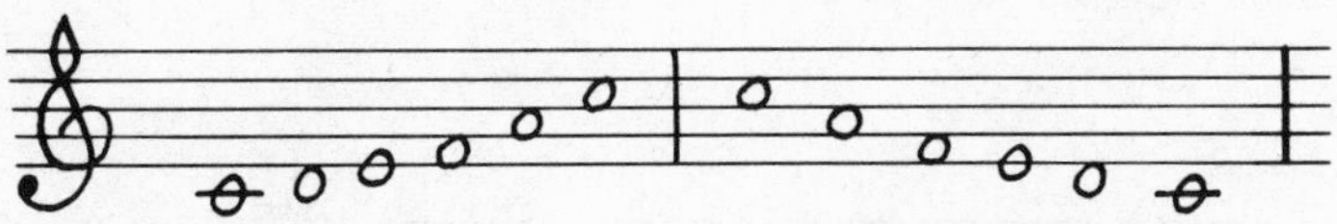

The notes *PA* (G) and *NI* (Bb) are avoided entirely.

(48) *Āndhāḷi*

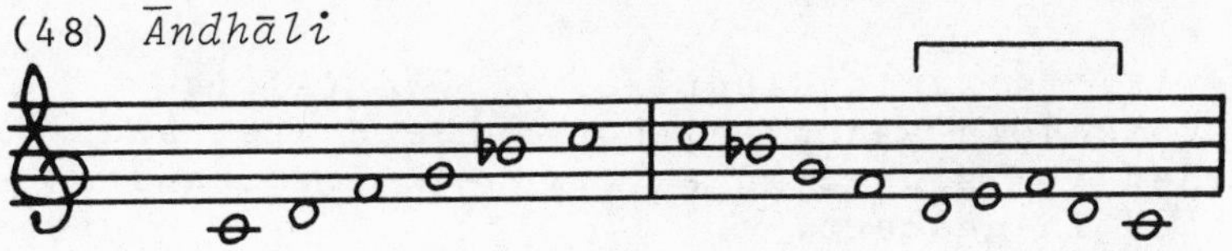

The note *DHA* (A) is avoided entirely. *GA* (E) is omitted in ascent, and the descent shows one extended *vakra* feature.

The SD (I, 17) states that the scale

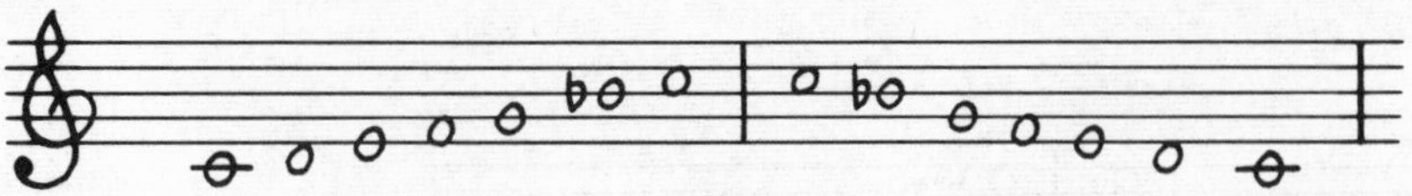

"given for this *rāga* in the *Saṅgīta Sampradāya Pradarśinī* [by Subbarāma Dīkshitar] is not supported by *lakshya*."

Āndhāḷi is an old and well-known *rāga*.

ĀNDHĀLI (*Triputa-tāla*) SCM, 153-54

(49) *Āndhōliki*

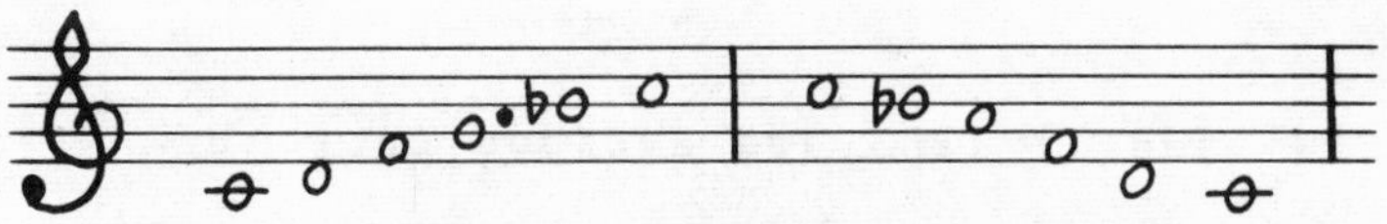

The note *GA* (E) is avoided entirely. *DHA* (A) is generally avoided in ascent although there are rare instances when it is used in a very weak form, and *PA* (G) is omitted in descent.

(50) *Aṅgalatā*

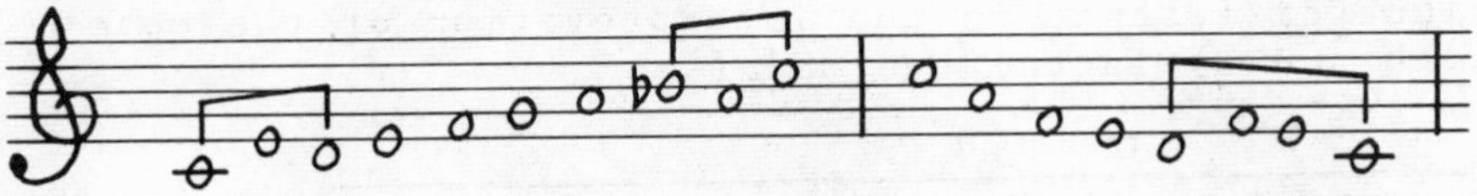

Ascent: *sampūrṇa*; two *vakra* features are shown.
Descent: the notes *NI* (Bb) and *PA* (G) are avoided; one extended *vakra* feature is shown.

(51) *Arkavardhani*

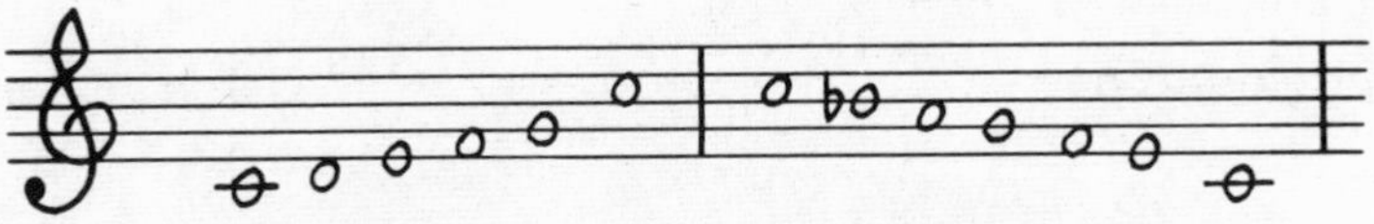

Ascent: the notes *DHA* (A) and *NI* (Bb) are avoided.
Descent: the note *RI* (D) is omitted.

(52) *Aruṇakāntam*

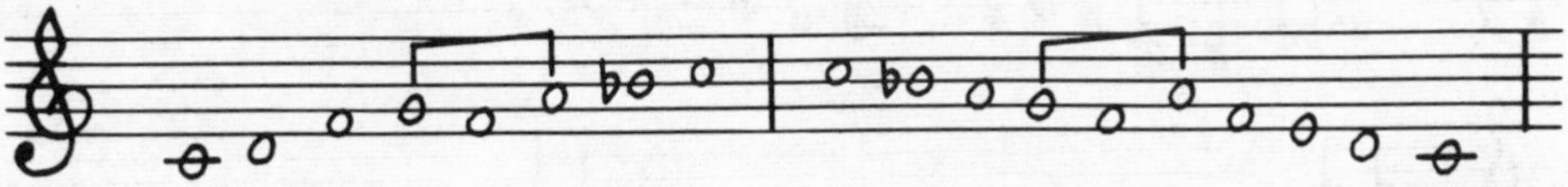

Ascent: the note *GA* (E) is avoided; one *vakra* feature is shown.
Descent: *sampūrṇa*; one *vakra* feature (the same as in ascent) is used.

(53) *Bāgēśvari*

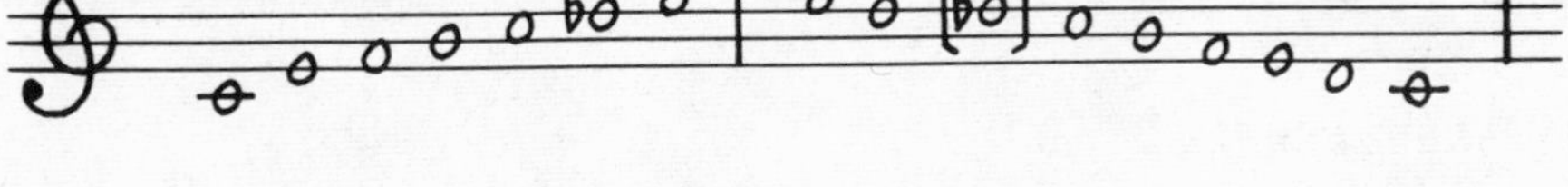

Ascent: the note *RI* (D) is avoided.
Descent: *krama sampūrṇa*.

(54) *Baṅgāḷa*

This ancient *rāga* is usually ascribed to the 29. *mēḷa* (10). It is mentioned here because a *Baṅgāḷa* melody pattern, ascribed to the 28. *mēḷa*, is offered in the SCM (#22, p. 156). Another reason for showing this *rāga* already here is the fact that occasionally there can be a slight difference between the *Baṅgāḷa* ascents of the 28. and 29. *mēḷas*, not taking into account the obvious difference in the interpretation of the note *NI* (Bb and B) in the two *mēḷas*.

The note *DHA* (A) is avoided entirely. *NI* (Bb) is omitted in ascent. There appear two *vakra* features, one in ascent and one in descent.

BAṄGĀḶA (*Triputa-tāla*) SCM, 156

(55) *Bhavasindhu*

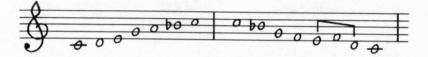

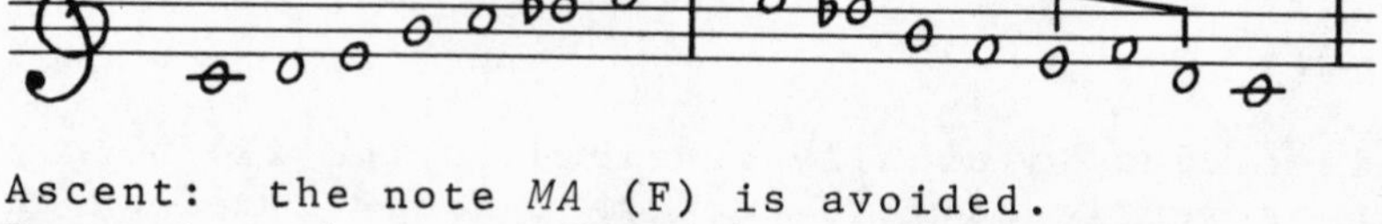

Ascent: the note *MA* (F) is avoided.
Descent: the note *DHA* (A) is omitted; one *vakra* feature is used.

(56) *Bhinna Vikriya*

The note *NI* (Bb) is avoided entirely. *GA* (E) is omitted in descent.

(57) *Bhōgi Bhairavī*

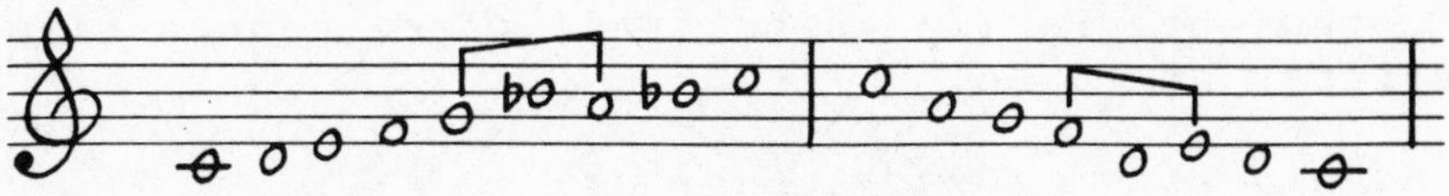

Ascent: *sampūrṇa*; one *vakra* feature is shown.
Descent: the note *NI* (Bb) is avoided; one *vakra* feature is used.

(58) *Bhūshaṇi* (*Bhūṣaṇi*)

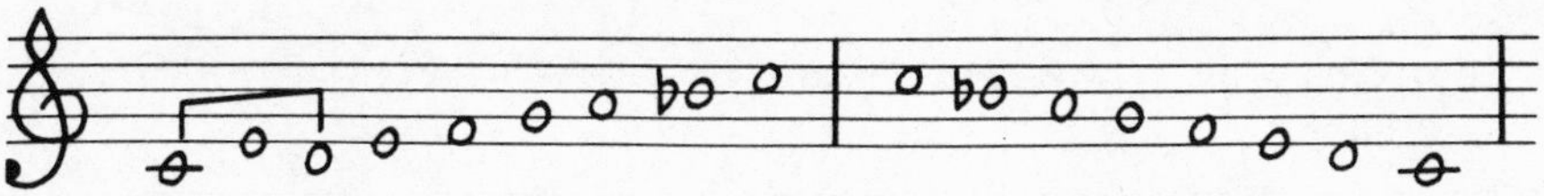

Ascent: *sampūrṇa*; one *vakra* feature is shown.
Descent: *krama sampūrṇa*.

(59) *Byāg*

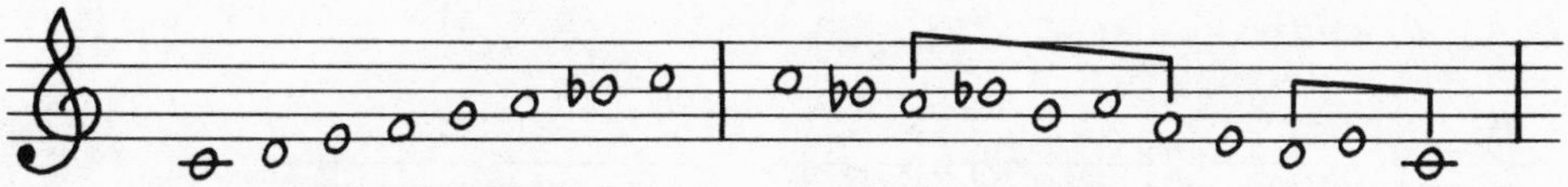

Ascent: *krama sampūrṇa*.
Descent: *sampūrṇa*; two *vakra* features are shown.

This *rāga* can be performed at all times. See also the *rāgas Byāg* (29, 22) and *Behag* (29, 12).

(60) *Chākāri* (*Cākāri*)

Ascent: the note *MA* (F) is avoided; one *vakra* feature is shown.
Descent: *krama sampūrṇa.*

(61) *Champaka Vidāri* (*Campaka Vidāri*)

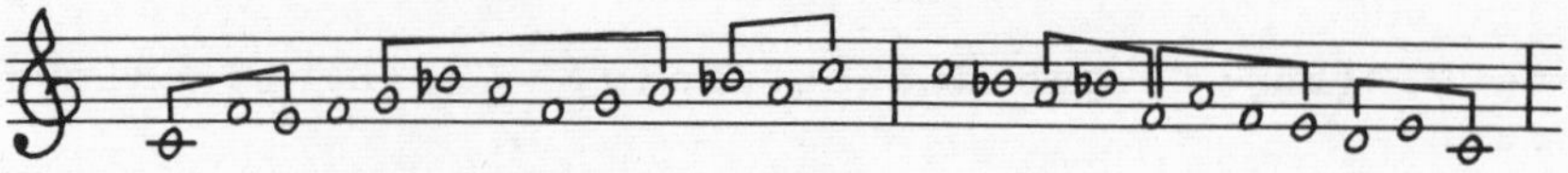

Ascent: the note *RI* (D) is avoided; three *vakra* features (the second one extended) are shown.
Descent: the note *PA* (G) is omitted; three consecutive *vakra* features are used.

(62) *Chandra Hasitam* (*Candra Hasitam*)

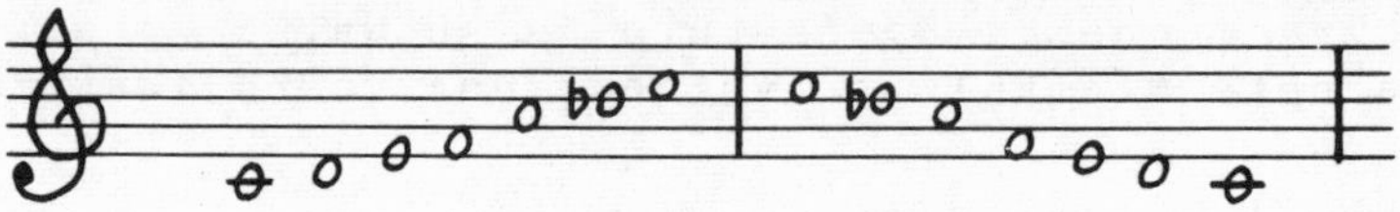

The note *PA* (G) is avoided entirely.

(63) *Chandra Śrī* (*Candra Śrī*)

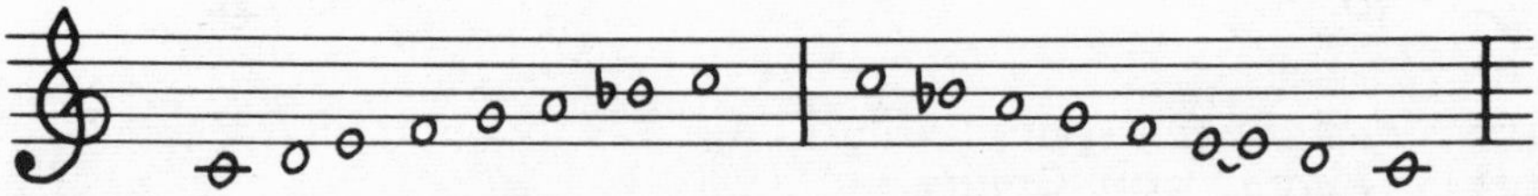

The scale is *krama sampūrṇa* in ascent and descent.

(64) *Chāndrikya* (*Cāndrikya*)

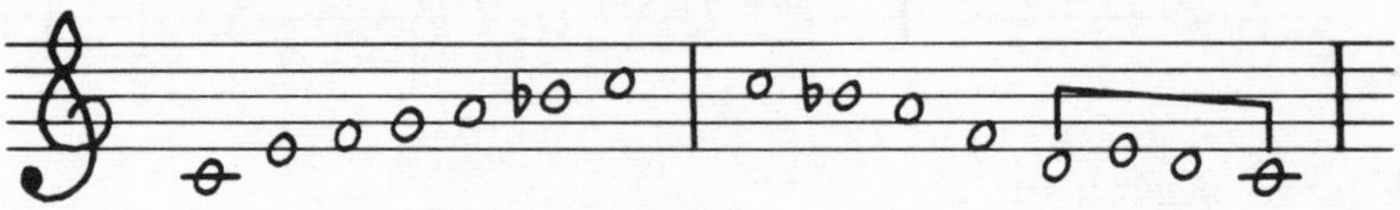

Ascent: the note *RI* (D) is avoided.
Descent: the note *PA* (G) is omitted; one extended *vakra* feature is shown.

(65) *Cheñchu Kāmbhōji* (*Ceñcu Kāmbhōji*)

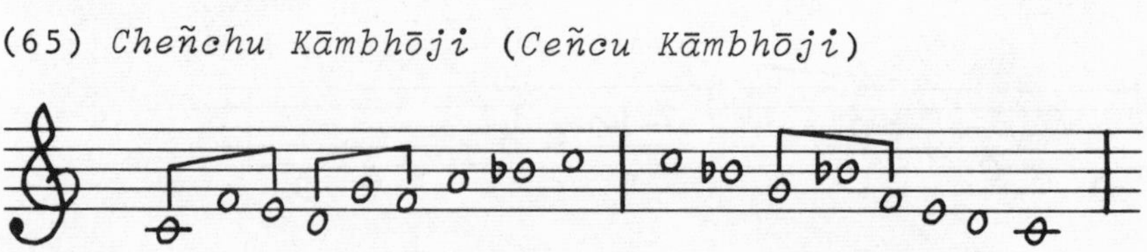

Ascent: *sampūrṇa*; two *vakra* features are shown.

Descent: the note *DHA* (A) is avoided; one *vakra* feature is used.

(66) *Dankāmaṇi*

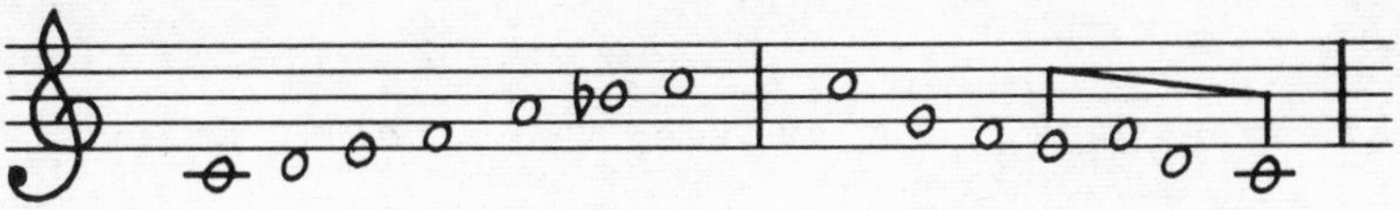

Ascent: the note *PA* (G) is avoided.
Descent: the notes *NI* (Bb) and *DHA* (A) are omitted; one *vakra* feature is used.

(67) *Darārdhari*

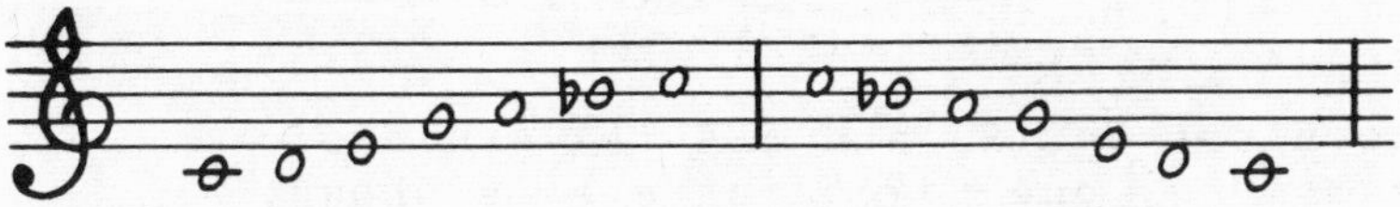

The note *MA* (F) is avoided entirely.

(68) *Dāsumukhi*

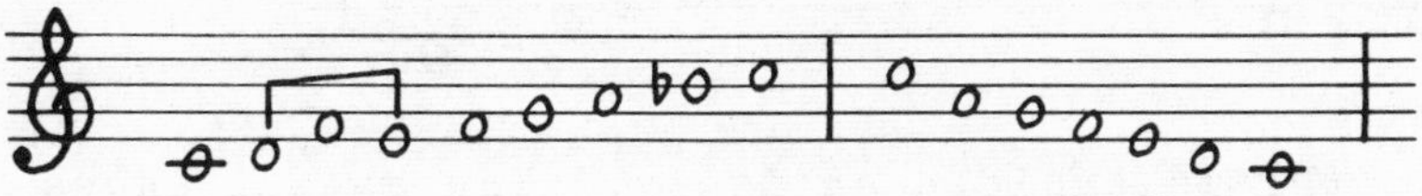

Ascent: *sampūrṇa*; one *vakra* feature is shown.
Descent: the note *NI* (Bb) is avoided.

(69) *Daṭi Māñji*

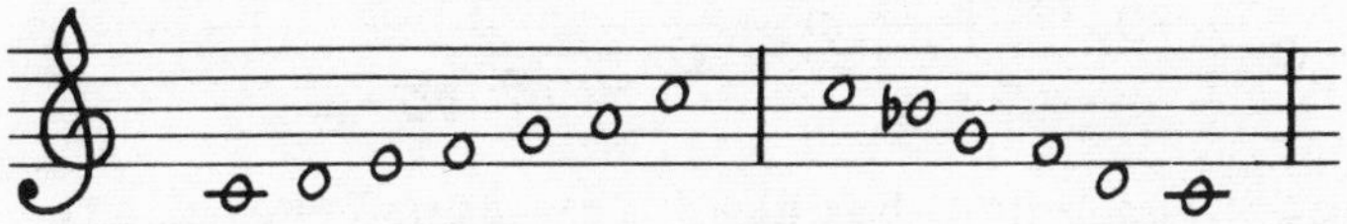

Ascent: the note *NI* (Bb) is avoided.
Descent: the notes *DHA* (A) and *GA* (E) are omitted.

(70) *Dayarañjani*

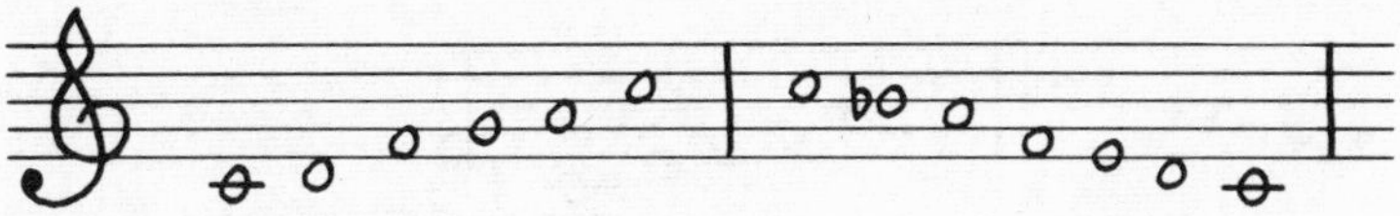

Ascent: the notes *GA* (E) and *NI* (Bb) are avoided.
Descent: the note *PA* (G) is omitted.

(71) *Dayāsyani*

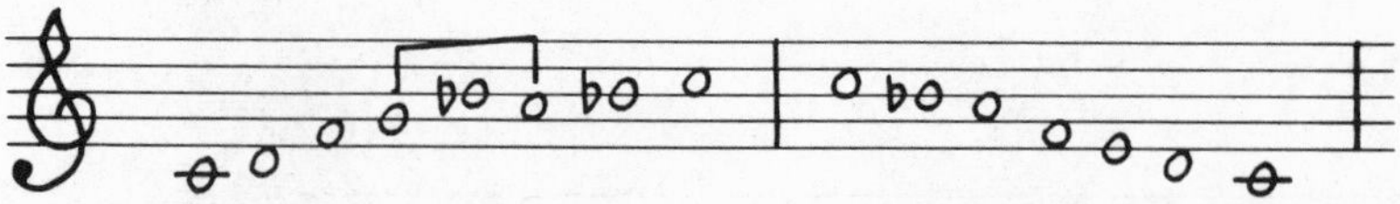

Ascent: the note *GA* (E) is avoided; one *vakra* feature is shown.
Descent: the note *PA* (G) is omitted.

(72) *Dēśī*

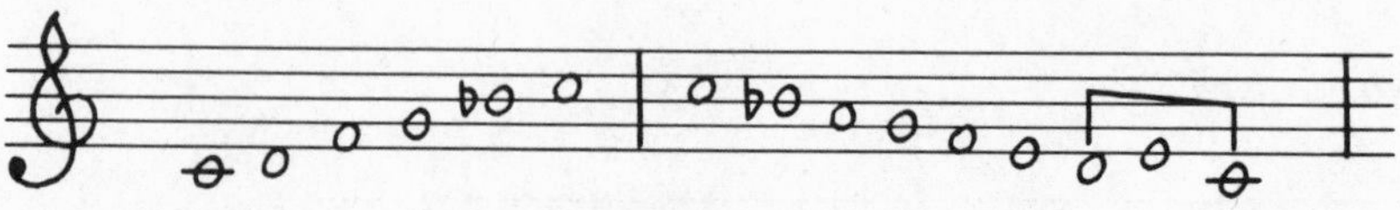

Ascent: the notes *GA* (E) and *DHA* (A) are avoided.
Descent: *sampūrṇa*; one *vakra* feature is shown.

(73) *Dēśya Kamās*

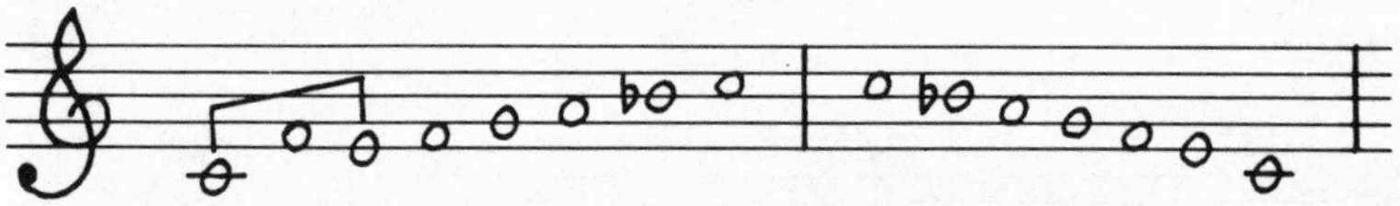

The note *RI* (D) is avoided entirely. The ascent shows one *vakra* feature.

(74) *Dēva Ghōsha Priya* (*Dēva Ghōṣa Priya*)

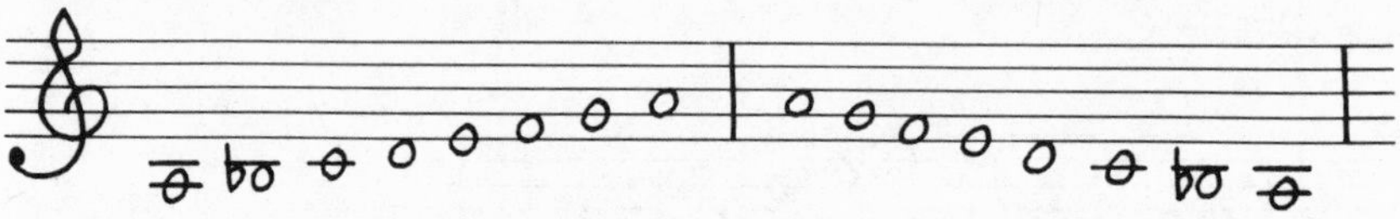

This is a *dhaivatāntya rāga* because its *sampūrṇa* scale begins with *DHA* (A) of the lowest octave region (*mandra saptaka*) and ends one octave higher with *DHA* (A) of the middle octave range.

(75) *Dēvaguptam* (*Dēvagupti*)

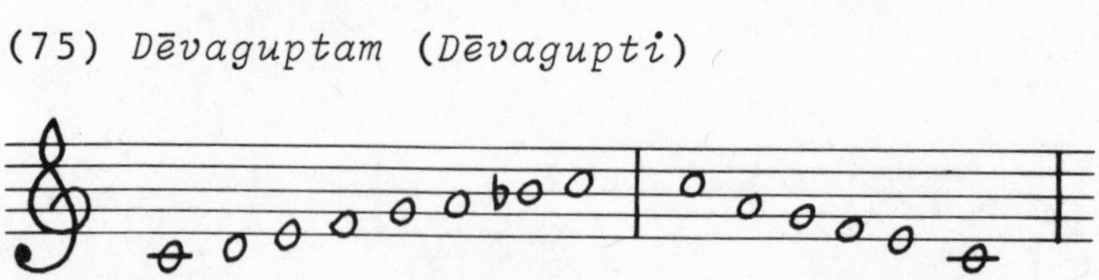

Ascent: *krama sampūrṇa*.
Descent: the notes *NĪ* (Bb) and *RI* (D) are avoided.

(76) *Dēvamukhi*

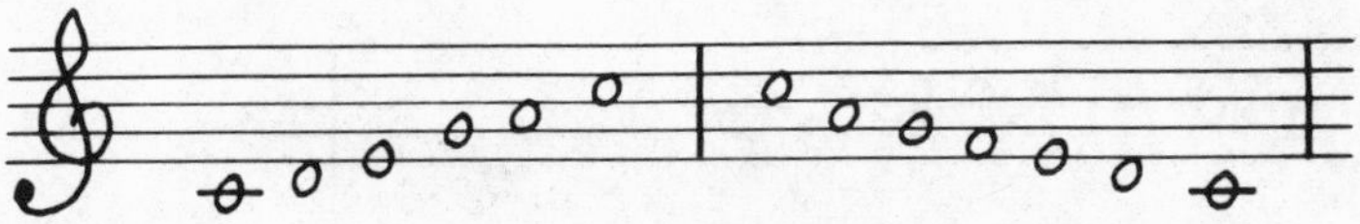

The note *NI* (Bb) is avoided entirely. In ascent the note *MA* (F) is omitted.

(77) *Dēvarañjani*

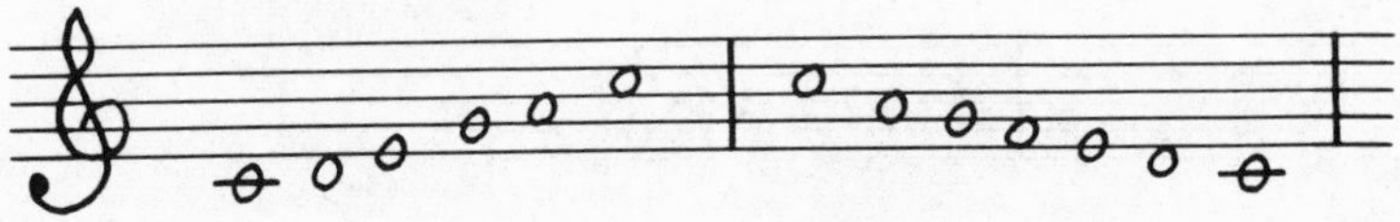

The scale of this *rāga* is identical with that of *Dēvamukhi* (28, 76).

Another *rāga Dēvarañjani* appears under the heading of the 22. *mēḷa* (36).

(78) *Dhāṭi Mañjari*

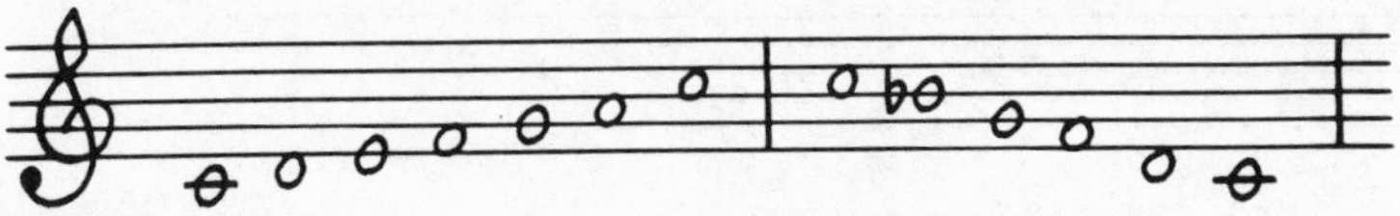

Ascent: the note *NI* (Bb) is avoided.
Descent: the notes *DHA* (A) and *GA* (E) are omitted.

(79) *Dūrdha Khyāyam*

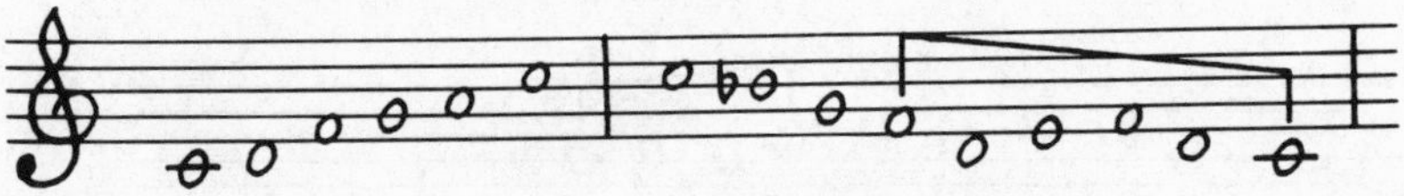

Ascent: the notes *GA* (E) and *NI* (Bb) are avoided.
Descent: the note *DHA* (A) is omitted; one extended *vakra* feature is shown.

(80) *Durita Nivāriṇī*

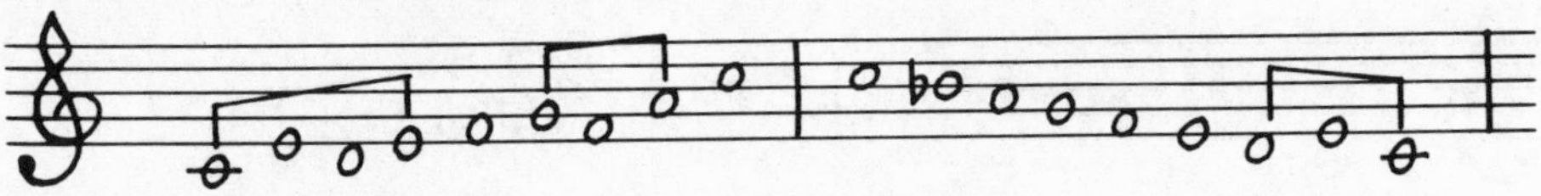

Ascent: the note *NI* (Bb) is avoided; two *vakra* features are shown.
Descent: *sampūrṇa*; one *vakra* feature is used.

(81) *Dvaita Chintāmaṇi* (*Dvaita Cintāmaṇi*)

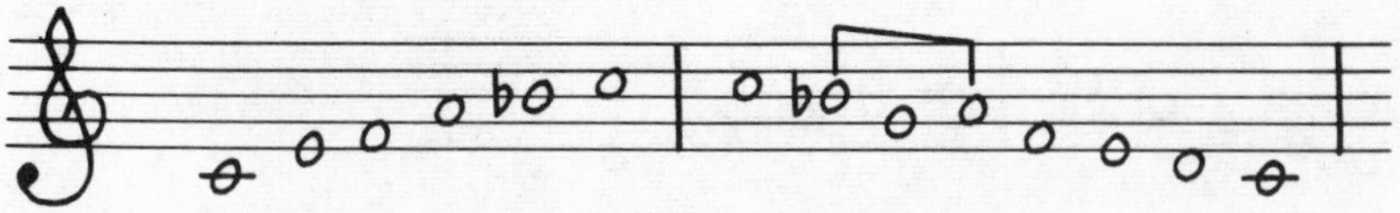

Ascent: the notes *RI* (D) and *PA* (G) are avoided.
Descent: *sampūrṇa*; one *vakra* feature is shown.

(82) *Dvaitānandi*

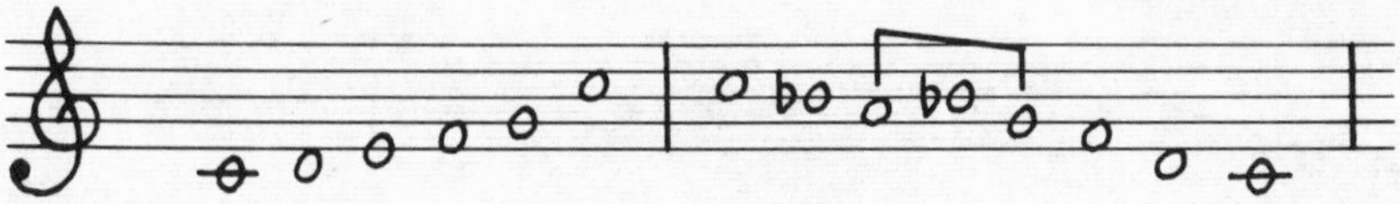

Ascent: the notes *DHA* (A) and *NI* (Bb) are avoided.
Descent: the notes *GA* (E) is omitted; one *vakra* feature is shown.

(83) *Dvaita Paripūrṇi*

This is a *niṣādāntya rāga* because the highest note of its ascending scale is *NI* (Bb). The descent, from *DHA* (A) to *SA* (C), shows one vakra feature.

(84) *Dvandvōtpala*

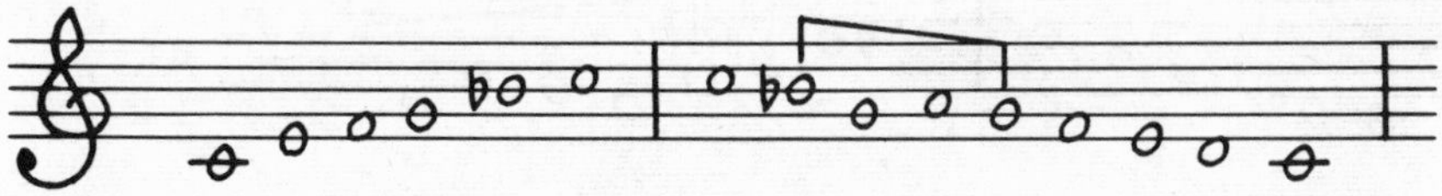

Ascent: the notes *RI* (D) and *DHA* (A) are avoided.
Descent: *sampūrṇa*; one *vakra* feature is shown.

(85) *Ēkāghrauṇi* (*Ēkāgraṇi*)

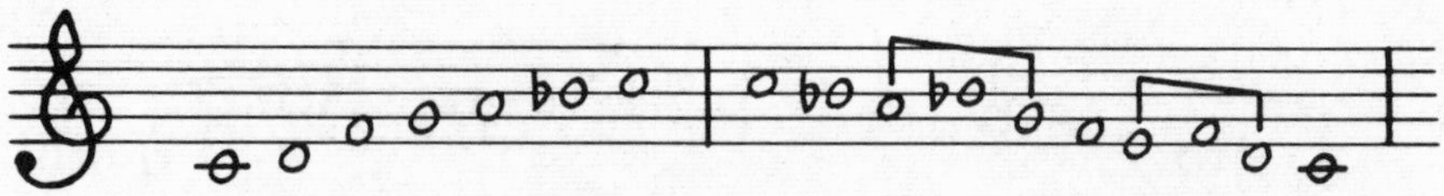

Ascent: the note *GA* (E) is avoided.
Descent: *sampūrṇa*; two *vakra* features are shown.

(86) *Ghanāndōlika*

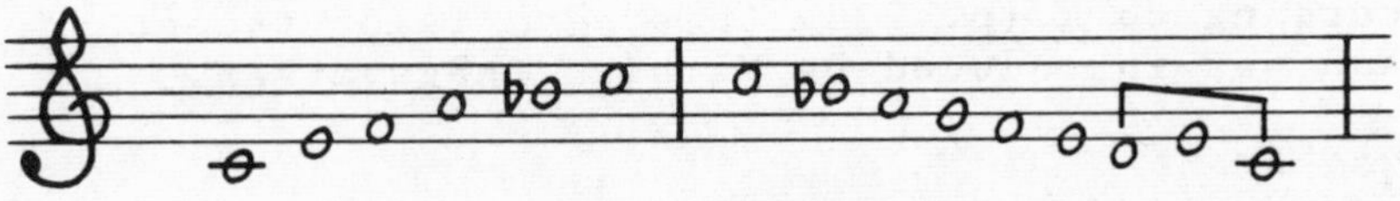

Ascent: the notes *RI* (D) and *PA* (G) are avoided.
Descent: *sampūrṇa*; one *vakra* feature is shown.

(87) *Giridhara*

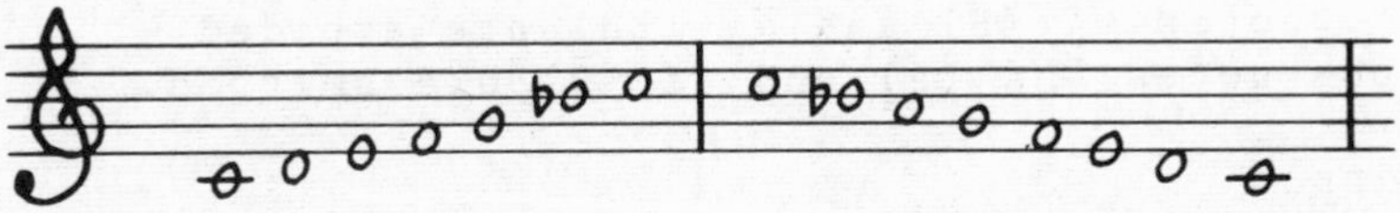

Ascent: the note *DHA* (A) is avoided.
Descent: *krama sampūrṇa*.

(88) *Gītālambana*

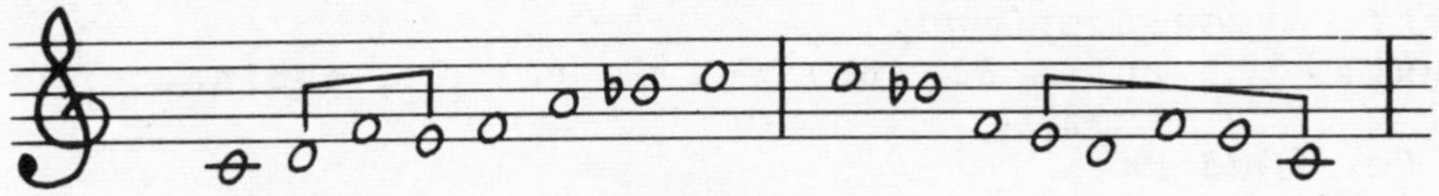

The note *PA* (G) is avoided entirely. In descent the note *DHA* (A) is omitted. Two *vakra* features are shown, one in ascent and an extended one in descent.

(89) *Gōmaṇḍalam*

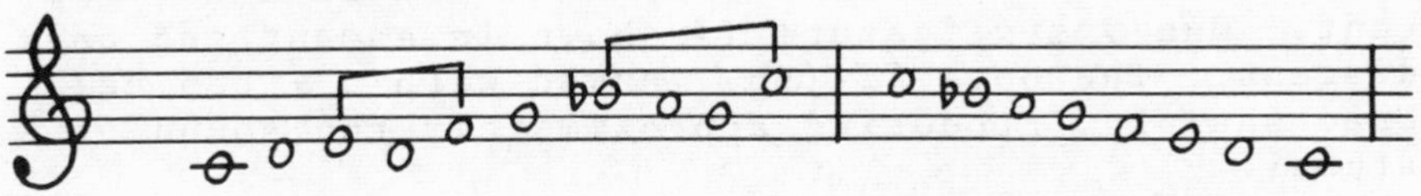

Ascent: *sampūrṇa*; two *vakra* features are shown.
Descent: *krama sampūrṇa*.

(90) *Guharañjanī*

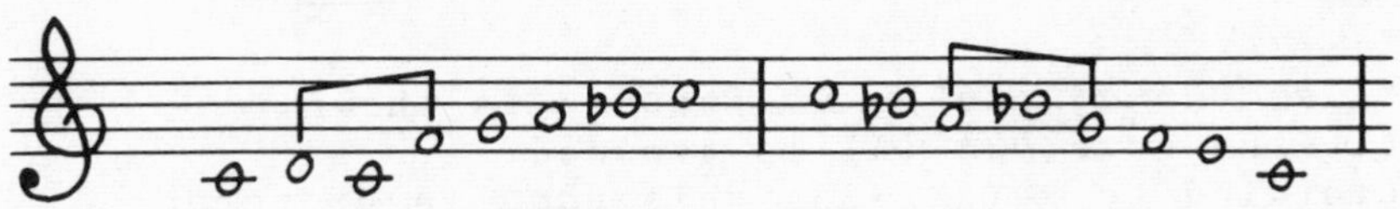

Ascent: the note *GA* (E) is avoided; one *vakra* feature is shown.

Descent: the note *RI* (D) is omitted; one *vakra* feature is used.

According to R (p. 223) this *rāga* is of recent origin and was introduced by Muthiah Bhāgavathar.

(91) *Haṃsa Śrēṇi*

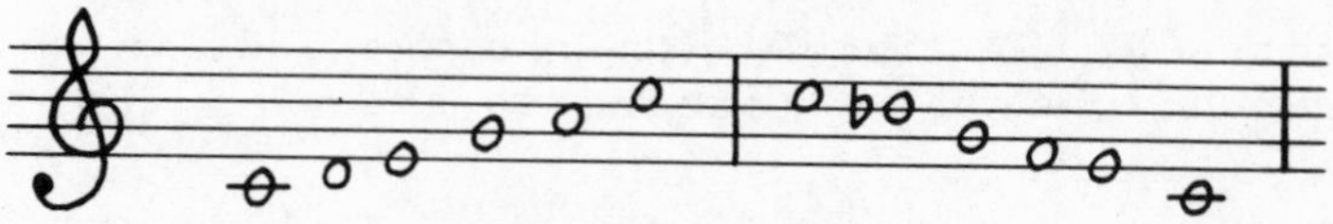

Ascent: the notes *MA* (F) and *NI* (Bb) are avoided.
Descent: the notes *DHA* (A) and *RI* (D) are omitted.

(92) *Haridarpam*

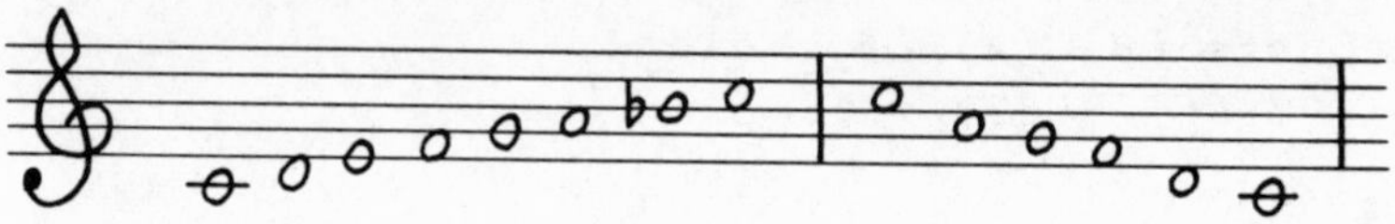

Ascent: *krama sampūrṇa.*
Descent: the notes *NI* (Bb) and *GA* (E) are avoided.

(93) *Harikēdāram*

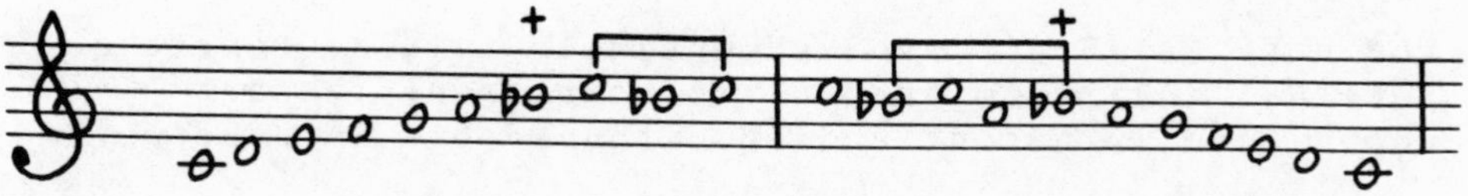

The scale of this *rāga* is *sampūrṇa* in ascent and descent. One *vakra* feature is shown in ascent and one in descent. The note *NI* (Bb) marked with a + can be intoned sharply, producing approximately the sound of B natural.

(94) *Harinārāyaṇī*

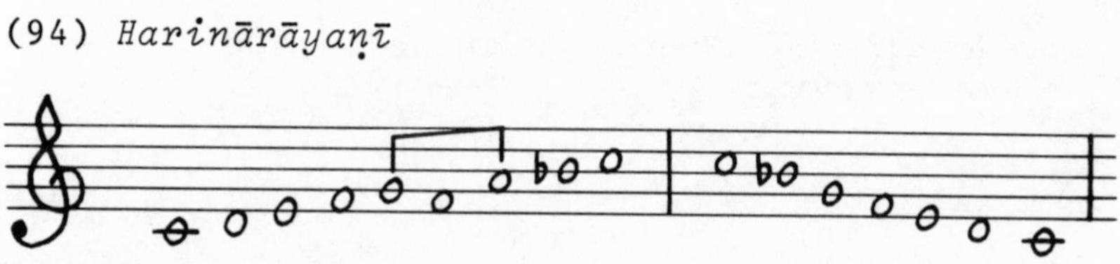

Ascent: *sampūrṇa*; one *vakra* feature is shown.
Descent: the note *DHA* (A) is avoided.

According to R (222-23) this *rāga* is of recent origin and was introduced by Muthiah Bhāgavathar.

Another *rāga* with the same name is listed under the heading of the 22. *mēḷa* (48).

(95) *Hāṭaka Varāḷi*

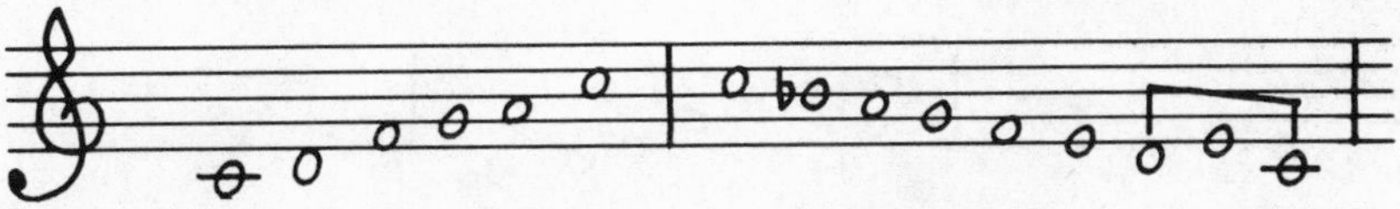

Ascent: the notes *GA* (E) and *NI* (Bb) are avoided.
Descent: *sampūrṇa*; one *vakra* feature is shown.

(96) *Hēma Māndāra*

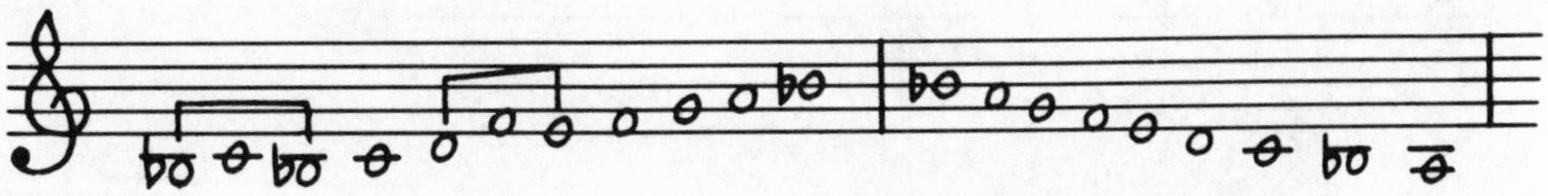

This is a *niṣādāntya rāga* because its highest note is *NI* (Bb). The ascent shows two *vakra* features; the descent progresses in a straight line.

(97) *Hēma Sāraṅga*

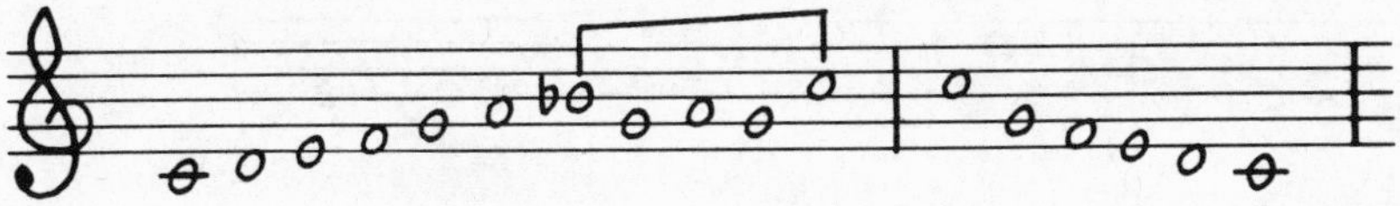

Ascent: *sampūrṇa*; one extended *vakra* feature is shown.
Descent: the notes *NI* (Bb) and *DHA* (A) are avoided.

(98) *Hitapriya*

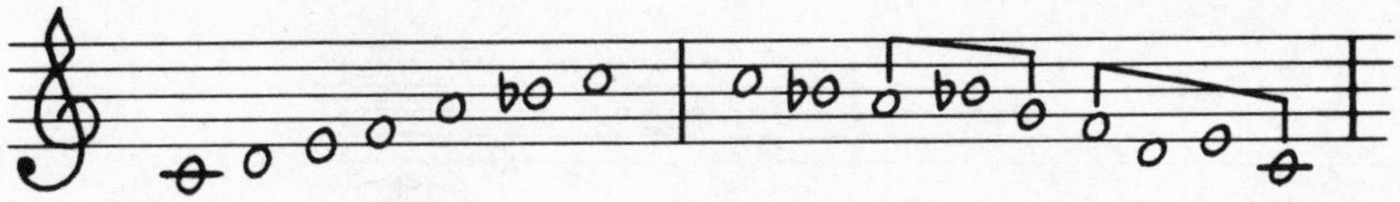

Ascent: the note *PA* (G) is avoided.
Descent: *sampūrṇa*; two *vakra* features are shown.

(99) *Indu Gauḷika*

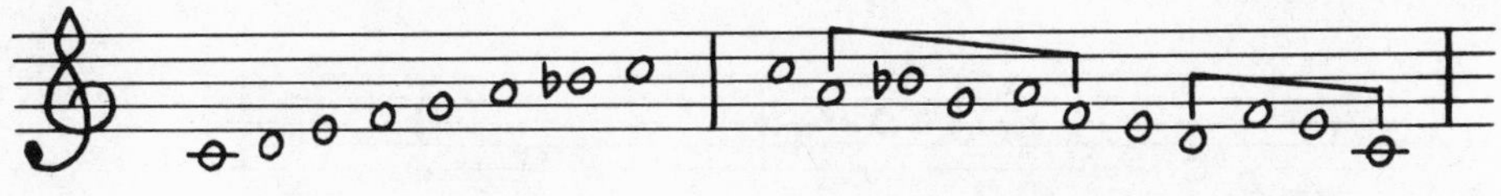

Ascent: *krama sampūrṇa*.
Descent: *sampūrṇa*; two extended *vakra* features are shown.

(100) *Janasammōdini*

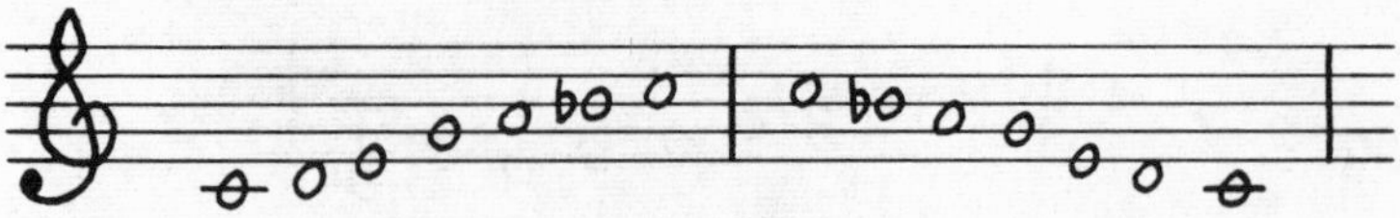

The note *MA* (F) is avoided entirely.

(101) *Jānudvaya*

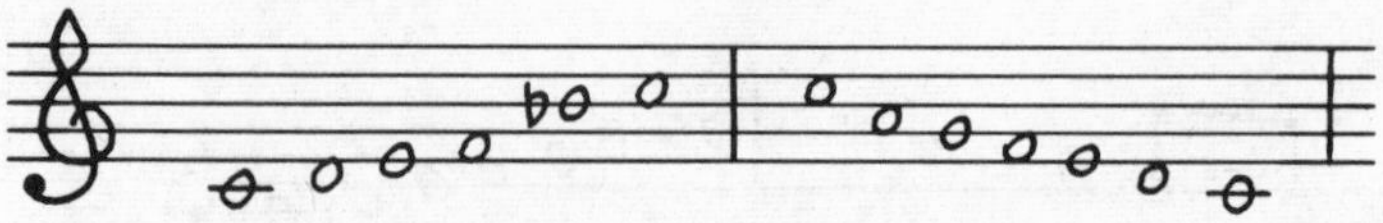

Ascent: the notes *PA* (G) and *DHA* (A) are avoided.
Descent: the note *NI* (Bb) is omitted.

(102) *Jaraśēkharam*

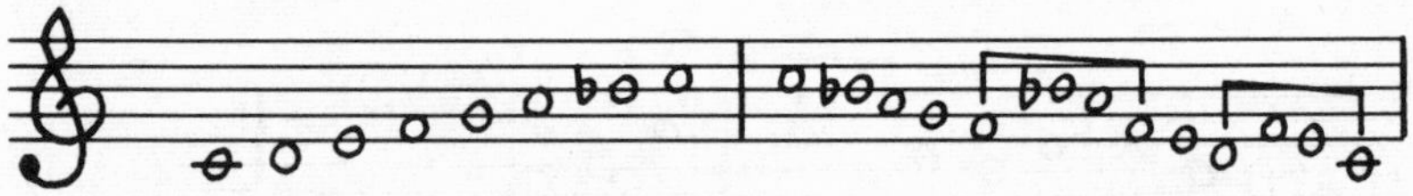

Ascent: *krama sampūrṇa*.
Descent: *sampūrṇa*; two extended *vakra* features are shown.

(103) *Jayaramā (Jayarāma)*

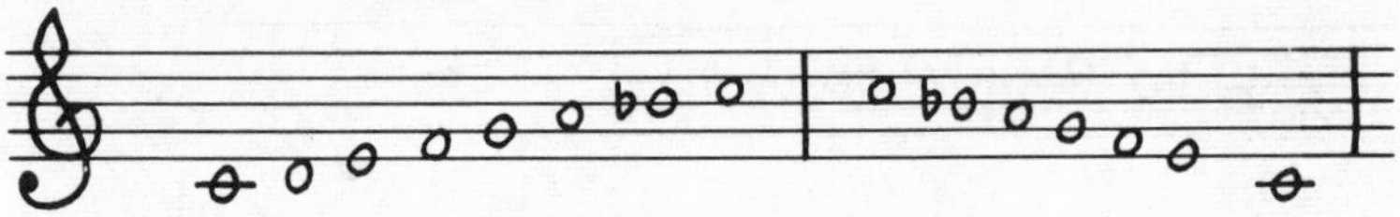

Ascent: *krama sampūrṇa*.
Descent: the note *RI* (D) is avoided.

(104) *Jogibhairavī*

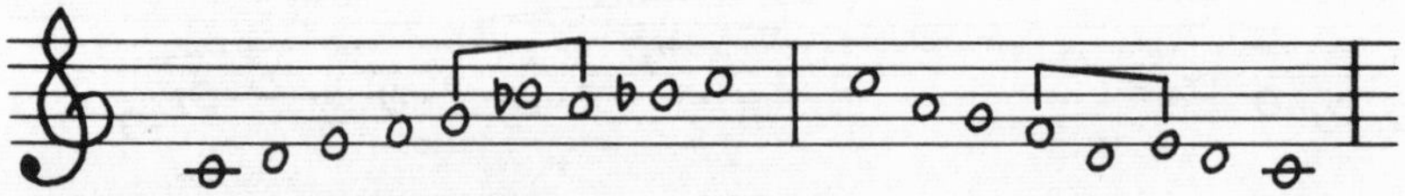

Ascent: *sampūrṇa*; one *vakra* feature is shown.
Descent: the note *NI* (Bb) is avoided; one *vakra* feature is used.

(105) *Jūṡaṅgadā*

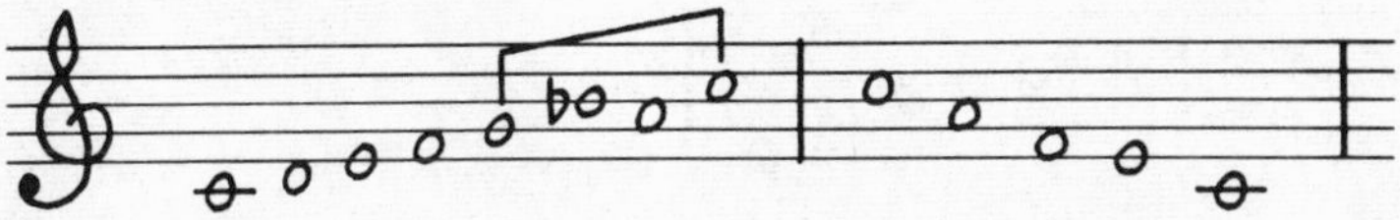

Ascent: *sampūrṇa*; one *vakra* feature is shown.
Descent: the notes *NI* (Bb), *PA* (G), and *RI* (D) are avoided.

(106) *Kalābharaṇam*

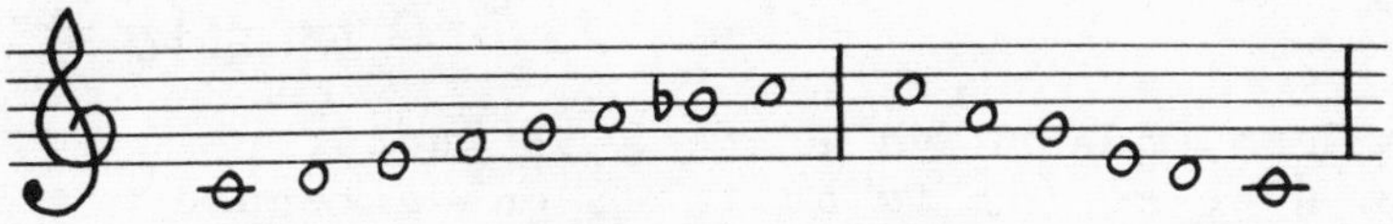

Ascent: *krama sampūrṇa*.
Descent: the notes *Nİ* (Bb) and *MA* (F) are avoided.

(107) *Kamala Mōhanam*

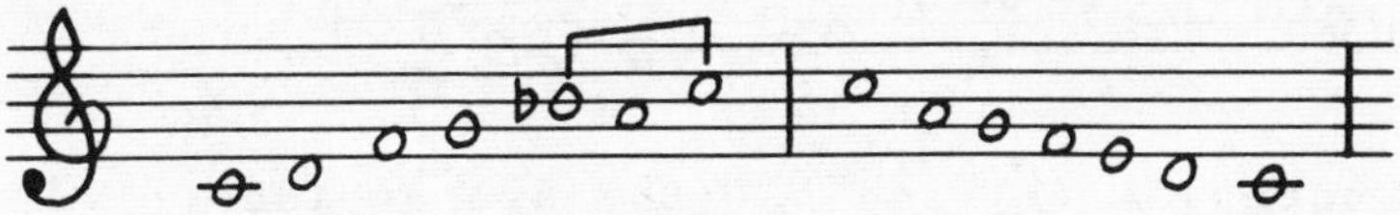

Ascent: the note *GA* (E) is avoided; one *vakra* feature is shown.
Descent: the note *NI* (Bb) is omitted.

(108) *Kammaji*

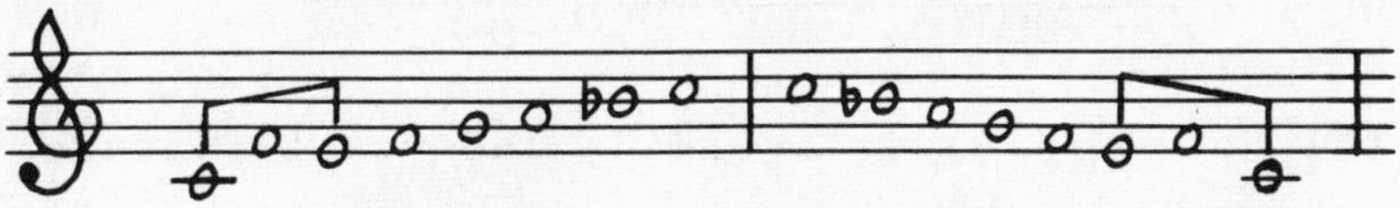

The note *RI* (D) is avoided entirely. One *vakra* feature appears in ascent and one in descent.

(109) *Kanaka Chandrikā* (*Kanaka Candrikā*)

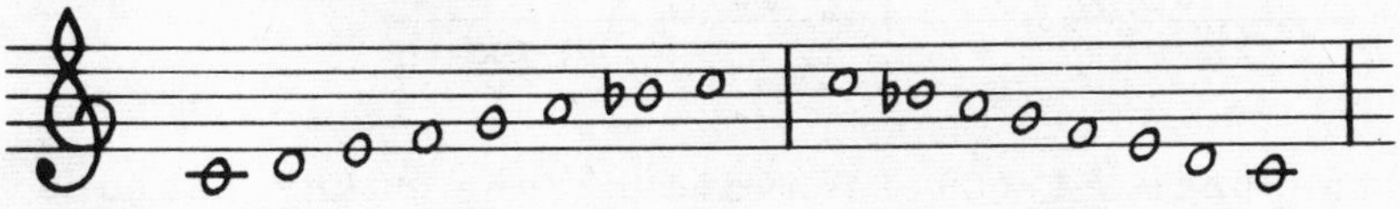

This scale, which is *krama sampūrṇa* in ascent and descent, is identical with that of the primary *rāga Hārikāmbhoji*.

(110) *Karañjakam*

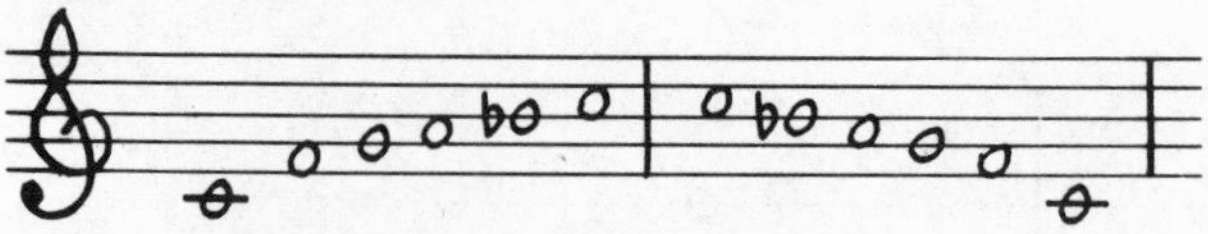

The notes *RI* (D) and *GA* (E) are avoided entirely.

(111) *Khararañjani*

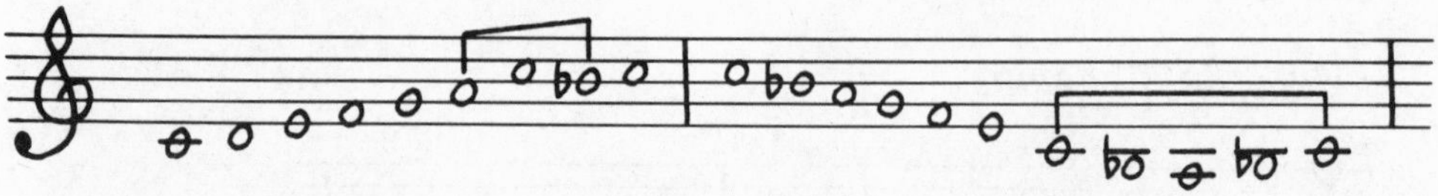

Ascent: *sampūrṇa*; one *vakra* feature is shown.
Descent: the note *RI* (D) is avoided; one extended *vakra* feature is used.

(112) *Kōkilavarāli*

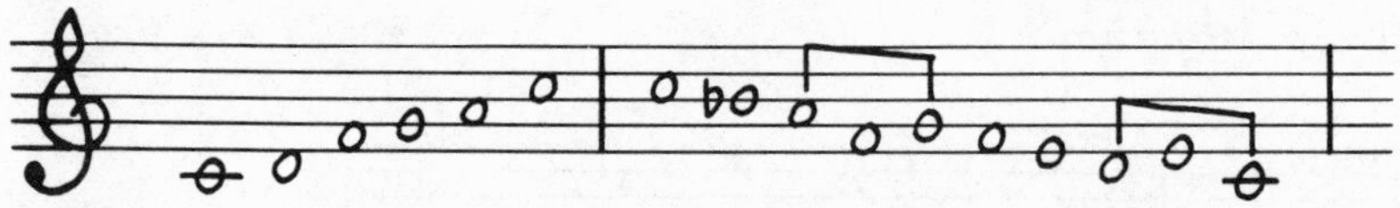

Ascent: the notes *GA* (E) and *NI* (Bb) are avoided.
Descent: *sampūrṇa*; two *vakra* features are shown.

(113) *Kulapavitri* (*Kulapavitra*)

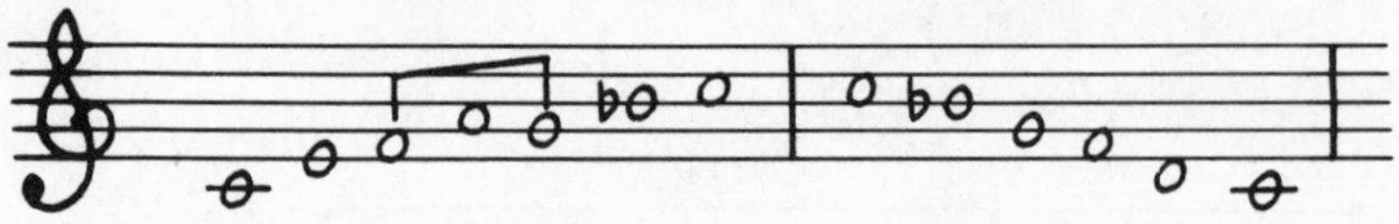

Ascent: the note *RI* (D) is avoided; one *vakra* feature is shown.
Descent: the notes *DHA* (A) and *GA* (E) are omitted.

(114) *Kumāradyuti*

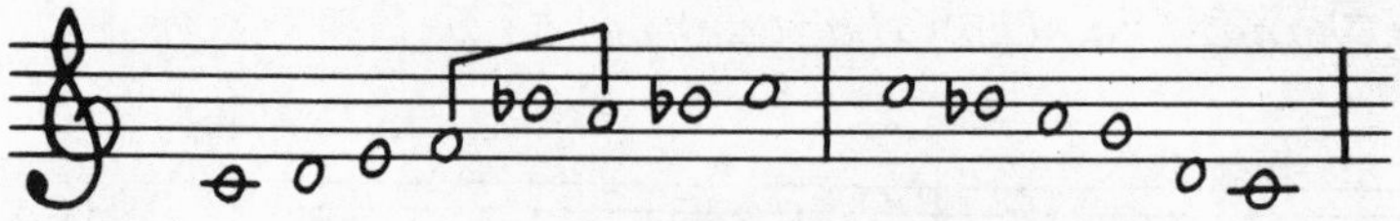

Ascent: the note *PA* (G) is avoided; one *vakra* feature is shown.
Descent: the notes *MA* (F) and *GA* (E) are omitted.

(115) *Madhurālāpa*

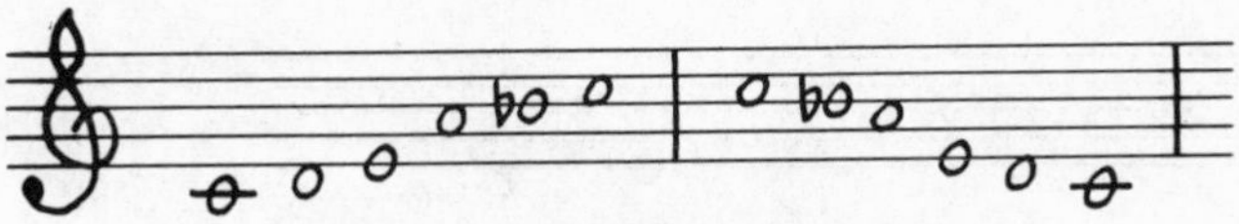

The notes *MA* (F) and *PA* (G) are avoided entirely.

(116) *Māyātaraṅgiṇi*

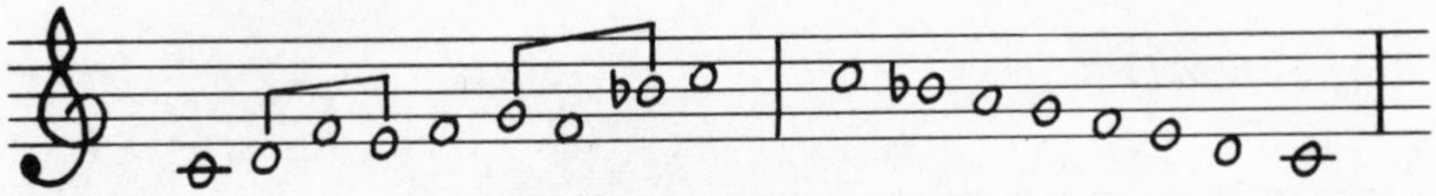

Ascent: the note *DHA* (A) is avoided; two *vakra* features are shown.
Descent: *krama sampūrṇa*.

(117) *Nartaki*

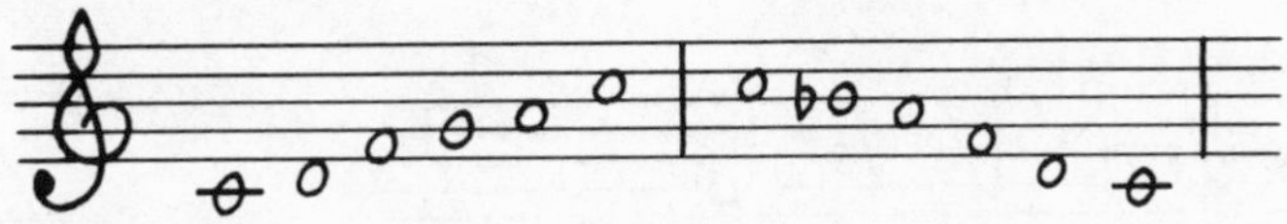

The note *GA* (E) is avoided entirely. *NI* (Bb) is omitted in ascent and *PA* (G) in descent.

(118) *Pratāpachintāmani* (*Pratāpacintāmani*)

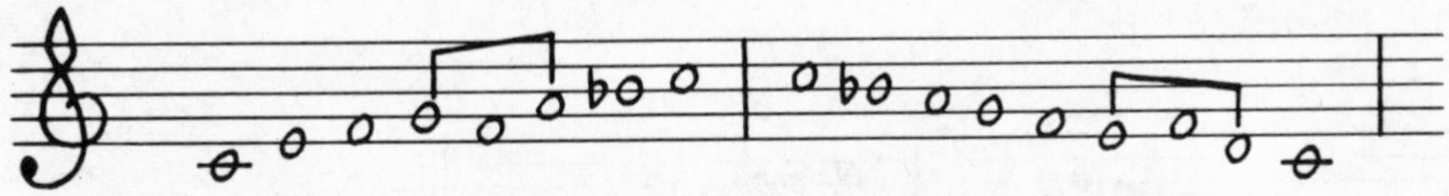

The scale of this little-known *rāga* avoids the note *RI* (D) in ascent and is *sampūrna* in descent. One *vakra* feature appears in ascent and one in descent.

(119) *Pratāpanāṭa*

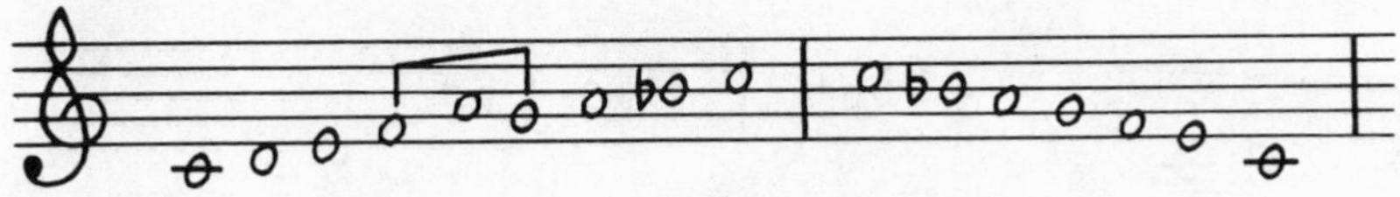

Ascent: *sampūrṇa*; one *vakra* feature is shown.
Descent: the note *RI* (D) is avoided.

(120) *Pratāparudhri*

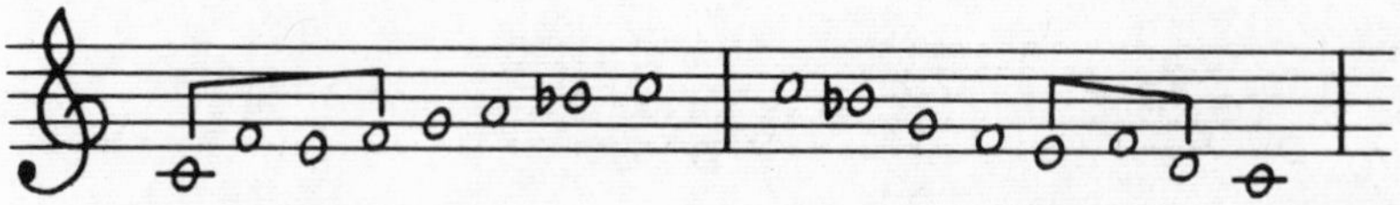

Ascent: the note *RI* (D) is avoided; one *vakra* feature is shown.
Descent: the note *DHA* (A) is omitted; one *vakra* feature is used.

(121) *Rāgavinodini*

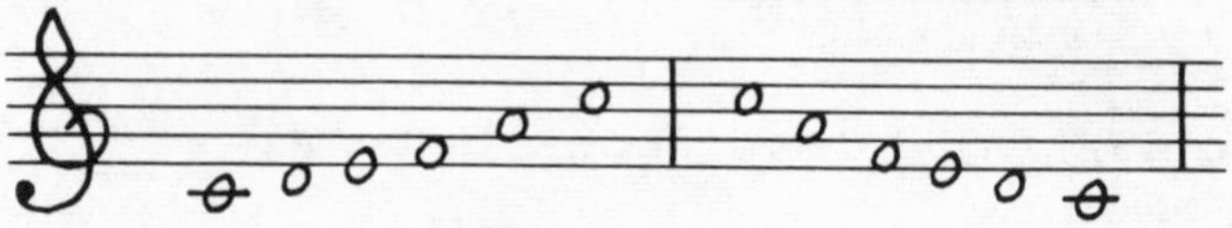

The notes *PA* (G) and *NI* (Bb) are avoided entirely.

(122) *Ratnakari*

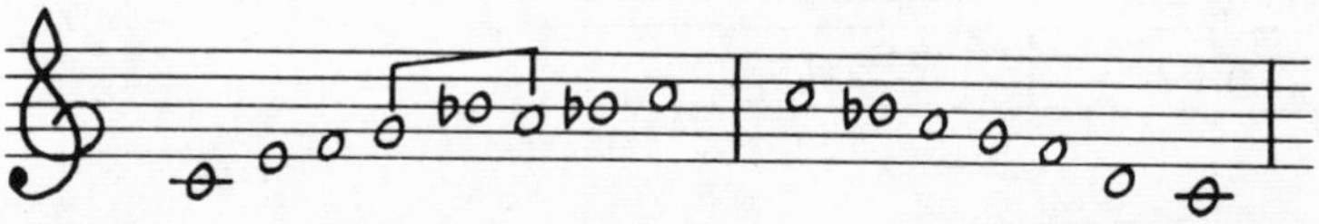

Ascent: the note *RI* (D) is avoided; one *vakra* feature is shown.
Descent: the note *GA* (E) is omitted.

(123) *Rōrañjakam*

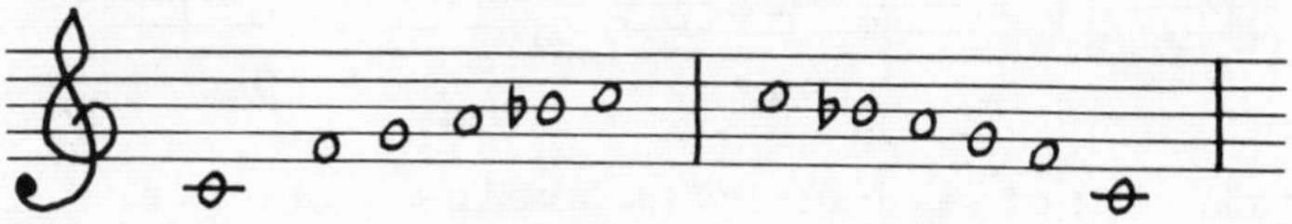

The notes *RI* (D) and *GA* (E) are avoided entirely.

(124) *Sajjukāmbhōji*

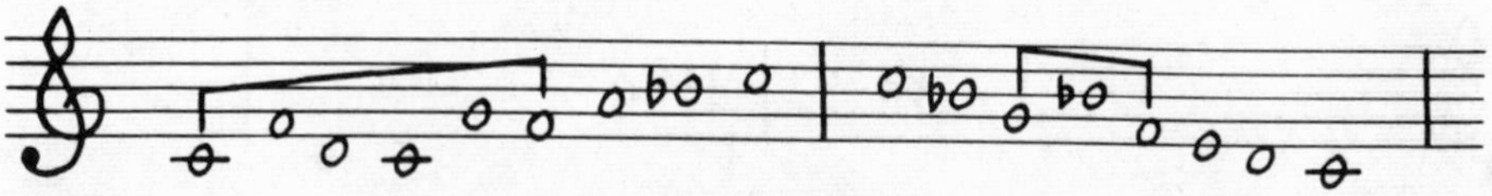

Ascent: the note *GA* (E) is omitted; one extended *vakra* feature is shown.
Descent: the note *DHA* (A) is avoided; one *vakra* feature is used.

(125) *Sāvitri*

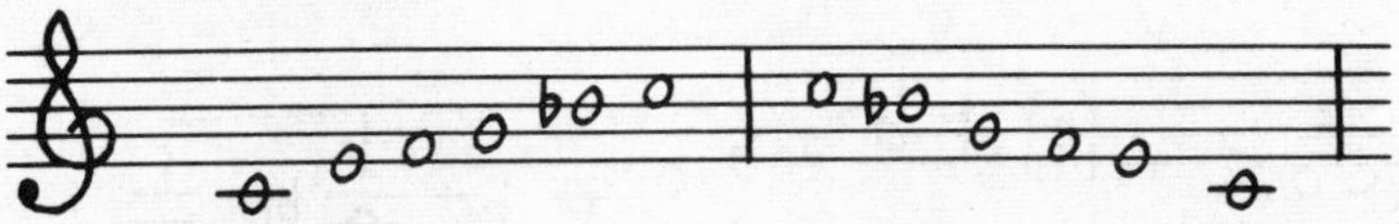

The notes *RI* (D) and *DHA* (A) are avoided entirely.

(126) *Śuddhamallār*

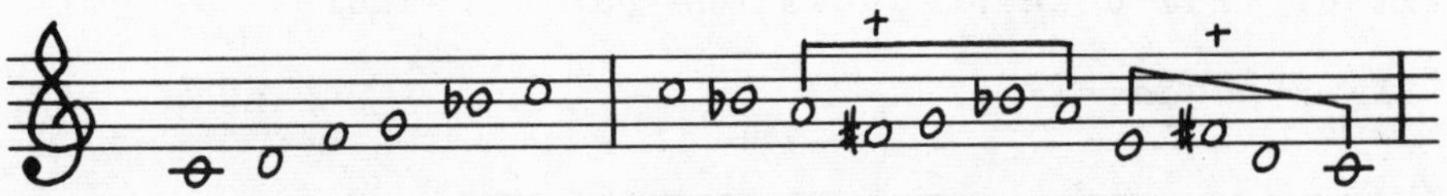

Ascent: the notes *GA* (E) and *DHA* (A) are avoided.
Descent: *sampūrṇa*; occasionally the note *MA* becomes F# in the two indicated extended *vakra* features.

(127) *Śuddhavarāli*

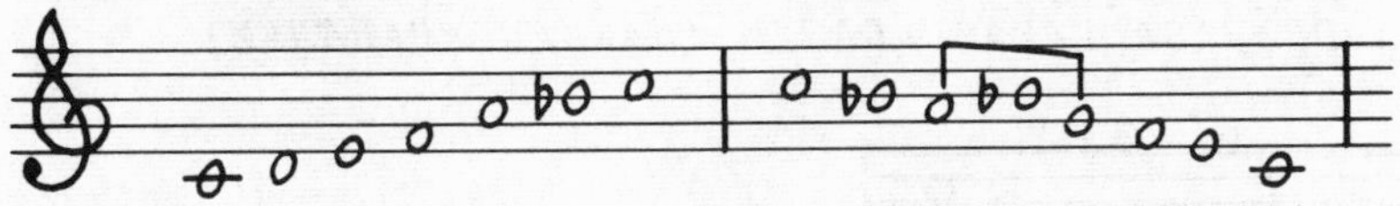

Ascent: the note *PA* (G) is avoided.
Descent: the note *RI* (D) is omitted; one *vakra* feature is shown.

(128) *Sumanapriyā*

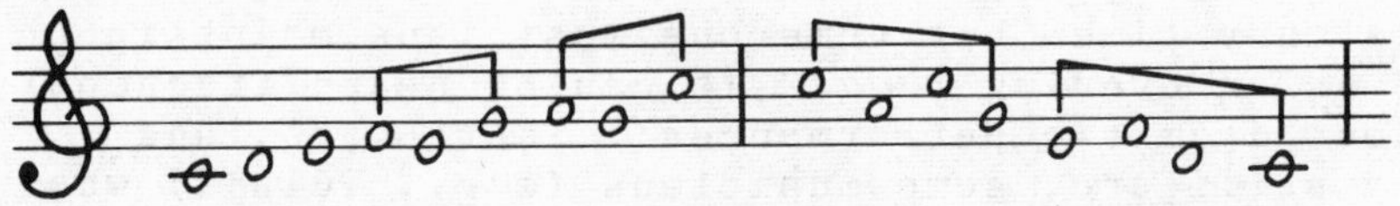

The note *NI* (Bb) is avoided entirely. Two *vakra* features appear in ascent and two in descent.

According to R (p. 223) this is a *rāga* of recent origin. It was introduced by Muthiah Bhāgavathar.

(129) *Surabhairavī*

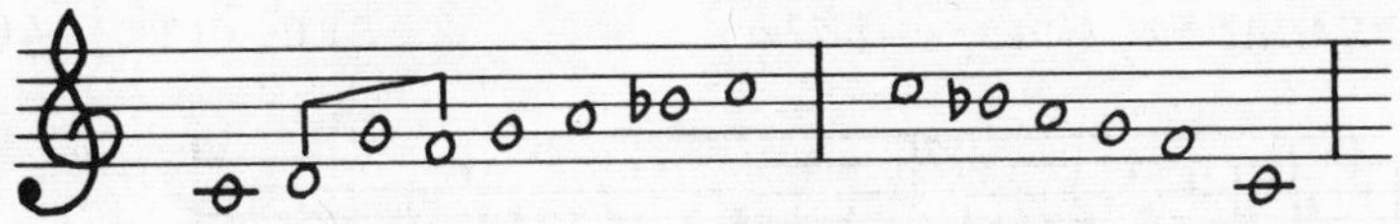

The note *GA* (E) is avoided entirely. The ascent shows one *vakra* feature. The note *RI* (D) is omitted in descent.

(130) *Vēdaghōshapriya* (*Vēdaghōṣapriya*)

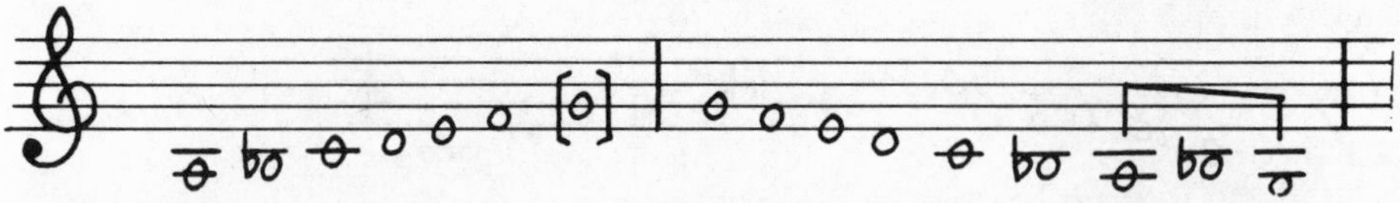

The scale of this *rāga* has *pañchamāntya* character because its highest note is *PA* (G) of the middle octave region. The descent shows one *vakra* feature.

(131) *Vīnavādini*

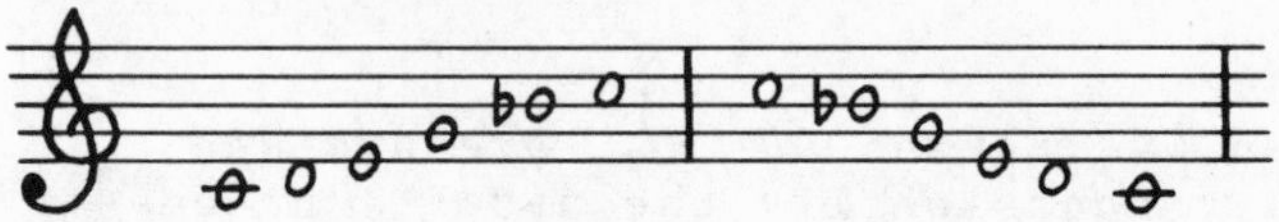

The notes *MA* (F) and *DHA* (A) are avoided entirely.

29. *MĒḶA DHĪRAŚAṄKARĀBHARAṆAM* (*ŚAṄKARĀBHARAṆAM*)

Dhīraśaṅkarābharaṇam is one of the most popular *rāgas* of the South. The prefix *Dhīra* is added to *Śaṅkarābharaṇam* in order to make it fit into the *kaṭapayādi saṅkhyā*. *Dhīraśaṅkarābharaṇam* may be performed at any time, but numerous musicians maintain that it is an evening *rāga*. It can be heard frequently at various dramatic performances. There were, and probably still are, some musicians (e.g., Tuḷajā) who make a distinction between *Dhīraśaṅkarābharaṇam* and *Śaṅkarābharaṇam*. Other, particularly contemporary musicians are of the opinion that both names represent one and the same *rāga*. While the former name represents, of course, the primary *rāga* in its *sampūrṇa* form, the latter appears now as a *janya rāga* (29,1) with *sampūrṇa* ascent and six notes in descent.

DHĪRAŚANKARĀBHARAṆAM (*Matya-tāla*) SPC, III, 40

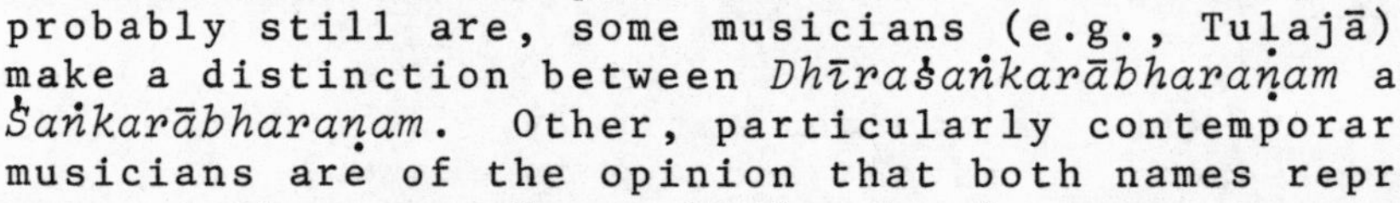

Janya Rāgas of the 29. Mēḷa

As to be expected, the very popular *mēḷa Dhīraśaṅkarābharaṇam* possesses a large number of *janya rāgas*, many subject to various changes of the intonation of the notes *RI*, *GA*, *DHA*, and *NI* (D, E, A, and B) by individual performers.

(1) *Śaṅkarābharaṇam*

As already stated, the opinions concerning the tone materials of *Dhīraśaṅkarābharaṇam* and *Śaṅkarābharaṇam* are divided. If *Śaṅkarābharaṇam* is considered to be a *janya rāga* of the 29. *mēḷa*, the following scale is in use. The *Rāga Lakṣaṇa*, the above-mentioned Tanjore manuscript referred to by R (p. 164), supports this view.

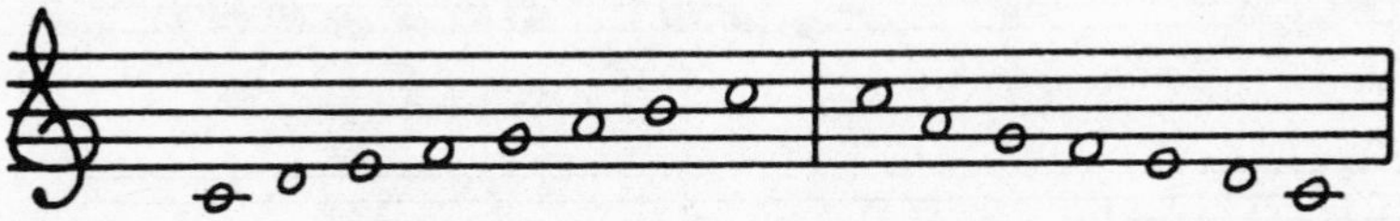

This scale is *krama sampūrṇa* in ascent and avoids the note *NI* (B) in descent. But the omission of this note is not always applied. In the following song specimen, which represents *Śaṅkarābharaṇam*, the note *NI* (B) appears in descent. This song example is set in the longest *tāla* of the South, *Siṁhanandana* which contains 128 rhythmic units in each measure and begins with an "upbeat" of 28 units (4+8+8+4+4). In the following transcription each unit is represented by an eighth note:

ŚAṄKARĀBHARAṆAM (*Siṁhanandana-tāla*) SPC, III, 37

(2) *Āhirinaṭa*

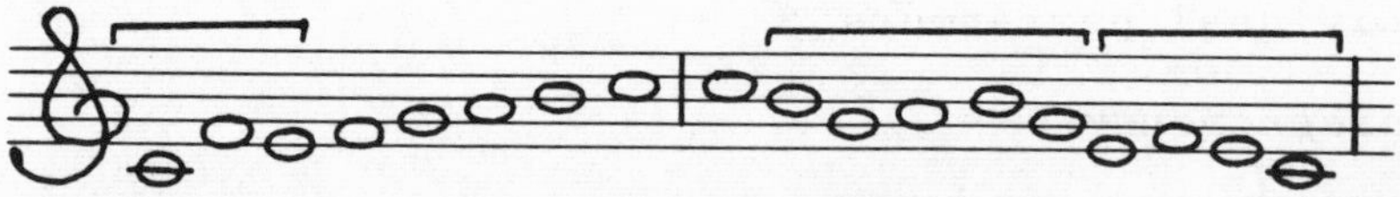

The note *RI* (D) is avoided entirely. The ascent shows one, the descent two *vakra* features.

ĀHIRINĀṬA (*Triputa-tāla*) SCM, 168

(3) *Amritalahari*

Ascent: the note *DHA* (A) is avoided and one *vakra* feature is shown.
Descent: *krama sampūrṇa.*

Another *rāga* with the same name appears under the heading of the 46. *mēḷa* (1).

(4) *Ānanda Laharī*

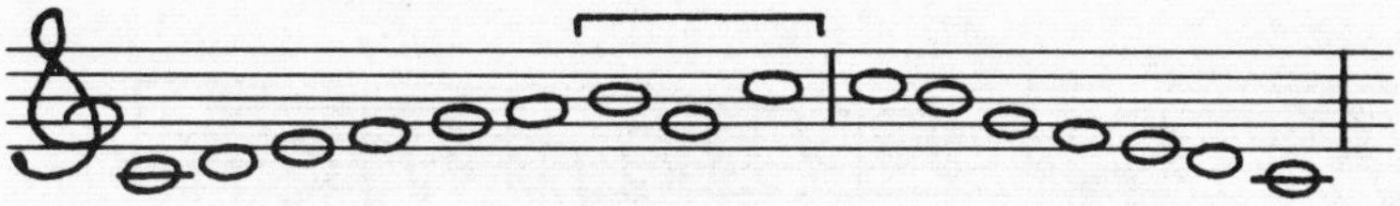

Ascent: *sampūrṇa*; one *vakra* feature is shown.
Descent: the note *DHA* (A) is avoided.

(5) *Ānandamukhi*

Ascent: the note *RI* (D) is avoided; two *vakra* features are shown.
Descent: *krama sampūrṇa.*

(6) *Antar Vāhini (Antara Vāhini)*

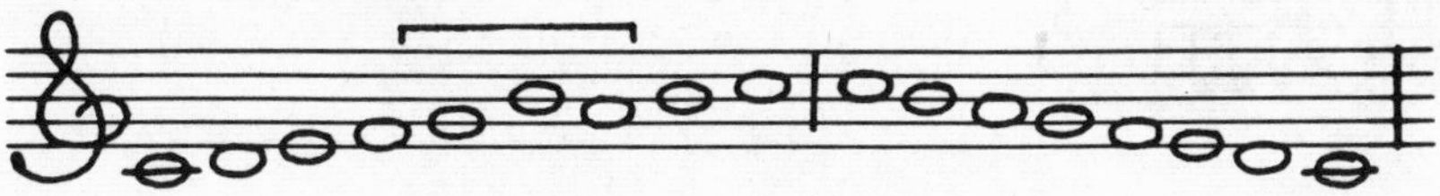

Ascent: *sampūrṇa*; one *vakra* feature is shown.
Descent: *krama sampūrṇa.*

(7) *Ārabhī*

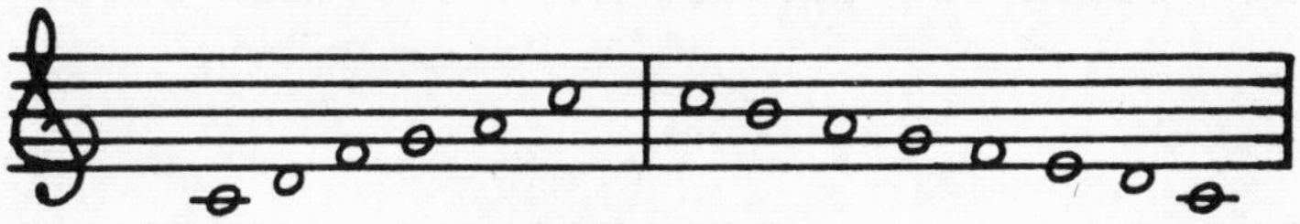

Ascent: the notes *GA* (E) and *NI* (B) are avoided.
Descent: *krama sampūrṇa.*

Ārabhī can be performed at any time. Its stressed notes are *RI* (D), *MA* (F), and *DHA* (A). *RI* (D) was supposed to be the *amśa*, which at the present time is more or less ignored. Weak notes of this *rāga* are *NI* (B) and *GA* (E) in descent.

The following song example comes from a palm-leaf manuscript. Neither date, author, nor place of preservation is given.

ĀRABHĪ RĀGA (*Triputa-tāla*) SPC, II, 40

The several passages shown below come from a *Gīta Govinda* performance, recorded by Wayne Howard in Kerala in 1972. In these passages the notes *NI* (B) and *GA* (E) are also avoided in descent. Furthermore the melody does not begin with the important notes *RI* (D), *MA* (F), and *DHA* (A), as stated before, but with the weak note *PA* (G).

In the Kerala performance the note *DHA* is often intoned low, and instead of the pitch A, Ab can be observed. Similarly, the note *MA* is occasionally lowered from F to E.

These are liberties which an orthodox musician would reject, yet they do occur and have to be reported.

(8) *Asambāda*

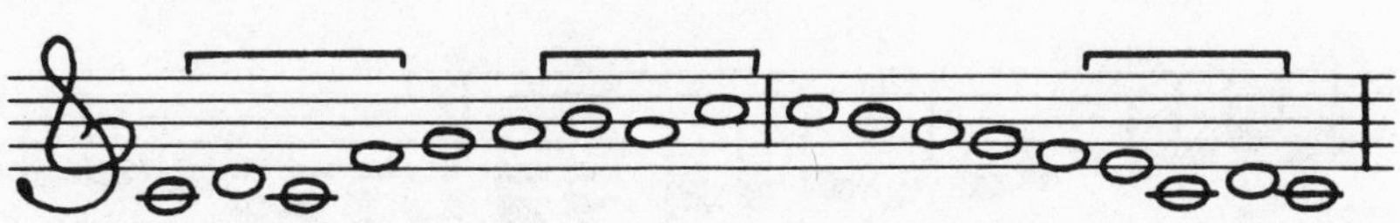

Ascent: the note *GA* (E) is avoided; two *vakra* features are shown.
Descent: *sampūrṇa*; one *vakra* feature is used.

(9) *Aṭhāṇā*

Ascent: the notes *GA* (E) and *DHA* (A) are avoided.
Descent: *sampūrṇa*; one *vakra* feature can be used.

According to SD (I, 31) the note *GA* can be interpreted as Eb occasionally in the following phrases:

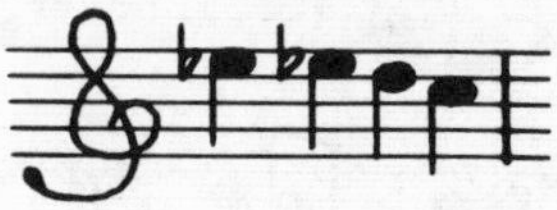

The note *NI*, too, can be interpreted as Bb in the following passages:

Passages such as *GA-MA-PA* (Eb-F-G) and *PA-DHA-NI* (G-A-Bb) are unlikely to occur, because the correct ascent does not use *GA* (E, or here Eb) or *DHA* (A). It can be assumed that the two foreign notes (Eb and Bb) are merely liberties taken by performers in very popular *rāgas*.

Aṭhāṇā can be performed at any time.

AṬHĀṆĀ (*Triputa-tāla*) SCM, 177

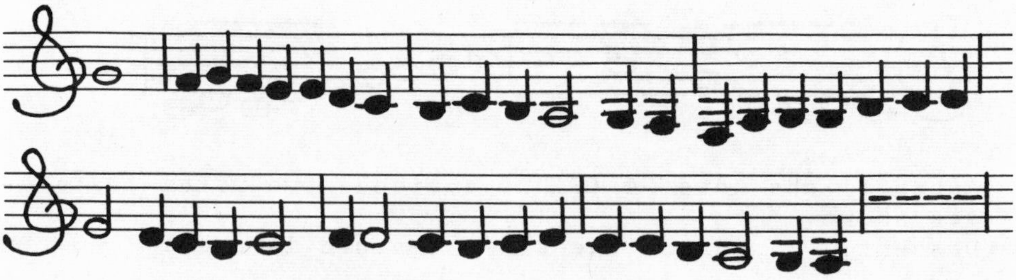

(10) *Baṅgāḷa*

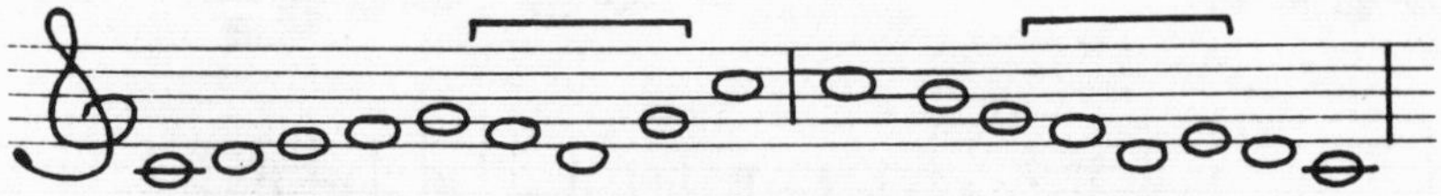

The note *DHA* (A) is avoided entirely. In ascent *NI* (B) is avoided; one *vakra* feature is shown. In descent one *vakra* feature is used. The notes *PA* (G) and *RI* (D) are stressed. *Baṅgāḷa* can be performed at any time.

When comparing this *rāga* with *Baṅgāḷa* of the 28. *mēḷa* (54) the difference of the two ascents can be noticed. The descent of the two *Baṅgāḷa* types is practically the same.

(11) *Bēgaḍa* (*Byāgaḍa*)

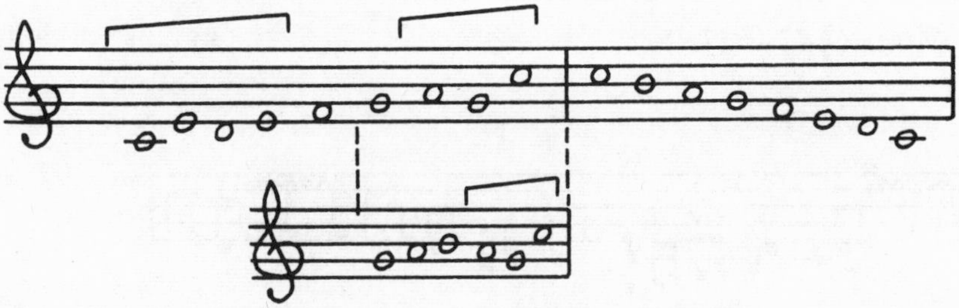

The ascent of *Bēgaḍa* can be performed in two ways: either without or with the note *NI* (B). In both forms of the ascent appear the two indicated *vakra* features showing the interval of a rising fourth from *PA* (G) to *SA* (c). The descent is *krama sampūrṇa*.

The SD (I, 40) states that "in the phrases *DHA-PA-MA* [A-G-F] and *PA-DHA-NI-DHA-PA* [G-A-B-A-G] a slightly sharpened form of *śuddha madhyama* [F] and a slightly flattened form of the *kākali nishada* [B] are used."

Songs in this *rāga* usually begin with one of the following notes: *GA* (E), *MA* (F), *DHA* (A), or *NI* (B).

BĒGAḌA (Triputa-tāla) SCM, 182-83

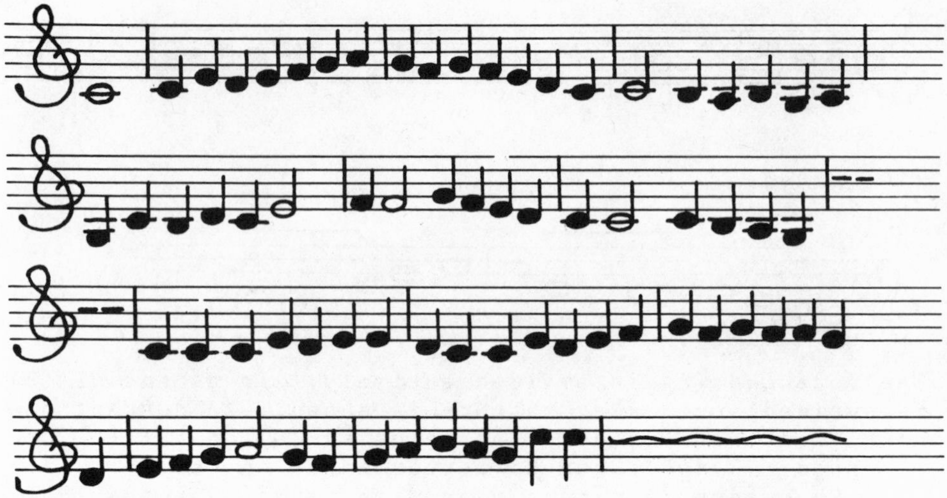

The following song example, composed by Vinai Kuppaiyer (1850- ?) shows *Bēgaḍa* with the prescribed ascending step *PA-SA* (G-c) in measures 1, 4, and 11, but shows also the "modern" straight-rising progression *DHA-NI-SA* (A-B-c) in measures 4 and 12.

BĒGAḌA RĀGA (Ādi-tāla) SPC III, 58

Pallavi

Anupallavi

(12) *Behāg* (*Byāg*, *Byāgu*, *Hindusthāni Behāg*)

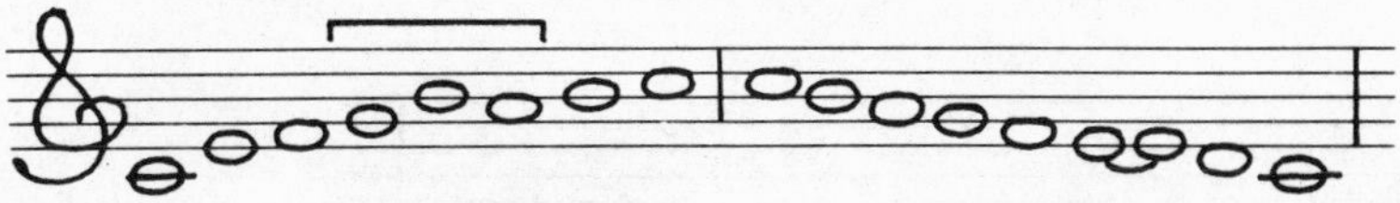

Ascent: the note *RI* (D) is avoided. *DHA* (A) appears only in the indicated *vakra* feature (*PA-NI-DHA* [G-B-A]).
Descent: *krama sampūrṇa*.

The middle note of the passage *PA-MA-PA* (G-F-G), also of the passage *GA-MA-GA* (E-F-E), is often raised to F#. In *PA-MA-MA-GA* (G-F-F-E), for instance, the first *MA* is often interpreted as F# while the second *MA* remains F natural. The note *NI* (B) is often taken flat and becomes Bb in descent. The notes *GA* (E) and *PA* (G) are stressed and appear frequently.

Songs in this *rāga* generally begin with one of the following notes: *SA* (C), *GA* (E), *PA* (G), or *NI* (B).

BYĀGU [*BEHĀG*] (*Triputa-tāla*) SCM, 172-73

(13) *Bhadragāndhāri*

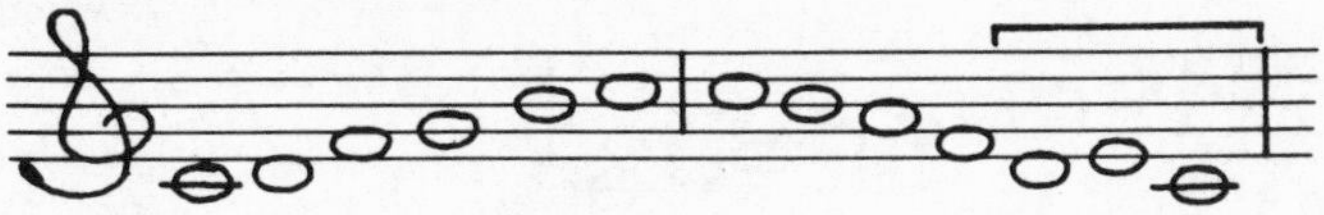

Ascent: the notes *GA* (E) and *DHA* (A) are avoided.
Descent: the note *PA* (G) is omitted; one *vakra* passage is shown.

(14) *Bhānuta*

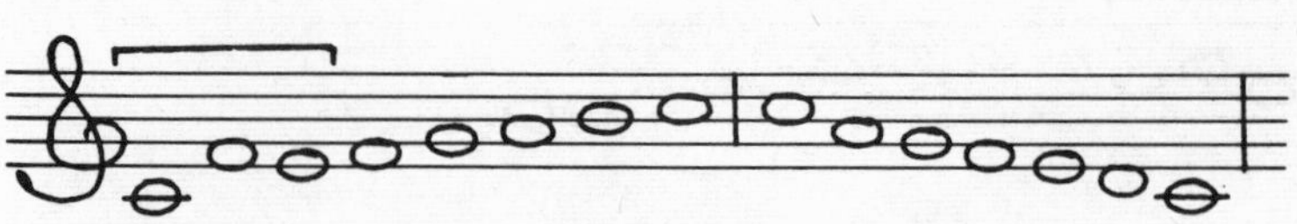

Ascent: the note *RI* (D) is avoided; one *vakra* feature is shown.
Descent: the note *NI* (B) is omitted.

(15) *Bhavā Bharaṇam*

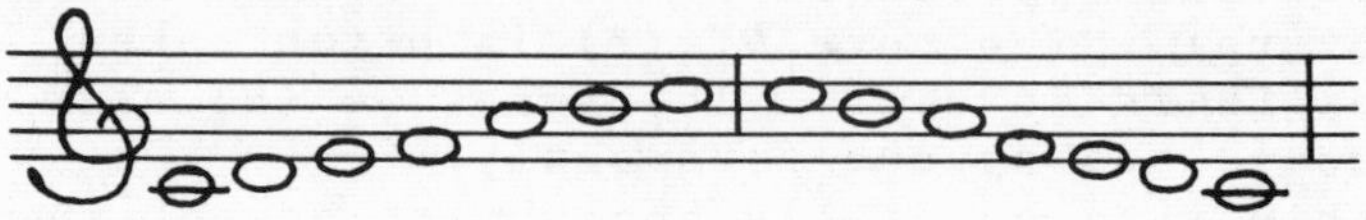

The note *PA* (G) is avoided entirely.

(16) *Bhinna Vikrama*

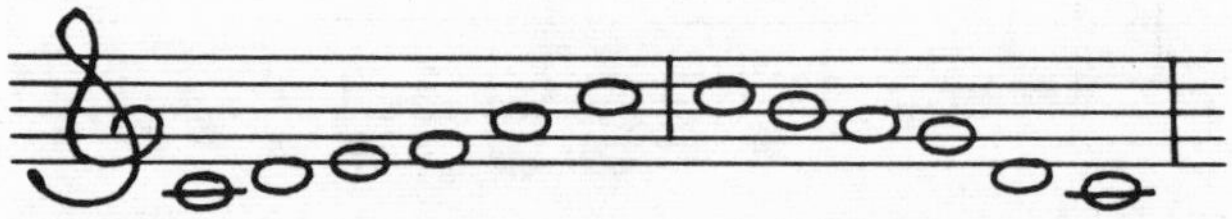

Ascent: the notes *PA* (G) and *NI* (B) are avoided.
Descent: the notes *MA* (F) and *GA* (E) are omitted.

(17) *Bhūpkalyāṇ*

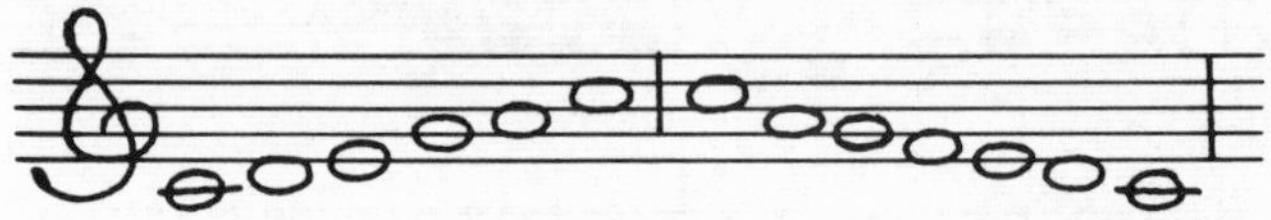

The note *NI* (B) is avoided entirely. *MA* (F) is omitted in ascent.

(18) *Bhuvana Sundari*

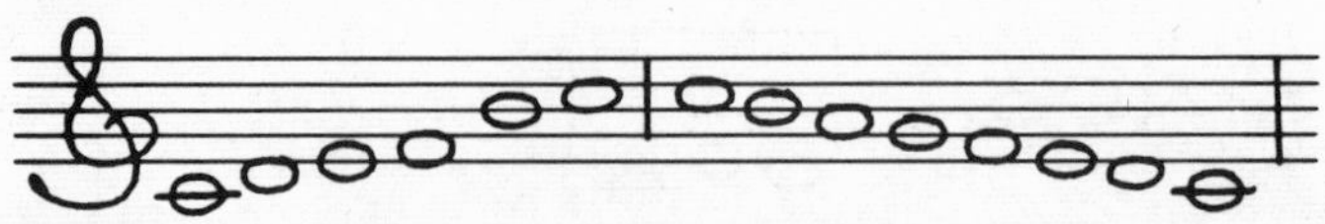

Ascent: the notes *PA* (G) and *DHA* (A) are avoided.
Descent: *krama sampūrṇa*.

(19) *Bilaharī* (*Bilahurī*, *Balaharī*)

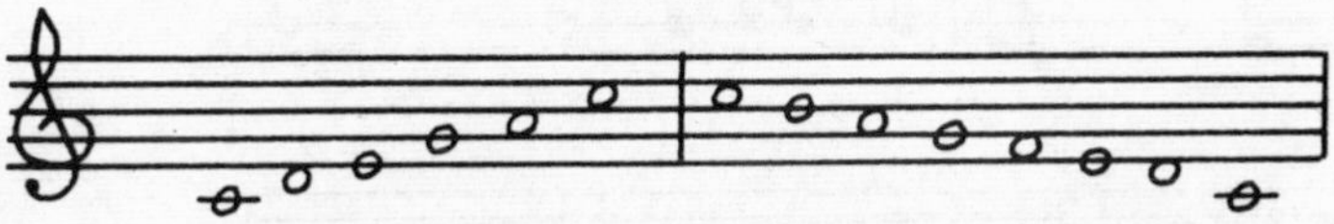

Ascent: the notes *MA* (F) and *NI* (B) are avoided.
Descent: *krama sampūrṇa*.

In descending motion the note *NI* can be taken slightly flat. This change has been described by musicians as "*NI* (B) lowered by only one *śruti*;" in common practice *NI* is usually intoned as low as Bb.

Bilaharī is to be performed in the morning, but this rule has lost its significance. At the present time this *rāga*, representing and possessing a joyful *rasa*, can be heard at other times of the day as well. The notes *DHA* (A) and *NI* (B) are supposed to be stressed, particularly in descent.

Veṅkaṭamakhin called this *rāga Bilahurī*, in which the note *NI* (B) may be employed in ascent and *MA* (F) may appear in a *vakra* feature.

There is a *janya rāga* of the 29. *mēḷa* (49), called *Garudadhvani* (see below), in which the descent utilizes the notes of the ascent of *Bilaharī* and the ascent of *Garudadhvani* employs the notes of *Bilaharī*.

BILAHARĪ RĀGA (*Ādi-tāla*) SPC II, 51-52

Pallavi

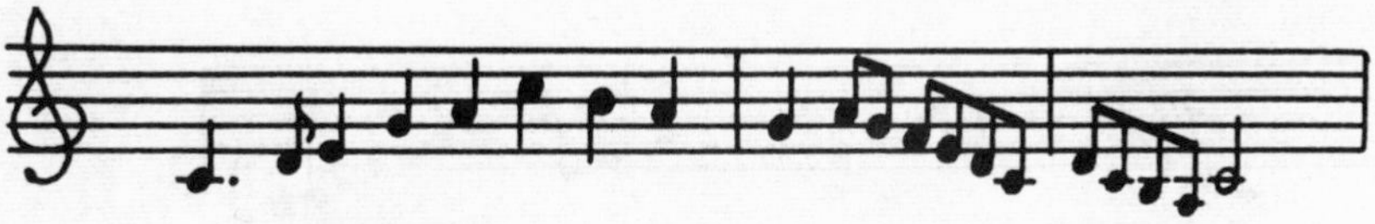

Anupallavi

Charana

BILAHARĪ (*Triputa-tāla*) SCM, 179-80

(20) *Bīṭāl*

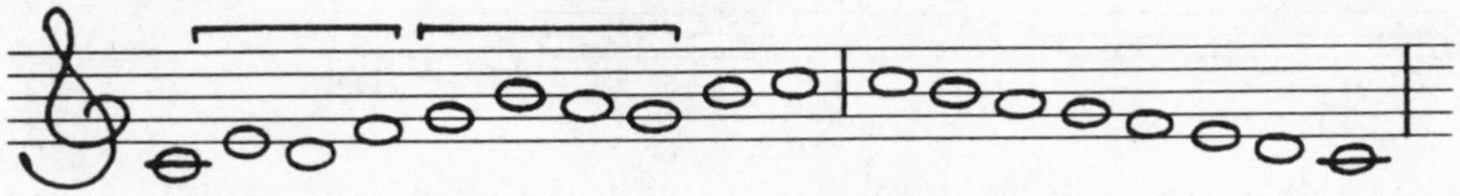

Ascent: *sampūrṇa*; two *vakra* features are shown.
Descent: *krama sampūrṇa*.

(21) *Budhamanōharī*

The notes *DHA* (A) and *NI* (B) are avoided entirely. The ascent shows one *vakra* feature.

Another *Budhamanōharī* which avoids the note *RI* (D) in ascent is listed under the heading of the 28. *mēḷa* (9).

(22) *Byāg*

This name stands for *Behāg* and may indicate *Hindusthāni* or *Karnāṭaka Behāg*. As shown (29,12 and 28,17) the two *rāgas* differ and the sole use of the name *Byāg*, although frequently employed, does not clearly indicate which of the two *rāgas* is meant.

(23) *Chandra Chūḍa (Candra Cūḍa)*

The note *RI* (D) is avoided entirely.

(24) *Chandrakauśika (Candrakauśika)*

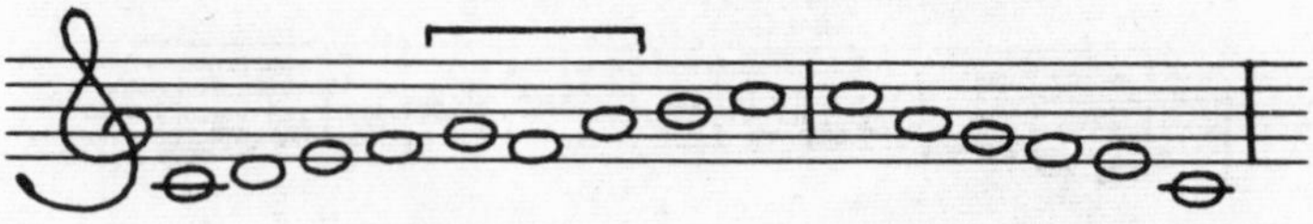

Ascent: *sampūrṇa*; one *vakra* feature is shown.
Descent: the notes *NI* (B) and *RI* (D) are avoided.

(25) *Chandravadana (Candravadana)*

Ascent: the note *DHA* (A) is avoided; one *vakra* feature is shown.
Descent: *krama sampūrṇa*.

(26) *Charavibhāsini (Caravibhāsini)*

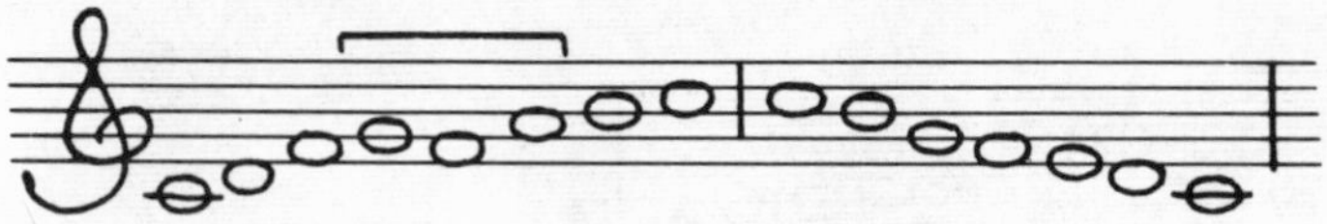

Ascent: the note *GA* (E) is avoided; one *vakra* feature is shown.
Descent: the note *DHA* (A) is omitted.

(27) *Chaturambhā (Caturambhā)*

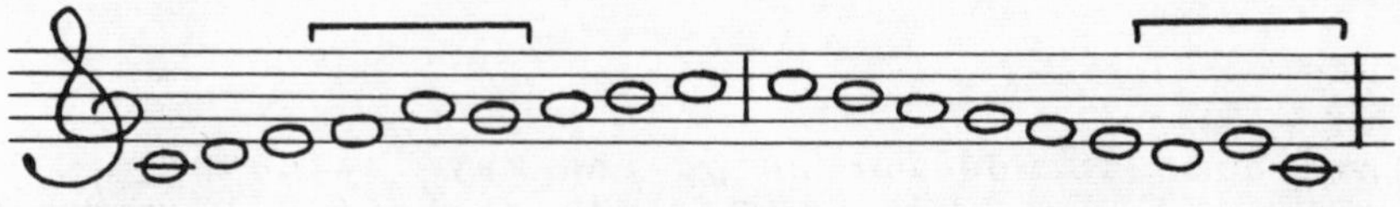

The scale is *sampūrṇa* in ascent and descent; each shows one *vakra* feature.

(28) *Chhāyā Rudra* (*Chāyā Rudra*)

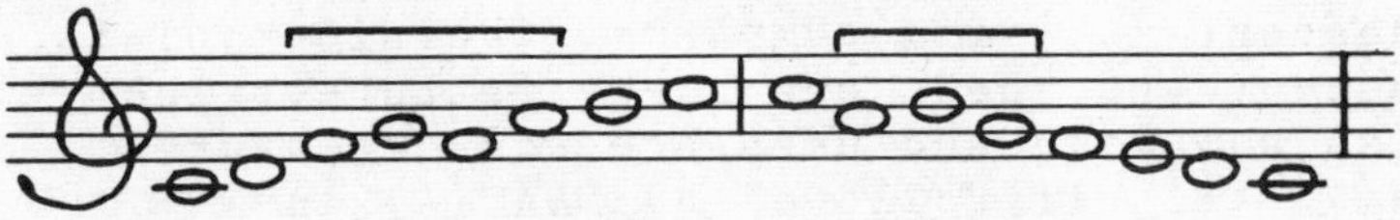

Ascent: the note *GA* (E) is avoided; one *vakra* feature is shown.
Descent: *sampūrṇa*; one *vakra* feature is used.

(29) *Chūḍāmaṇi* (*Cūḍāmaṇi*)

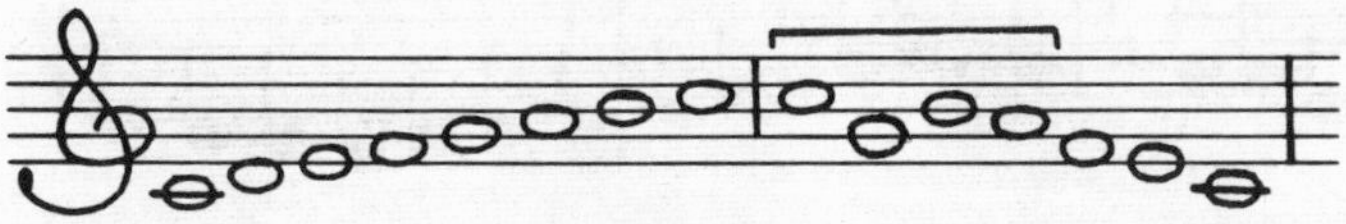

Ascent: *krama sampūrṇa*.
Descent: the note *RI* (D) is avoided; one *vakra* passage is shown.

(30) *Dākshāyaṇi* (*Dākṣāyaṇi*)

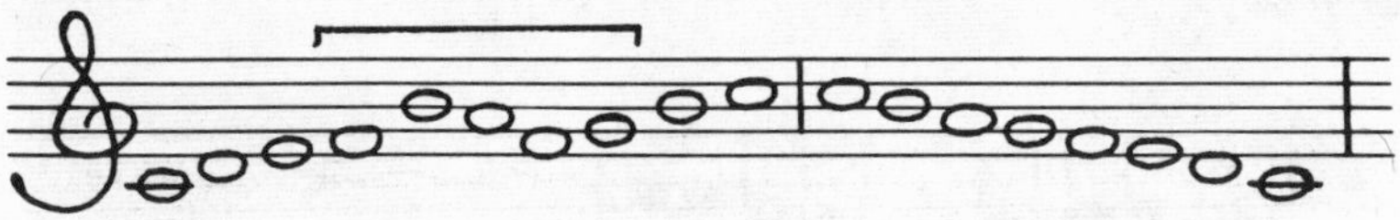

Ascent: *sampūrṇa*; one *vakra* passage is shown.
Descent: *krama sampūrṇa*.

Another *rāga* with the same name is listed under the heading of the 15. *mēḷa* (52).

(31) *Dēśakshi* (*Dēśakṣi*)

For the description of this *rāga* see *Dēśakshi* under the heading of the 28. *mēḷa* (11).

(32) *Dēvagāndhāri*

There are two versions of the *Dēvagāndhāri* scale. Version (a) avoids the notes *GA* (E) and *NI* (B) in ascent; its descent is *krama sampūrṇa*. Version (b) is *sampūrṇa* in ascent and shows one *vakra* feature. The descent is also *sampūrṇa* and uses one *vakra* feature.

The note *NI* (B), if followed by *DHA* (A) in descent, can be interpreted as Bb.

The following melody pattern shows the (b) ascent and the (a) descent:

DĒVAGĀNDHĀRI (*Triputa-tāla*) SCM, 174-75

(33) *Dharaṇi Manōharī*

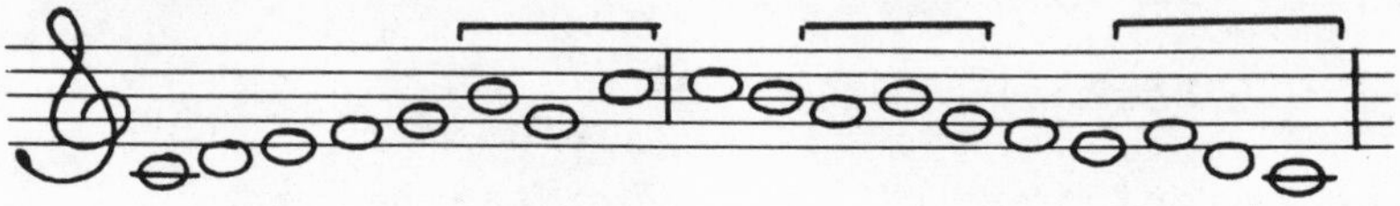

Ascent: the note *DHA* (A) is avoided; one *vakra* feature is shown.
Descent: *sampūrṇa*; two *vakra* features are used.

(34) *Dhīramati*

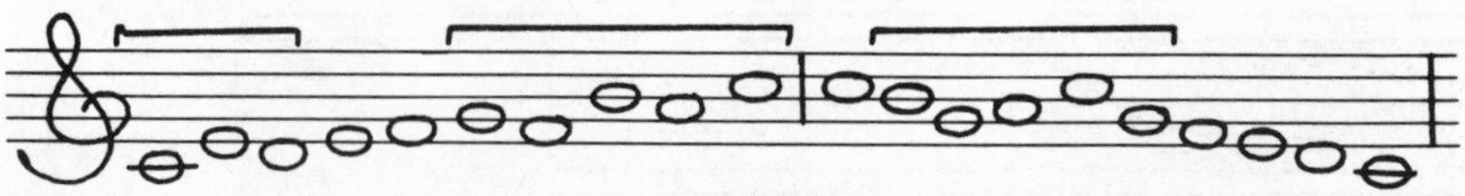

Ascent: *sampūrṇa*; two *vakra* features are shown.
Descent: *sampūrṇa*; one extended *vakra* feature is used.

Another *rāga* with the same name is listed under the heading of the 13. *mēḷa* (7).

(35) *Dhruti Vardhani (Druta Vardhanam)*

Ascent: the notes *RI* (D) and *NI* (B) are avoided.
Descent: *sampūrṇa*; one *vakra* feature is shown.

(36) *Dhūrvāṅki*

Ascent: the notes *GA* (E) and *NI* (B) are avoided.
Descent: *sampūrṇa*; one *vakra* feature is shown.

(37) *Dhvajōnnatam*

Ascent: the note *PA* (G) is avoided.
Descent: the notes *NI* (B) and *DHA* (A) are omitted.

(38) *Dhvaujeṅkaram*

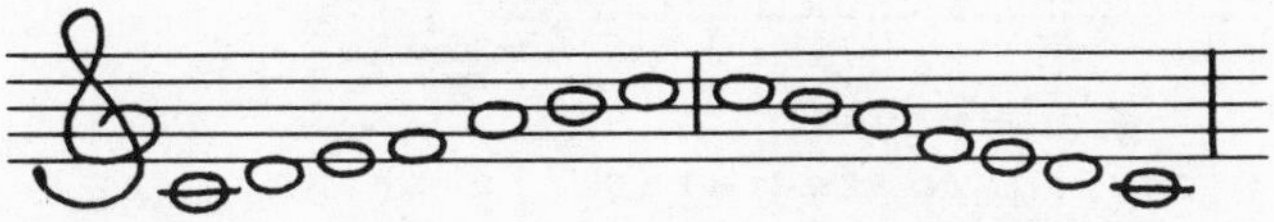

The note *PA* (G) is avoided entirely.

(39) *Dūrvāhi*

Ascent: the notes *GA* (E) and *NI* (B) are avoided.
Descent: *sampūrṇa*; one *vakra* feature is shown.

(40) *Ēlaprabhāvam*

Ascent: *sampūrṇa*; one *vakra* feature is shown.
Descent: *sampūrṇa*; one *vakra* feature is used.

(41) *Gaganāmbari*

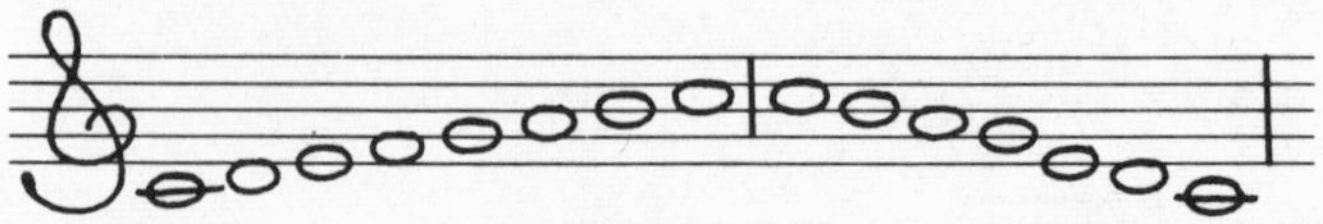

Ascent: *krama sampūrṇa*.
Descent: the note *MA* (F) is avoided.

(42) *Gaja Vardhanam* (*Gaja Vardhani*)

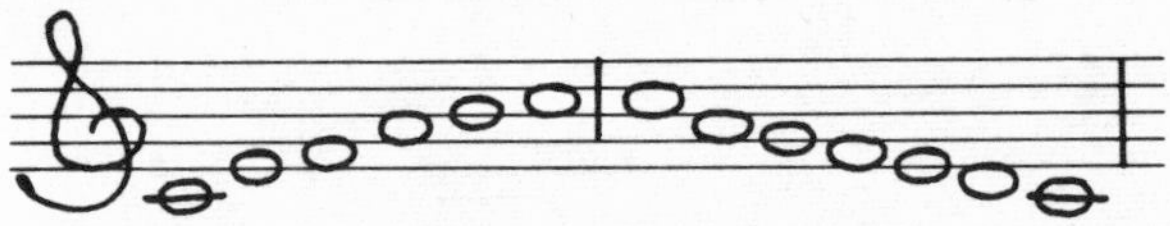

Ascent: the notes *RI* (D) and *PA* (G) are avoided.
Descent: the note *NI* (B) is omitted.

(43) *Gaja Vilaśita*

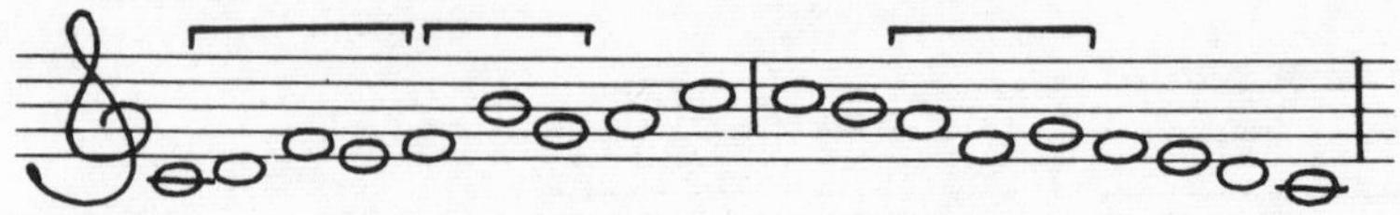

Ascent: *sampūrṇa*; two *vakra* features are shown.
Descent: *sampūrṇa*; one *vakra* feature is used.

(44) *Gamana Bhāskara(m)*

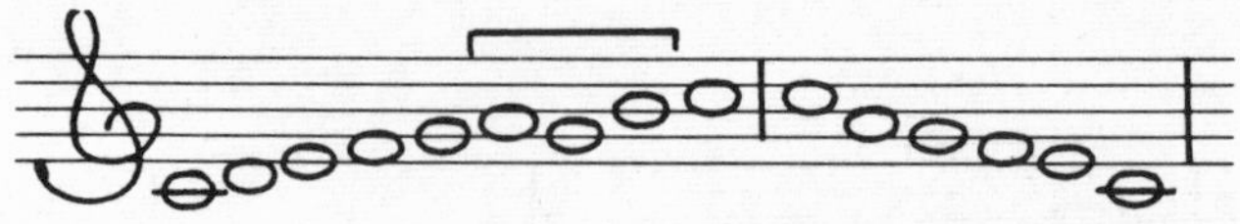

Ascent: *sampūrṇa*; one *vakra* feature is shown.
Descent: the notes *NI* (B) and *RI* (D) are avoided.

(45) *Gāna Lōlam*

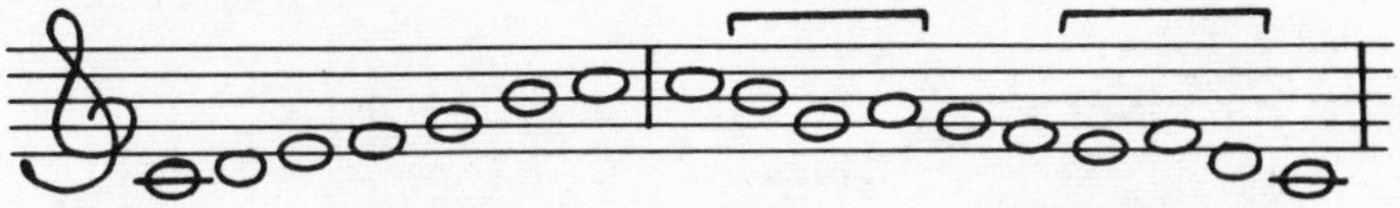

Ascent: the note *DHA* (A) is avoided.
Descent: *sampūrṇa*; two *vakra* features are shown.

(46) *Ganda Taraṅgiṇi*

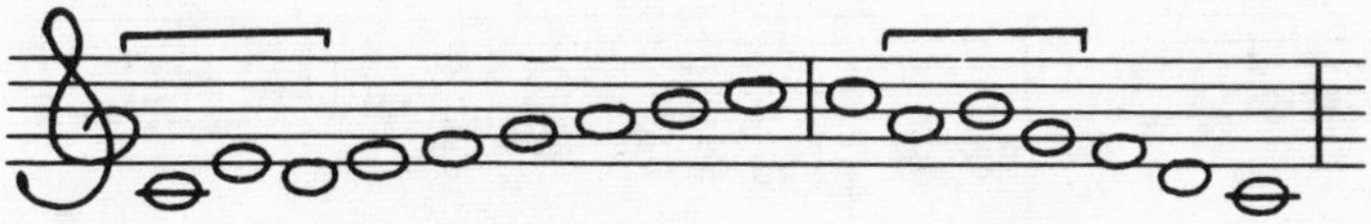

Ascent: *sampūrṇa*; one *vakra* feature is shown.
Descent: the note *GA* (E) is avoided; one *vakra* feature is shown.

(47) *Garuḍadhvani*

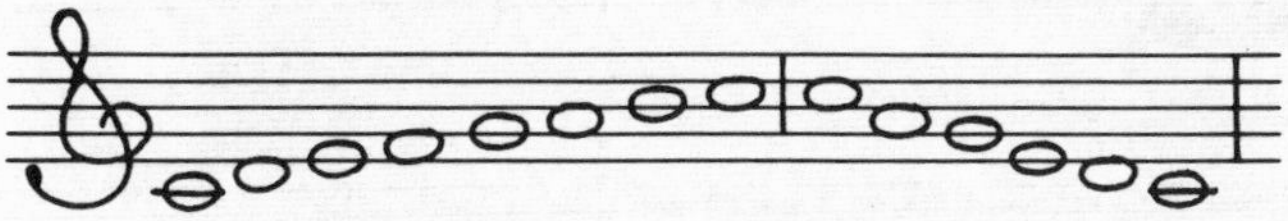

Ascent: *krama sampūrṇa*.
Descent: the notes *NI* (B) and *MA* (F) are avoided.

In its popular form, *Garuḍadhvani* shows several features that display deviations from the given scale. The ascent is not in all performances *sampūrṇa*. There are instances when the notes *RI* (D), *DHA* (A), and *NI* (B) are scarcely, or not at all, used and when the note *MA* (F) is employed in a stressed manner or as a "finalis."

The note *tāra RI* (d of the upper octave) is frequently approached by means of a lightly performed glide from above:

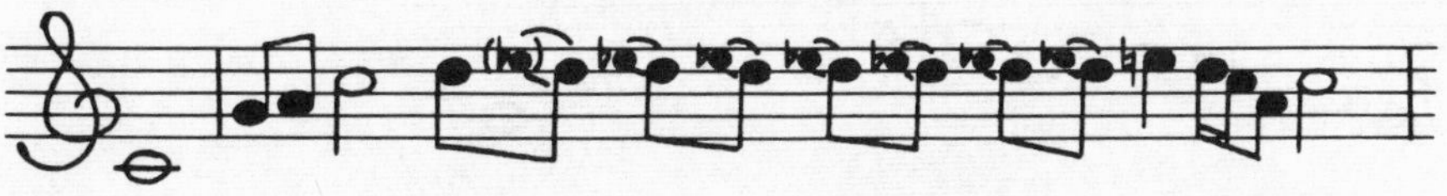

(48) *Gauḍa Mallāri* (*Gauḍa Mallāru*, *Gauḷa Mallār*)

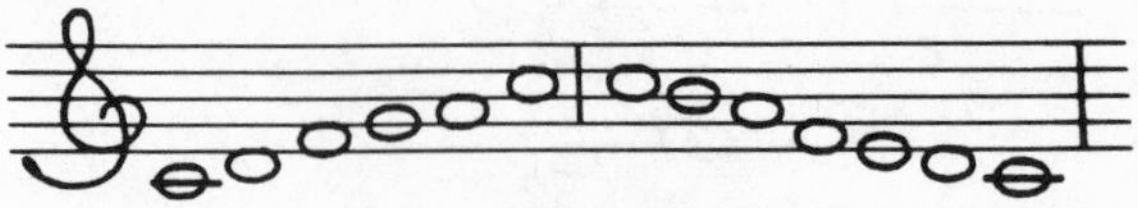

Ascent: the notes *GA* (E) and *NI* (B) are avoided.
Descent: the note *PA* (G) is omitted.

GAUḌMALLĀR (*Triputa-tāla*) SCM, 186

(49) *Gāyakarañjani*

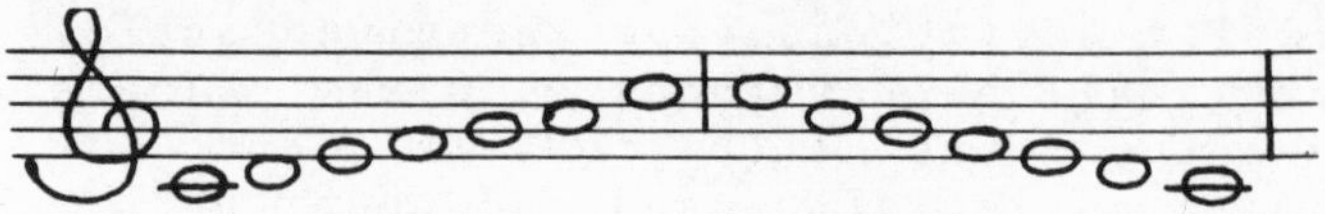

The note *NI* (B) is avoided entirely.

(50) *Ghana Taraṅgiṇi*

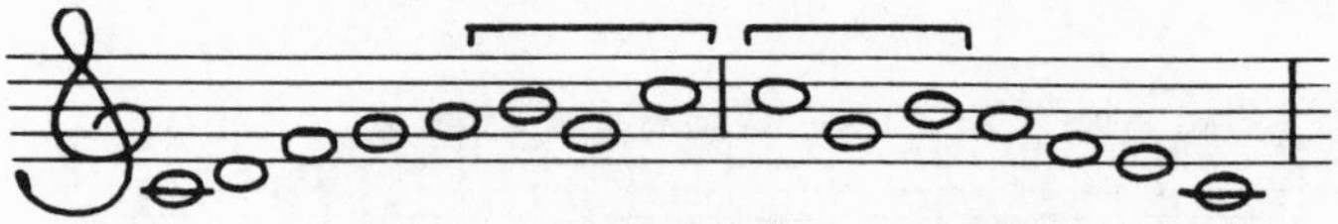

Ascent: the note *GA* (E) is avoided; one *vakra* feature is shown.
Descent: the note *RI* (D) is omitted; one *vakra* feature (being the inversion of the *vakra* feature in the ascending line) is used.

(51) *Gīrvāṇapriya*

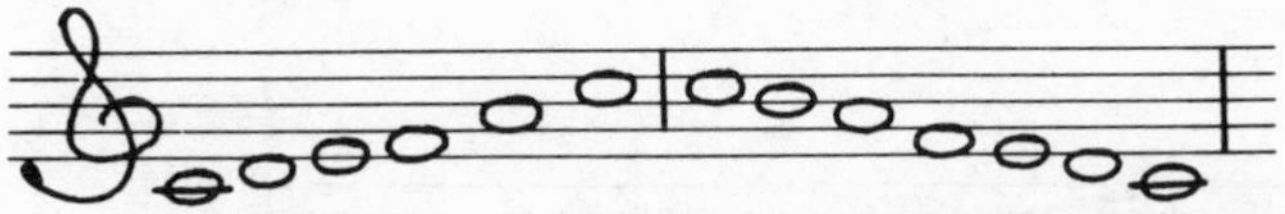

The note *PA* (G) is avoided entirely. In ascent the note *NI* (B) is avoided.

(52) *Grandha Taraṅgiṇi*

Ascent and descent are *sampūrṇa*; the scale shows one *vakra* feature in ascent and one in descent.

(53) *Gumyadyuti*

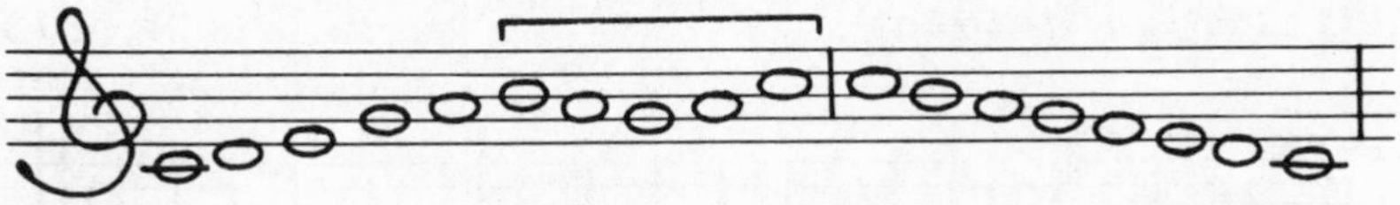

Ascent: the note *MA* (F) is avoided; one extended *vakra* passage is shown.
Descent: *krama sampūrṇa*.

(54) *Haṃsadhvani*

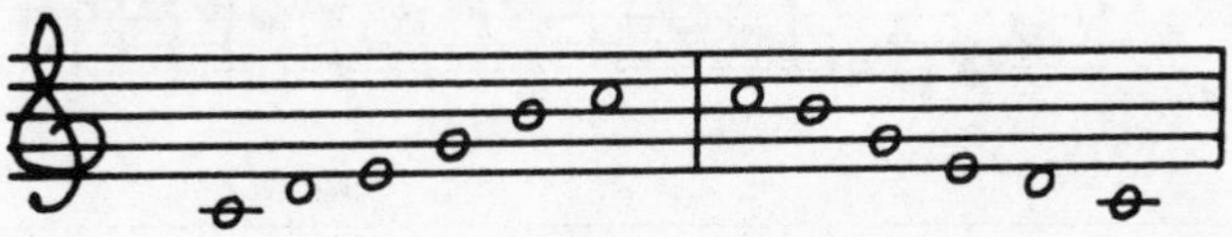

The notes *MA* (F) and *DHA* (A) are avoided entirely.

The SD (II, 222) remarks that *Haṃsadhvani*'s "*PA* [G] as *ṣaḍja* [*SA*, C] gives the *rāga Nāgasvarāvaḷi* [28, 22]"—a statement that if checked carefully is open to some doubts.

The following song example was composed by M. Veṅkaṭasubhaiyer, a relative and disciple of Thiagaiyer. The composer was born at Manambuchavadi; dates of birth and death are uncertain.

HAṂSADHVANI RĀGA (*Ādi-tāla*) SPC, III, 49

Pallavi

Anupallavi

HAṂSADHVANI (*Triputa-tāla*) SCM, 173

(55) *Haṃsanibhōgi*

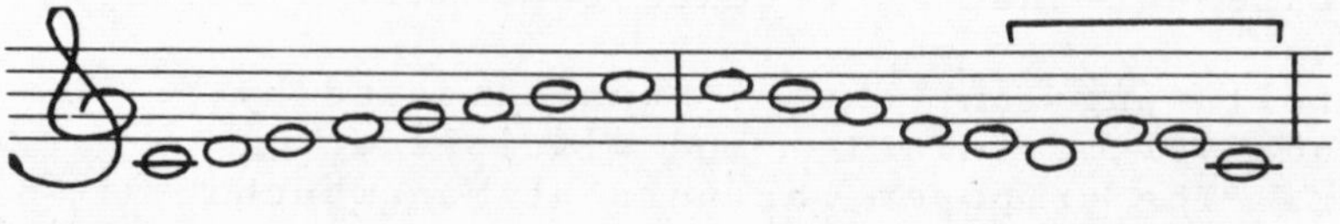

Ascent: *krama sampūrṇa*.
Descent: the note *PA* (G) is avoided; one *vakra* feature is shown.

(56) *Haṃsa Vinōdini*

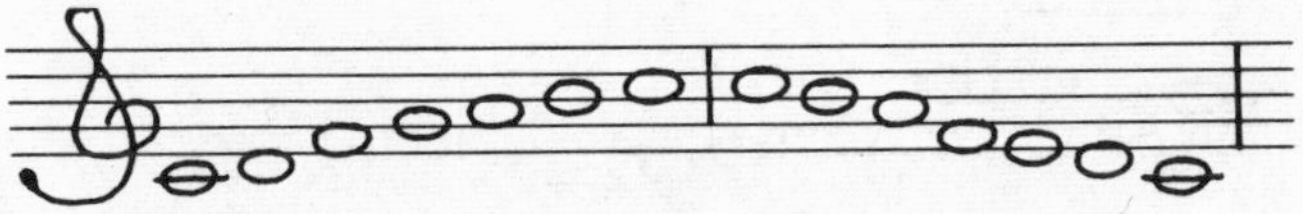

Ascent: the note *GA* (E) is avoided.
Descent: the note *PA* (G) is omitted.

(57) *Harṇōtrikam*

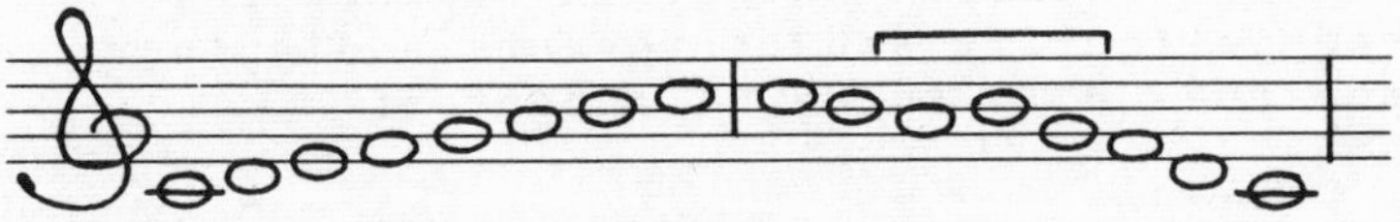

Ascent: *krama sampūrṇa.*
Descent: the note *GA* (E) is avoided; one *vakra* feature is shown.

(58) *Hēlaprabhāta*

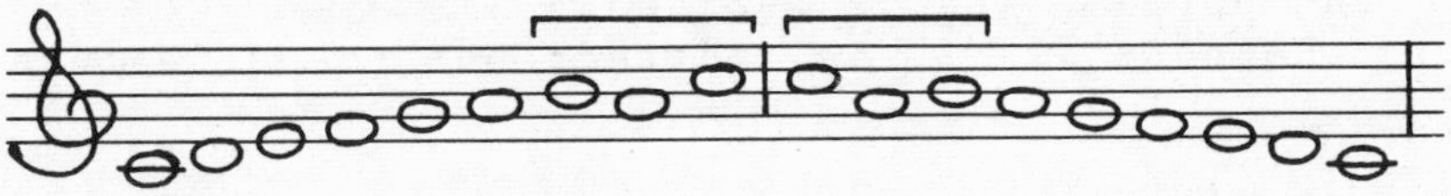

Ascent: *sampūrṇa*; one *vakra* feature is shown.
Descent: *sampūrṇa*; one *vakra* feature is used.

(59) *Indravaṃsa*

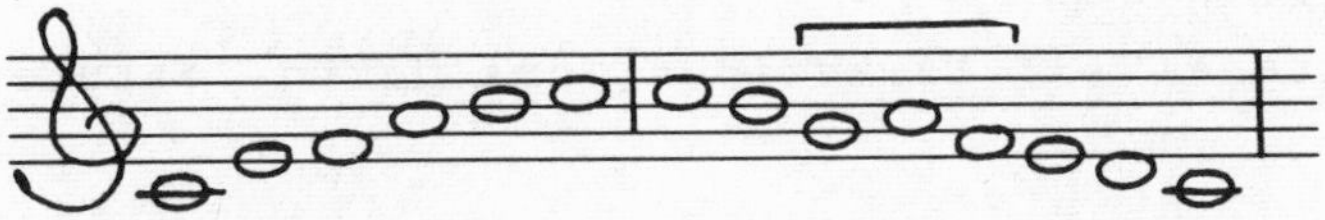

Ascent: the notes *RI* (D) and *PA* (G) are avoided.
Descent: *sampūrṇa*; one *vakra* feature is shown.

(60) *Indravardhanam*

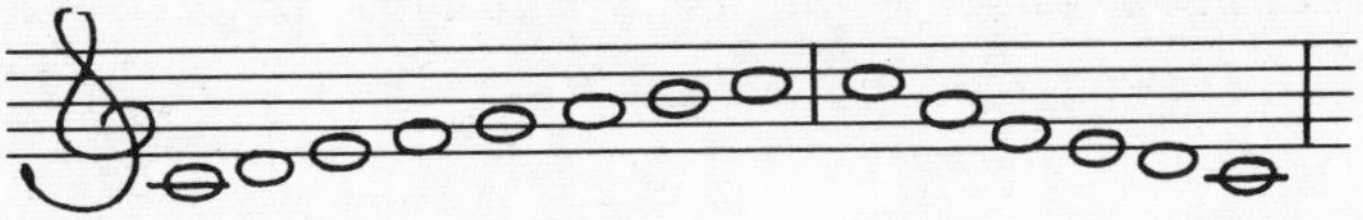

Ascent: *krama sampūrṇa.*
Descent: the notes *NI* (B) and *PA* (G) are avoided.

(61) *Induvardhanam*

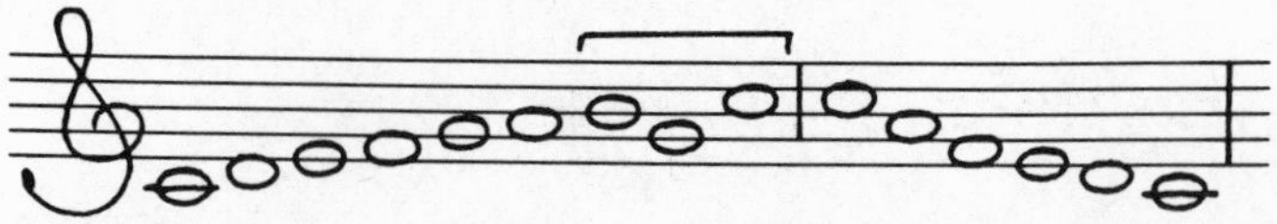

Indravardhanam (29,60) and *Induvardhanam*, the *rāga* under consideration probably are identical. The reason for keeping them apart is the fact that the SD (II, 233 and 234) lists them separately. It states that *Induvardhanam* shows the one indicated *vakra* feature in ascent. It is impossible to ascertain whether this *vakra* is indeed obligatory and represents a distinct difference from the *krama sampūrṇa* ascent of *Indravardhanam*.

(62) *Jaganmanōharī*

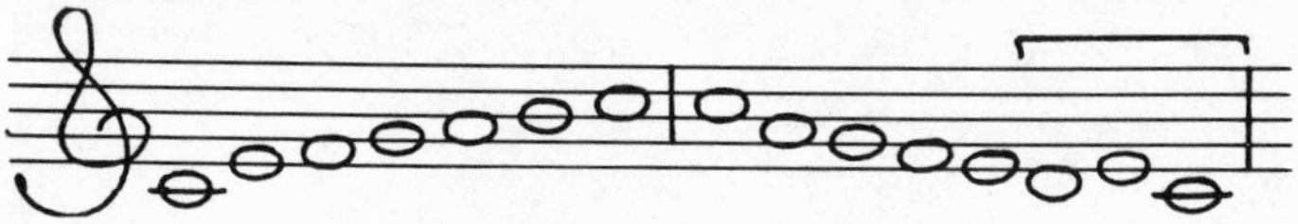

Ascent: the note *RI* (D) is avoided.
Descent: the note *NI* (B) is omitted; one *vakra* feature is used.

(63) *Jājīvasantam*

Ascent: *krama sampūrṇa*
Descent: the note *NI* (B) is avoided; one *vakra* feature is shown.

(64) *Jālaprabala*

SD (II, 240) describes this *rāga* as a *madhyamāntya* type

because its highest note is *MA* (F) of the middle octave range.

(65) *Jalōddhati*

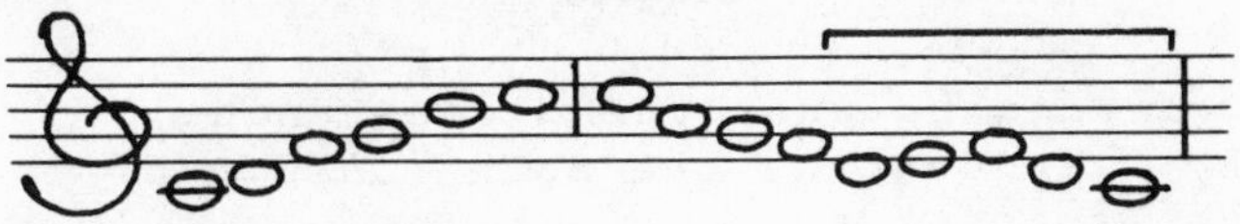

Ascent: the notes *GA* (E) and *DHA* (A) are avoided.
Descent: the note *NI* (B) is omitted; one extended *vakra* passage is used.

(66) *Jambukriya*

The note *DHA* (A) is avoided entirely. The ascent shows one *vakra* feature and the descent uses one.

(67) *Janarañjaṇi*

Ascent: *sampūrṇa*; one *vakra* feature is shown.
Descent: the notes *NI* (B) and *GA* (E) are avoided.

JANARAÑJAṆI (*Triputa-tāla*) SCM, 171-72

(68) *Jaṅgala*

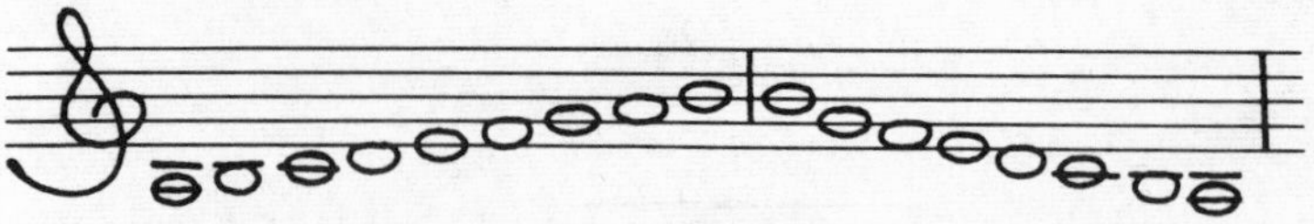

This is a *niṣādāntya rāga* because the highest note of its scale is *NI* (B). In descent the note (*DHA*) A of the middle octave range is omitted.

(69) *Javōnnati*

Ascent: the note *MA* (F) is avoided; one *vakra* feature is shown.
Descent: *sampūrṇa*; one *vakra* feature is used.

(70) *Jhaṅkāra Śīla*

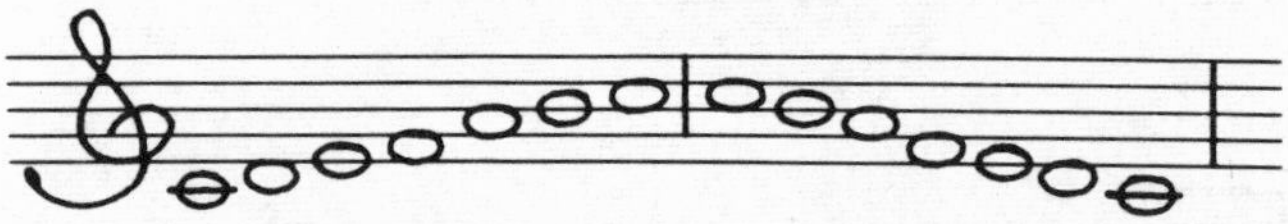

The note *PA* (G) is avoided entirely.

(71) *Jharālata*

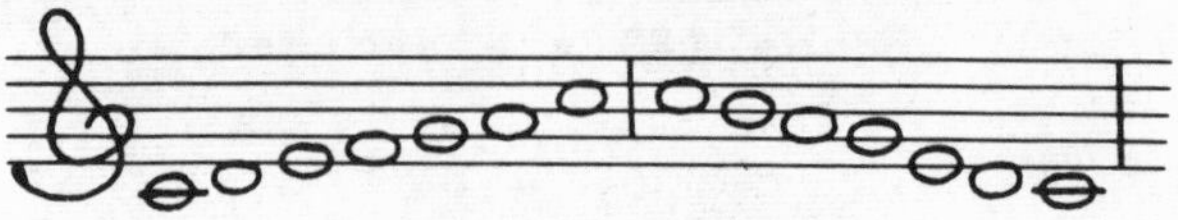

Ascent: the note *NI* (B) is avoided.
Descent: the note *MA* (F) is omitted.

(72) *Julāv*

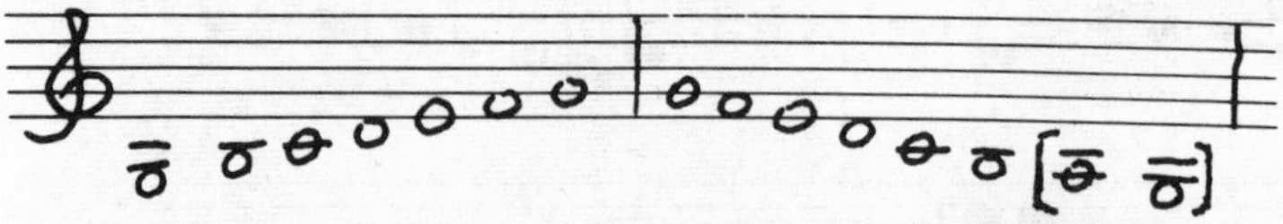

This *rāga* is a *pañcamāntya* type because the highest note of its scale is the note *PA* (G).
Ascent: the note *DHA* (A) of the *mandra saptaka* (low octave range) is avoided.
Descent: *krama sampūrṇa*.

(73) *Julāvu*

Despite the fact that *rāgas Julāv* (29, 72) and *Julāvu* are practically the same, the SD (II, 264) lists them separately. One possible difference between the two *rāgas* can be the entire omission of the note *DHA* (A), but this does not appear to be a fixed rule.

JULĀVU (*Triputa-tāla*) SCM, 178

(74) *Jvālākēśari*

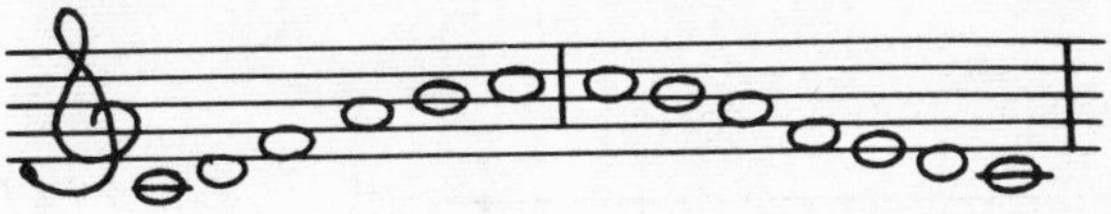

The note *PA* (G) is avoided entirely and *GA* (E) is omitted in ascent.

(75) *Kadana Kutūhalam* (*Kathana Kutūhalam*)

The SD (II, 278) states that this *rāga* was created by Pattaṇam Subramaṇya Ayyar (see *rāga Ābhōgi*, 22, 2).
Two forms of ascent are possible: (a) is given in the SD and (b) is frequently used.
Ascent (a): *sampūrṇa*; one extended *vakra* passage is shown.
Ascent (b): the note *GA* (E) is avoided; one extended *vakra* passage is used.
Descent: *krama sampūrṇa*.

(76) *Kamala Vilasita*

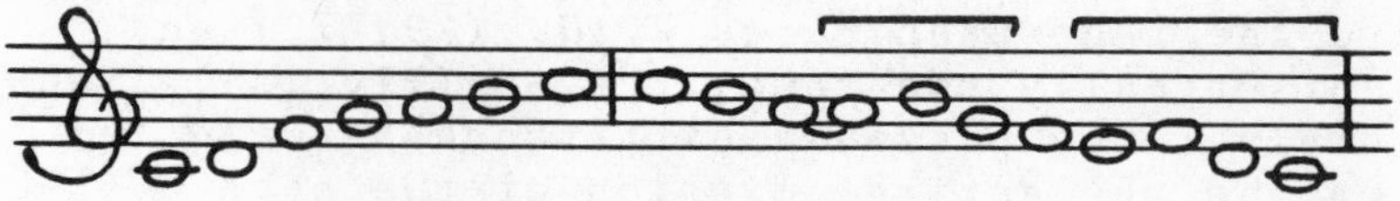

Ascent: the note *GA* (E) is avoided.
Descent: *sampūrṇa*; two *vakra* features are shown.

(77) *Kāndadruma*

The note *PA* (G) is avoided entirely.
Ascent: *RI* (D) is omitted; one *vakra* feature is shown.
Descent: *DHA* (A) is avoided. (See also 29, 80.)

(78) *Kañja Mālini*

Ascent: *sampūrṇa*; two *vakra* features are shown.
Descent: the note *PA* (G) is avoided.

(79) *Kannaḍa*

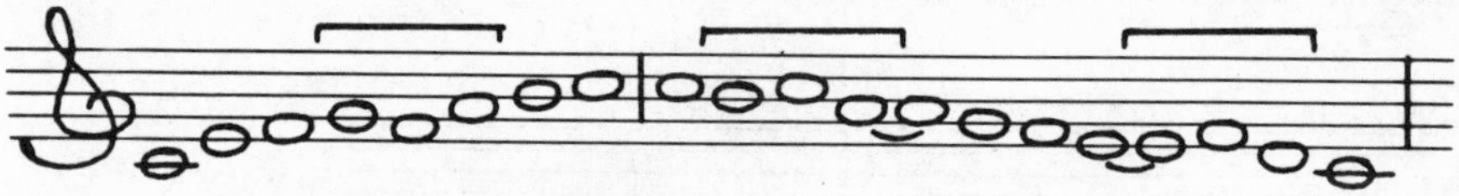

Ascent: the note *RI* (D) is avoided; one *vakra* feature is shown.
Descent: *sampūrṇa*; two *vakra* features are used.

The note *DHA* (A) is often performed with a vibrato. Songs in this *rāga* usually begin with one of the following notes: *SA* (C), *GA* (E), or *DHA* (A). *Kannaḍa* can be performed at any time.

In the following melody pattern the note *RI* (D) can appear in ascent (e.g., measures 4 and 5). In the SCM (128) the tone material of this *rāga* is given as:

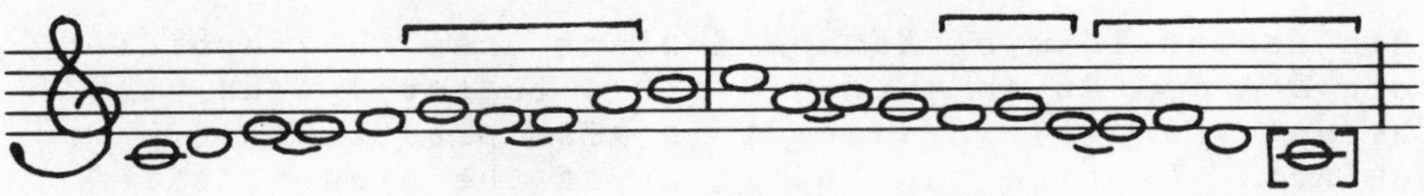

Here the descent shows two consecutive *vakra* passages.

KANNAḌA (*Triputa-tāla*) SCM, 178-79

(80) *Kānta Dhruma*

This *rāga* is the same as *Kāndadruma* (29, 77). *Kānta Dhruma* is mentioned here again because the SD lists the two names separately (II, 295 and II, 299). This may lead the reader to assume that despite the fact that the tone material of both *rāgas* is the same, there could exist some obscure difference between the two.

(81) *Kēdāra* (*Kēdāram*)

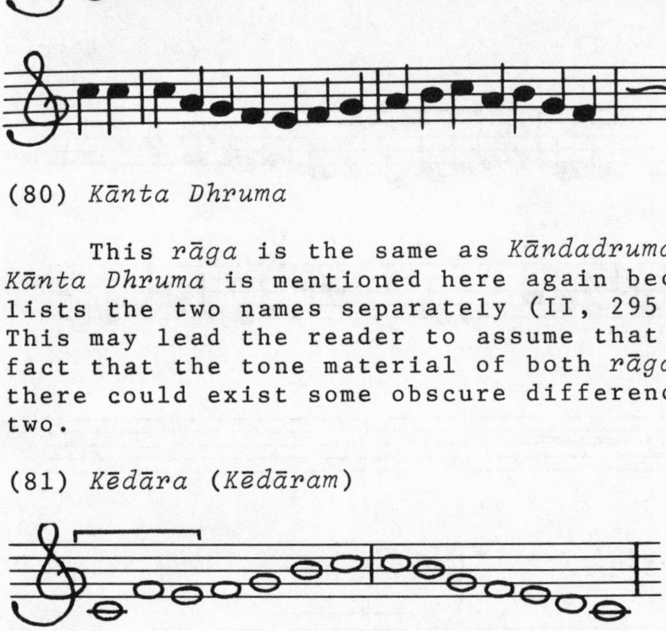

The note *DHA* (A) is avoided entirely.
Ascent: the note *RI* (D) is avoided and one *vakra* feature is shown.
A descent other than the one shown above is:

This second form of *Kēdāra* descent uses the forbidden note *DHA* (A) in an extended *vakra* feature. The use of the note *DHA* (A) in descent is also prescribed by Govinda. Despite the fact that at the present time this note is avoided, the following forms of descent can be observed occasionally:

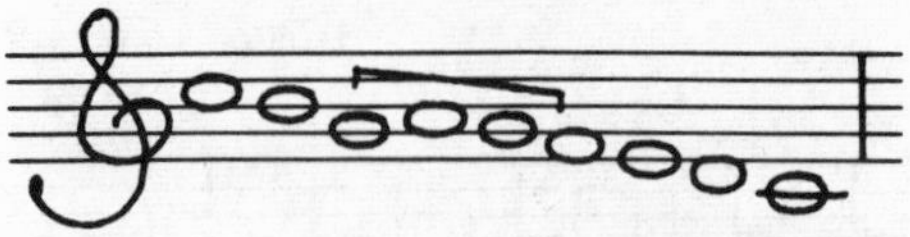

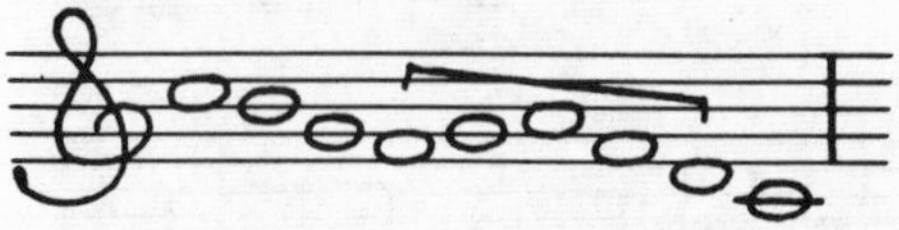

There are some musicians who refuse to call the forbidden *DHA*, when it is used, by its proper name and speak of *śuddha NI* (Bbb) instead.

KĒDĀRA (*Triputa-tāla*) SCM, 168-69

(82) *Kōkila Bhāshiṇi* (*Kōkilabhāṣiṇi*, *Kōkilabhāshaṇi*)

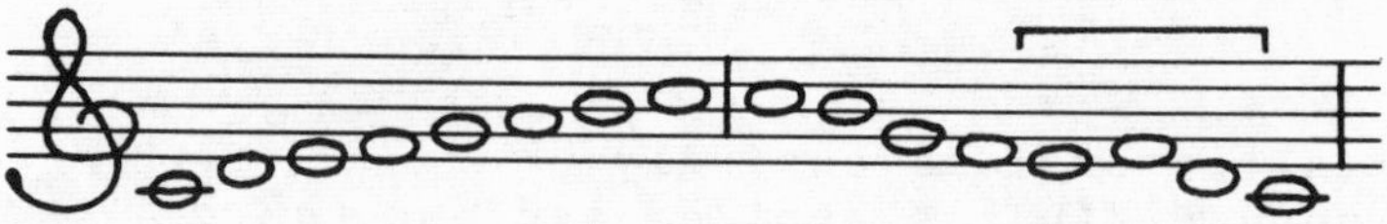

Ascent: *krama sampūrṇa*.
Descent: the note *DHA* (A) is avoided; one *vakra* feature is shown.

(83) *Kōlāhala(m)*

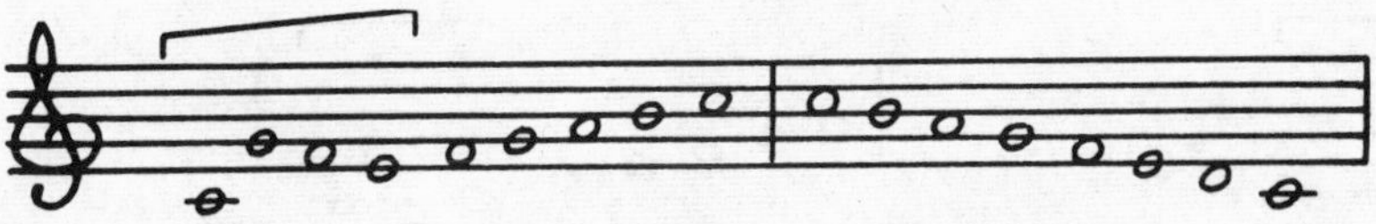

Ascent: the note *RI* (D) is avoided; one extended *vakra* passage is shown.
Descent: *krama sampūrṇa*.
Another ascent of this *rāga* can be:

KŌLĀHALA (*Triputa-tāla*) SCM, 170-71

(84) *Kshapā* (*Kṣapā*)

The note *DHA* (A) is avoided entirely. *PA* (G) is omitted in descent.

(85) *Kumāra Vilasita*

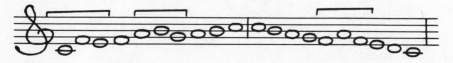

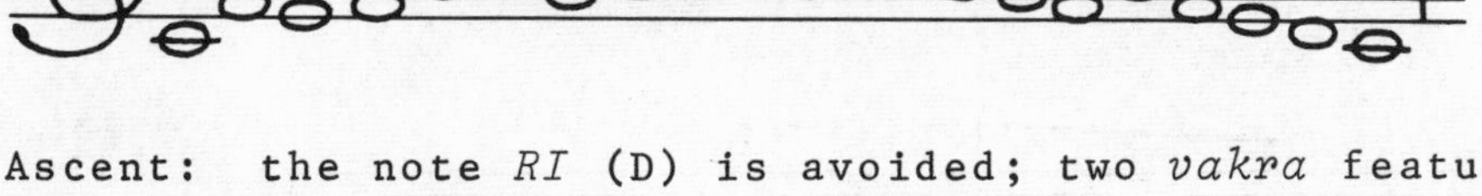

Ascent: the note *RI* (D) is avoided; two *vakra* features are shown.
Descent: *sampūrṇa*; one *vakra* feature is used.

(86) *Kurañjī*

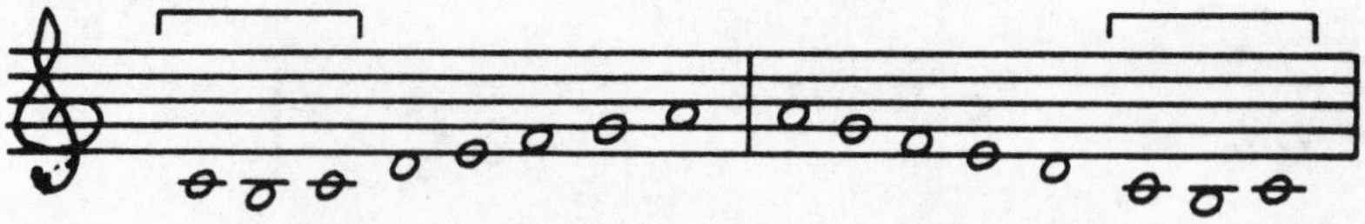

This is a *dhaivatāntya rāga* because its highest note is *DHA* (A).

The note *NI* of the low octave range is taken flat in passages such as:

or

KURAÑJĪ (*Triputa-tāla*) SCM, 167

(87) *Kusuma Vichitra* (*Kusuma Vicitra*)

Ascent and descent are *sampūrṇa*; each shows two *vakra* features.

(88) *Kutūhalam*

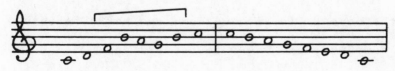

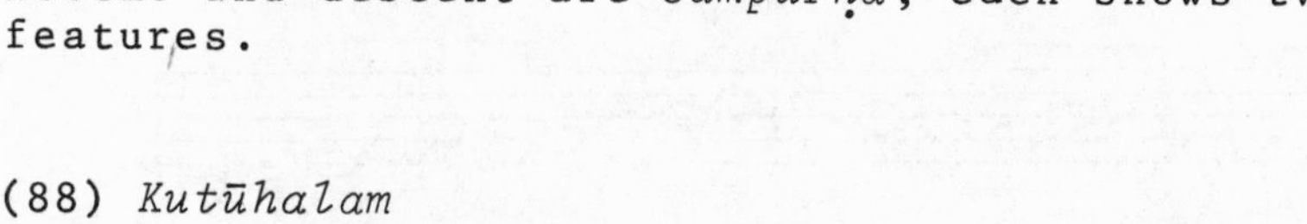

Ascent: the note *GA* (E) is avoided; one extended *vakra* feature is shown.
Descent: *krama sampūrṇa*.

(89) *Mahuri*

This is a *niṣadāntya rāga* because its highest note is *NI* (B). The ascent avoids the note *DHA* (A) and shows one *vakra* feature.

MAHURI (*Triputa-tāla*) SCM, 170

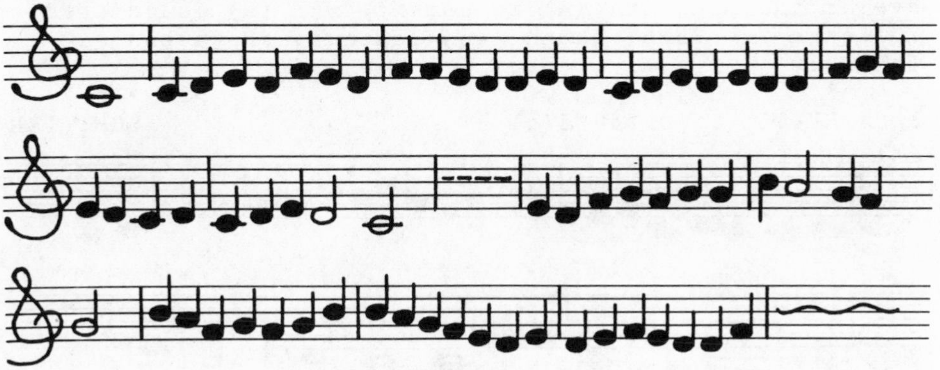

(90) *Mānd*

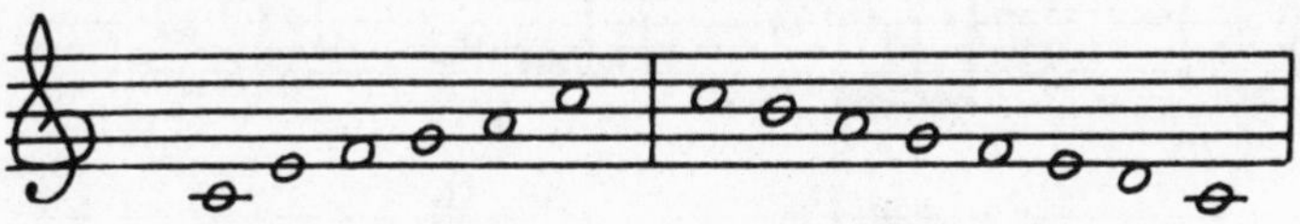

Ascent: the notes *RI* (D) and *NI* (B) are avoided.
Descent: *krama sampūrṇa*.

(91) *Nāgabhūṣaṇī*

The note *GA* (E) is avoided entirely. In ascent *NI* (B) is omitted.

R (p. 223) states that this *rāga* is of recent origin and was introduced by Muthiah Bhāgavathar.

(92) *Nāgadhvani*

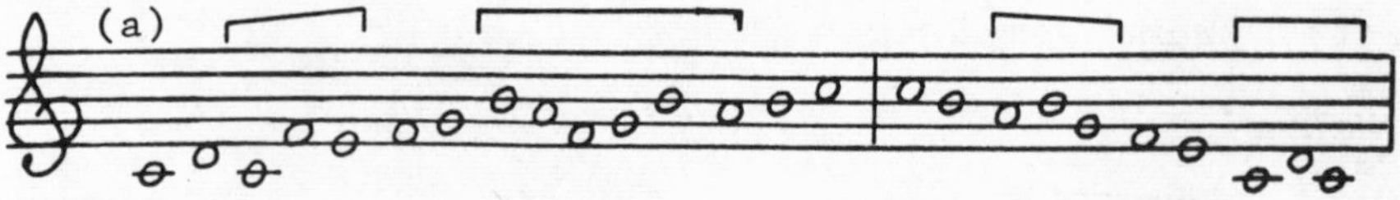

This *rāga* can be represented by two scales. Scale (a) is *sampūrṇa* in ascent and descent and shows two extended *vakra* passages in ascent and two shorter *vakra* features in descent. Scale (b) is less complex and avoids the note *DHA* (A) in ascent. *RI* (D) is omitted in descent. Each, ascent and descent, shows one *vakra* feature.

NĀGADHVANI (*Triputa-tāla*) SCM, 181

(93) *Navaroj* (*Navaroju*)

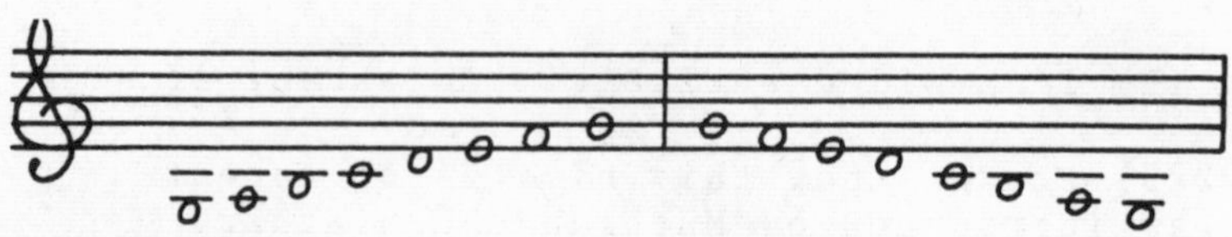

This is a *pañcamāntya rāga* because its highest note is *PA* (G).

NAVAROJU (*Triputa-tāla*) SCM, 176-77

(94) *Parōdha*

The notes *GA* (E) and *PA* (G) are avoided entirely.

(95) *Paśupatipriya*

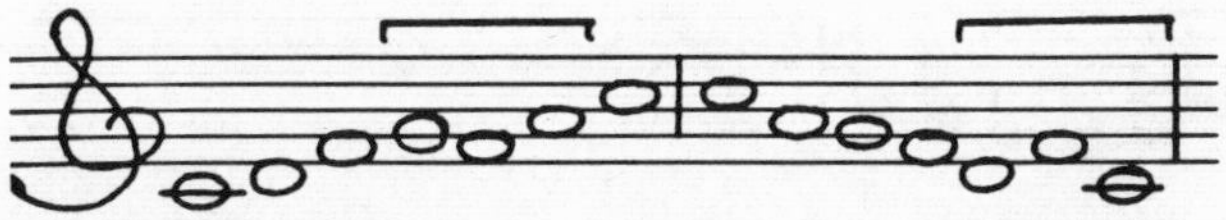

The notes *GA* (E) and *NI* (B) are avoided entirely. One *vakra* feature appears in ascent and one in descent.

R (p. 223) states that this *rāga* is of recent origin and was introduced by Muthiah Bhāgavathar.

(96) *Pūrṇachandrikā* (*Pūrṇacandrikā*)

Ascent: the note *NI* (B) is avoided; one *vakra* feature is shown.
Descent: there are several forms, two are shown here as (a) and (b). Descent (a): the note *DHA* (A) is

avoided; one extended *vakra* passage is shown. Descent (b): *sampūrṇa*; two *vakra* features are shown.

In the low octave region (*mandra saptaka*) the progression *DHA-NI-SA* (A-B-C) is permitted. The same applies to *DHA-RI-SA-NI* (A-D-C-B).

PŪRṆACHANDRIKĀ (*Triputa-tāla*) SCM, 174

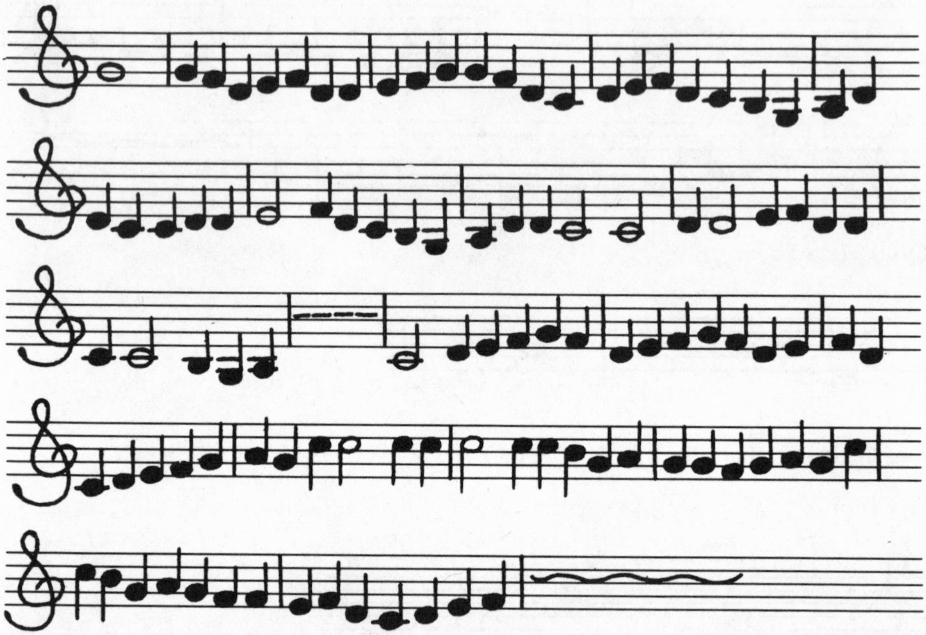

(97) *Pūrvagauḷa*

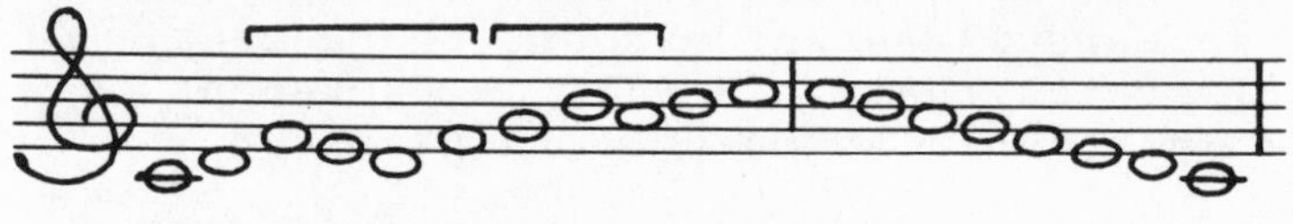

Ascent: *sampūrṇa*; two *vakra* features are shown.
Descent: *krama sampūrṇa*.

PŪRVAGAUḶA (*Triputa-tāla*) SCM, 185

(98) *Putrika*

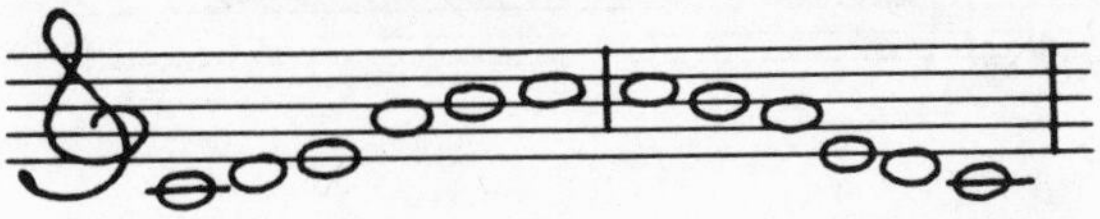

The notes *MA* (F) and *PA* (G) are avoided entirely.

(99) *Śaṅkarī*

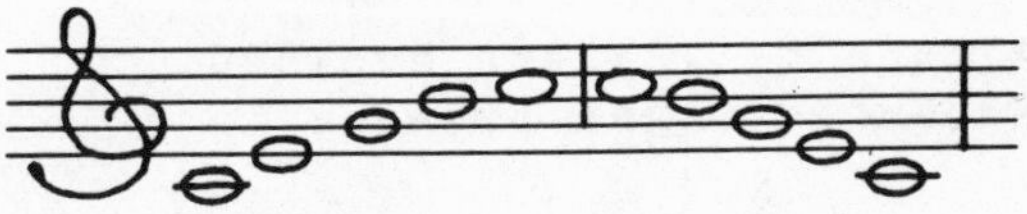

The notes *RI* (D), *MA* (F), and *DHA* (A) are avoided entirely.

(100) *Siṃhelavarāli*

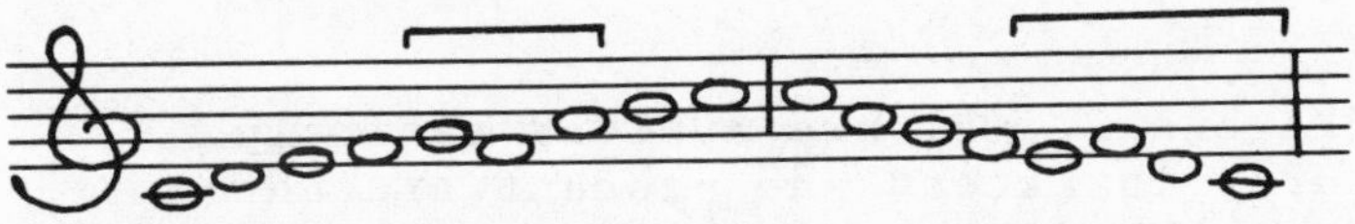

Ascent: *sampūrṇa*; one *vakra* feature is shown.
Descent: the note *NI* (B) is avoided; one *vakra* feature is used.

(101) *Sindhu*

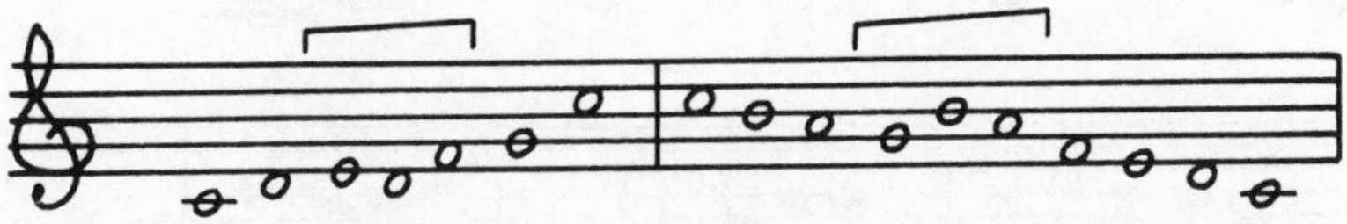

Ascent: the notes *DHA* (A) and *NI* (B) are avoided; one *vakra* feature is shown.
Descent: *sampūrṇa*; one *vakra* feature is used.

SINDHU (*Triputa-tāla*) SCM, 184-85

(102) *Sindhu Mandāri*

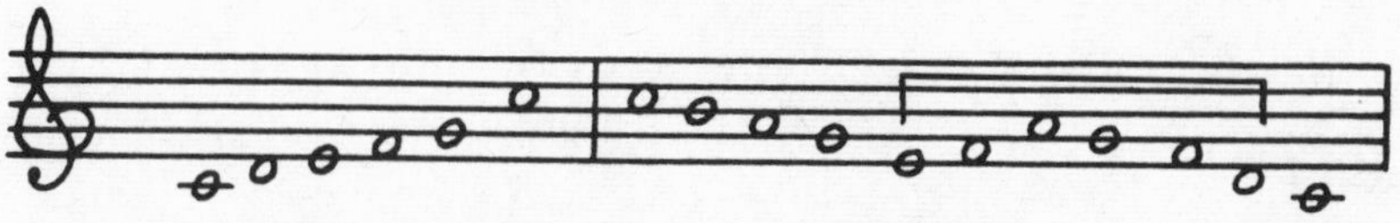

Ascent: the notes *DHA* (A) and *NI* (B) are avoided.
Descent: *sampūrṇa*; one extended *vakra* passage is shown.

(103) *Śuddhasāveri*

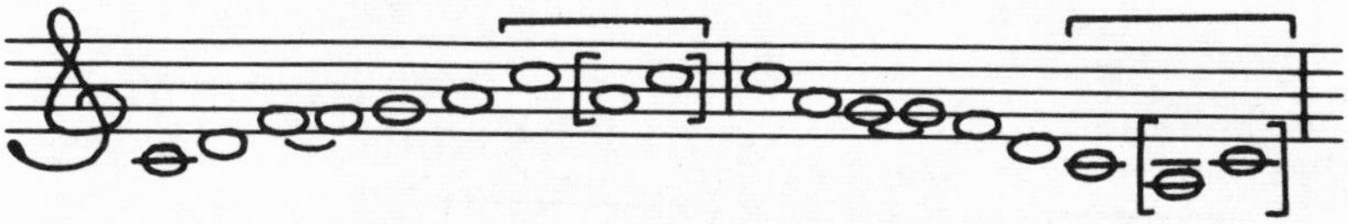

The notes *GA* (E) and *NI* (B) are avoided entirely. The *vakra* features in ascent and descent are not obligatory and can be disregarded.

ŚUDDHASĀVERI (*Triputa-tāla*) SCM, 180-81

ŚUDDHASĀVERI RĀGA (*Triputa-tāla*) SPC, II, 37

(104) *Śuddhavasanta*

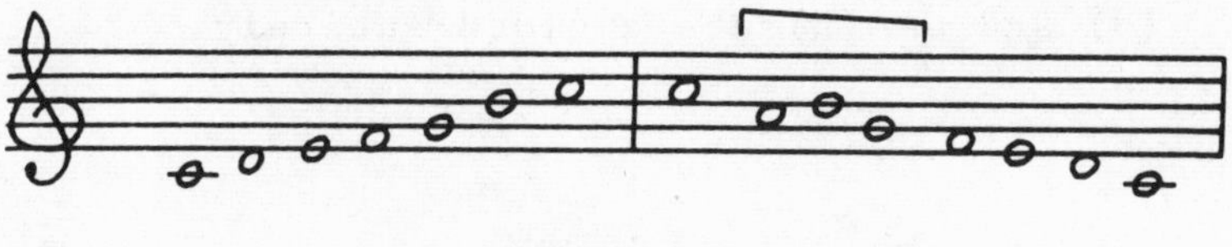

Ascent: the note *DHA* (A) is avoided.
Descent: *sampūrṇa*; one *vakra* feature is shown.

ŚUDDHAVASANTA (*Triputa-tāla*) SCM, 182

(105) *Suramandini*

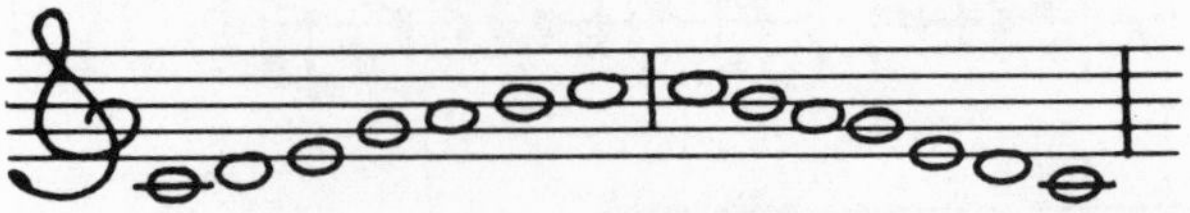

The note *MA* (F) is avoided entirely.

(106) *Svambhuṣvara*

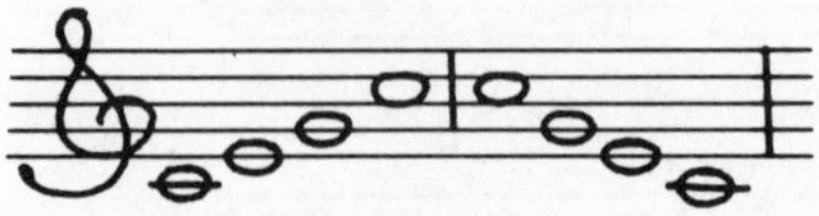

The scale of this unusual four-note *rāga* avoids the notes *RI* (D), *MA* (F), *DHA* (A), and *NI* (B) entirely.

According to R (222-23) this *rāga* is of recent origin. It is obvious that with the limited tone material little elaboration can be achieved.

(107) *Tāmalaki*

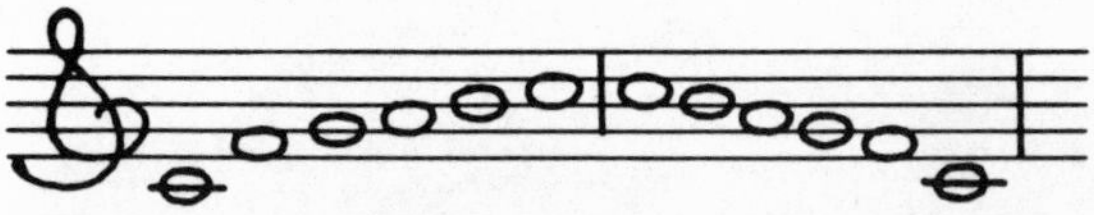

The notes *RI* (D) and *GA* (E) are avoided entirely.

(108) *Taṇḍavam*

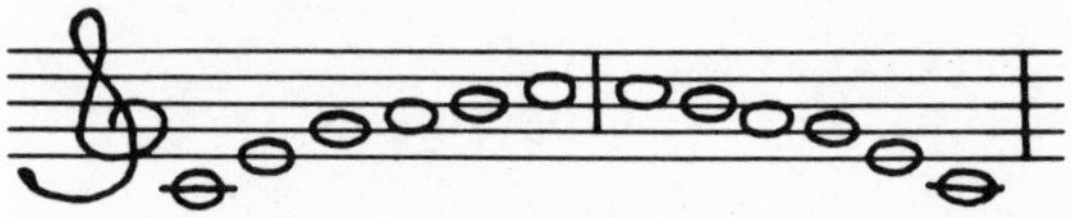

The notes *RI* (D) and *MA* (F) are avoided entirely.

(109) *Tōmaratārini*

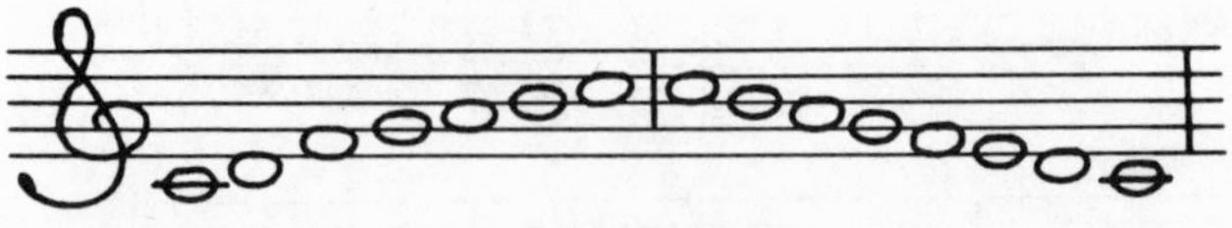

Ascent: the note *GA* (E) is avoided.
Descent: *krama sampūrṇa*.

(110) *Vasantaghōshi* (*Vasantaghōṣi*)

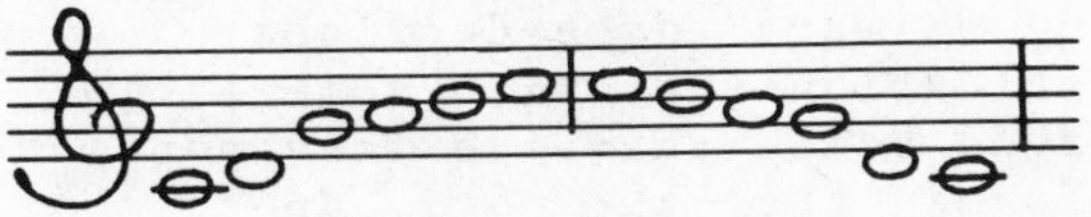

The notes *GA* (E) and *MA* (F) are avoided entirely.

(111) *Vēdandagāmini*

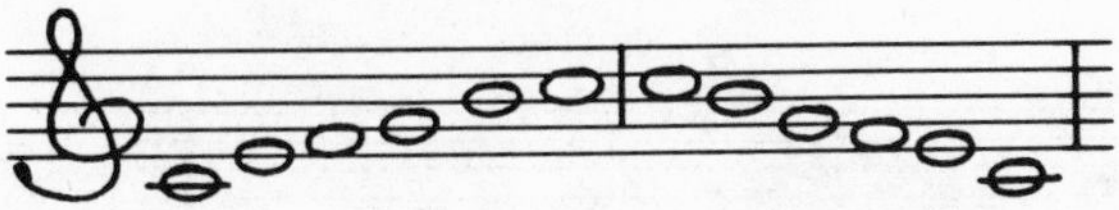

The notes *RI* (D) and *DHA* (A) are avoided entirely.

(112) *Vivardhani* (*Vardhani*)

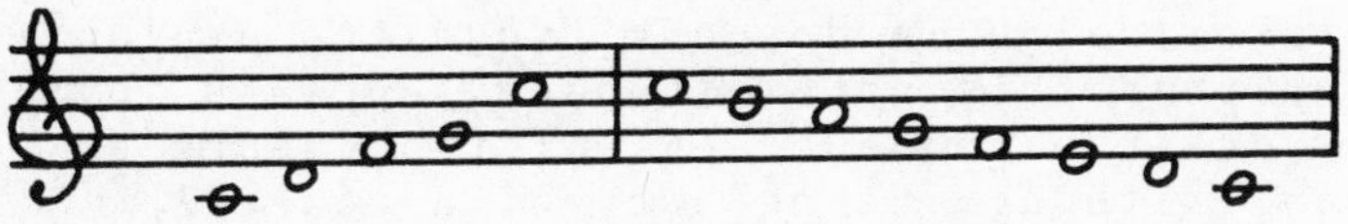

Ascent: the notes *GA* (E), *DHA* (A), and *NI* (B) are avoided.
Descent: *krama sampūrṇa*.

VIVARDHANI (*Triputa-tāla*) SCM, 183-84

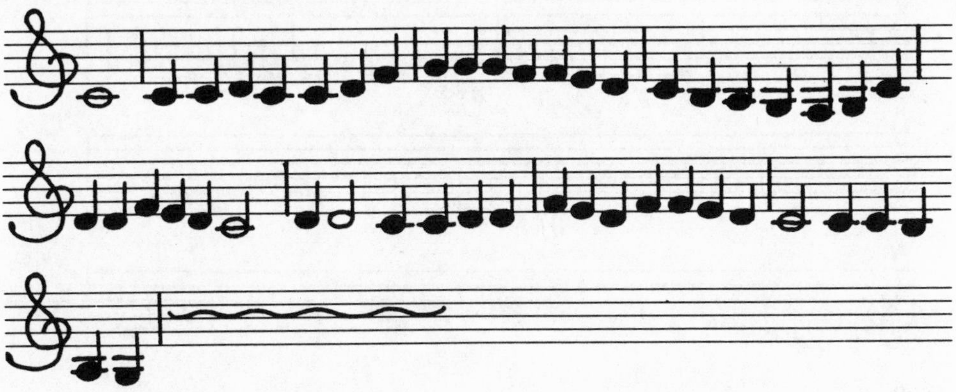

30. *MĒḶA NĀGĀNANDĪ* (*NĀGĀNANDINĪ*)

Beginning with *mēḷa* 30 the number of *janya rāgas* ascribed to the following primary *rāgas* declines markedly. This is an indication that with some exceptions which can be observed below they are less popular and less frequently performed than the *rāgas* up to *mēḷa* 29.

Veṅkaṭamakhin calls this *rāga Nāgābharaṇam*, with *DHA* (A#) in an ascending *vakra* feature and a low intoned *DHA* (approximately A) in descent. The SCM (p. 130) states the following scale:

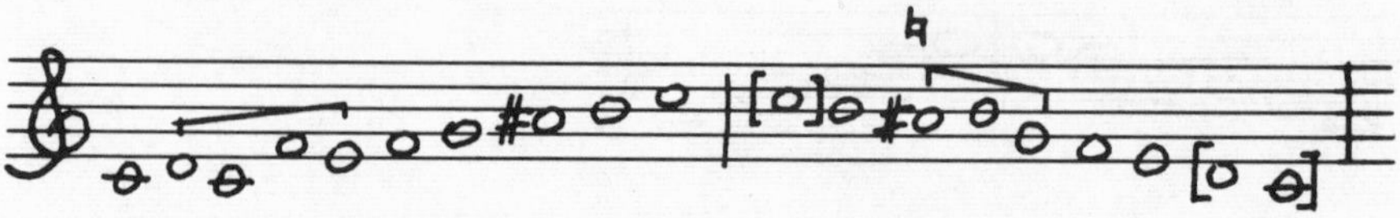

R. (p. 197) states that Veṅkaṭamakhin speaks of a "*vakra d* [*DHA*] in *arohana* [ascent] and no *d* [*DHA*] in descent." The discrepancy between the use of *DHA* (low intoned) and its omission in descent finds its explanation in the fact that this note, if used, appears in a *vakra* feature where the sequence *DHA-NI* represents an ascending motion (although being part of a general descent). The second possiblity of avoiding *DHA* in descent probably indicates a variant in use at Veṅkaṭamakhin's time.

NĀGĀNANDINĪ (*Triputa-tāla*) SCM, 186-7

Janya Rāgas of the 30. Mēḷa

(1) *Bhānukriya*

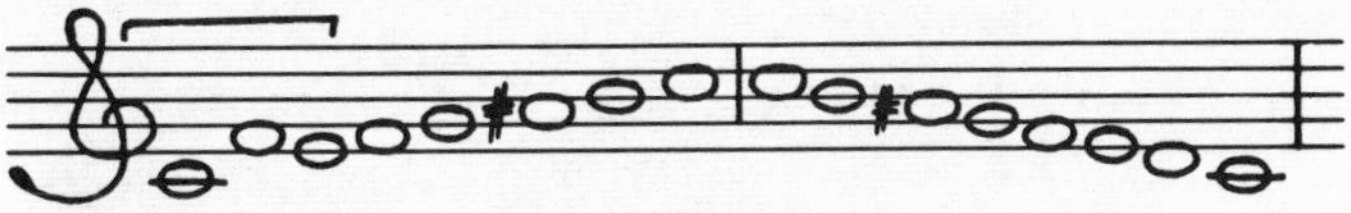

Ascent: the note *RI* (D) is avoided; one *vakra* feature is shown.
Descent: *krama sampūrṇa*.

(2) *Barhidhvaja*

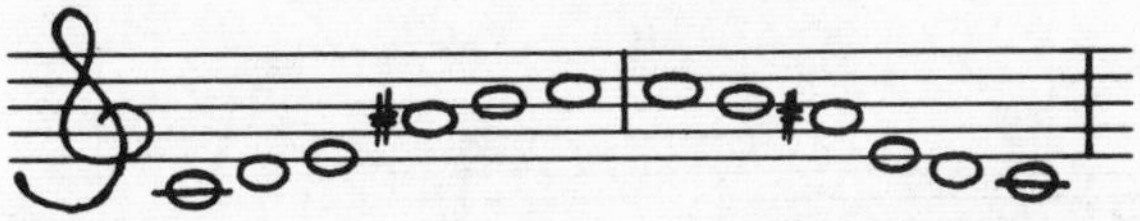

The notes *MA* (F) and *PA* (G) are avoided entirely.

(3) *Bharmāmbari*

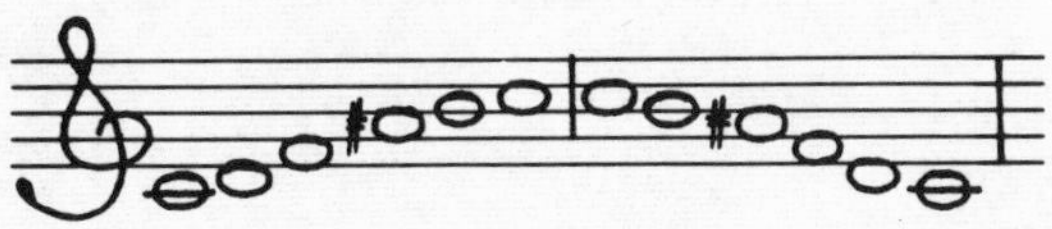

The notes *GA* (E) and *PA* (G) are avoided entirely.

(4) *Chitraravam (Citraravam)*

Ascent: *sampūrṇa*; one *vakra* feature is shown.
Descent: the note *RI* (D) is avoided.

(5) *Chitrasaurabham (Citrasaurabham)*

The scale of this *rāga* is identical with that of *rāga Chitraravam* (30,4). *Chitrasaurabham* is listed here because the SD (I, 90) presents the two *rāgas* separately; hence there seems to be an implication that some fine distinction between the two *rāgas* may exist.

(6) *Dhūrjaṭipriya*

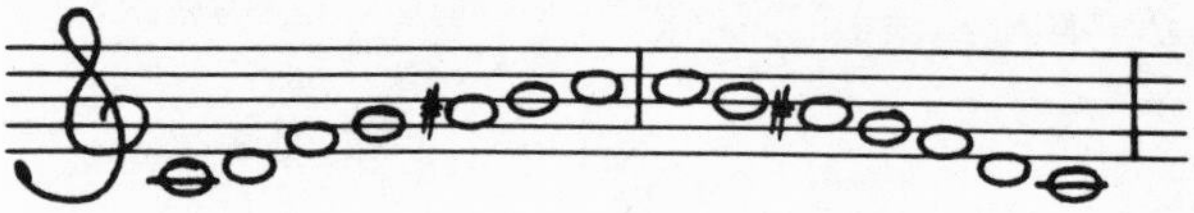

The note *GA* (E) is avoided entirely.

(7) *Gajānandini*

The note *PA* (G) is avoided entirely.

(8) *Gambhīra Vāṇi*

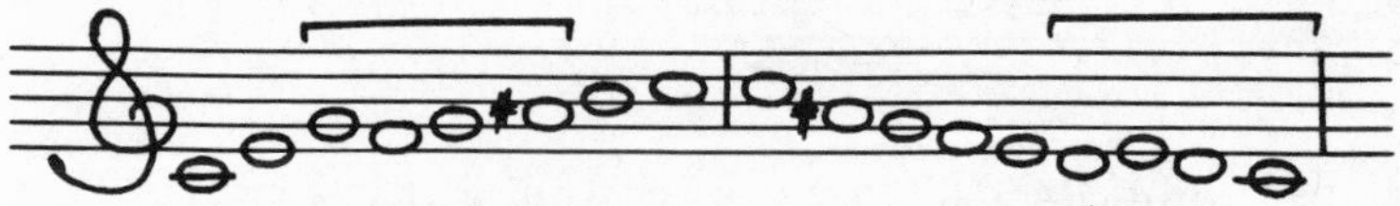

Ascent: the note *RI* (D) is avoided; one *vakra* feature is shown.
Descent: the note *NI* (B) is omitted; one *vakra* feature is used.

(9) *Gayakālāsini*

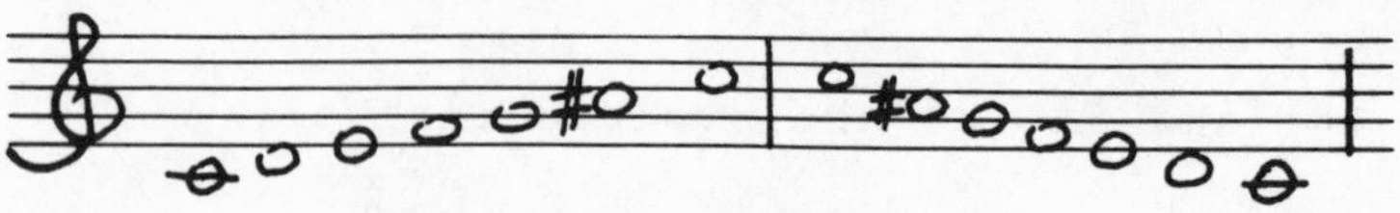

The note *NI* (B) is avoided entirely.

This *rāga* is also called *Gayakālāpini* (cf. N).

(10) *Haṃsa Gandharvam*

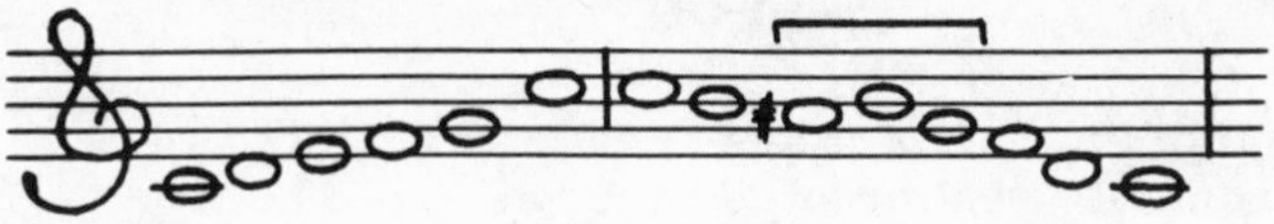

Ascent: the notes *DHA* (A#) and *NI* (B) are avoided.
Descent: the note *GA* (E) is omitted; one *vakra* feature is shown.

(11) *Jaganmāta*

The notes *RI* (D) and *MA* (F) are avoided entirely.

(12) *Kamalini*

The note *PA* (G) is avoided entirely. *RI* (D) is omitted in ascent.

Another *rāga* with the same name is listed under the heading of *mēḷa* 1 (11).

(13) *Karpūramu*

The notes *RI* (D) and *GA* (E) are avoided entirely.

(14) *Kōlaphaṇi*

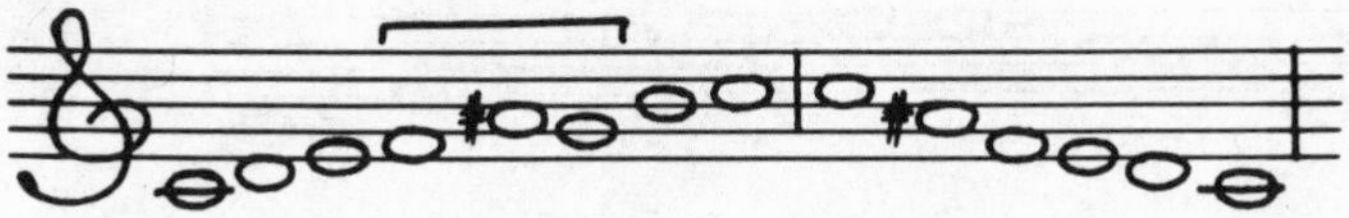

Ascent: *sampūrṇa*; one *vakra* feature is shown.
Descent: the notes *NI* (B) and *PA* (G) are avoided.

(15) *Lalitaghāndravam*

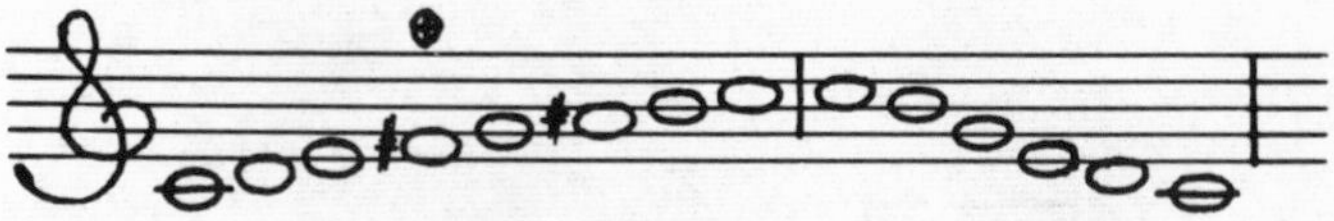

Ascent: *krama sampūrṇa*. The note *MA*, basically an F natural, is occasionally intoned sharp as an F#.
Descent: the notes *DHA* (A#) and *MA* (F) are avoided.

(16) *Nāgabāṣiṇi*

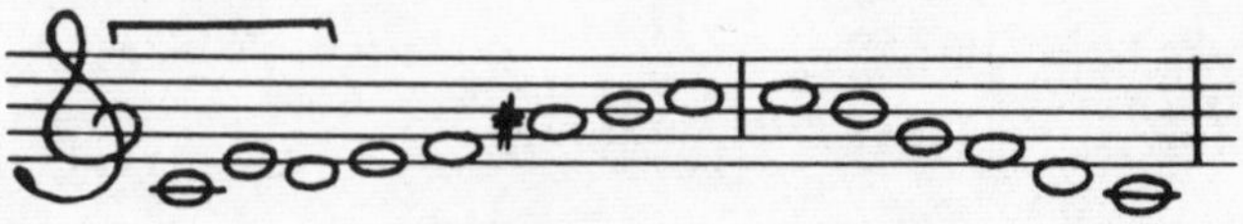

Ascent: the note *PA* (G) is avoided; one *vakra* feature is shown.
Descent: the notes *DHA* (A#) and *GA* (E) are omitted.

(17) *Nirmalāṅgi*

Ascent: the notes *GA* (E) and *NI* (B) are avoided.
Descent: *sampūrṇa*; one *vakra* feature is shown.

(18) *Pratāpakōkilam*

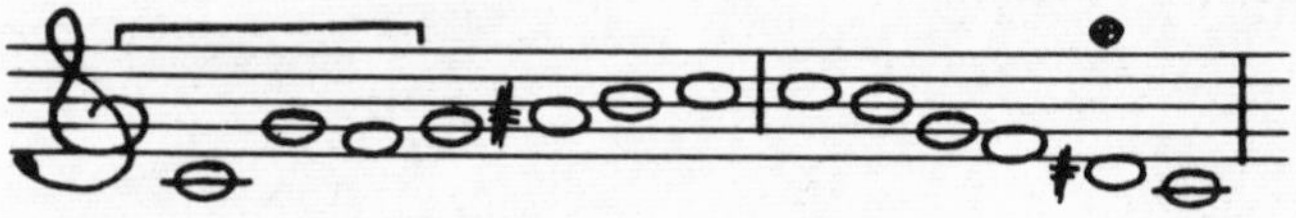

The note *GA* (E) is avoided entirely. The ascent omits the note *RI* (D) and the descent omits *DHA* (A#). The note *RI* is often intoned as sharp as D#.

(19) *Sāmant*

The scale of this *rāga* is *sampūrṇa* and shows one *vakra* feature in ascent and one in descent. *Sāmant* can be heard more frequently than any other *janya rāgas* of the 30. *mēḷa*.

SĀMANT (*Triputa-tāla*) SCM, 187-88

(20) *Siṃhēlasāvēri*

The note *RI* (D) is avoided entirely. The scale shows one *vakra* feature in ascent and one in descent.

(21) *Sōmabhūpāḷam*

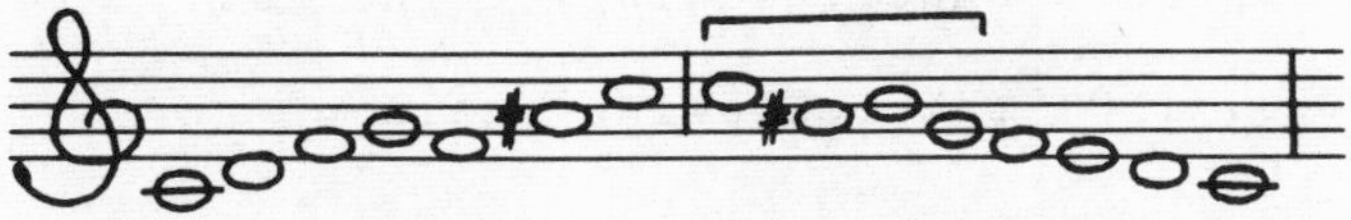

Ascent: the notes *GA* (E) and *NI* (B) are avoided.
Descent: *sampūrṇa*; one *vakra* feature is shown.

(22) *Trilōchanapriya* (*Trilōcanapriya*)

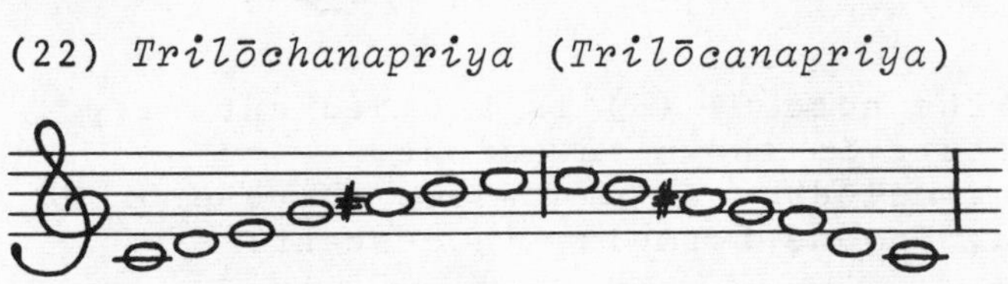

Ascent: the note *MA* (F) is avoided.
Descent: the note *GA* (E) is omitted.

Chakra VI

31. *MĒḶA YĀGAPRIYĀ*

Veṅkaṭamakhin called this *rāga Kalāvatī* in the *asampūrṇa mēḷa* system. R (p. 197) reports that Veṅkaṭamakhin's *Kalāvatī* avoided the note *NI* (Bbb) in ascent and used *GA* (E) in a *vakra* feature in descent. The SD (II, 286) presents the following *Kalāvatī* scale:

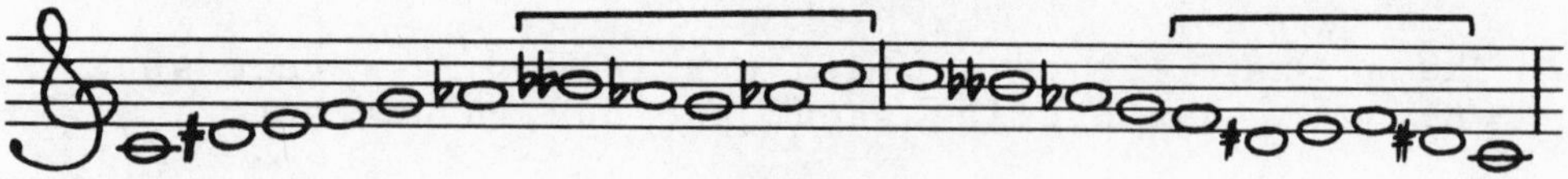

Another *Kalāvatī* appears under heading of the 16. *mēḷa* (2).

In the SCM (p. 130) the following scale of *Yāgapriyā* is given:

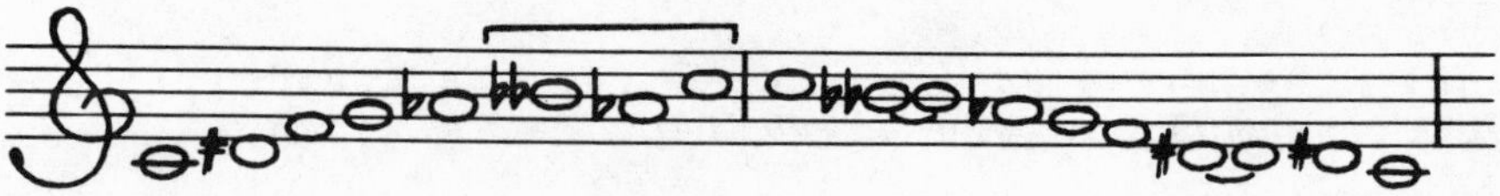

In this instance the note *GA* (E) is avoided entirely and one *vakra* feature is shown in ascent.

The following melody specimen shows the use of *GA* (E) in ascent and, in one formula, in descent:

YĀGAPRIYĀ (*Triputa-tāla*) SCM, 188-9

Janya Rāgas of the 31. Mēḷa

(1) *Biḍājapriya*

The notes *MA* (F) and *PA* (G) are avoided entirely.

(2) *Ḍamarukapriya*

The note *MA* (F) is avoided entirely.

(3) *Dēśa Rañjani*

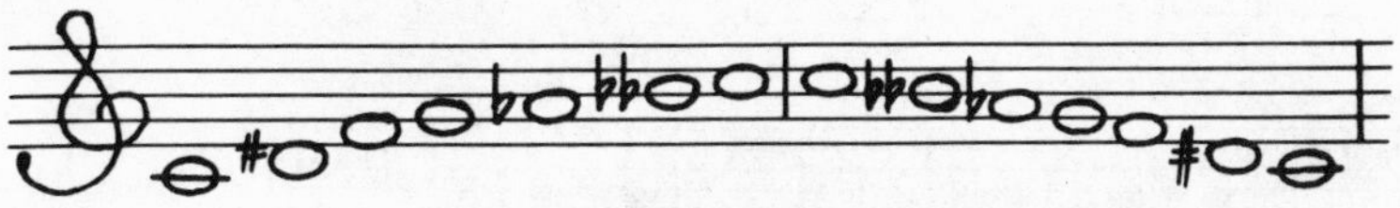

The note *GA* (E) is avoided entirely.

(4) *Gandharva Kannaḍa*

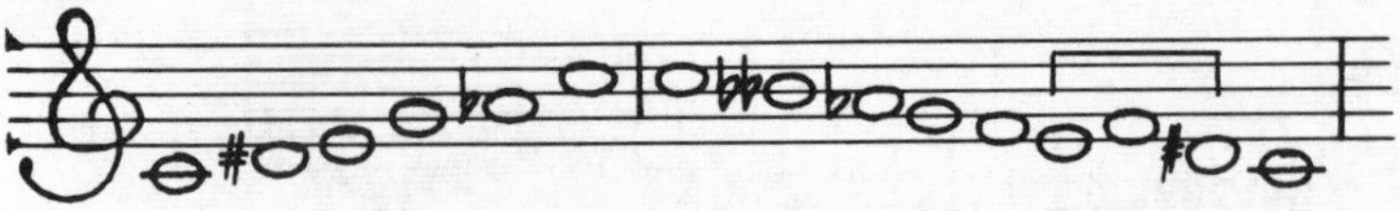

Ascent: the notes *MA* (F) and *NI* (Bbb) are avoided.
Descent: *sampūrṇa*; one *vakra* feature is shown.

(5) *Hindōḷa Kannaḍa*

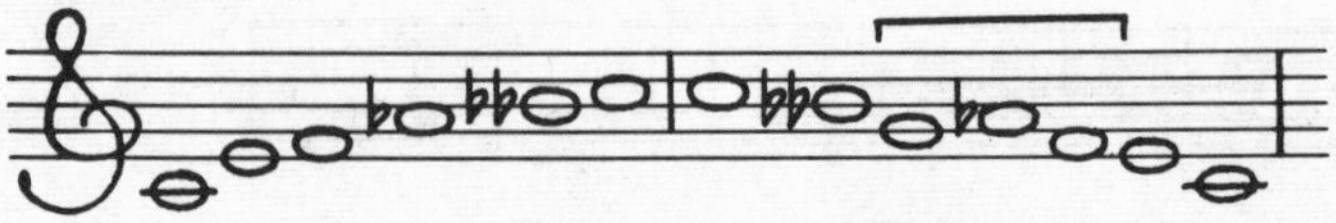

The note *RI* (D#) is avoided entirely. In ascent the note *PA* (G) is avoided and the descent shows one *vakra* feature.

(6) *Kalahans* (*Kalahaṃsa*)

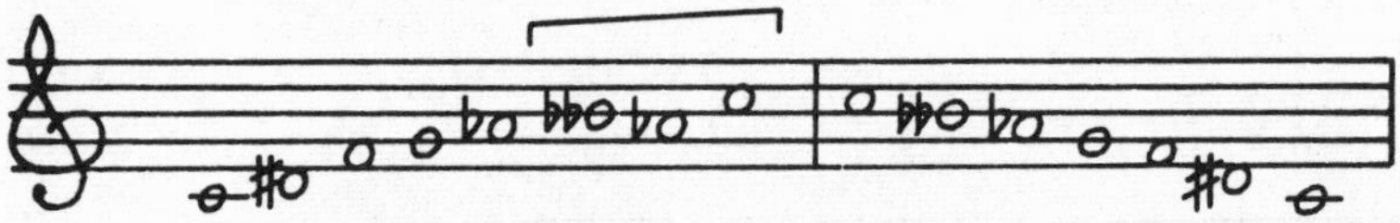

The note *GA* (E) is avoided entirely and the ascent shows one *vakra* feature.

This scale is identical with the *Yāgapriyā* material as it is shown in the SCM (130) shown above in the description of *rāga Yāgapriya* (31, ¯). [notation for material before 31, 1] The following melody specimen avoids the note *GA* (E) in ascent and descent. The sequence *PA-DHA-PA-MA* (G-Ab-G-F) is of some importance.

KALAHANS (*Triputa-tāla*) SCM, 189

(7) *Kallōla Baṅgala*

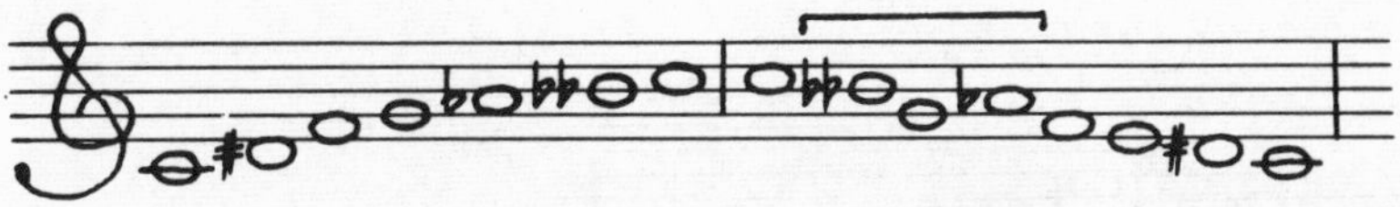

Ascent: the note *GA* (E) is avoided.
Descent: *sampūrṇa*; one *vakra* feature is shown.

(8) *Kanakachāri* (*Kanakacāri*)

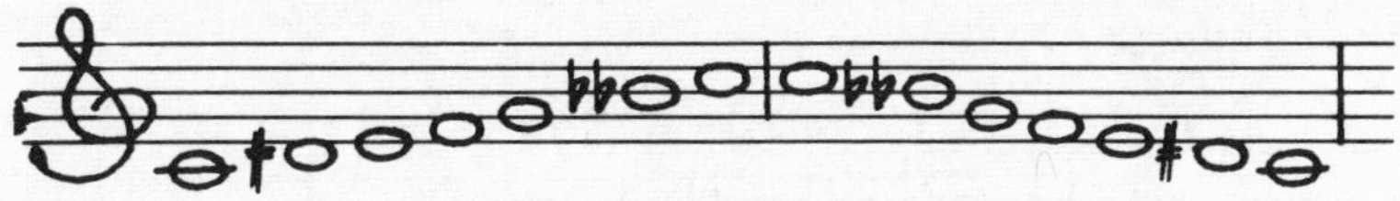

The note *DHA* (Ab) is avoided entirely.

(9) *Kānchani* (*Kāncani*)

The note *DHA* (Ab) is avoided entirely. This scale is identical with that of *rāga Kanakachāri* (31,8). N lists the two *rāga* names separately.

(10) *Kantimati*

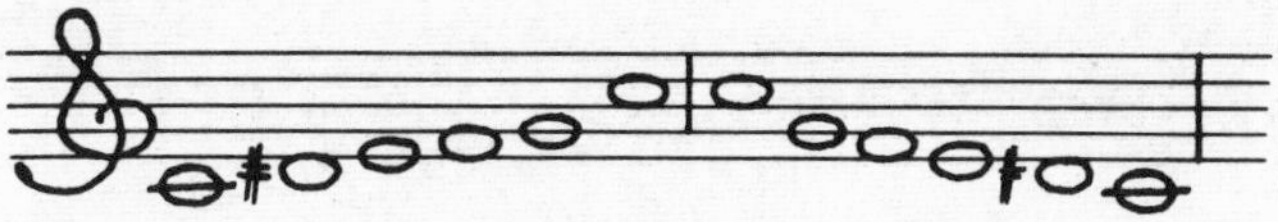

The notes *DHA* (Ab) and *NI* (Bbb) are avoided entirely.
Another *rāga* with the same name appears under the heading of the 60. *mēḷa* (10).

(11) *Kanyāvitāna*

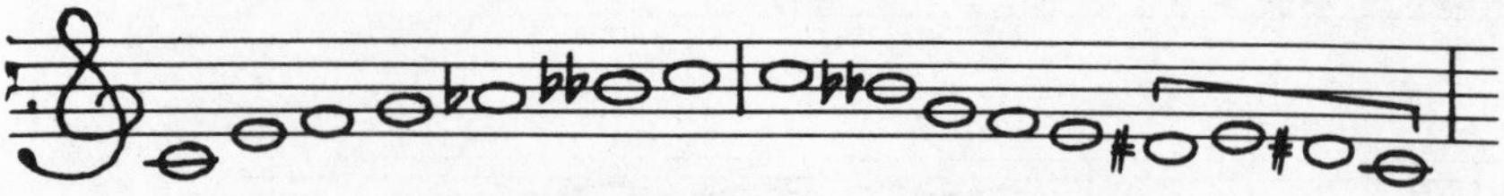

Ascent: the note *RI* (D#) is avoided.
Descent: the note *DHA* (Ab) is omitted; one *vakra* feature is shown.

(12) *Kōkila Gāndharvam*

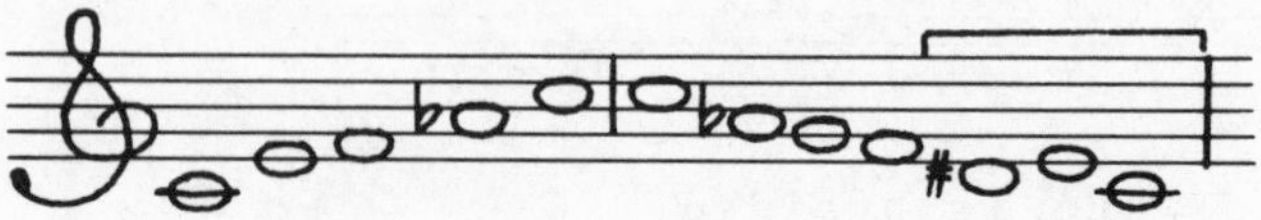

The note *NI* (Bbb) is avoided entirely. In ascent the notes *RI* (D#) and *PA* (G) are omitted. The descent shows one *vakra* feature.

(13) *Nāgagāndharvam*

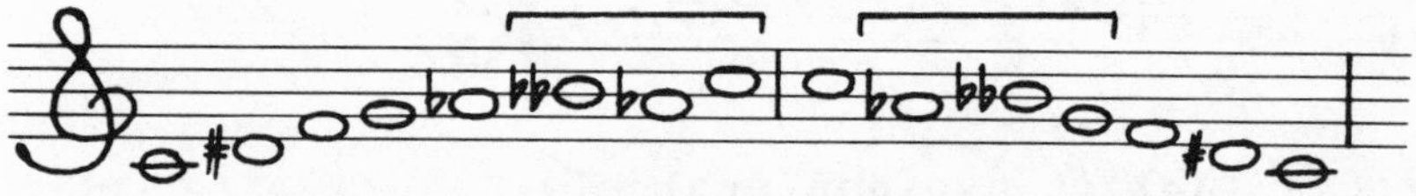

The note *GA* (E) is avoided entirely. One *vakra* feature is shown in ascent and one in descent.

(14) *Nirjhārini*

The notes *GA* (E) and *MA* (F) are avoided entirely.

(15) *Pratāpahaṃsi*

Ascent: the note *RI* (D#) is avoided; one *vakra* feature is shown.
Descent: *sampūrṇa*; one *vakra* feature is used.

(16) *Sahavāsiṇi*

The notes *MA* (F) and *DHA* (Ab) are avoided entirely.

(17) *Sarasāvāṇi*

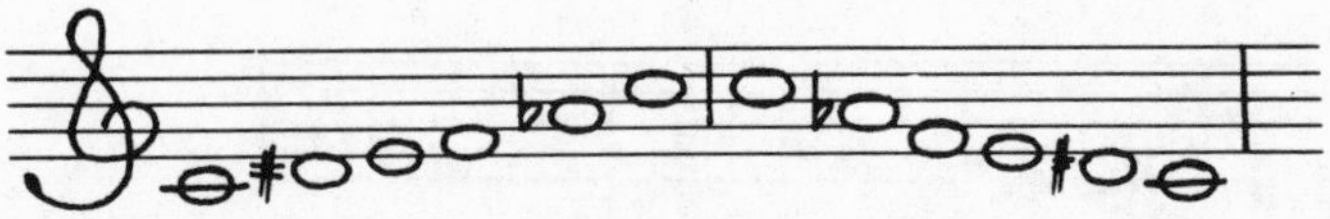

The notes *PA* (G) and *NI* (Bbb) are avoided entirely.

(18) *Sōmakriya*

Ascent: *sampūrṇa*; one *vakra* feature is shown.
Descent: the note *NI* (Bbb) is avoided; one *vakra* feature is used.

(19) *Sukhatāyini*

The notes *GA* (E) and *MA* (F) are avoided entirely.

32. *MĒḶA RĀGAVARDHANĪ*

In the past this *rāga* was called *Rāgachūḍamaṇi* (*Rāgacūḍamaṇi*). At the present time *Rāgachūḍamaṇi* is considered to be a *janya rāga* of *mēḷa* 32 (12) and will be described below.

RĀGAVARDHANĪ (*Triputa-tāla*) SCM, 190

Janya Rāgas of the 32. Mēḷa

(1) *Chitrapādita* (*Citrapādita*)

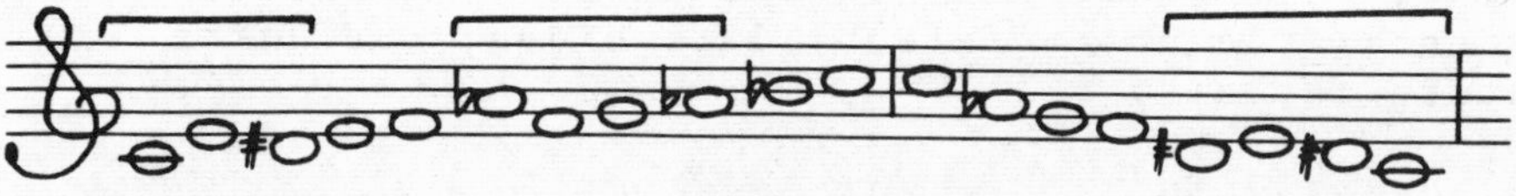

Ascent: *sampūrṇa*; two *vakra* features are shown.
Descent: the note *NI* (Bb) is avoided; one *vakra* feature is shown.

(2) *Ḍaumya*

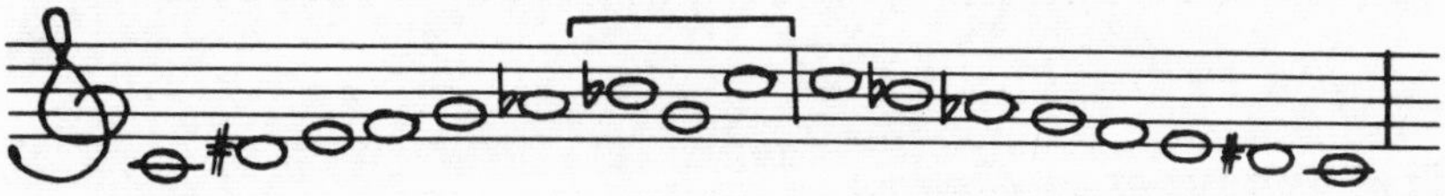

Ascent: *sampūrṇa*; one *vakra* feature is shown.
Descent: *krama sampūrṇa*.

(3) *Ghōshākari* (*Ghōṣākari*)

The note *NI* (Bb) is avoided entirely.

(4) *Haṃsa Nisāri*

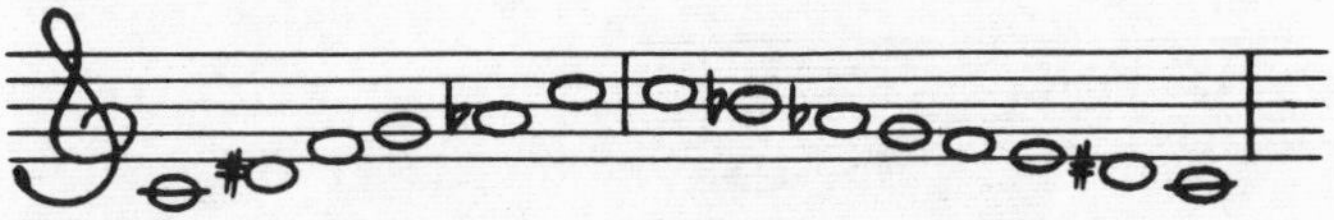

Ascent: the notes *GA* (E) and *NI* (Bb) are avoided.
Descent: *krama sampūrṇa*.

(5) *Hindōḷa Darbār*

Ascent: the notes *RI* (D#), *DHA* (Ab), and *NI* (Bb) are avoided.
Descent: the note *GA* (E) is omitted.

(6) *Hindōḷa Kāpi*

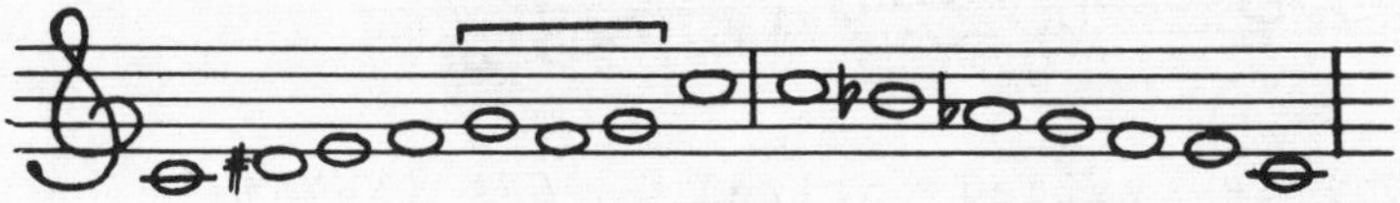

Ascent: the notes *DHA* (Ab) and *NI* (Bb) are avoided; one *vakra* feature is shown.
Descent: the note *RI* (D#) is omitted.

(7) *Hindōḷa Sāraṅga*

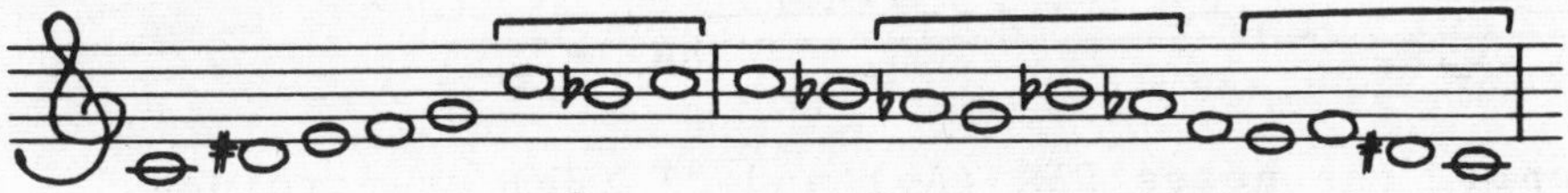

Ascent: the note *DHA* (Ab) is avoided; one *vakra* feature is shown.
Descent: *sampūrṇa*; two *vakra* features are used.

(8) *Jiṅglābhairavī* (*Jiṅgalābhairavī*)

Ascent: the notes *RI* (D#) and *NI* (Bb) are avoided; one *vakra* feature is shown.
Descent: *sampūrṇa*; one *vakra* passage is used.

(9) *Khadyōta Kānti*

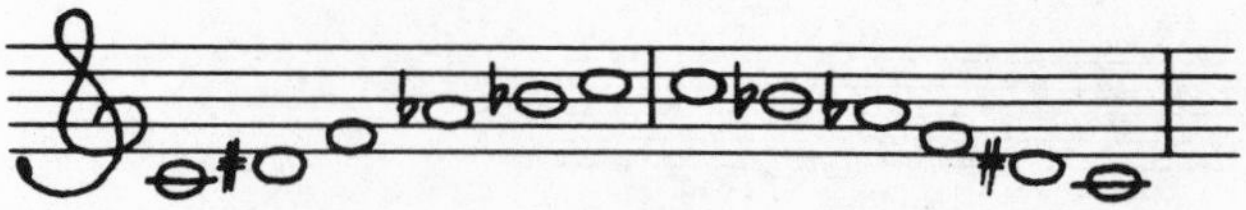

The notes *GA* (E) and *PA* (G) are avoided entirely.

(10) *Kusumachandrikā* (*Kusumacandrikā*)

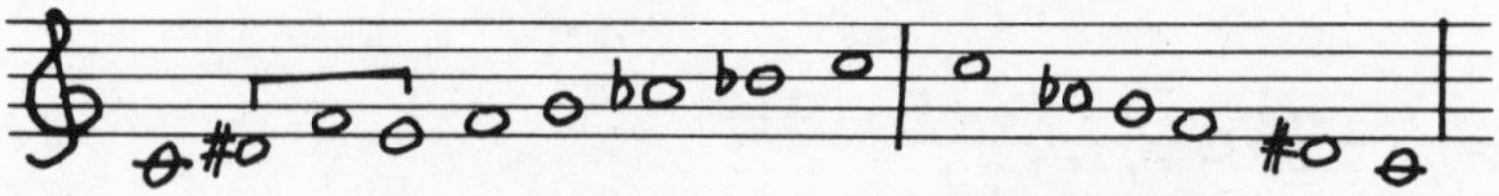

Ascent: *sampūrṇa*; one *vakra* feature is shown.
Descent: the notes *NI* (Bb) and *GA* (E) are avoided.

(11) *Kusumakallōlam*

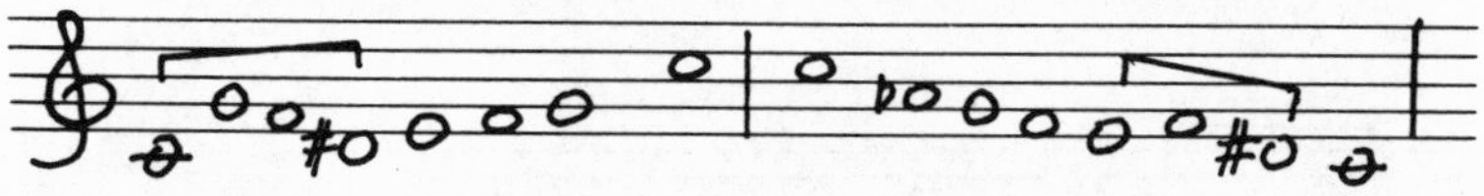

The note *NI* (Bb) is avoided entirely. *DHA* (Ab) is omitted in ascent. Two *vakra* passages appear, one in ascent and one in descent.

(12) *Rāgachūdāmaṇī* (*Rāgacūdāmaṇī*)

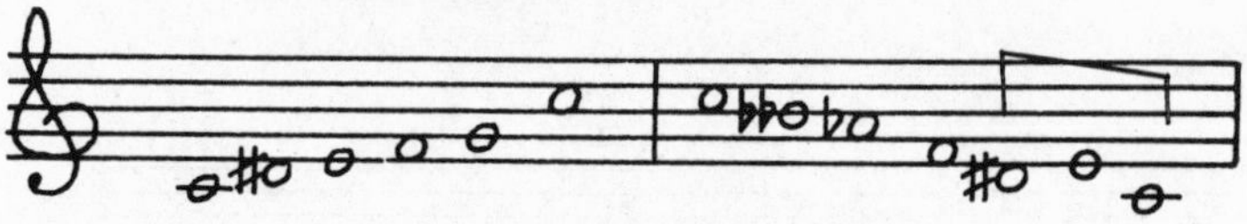

Ascent: the notes *DHA* (Ab) and *NI* (Bb) are avoided.
Descent: the note *PA* (G) is omitted; one *vakra* feature is shown.

R (p. 198) reports that in Veṅkaṭamakin's description of this *rāga* it is stated that the note *GA* (E) is to be avoided in ascent and *ṘI* (D#) in descent. This results in a scale noticeably different from the one used at the present time.

The following melody specimen, taken from the SCM, does not tally with R's report, because in it the note *GA* (E) is shown in ascent.

RĀGACHŪDĀMAṆĪ (*Triputa-tāla*) SCM, 190-91

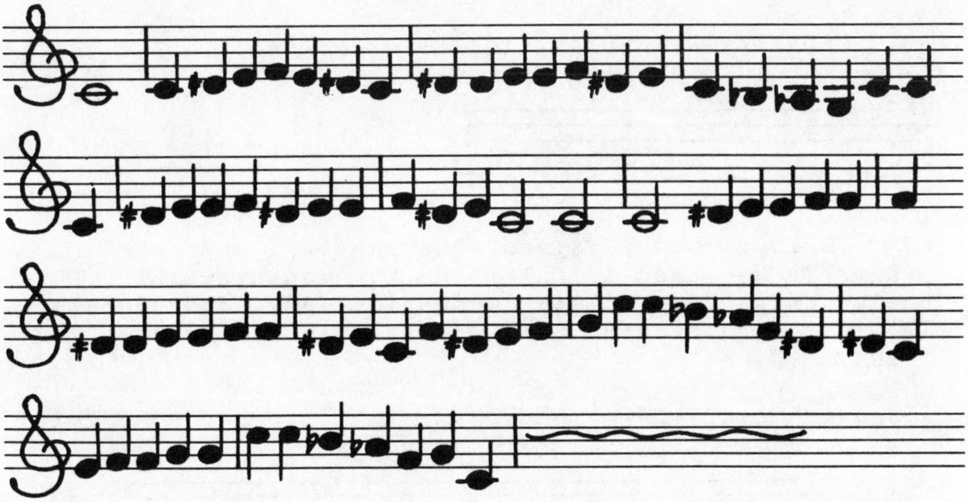

(13) *Rīṃkari*

The note *DHA* (Ab) is avoided entirely. The ascent shows one *vakra* feature and the descent omits the note *GA* (E).

(14) *Sāmantagiṅgala*

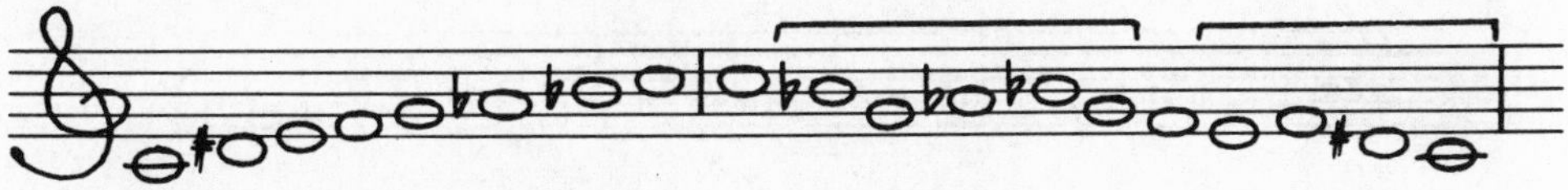

Ascent: *krama sampūrṇa*.
Descent: *sampūrṇa*; two extended *vakra* passages are shown.

(15) *Vipula*

The notes *MA* (F) and *NI* (Bb) are avoided entirely.

33. *MĒḶA GĀṄGEYABHUṢANĪ (GĀṄGEYABHUSHANĪ)*

Rāga Gāṅgeyabhuṣanī gained some popularity after Tyāgarāja had used it in his work. Veṅkaṭamakhin called this *rāga Gāṅgātaraṅgiṇī* (or *Gāṅgeyataraṅginī*). It will be considered below (33, 7) in its present form.

Gāṅgeyabhuṣanī (Triputa-tāla) SCM, 191-2

Janya Rāgas of the 33. Mēḷa

(1) *Ānanda Līlā*

Ascent: the note *DHA* (Ab) is avoided.
Descent: *krama sampūrṇa*.

(2) *Bhadrakara*

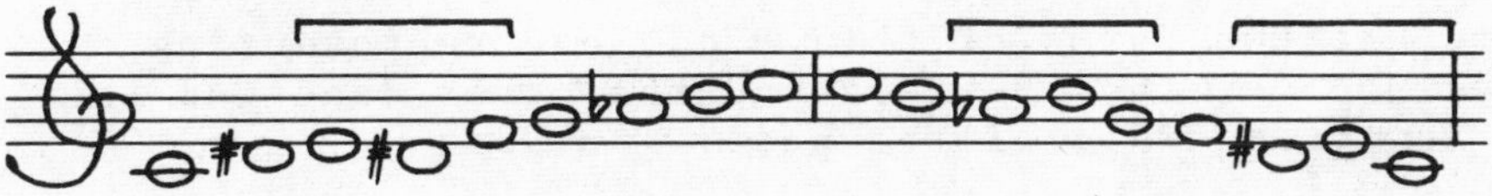

Ascent: *sampūrṇa*; one *vakra* feature is shown.
Descent: *sampūrṇa*; two *vakra* features are used.

(3) *Bharmāṅgi*

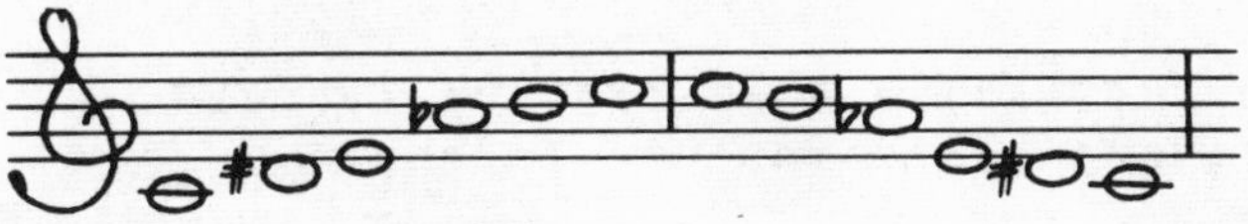

The notes *MA* (F) and *PA* (G) are avoided entirely.

(4) *Bhūpāḷa Rañjani*

The note *GA* (E) is avoided entirely.

(5) *Dēvamaṇi*

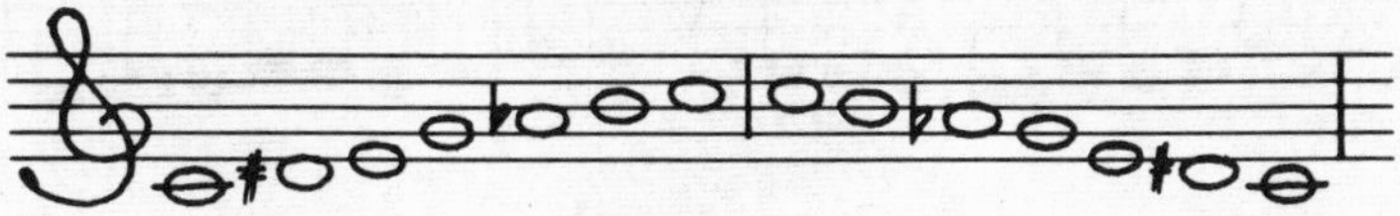

The note *MA* (F) is avoided entirely.

(6) *Gāmbhirya Nāṭa*

The note *DHA* (Ab) is avoided entirely. *RI* (D#) is avoided in ascent and *GA* (E) in descent.

Another *rāga* with the same name appears under the heading of the 36. *mēḷa* (5); it has the same ascent as 33, 6, but differs slightly in descent as will be shown below.

(7) *Gaṅgā Taraṅgiṇi* (*Gaṅgeya Taraṅgiṇi*)

There are two forms of this *rāga*: one representing a *janya rāga* of the 33. *mēḷa* and the other denoting the 33. *asampurna mēḷa* of the past.

(a) *Janya rāga Gaṅgā Taraṅgiṇi*:

Ascent: the notes *DHA* (Ab) and *NI* (B) are avoided.
Descent: *sampūrṇa*; one *vakra* feature is shown.

(b) SD (II, 180) states that Subbarama Dikṣitar in his *Saṅgīta Sampradāya-Pradarśinī* (see n. 4 of my Chapter on *Mēḷas* and *Rāgas*) presents the following scale of the 33. *aṡampūrṇa mēḷa*:

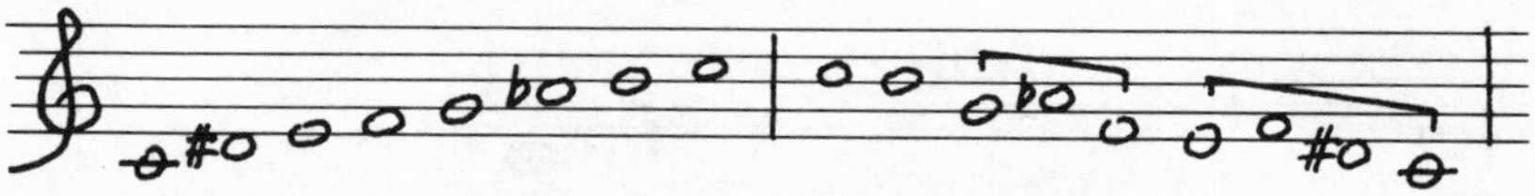

GAṄGĀTARAṄGIṆI (*Triputa-tāla*) SCM, 192-93

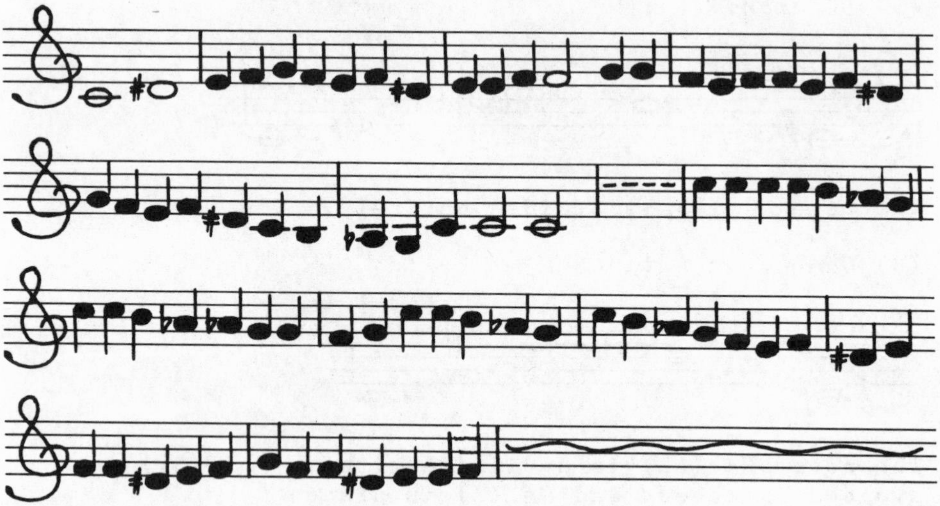

(8) *Ghavavati*

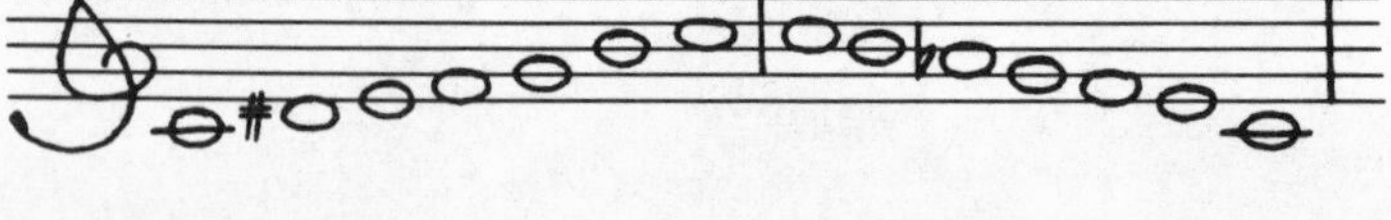

Ascent: the note *DHA* (Ab) is avoided.
Descent: the note *RI* (D#) is omitted.

(9) *Gītamūrti*

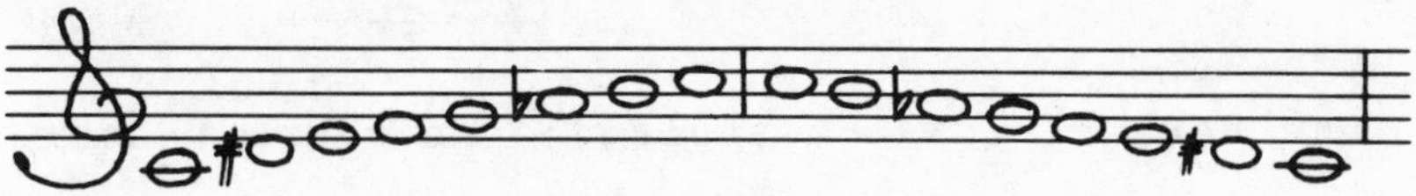

The scale of this *rāga* is identical with that of the primary *rāga Gāṅgeyabhuṣanī*.

(10) *Halamukhi*

Ascent: the note *GA* (E) is avoided.
Descent: the note *PA* (G) is omitted.

(11) *Hēma Bhūṣaṇi*

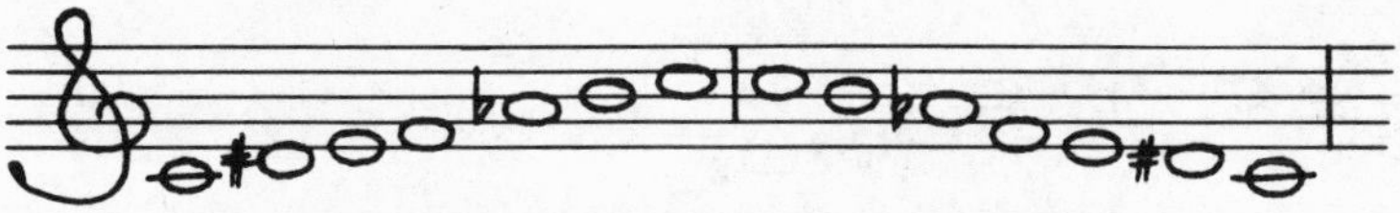

The note *PA* (G) is avoided entirely.

(12) *Hindōḷa Māḷavi*

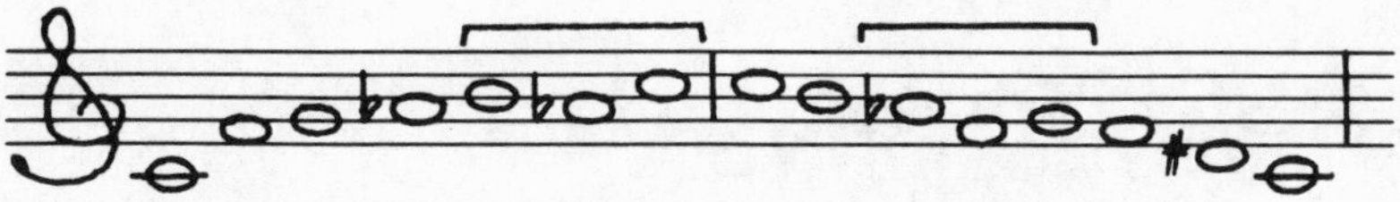

The note *GA* (E) is avoided entirely.
Ascent: the note *RI* (D#) is avoided; one *vakra* feature is shown.
Descent: one *vakra* feature is used.

(13) *Hinḍōḷa Nāyaki*

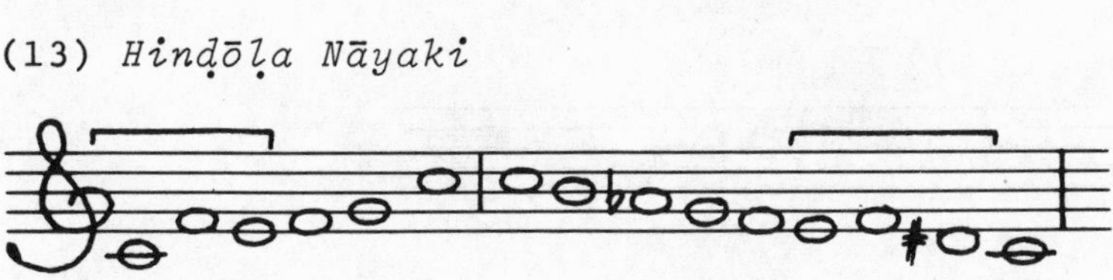

Ascent: the notes *RI* (D#), *DHA* (Ab), and *NI* (B) are avoided; one *vakra* feature is shown.
Descent: *sampūrṇa*; one *vakra* feature is used.

(14) *Hindōḷa Sāvēri*

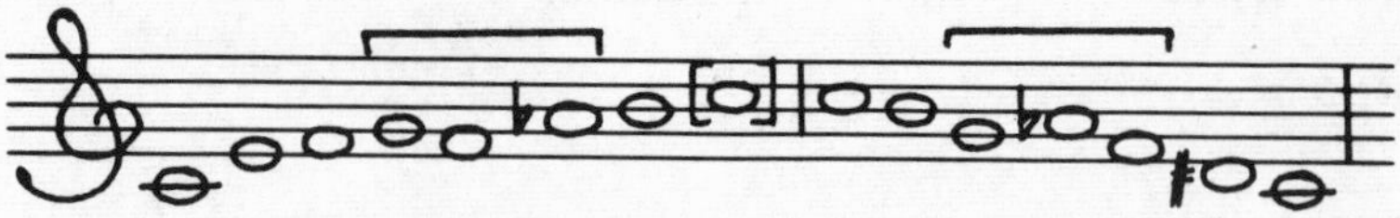

Ascent: the note *RI* (D#) is avoided; one *vakra* feature is shown.
Descent: the note *GA* (E) is omitted; one *vakra* feature is shown.

(15) *Kannaḍa Darbar*

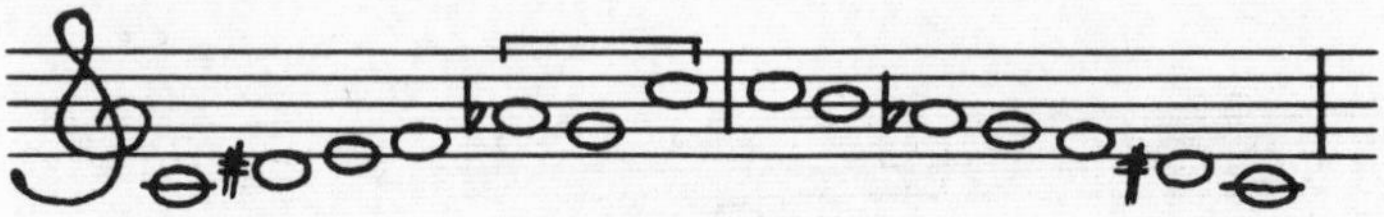

Ascent: the note *NI* (B) is avoided; one *vakra* feature is shown.
Descent: the note *GA* (E) is omitted.

(16) *Nādika*

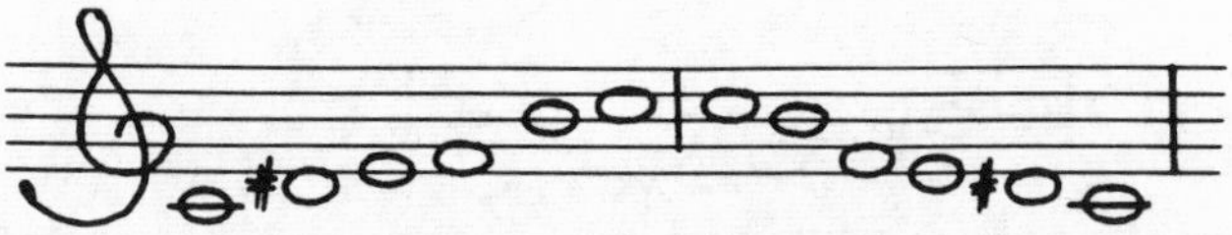

The notes *PA* (G) and *DHA* (Ab) are avoided entirely.

(17) *Nāgahindōḷam*

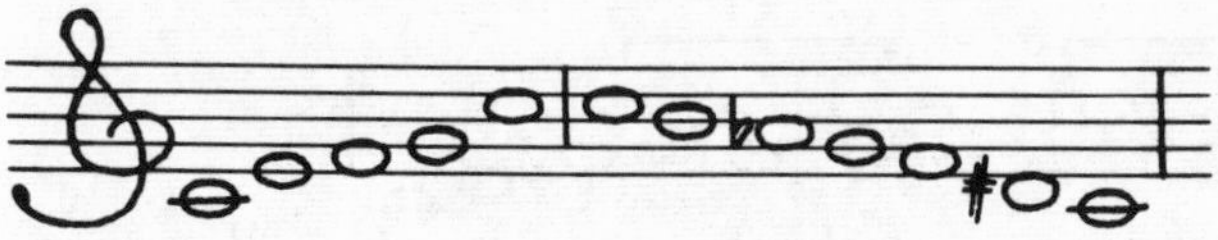

Ascent: the notes *RI* (D#), *DHA* (Ab), and *NI* (B) are avoided.
Descent: the note *GA* (E) is omitted.

(18) *Nirhāri*

The notes *GA* (E) and *PA* (G) are avoided entirely.

(19) *Śubhakari*

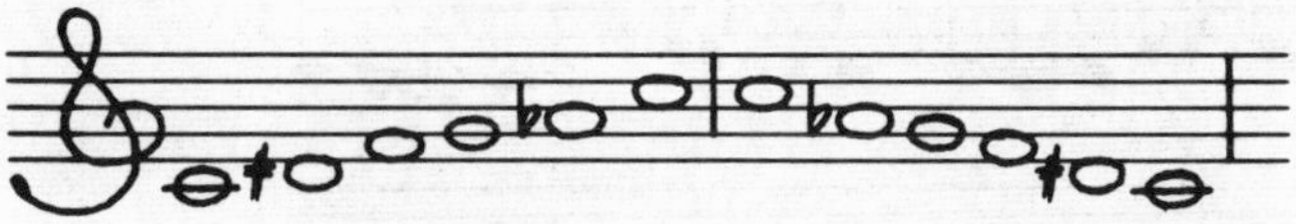

The notes *GA* (E) and *NI* (B) are avoided entirely.

(20) *Śuddhajiṅgala*

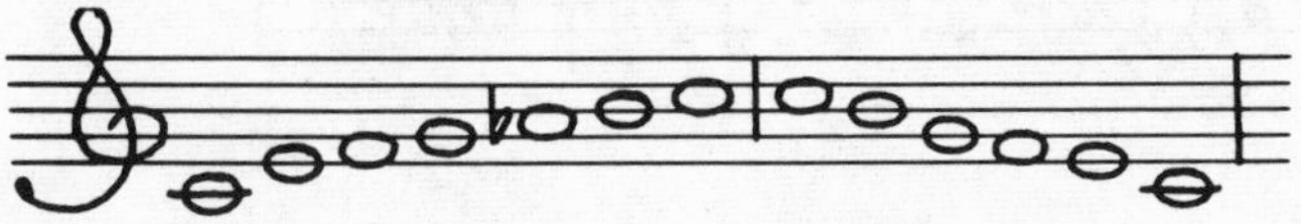

The note *RI* (D#) is avoided entirely. *DHA* (Ab) is omitted in descent.

(21) *Vādityavinōdini*

The notes *GA* (E) and *MA* (F) are avoided entirely.

34. *MĒḶA VĀGADHĪŚVARĪ (VĀGADHĪSHVARĪ)*

In the old *asampūrṇa mēḷa* system this *mēḷa* was called *Bhōgachhāyānāṭa*. *Chhāyānāṭa* is the name of the *rāga*, and *Bhōga* represents the *kaṭapayādi* prefixes.

At the present time *(Bhōga)chhāyānāṭa* is a *janya rāga* which will be considered below as 34, 4.

VĀGADHĪŚVARĪ (*Triputa-tāla*) SCM, 192-3

Janya Rāgas of the 34. Mēḷa

(1) *Bhānu Dīparam*

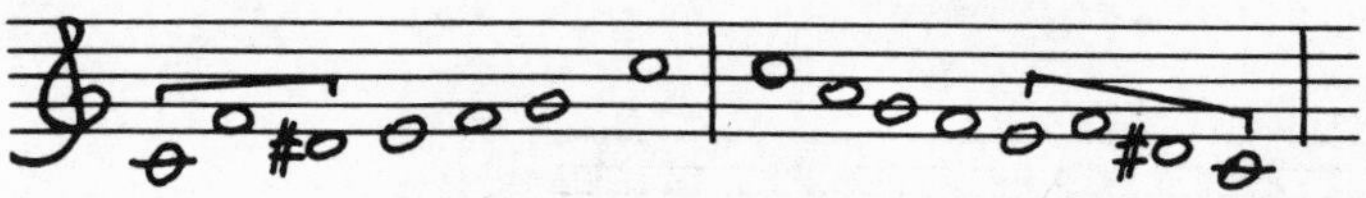

The note *NI* (Bb) is avoided entirely. *DHA* (A) is omitted in ascent which shows one *vakra* feature. The descent uses one *vakra* passage.

(2) *Bhānumañjari*

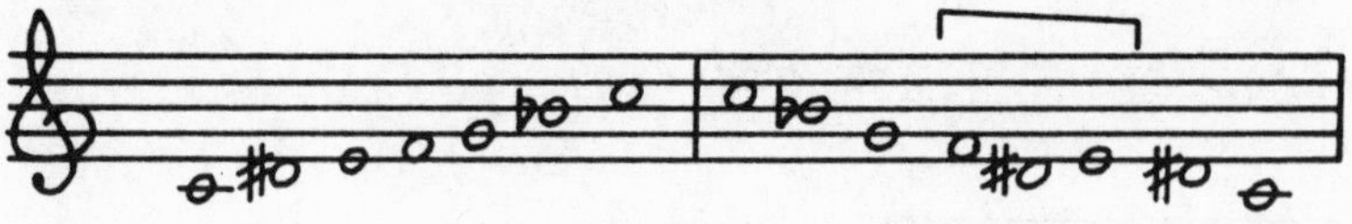

The note *DHA* (A) is avoided entirely. The descent shows one *vakra* feature.

BHĀNUMAÑJARI (*Triputa-tāla*) SCM, 195

(3) *Bhānu Tivra*

Ascent: identical with the ascent of *Bhānu Dīparam* (34,1).
Descent: *sampūrṇa*; one extended *vakra* passage is shown.

(4) *Chhāyānāṭa* (*Bhōgachhāyānāṭa*)

Ascent: the notes *DHA* (A) and *NI* (Bb) are avoided; one *vakra* feature is shown.
Descent: the note *GA* (E) is omitted; one *vakra* feature is used.
(See remark to the 34. *mēḷa Vāgadhīśvarī*.)

CHHĀYĀNĀṬA (*Triputa-tāla*) SCM, 131

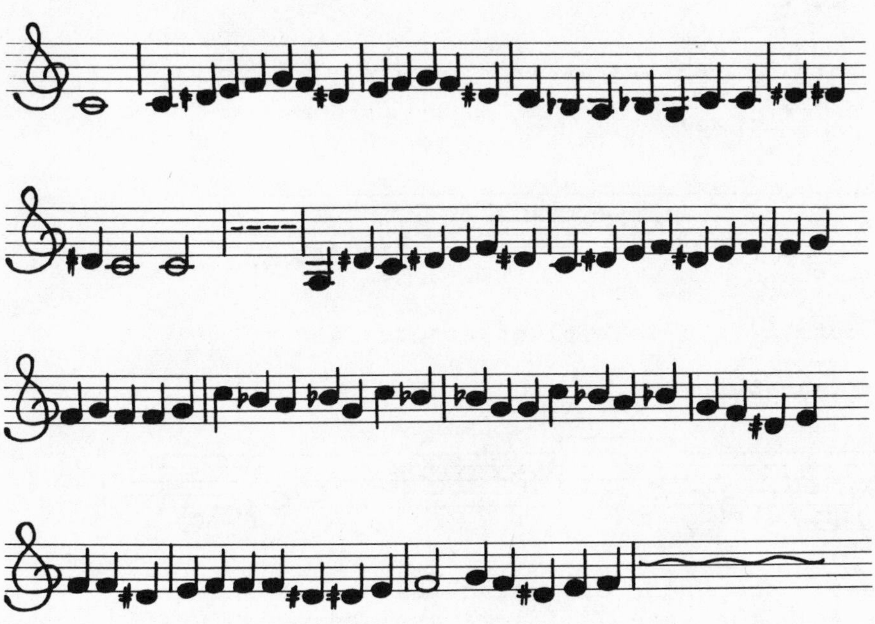

(5) *Dhrutarūpa*

The note *NI* (Bb) is avoided entirely. *DHA* (A) is omitted in descent where one extended *vakra* passage is used.

(6) *Gāna Vāridhi*

Ascent: *sampūrṇa*; one *vakra* feature is shown.
Descent: the note *GA* (E) is avoided; one *vakra* feature is used.

This *rāga* is occasionally ascribed to the 35. *mēḷa* in which the note *NI* is interpreted as B natural.

(7) *Ghōshavinōdini* (*Ghōṣavinōdini*)

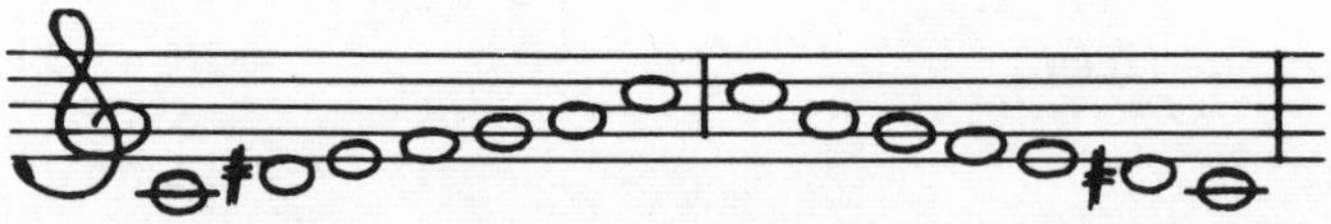

The note *NI* (Bb) is avoided entirely.

(8) *Jagadīśvari*

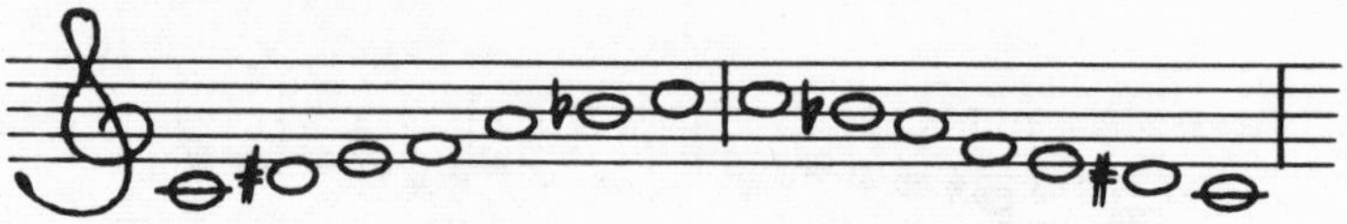

The note *PA* (G) is avoided entirely.

(9) *Kusumabhramari*

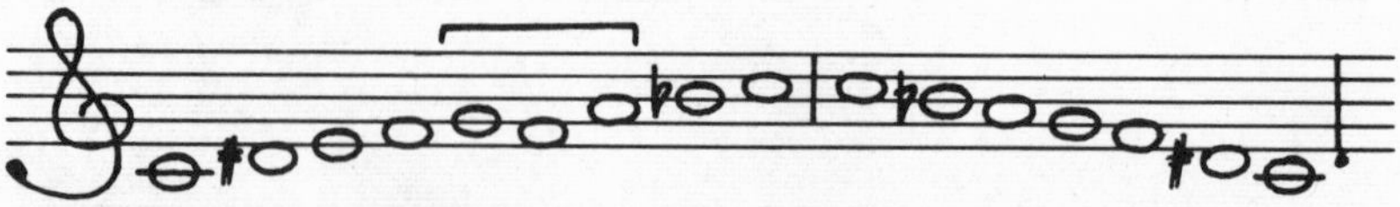

Ascent: *sampūrṇa*; one *vakra* feature is shown.
Descent: the note *GA* (E) is avoided.

(10) *Māgadhi*

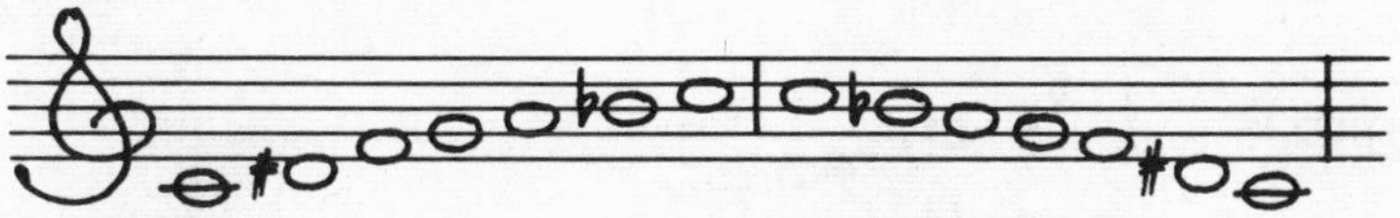

The note *GA* (E) is avoided entirely.

(11) *Māyāvinōdini*

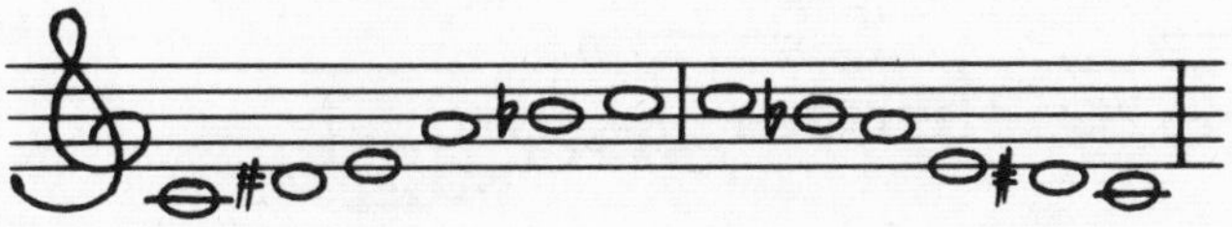

The notes *MA* (F) and *PA* (G) are avoided entirely.

(12) *Mēchagāndhāri* (*Mēcagāndhāri*)

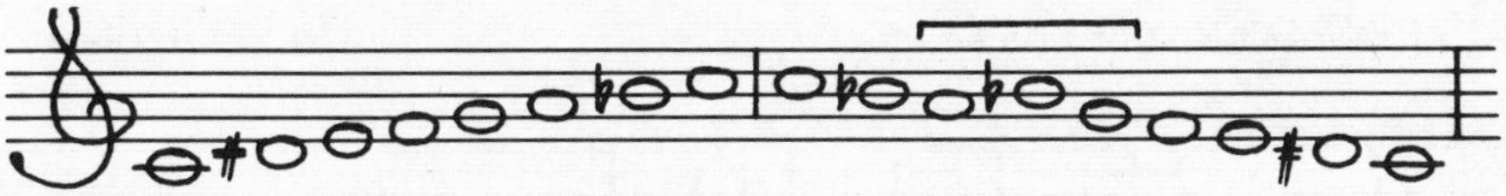

Ascent: *krama sampūrṇa*.
Descent: *sampūrṇa*; one *vakra* feature is shown.

(13) *Nalinasukhi*

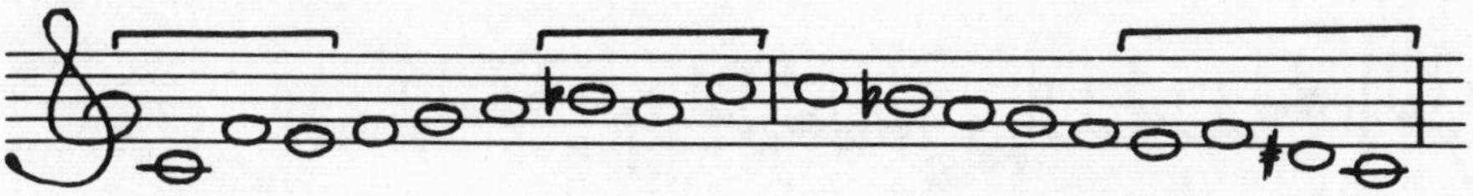

Ascent: the note *RI* (D#) is avoided and two *vakra* features are shown.
Descent: *sampūrṇa*; one *vakra* feature is used.

(14) *Nīlakaṇṭhapriya*

The note *MA* (F) is avoided entirely.

(15) *Saptāsvaktīrani*

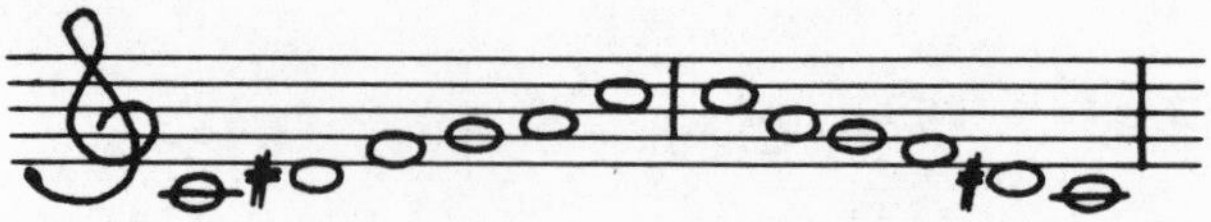

The notes *GA* (E) and *NI* (Bb) are avoided entirely. (See 34, 18.)

(16) *Śāradabharaṇam*

Ascent: the note *RI* (D#) is avoided; two *vakra* features are shown.
Descent: the note *GA* (E) is omitted; one *vakra* feature is used.

ŚĀRADABHARAṆAM (*Triputa-tāla*) SCM, 195-96

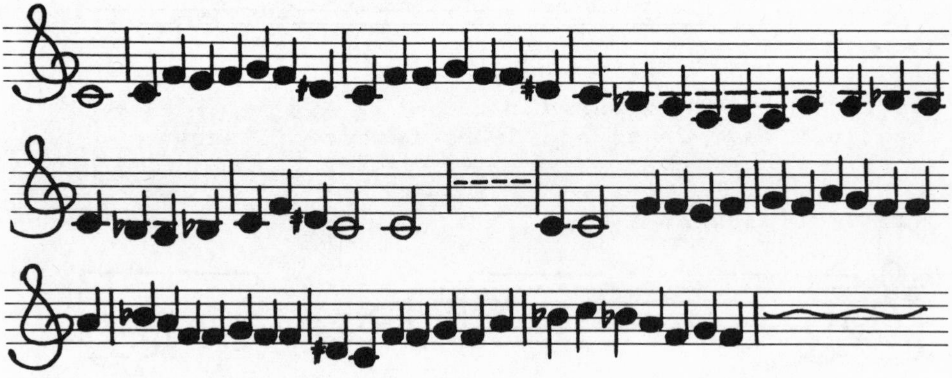

(17) *Sarasabhāṣiṇi*

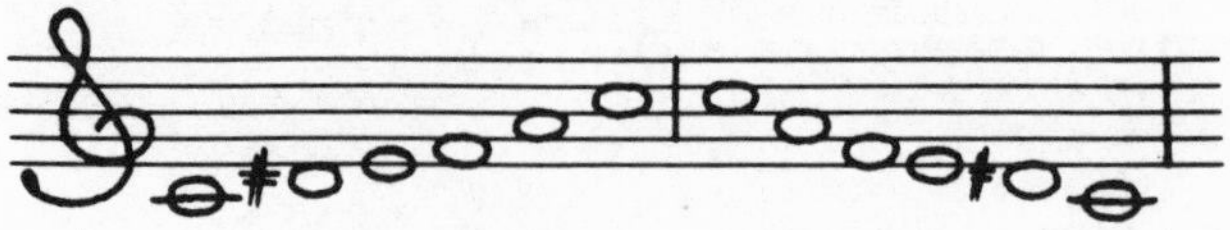

The notes *PA* (G) and *NI* (Bb) are avoided entirely.

(18) *Sarasīruhapriya*

The notes *GA* (E) and *NI* (Bb) are avoided entirely (see also 34,15). *Sarasīruhapriya* can also be listed under the heading of the 35. *mēḷa*.

(19) *Śuddhaghaṇṭānam*

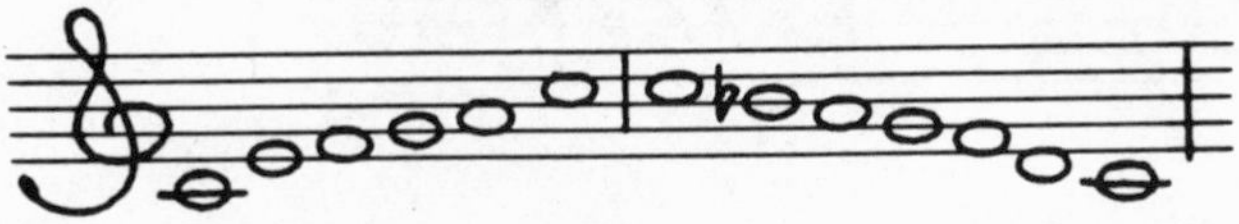

Ascent: the notes *RI* (D#) and *NI* (Bb) are avoided.
Descent: the note *GA* (E) is omitted.

(20) *Vimali*

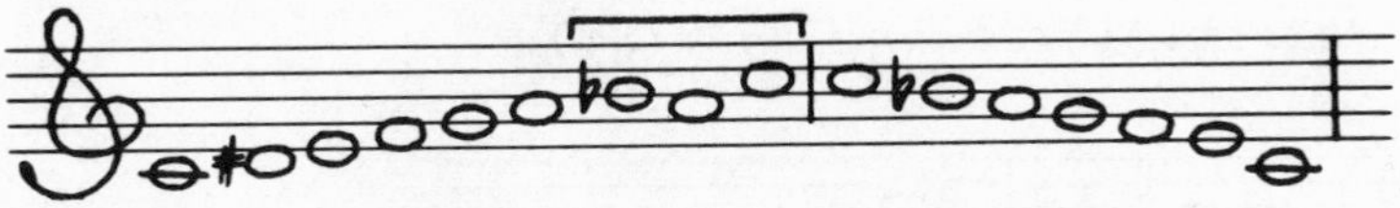

Ascent: *sampūrṇa*; one *vakra* feature is shown.
Descent: the note *RI* (D#) is avoided.

35. *MĒḶA ŚŪLINĪ*

Veṅkaṭamakhin called this *rāga Śailadēśākṣi*, in which the notes *RI* (D#) and *NI* (B) are to be avoided in ascent and *GA* (E) in descent. *Rāga Dēśākṣi* (*Dēśākṣirī* or *Dēśākṣarī*) will be shown below as 35, 3̇.

ŚŪLINĪ (*Triputa-tāla*) SCM, 196-7

Janya Rāgas of the 35. Mēḷa

(1) *Bhūṣaṇa Dhāriṇi* (*Bhūshaṇa Dhāriṇi*)

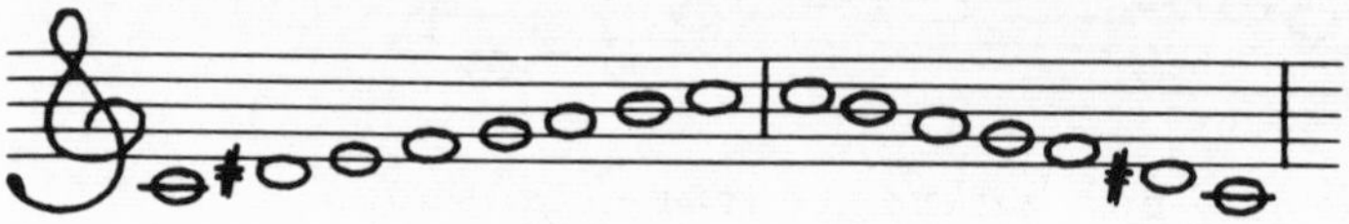

Ascent: *krama sampūrṇa*.
Descent: the note *GA* (E) is avoided.

(2) *Chalanī* (*Calanī*)

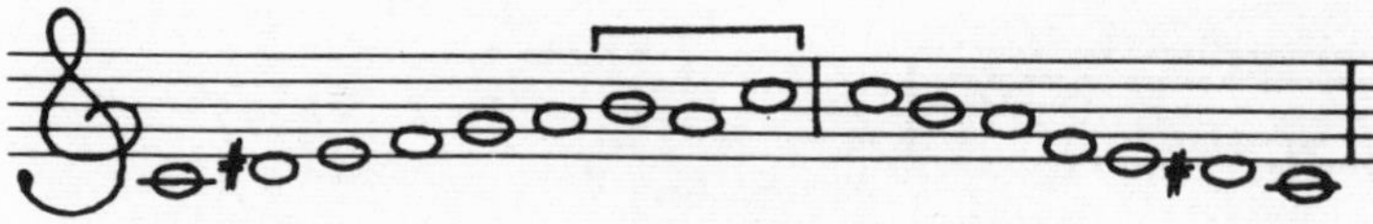

Ascent: *sampūrṇa*; one *vakra* feature is shown.
Descent: the note *PA* (G) is avoided.

(3) *Dēśākṣirī* (*Dēśākṣarī*)

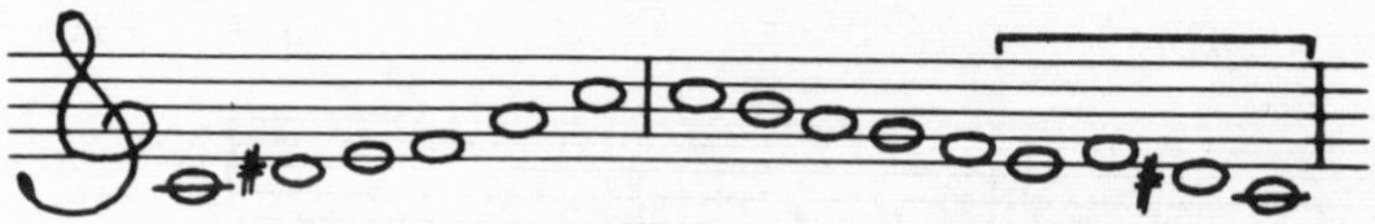

This *rāga*, at times also called *Dēśākṣī*, is related to Veṅkaṭamakhin's *Śailadēśākṣī* (see remark to the 35. *mēḷa Śūlinī*). The use of the name *Dēśākṣī* in this instance causes readers to refer to *rāgas* 28, 11 or 29, 31, hence it is advisable to call *rāga* 35, 3 by the name of *Dēśākṣirī*. Even a superficial comparison of the scales of 35, 3 with 28, 11 shows noticeable differences in ascent and descent.

The *Dēśākṣirī* ascent avoids the notes *PA* (G) and *NI* (B), the *sampūrṇa* descent uses one *vakra* passage.

(4) *Haṃsa Ghaṇṭanam*

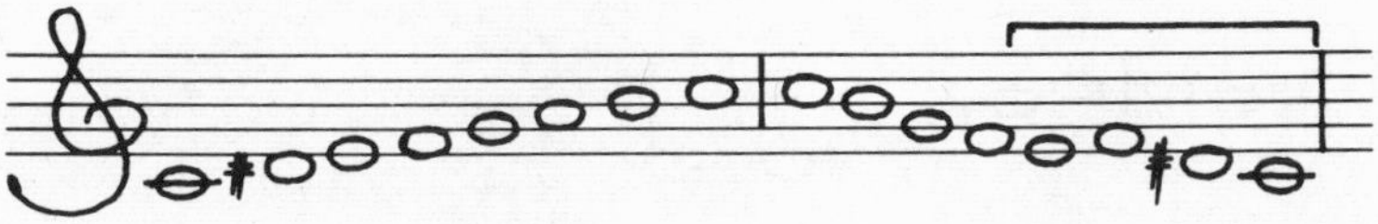

Ascent: *krama sampūrṇa*.
Descent: the note *DHȦ* (A) is avoided; one *vakra* feature is shown.

(5) *Haranarthana*

Ascent: the note *GA* (E) is avoided; two *vakra* features are shown.
Descent: the note *PA* (G) is omitted; two *vakra* features are used.

(6) *Kinnarāvaḷi*

The note *MA* (F) is avoided entirely.

(7) *Māruvakannaḍa*

The note *DHA* (A) is avoided entirely. One *vakra* feature is shown in ascent and one in descent.

(8) *Nalinahaṃsi*

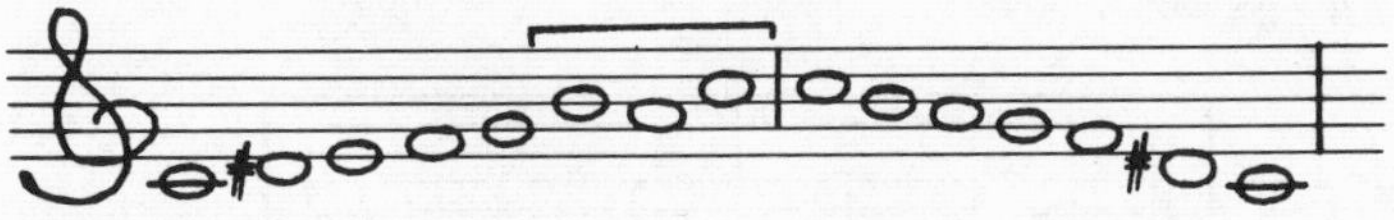

Ascent: *sampūrṇa*; one *vakra* feature is shown.
Descent: the note *GA* (E) is avoided.

(9) *Pratiti*

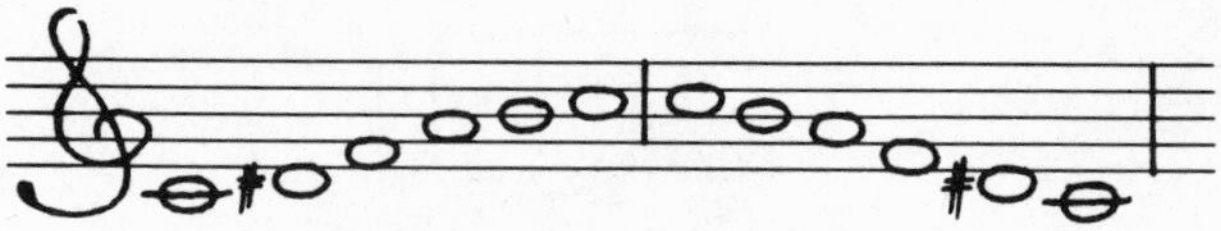

The notes *GA* (E) and *PA* (G) are avoided entirely.

(10) *Śuddhanilāmbari*

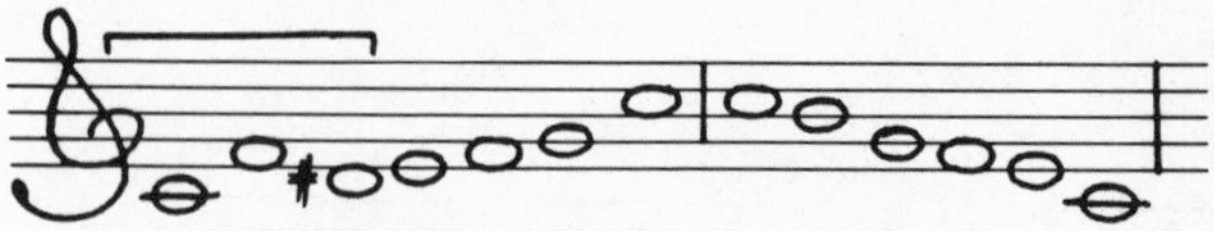

The note *DHA* (A) is avoided entirely. The ascent omits *NI* (B) and shows one *vakra* feature; the descent avoids *RI* (D#).

(11) *Tāṇḍavōllāsini*

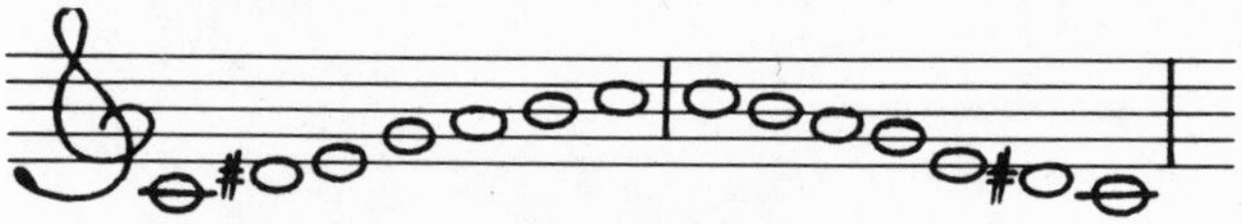

The note *MA* (F) is avoided entirely.

36. *MĒḶA CHALANĀṬA (CALANĀṬA)*

CHALANĀṬA (*Triputa-tāla*) SCM, 198-9

Janya Rāgas of the 36. Mēḷa

(1) *Achala Nāṭa (Acala Nāṭa)*

The note *PA* (G) is avoided entirely.

(2) *Ashṭamūrti (Aṣṭamūrti)*

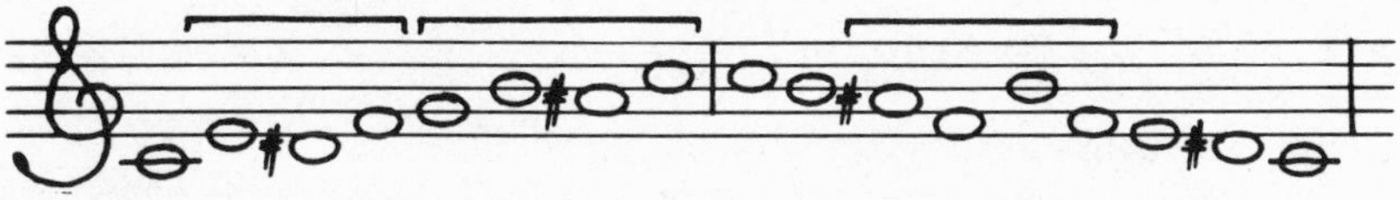

Ascent: *sampūrṇa*; two *vakra* features are shown.
Descent: the note *PA* (G) is avoided; one *vakra* feature is shown.

(3) *Bhāskarapriya*

The note *GA* (E) is avoided entirely.

(4) *Chidānandi (Cidānandi)*

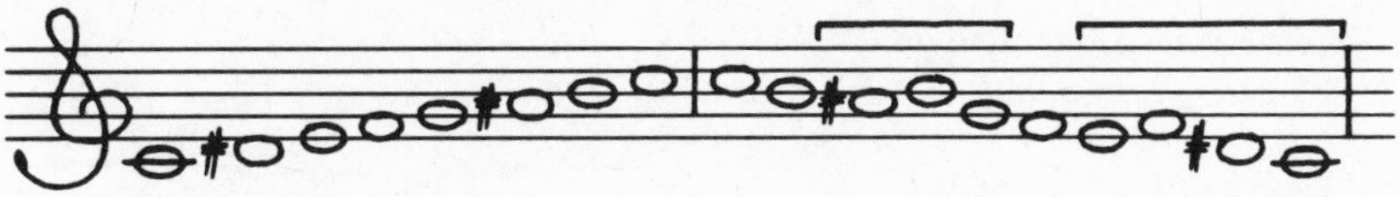

Ascent: *krama sampūrṇa*.
Descent: *sampūrṇa*; two *vakra* features are shown.

(5) *Gambhīra Nāṭa* (*Gambhīrya Nāṭa*)

The notes *RI* (D#) and *DHA* (A#) are avoided entirely. These two notes represent the characteristic feature of the 36. *mēḷa* and their omission can cause a placing of this *rāga* under the headings of other appropriate *mēḷas*. One similar *rāga* with the same name appears under the heading of the 33. *mēḷa* (6).

The SD (II, 174) remarks that "this is a *vīra* (heroic) *rasa rāga*. The tune called *Mallāri* played by nāgasvaram players at the commencement of temple processions is in this *rāga*."

(6) *Ghōradarśiṇi*

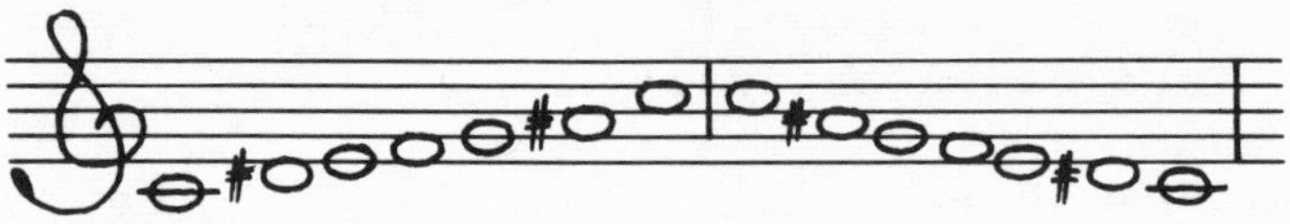

The note *NI* (B) is avoided entirely.

(7) *Hindōḷa Mōhanam*

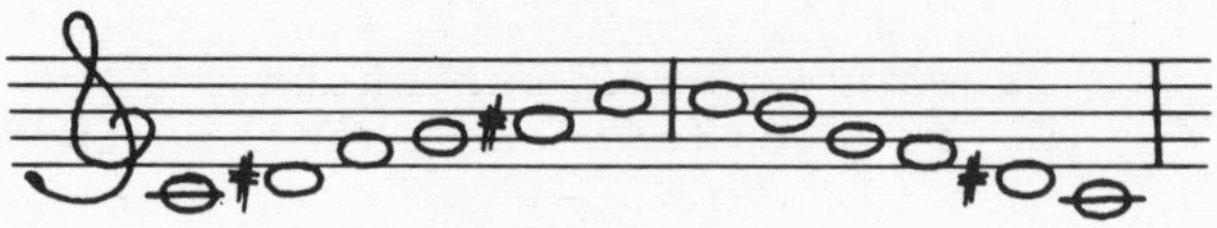

The note *GA* (E) is avoided entirely. *NI* (B) is avoided in ascent and *DHA* (A#) in descent.

(8) *Kōkilanāṭa*

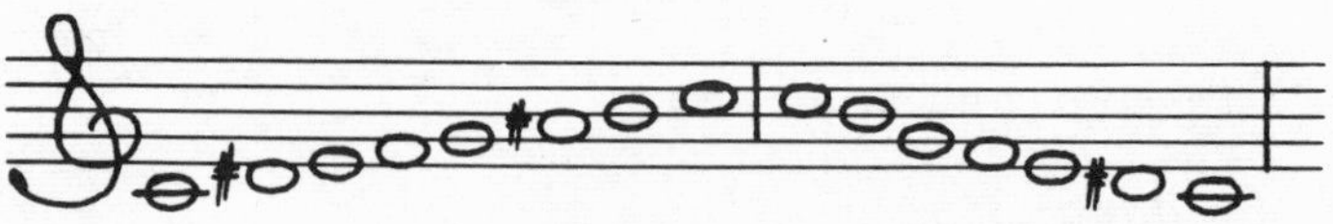

Ascent: *krama sampūrṇa*.
Descent: the note *DHA* (A#) is avoided.

(9) *Lōlākchi* (*Lōlākci*)

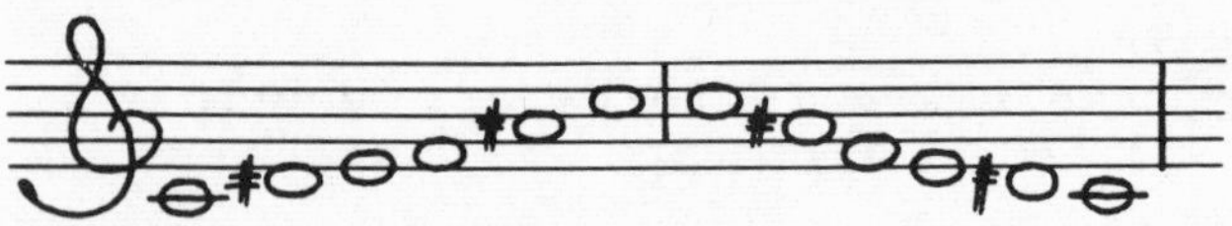

The notes *PA* (G) and *NI* (B) are avoided entirely.

(10) *Mañjula*

The scale of this *rāga* is identical with that of the primary *rāga Chalanāṭa* (36. *mēḷa*). Here *rāga Mañjula* is listed separately because some southern authors (e.g., N) employ the same method.

(11) *Nāṭa*

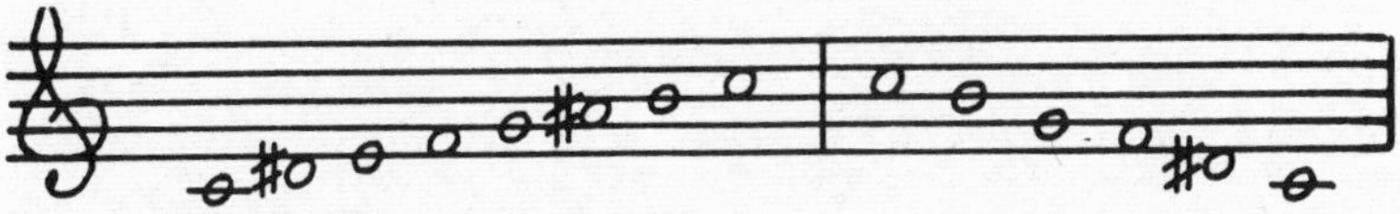

Ascent: *krama sampūrṇa*.
Descent: the notes *DHA* (A#) and *GA* (E) are avoided.

The note *DHA* (A#) although permissible in ascent is often avoided entirely or is treated so weakly that its use is hardly noticed, as can be observed in the melody specimen shown below. This specimen, a song, was composed by Appaya Dikṣitar, who was born in Adapalayam, Madras State and died in 1593. (Another source states that he was born in 1552 and died in 1624.)

NĀṬA RĀGA (*Eka-tāla*) SPC, II, 38

(12) *Nēpāli (Nēipāli)*

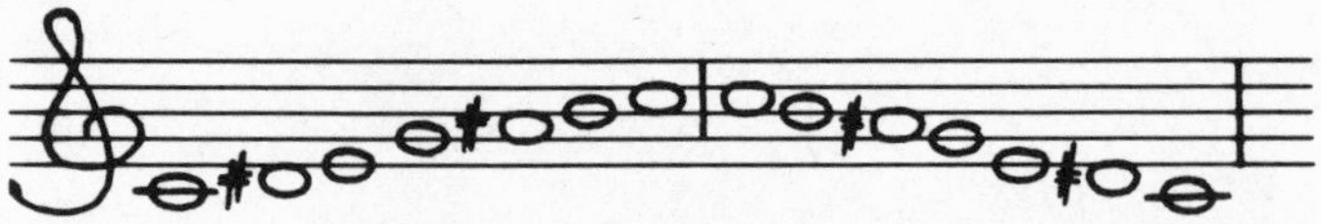

The note *MA* (F) is avoided entirely.

(13) *Rēva (Rēwa)*

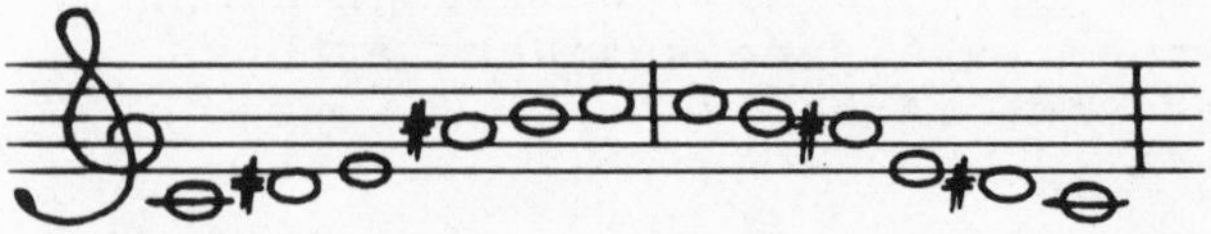

The notes *MA* (F) and *PA* (G) are avoided entirely.

(14) *Ruchirangi (Rucirangi)*

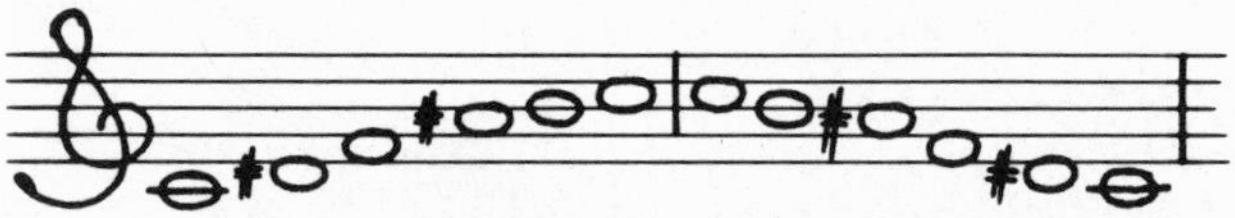

The notes *GA* (E) and *PA* (G) are avoided entirely.

(15) *Sāyujyatāyini*

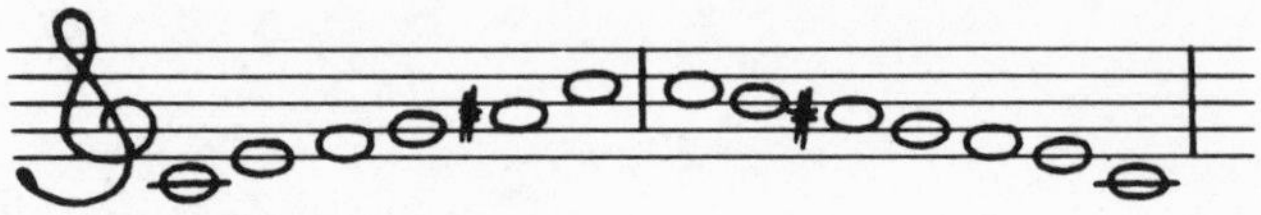

The note *RI* (D#) is avoided entirely. *NI* (B) is omitted in ascent.

(16) *Śrīmañjula*

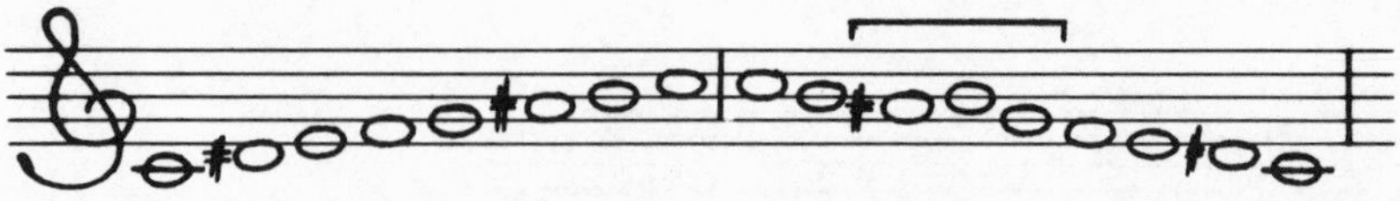

Ascent: *krama sampūrṇa*.
Descent: *sampūrṇa*; one *vakra* feature is shown.

(17) *Surarañjaṇi*

The notes *MA* (F) and *DHA* (A#) are avoided entirely.

(18) *Śuddhanāṭa*

The notes *RI* (D#) and *DHA* (A#), both characteristic of the 36. *mēḷa*, are avoided entirely.

(19) *Varṇakariṇa*

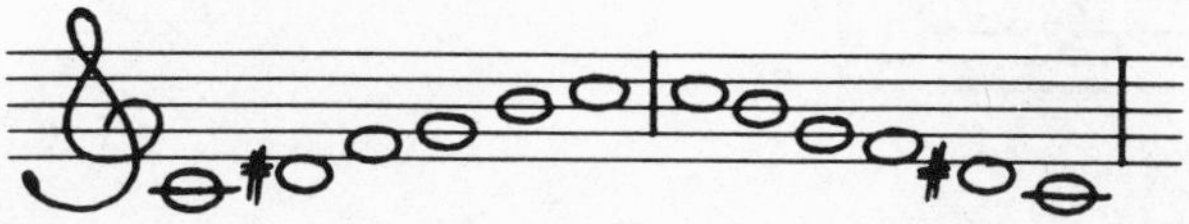

The notes *GA* (E) and *DHA* (A#) are avoided entirely. This scale is identical with that of *rāga Vasantatāriṇi* (36, 20).

(20) *Vasantatāriṇi*

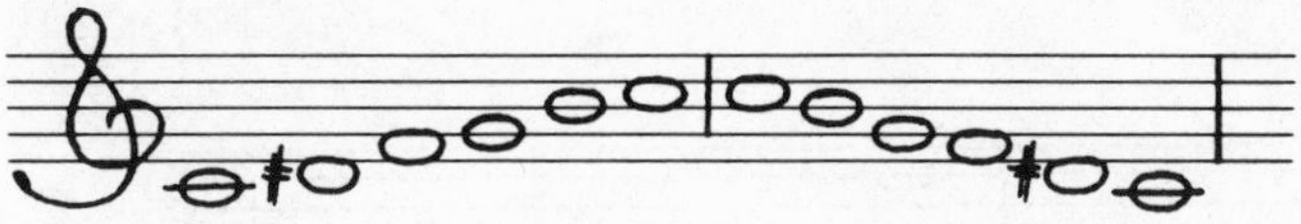

The notes *GA* (E) and *DHA* (A#) are avoided entirely. This scale is identical with that of *rāga Varṇakariṇa* (36, 19).

(21) *Vijayaprata*

The note *PA* (G) is avoided entirely. *NI* (B) is omitted in ascent and *DHA* (A#) in descent.

Chakra VII

37. *MĒḶA SĀLAGA*

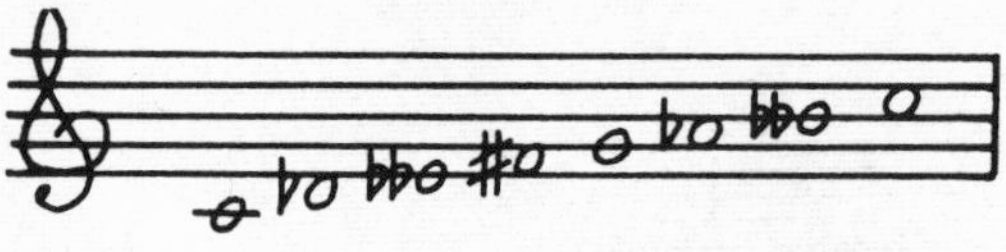

Although it is well known and has been stated before, it may be repeated here once more that the sequence of the tone materials of *mēḷas* 1-36 is repeated in the same order in *mēḷas* 37-72. The only difference is that in the sequence 1-36 the note *MA* (F) is used, while in the sequence 37-72 *prati MA* (F#) is employed.

SĀLAGA (*Triputa-tāla*) SCM, 200

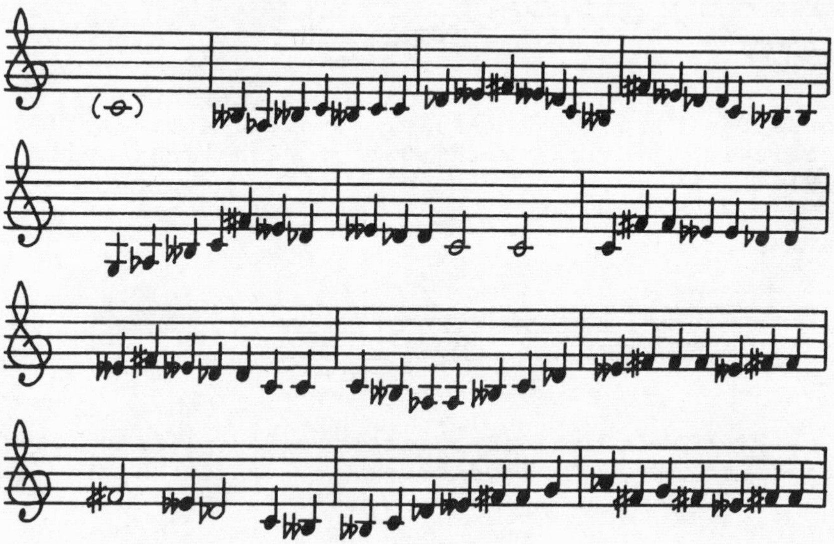

Janya Rāgas of the 37. Mēḷa

(1) *Ālāpi*

This scale is identical with that of the primary *rāga* *Sālaga*, *mēḷa* 37.

(2) *Alaru*

The notes *RI* (Db) and *PA* (G) are avoided entirely.

(3) *Bhārgavī*

The note *RI* (Db) is avoided entirely.
Another *rāga* with the same name appears under the heading of the 9. *mēḷa* (4).

(4) *Bhōga Sāvēri*

This *rāga* has *niṣādāntya* character. In its ascending scale the note *GȦ* (Ebb) is avoided. Occasionally also *MA* (F#) can be omitted.

The following melody specimen uses the note *MA* in ascent:

BHŌGASĀVĒRI (*Triputa-tāla*) SCM, 201-2

(5) *Bhōga Varāḷi*

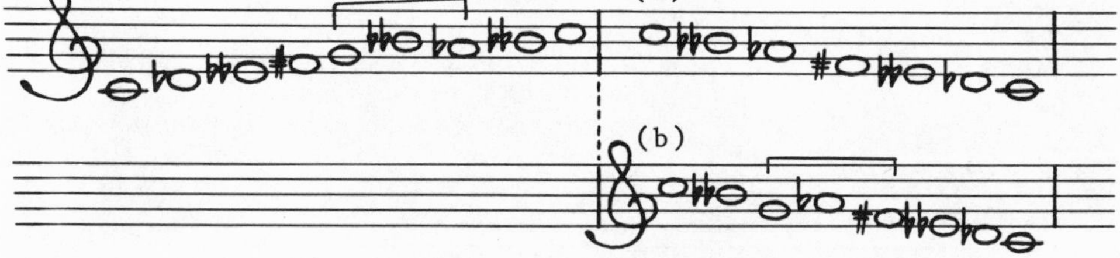

Ascent: *sampūrṇa*; one *vakra* feature is shown.
Descent: two forms are in use:
(a) the note *PA* (G) is avoided.
(b) *sampūrṇa*; one *vakra* feature is used.
Another *rāga* with the same name appears under the heading of the 12. *mēḷa* (3).

(6) *Bhōga Vardhani*

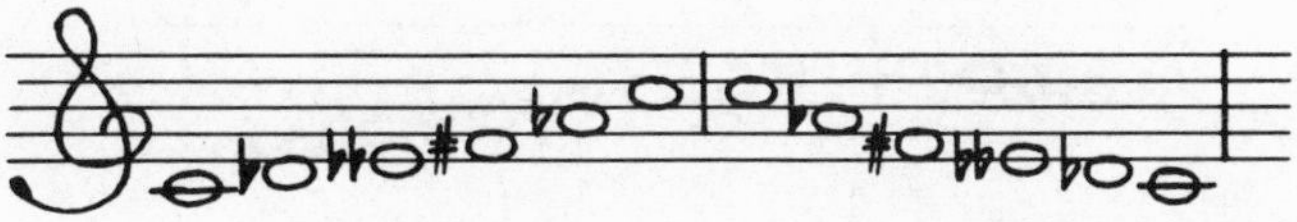

The notes *PA* (G) and *NI* (Bbb) are avoided entirely.

(7) *Ēlāṅka Manōharī*

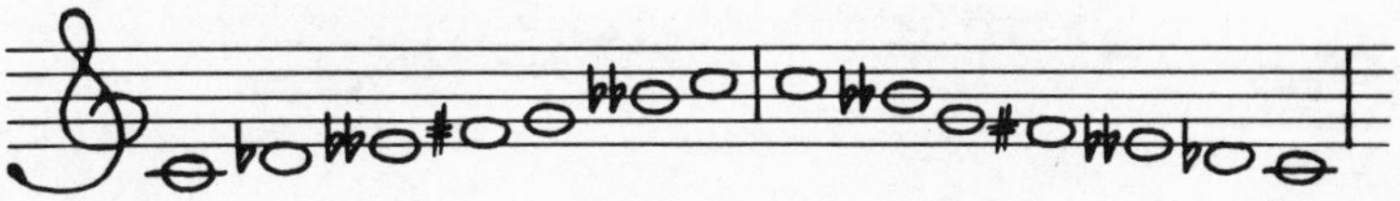

The note *DHA* (Ab) is avoided entirely.

(8) *Guṇabhūṣaṇi*

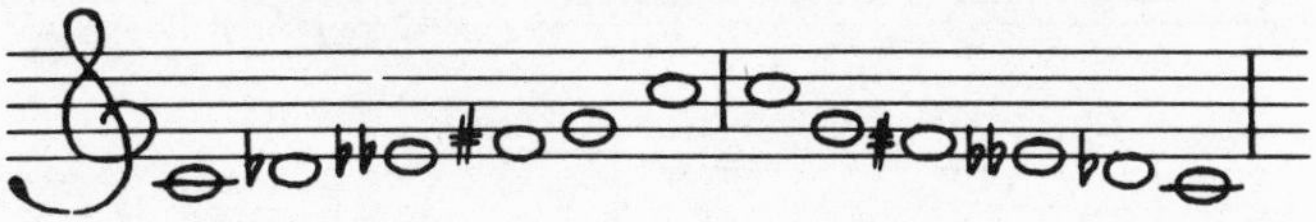

The notes *DHA* (Ab) and *NI* (Bbb) are avoided entirely.

(9) *Hāradhāriṇi*

The notes *RI* (Db) and *NI* (Bbb) are avoided entirely.

(10) *Hastini*

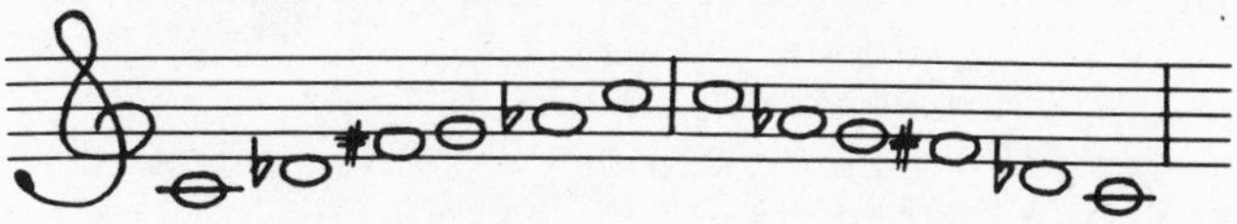

The notes *GA* (Ebb) and *NI* (Bbb) are avoided entirely.

(11) *Kamala Vasantam*

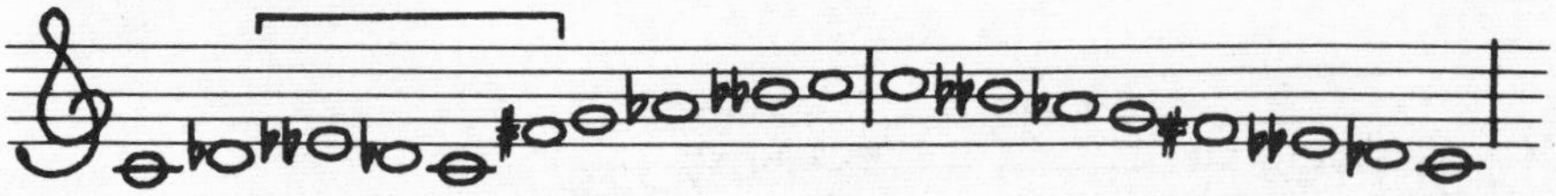

Ascent: *sampūrṇa*; one extended *vakra* passage is shown.
Descent: *krama sampūrṇa*.

(12) *Kamalika Vasantam*

Ascent: *sampūrṇa*; one *vakra* feature is shown.
Descent: the note *PA* (G) is avoided.

(13) *Kānta Mañjari*

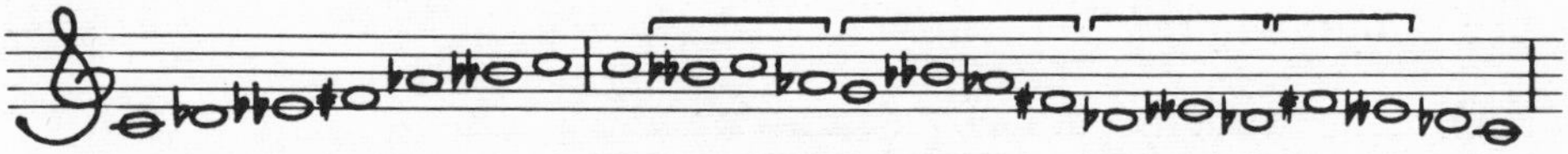

Ascent: the note *PA* (G) is avoided.
Descent: *sampūrṇa*; four *vakra* features are shown.

(14) *Karuṇapriya*

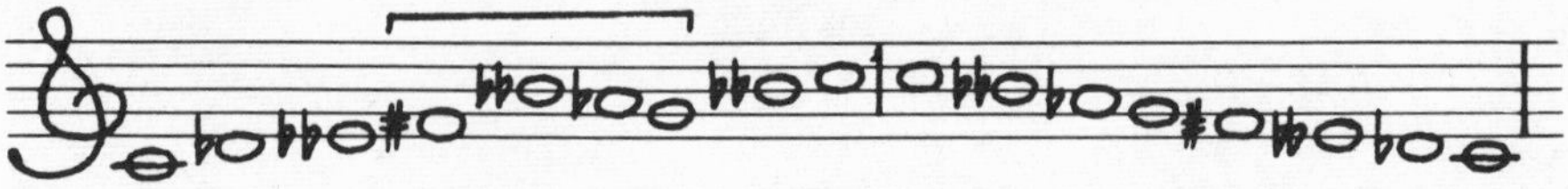

Ascent: *sampūrṇa*; one extended *vakra* feature is shown.
Descent: *krama sampūrṇa*.

(15) *Kusumarañjani*

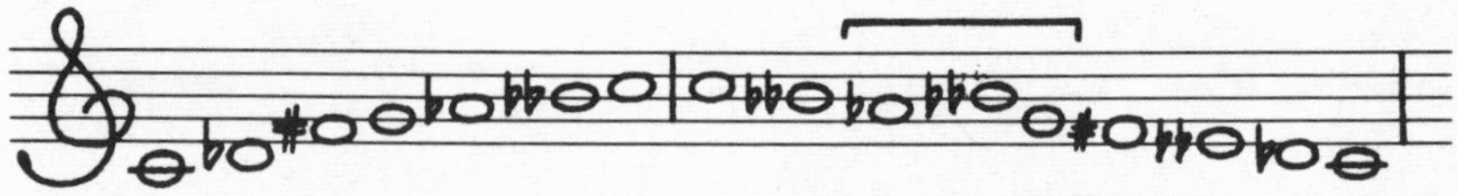

Ascent: the note *GA* (Ebb) is avoided.
Descent: *sampūrṇa*; one *vakra* feature is shown.

(16) *Lalitamāruva*

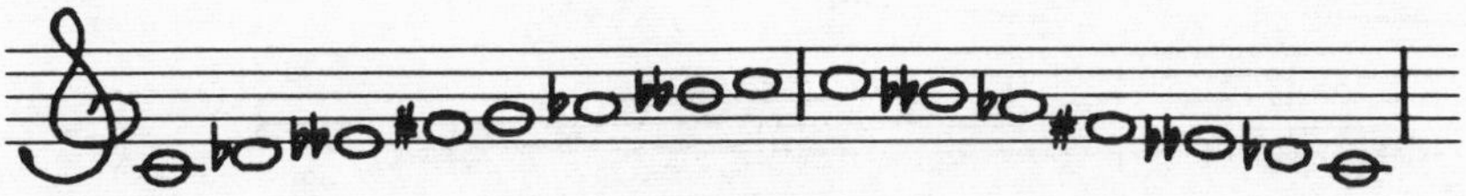

Ascent: *krama sampūrṇa*.
Descent: the note *PA* (G) is avoided.

(17) *Mēlagam*

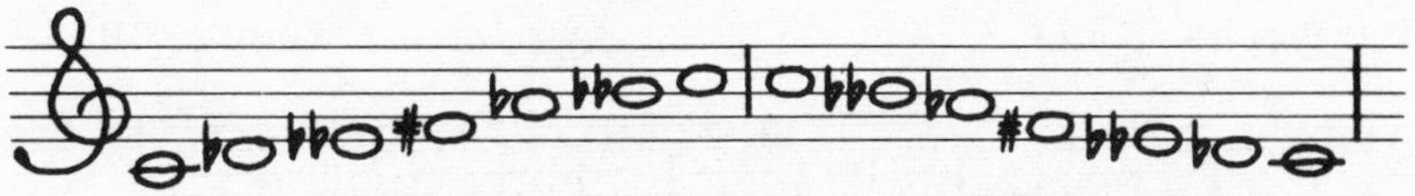

The note *PA* (G) is avoided entirely.

(18) *Nādabhramari*

The ascent of this *niṣādāntya rāga* shows one *vakra* feature. The descent is *sampūrṇa*.

(19) *Raṅgavalli*

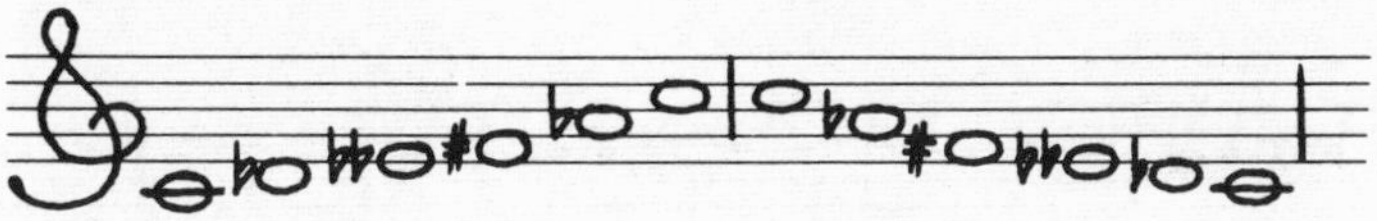

The notes *PA* (G) and *NI* (Bbb) are avoided entirely.

(20) *Sālavāṅgam*

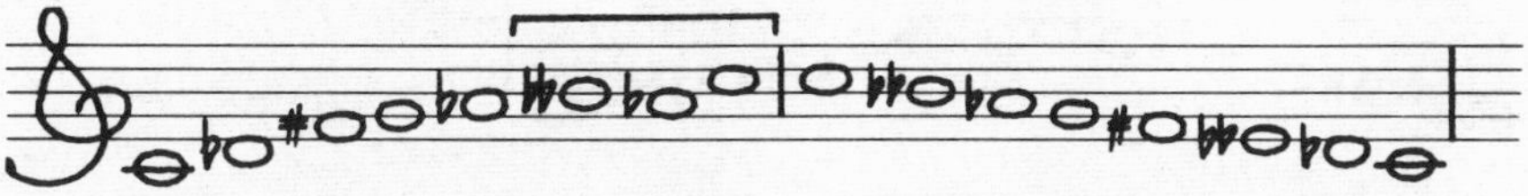

Ascent: the note *GA* (Ebb) is avoided; one *vakra* feature is shown.
Descent: *krama sampūrṇa*.

(21) *Sālavi*

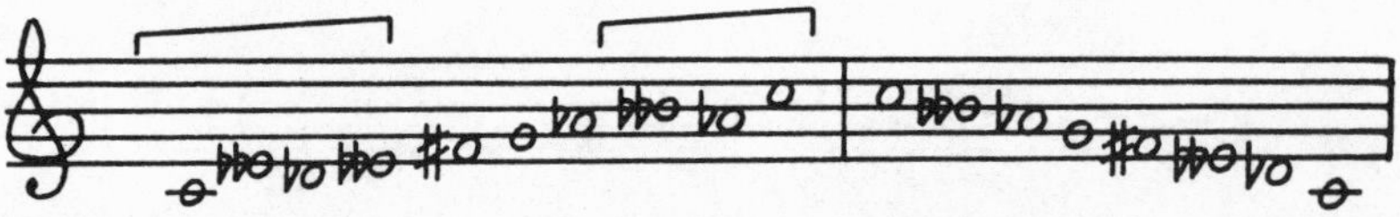

Ascent: *sampūrṇa*; two *vakra* features are shown.
Descent: *krama sampūrṇa*.

Sālavi is better known and more frequently performed than all other *janya rāgas* of the 37. *mēḷa*.

SĀLAVI (*Triputa-tāla*) SCM, 200-01

(22) *Sāmālāpini*

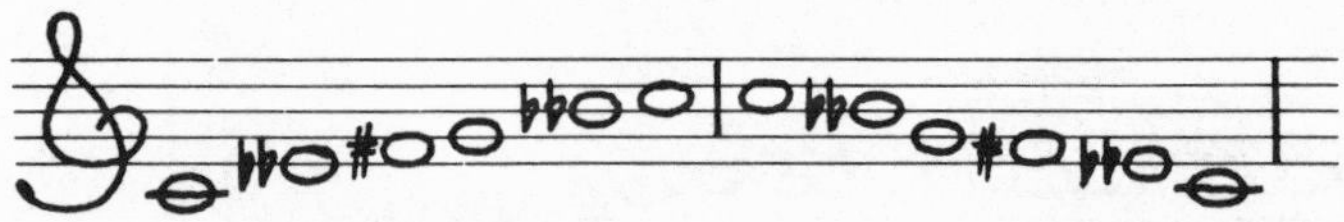

The notes *RI* (Db) and *DHA* (Ab) are avoided entirely.

(23) *Sindhughaṇṭānam*

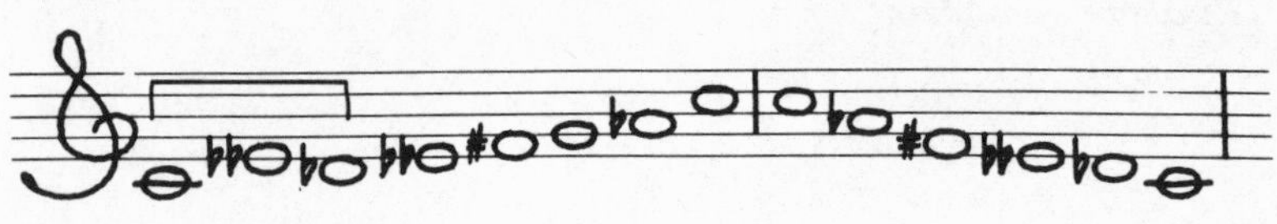

The note *NI* (Bbb) is avoided entirely. The ascent shows one *vakra* feature and the descent omits the note *PA* (G).

(24) *Sōmaprabhāvali*

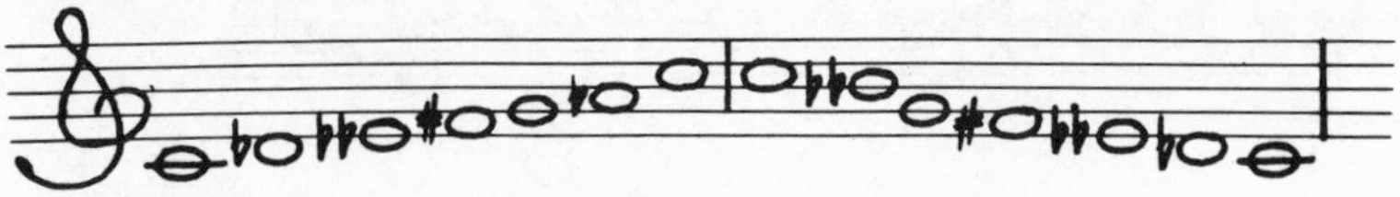

Ascent: the note *NI* (Bbb) is avoided.
Descent: the note *DHA* (Ab) is omitted.

(25) *Śuddhabhōgi*

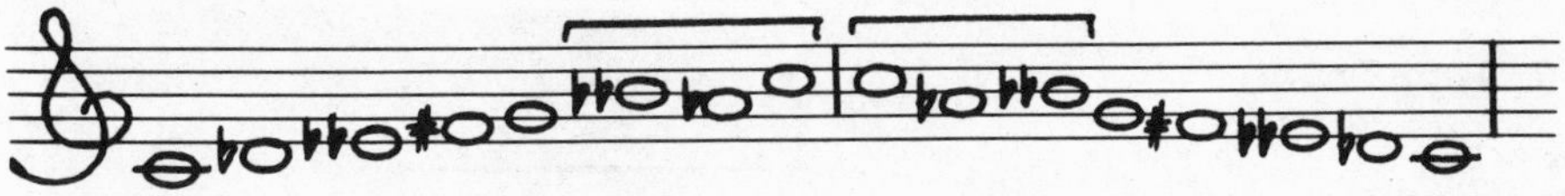

Ascent: *sampūrṇa*; one extended *vakra* passage is shown.
Descent: *sampūrṇa*; one extended *vakra* passage is used.

(26) *Yakshāpriya (Yakṣāpriya)*

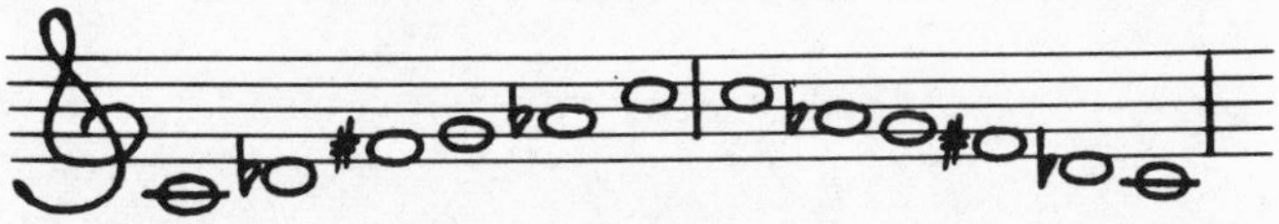

The notes *GA* (Ebb) and *NI* (Bbb) are avoided entirely.

38. *MĒḶA JALĀRṆAVA*

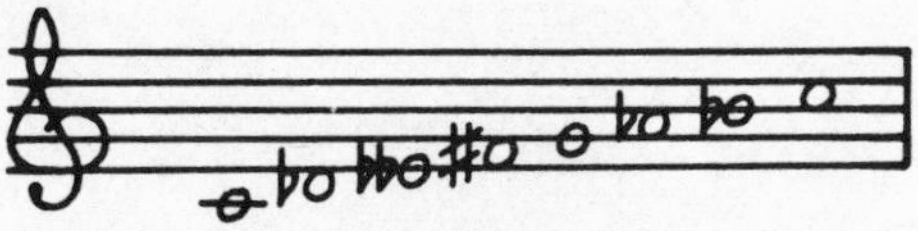

JHALĀRṆAVA (Triputa-tāla) SCM, 202

Janya Rāgas of the 38. Mēḷa

(1) *Aruṇāmbari*

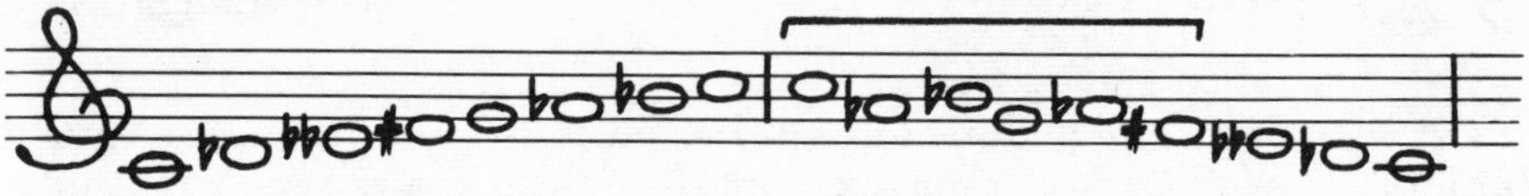

Ascent: *krama sampūrṇa*.
Descent: *sampūrṇa*; one extended *vakra* passage is shown.

(2) *Bhōga Rasāḷi* (*Bhōga Rasāvaḷi*)

Ascent and descent are *sampūrṇa*; each shows one *vakra* feature.

(3) *Haṃsa Bhōgi*

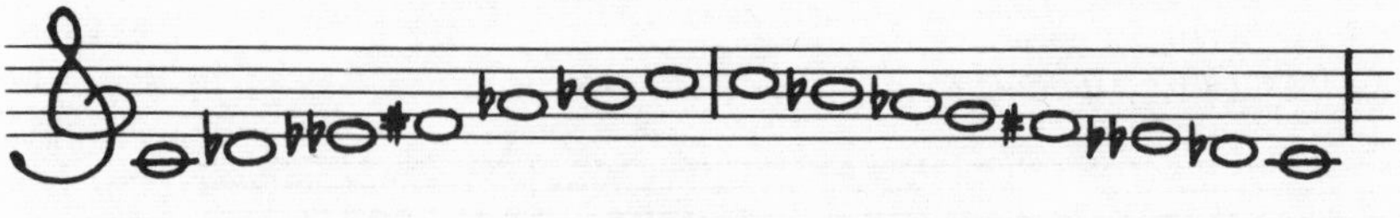

Ascent: the note *PA* (G) is avoided.
Descent: *krama sampūrṇa*.

(4) *Jaganmōhanam*

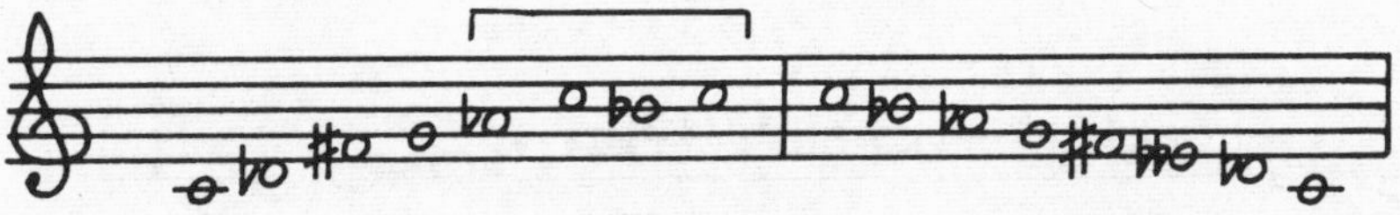

Ascent: the note *GA* (Ebb) is avoided; one *vakra* feature is shown.
Descent: *krama sampūrṇa*.

JAGANMŌHANAM (*Triputa-tāla*) SCM, 203

(5) *Jalasugandhi*

The note *NI* (Bb) is avoided entirely.

(6) *Jīvaratnabhūṣaṇi*

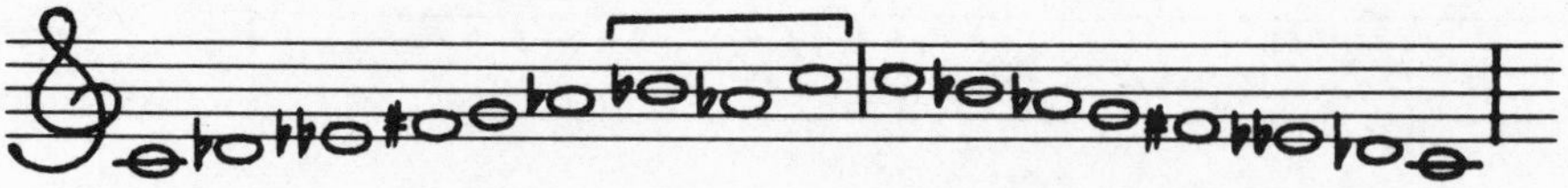

Ascent and descent are *sampūrṇa*. The ascent shows one *vakra* feature.

(7) *Kamalasūna*

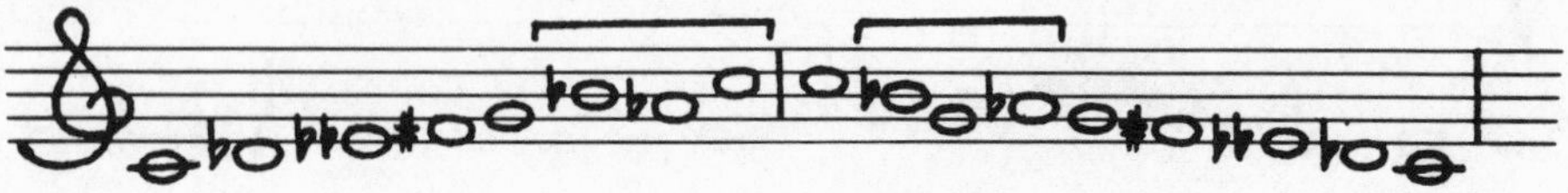

Ascent and descent are *sampūrṇa*; each shows one *vakra* feature.

(8) *Kannaḍamu*

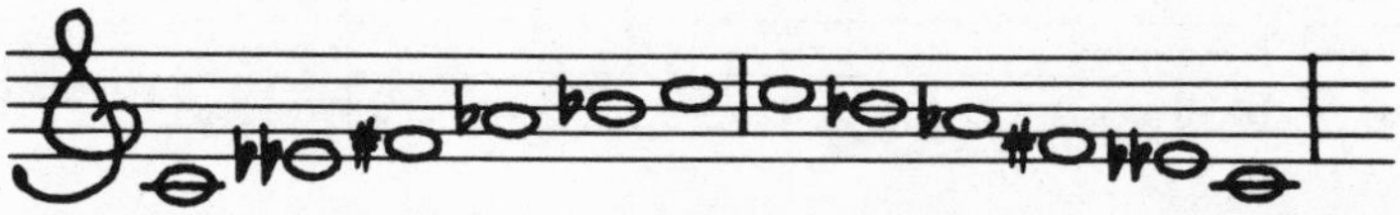

The notes *RI* (Db) and *PA* (G) are avoided entirely.

(9) *Kānti*

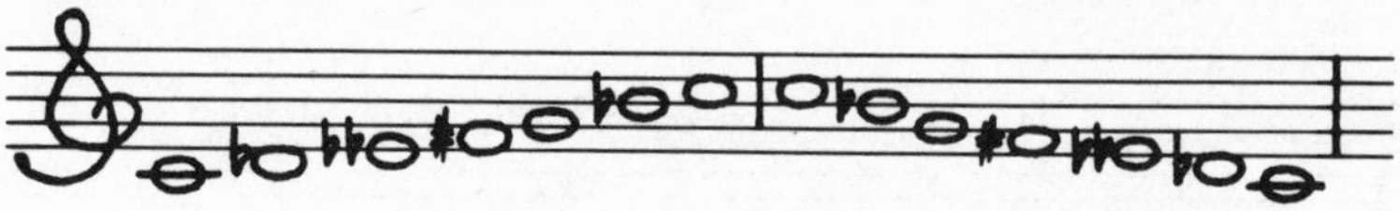

The note *DHA* (Ab) is avoided entirely.

(10) *Kumudābharaṇam*

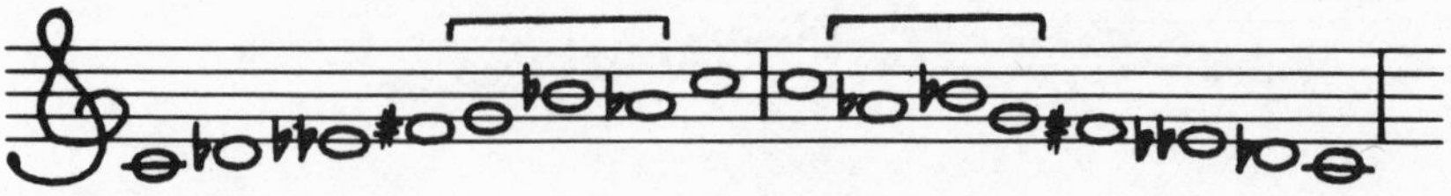

Ascent and descent are *sampūrṇa*; each shows one *vakra* feature.

(11) *Kusumāvaḷi*

The scale of this *rāga* has *niṣādāntya* character. Another *rāga* with the same name appears under the heading of the 71. *mēḷa* (5).

(12) *Marakatabhūṣaṇi*

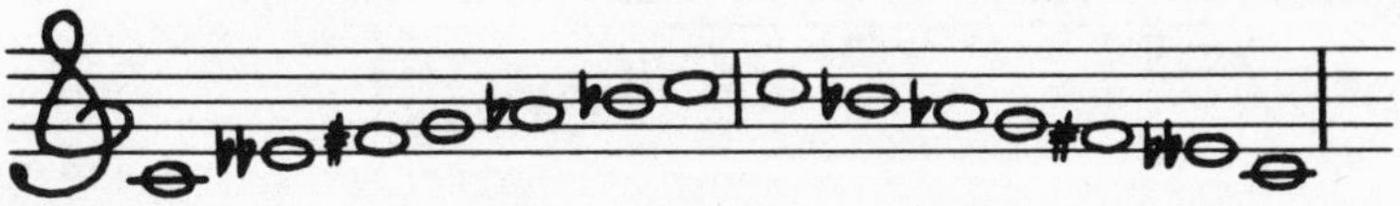

The note *RI* (Db) is avoided entirely.

(13) *Māruvachandrikā* (*Māruvacandrikā*)

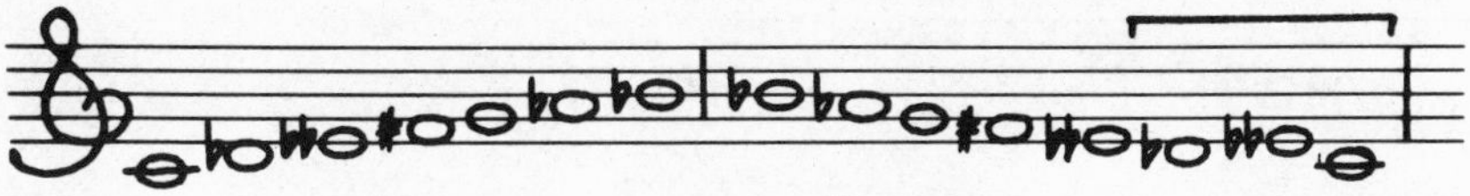

This *rāga* has *niṣādāntya* character. Its highest note is *NI* (Bb). Its descent shows one *vakra* feature.

(14) *Nāgadīparam*

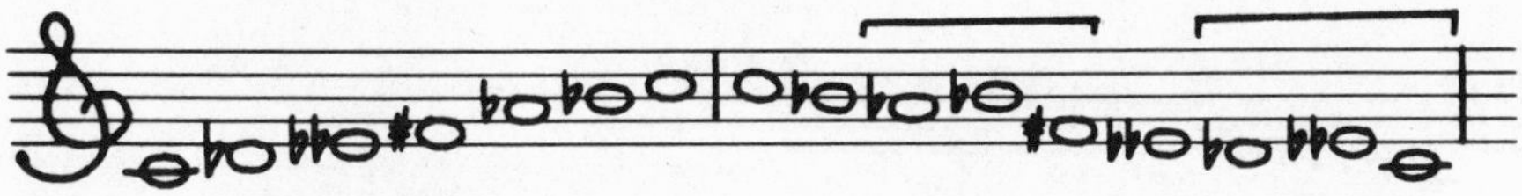

The note *PA* (G) is avoided entirely. The descent shows two *vakra* features.

(15) *Raviprabhāvali*

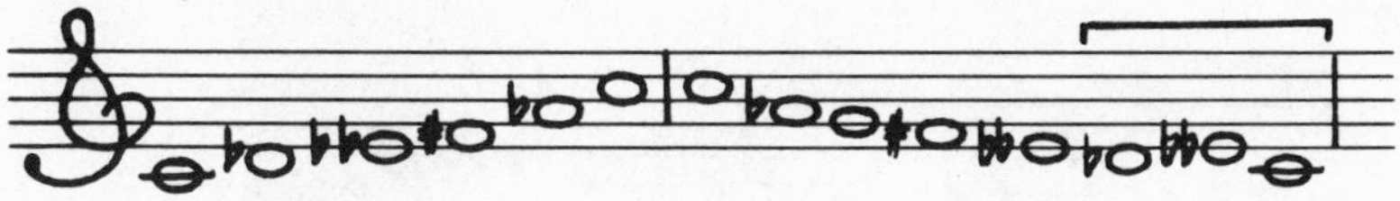

The note *NI* (Bb) is avoided entirely. *PA* (G) is omitted in ascent and one *vakra* feature is shown in descent.

(16) *Siṃhanādam*

The note *PA* (G) is avoided entirely. *GA* (Ebb) is avoided in ascent and *RI* (Db) in descent.

(17) *Sutāsāgaram*

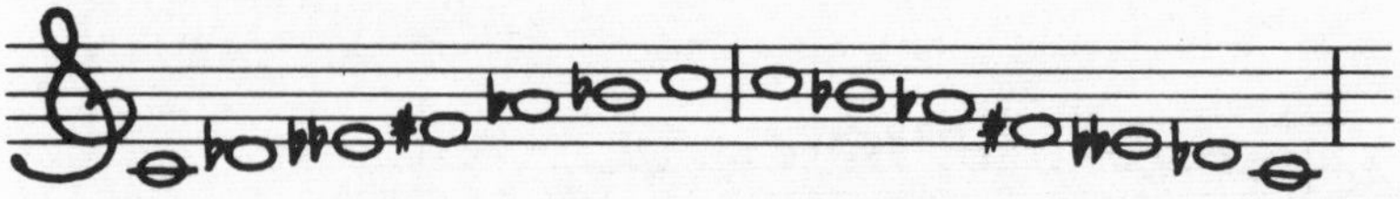

The note *PA* (G) is avoided entirely.

(18) *Vanajamukhi*

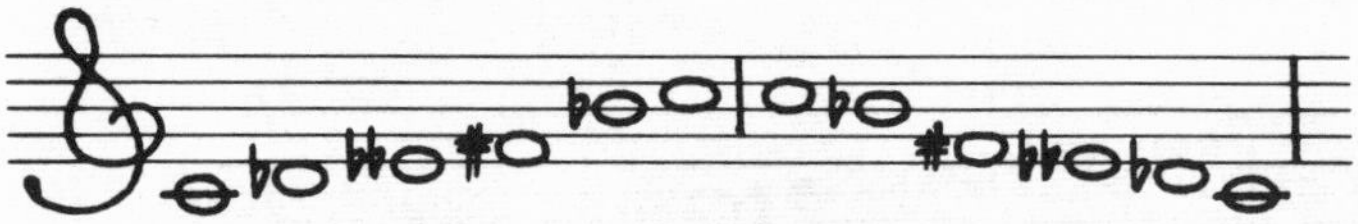

The notes *PA* (G) and *DHA* (Ab) are avoided entirely.

39. *MĒḶA JHĀLAVARĀḶI*

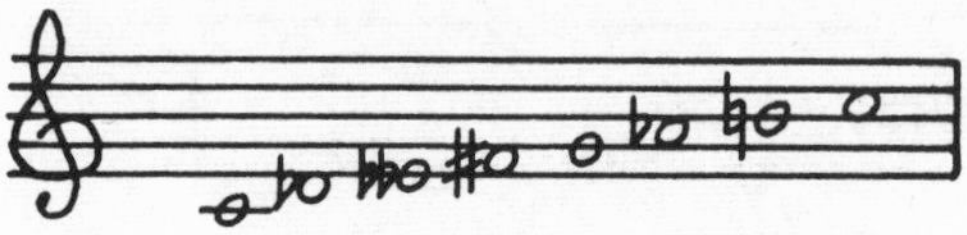

Veṅkaṭamakhin used for his 39. *mēḷa* (of the *asampūrṇa* system), the name *Dhālivarāḷi*.

JHĀLAVARĀḶI (*Triputa-tāla*) SCM, 203-4

Janya Rāgas of the 39. Mēḷa

(1) *Ādi Dēśya*

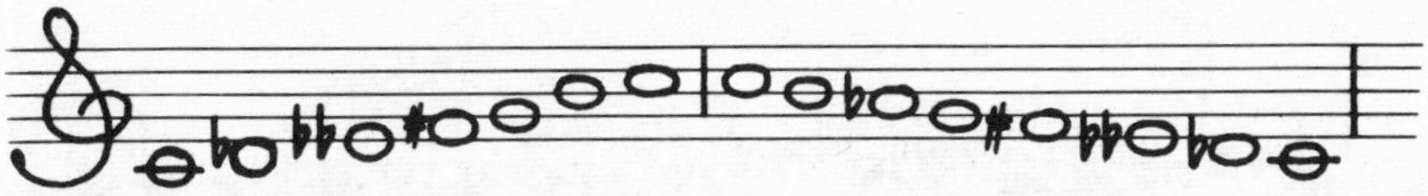

Ascent: the note *DHA* (Ab) is avoided.
Descent: *krama sampūrṇa*.

(2) *Amritavarśiṇi* (*Amrita Varśaṇi*)

The scale of this *rāga* is *sampūrṇa* in ascent and descent. One *vakra* feature is shown in ascent and one in descent. Another *rāga* with the same name appears under the heading of the 66. *mēḷa* (1).

(3) *Anaṅgādhari*

Ascent: *sampūrṇa*; two *vakra* features are shown.
Descent: *sampūrṇa*; two *vakra* features are used.

(4) *Bhōga Dhvajā*

Ascent: *krama sampūrṇa.*
Descent: the notes *NĪ* (B) and *GA* (Ebb) are avoided.
A *rāga* called *Bhōga Dhvaji* appears under the heading of the 47. *mēḷa* (4).

(5) *Bhūpāḷa Pañchama (Bhūpāḷa Pañcama)*

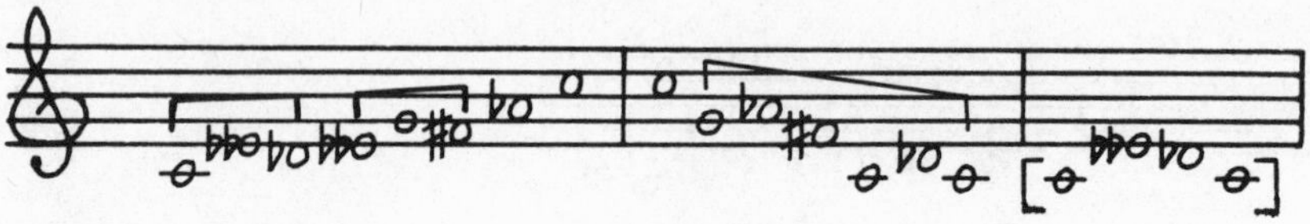

The note *NI* (B) is avoided entirely. The ascent shows two, the descent one *vakra* feature.

BHŪPĀḶAPAÑCHAMA (*Triputa-tāla*) SCM, 205

(6) *Bhūteśapriya*

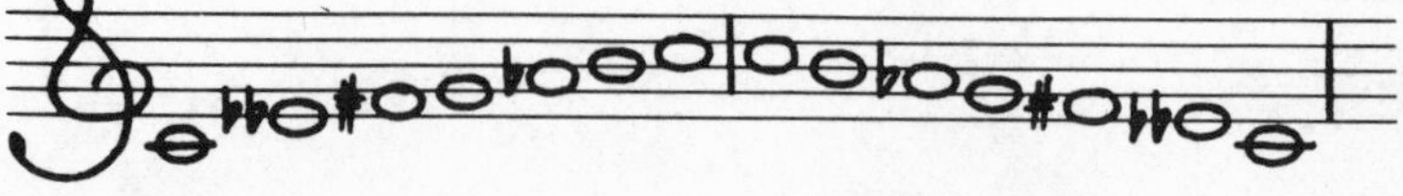

The note *RI* (Db) is avoided entirely.

(7) *Ēkaśruṅgi*

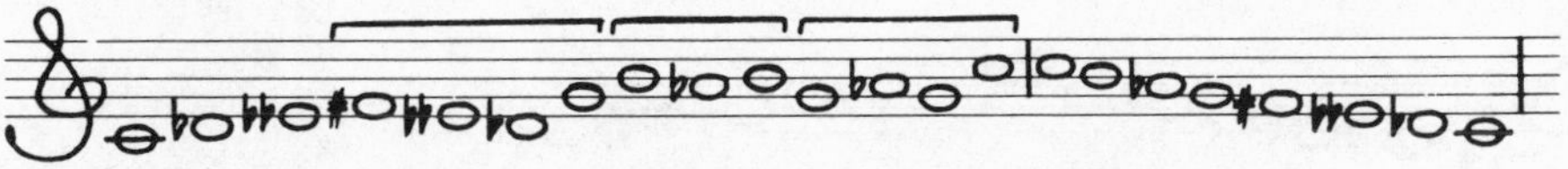

Ascent: *sampūrṇa*; three *vakra* features are shown.
Descent: *krama sampūrṇa*.

(8) *Girīśapriya*

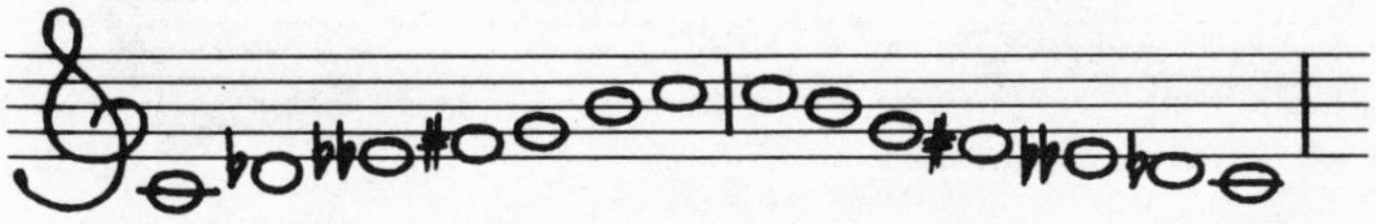

The note *DHA* (Ab) is avoided entirely.

(9) *Godāri*

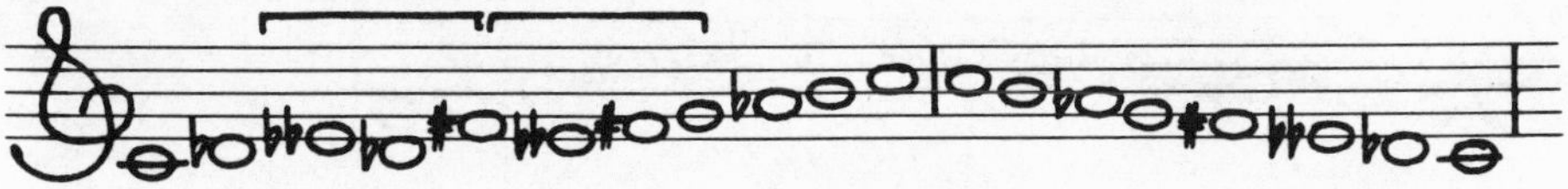

Ascent: *sampūrṇa*; two *vakra* features are shown.
Descent: *krama sampūrṇa*.

(10) *Haṃsa Nīlāmbari*

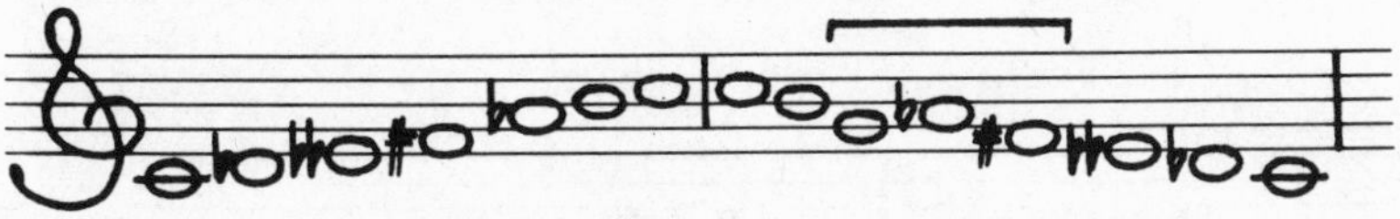

Ascent: the note *PA* (G) is avoided.
Descent: *sampūrṇa*; one *vakra* feature is shown.

(11) *Hārabhūṣaṇi*

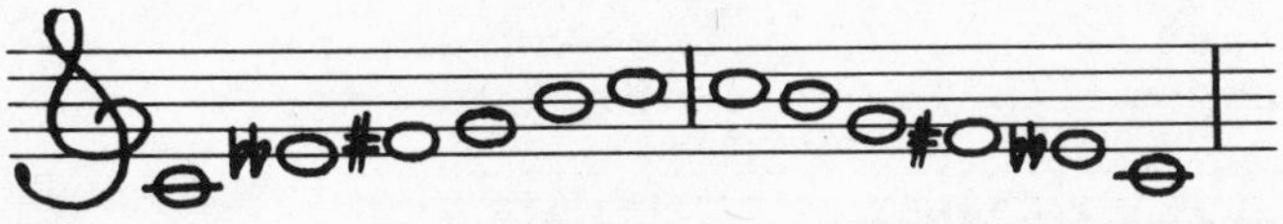

The notes *RI* (Db) and *DHA* (Ab) are avoided entirely.

(12) *Inavardhani*

Ascent: the note *NI* (B) is avoided.
Descent: the note *RI* (Db) is omitted.

(13) *Jhīnāvaḷi*

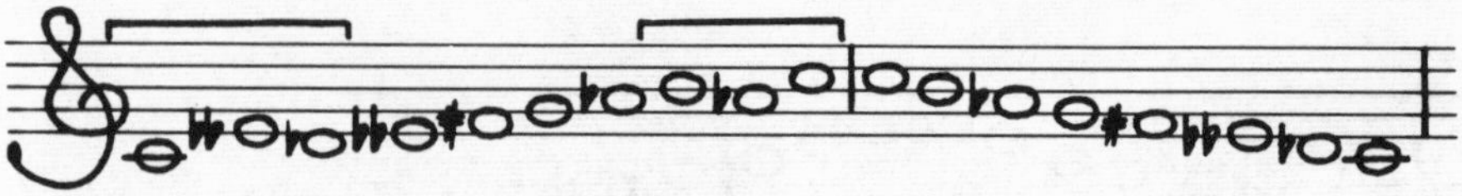

Ascent: *sampūrṇa*; two *vakra* features are shown.
Descent: *krama sampūrṇa*.

(14) *Kalyāṇa Gauri*

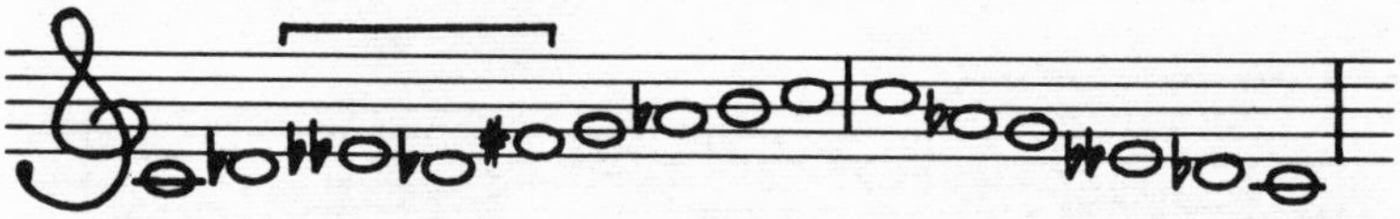

Ascent: *sampūrṇa*; one *vakra* feature is shown.
Descent: the notes *NI* (B) and *MA* (F#) are avoided.

(15) *Kōkila Pañcham*(*am*) (*Kōkila Pañcam*[*am*])

According to one source (*Saṅgīta Svara Prastāra Sāgaram* by Nadamuni Panditar, n.d.) the scale of this *rāga* is:

Ascent: the note MA (F#) is avoided and one extended *vakra* passage is shown.
Descent: *krama sampūrṇa*; the note *GA* (Ebb) is stressed.
According to another source (*Saṅgīta Kaumudi* by Tiruvaiya Subramanyam (in Telugu; n.d.) the scale is:

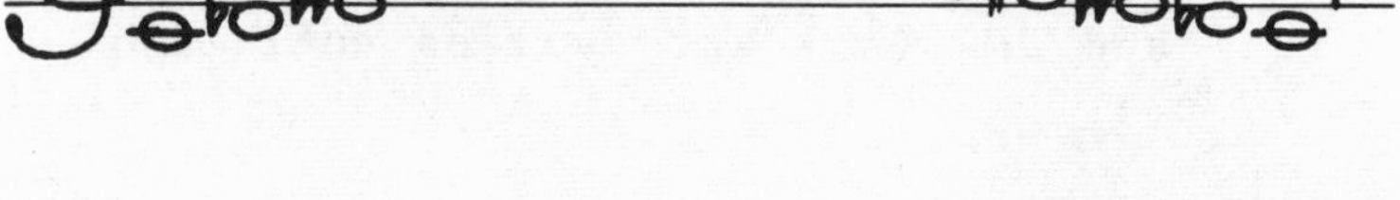

Ascent: the note *MA* (F#) is avoided. No *vakra* passage is used.
Descent: the same as in the first version.

In the list of *rāga* scales appended to the SCM (1938 edition, p. 331, Madras) the following limited tone material of *Kōkila Pañcham* is given:

The material shown in the SCM indicates that the range of melodies in this *rāga* can be confined to the lower and middle octave regions. A few phrases may provide a picture of this version of *Kōkila Pañcham*:

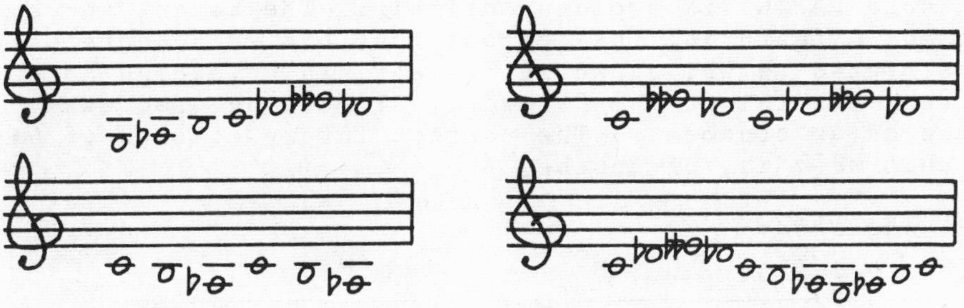

KŌKILA PAÑCHAM (*Triputa-tāla*) SCM, 204-05

(16) *Māruvabaṅgaḷa* (*Mārtāndapriya*)

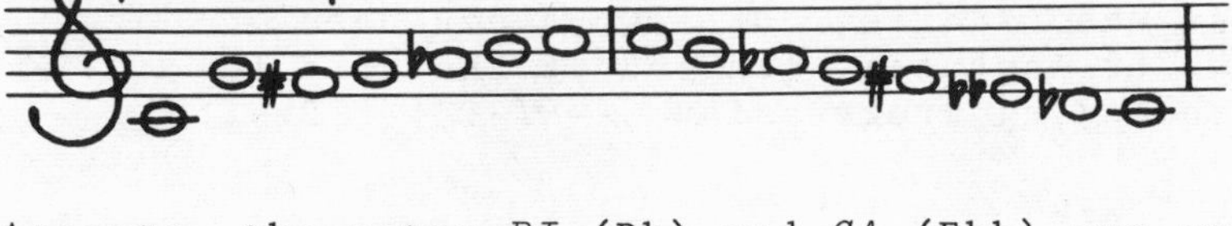

Ascent: the notes *RI* (Db) and *GA* (Ebb) are avoided; one *vakra* feature is shown.
Descent: *krama sampūrṇa*.

(17) *Nāṭanavēlāvaḷi*

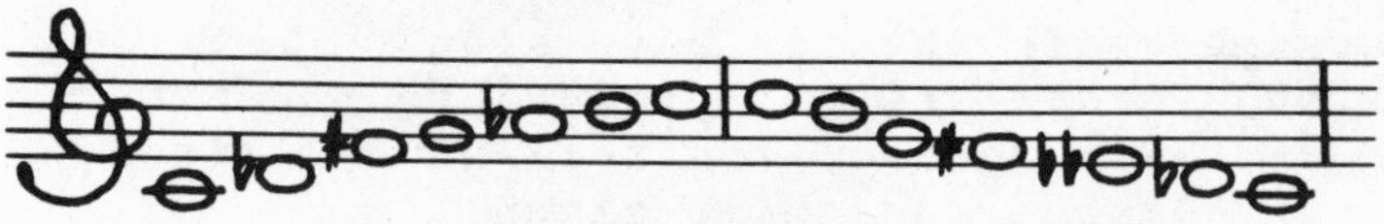

Ascent: the note *GA* (Ebb) is avoided.
Descent: the note *DHA* (Ab) is omitted.

(18) *Nāgaghaṇṭam*

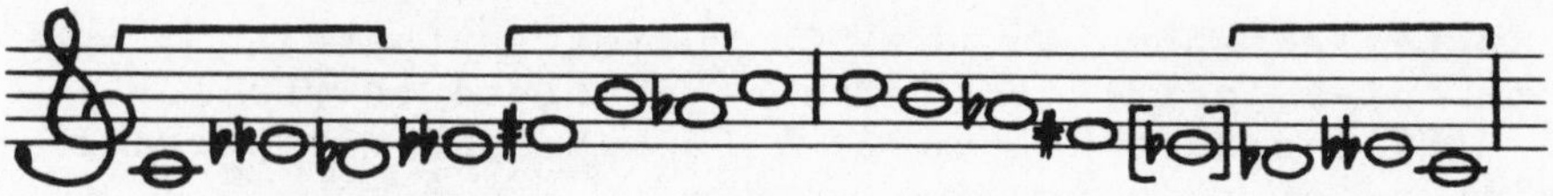

The note *PA* (G) is avoided entirely. The ascent shows two *vakra* features, the descent uses one. The note *GA*, interpreted as Eb, shown in descent, is a foreign note to the material of the 39. *mēḷa*. It can be used at times as an ornament. The correct interpretation of *GA* in this *mēḷa* is, of course, Ebb.

(19) *Nāgabhōgi*

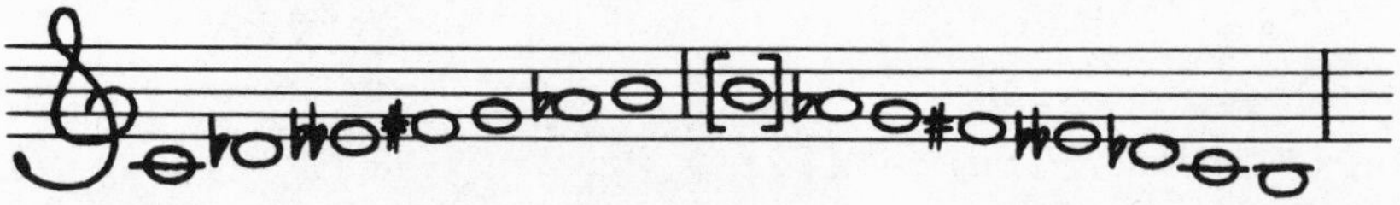

This is a *niṣadāntya rāga* and shows neither *vakra* features nor omitted notes.

(20) *Varāḷi*

Veṅkaṭamakhin calls the primary *rāga* of this *mēḷa* *Dhālivaraḷi* (in the *asampūrṇa* system.)

The *Varāḷi* scale of the present time is identical with that of the primary *rāga*, *Jhālavarāḷi*. Some musicians maintain that, in contrast to *rāga Jhālavarāḷi*, there appears a characteristic *vakra* phrase in the ascent of *Varāḷi*: *SA-GA-RI-GA-MA* (C-Ebb-Db-Ebb-F#). This phrase was, and is, not always employed. Tyāgarāja, for instance, ignored it and used the straight ascending progression *SA-RI-GA* (C-Db-Ebb).

(21) *Varuṇātmaja*

The notes *RI* (Db) and *PA* (G) are avoided entirely.

(22) *Yāmi*

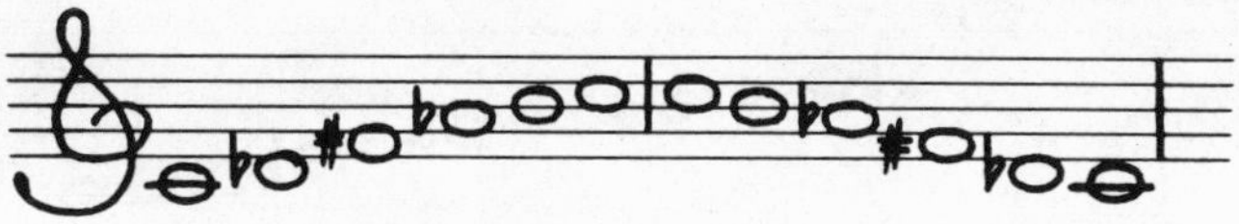

The notes *GA* (Ebb) and *PA* (G) are avoided entirely.

40. *MĒḶA NAVANĪTAM*

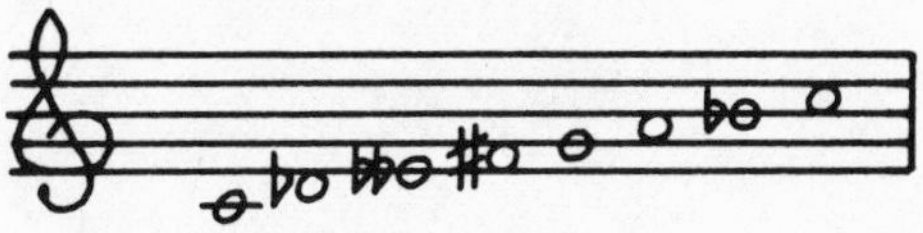

NAVANĪTAM (*Triputa-tāla*) SCM, 206

Janya Rāgas of the 40. Mēḷa

(1) *Dīrghānandiṇi*

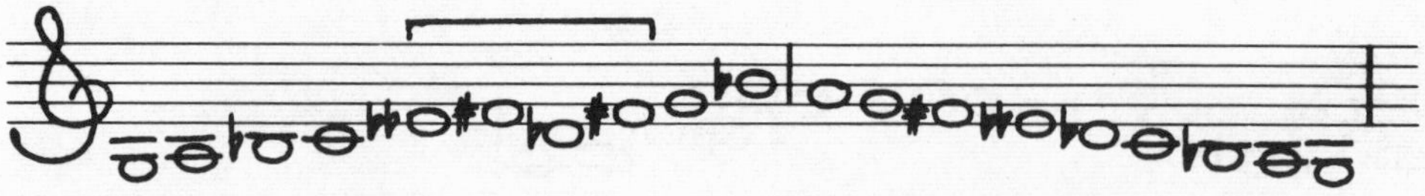

Ascent: the scale begins with the note *PA* (G) of the low octave range and extends to *NI* (Bb) of the middle octave range. One *vakra* feature is shown. Although the low note *DHA* (A) is used, its upper octave (in the middle range) is avoided.
Descent: the scale is straight and begins with *DHA* (A) of the middle octave range. It descends to the low *PA* (G).

(2) *Divyamati*

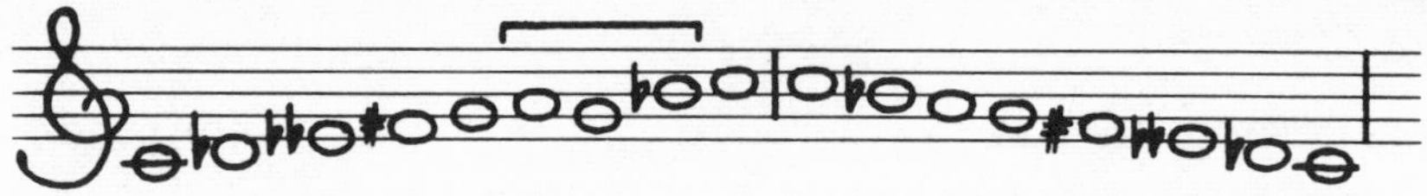

Ascent: *sampūrṇa*; one *vakra* feature is shown.
Descent: *krama sampūrṇa*.

(3) *Divyāmbari*

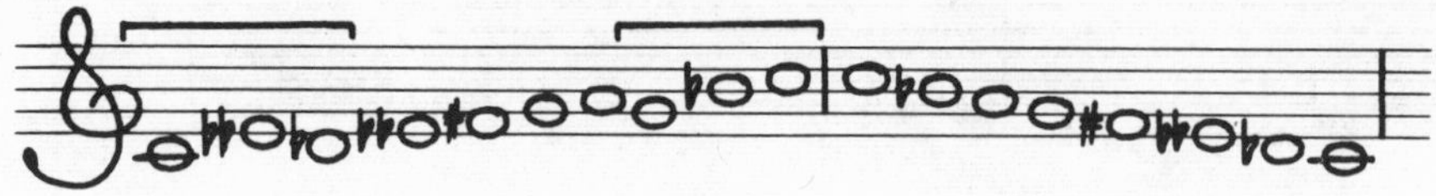

Ascent: *sampūrṇa*; two *vakra* features are shown.
Descent: *krama sampūrṇa*.
Another *rāga* with the same name appears under the heading of the 27. *mēḷa* (12).

(4) *Gagana Gāndhāri*

Ascent: *sampūrṇa*; two *vakra* features are shown.
Descent: *krama sampūrṇa*.

(5) *Haiyaṅgavīnam*

The note *PA* (G) is avoided entirely.

(6) *Janānandi*

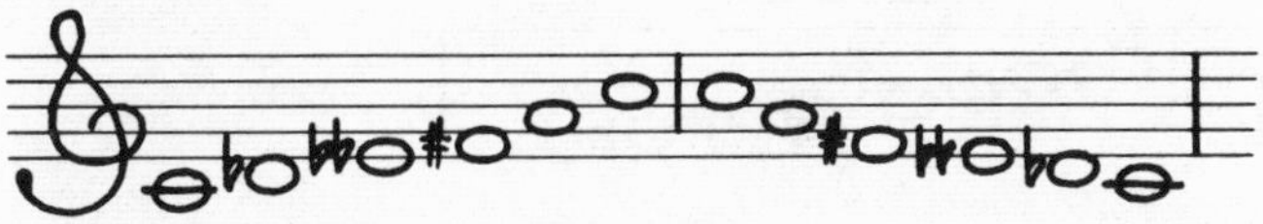

The notes *PA* (G) and *NI* (Bb) are avoided entirely.

(7) *Mallikāmōda*

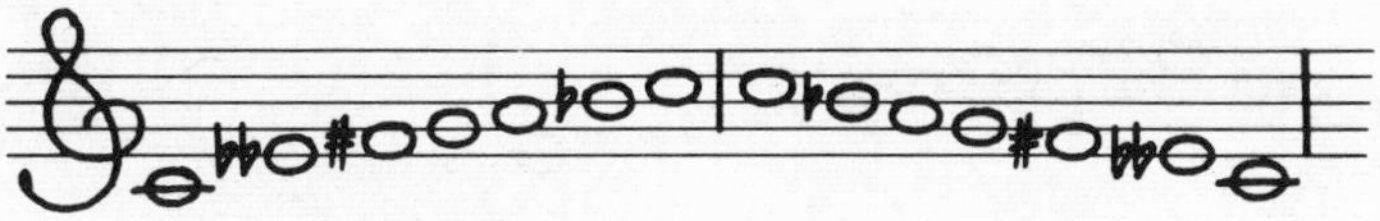

The note *RI* (Db) is avoided entirely.

(8) *Nabhomani*

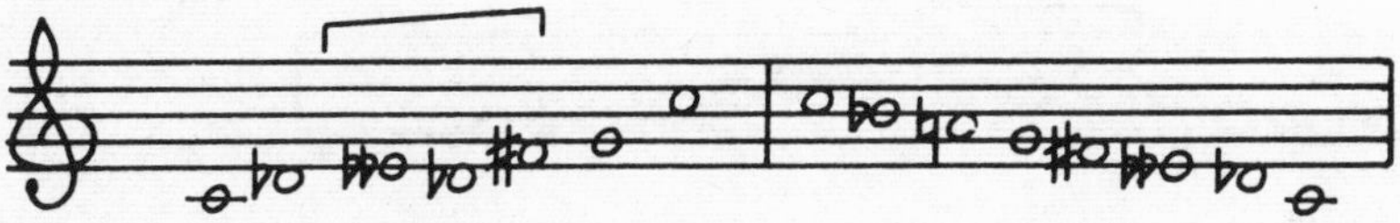

Ascent: the notes *DHA* (A) and *NI* (Bb) are avoided; one *vakra* feature is shown.
Descent: *krama sampūrṇa*.

NABHOMANI (*Triputa-tāla*) SCM, 206-07

(9) *Navarasakuntavarāḷi*

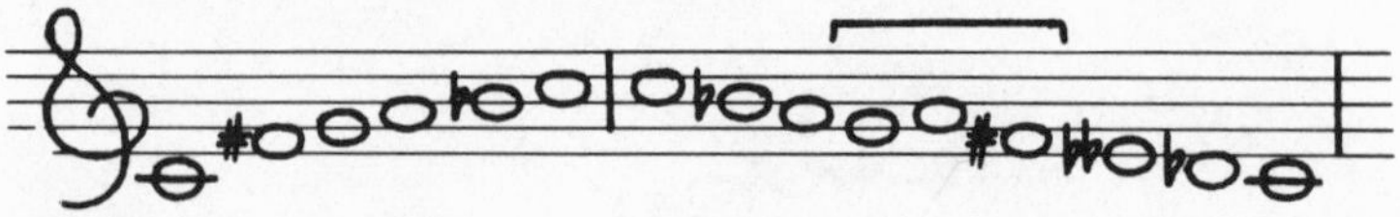

Ascent: the notes *RI* (Db) and *GA* (Ebb) are avoided.
Descent: *sampūrṇa*; one *vakra* feature is shown.

(10) *Nāgavēlāvali*

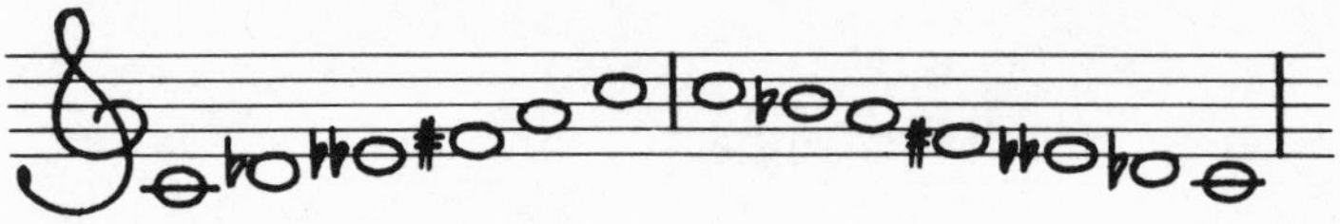

The note *PA* (G) is avoided entirely. *NI* (Bb) is omitted in ascent.

(11) *Sindhunāṭakurañji*

Ascent: the note *PA* (G) is avoided; one *vakra* feature is shown.
Descent: *krama sampūrṇa*.

(12) *Sōmaghaṇṭānam*

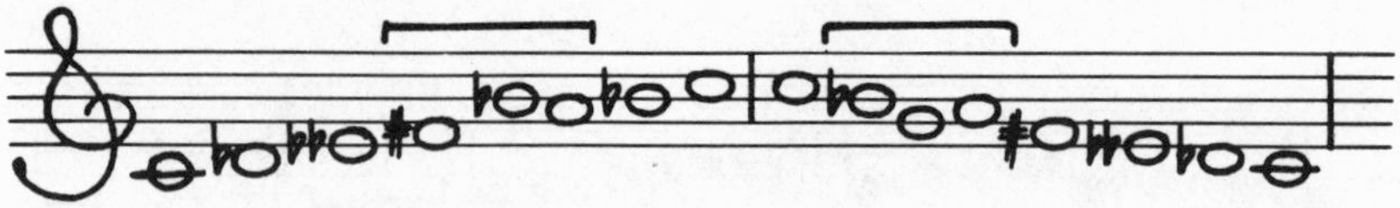

Ascent: the note *PA* (G) is avoided; one *vakra* feature is shown.
Descent: *sampūrṇa*; one *vakra* feature is used.

(13) *Sukhanīlāmbari*

Ascent: the note *NI* (Bb) is avoided; one *vakra* feature is shown.
Descent: *krama sampūrṇa*.

(14) *Tālamu*

The notes *RI* (Db) and *PA* (G) are avoided entirely.
See also *rāga Tālam* listed under the heading of the 64. *mēḷa* (31).

41. *MĒḶA PĀVANI*

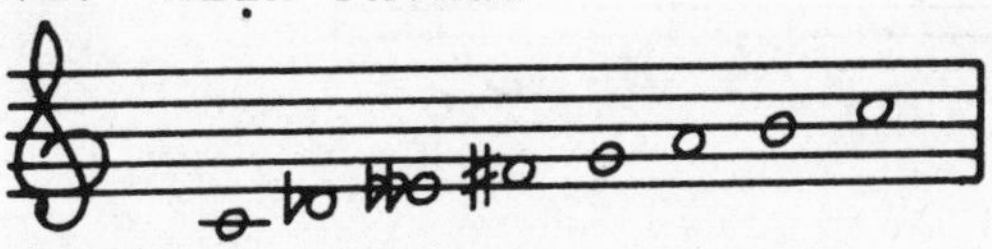

PĀVANI (*Triputa-tāla*) SCM, 207-8

Janya Rāgas of the 41. Mēḷa

(1) *Ādi Vasu*

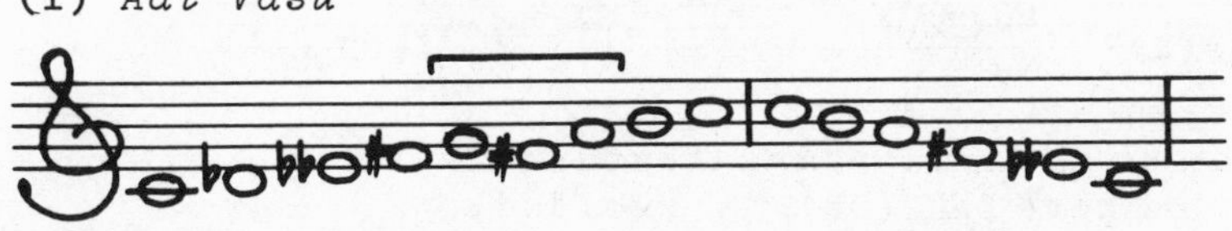

Ascent: *sampūrṇa*; one *vakra* feature is shown.
Descent: the notes *PA* (G) and *RI* (Db) are avoided.

(2) *Bogīni*

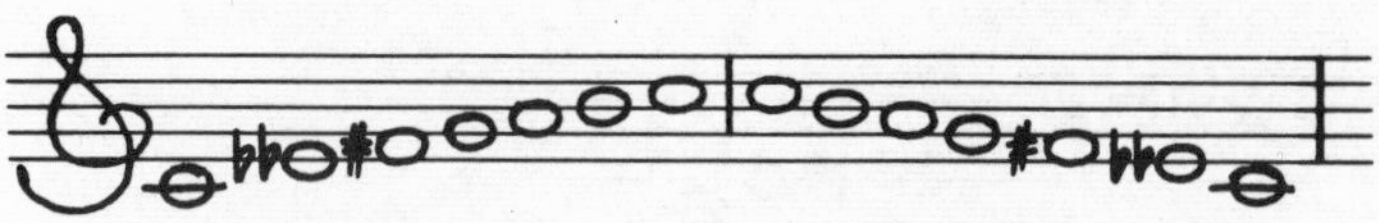

The note *RI* (Db) is avoided entirely.

(3) *Chandrajyōti* (*Candrajyōti*)

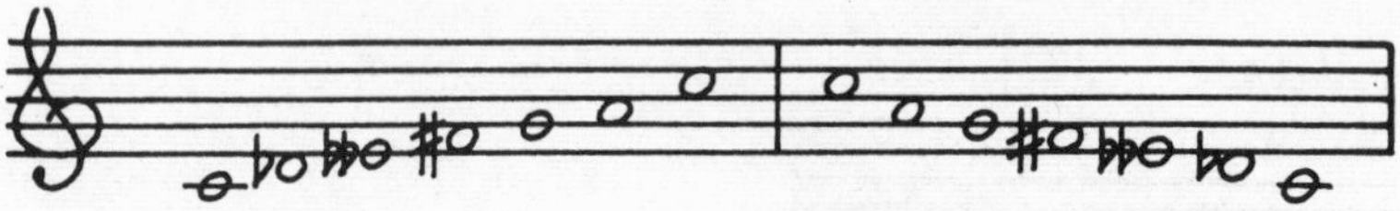

The note *NI* (B) is avoided entirely.

CHANDRAJYŌTI (*Triputa-tāla*) SCM, 209

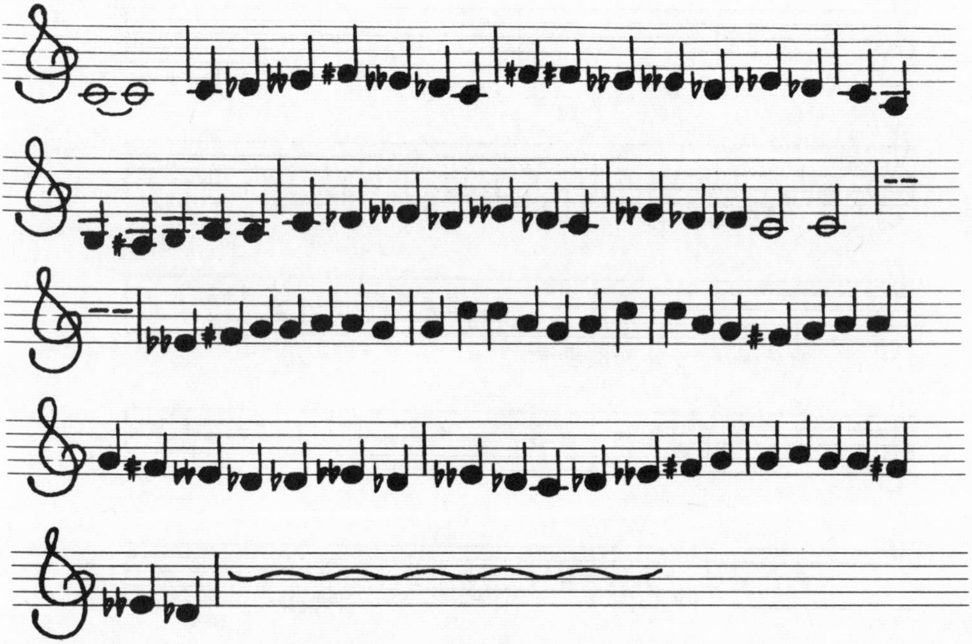

(4) *Haṃsa Rasāḷi* (*Haṃsa Rasāvaḷi*)

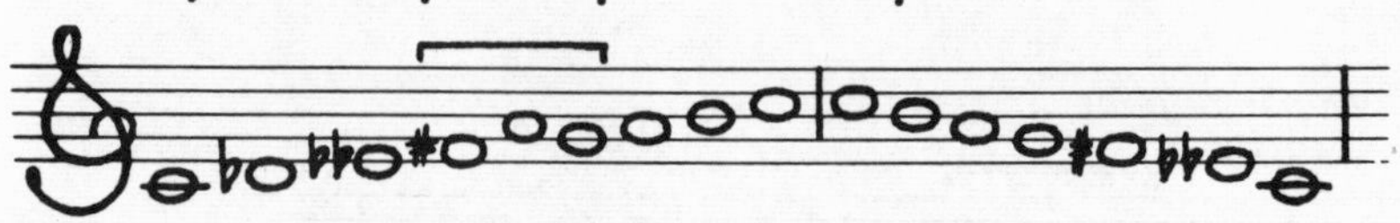

Ascent: *sampūrṇa*; one *vakra* feature is shown.
Descent: the note *RI* (Db) is avoided.

(5) *Hēmapiṅgaḷa*

Ascent: *sampūrṇa*; three *vakra* features are shown.
Descent: the notes *NI* (B) and *DHA* (A) are avoided.

(6) *Kōkila Svarāvaḷi*

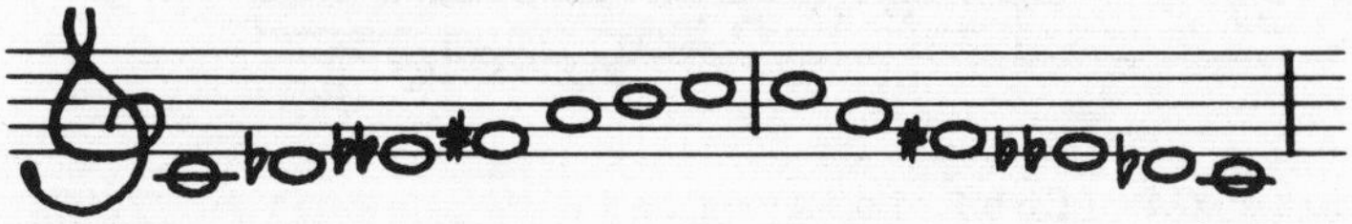

The note *PA* (G) is avoided entirely. *NI* (B) is omitted in descent.

(7) *Kumbhiṇi*

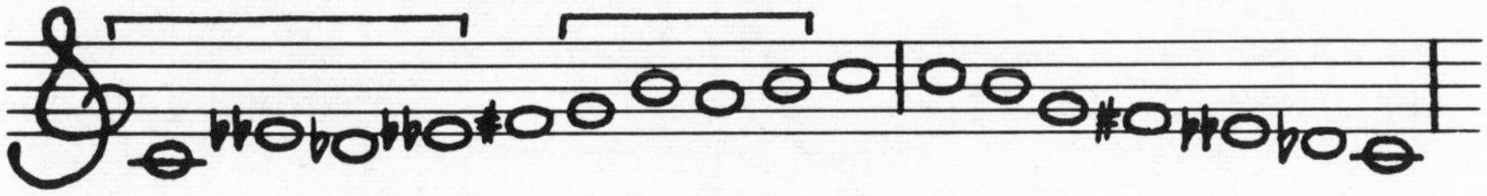

Ascent: *sampūrṇa*; two *vakra* features are shown.
Descent: the note *DHA* (A) is avoided.

Another *rāga* with the same name appears under the heading of the 2. *mēḷa* (10).

(8) *Kuntala Bhōgi*

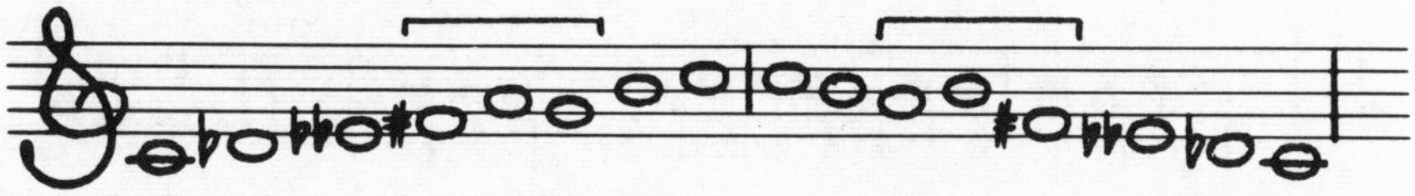

Ascent: *sampūrṇa*; one *vakra* feature is shown.
Descent: the note *PA* (G) is avoided; one *vakra* feature is used.

(9) *Nīvāram*

The notes *RI* (Db) and *PA* (G) are avoided entirely.

(10) *Pāvanakari*

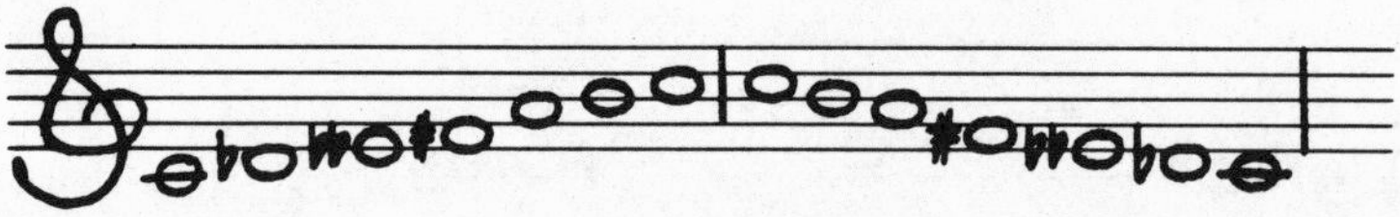

The note *PA* (G) is avoided entirely.

(11) *Prabhavali*

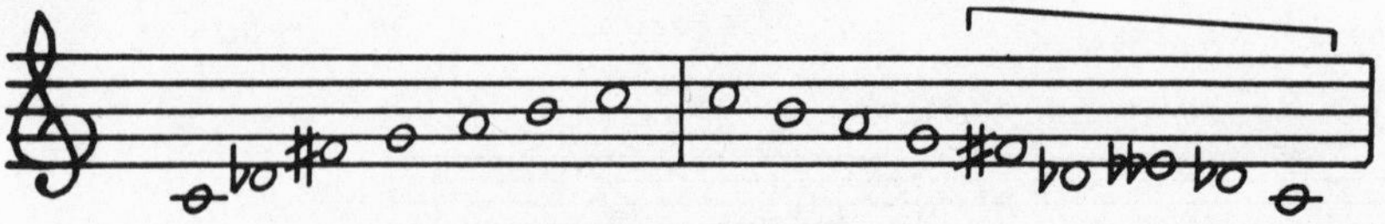

Ascent: the note *GA* (Ebb) is avoided.
Descent: *sampūrṇa*; one extended *vakra* passage is used.
Another descent of *Prabhavali* is:

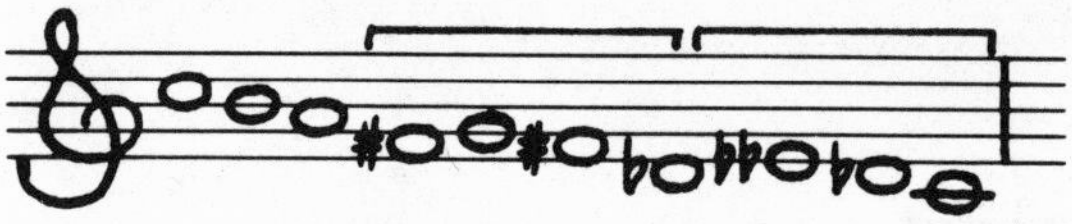

PRABHAVALI (*Triputa-tāla*) SCM, 208-09

(12) *Sōmakiraṇi*

The notes *GA* (Ebb) and *NI* (B) are avoided entirely.

(13) *Śuddhagīrvaṇi*

Ascent: *krama sampūrṇa*.
Descent: the notes *DHA* (A) and *RI* (Db) are avoided.
The note *MA*, which is F# in the 41. *mēḷa*, becomes F in the descending scale of this *rāga*.

(14) *Śyāmanīlāmbari*

Ascent: *krama sampūrṇa*.
Descent: the note *PA* (G) is avoided; one *vakra* feature is shown.

(15) *Vijayaśrī*

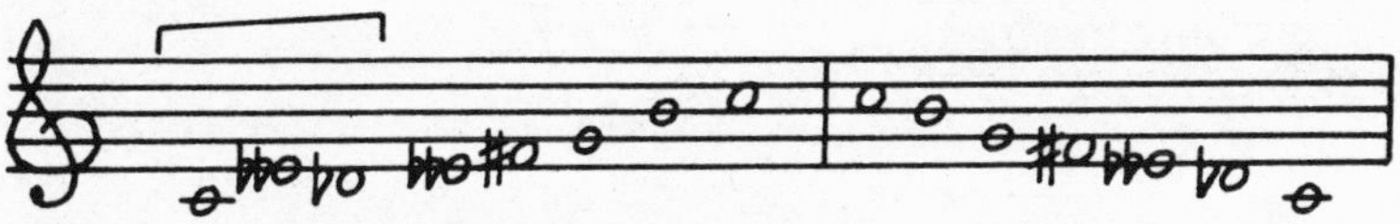

The note *DHA* (A) is avoided entirely. One *vakra* feature appears in ascent.

42. *MĒḶA RAGHUPRIYĀ*

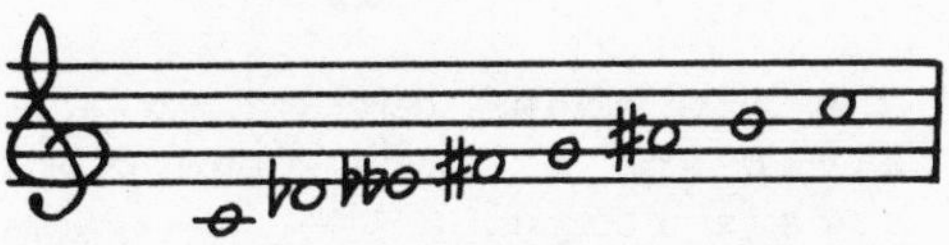

RAGHUPRIYĀ (*Triputa-tāla*) SCM, 210

Janya Rāgas of the 42. Mēḷa

(1) *Alava*

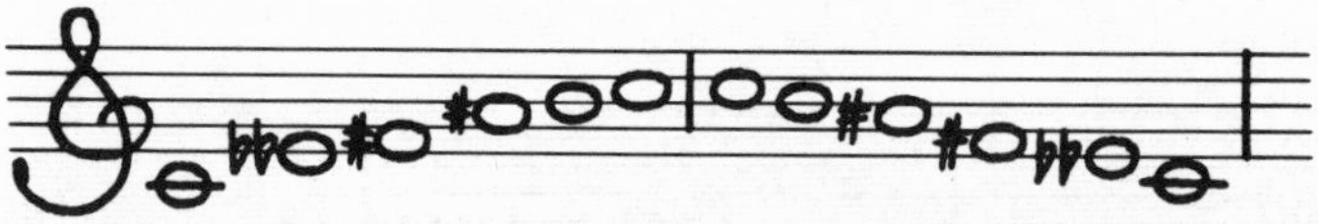

The notes *RI* (Db) and *PA* (G) are avoided entirely.

(2) *Ānandhabhōgi* (*Ānandabhōgi*)

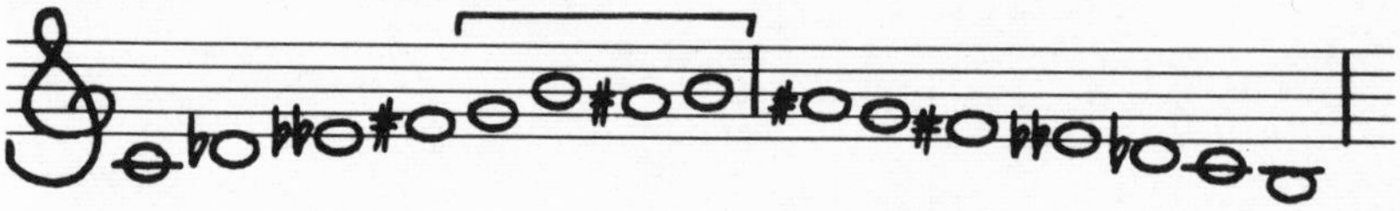

The ascent of this *niṣādāntya* scale shows one *vakra* feature. The descent is straight and extends from *DHA* (A#) to *NI* (B) of the lower octave range.

(3) *Chandra Prabhā* (*Candra Prabhā*)

The note *NI* (B) is avoided entirely.

(4) *Dhūmāla*

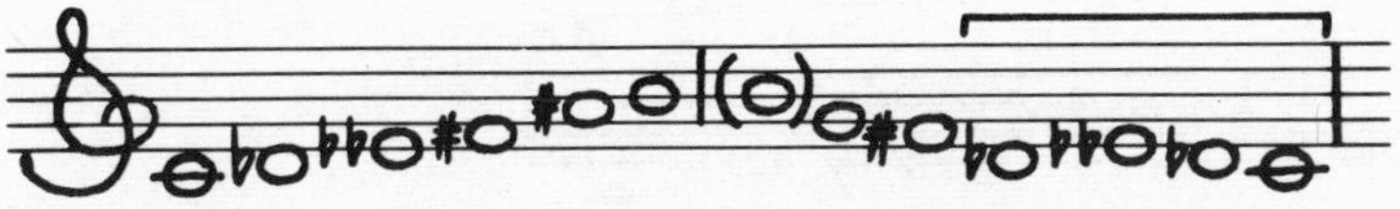

This *niṣādāntya* scale avoids in ascent *PA* (G), and in descent *DHA* (A#) where one *vakra* passage is used.

(5) *Gāndharvam*

The lowest note of this unusual scale is the low *MA* (F#), the highest is *GA* (Ebb). While the ascent is straight, the descent avoids the low note *DHA* (A#).

GĀNDHARVA (*Triputa-tāla*) SCM, 211-12

(6) *Gopati*

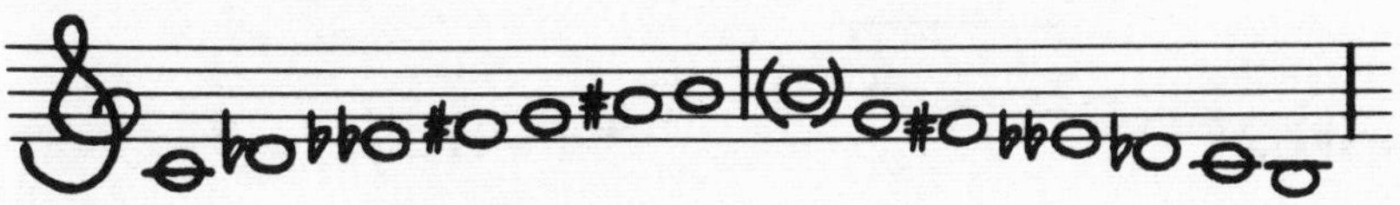

This *niṣādāntya* scale is straight in ascent and avoids the note *DHA* (A#) in descent.

A variant of the *Gopati* scale is:

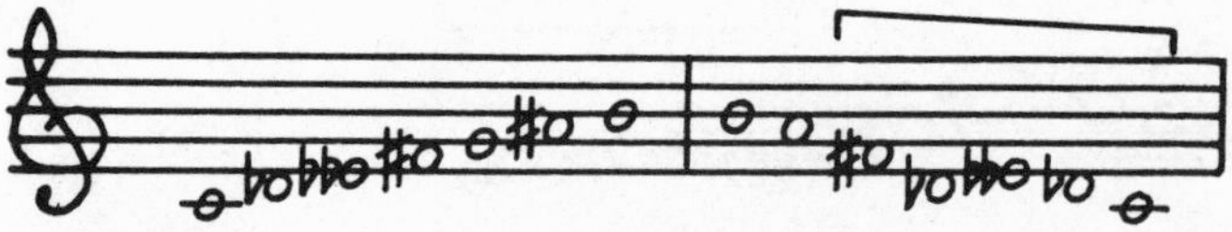

The ascent remains unchanged but the descent shows one extended *vakra* passage.

GOPATI (*Triputa-tāla*) SCM, 212-13

(7) *Haṃsa Dīparam*

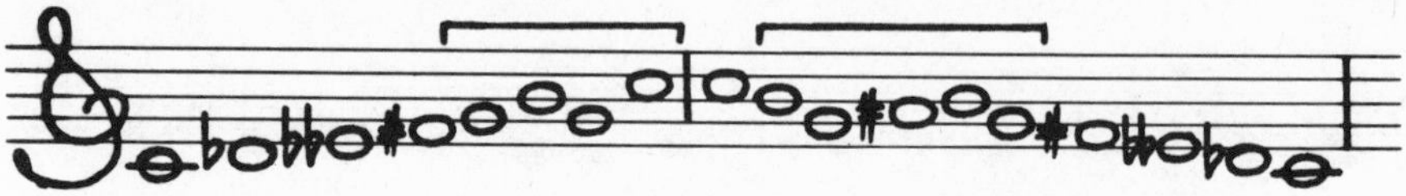

Ascent: the note *DHA* (A#) is avoided; one *vakra* feature is shown.
Descent: *sampūrṇa*; one extended *vakra* feature is used.

(8) *Haṃsa Vēḷāvaḷi*

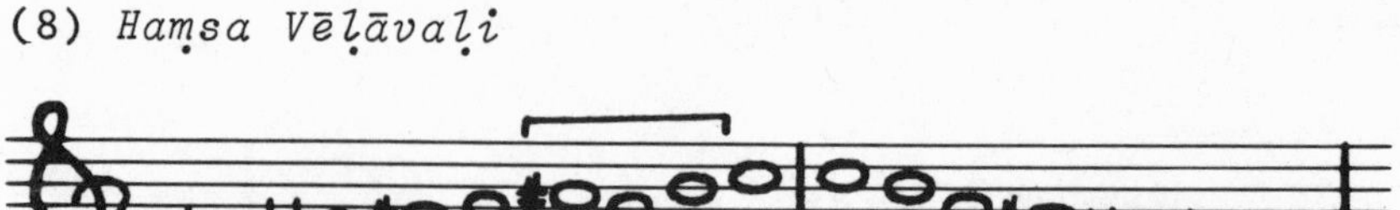

Ascent: *sampūrṇa*; one *vakra* feature is shown.
Descent: the note *DHA* (A#) is avoided.

(9) *Harēnapi*

The notes *RI* (Db) and *NI* (B) are avoided entirely.

(10) *Indu Gīrvāṇi*

Ascent: the notes *DHA* (A#) and *NI* (B) are avoided.
Descent: *sampūrṇa*; one extended *vakra* passage is shown.

(11) *Jagāṅgana*

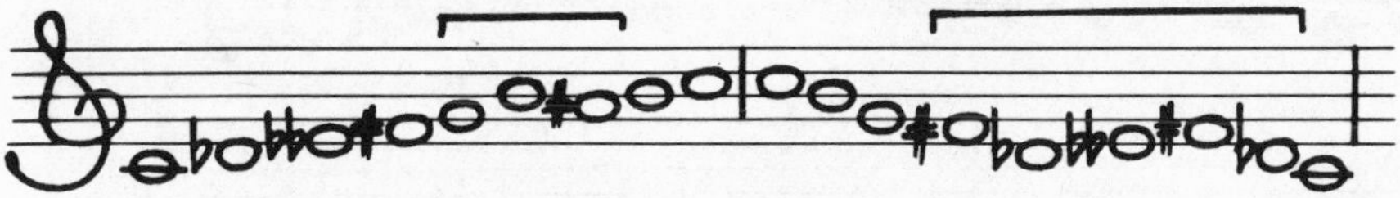

Ascent: *sampūrṇa*; one *vakra* feature is shown.
Descent: the note *DHA* (A#) is avoided; one extended *vakra* feature is used.

(12) *Lalitadīparam*

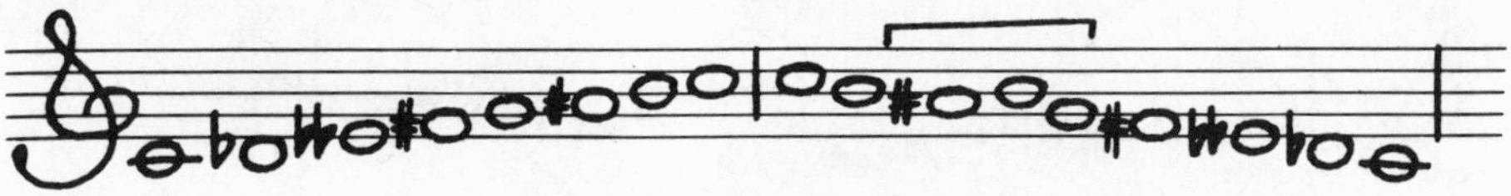

Ascent: *krama sampūrṇa*.
Descent: *sampūrṇa*; one *vakra* feature is shown.

(13) *Mēchasāvēri* (*Mēcasāvēri*)

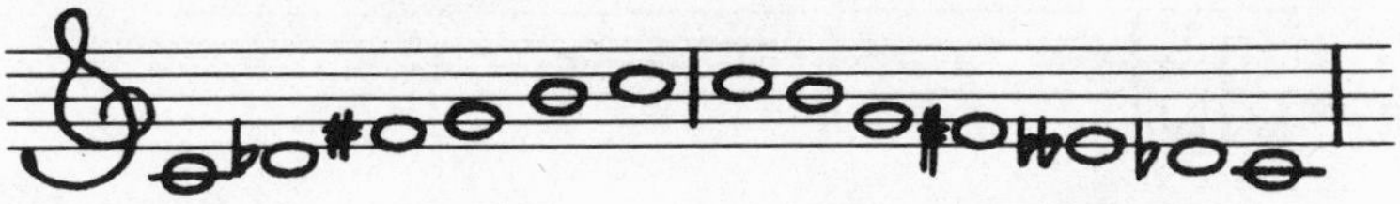

The note *DHA* (A#) is avoided entirely. *GA* (Ebb) is omitted in ascent.

(14) *Raghulīlā*

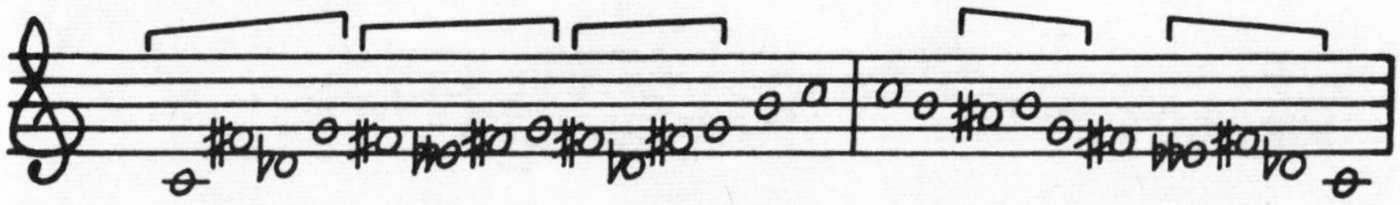

Ascent: the note *DHA* (A#) is avoided; three *vakra* features are shown.
Descent: *sampūrṇa*; two *vakra* features are used.
Another descent of *Raghulīlā* can be:

RAGHULĪLĀ (*Triputa-tāla*) SCM, 210-11

(15) *Ruṣabhavāhiṇi* (*Rushabhavāhiṇi*)

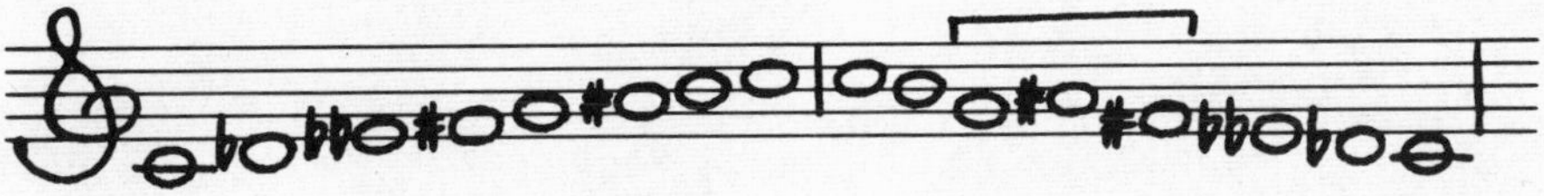

Ascent: *krama sampūrṇa*.
Descent: *sampūrṇa*; one *vakra* feature is shown.

(16) *Sarasvatīraṅgani*

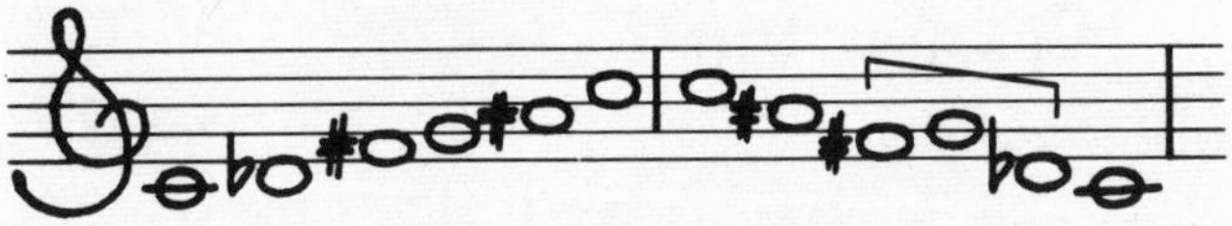

The notes *GA* (Ebb) and *NI* (B) are avoided entirely. The descent shows one *vakra* feature.

Chakra VIII

43. *MĒḶA GAVĀMBHODI*

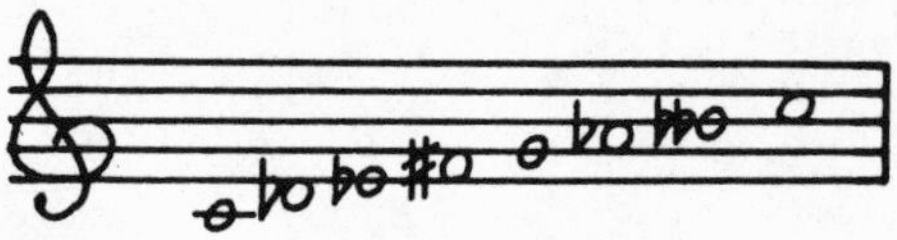

GAVĀMBHODHI (*Triputa-tāla*) SCM, 213

Janya Rāgas of the 43. Mēḷa

(1) *Añjanāvati*

The note *NI* (Bbb) is avoided entirely.

(2) *Dēva Mālāka*

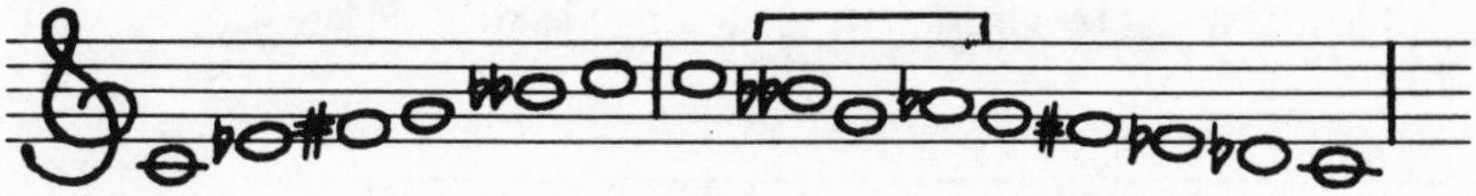

Ascent: the notes *RI* (Db) and *DHA* (Ab) are avoided.
Descent: *sampūrṇa*; one *vakra* feature is shown.

(3) *Druva Kīrṇavam*

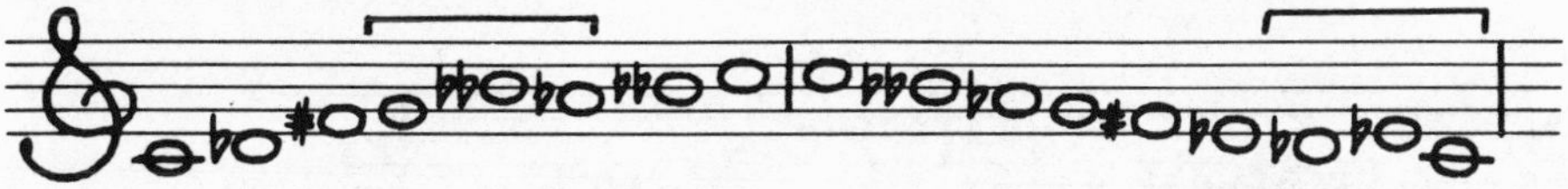

Ascent: the note *GA* (Eb) is avoided; one *vakra* feature is shown.
Descent: *sampūrṇa*; one *vakra* feature is used.

(4) *Gīrvāṇi*

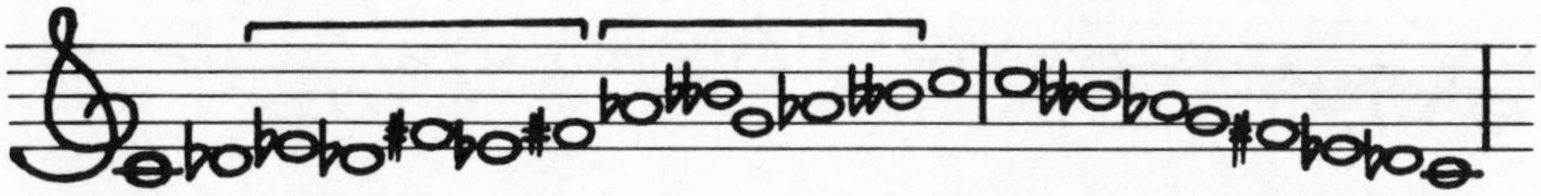

Ascent: *sampūrṇa*; two extended *vakra* features are shown.
Descent: *krama sampūrṇa*.

Another, similar, ascent of this *rāga* can be:

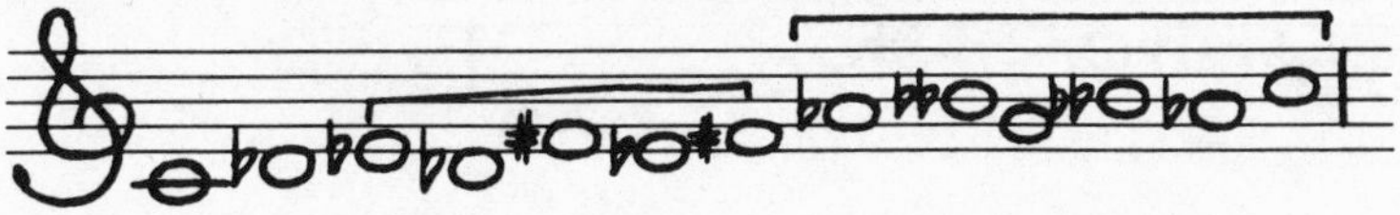

Gīrvāṇi is also the name of the 43. *rāga* of the *asampūrṇa* system.

GĪRVĀṆI (*Triputa-tāla*) SCM, 214

(5) *Gōpikābharaṇam*

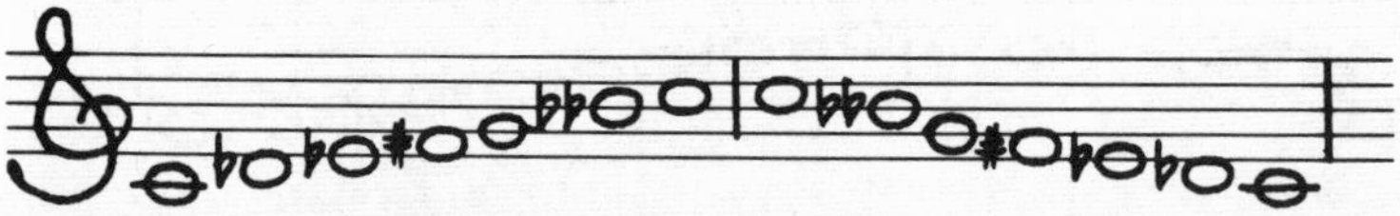

The note *DHA* (Ab) is avoided entirely.

(6) *Jayavēlāvaḷi*

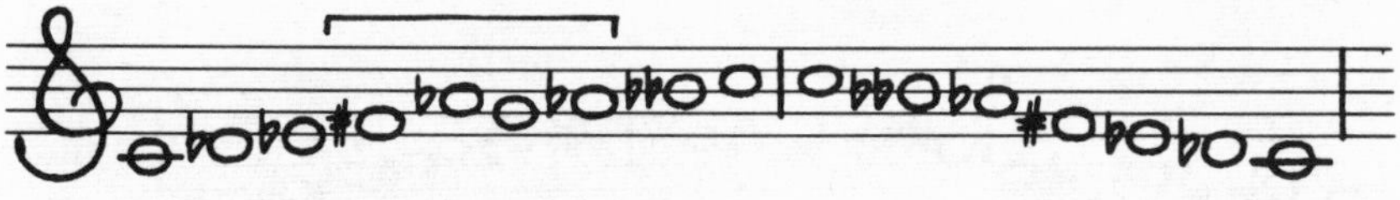

Ascent: *sampūrṇa*; one *vakra* feature is shown.
Descent: the note *PA* (G) is avoided.

(7) *Kalāvasanta* (*Kalika Vasanta*)

The note *RI* (Db) is avoided entirely. *DHA* (Ab) is omitted in descent.

KALĀVASANTA (*Triputa-tāla*) SCM, 214-15

(8) *Kalivasantam*

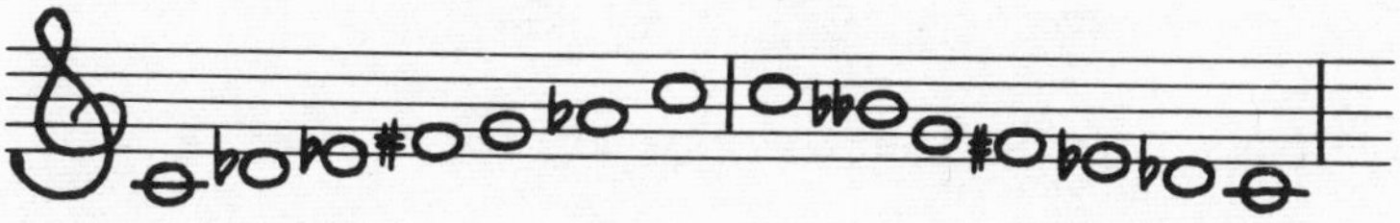

Ascent: the note *NI* (Bbb) is avoided.
Descent: the note *DHA* (Ab) is omitted.

(9) *Kavardham*

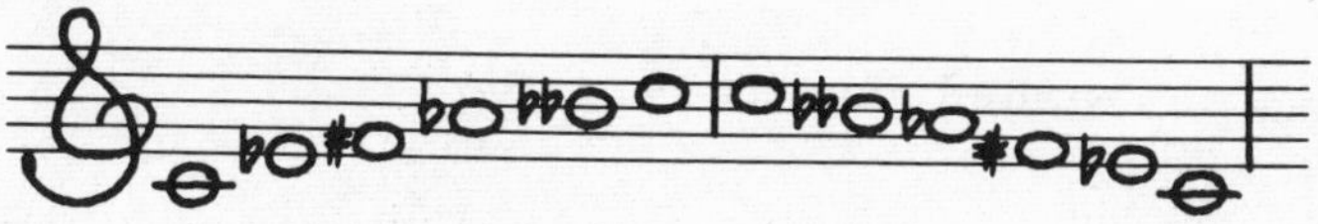

The notes *RI* (Db) and *PA* (G) are avoided entirely.

(10) *Kōkila Dīparam*

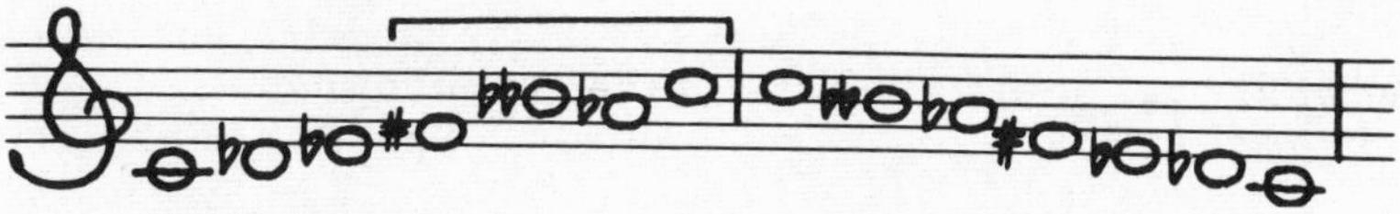

The note *PA* (G) is avoided entirely. The ascent shows one *vakra* feature.

(11) *Kōkila Dīptam*

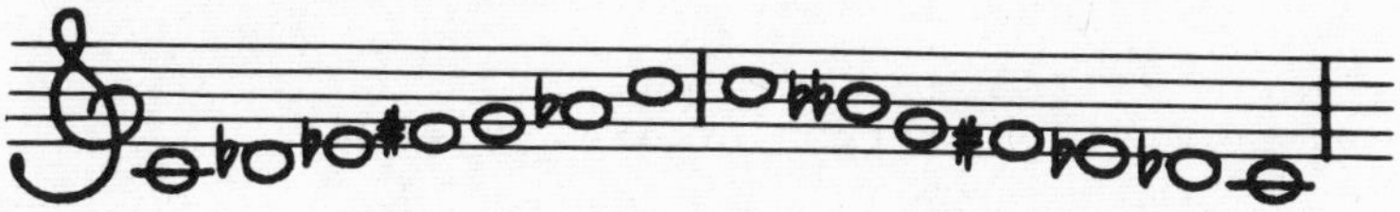

Ascent: the note *NI* (Bbb) is avoided.
Descent: the note *DHA* (Ab) is omitted.

(12) *Kōkila Gīrvāṇi*

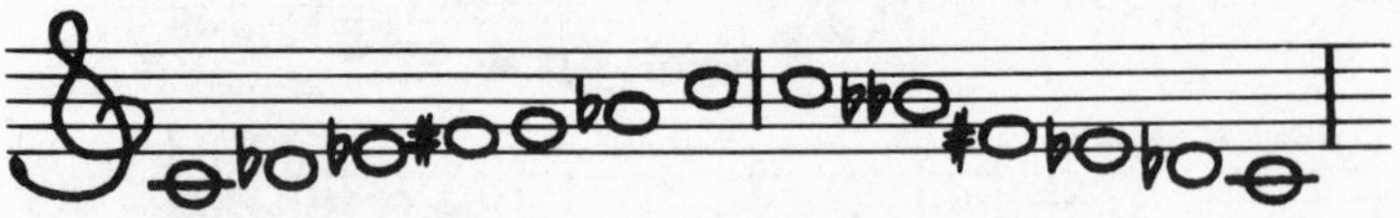

Ascent: the note *NI* (Bbb) is avoided.
Descent: the notes *DHA* (Ab) and *PA* (G) are omitted.

(13) *Lāsyapriya*

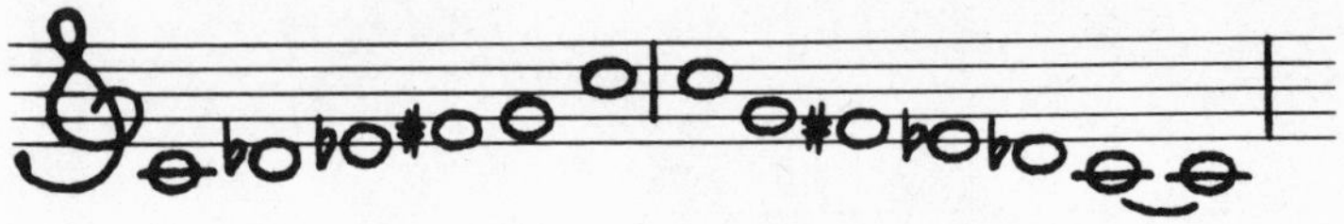

The notes *DHA* (Ab) and *NI* (Bbb) are avoided entirely.

(14) *Mahati*

The note *RI* (Db) is avoided entirely.

(15) *Māruvagauḷa*

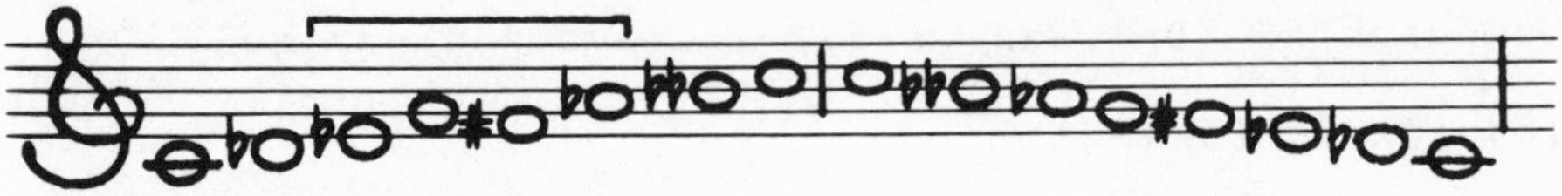

Ascent: *sampūrṇa*; one *vakra* feature is shown.
Descent: *krama sampūrṇa*.

(16) *Mēchakāmbhōji* (*Mēcakāmbhōji*)

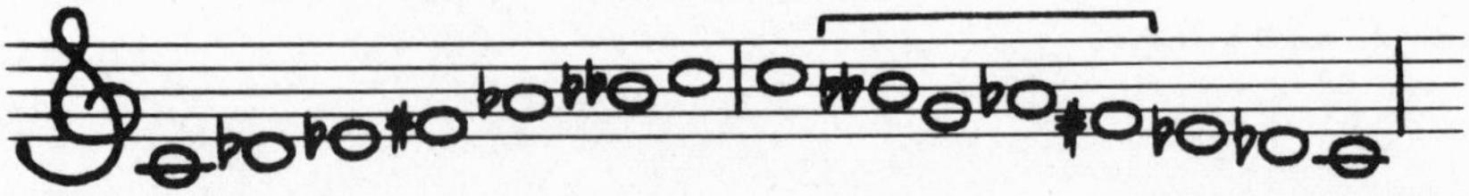

Ascent: the note *PA* (G) is avoided.
Descent: *sampūrṇa*; one *vakra* feature is shown.

(17) *Sāmansvarāḷi*

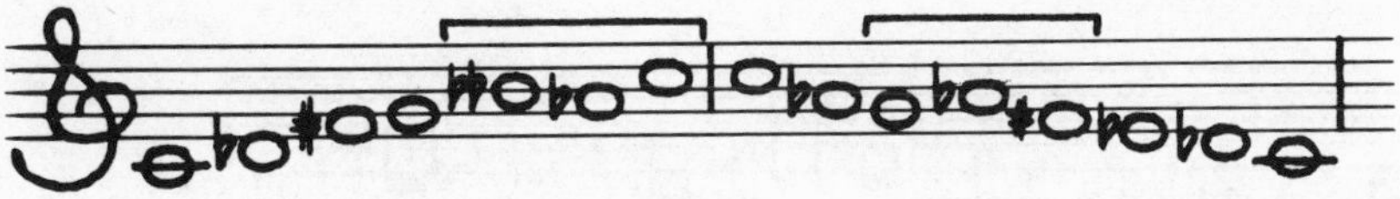

Ascent: the note *GA* (Eb) is avoided; one *vakra* feature is shown.
Descent: the note *NI* (Bbb) is omitted; one *vakra* feature is used.

(18) *Siṃhamadhyama*

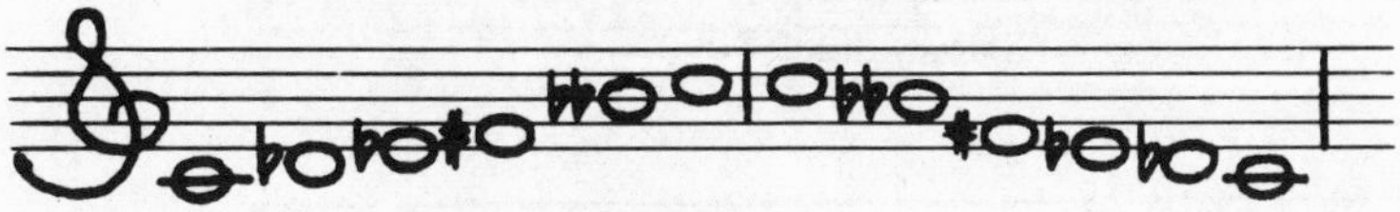

The notes *PA* (G) and *DHA* (Ab) are avoided entirely.

(19) *Śuddhāmbhodhi* (*Śudhāmbhodhi*)

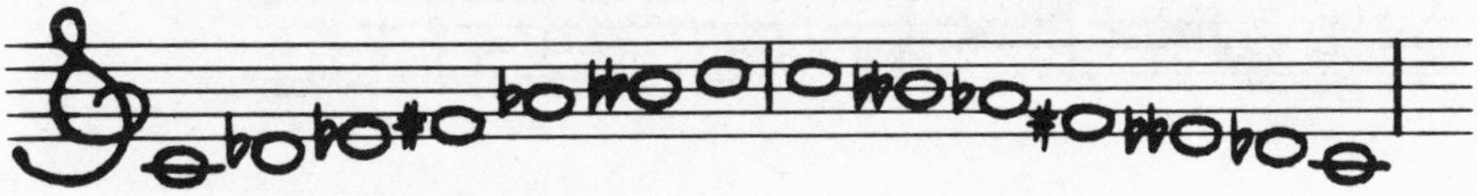

The note *PA* (G) is avoided entirely.

(20) *Vijayabhūshāvaḷi* (*Vijayabhūṣāvaḷi*)

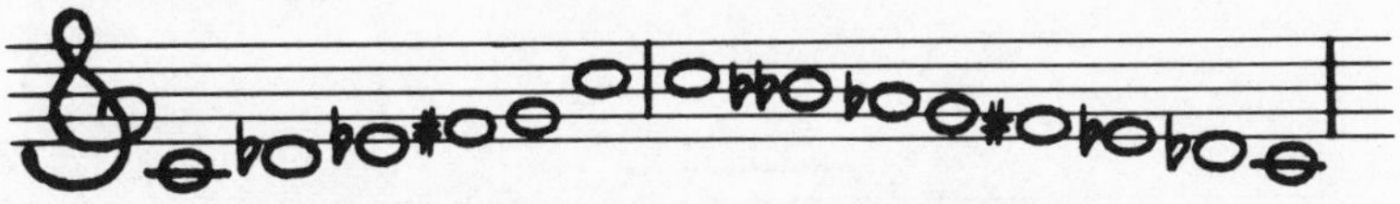

Ascent: the notes *DHA* (Ab) and *NI* (Bbb) are avoided.
Descent: *krama sampūrṇa*.

44. *MĒLA BHĀVAPRIYĀ*

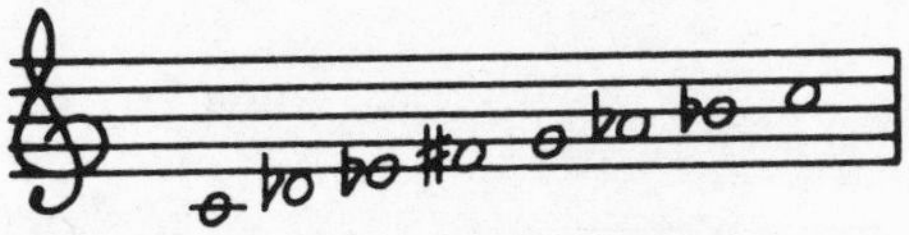

Rāga Bhāvapriyā can be performed at any time.

BHĀVAPRIYĀ (*Triputa-tāla*) SCM, 215

Janya Rāgas of the 44. Mēḷa

(1) *Ambhōruham*

Ascent: the note *MA* (F#) is avoided.
Descent: *sampūrṇa*; one *vakra* feature is shown.

(2) *Bhānukatayam*

The note *RI* (Db) is avoided entirely.

(3) *Bhārati*

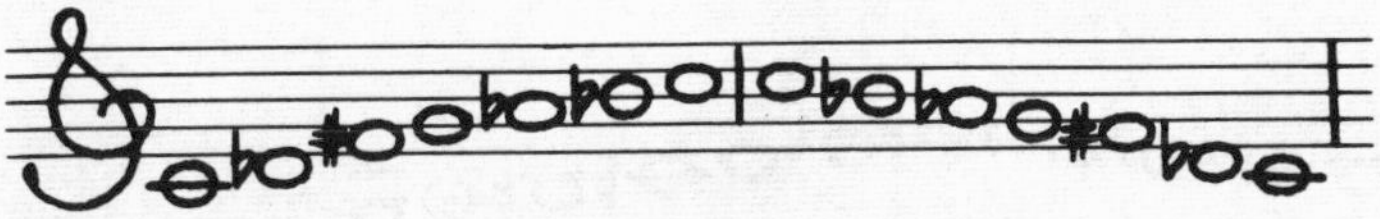

The note *GA* (Eb) is avoided entirely.

(4) *Bhavāni*

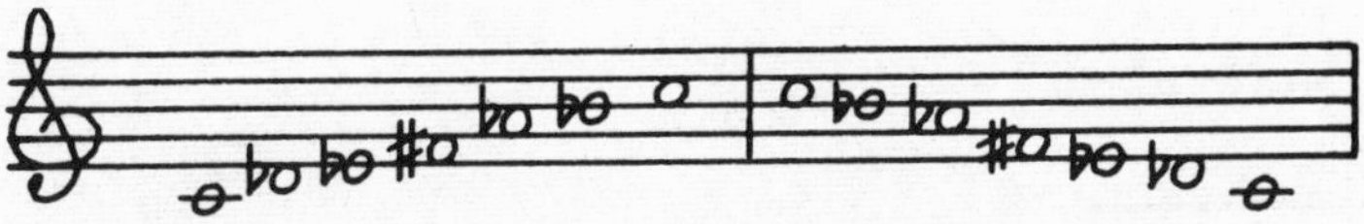

The note *PA* (G) is avoided entirely. *Bhavāni* is also the name of the 44. *rāga* in the *asampūrṇa mēḷa* system.

BHAVĀNI (*Triputa-tāla*) SCM, 216

(5) *Bhāvukadāyini*

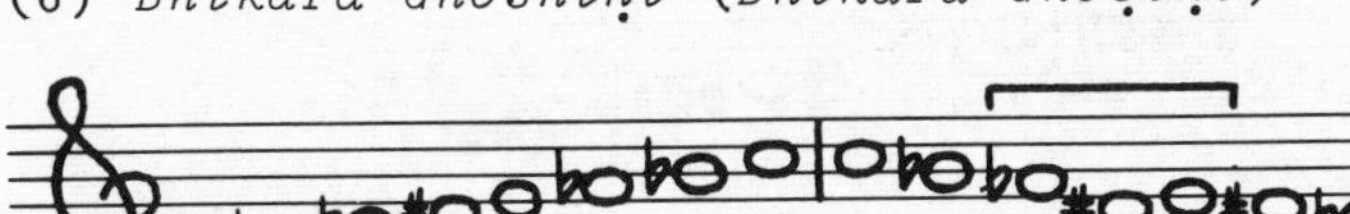

The note *RI* (Db) is avoided entirely.

(6) *Bhīkara Ghōshiṇi* (*Bhīkara Ghōṣiṇi*)

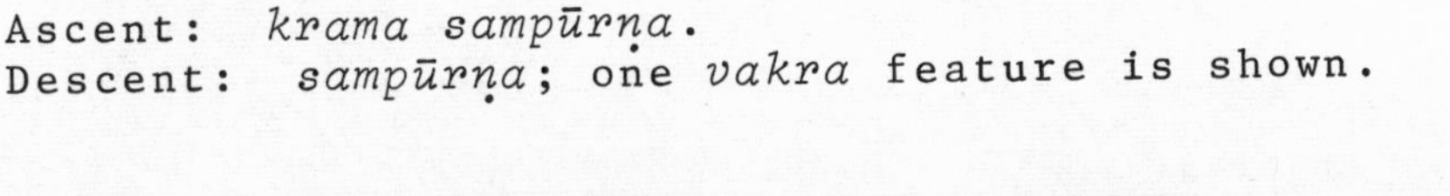

Ascent: *krama sampūrṇa*.
Descent: *sampūrṇa*; one *vakra* feature is shown.

(7) *Bhramarabhōgi*

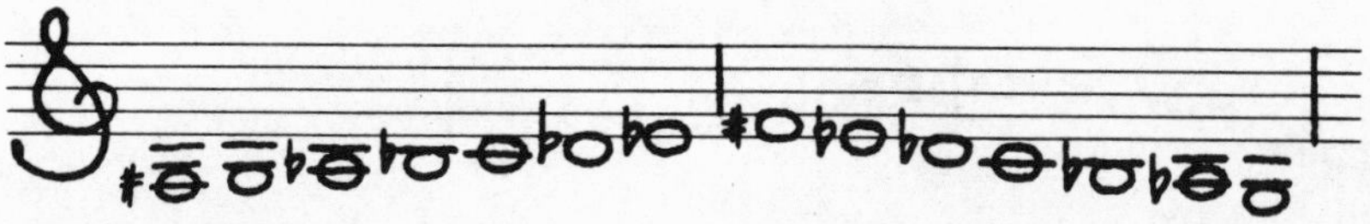

The lowest note of this scale is *MA* (F#) of the low octave range, the highest is *MA* (F#) of the middle octave range. The scale is straight in ascent and descent.

(8) *Dhavaḷa Sarasīruham*

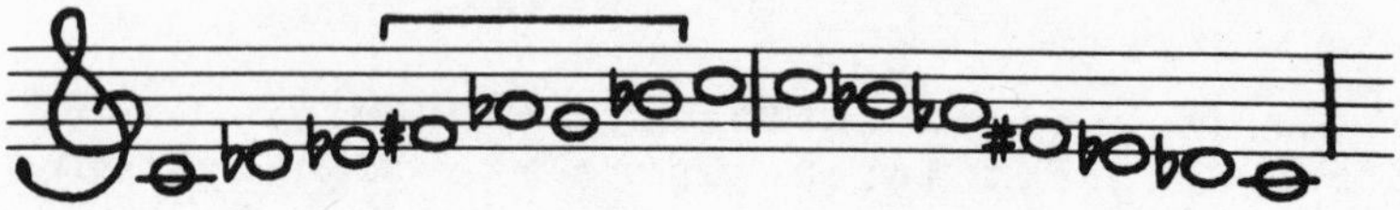

Ascent: *sampūrṇa*; one *vakra* feature is shown.
Descent: the note *PA* (G) is avoided.

(9) *Hālāyudhapriya*

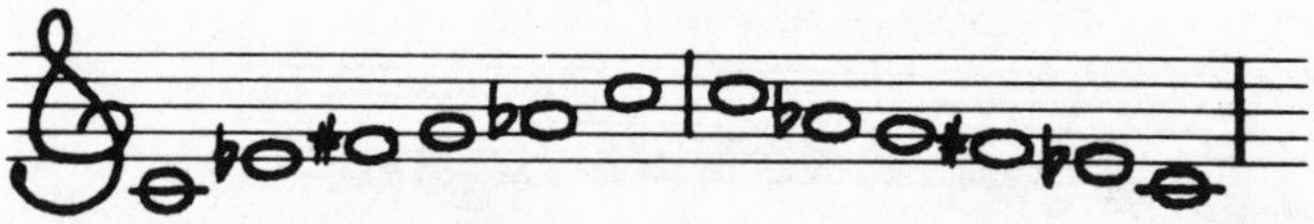

The notes *RI* (Db) and *NI* (Bb) are avoided entirely.

(10) *Kalāmūrti*

Ascent: the notes *DHA* (Ab) and *NI* (Bb) are avoided.
Descent: *krama sampūrṇa*.

(11) *Kāñchanāvati* (*Kāñcanāvati*)

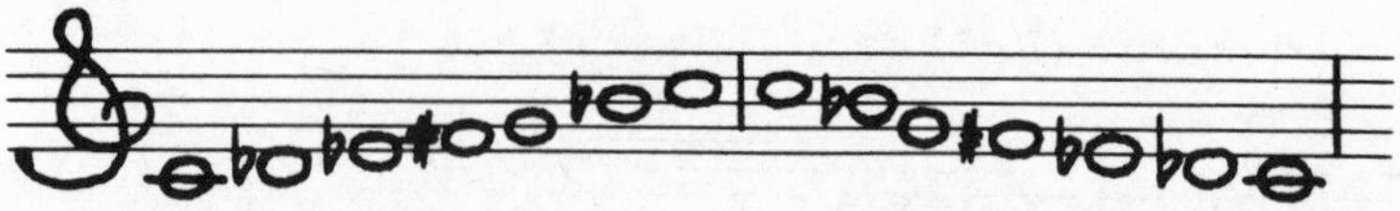

The note *DHA* (Ab) is avoided entirely.

(12) *Kannaḍa Dīparam*

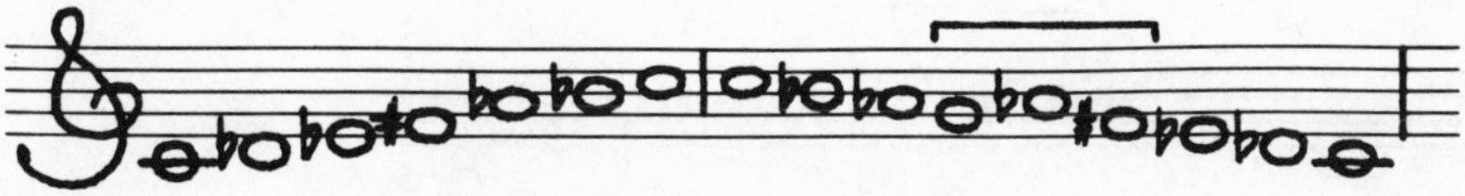

Ascent: the note *PA* (G) is avoided.
Descent: *sampūrṇa*; one *vakra* feature is shown.

(13) *Karmuvu*

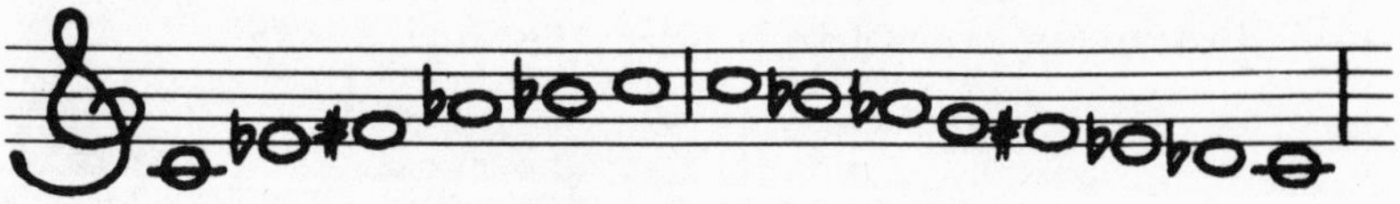

Ascent: the notes *RI* (Db) and *PA* (G) are avoided.
Descent: *krama sampūrṇa*.

(14) *Mechabaṅgāḷa* (*Mecabaṅgāḷa*)

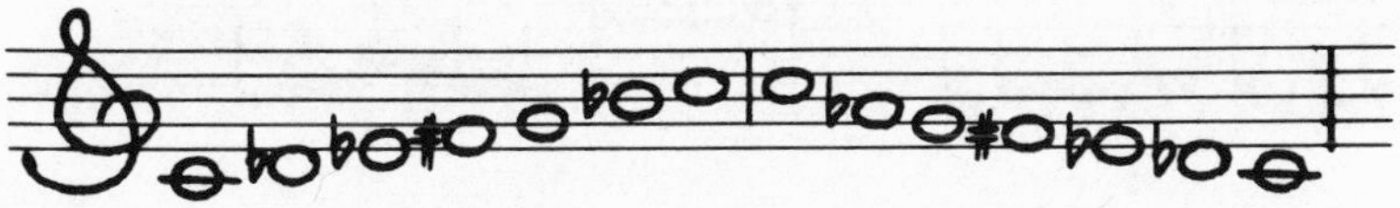

Ascent: the note *DHA* (Ab) is avoided.
Descent: the note *NI* (Bb) is omitted.

(15) *Sāmantvēlāvaḷi*

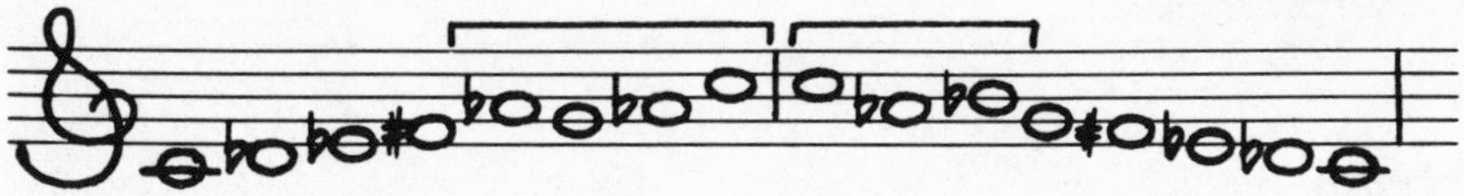

Ascent: the note *NI* (Bb) is avoided; one *vakra* feature is shown.
Descent: *sampūrṇa*; one *vakra* feature is used.

(16) *Sāraṅgamāruva*

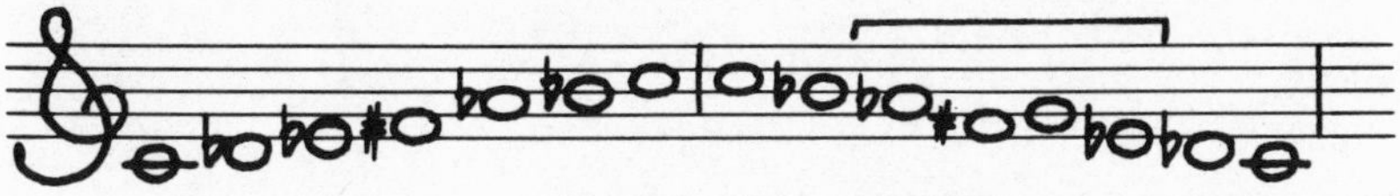

Ascent: the note *PA* (G) is avoided.
Descent: *sampūrṇa*; one *vakra* feature is shown.

(17) *Sarasīruham*

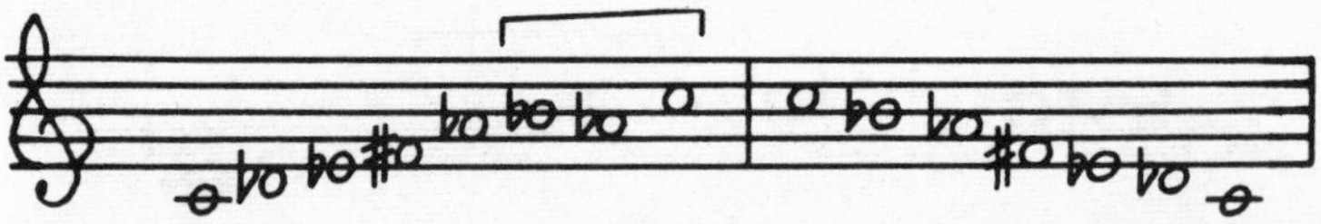

The note *PA* (G) is avoided entirely. The ascent shows one *vakra* feature.

The difference between *Dhavaḷa Sarasīruham* (44, 17) and the *rāga* under consideration, *Sarasiruham*, appears in the formations of the two ascents. Tone material and descents are identical in both *rāgas*.

SARASĪRUHAM (*Triputa-tāla*) SCM, 217

(18) *Śivapriya*

The note *PA* (G) is avoided entirely.

(19) *Vēdika*

The notes *PA* (G) and *DHA* (Ab) are avoided entirely.

45. *MĒḶA ŚUBHAPANTUVARĀLĪ*

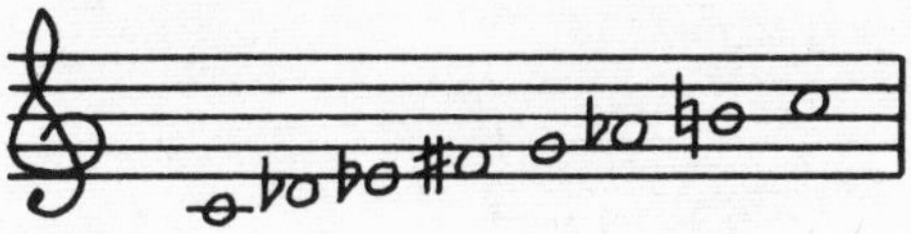

Veṅkaṭamakhin called this *rāga Śaivapantuvarālika* and Tulaja derived it from *rāga Sindhuramakriya*.

ŚUBHAPANTUVARĀLĪ Triputa-tāla SCM, 217-8

Janya Rāgas of the 45. Mēḷa

(1) *Airāvati*

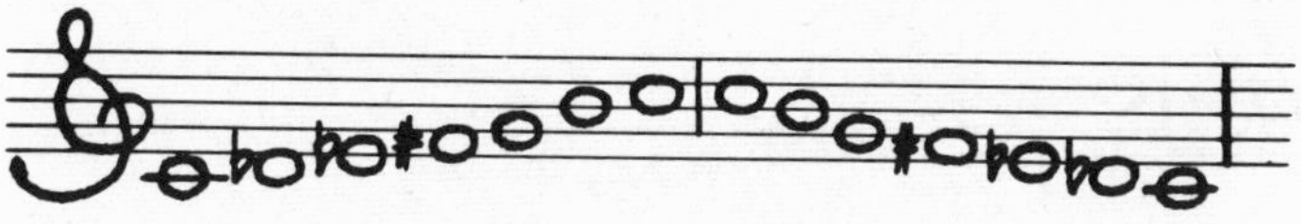

The note *DHA* (Ab) is avoided entirely.

Another *rāga* with the same name appears under the heading of the 64. *mēḷa* (1).

(2) *Bauḷāmukhi*

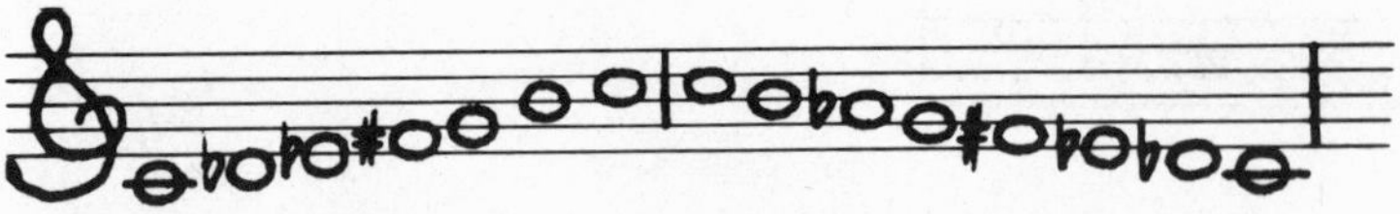

Ascent: the note *DHA* (Ab) is avoided.
Descent: *krama sampūrṇa*.

(3) *Bhānu Dhanyāsi*

This *niṣādāntya* scale avoids the note *PA* (G) in ascent. It shows two *vakra* features, one in ascent and one in descent.

(4) *Bhānu Gīrvāṇi*

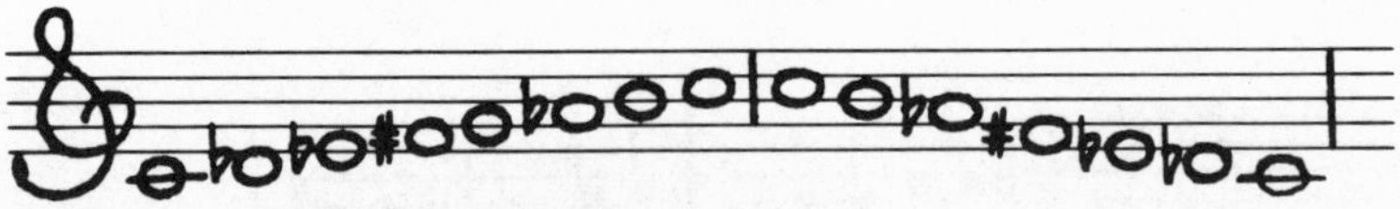

Ascent: *krama sampūrṇa*.
Descent: the note *PA* (G) is avoided.

(5) *Dhaurēyaṇi*

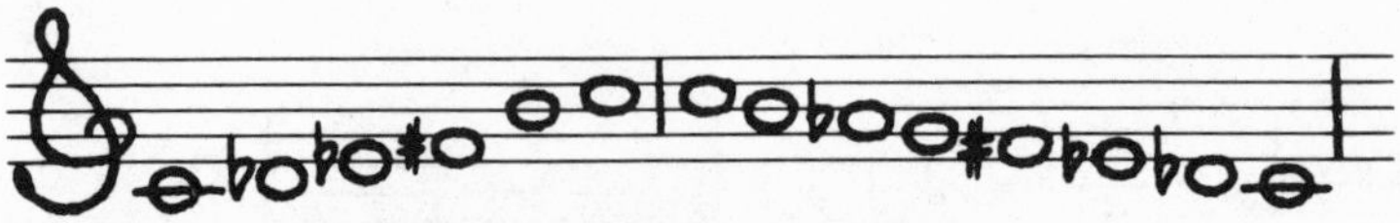

Ascent: the notes *PA* (G) and *DHA* (Ab) are avoided.
Descent: *krama sampūrṇa*.

(6) *Gamaka Sāmantam*

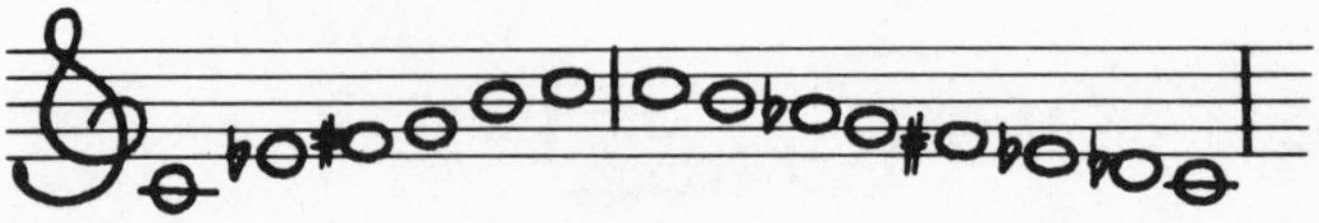

Ascent: the notes *RI* (Db) and *DHA* (Ab) are avoided.
Descent: *krama sampūrṇa*.

(7) *Garuḍapriya*

Ascent: the notes *RI* (Db) and *GA* (Eb) are avoided.
Descent: *sampūrṇa*; two *vakra* features are shown.

(8) *Garuḍavardhani*

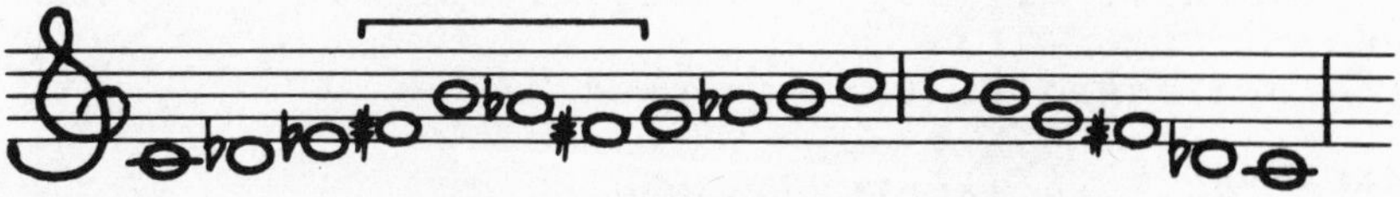

Ascent: *sampūrṇa*; one extended *vakra* feature is shown.
Descent: the notes *DHA* (Ab) and *GA* (Eb) are avoided.

(9) *Gōvardhani*

Ascent: the notes *MA* (F#) and *NI* (B) are avoided.
Descent: *krama sampūrṇa*.

(10) *Jhālakēśari*

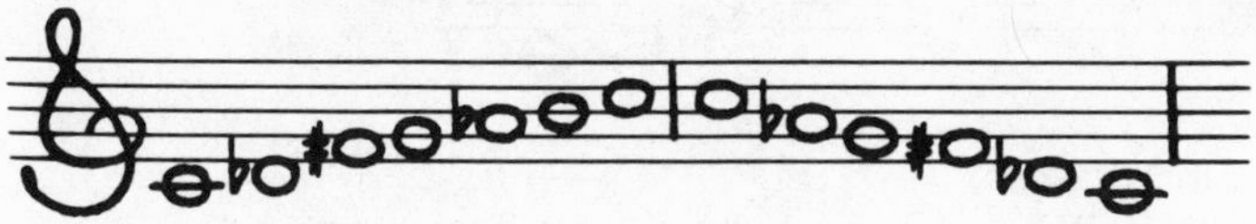

The note *GA* (Eb) is avoided entirely. *NI* (B) is omitted in descent.

(11) *Kamalābharaṇam*

The scale of this *rāga* is *sampūrṇa* and shows one *vakra* feature in ascent and one in descent.

(12) *Kāmarañjari*

Ascent: *sampūrṇa*; one *vakra* feature is shown.

Descent: the note *PA* (G) is avoided; one *vakra* feature is used.

(13) *Kanaka Dīparam*

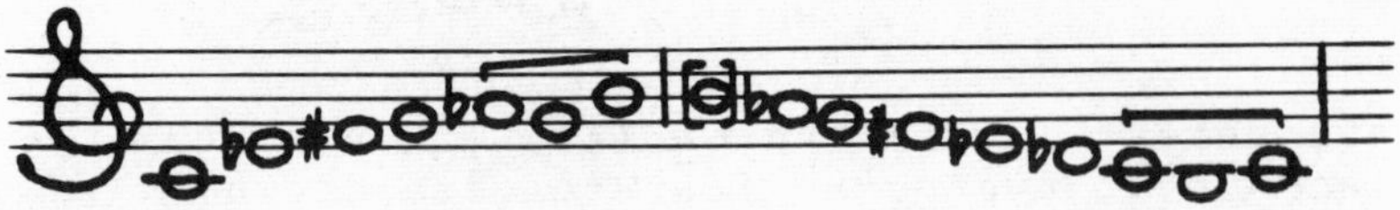

The scale of this *rāga* has *niṣādāntya* character.
Ascent: the note *RI* (Db) is avoided; one *vakra* feature is shown.
Descent: one *vakra* feature is used.

(14) *Kānta Rākshasa* (*Kānta Rākṣasa*)

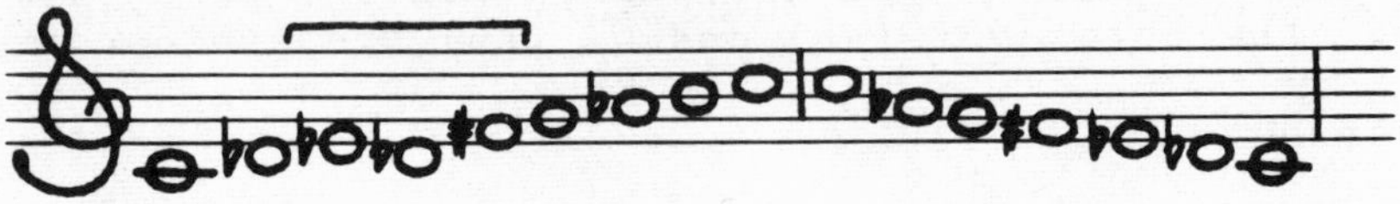

Ascent: *sampūrṇa*; one *vakra* feature is shown.
Descent: the note *NI* (B) is omitted.

(15) *Kriḍāmati*

Ascent: *krama sampūrṇa*.
Descent: the notes *NI* (B) and *MA* (F#) are avoided.

(16) *Mayūradhvani*

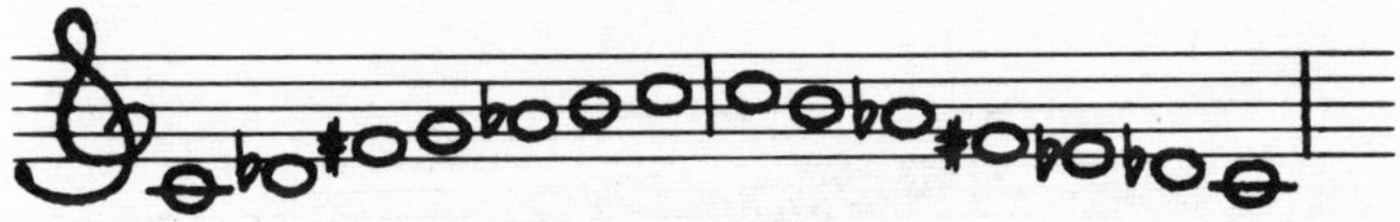

Ascent: the note *GA* (Eb) is avoided.
Descent: the note *PA* (G) is omitted.

(17) *Mālavatāriṇi*

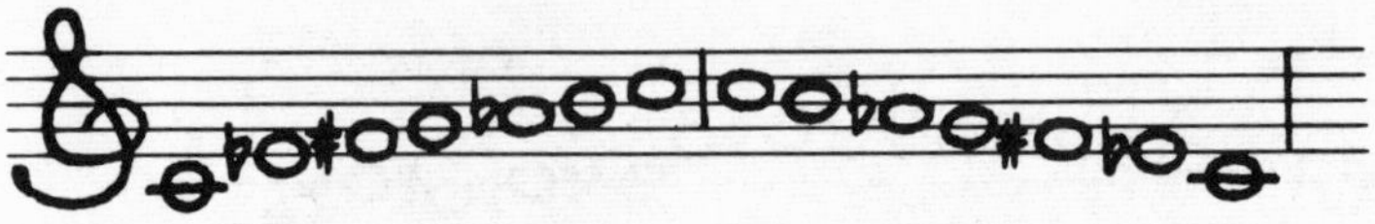

The note *RI* (Db) is avoided entirely.

(18) *Māruvavasantam*

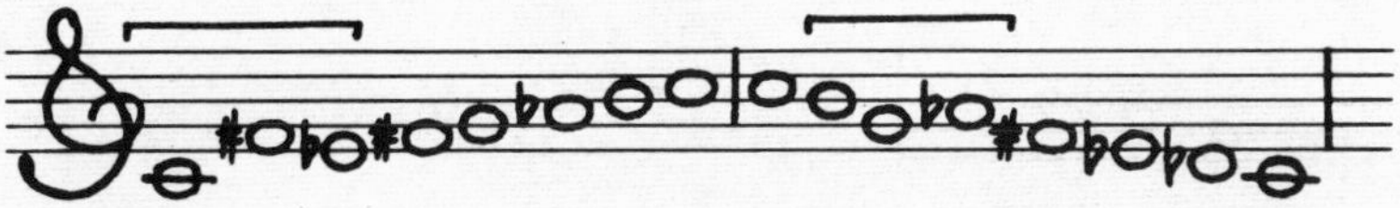

Ascent: the note *RI* (Db) is avoided; one *vakra* feature is shown.
Descent: *sampūrṇa*; one *vakra* feature is used.

(19) *Mēchamanōharī* (*Mēcamanōharī*)

Ascent: the note *RI* (Db) is avoided; one *vakra* feature is shown.
Descent: the note *PA* (G) is omitted.

(20) *Ratnagarbha*

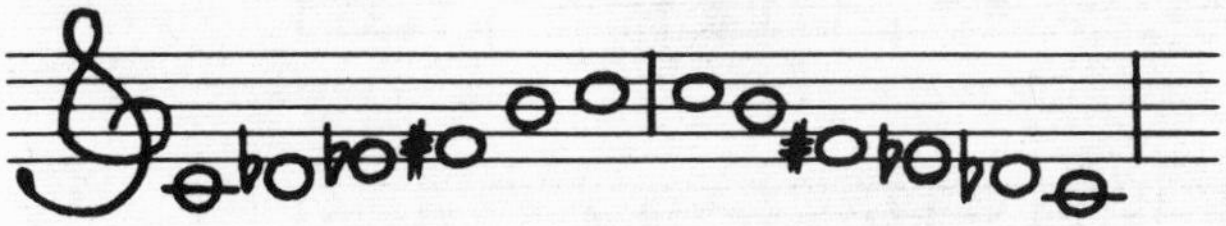

The notes *PA* (G) and *DHA* (Ab) are avoided entirely.

(21) *Śubhāli*

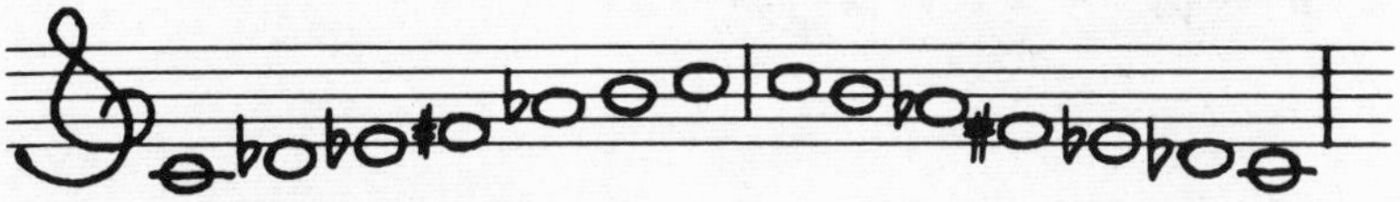

The note *PA* (G) is avoided entirely.

(22) *Śuddhasvarāvaḷi*

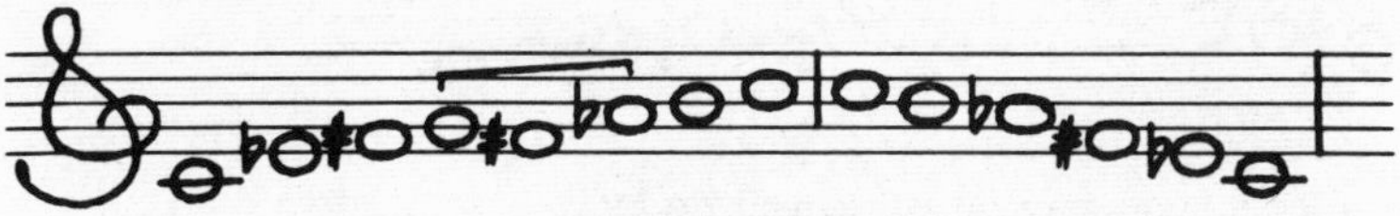

The note *RI* (Db) is avoided entirely. The ascent shows one *vakra* feature; the descent omits the note *PA* (G).

46. *MĒḶA ṠAḌVIDHAMĀRGIṆĪ (ṠAḌVIDHAMĀRGAṆĪ)*

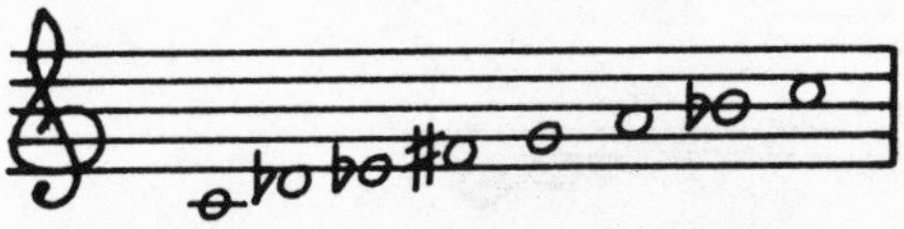

ṠAḌVIDHAMĀRGIṆĪ (Triputa-tāla) SCM, 219

Janya Rāgas of the 46. Mēḷa

(1) *Amritalaharī (Amrutalaharī)*

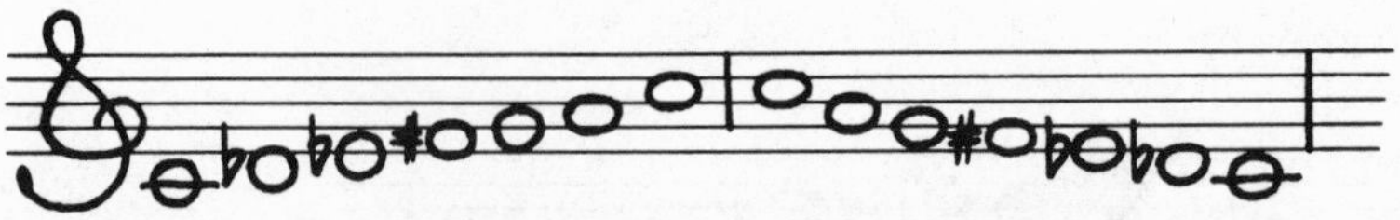

The note *NI* (Bb) is avoided entirely.

Another *rāga* with the same name appears under the heading of the 29. *mēḷa* (3).

(2) *Bahumāriṇi*

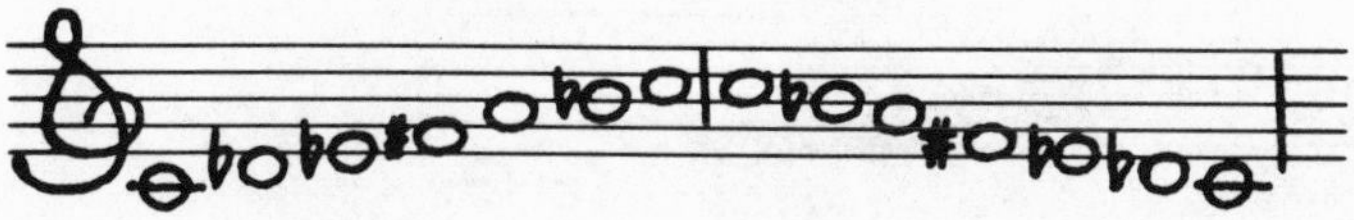

The note *PA* (G) is avoided entirely.

(3) *Bhavāḷi*

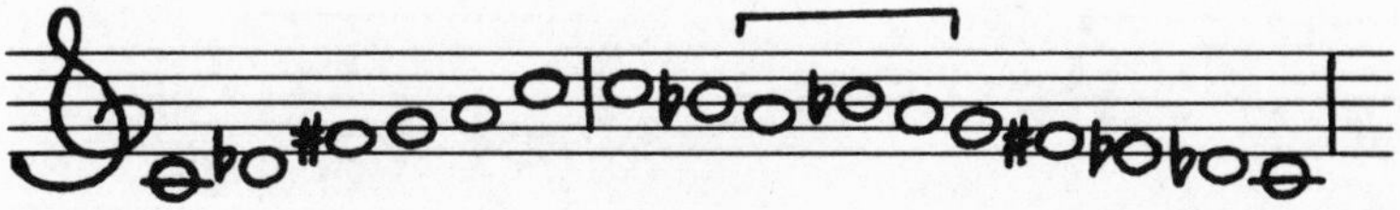

Ascent: the notes *GA* (Eb) and *NI* (Bb) are avoided.
Descent: *sampūrṇa*; one *vakra* feature is shown.

(4) *Brāhmi*

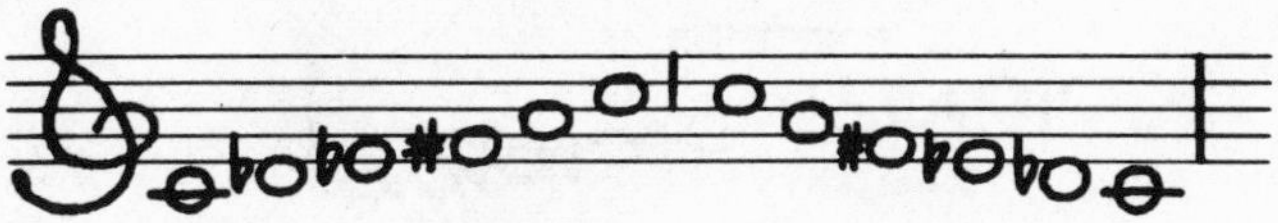

The notes *PA* (G) and *NI* (Bb) are avoided entirely.

(5) *Dāna Mañjari*

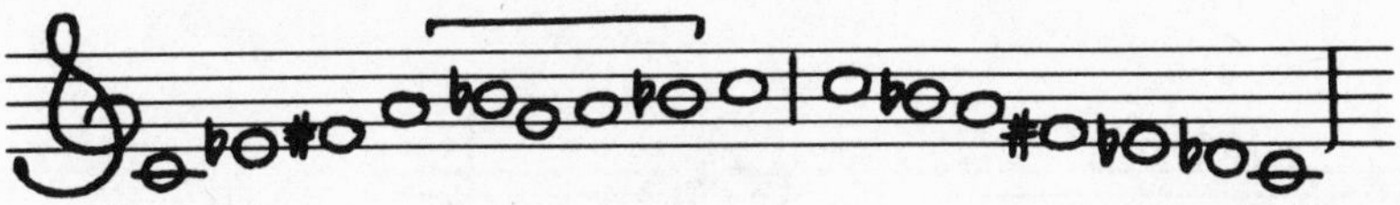

Ascent: the note *RI* (Db) is avoided; one *vakra* feature is shown.
Descent: the note *PA* (G) is omitted.

(6) *Dīkshāṅgi* (*Dīkṣāṅgi*)

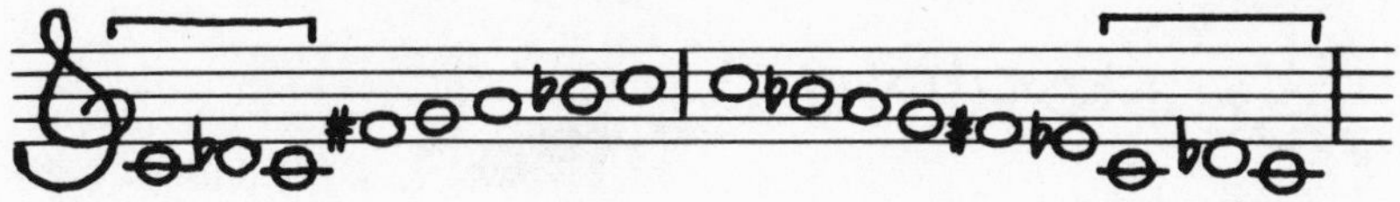

Ascent: the note *GA* (Eb) is avoided; one *vakra* feature is shown.
Descent: *sampūrṇa*; the same *vakra* feature that appears in ascent is used in descent.

(7) *Esāndhōḷi*

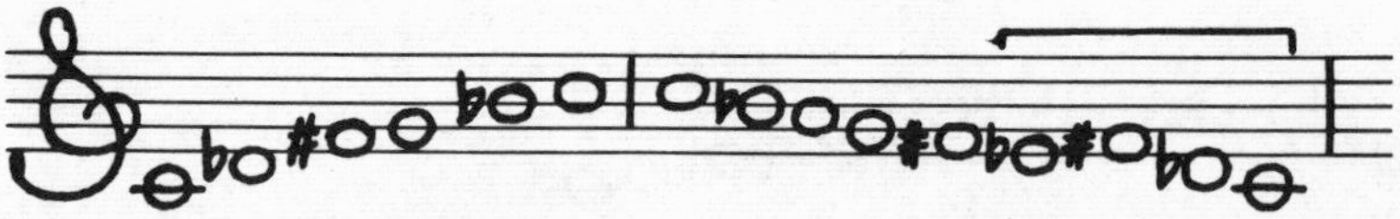

Ascent: the notes *GA* (Eb) and *DHA* (A) are avoided.
Descent: *sampūrṇa*; one *vakra* feature is shown.

(8) *Garbha Līla*

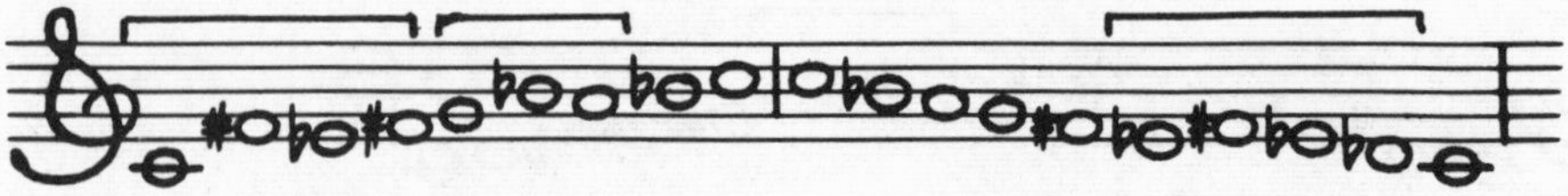

Ascent: the note *RI* (Db) is avoided; two *vakra* features are shown.
Descent: *sampūrṇa*; one *vakra* feature is used.

(9) *Indubhōgi*

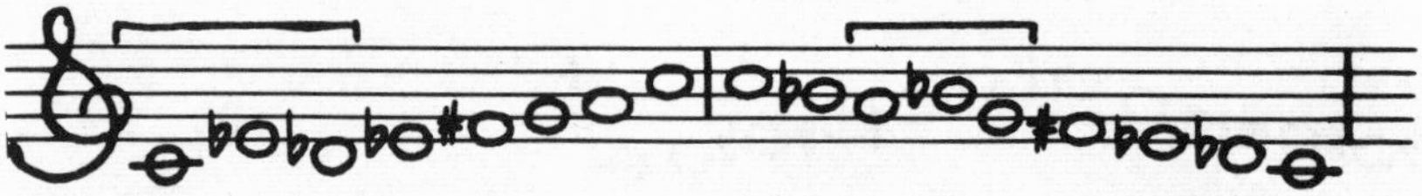

Ascent: the note *NI* (Bb) is avoided; one *vakra* feature is shown.
Descent: *sampūrṇa*; one *vakra* feature is shown.

(10) *Indu Dhanyāsi*

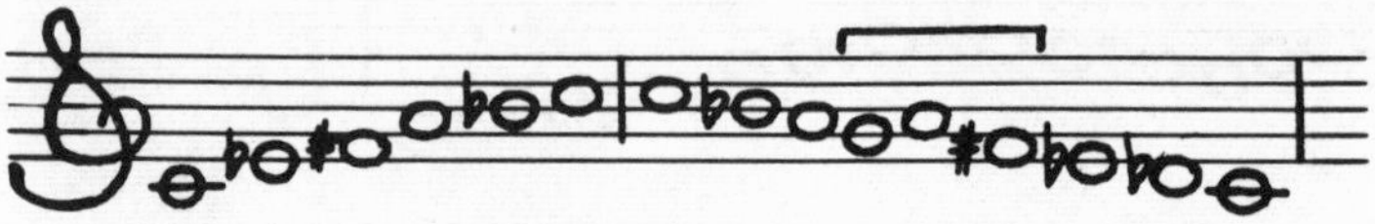

Ascent: the notes *RI* (Db) and *PA* (G) are avoided.
Descent: *sampūrṇa*; one *vakra* feature is shown.

(11) *Jayaśrīkanthi*

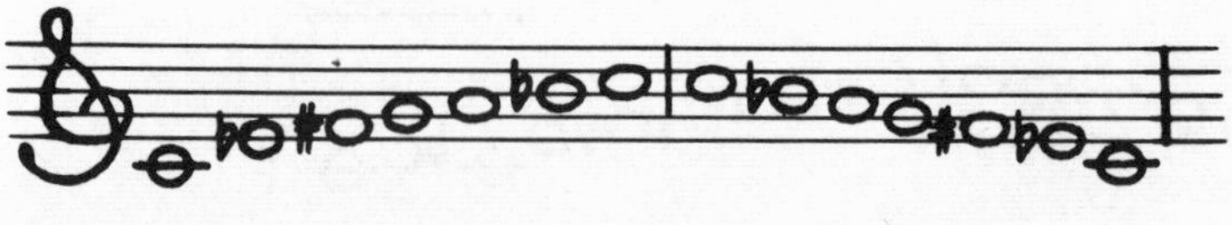

The note *RI* (Db) is avoided entirely.

(12) *Kañja Puñji*

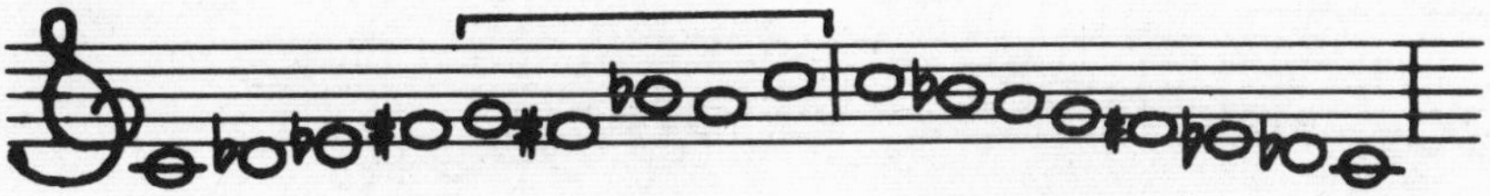

Ascent: *sampūrṇa*; one extended *vakra* feature is shown.
Descent: *krama sampūrṇa*.

(13) *Karalādhari*

The note *PA* (G) is avoided entirely.

(14) *Kshadrākshi* (*Kṣadrākṣi*)

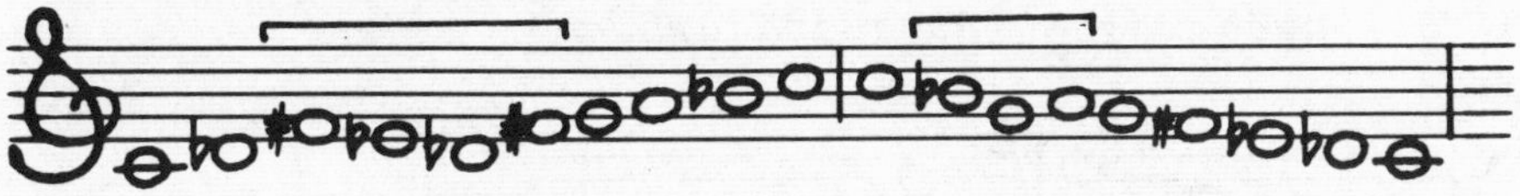

Ascent: *sampūrṇa*; one *vakra* feature is shown.
Descent: *sampūrṇa*; one *vakra* feature is used.

(15) *Kuntala Svarāvali*

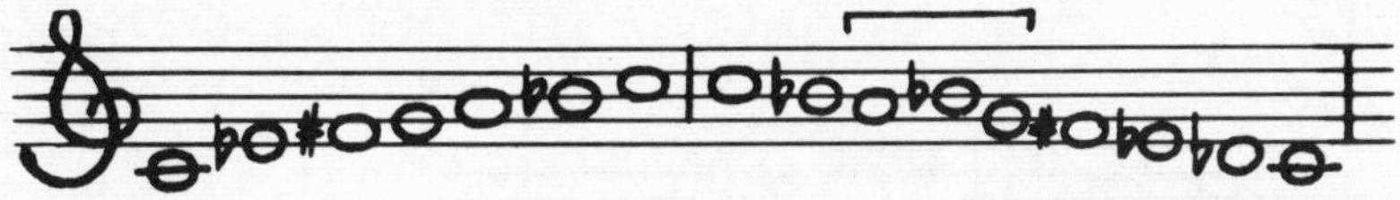

Ascent: the note *RI* (Db) is avoided.
Descent: *sampūrṇa*; one *vakra* feature is shown.

(16) *Lōkadīparam*

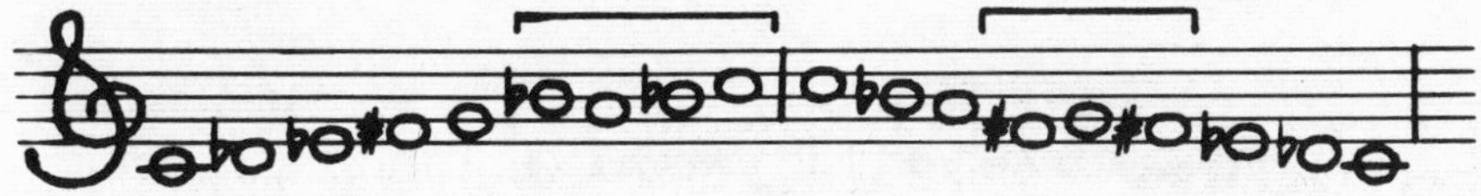

The scale of this *rāga* is *sampūrṇa*; it shows two *vakra* features, one extended one in ascent and one in descent.

(17) *Māruvagauri*

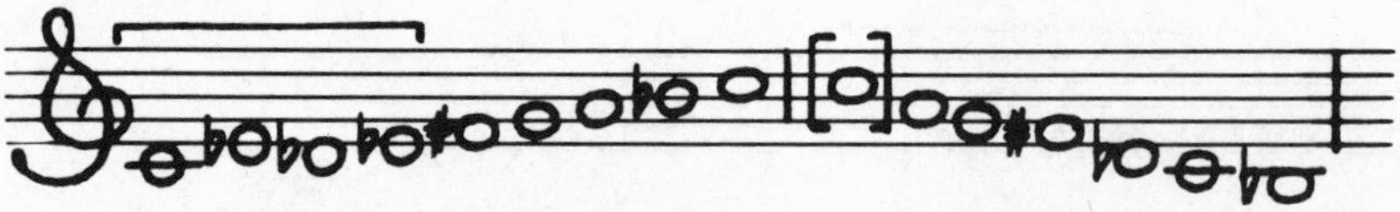

Ascent: *sampūrṇa*; one *vakra* feature is shown.
Descent: the note *NI* (Bb) of the middle octave range and *GA* (Eb) are avoided; the note *NI* (Bb) of the low octave range can be used.

(18) *Pratihari*

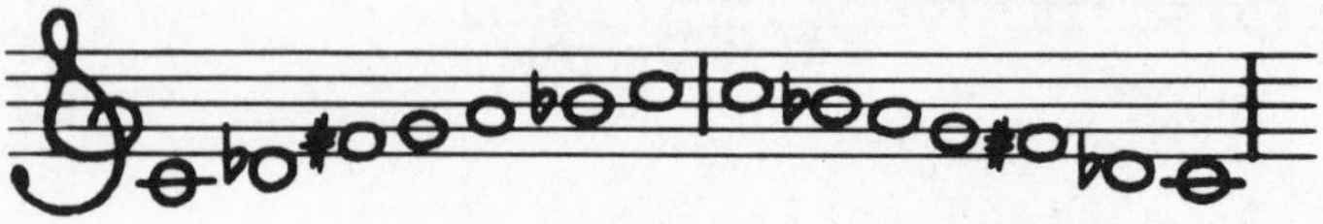

The note *GA* (Eb) is avoided entirely.

(19) *Stavarājarāgam* (*Sthavarājarāgam*)

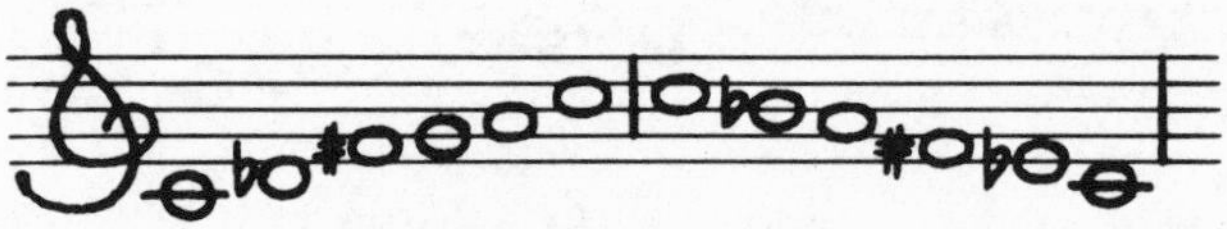

Ascent: the notes *GA* (Eb) and *NI* (Bb) are avoided.
Descent: the notes *PA* (G) and *RI* (Db) are omitted.

(20) *Śrīkanti*

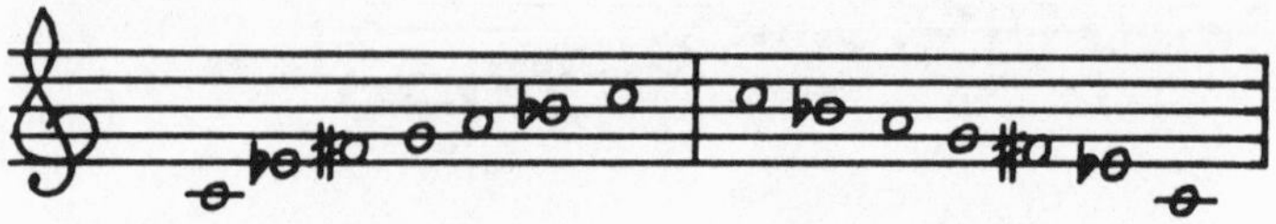

The note *RI* (Db) is avoided entirely.

ŚRĪKANTI (*Triputa-tāla*) SCM, 220

(21) *Suktijapriya*

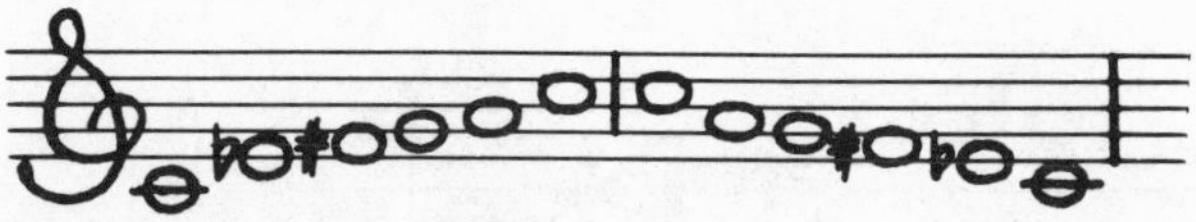

The notes *RI* (Db) and *NI* (Bb) are avoided entirely.

(22) *Tivravahiṇi*

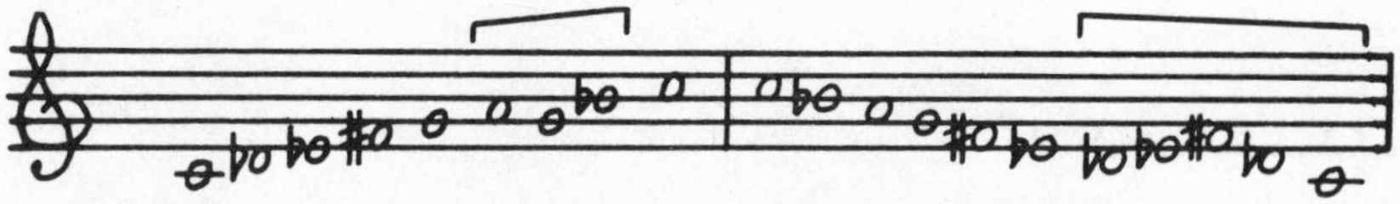

The scale of this *rāga* is *sampūrṇa*. It shows two *vakra* features, one in ascent and one in descent.

TIVRAVAHIṆI RĀGA (*Triputa-tāla*) SCM, 219

(23) *Vijayābhīru*

Ascent: *sampūrṇa*; two *vakra* features are shown.
Descent: the note *NI* (Bb) is avoided.

47. *MĒḶA SUVARṆĀṄGĪ*

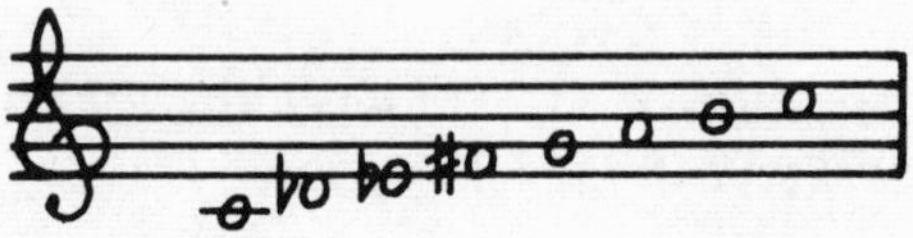

SUVARṆĀṄGĪ (*Triputa-tāla*) SCM, 221

Janya Rāgas of the 47. Mēḷa

(1) *Ābhiru*

Ascent: the note *DHA* (A) is avoided; one *vakra* feature is shown.
Descent: the notes *NI* (B) and *RI* (Db) are omitted.

The SCM (136) presents the following form of *Ābhiru*:

The following melody specimen represents this latter version:

ĀBHIRU (*Triputa-tāla*) SCM, 223-24

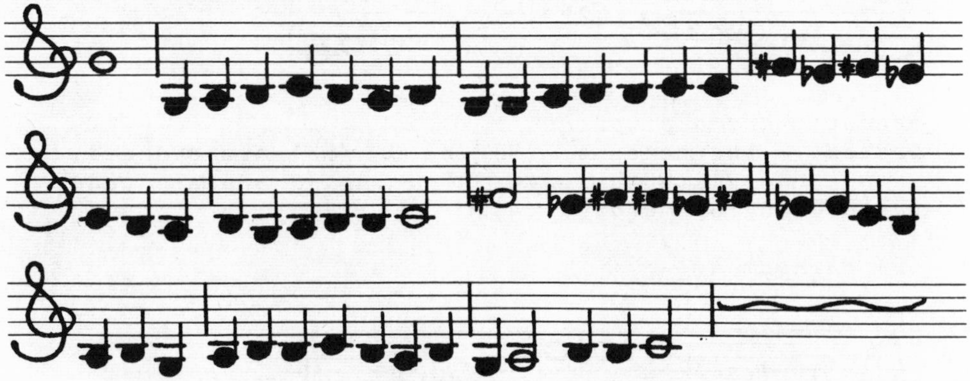

Another form of *Ābhiru* can be:

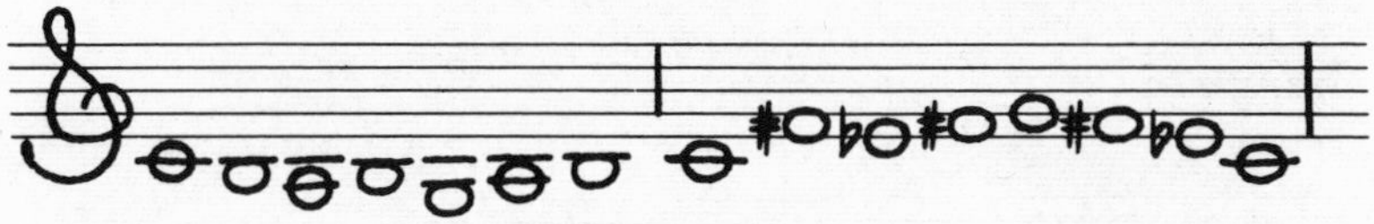

In the latter two versions of this *rāga* the note *RI* (Db) is avoided entirely and the scales assume either *dhaivatāntya* or *pañcamāntya* character respectively.

(2) *Anughaṇṭa*

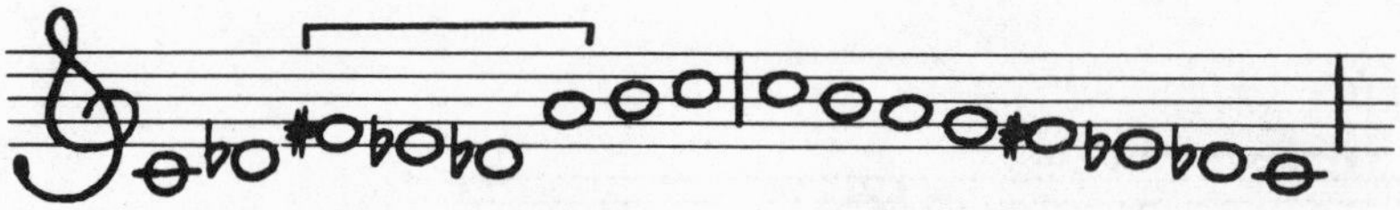

Ascent: *sampūrṇa*; one *vakra* feature is shown.
Descent: *krama sampūrṇa*.

(3) *Bhaka Mañjari*

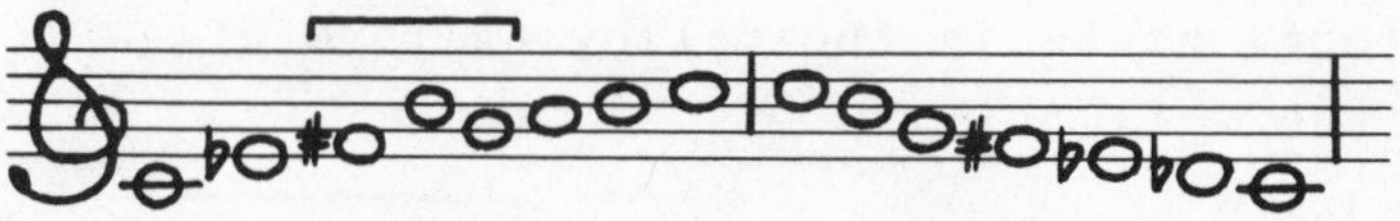

Ascent: the note *RI* (Db) is avoided; one *vakra* feature is shown.
Descent: the note *DHA* (A) is omitted.

(4) *Bhōga Dhvaji*

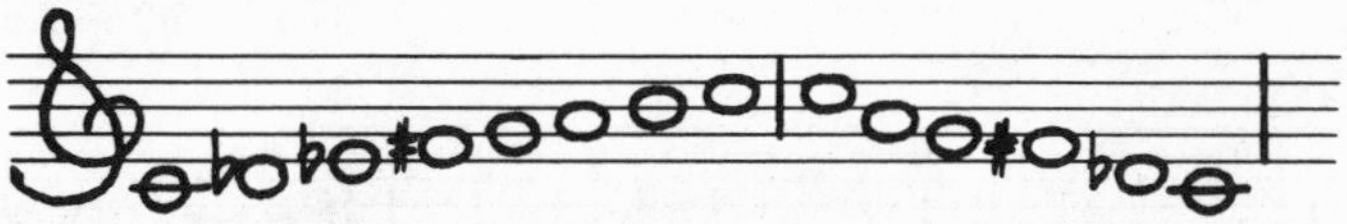

Ascent: *krama sampūrṇa*.
Descent: the notes *NĪ* (B) and *GA* (Eb) are avoided.

A *rāga* with the name *Bhōga Dhvaja* appears under the heading of *mēḷa* 39 (4).

(5) *Bhṛngamōhi*

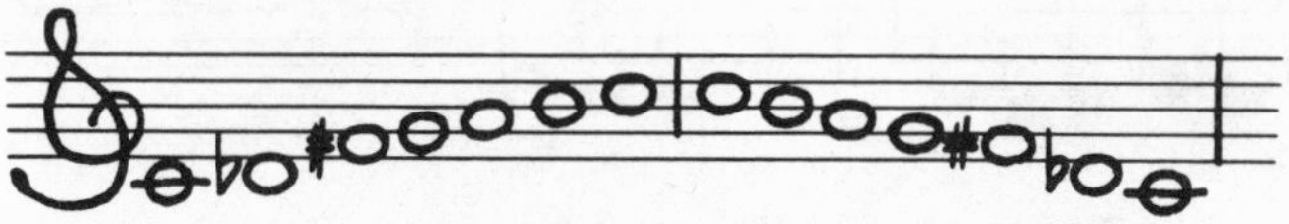

The note *GA* (Eb) is avoided entirely.

(6) *Dīrghamaṅgali*

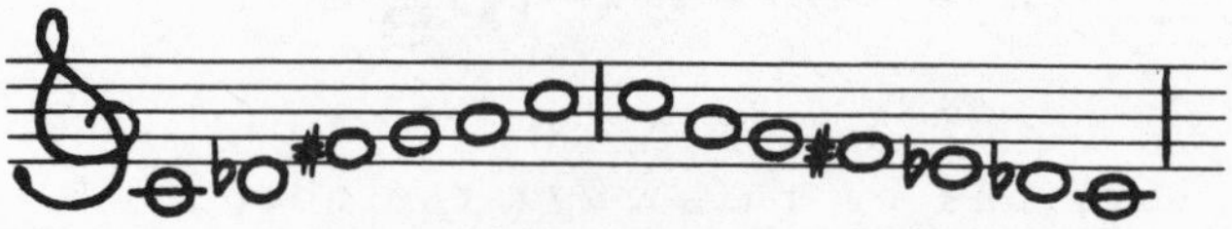

The note *NI* (B) is avoided entirely. *GA* (Eb) is omitted in ascent.

(7) *Haṭakaṅgi*

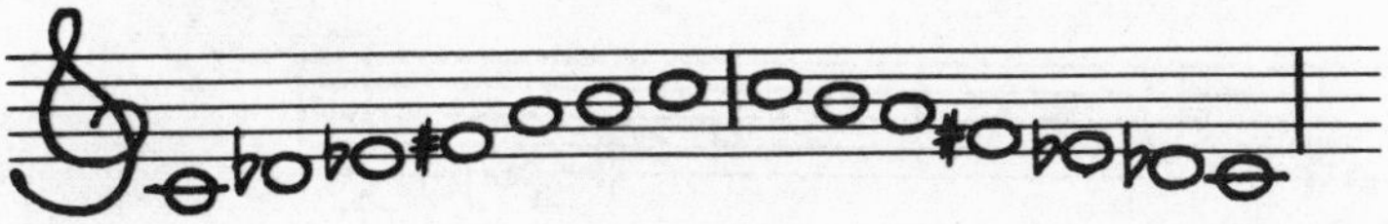

The note *PA* (G) is avoided entirely.

(8) *Kuntala Dhanyāsi*

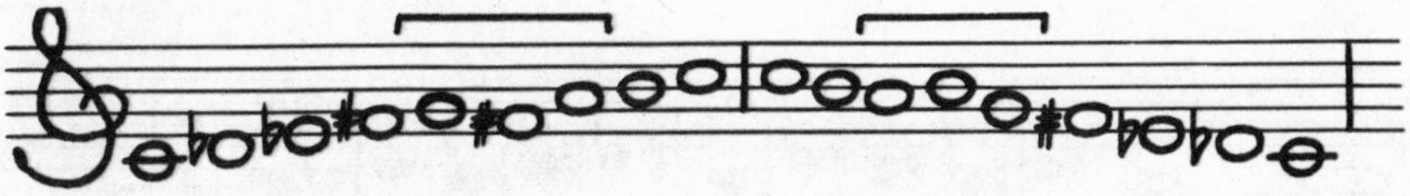

The scale of this *rāga* is *sampūrṇa* and shows two *vakra* features, one in ascent and one in descent.

(9) *Mānini*

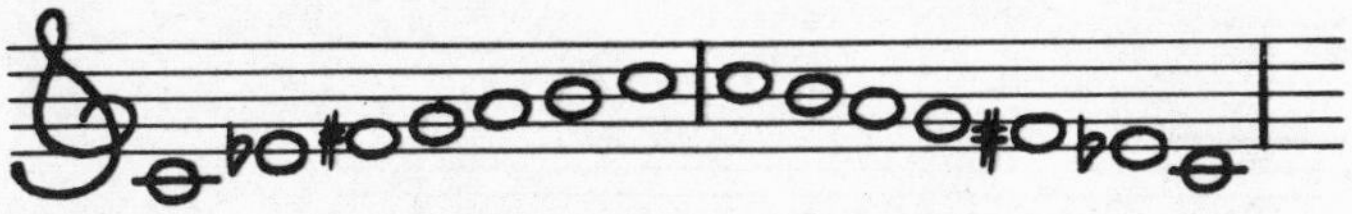

The note *RI* (Db) is avoided entirely.

Another *rāga* with the same name appears under the heading of the 66. *mēḷa* (13).

(10) *Māruvanārāyaṇi*

Ascent: the note *NI* (B) is avoided.
Descent: *sampūrṇa*; two *vakra* features are shown.

(11) *Navarasabaṅgāḷa*

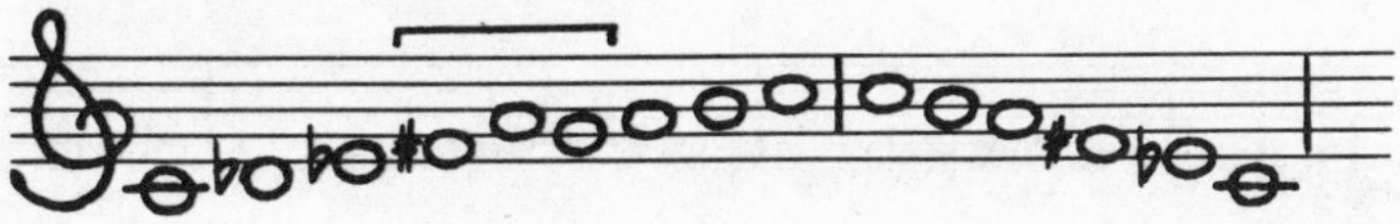

Ascent: *sampūrṇa*; one *vakra* feature is shown.
Descent: the notes *PA* (G) and *RI* (Db) are avoided.

(12) *Ratika*

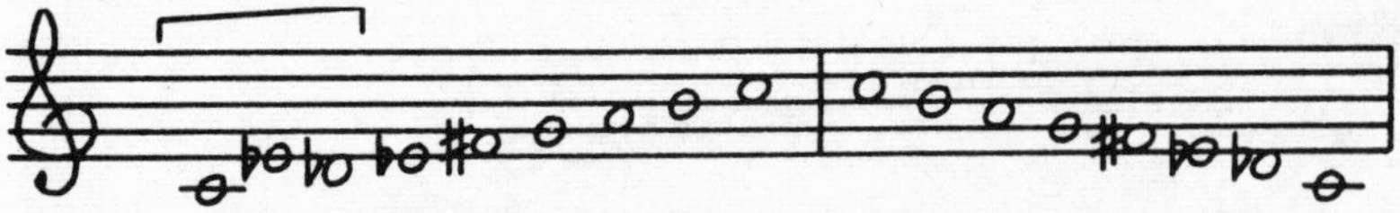

Ascent: *sampūrṇa*; one *vakra* feature is shown.
Descent: *krama sampūrṇa*.

RATIKA (*Triputa-tāla*) SCM, 222-23

(13) *Sālagavēḷāvaḷi*

Ascent: *sampūrṇa*; one *vakra* feature is shown.
Descent: the note *RI* (Db) is avoided.

(14) *Sauvira*

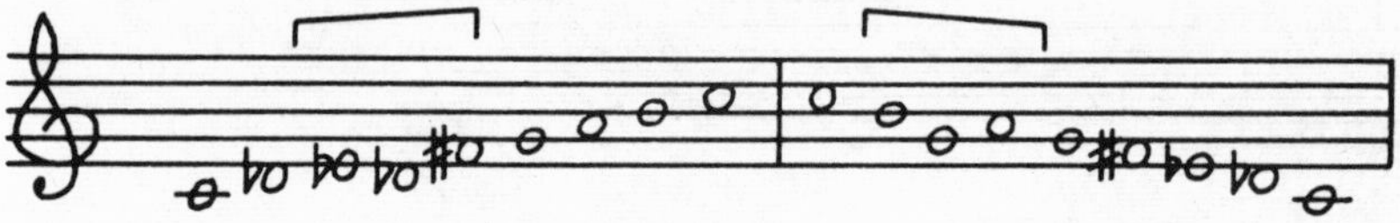

The scale of this *rāga* is *sampūrṇa* and shows two *vakra* features, one in ascent and one in descent.

SAUVIRA (*Triputa-tāla*) SCM, 221-22

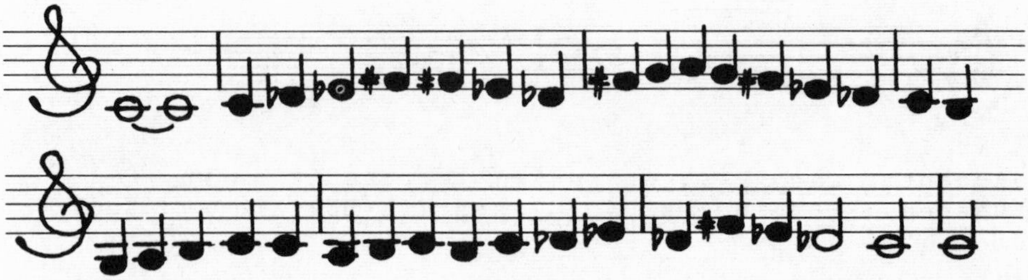

(15) *Sēnāmanoharī*

The scale of this *rāga* is *sampūrṇa* and shows two *vakra* features, one in ascent and one in descent.

48. *MĒḶA DIVYAMAṆĪ*

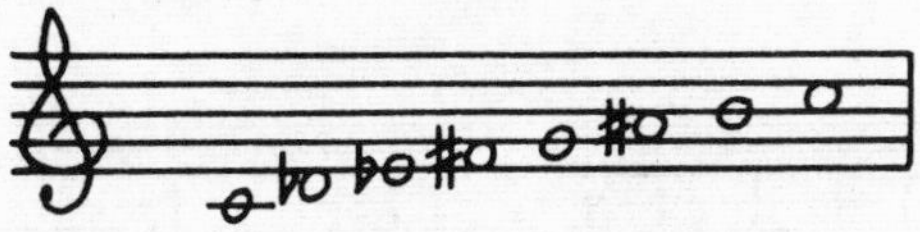

DIVYAMAṆĪ (*Triputa-tāla*) SCM, 224

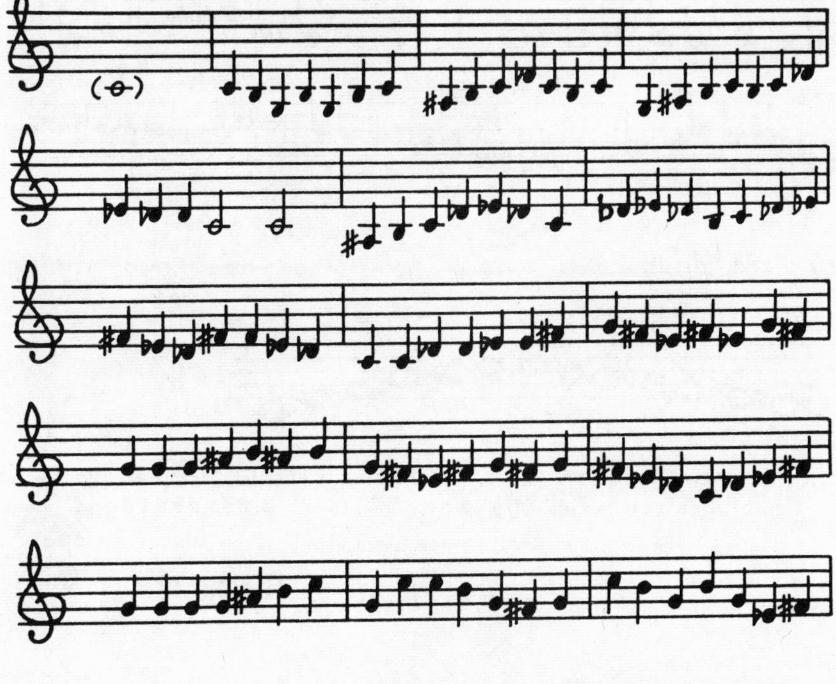

Janya Rāgas of the 48. Mēḷa

(1) *Ādi Pañchama (Ādi Pañcama)*

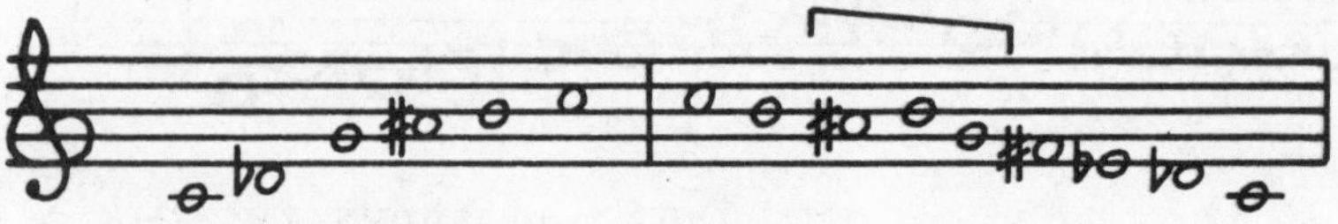

Ascent: the notes *GA* (Eb) and *MA* (F#) are avoided.
Descent: *sampūrṇa*; one *vakra* feature is shown.

ĀDI PAÑCHAMA (*Triputa-tāla*) SCM, 227-28

(2) *Āma Pañchamam*

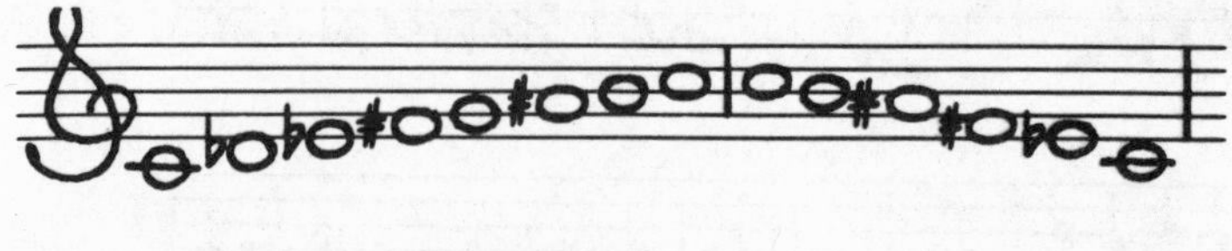

Ascent: *krama sampūrṇa*.
Descent: the notes *PA* (G) and *RI* (Db) are avoided.

(3) *Āmra Pañchamam*

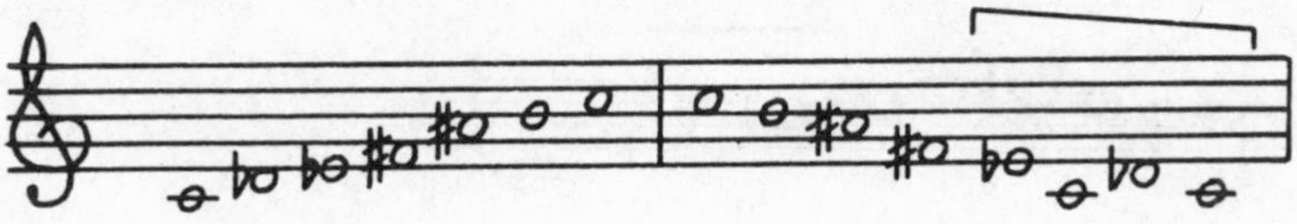

This is a variant of 48, 2.
The note *PA* (G) is avoided entirely. The note *RI* (Db) can be omitted in descent.

ĀMRA PAÑCHAMAM (*Triputa-tāla*) SCM, 226-27

(4) *Amrita Pañchamam*

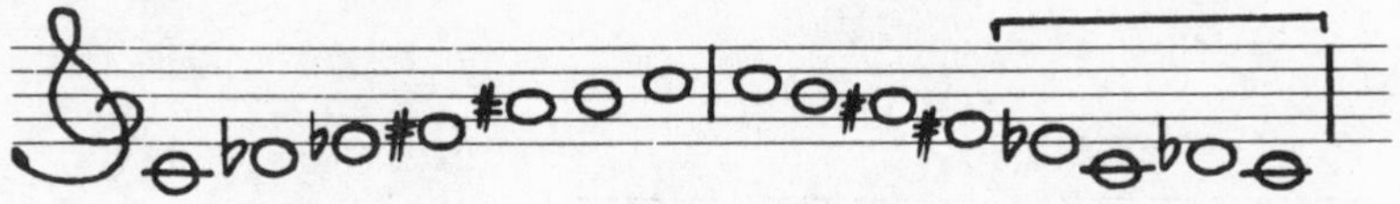

The scale of this *rāga* is identical with that of 48, 3. It is presented here because the SD (I, 14) lists *Āmra Pañchamam* and *Amrita Pañchamam* separately.

(5) *Bhōga Dhanyāsi*

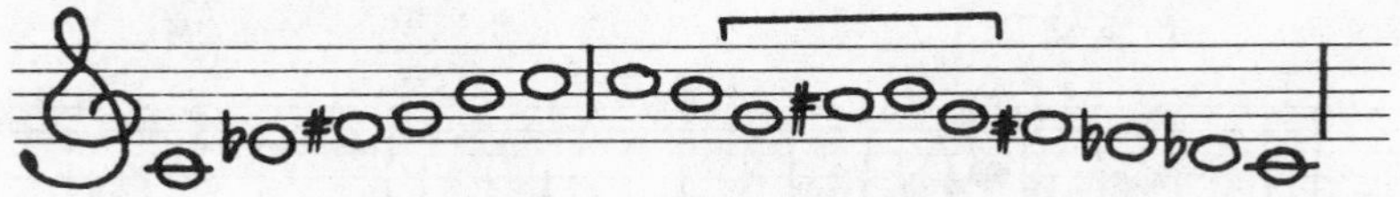

Ascent: the notes *RI* (Db) and *DHA* (A#) are avoided.
Descent: *sampūrṇa*; one extended *vakra* feature is shown.

(6) *Bhōgi Sindhu*

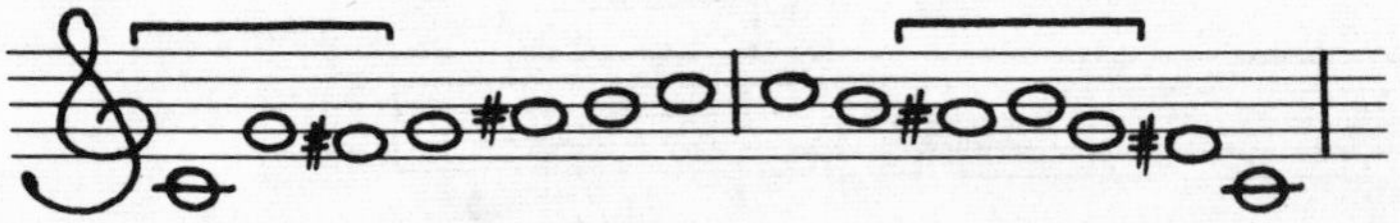

The notes *RI* (Db) and *GA* (Eb) are avoided entirely. Two *vakra* features are shown, one in ascent and one in descent.

(7) *Divya Kuntala*

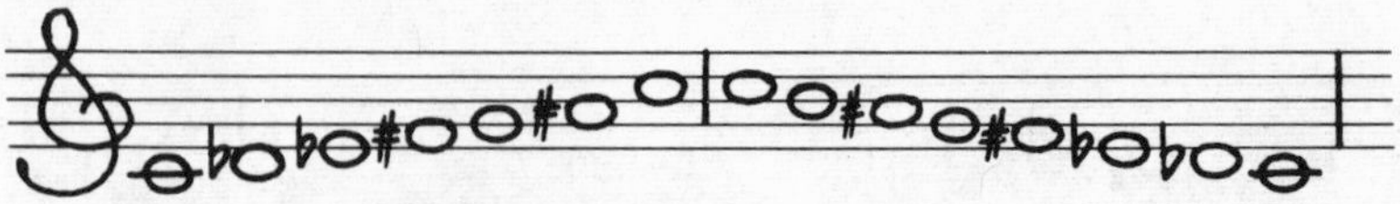

Ascent: the note *NI* (B) is avoided.
Descent: *krama sampūrṇa*.

(8) *Dundubhipriya*

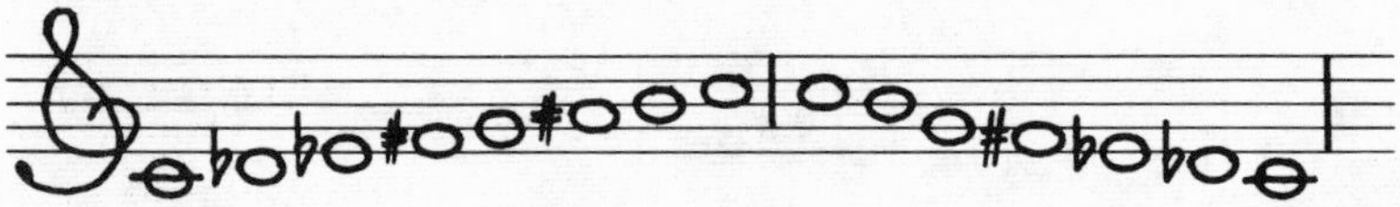

Ascent: *krama sampūrṇa*.
Descent: the note *DHA* (A#) is avoided.

(9) *Jīvantini*

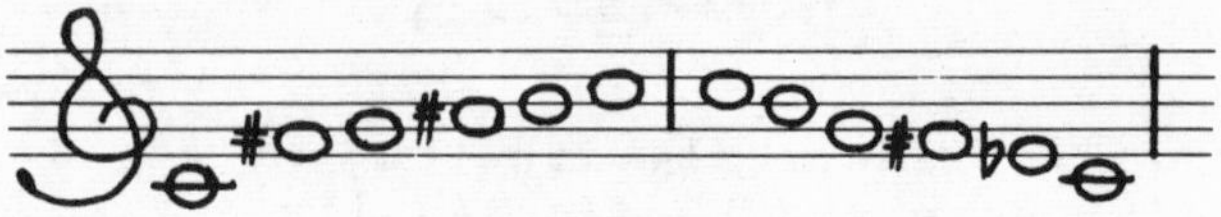

The note *RI* (Db) is avoided entirely. *GA* (Eb) is omitted in ascent and *DHA* (A#) in descent.

JĪVANTINI (*Triputa-tāla*) SCM, 225

(10) *Kannaḍa Vēḷāvaḷi*

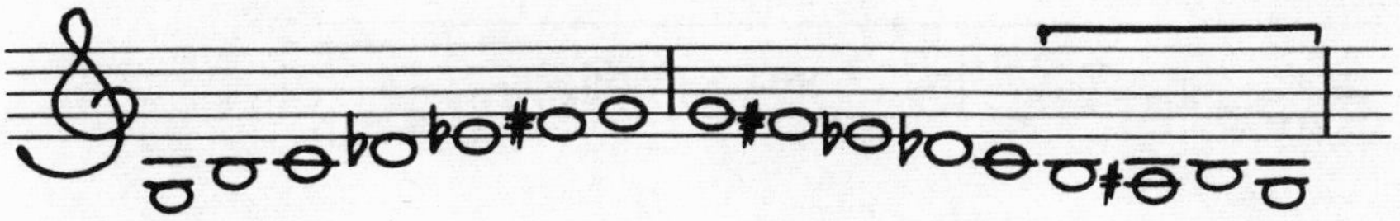

This *pañchamāntya* scale avoids *DHA* (A#) in ascent and shows one *vakra* feature in descent.

(11) *Kuntala Dīparam*

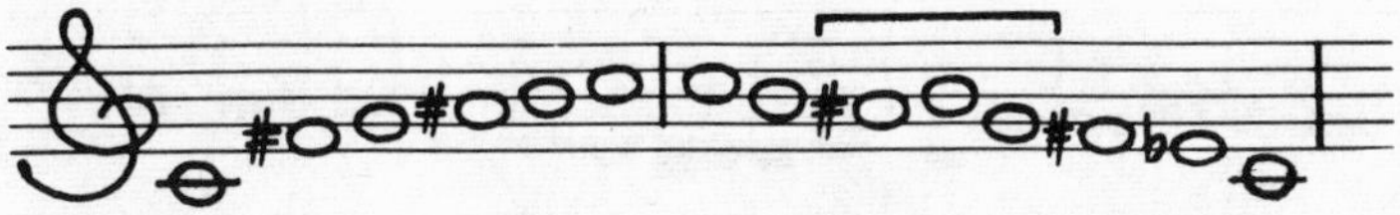

The note *RI* (Db) is avoided entirely. *GA* (Eb) is avoided in ascent. The descent shows one *vakra* feature.

(12) *Mangalapratha*

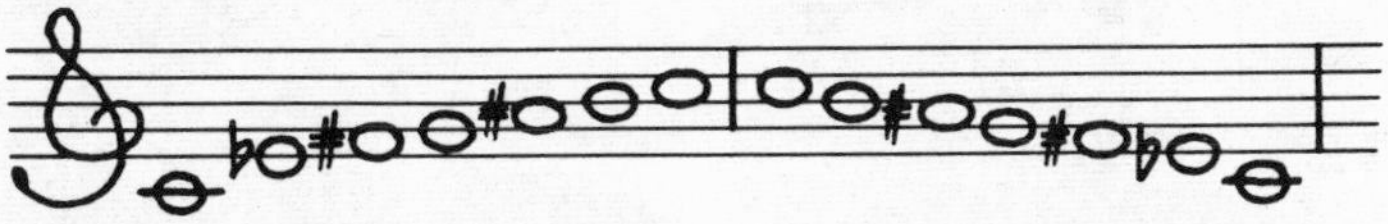

The note *RI* (Db) is avoided entirely.

(13) *Māruvadēśi*

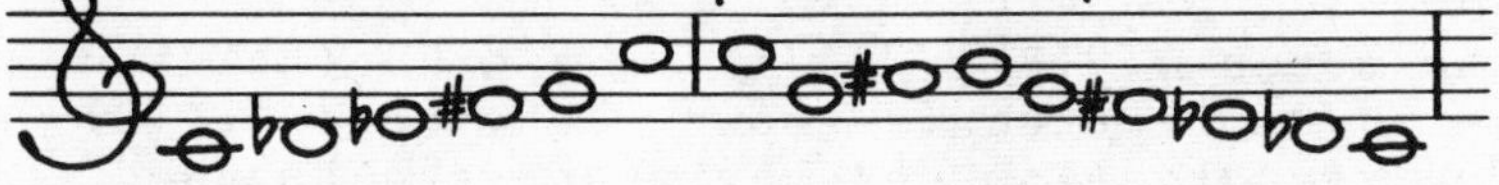

Ascent: the notes *DHA* (A#) and *NI* (B) are avoided.
Descent: *sampūrṇa*; one extended *vakra* feature is shown.

This *rāga* must not be mistaken for *rāga Māruvadēśika* of the 11. *mēḷa* (8).

(14) *Pātaladhari*

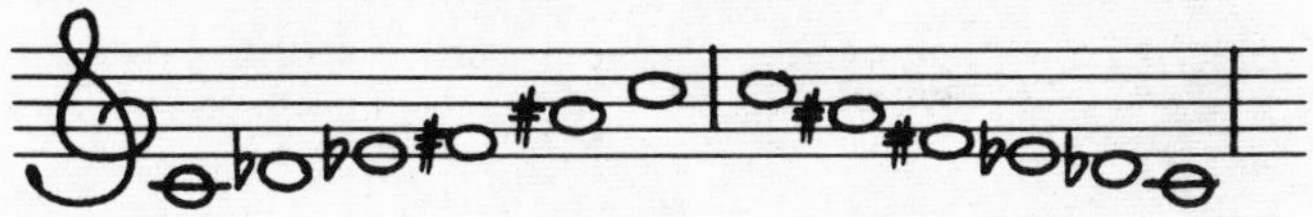

The notes *PA* (G) and *NI* (B) are avoided entirely.

(15) *Śuddhagāndhāri*

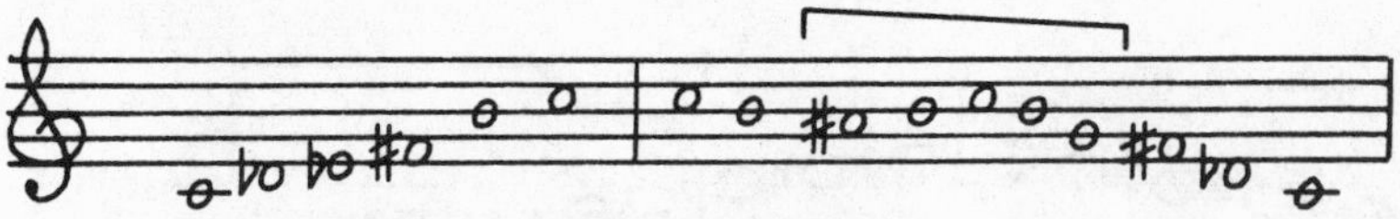

Ascent: the notes *PA* (G) and *DHA* (A#) are avoided.
Descent: the note *GA* (Eb) is omitted; one extended *vakra* feature is shown.

ŚUDDHAGĀNDHĀRI (*Triputa-tāla*) SCM, 226

(16) *Sukasvarāḷi*

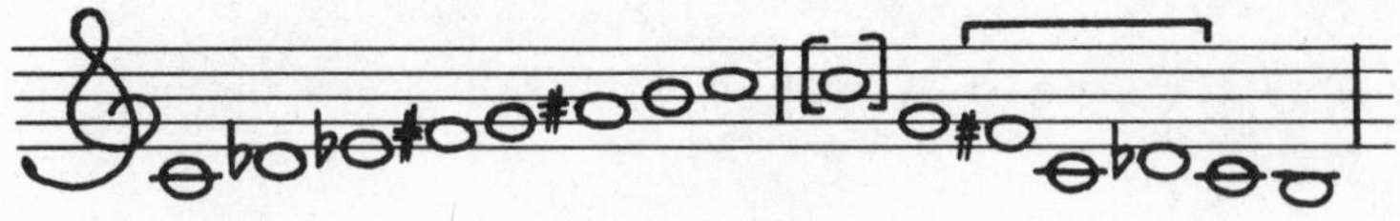

Ascent: *krama sampūrṇa*.
Descent: the notes *NI* (B), *DHA* (A#), and *GA* (Eb) are avoided; one *vakra* feature is shown. The note *NI* (B) of the *mandra saptaka* (low octave range) can be used.

(17) *Suramani*

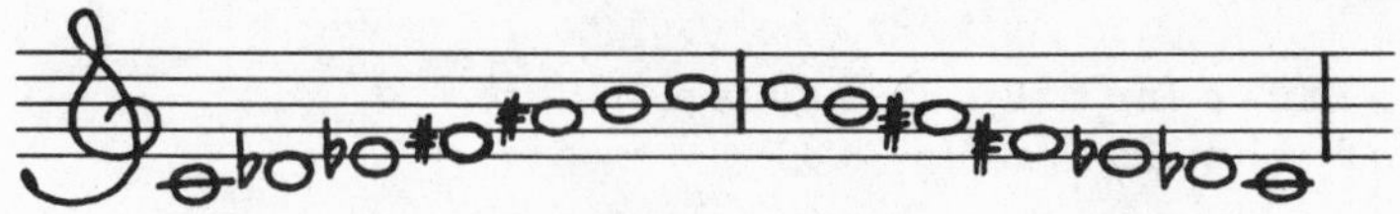

The note *PA* (G) is avoided entirely.

Chakra IX

49. *MĒḶA DHAVALĀMBARĪ*

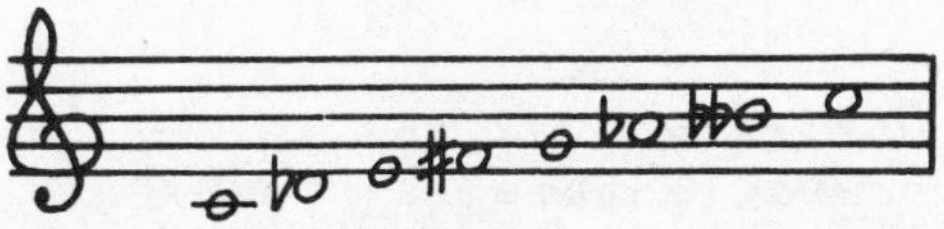

DHAVALĀMBARĪ (*Triputa-tāla*) SCM, 228-9

The name of the 49. *mēḷa* in the *asampūrṇa* system was *Dhavaḷangam*. Its scale avoids the note *ṄI* (Bbb) in ascent and is *krama sampūrṇa* in descent:

Janya Rāgas of the 49. Mēḷa

(1) *Bhinna Hērāḷi*

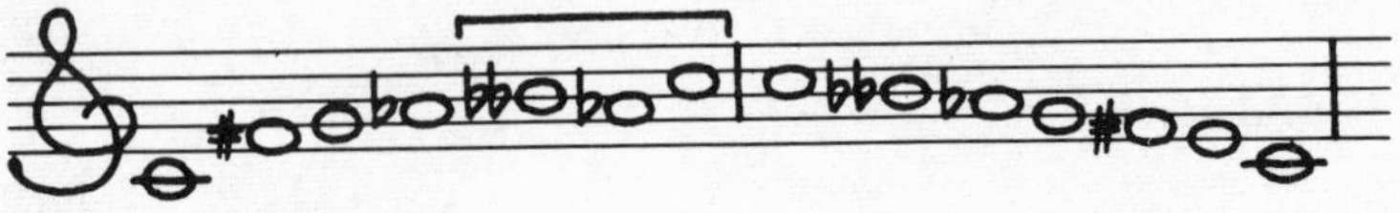

The note *RI* (Db) is avoided entirely. *GA* (E) is omitted in ascent where one *vakra* feature is shown.

(2) *Bhinna Paurāḷi*

The SD (I, 57) states that this "raga [is] mentioned in the *Sangīta Ratnākara* as a *bhāshā* of *Hindola*. The *Sangīta Samaya* mentions this as a *bhāshānga sampūrṇa rāga*." The scale of this old and obscure form is not given.

The SCM (230) presents one melody specimen which is shown below:

BHINNAPAURĀḶI (*Triputa-tāla*) SCM, 230

If a scale were derived from the foregoing specimen, the following form could be established:

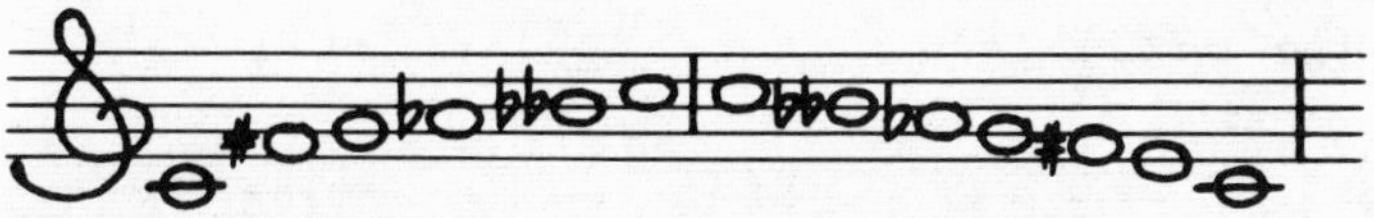

The note *RI* (Db) is avoided entirely and *GA* (E) is omitted in ascent. The *vakra* feature of *Bhinna Hērāḷi* (49,1) is not in use.

(3) *Bhinna Varāḷi*

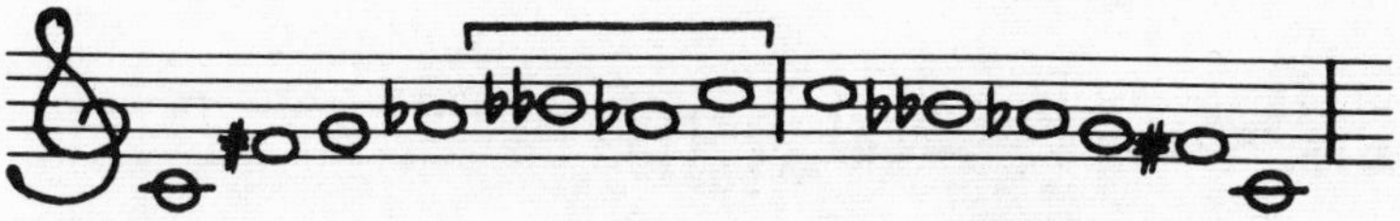

The notes *RI* (Db) and *GA* (E) are avoided entirely. The ascent shows one *vakra* feature.

(4) *Chhāyā Māruva*

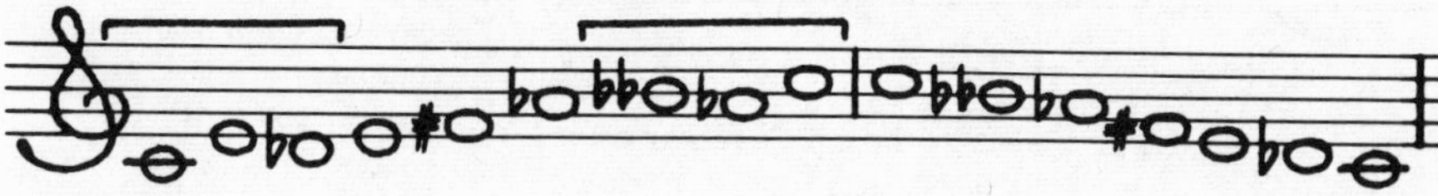

The note *PA* (G) is avoided entirely. The ascent shows two *vakra* features.

(5) *Dēvābharaṇam*

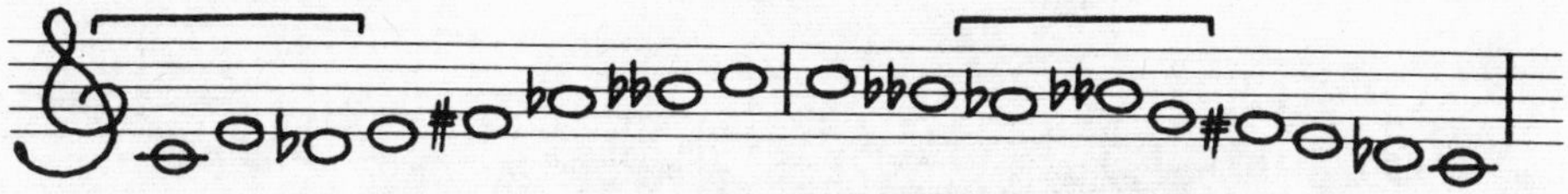

Ascent: the note *PA* (G) is avoided; one *vakra* feature is shown.
Descent: *sampūrṇa*; one *vakra* feature is used.

(6) *Dēvagiri*

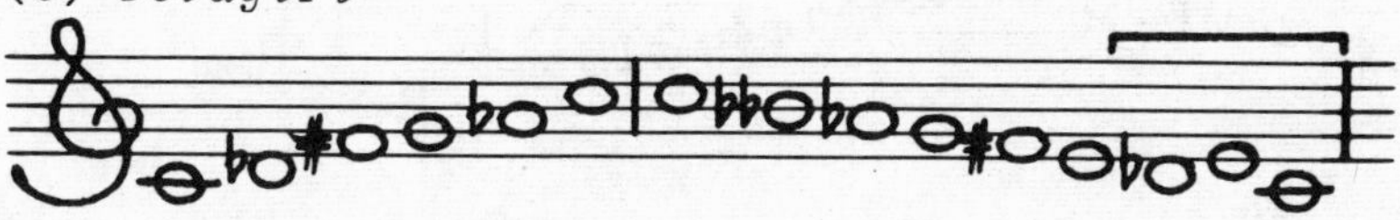

Ascent: the notes *GA* (E) and *NI* (Bbb) are avoided.
Descent: *sampūrṇa*; one *vakra* feature is shown.

Another *rāga* with the same name is listed under the heading of the 51. *mēḷa* (10).

The following melody specimen of *Dēvagiri* (49, 6) shows that the use of the *vakra* feature in descent (as shown above) is not obligatory.

DĒVAGIRI (*Triputa-tāla*) SCM, 230-31

(7) *Dharmāṇi* (*Dharmiṇi*)

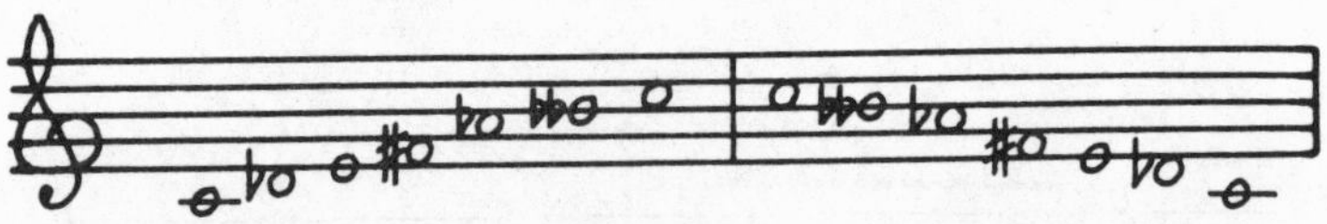

The note *PA* (G) is avoided entirely.

DHARMĀṆI (*Triputa-tāla*) SCM, 231-32

(8) *Dhavaḷāṅgi*

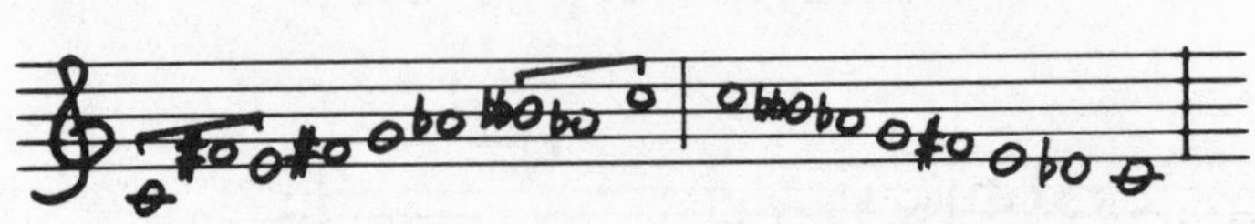

Ascent: the note *RI* (Db) is avoided; two *vakra* features are shown.
Descent: *krama sampūrṇa.*

Another *rāga* with the same name is listed under the heading of the 15. *mēḷa* (58).

DHAVAḶĀṄGI (Triputa-tāla) SCM, 229

(9) *Dhīra Svarūpi (Dhīra Svarūpiṇi)*

Ascent: *krama sampūrṇa.*
Descent: the note *RI* (Db) is avoided; one *vakra* feature is shown.

(10) *Dhīvakriya*

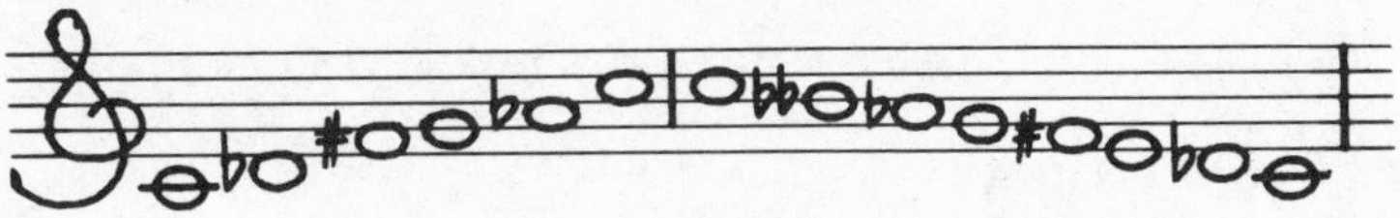

Ascent: the notes *GA* (E) and *NI* (Bbb) are avoided.
Descent: *krama sampūrṇa.*

(11) *Kāñchanamāla (Kāñcanamāla)*

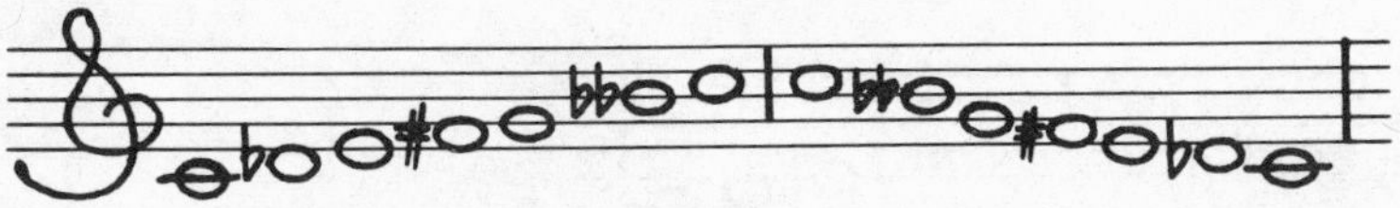

The note *DHA* (Ab) is avoided entirely.

(12) *Kannaḍa Kurañji*

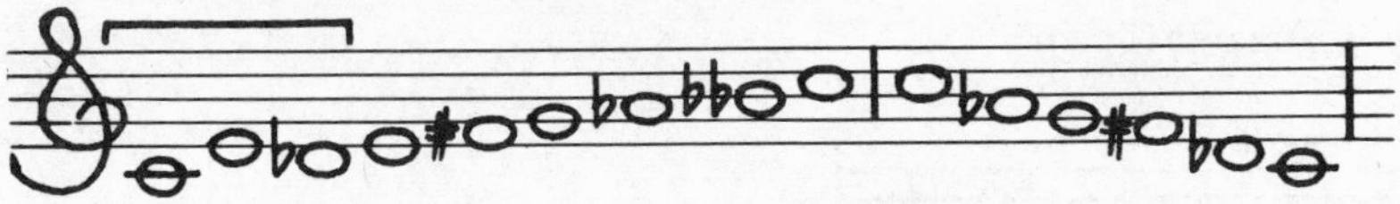

Ascent: *sampūrṇa*; one *vakra* feature is shown.
Descent: the notes *NI* (Bbb) and *GA* (E) are avoided.

(13) *Navarasāndhāḷi*

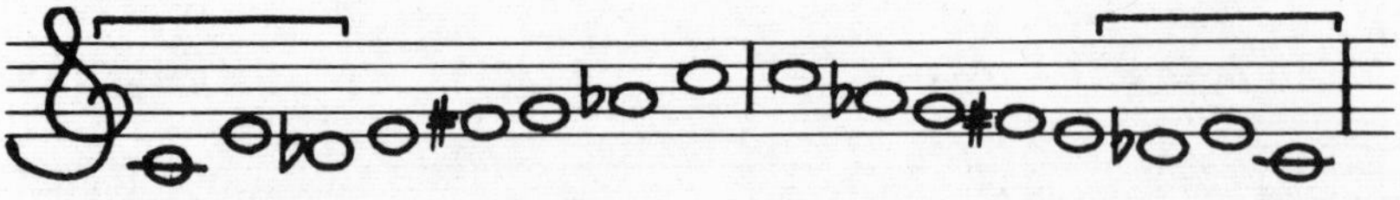

The note *NI* (Bbb) is avoided entirely. Two *vakra* features are shown, one in ascent and one in descent.

(14) *Svarābharaṇam*

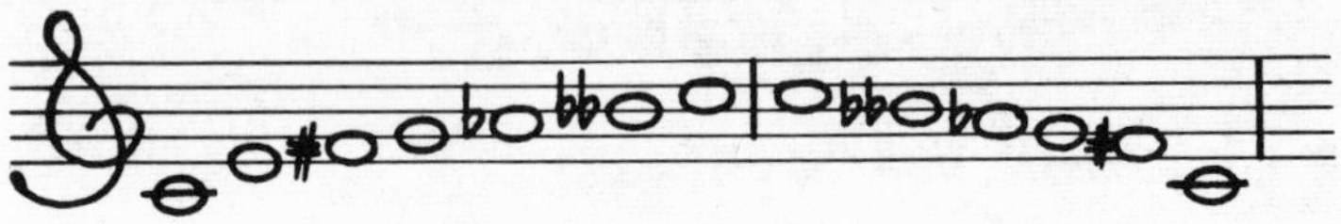

The note *RI* (Db) is avoided entirely. *GA* (E) is omitted in descent.

(15) *Śaṅkarapriya* (*Shaṅkarapriya*)

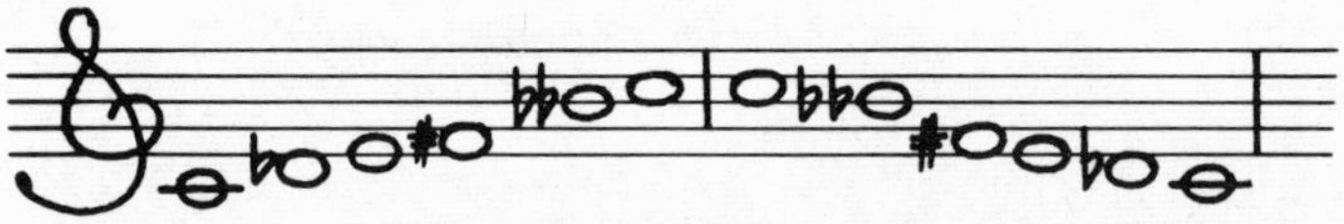

The notes *PA* (G) and *DHA* (Ab) are avoided entirely.

(16) *Śantamūrti* (*Shantamūrti*)

This *rāga* is identical with *rāga Śaṅkarapriya* (49, 15).

(17) *Tāṇḍavapriya*

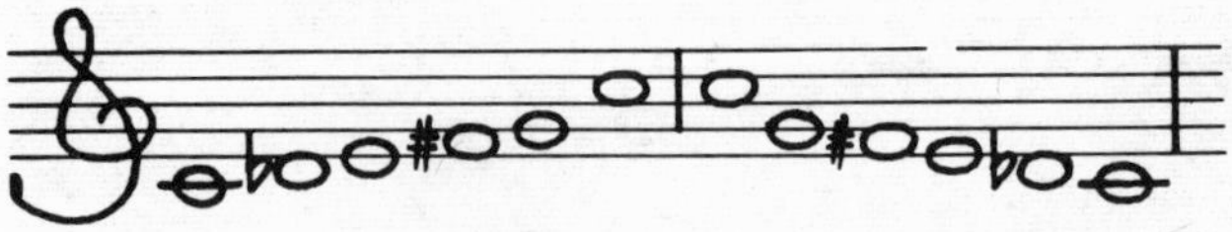

The notes *DHA* (Ab) and *NI* (Bbb) are avoided entirely.

50. *MĒḶA NĀMANĀRĀYAṆĪ*

NĀMANĀRAYAṆĪ (*Triputa-tāla*) SCM, 232

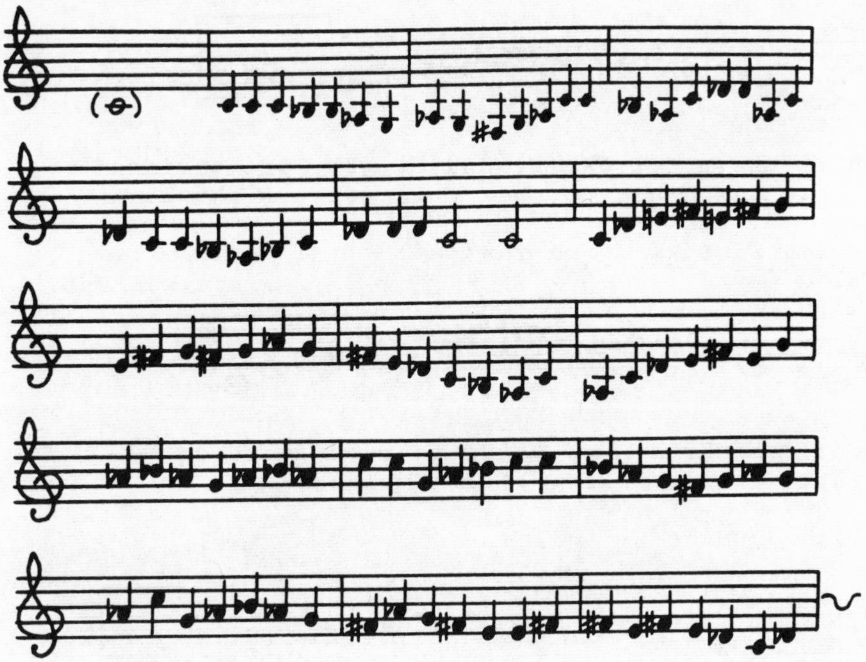

Janya Rāgas of the 50. Mēḷa

(1) *Daṇḍayāna*

Ascent: the note *MA* (F#) is avoided; one *vakra* feature is shown.
Descent: *sampūrṇa*; one *vakra* feature is used.

(2) *Dēvakōṭi*

Ascent: the note *DHA* (Ab) is avoided; one *vakra* feature is shown.
Descent: the note *NI* (Bb) is omitted; one *vakra* feature is used.

(3) *Gaurīmāruva*

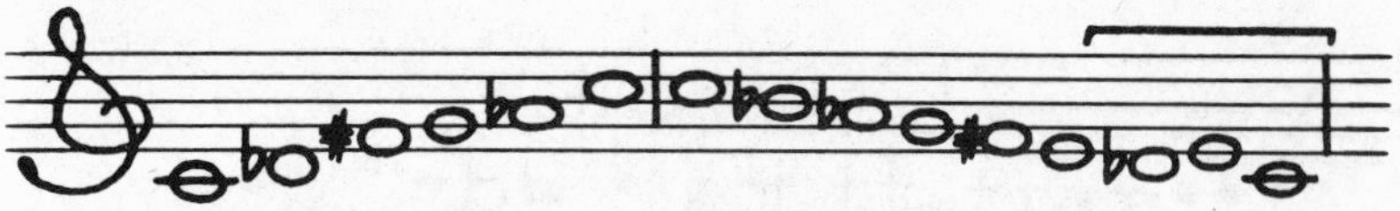

Ascent: the notes *GA* (E) and *NI* (Bb) are avoided.
Descent: *sampūrṇa*; one *vakra* feature is shown.

(4) *Hrida Tāntiṇi* (*Hṛda Tāntiṇi*)

Ascent: *sampūrṇa*; one *vakra* feature is shown.
Descent: the note *RI* (Db) is avoided.

(5) *Kannaḍa Bhōgi*

Ascent: *sampūrṇa*; one *vakra* feature is shown.
Descent: the note *PA* (G) is avoided; one *vakra* feature is used.

(6) *Kusumabhōgi*

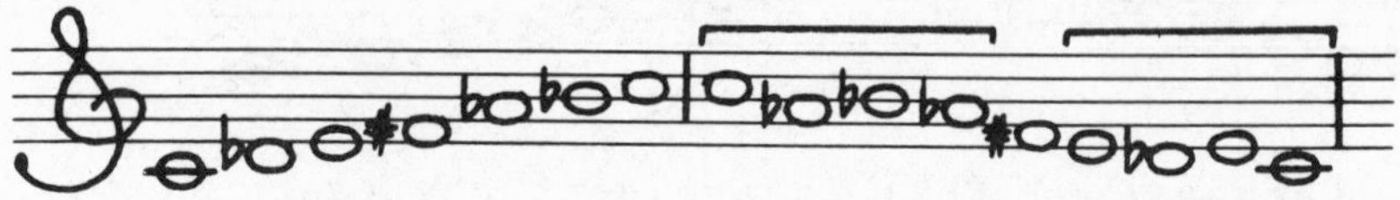

The note *PA* (G) is avoided entirely. In descent appear two extended *vakra* features.

(7) *Madhukāri*

The scale of this *rāga* is *krama sampūrṇa* in ascent and descent and is therefore identical with that of its primary *rāga Namanārāyaṇi*.

(8) *Mandāri*

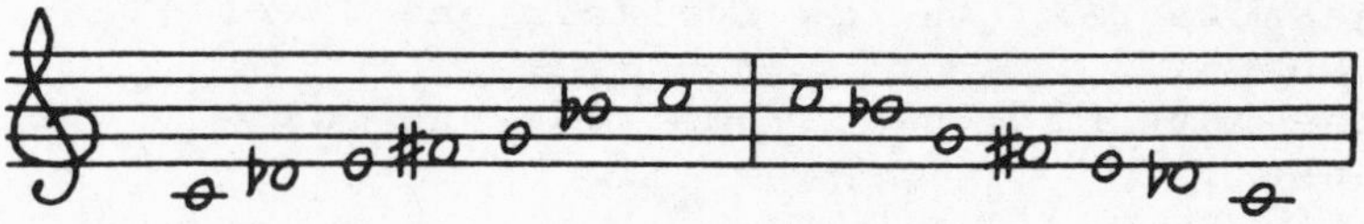

The note *DHA* (Ab) is avoided entirely. Occasionally the note *NI* (theoretically Bb) is raised to B. This causes musicians to place this *rāga* under the heading of the 51. *mēḷa* (27).

MANDĀRI (*Triputa-tāla*) SCM, 233-34

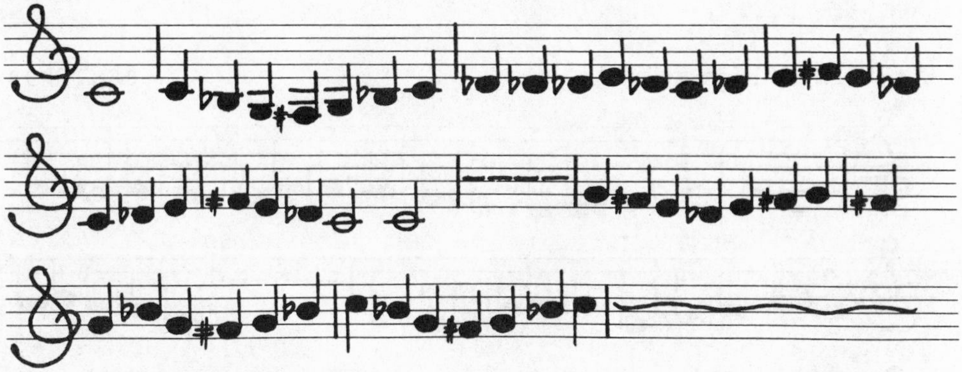

(9) *Māranārāyaṇi*

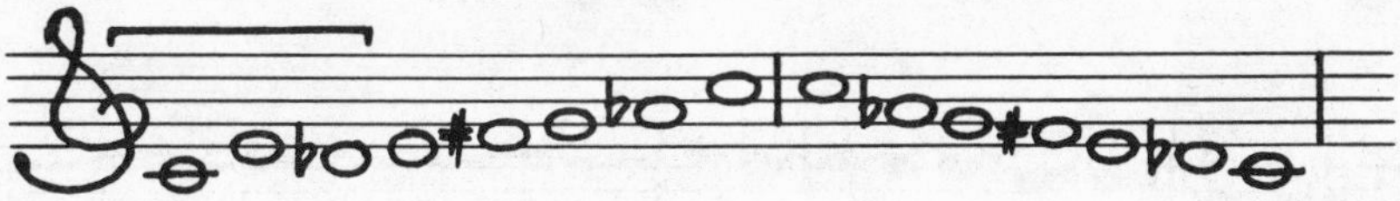

The note *NI* (Bb) is avoided entirely. One *vakra* feature appears in ascent.

(10) *Mēchakannaḍa* (*Mēcakannaḍa*)

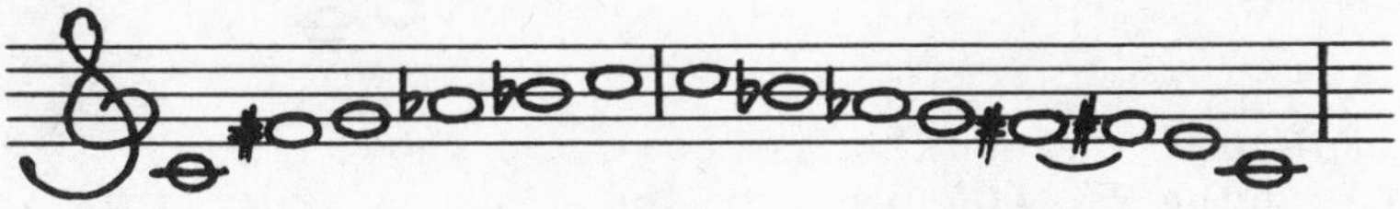

The note *RI* (Db) is avoided entirely. *GA* (E) is omitted in ascent.

(11) *Narmadā*

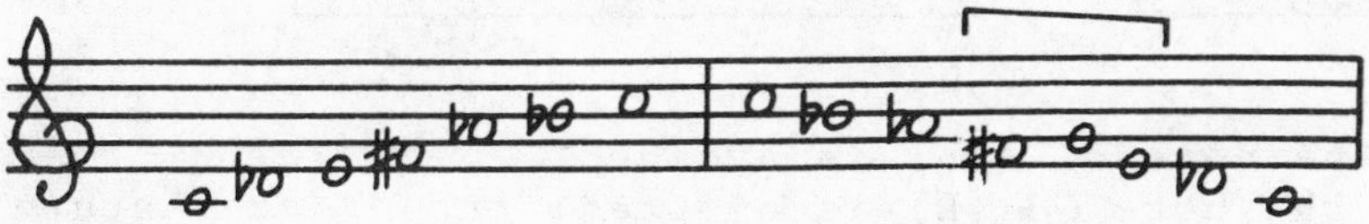

The note *PA* (G) is usually avoided in ascent. The descent is *sampūrṇa* and shows one *vakra* feature.

A second form of descent can be:

The following melody specimen shows the rare use of the note *PA* (G) in ascent:

NARMADĀ (*Triputa-tāla*) SCM, 233

(12) *Navarasagāndhāri*

Ascent: *sampūrṇa*; one *vakra* feature is shown.
Descent: the note *PA* (G) is avoided.

(13) *Pratāpa*

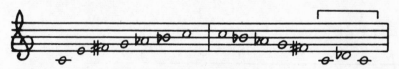

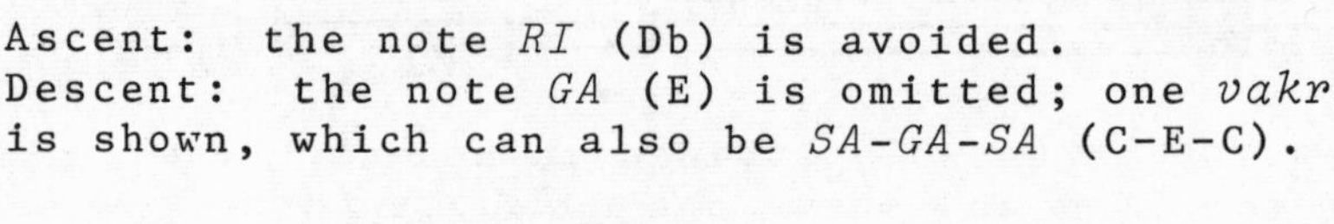

Ascent: the note *RI* (Db) is avoided.
Descent: the note *GA* (E) is omitted; one *vakra* feature is shown, which can also be *SA-GA-SA* (C-E-C).

PRATĀPA (*Triputa-tāla*) SCM, 234-35

(14) *Sātvi*

The notes *RI* (Db) and *PA* (G) are avoided entirely.

(15) *Śrīmadhukari*

The scale of this *rāga* is identical with that of the primary *rāga Namanārāyaṇi* and with that of *rāga Madhukāri* (50,7).

(16) *Suvarṇāmbari*

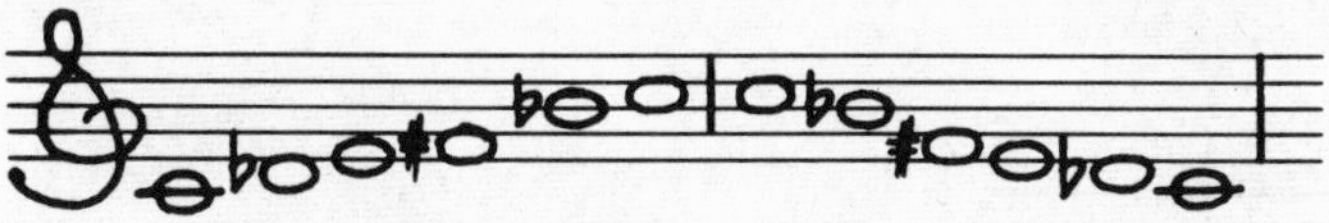

The notes *PA* (G) and *DHA* (Ab) are avoided entirely.

51. *MĒḶA KĀMAVARDHANĪ*

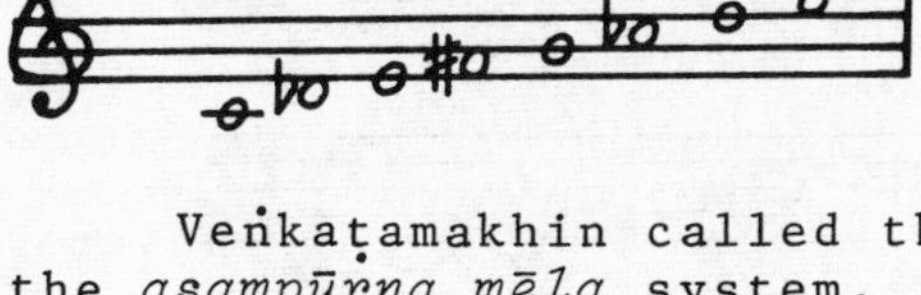

Veṅkaṭamakhin called this *rāga Kaśīrāmakriyā* in the *asampūrṇa mēḷa* system.

KĀMAVARDHANĪ (*Triputa-tāla*) SCM, 235

Janya Rāgas of the 51. Mēḷa

(1) *Badarika*

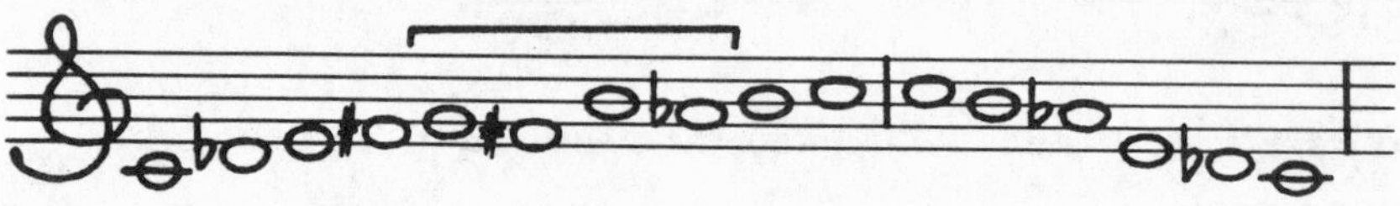

Ascent: *sampūrṇa*; one *vakra* feature is shown.
Descent: the notes *PA* (G) and *MA* (F#) are avoided.

(2) *Bahudāmani*

Ascent: *sampūrṇa*; one *vakra* feature is shown.
Descent: the note *PA* (G) is avoided.

(3) *Bhōga Sāmantam*

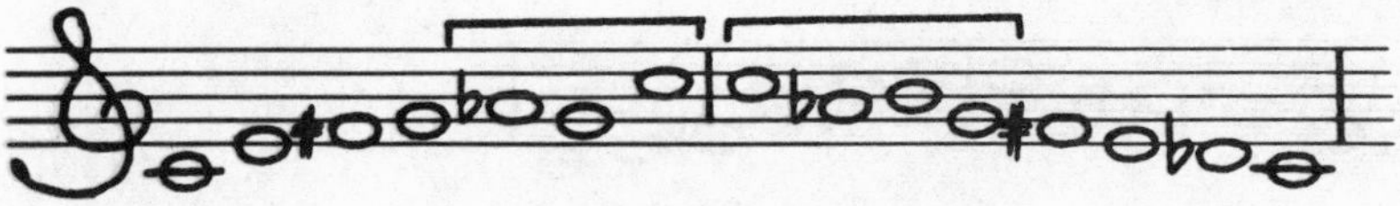

Ascent: the notes *RI* (Db) and *NI* (B) are avoided; one *vakra* feature is shown.
Descent: *sampūrṇa*; one *vakra* feature is used.

(4) *Bhōga Vasantam*

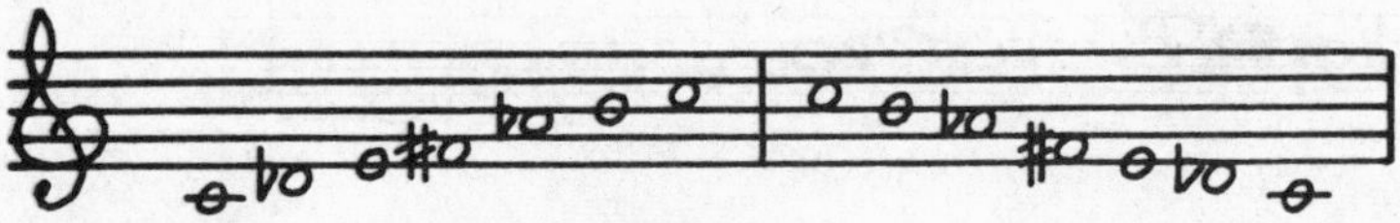

The note *PA* (G) is avoided entirely.

BHŌGAVASANTAM (Triputa-tāla) SCM, 237-38

(5) *Bramā Taranganị*

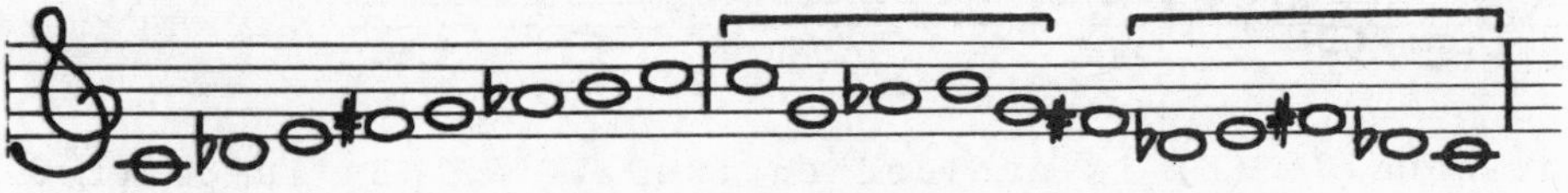

Ascent: *krama sampūrṇa*.
Descent: *sampūrṇa*; two extended *vakra* features are shown.

(6) *Chara Chanḍini (Cara Canḍini)*

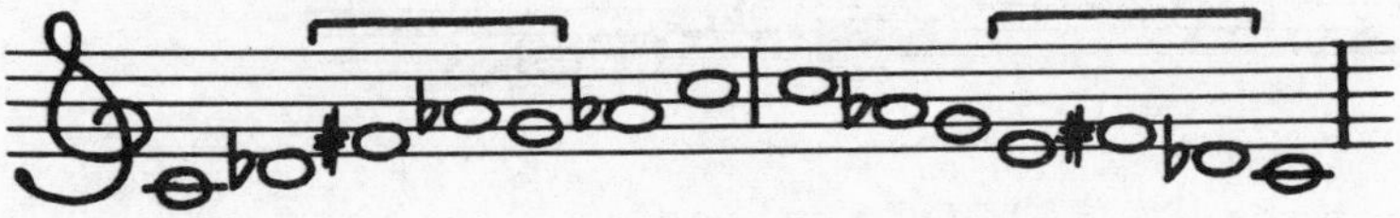

The note *NI* (B) is avoided entirely. *GA* (E) is avoided in ascent and one *vakra* feature is shown. In descent one *vakra* feature is used.

(7) *Dambōḷi*

Ascent: the note *MA* (F#) is avoided.
Descent: the notes *DHA* (Ab) and *PA* (G) are omitted.

(8) *Danti Vasantam*

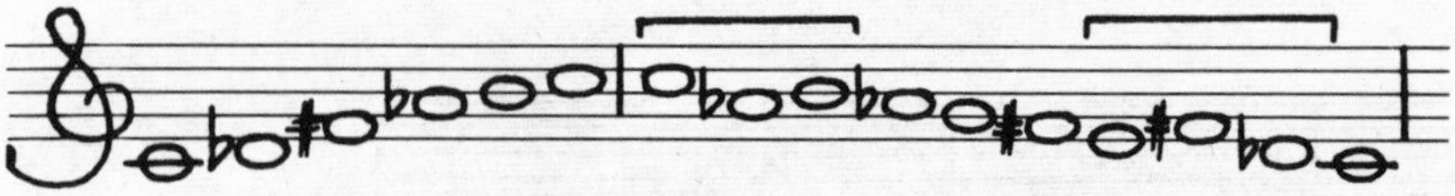

Ascent: the notes *GA* (E) and *PA* (G) are avoided.
Descent: *sampūrṇa*; two *vakra* features are shown.

(9) *Dāṭika Pañchamam* (*Dāṭika Pañcamam*)

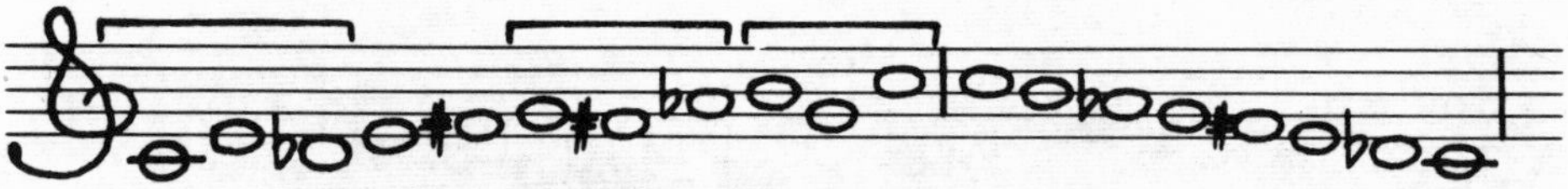

Ascent: *sampūrṇa*; three *vakra* features are shown.
Descent: *krama sampūrṇa*.

(10) *Dēvagiri*

The note *GA* (E) is avoided entirely. *NI* (B) is omitted in ascent. The descent shows one *vakra* feature.

Another *rāga* with the same name appears under the heading of the 49. *mēḷa* (6).

(11) *Dharmiṇi*

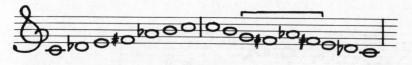

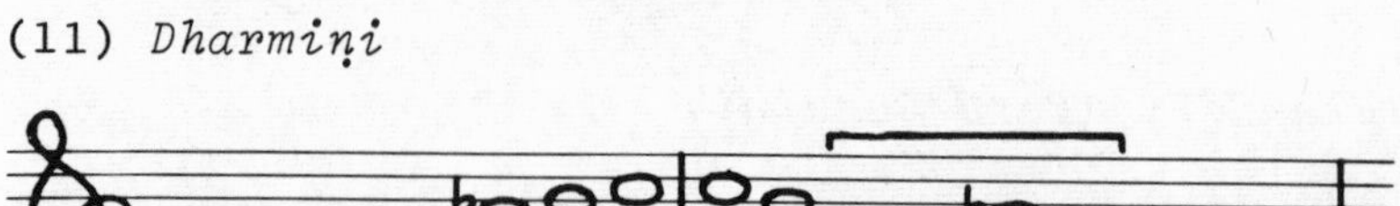

Ascent: the note *PA* (G) is avoided.
Descent: *sampūrṇa*; one extended *vakra* feature is shown.

(12) *Dīpakam*

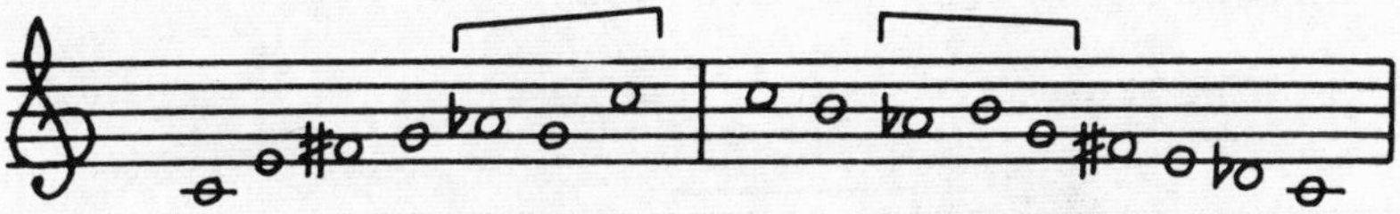

Ascent: the notes *RI* (Db) and *NI* (B) are avoided; one *vakra* feature is shown.
Descent: *sampūrṇa*; one *vakra* feature is used.

DĪPAKAM (*Triputa-tāla*) SCM, 236-37

(13) *Gagana Mayūri*

Ascent: the notes *RI* (Db) and *PA* (G) are avoided; one *vakra* feature is shown.
Descent: *sampūrṇa*; one extended *vakra* feature is used.

The SD (II, 176) mentions another *rāga* with the name *Gana Mayūri*, which appears to be a variant of *Gagana Mayūri*. The scale of *Gana Mayūri* is:

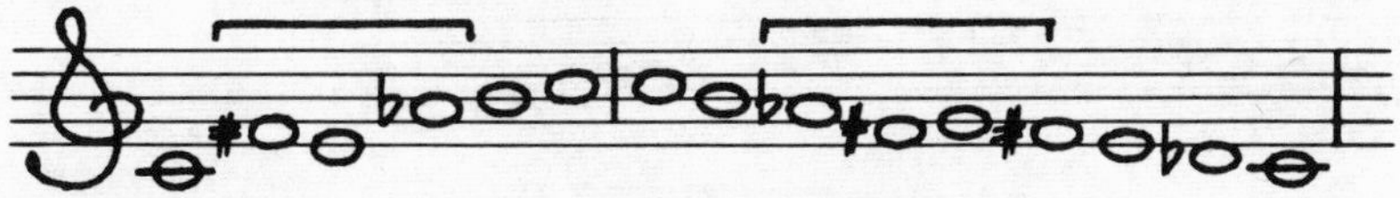

The ascents of the two scales are identical. The descent of *Gana Mayūri* differs from that of *Gagana Mayūri* only in the omission of the second use of the sequence *MA-PA* (F#-G).

(14) *Gamakapriya*

Ascent: *sampūrṇa*; one *vakra* feature is shown.
Descent: the note *NI* (B) is avoided.

(15) *Garbha Śārdūlam*

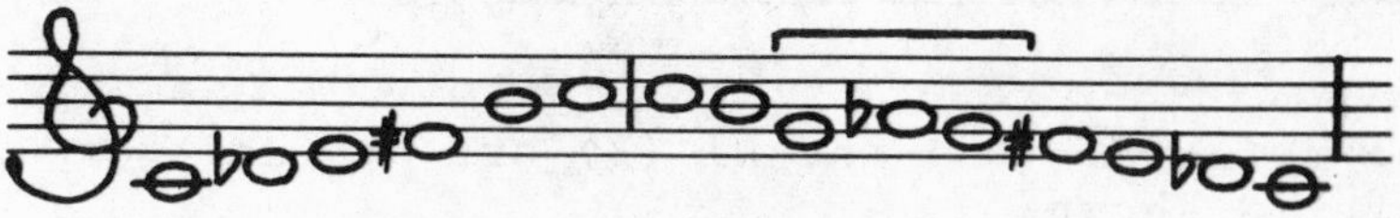

Ascent: the notes *PA* (G) and *DHA* (Ab) are avoided.
Descent: *sampūrṇa*; one *vakra* feature is shown.

(16) *Gaurī Pantu*

Ascent: the notes *GA* (E) and *DHA* (Ab) are avoided.
Descent: *sampūrṇa*; one *vakra* feature is shown.

(17) *Haṃsa Nārāyaṇi*

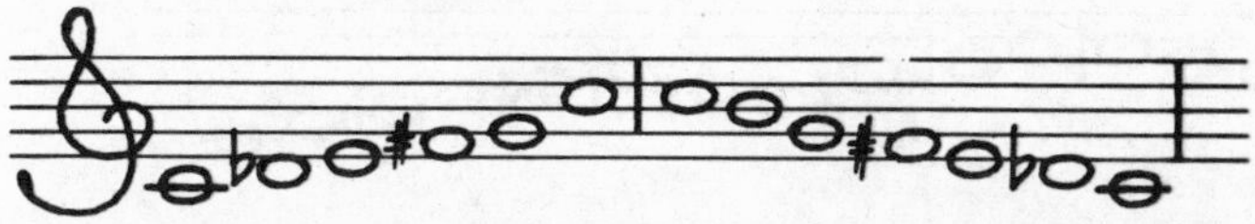

The note *DHA* (Ab) is avoided entirely. *NI* (B) is omitted in ascent.

(18) *Hēmārṇavam*

Ascent: the note *RI* (Db) is avoided.
Descent: the note *PA* (G) is omitted.

(19) *Indumati*

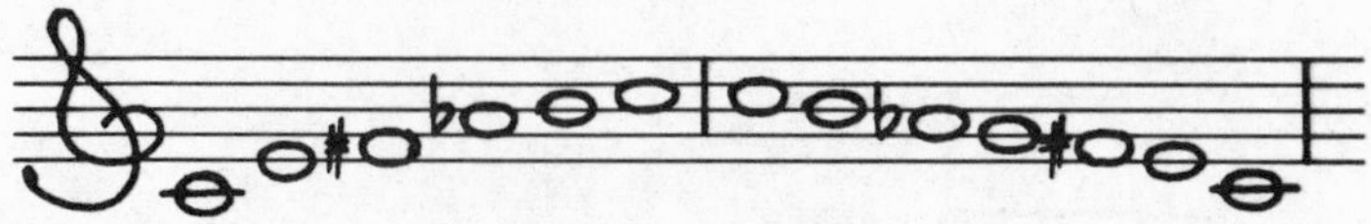

The note *RI* (Db) is avoided entirely. *PA* (G) is omitted in ascent.

(20) *Kamalāptapriya*

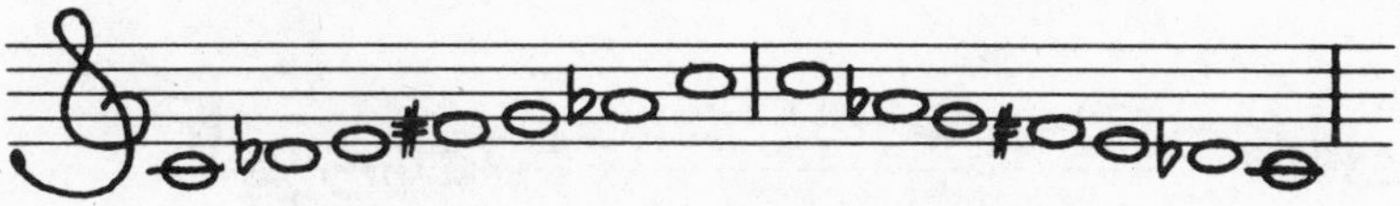

The note *NI* (B) is avoided entirely.

(21) *Kanaka Rasāḷi*

Ascent: the note *PA* (G) is avoided.
Descent: the note *NI* (B) is omitted.

(22) *Kāṇḍajvalana*

Ascent: the notes *GA* (E) and *DHA* (Ab) are avoided.
Descent: *krama sampūrṇa*.

(23) *Kāshīrāmakriya* (*Kāśīrāmakriya*)

Ascent: *sampūrṇa*; one *vakra* feature is shown.
Descent: *krama sampūrṇa*.

(24) *Kēśarikriya*

Ascent: *sampūrṇa*; one *vakra* feature is shown.
Descent: the note *DHA* (Ab) is avoided; one *vakra* feature is used.

(25) *Kiraṇi*

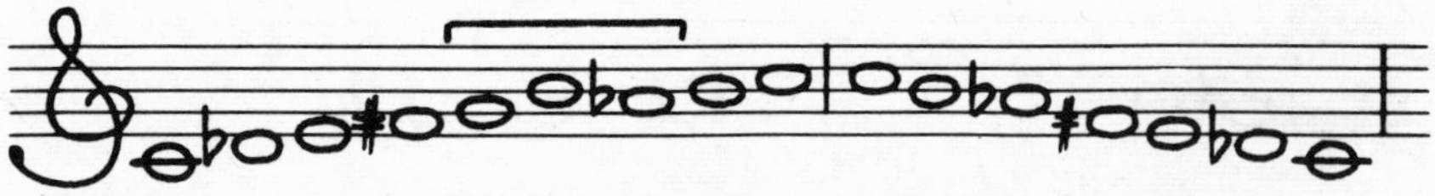

Ascent: *sampūrṇa*; one *vakra* feature is shown.
Descent: the note *PA* (G) is avoided.

(26) *Kumudapriya*

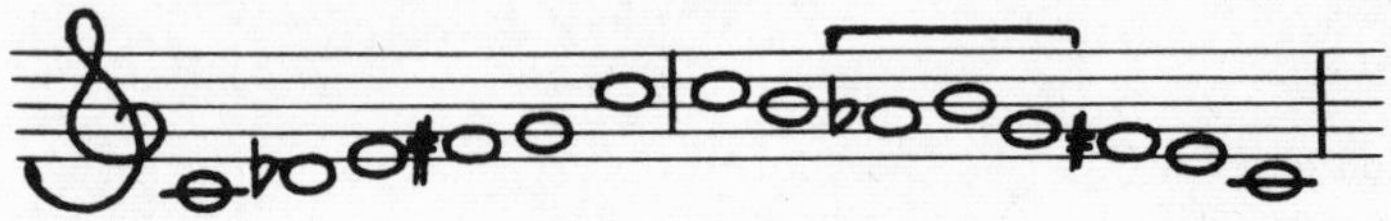

Ascent: the notes *DHA* (Ab) and *NI* (B) are avoided.
Descent: the note *RI* (Db) is omitted; one *vakra* feature is shown.

Another *rāga* with the same name appears under the heading of the 22. *mēḷa* (83).

(27) *Mandāri*

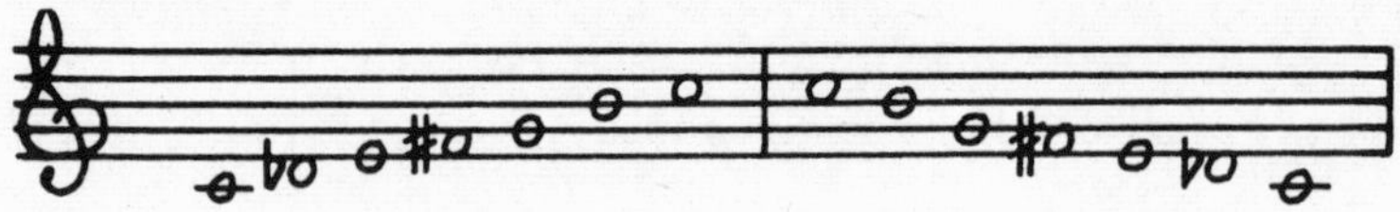

The note *DHA* (Ab) is avoided entirely.

Mandāri can also be listed under the heading of the 50. *mēḷa* (8) whenever the note *NI* is interpreted as Bb.

(28) *Māruva* (*Māru*)

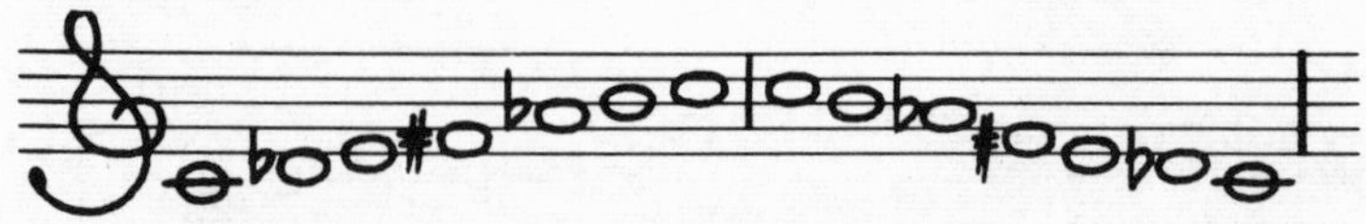

The note *PA* (G) is avoided entirely.

Another *rāga* with the same name appears under the heading of the 15. *mēḷa* (31).

(29) *Nīharam*

The notes *RI* (Db) and *PA* (G) are avoided entirely.

(30) *Pantuvarāli*

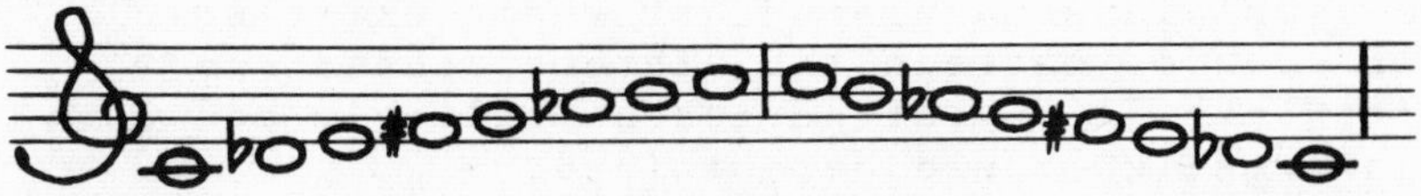

The scale of this *rāga* is identical with that of its primary *rāga*, *Kāmavardhanī*.

The following song example was composed by Sankarabharanam Narasayya, a nineteenth-century court musician of the Sarfoji Maharaja of Tanjore:

PANTUVARĀLI RĀGA (*Ādi-tāla*) SPC, III, 60-61

Pallavi

The foregoing melody shows in measures 2, 5, and 7-8 the *vakra* sequence *NI-DHA-SA* (B-Ab-c) which is believed to add a characteristic flavor to this *rāga*, although this feature is not always in use. There are musicians who occasionally perform *Pantuvarāli* with the note *sādharana GA* (Eb), a procedure that equates this *rāga* with the 45. *mēḷa-rāga Śubhapantuvarālī*.

At one Madras Music Conference (Dec. 12, 1943) the suggestion was made to call *Pantuvarālī* with *antara GA* (E) by the old name *Rāmakriyā* in order to establish a distinction between the two forms. Although the resolution was approved and accepted, no further steps were taken to effect the changes in name.

Therefore *Rāmakriyā* will be listed here as a separate *rāga* of the 51. *mēḷa* (31).

(31) *Rāmakriyā*

As already pointed out in the discussion of 51, 30 the scale of *Rāmakriyā* is *krama sampūrṇa* in ascent and descent. There is no apparent difference between this scale and the ones of *Kāmavardhani* (the 51. *mēḷa-rāga*) and *Pantuvarāḷī* (51, 30).

A few musicians maintain that there exist some subtle differences between the aforementioned *rāgas*, but despite careful investigation no reliable and convincing information could be obtained.

RĀMAKRIYĀ (*Triputa-tāla*) SCM, 236

(32) *Ṡadananapriya*

The notes *PA* (G) and *DHA* (Ab) are avoided entirely.

(33) *Stavapriya (Sthavapriya)*

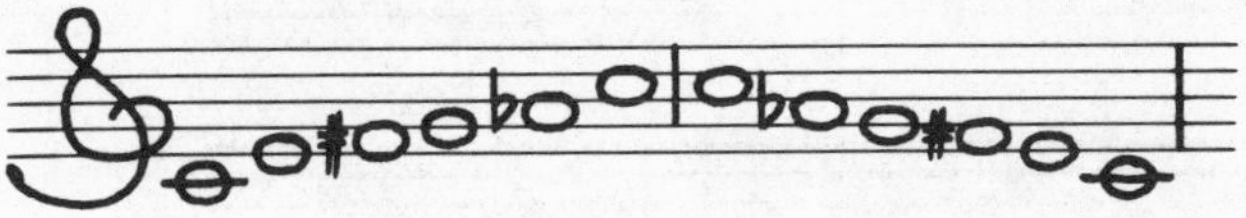

The notes *RI* (Db) and *NI* (B) are avoided entirely.

(34) *Vasantamāruva*

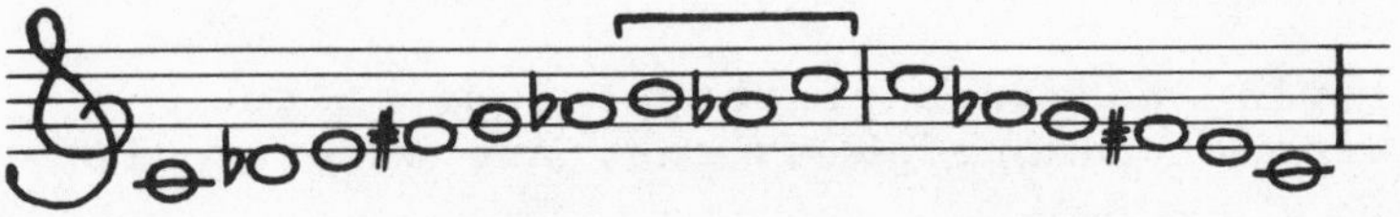

Ascent: *sampūrṇa*; one *vakra* feature is shown.
Descent: the notes *NI* (B) and *RI* (Db) are avoided.

52. *MĒḶA RĀMAPRIYĀ*

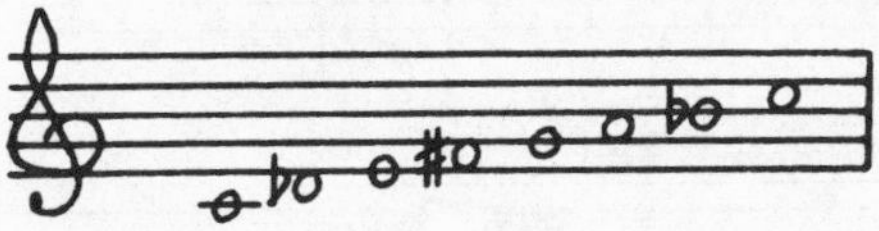

RĀMAPRIYĀ (Triputa-tāla) SCM, 238

The following passages represent some of the various features of *Rāmapriyā* as they are used at the present time:

One can observe in the foregoing material that:

RI (Db) is rare in ascent

MA (F#) is rare in ascent; in descent it is practically avoided except in quickly moving passages such as the one marked with the sign ⊗

DHA (A) is rare in descent

NI (Bb) is rare in ascent

None of these features represents strict rules, and musicians will employ various interpretations when performing this *rāga*.

Janya Rāgas of the 52. Mēḷa

(1) *Bhairavadhvani*

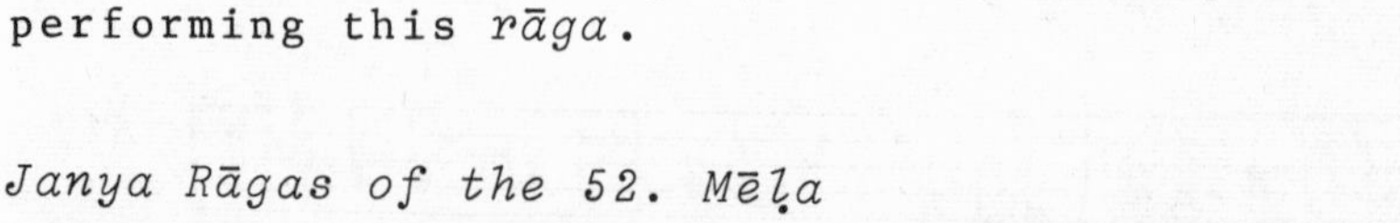

Ascent: *sampūrṇa*; one extended *vakra* feature is shown.
Descent: the note *NI* (Bb) is avoided.

(2) *Chintāramaṇi* (*Cintāramaṇi*)

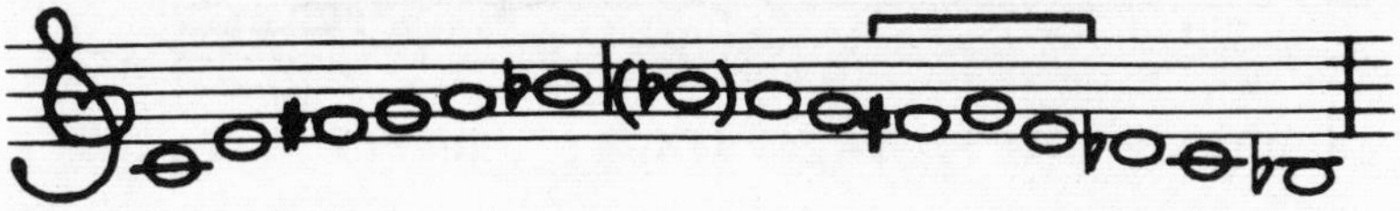

This *niṣādāntya* scale avoids the note *RI* (Db) in ascent and shows one *vakra* feature in descent.

(3) *Dhīkaruṇi*

Ascent: *sampūrṇa*; two extended *vakra* passages are shown.
Descent: *krama sampūrṇa*.

(4) *Gāmbhīrya Ghōṣani*

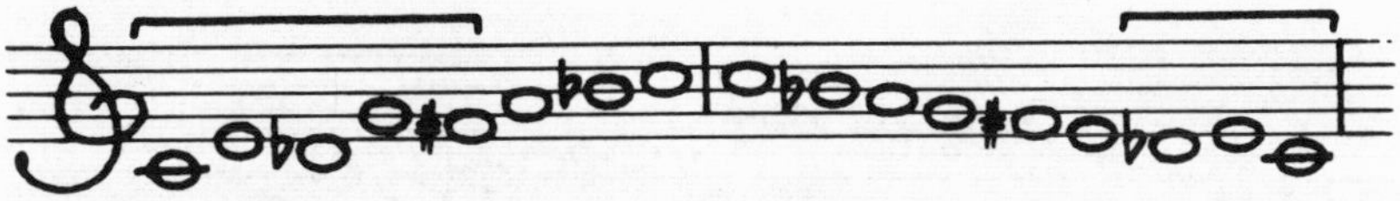

Ascent: *sampūrṇa*; one extended *vakra* feature is shown.
Descent: *sampūrṇa*; one *vakra* feature is used.

(5) *Ghōshamañjari* (*Ghōṣamañjari*)

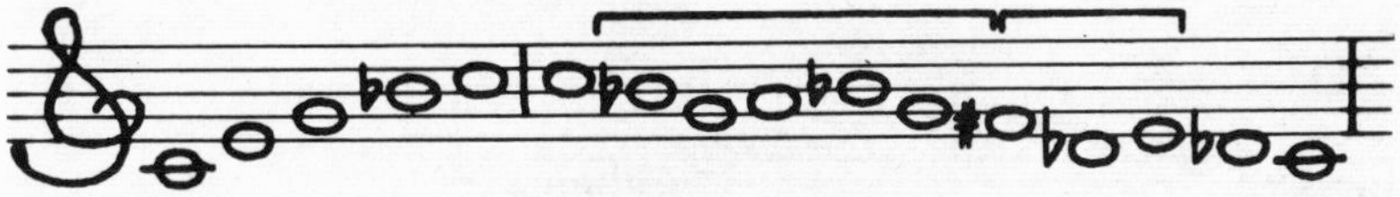

Ascent: the notes *RI* (Db), *MA* (F#), and *DHA* (A) are avoided.
Descent: *sampūrṇa*; one extended and one brief *vakra* features are shown.

(6) *Gōvinda Nārāyaṇi*

Ascent: the note *RI* (Db) is avoided.
Descent: the note *MA* (F#) is omitted.

(7) *Haṃsa Gamani*

Ascent: the note *RI* (Db) is avoided; one *vakra* feature is shown.
Descent: *sampūrṇa*; one *vakra* passage is used.

(8) *Jagadambari*

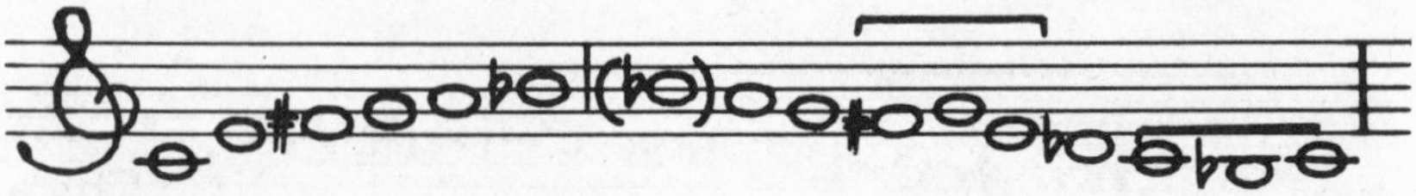

This is a *niṣādāntya rāga*.
Ascent: the note *RI* (Db) is avoided.
Descent: two *vakra* features are shown.

There exists a striking similarity between this *rāga* and *rāga Chintāramaṇi* (52, 2).

(9) *Janani*

Ascent: *krama sampūrṇa*.
Descent: *sampūrṇa*; one *vakra* feature is shown.

(10) *Jaṭādhari*

Ascent: *sampūrṇa*; one *vakra* feature is shown.
Descent: the note *MA* (F#) is avoided.

(11) *Kalābharaṇi*

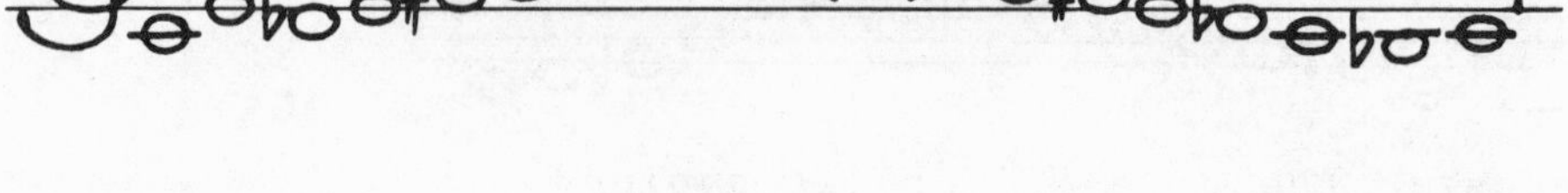

This is a *niṣādāntya rāga*.
Ascent: two *vakra* features are shown.
Descent: one *vakra* feature is used.

(12) *Kāmarupi*

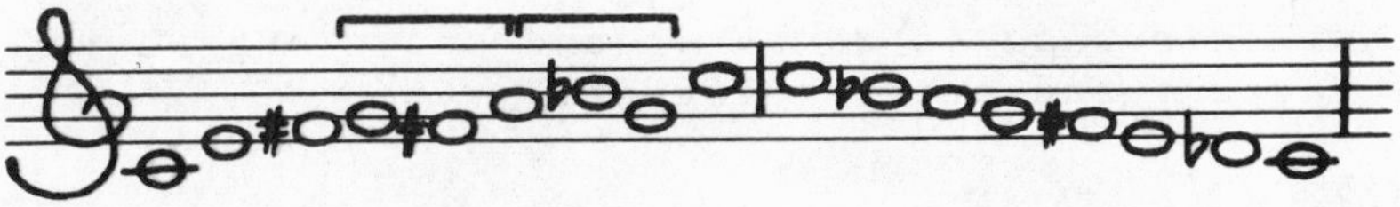

Ascent: the note *RI* (Db) is avoided; two *vakra* features are shown.
Descent: *krama sampūrṇa*.

(13) *Kaṅkaṇālaṅkāri*

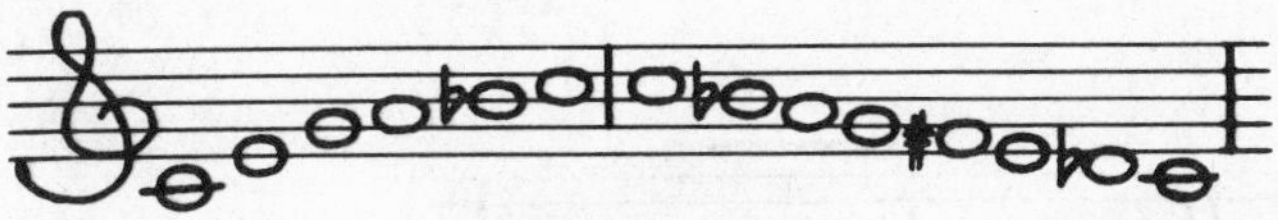

Ascent: the notes *RI* (Db) and *MA* (F#) are avoided.
Descent: *krama sampūrṇa*.

(14) *Lokarañjani*

Ascent: the note *RI* (Db) is avoided; one *vakra* feature is shown.
Descent: *sampūrṇa*; one *vakra* feature is used.

(15) *Mandhāsini*

Ascent: *sampūrṇa*; one *vakra* feature is shown.
Descent: *sampūrṇa*; one *vakra* feature is used.

(16) *Nakhaprakāśini*

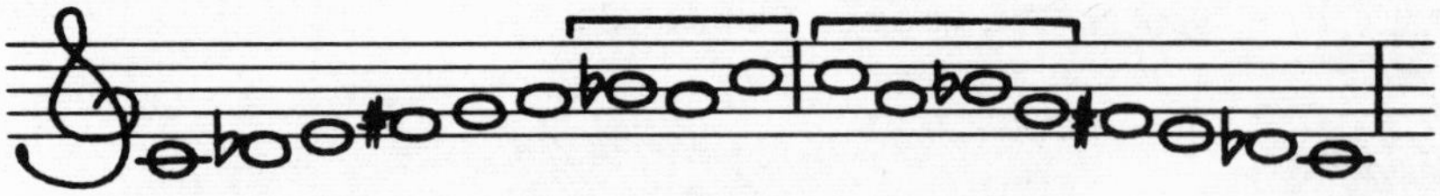

The scale of this *rāga* is *sampūrṇa* and shows one *vakra* feature in ascent and one in descent.

(17) *Pātalāmbari*

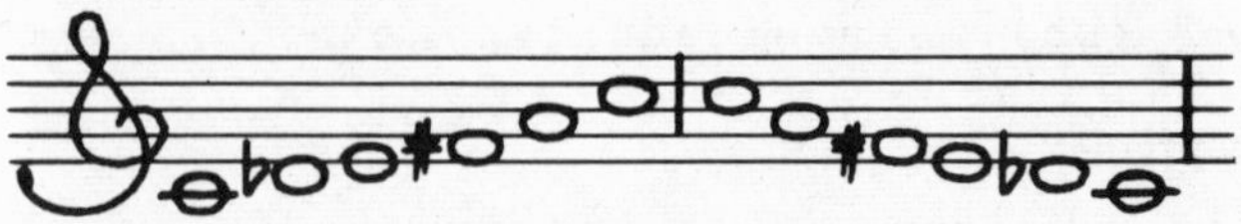

The notes *PA* (G) and *NI* (B) are avoided entirely.

(18) *Raktimārgaṇi*

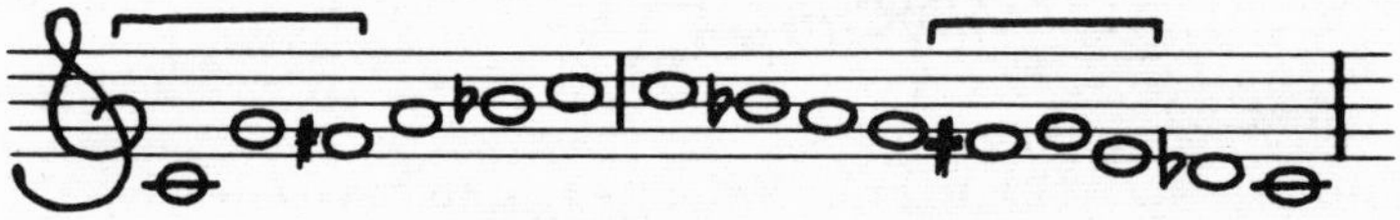

Ascent: the notes *RI* (Db) and *GA* (E) are avoided; one *vakra* feature is shown.
Descent: *sampūrṇa*; one *vakra* feature is shown.

(19) *Ramāmanoharī*

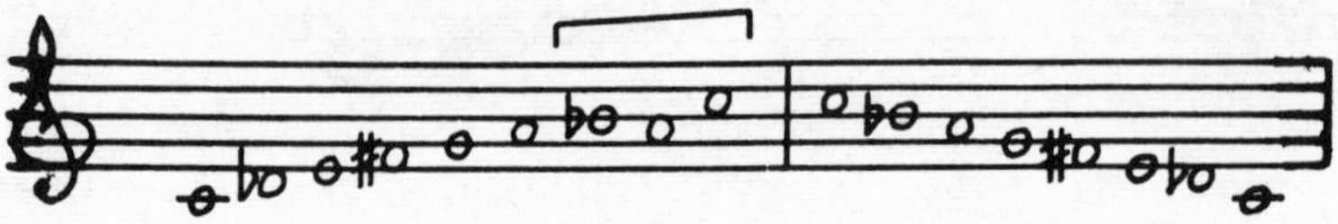

Ascent: *sampūrṇa*; one *vakra* feature is shown.
Descent: *krama sampūrṇa*.

The following melody specimen shows that the *vakra* feature in ascent need not appear regularly:

RAMĀMANOHARĪ (*Triputa-tāla*) SCM, 239

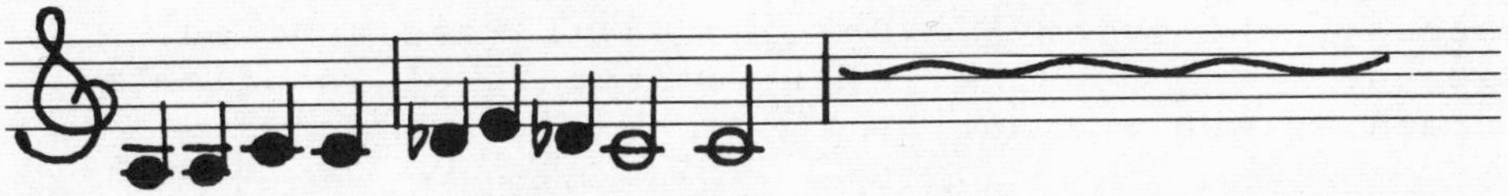

(20) *Rasavinōdini*

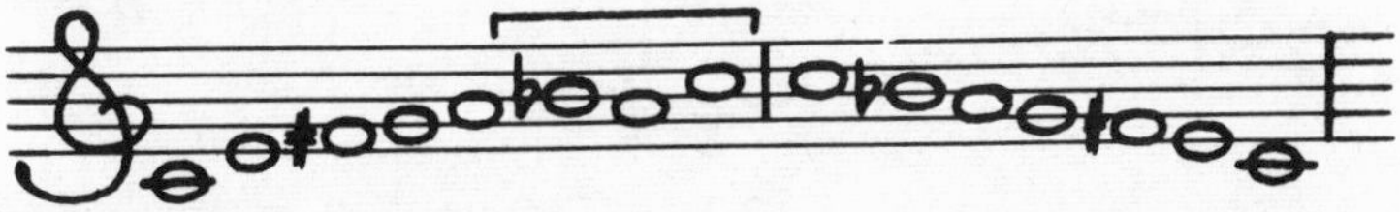

The note *RI* (Db) is avoided entirely. The ascent shows one *vakra* feature.

(21) *Ratichandrikā* (*Raticandrikā*, *Rīticandrikā*)

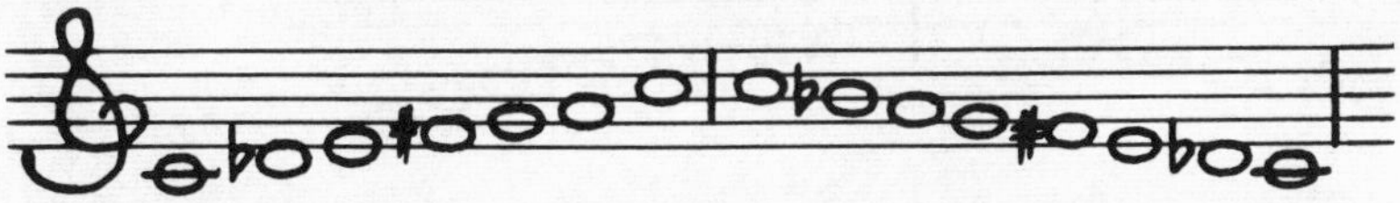

Ascent: the note *NI* (Bb) is avoided.
Descent: *krama sampūrṇa*.

(22) *Sīmantinipriya*

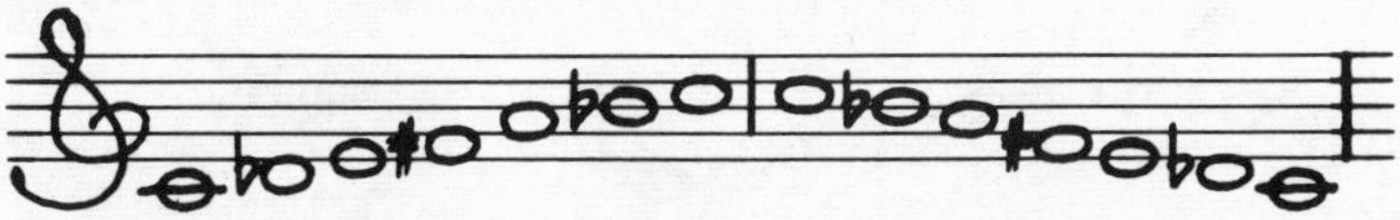

The note *PA* (G) is avoided entirely.

(23) *Śrīkari*

Ascent: the note *MA* (F#) is avoided.
Descent: the note *RI* (Db) is omitted.

(24) *Sukhakari*

Ascent: the notes *RI* (Db) and *GA* (E) are avoided.
Descent: the note *PA* (G) is omitted. *GA* is often performed as Ebb and not as E.

(25) *Tapasvini*

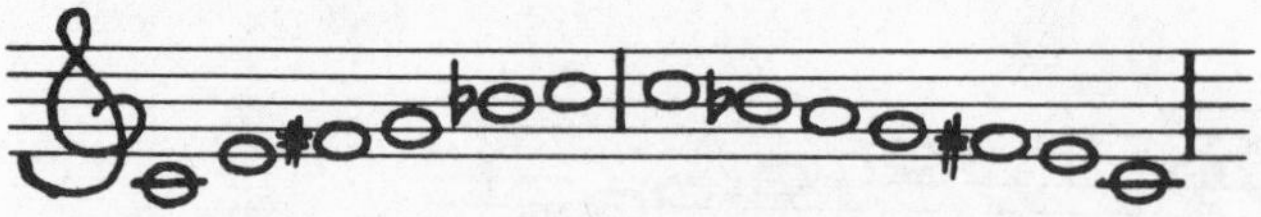

The note *RI* (Db) is avoided entirely. *DHA* (A) is omitted in ascent.

(26) *Vēdasvarūpi*

Ascent: *sampūrṇa*; one *vakra* feature is shown.
Descent: the note *RI* (Db) is avoided; one *vakra* feature is used.

(27) *Vishupati* (*Viṣupati*)

The notes *GA* (E) and *PA* (G) are avoided entirely.

(28) *Yōgānandi*

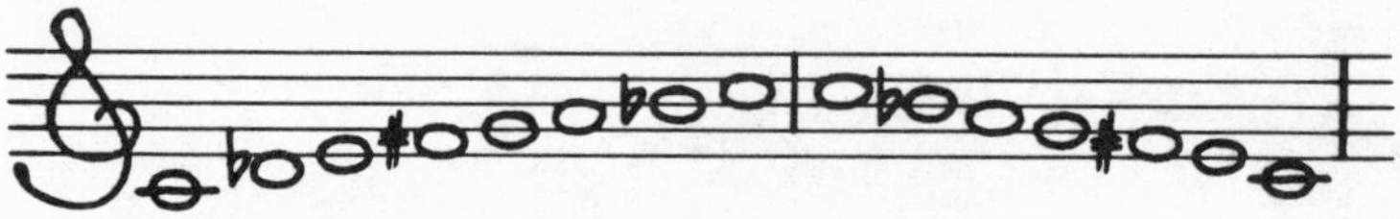

Ascent: *krama sampūrṇa*.
Descent: the note *RI* (Db) is avoided.

53. *MĒḶA GAMANAŚRAMA (GAMANAPRIYA)*

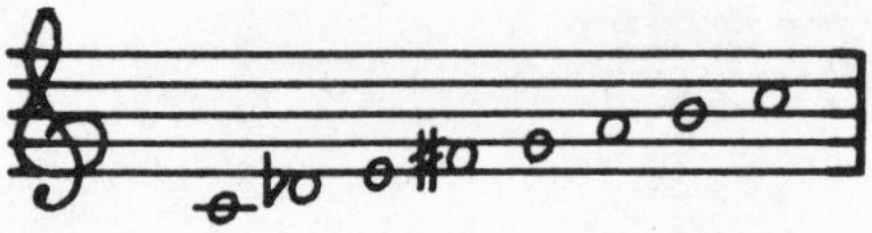

Veṅkaṭamakhin called this *rāga Gamakakriyā*, a name

that at the present time represents a *janya rāga* of the 53. *mēḷa* (9).

GAMANAŚRAMA (Triputa-tāla) SCM, 240

Janya Rāgas of the 53. Mēḷa

(1) *Anilamadhya*

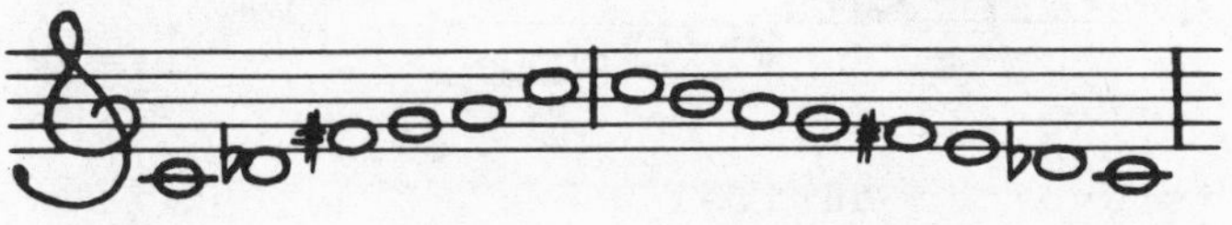

Ascent: the notes *GA* (E) and *NI* (B) are avoided.
Descent: *krama sampūrṇa*.

(2) *Balivalam*

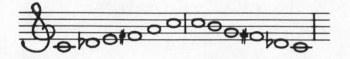

Ascent: the notes *PA* (G) and *NI* (B) are avoided.
Descent: the notes *DHA* (A) and *GA* (E) are omitted.

(3) *Bhavamanōharī*

Ascent: *sampūrṇa*; one *vakra* feature is shown.
Descent: *sampūrṇa*; two *vakra* features are used.

(4) *Dāna Rakshasa* (*Dāna Rakṣasa*)

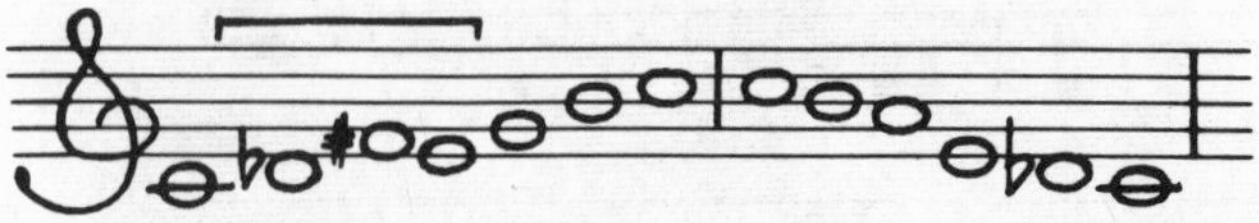

Ascent: the note *DHA* (A) is avoided; one *vakra* feature is shown.
Descent: the notes *PA* (G) and *MA* (F#) are omitted.

(5) *Darphamañjari*

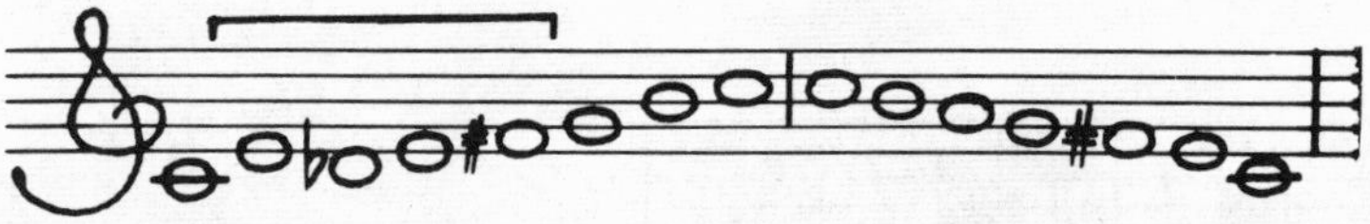

Ascent: the note *DHA* (A) is avoided; one *vakra* feature is shown.
Descent: the note *RI* (Db) is omitted.

(6) *Daurēyaṇi*

The note *PA* (G) is avoided entirely.

This *rāga* is identical with the *rāgas Haṃsānandi* (53, 14) and *Dēvāśramam* (53, 7).

(7) *Dēvāśramam*

As already stated, this *rāga* is identical with the *rāgas Daurēyaṇi* (53, 6) and *Haṃsānandi* (53, 14).

(8) *Gagana Sarasīruham*

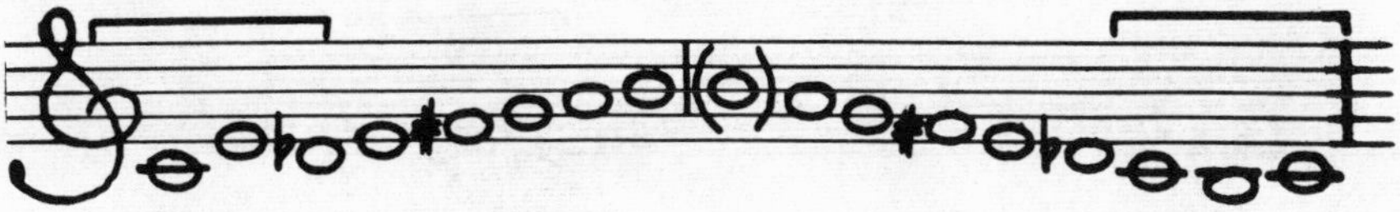

The scale of this *niṣadantya rāga* shows one *vakra* feature in ascent and one in descent.

(9) *Gamakakriya*

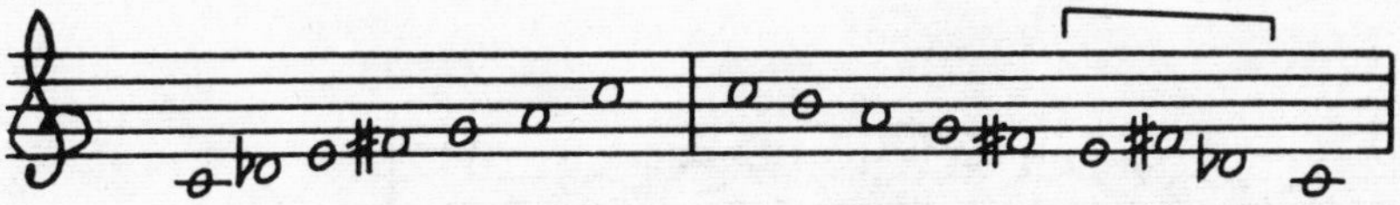

Ascent: the note *NI* (B) is generally avoided and *GA* (E) appears rarely.
Descent: *sampūrṇa*; one *vakra* feature is shown.

As mentioned before (see remark concerning the 53. *mēḷa Gamanaśrama*), *Gamakakriya* was the name of the 53. *mēḷa* of Veṅkaṭamakhin's *asampūrṇa* system. At present *Gamakakriya* is a *janya rāga*.

It can be seen that in the following melody specimen the note *NI* (B) can be used in ascent, a feature that brings modern *Gamakakriya* close to its primary *rāga*. The only noticeable difference is the characteristic *vakra* feature of the *Gamakakriya* descent.

GAMAKAKRIYA (*Triputa-tāla*) SCM, 240-41

(10) *Gamanakriya*

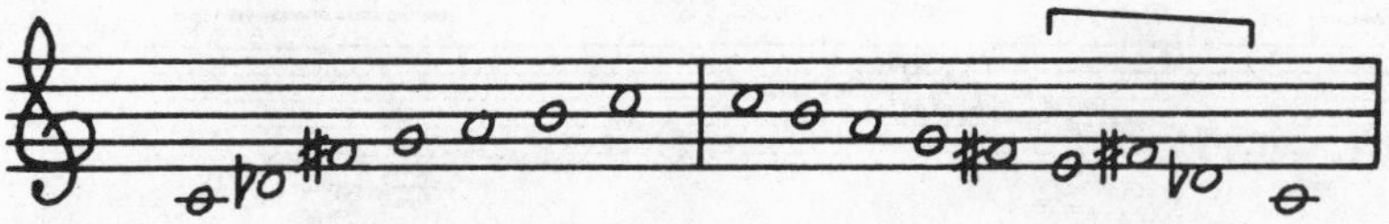

Ascent: the note *GA* (E) is avoided.
Descent: *sampūrṇa*; one *vakra* feature is shown.

(11) *Gamana Nirmaḷa*

Ascent: *krama sampūrṇa*.
Descent: the notes *DHA* (A) and *GA* (E) are avoided.

(12) *Ganda Madanam*

Ascent: the notes *GA* (E) and *NI* (B) are avoided.
Descent: *sampūrṇa*; one *vakra* feature is shown.

(13) *Gītanāṭaṇi*

Ascent: *sampūrṇa*; one *vakra* feature is shown.
Descent: the note *GA* (E) is avoided.

(14) *Haṃsānandi*

The note *PA* (G) is avoided entirely.
The *rāgas Daurēyaṇi* (53, 6) and *Dēvaśramam* (53, 7) are identical with *Haṃsānandi*.

Another *rāga* with the same name appears under the heading of the 8. *mēḷa* (25).

The following *Haṃsānandi* phrases are taken from a *Gīta Govinda* performance in Kerala (recorded by Wayne Howard in 1972):

The last phrase shows the use of the notes *PA* (G) and *DHA* interpreted here as Ab.

(15) *Indu Kānti*

The note *NI* (B) is avoided entirely.

(16) *Jayamōhanam*

Ascent: the notes *RI* (Db) and *NI* (B) are avoided.
Descent: *krama sampūrṇa*.

(17) *Kannaḍa Māruva*

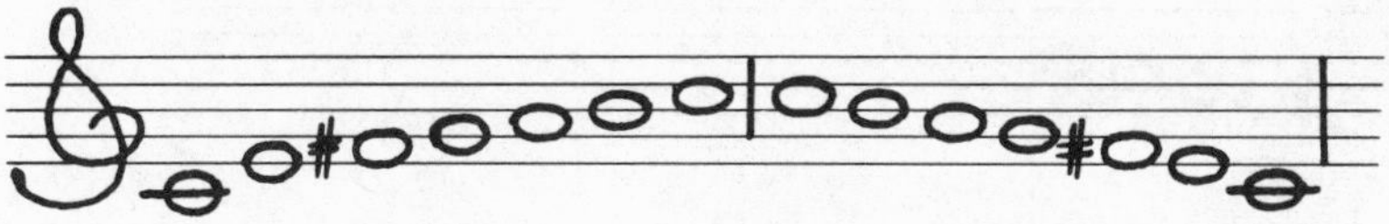

The note *RI* (Db) is avoided entirely.

SD (II, 298) remarks that "some scholars give the *janaka mēḷa* of this *rāga* as *Mēchakalyāṇī* [65. *mēḷa*] but it makes no difference, since *RI* [Db] is deleted in *Kannaḍa Māruva* and the other notes are common to both *mēḷas*."

(18) *Karṇāṭa Kadamba*

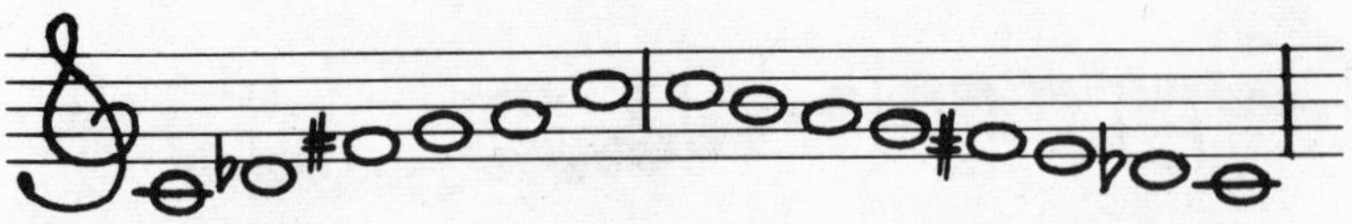

Ascent: the notes *GA* (E) and *NI* (B) are avoided.
Descent: *krama sampūrṇa*.

(19) *Kuntala Rāma*

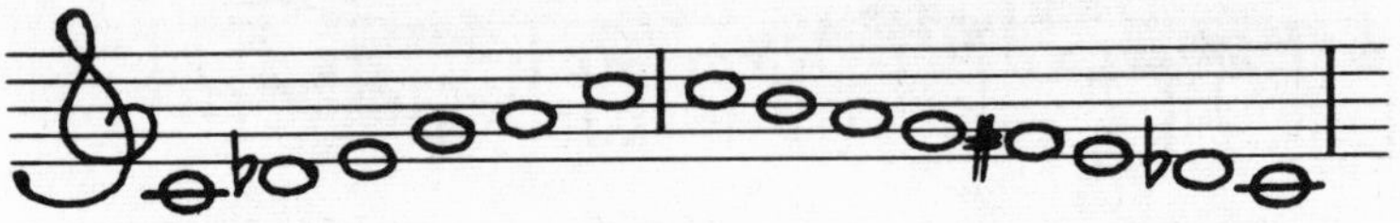

Ascent: the notes *MA* (F#) and *NI* (B) are avoided.
Descent: *krama sampūrṇa*.

(20) *Mechakaṅgi (Mecakaṅgi)*

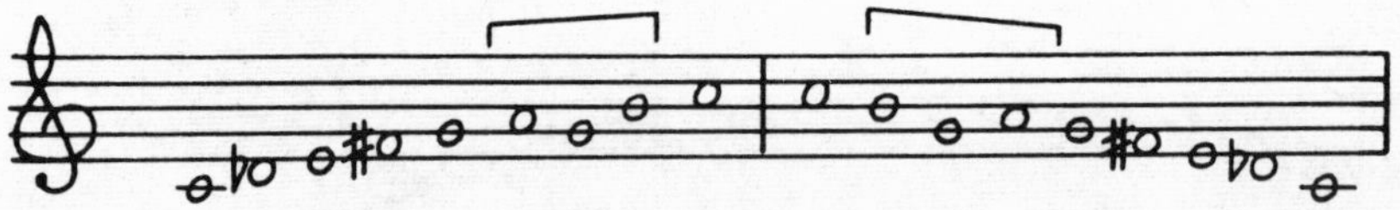

Ascent: *sampūrṇa*; one *vakra* feature is shown.
Descent: *sampūrṇa*; one *vakra* feature is used.

(21) *Pūrvakalyāṇī (Pūrvikalyāṇī)*

There are two forms of this *rāga*, which are distinguished by their ascending scales:

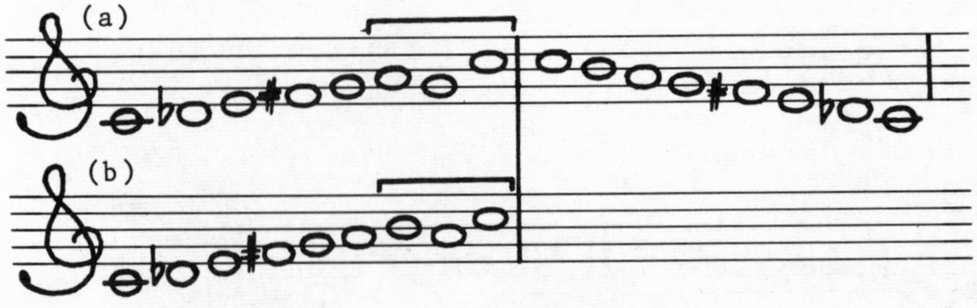

The ascent (a) avoids the note *NI* (B), and ascent (b) is *sampūrṇa*. Each of the two ascents shows one *vakra* feature. The descent of both scales is *krama sampūrṇa*.

Occasionally one can observe the straight ascent *PA-DHA-SA* (G-A-c). *Pūrvakalyāṇī* is supposed to be performed in the evening. Its melodies usually begin with *SA* (C) or *PA* (G). The similarity between this *rāga* and *Gamakakriya* (53, 9) is noticeable. The only difference between the two *rāgas* is the appearance of the indicated *vakra* feature in the ascent of *Pūrvakalyāṇi* and in the descent of *Gamakakriya*.

PŪRVAKALYĀṆĪ (*Triputa-tāla*) SCM, 241-42

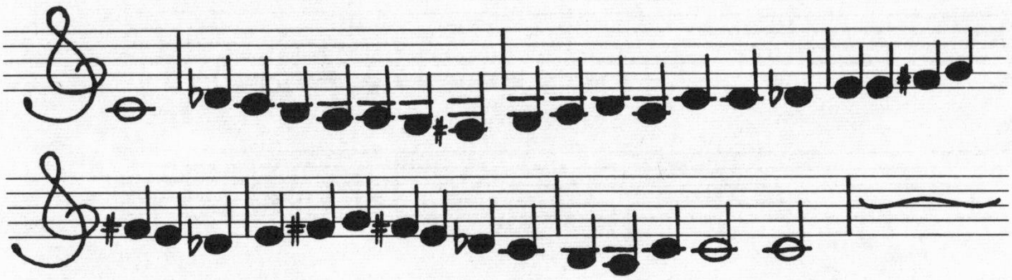

(22) *Sukadhvani*

Ascent: the note *RI* (Db) is avoided.
Descent: *krama sampūrṇa*. The note *RI* in descent is rarely intoned as Db, as is required in the 53. *mēḷa*, but is taken sharp, approximately as D natural.

(23) *Śubika*

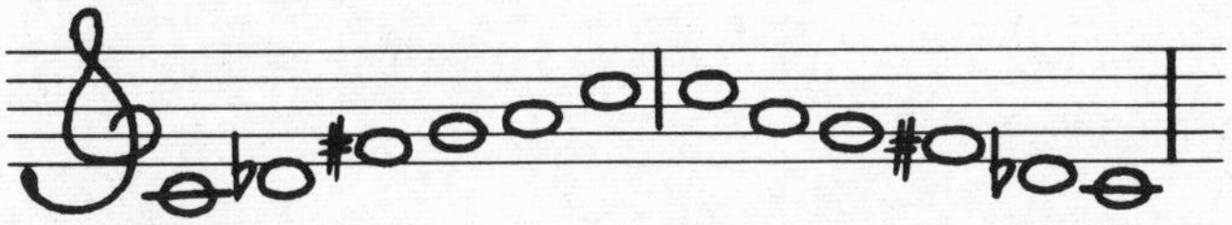

The notes *GA* (E) and *NI* (B) are avoided entirely.

(24) *Śuddharasāḷi*

The notes *RI* (Db) and *NI* (B) are avoided entirely.

54. *MĒḶA VIŚVAMBHARĪ*

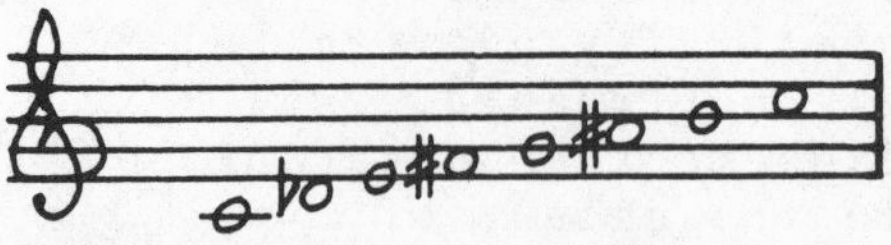

VIŚVAMBHARĪ (*Triputa-tāla*) SCM, 242-3

Janya Rāgas of the 54. Mēḷa

(1) *Balabi*

Ascent: the note *RI* (Db) is avoided; two *vakra* features are shown.
Descent: *krama sampūrṇa*.

(2) *Bhramara Dhvani*

Ascent: the notes *RI* (Db) and *PA* (G) are avoided.
Descent: *sampūrṇa*; one *vakra* feature is shown.

(3) *Bhramara Nārāyaṇi*

Ascent: *sampurṇa*; one *vakra* feature is shown.
Descent: the notes *DHA* (A#) and *PA* (G) are avoided.

(4) *Bhūshā Kalyāṇi* (*Bhūṣa Kalyāṇi*)

Ascent: *krama sampūrṇa*.
Descent: the note *DHA* (A#) is avoided.

(5) *Dēśya Māruva*

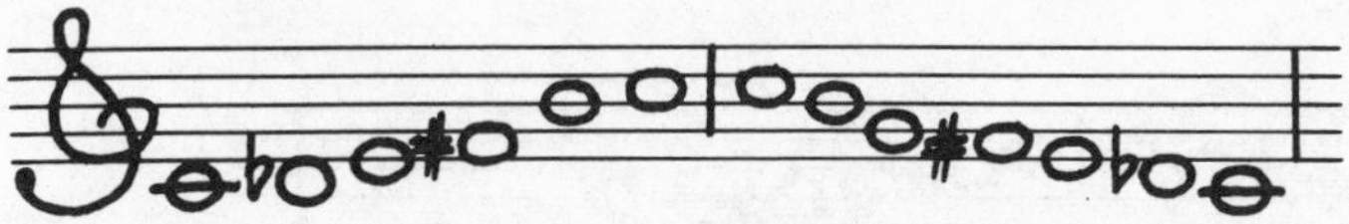

The note *DHA* (A#) is avoided entirely. *PA* (G) is omitted in ascent.

(6) *Gaganādari*

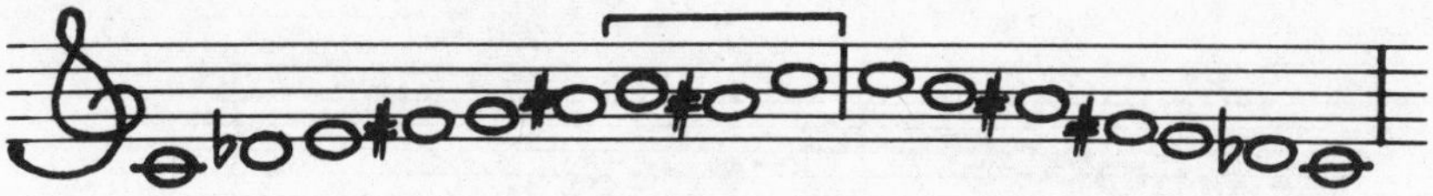

Ascent: *sampūrṇa*; one *vakra* feature is shown.
Descent: the note *PA* (G) is avoided.

(7) *Hēmāṅgi*

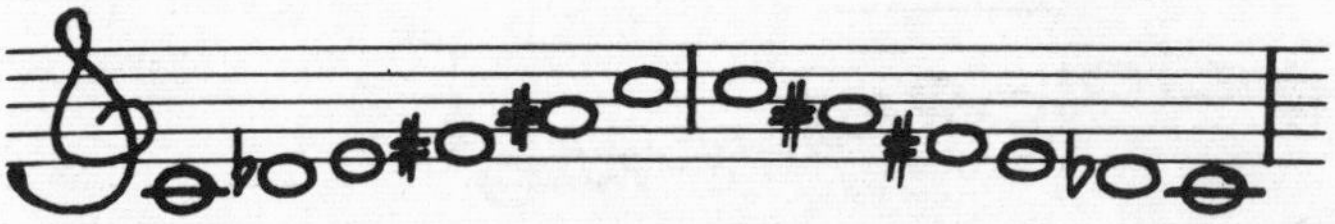

The notes *PA* (G) and *NI* (B) are avoided entirely.

(8) *Indrapriya*

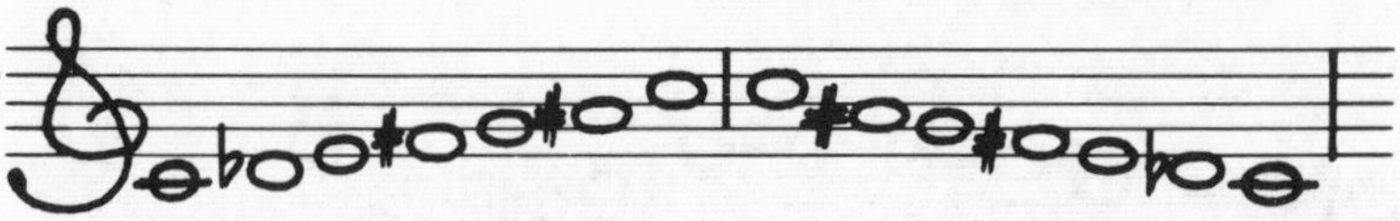

The note *NI* (B) is avoided entirely.

Two other *rāgas*, each with the same name, are listed as 1,10 and 24,14.

(9) *Jagadbari*

The scale of this *niṣādāntya rāga* avoids in ascent the note *RI* (Db) and shows two *vakra* features in descent.

(10) *Karṇāṭaka Mañjari*

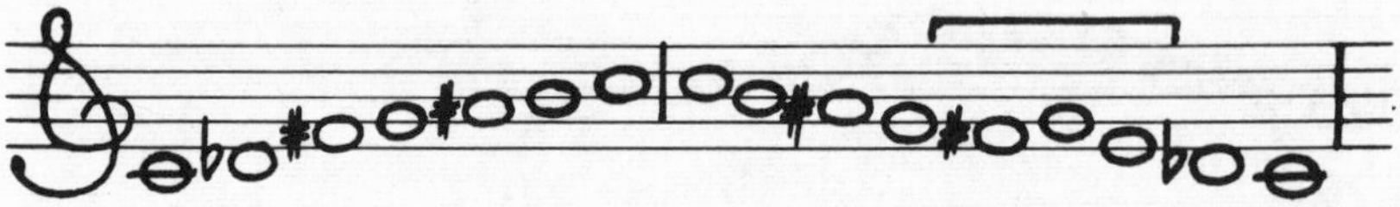

Ascent: the note *GA* (E) is avoided.
Descent: *sampūrṇa*; one *vakra* feature is shown.

(11) *Kriyāvati*

Ascent: *krama sampūrṇa*.
Descent: *sampūrṇa*; one *vakra* feature is shown.

(12) *Nāgasarasīrūham*

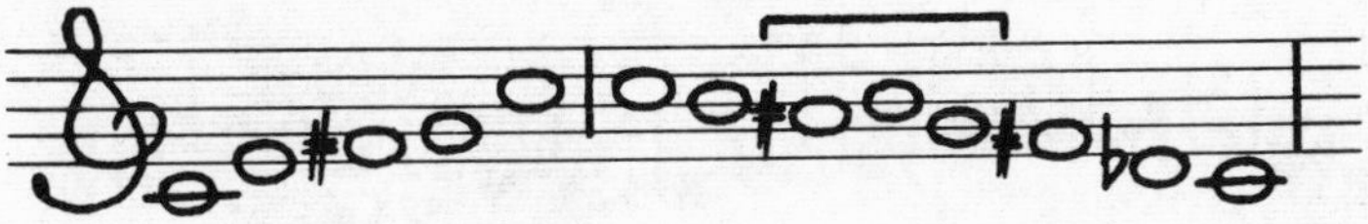

Ascent: the notes *RI* (Db), *DHA* (A#), and *NI* (B) are avoided.
Descent: the note *GA* (E) is omitted; one *vakra* feature is shown.

(13) *Pusha Kalyāṇi* (*Puṣakalyāṇi*)

Ascent: *krama sampūrṇa*.
Descent: the note *DHA* (A#) is avoided.

(14) *Sindhumāruva*

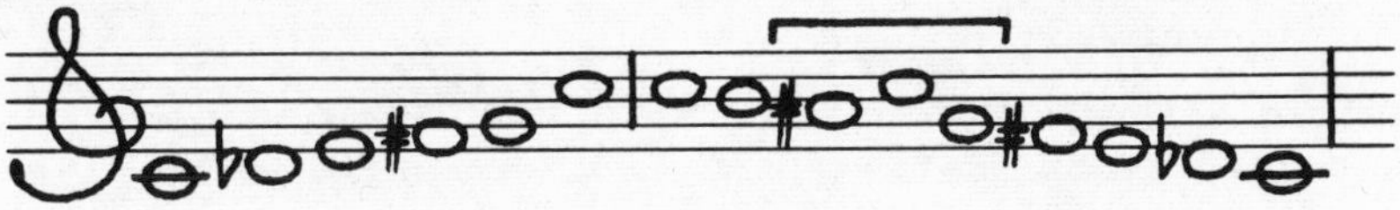

Ascent: the notes *DHA* (A#) and *NI* (B) are avoided.
Descent: *sampūrṇa*; one *vakra* feature is shown.

(15) *Śrīkhandalilepani*

The notes *GA* (E) and *PA* (G) are avoided entirely.

(16) *Vaiśākha*

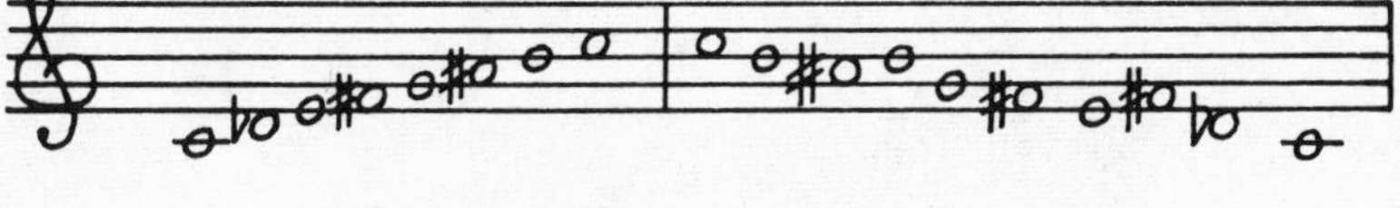

Ascent: *krama sampūrṇa*.
Descent: *sampūrṇa*; two *vakra* features are shown.

VAIŚĀKHA (*Triputa-tāla*) SCM, 243-44

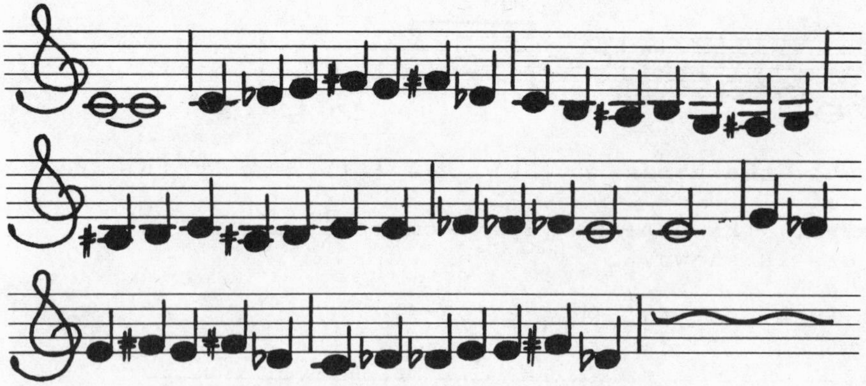

(17) *Vijayavasanta*

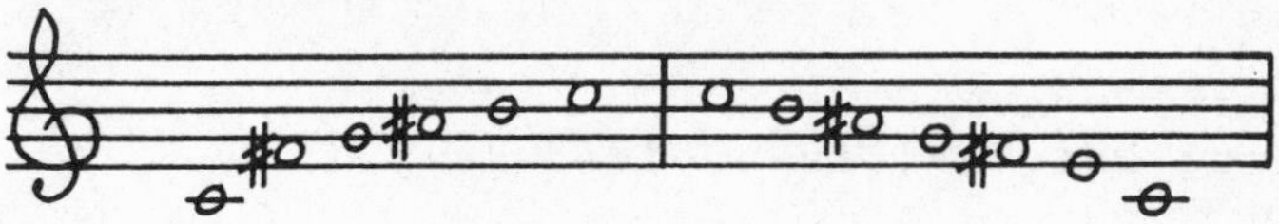

The note *RI* (Db) is avoided entirely. *GA* (E) is omitted in ascent.

Chakra X

55. *MĒḶA ŚYĀMALĀṄGĪ*

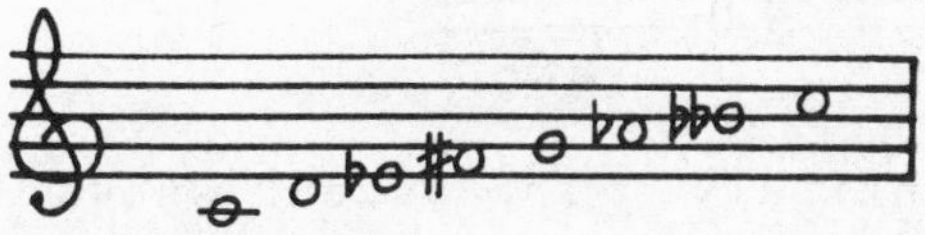

ŚYĀMALĀṄGĪ (*Triputa-tāla*) SCM, 244

Janya Rāgas of the 55. Mēḷa

(1) *Baṅgāḷa Gauḷa*

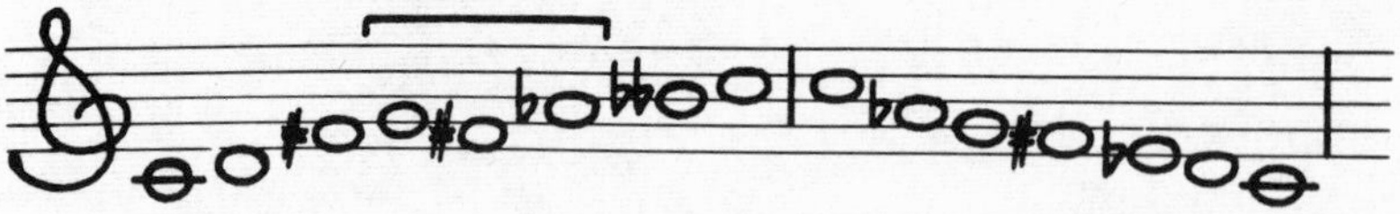

Ascent: the note *GA* (Eb) is avoided; one *vakra* feature is shown.
Descent: the note *NI* (Bbb) is omitted.

(2) *Dēśā Vāḷi*

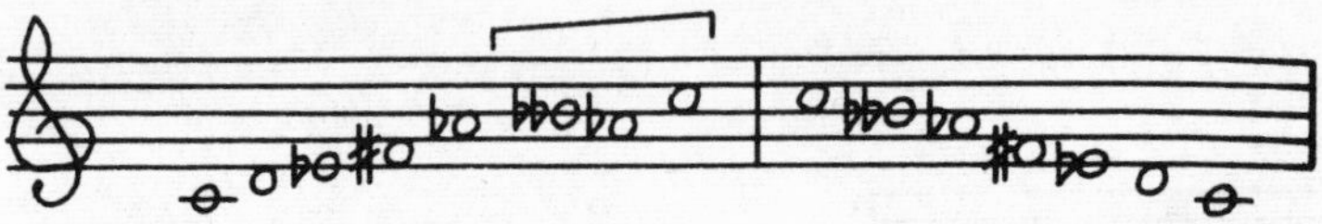

The note *PA* (G) is avoided entirely. The ascent shows one *vakra* feature.

DĒŚĀ VĀḶI (*Triputa-tāla*) SCM, 245-46

(3) *Dēśya Nāṭakurañji*

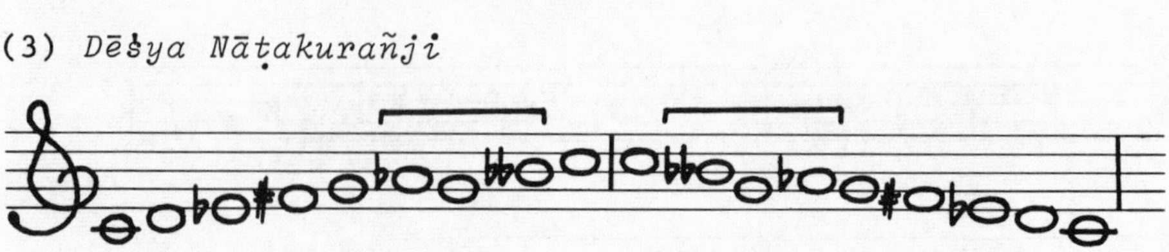

Ascent and descent are *sampūrṇa*; each shows one *vakra* feature.

(4) *Haṃsa Bhūshavāḷi* (*Haṃsa Bhūṣavāḷi*)

The scale of this *niṣādāntya rāga* shows two *vakra* features, one in ascent and one in descent. (Cf. *Haṃsa Prabhāvaḷi*, 55,6.)

(5) *Haṃsa Gīrvāṇi*

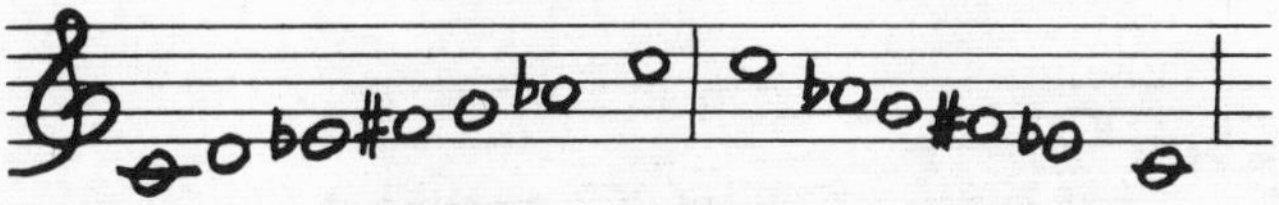

The note *NI* (Bbb) is avoided entirely. *RI* (D) is omitted in descent.

(6) *Haṃsa Prabhāvaḷi*

This *rāga* is identical with *Haṃsa Bhūshavāḷi* (55,4).

(7) *Hēmāmbari*

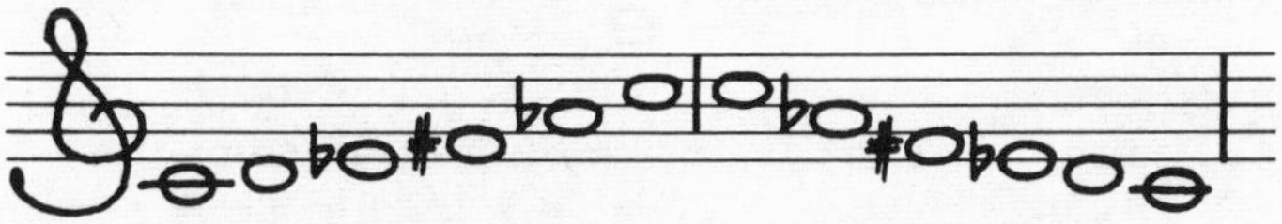

The notes *PA* (G) and *NI* (Bbb) are avoided entirely. See also *rāga Hēmāmbari* (58,8).

(8) *Kākali*

The note *DHA* (Ab) is avoided entirely.

(9) *Kamala Nārāyaṇi*

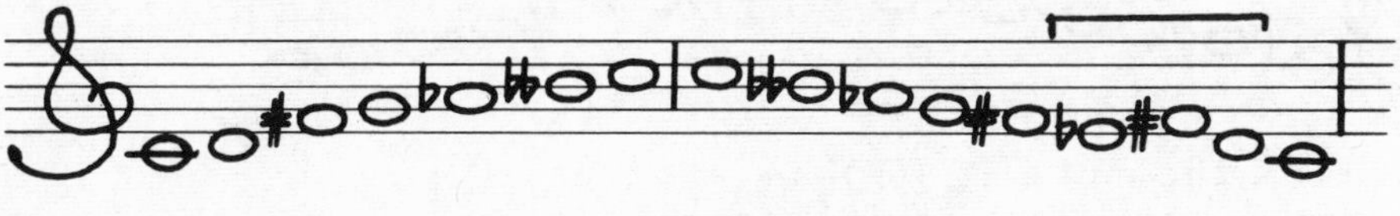

Ascent: the note *GA* (Eb) is avoided.
Descent: *sampūrṇa*; one *vakra* feature is shown.

(10) *Kamaṭadhvajam*

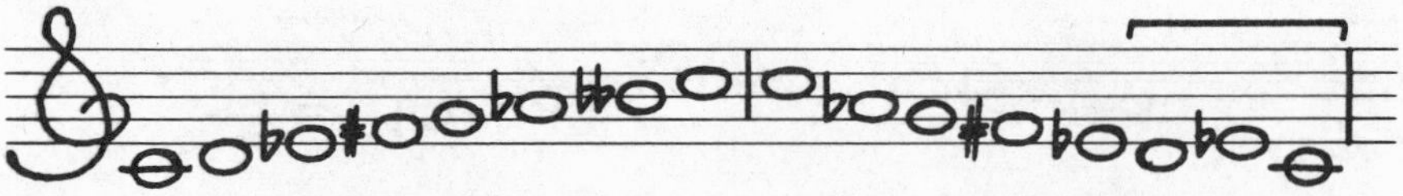

Ascent: *krama sampūrṇa*.
Descent: the note *NI* (Bbb) is avoided; one *vakra* feature is shown.

(11) *Kānchanāṅgi* (*Kāncanāṅgi*)

The note *NI* (Bbb) is avoided entirely.

Another *rāga* with the same name appears under the heading of the 19. *mēḷa* (14).

(12) *Līlāvati*

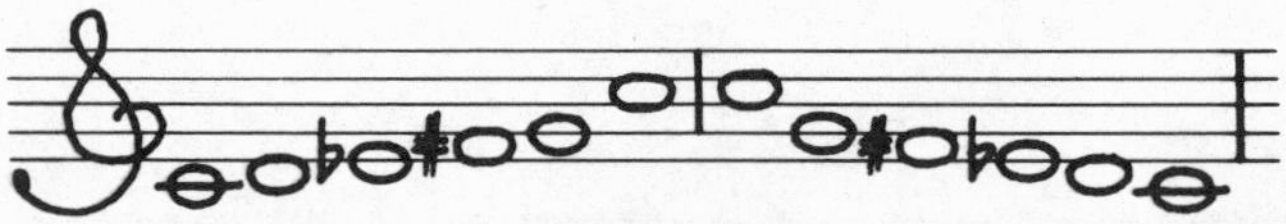

The notes *DHA* (Ab) and *NI* (Bbb) are avoided entirely.

(13) *Nāgagīrvāṇi*

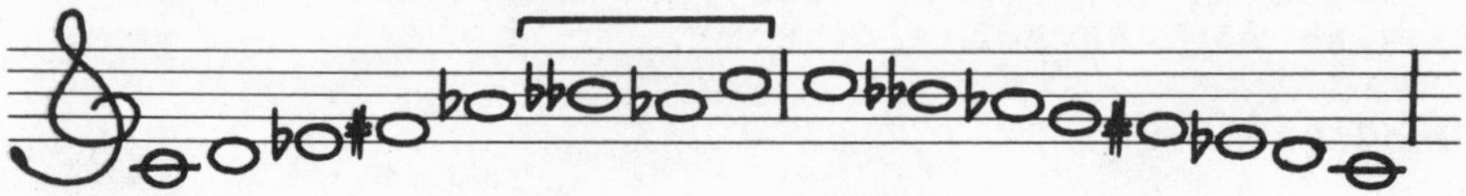

Ascent: the note *PA* (G) is avoided; one *vakra* feature is shown.
Descent: *krama sampūrṇa*.

(14) *Nāgaprabhāvali*

Ascent: the note *RI* (D) is avoided.
Descent: the note *PA* (G) is omitted.

(15) *Nīlāṅgi*

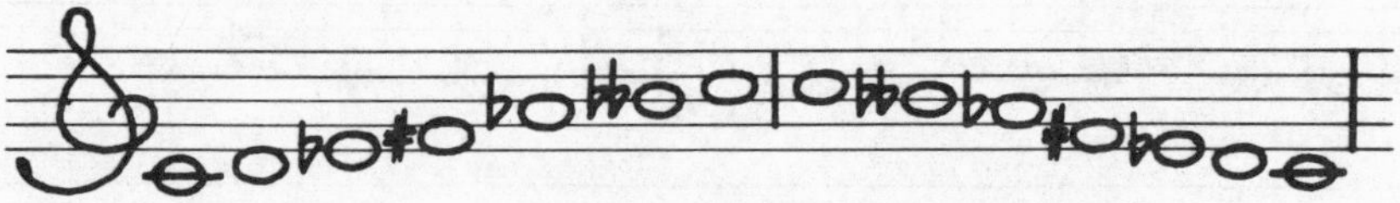

The note *PA* (G) is avoided entirely.

(16) *Śārvari*

The notes *PA* (G) and *DHA* (Ab) are avoided entirely.

(17) *Shītakiraṇi* (*Śītakiraṇi*)

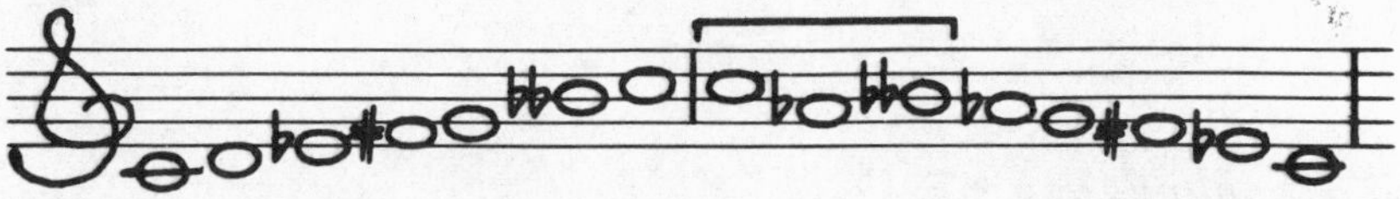

Ascent: the note *DHA* (Ab) is avoided.
Descent: the note *RI* (D) is omitted; one *vakra* feature is shown.

(18) *Śyāmala* (*Śyāmali*)

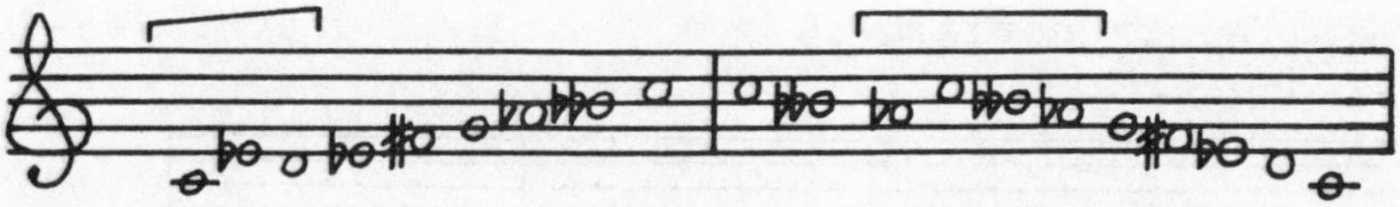

The scale of this *rāga* is *sampūrṇa* and shows two *vakra* features, one in ascent and one in descent.

A second form of the *Śyāmala* scale is:

In this scale the ascent shows two *vakra* features; the descent is *krama sampūrṇa*.

ŚYĀMALA (*Triputa-tāla*) SCM, 245

56. *MĒḶA ŚAṆMUKHAPRIYĀ*

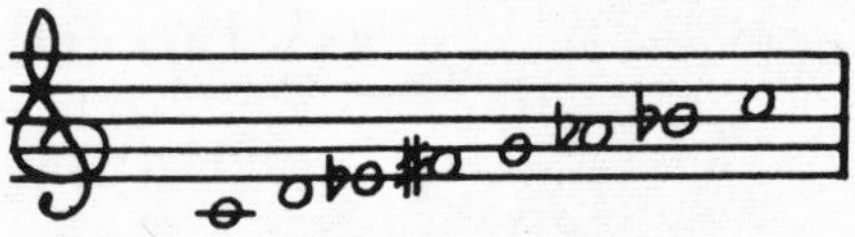

ŚAṆMUKHAPRIYĀ (*Triputa-tāla*) SCM, 246-7

The following *Śaṇmukhapriyā* phrases are taken from a *Gīta Govinda* performance in Kerala, recorded in 1972 by Wayne Howard:

The note *MA* (F#) is practically avoided and appears only as an insignificant and very lightly touched upon ornament before *PA* (G) in ascent. The note *DHA* (Ab) is used very rarely in descent.

Janya Rāgas of the 56. Mēḷa

(1) *Bhāshiṇi* (*Bhāṣiṇi*)

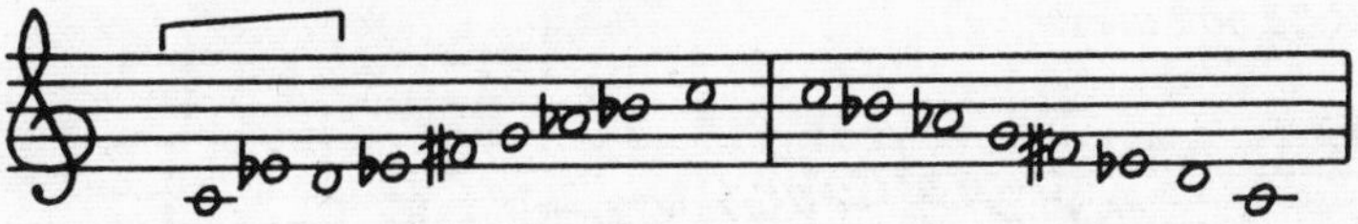

Ascent: *sampūrṇa*; one *vakra* feature is shown.
Descent: *krama sampūrṇa*.

BHAṢIṆI (*Triputa-tāla*) SCM, 248-49

(2) *Bhramara Kusumam*

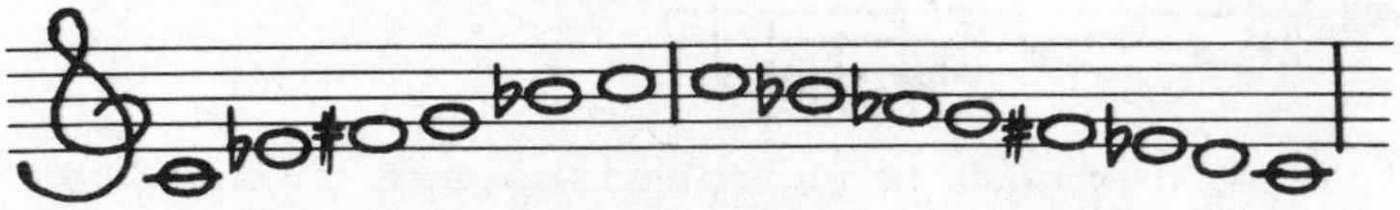

Ascent: the notes *RI* (D) and *DHA* (Ab) are avoided.
Descent: *krama sampūrṇa*.

(3) *Bhramara Sāraṅga*

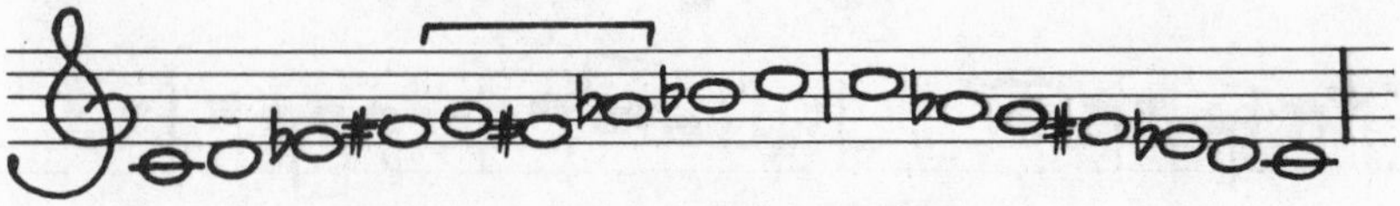

Ascent: *sampūrṇa*; one *vakra* feature is shown.
Descent: the note *NI* (Bb) is avoided.

(4) *Chakra Mañjari* (*Cakra Mañjari*)

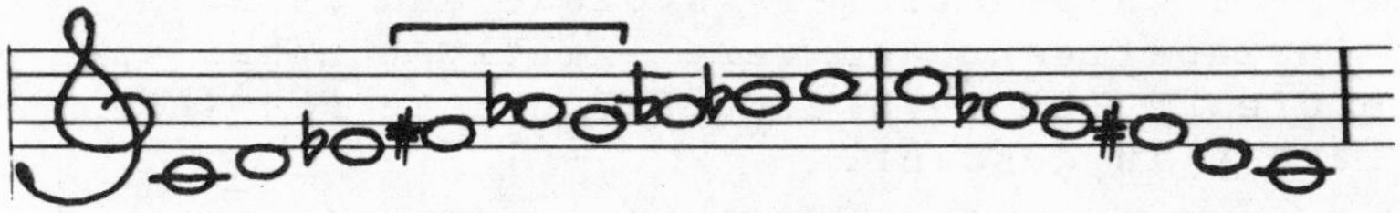

Ascent: *sampūrṇa*; one *vakra* feature is shown.
Descent: the notes *NI* (Bb) and *GA* (Eb) are avoided.

(5) *Chāmaram* (*Cāmaram*)

Ascent: the note *DHA* (Ab) is avoided; one *vakra* feature is shown.
Descent: *krama sampūrṇa*.

The name *Chāmaram* was also applied to the 56. *mēḷa* of the old *asampūrṇa* system.

(6) *Chandradēśika* (*Candradēśika*)

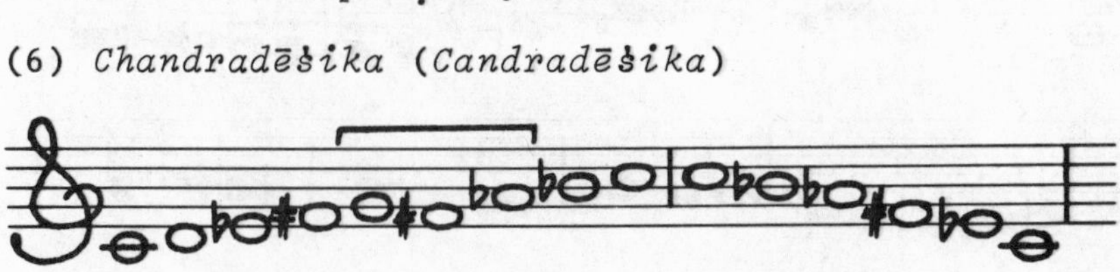

Ascent: *sampūrṇa*: one *vakra* feature is shown.
Descent: the notes *PA* (G) and *RI* (D) are avoided.

(7) *Chintāmaṇi* (*Cintāmaṇi*)

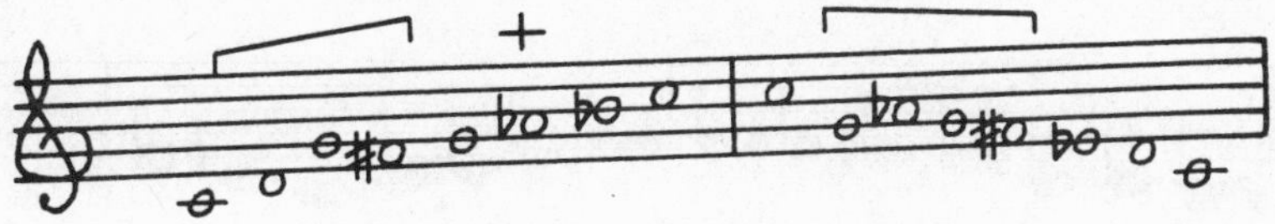

Ascent: the note *GA* (Eb) is avoided; one *vakra* feature is shown.
Descent: the note *NI* (Bb) is omitted; one *vakra* feature is used.

SD (I, 89) remarks that "the only foreign note, *chatuśśruti dhaivata* [the four-*śruti* *DHA*, interpreted approximately as A natural] occurs in the phrase *PA-DHA-NI-SA* [G-A-Bb-c]."

Chintāmaṇi is to be performed at night. Two other *rāgas* with the name *Chintāmaṇi* (or *Bhōga Chintāmaṇi*) appear under the headings of the 1, 5 and 7, 3 *mēḷas*.

(8) *Chūtāvaḷi* (*Cūtāvaḷi*)

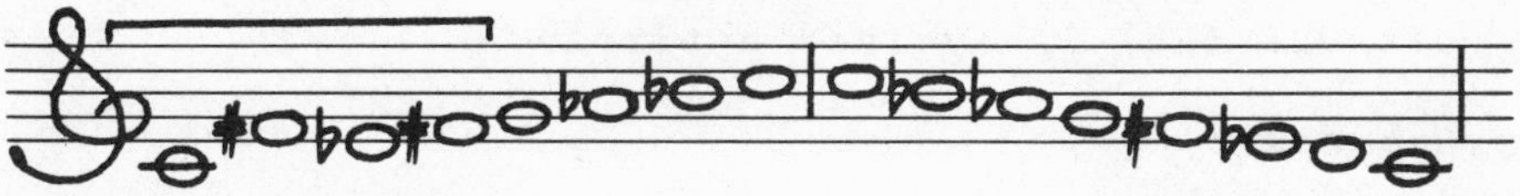

Ascent: the note *RI* (D) is avoided; one *vakra* feature is shown.
Descent: *krama sampūrṇa*.

(9) *Dēva Māḷavi*

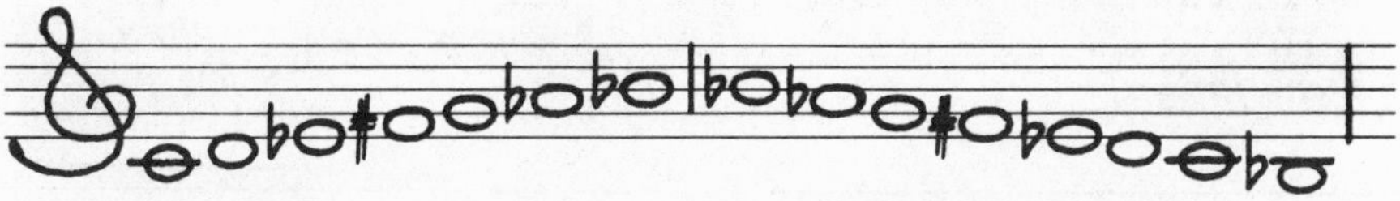

The scale of this *rāga* has *niṣādāntya* character. Excepting the upper *SA* (c) which is always omitted in *niṣādāntya rāgas*, no other notes are avoided.

(10) *Garigadya*

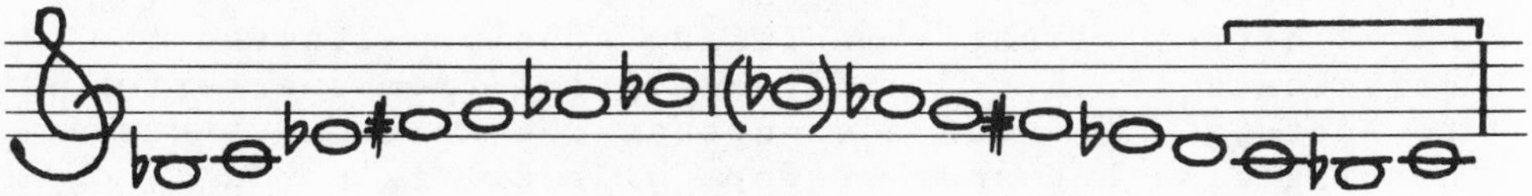

The *niṣādāntya* scale of this *rāga* avoids the note *RI* (D) in ascent and shows one *vakra* feature in descent.

GARIGADYA (*Triputa-tāla*) SCM, 249-50

(11) *Gōpikā Tilakam*

The note *DHA* (Ab) is avoided entirely.

(12) *Gummāvaḷi*

Ascent: the note *MA* (F#) is avoided.
Descent: the note *NI* (Bb) is omitted.

(13) *Gurugadya*

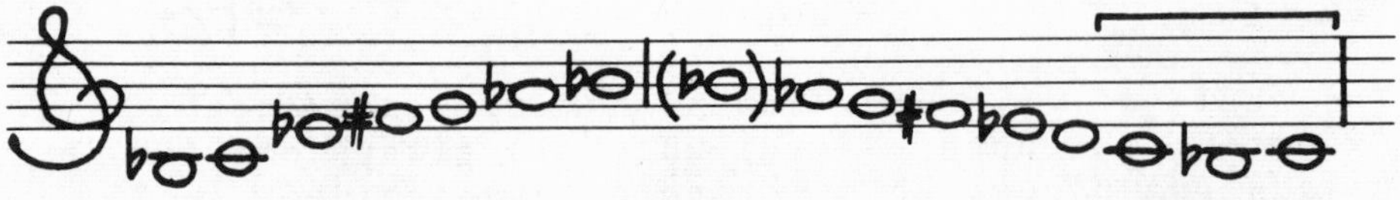

The scale of this *rāga* appears to be identical with that of *Garigadya* (56, 10). It is shown again because there are some musicians who maintain that the two *rāgas* differ slightly in interpretation although the difference shown is vague and varies from one performer to another. One can assume that the name *Gurugadya* is nothing else but another form of spelling of *Garigadya*.

(14) *Karatoyam*

The notes *RI* (D) and *GA* (Eb) are avoided entirely.
See also *rāga Karatoyam* listed as 7, 17.

(15) *Kōkilānandi*

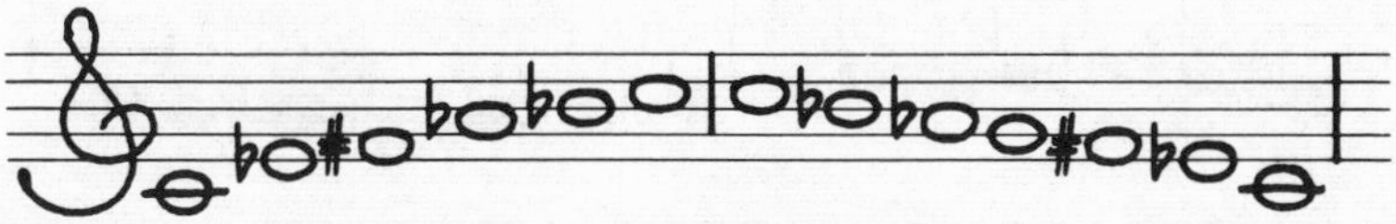

The note *RI* (D) is avoided entirely. *PA* (G) is omitted in ascent.

(16) *Kusumasāraṅga*

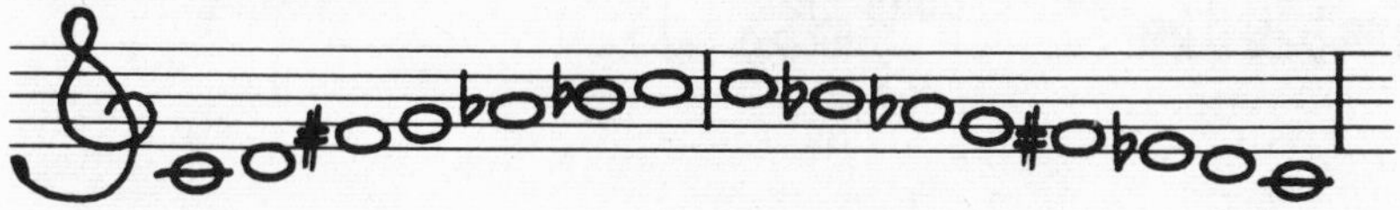

Ascent: the note *GA* (Eb) is avoided.
Descent: *krama sampūrṇa*.
Another *rāga* with the same name is 27, 22.

(17) *Sāraṅgabharaṇam*

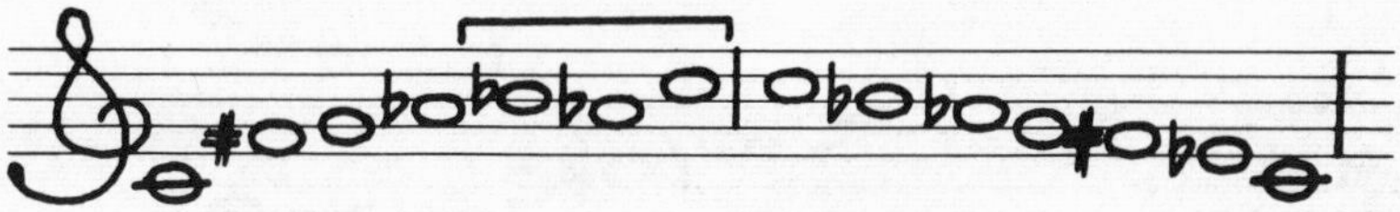

The note *RI* (D) is avoided entirely. In ascent the note *GA* (Eb) is omitted and one *vakra* feature is shown.

(18) *Sumanisarañjaṇi*

The notes *RI* (D) and *DHA* (Ab) are avoided entirely.

(19) *Trimūrti*

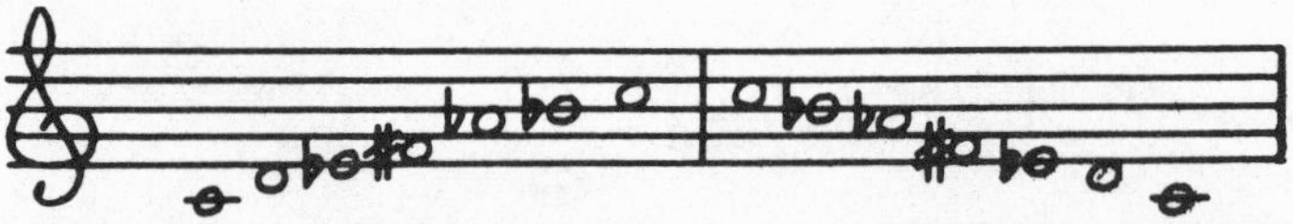

The note *PA* (G) is avoided entirely.

TRIMŪRTI (*Triputa-tāla*) SCM, 246

(20) *Vasugarbha*

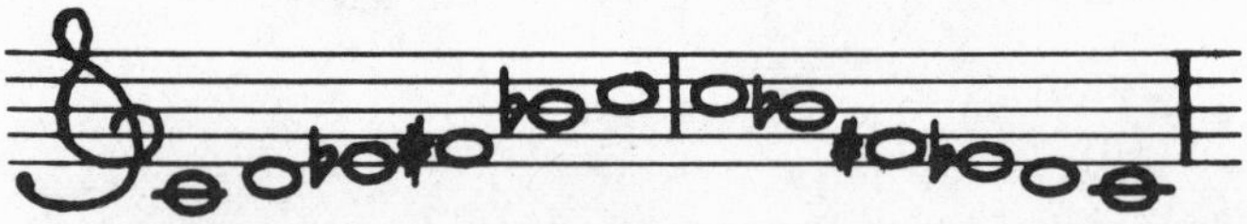

The notes *PA* (G) and *DHA* (Ab) are avoided entirely.

(21) *Vasukari*

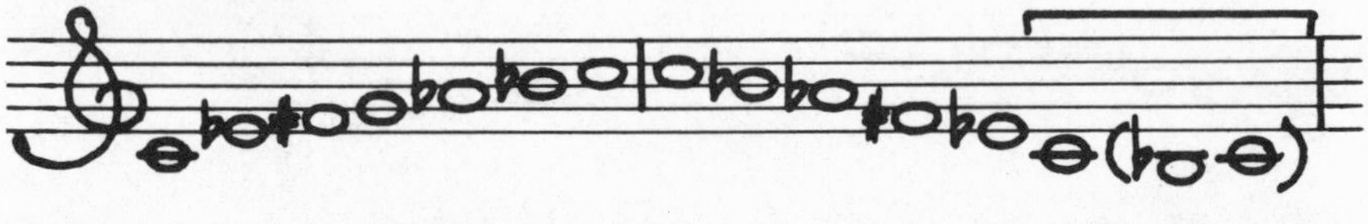

The note *RI* (D) is avoided entirely. *PA* (G) is omitted in descent where one *vakra* feature is shown.

VASUKARI (*Triputa-tāla*) SCM, 248

57. *MĒḶA SIṂHENDRAMADHYAMA*

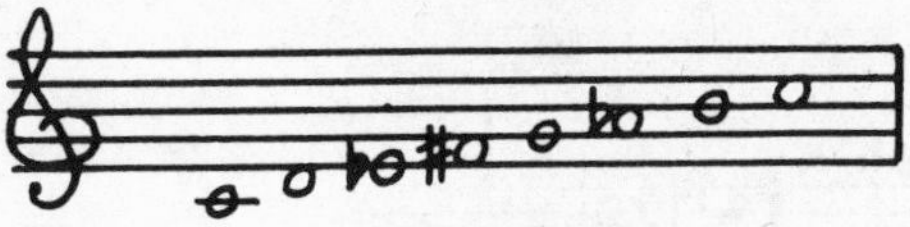

Rāga Siṃhendramadhyama can be performed at any time. Frequently the notes *RI* (D) and *PA* (G) are stressed.

SIṂHENDRAMADHYAMA (*Triputa-tāla*) SCM, 250

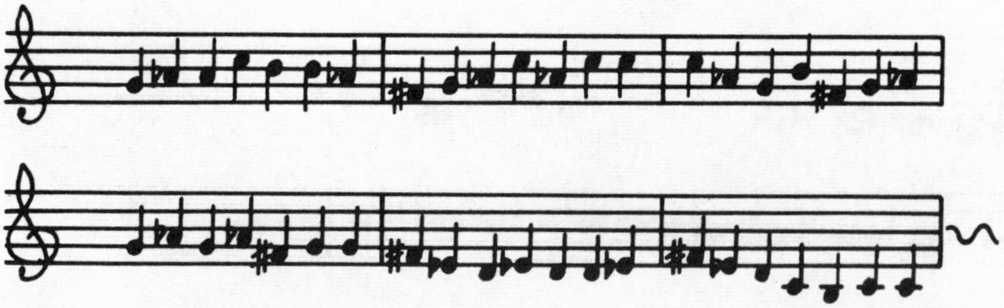

Janya Rāgas of the 57. Mēḷa

(1) *Ādi Varāḷi*

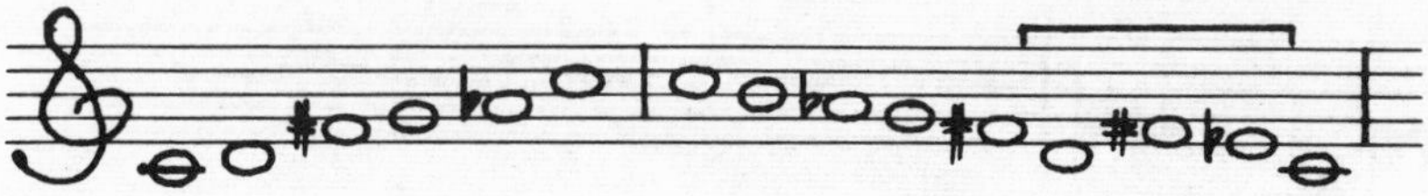

Ascent: the notes *GA* (Eb) and *NI* (B) are avoided.
Descent: *sampūrṇa*; one *vakra* feature is shown.

(2) *Amrita Vasantam*

Ascent: the note *MA* (F#) is avoided.
Descent: the notes *PA* (G) and *RI* (D) are omitted.

(3) *Aruṇakriya*

Ascent: the notes *GA* (Eb) and *DHA* (Ab) are avoided.
Descent: *krama sampūrṇa*.

(4) *Bhramara Haṃsi*

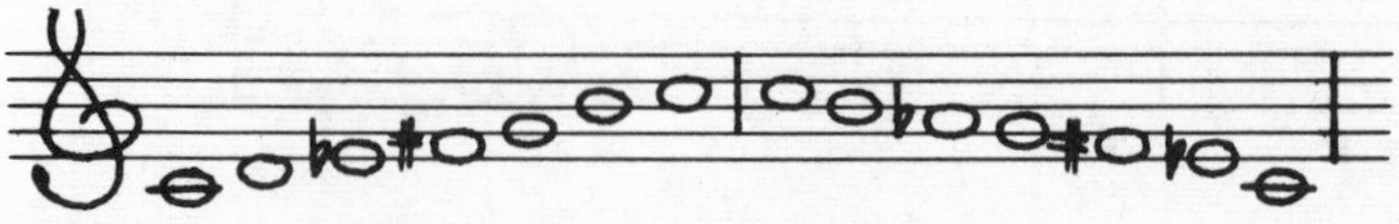

Ascent: the note *DHA* (Ab) is avoided.
Descent: the note *RI* (D) is omitted.

(5) *Bhramara Kōkilam*

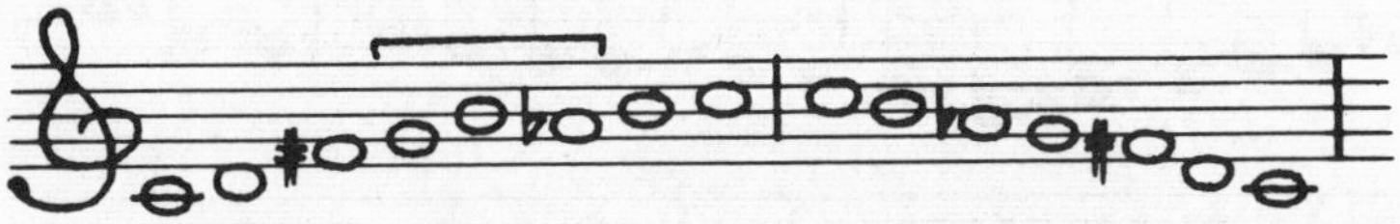

The note *GA* (Eb) is avoided entirely. The ascent shows one *vakra* feature.

(6) *Bhramara Sukhi*

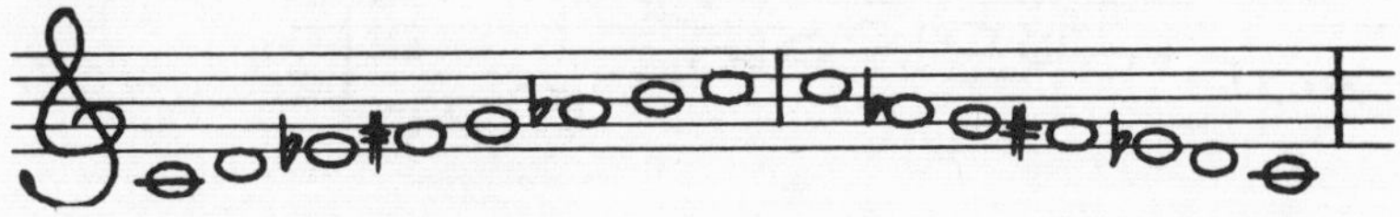

Ascent: *krama sampūrṇa*.
Descent: the note *NI* (B) is avoided.

(7) *Dhavaḷa Haṃsi*

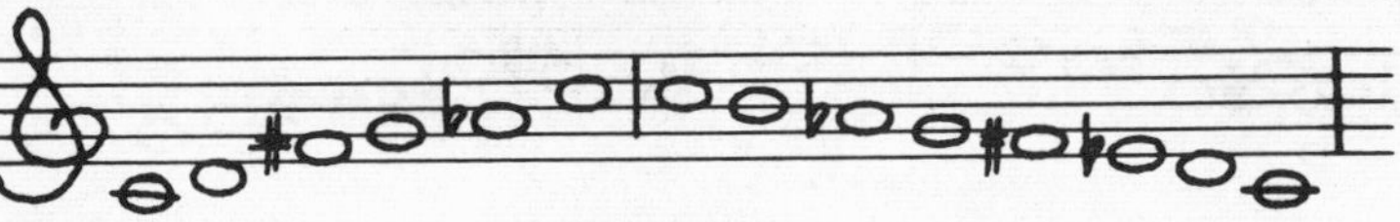

Ascent: the notes *GA* (Eb) and *NI* (B) are avoided.
Descent: *krama sampūrṇa*.

(8) *Ghaṇṭāṇaman* (*Ghottāṇam*)

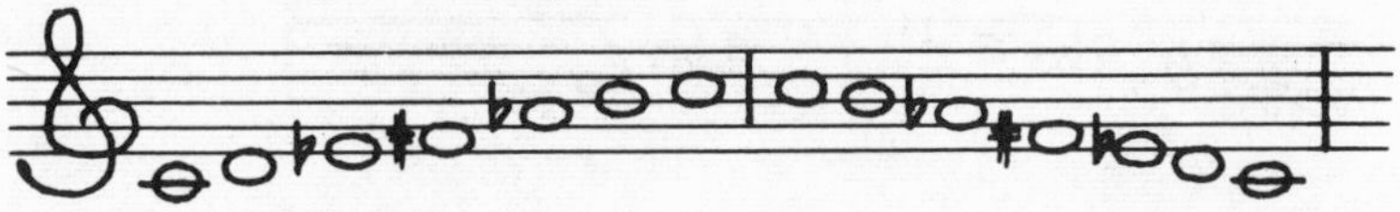

The note *PA* (G) is avoided entirely.

Occasionally the name *Ghaṇṭāṇam* (or *Ghaṇṭāravam*) is used to denote *rāga Ghaṇṭā* (8,9); (see also 2,3).

GHAṆṬĀNAM (*Triputa-tāla*) SCM, 253-54

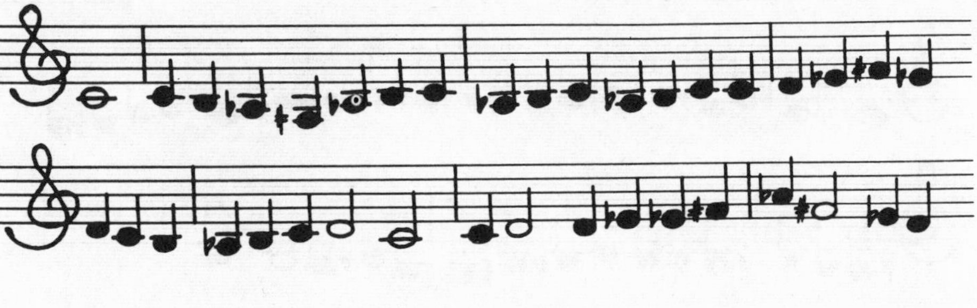

(9) *Ghoshpānī* (*Ghoṣpānī*)

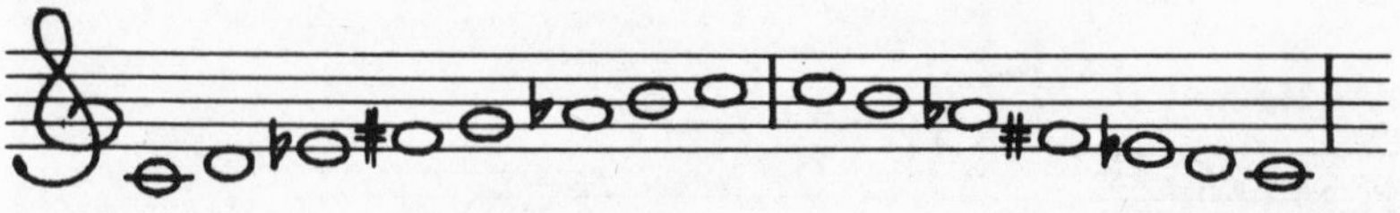

Ascent: *krama sampūrṇa*.
Descent: the note *PA* (G) is avoided.

(10) *Jayasāraṅga*

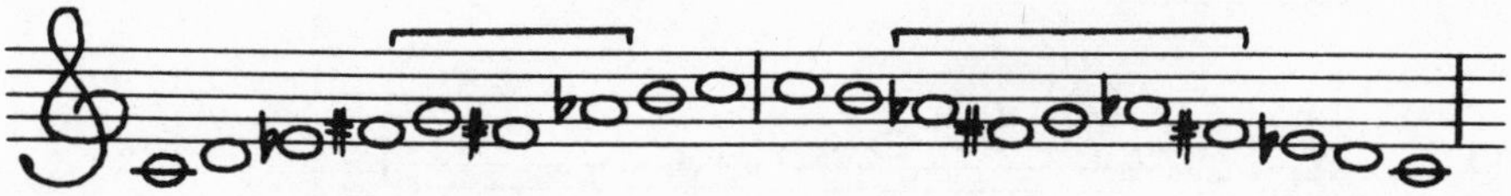

Ascent: *sampūrṇa*; one *vakra* feature is shown.
Descent: *sampūrṇa*; one extended *vakra* passage is used.

(11) *Madhavamanōharī*

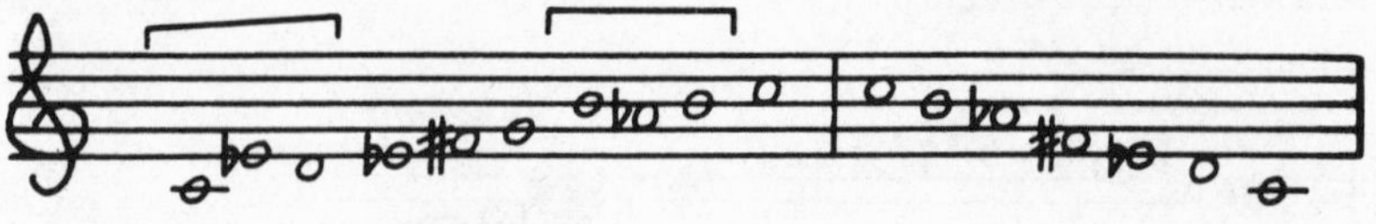

Ascent: *sampūrṇa*; two *vakra* features are shown.
Descent: the note *PA* (G) is avoided.

Veṅkaṭamakhin placed this *rāga* under the heading of his 22. *mē̤la*, in which the note *MA* appeared in its *śuddha* form (F natural).

MADHAVAMANŌHARĪ (*Triputa-tāla*) SCM, 252

(12) *Padmamukhi*

Ascent: the note *PA* (G) is avoided.
Descent: the notes *NI* (B) and *RI* (D) are omitted.

(13) *Ravipriya*

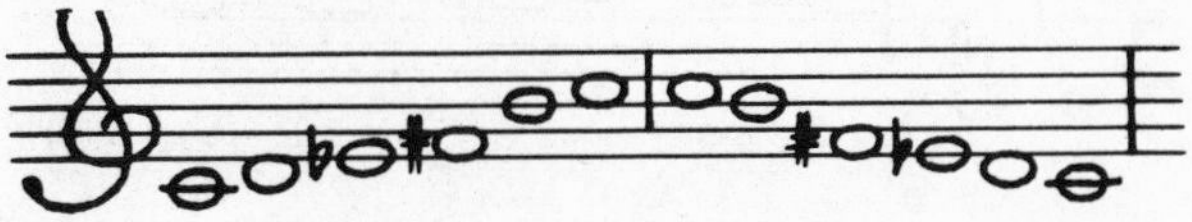

The notes *PA* (G) and *DHA* (Ab) are avoided entirely.

(14) *Savaraṅgi*

The note *PA* (G) is avoided entirely.
Ascent: the note *GA* (Eb) is omitted.
Descent: one *vakra* feature is shown.

SAVARAṄGI (*Triputa-tāla*) SCM, 254-55

(15) *Śeshānada (Śeṣānada)*

Ascent: the note *NI* (B) is avoided.
Descent: *krama sampūrṇa*.

ŚEṢĀNADA (*Triputa-tāla*) SCM, 252-53

(16) *Sīmantī*

Ascent: *krama sampūrṇa*.
Descent: the notes *NĪ* (B) and *DHA* (Ab) are avoided.

SĪMANTĪ (*Triputa-tāla*) SCM, 251

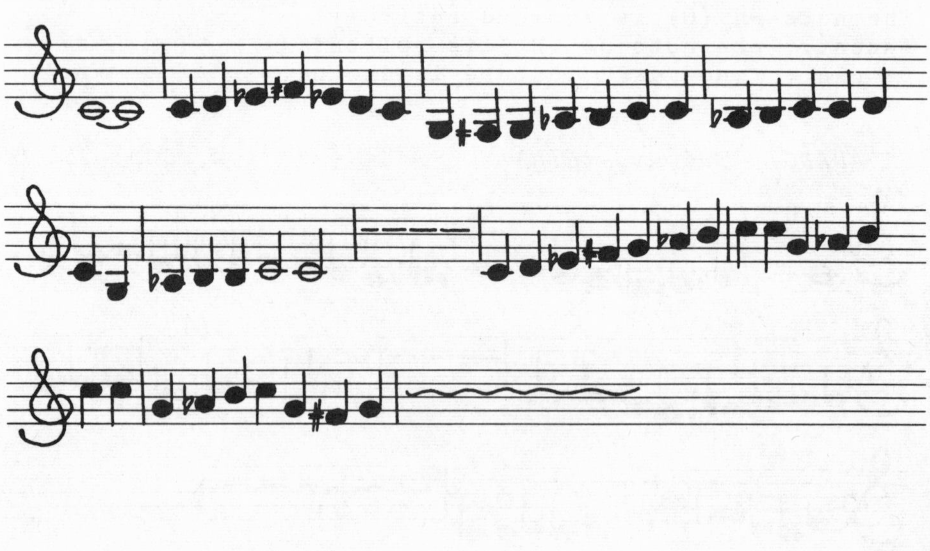

(17) *Śuddharāga*

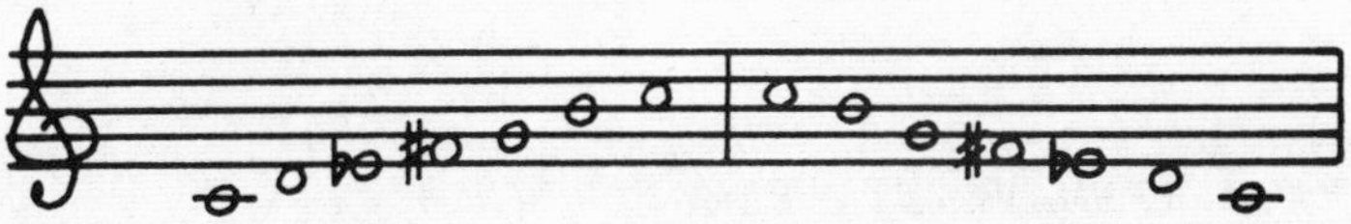

The note *DHA* (Ab) is avoided entirely.
See also *rāga Ūrmika* (57,19).

ŚUDDHARĀGA (*Triputa-tāla*) SCM, 255

(18) *Sundarapriya*

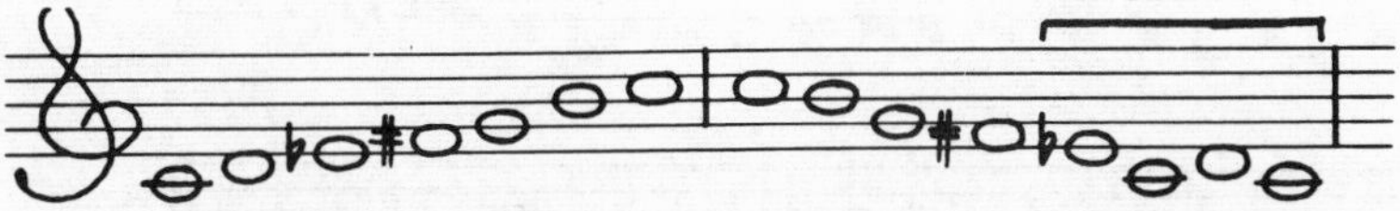

The note *DHA* (Ab) is avoided entirely. One *vakra* feature is shown in descent.

(19) *Ūrmika*

The scale of this *rāga* is identical with that of *Śuddharāga* (57,17). According to R (223), *Ūrmika* is of recent origin and was introduced by Muthiah Bhāgavathar (see n.1, p. 696).

(20) *Vijayasarasvatī*

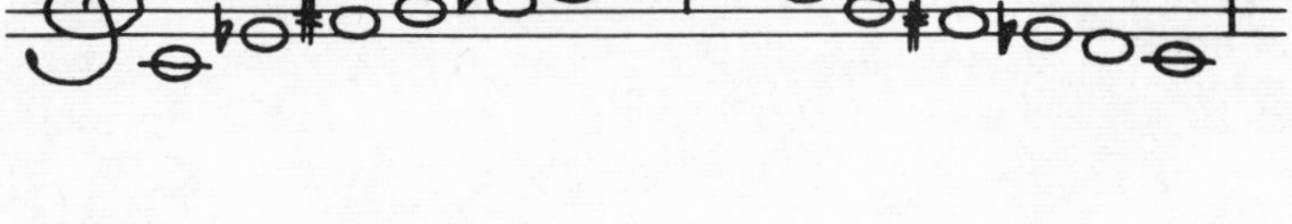

Ascent: the note *RI* (D) is avoided.
Descent: the note *DHA* (Ab) is omitted.

58. *MĒḶA HEMĀVATĪ* (*HEMĀVANTI*, *HEMĀVANTIṆI*)

Rāga Hemāvatī can be performed at any time.

HEMĀVATĪ (*Triputa-tāla*) SCM, 256

Janya Rāgas of the 58. Mēḷa

(1) *Bhramara Puttari*

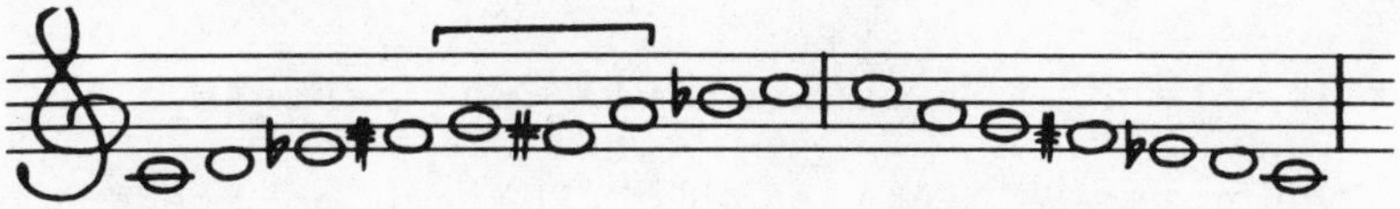

Ascent: *sampūrṇa*; one *vakra* feature is shown.
Descent: the note *NI* (Bb) is avoided.

(2) *Buktipriya*

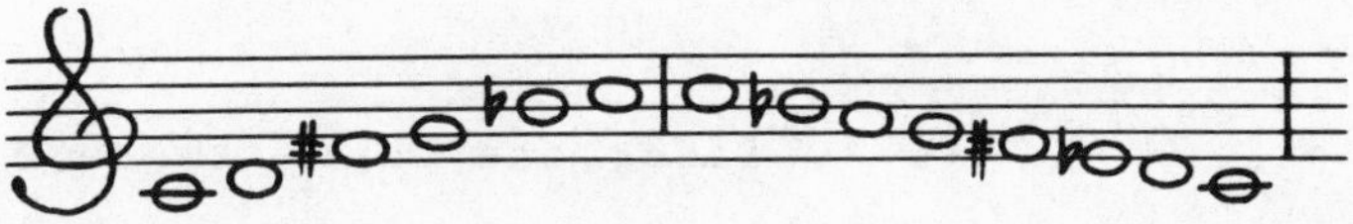

Ascent: the notes *GA* (Eb) and *DHA* (A) are avoided.
Descent: *krama sampūrṇa*

(3) *Chandrarēkhā* (*Chandrarēkhi*, *Candrarēkhā*, *Candrarēkhi*)

The note *NI* (Bb) is avoided entirely.

Another *rāga* with the same name appears under the heading of the 15. *mēḷa* (46).

(4) *Dēśya Śrī*

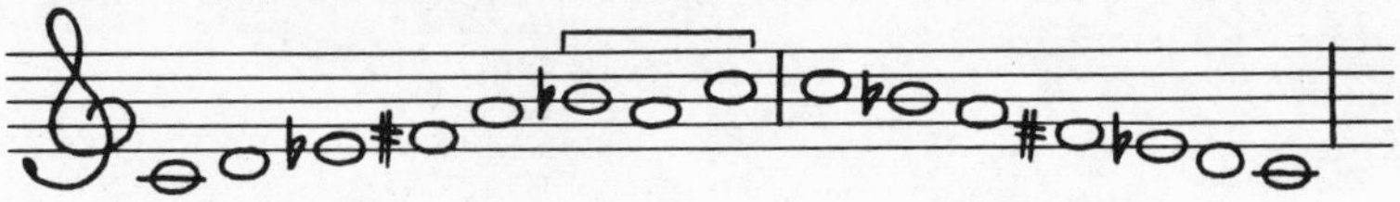

The note *PA* (G) is avoided entirely. One *vakra* feature is shown in ascent.

(5) *Dēvakānta*

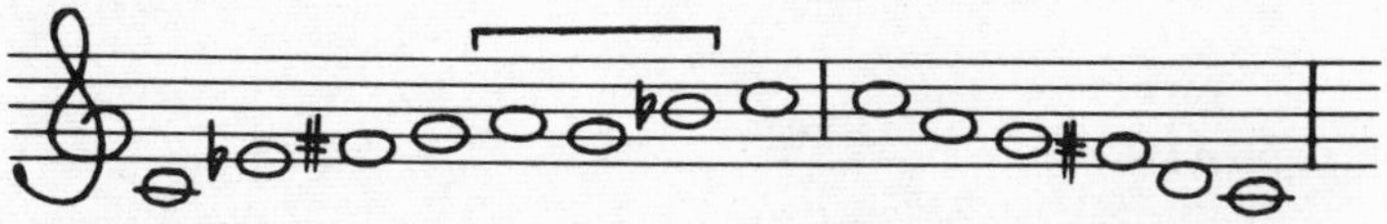

Ascent: the note *RI* (D) is avoided; one *vakra* feature is shown.
Descent: the notes *NI* (Bb) and *GA* (Eb) are omitted.

(6) *Divyasēnā*

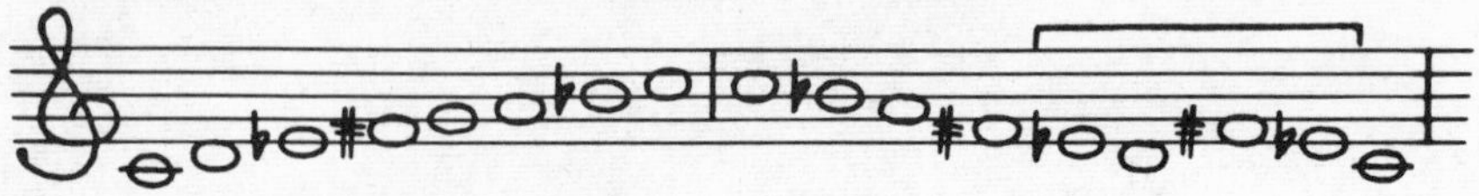

Ascent: *krama sampūrṇa*.
Descent: the note *PA* (G) is avoided; one *vakra* feature is shown.

(7) *Haṃsabhramari*

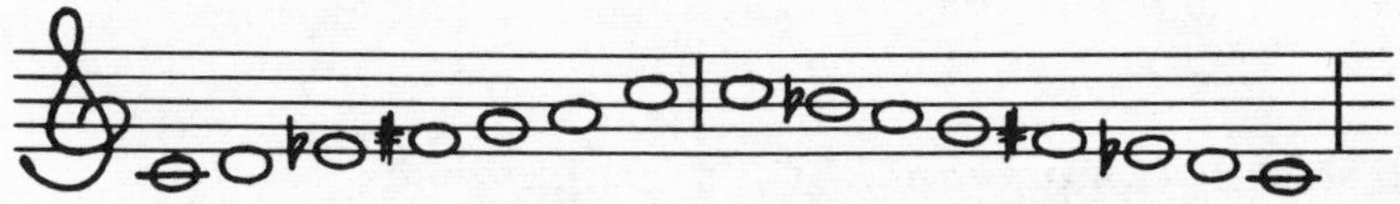

Ascent: the note *NI* (Bb) is avoided.
Descent: *krama sampūrṇa*.

(8) *Hēmāmbari*

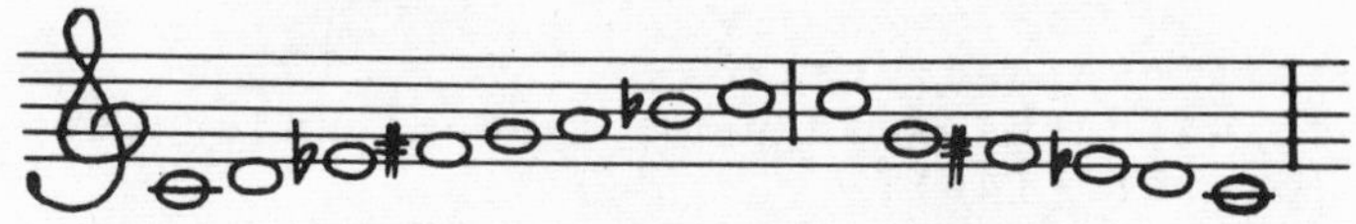

Ascent: *krama sampūrṇa*.
Descent: the notes *NI* (Bb) and *DHA* (A) are avoided.
Another *rāga* with the same name appears under the heading of the 55. *mēḷa* (7).

(9) *Hēmāpriya*

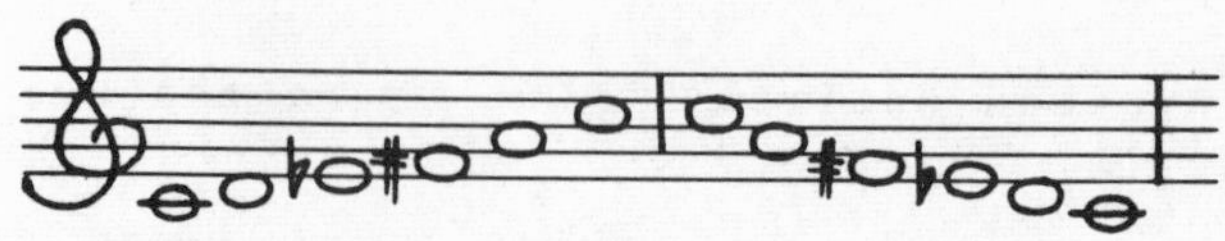

The notes *PA* (G) and *NI* (Bb) are avoided entirely.

(10) *Hēmāvāhini*

Ascent: the note *GA* (Eb) is avoided; one *vakra* feature is shown.
Descent: the notes *NI* (Bb) and *RI* (D) are omitted.

(11) *Kaivasi*

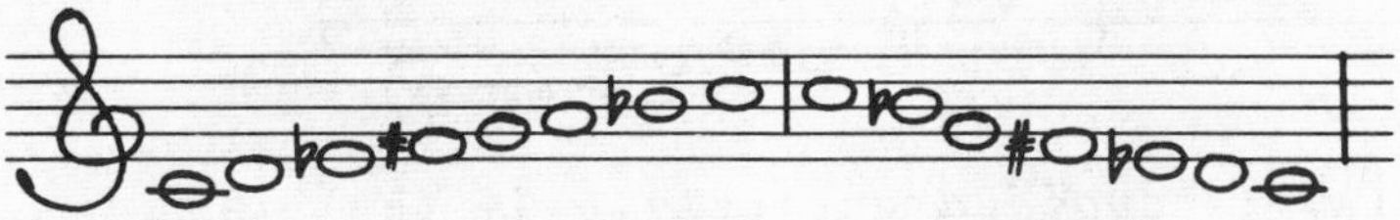

Ascent: *krama sampūrṇa.*
Descent: the note *DHA* (A) is avoided.

(12) *Kanaka Bhūṣavāḷi*

The scale of this *rāga* is identical with that of its primary *rāga Hēmāvati* (58. *mēḷa*). There are a few musicians who maintain that there exists a slight difference between the two *rāgas*, but the descriptions of the difference were too vague to enable me to record them.

(13) *Kēsarāvalōkam*

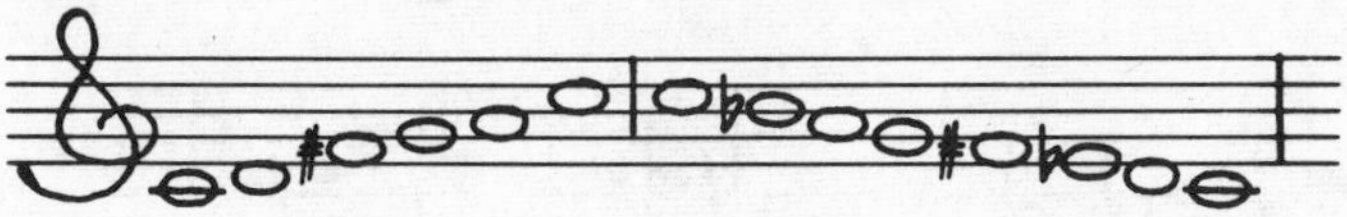

Ascent: the notes *GA* (Eb) and *NI* (Bb) are avoided.
Descent: *krama sampūrṇa.*

(14) *Kshēmakari* (*Kṣēmakari*)

The notes *GA* (Eb) and *PA* (G) are avoided entirely.

(15) *Nalinābhūmaṇi*

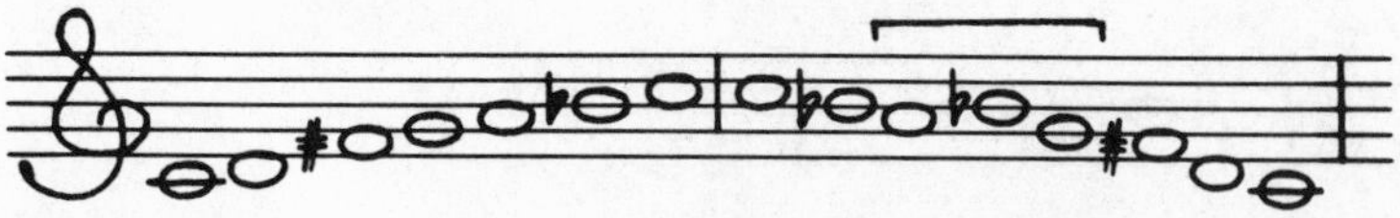

The note *GA* (Eb) is avoided entirely. The descent shows one *vakra* feature.

(16) *Siṃhārava* (*Sinhārava*)

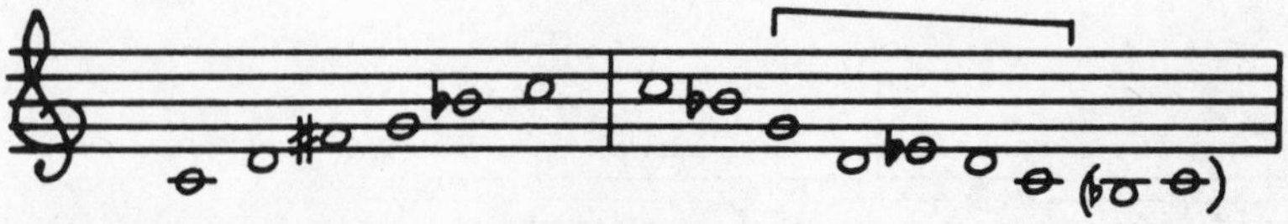

The note *DHA* (A) is *avoided* entirely. *GA* (Eb) is omitted in ascent, *MA* (F#) in descent. One *vakra* feature is shown in descent.

Another descent of this *rāga* can be:

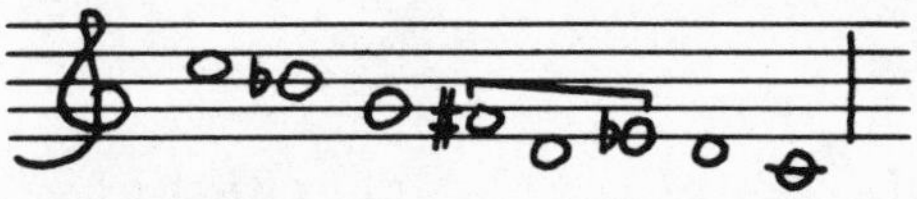

N calls this latter form *Dēśīsiṃhāravam*.

SIṂHĀRAVA (*Triputa-tāla*) SCM, 256-57

(17) *Varata*

The notes *GA* (Eb) and *DHA* (A) are avoided entirely.

(18) *Vijayanāgari*

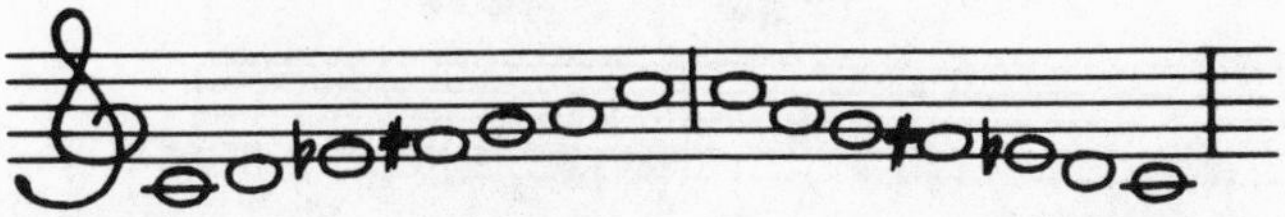

The note *NI* (Bb) is avoided entirely.

(19) *Vijayasāmantam*

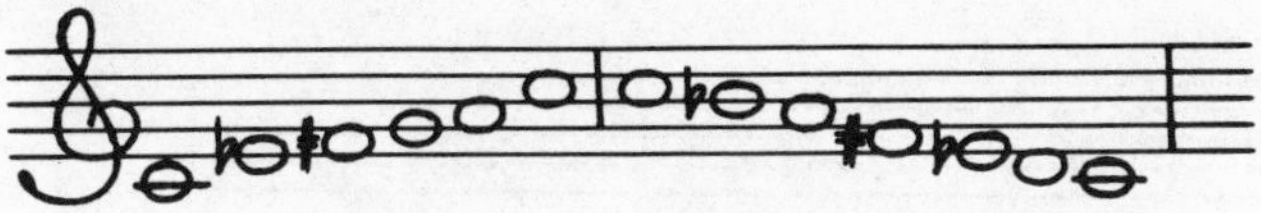

Ascent: the notes *RI* (D) and *NI* (Bb) are avoided.
Descent: the note *PA* (G) is omitted.

Another *rāga* with the same name is listed as 54, 17.

(20) *Yāgiṇi*

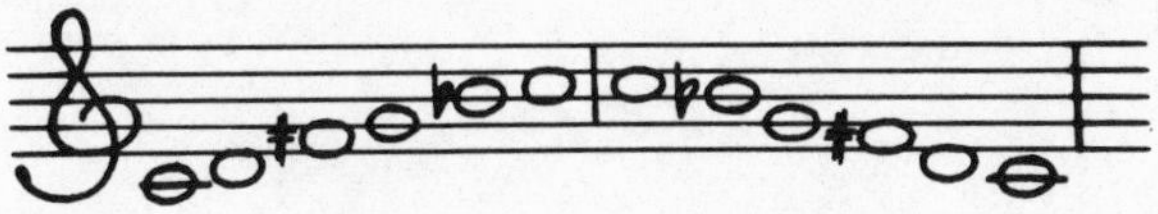

The notes *GA* (Eb) and *DHA* (A) are avoided entirely.

59. *MĒḶA DHARMAVATĪ*

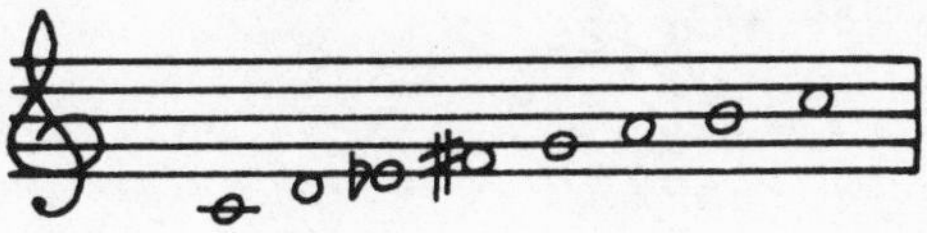

DHARMAVATĪ (*Triputa-tāla*) SCM, 257-8

Janya Rāgas of the 59. Mēḷa

(1) *Aruṇajvalita*

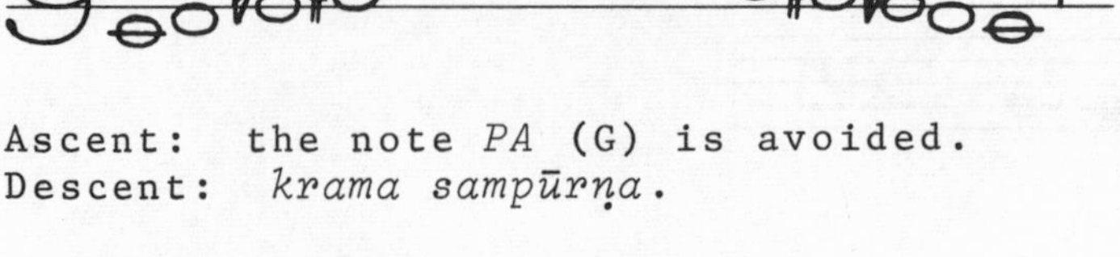

Ascent: the note *PA* (G) is avoided.
Descent: *krama sampūrṇa*.

(2) *Asati*

The notes *RI* (D) and *PA* (G) are avoided entirely.

(3) *Bāla Gambhīrya*

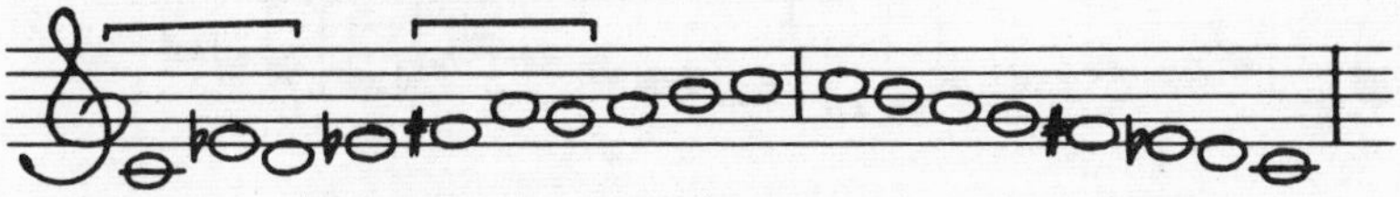

Ascent: *sampūrṇa*; two *vakra* features are shown.
Descent: *krama sampūrṇa*.

(4) *Bhūpāvaḷi*

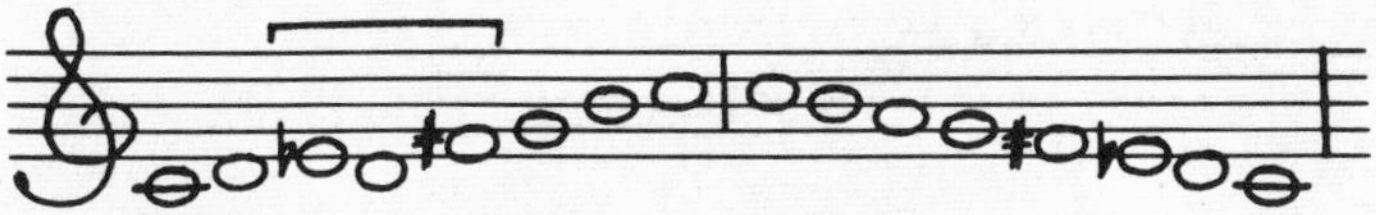

Ascent: the note *DHA* (A) is avoided; one *vakra* feature is shown.
Descent: *krama sampūrṇa*.

(5) *Dāmya*

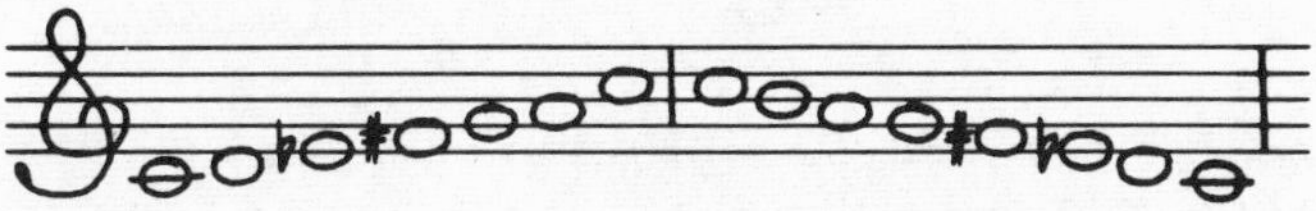

Ascent: the note *NI* (B) is avoided.
Descent: *krama sampūrṇa*.

See *rāga Dhaumya* (59,6).

(6) *Dhaumya Rāgam* (*Dhaumiya Rāgam*)

The *rāgas Damya* (59,5) and *Dhaumya* (59,6) are identical.

DHAUMYA (*Triputa-tāla*) SCM, 258-59

(7) *Dhīrākāri*

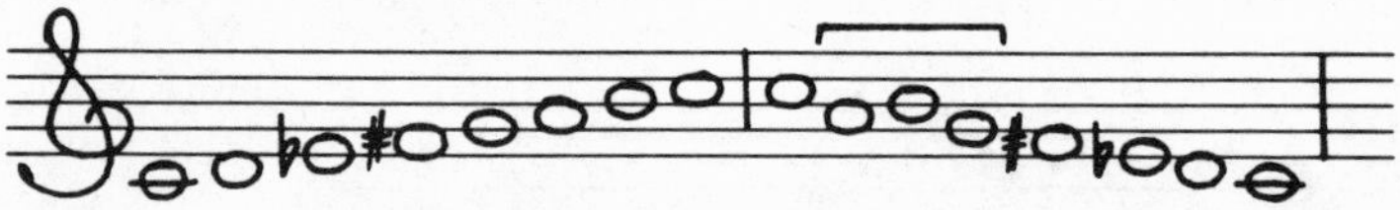

Ascent: *krama sampūrṇa*.
Descent: *sampūrṇa*; one *vakra* feature is shown.

(8) *Dhīra Kuntaḷi*

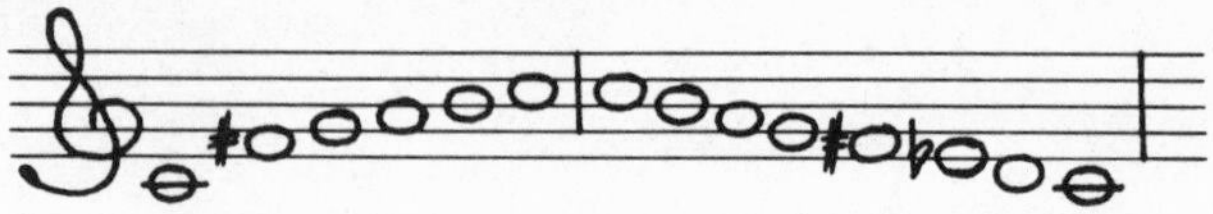

Ascent: the notes *RI* (D) and *GA* (Eb) are avoided.
Descent: *krama sampūrṇa*.

(9) *Garuḍa Varāḷi*

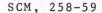

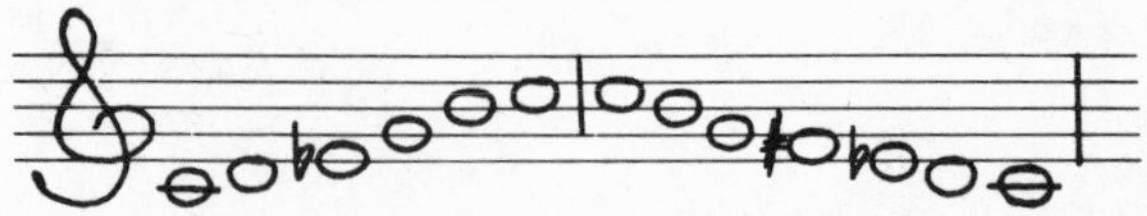

The note *DHA* (A) is avoided entirely. *MA* (F#) is omitted in ascent.

(10) *Kārmukhāvati*

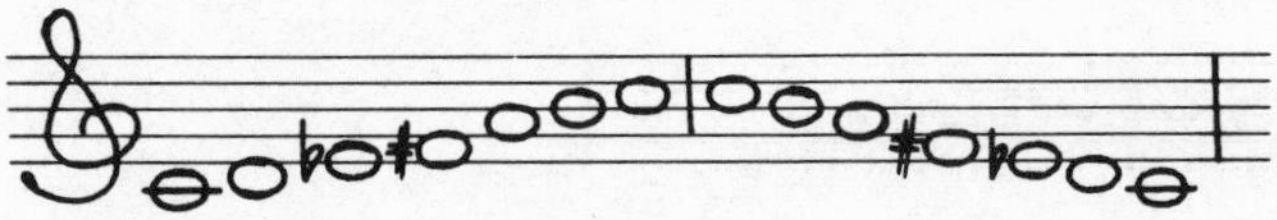

The note *PA* (G) is avoided entirely.

(11) *Lalitasiṃhāravam*

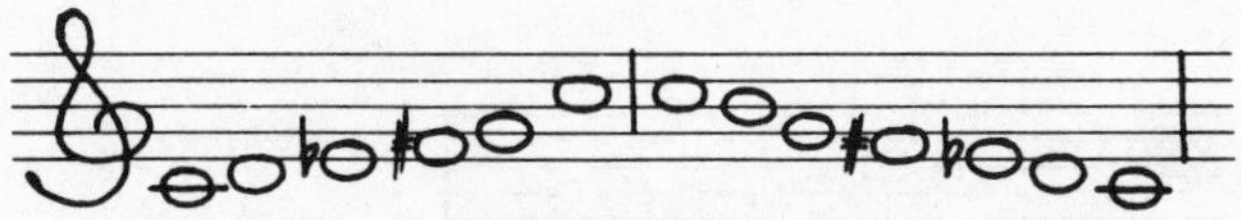

The note *DHA* (A) is avoided entirely. *NI* (B) is omitted in ascent.

Another *rāga* with the same name appears under the heading of the 9. *mēḷa* (13).

(12) *Rañjani*

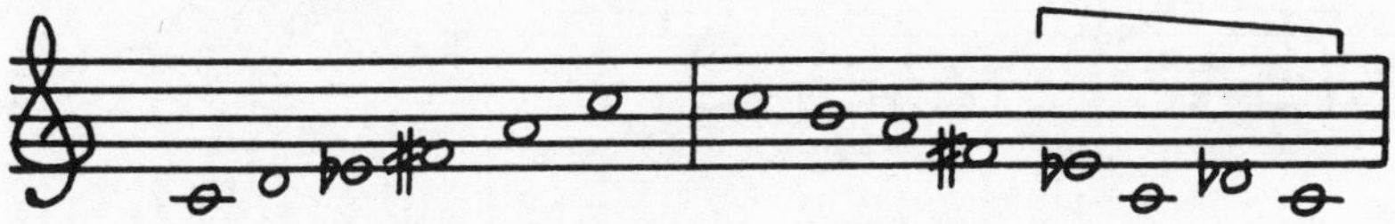

The note *PA* (G) is avoided entirely. *NI* (B) is omitted in ascent. The descent shows one *vakra* feature.

RAÑJANI (*Triputa-tāla*) SCM, 259-60

(13) *Śuddhanavanītam*

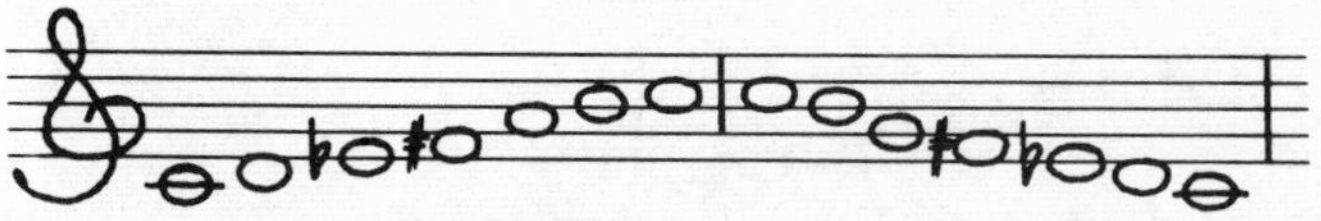

Ascent: the note *PA* (G) is avoided.
Descent: the note *DHA* (A) is omitted.

(14) *Vasantagīrvāṇi*

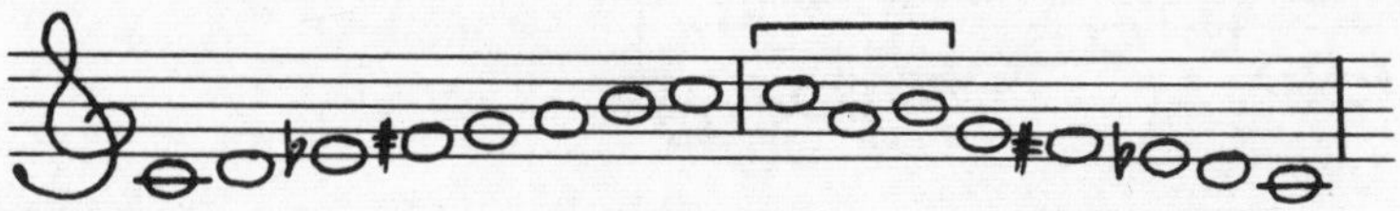

Ascent: *krama sampūrṇa*.
Descent: *sampūrṇa*; one *vakra* feature is shown.

(15) *Vijayaśrīkaṇṭhi*

Ascent: the notes *RI* (D), *DHA* (A), and *NI* (B) are avoided.
Descent: the note *PA* (G) is omitted.

60. *MĒḶA NĪTIMATĪ*

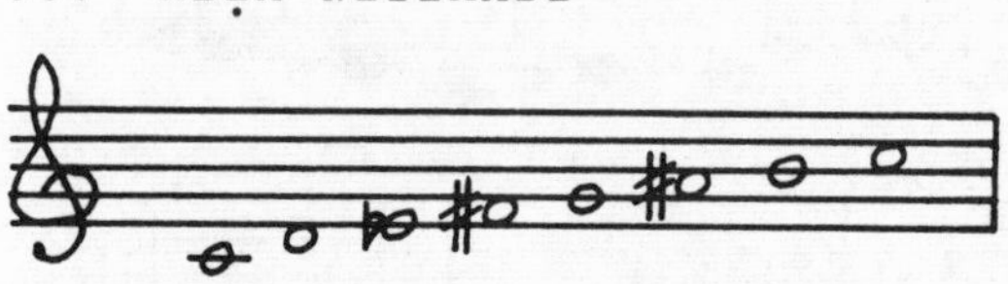

NĪTIMATĪ (*Triputa-tāla*) SCM, 260

Janya Rāgas of the 60. Mēḷa

(1) *Bālacharitra* (*Bālacaritra*)

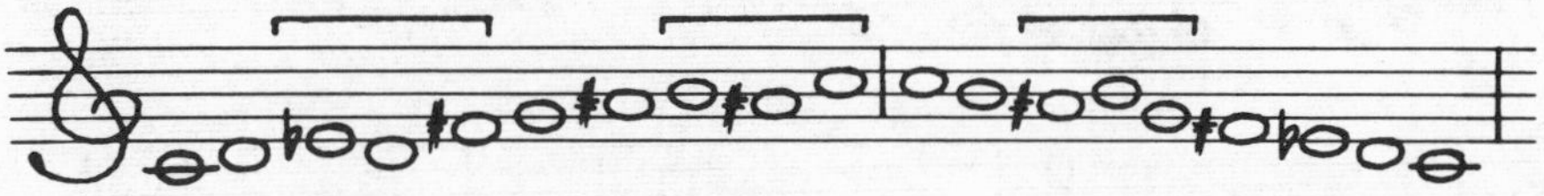

Ascent: *sampūrṇa*; two *vakra* features are shown.
Descent: *sampūrṇa*; one *vakra* feature is used.

(2) *Dēśya Gānavāridhi*

Ascent: *sampūrṇa*; one *vakra* feature is shown.
Descent: the note *DHA* (A#) is avoided; one *vakra* feature is used.

(3) *Dēva Kusumāvaḷi*

The note *DHA* (A#), a characteristic feature of the 60. *mēḷa* and its *janya rāgas*, is avoided entirely; hence this *rāga* can also be ascribed to the 59. *mēḷa*. In ascent the notes *RI* (D) and *NI* (B) are omitted and one *vakra* feature is used.

(4) *Gaurī Kriya*

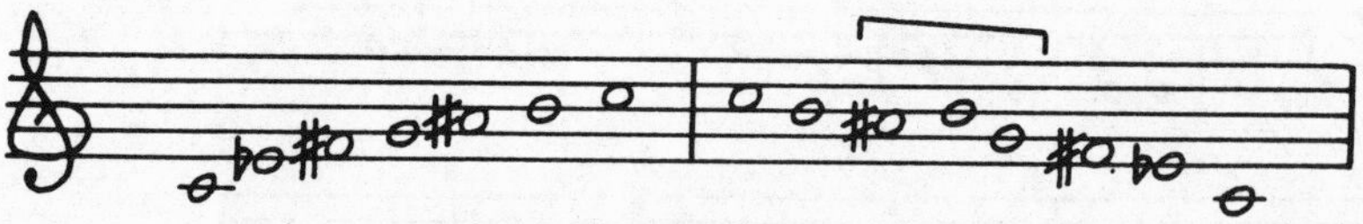

The note *RI* (D) is avoided entirely. The descent shows one *vakra* feature.

GAURĪKRIYA (*Triputa-tāla*) SCM, 262

(5) *Haṃsa Nādam*

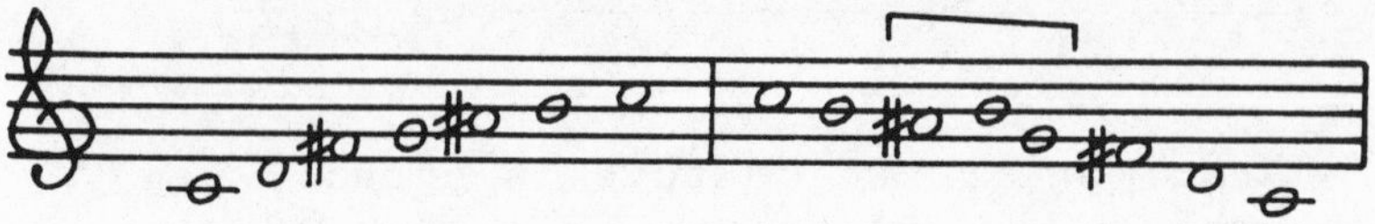

The note *GA* (Eb) is avoided entirely, hence this *rāga* can also be ascribed to the 66. *mēḷa*. The descent shows one *vakra* feature.

HAṂSANĀDAM (*Triputa-tāla*) SCM, 262

(6) *Hēmalatā*

The notes *PA* (G) and *NI* (B) are avoided entirely.

(7) *Kaikavaśi*

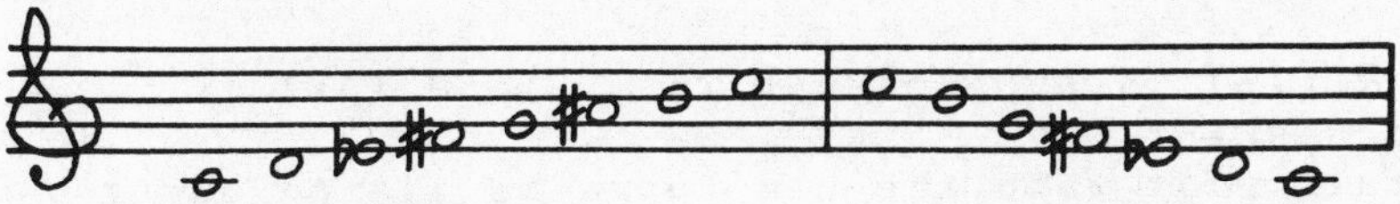

Ascent: *krama sampūrṇa*.
Descent: the note *DHA* (A#) is avoided.

KAIKAVAŚI (*Triputa-tāla*) SCM, 263

(8) *Kamalu*

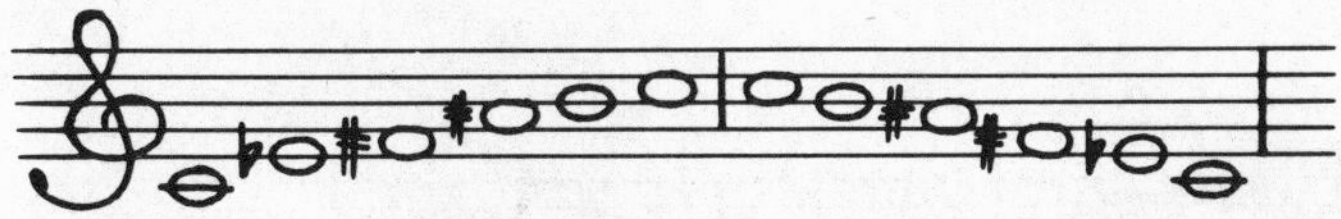

The notes *RI* (D) and *PA* (G) are avoided entirely.

(9) *Kanaka Śrīkaṇṭhi*

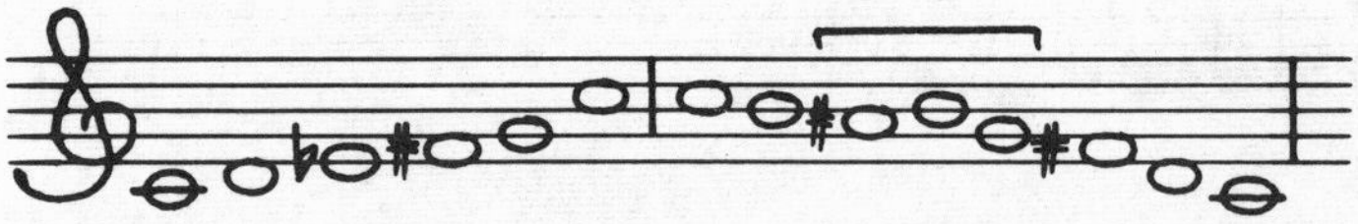

Ascent: the notes *DHA* (A#) and *NI* (B) are avoided.
Descent: the note *GA* (Eb) is omitted; one *vakra* feature is shown.

(10) *Kantimati*

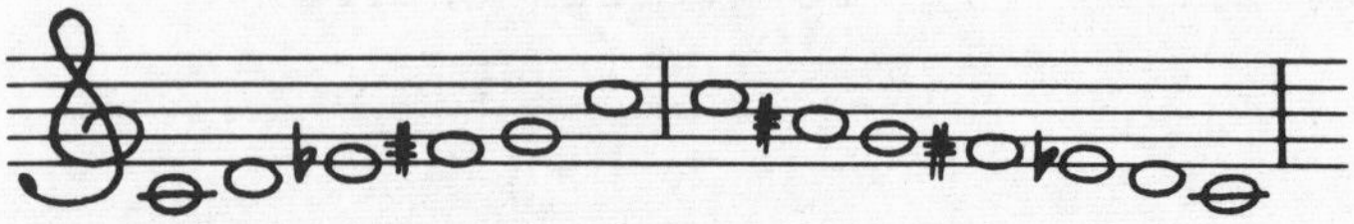

The note *NI* (B) is avoided entirely. *DHA* (A#) is omitted in ascent.

Another *rāga* with the same name is listed under the heading of the 31. *mēḷa* (10).

(11) *Kētāramañjari*

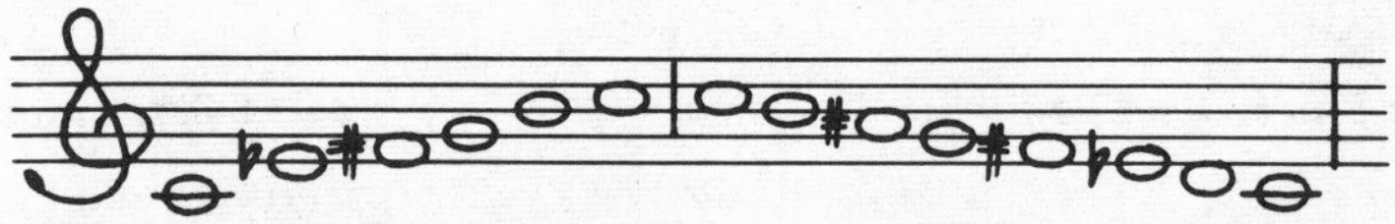

Ascent: the notes *RI* (D) and *DHA* (A#) are avoided.
Descent: *krama sampūrṇa*.

(12) *Niṣāda*

Ascent: the notes *DHA* (A#) and *NI* (B) are avoided; one *vakra* feature is shown.
Descent: *sampūrṇa*; one extended *vakra* feature is used.

NIṢĀDA (*Triputa-tāla*) SCM, 261

(13) *Śuddhagaurīkriya*

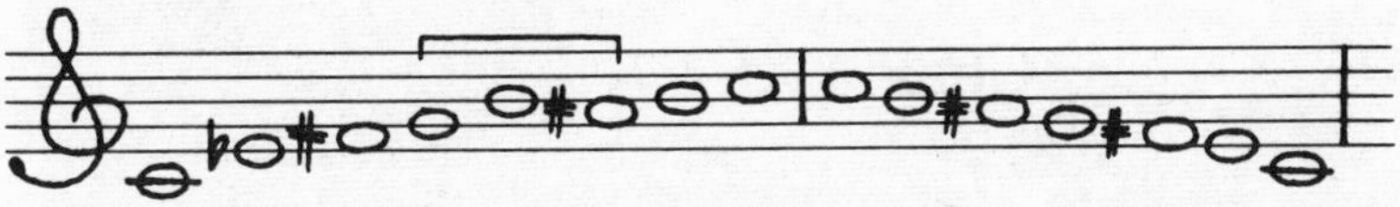

The note *RI* (D) is avoided entirely. One *vakra* feature appears in ascent.

(14) *Vijayanāgari*

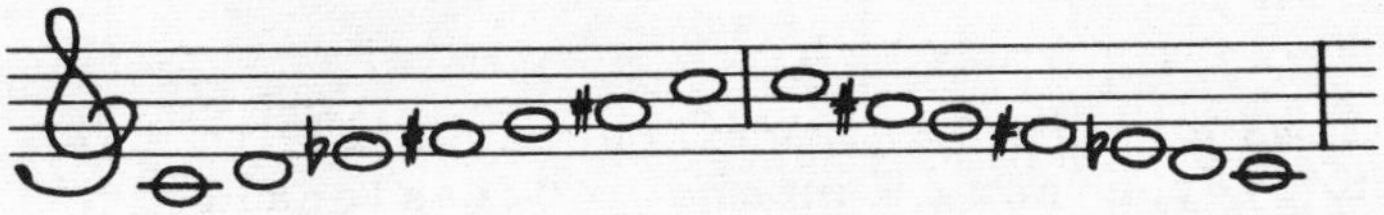

The note *NI* (B) is avoided entirely.

Chakra XI

61. *MĒḶA KĀNTĀMAṆI*

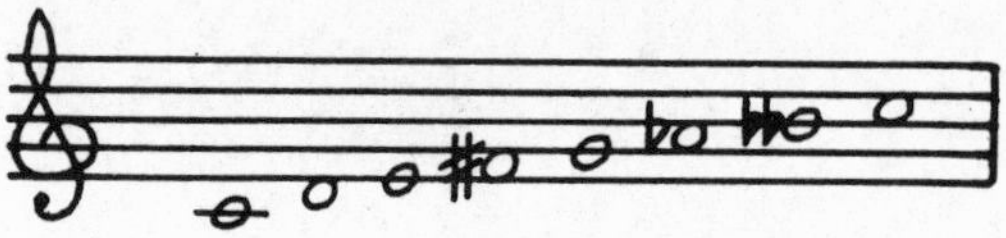

The current *mēḷa Kāntāmaṇi* was represented in the *asampūrṇa* system by the name *Kuntala*. Occasionally the name *Kuntala* is still employed at the present time whenever the tone material of *Kāntāmaṇi* is used. The scale of *rāga Kuntala*, in contrast to the *krama sampūrṇa* character of the *Kāntāmaṇi* scale, is characterized by two *vakra* features which need not appear at every possible opportunity. The features are: *NI-DHA-SA* (Bbb-Ab-c) in ascent and *GA-MA-RI-SA* (E-F#-D-C) in descent.

The first of the following melody specimens (called *Kāntāmaṇi* in SCM) shows the typical *Kuntala vakra* feature in ascent. The second short specimen shows the other *vakra* feature of *Kuntala* in descent.

Another *rāga Kuntala*, structurally but not tonally related to *Kāntāmaṇi*, is listed as 16, 29.

KĀNTĀMAṆI (*Triputa-tāla*) SCM, 264-5

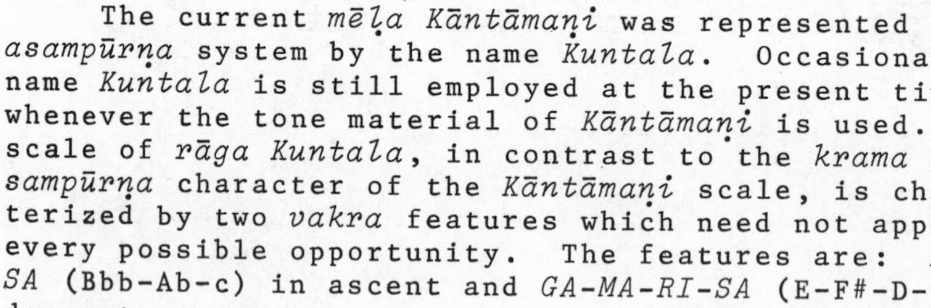

KUNTALA (*Triputa-tāla*) SCM, 265

Janya Rāgas of the 61. Mēḷa

(1) *Bhāmāmaṇi*

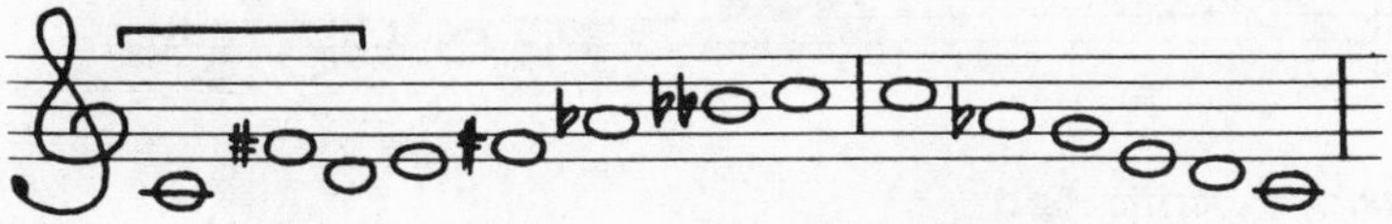

Ascent: the note *PA* (G) is avoided; one *vakra* feature is shown.
Descent: the notes *NI* (Bbb) and *MA* (F#) are omitted.

Another *rāga* with the same name is listed under the heading of the 15. *mēḷa* (39).

(2) *Chambaulani* (*Cambaulani*)

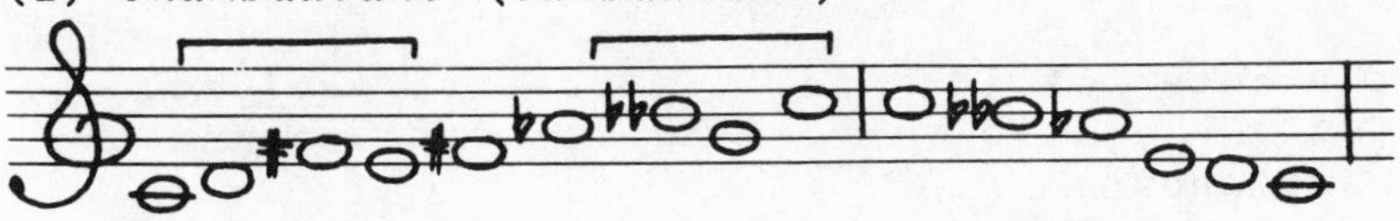

Ascent: *sampūrṇa*; two *vakra* features are shown.
Descent: the notes *PA* (G) and *MA* (F#) are avoided.

(3) *Divya Tōraṇi*

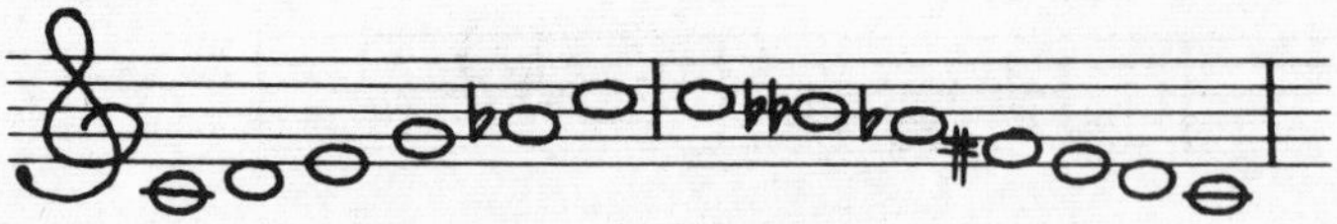

Ascent: the notes *MA* (F#) and *NI* (Bbb) are avoided.
Descent: the note *PA* (G) is omitted.

(4) *Dvipavati*

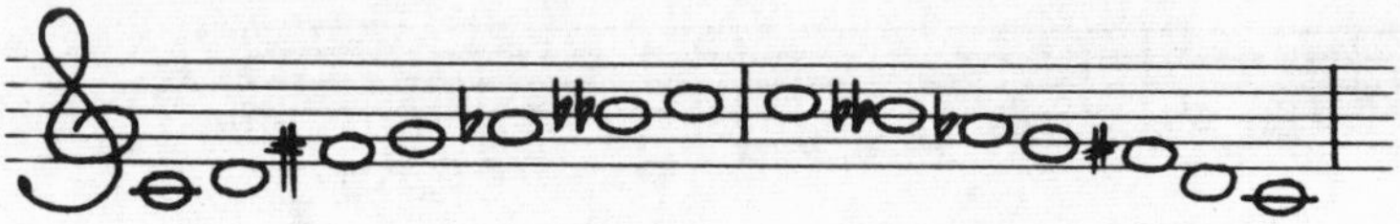

The note *GA* (E) is avoided entirely.

(5) *Gurujyōti*

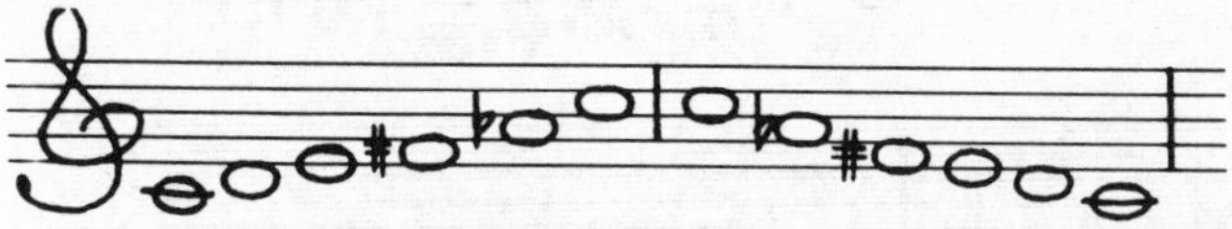

The notes *PA* (G) and *NI* (Bbb) are avoided entirely.

(6) *Jyōtīrañjani*

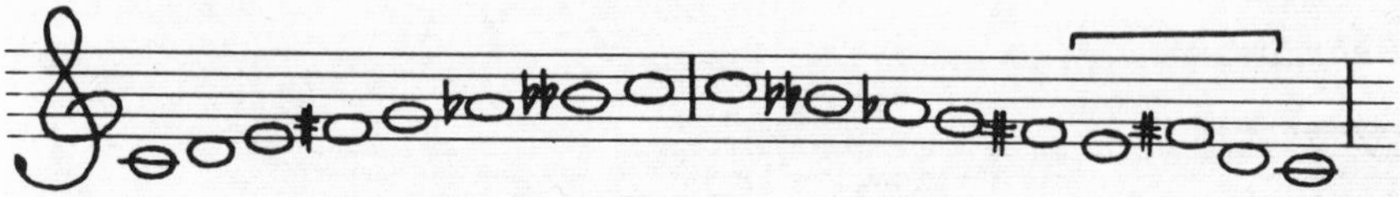

Ascent: *krama sampūrṇa*.
Descent: *sampūrṇa*; one *vakra* feature is shown.

(7) *Kaivēṇi*

Ascent: the notes *GA* (E) and *NI* (Bbb) are avoided.
Descent: *sampūrṇa*; two *vakra* features, the second one extended, are shown.

(8) *Kanaka Kusumāvaḷi*

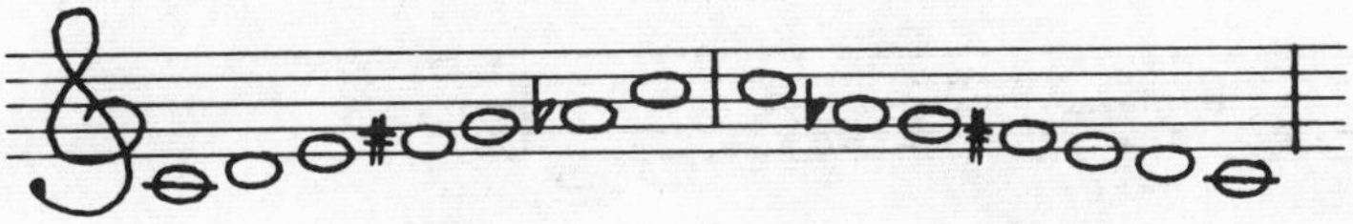

The note *NI* (Bbb) is avoided entirely. This omission allows musicians and theorists to ascribe this *rāga* also to the 62. *mēḷa*.

(9) *Kanaka Siṃhāravam*

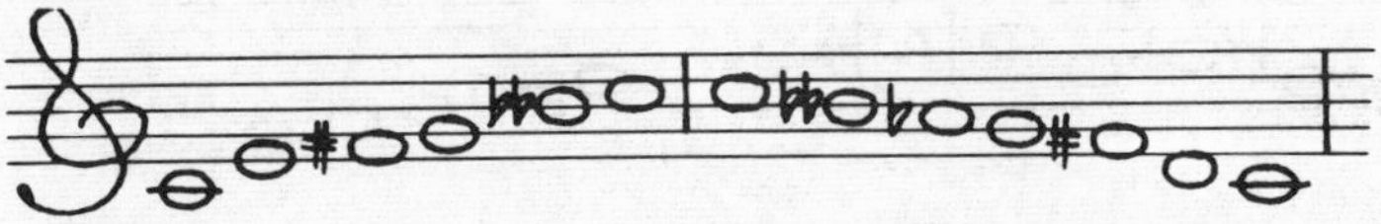

Ascent: the notes *RI* (D) and *DHA* (Ab) are avoided.
Descent: the note *GA* (E) is omitted.

(10) *Kandāvaḷi*

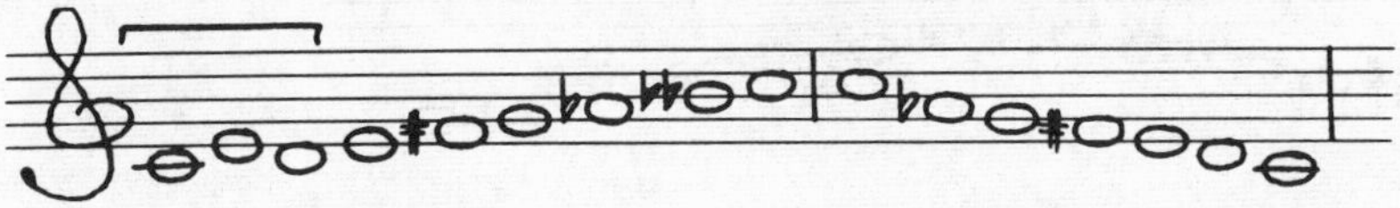

Ascent: *sampūrṇa*; one *vakra* feature is shown.
Descent: the note *NI* (Bbb) is avoided.

(11) *Kāntā Ratna*

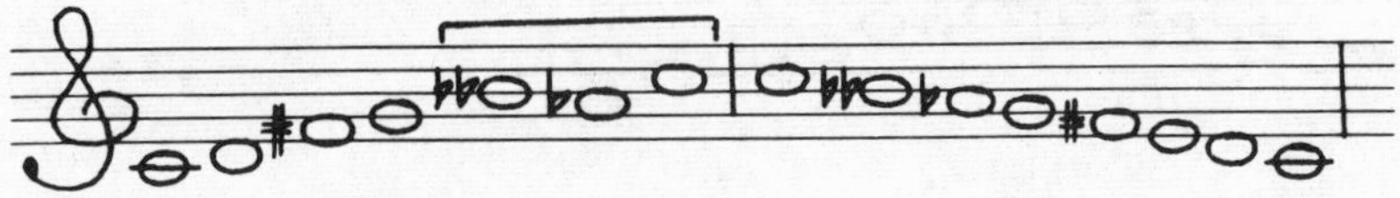

Ascent: the note *GA* (E) is avoided; one *vakra* feature is shown.
Descent: *krama sampūrṇa*.

(12) *Kantisvarūpiṇi*

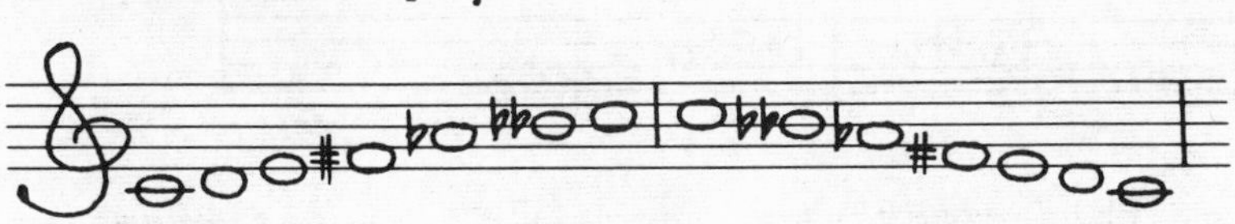

The note *PA* (G) is avoided entirely.

(13) *Karṇāṭaka Taraṅgiṇi*

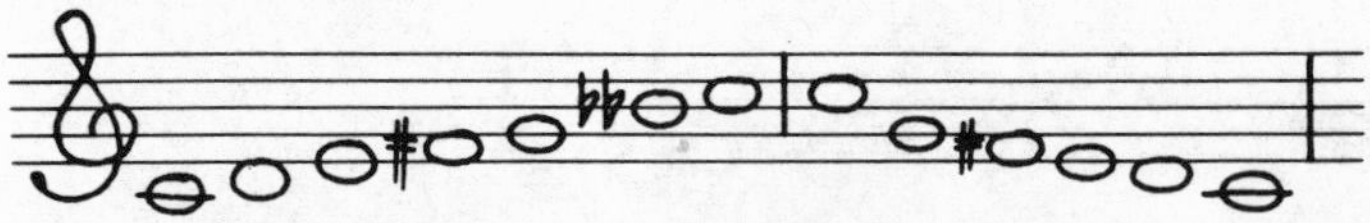

The note *DHA* (Ab) is avoided entirely. *NI* (Bbb) is omitted in descent.

(14) *Kīrtivijaya*

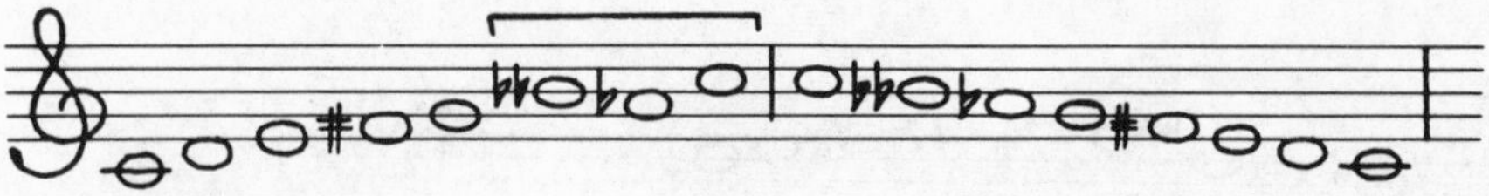

Ascent: *sampūrṇa*; one *vakra* feature is shown.
Descent: *krama sampūrṇa*.

(15) *Rāmakusumāvaḷi*

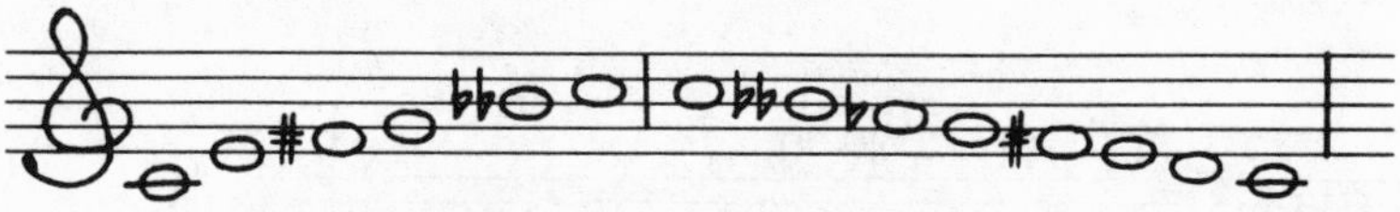

Ascent: the notes *RI* (D) and *DHA* (Ab) are avoided.
Descent: *krama sampūrṇa*.

(16) *Sputalāpiṇi*

The notes *RI* (D) and *DHA* (Ab) are avoided entirely.

Another *rāga* with the same name appears under the heading of the 72. *mēḷa* (11).

(17) *Śrutirañjaṇi*

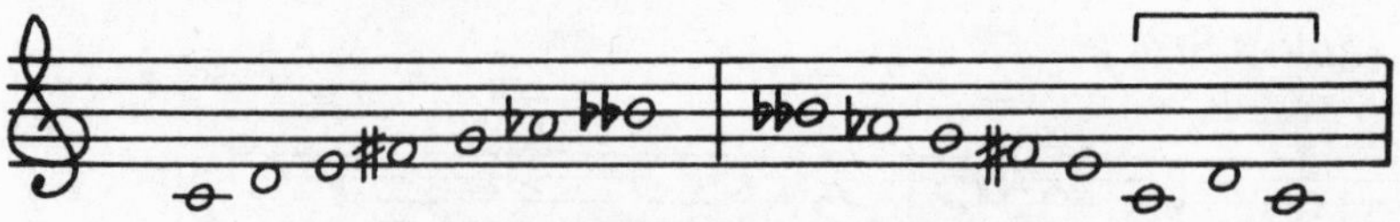

The scale of this *niṣādāntya rāga* is in ascent *krama sampūrṇa*. In descent it is *sampūrṇa*; one *vakra* feature is shown.

The following melody specimen does not show the indicated *vakra* feature in descent:

ŚRUTIRAÑJAṆI (*Triputa-tāla*) SCM, 266

(18) *Śuddhajyotiṣmati*

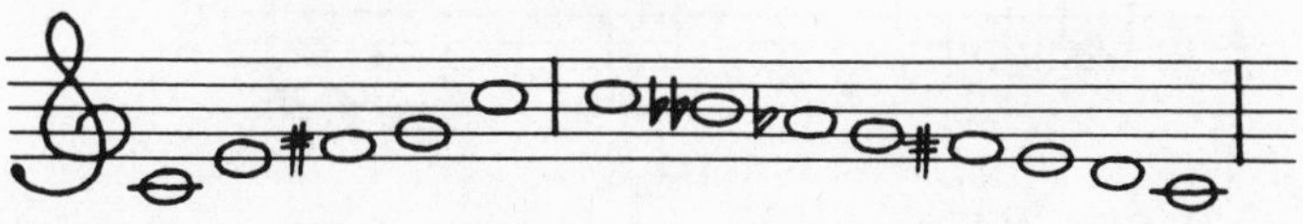

Ascent: the notes *RI* (D), *DHA* (Ab), and *NI* (Bbb) are avoided.
Descent: *krama sampūrṇa*.

(19) *Vijayadīpika*

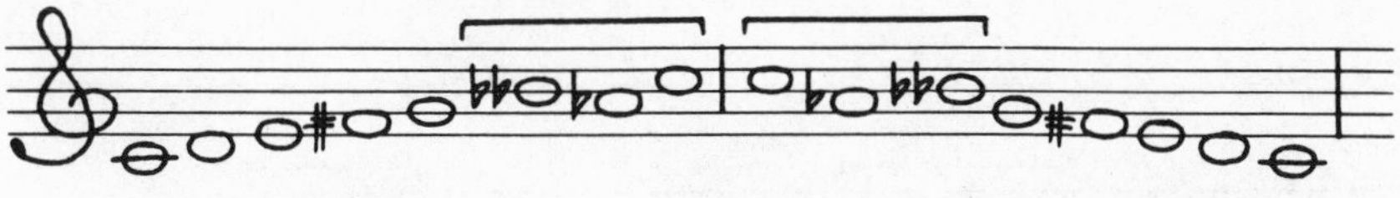

The scale of this *rāga* is *sampūrṇa* and shows two *vakra* features, one in ascent and one in descent.

62. *MĒḶA RIṢABHAPRIYĀ* (*RUṢABHAPRIYĀ*)

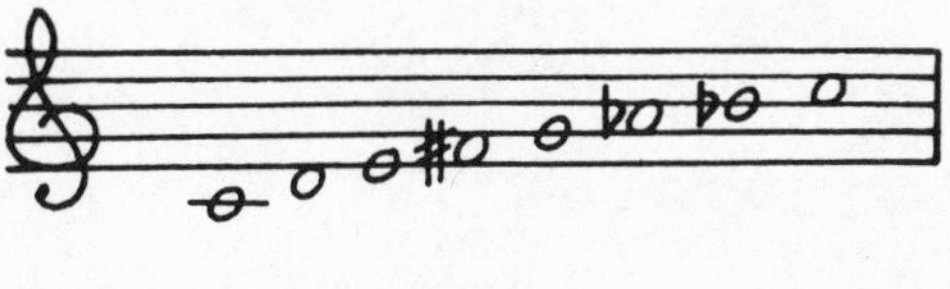

RIṢABHAPRIYĀ (*Triputa-tāla*) SCM, 266-7

Janya Rāgas of the 62. Mēḷa

The names of the first three *janya rāgas*, *Ābradēśi*, *Āmradēśi*, and *Āpradēśi*, represent variants of the same *rāga*. The differences between the three forms appear in the descents. In practice they are not always clearly distinguished from each other and occasionally some confusion can be observed.

(1) *Ābradēśi*

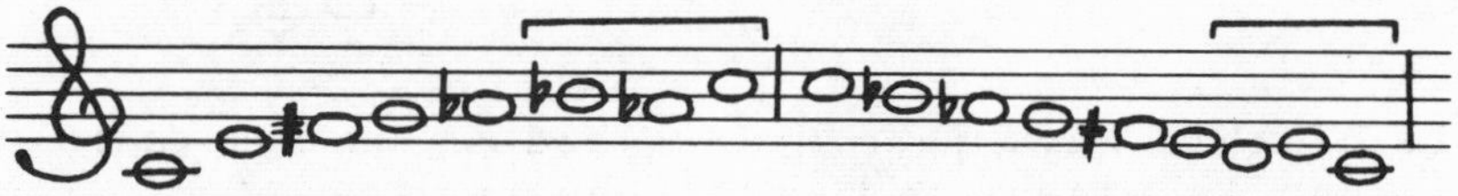

Ascent: the note *RI* (D) is avoided; one *vakra* feature is shown.
Descent: *sampūrṇa*; one *vakra* feature is used.

(2) *Āmradēśi*

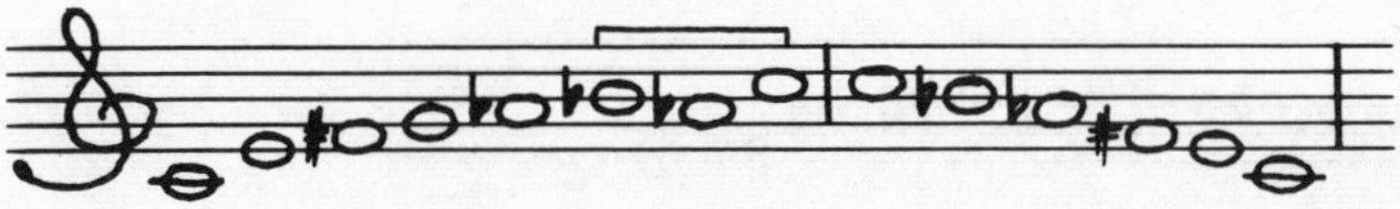

The note *RI* (D) is avoided entirely. One *vakra* feature appears in ascent and the note *PA* (G) is omitted in descent.

(3) *Āpradēśi*

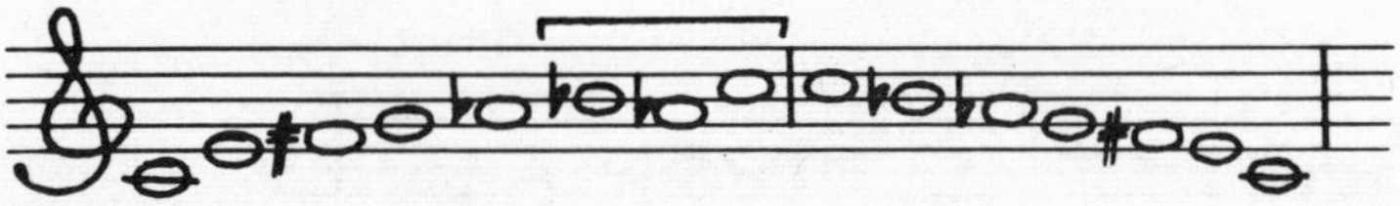

The note *RI* (D) is avoided entirely; one *vakra* feature is shown in ascent.

(4) *Bhṛngadhvani* (*Bhringadhvani*)

The note *RI* (D) is avoided entirely.

(5) *Bṛndāvana Deśākshi* (*Brindavana Deśākṣi*)

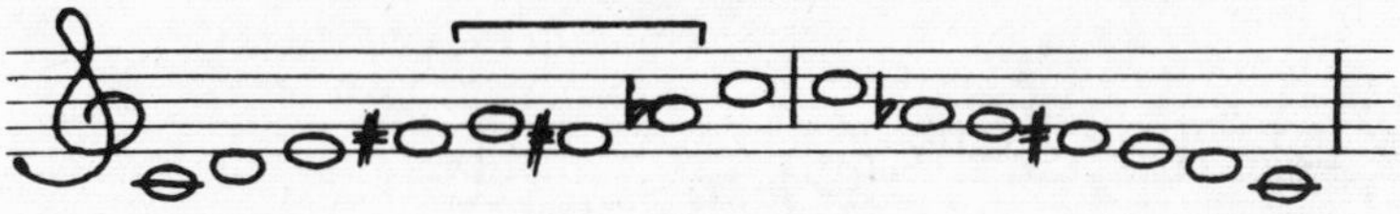

The note *NI* (Bb) is avoided. One *vakra* feature is shown in ascent.

(6) *Gōkulamūrti*

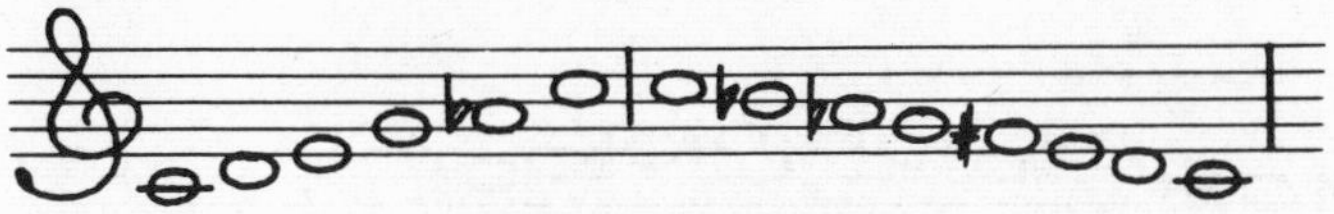

Ascent: the notes *MA* (F#) and *NI* (Bb) are avoided.
Descent: *krama sampūrṇa*.

(7) *Gōpriya*

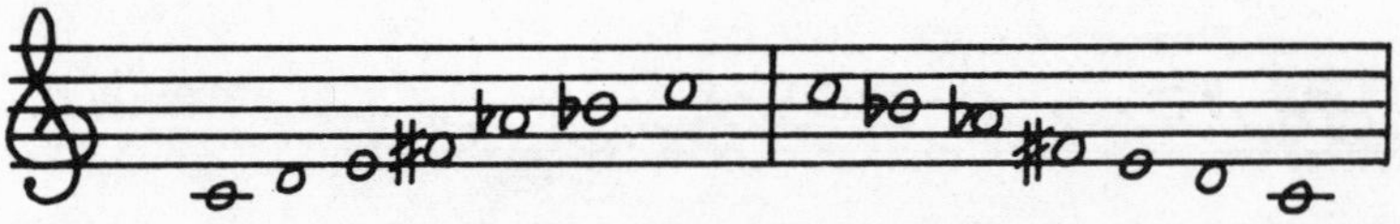

The note *PA* (G) is avoided entirely. This scale can be compared with the western whole-tone scale. As far as I know not one single known song has been created in this *rāga*.

(8) *Kanaka Nāsāmani*

Ascent: *sampūrṇa*; one *vakra* feature is shown.
Descent: *krama sampūrṇa*.

(9) *Katyayanī*

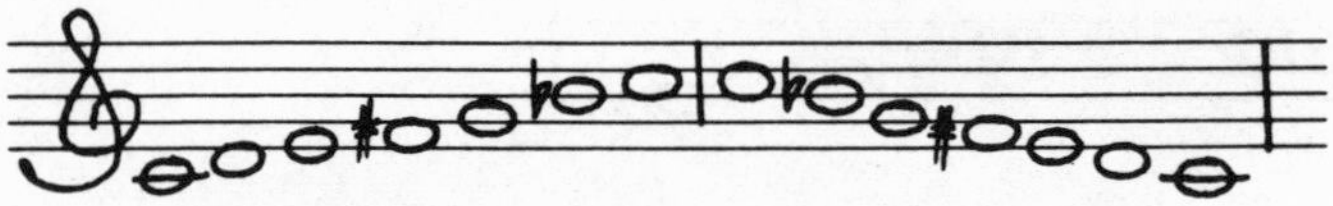

The note *DHA* (Ab) is avoided entirely.

(10) *Padmakānti*

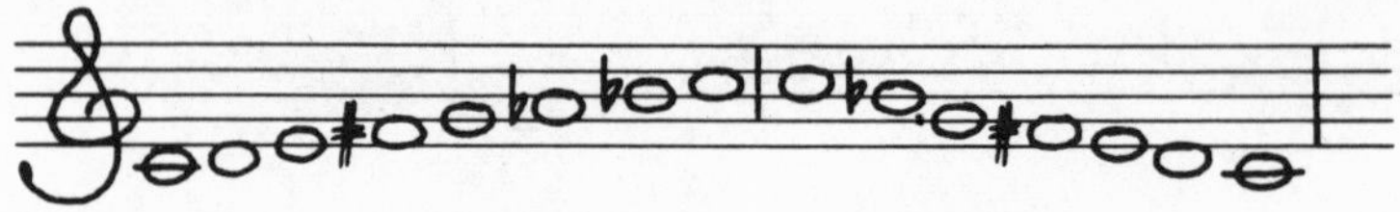

Ascent: *krama sampūrṇa*.
Descent: the note *DHA* (Ab) is avoided.

(11) *Ratipriya*

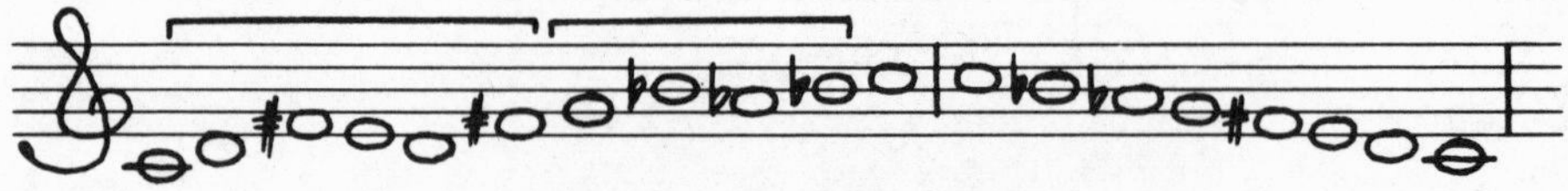

Ascent: *sampūrṇa*; two extended *vakra* features are shown.
Descent: *krama sampūrṇa*.

(12) *Ratnabhānu*

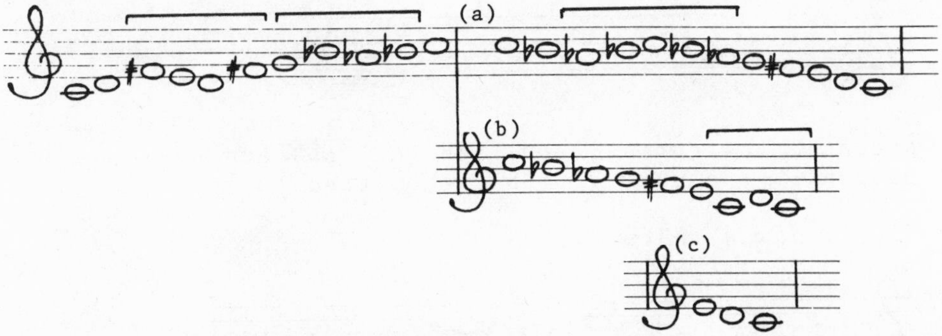

Ascent: *sampūrṇa*; two extended *vakra* features are shown.
Descent (a) *sampūrṇa*; one extended *vakra* feature is used.
(b) *sampūrṇa*; one *vakra* feature is used.
(c) *krama sampūrṇa*.

RATNABHĀNU (*Triputa-tāla*) SCM, 267-68

(13) *Ruchiramaṇi* (*Ruciramaṇi*)

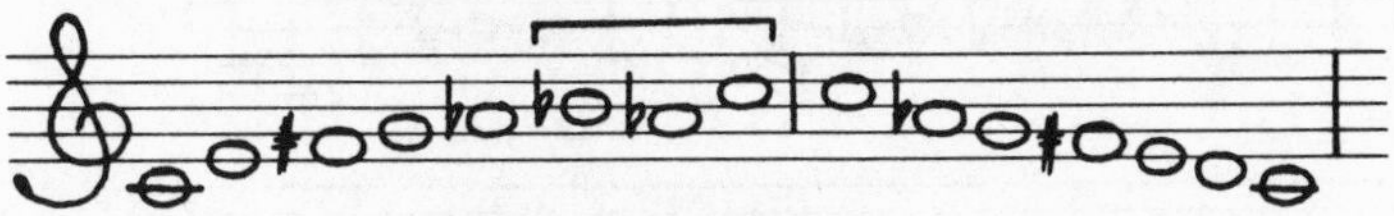

Ascent: the note *RI* (D) is avoided; one *vakra* feature is shown.
Descent: the note *NI* (Bb) is omitted.

(14) *Śuddhasāraṅga*

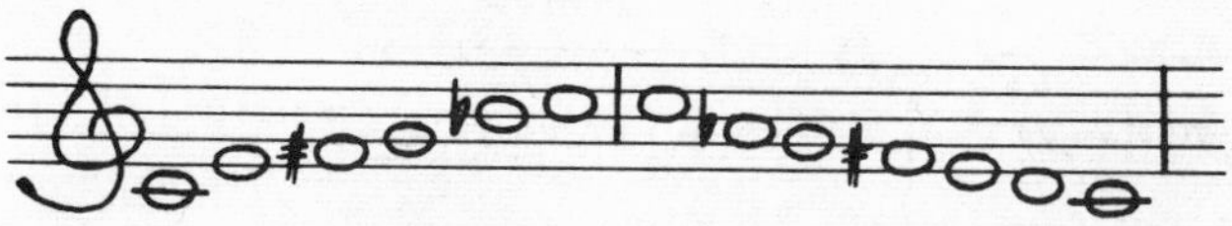

Ascent: the notes *RI* (D) and *DHA* (Ab) are avoided.
Descent: the note *NI* (Bb) is omitted.

(15) *Vijayagōtrāri*

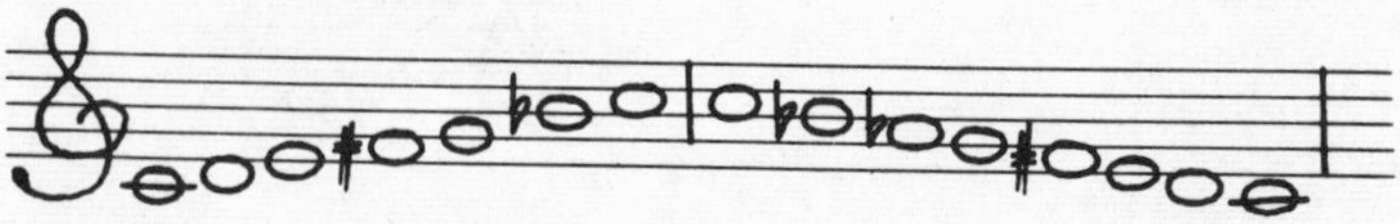

Ascent: the note *DHA* (Ab) is avoided.
Descent: *krama sampūrṇa*

63. *MĒḶA LATĀṄGĪ*

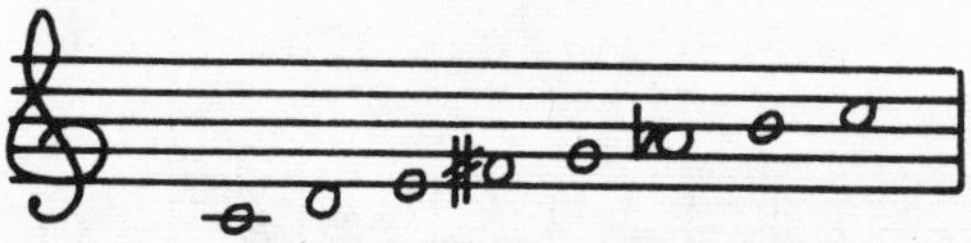

LATĀṄGĪ (*Triputa-tāla*) SCM, 268-69

Janya Rāgas of the 63. Mēḷa

(1) *Bhinna Niṣāda*

The scale of this *rāga* has *niṣādāntya* character.
Another *rāga* with the same name appears under the heading of the 6. *mēḷa* (2).

(2) *Chāmuṇḍi* (*Cāmuṇḍi*)

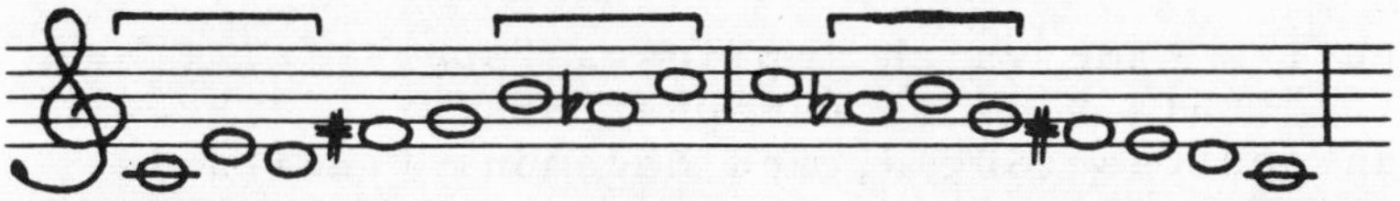

Ascent: *sampūrṇa*; two *vakra* features are shown.
Descent: *sampūrṇa*; one *vakra* feature is used.

(3) *Chandradāri* (*Candradāri*, *Chhatradhāri*)

Ascent: the notes *DHA* (Ab) and *NI* (B) are avoided.
Descent: *krama sampūrṇa*.

(4) *Chitra Chandrikā* (*Citra Candrikā*)

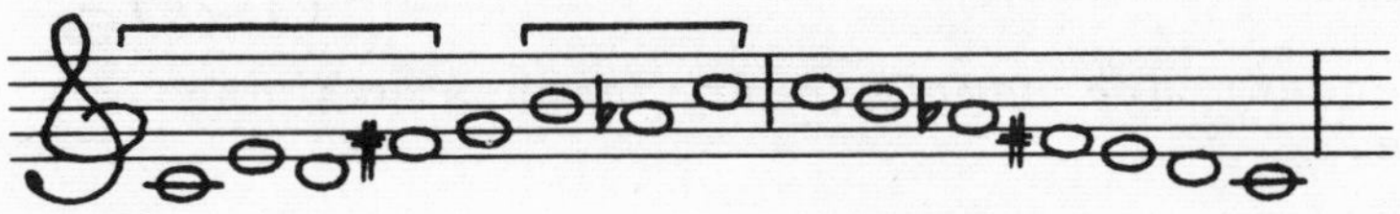

Ascent: *sampūrṇa*; two *vakra* features are shown.
Descent: the note *PA* (G) is avoided.

(5) *Dhātri*

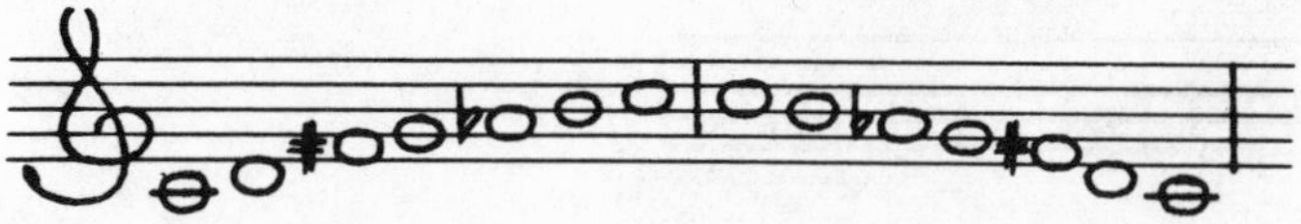

The note *GA* (E) is avoided entirely.

(6) *Dhātupriya*

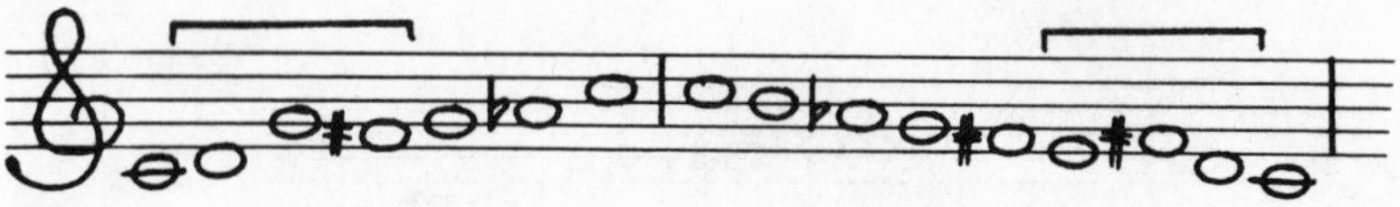

Ascent: the notes *GA* (E) and *NI* (B) are avoided; one *vakra* feature is shown.
Descent: *sampūrṇa*; one *vakra* feature is used.
Another *rāga* with the same name appears as 69,7.

(7) *Dōsharahita Svarūpiṇī* (*Dōṣarahita Svarūpiṇī*)

Despite its name which implies a "*Svarūpiṇī* free of any fault," this *rāga* is somewhat obscure. Three South Indian sources (SD, N, and Nadamuni Panditar's *Saṅgīta Svara Prastāra Sāgaram*) do not specify whether the scale covers the lower and middle or the middle and upper ranges of the octave. The ascent, extending from *MA* (F#) to *GA* (E), avoids the note *RI* (D) and shows one *vakra* feature. The descent, beginning with *RI* (D) and ending with *MA* (F#) below, uses the same *vakra* feature as that shown in ascent.

(8) *Gītapriya*

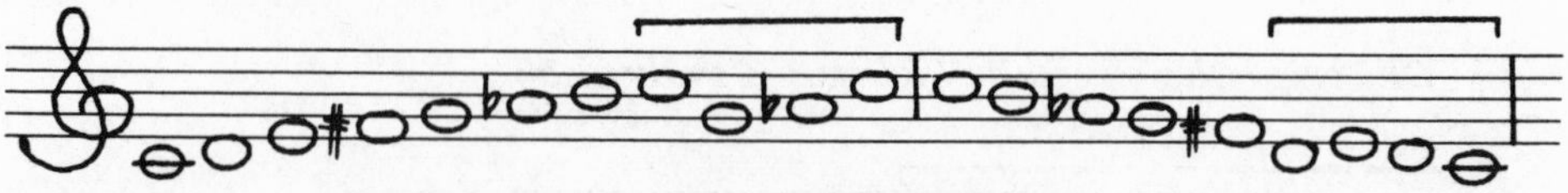

Ascent and descent are *sampūrṇa* and each shows one *vakra* feature.

Another *rāga* with the same name appears under the heading of the 13. *mēḷa* (10). The name *Gītapriya* was also used in the past to indicate the 63. *mēḷa* of the *asampūrṇa* system.

(9) *Gōtrāri*

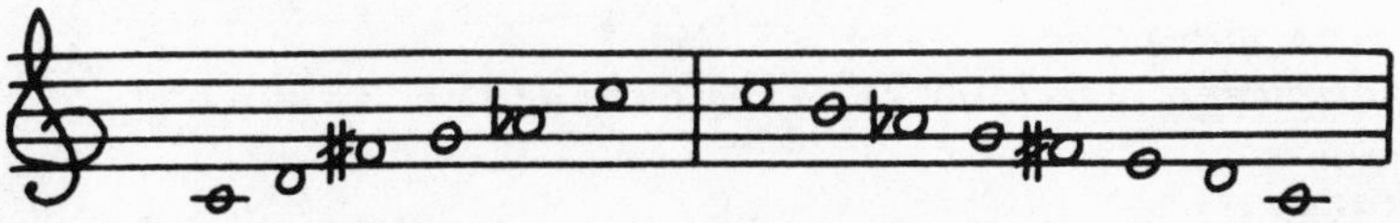

Ascent: the notes *GA* (E) and *NI* (B) are avoided.
Descent: *krama sampūrṇa*.

GŌTRĀRI (*Triputa-tāla*) SCM, 269

(10) *Gōvinda Dhanyāsi*

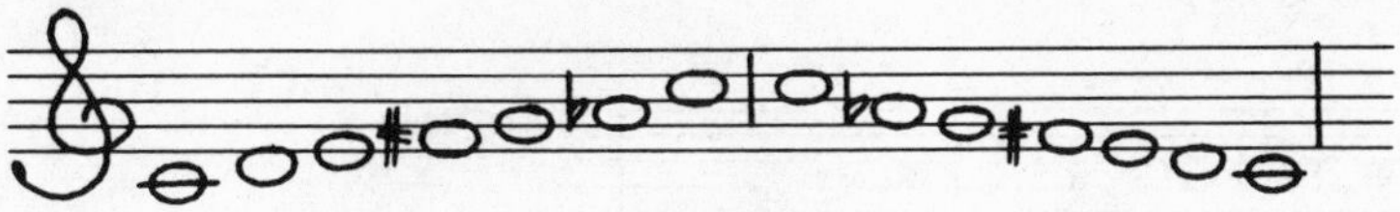

The note *NI* (B) is avoided entirely.

(11) *Jalōdharam*

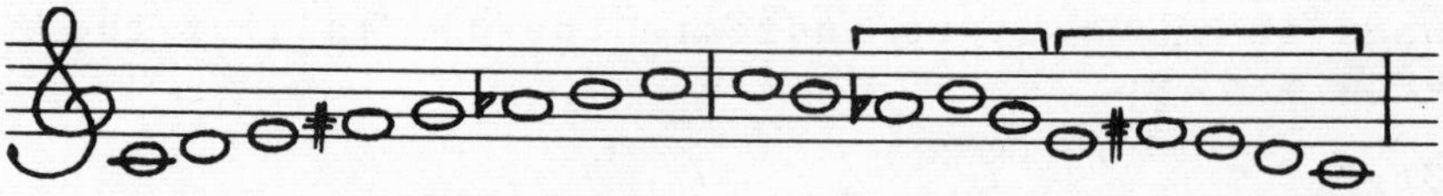

Ascent: *krama sampūrṇa*.
Descent: *sampūrṇa*; two *vakra* features are shown.

(12) *Jhaṇākāri*

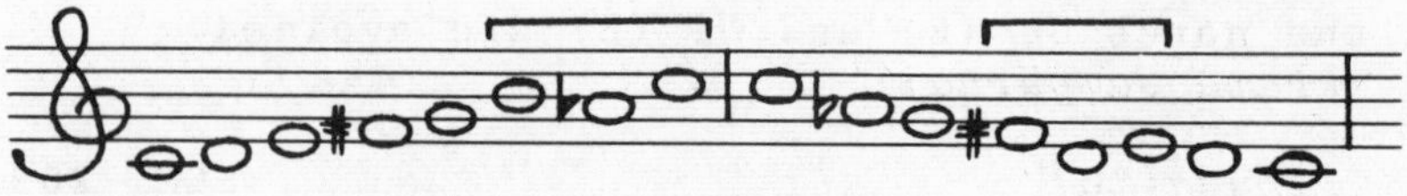

Ascent: *sampūrṇa*; one *vakra* feature is shown.
Descent: the note *NI* (B) is avoided; one *vakra* feature is shown.

(13) *Kālanirnika*

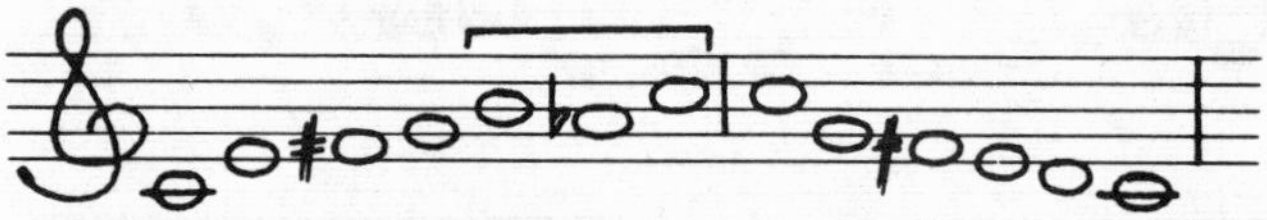

Ascent: the note *RI* (D) is avoided; one *vakra* feature is shown.
Descent: the notes *NI* (B) and *DHA* (Ab) are omitted.

(14) *Kannapriya* (*Kanaḍapriya*)

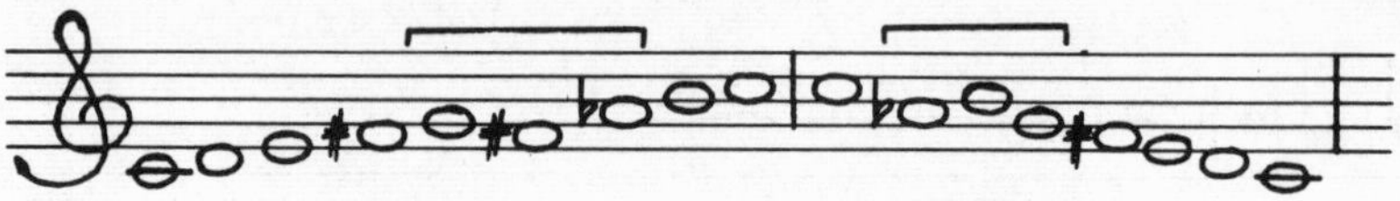

The scale of this *rāga* is *sampūrṇa* and shows one *vakra* feature in ascent and one in descent.

(15) *Karunakai*

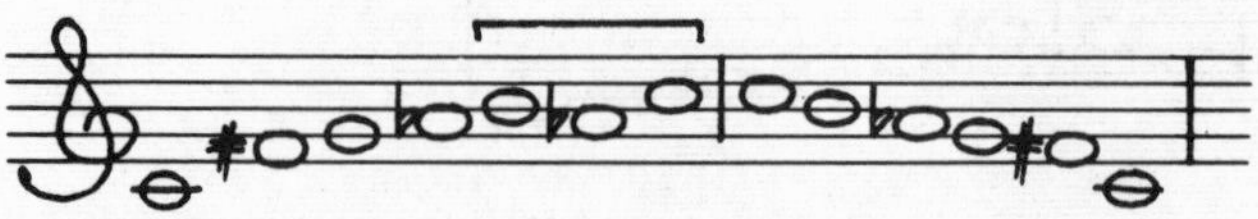

The notes *RI* (D) and *GA* (E) are avoided entirely. One *vakra* feature appears in ascent.

(16) *Kattalam*

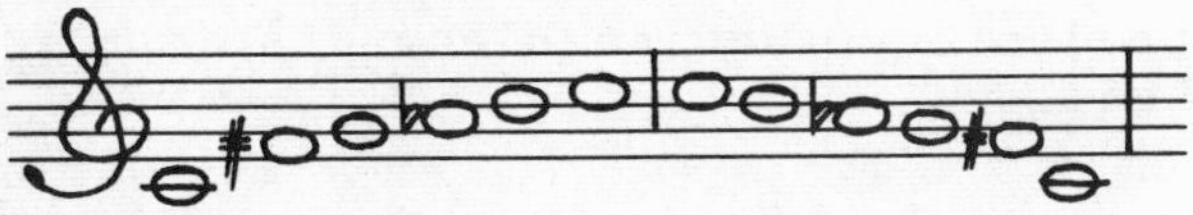

The notes *RI* (D) and *GA* (E) are avoided entirely.

(17) *Kōmali*

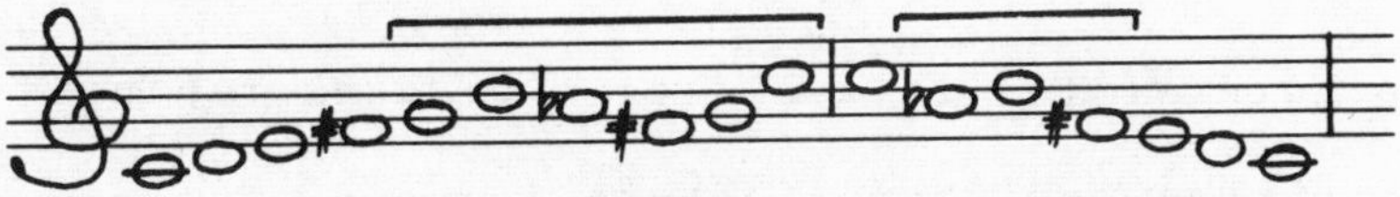

Ascent: *sampūrṇa*; one extended *vakra* feature is shown.
Descent: the note *PA* (G) is avoided; one *vakra* feature is used.

(18) *Līlāvinōdiṇi*

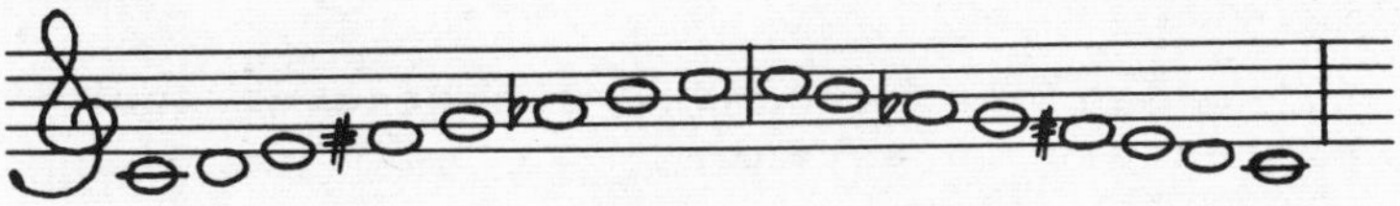

The scale of this *rāga* is *krama sampūrṇa* in ascent and descent. There appears to be no noticeable difference between this *rāga* and its primary *rāga*, *Latāṅgī*. A few musicians maintain, however, that there exist some vague characteristics of *Līlāvinōdiṇi* that cannot be determined with any certainty.

(19) *Navaratnabhūṣaṇi*

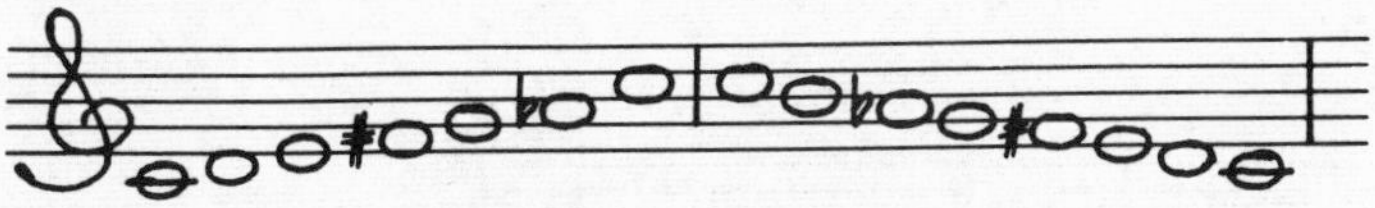

Ascent: the note *NI* (B) is avoided.
Descent: *krama sampūrṇa*.

(20) *Nāgavāhiṇi*

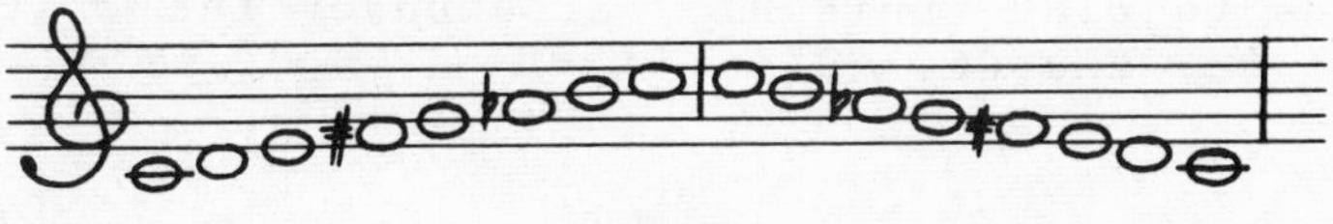

The scale of this *rāga* is *krama sampūrṇa* in ascent and

descent. Interpretational differences between this *rāga* and its primary *rāga* and *rāga Līlāvinōdiṇi* (63,18) are so vague and contradictory that no clear distinction can be established.

(21) *Nīmapriya*

Ascent: the note *NI* (B) is avoided; two *vakra* features are shown.
Descent: *sampūrṇa*; one *vakra* feature is used.

(22) *Pūrnaniṣādam*

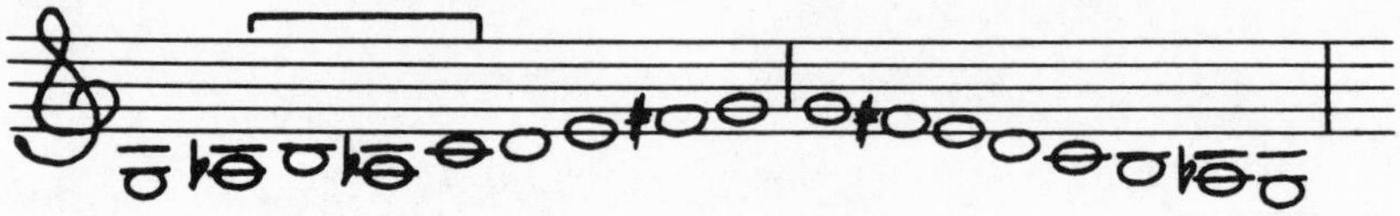

The scale of this *rāga* has *pañcamāntya* character and shows one *vakra* feature in ascent.

(23) *Ramanī*

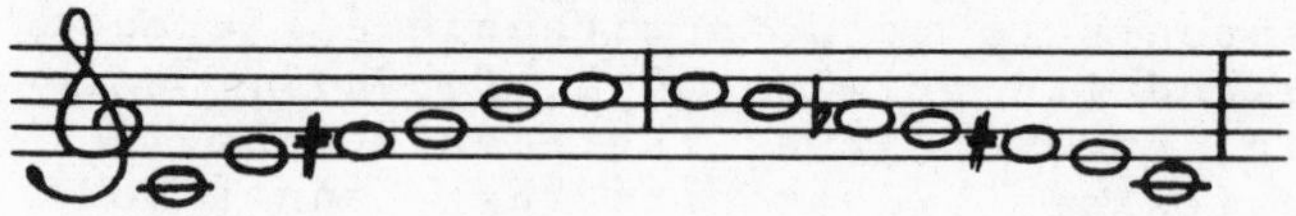

The note *RI* (D) is avoided entirely. *DHA* (Ab) is omitted in ascent.

(24) *Ratnakānti*

The note *DHA* (Ab), one of the characteristic notes of the 63. *mēḷa*, is avoided entirely. This omission allows musicians to place this *rāga* also under the headings of the 65. and 66. *mēḷas*.

(25) *Ravisvarūpiṇī*

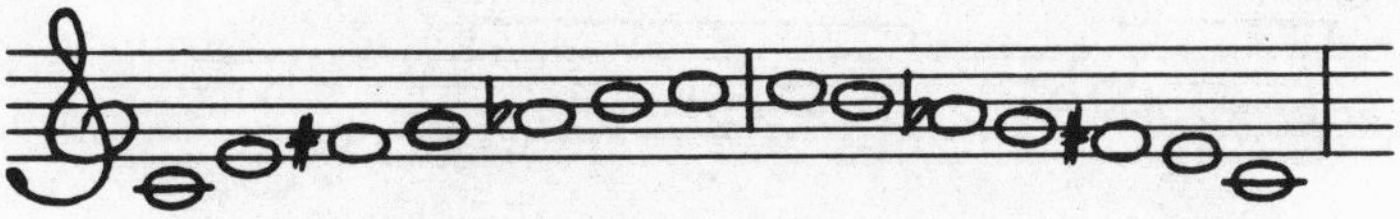

The note *RI* (D) is avoided entirely.

(26) *Śrutiprakāśini*

The notes *GA* (E) and *PA* (G) are avoided entirely.

(27) *Sujanarañjaṇi*

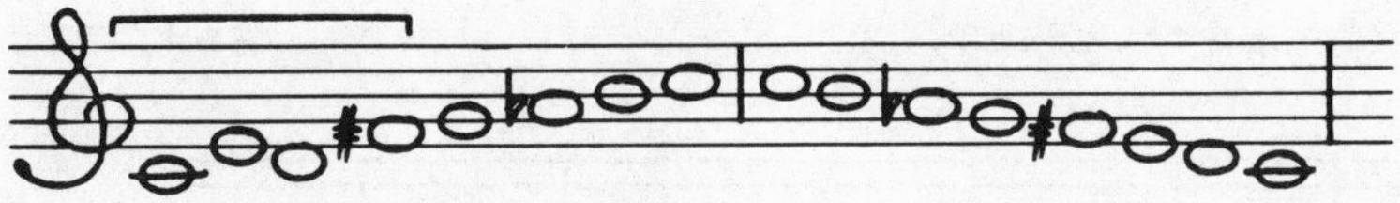

Ascent: *sampūrṇa*; one *vakra* feature is shown.
Descent: *krama sampūrṇa*.

(28) *Śadvidhasvarūpiṇi*

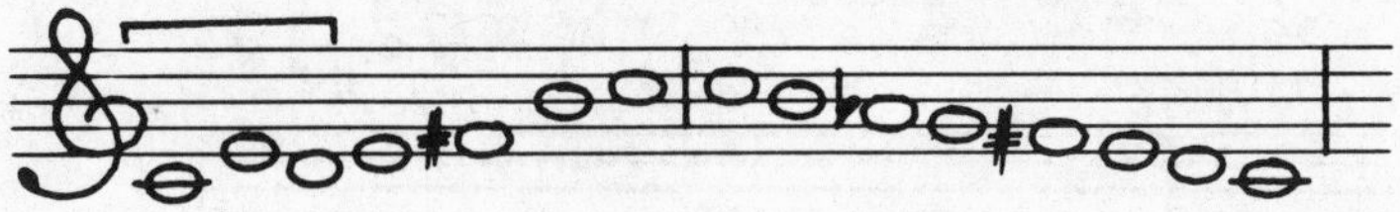

Ascent: the notes *PA* (G) and *DHA* (Ab) are avoided; one *vakra* feature is shown.
Descent: *krama sampūrṇa*.

(29) *Śuddhakalānidhi*

The scale of this *rāga* has *niṣādāntya* character. The note *RI* (D) is avoided in ascent.

(30) *Tāmasarañjani*

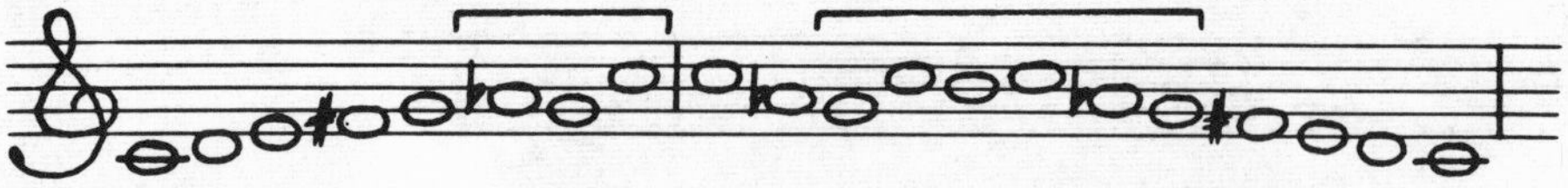

Ascent: the note *NI* (B) is avoided; one *vakra* feature is shown.
Descent: *sampūrṇa*; one extended *vakra* feature is used.

64. *MĒḶA VĀCHASPATI* (*VĀCASPATI*)

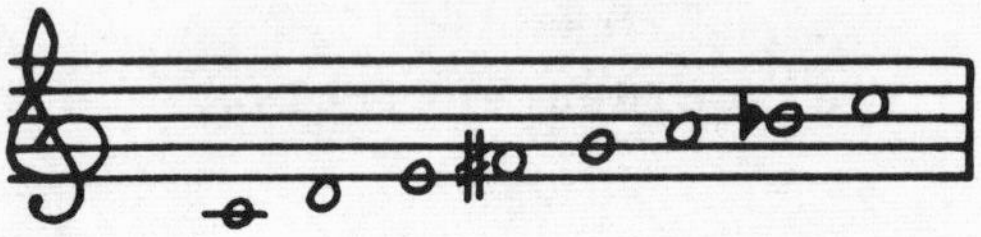

VĀCHASPATI (*Triputa-tāla*) SCM, 270

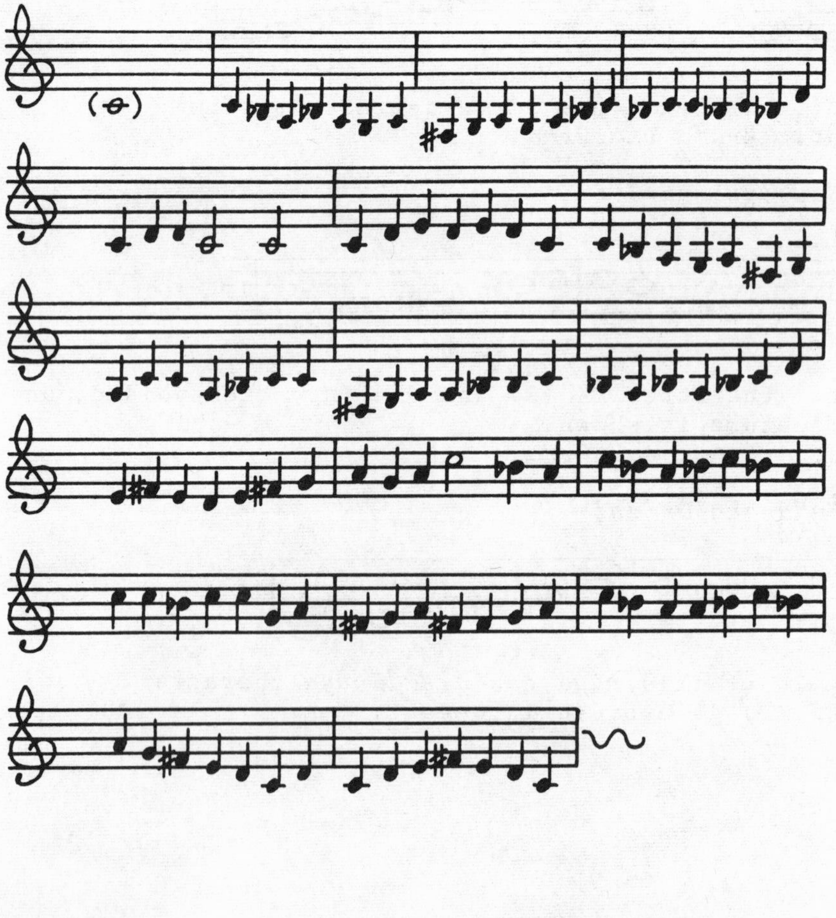

Janya Rāgas of the 64. Mēḷa

(1) *Airāvati*

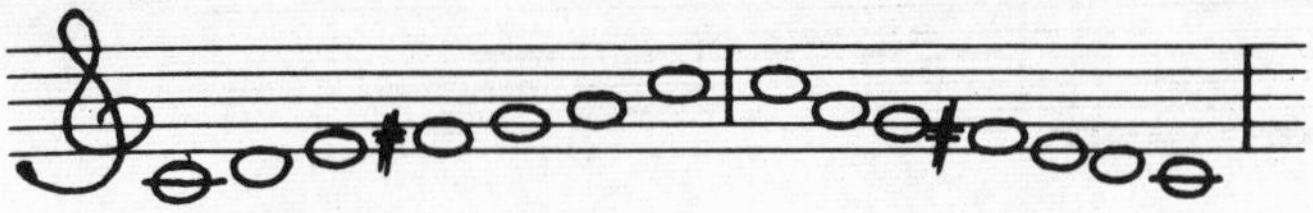

The note *NI* (Bb) is avoided entirely.
Another *rāga* with the same name appears under the heading of the 45. *mēḷa* (1).

(2) *Aruṇagiri*

The notes *PA* (G) and *NI* (Bb) are avoided entirely.

(3) *Barbarā* (*Bharbarā*, *Bharbharā*)

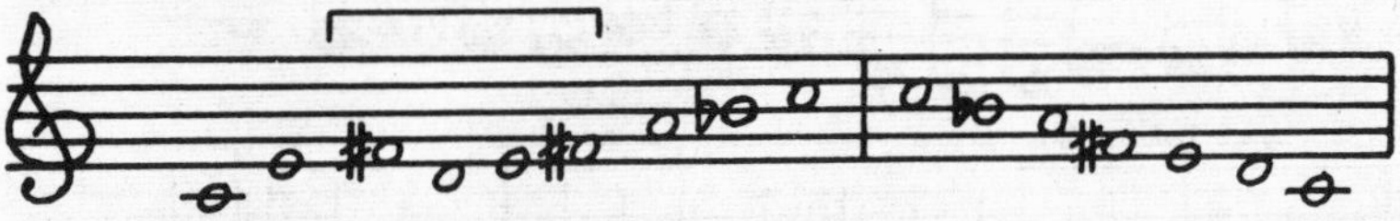

The note *PA* (G) is avoided entirely. The ascent shows one extended *vakra* feature.
Another form (also called *Bharbharā*) is presented, according to PS, in SD (I, 52) as:

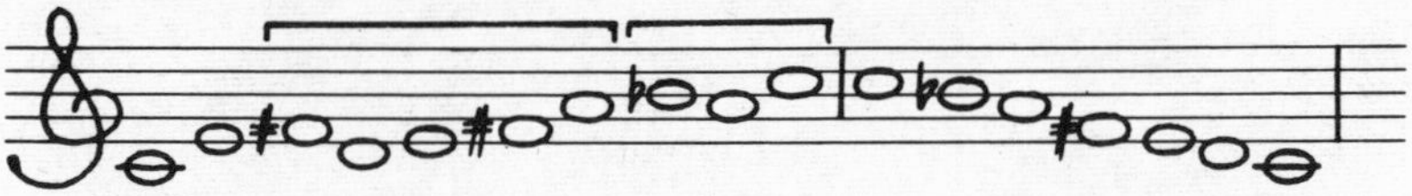

which is doubtlessly the same as the first form, although it shows a second *vakra* feature in ascent.

BARBARĀ (*Triputa-tāla*) SCM, 270-71

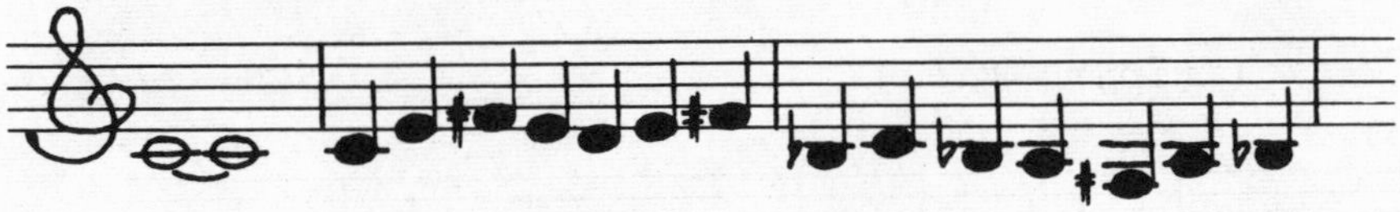

(4) *Bhōgīśvari* (*Bhōgēśvari*)

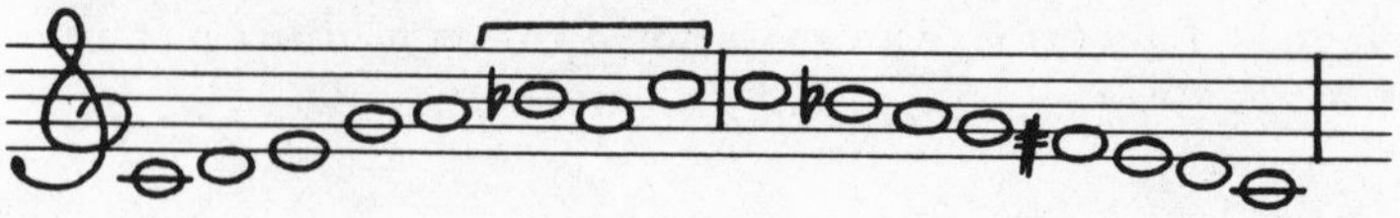

Ascent: the note *MA* (F#) is avoided; one *vakra* feature is shown.
Descent: *krama sampūrṇa*.

BHŌGĪŚVARI (*Triputa-tāla*) SCM, 274-75

(5) *Bhūṣāvaḷi*

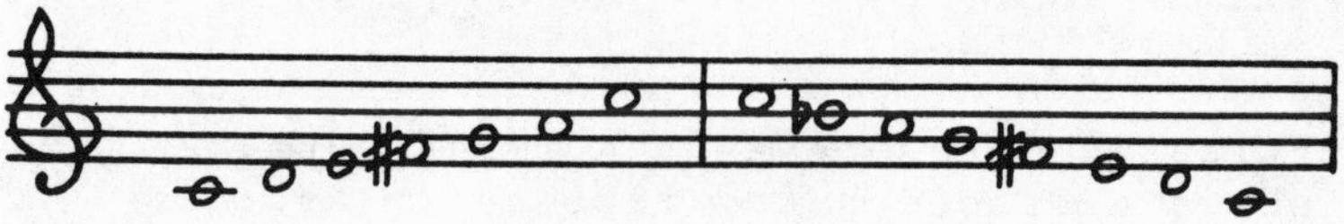

Ascent: the note *NI* (Bb) is avoided.
Descent: *krama sampūrṇa*.

BHŪṢĀVAḶI (*Triputa-tāla*) SCM, 272-73

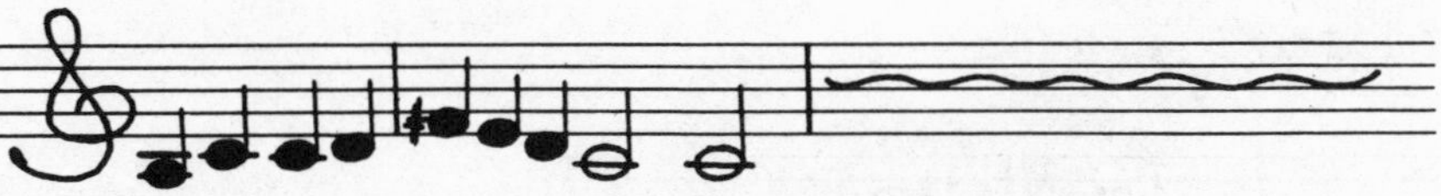

(6) *Dēvamṛta Vāhiṇi* (*Dēvamrita Vāhiṇi*)

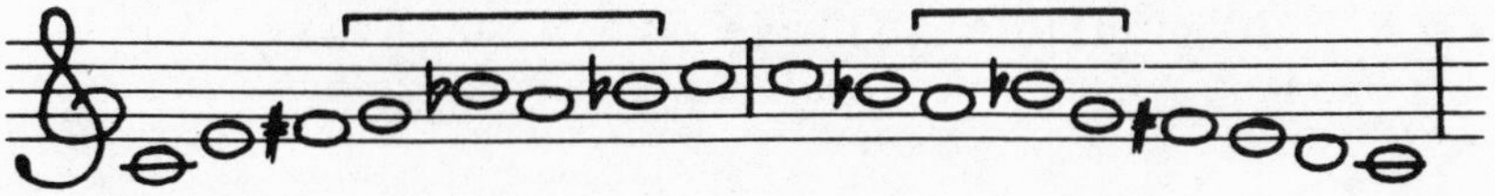

Ascent: the note *RI* (D) is avoided; one *vakra* feature is shown.
Descent: *sampūrṇa*; one *vakra* feature is used.

(7) *Gagana Mōhini*

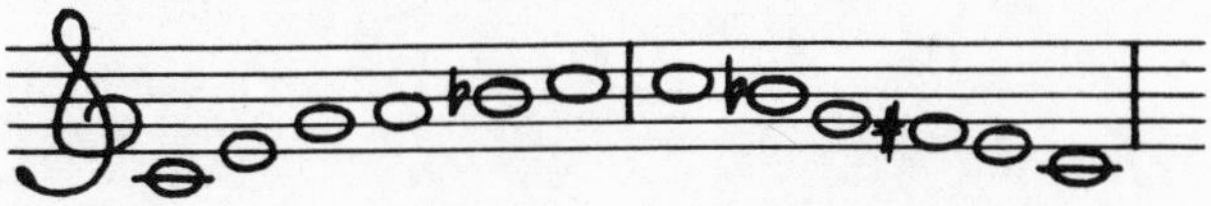

The note *RI* (D) is avoided entirely. *MA* (F#) is omitted in ascent and *DHA* (A) in descent.

(8) *Ghaṭita*

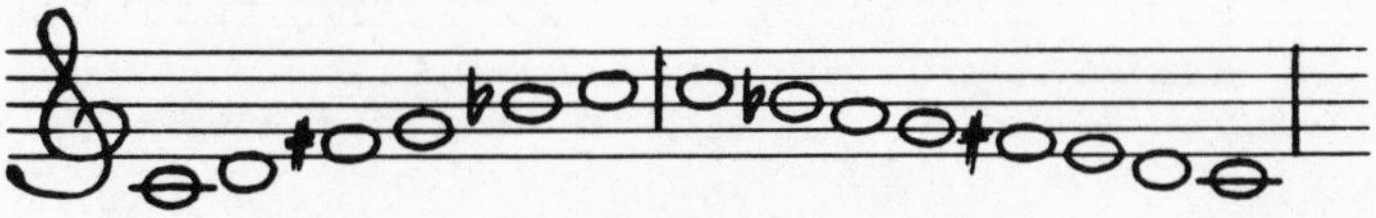

Ascent: the notes *GA* (E) and *DHA* (A) are avoided.
Descent: *krama sampūrṇa*.

(9) *Gurupriya*

The note *PA* (G) is avoided entirely.

(10) *Hiradhāriṇi*

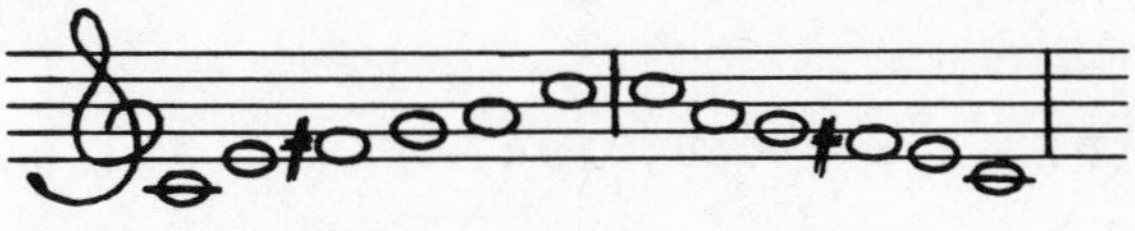

The notes *RI* (D) and *NI* (Bb) are avoided entirely.

(11) *Hlādiṇi*

The notes *RI* (D) and *DHA* (A) are avoided entirely.

(12) *Īravati*

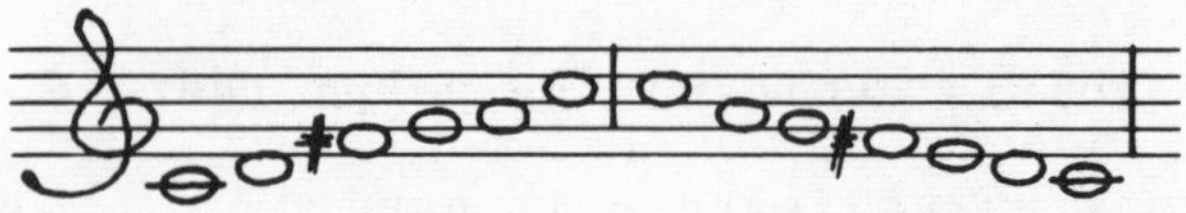

The note *NI* (Bb) is avoided entirely. *GA* (E) is omitted in ascent.

(13) *Jagābharaṇam*

The scale of this *rāga* is *sampūrṇa*. Two *vakra* features are shown, one in ascent and one in descent.

(14) *Ketakapriya*

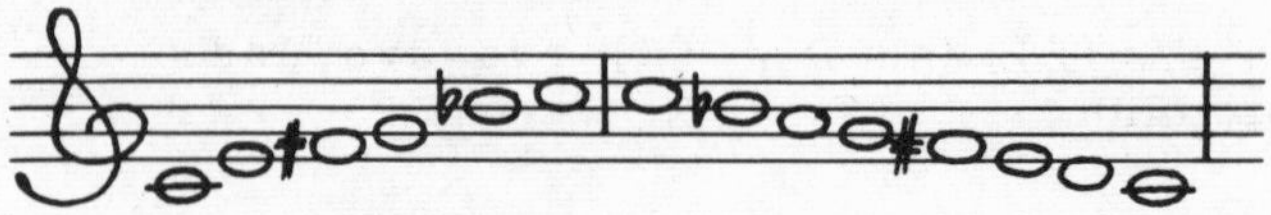

Ascent: the notes *RI* (D) and *DHA* (A) are avoided.
Descent: *krama sampūrṇa*.

(15) *Kuṭumbini*

Ascent: the note *RI* (D) is avoided; one *vakra* feature is shown.
Descent: the note *DHA* (A) is omitted.

(16) *Maṅgalakari*

The note *GA* (E) is avoided entirely.
Ascent: one *vakra* feature is shown.
Descent: the note *MA* (F#) is omitted; one *vakra* feature is used.

(17) *Muktitāyani*

The note *RI* (D) is avoided entirely.

(18) *Nādabhramam*

The note *RI* (D) is avoided entirely. The notes *GA* (E) and *DHA* (A) are omitted in ascent where one *vakra* feature is shown.

(19) *Pañcamūrti*

The scale of this *rāga* has *niṣādāntya* character. Its descent shows one *vakra* feature.

(20) *Puttari*

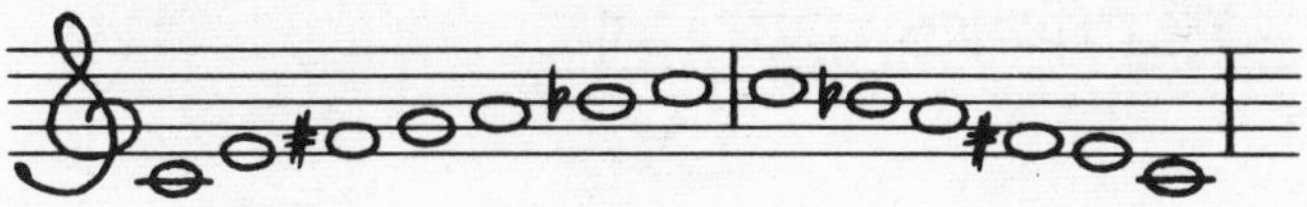

The note *RI* (D) is avoided entirely. *PA* (G) is omitted in descent.

(21) *Praṇavākari*

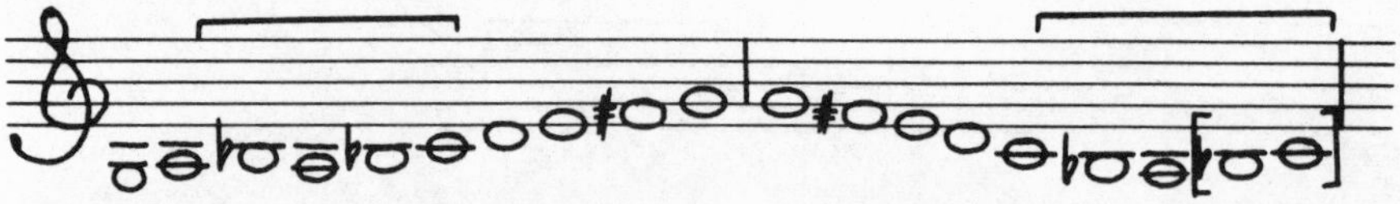

The scale of this *rāga* has *pañcamāntya* character. It shows one *vakra* feature in ascent, a feature that can also appear in descent.

(22) *Phaladāyaki*

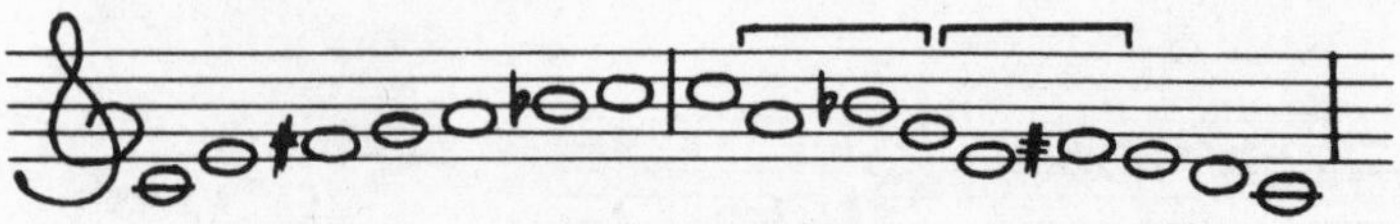

Ascent: the note *RI* (D) is avoided.
Descent: *sampūrṇa*; two *vakra* features are shown.

(23) *Ratnāmbari*

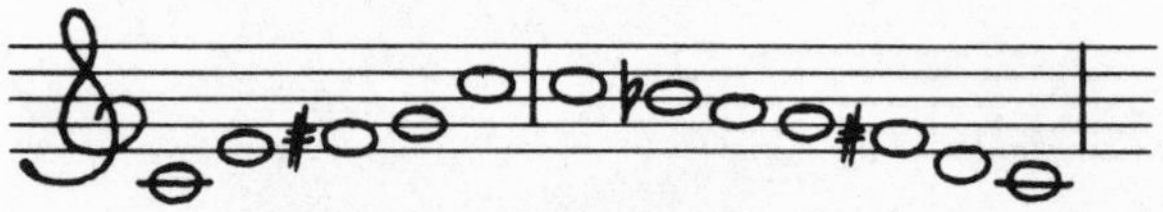

Ascent: the notes *RI* (D), *DHA* (A), and *NI* (Bb) are avoided.
Descent: the note *GA* (E) is omitted.

(24) *Santānika*

The notes *PA* (G) and *DHA* (A) are avoided entirely.

(25) *Sāmantasikhāmani*

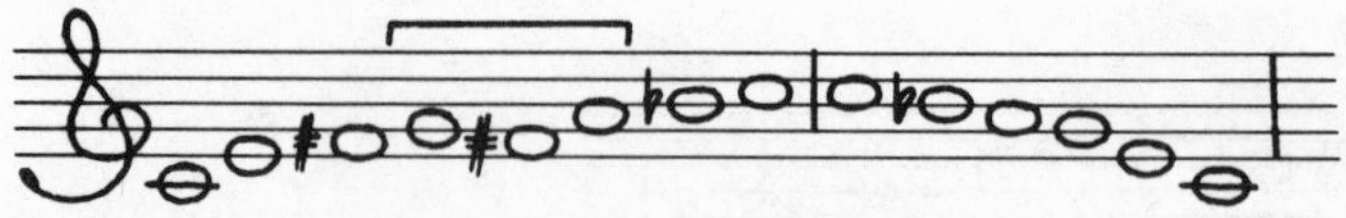

The note *RI* (D) is avoided entirely.
Ascent: one *vakra* feature is shown.
Descent: the note *MA* (F#) is omitted.

(26) *Śāradindumukhi*

Ascent: the note *RI* (D) is avoided; one extended *vakra* feature is shown.
Descent: *krama sampūrṇa*.

(27) *Sāraṅga*

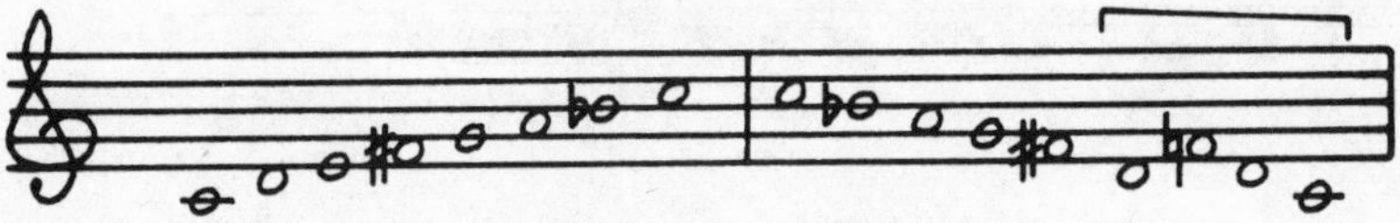

Ascent: *krama sampūrṇa*.
Descent: the note *GA* (E) is avoided; one characteristic *vakra* feature, in which the note *MA* is lowered to F natural, is used.

Occasionally *Sāraṅga* appears under the heading of the 65. *mēḷa* in which the note *NI* is raised to B natural.

SĀRAṄGA RĀGA (*Ādi-tāla*) SPC, III, 63

Pallavi

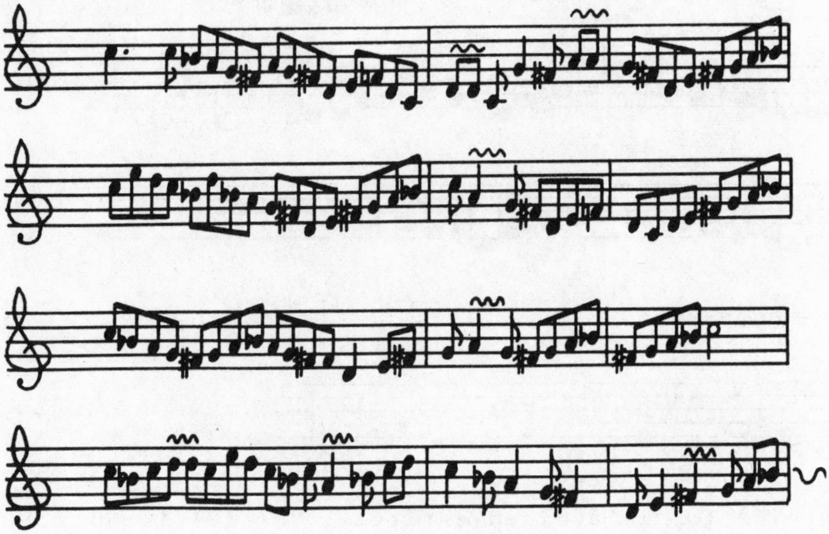

SĀRAṄGA (*Triputa-tāla*) SCM, 273

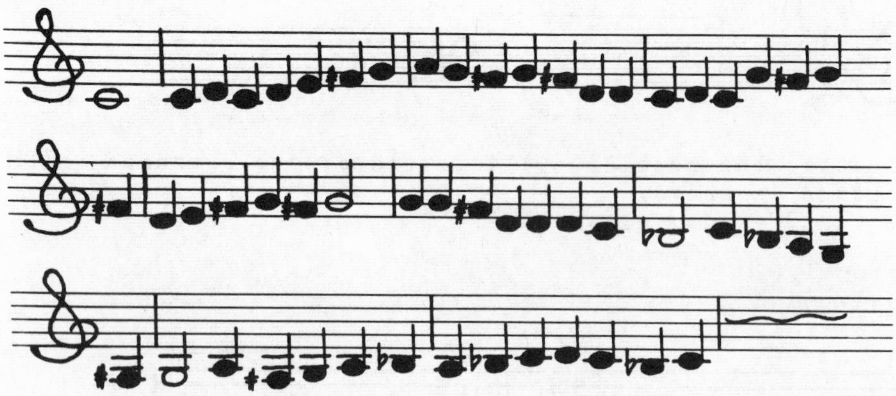

(28) *Sarasvati*

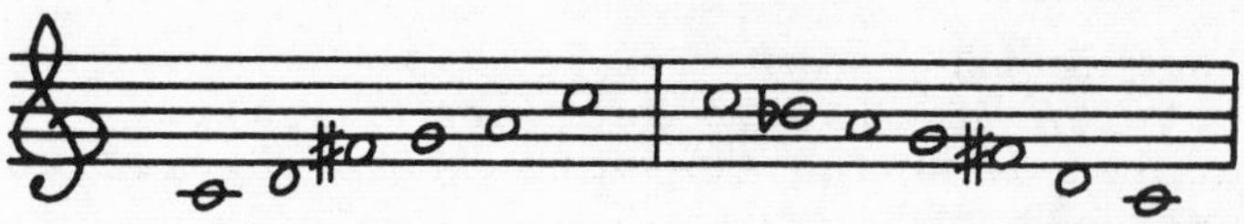

The note *GA* (E) is avoided entirely. *NI* (Bb) is omitted in ascent.

SARASVATI (*Triputa-tāla*) SCM, 274

(29) *Siṃhasvarūpi*

The note *RI* (D) is avoided entirely. *PA* (G) is omitted in ascent and *DHA* (A) in descent.

(30) *Śuddhalahari (Śudhalahari)*

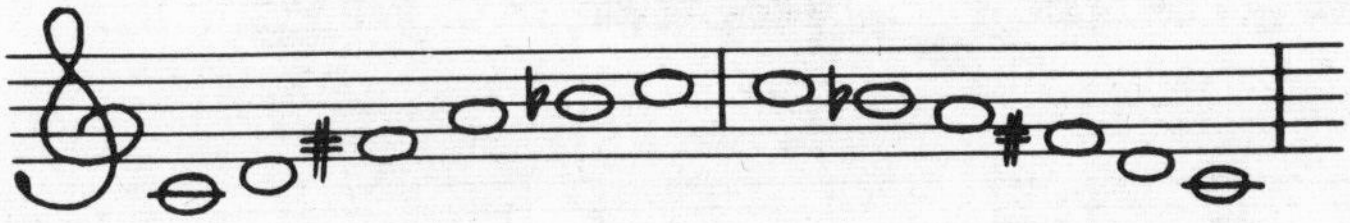

The notes *GA* (E) and *PA* (G) are avoided entirely.

(31) *Tālam*

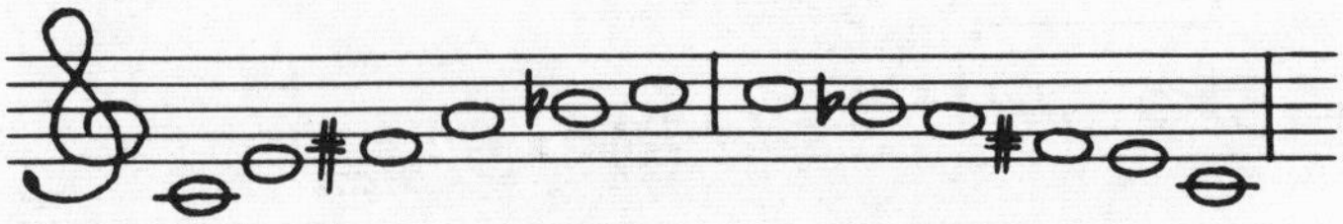

The notes *RI* (D) and *PA* (G) are avoided entirely.
Another *rāga* with the same name is listed under the heading of the 40. *mēḷa* (14).

(32) *Taruṇipriya*

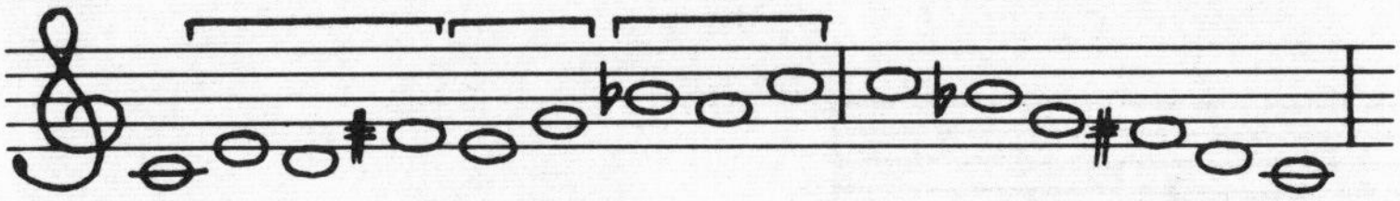

Ascent: *sampūrṇa*; three *vakra* features are shown.
Descent: the notes *DHA* (A) and *GA* (E) are avoided.

(33) *Uttari*

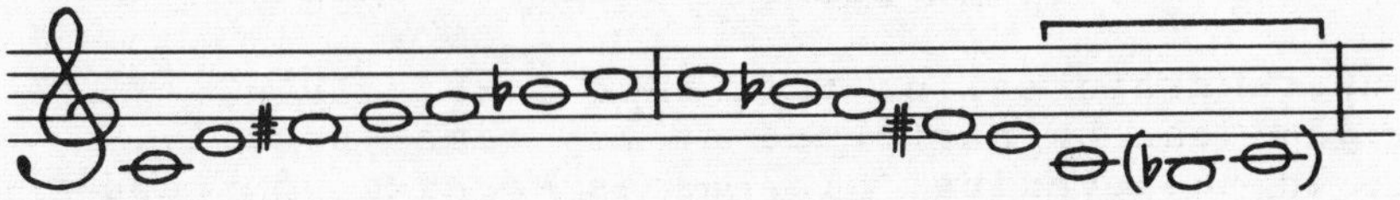

The note *RI* (D) is avoided entirely. *PA* (G) is omitted in descent where, occasionally, one *vakra* feature can be used.

UTTARI (*Triputa-tāla*) SCM, 271-72

(34) *Vijayābharaṇi*

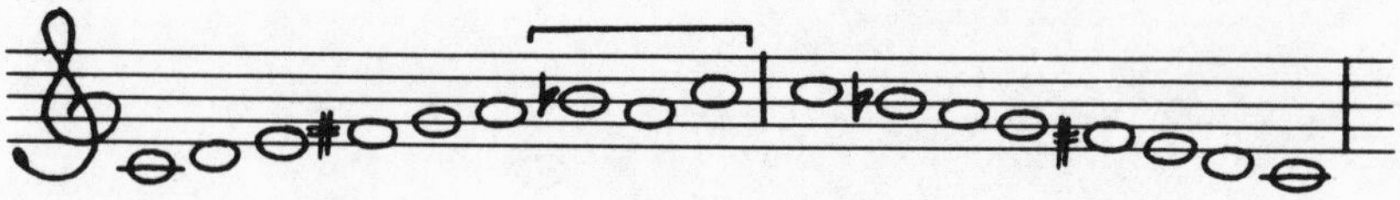

Ascent: *sampūrṇa*; one *vakra* feature is shown.
Descent: *krama sampūrṇa*.

65. *MĒḶA MECHAKALYĀṆĪ* (*MECAKALYĀṆĪ*, *KALYĀṆĪ*)

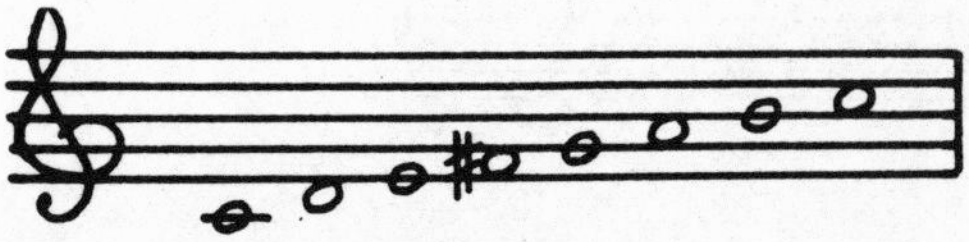

Among the primary *rāgas* that employ the note *prati MA* (F#), *Mechakalyāṇī* is the most popular. This is shown not only by its frequent performances but also by the comparatively large number of subordinate *janya rāgas*.

Veṅkaṭamakhin called this *rāga Śantakalyāṇī*. *Mechakalyāṇī* can be performed at any time—usually, however, in the evening. The names *Mechakalyāṇī* and *Kalyāṇī* generally refer to the same *rāga*. There are a few musicians who make distinctions between the two *rāgas*, but they are too vague and contradictory to represent two different forms.

MECHAKALYĀṆĪ (*Triputa-tāla*) SCM, 275-6

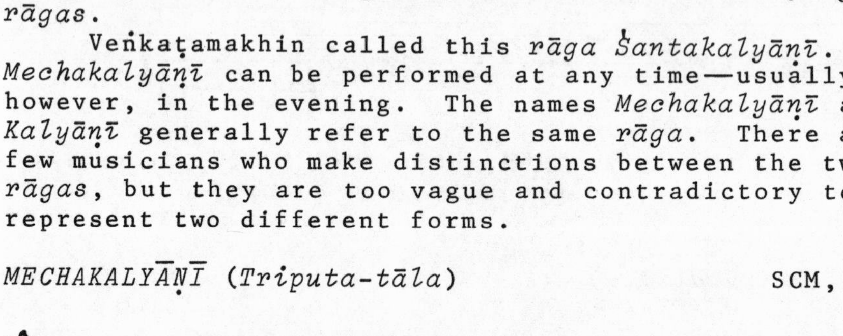

KALYĀṆĪ RĀGA (Triputa-tāla) SPC, II, 43

The second of the foregoing examples, a song in *Kalyāṇī*, does not show any significant differences from *Mechakalyāṇī*. Occasional *vakra* passages such as *MA-PA-GA-RI-SA* (F#-G-E-D-C) in measures 10-12, 28-30, or, in a smaller form, *MA-PA-GA* (F#-G-E) in measures 6-7, 10-11, 27-28, 31-32 are opposed by straight descents as in measures 16-18 and 37-39. Of some interest is the stressing of the note *DHA* (A) performed with a vibrato. But all these and similar phenomena occur in the majority of popular *rāgas* and it is doubtful whether they represent any real distinction between *Mechakalyāṇī* and *Kalyāṇī*.

Janya Rāgas of the 65. Mēḷa

(1) *Aprameyam*

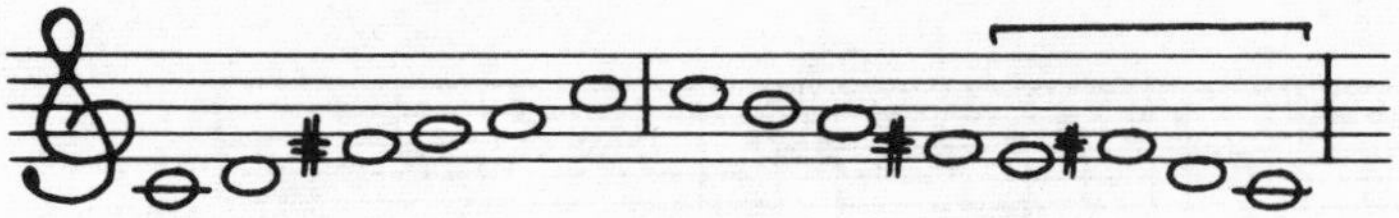

Ascent: the notes *GA* (E) and *NI* (B) are avoided.
Descent: the note *PA* (G) is omitted; one *vakra* feature is shown.

(2) *Bhūpa Kalyāṇī*

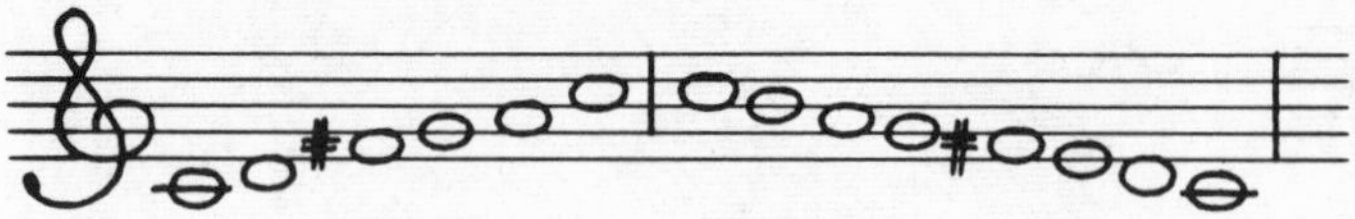

Ascent: the notes *GA* (E) and *NI* (B) are avoided.
Descent: *krama sampūrṇa*.

(3) *Bhūrañjani*

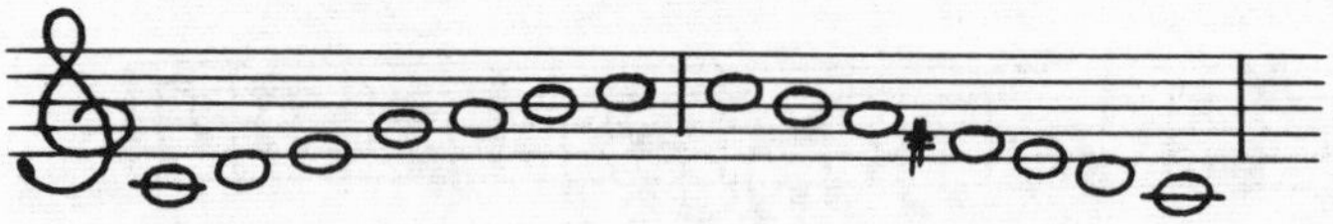

Ascent: the note *MA* (F#) is avoided.
Descent: the note *PA* (G) is omitted.

(4) *Chakra Tulyam* (*Cakra Tulyam*)

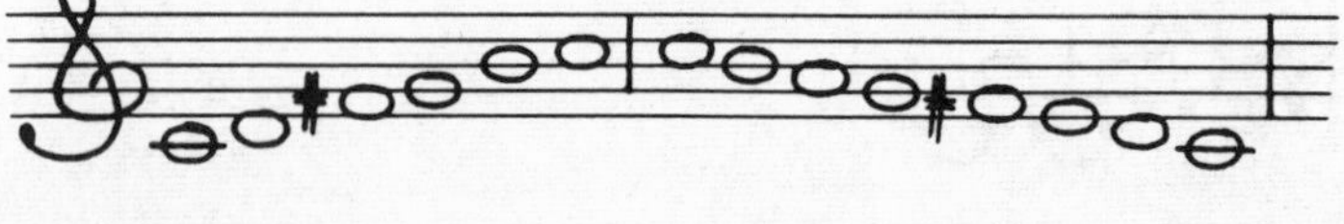

Ascent: the notes *GA* (E) and *DHA* (A) are avoided.
Descent: *krama sampūrṇa*.

(5) *Chandrakāntam* (*Chandrakānti*, *Candrakānti*)

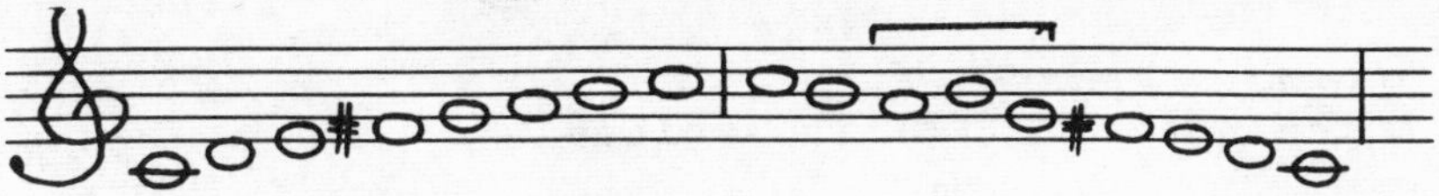

Ascent: *krama sampūrṇa*.
Descent: *sampūrṇa*; one *vakra* feature is shown.

(6) *Charavibhāsitam* (*Caravibhāsitam*)

Ascent: the note *RI* (D) is avoided.
Descent: the note *NI* (B) is omitted.

(7) *Chētulāvaḷi* (*Cētulāvaḷi*)

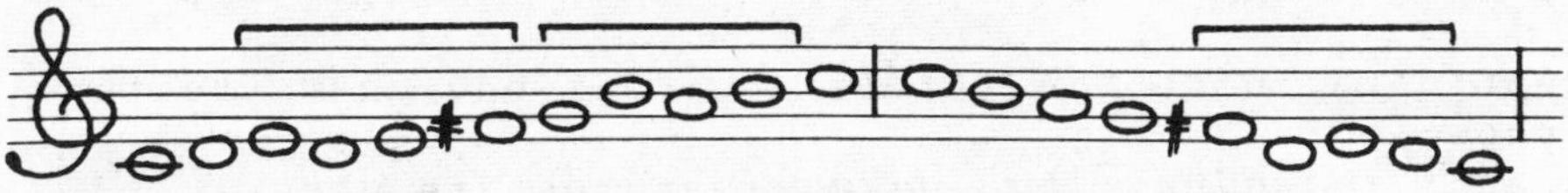

Ascent: *sampūrṇa*; two *vakra* features are shown.
Descent: *sampūrṇa*; one *vakra* feature is used.

(8) *Chittadyuti* (*Cittadyuti*)

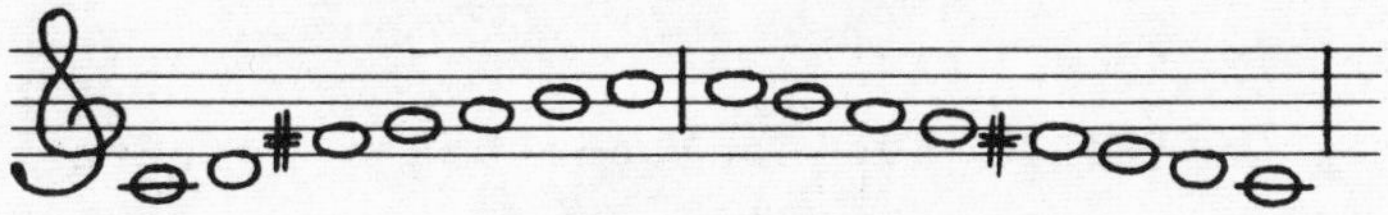

Ascent: the note *GA* (E) is avoided.
Descent: *krama sampūrṇa*.

(9) *Dambhā Kauśikam*

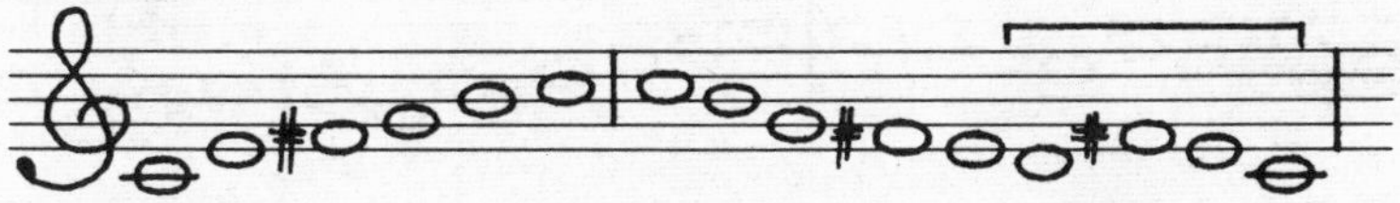

The note *DHA* (A) is avoided entirely.
Ascent: the note *RI* (D) is omitted.
Descent: one *vakra* feature is shown.

(10) *Dāṭi Balam*

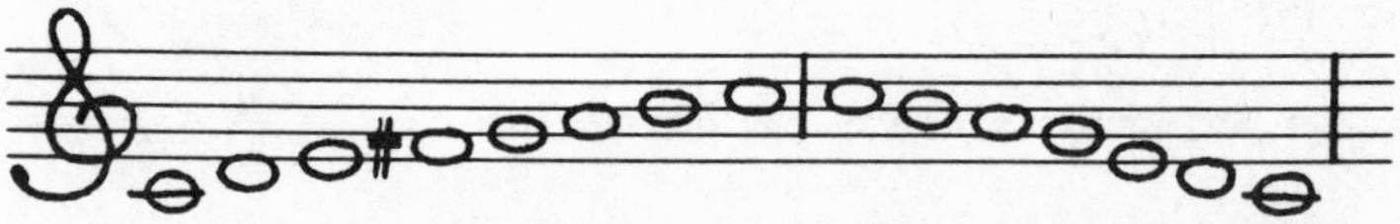

Ascent: *krama sampūrṇa*.
Descent: the note *MA* (F#) is avoided.

(11) *Dēśya Kalyāṇī*

Ascent: *sampūrṇa*; one *vakra* feature is shown.
Descent: the notes *NI* (B) and *GA* (E) are avoided.

(12) *Dhara Pallavam*

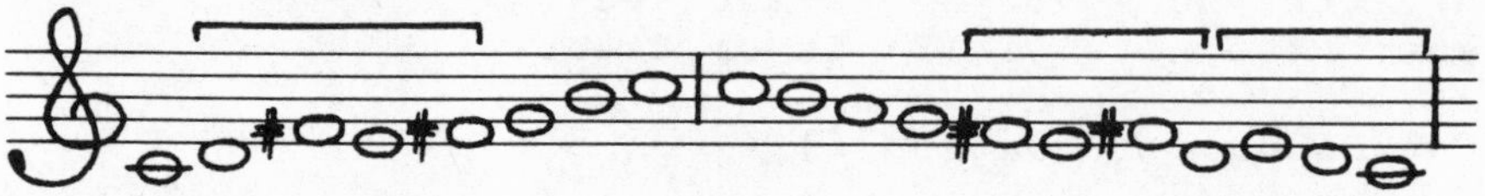

Ascent: the note *DHA* (A) is avoided; one *vakra* feature is shown.
Descent: *sampūrṇa*; two *vakra* features are used.

(13) *Dīrghadarśi*

Ascent: the note *GA* (E) is avoided; one *vakra* feature is shown.
Descent: the note *RI* (D) is omitted; one *vakra* feature is used.

(14) *Druti*

Ascent: *sampūrṇa*; two *vakra* features, the second one in an extended form, are shown.
Descent: *sampūrṇa*; one extended *vakra* feature is used.

(15) *Dvimukhapriya*

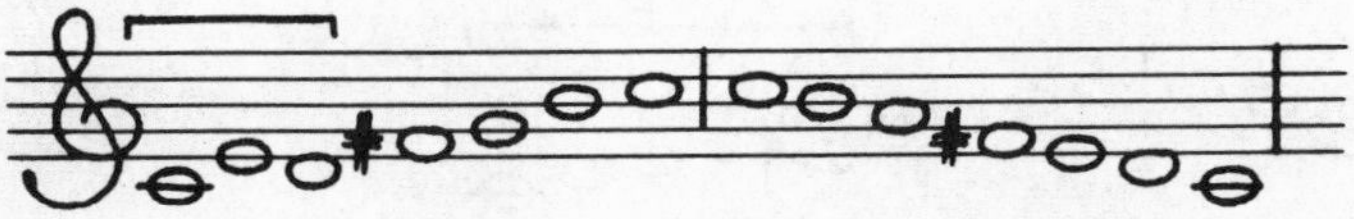

Ascent: the note *DHA* (A) is avoided; one *vakra* feature is shown.
Descent: the note *PA* (G) is omitted.

(16) *Garalāri*

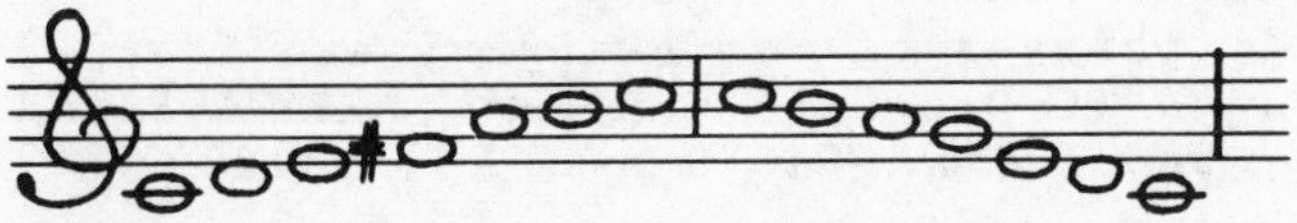

Ascent: the note *PA* (G) is avoided.
Descent: the note *MA* (F#) is omitted.

(17) *Gargēśvari*

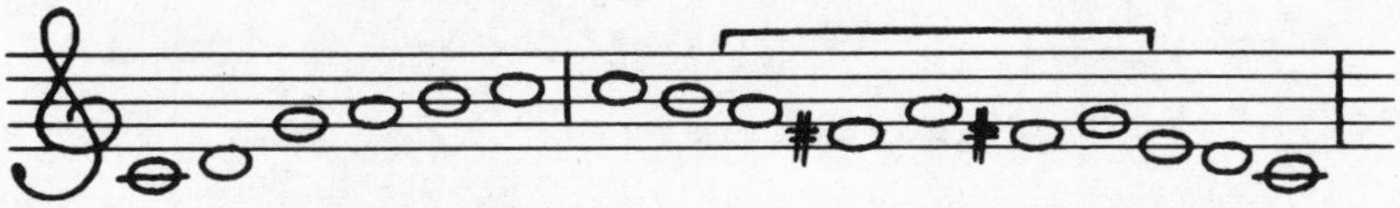

Ascent: the notes *GA* (E) and *MA* (F#) are avoided.
Descent: *sampūrṇa*; one extended *vakra* feature is used.

(18) *Ghana Nāyaki*

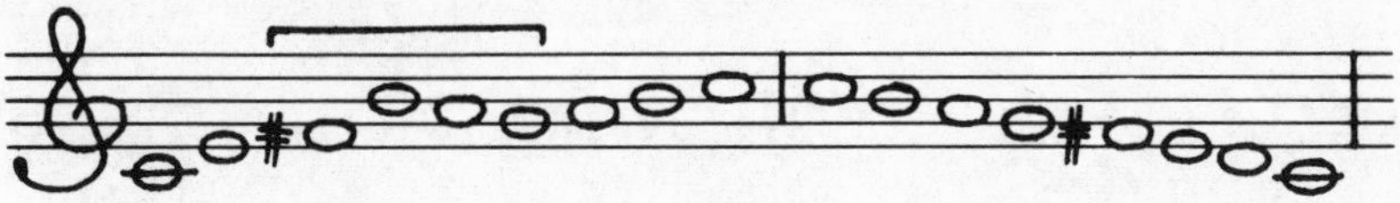

Ascent: the note *RI* (D) is avoided; one *vakra* feature is shown.
Descent: *krama sampūrṇa*.

(19) *Ghana Suprabhātam*

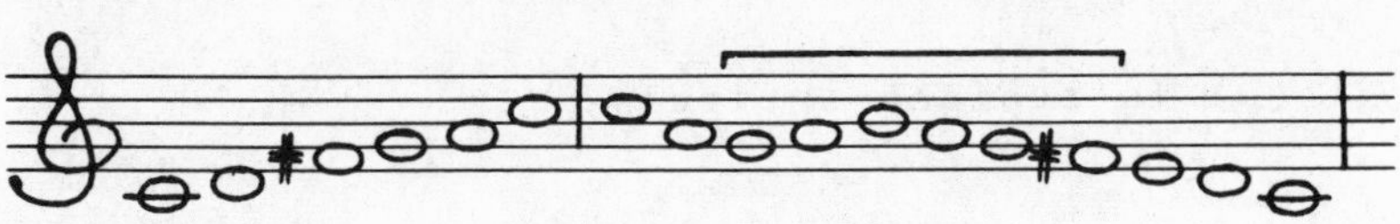

Ascent: the notes *GA* (E) and *NI* (B) are avoided.
Descent: *sampūrṇa*; one extended *vakra* feature is shown.

(20) *Hamīrkalyāṇī*

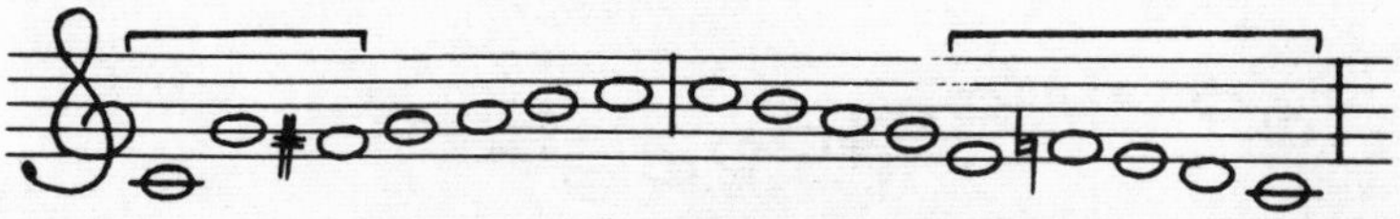

Ascent: the notes *RI* (D) and *GA* (E) are usually avoided; one *vakra* feature is shown. In a few instances the ascent of this *rāga* is *sampūrṇa*.
Descent: *sampūrṇa*; the note *prati MA* (F#) is generally lowered to *MA śuddha* (F natural) whenever it appears in the indicated extended *vakra* passage.

Characteristic phrases of *Hamīrkalyāṇī* are *SA-RI-SA-PA-MA-PA-DHA-NI-SA* (C-D-C-G-F#-G-A-B-c), *GA-MA-RI-SA* (E-F natural-D-C), and *PA-DHA-SA* (G-A-c).

(21) *Kalyāṇa Dāyini*

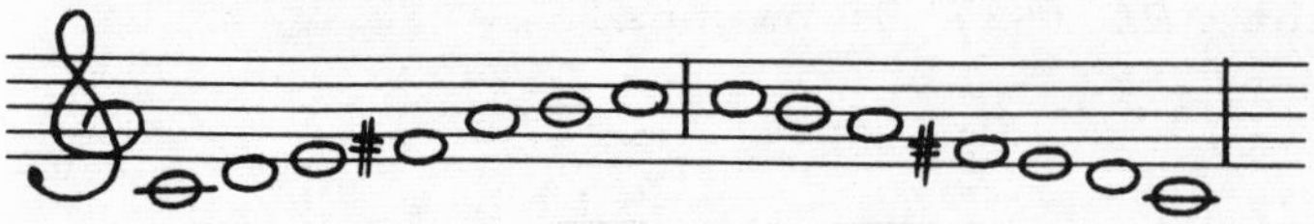

The note *PA* (G) is avoided entirely.

(22) *Kamalōttaram*

The notes *RI* (D) and *GA* (E) are avoided entirely.

(23) *Kāmodamāruva*

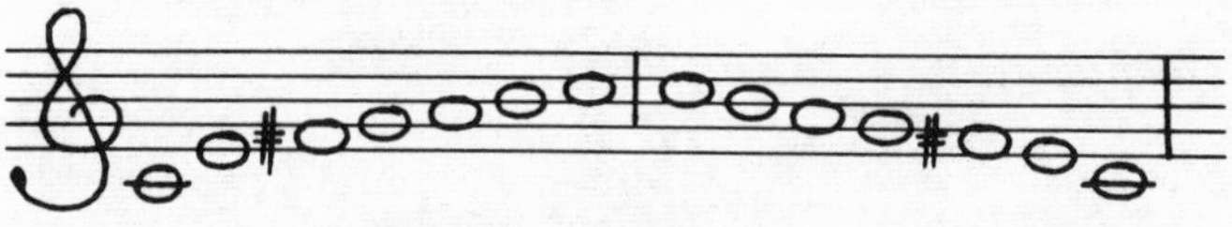

The note *RI* (D) is avoided entirely.

(24) *Kāmodnāṭ*

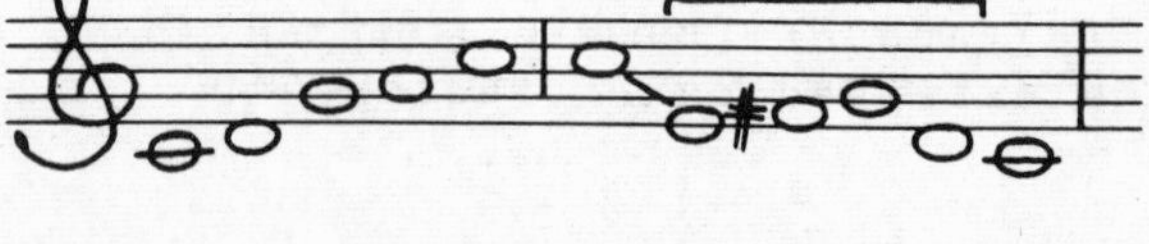

Ascent: the notes *GA* (E), *MA* (F#), and *NI* (B) are avoided.
Descent: the glide *SA-GA* (c-E) is characteristic. One extended *vakra* feature is used.

(25) *Kanaka Ghaṇṭa*

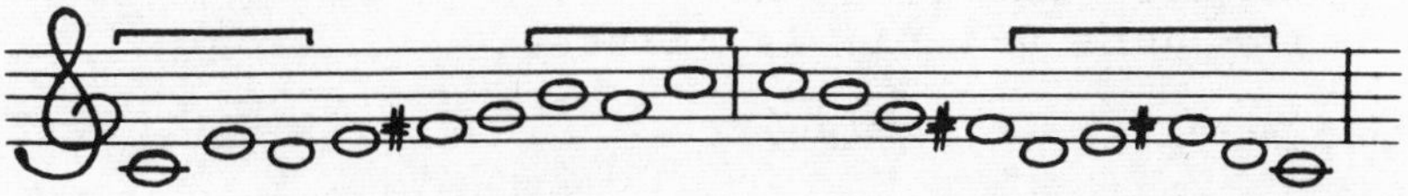

Ascent: *sampūrṇa*; two *vakra* features are shown.
Descent: the note *DHA* (A) is avoided; one extended *vakra* feature is used.

(26) *Kaumōda*

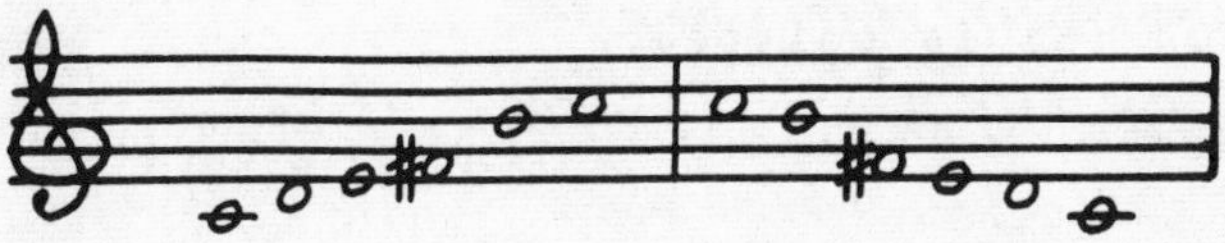

The notes *PA* (G) and *DHA* (A) are avoided entirely.

KAUMŌDA (*Triputa-tāla*) SCM, 276-77

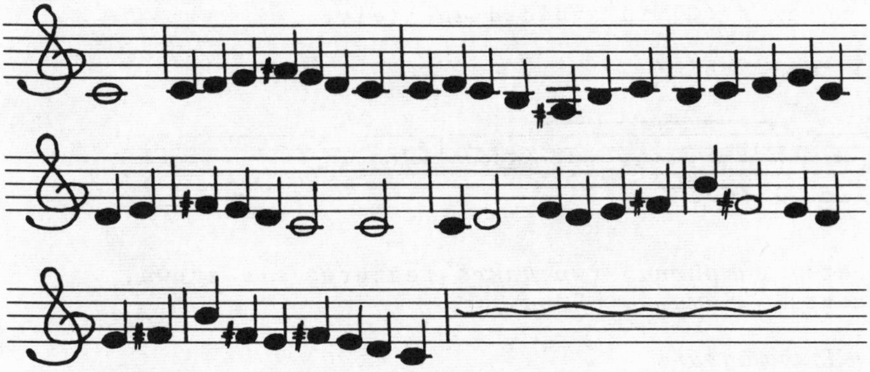

(27) *Kuntala Kusumāvaḷi*

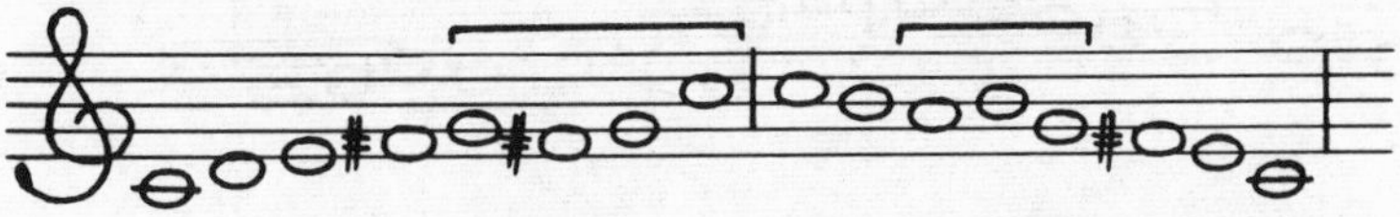

Ascent: the notes *DHA* (A) and *NI* (B) are avoided; one extended *vakra* feature is shown.
Descent: the note *RI* (D) is omitted; one *vakra* feature is used.

(28) *Kuntala Śrīkaṇṭhi*

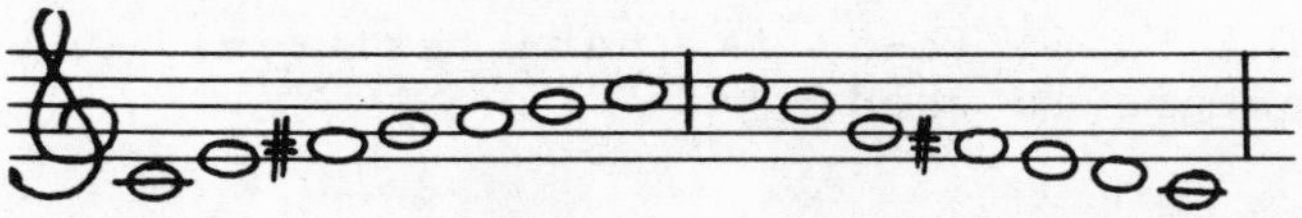

Ascent: the note *RI* (D) is avoided.
Descent: the note *DHA* (A) is omitted.

(29) *Kūrēśam*

Ascent: the note *DHA* (A) is avoided.
Descent: the note *GA* (E) is omitted.

(30) *Kurudēśyam*

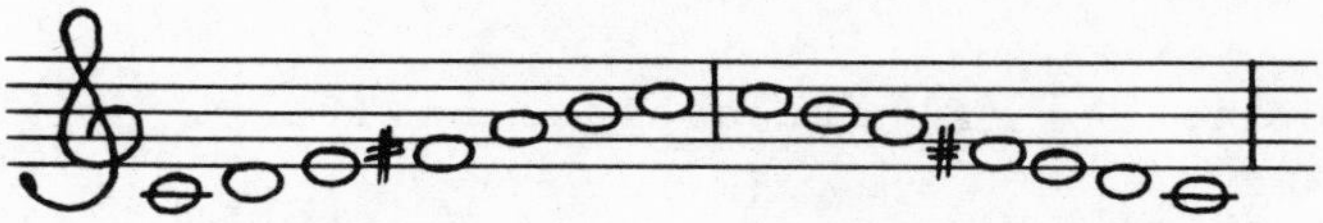

The note *PA* (G) is avoided entirely.

(31) *Kuśa Vāhiṇi*

Ascent: *sampūrṇa*; two *vakra* features are shown.
Descent: *krama sampūrṇa*.

(32) *Kusumāgraṇi*

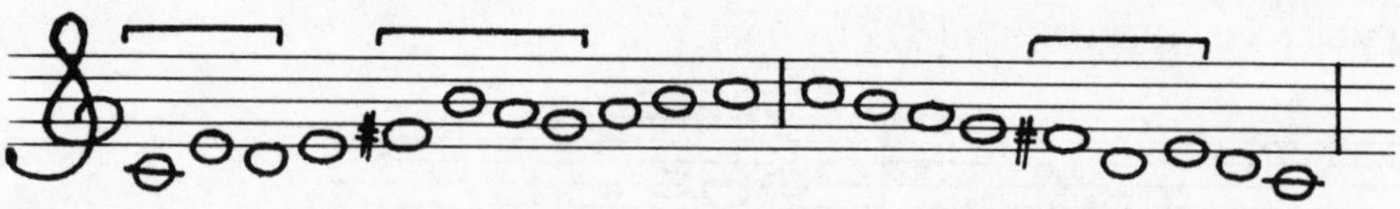

Ascent: *sampūrṇa*; two *vakra* features are shown.
Descent: *sampūrṇa*; one *vakra* feature is used.

(33) *Mitrabhāviṇi*

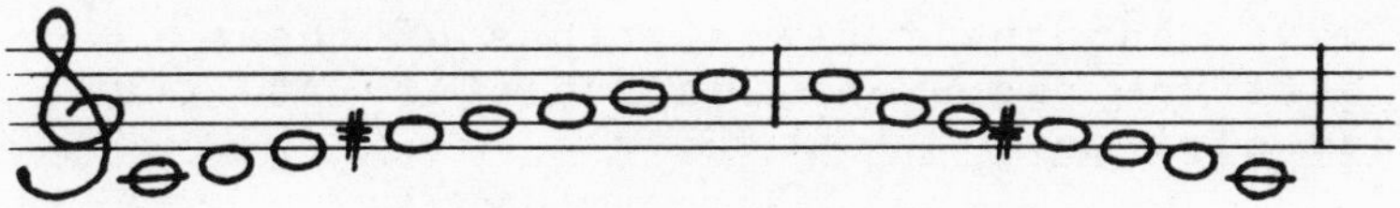

Ascent: *krama sampūrṇa.*
Descent: the note *NI* (B) is avoided.

(34) *Nishādi* (*Niṣādi*)

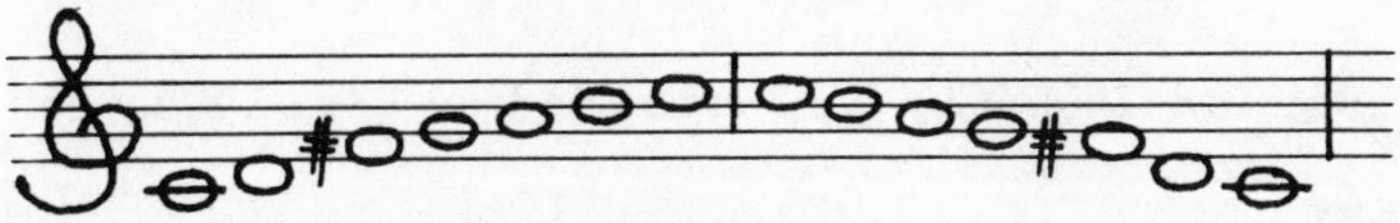

The note *GA* (E) is avoided entirely.

(35) *Sundaravinōdiṇi*

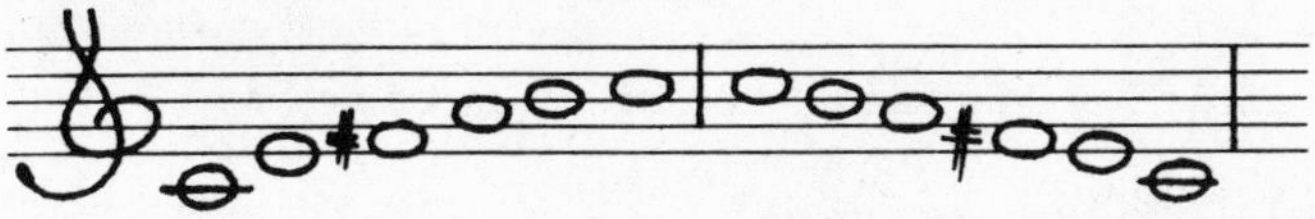

The notes *RI* (D) and *PA* (G) are avoided entirely.

(36) *Suraṭavinodiṇi*

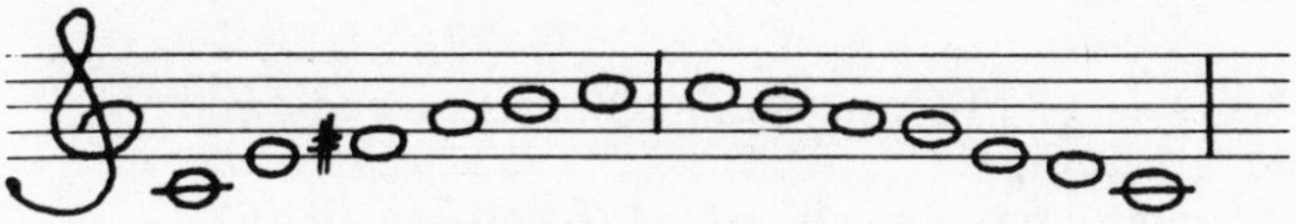

Ascent: the notes *RI* (D) and *PA* (G) are avoided.
Descent: the note *MA* (F#) is omitted.

(37) *Śantakalyāṇī*

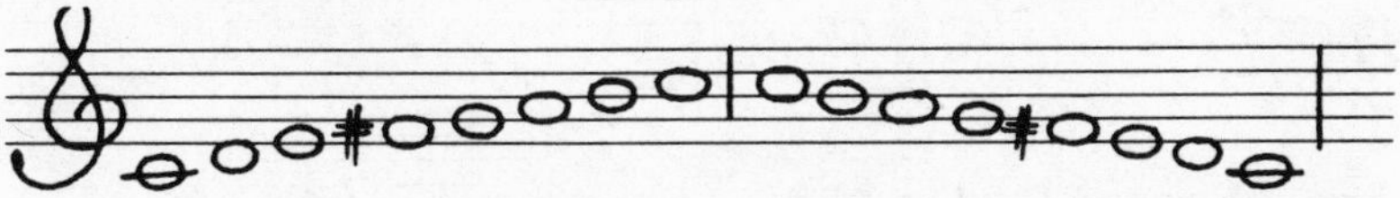

The scale of this *rāga* is identical with that of its primary *rāga*, *Mechakalyāṇī*. In the past *Śantakalyāṇī* was the name of the later 65. *asampūrṇa mēḷa* (with *kaṭapayādi* prefixes).

A few musicians maintain that at the present time there are some slight differences between *Śantakalyāṇī* and *Mechakalyāṇī*, but their descriptions of these differences were too vague and contradictory and could not be defined clearly.

(38) *Shīlāṅgi* (*Śīlāṅgi*)

The notes *RI* (D) and *DHA* (A) are avoided entirely.

(39) *Śubhavāsini*

The notes *GA* (E) and *PA* (G) are avoided entirely.

(40) *Śuddhakalyāṇī* (*Mōhanakalyāṇī*)

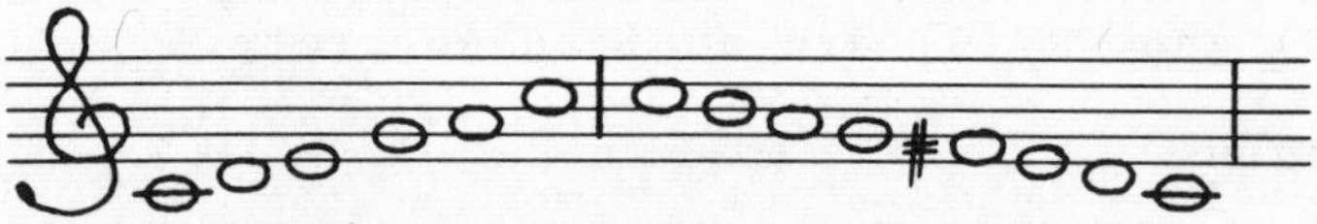

Ascent: the notes *MA* (F#) and *NI* (B) are avoided.
Descent: *krama sampūrṇa*.

Another *rāga* with the name of *Mohanakalyāṇī* appears under the heading of the 28. *mēḷa* (3).

(41) *Śuddhakōsala*

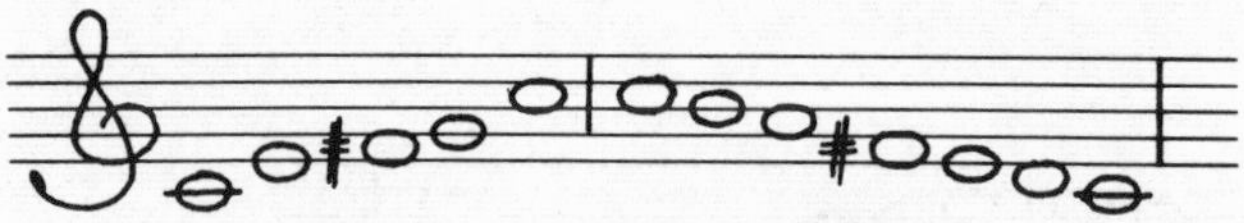

Ascent: the notes *RI* (D), *DHA* (A), and *NI* (B) are avoided.
Descent: the note *PA* (G) is omitted.

(42) *Śuddharatnabhānu*

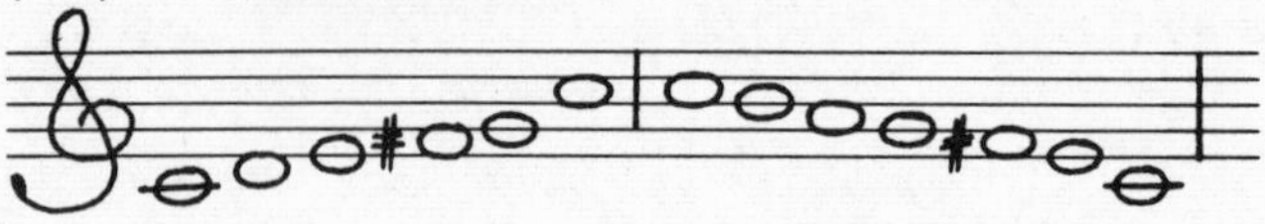

Ascent: the notes *DHA* (A) and *NI* (B) are avoided.
Descent: the note *RI* (D) is omitted.

(43) *Vandanadhāriṇi*

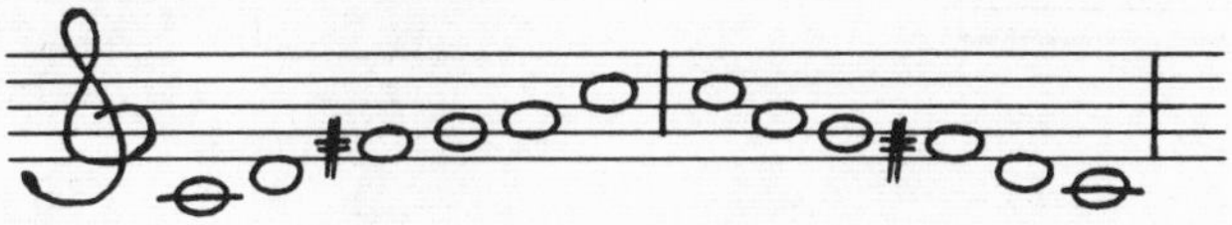

The notes *GA* (E) and *NI* (B) are avoided entirely.

(44) *Yamunakalyāṇī*

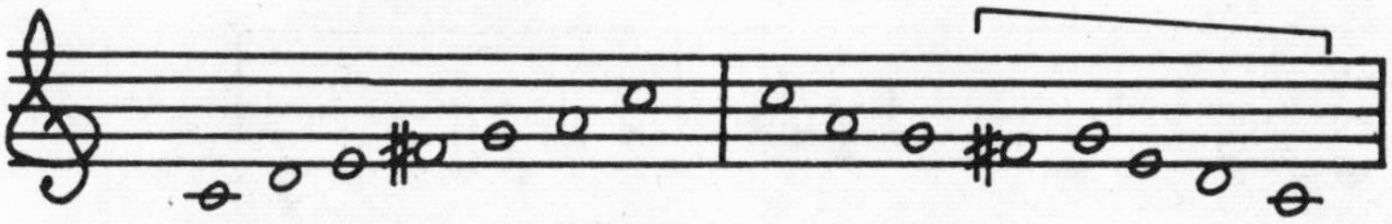

The note *NI* (B) is avoided entirely and the descent shows one extended *vakra* passage.

Occasionally the note *NI* (B) can be used slightly. Veṅkatamakhin speaks of the "*sampūrṇa scale*" of this *rāga*. The note *MA śuddha* (F natural) can appear as a brief feature, usually in descent as first note of the extended *vakra* passage.

Another form of the *Yamunakalyāṇī* ascent is:

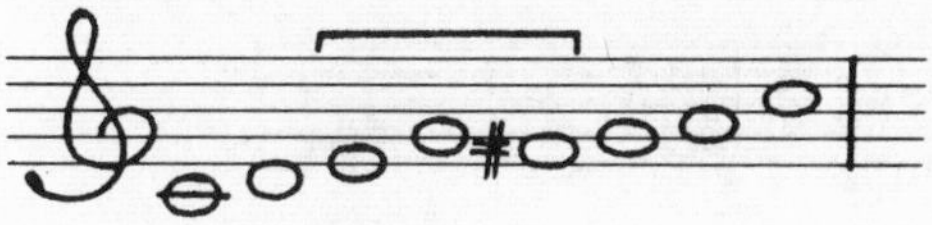

YAMUNAKALYĀṆĪ (*Triputa-tāla*) SCM, 277-78

66. *MĒḶA CHITRĀMBARĪ (CITRĀMBARĪ)*

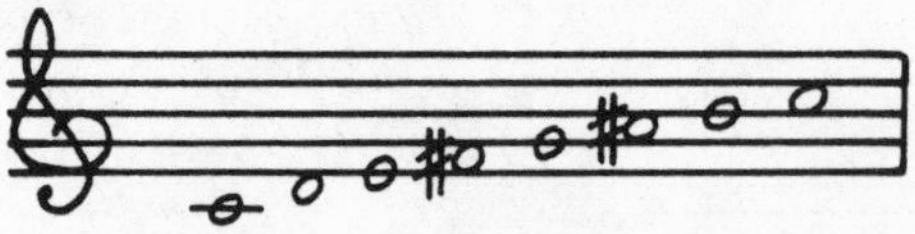

CHITRĀMBARĪ (Triputa-tāla) SCM, 278

Janya Rāgas of the 66. Mēḷa

(1) *Amritavarṡiṇi*

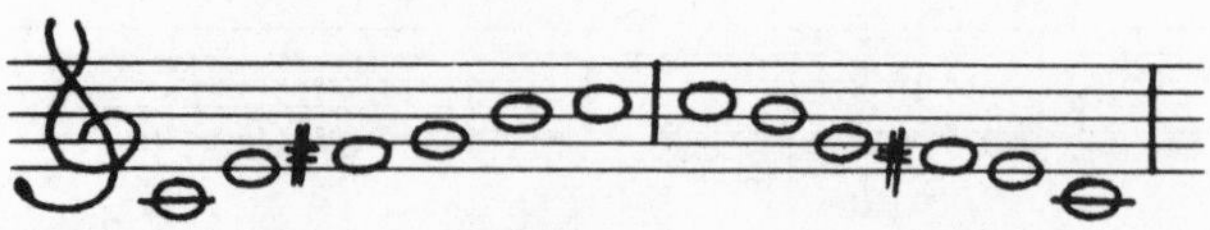

The notes *RI* (D) and *DHA* (A#) are avoided entirely.

Another *rāga* with the same name is listed under the heading of the 39. *mēḷa* (2).

(2) *Chandhikam*

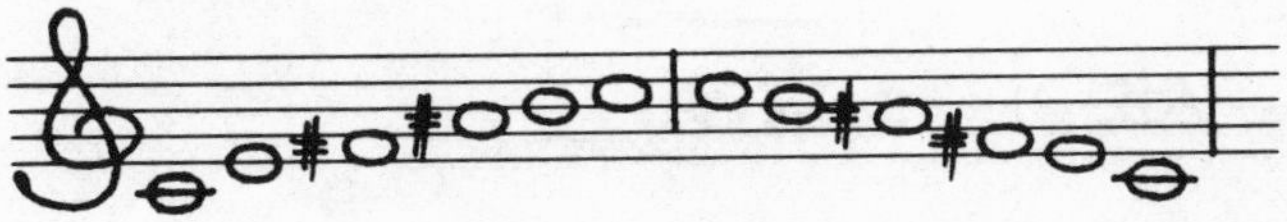

The notes *RI* (D) and *PA* (G) are avoided entirely.

(3) *Chaturaṅgiṇī* (*Caturaṅgiṇī*)

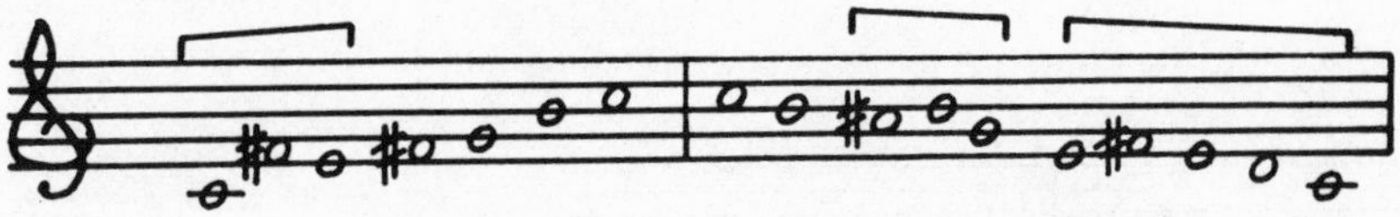

Ascent: the notes *RI* (D) and *DHA* (A#) are avoided; one *vakra* feature is shown.
Descent: *sampūrṇa*; two *vakra* features, the second one extended, are used.

The name *Chaturaṅgiṇī* was applied in the past to the 66. *mēḷa* of the *asampūrṇa mēḷa* system. According to SD (I, 77) its scale is given as:

in which the ascent is *krama sampūrṇa* and the descent avoids the note *DHA* (A#).

CHATURAṄGIṆĪ (*Triputa-tāla*) SCM, 279

(4) *Chitta Rañjillini* (*Citta Rañjillini*)

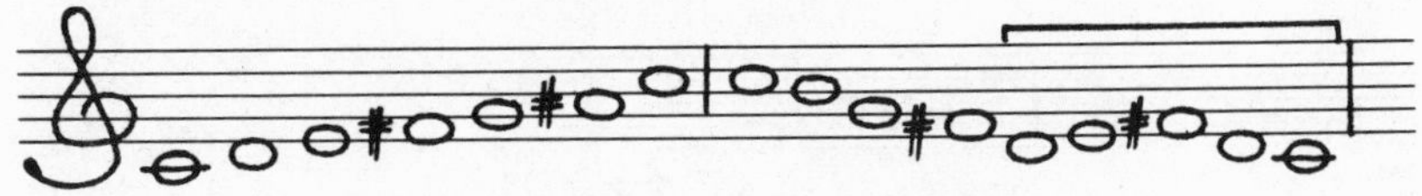

Ascent: the note *NI* (B) is avoided.
Descent: the note *DHA* (A#) is omitted; one extended *vakra* passage is shown.

(5) *Chūrṇika Vinōdini* (*Cūrṇika Vinodini*)

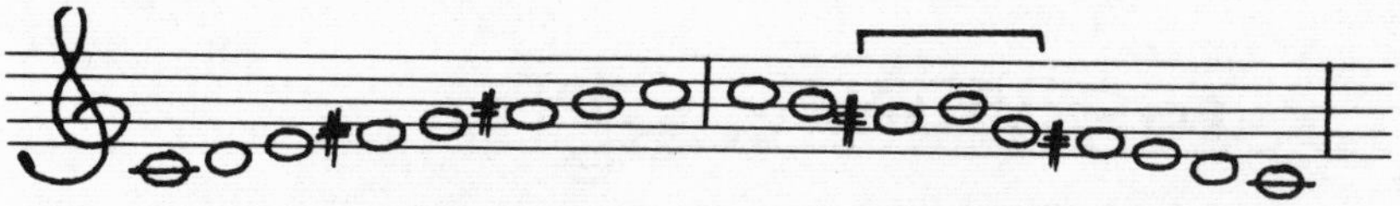

Ascent: *krama sampūrṇa*.
Descent: *sampūrṇa*; one *vakra* feature is shown.

(6) *Dēvagīrvāṇi*

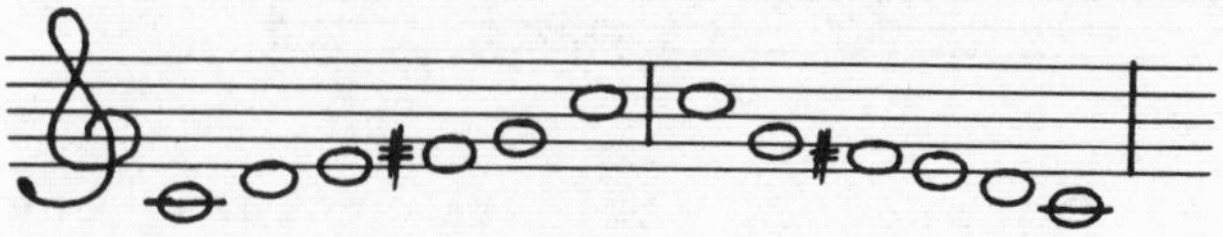

The notes *DHA* (A#) and *NI* (B) are avoided entirely.

(7) *Dviradagāmiṇi*

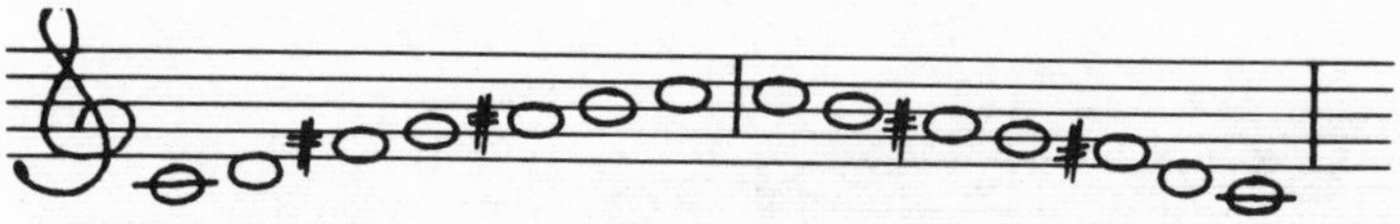

The note *GA* (E) is avoided entirely.

(8) *Gagana Rañjani*

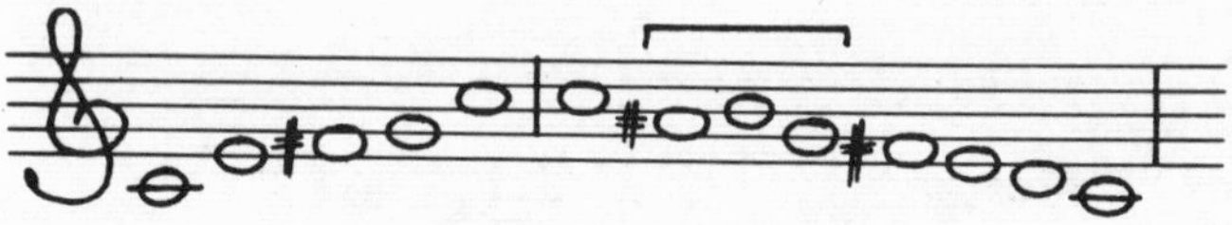

Ascent: the notes *RI* (D), *DHA* (A#), and *NI* (B) are avoided.
Descent: *sampūrṇa*; one *vakra* feature is shown.

(9) *Hērambhapriya*

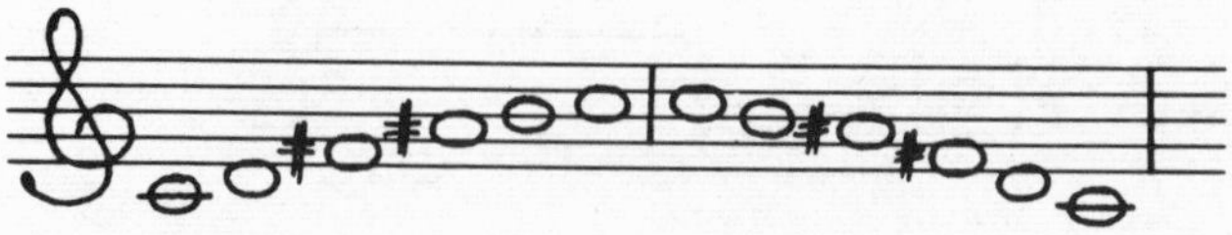

The notes *GA* (E) and *PA* (G) are avoided entirely.

(10) *Īśapriya*

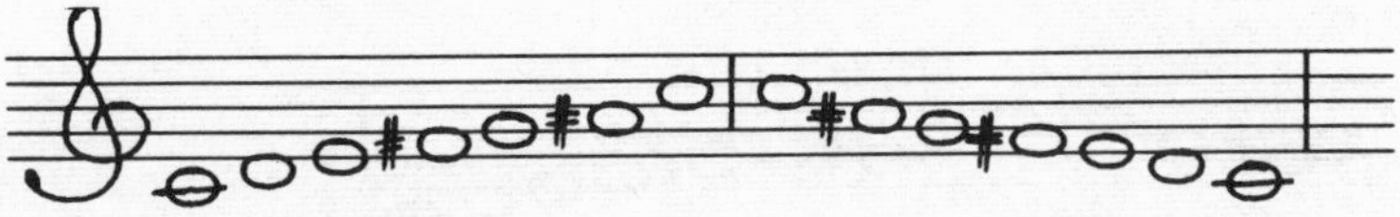

The note *NI* (B) is avoided entirely.

(11) *Kanaka Bhavāni*

Ascent: the note *RI* (D) is avoided; one *vakra* feature is shown.
Descent: the notes *DHA* (A#) and *GA* (E) are omitted.

(12) *Kanakagiri*

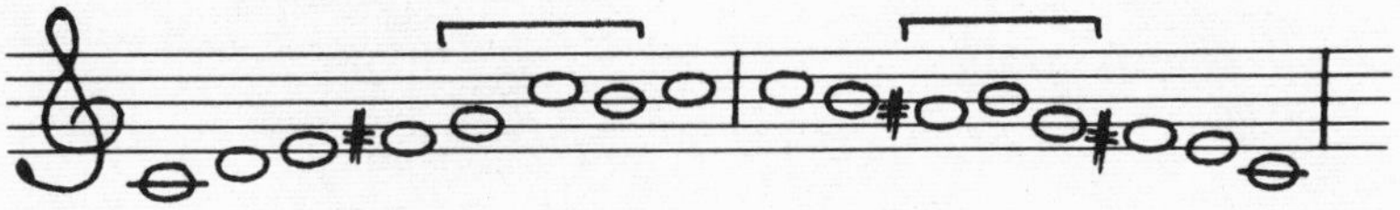

Ascent: the note *DHA* (A#) is avoided; one *vakra* feature is shown.
Descent: the note *RI* (D) is omitted; one *vakra* feature is used.

(13) *Mānini*

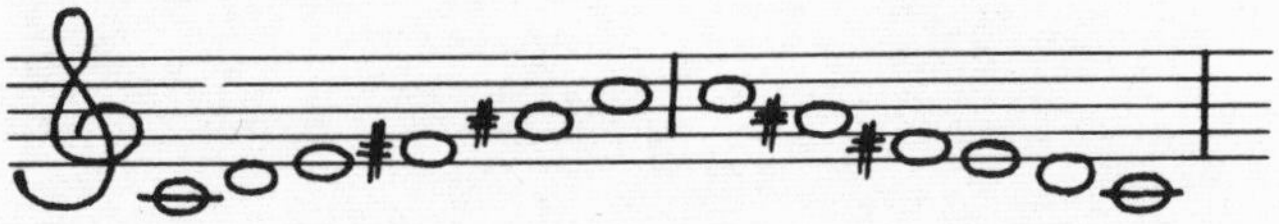

The notes *PA* (G) and *NI* (B) are avoided entirely.
Another *rāga* with the same name is listed under the heading of the 47. *mēḷa* (9).

(14) *Nāgakuntali*

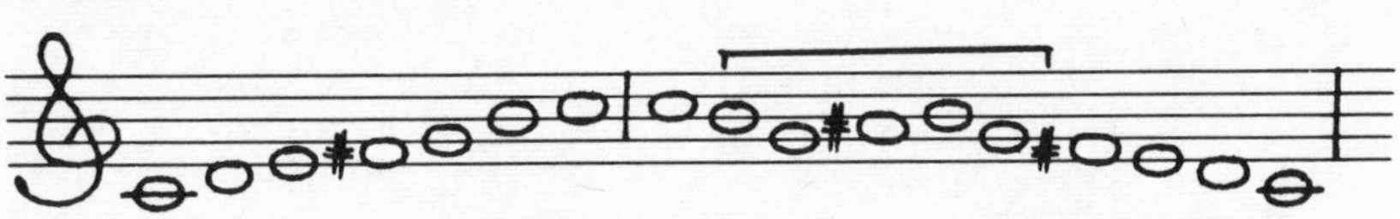

Ascent: the note *DHA* (A#) is avoided.
Descent: *sampūrṇa*; one extended *vakra* feature is shown.

(15) *Sarati*

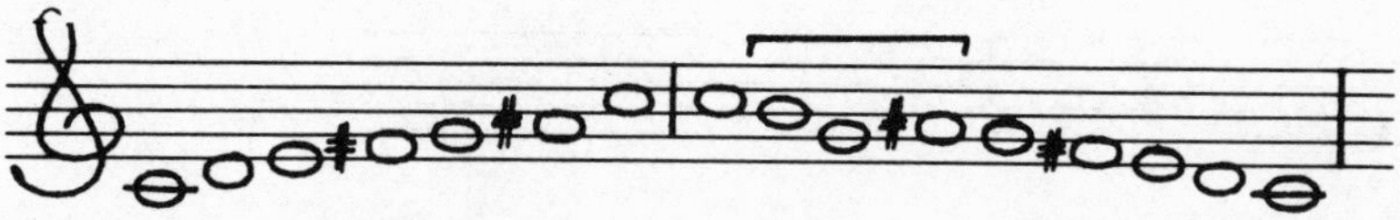

Ascent: the note *NI* (B) is avoided.
Descent: *sampūrṇa*; one *vakra* feature is shown.

(16) *Vijayakōsalam*

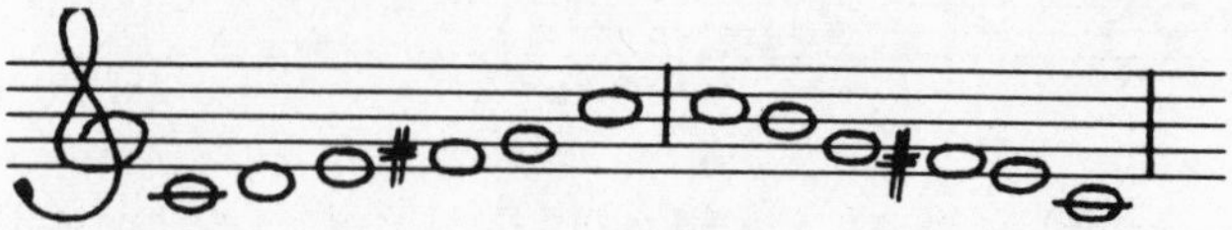

The note *DHA* (A#), a characteristic feature of the 66. *mēḷa*, is avoided entirely. *NI* (B) is avoided in ascent and *RI* (D) in descent.

Chakra XII

67. *MĒḶA SUCHARITRA* (*SUCARITRA*)

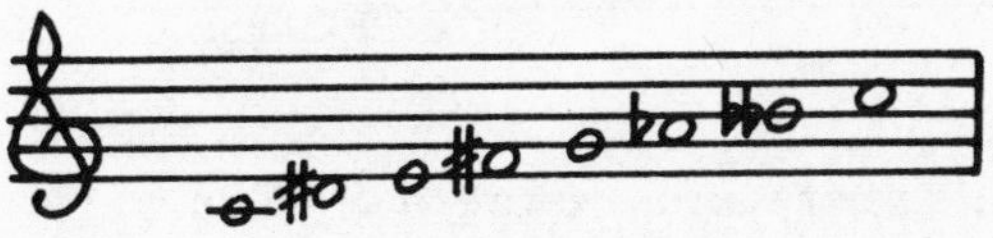

SUCHARITRA (*Triputa-tāla*) SCM, 280

Janya Rāgas of the 67. Mēḷa

(1) *Āśrita Rañjani*

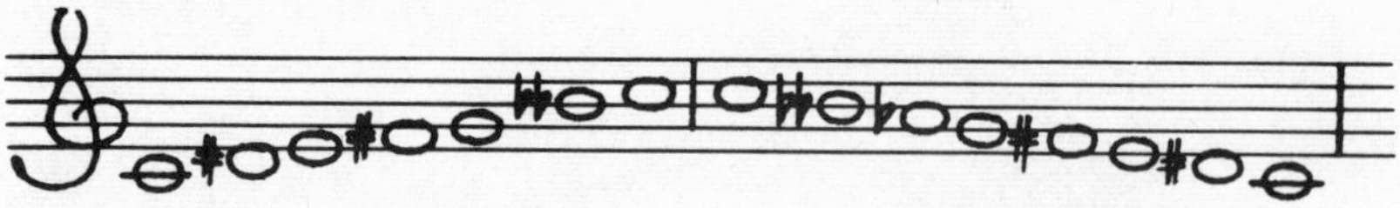

Ascent: the note *DHA* (Ab) is avoided.
Descent: *krama sampūrṇa*.

(2) *Bhānu Jyōtiṣmati*

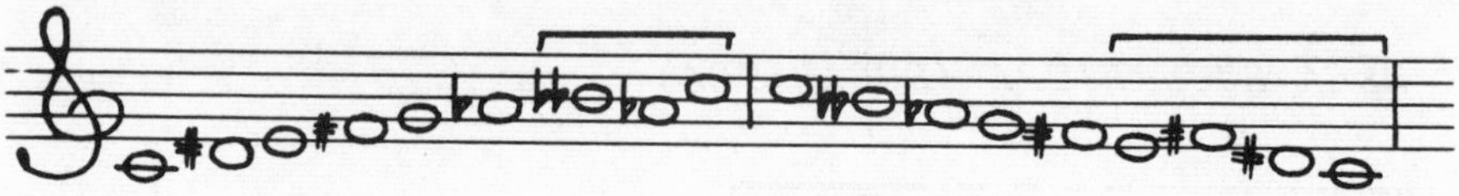

This scale is *sampūrṇa* in ascent and descent. Two *vakra* features are shown, one in ascent and one in descent.

(3) *Biṅkāvati*

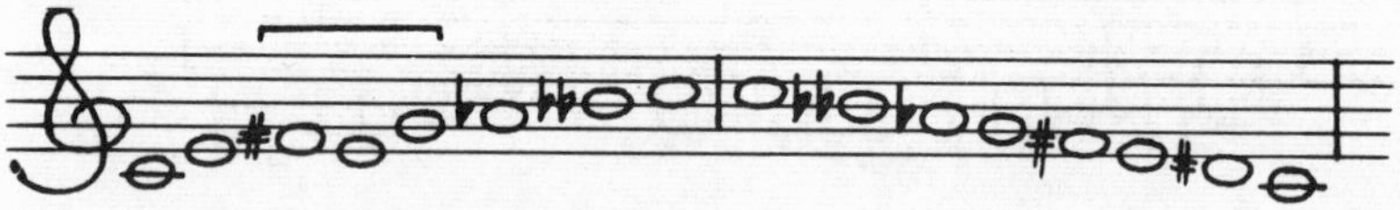

Ascent: the note *RI* (D#) is avoided; one *vakra* feature is shown.
Descent: *krama sampūrṇa*.

(4) *Gōpikāmanōrañjani*

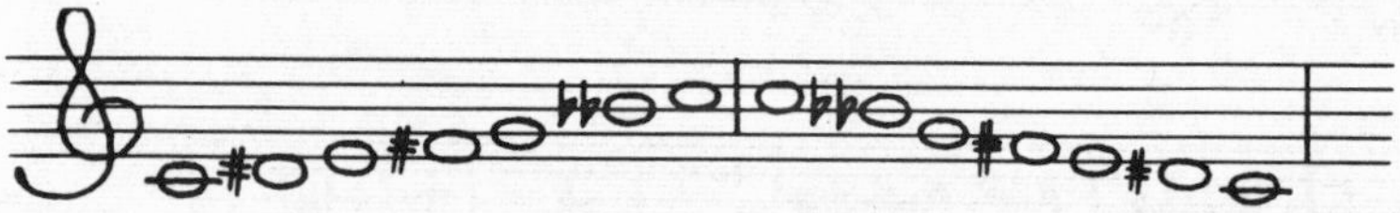

The note *DHA* (Ab) is avoided entirely.

(5) *Kanaka Gīrvāṇi*

The note *GA* (E) is avoided entirely.

Ascent: one *vakra* feature is shown.
Descent: the note *NI* (Bbb) is omitted.

(6) *Kanaka Nirmada*

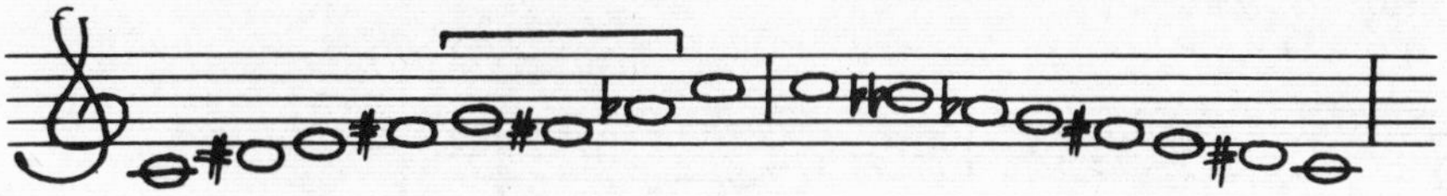

Ascent: the note *NI* (Bbb) is avoided; one *vakra* feature is shown.
Descent: *krama sampūrṇa*.

(7) *Kētanāvaḷi*

Ascent: *sampūrṇa*; one *vakra* feature is shown.
Descent: the note *RI* (D#) is avoided; one *vakra* feature is used.

(8) *Kīrtibhānu*

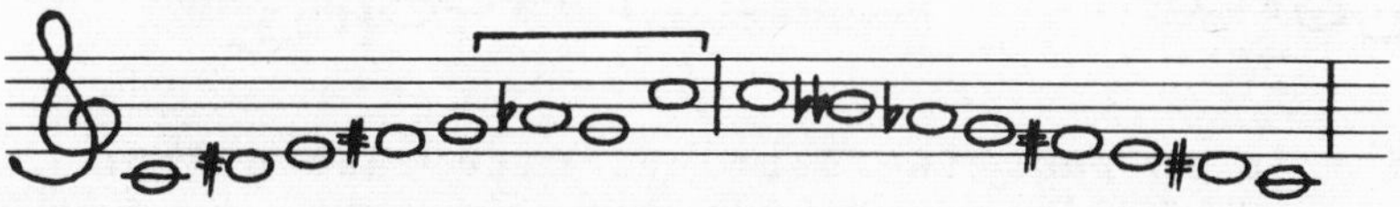

Ascent: the note *NI* (Bbb) is avoided; one *vakra* feature is used.
Descent: *krama sampūrṇa*.

(9) *Kumuthiṇi*

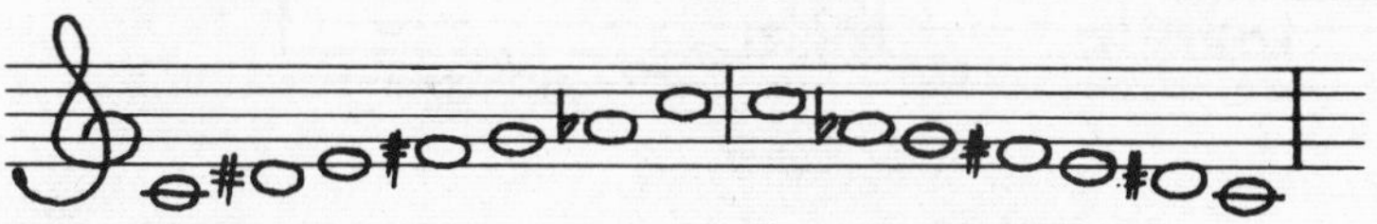

The note *NI* (Bbb) is avoided entirely.

(10) *Kuntala Bhavāni*

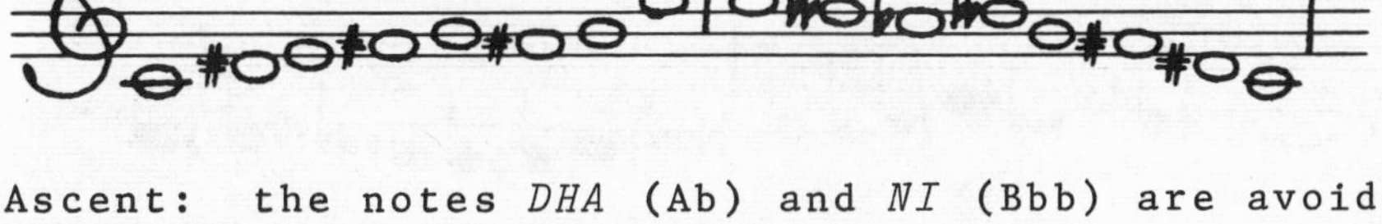

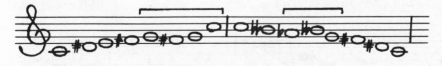

Ascent: the notes *DHA* (Ab) and *NI* (Bbb) are avoided;

one *vakra* feature is shown.
Descent: the note *GA* (E) is omitted; one *vakra* feature is used.

(11) *Ramkavāmbari*

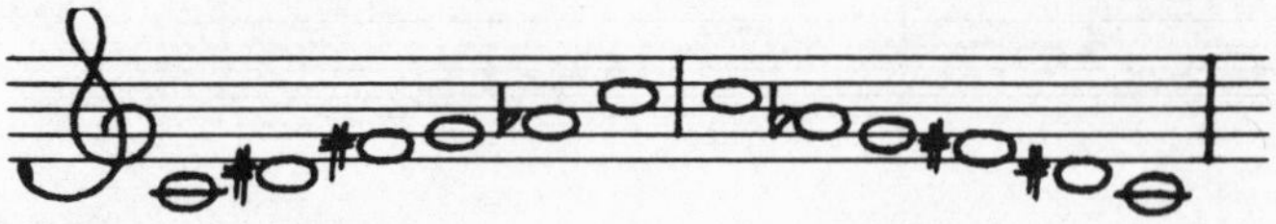

The notes *GA* (E) and *NI* (Bbb) are avoided entirely.

(12) *Rāmakuntala*

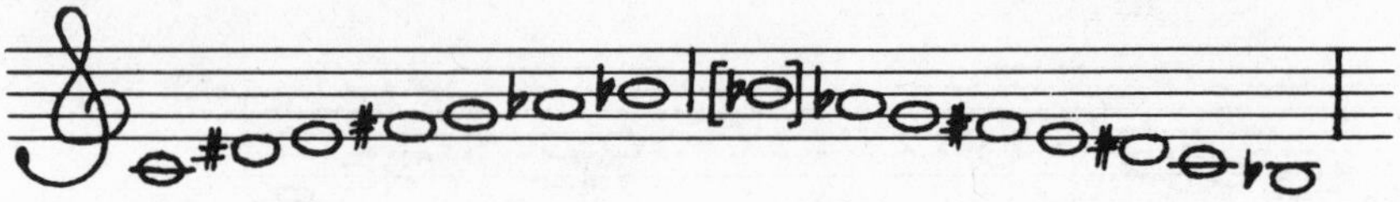

The scale of this *rāga* has *niṣādāntya* character.

(13) *Santānamañjari*

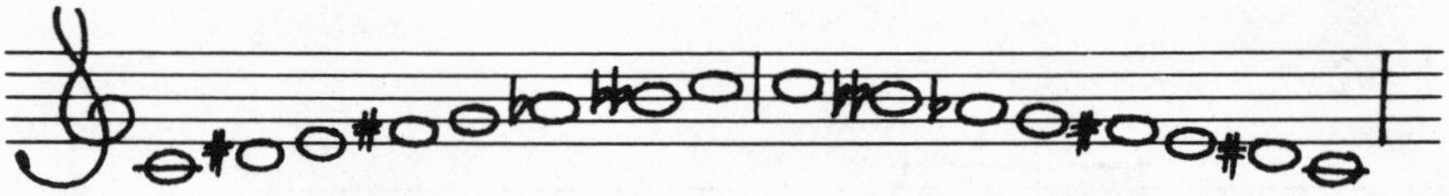

The scale of this *rāga* is identical with that of the primary *rāga Sucharitra*. Despite the fact that a few musicians speak of slight differences between the two *rāgas*, none could be noticed.

(14) *Satyavatī*

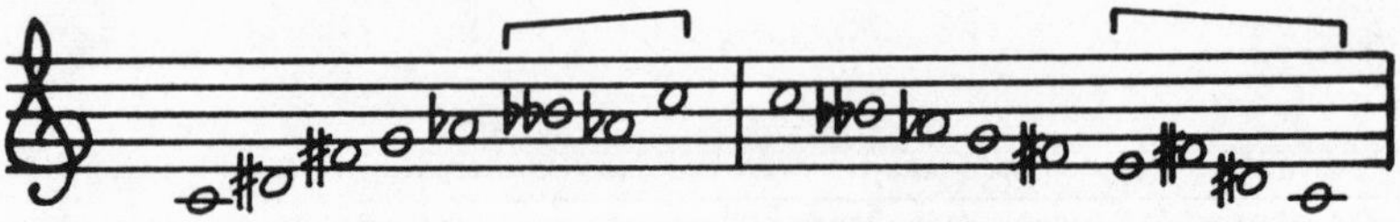

Ascent: the note *GA* (E) is avoided; one *vakra* feature is shown.
Descent: *sampūrṇa*; one *vakra* feature is used.

SATYAVATĪ (*Triputa-tāla*) SCM, 280-81

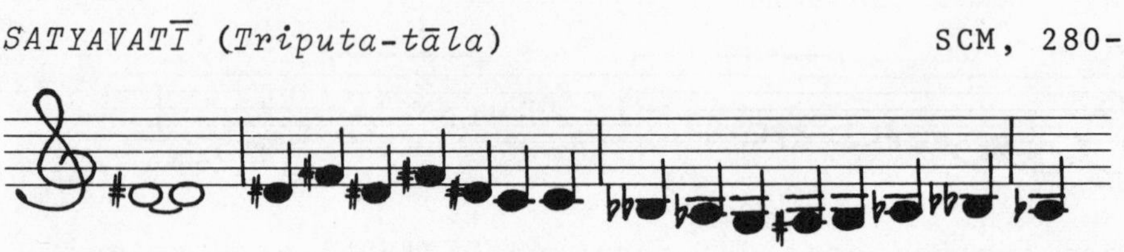

(15) *Sēnājayanti*

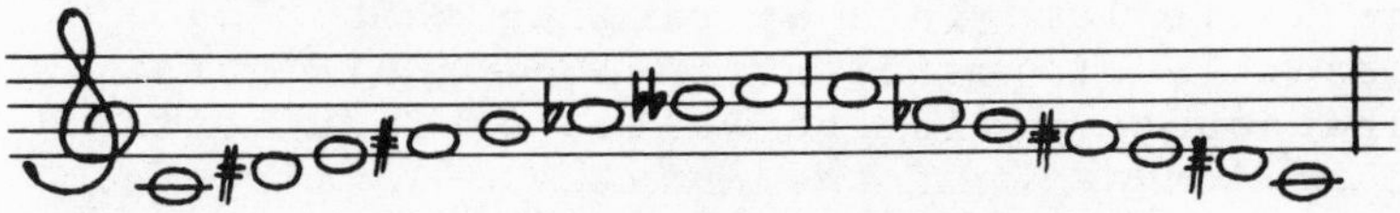

Ascent: *krama sampūrṇa*.
Descent: the note *NI* (Bbb) is avoided.

(16) *Sōmamañjari*

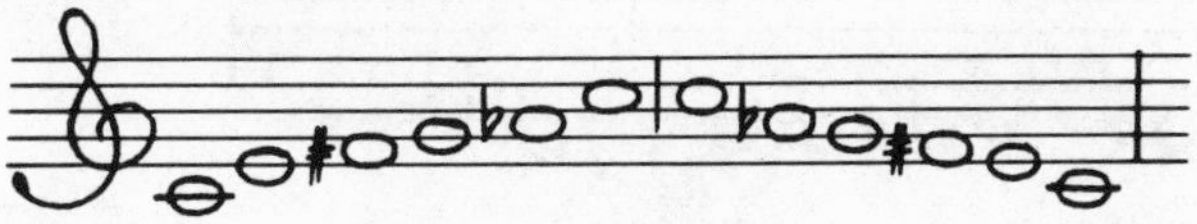

The notes *RI* (D#) and *NI* (Bbb) are avoided entirely.

(17) *Śāmbhavi*

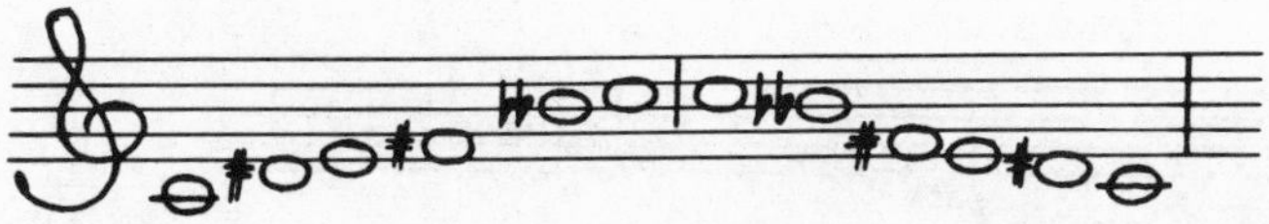

The notes *PA* (G) and *DHA* (Ab) are avoided entirely.

(18) *Śuddhasiṃhāravam*

Ascent: *sampurṇa*; one *vakra* feature is shown.
Descent: the note *GA* (E) is avoided; one *vakra* feature is used.

(19) *Śyāmaḷavarṇi*

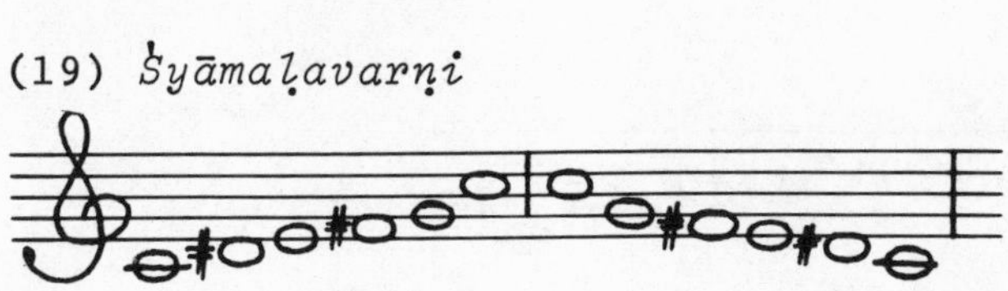

The notes *DHA* (Ab) and *NI* (Bbb) are avoided entirely.

68. *MĒḶA JYŌTISVARŪPIṆĪ*

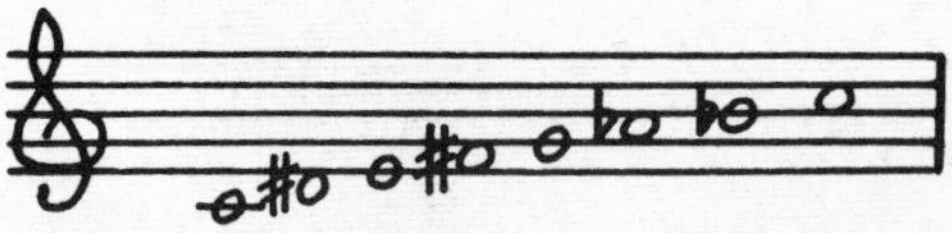

SD (II, 265) relates that "Tyāgarāja...is reputed to have made an unlit lamp burn by singing this *rāga* before an assembly of musicians including his guru, Sonti Veṅkaṭaramanayya, in the Palace of Pudukkottai (see p. 870 of *A Manual of the Pudukkotai State*, Vol. II, Part I, second revised edition, 1940)."

JYŌTISVARŪPIṆĪ (*Triputa-tāla*) SCM, 281-2

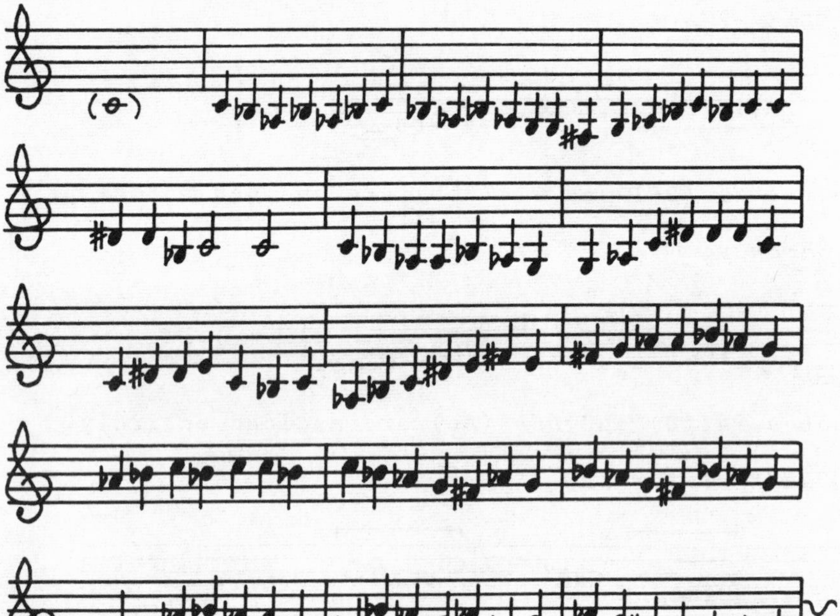

Janya Rāgas of the 68. Mēḷa

(1) *Bhuvana Kuntali*

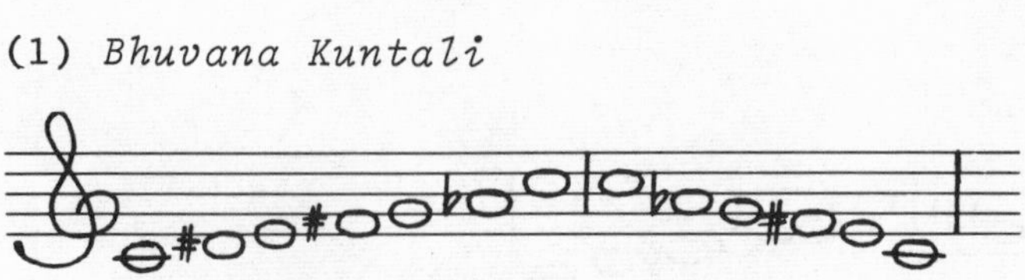

The note *NI* (Bb) is avoided entirely; *RI* (D#) is omitted in descent.

(2) *Buddhavāhiṇi*

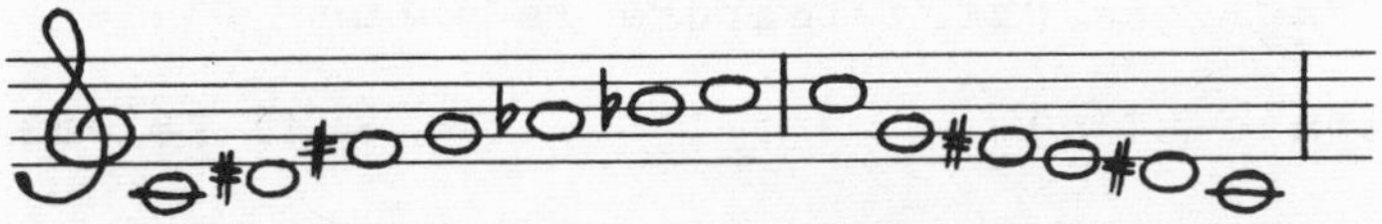

Ascent: the note *GA* (E) is avoided.
Descent: the notes *NI* (Bb) and *DHA* (Ab) are omitted.

(3) *Gauḷa Gāndhāri*

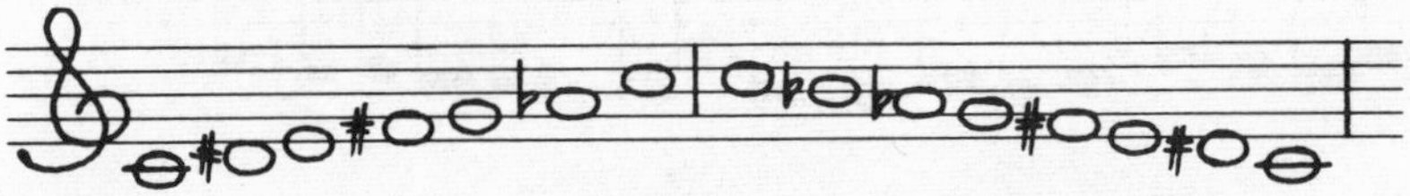

Ascent: the note *NI* (Bb) is avoided.
Descent: *krama sampūrṇa*.

(4) *Hindōḷa Dēśākṣi*

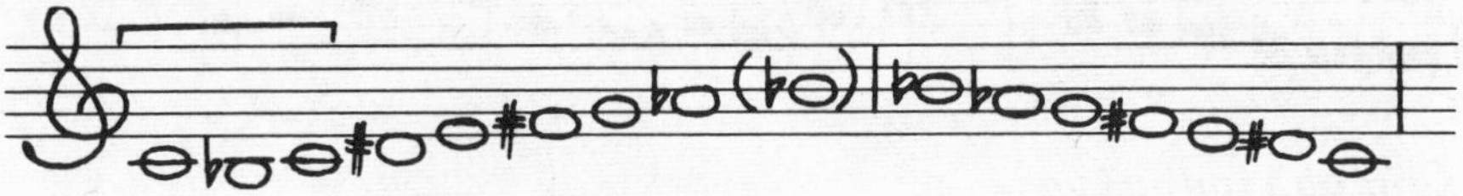

The scale of this *niṣādāntya rāga* shows one *vakra* feature in ascent.

(5) *Jalajamukhi*

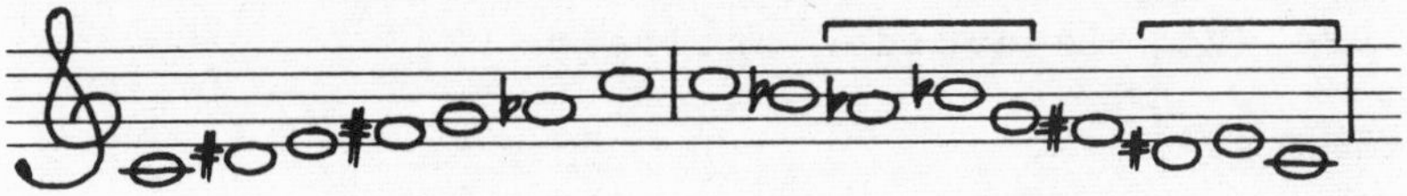

Ascent: the note *NI* (Bb) is avoided.
Descent: *sampūrṇa*; two *vakra* features are shown.

(6) *Jauḍa Gāndhāri*

Ascent: the note *NI* (Bb) is avoided.
Descent: *krama sampūrṇa*.

(7) *Jyōtiṣmati*

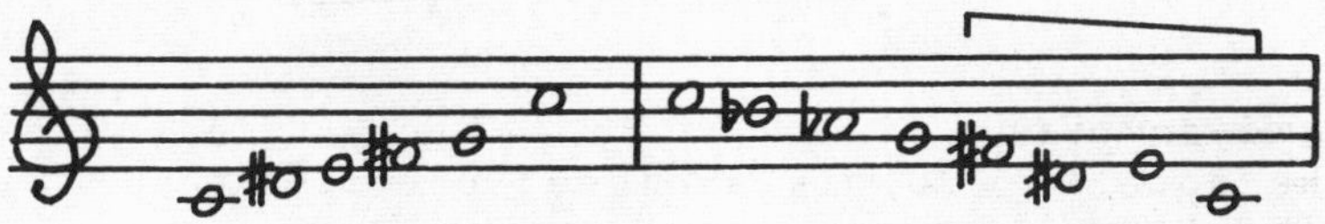

Ascent: the notes *DHA* (Ab) and *NI* (Bb) are avoided.
Descent: *sampūrṇa*; one *vakra* feature is shown.

JYŌTIṢMATI (*Triputa-tāla*) SCM, 282-83

(8) *Kañjabhavapriya*

The note *DHA* (Ab) is avoided entirely.

(9) *Kētakāṃkuśa*

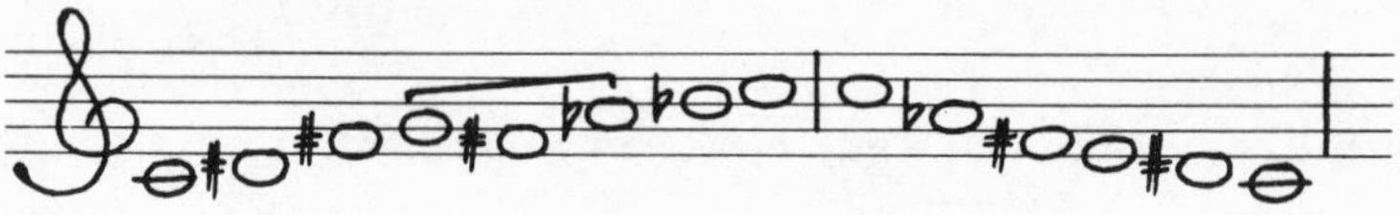

Ascent: the note *GA* (E) is avoided and one *vakra* feature is shown.
Descent: the notes *NI* (Bb) and *PA* (G) are omitted.

(10) *Kuntala Gīrvāṇi*

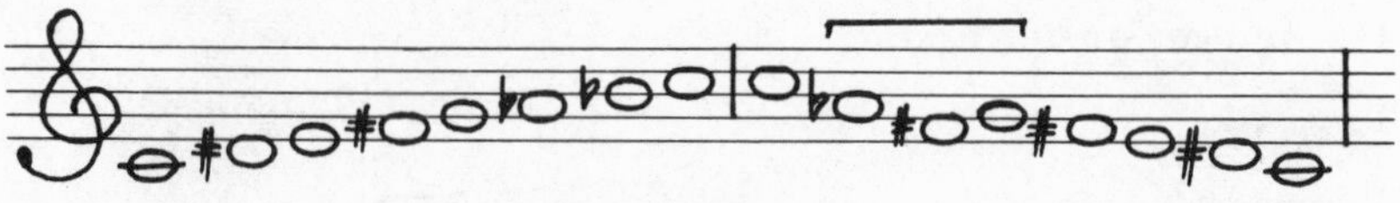

Ascent: *krama sampūrṇa*.
Descent: the note *NI* (Bb) is avoided; one *vakra* feature is shown.

(11) *Kuntala Rañjaṇi*

Ascent: the note *GA* (E) is avoided; one *vakra* feature is shown.
Descent: *krama sampūrṇa*.

(12) *Kusuma Bhavāni*

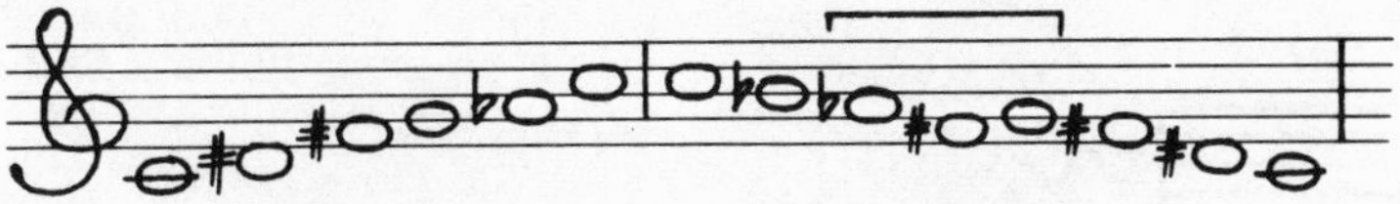

The note *GA* (E) is avoided entirely.
Ascent: the note *NI* (Bb) is omitted.
Descent: one *vakra* feature is shown.

(13) *Rāmgiri*

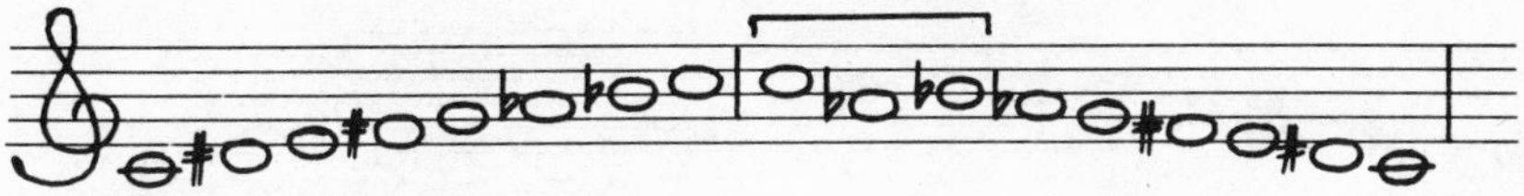

Ascent: *krama sampūrṇa*.
Descent: *sampūrṇa*; one *vakra* feature is shown.

69. *MĒḶA DHĀTUVARDHANĪ*

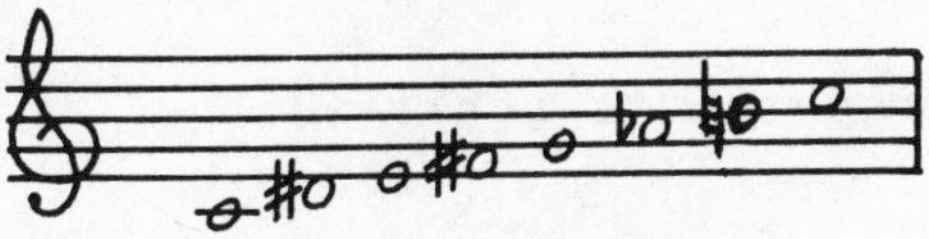

DHĀTUVARDHANĪ (*Triputa-tāla*) SCM, 283

The name *Dhauta Pañchamam* represents the 69. *mēḷa* of the *asampūrṇa* system of the past. *Rāga Dhauta Pañchamam*, at the present time, has the following scale:

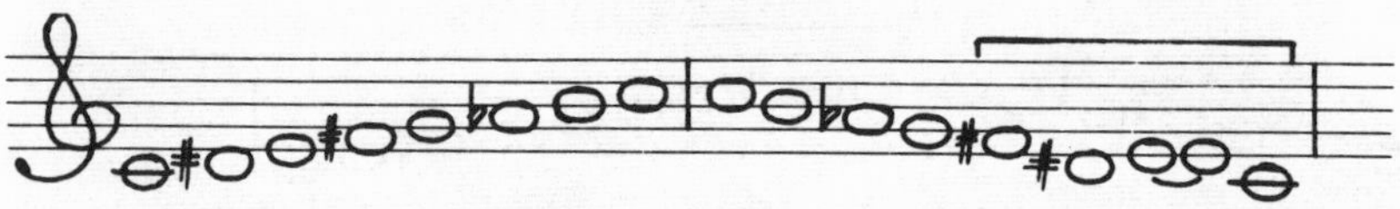

SD (I, 113) mentions the following characteristic phrases of this *rāga*:

R (p. 216) presents the *Dhautapañchama* scale in the following manner:

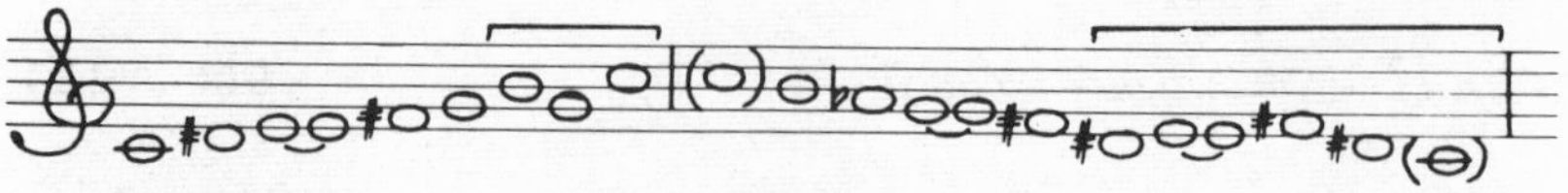

DHAUTAPAÑCHAM (*Triputa-tāla*) SCM, 284

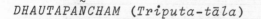

Janya Rāgas of the 69. Mēḷa

(1) *Bṛndāvana Kannaḍa* (*Brindāvana Kannaḍa*)

The note *NI* (B), a characteristic feature of the 69. *mēḷa*, is avoided entirely. Hence this *rāga* could also be listed under the headings of the 67. and 68. *mēḷas*. The ascent avoids the note *RI* (D#).

(2) *Chhāyā Vardhini*

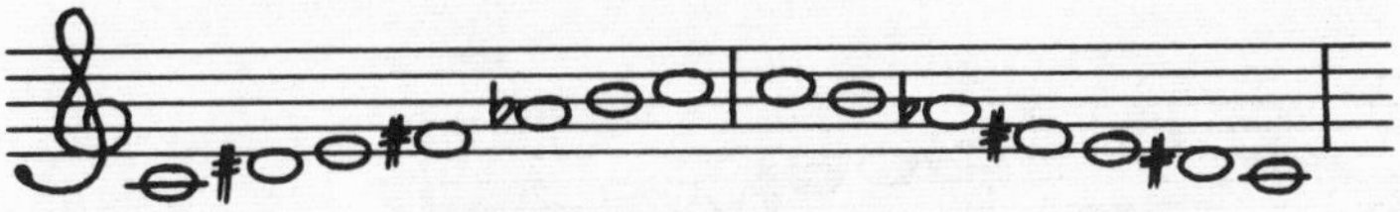

The note *PA* (G) is avoided entirely.

(3) *Dēva Nāyaki*

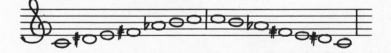

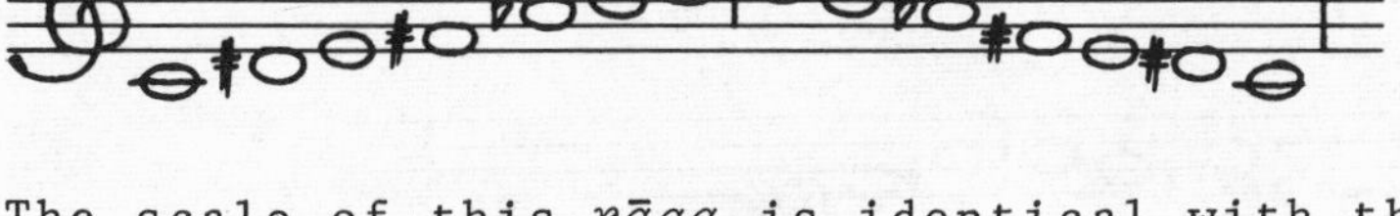

The scale of this *rāga* is identical with that of *Chhāyā Vardhini* (69, 2). Despite some vague and confusing statements to the contrary, no differences in performance practice can be observed.

(4) *Dēvarāṣṭram*

Ascent: the note *DHA* (Ab) is avoided.
Descent: *krama sampūrṇa*.

(5) *Dhanupriya*

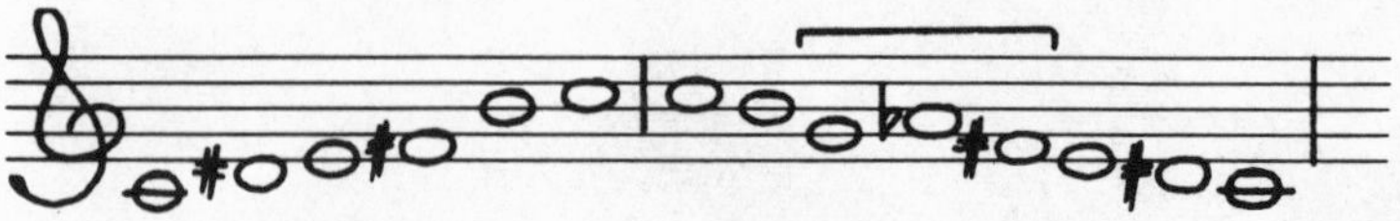

Ascent: the notes *PA* (G) and *DHA* (Ab) are avoided.
Descent: *sampūrṇa*; one *vakra* feature is shown.

(6) *Dhātu Pañchamam* (*Dhātu Pañcamam*)

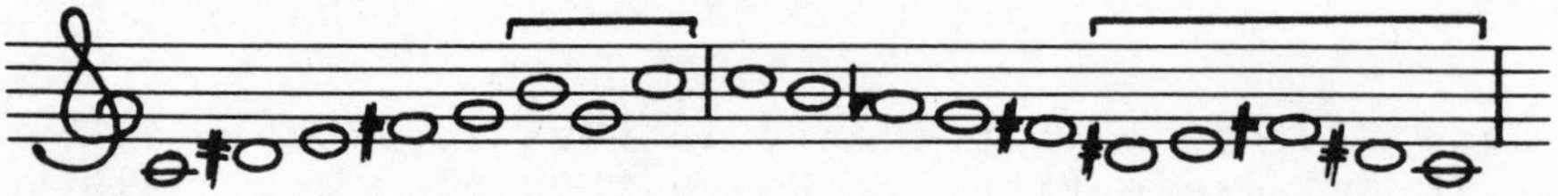

Ascent: the note *DHA* (Ab) is avoided; one *vakra* feature is shown.
Descent: *sampūrṇa*; one extended *vakra* passage is used.

(7) *Dhātupriya*

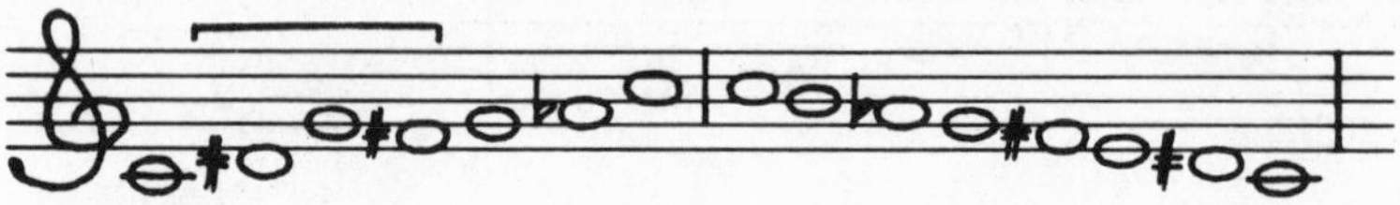

Ascent: the notes *GA* (E) and *NI* (B) are avoided.
Descent: *krama sampūrṇa*.

Another *rāga* with the same name is listed under the heading of the 63. *mēḷa* (6).

(8) *Dhīrasāvēri*

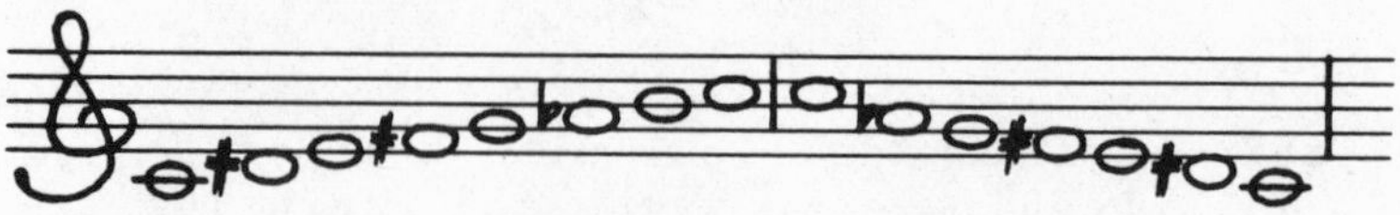

Ascent: *krama sampūrṇa*.
Descent: the note *NI* (B) is avoided.

(9) *Dvitīya Pañchamam (Dvitīya Pañcamam)*

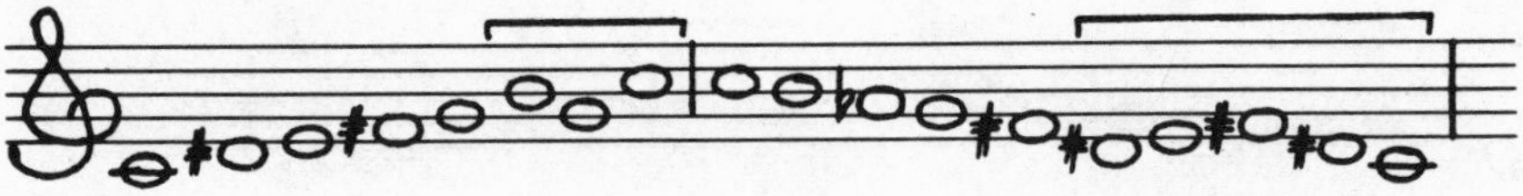

Ascent: the note *DHA* (Ab) is avoided; one *vakra* feature is shown.
Descent: *sampūrṇa*; one extended *vakra* passage is used.

(10) *Hāvavilāsini*

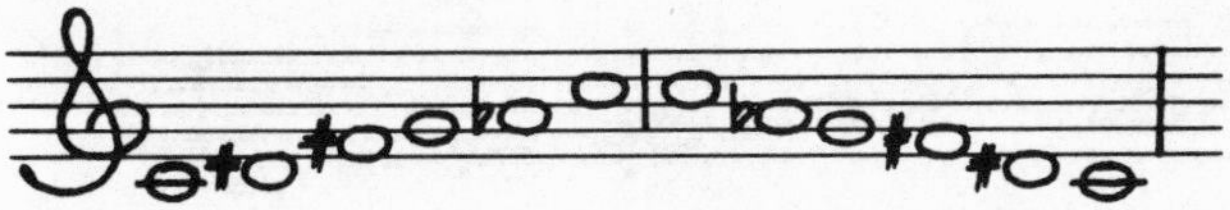

The notes *GA* (E) and *NI* (B) are avoided entirely.

(11) *Īśagiri*

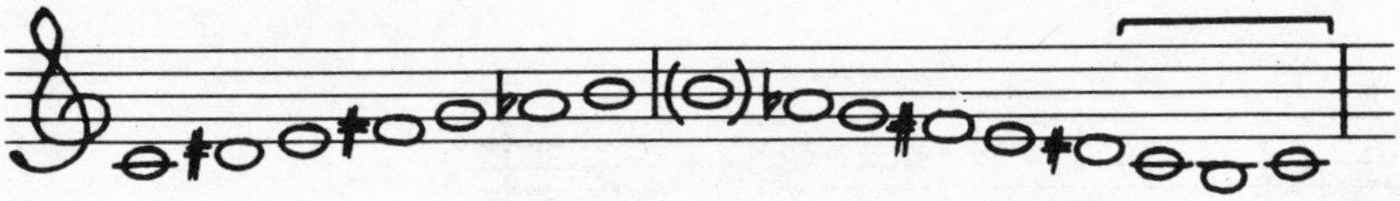

The *niṣādāntya* scale of this *rāga* ascends and descends in a straight manner and shows at the lowest point of its descent one *vakra* feature.

(12) *Kalābhogi*

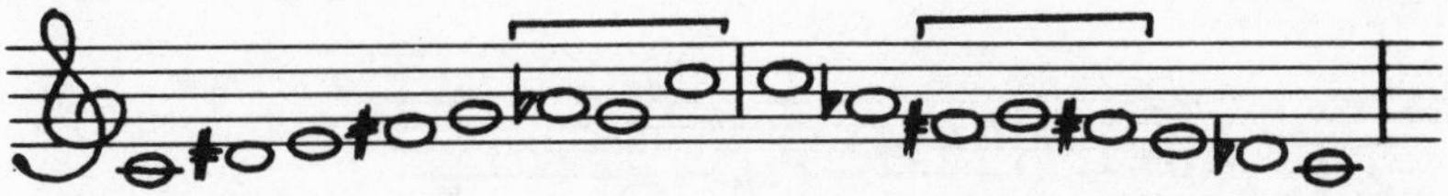

The note *NI* (B) is avoided entirely. The scale shows two *vakra* features, one in ascent and one in descent.

(13) *Kuntala Siṃhāravam*

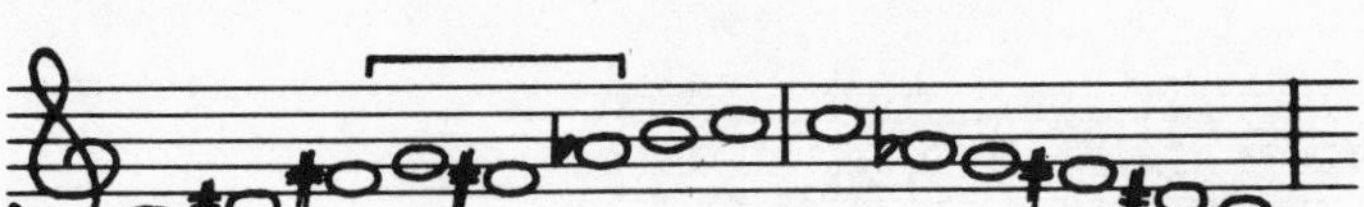

The note *GA* (E) is avoided entirely.
Ascent: one *vakra* feature is shown.
Descent: the note *NI* (B) is omitted.

(14) *Kusuma Jyōtiṣmati*

Ascent: *sampūrṇa*; one *vakra* feature is shown.
Descent: the note *GA* (E) is avoided; one *vakra* feature is used.

(15) *Lalitakōsaḷi*

The scale of this *rāga* is *sampūrṇa* and shows one *vakra* feature in ascent and one in descent.

(16) *Nalinakusumāvaḷi*

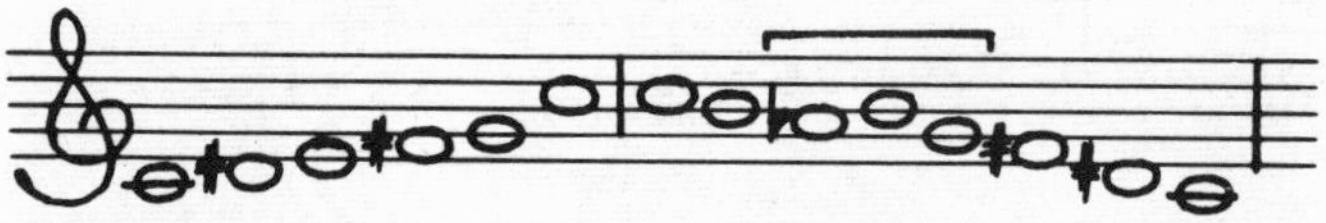

Ascent: the notes *DHA* (Ab) and *NI* (B) are avoided.
Descent: the note *GA* (E) is omitted; one *vakra* feature is shown.

(17) *Padmabhavāni*

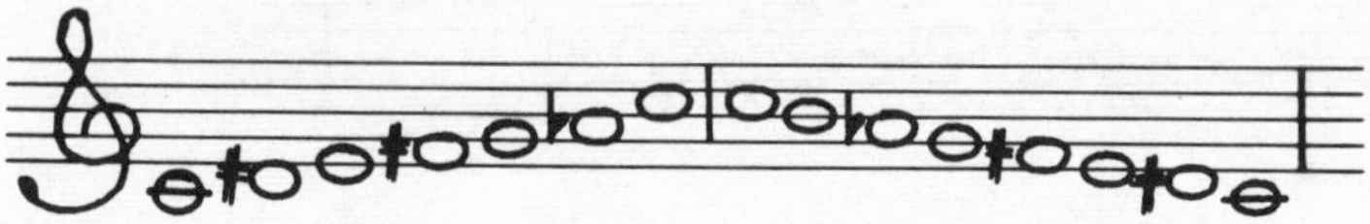

Ascent: the note *NI* (B) is avoided.
Descent: *krama sampūrṇa*.

(18) *Paridhi*

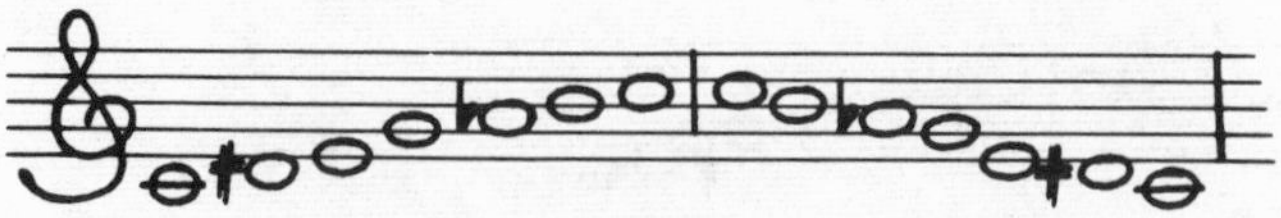

The note *MA* (F#) is avoided entirely.

(19) *Samavēṣiṇi*

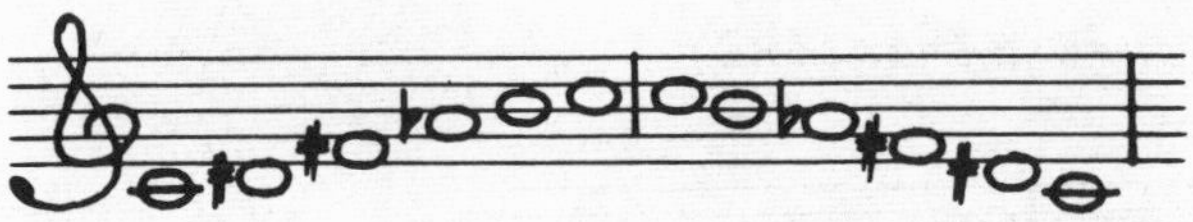

The notes *GA* (E) and *PA* (G) are avoided entirely.

70. *MĒḶA NĀSIKABHŪṢAṆĪ*

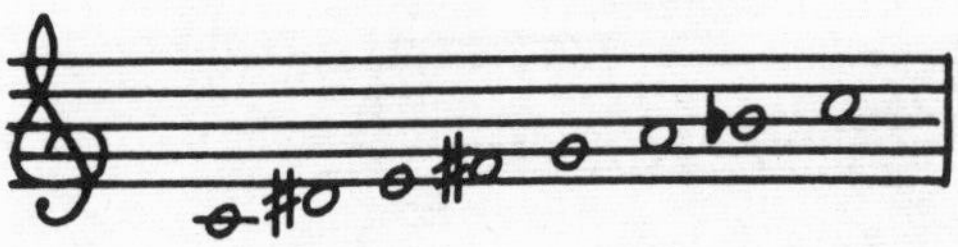

NĀSIKABHŪṢAṆĪ (*Triputa-tāla*) SCM, 284-5

Janya Rāgas of the 70. Mēḷa

(1) *Gaurī Sīmanti (Gaurī Sīmantini)*

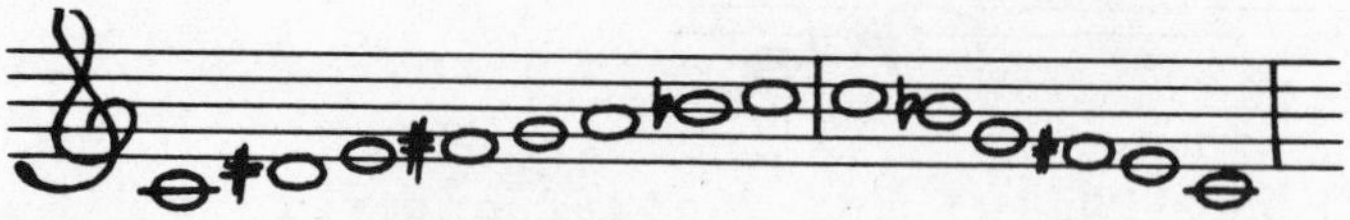

Ascent: *krama sampūrṇa*.
Descent: the notes *DHA* (A) and *RI* (D#) are avoided.

(2) *Haṃsa Kōsali (Haṃsa Kōsala)*

Ascent: *sampūrṇa*; one *vakra* feature is shown.
Descent: the note *RI* (D#) is avoided; one *vakra* feature is used.

(3) *Hariṇākṣi*

The notes *GA* (E) and *PA* (G) are avoided entirely.

(4) *Kamalapāṇi*

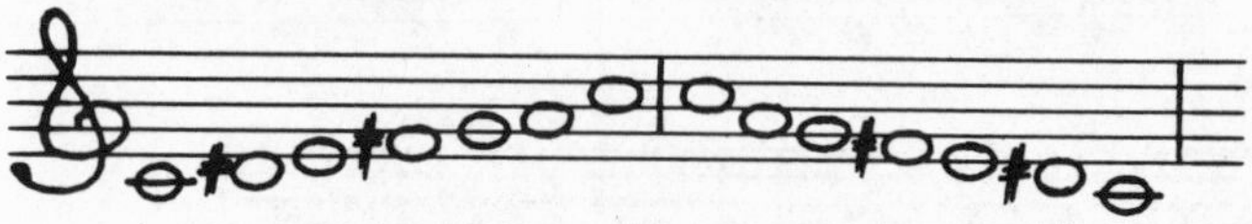

The note *NI* (Bb), a characteristic of the 70. *mēḷa*, is avoided entirely. Therefore this *rāga* can be ascribed to the 71. *mēḷa* as well.

(5) *Kannaḍa Bhōmaṇi*

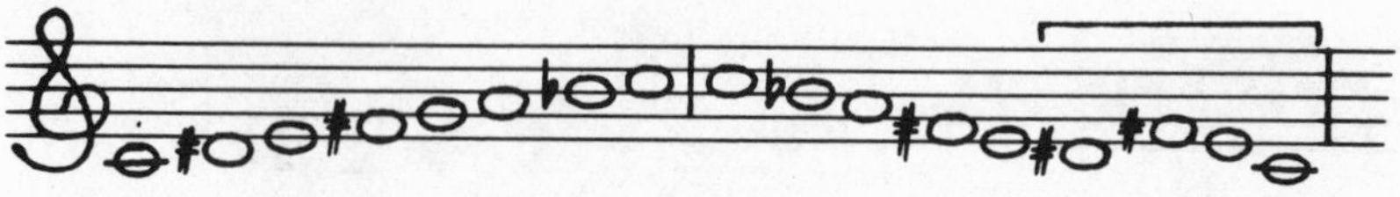

Ascent: *krama sampūrṇa*.

Descent: the note *PA* (G) is avoided; one extended *vakra* feature is shown.

(6) *Karṇabhūṣaṇi*

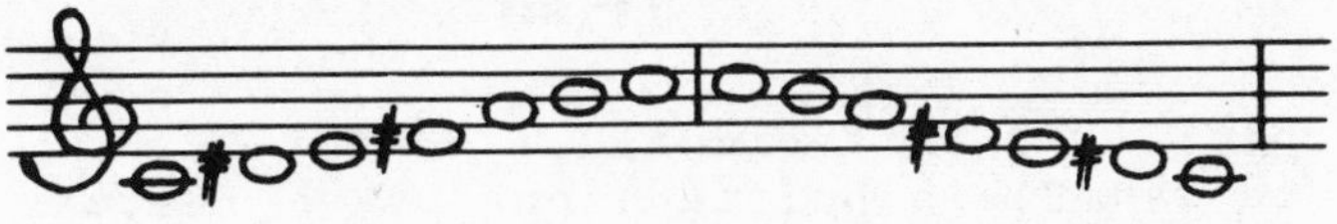

The note *PA* (G) is avoided entirely.

Another *rāga* with the same name is listed under the heading of the 16. *mēḷa* (26).

(7) *Kuntala Ghaṇṭāṇam*

The note *DHA* (A) is avoided entirely.
Ascent: the note *NI* (Bb) is avoided; one extended *vakra* feature is shown.
Descent: the note *GA* (E) is omitted.

(8) *Nāsāmaṇi*

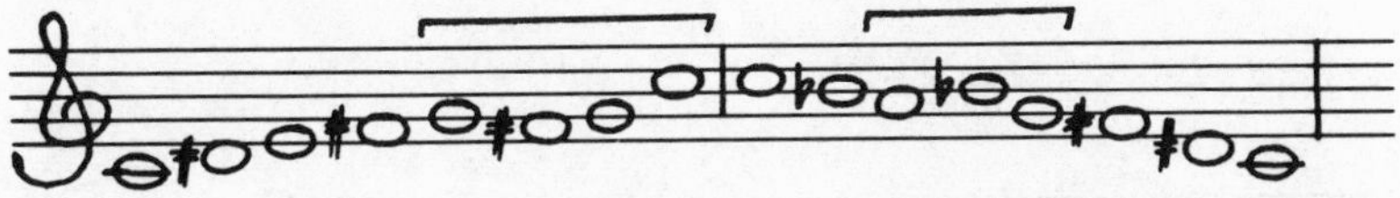

The ascent of this *rāga* is identical with that of *rāga Kuntala Ghaṇṭaṇam* (70, 7). The descent avoids the note *GA* (E) and shows one *vakra* feature.

NĀSĀMAṆI (*Triputa-tāla*) SCM, 285-86

(9) *Nigamasañjāri*

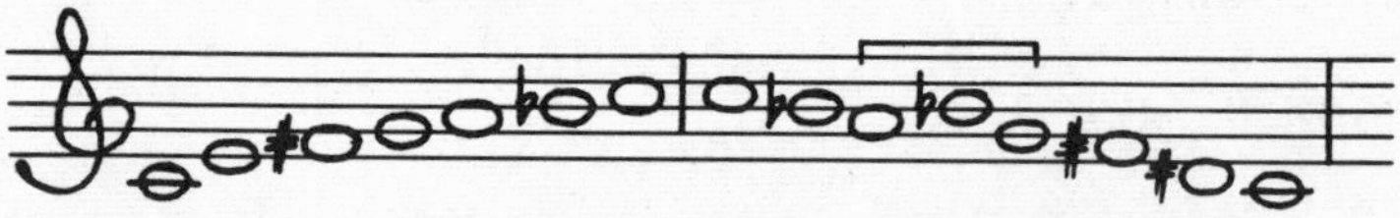

Ascent: the note *RI* (D#) is avoided.
Descent: the note *GA* (E) is omitted; one *vakra* feature is shown.

(10) *Pākasanapriya*

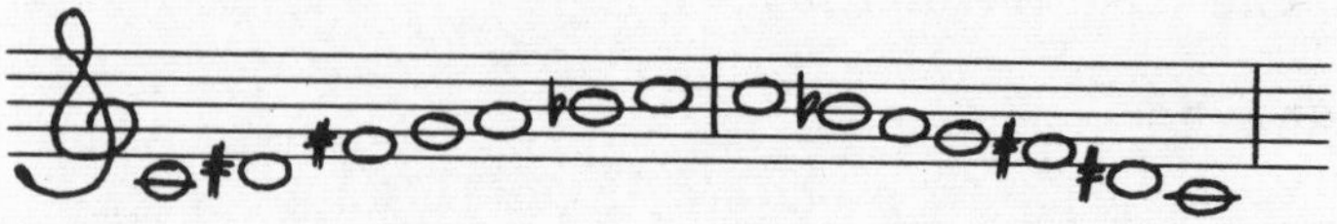

The note *GA* (E) is avoided entirely.

(11) *Raṅgārōhiṇi*

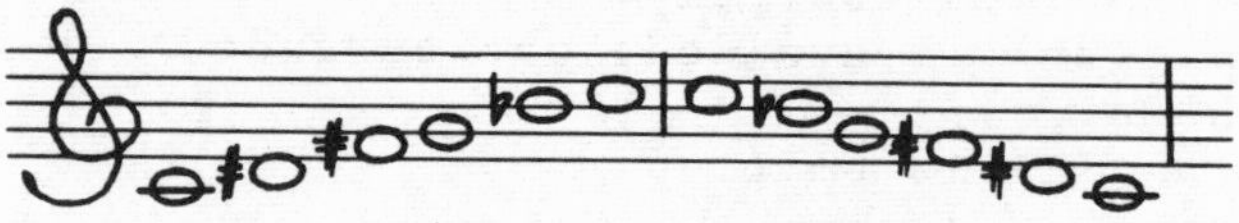

The notes *GA* (E) and *DHA* (A) are avoided entirely.

(12) *Ravipratāpi*

The notes *PA* (G) and *NI* (Bb) are avoided entirely.

(13) *Ṡatpadhadhvani*

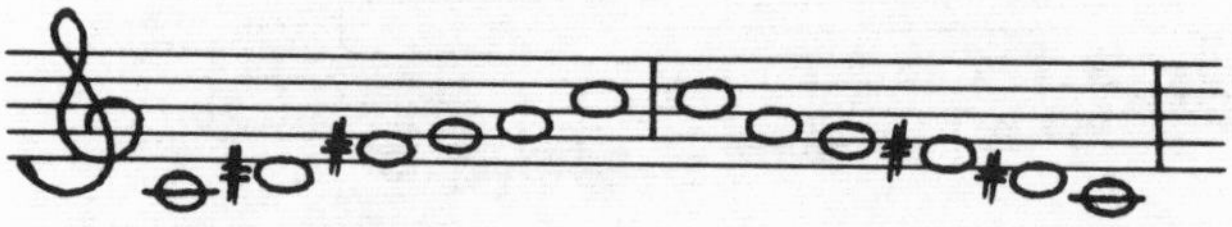

The notes *GA* (E) and *NI* (Bb) are avoided entirely.

71. *MĒḶA KŌSALA*(*M*) (*KŌSALAPRIYA*)

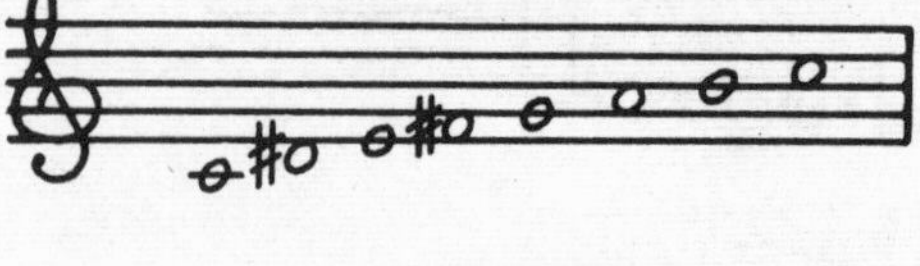

KŌSALA (Triputa-tāla) SCM, 286-7

Janya Rāgas of the 71. Mēḷa

(1) *Bahula*

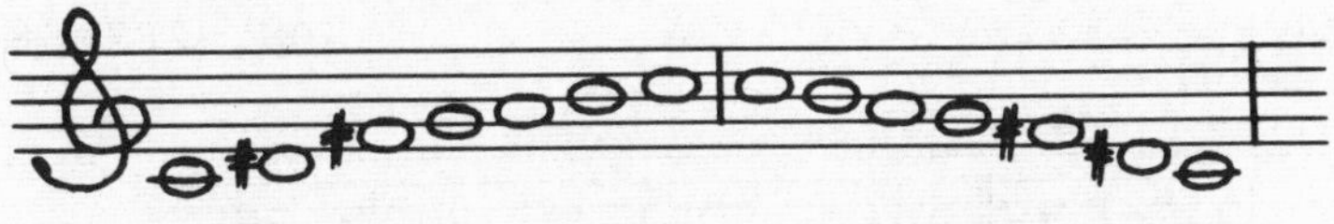

The note *GA* (E) is avoided entirely.

Bahula must not be mistaken for *Bahuli* which is another name for *Bauḷi* of the 15. *mēḷa* (11).

(2) *Gaurī Niṣādam*

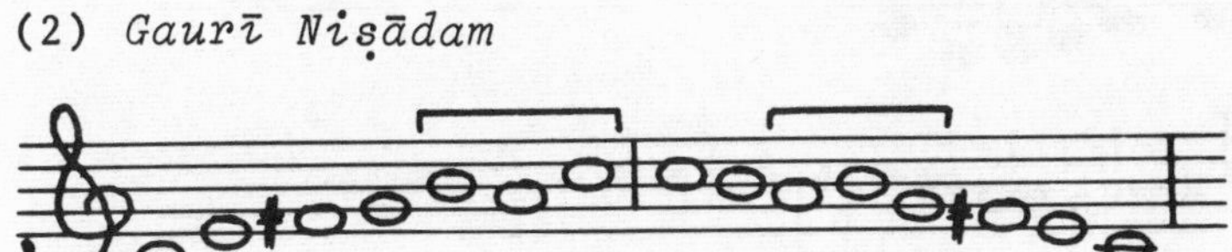

The note *RI* (D#) is avoided entirely. The scale shows two *vakra* features, one in ascent and one in descent.

(3) *Jayaśuka*

Ascent: *krama sampūrṇa*.
Descent: the note *NI* (B) is avoided; one extended *vakra* feature is shown.

(4) *Kaustubhapriya*

This scale is identical with that of *rāga Jayaśuka* (71, 3). A few musicians believe that the two *rāgas* differ in some slight details of performance practice. These details were expressed vaguely, even contradictorily, hence no clear description can be offered.

(5) *Kusumāvaḷi* (*Kusumākara*)

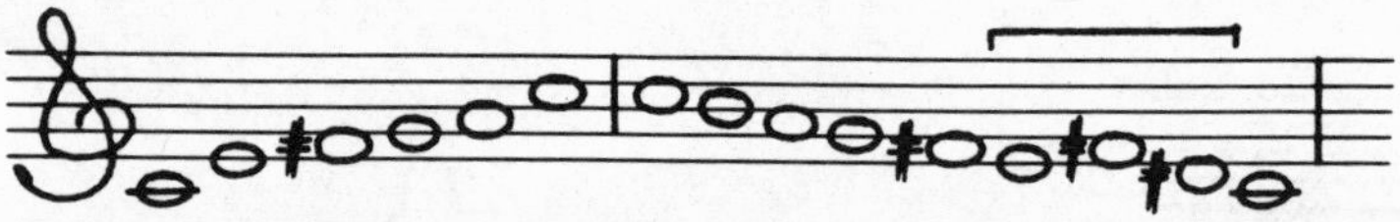

Ascent: the notes *RI* (D#) and *NI* (B) are avoided.
Descent: *sampūrṇa*; one *vakra* feature is shown.

Another *rāga* with the same name appears under the heading of the 38. *mēḷa* (11).

KUSUMĀVAḶI (*Triputa-tāla*) SCM, 287-88

(6) *Nāgagiri*

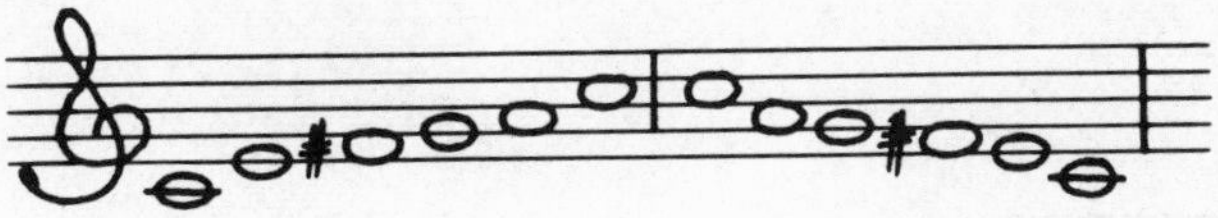

The notes *RI* (D#) and *NI* (B) are avoided entirely.

(7) *Pratāpasāraṅga*

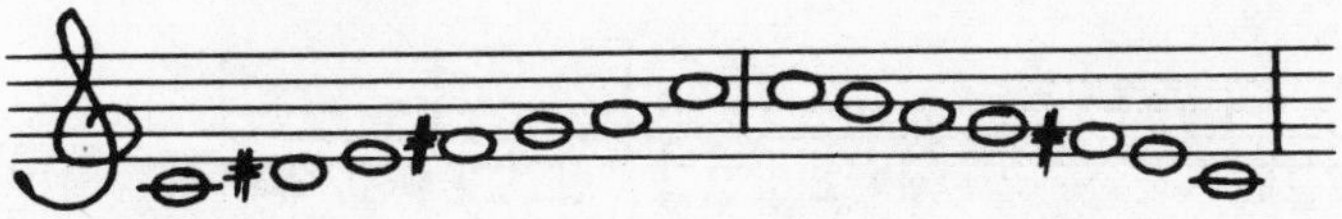

Ascent: the note *NI* (B) is avoided.
Descent: the note *RI* (D#) is omitted.

(8) *Saravamaṅgala*

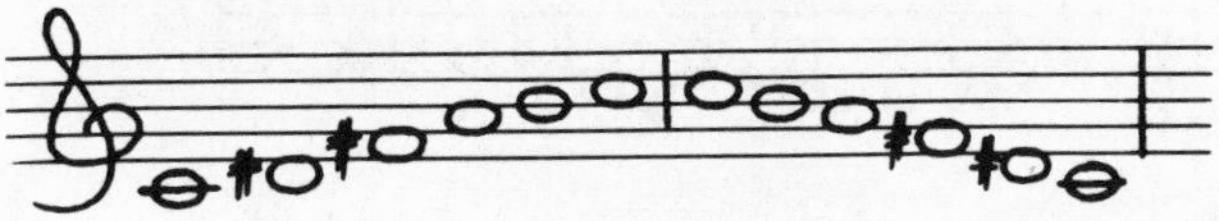

The notes *GA* (E) and *PA* (G) are avoided entirely.

(9) *Satyabhūṣaṇi*

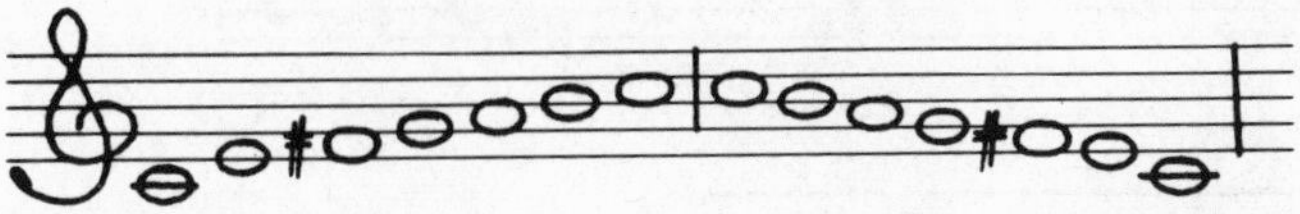

The note *RI* (D#) is avoided entirely.

(10) *Vaṅgam*

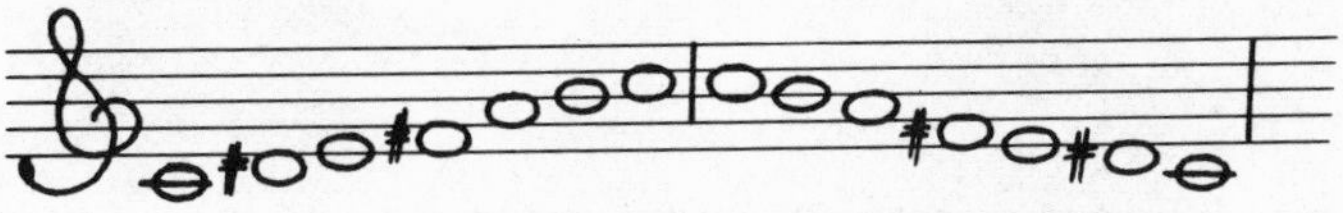

The note *PA* (G) is avoided entirely.

72. *MĒḶA RASIKAPRIYĀ*

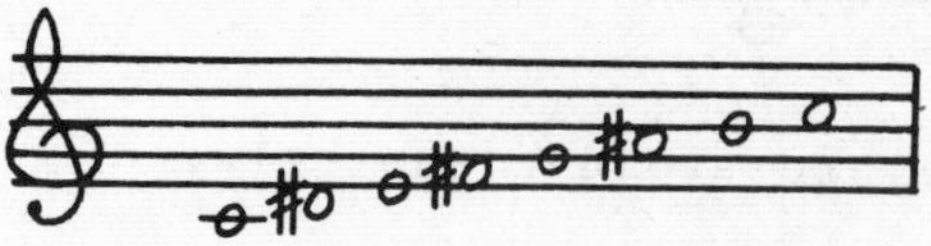

RASIKAPRIYĀ (*Triputa-tāla*) SCM, 288

Janya Rāgas of the 72. Mēḷa

(1) *Amrita Svarūpiṇi*

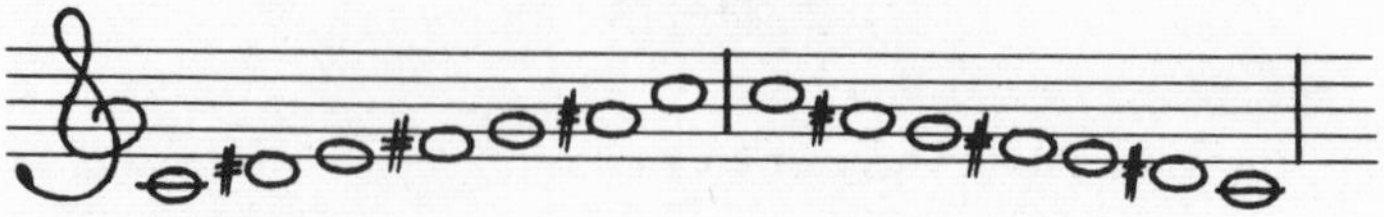

The note *NI* (B) is avoided entirely.

(2) *Giri Kuntaḷi*

Ascent: the notes *DHA* (A#) and *NI* (B) are avoided; one extended *vakra* feature is shown.
Descent: the note *RI* (D#) is omitted; one *vakra* feature is used.

(3) *Gīrvāṇa Padam*

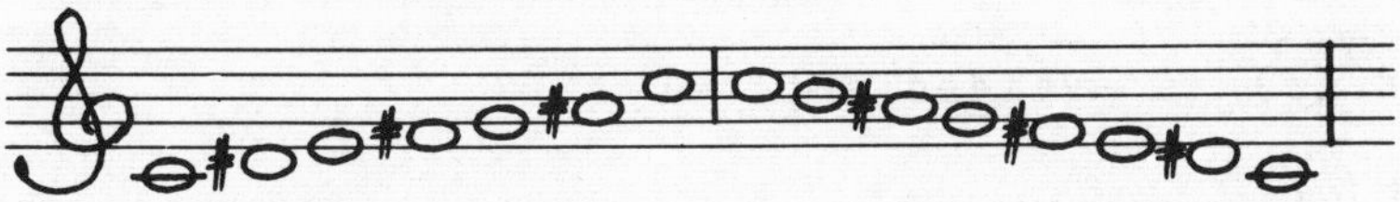

Ascent: the note *NI* (B) is avoided.
Descent: *krama sampūrṇa*.

(4) *Haṃsagiri*

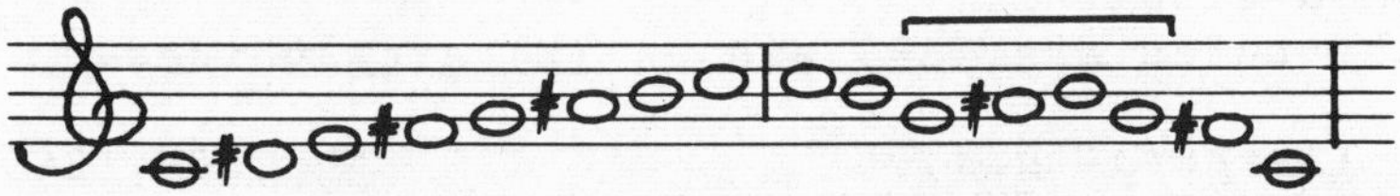

Ascent: *krama sampūrṇa*.
Descent: the notes *GȦ* (E) and *RI* (D#) are avoided; one extended *vakra* feature is shown.

(5) *Harichandanapriya (Haricandanapriya)*

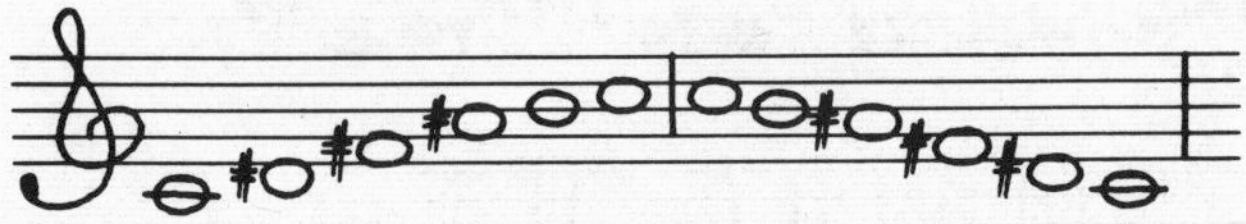

The notes *GA* (E) and *PA* (G) are avoided entirely.

(6) *Kanaka Jyōtiṣmati*

The notes *RI* (D#) and *GA* (E) are avoided entirely.

(7) *Nantanapriya*

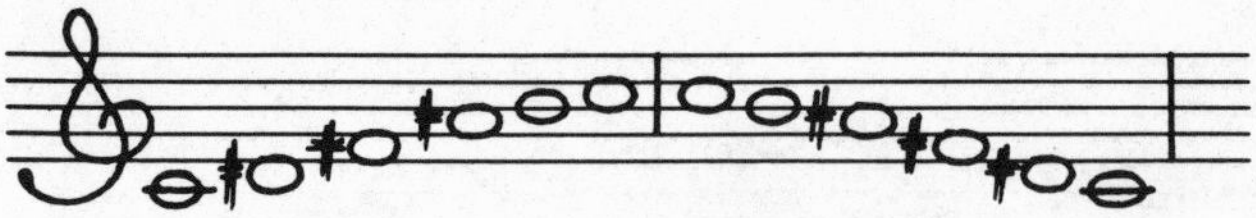

The notes *GA* (E) and *PA* (G) are avoided entirely.

(8) *Pārvati*

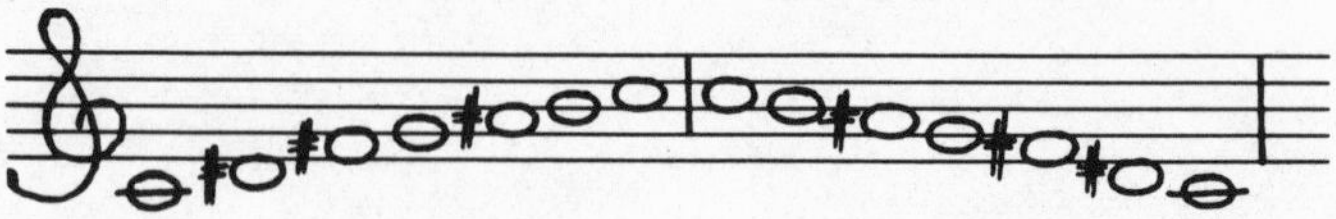

The note *GA* (E) is avoided entirely.

(9) *Rasamañjari*

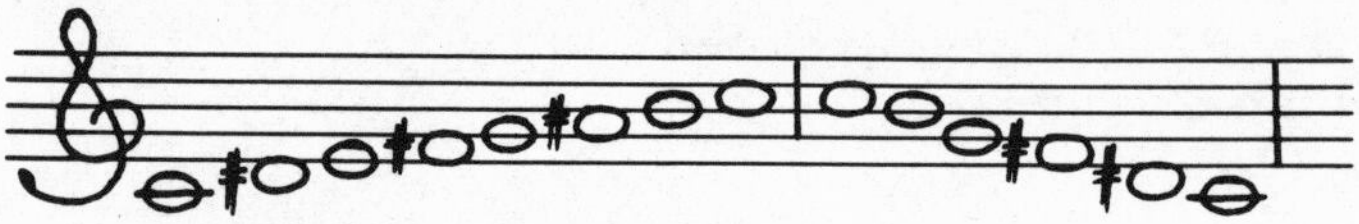

Ascent: *krama sampūrṇa*.
Descent: the notes *DHA* (A#) and *GA* (E) are avoided.

RASAMAÑJARI (*Triputa-tāla*) SCM, 289

(10) *Sarasapriya*

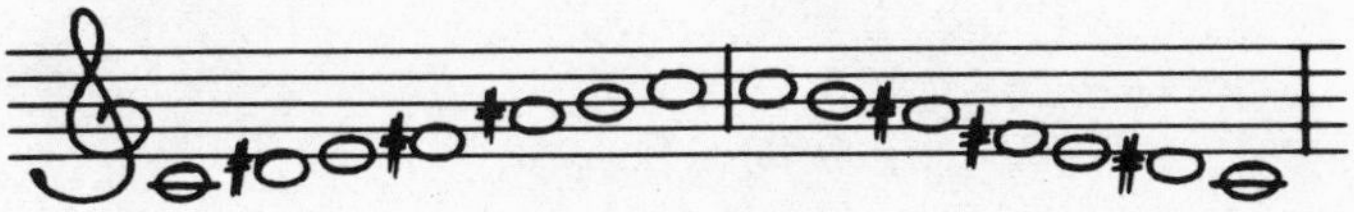

The note *PA* (G) is avoided entirely.

Another *rāga* with the same name appears under the heading of the 27. *mēḷa* (36).

(11) *Sputalāpini*

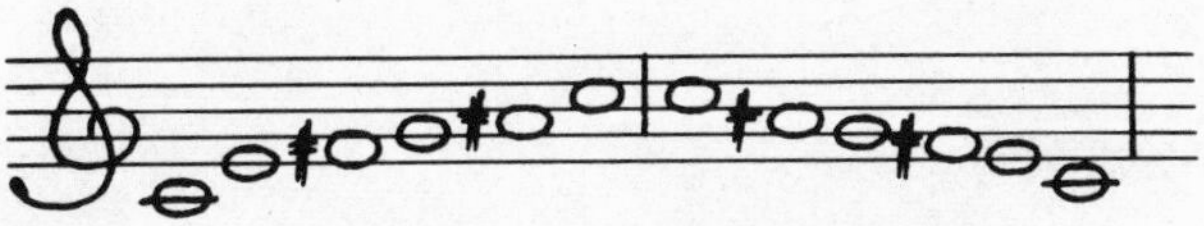

The notes *RI* (D#) and *NI* (B) are avoided entirely.

Another *rāga* with the same name appears under the heading of the 61. *mēḷa* (16).

(12) *Vāridarañjani*

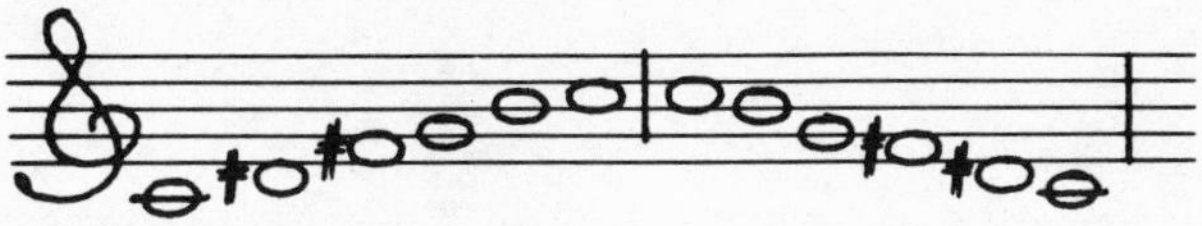

The notes *GA* (E) and *DHA* (A#) are avoided entirely.

CONCLUDING REMARKS

At the end of this somewhat sizeable and yet never totally complete array of representative scales, some of which are identical, one would feel inclined to start comparisons and other examinations from various points of view. One could compare the scales of *janya rāgas* and investigate how many have the same tone material, or how many employ the same *vakra* features, how many avoid this and that note in ascent or descent; one could endeavour to find out which scales result if the tonic (*SA*) is shifted to the *RI*-, *GA*-, *MA*-, etc., positions, how and where they are being used; one could make a comparison between northern and southern scales, particularly those that have the same or similar names; one could establish an investigation of ornaments used at the present time, examine the types and frequency of appearance of characteristic phrases, and so forth.

Such and similar investigations could be made rather easily with the help of an electronic computer. But these endeavours cannot be contemplated within the already rather extended framework of this study, and furthermore, the question arises as to how much significant information can be gained by such examinations. It probably would be the same as if we fed the first few measures of the main theme of the first movement of the Eroica and the same number of corresponding measures of the opening of Mozart's *Bastien und Bastienne* into the computer. We would be informed that both are the same. However, beside the printed notes, how much is there in common between the two excerpts? The first represents the heroic, revolutionary, driving power of the mature Beethoven, and the second shows the opening of a little, charming Singspiel of a twelve-year-old boy. One would have to say that the difference between the two lies predominantly in the *rasas* employed.

Rasa in the art music of India is, most probably, of greater importance than it is in the West. And it is exactly these subtle but essential phenomena that cannot be fed on punched cardboard slips into a computer.

But even without the help of a computer we should have no difficulties in pointing out obvious parallels such as the basic scale materials of the northern *Bilaval* and the southern *Dhīraśankarābharaṇam*. Or, we could show the sameness of the northern *Durga* (*Bilaval*) and the southern *Hanumattōḍi*; the northern *Kafi* and the southern *Kharaharapriyā*; the northern *Bhairav* and the southern *Māyāmāḷavagauḷa*; and so forth. But with this correlation the matter ends; additional features would have to be considered. For instance, the northern *Bilaval* (see RNI, 117-21) requires for a satisfactory performance the most significant, but extremely subtle trace of *NI komal* (Bb) which is absent in the southern *Dhīraśankarābharaṇam*. Similar differences, often extremely subtle, are nevertheless of decisive importance in the proper rendition of the various *rāgas* and cannot be ignored.

As a final remark it has to be stated that despite its comparatively clear organization, the system of the 72 *mēḷas* and their subordinate *janya rāgas* is not absolutely perfect. Many South Indian musicians are aware of the shortcomings and are working toward an improvement of the system. Of great value are the numerous Madras Music Conferences where ambiguities of the system in general and of specific *rāgas* in detail are discussed. As an example of these activities may serve my description of *rāga Pantuvarāli* (51, 30) where several suggestions made during two of these Conferences are reported. The fields in which improvements of the system of the 72 *mēḷas* are aimed at, are the scales, performance practice in various aspects, and occasionally the entire matter of *rāga* classification. Some scholars (e.g., Dr. B. Chaitanya Deva) suggest the use of entire new systems for both northern and southern *rāgas*, but only time will show whether these new ideas will receive recognition and eventually will come into general use.

NOTES

Preface and Introduction

1. Walter Kaufmann, *The Ragas of North India* (Bloomington: Indiana University Press, 1968).

2. W. Kaufmann, *Musical Notations of the Orient* (Bloomington: Indiana University Press, 1967), pp. 188-194.

3. See RNI, pp. 402-4.

4. See RNI, pp. 9, 39.

5. See RNI, p. 42.

6. The *Śilappadikāram* mentions several modes such as *padumalai*, *shevvali*, *vilari*, *mershem*. Each mode has its own tone material and its prescribed *graha* (initial note). See: Prince Ilango Adigal, *Shilappadikaram*, trans. by Alain Daniélou (New York, 1965). See also: Swami Prajnanananda, *A History of Indian Music* (Calcutta, 1963), pp. 180-1.

7. Ed. by Pandit V. N. Bhatkhande (with commentary in Mahratti), (Bombay, 1910). See also: M. S. Ramaswami Aiyar (ed.), Annamalai University, 1932.

8. See RNI, pp. 42-44.

9. See RNI, pp. 14-15.

10. According to O. C. Gangoly, *Rāgas and Rāginīs* (Bombay, 1935), pp. 107-8 (as quoted from M. S. Ramaswami Aiyar's edition of the *Svaramēḷakalānidhi* (1932), p. xliv.

11. See RNI, p. 52.

12. See Gangoly, *op. cit.*, p. 88.

13. Ed. by P. S. Sundaram Aiyar and Pandit S. Subrahmanya Śāstri, *The Music Academy Series* (Madras, 1930).

14. Ed. by Joshi and Sukthankar (Poona: Arya Bhusan Press, 1918). Repr. *Music Academy Series* (in Sanskrit and Tamil), Madras, 1934.

15. Recently questions have been raised concerning the authenticity of the *dhrūpads*.

16. *The Ragas of Karnatic Music*, Madras, 1938, p. 14.

17. See: V. Raghavan. "Venkatamakhin and the 72 Melas," *Journal of the Music Academy Madras*, XII (1-4), Madras, 1941.

18. K. V. Ramachandran. "The Melakarta, A Critique," *Journal of the Music Academy Madras*, IX (1-4), Madras, 1938, pp. 31-3.

19. Adyar Library, Madras, 1938.

Mēḷas and Rāgas

1. L. Muthiah Bhagavathar (1877-1945) was born in Arikesanallore, Tirunelveli district, Madras State. He was appointed as court musician to the Maharaja of Mysore in 1924. He composed numerous songs to texts in Kannada, Tamil and 142 songs in Sanskrit. He has created several new *rāgas* such as *Valajibudamanohari*, *Pasupatipriyaalankari*, and *Sarangamallar*.

2. There are four forms of *chāpu tāla*:
   (a) *misra chāpu*: 3+4 (also 4+3)
   (b) *khaṇḍa chāpu*: 2+3 (representing half of *jhampa tala*)
   (c) *tisra chāpu*: 1+2
   (d) *sankīrṇa chāpu*: 4+5 (rare)

If the word *chāpu* is used alone it always implies the *misra chāpu* form.

3. Kshetrayya (Kshetrajna, Kshetriyulu) was a musician who lived some time between the seventeenth and eighteenth centuries. Exact dates of his birth and death are not known. He came either from Muvvapuri or from Muvva, both located in Andhra State, South India. He was called Kshetrayya because he was deeply devoted to visiting sacred shrines (*kshetras*). Kshetrayya excelled in composing *padas* in which the subtleties of the text and perfectly shaped melodies created the *rasas* of love and devotion. His favorite *tala* was *triputa* (3+2+2).

4. Subbarama Diksitar in his work *Saṅgīta-Ṣampradāya-Pradarśinī* (cf. R, 163) describes the *Śrīrāga* scale (using descent (a)) as a variant of *Kharaharapriya*.

5. The *ankitam* (signature) of Garbapuriyar has been used by two men: Karur Dakshinamurti Sastri and Karur Devudayya. (Dates concerning their lives are uncertain.) The former of the pair, a school teacher at Karur, wrote the texts, and the latter, a gifted string player set them to music.

6. As indicated in the name (Tiruvarur Thiagaiyer, 1767-1847) the composer was born at Tiruvarur, Tanjore District, Madras State. He is considered to be one of the most important figures of

Carnatic music.

7. See n. 1 to Notes on *Mēḷas* and *Rāgas* (p. 696).

8. Fiddle Ponnuswami was an associate of the musician Tiruvattur Kuppaiyer. He was the composer of numerous *varnas*. Dates of his birth and death are uncertain.

9. A court poet and singer under the Marasing and Sarfoji rulers of Tanjore in the nineteenth century, Kuppuswami composed numerous *kirtanas* in the *rasa* of love (*śringāra*). It is said that he was the great-grandson of the famous Śyāma Śāstri.

REGISTER OF MĒḶAS AND RĀGAS

The two numbers placed after each *rāga* name indicate *mēla* and *janya-rāga* numbers. A single number refers to a *mēḷa*.)

Ābhēri 20, 8
Ābhēri 22, 6
Abhimāniṇi 5, 2
Ābhiru 47, 1
Ābhōgi 22, 2
Ābradēśi 62, 1
Achala Nāṭa 36, 1
Adbodham 8, 12
Ādi Bhairavī 20, 27
Ādi Dēśya 39, 1
Ādi Pañchama 48, 1
Ādi Varāḷi 57, 1
Ādi Vasu 41, 1
Agnikōpam 20, 28
Āhiri 14, 3
Āhiri. See *Āhiri Tōḍi*
Āhirināṭa 29, 2
Āhiri Tōḍi 8, 7
Āhōri 20, 29
Airāvati 45, 1
Airāvati 64, 1
Alakavarāḷi 28, 45
Alankārapriya 10, 4
Ālāpi 37, 1
Alaru 37, 2
Alava 42, 1
Alivardhani 17, 4
Āma Pañchamam 48, 2
Amaravali 28, 46
Ambāmanōharī 23, 2
Ambhōgiṇi 28, 47
Ambhōruham 44, 1
Āmradēśi 62, 2
Āmra Pañchamam 48, 3
Amrita Dhanyāsi 8, 11
Amrita Laharī 29, 3
Amritalaharī (*Amrutalahari*) 46, 1
Amrita Pañchamam 48, 4
Amrita Svarūpiṇi 72, 1
Amrita Rañjaṇī. See *Amrita Taraṅgiṇī*
Amrita Taraṅgiṇī 19, 3
Amritavāhiṇi 20, 24
Amritavarśiṇi (*Amritavarśaṇi*) 39, 2
Amritavarśiṇi 66, 1
Amrita Vasantam 57, 2
Amrutalahari. See *Amritalahari*
Ānandabhairavī 20, 9
Ānandabhōgi 42, 2
Ānanda Laharī 29, 4
Ānanda Līlā 33, 1
Ānandamukhi 29, 5
Ānanda Nāṭanī 2, 4
Ānanda Vāridhi 22, 7
Anaṅgādhari 39, 3
Ananta 17, 5
Āndhāḷi 28, 48

Ēkāgraṇi. See *Ēkāghrauṇi*
Ēkākṣari. See *Ēkākshari*
Ēkākśhari 15, 61
Ēkalīlā 15, 62
Ēkanika 15, 63
Ēkaśruṅgi 39, 7
Ēlānka Manōharī 37, 7
Ēlaprabhāvam 29, 40
Ēsandhōli 46, 7
Ēsāri 13, 9

Gagana Bhūpāḷam 21, 9
Gagana Bhūpāḷi. See *Gagana Bhūpāḷam*
Gaganādari 54, 6
Gagana Gāndhāri 40, 4
Gagana Mayūri 51, 13
Gaganāmbari 29, 41
Gagana Mōhiṇi 64, 7
Gagana Rañjani 66, 8
Gagana Sarasīruham 53, 8
Gajānandiṇi 30, 7
Gaja Sāri 9, 8
Gaja Vardhanam 29, 42
Gaja Vardhani. See *Gaja Vardhanam*
Gaja Vilaśita 29, 43
Gamakakriya 53, 9
Gamakapriya 51, 14
Gamaka Sāmantam 45, 6
Gāmākyam 23, 5
Gamana Bhāskara(m) 29, 44
Gamanakriya 53, 10
Gamana Lalita 15, 64
Gamana Nirmaḷa 53, 11
Gamanapriya. See *Gamanaśrama*
Gamanaśrama 53, -
Gamana Taraṅgiṇī 20, 52
Gambhīra Nāṭa 36, 5
Gambhīra Vāṇi 30, 8
Gambhīra Vasantam 8, 23
Gambhīriṇi 23, 6
Gāmbhīrya Ghōṣaṇi 52, 4
Gāmbhīrya Nāṭa 33, 6
Gāna Lalita 3, 9
Gāna Lōlam 29, 45
Gāna Mayūri. See *Gagana Mayūri*
Gānamūrti 3, -
Gānāṅgi 20, 53
Gānapriya 19, 10
Gāna Sindhu 15, 65
Gāna Svabhāva 15, 66
Gāna Śyāmala 5, 5
Gāna Vāridhi 34, 6
Gāna Vasantam 22, 40
Ganda Madanam 53, 12
Ganda Taraṅgiṇī 29, 46
Gāndhāra Gauḷa 15, 67
Gāndhārapriya 20, 54
Gāndharva Kannaḍa 31, 4
Gāndharvam 42, 5
Gāndharvam Manōharī 26, 6
Gāndharva Nārāyaṇi 24, 6
Gaṅgataraṅgiṇī 33, 7
Gāṅgeyabhūṣanī 33, -
Gaṅgeya Taraṅgiṇī. See *Gaṅgātaraṅgiṇi*
Gaṇita Vinōdiṇi 16, 18
Gāpriyanagam 12, 5
Garalāri 65, 16
Gārava Siṃhala 22, 41
Garbha Līla 46, 8
Garbha Śārdūlam 51, 15
Gargeśvari 65, 17
Garigadya 56, 10
Garjam 17, 10
Garuḍadhvani 29, 47
Garuḍapriya 45, 7
Garuḍa Varāḷi 59, 9
Garuḍavardhani 45, 8
Gauḍa Mallāri 29, 48
Gauḍa Mallāru. See *Gauḍa Mallāri*
Gauḍīpantu. See *Gauḷīpantu*
Gauḷa 15, 2
Gauḷa Chandrika 7, 15
Gauḷa Gāndhāri 68, 3
Gauḷa Mālavi 6, 7
Gauḷa Mallār. See *Gauḍa Mallāri*
Gauḷa Pañchamam 24, 7
Gauḷīpantu 15, 5
Gaurī 15, 12
Gaurī Baṅgāḷa 9, 9
Gaurī Gāndhāri 2, 6
Gaurī Kriya 60, 4
Gaurīmanōharī 23, -